Catholic Bible Dictionary

GENERAL EDITOR, SCOTT HAHN

DOUBLEDAY

New York   London   Toronto   Sydney   Auckland

DD

DOUBLEDAY

Published in the United States by Doubleday Religion, an imprint of
the Crown Publishing Group, a division of Random House, Inc., New York.
www.doubleday.com

DOUBLEDAY and the DD colophon
are registered trademarks of Random House, Inc.

Nihil Obstat: Monsignor Michael F. Hull, STD, Censor Librorum.
Imprimatur: Most Reverend Dennis J. Sullivan, Auxiliary Bishop and Vicar General,
Archdiocese of New York.

The *Nihil Obstat* and *Imprimatur* are official declarations that a book or pamphlet is free of
doctrinal or moral error. No implication is contained therein that those who have granted the
Nihil Obstat and the *Imprimatur* agree with the content, opinions, or statements expressed.

Book design by Nancy Campana

Library of Congress Cataloging-in-Publication Data
Hahn, Scott.
    Catholic Bible dictionary / general editor, Scott Hahn. — 1st ed.
        p.   cm.
1. Bible—Dictionaries.   2. Catholic Church—Doctrines.   I. Title.
BS440.H23 2008
220.3—dc22
2008020687

ISBN 978-0-385-51229-9

PRINTED IN THE UNITED STATES OF AMERICA

10   9   8   7   6   5   4

First Edition

TO MIKE AQUILINA

CONTENTS

A dictionary is, by definition, a reference book listing terms important to a particular subject along with a discussion of their meanings and applications.

If the Bible is what Christians say it is, can there be any task more daunting than the compiling of a Bible dictionary? For we believe that the Bible is the written Word of God. We believe it is "inspired by God" (2 Tim 3:16). We believe it is not a dead letter, but "living and active" (Heb 4:12). We believe it "must be fulfilled" (Luke 22:37) and "cannot be broken" (John 10:35). What's more, it is not subject merely to private interpretation (2 Pet 1:20), but to the discernment of the Church. For people can easily "twist" Scripture "to their own destruction" (2 Pet 3:16).

The Bible is as sharp as any two-edged sword (Heb 4:12), and thus it should be handled with care.

Yet it should indeed be handled. The Bible itself exhorts us to attend to its study (1 Tim 4:13) and praises those who "examine the Scriptures daily" (Acts 17:11).

We live in a time of unprecedented opportunities for Bible study. In the 1970s the Catholic Church revised its lectionary—the order of scriptural readings for the Mass. The readings now unfold in a three-year cycle and include all the books of both testaments of the Bible. The schema proved so effective in communicating the Word of God that it has been adopted and adapted by many Protestant bodies as well. Historians may one day judge the new lectionary to be the most significant ecumenical advance of the twentieth century.

The Mass is the one thing that Catholics experience on a weekly basis all their lives, and the Bible is the one book that they will hear at every Mass. Since Masses on Sundays and holy days usually include three readings from the two testaments, plus a fourth from the book of Psalms, the average faithful Catholic spends about fifteen hours a year in focused Bible study. If you include the other overtly biblical parts of the Mass (the "Holy, Holy, Holy," the "Lamb of God," the "Lord, Have Mercy," and so on), the average time per annum doubles or triples. For the Catholic who goes to daily Mass, the times are quite impressive, rivaling even the hours spent by some scholars.

What does the lectionary mean, practically speaking? It means that Catholics who keep to their minimum obligations—attendance at Mass on Sundays and holy days—are immersed in the Bible. What's more, since the lectionary itself is held in common by a growing number of Christians, we find that Catholics and Protestants may find, more and more, that they are "on the same page," so to speak.

The lectionary is the greatest, but surely not the only great new opportunity for Bible study. The Bible is not only fully divine, but also fully human; and so we have to work with its literary sense and historical background in order to get to the theological meaning. And, again, we are blessed to live in a season of abundance.

Of the making of new books—and Bibles—there is no end. Publishing in the fields of biblical studies and translation is at an all-time high. The airwaves are thick with television and radio shows that claim to represent a biblical worldview. Software packages enable us to search the Scriptures with the speed and accuracy that ancient monks imagined to be impossible this side of heaven.

Yet even with all these tools, major longitudinal studies seem to indicate that biblical literacy—among all Christians—is not advancing, but declining. Thus, there is a widespread need for a fresh statement of the basic terms we encounter in reading the Bible.

More than a generation has passed since the appearance of the last major Catholic Bible dictionary. It has been a fertile generation for biblical scholarship. It has been an eventful time for biblical archaeology. It has been a fruitful time for the Church's interpretation of the Bible. It is time for a new resource. I pray that my colleagues and I have lived up to our task. I pray, too, that our readers will live up to theirs.

In this book, our range is catholic and inclusive, and so we privilege the Church's ancient canon, which was ratified at the Council of Trent. We treat the "deuterocanonical books"—Tobit, Baruch, Judith, Wisdom, Ecclesiasticus (Sirach), 1 Maccabees, and 2 Maccabees—as inspired Scriptures. We also recognize the longer forms of Daniel and Esther. We have been pleased to assimilate the great contributions of historical-critical scholarship, but we have also relied upon the Church's interpretive tradition and Magisterium.

Responding to the call of the magisterium, we have produced this book. The Church, after all, "forcefully and specifically exhorts all the Christian faithful . . . to learn the surpassing knowledge of Jesus Christ, by frequent reading of the divine Scriptures." So says the Catechism of the Catholic Church, and then it concludes by quoting the great Scripture scholar of the first millennium, St. Jerome: *Ignorance of the Scriptures is ignorance of Christ.*

Scott W. Hahn, Ph.D.
September 30, 2008
Feast of St. Jerome

ACKNOWLEDGMENTS

It is difficult to send this book off. The project has been very much a part of my life for a decade, and it has been a good excuse for close collaboration with colleagues and friends whose work and company I enjoy. I would especially like to thank Dr. Matthew Bunson, Curtis J. Mitch, Dr. John S. Bergsma, Dr. Brant Pitre, and Christopher Bailey. Their hard work, expertise, and editorial assistance were indispensable.

I also want to recognize the St. Paul Center for Biblical Theology for generously funding much of the research that went into this project. The St. Paul Center promotes biblical literacy for all Catholics and biblical fluency for clergy and teachers. I pray that this volume fulfills the Center's mission on every page.

The Old Testament

Gen	The Book of Genesis
Exod	The Book of Exodus
Lev	The Book of Leviticus
Num	The Book of Numbers
Deut	The Book of Deuteronomy
Josh	The Book of Joshua
Judg	The Book of Judges
Ruth	The Book of Ruth
1, 2 Sam	First, Second Book of Samuel
1, 2 Kgs	First, Second Book of Kings
1, 2 Chr	First, Second Book of Chronicles
Ezra	The Book of Ezra
Neh	The Book of Nehemiah
Tob	The Book of Tobit
Jdt	The Book of Judith
Esth	The Book of Esther
1, 2 Macc	First, Second Book of Maccabees
Job	The Book of Job
Ps	The Book of Psalms
Prov	The Book of Proverbs
Eccl	The Book of Ecclesiastes
Song	The Song of Songs
Wis	The Book of Wisdom

Sir	The Book of Sirach
Isa	The Book of Isaiah
Jer	The Book of Jeremiah
Lam	The Book of Lamentations
Bar	The Book of Baruch
Ezek	The Book of Ezekiel
Dan	The Book of Daniel
Hos	The Book of Hosea
Joel	The Book of Joel
Amos	The Book of Amos
Obad	The Book of Obadiah
Jonah	The Book of Jonah
Mic	The Book of Micah
Nah	The Book of Nahum
Hab	The Book of Habakkuk
Zeph	The Book of Zephaniah
Hag	The Book of Haggai
Zech	The Book of Zechariah
Mal	The Book of Malachi

The New Testament

Matt	Gospel of Matthew
Mark	Gospel of Mark
Luke	Gospel of Luke
John	Gospel of John
Acts	Acts of the Apostles

Rom   Letter to the Romans

1, 2 Cor   First, Second Letter to the Corinthians

Gal   Letter to the Galatians

Eph   Letter to the Ephesians

Phil   Letter to the Philippians

Col   Letter to the Colossians

1, 2 Thess   First, Second Letter to the Thessalonians

1, 2 Tim   First, Second Letter to Timothy

Titus   Letter to Titus

Phlm   Letter to Philemon

Heb   Letter to the Hebrews

Jas   Letter of James

1, 2 Pet   First, Second Letter of Peter

1, 2, 3 John   First, Second, Third Letter of John

Jude   Letter of Jude

Rev   Revelation

Old Testament Pseudigrapha

1, 2 Enoch   *First, Second Book of Enoch*

T. Lev.   *The Testament of Levi*

T. Sol.   *The Testament of Solomon*

Jub.   *The Book of Jubilees*

Apostolic Fathers

1, 2 Clem.   *First, Second Letter of Clement*

Did.   *Didache*

Ign. *Rom.*   Ignatius, *To the Romans*

Ign. *Eph.*   Ignatius, *To the Ephesians*

Ign. *Smyrn.*   Ignatius, *To the Smyrnaeans*

Ign. *Magn.*   Ignatius, *To the Magnesians*

Classical and Ancient Christian Writings

Canones Apostolicae

Can. Ap.   *Canones Apostolicae (Apostolic Canons)*

Clement of Alexandria

Strom.   *Stromata (Miscellanies)*

Eusebius

Hist. Eccl.   *Historia Ecclesiastica (Ecclesiastical History)*

Onom.   *Onomasticon*

Herodotus

Hist.   *Historiae (Histories)*

Hippolytus

Haer.   *Refutatio Omnium Haeresium (Refutation of All Heresies)*

Josephus

Ant.   *Jewish Antiquities*

B.J.   *Bellum Judaicum (The Jewish War)*

C. Ap.   *Contra Apionem*

Justin Martyr

Dial.   *Dialogus cum Tryphone (Dialogue with Trypho)*

1, 2 Apol.   *Apologia i–ii (First, Second Apology)*

Origen

Comm. Rom.   *Commentarii in epistulam ad Romanos (Commentary on the Letter to the Romans)*

Pausanias

Descr.   *Graeciae Descriptio (Description of Greece)*

Philo

Moses 1, 2   *De Vita Mosis 1, 2 (On the Life of Moses 1, 2)*

Her.   *Quis Rerum Divinarum Heres Sit*

Philostratus

Vit. Apoll.   *Vita Apollonii (Life of Apolonius of Tyana)*

Pliny the Elder

Nat.   *Naturalis Historia (Natural History)*

St. Augustine

Enarrat. Ps.   *Enarrationes in Psalmos (Ennarations on the Psalms)*

Faust.   *Contra Faustus Manichaeum (Against Faustum the Manichean)*

Gen. litt.   *De Genesi ad litteram (On Genesis Literally Interpreted)*

Quaest. Hept.   *Quaestiones in Heptateuchum*

Serm. Dom.   *De Sermone Domini in Monte (The Sermon on the Mount)*

St. Jerome

Comm. Am.   *Commentariorum in Amos (Commentary on Amos)*

Comm. Gal.   *Commentariorum in Epistolam ad Galatas (Commentary of the Letter to the Galatians)*

Comm. Jon.   *Commentariorum in Jonam (Commentary on Jonah)*

Epist.   *Epistulae (Letters)*

Tract. Ps.   *Tractatus in Psalmos (Tract on Psalms)*

Vir. Ill.   *De Viris Illustribus (On Illustrious Men)*

St. John Chrysostom

Hom. 1 Cor.   *Homiliae in epistulam I ad Corinthios (Homily on the First Letter to the Corinthians)*

Strabo

Geogr.   *Geographica (Geography)*

Suetonius

Claud.   *Divus Claudius*

Tacitus

Ann.   *Annales*

Hist.   *Historiae*

Tertullian

An.   *De Anima (The Soul)*

Or.   *De Oratione (Prayer)*

Pud.   *De Pudicitia (Modesty)*

Scorp.   *Scorpiace (Antidote for the Scorpion's Sting)*

Documents and Offices of the Catholic Church

CCC   Catechism of the Catholic Church

CDF   Congregation for the Doctrine of the Faith

CSEL   Corpus Scriptorum Ecclesiasticorum Latinorum (Vienna, 1866–)

DS	Denzinger-Schönmetzer, *Enchiridion Symbolorum, definitionum et declarationum de rebus fidei et morum* (1965)
DV	*Dei Verbum*
EB	Enchiridion Biblicum
GS	*Gaudium et Spes*
LG	*Lumen Gentium*
PBC	Pontifical Biblical Commission
PG	J. P. Migne, ed., Patrologia Graeca (Paris: 1841–1855)
PL	J. P. Migne, ed., Patrologia Latina (Paris: 1857–1866)
VS	*Veritatis Splendor*

Abbreviations of Common Translations of the Bible

Douai	Douay-Rheims Bible
JB	Jerusalem Bible
KJV	King James Version
NAB	New American Bible
NIV	New International Version
NJB	New Jerusalem Bible
NKJV	New King James Version
NRSV	New Revised Standard Version
RSV	Revised Standard Version

Technical Abbreviations

A.D.	*anno domini* (the year of the Lord)
B.C.	before Christ
ca.	circa
cf.	*confer* (compare)
chap(s).	chapter(s)
d.	died
e.g.	*exempli gratia* (for example)
esp.	especially
etc.	*et cetera* (and the rest)
f(f).	and the following one(s)
i.e.	*id est* (that is)
ibid.	*ibidem* (in the same place)
LXX	Septuagint (the Greek OT)
MS(s)	Manuscript(s)
MT	Masoretic Text (of the OT)
no(s).	number(s)
NT	New Testament
OT	Old Testament
pl.	plural
r.	reigned
SP	Samaritan Pentateuch
v(v).	verse(s)
vs.	versus

Catholic Bible Dictionary

A

A The symbol commonly used for Codex Alexandrinus (*see* **Codex**).

AARON Elder brother of **Moses**, and first high priest of Israel; ancestor of the priestly Aaronites (Exod 6:20; 7:7; 15:20).

I. THE LIFE OF AARON

Aaron, like Moses, was the son of Amram and Jochebed. His wife was Elisheba, and their sons were **Nadab**, **Abihu**, **Eleazar**, and Ithamar. (Nadab and Abihu died offering "unholy fire" contrary to the Law; see Lev 10:1–2. Eleazar therefore was Aaron's heir and successor as high priest.)

Aaron is first mentioned in Exod 4:14, where he is called "the Levite." He was divinely appointed to serve as Moses's spokesman before Pharaoh (Exod 4:14–16; 5:1–4) and with the Israelites in Egypt (Exod 4:27–31).

Once the Israelites were freed from Egypt, Aaron remained at Moses's side. With Hur, he held up Moses's outstretched arms during the battle with the Amalekites (Exod 17:10–12), and he shared Moses's meal with Jethro, along with the elders (Exod 18:12). With Moses, the seventy elders, and Nadab and Abihu, he ascended Mount Sinai and took part in the covenant meal held in the presence of the Lord (Exod 19:24; 24:1–2, 9–11).

While Moses remained on the mountain for forty days, Aaron and Hur were given the task of caring for the people. When the unruly people demanded that he make them visible gods, Aaron complied, crafting the **golden calf**—Israel's first act of national apostasy (Exod 32:1–4, 15–24). Aaron might have been killed that very day had Moses not intervened on his behalf (Exod 32:28; Deut 9:20).

With Miriam, Aaron opposed Moses over the Cushite (or Ethiopian) woman Moses had married (Num 12) and suffered a severe rebuke; Miriam was punished with leprosy, and Aaron's punishment was mitigated only because he confessed his wrongdoing.

Aaron was prohibited from entering the Promised Land, and thus shared Moses's punishment for unbelief at Meribah (Num 20:12). Warned of his coming death, Aaron went up to Mount Hor with Moses and Eleazar. Moses stripped Aaron of his sacred vestments and put them on Eleazar, and Aaron died on the top of the mountain. The Israelites mourned his passing for thirty days (Num 20:22–29).

II. AARON AS HIGH PRIEST

In the Exodus, Aaron spoke and acted as his brother Moses's assistant. He was always subordinate to Moses, as a prophet is to God (Exod 7:1). When Aaron questioned Moses's choice of a wife (Num 12:1–15), God rebuked him and made it clear that Aaron's place was secondary to that of his brother, who was God's covenant mediator and lawgiver. Moses's special relationship with God gave him authority even over Israel's anointed priests.

Despite his sins, Aaron remained God's choice to be Israel's first high priest. Aaron was installed as high priest and his sons as priests to minister in the wilderness and to maintain the tabernacle. Aaron was anointed by Moses (Lev 8:1–12) and was dressed in sacred vestments made according to divine instructions (Exod 28). His turban was adorned with a crown of pure gold, engraved with the signet "Holy to the Lord" (Exod 28:36). Of special importance for the fulfillment of his priestly function was the Day of Atonement (Lev 16; see **Atonement, Day of**).

Aaron's rod was the symbol of his authority. In the time of the Exodus, it was the instrument of miraculous events intended to convince Pharaoh of the divine commandment to free the Israelites (Exod 7:9–10). Thus the rod was used to defeat the serpents of the Egyptian magicians, to change the waters of the Nile into blood, to bring the plague of frogs, to launch the plague of gnats (Exod 7–8), and to divide the Red Sea (Exod 14:15–21). During the rebellion of **Korah**, Aaron's rod alone sprouted buds, blossoms, and almonds when the rods of the rebels did not, signifying that

Aaron's authority was divinely instituted (Num 17:1–8). His rod was placed in the ark and kept alongside the tablets of the covenant (Heb 9:4). (*See* **Priest and priesthood**.)

The Aaronite priests claimed descent from Levi through Aaron and were described as the "sons of Aaron" (cf. Lev 3:8, 21:1; Num 10:8; Josh 21:4; 1 Chr 24:1; Neh 12:47) or "belonging to Aaron" (cf. 1 Chr 12:28, 27:17).

In the New Testament, Aaron is described as the ancestor of Elizabeth, mother of John the Baptist (Luke 1:5). In Hebrews, the priesthood of Aaron is compared to Christ's priesthood (5:4), and the transitional and provisional nature of the earlier priesthood is contrasted with the perfect and eternal priesthood of Christ (Heb 9:1–14; cf. 7:11), "who through the eternal Spirit offered himself without blemish to God" (Heb 9:14).

AARON'S ROD *See under* **Aaron**.

AB The fifth month of the Hebrew calendar (corresponding to July/August). The month was noted especially for the traditional harvesting of grapes and figs. The ninth day of Ab is kept as a day of fast to mark the destruction of the **Temple** in Jerusalem by **Nebuchadnezzar** in 586 B.C. and again by Titus in A.D. 70.

ABADDON (Hebrew, "destruction") The name is used with several meanings. These include ruin and destruction in a broad sense (Job 31:12), a place of destruction, and the **abyss** in the sense of the abode of the dead (Job 26:6; Prov 15:11). Other references are found in Psalms (88:11) and Job (28:22). Abaddon is personified in the New Testament (Rev

9:11, presented in the Greek as *Apollyōn*) as an angel with authority over hell. Abaddon in this sense is the ruler and author of havoc and destruction on earth. (*See also* **Asmodeus** and **Sheol**.)

ABAGTHA One of the seven eunuchs in the service of the Persian king **Ahasuerus** as chamberlains (Esth 1:10).

ABANA A river that feeds the Ghouta oasis, and hence one of the rivers of the city of **Damascus**, along with the Pharpar River to the south (2 Kgs 5:12). The Abana is identified with the modern river Barada.

ABARIM A mountain range directly northeast of the Dead Sea (Num 27:12; Jer 22:20). The Israelites passed through the Abarim as they neared Canaan, camping there before their entry into the plains of Moab (Num 33:47–48). Moses stood upon the highest peak of **Mount Nebo**, the peak Pisgah, and gazed down upon the Promised Land (Deut 32:49). Jeremiah also hid the **ark** (2 Macc 2:4–5) in the range.

ABBA The Aramaic term for "Father" that occurs three times in the New Testament (Mark 14:36; Rom 8:15; Gal 4:6). Each time it is used, the Greek translation is attached to it, giving us "Abba, Father" in the English translation. In the Bible, the term was first uttered by Jesus (Mark 14:36) and was thereafter used by Christians (Rom 8:15; Gal 4:6) as adoptive children of God. It was a familiar form of address used especially by children, and thus de-

notes a level of intimacy between Christ and the Father that is now made available to the members of the Church (CCC 683, 742, 1303, 2766, 2777).

ABDON There are four men by the name of Abdon in the Old Testament.

1. One of the minor judges, the son of Hillel of Pirathon and a judge over Israel for eight years. According to Judg 12:13–15, his forty sons and thirty grandsons rode on seventy asses as a demonstration of his enormous wealth.

2. The son of Jeiel and his wife, Maacah, and an ancestor of Saul (1 Chr 8:30; 9:36).

3. The son of Shashak counted among the descendants of Benjamin (1 Chr 8:23).

4. The son of Micah and a member of the court of **Josiah** of Judah (2 Chr 34:20); he is also listed in 2 Kgs 22:12 as Achbor.

5. Abdon was also a Levitical city in the tribal region of Asher (Josh 21:30; 1 Chr 6:74).

ABEDNEGO (Akkadian, "servant of Nego," or "servant of Nabû," the personal god of King Nebuchadnezzar) One of the three Israelites (with **Shadrach** and **Meshach**) who were companions of **Daniel** at the court of **Nebuchadnezzar** (Dan 1:7). Abednego was originally named Azariah, but the chief eunuch at the court gave him a Babylonian name. When Daniel was named governor of the province of Babylon, the three were appointed administrators (Dan 2:48–49). When, however, they refused to worship a golden image set up by Nebuchadnezzar, they were thrown into the fiery furnace. For their faithfulness, they were miraculously saved by a messenger of God and subsequently honored by Nebuchadnezzar (Dan 3:12–97; 1 Macc 2:59). (*See also* **Furnace**.)

ABEL Second son of Adam and Eve (Gen 4:2) and brother of **Cain**. Whereas Cain became a tiller of the ground, Abel was a herdsman and willingly gave as a sacrifice to the Lord the firstborn of his flock as well as their fat portions. Yahweh found Abel's sacrifice acceptable and rejected that of Cain. Succumbing to the sin of envy, Cain murdered Abel in a field (Gen 4:8).

In the New Testament, Abel is seen as one whose faith made his sacrifice acceptable to God and who is a model of righteousness (Matt 23:35; Luke 11:51; Heb 11:4; 1 John 3:12) (CCC 58, 401, 2559).

ABEL OF BETH-MAACAH A city in David's kingdom located in northern Palestine, north of Lake Huleh. The city was in the tribal territory of Naphtali and was the site where Sheba took refuge following his failed revolt against David (2 Sam 20:14–18). It was also conquered by Ben-hadad some eight decades later (1 Kgs 15:20; 2 Chr 16:4) and again around 733–732 B.C. by the Assyrian king Tiglath-pileser III. The latter carried off the inhabitants to Assyria (2 Kgs 15:29). At its height, Abel of Beth-Maacah was a thriving center for commerce and travel into ancient Israel from the north, especially Phoenicia. It is identified today with Tell Abil al-Qamh.

ABEL-KERAMIM (Hebrew, "meadow of the vineyards") A city in Ammon, east of the Jordan. Jephthah defeated the Ammonites and pursued them to Abel-Keramim (Judg 11:32–33).

ABEL-MEHOLAH (Hebrew, "meadow of dancing") A city east of the Jordan; its exact location has not been identified. Gideon drove the Midianites to the region of Abel-Meholah (Judg 7:22). The name Meholathites was also used apparently for the inhabitants (1 Sam 18:19; 2 Sam 21:8). Part of the administrative system of King Solomon, it was situated on the frontier of the fifth district (1 Kgs 4:12). The city was the birthplace of Elisha (1 Kgs 19:16), and there he was named the successor to Elijah (1 Kgs 19:19–21).

ABEL-MIZRAIM (Hebrew, "meadow of Egypt") A place east of the Jordan where the funeral procession of Jacob stopped and where Joseph, in the company of Egyptian officials, mourned his father for seven days (Gen 50:11). The story involves a play on the Hebrew word for "meadow," which closely resembles the word for "mourning." (*See also* **Atad**.)

ABEL-SHITTIM *See* **Shittim**.

ABIA *See* **Abijah**.

ABIATHAR A descendant of Ithamar, the youngest son of Aaron, and the son of Ahimelech of the family of Eli (1 Sam 22:2–23; 1 Kgs 2:27; 1 Chr 24:3). Abiathar served as a priest at Nob with Ahimelech and was the sole survivor of the massacre of the priests of Nob ordered by Saul (1 Sam 22:20). He fled to David, taking with him the **ephod** (1 Sam 23:6; *see* also **Urim and Thummim**), and subsequently served as David's chief priest during the period of difficulty with Saul. His duties during this time are uncertain, but he was firm in his loyalty to David during the rebellion of Absalom (2 Sam 15:1–12). After the rebellion, Abiathar remained at David's command in Jerusalem with **Zadok**. Throughout David's reign, Abiathar was counted as one of his two chief priests (cf. 1 Chr 15:11; 2 Sam 20:25).

When David was near death, Abiathar gave his support not to Solomon but to **Adonijah**, while Zadok backed Solomon (1 Kgs 1–2, 19, 25; 2:22). Once installed, Solomon expelled Abiathar from his priestly office and banished him to Anathoth; Abiathar was not put to death solely because of his many years of service to David (1 Kgs 2:26–27). Zadok was given Abiathar's place (1 Kgs 2:35). The end of Abiathar's time as priest thus fulfilled the prediction made nearly 150 years before (1 Sam 2:27–36) that the priestly house of Eli would be ended for its infidelities.

ABIB (Hebrew, "ear of corn") The original name for the first month (March/April) of the Israelite liturgical calendar (Exod 13:4; 23:15; 34:18). After the **Exile**, the name was changed to **Nisan** (Neh 2:1; Esth 3:7).

ABIEL (Hebrew, "God is my father") The grandfather of King Saul and the father of Kish (1 Sam 9:1; 14:51).

ABIEZER (Hebrew, "my father is help")

1. A descendant of Manasseh, as noted in the genealogies of 1 Chr 7:18, Josh 17:2, and Num 26:30. Gideon was a member of the family of Abiezer (Judg 6:11–12; 8:2, 32). In various translations, he is also known also as Iezer and Jeezer.

2. A member of the army of David, from Anathoth. Abiezer commanded the ninth division of David's forces (2 Sam 23:27; 1 Chr 11:28; 27:12).

ABIGAIL (Hebrew, "my father rejoices")

1. The wife of **Nabal** of Carmel in Judah and, after Nabal's death, of David (1 Sam 25; 2 Sam 3:3). She is described as an attractive and sensible woman (1 Sam 25:3). While married to Nabal, Abigail prevented David's massacre of Nabal and his household when her husband refused to assist David (1 Sam 25). Nabal died shortly after (1 Sam 25:38), and David took Abigail as his wife (1 Sam 25:39–42). Later she was among those captured in a raid by the Amalekites upon David's fortress at Ziklag (1 Sam 30:5), then rescued (1 Sam 30:18). When David went to Hebron for his accession, she accompanied him (2 Sam 2:2), and there she bore David's second son, named variously Chileab (2 Sam 3:3), Daniel (1 Chr 3:1), and Daluiah (2 Sam 3:3; *see* **LXX**).

2. The sister (or half sister) of David (1 Chr 2:16), wife of Ithra the Ishmaelite (2 Sam 17:25, also called Jether the Ishmaelite in 1 Chr 2:17), and mother of Amasa, leader of the forces of Absalom. Abigail was the daughter of Nahash (2 Sam 17:25).

ABIHAIL (Hebrew, "my father's strength") There are three men and two women by the name of Abihail in the Old Testament.

1. A Levite of the family of Merari and the father of Zuriel (Num 3:35).

2. The wife of Abishur, of the tribe of Judah (1 Chr 2:29).

3. A member of the tribe of Gad in Gilead (1 Chr 5:14). He had seven sons.

4. The daughter of David's oldest brother Eliab and the wife of David's son Jerimoth. Her daughter, Mahalath, became the wife of King Rehoboam of Judah (2 Chr 11:18).

5. The father of Queen Esther (Esth 2:15; 9:29) and uncle of Mordecai.

ABIHU (Hebrew, "he is my father") The second son of Aaron and Elisheba (Exod 6:23; Num 3:2, 26:60; 1 Chr 5:29, 24:1) and brother of Nadab, Eleazar, and Ithamar. With his brother Nadab, Abihu was permitted to accompany Moses, Aaron, and the seventy elders to the theophany on Mount Sinai (Exod 24:1), and he and Nadab were appointed priests (with their father). Both sons, however, died when they "offered unholy fire before the Lord, such as he had not commanded them" (Lev 10:1–3). The priestly succession thus passed to **Eleazar**, the elder of Aaron's two remaining sons.

ABIJAH (Hebrew, "Yahweh is my father")

1. The king of Judah (ca. 913–911 B.C.), the son and successor of King Rehoboam (2 Chr 13:2); also called Abijam in 1 Kgs 15. His brief reign is judged harshly in 1 Kgs 15:1–8, owing probably to his religious habits (*see* 1 Kgs 15:3–5), but the author of Chronicles treats him more favorably. His battle with Jeroboam in 2 Chr 13:1–22 is documented in some detail; Abijah's speech to the enemy, including his pious proclamation of his devotion to Yahweh, is preserved in 2 Chr 13:4–12. With God's help, Abijah escaped the ambush of his enemy, defeated Jeroboam, and recaptured the cities of Bethel, Ephron, and Jeshanah (1 Chr 13:15–20). Abijah had fourteen wives, sixteen daughters, and twenty-two sons (2 Chr 13:21).

2. The second son of Samuel (1 Sam 8:2) who, with his brother Joel, served as a judge in Beer-sheba. With his brother, he fell into corruption (1 Sam 8:2–3).

3. The son of King Jeroboam I of Israel. As a child, he fell ill, and his father sent his wife in disguise to the prophet Ahijah at Shiloh. The deception was a failure, and Abijah died in Tirzah as had been predicted. The death was the occasion of Ahijah's denunciation of the king (1 Kgs 14).

4. The wife of Ahaz and mother of King Hezekiah of Judah (2 Chr 29:1); in 2 Kgs (18:2), she is also called Abi.

5. The son of Becher and a member of the tribe of Benjamin (1 Chr 7:6, 8).

6. The name of three priests: the leader of the eighth division of priests (1 Chr 24:10); the head of a group of priests returning from Babylonia (Neh 12:4); and a priest who signed the renewed covenant at the time of Nehemiah (Neh 10:8).

ABILENE A district or tetrarchy situated around Abila, almost twenty miles northwest of Damascus, in the valley of the Barada. At the start of the public ministry of Jesus, Abilene was ruled by Lysanias (Luke 3:1). It was subsequently granted to Herod Agrippa I around A.D. 34–37.

ABIMELECH (Hebrew, "the king is my father")

1. A Canaanite king of Gerar (Gen 20:1–

18; 26:1–33). When Abraham pretended that Sarah was his sister and not his wife, Abimelech took her into his harem. The ruler was warned by God in a dream and delivered her back into Abraham's keeping. Abraham subsequently reached a covenant with Abimelech for possession of a well and rights to pasture land in the Negeb. Another king named Abimelech also took into his harem the wife of Isaac, a ruse that was again discovered (Gen 26:1–16); likewise, there is a dispute over water supply in Beer-sheba (Gen 26:26–33). "Abimelech" might be a throne name or dynastic name rather than a personal name, which would explain why both monarchs were called Abimelech.

2. One of the sons of Gideon by a Canaanite concubine from the city of Shechem (Judg 8:31). He was ambitious, driven by a lust for power rather than genuine public service. Using his ties to the people of Shechem by birth, Abimelech convinced the people of Shechem to support his uprising against the brothers of Gideon. He was thus able to kill the seventy brothers, except for Jotham (Judg 9:1–5). Abimelech then became king of Shechem, and Jotham reacted by stirring up a revolt of the Shechemites against him (Judg 9:7–21). The people came under the leadership of Gaal, son of Ebed, and revolted against Zebul, Abimelech's governor while he was at Arumah (Judg 9:41). In retribution, Abimelech destroyed the city and sowed it with salt (Judg 9:26–45); he also burned down the temple El-berith where the last survivors had fled for safety. Abimelech, however, was soon killed while leading an attack on the city of Thebez: he was crushed by a millstone dropped from above by a woman (Judg 9:50–55), a death that became proverbial (2 Sam 11:21).

ABINADAB (Hebrew, "my father is noble")

1. In 1 Sam 7:1, a man from Kiriath-jearim whose house was used to store the **ark of the covenant** after it had been recovered from the Philistines and brought from Beth-shemesh. His son, **Eleazar**, was consecrated and given responsibility for the ark.

2. The second son of Jesse (1 Sam 16:8; 1 Chr 2:13). He served in the army of Saul against the Philistines at Elah (1 Sam 17:13).

3. The third son of Saul (1 Chr 8:33; 9:39). He was killed with his brothers Jonathan and Malchishua at Mount Gilboa by the Philistines (1 Sam 31:2; 1 Chr 10:2).

ABINOAM (Hebrew, "my father is delight") The father of Barak, a warrior of the tribe of Naphtali during the time of the Judges (Judg 4:6; 5:1, 12).

ABIRAM (Hebrew, "my father is exalted")

1. A Reubenite and son of Eliab (Num 16:1). With his brother Dathan, his Reubenite cousin On, and the Levite Korah, Abiram helped organize some 250 tribal leaders in a rebellion against **Moses** and **Aaron** (Num 16:1–35). Abiram and Dathan were summoned to appear before Moses but refused, using as their excuse that Moses had failed to lead them to a land of milk and honey and fields and vineyards. Abiram, Dathan, and Korah, as well as their families and possessions save for the sons of Korah, were swallowed by the earth (Num 16:31–33), and the rebel followers were consumed by fire (Num 16:35, 26:9; Deut 11:6; Ps 106:17).

2. The firstborn son of Hiel the Bethelite (1 Kgs 16:34). He rebuilt Jericho, and his death was attributed to Joshua's curse on anyone who rebuilt the city (Josh 6:26).

ABISHAG A young Shunammite woman who ministered to King David in his old age (1 Kgs 1:4, 15). Although she slept with David to keep him warm, she did not have sexual relations with him. Nevertheless, Solomon considered her to be one of David's harem. When **Adonijah** asked to marry Abishag, Solomon saw the request as an effort to seize the throne and had Adonijah executed for treason (1 Kgs 2:13–25).

ABISHAI One of the three sons of Zeruiah, the sister of David; the other two were **Joab** and **Asahel** (1 Sam 26:6). He was a close supporter of David and held trusted positions as a soldier and advisor during his reign; he was also one of the most famous of the elite warriors in the service of David. In his long career, Abishai participated in a host of battles and engagements, including the pursuit of **Abner** with Joab after Abner had slain Asahel in battle (2 Sam 2:24); command of the army under Joab; conspicuous achievement at the siege of Rabbah where he held back the Ammonites while Joab assaulted the Arameans (2 Sam 10:9–14); and, with Joab and **Ittai**, command of the forces against Absalom (2 Sam 18:2; 20:10). In the wars with the Philistines, Abishai saved David's life (2 Sam 21:16–17) and was accounted as the chief of the thirty "mighty men" of David. He also waged a successful campaign into Edom, establishing a number of garrisons (2 Sam 23:12–19), an ex-

pedition generally not considered synonymous with that of Joab (1 Kgs 11:15). Twice Abishai asked David's permission to kill (first Saul, 1 Sam 26; and then **Shimei**, 2 Sam 19:19–23), but twice was forbidden. He and Joab as men of vengeance and blood (they are denounced by David in 2 Sam 3:39 and 16:10) thus stood in contrast to David, a man of mercy (1 Sam 26:6–12; 2 Sam 16:9–14). It is possible, if not likely, that Abishai was dead by the time of the struggle between Solomon and Adonijah following David's death.

ABITAL One of the wives of King David (2 Sam 3:4; 1 Chr 3:3). She was the mother of his fifth son, Shephatiah.

ABIUD The son of Zerubbabel. He is mentioned as an ancestor of Jesus in the genealogy of Matthew (1:13).

ABNER (Hebrew, possibly "father is a lamp") The son of Ner and a cousin of King Saul. He served as commander of Saul's army (1 Sam 14:50–51), although there is little information on his activities. It is known that he waged a war against the Philistines (1 Sam 17:55–57), a campaign against David (1 Sam 26:5), and apparently wielded considerable influence in Saul's court (1 Sam 20:25). David rebuked Abner for permitting him to enter Saul's camp at night (1 Sam 26:14–25), especially as Abner perhaps served as a private guard to the king.

Following Saul's death at Gilboa, Abner took **Ishbaal**—Saul's only surviving son—across the Jordan to Mahanaim and proclaimed Ishbaal the king of Israel (2 Sam 2:8–10). In the two-year reign that followed,

Abner continued to command the royal army and thus was leader against David once hostilities erupted between Judah and Israel at the pool of Gibeon (2 Sam 2:12). In the engagement, Abner killed **Asahel**, despite warning Asahel not to pursue him following the retreat after the skirmish (2 Sam 2:12–32). The death set off a blood feud between Abner and Asahel's brothers **Joab** and **Abishai** that would end with Abner's death.

In the ensuing campaign, the cause of Ishbaal declined rapidly, and Ishbaal alienated his most important supporter by rebuking Abner for consorting with one of Saul's concubines, Rizpah; Ishbaal interpreted Abner's action as an effort to place himself in a position to usurp Saul's kingship. Abner then abandoned Ishbaal and entered into negotiations with David (2 Sam 3:12–16). The precise reasons for Abner's defection are unclear, but he might have had ambitions toward the throne or, more likely, considered himself a likely replacement for Joab as commander of David's army. It is also likely that Abner considered the position of the house of Saul to be untenable and saw that the only hope for Israel rested in a unified kingdom under David.

Abner soon proved a leading voice among the Israelites for the unification of the kingdoms and for recognizing David as sole king, especially among the tribe of Benjamin, which was Saul's tribe (2 Sam 3:17–19). David made additional demands, but once satisfied, he agreed to meet with Abner at Hebron.

After the meeting, Abner was murdered by the brothers of Asahel, Joab and Abishai (2 Sam 3:23–27). The murder was condemned by David, who publicly declared that he was not involved. Nevertheless, David benefited from the death and did not punish Joab, whose personal loyalty was beyond reproach.

In Abner's honor, David composed an elegy (2 Sam 3:33–34). Abner had at least one son, Jaasiel, whom David appointed as a leader over the tribe of Benjamin (1 Chr 27:21).

ABRAHAM (Hebrew *'abrām*, "exalted father"; *'abrāhām*, "father of a multitude") Son of Terah; husband of Sarah and, later, Keturah; a descendant of Shem and father to Isaac, Ishmael, and others. Abraham is revered as the great-grandfather of tribal Israel. He lived around 2000 B.C. God established a covenant so that Abraham might become the father of nations and through him "all the nations of the earth shall be blessed" (Gen 17:5). The complete account of Abraham is presented in Gen 11:26–25:18. He is known as Abram from Gen 11:26 to 17:4 and thereafter as Abraham (see below). The etymological origin of the name *Abram* is uncertain, but *Abraham* is perhaps a dialectical form of *Abram*.

I. *The Life of Abraham*
    A. *The Promise*
    B. *Travels in Canaan and Egypt*
    C. *The Promised Heir*
    D. *The Test of Faith*
    E. *The End of Abraham's Life*
II. *The Abrahamic Covenant*
    A. *Three Promises*
    B. *The Abrahamic Covenant Anticipates Later Covenants*
III. *Abraham's Faith and Obedience*
    A. *The Model of Faith*
    B. *Abraham, the Friend of God*

I. THE LIFE OF ABRAHAM

A. *The Promise*

Abram came from **Ur of the Chaldeans** in Mesopotamia, as part of the clan of Terah (Gen 11:28). With his wife Sarai, his father, his brothers, and his nephew **Lot**, Abram moved from Ur to Haran in northern Mesopotamia (Gen 11:31). When Abram was seventy-five years old, he received a command from the Lord to leave his homeland and the surety of his father's household and set out for Palestine and the land of Canaan.

B. *Travels in Canaan and Egypt*

The trip of Abram and his family—including Sarai and Lot—took him through **Canaan**, which the Lord promised Abram that his descendants would possess (Gen 12:7), then into **Egypt**, then back to Canaan, where he settled. Lot settled near Sodom, while Abram chose to remain in the hills of Canaan (Gen 13), moving to **Hebron** and the Oaks of Mamre. Here he was forced to take on the role of military commander to rescue Lot from the clutches of the Mesopotamians (Gen 14:13–16). That rescue set up his encounter with King **Melchizedek** of Salem at the Valley of Shaveh (the King's Valley), where Melchizedek offered Abram bread and wine as a priest of God Most High and blessed Abram. Abram acknowledged Melchizedek as priest by paying him a tithe (Gen 14:18–20).

As patriarch of his migrant household, Abraham also fulfilled the leadership roles associated with natural religion. Like other fathers in the patriarchal era (Isaac, Jacob), he functioned as a *priest*, performing cultic services on behalf of the family. Abraham built altars (Gen 12:7), called on the name of the Lord (Gen 12:8), offered sacrifice (Gen 22:13), and served as a mediator between God and men (18:23). Abraham is also the first person in Scripture identified as a "prophet" (Gen 20:7).

C. *The Promised Heir*

Abram was wealthy and powerful, but he still had no heir to make the fulfillment of the divine promises possible. God nevertheless assured Abram of the promise, and established his first **covenant** with Abram, solemnly promising the land of Canaan to Abram's descendants in a striking covenant ritual. (*For more on the significance of that ritual, see* **covenant**.)

Sarai remained barren, so she encouraged Abraham to father an heir by her Egyptian servant **Hagar**, who conceived and bore **Ishmael**. He was born when Abraham was eighty-six. Nevertheless, Ishmael was not the promised heir. When Abram was ninety-nine, the Lord renewed the covenant promise: "You shall be the ancestor of a multitude of nations" (Gen 17:4). To signify the moment, God changed Abram's name to Abraham and Sarai's name to **Sarah**, who "shall give rise to nations; kings of peoples shall come from her" (Gen 17:16). Incredible as it might seem, ninety-year-old Sarah would be the mother of Abraham's heir: "Sarah shall bear you a son, and you shall name him **Isaac**. I will establish my covenant with him as an everlasting covenant for his offspring after him" (Gen 17:19). The sign of the covenant would be **circumcision**.

The change in names bespeaks a change in mission. Abraham will be the father not only of a son who will be his heir, but of a whole multitude of descendants who will look to him as their ancestor and forefather.

In due course, Isaac was born, but his birth was the source of division in the household, as usually happens in the case of polygamy in Scripture (see **Marriage**). Abraham was forced to send away Hagar and Ishmael. Although God promised to make a great nation of Ishmael as well, Isaac was the promised heir (Gen 17:13, 18).

D. The Test of Faith

Abraham finally had the heir he had prayed for for so long. Now comes the climax of the whole Abraham cycle: "After these things God tested Abraham" (Gen 22:1).

Abraham was ordered to take Isaac to the land of **Moriah** and offer him there as a burnt offering. The ancient rabbis refer to this event as the *Aqedah* or Binding of Isaac, because Abraham "bound" his son for sacrifice (Gen 22:9). The ordeal is deliberately staged by God to test the faith of Abraham (CCC 145, 2572).

Obedient in his faith, Abraham prepared to make the sacrifice. His hand was stayed, however, and God gave him a ram to use as a burnt offering in the place of his son.

Now God gave Abraham a third promise, one that serves as the climax of the Abrahamic narrative (Gen 22:16–18): "Because you have done this, and have not withheld your son, your only son, I will indeed bless you,

and I will make your offspring as numerous as the stars of heaven and as the sand that is on the seashore. And your offspring shall possess the gate of their enemies, and by your offspring shall all the nations of the earth gain blessing for themselves, because you have obeyed my voice." (*For more on the binding of Isaac, see* **Isaac**.)

E. The End of Abraham's Life

Among the last acts of Abraham were the burial of Sarah (Gen 22:19–20), the arrangement of Isaac's marriage (24:1–9), and Abraham's own marriage to Keturah. This second wife bore him Zimran, Jokshan, Medan, Midian, Ishbak, and Shuah. From these sons descended great tribes and nations that settled in the Arabian Peninsula (e.g., the Midianites). Nevertheless, Abraham bequeathed all that he had to Isaac, except for gifts he gave to the sons of his concubines (Gen 25:1–6). Abraham died at the age of 175 and was buried in the cave of Machpelah (Gen 25:7–11). The details of his story are consistent with what ancient Near Eastern archaeology and literature tell us about the cultural and religious milieu of the early second millennium.

II. THE ABRAHAMIC COVENANT

A. Three Promises

The Lord made three promises to Abram: [1] "I will make of you a great nation"; [2] "I will bless you, and make your name great, so that you will be a blessing. I will bless those who bless you, and the one who curses you I will curse"; and [3] "in you all the families of the earth shall be blessed" (Gen 12:2–3). These three promises outline the entire future course of salvation history (CCC 59, 72, 762).

The three promises of the blessings correspond to the narrative sequence of the three covenant episodes in Genesis (in chaps. 15, 17, and 22 respectively). The blessing of Abraham's descendants as a nation is implied in the episode of the divided animals (Gen 15); the blessing of a dynasty in Abraham's great name is a central theme in the circumcision covenant (Gen 17); and the blessing to all nations is seen in the promise made after the events on Moriah (Gen 22:16–18).

B. The Abrahamic Covenant Anticipates Later Covenants

Seen in the wider context of covenant history, the Abrahamic covenant anticipates the pattern of divine dealings with Israel and the nations in salvation history and the gradual fulfillment of the covenants in the Mosaic, Davidic, and New covenants:

The promise of *land and a nation* is more fully realized in the Mosaic covenant, through which Israel—Abraham's descendants—became a nation. The promised land is significant because it is the place where God will be worshipped in truth.

The promise of *a kingdom and a dynasty* anticipates the Davidic covenant, in which God promised an everlasting dynasty and a kingdom that would lead the nations.

The promise of *universal blessing* will be fulfilled in Jesus Christ, the mediator through whom the blessings of Abraham's righteousness and faith reach the Gentiles and all nations (CCC 72, 422, 705, 706, 992, 1222, 1716, 1725, 2571, 2619).

Abraham is himself a type foreshadowing Israel. He goes to Egypt, where Pharaoh claims Sarah, triggering divine judgment in the form of plagues. He leaves Egypt and resettles in Canaan. Abraham's story is a prefiguration of what Israel would undergo at a corporate, national level in the Exodus.

III. ABRAHAM'S FAITH AND OBEDIENCE

A. The Model of Faith

Abraham is the model of faith for all God's people (cf. 1 Macc 2:52). He proclaimed his faith in the Lord in many ways (cf. Gen 14:22; 15:14; 17:1; 18:25; 21:33; 24:3) and was above all obedient to the command he was given. On faith he set out from Ur (Gen 11:31, 15:7; cf. Acts 7:2–4), with an unknown land as his destination. Led by God's prompting, he continued in migrations covering many hundreds of miles, beset often by plagues, famine, and hostile men. When God told him he would have an heir—and even descendants as numerous as the stars—he believed God. Abraham proved his faith ultimately by his willingness to sacrifice his own son, even when he knew that such an act would render impossible the very promises that had been made to him by God. He trusted that, if necessary, God would raise his son from the dead (Heb 11:19).

In a deepening relationship, God called Abraham to make increasingly greater sacrifices and greater acts of faith—first sacrificing his homeland, then his own flesh (in circumcision), and then his beloved son.

It is precisely because Abraham exercised

this highest degree of faith that God swears his oath to bless all nations through Abraham.

B. Abraham, the Friend of God

The faith of Abraham found expression in his dedicated monotheism, a devotion that placed him in contrast both with his contemporaries and with his own ancestors (Josh 24:2). He built altars to the Lord and called upon his name (Gen 12:8; 13:4, 18). He also enjoyed a deeply personal communion with the Lord (Gen 18:33, 24:40, 48:15; Exod 6:3), received special visions (Gen 15:1), and showed hospitality to the divine when it appeared in human and angelic form (Gen 18:1; 22:11, 15). Abraham likewise used his special relationship not for his own benefit but for the assistance of others, such as Ishmael (Gen 17:20) and Lot (Gen 18:27–33), and most strikingly for the benefit of the people of Sodom. When God informed Abraham that Sodom would be destroyed, Abraham negotiated with God, finally winning an agreement that Sodom would be spared even if only ten righteous people were found there. (*For more on the destruction of Sodom and Gomorrah, see* **Sodom**.)

IV. ABRAHAM IN THE NEW TESTAMENT

A. Who Is a Descendant of Abraham?

The New Testament begins with Matthew tracing the genealogy of Jesus Christ back to Abraham (Matt 1:1–17). As the founder of the faith of the Israelites, Abraham is also the human founder of the Christian faith.

The NT, following a precedent set by Jesus himself, is careful to distinguish what it means to be a descendant of Abraham.

On the one hand, Abraham is the direct ancestor of the Jews in particular. Thus Jesus calls Zacchaeus "a son of Abraham" (Matt 19:9), and a Jewish woman who came to be cured "a daughter of Abraham" (Luke 13:16).

On the other hand, when some of the Jews boast that "Abraham is our father," Jesus warns them that genealogy is not enough to make them descendants of Abraham. "If you were Abraham's children, you would do what Abraham did, but now you seek to kill me, a man who has told you the truth which I heard from God; this is not what Abraham did" (John 8:39–40). Nominally, all the Jews are descendants of Abraham, but to be a *true* descendant of Abraham requires having Abraham's faith.

Genealogical descent from Abraham is not determinative of Abrahamic sonship; what is crucial—even indispensable—is holding the faith of Abraham and living by his example. "Bear fruit that befits repentance," John the Baptist warned the Pharisees and Sadducees, "and do not presume to say to yourselves, 'We have Abraham as our father'; for I tell you, God is able from these stones to raise up children to Abraham" (Matt 3:8–9).

B. The Promise of Universal Blessing Fulfilled

But if it is faith that matters, rather than genealogy, then faithful Gentiles might also claim Abraham as their father. This is exactly the radical conclusion Paul comes to: "Thus Abraham 'believed God, and it was reckoned to him as righteousness.' So you see that it is men of faith who are the sons of Abraham" (Gal 3:6–7).

"Men of faith" come from all nations, for

God promised that in Abraham all the nations would be blessed. "And the scripture, foreseeing that God would justify the Gentiles by faith, preached the gospel beforehand to Abraham, saying, 'In you shall all the nations be blessed.' So then, those who are men of faith are blessed with Abraham who had faith" (Gal 3:8–9). In Jesus Christ, the promise of the Abrahamic covenant is perfectly fulfilled.

C. Abraham, the Model of Faith

"Abraham believed God, and it was reckoned to him as righteousness" (Rom 4:3): this is the centerpiece of Paul's theology of **justification**. Paul carefully points out that Abraham's faith "was reckoned to him as righteousness" before Abraham was circumcised. It is not "works" of the Law but faith that brings righteousness.

James uses exactly the same quotation (Jas 2:23) to counter those who twisted Paul's arguments into an excuse for not doing good works. He recalls Abraham's willingness to sacrifice Isaac: "You see that faith was active along with his works, and faith was completed by works" (Jas 2:22). Abraham's faith requires doing what God commands: "For as the body apart from the spirit is dead, so faith apart from works is dead" (Jas 3:26).

ABRAHAM'S BOSOM

Also "Abraham's embrace." In Jesus's parable of the rich man and Lazarus (Luke 16:22), Abraham's bosom is a resting place for the righteous dead, separated from the sufferings of the unrighteous dead. In Jesus's time, it was usual for diners to recline on couches at table. Normally, guests leaned on their left elbows and used the right arm to eat or drink. By such an arrangement, the head of one diner was said "to rest in the bosom" of the other, and a place of honor was recognized for the guest who rested in the bosom of the host of the feast (cf. John 13:23). Thus to be in Abraham's bosom was to be honored after death. The Fathers of the Church understood "Abraham's bosom" to be the abode of the righteous dead of Old Testament times before they were granted the beatific vision after the death of Jesus—so Abraham's bosom was an Old Covenant **type** of the heaven of the New Covenant. (*See also* **Death**; **Heaven**; **Sheol**.)

ABRAM

The original name of Abraham. (*See* **Abraham**.)

ABRONAH

A site near Ezion-geber at the northern tip of the Gulf of Aqaba. It was used by the Israelites as a stopping point during their wanderings in the wilderness (Num 33:34–35).

ABSALOM

(Hebrew, "the father is peace") The third son of David; his mother was the foreigner Maacah, daughter of Talmai, king of Geshur (2 Sam 3:3; 1 Chr 3:2). When Absalom's full sister, Tamar, was raped by his half brother Amnon (2 Sam 13), Absalom planned and achieved bloody revenge by luring Amnon to his death at the festival at Baal-hazor, near Ephraim, during the time of sheepshearing (2 Sam 13:23–29). Absalom then fled to Geshur, where he remained for three years (2 Sam 13:30–39) until Joab, David's general and nephew, arranged for his return to the court (2 Sam 14). Even so, Absalom was not permitted into the presence of the king for two years (2 Sam 14:28), after which time some reconciliation was achieved (2 Sam 14:29–33).

Immediately after his reconciliation Absalom began to ingratiate himself with the people, and so acquired popularity while speaking against his father (2 Sam 15:1–6). At last, convinced of his own political strength, Absalom went to Hebron to proclaim himself king and so began a revolt (2 Sam 15:7–12). David fled from Jerusalem (2 Sam 15:13–16). At the urging of Ahithophel, one of David's former counselors, Absalom entered the city and took possession of his father's harem "in the sight of all Israel" (2 Sam 16:21–22)—a symbolic proclamation that he had replaced David as king. Ahithophel next called on Absalom to move immediately to finish off his father; this counsel was opposed by Hushai, who was secretly working for David. Absalom listened to the latter, and Ahithophel, sensing this to be a fatal error, hanged himself in despair (2 Sam 17:23).

Absalom marched at last across the Jordan to attack his father but was defeated in the forest of Ephraim. Absalom fled from the field upon a mule, but his hair—famous for its length and beauty (2 Sam 14:25–26)—became entangled in the branches of an oak tree. Contrary to David's orders, Absalom was slain by Joab. David mourned so bitterly for his dead son that Joab rebuked the king for neglecting his faithful followers (2 Sam 18:33; 19:1–4). Absalom was buried in a pit, although in his lifetime he had built a pillar to keep his name in memory (2 Sam 18:17–18).

ABYSS Also "the deep," "depth of the sea," or "bottomless pit." These terms are used primarily to mean a great depth (Wis 10:19; Job 38:16). The Greek *abyssos* is used some thirty times in the Septuagint as an equivalent of the Hebrew *tĕhôm* ("waters of the deep"), and in other senses to imply deep places and floods. In the New Testament, "abyss" is understood as the abode of the dead (Rom 10:7), as well as the abode of evil spirits (Luke 8:31). It is from the abyss, for example, that the beast emerges (Rev 11:7–8), and the angel who carries the keys of the abyss unleashes its destructive powers (Rev 9:1–2).

ABADDON is considered the angel of the abyss.

ACCO A Syrian seaport on the Mediterranean, north of Mount Carmel; best known now for the medieval fortress of Acre. While Acco is mentioned only sporadically in the Bible, its prominence is attested by other ancient sources.

Acco was founded by the Canaanites, but it later passed to the Phoenicians. It was allotted to the tribe of Asher (Judg 1:31), but it was not conquered. Sacked by the forces of Sennacherib the Assyrian (705–681 B.C.), it fell into the hands of Tyre and then the Seleucid kings of Syria. At the time of the Maccabees (1 Macc 5:15, 22, 55), it was the center of activity for Alexander and Tryphon (1 Macc 10:1, 39, 56–60; 11:22, 24; 13:12; 2 Macc 13:24). Under the Ptolemies, the name was changed to Ptolemais.

Pompey the Great conquered the city in 63 B.C., and Emperor Claudius (d. A.D. 48) granted Roman municipal rights to the town; hence it received the name Colonia Claudii

Ptolemais (Caesaris). Saint Paul visited its nascent Christian community (Acts 21:7).

ACCOMMODATED SENSE *See* "Senses of Scripture" *under* **Interpretation of the Bible**.

ACELDAMA *See* **Akeldama**.

ACHAB *See* **Ahab**.

ACHAIA The region of lower Greece south of the Gulf of Corinth (also spelled "Achaea"). The territory was conquered by the Romans in 146 B.C. following the defeat of the Achaean League. The Romans placed Achaia under the control of the province of **Macedonia**. In 27 B.C., Emperor Augustus declared Achaia a senatorial province under the massive reorganization of the empire. The Romans often considered Achaia to be synonymous with Greece itself, especially as the province encompassed the ancient and leading cities of **Athens** and **Corinth** (the provincial capital).

Achaia, and Corinth in particular, is mentioned frequently in the New Testament (Acts 18:27; Rom 15:26; 1 Cor 16:15; 2 Cor 1:1, 9:2, 11:2; 1 Thess 1:7–8). Achaia was visited by Paul during his second (Acts 17:15; 18:18) and third (Acts 19:21) missionary journeys. The governor of the province at the time of Paul was a proconsul; the office was held by Gallio, brother of the philosopher Seneca (Acts 18:12).

ACHAICUS A Christian from Corinth. He was sent by the Corinthian Christian community to Saint Paul in Ephesus (1 Cor 16:17).

ACHAN A rebel Israelite in the days of Joshua. He was a member of the tribe of Judah (Josh 7:1) and the son of Carmi, son of Zabdi. God had forbidden taking any plunder from **Jericho** (Josh 6:18), but Achan took silver, gold, and a mantle of Shinar after the conquest and destruction of the city. When the Israelites were repelled in their next engagement, against Ai, Joshua prayed and was told that the defeat had happened because someone had violated the sacred ban on confiscating spoils from Jericho. Achan was discovered and confronted, and then confessed. The stolen goods were found buried beneath his tent. Joshua led Achan and his family into the Valley of **Achor**, where they were stoned to death and their possessions were burned (Josh 7:25–26).

ACHBOR A court official of King **Josiah**. In about 622 B.C., he was sent to the prophetess **Huldah** to consult with her about the book of the Law found in the Temple (2 Kgs 22:12, 14; in 2 Chr 34:20 he is known as Abdon).

ACHIOR According to Jdt 5:5–21, the commander of the Ammonites. Achior served under the general Holofernes and attempted to dissuade him from launching a campaign against the Israelites by recounting the conquest of Canaan and the acts of favor shown to the Israelites by God. Holofernes and his officers discounted Achior's warning and ordered him bound to be executed after the conquest of Bethulia. After Holofernes was beheaded by Judith, Achior declared his belief in the God of Israel, accepted circumcision, and became a member of the community of Israel (Jdt 14:10).

ACHISH The Philistine king of the city of Gath during the time of David; he is identified as the king of Gath in 1 Sam 27:2 and 1 Kgs 2:39. When he fled from Saul, David took refuge in Gath, but he was recognized as a dangerous military leader and pretended insanity to escape (1 Sam 21:10–13). David took refuge a second time in Gath, receiving from Achish the city of Ziklag. Achish placed his trust in David, so much so that David and his warriors were used as bodyguards. For his part, David conducted raids against the enemies of Israel in southern Palestine, although he reported to Achish that he had been raiding Judah (1 Sam 27:6–12). Achish placed such trust in David that he included him and his troops in the Philistine army gathered at Aphek for a campaign against Saul (1 Sam 29). The other Philistine leaders, however, refused to have David among them and demanded that he leave. David soon after became king of Judah and was no longer the vassal of Achish. Achish remained ruler over Gath for many years (1 Kgs 2:39–40) and was still king there in the early time of the reign of King Solomon.

ACHOR The valley where **Achan** and his family were stoned to death for plundering forbidden spoils from Jericho (Josh 7:24–26). Achor was located southwest of Jericho on the northern boundary of Judah, although the exact site is not known with certainty. The valley's name means "trouble," in memory of the trouble brought on Israel by Achan's thiev-ery. However, prophets later declared that this place of "trouble" would become a "door of hope" (Hos 2:15; cf. Isa 65:10).

ACHSAH The only daughter of **Caleb**; she was given in marriage as a prize to anyone able to capture the city of Keriath-sephir (Debir). She was then granted as wife to Othniel, Caleb's nephew, after his successful conquest of the city. Her dowry included a portion of the Negeb, but she also asked as a wedding gift from Caleb the upper and lower springs of Gullath, near Hebron (Josh 15:16–19; Judg 1:12–15).

ACHSHAPH A Canaanite city-state approximately ten miles southeast of **Acco** that entered into an alliance with Jabin of Hazor against Joshua and the Israelites (Josh 11:1–5). Joshua defeated that alliance near Merom (Josh 11:6–9; 12–20).

ACHZIB The name of two cities.

1. A city of Judah in the **Shephelah**, the low hills of western Palestine (Josh 15:44; also Mic 1:14).

2. A city of northwestern Palestine on the Mediterranean coast, approximately fourteen miles north of **Acco**. It enjoyed considerable early prominence and was given to the tribe of Asher (Josh 19:29). Asher did not displace the original Canaanite inhabitants, so they resided among them (Judg 1:31–32).

ACRE *See* **Acco**.

ACTS OF THE APOSTLES The fifth book of the New Testament. Traditionally accepted as the work of Saint **Luke**, the Acts of the Apostles is a continuation of the narrative of Luke's Gospel, presenting a history of the Church from the Ascension of Christ and the descent of the Holy Spirit to the period when Saint Paul preached in Rome.

I. Authorship and Date

II. Contents

III. Purpose and Themes

    A. The Holy Spirit

    B. Peter and Paul

    C. A Universal Church

    D. The Kingdom Restored

    E. History

I. AUTHORSHIP AND DATE

Tradition has always identified Acts as the work of Luke. His authorship has been attested by many Christian writers, including Saint Irenaeus, Tertullian, Saint Clement of Alexandria, Eusebius, and the Muratorian Canon. That Luke and Acts are by the same author is very likely: both writings are addressed to "Theophilus" (Acts 1:1; Luke 1:1–4); Acts mentions "the first book" at the beginning and then gives a brief summary of it (Acts 1:1–2). That the author of both books (unnamed in the books themselves) was Luke "the beloved physician" (Col 4:14) is strongly suggested by the medical details that sometimes appear in stories of healings (Acts 9:18, 28:6, 8; cf. Luke 4:38, 8:43–44). In several episodes in Paul's journeys, the author uses the first person ("we"), suggesting that he was actually part of the events recounted (Acts 16:10–17; 20:5–16; 21:1–8; 27:1–28:16). Considering both the unanimous voice of tradition and the indica-

tions in the work itself, it seems safe to call the author Luke.

Acts was most likely written around A.D. 63, which is when the narrative breaks off after Paul had been under house arrest in Rome for two years (Acts 28:30). There is no reference to the great fire of A.D. 64 in Rome that led to the great persecution of the Christians there—a persecution in which Peter and Paul, the chief protagonists of Acts, were heroically martyred. Nor is there any mention made of the destruction of Jerusalem by the Romans in A.D. 70, another momentous event for the early Church.

II. CONTENTS

Jesus himself gives the broad outline of the book in his last words to the apostles (Acts 1:8): "you will receive power when the Holy Spirit has come upon you; and you will be my witnesses in Jerusalem, in all Judea and Samaria, and to the ends of the earth." This is exactly the course the narrative follows. The apostles preach in Jerusalem (chaps. 1–7), extend the proclamation of the Gospel to Judea and Samaria (chaps. 8–12), and then take the message to the Gentiles, ending up at Rome, the capital of the world (chaps. 13–28):

I. Preface (1:1–5)

II. Up to the Coming of the Holy Spirit (1:6–2:13)

    A. The Ascension of Christ (1:6–11)

    B. The Calling of Matthias (1:12–26)

    C. Pentecost (2:1–13)

III. In Jerusalem (2:14–8:3)

    A. The Preaching of Peter (2:14–47)

    B. Peter's Ministry (3:1–4:31)

    C. The Early Community (4:32–5:11)

III. PURPOSE AND THEMES

The stated purpose of Acts is to pick up where Luke's Gospel left off, telling us what happened after Jesus was "taken up" (Acts 1:2). But the book is more than a simple history: the events in it demonstrate that the Holy Spirit guides the Church. The rapid spread of the Good News is part of the divine plan, not merely the dedicated work of the apostles.

A. The Holy Spirit

Throughout the work, the author shows us the important role of the Holy Spirit in guiding the ministry of the apostles (Acts 2:1–13; 5:12–16; and 8:26–40). The Spirit makes possible the stunning success of the Gospel across the Roman world and the development of the Church in the cities of the empire (cf. Acts 2:41, 47; 4:4, 31; 6:7; 13:2; 15:8, 28; 16:6–10; 20:23).

B. Peter and Paul

The title "Acts of the Apostles" was given to the book at least by the second century A.D., but the book focuses chiefly on two main apostles: Peter and Paul. The entire book can, in fact, be divided into two major sections, the first following the leadership of Peter (chaps. 1–12) and the second the labors of Paul (chaps. 13–28). On the one hand, the book presupposes Peter's unquestioned authority as leader of the Church; on the other hand, a series of literary parallels shows that Paul also has apostolic authority. Both Peter and Paul, for example, preach their first sermons on the fulfillment of the Davidic covenant (Acts 2:22–36; 13:26–41). Both heal men who are crippled (Acts 3:1–10; 14:8–10). Both confer the Holy Spirit by the laying on of hands (Acts 8:14–17; 19:6). Both confront magicians (Acts 8:18–24; 13:6–11). Both raise the dead (Acts 9:36–41; 20:9–12). Both are hailed as gods but refuse to accept divine worship (Acts 10:25–26; 14:11–15). Both are freed miraculously from jail (Acts 12:6–11; 16:25–34). With these parallels, Luke presents a strong case to authenticate the apostleship of Paul.

Luke was aware (as a companion of the

apostle, Acts 16:10) that there were those who denied Paul's claim to apostleship (cf. 2 Cor 11:4–6, 12:11; Gal 6:12). This book is Luke's clear answer to those people. Luke leaves no question in the minds of his readers that Paul was called by Jesus and sent as his messenger to proclaim the Good News (Acts 9:1–19; 22:3–16; 26:2–18) to every nation.

C. A Universal Church

In the thirty-some years covered by Acts, the Church spreads from Palestine to Italy. Credit for this immense achievement of evangelization is due to Paul's three missionary journeys: Cyprus and Asia Minor (Acts 13:1–14:28); Asia Minor, Greece, and Ephesus (Acts 15:36–18:22); and Ephesus and the western coast of Asia Minor (Acts 18:23–21:15).

But the quick spread of the Good News brought up vital questions: Did a follower of Christ need to convert to Judaism? Did Gentile converts need to be circumcised and follow the whole **Law** of Moses, including all the ritual actions proper to the Old Covenant?

The questions come to a head almost exactly in the middle of the book of Acts. At the Council of Jerusalem, the apostles, led by Peter, proclaim that the Church is open to all. It is not a national Church but a universal one.

Throughout Acts we see this conclusion as guided by the Holy Spirit. **Stephen**, the first martyr, who was "full of the Holy Spirit" (Acts 7:55), declared that the Law and Temple could be dispensed with through the coming of Christ. Peter's rooftop vision declared all foods clean (Acts 10:9–17). The Holy Spirit led Peter to **Cornelius**, a Gentile, and the Spirit came to the Gentiles at Cornelius's house before Peter decided to baptize them (Acts 10:44–48; 11:15–16). Thus the ritual actions distinctive to Judaism are set aside in the New Covenant because they no longer serve their original purpose of making Israel separate and distinct from the Gentiles.

D. The Kingdom Restored

Luke presents the universal Church, not as a new idea, but as the fulfillment of the covenant with **David**. The Church is the long-promised restoration of the Davidic kingdom, as well as the Kingdom of God in history.

At the start of Acts, the apostles ask the risen Jesus, "Lord, will you at this time restore the kingdom to Israel?" (Acts 1:6). Here they still seem to be thinking of a political kingdom. But with the coming of the Holy Spirit at Pentecost, Peter is able to understand—and explain to the crowd—how the promises made to David are fulfilled only in Jesus Christ (Acts 2:25–36). Paul makes the same argument in his first sermon (Acts 13:34–37). And when James sums up the conclusion of the Council of Jerusalem, he remembers the words of the prophets, who foretold that the kingdom of David would be restored "that the rest of men may seek the Lord, and all the Gentiles who are called by my name" (Acts 15:17).

E. History

Even as we appreciate Luke's profound *interpretation* of history, we should not forget that his intent was to write history. He interprets the events, but he records them accurately and with acute observation. Acts is immensely valuable to us as a record of the very beginnings of Christianity. For many events it is our only source; but wherever it intersects with the other historical records we have, we can confirm that Luke was an uncommonly accurate historian who took care to get his facts straight. Luke's skill in description is evident everywhere: in a few brief strokes he gives us a vivid portrait of **Athens** in its dotage (Acts 17:16–33), and his description of a shipwreck (chap. 27) is one of the finest pieces of nautical writing we have from the ancient world. The more we know about the times from archaeology and scholarship, the more apparent it becomes that Acts is a reliable record of actual historical events.

ADADAH A town in southern Judah (Josh 15:22).

ADAH (Hebrew, "ornament") The name of two women in the book of Genesis.

1. One of the two wives of Lamech (Gen 4:19). She was the mother of Jabal and Jubal (Gen 4:21–23).

2. The daughter of Elon the Hittite and the wife of Esau (Gen 36:2, 4, 10, 12, 16).

ADAIAH The name of several men in the Old Testament.

1. The father of Maaseiah, a leader of the "hundreds" used by Jehoiada the priest in his uprising against Queen Athaliah (2 Chr 23:1).

2. The grandfather of King Josiah (2 Kgs 22:1); he was from Bozkath.

3. The son of Jeroham, of the family of Malchijah (1 Chr 9:12; Neh 11:12); he served as a priest.

Other individuals by this name are men-

tioned in 1 Chr 6:41, 8:21; Ezra 10:29, 39; Neh 11:5.

ADAM The first human being; his name in Hebrew is both a personal name and a common noun meaning "human being" or "mankind." Thus he is himself the archetypal man and the father of humanity. In Genesis he is referred to as "the man" until Gen 3:17, when the word *Adam* is first used as a proper name. The meaning of the name is subject to uncertainty, but the etymology suggests a connection with the root ʾdm, "red," perhaps referring to the color of human skin. Genesis 2:7 and 3:19 involve a wordplay between ʾādām and ʾădāmâ ("ground, earth"), showing the connection between the first man and the earth from which he was made (Sir 33:10). Adam's wife, Eve, was created from his rib (Gen 3:21–22). Eve bore Adam's children: Cain, Abel, Seth, and others who are unnamed in Scripture (Gen 5:4). According to Gen 5:5, Adam lived 930 years.

I. Adam in the Old Testament
  A. The Vocation of Adam
  B. The Testing of Adam
II. Adam in the New Testament

I. ADAM IN THE OLD TESTAMENT

A. The Vocation of Adam

In the first creation narrative, Adam and Eve were created by God in the divine image and likeness (Gen 1:26). In ancient Near Eastern literature, the "image" motif is commonly associated with kings, who required that vassal states or provinces prominently display an image of the king as a symbol of his dominion. Created in God's image, Adam and Eve are given dominion over all the earth and sky. They are established as vice-regents who rule creation under the authority of God.

"Image and likeness" also connote sonship. In successive verses, Gen 5:2–3, God creates man "in the likeness of God," and Adam then begets a son "in his likeness." Thus as Seth is a son of Adam, Adam is analogously a son of God.

This divine image implies that man resembles God in ways that set him above the animals. He possesses intelligence, conscience, and a capacity for communion with God (CCC 343, 355–58).

Adam's vocation is exalted, though he has been called forth from humble matter. God "formed man from the dust of the ground, and breathed into his nostrils the breath of life; and the man became a living being" (Gen 2:7). In this way, Adam received a soul that animated his body, making him a combination of matter and spirit (CCC 362–66). The infusion of the soul, as the Church teaches, filled Adam with natural life as well as the supernatural life of holiness and justice, so that Adam was in harmony with himself, with the created order, and with the Creator who made him (CCC 374–76). He was to share in a covenant relationship that would unite the whole human family with God in a state of blessing.

Adam was thus more than a mere creature. From the first moment, he stood in God's presence as an adopted son of the divine Father. His vocation was to exercise dominion over creation. The sign of God's covenant with creation was the Sabbath, the seventh day of crea-

tion (cf. Gen 2:2–3; Exod 31:12–17). Indeed, the Hebrew word "to swear a covenant" (in Hebrew, *šābaʾ*) is related to the Hebrew word for "seven" (*šebaʾ*).

The first covenant established between God and creation was intended to unite the human family with God in a state of blessing (CCC 288). Several details in Genesis suggest that the Garden of Eden was the primeval sanctuary and Adam the first priest. The description of the Garden resembles, in many ways, the biblical accounts of the Tabernacle and Temple of later times. Both are entered from the east (3:24; Exod 27:13; Ezek 47:1), home to angels (3:24; 1 Kgs 6:23–28), decorated with trees (2:9; Josh 24:26; 1 Kgs 6:29–32), the source of sacred waters (Gen 2:10; Ezek 47:1–12; Joel 3:18), and the place where God walks upon the earth (Gen 3:8; Lev 26:12; 2 Sam 7:6). God placed Adam in the garden to "till and keep" it (Gen 2:15). This same pair of words (in Hebrew, *ʿābad* and *šāmar*) appears elsewhere in the Law to describe the ritual duties of the priests and Levites of Israel (Num 8:26, translated "minister" and "keep" in the RSV). That he was to "keep" (a better translation might be "guard") the garden suggests that he should be ready to defend it from a powerful enemy and protect it from desecration. The implication of these cultic details is that man is made for worship.

Adam was also made for companionship with his wife, Eve, as her husband and protector.

Having established Adam in the Garden of Eden, God marked out the limits of obedience: "You may freely eat of every tree of the garden; but of the tree of the knowledge of good and evil you shall not eat, for in the day that you eat of it you shall die" (Gen 2:17).

B. The Testing of Adam

A powerful enemy soon arrived, and Adam's obedience faced a test, a trial, an ordeal. Adam failed to fulfill his duty and vocation (Gen 3:1–7). Confronted by the serpent—who was Satan in disguise (Rev 12:9)—Adam abused the freedom given to him. Instead of defending the garden (and his wife) from the enemy, he ruptured the covenant by rebellion. Eve was tempted first, but Adam was there, too. The Hebrew text of Gen 3:6 states that the woman gave the fruit to her husband, "who was with her." Moreover, in the Hebrew text of Gen 3:4–5, the serpent speaks in the plural to both Eve and Adam when telling them "You will not die." Adam was there, but he did nothing. He remained silent during the serpent's encroachment. He not only failed to help Eve resist temptation, but he fell to temptation himself. He failed to cooperate with grace and refused to offer himself sacrificially for his covenant bride, who was in danger from the lies of the serpent. In his sin Adam preferred himself to God and wanted to be like God (CCC 397–98).

As the father of the human family, Adam turned away from God on behalf of all mankind. His rebellion was thus a representative act that not only injured him personally, but dragged all of humanity into suffering and separation from God.

The Fall transformed the covenant blessings into covenant curses (Gen 3:16–19). But with the curses came a promise—what the Fathers of the Church called the "Protevangelium," or "first Gospel." In cursing the serpent, God promised that the "seed" of the woman would overcome the serpent in the future, though not without sacrifice: "he shall bruise your head, and you shall bruise his heel" (Gen 3:15).

Driven from the Garden of Eden (Gen 3:22–24), Adam and Eve lived to see evil fill the world, beginning with the murder of their son Abel by his brother Cain (CCC 400, 1609). According to Genesis, Adam lived to the age of 930.

The OT says very little else about Adam. There is a passing reference in a genealogy at 1 Chr 1:1. In Tob 8:6, Tobias situates the origin of marriage with Adam and Eve. Sirach invokes Adam as the common ancestor of humanity (Sir 33:10; 40:1) and calls him "honored . . . above every living being in the creation" (Sir 49:16).

In the intertestamental literature, Adam returned intermittently as the focus of Jewish speculative thought.

II. ADAM IN THE NEW TESTAMENT

It is in the New Testament, however, that Adam rises to theological prominence.

Luke (3:38) traces Jesus's ancestry back to Adam, thus indicating a radical and universal mission of redemption, a restoration and fulfillment of God's original covenant with creation. John's gospel begins by drawing literary parallels between Jesus's origins and Adam's, "in the beginning" (John 1:1, Gen 1:1). In Matt 19:4 and 8, Jesus speaks of Adam and Eve as the exemplars of lifelong monogamy, with greater authority than Moses's provisional legislation that permitted divorce.

For the Christian, the tragedy of Adam's sin is reversed by the redemptive obedience of Christ. Saint Paul identifies Adam as a "type" of Christ (Rom 5:14). Following Paul, the Church Fathers noted many parallels between Adam and Jesus. Both men are sons of God whose vocation was to establish God's family upon earth. Both men entered the world in a state of purity and grace. The disobedience of Adam led the world to catastrophe; the obedience of Christ repaired the damage. The actions of these two men reverberate through all humanity and all the cosmos. All of creation is either disturbed or restored through the actions of these men. Adam's legacy is death; Christ's is life.

Where Adam failed, Christ succeeded. By his suffering and death upon the Cross, Christ canceled the rebellion of Adam and repaired the damage done by sin (Rom 5:12–21; 1 Cor 15:20–22, 45–49). Christ is the "Last Adam" who is perfectly obedient, even to death.

Paul develops the typology of Adam at length in Rom 5:12–21. He compares and contrasts Christ and Adam. Sin and death came into the world through the rebellion of one man; they are defeated by the perfect obedience of one man, Jesus Christ. Through abundant grace, Jesus Christ overcomes our many sins to bring life, where Adam's single sin brought death to all. "For as in Adam all die, so also in Christ shall all be made alive" (1 Cor 15:22).

The coming of Christ gives mankind the chance to escape from the curse. "The first man was from the earth, a man of dust; the second man is from heaven. As was the man of dust, so are those who are of the dust; and as is the man of heaven, so are those who are of heaven. Just as we have borne the image of the man of dust, we will also bear the image of the man of heaven" (1 Cor 15:45–49; cf. Heb 5:7–9).

ADAR The twelfth month of the Hebrew calendar, corresponding to February/March (Ezra 6:15). During Adar the feast of Purim was celebrated (Esth 9:17, 19, 21).

ADASA A town on the main highway between Jerusalem and Beth-horon (according to Flavius Josephus, *Ant.* 12.10.5); probably modern Khirbet Addaseh. Judas Maccabeus defeated the Seleucid general Nicanor in 161 B.C. at Adasa (1 Macc 7:40–45).

ADMAH One of the "cities of the plain" near the southern end of the Dead Sea (Gen 10:19); it was destroyed with Sodom. The ruler of Admah, Shinab, joined in an alliance with other local kings—notably of Sodom, Gomorrah, and Zeboiim—against the foreign kings of Shinar, Ellasar, Elam, and the Goiim. The Lord rained fiery judgment on Admah along with Sodom and Gomorrah "and all the valley" (Gen 19:25). Admah is mentioned with Zeboiim (Deut 29:23; Hos 11:8) as a model of the fate of those who defy the Lord and revel in wanton iniquity.

ADONAI *See* **God.**

ADONIBEZEK The Canaanite king of Bezek who was defeated and mutilated by the tribe of Judah. Adonibezek had his thumbs and toes cut off because he had mutilated seventy other kings. He was then taken to Jerusalem, where he died (Judg 1:5–7). Some scholars think that Adonibezek may be the same as **Adonizedek**, king of Jerusalem in Josh 10:1, but this is unlikely.

ADONIJAH (Hebrew, "my Lord is Yahweh") The fourth son of David, born at Hebron of his wife Haggith (2 Sam 3:4). When King David was very old, Adonijah tried to take the throne before Solomon, his younger brother and the designated heir, could be installed. Adonijah was supported in his court intrigue by **Joab** and the priest **Abiathar**, but Solomon counted among his party **Bathsheba, Zadok, Nathan**, and **Benaiah** (1 Kgs 1:5–31).

When Adonijah was defeated, Solomon spared his life. But when Adonijah asked for the hand in marriage of **Abishag** the Shunammite, who had ministered to King David in his last days, Solomon interpreted the request as a backdoor scheme on Adonijah's part to claim the kingship by marrying the former wife of the king. Solomon therefore ordered Benaiah to put Adonijah and Joab to death; Abiathar was sent into exile (1 Kgs 2:13–25).

ADONIRAM (Hebrew, "my Lord is exalted") Also called Adoram and Hadoram. The son of Abda and the official in charge of the forced labor in the court of Kings David, Solomon, and Rehoboam (1 Kgs 4:6; 5:13, 14). Under King Rehoboam, Adoniram was sent to negotiate with the rebellious northern tribes of Israel, but he was stoned to death, and the break between Israel and Judah was never healed (1 Kgs

12:18; 2 Chr 10:18). It is possible that there was more than one official named Adoniram in the long reigns of David and Solomon.

ADONIZEDEK (Hebrew, "my Lord is righteousness") The Canaanite king of Jerusalem, during the time of Joshua's invasion. Adonizedek entered into an alliance with four other Canaanite kings of the region to wage war upon Gibeon after the town made peace with Joshua and the Israelites (Josh 10:1–26). Joshua rushed to the defense of Gibeon and defeated the Canaanite alliance, and the five kings were discovered hiding in a cave. All five were hanged on trees until sunset, and then buried in the cave in which they were found. Some scholars believe that **Adonibezek** in Judg 1:5–7 is the same person, but this is unlikely.

ADOPTION See **Covenant; Family**.

ADORAM See **Adoniram**.

ADRAMMELECH (Hebrew, "the Glorious One is King")

1. A deity worshipped by the Sepharvaim, a people settled by Sargon II of Assyria in central Palestine after the conquest of Samaria in 722 B.C. (2 Kgs 17:31). Adrammelech may be the same as **Hadad**, the Semitic storm god.

2. One of the sons of the Assyrian king **Sennacherib**. With his brother, Sarezer, Adrammelech murdered Sennacherib in 681 B.C. while their father was at prayer in the temple of Nisroch (2 Kgs 19:37).

ADRAMYTTIUM A seaport in Mysia, on the northwestern coast of Asia Minor; modern

Edremit, Turkey. While being taken to Rome, Saint Paul traveled from Caesarea to Myra on a ship whose home port was Adramyttium (Acts 27:1–6).

ADRIA The waters east and south of the Italian peninsula. In Roman antiquity the Sea of Adria was said to extend southwest to Sicily and Malta and southeast to the island of Crete. The ship carrying Saint Paul to Rome was wrecked while sailing through Adria (Acts 27:27).

ADRIEL The son of Barzillai the Meholathite and husband of **Merab**, daughter of Saul. Adriel was given Merab for his wife despite the fact that Saul had already promised her to David (1 Sam 18:19). To atone for the guilt of Saul, David later handed Adriel's five sons into the hands of the Gibeonites, who executed them (2 Sam 21:8).

ADULLAM A fortified town in Judah, southwest of Jerusalem (Josh 15:35), identified with the modern Tell esh-Sheik Madkar. Adullam was conquered by Joshua (Josh 12:15), and the town was part of the story of Judah and Tamar (Gen 38:1, 12, 20). David stayed in a cave of Adullam while seeking refuge from Saul (1 Sam 22:12), and again during the campaign against the Philistines. Three of David's "mighty men" penetrated into Philistine territory and returned to Adullam with water from the well or spring of Bethlehem (2 Sam 23:13; 1 Chr 11:15). Adullam was subsequently fortified further by King Rehoboam (2 Chr 11:7) as part of his preparations for the defense of

Judah against an impending invasion by the Egyptian pharaoh Shishak; it was reoccupied after the Jews returned from the Exile in Babylon (Neh 11:30). It was also a place where Judas Maccabeus and his followers rested following their engagement with the governor of Idumea (2 Macc 12:38).

ADULTERY *See under* **Marriage**.

ADUMMIM A mountain pass, described as the "ascent of Adummim," on the road from Jericho to Jerusalem. It marked the boundary between Judah and Benjamin (Josh 15:7; 18:17). It was called Adummim, referring to redness or red rocks, because of its distinctive red limestone rock.

ADVOCATE *See* **Paraclete**.

AENEAS The name of a paralyzed man in Lydda who was bedridden for eight years before being healed by Saint Peter (Acts 9:33–35).

AENON A site on the west bank of the Jordan associated with the ministry of John the Baptist (John 3:23). The exact location of Aenon has not been identified. John the Evangelist locates it near Salim (John 3:23); Eusebius (*Onom.* 40.1–4) puts it south of Beth-shan.

AGABUS A Jewish-Christian prophet mentioned in Acts 11:27–30 and 21:10–11. While at Antioch, Agabus predicted that a terrible famine would strike the Roman Empire, a claim that was fulfilled during the reign of Emperor Claudius in A.D. 49. In the year 58, Agabus correctly predicted that Saint Paul would soon face imprisonment, although he could not convince the apostle to avoid Jerusalem (Acts 21:10–11). According to Christian tradition, Agabus was one of the seventy disciples chosen by Jesus (Luke 10:1), and one of the martyrs who died at Antioch. The *Roman Martyrology* listed his name on February 13.

AGAG The name of two Amalekite kings; it may be a throne name—the name of a dynasty of rulers—rather than a personal name. It is also possible that there is only one king, mentioned in two different times and places. The first is mentioned in Num 24:7, where Balaam predicts that the future kings of Israel will be more highly exalted than Agag. The second was an Amalekite ruler defeated by Saul. Because of the evil deeds of the Amalekites during the Exodus, God had commanded through the prophet Samuel that none of them should be spared (1 Sam 15:3). But Saul spared Agag's life (1 Sam 15:8–9). Samuel therefore pronounced God's judgment against Saul and then slew Agag himself "before the Lord" (1 Sam 15:32–33). (*See also* **Gog**.)

AGAPE *See under* **Love**.

AGORA The conventional name for the town center or town square during the Greco-Roman period. It was used especially as a gathering place for markets and civic assemblies (Matt 11:16, 20:3; Mark 6:56; Acts 16:19, 17:17).

AGRIPPA I *See* **Herod Agrippa I**.

AGRIPPA II *See* **Herod Agrippa II**.

AGUR The son of **Jakeh** and the author (or assembler) of a collection of proverbs (Prov 31:1). He was from the same land as Lemuel, king of Massa (Prov 31:1).

AHAB (Hebrew, possibly "father's brother") Son and successor of **Omri** and king of Israel from around 874 to 853 B.C. (although the dates of his reign are disputed among scholars). The chief source on his reign is 1 Kgs 16:29–22:40. His marriage to the pagan **Jezebel** brought him into conflict with the prophets of God, in particular **Elijah**, and this conflict dominates the account of his reign.

Politically, Ahab was an able king and administrator. When **Ben-hadad** of Syria invaded Israel and besieged Samaria, Ahab managed to defeat the invader (1 Kgs 20:1–21). The following year, Ben-hadad returned and was again defeated, this time at Aphek. Ahab spared his life, in return for which the Syrians restored cities that had been taken under Omri and accepted several commercial agreements that were favorable to the Israelites (1 Kgs 20:26–34).

But the political successes of Ahab are overshadowed in 1 Kings by his religious failures. Even his advantageous peace with Ben-hadad is shown to be contrary to the will of God: an unnamed prophet pronounces God's judgment against Ahab for letting Ben-hadad live (1 Kgs 20:35–43).

When Ahab wed **Jezebel**, daughter of Ethbaal of Tyre (1 Kgs 16:31), the union brought idolatry with it. In fact, Jezebel is often portrayed as the real power in Israel. Ahab gave official approval to the cults of Baal and Astarte and allowed Jezebel to persecute the prophets of God. The prophet Elijah stood firm in the defense of the true God and suffered persecution from Jezebel (1 Kgs 19:1–18). Elijah remained a critic of the king, even extracting penance from Ahab for his complicity in the scandalous episode of the vineyard of **Naboth** (1 Kgs 21).

Other prophets besides Elijah are mentioned in Ahab's reign. In just the account of Ahab's preparation for a war against the Arameans, we see four hundred court prophets in attendance to Ahab, Zedekiah son of Chenaanah, and Micaiah (1 Kgs 22:5–28). This last prophet, Micaiah, who "never prophesies good" for Ahab (1 Kgs 22:8), forecasts defeat, though the four hundred court prophets had forecast victory. Micaiah's prophecy came true, as Ahab died from wounds received in the war against the Syrians to recover Ramoth-gilead (1 Kgs 21:34–35).

AHASUERUS (Greek *Xerxes*) The king who made the Jewish woman Esther the queen of Persia; it is an alternate name for the Persian ruler Xerxes I (r. 486–465 B.C.). (*See under* **Xerxes** for details.)

AHAZ (A shortened form of the Hebrew name Ahaziah, meaning "Yahweh holds") King of Judah from around 735 to 715 B.C. and the son and successor of King **Jotham**. His reign is documented in several sources (2 Kgs 16; 2 Chr 28; and Isa 7).

Almost immediately after coming to the throne, Ahaz found himself faced with the rising threat of Assyria. King Rezin of Damascus and King Pekah of Israel pressured Ahaz to enter with them into an alliance against Tiglathpileser III (2 Kgs 16:1–6). When Ahaz declined their offer, the two kings tried to force his compliance by invading Judah and attacking Jerusalem. Ahaz sought the help of Assyria (2 Kgs 16:7–9), offering submission and tribute to **Tiglath-Pileser**. His policy was opposed vigorously by **Isaiah**, who counseled neutrality for the kingdom and trust in Yahweh (Isa 7:3). The Assyrians conquered northern Israel and the Transjordan in about 734 B.C. (2 Kgs 15:29) and Damascus in 732 B.C., and the vassal status of the king brought religious implications exemplified by syncretist tendencies and the spread of foreign cults (2 Kgs 16:10–18; 2 Chr 28:33). For this reason, Ahaz is judged harshly in the account of 2 Kings and 2 Chronicles.

AHAZIAH (Hebrew, "Yahweh holds")

1. The king of Israel (r. ca. 853–852 B.C.) and the son and successor of **Ahab**. Ahaziah reigned for barely one year (1 Kgs 22:40, 50, 52–54; 2 Kgs 1:1–18; 2 Chr 20:35, 37). The chief event of his reign was the failed joint commercial effort undertaken with **Jehoshaphat** of Judah to **Ophir** using a fleet of merchant vessels constructed at Ezion-geber (2 Chr 20:35; 1 Kgs 22:48). His reign was ended abruptly when he fell from a window. To recover from his injuries, he sought assistance from Baalzebul, the god of the city of Ekron. For this idolatrous superstition, he was condemned by **Elijah** and died soon after (2 Kgs 1:2–18).

2. King of Judah around 841, the son and successor of **Jehoram**. He succeeded to the throne at the age of twenty-two, and his brief reign was taken up chiefly in his campaign

against Syria in alliance with **Jehoram** of Israel. Jehoram, however, was killed and Ahaziah was gravely wounded during the rebellion of **Jehu**. Ahaziah fled, but died of his wounds at Megiddo (2 Kgs 9:27; cf. 2 Chr 22:7–9).

AHIJAH (Hebrew, "Yahweh is my brother or kinsman") A prophet from Shiloh who foretold that Solomon's kingdom would be divided and that **Jeroboam** would be king of the ten northern tribes (1 Kgs 11:29–31, 12:15; 2 Chr 10:15). Ahijah tore his robe into twelve pieces and handed ten of them to Jeroboam, symbolizing the division. The prophecy came true after Solomon's death, when the ten northern tribes rebelled against **Rehoboam**. But when Jeroboam turned to idolatry, Ahijah spoke out against him. Thus when Jeroboam's son fell ill and the king sent his wife to Ahijah to learn his son's fate, Ahijah forecast death (1 Kgs 14:2–18; 15:29–30) as well as the eventual extinction of Jeroboam's line. There are also seven other individuals with the name Ahijah in the Old Testament, including the son of Ahitub, the great-grandson of Eli, and a priest in Shiloh (1 Sam 14:3, 18–19); the son of Shisha, a scribe to King Solomon (1 Kgs 4:3); a member of the tribe of Judah (1 Chr 2:25); and a member of the tribe of Issachar and the father of King Baasha of Israel (1 Kgs 15:27, 33, 21:22; 2 Kgs 9:9).

AHIKAM (Hebrew, "my brother has risen") A court official under King **Josiah** and his two sons. The son of Shaphan (2 Kgs 22:12), a scribe, he was the father of Gedaliah (2 Kgs 25:22) and was among the officials sent by Josiah to the prophetess **Huldah** concerning the newly discovered book of law (2 Kgs 22:14; 2 Chr 34:20). He later protected **Jeremiah** from **Jehoiakim** (Jer 26:24). His son was governor of Judah under **Nebuchadnezzar** (ca. 587 B.C.) and was eventually assassinated (Jer 41:1–4).

AHIMAAZ

1. The son of the priest **Zadok** who remained loyal to King David during the rebellion of **Absalom**. Ahimaaz was given the task, with Jonathan, son of Abiathar, of bringing David the reports from Hushai concerning the plans of Absalom (2 Sam 15:27, 36; 17:20). Ahimaaz and Jonathan hid at En-rogel, and at one point took refuge in a well at Bahurim, with the help of a family who was supporting David (2 Sam 17:17–19). Ahimaaz requested the privilege of bringing to David the news of Absalom's death, but once he reached the king he was unable to bring himself to announce the event. Instead he proclaimed only the victory and left it to another messenger to announce Absalom's death (2 Sam 18:19–30).

2. One of the twelve officers or administrators of Solomon; he was in charge of the district of Naphtali, with the duty of supplying provisions for the king (1 Kgs 4:15). He was married to Basemath, a daughter of Solomon.

3. The father of Ahinoam, wife of Saul (1 Sam 14:50).

AHIMAN A descendant of Anak and one of the giants (the Anakim) of Hebron who lived in Palestine before the time of the Israelites (Num 13:22). He was driven out of Hebron by Caleb (Josh 15:14; Judg 1:10).

AHIMELECH (Hebrew, "my brother is king") The son of Ahitub, of the priestly house of **Eli**

(1 Sam 22:9), the father of **Abiathar** (1 Sam 30:7), and the high priest at Nob during the reign of Saul (1 Sam 21:1). Ahimelech gave sanctuary to David at the time he was fleeing from Saul (1 Sam 21:1–9) and offered the showbread (the holy bread of the sanctuary) to sustain David and his followers (Matt 12:3–4; Luke 6:3–4). He also gave David the sword of Goliath (1 Sam 21:1–10). Saul, however, was informed of Ahimelech's actions by Doeg the Edomite. In revenge, Saul ordered Ahimelech and all the priests at Nob to be massacred (1 Sam 22:11–19). The slaughter thus fulfilled the prophecy that the house of Eli would be extinct (1 Sam 2:27–36, 3:10–14; cf. Ps 52). Ahimelech's grandson, by the same name, became a priest with **Zadok** during the time of King David (2 Sam 8:17; 1 Chr 24:6).

AHINADAB One of the twelve officers or administrators of Solomon; he was in charge of the district of Mahanaim and had the duty of supplying provisions for the king (1 Kgs 4:14).

AHINOAM (Hebrew, "my brother is delight")

1. The daughter of Ahimaaz and the wife of King Saul (1 Sam 14:50). It is possible that she was the mother of all of Saul's children (1 Sam 14:49; 1 Chr 8:33, 9:39).

2. A wife of David, a woman of Jezreel, and the mother of David's firstborn, Amnon (2 Sam 3:2). She was with David on his visit to the Philistines (1 Sam 25:43; 27:3) but was captured in a raid by the Amalekites upon Ziklag (1 Sam 30:5). Rescued from her captivity, she went with David to Hebron (2 Sam 2:2); there David was crowned king of Judah (2 Sam 2:1–4).

AHIO A son of **Abinidab** and brother of **Uzzah** (2 Sam 6:3–4; 1 Chr 13:7). With Uzzah, Ahio helped to transport the ark of the covenant at the command of David. The ark was transported on a cart, with Uzzah walking at the side of the cart and Ahio leading the oxen. Uzzah was killed after touching the ark (2 Sam 6:6–7).

AHITHOPHEL A respected counselor in the court of King David (1 Chr 27:33). Ahithophel was originally from the town of Giloh in Judah and enjoyed a position of influence at the court. He turned his back on the king, however, and became a leading figure in the rebellion of **Absalom** (2 Sam 15:12). It was on his advice that Absalom seized and violated David's harem—symbolically laying claim to the kingship (2 Sam 16:20–22). Once David had fled, Ahithophel strategically deduced the value of pursuing David with troops and finishing him off quickly before the king had time to regroup. This plan, however, was overruled by Absalom, who instead heeded the advice of **Hushai**, a secret supporter of David. The latter urged Absalom to gather a larger force and to have the king himself, rather than Ahithophel, command the force (2 Sam 17:1–14). Ahithophel perceived that Absalom's chance for victory had passed and so committed suicide by hanging (2 Sam 17:23).

Ahithophel is never directly mentioned in the New Testament, but his treachery against David prefigures **Judas Iscariot**'s treachery against the Son of David, Jesus Christ. Both were trusted friends who betrayed the Lord's Anointed; both planned to send soldiers at night to capture their victims (2 Sam 17:1–4;

Matt 26:47–48); and both hanged themselves in a final act of despair (2 Sam 17:23; Matt 27:5).

AHITUB The father of **Ahimelech** (1 Sam 22:9) and **Ahijah** (1 Sam 14:3). Ahitub was the brother of Ichabod and the grandson of **Eli** the priest.

AHUZZATH An advisor to King **Abimelech** of Gerar (Gen 26:26–31). He accompanied the king in the effort to establish a covenant with Isaac.

AI (Hebrew, "the ruin") A city east of Bethel, usually identified with modern Et-Tell. Abram (the later **Abraham**) camped between Bethel and Ai on his journey into Canaan and established an altar there (Gen 12:8; 13:3). **Joshua** conquered the city after an initial failure caused by the disobedience of **Achan** (Josh 7–8).

AIJALON A town in the **Shephelah**, the western lowlands of Canaan, that was strategically important because of its location on a main road to Jerusalem. The city is listed as a possession of the tribe of Dan and a Levitical town (Josh 19:42; 21:24); for reasons that are partly unclear, it is later listed as a Levitical town of Ephraim (1 Chr 6:69) and a settlement occupied by Benjamin (1 Chr 8:13). Its strategic importance was attested by Joshua's victory over the alliance of Canaanite kings (Josh 10:12) and Saul's triumph over the Philistines (1 Sam 14:31). It was fortified by Rehoboam (2 Chr 11:10) and was captured by the Philistines in the reign of Ahaz (2 Chr 28:18).

AKELDAMA (Aramaic, "field of blood") A plot of land in the Hinnom Valley, south of Jerusalem, that was set aside as a place to bury strangers. The name Field of Blood became attached to the site after it was purchased for the burial of **Judas Iscariot**, who betrayed innocent blood. According to Acts 1:18, Judas died in the field, his blood and his bowels pouring out upon the ground. In the account recorded in Matt 27:3–10, the land was known originally as the Potter's Field and was purchased by the high priests with the "blood money" returned to them by Judas (cf. Zech 11:12–13).

AKKUB The name of four men in the Old Testament.

1. A son of **Elioenai** (1 Chr 3:24); he was of the royal line of David that survived after the **Exile**.

2. The head of a Levitical family that held the post of gatekeepers in the Temple (1 Chr 9:17; Ezra 2:42; Neh 7:45, 11:19, 12:25).

3. The head of a family of servants or slaves who served in the Temple (Ezra 2:45).

4. A Levite who interpreted the **Law** of Moses for laypeople in the days of **Ezra** (Neh 8:7).

AKRABATTENE A district in southern Judah, where Judas Maccabeus defeated the Idumeans (1 Macc 5:3).

ALCIMUS (Greek *Alkmos*) A high priest in Jerusalem who was leader of the Hellenizing party and an opponent of the revolt by Judas Maccabeus (1 Macc 7; 2 Macc 14). According to Josephus (*Ant.* 12.385), Alcimus was appointed high priest in Jerusalem by the Seleucid king Antiochus V Eupator around 162 B.C.; he was confirmed as high priest (ca. 161 B.C.) by Demetrius I Soter (1 Macc 7:5–7) and threw his support behind Bacchides, the general in charge of Syrian troops in the region. In return, Bacchides gave him protection. Alcimus was involved in the slaughter of sixty Hasideans (1 Macc 7:12–16) and was implicated in the atrocities of General Nicanor—the Greek military officer commissioned to suppress the Jewish revolt—and Bacchides. Alcimus was preparing to tear down the wall of the inner court of the Temple when he was stricken suddenly by paralysis and died around 153 B.C. (1 Macc 9:54–57). His torment and death were considered punishment for his impiety.

ALEMA A city in Gilead, east of the Jordan. A Hellenic community, Alema became a place of imprisonment for the Jewish population at the hands of the Gentiles until liberated by Judas Maccabeus (1 Macc 5:26–45).

ALEPH The first letter in the Hebrew alphabet (א). The letter א is also used to represent Codex Sinaiticus, an ancient Greek version of the Scriptures that dates back to the fourth century A.D. (*See also* **Languages of the Bible**.)

ALEXANDER BALAS Also known as Alexander Epiphanes, a usurper and later king of the Seleucids from 150 to 145 B.C. (1 Macc 10:1; 11:1–17; 15:21, 47–67, 88–89). Alexander was the son of **Antiochus IV** Epiphanes and hence the rightful heir to the throne (1 Macc 10:1), although many ancient historians doubted his legitimacy. In the subsequent struggle with Seleucid king **Demetrius I Soter**, Alexander won the assistance of **Jonathan Maccabeus** through his appointment of Jonathan as high priest (1 Macc 10:15–21, 47). When King Ptolemy VI of Egypt invaded Alexander's kingdom and won the support of Demetrius I, Alexander fled to Arabia, where he was beheaded by the chieftain Zabdiel (1 Macc 11:16–17).

ALEXANDER THE GREAT Mentioned by name only twice in the Bible (1 Macc 1:1–9; 6:2), Alexander left a major mark on the history of Asia Minor and Palestine through his campaign to spread the culture of **Hellenism** throughout the eastern Mediterranean world.

Alexander (356–323 B.C.) was one of the most successful conquerors in history. Succeeding to the throne in 336 B.C., he set out to end the perennial Persian threat against Greece. Ultimately he conquered not only Persia but also Asia Minor, Tyre, Gaza, Egypt, and even part of India. By the time he died his empire stretched from Greece to India and from Egypt to Asia Minor. His reign spread Greek ideas, customs, and language throughout Asia and the eastern Mediterranean; he is thus fittingly introduced as the backdrop for the story of the Maccabees (1 Macc 1–7).

The book of **Daniel** seems to allude to Alexander as the "great horn" (Dan 8:5–8) and the "mighty king" (Dan 11:3), although his name is never mentioned there.

ALEXANDER JANNEUS *See* **Hasmonean Dynasty**.

ALEXANDRIA A city of Egypt founded by **Alexander the Great** in 331 B.C. The city was established on the Mediterranean near Lake Mareotis on the site of the native Egyptian village of Rhakotis. Following the death of Alexander in 323 B.C., Egypt fell under the authority of the Macedonian general Ptolemy, who became Ptolemy I Soter and founded the Ptolemaic Dynasty. Alexandria became the capital of Egypt, although its distinctly Hellenic culture set it apart from the rest of Egypt. It remained the chief city of Egypt under the Romans. By the time of Roman occupation, the city was the foremost intellectual center in the ancient world and one of the principal cities of the entire Roman Empire.

There may have been a Jewish presence in Alexandria as early as Ptolemy I; there certainly was in the time of Ptolemy II in the third century B.C. By the first century A.D. there were perhaps as many as a million Jews in Egypt, many of them living in Alexandria. The city had the largest Jewish community of the **Dispersion**, and the community maintained close ties with Jerusalem, at least until the time of the destruction of the holy city in A.D. 70. It was in Alexandria that the Greek translation of the Hebrew Bible, the **Septuagint**, was undertaken (*see also* **Wisdom, book of**).

The exact date of the arrival of Christianity is not known with certainty, but early Christian tradition holds that Mark, the second evangelist, established the church in Alexandria by his preaching. Alexandria was mentioned in Acts as the home of **Apollos**, a companion to Paul on his journey to Rome (Acts 18:24). It was also the home port of several ships that transported Paul (Acts 27:6; 28:11). Alexandrian Jews had their own synagogue in Jerusalem and were counted among the opponents of **Stephen**, the first Christian martyr (Acts 6:9).

ALEXANDRINUS, CODEX *See under* **Codex**.

ALLEGORICAL SENSE *See* **Interpretation of the Bible**.

ALLELUIA *See* **Hallelujah**.

ALLIANCES *See* **Covenant**.

ALLON-BACUTH (Hebrew, "oak of weeping") A place near Bethel where Deborah, the nurse of Rebekah, was buried (Gen 35:8).

ALMIGHTY (Hebrew *šadday*) One of the names for God in the Hebrew Old Testament. El Shaddai, or God Almighty, was the name of God known in the patriarchal period (Gen 17:1, 28:3, 35:11; Exod 6:3). It was translated as *pantokratōr* in the Greek **Septuagint**, meaning "almighty, all-powerful."

ALMON-DIBLATHAIM A place that served as a campsite for the Israelites during their wanderings in the wilderness (Num 33:46, 47). The precise location is unknown.

ALMS Gifts, usually of money, given to the poor. The duty to give to the poor is not mentioned in the early books of the Old Testament; rather, it finds development in the later writings, in particular Tobit (4:6–11), Sirach (3:30–4:10; cf. Dan 4:24), and also in Proverbs (3:27; 22:9; 28:27). In the New Testament, Christ called upon his followers to give to the poor (Matt 6:2–4; Luke 11:41, 12:43) and noted that giving away one's possessions was a mark of authentic Christian discipleship (Matt 19:21; Mark 10:21; Luke 18:22). In Acts, **Tabitha** (Acts 9:36) and **Cornelius** (Acts 10:2) are praised for their almsgiving, and Paul speaks of almsgiving in Jerusalem (Acts 24:17). Such giving, however, is useless unless it is an expression of love (1 Cor 13:3).

ALOE An aromatic oil derived from the trees of southeast Asia and India. It was highly prized in Palestine and was used especially as a perfume (Prov 7:17). Aloe was used with myrrh to embalm the body of Jesus (John 19:39).

ALPHA AND OMEGA The first and last letters of the Greek alphabet (A, Ω). The expression is a divine title in the book of Revelation, where it means that everything in creation begins and ends with God, who is Lord of all (Rev 22:13). Compare Isaiah 41:4, 44:6, and 48:12, where the same idea is expressed.

ALPHABET *See* **Languages of the Bible**; *see also* **Greek**; **Hebrew**.

ALPHAEUS (Greek *Halphaios*) The father of the apostle **James the Less** (Matt 10:3; Mark 3:18; Luke 6:15; Acts 1:13). A man named Alphaeus is also mentioned as the father of Levi the tax collector (see **Matthew**), but this is almost certainly a different person from Alphaeus, the father of James (Mark 2:14).

ALTAR (Hebrew *mizbēaḥ*; Greek *thysiastērion*) A cultic platform used for sacrifice. In the Old Testament the term used is invariably *mizbēaḥ* (some four hundred times), derived from the root "to slaughter." Before the Law of Moses and the establishment of a national priesthood, erecting altars and performing ritual acts of sacrifice was the responsibility of the head of the family or clan, as we see in the stories of **Noah**, **Abraham**, and other patriarchs (Gen 8:20; 12:8; 13:18; 22:9). The oldest prescribed form of altar is in Exod 20:24–25, where the altar is to be made of earth or unhewn stone and without steps. The altar of the Tabernacle, described in Exod 27:1–8, is a square frame of acacia wood overlaid with bronze, with horns on the four corners. The enormous bronze altar in the forecourt of the **Temple** of Solomon (1 Kgs 8:64; 2 Chr 4:1) was also square. In the eighth century B.C. King **Ahaz** added the "great altar," based on what he had seen in Damascus. The great altar assumed the role of Solomon's altar for some unspecified period of time, but Ahaz kept Solomon's altar "to inquire by" (2 Kgs 16:10–16). The great altar was where regular sacrifices were conducted and was called the "altar of burnt offering." Solomon's altar was also sometimes called the Lord's "table" (Ezek 41:22; Mal 1:7, 12)—a name that would have particular significance in Paul's theology of the Eucharist (1 Cor 10:21).

There was also an incense altar in the Tabernacle and the Temple; it was overlaid with gold (1 Kgs 6:20; 1 Chr 28:18; 2 Chr 26:16–20).

Altars are mentioned several times in the New Testament (Matt 23:35; Luke 11:51; Rom 11:3; Jas 2:21), including reference to the altar in Herod's temple (Matt 23:18–20; 1 Cor 9:13). The sole direct reference to a Christian altar is in Heb 13:10. Most likely this refers to the Eucharistic altar of the Church (CCC 1182). (*See* **Liturgy**; **Sacrifice**.)

ALUSH A place that became a campsite for the Israelites in the wilderness during their wanderings toward Canaan (Num 33:13–14). It was situated between **Rephidim** and **Dophkah**, although its exact location is not known with certainty.

AMALEKITES A nomadic people remembered as one of the traditional enemies of Israel. They derived their name from Amalek, one of the six sons of Eliphaz and Timna, a grandson of Esau (Gen 36:11, 12; cf. 1 Chr 1:36), and one of the chiefs of Eliphaz in the land of Edom (Gen 36:15, 16). The Amalekites moved about in the Sinai Peninsula and in the **Negeb** of southern Canaan (1 Sam 15:5). The Old Testament shows them as determined enemies of the Israelites. They first attacked the Israelites during the passage out of Egypt at Rephidim (Exod 17:8) and again at Hormah (Num 14:45)—attacks that Israel was told not to forget (Exod 17:16; Deut 25:17–19).

The prophet Samuel ordered the recently anointed Saul to launch a war of extermination against the Amalekites and their king, **Agag**, fulfilling the orders of Deut 25:17–19. But when Saul failed to carry out the war to its conclusion—despite a great victory—he was punished (1 Sam 15:1–35). Later, Amalekites attacked Ziklag, burned the city, and carried off all of the women and children, including David's own family. In revenge, David pursued the Amalekites and defeated them, leaving alive only four hundred men. After that, the Amalekites all but disappear from history (cf. 1 Chr 4:43).

AMANA A mountain in the Anti-Lebanon range north of Palestine. It is situated near the Amana River (Song 4:8).

AMARIAH There are numerous men named Amariah in the Old Testament, most of them priests.

1. A descendant of Eleazar and Phinehas (1 Chr 6:7, 52) who became a priest.

2. A priest in the Temple of Solomon and the son of Azariah (1 Chr 6:10–11).

3. The second son of Hebron who was mentioned in the genealogy of the tribe of Levi (1 Chr 23:19; 24:23). He was also a cousin of Moses and Aaron.

4. A high priest during the reign of King Jehoshaphat. He served in the Temple in Jerusalem (2 Chr 19:11).

5. A Levite during the reign of King Hezekiah (2 Chr 31:15).

6. The great-grandfather of the prophet Zephaniah (Zeph 1:1).

7. A priest in the period of Nehemiah (Neh 10:3).

8. A Judahite whose great-grandson was a prominent figure in Jerusalem after the **Exile** (Neh 11:4).

AMASA A nephew of King **David**; the son of Ithra the Ishmaelite (2 Sam 17:25, or Jether the Ishmaelite, 1 Chr 2:17) and Abigail, the sister of David. Amasa supported **Absalom** in his rebellion against David, and Absalom named him commander of the army (2 Sam 17:25) in place of **Joab**, who had fled with the king. After the defeat of Absalom, Amasa sought to restore himself to King David's good graces, succeeding in part because of his efforts to convince the supporters of Absalom to return to David's cause (2 Sam 19:14). David retained him as head of the army in place of Joab, but when Amasa was sent to suppress an uprising of **Sheba**, the son of Bichri (2 Sam 20:4), Joab murdered Amasa at Gibeon (2 Sam 20:7–10). The body was left on the road until the troops passing by stopped to stare at the remains (2 Sam 20:12). Joab once more became head of the army until his own death at the hands of Benaiah for the murders of Amasa and Abner (1 Kgs 2:5, 32).

AMASAI The leader of David's thirty "mighty men" (1 Chr 12:18). Some scholars suggest that Amasai should be considered the same person as Amasa. Neither name is listed, however, in the roster of the thirty in 2 Samuel (23:18–39) and 1 Chronicles (11:26–47). There are several other individuals by the name of Amasai, including an ancestor of Samuel (1 Chr 6:25, 35); one of the priests who blew a trumpet to mark the return of the **ark of the covenant** to Jerusalem (1 Chr 15:24); and a Levite who helped to cleanse the Temple in the days of Hezekiah (2 Chr 29:12).

AMASIAH Son of Zichri, a soldier in the army of King **Jehoshaphat** of Judah (2 Chr 17:16). He was "a volunteer for the service of the LORD" and was named commander of a division of warriors from Judah.

AMAZIAH (Hebrew, "Yahweh is mighty") The son of **Joash** and the king of Judah (ca. 796–767 B.C.; 2 Kgs 14; 2 Chr 25). His reign began when his father was assassinated, and he ordered the assassins to be executed, although he permitted their sons to live (2 Kgs 14:5–6). The first significant event of his reign was his war against the Edomites in which he slaughtered ten thousand of the enemy in the Valley of Salt and killed ten thousand more by hurling them from the cliffs surrounding the valley (2 Chr 25:11–12). After the victory Amaziah brought back Edomite gods and began to worship them (2 Chr 25:14). The overconfident Amaziah then provoked a war with Jehoash, king of Israel (2 Chr 25:17–20), but Jehoash defeated him and brought him back to Jerusalem as a prisoner, tearing down part of the city wall and plundering the Temple. Nevertheless, Amaziah lived for fifteen years after Jehoash had died; eventually, like his father, he was assassinated by a court conspiracy (2 Kgs 14:17–20). He was succeeded by his son **Azariah**.

AMEN (Hebrew, "so be it," "so it is," or "it is true") A hallowed expression used extensively at the end of doxologies, prayers, blessings, and curses as an affirmation or acceptance of what has been said or gone before (Num 5:22; Deut 27:15–26; 1 Kgs 1:36; Jer 11:5; 28:6). "Amen" was a confirmation on the part of the speaker of the greatness of God (1 Chr 16:36; Neh 8:6). It was also used to confirm an oath (Num 5:22; Deut 27:15–26). "Amen" is especially significant in the Psalms (41:13; 72:19; 89:52; 106:48), where it affirms and emphasizes the praise of God.

In the New Testament, Jesus uses the word "Amen" (translated "truly" in the RSV) to give emphasis to his teachings (Matt 5:18, 26; 18:3; John 1:51). Outside of the Gospels, the term is used as a liturgical response by the congregation (1 Cor 14:16; cf. Rev 5:14, 7:12) and appears at the end of doxologies that proclaim God's glory (Rom 11:36; Gal 1:5; Eph 3:21). In Rev 3:14, Christ is called the "Amen" because he is the realization of all of the promises of God to humanity (2 Cor 1:20) (CCC 1061–65).

AMITTAI The father of **Jonah** the prophet (2 Kgs 14:25; Jonah 1:1). He came from Gath-hepher in Zebulun (lower **Galilee**).

AMMINADAB The father of Nahshon (Num 1:7; 2:3) and **Elisheba**, the wife of Aaron (Exod 6:23); and a leader of the tribe of Judah. He was named in the genealogies of David (Ruth 4:19–22) and Jesus (Matt 1:4; Luke 3:33). Another Amminadab was the head of the family of Uzziel and one of the Levites who assisted in transferring the ark to Jerusalem (1 Chr 15:10–11).

AMMIZABAD The son of **Benaiah**; he was a military officer in the time of King **David** (1 Chr 27:6).

AMMON *See* **Ammonites**.

AMMONITES Eastern neighbors of Israel who occupied a part of the Transjordan between the Arnon and Jabbok rivers. Scripture identifies them as descendants of Ammon, the son of Abraham's nephew Lot through an incestuous union with one of Lot's own daughters (Gen 19:36–38). In this way the Ammonites were related to the Israelites. They settled in the Transjordan by displacing the Rephaim (also called the Zamzummim; Deut 2:20) and encountered the Israelites during the Exodus (Num 21:24–35; Deut 2:16–37). They later joined an alliance with the **Moabites** and **Amalekites** against the Israelites during the period of the Judges (Judg 3:13), but the leader of the alliance was defeated by **Ehud** (Judg 3:15–23) and the Ammonites themselves were routed by **Jephthah** (Judg 11:32–33).

Saul defeated the Ammonites (1 Sam 11:1–15). David's relations with them were good at first, owing to the fact that they were both enemies of Saul. When the Ammonite king Nahash died, David sent ambassadors to "console" his son and successor Hanun. Hanun, however, treated David's ambassadors as spies and humiliated them (2 Sam 10:1–5). A long war followed (2 Sam 10:6–12:31), during which the incident of **Uriah** and **Bathsheba** took place. David finally routed the Ammonites and captured their chief city, Rabbah of the Ammonites (2 Sam 12:26–31).

After the Babylonian **Exile**, the Ammonites opposed the rebuilding of the walls of Jerusalem (Neh 2:19–20). That they remained politically significant well after the **Exile** is attested by the campaign of Judas Maccabeus (1 Macc 5:6).

AMNON (Hebrew, "faithful") The firstborn son of David; his mother was Ahinoam of Jezreel (2 Sam 3:2; 1 Chr 3:1). Amnon was born at Hebron. The prince developed an uncontrollable passion for his half sister Tamar, daughter of David and Maacah and thus the full sister of **Absalom**. Amnon eventually revealed his lust after feigning illness and requesting that David send Tamar to care for him (2 Sam 13:1–6). When Tamar refused his advances, Amnon raped her and then humiliated her further by throwing her out into the street (2 Sam 13:7–19). Absalom plotted revenge for the crime and brought his scheme to fruition two years later at a banquet celebrating the shearing of the flocks at Baal-hazor. When Amnon became drunk on wine, Absalom had him murdered (2 Sam 13:23–29). The murder was a significant foundation for the eventual breach between David and Absalom. This domestic chaos was the inevitable price of David's adultery and crimes as pronounced by **Nathan** (2 Sam 12:7–15).

AMON The son of **Manasseh** and king of Judah from around 642 to 640 B.C. (2 Kgs 21:19–26; 2 Chr 33:21–25). Amon is remembered for continuing his father's pro-Assyrian policy, and for endorsing his father's Assyrian-influenced idolatry (2 Kgs 21:20–22; 2 Chr 33:22). Amon was soon assassinated by a conspiracy in the palace and was replaced by his eight-year-old son **Josiah**.

AMORITES The name used for one of the nations inhabiting **Canaan** before the arrival of the Israelites (Gen 15:16, 19–21; Josh 7:10). Occasionally the name seems to designate all the peoples of Palestine in the time before the Israelites (Gen 15:16), but their relationship to the Canaanites is difficult to assess; Scripture usually refers to the Amorites as living in the

hills (Num 13:29) and the Canaanites as living in the valleys and plains (cf. Josh 5:1). The Amorite homeland was in northwestern Mesopotamia, in the region between Syria and Babylonia; many scholars posit an extensive migration of Amorites in the early second millennium B.C. to explain why the Amorites were distributed widely across Palestine. **Mamre**, an Amorite, was an ally of Abraham (Gen 14:13). At the time of Joshua, Amorite rulers were found in western Palestine (Josh 5:1), and the Amorites were defeated by the Israelites at Gibeon (Josh 10:1–19). Amorites also prevented the tribe of Dan from reaching the sea and kept control of the coastal plain (Judg 1:34–35).

AMOS, BOOK OF A collection of oracles attributed to an eighth-century B.C. prophet from Judah; the third of the twelve minor prophets. The prophet came from the southern kingdom of **Judah**, but his prophecies are addressed to the northern kingdom of **Israel**.

I. AUTHORSHIP AND DATE

Amos was a shepherd of Tekoa in Judah (Amos 1:1) and a "dresser of sycamore trees" (Amos 7:14). This background indicates that Amos was not a prophet by profession but gave his prophecies according to divine command. He lived during the reigns of King **Uzziah** of Judah and **Jeroboam II** of Israel during a time of relative peace and prosperity. The oracles date to the middle of the eighth century B.C., before the collapse of the northern kingdom. Nothing is known about the prophet except what is found in the book itself.

Traditionally, the book is attributed to

the prophet himself. Critical scholarship has reached no consensus in the matter, though many twentieth-century scholars envisioned an ancient core of Amos's oracles being supplemented over time by insertions and additions contributed by later editors (some before and some after the **Exile**). More recent scholarship has come to appreciate the book, not as a patchwork of original and supplemental material, but as a unified literary whole. Some are willing to grant that it represents the genius of Amos himself, written down in the eighth century B.C. by the prophet or one of his contemporaries.

II. CONTENTS

I. Introduction (1:1)

II. Judgments (1:2–2:16): Amos announces judgments upon Israel's neighbors, Judah, and Israel. The oracles speak against Damascus (1:3–5), Gaza (1:6–7), Tyre (1:9–10), Edom (1:11–120), Ammon (1:13–15), Moab (2:1–3), Judah (2:4–5), and Samaria (2:6–16). The judgments upon Judah and Israel are for transgressions of the divine law (2:4, 11–12).

III. Discourses (3:1–6:14): A series of discourses or addresses, each beginning with the formula, "Hear this word" (3:1; 4:1; 5:1). The purpose is to lament the sinfulness of Israel and its inevitable suffering because of its iniquities. The section contains the grim imagery of the day of the Lord, asking, "Is not the day of the LORD darkness, not light, and gloom with no brightness in it?" (5:20).

IV. Visions (7:1–9:10): Five visions of judgment are related, each with a symbol—locusts (7:1–3), fire (7:4–6), a plummet (7:7–9), summer fruit (8:1–14), and an altar beside which (or on which) Yahweh stands, followed by the threat of the total destruction of Israel (9:1–10).

V. Conclusion (9:11–15): The conclusion describes the restoration of David's kingdom.

III. THE PROPHETIC MESSAGE

The book of Amos may be the earliest prophetical writing in the Bible, and the first to predict the end of the northern kingdom of Israel (see **Israel, Kingdom of**). The style is simple and to the point, but the poetic rhythm is powerful and the metaphors colorful and striking.

Amos speaks against the corruption of wealth and the perversion of justice that will bring the **Day of the Lord**. Amos is the first to use the expression "Day of the Lord," signaling a truly dark time of defeat and suffering (5:18–20). The threat was already forming: **Assyria** would soon invade (about 734 B.C.), bringing immense suffering to Israel.

Amos declared the universal power of the Lord and his justice. The Lord rightly judges all the nations and controls their destinies (1:3–2:3; 2:9; 6:14; 9:7); above all he judges them when they violate the moral law. This message is directed especially at the northern kingdom and its capital, **Samaria**, which has been living in a state of perpetual religious apostasy. As Samaria has failed to remain faithful to the Lord and to uphold its **covenant** obligations, divine judgment will be imposed upon it (3:2). Put simply, the election of Israel does not lessen or annul the moral obligations of the Israelites; rather it places even more rigorous demands upon them. Moreover, worship without righteousness is an abomination, and the Lord stands ready at the altar to pass divine judgment (9:1–4).

But the prophecy is not only a message of gloom. The book of Amos ends on a hopeful note: Amos was the first to teach that a faithful remnant would survive the cataclysm (3:12). There would come a better day, a time of hope, when the Davidic Kingdom would be restored (9:11–15).

AMOZ (Hebrew, "he is strong") The father of the prophet Isaiah (2 Kgs 19:2; Isa 1:1). The name is a shortened form of Amaziah, meaning "Yahweh is strong," although he is also considered the brother of King Amaziah of Judah.

AMPHIPOLIS A Macedonian city on the Gulf of Strimon on the Aegean coast, east of Thessalonica and the port of Eion. In Roman times the city served as the capital of Macedonia Prima. Paul and Silas passed through Amphipolis during the second missionary journey (Acts 17:1).

AMPLIATUS A member of the Christian community in Rome who was greeted by Saint Paul as "my beloved in the Lord" (Rom 16:8).

AMRAM (Hebrew, "the kinsman") The father of Moses, Aaron, and Miriam (Exod 6:20; Num 26:59). He was a descendant of Levi and Kohath, and the husband of Jochebed (Exod 6:16–18; 1 Chr 6:1–3). His clan, the Amramites, belonged to the Levitical clan of the Kohathites, which had the task of transporting the furniture of the Tabernacle (Num 3:27; cf.

1 Chr 26:23–24). Little is known about Amram except that he lived to be over a hundred; his name appears only in genealogies.

AMRAPHEL The king of Shinar and one of the four Mesopotamian kings (the kings of the East)—with Arioch king of Ellasar, Tidal king of Goiim, and Chedorlaomer king of Elam—who jointly invaded Canaan and defeated the five kings of the Plains (Gen 14:1–9). In this campaign they plundered **Sodom** and **Gomorrah** and captured **Lot** and his family, together with a vast treasury (Gen 14:10–12). When Abram (later **Abraham**) heard the news, he attacked the four kings with 318 men and routed them in a single night. Lot and his family were rescued, and the plunder was returned (Gen 14:13–16).

Some scholars have identified Amraphel with the great Babylonian king Hammurabi, but most experts no longer accept that identification.

ANAB A city in the hill country of Judah where Joshua defeated the Anakim (Josh 11:21; 15:50).

ANAGOGICAL SENSE *See* **Interpretation of the Bible**.

ANAKIM The name given to a tribe in southern **Canaan**, near Hebron (Num 13:22). They were said to be descendants of the ancient **Nephilim** (Num 13:33), meaning that they were like giants. Three chiefs named Ahiman, Sheshai, and Talmai are mentioned specifically. The Israelites considered the Anakim fearfully tall (Num 13:33; "Anak" in Hebrew means "long-necked" or "giant"), and the spies sent by Moses into Canaan listed the "descendants of Anak" as one of the reasons that "we are not able to go up against the people" (Num 13:29–31). Joshua defeated the Anakim and destroyed their cities of Hebron, Debir, and Anab; the surviving Anakim settled in the lands of the Philistines around Gaza, Gath, and Ashdod (Josh 11:21–22; cf. 2 Sam 21:16–22). Joshua 15:14 says that Caleb was responsible for the defeat of Ahiman, Sheshai, and Talmai (cf. Judg 1:20).

ANALOGY OF FAITH The coherence of the truths of Christian faith among themselves and also within the entire plan of **Revelation** (CCC 114).

ANAMMELECH A deity to whom the **Sepharvaim** sacrificed human children (2 Kgs 17:31). One popular interpretation identifies Anammelech with the Mesopotamian sky god Anu. Anammelech was worshipped with **Adrammelech**; their cult came to Samaria with pagan immigrants settled there by **Sargon II** (2 Kgs 17:24).

ANANIAS The name of three men in the Acts of the Apostles.

1. The husband of Sapphira and a member of the earliest Christian community in Jerusalem (Acts 5:1–10). According to the account in Acts, Ananias and Sapphira withheld from the community some of the proceeds from the sale of land, though they claimed to have given the whole sum. When Peter confronted

him with the lie, Ananias died suddenly; the same thing happened to his wife a few hours later. "A great fear" descended upon the faithful who saw what happened.

2. A Jewish Christian of Damascus who played a role in the conversion of Saul of Tarsus, also known as **Paul** (Acts 9:10–18; 22:12–16). Ananias received a vision commanding him to go to Saul—who was then sitting blind in Damascus—and to lay hands upon him to cure him of his temporary blindness and to administer the sacrament of baptism. Paul gave confirmation of the actions of Ananias in Acts 22:12–16.

3. Ananias, son of Nedebaeus, high priest in A.D. 47–59. He was the high priest when Paul was arrested in Jerusalem. He had been appointed by King Herod Agrippa II and presided over the council hearing to which Paul was brought (Acts 23:2–5). Ananias ordered Paul to be struck on the mouth, receiving in turn a curse from the apostle. Ananias also took part in the trial of Paul before the Roman governor Marcus Antonius **Felix** (Acts 24:1).

ANATHOTH A Levitical city situated several miles northeast of Jerusalem, in the tribal territory of Benjamin (Josh 21:18; 1 Chr 7:8). **Abiathar**, a powerful priest of David, owned lands and estates there, and it was to Anathoth that he was banished by Solomon (1 Kgs 2:26–27). Two noted warriors of David also came from Anathoth: Abiezer (2 Sam 23:29) and Jehu (1 Chr 12:3). But the city's greatest fame was as the hometown of the prophet **Jeremiah** (Jer 1:1; 29:27), who owned a field there (32:7–9). Jeremiah also encountered severe opposition from some of the people of his native city (Jer 11:21–23), anticipating the saying that "no prophet is accepted in his own country." One hundred and twenty eight men of Anathoth also returned from Babylon, according to the lists in Ezra (2:23) and Nehemiah (7:27). The town was resettled after the **Exile** (Neh 11:32). The exact location of Anathoth is uncertain, but it may be the modern Anata, approximately five miles northeast of Jerusalem.

ANCHOR One of the best-known symbols of Christian **hope** (Heb 6:19–20). Early Christians also used it as a cryptic version of the **Cross**.

ANCIENT OF DAYS See under **Daniel, book of**.

ANDREW (Greek *Andreas*, "manly") Apostle, martyr, and brother of **Peter** (Matt 4:18; Mark 3:18; Luke 6:14). With his brother, Andrew was a Galilean fisherman from Bethsaida (Matt 4:18–20; Mark 1:16; John 1:44). He was a follower of John the Baptist before being called by Christ (John 1:35–42); he proclaimed to his brother that Jesus is "the Messiah." The first-called of the apostles, Andrew brought forward his brother Simon (renamed Peter by Jesus) and is always among the first four apostles listed in the Gospels (Matt 10:2; Mark 3:18; Luke 6:14). In John 6:8 Andrew calls attention to the boy with the loaves and the fishes; in John 12:22 Andrew and Philip (cf. John 1:40) serve as intermediaries between Jesus and the Greeks who had asked for an audience. In Mark 13:4 Andrew's

question about what sign to expect when the end is near brings out Jesus's long eschatological discourse (Mark 13:5–37).

Early Church historians (chiefly Eusebius of Caesarea) and apocryphal books (e.g., the *Acts of Andrew*) recorded that Andrew conducted missions in Cappadocia, Galatia, and Bithynia (all in modern Turkey), Scythia (from the northern Black Sea area to parts of Asia), and then in Byzantium (modern Istanbul). He also preached in Thrace, Macedonia, Thessaly, and Achaia (all in modern Greece). He was crucified on an X-shaped cross in Patrae, in Achaea, by order of the Roman governor, Aegeas. His martyrdom is believed to have taken place in the reign of Emperor Nero (r. 54–68), around A.D. 60.

In tradition, Andrew is the patron of Scotland, Russia, Greece, Burgundy, Spain, Sicily, Lower Austria, Naples, Ravenna, Brescia, Amalfi, Mantua, Manila, Bruges, Bordeaux, and Patra. He is also the patron of butchers, fishermen, miners, rope-makers, spinsters, water carriers, and weddings. Several orders of knighthood were established in his honor as well: the Order of the Golden Fleece in Spain, founded in 1429; King James's Order of Saint Andrew, founded in Scotland in 1540; and the Order of Saint Andrew of Czar Peter I, founded in 1698. His feast day is November 30.

ANDRONICUS (Greek, "victorious over men") The name of two men in the Bible.

1. An official under the **Seleucid** ruler Antiochus IV Epiphanes. He was named viceroy over Antioch and was soon embroiled in a bribery scandal involving Menelaus. When the

high priest Onias exposed the affair, Andronicus had him arrested and executed. Andronicus was then put to death by Antiochus (2 Macc 4:31–38). According to the historian Diodorus Siculus (*Bibliotheca Historica* 30.7.2–3), Andronicus was executed to hide his involvement in the death of the son of Seleucus IV.

2. A Jewish Christian in Rome who received greetings from Paul in Romans 16:7. Andronicus and Junias were fellow prisoners with Paul and were described by him as "prominent among the apostles."

ANER An Amorite who, with his brothers **Mamre** and Eshkol, helped **Abraham** in his swift battle against the four kings of the East who had sacked Sodom and Gomorrah and captured Lot and his family (Gen 14:13, 24).

ANGEL Literally a "messenger." Angels are pure spirits, created by God, who serve as messengers of the divine will; the name is used at times also for a human person who acts in the role of a messenger (translated as "messenger" or "envoy" in the RSV; e.g., Isa 18:2, 33:7; applied to John the Baptist, Matt 11:10). Angels have been present since creation, serving as heralds of the divine plan.

I. THE NATURE AND OFFICE OF ANGELS

A. Angels Are Pure Spirits

The existence of angels as spiritual, noncorporeal beings is a truth of faith that is supported by Scripture (Ps 90:11; Matt 18:10) and by long Catholic tradition (cf. CCC 328–36). Jewish tradition generally maintained a belief in angels, with the exception of the **Sadducees** (Acts 23:8). Pope Clement X (r. 1670–76) approved the devotion to **guardian angels** (cf. Dan 4:10, 20; 10:10, 13, 20; Matt 18:10; Acts 16:6).

B. The Difference Between Their Nature and Their Office

Saint Augustine declared: "'Angel' is the name of their office, not of their nature. If you seek the name of their nature, it is 'spirit'; if you seek the name of their office, it is 'angel': from what they are, 'spirit,' from what they do, 'angel.'"

C. Angels as God's Holy Retinue

Angels are often shown attending the divine throne, as was described vividly in Daniel (7:9–10; cf. Ps 96:7, 102:20; Isa 6). Reference is also made to the seven angels who have the special function of standing before the throne of God (Tob 12:15; Rev 8:2–5; also the "angel of the presence," Isa 63:9). The angels behold God (Matt 18:10). In the Old Testament the image is often presented of a holy retinue made up of the "holy ones" (Ps 89:6; Job 5:1; Dan 8:13) and the "sons *of elohim*" (God) or "sons *of elim*" (Ps 29:1, 89:7; Job 1:6, 2:1, 38:7) who surround the divine throne and praise Yahweh (Josh 5:14; 1 Kgs 22:19; Ps 103:20; 148:2). They are also called "sons of God" (Job 1:6; 38:7) and "ministers" of God's will (Ps 103:21; 104:4). Three angels are named specifically in Scripture: **Michael** (Dan 10:13, 21, 12:1; Jude 1:9; Rev 12:7), **Raphael** (Tob 5–11; 12:15), and **Gabriel** (Dan 8:16, 9:21; Luke 1:11, 19, 26ff.).

II. THE MINISTRY OF ANGELS

God sends angels to announce the divine will; to rebuke, encourage, assist, punish, and teach; and to execute divine judgment. They serve as key mediators between God and man.

A. Angels in the Old Testament

In the OT angels aid those who fear God (Ps 33:8; 90:11) and are sent by God to assist a large number of individuals: **Hagar** (Gen 16:7; 21:17), **Abraham** (Gen 18; 22:11), **Lot** (Gen 19:1–23), **Jacob** (Gen 28:12), **Elijah** (1 Kgs 19:5), the three children (Dan 3:49), **Daniel** (Dan 6:22), **Tobias** (Tob. 5:6–22).

An angel guided the people of Israel on their **Exodus** journey (Exod 23:20, 33:2; Num 20:16). Similarly, God sent an angel to keep **Balaam** from cursing God's people (Num 22:31–32), and sent another angel to **Joshua** (Josh 5:13–14). An angel censured the people (Judg 2:1–4) and appeared to **Gideon** (Judg 6:11–40; 7:1–7), **Samson**'s mother (Judg 13:3–21), and the prophet **Zechariah** (Zech 2–6); an angel punished **David** (2 Sam 24:16; 1 Chr

21:15), and explained visions to Daniel (Dan 8:16; 9:21; 10:5, 10, 16). Angels were also actively involved in the military actions of the OT, in defeating the Assyrians (2 Kgs 19:35), leading the forces of the Maccabees (2 Macc 11:6–13), and punishing **Heliodorus** (2 Macc 3:24–27). The particular expression "Angel of the Lord" in Genesis and Historical Books is often taken to imply a heavenly messenger who speaks and acts in the name of the Lord, thus an angelic mediator, but some scholars prefer to interpret the phrase as pointing to the direct intervention of God in human affairs (e.g., Gen 16:13, 21:18, 31:11, 32:24; Exod 14:19; Judg 6:14, 13:22).

B. Angels in the New Testament

In the NT angels play the same roles they played in the OT. Hebrews 1:14 asks rhetorically, "Are they not all ministering spirits sent forth to serve, for the sake of those who are to obtain salvation?"

An angel announces the birth of the Messiah to **Mary** (Luke 1:26–38), and angels are associated closely in the NT with Christ, from the infancy narratives to the Ascension. Thus angels proclaim their song of praise at the birth of Christ: "Glory to God in the highest!" (Luke 2:14) and an angel appears to **Joseph** (Matt 1:20; 2:13–19), **Zechariah** (Luke 1:11, 19–20), and the shepherds of Bethlehem (Luke 2:9, 15).

During the earthly life of Jesus, angels continued to fulfill the two traditional functions of messengers in salvation history and of members of the heavenly court, most particularly in their attendance upon Christ (Luke 12:8,

15:10; Matt 24:36). They ministered to Jesus in the desert (Matt 4:11) and gave him strength during the Agony in the Garden (Luke 22:43). After the Resurrection, angels descended from heaven, rolled back the stone of the tomb, and announced that Jesus had risen (Matt 28:2–7). In Matt 28:3, the angel's "appearance was like lightning, and his raiment white as snow."

Angels appeared to the disciples after the Ascension (Acts 1:10) and then to Peter (Acts 10:19; 12:7–11), Paul (Acts 27:23), Cornelius (Acts 10:3; 11:13), and the eunuch of Queen Candace (Acts 8:26–39). An angel released Peter and John from prison (Acts 5:19), an angel appeared to Paul in a dream during his voyage to Rome (Acts 27:23), and an angel struck Herod Agrippa with a terminal disease (Acts 12:23).

In the Epistles, angels witnessed the sufferings of the persecuted apostles (1 Cor 4:9) and in the context of the liturgy Paul declares that a woman should cover her head out of respect for the angels (1 Cor 11:10). The Law of Moses was given through angels (Acts 7:53; Heb 2:2; Gal 3:19). Even if an angel should preach another gospel, there should be no belief (Gal 1:8), nor are angels to be worshipped (Rev 19:9–10). An angel also mediated the visions in the **Revelation** to John (Rev 1:1; 22:8).

The role of angels in the end times is affirmed in several passages. Angels will summon men to judgment (Matt 24:31; 1 Thess 4:16); however, they do not know the day when that will come to pass (Mark 13:32). Nevertheless, they will come with Christ when he returns to judge the world (Matt 16:27; 2 Thess 1:7).

III. ORGANIZATION AND NUMBERS OF ANGELS

A. Ranks of Angels

Scripture lists various types of angels, and not all angels are equal (Dan 10:13; Rev 12:7). The recognized grades or choirs are named in different places: **seraphim** (Isa 6:2, 6); **cherubim** (Gen 3:24; Sir 49:10; Ezek 10:1–22); thrones (Col 1:16); dominions (or dominations; Col 1:16); virtues (1 Pet 3:22); authorities (or powers; Col 1:16; 1 Pet 3:22); principalities (Col 1:16); **archangels** (1 Thess 4:16); and angels. This listing was subject to variations by subsequent Christian writers, with extensive development provided by Dionysius the Areopagite in *De Coelesti Hierarchia (The Celestial Hierarchy)*, Saint Gregory the Great, and Saint Thomas Aquinas in the *Summa theologiae*.

B. Angels in Charge of Particular Places

According to Dan 10:12–21 various angels, described as princes, are responsible for different nations (e.g., Persia). A similar role is implied in Revelation, where the "angels of the seven churches" of Asia are mentioned (Rev 1:20).

C. The Number of Angels

The number of the angels is declared in Scripture to be enormous, "a thousand thousands served him, and ten thousand times ten thousand" (Dan 7:10; *also* Rev 5:11; Ps 67:18; Matt 26:53). (*See also* **Sabaoth**.)

IV. FALLEN ANGELS

Scripture also affirms the existence of fallen angels: those spirits who rebelled against

God, were cast out of heaven, and were condemned to the torments of hell (2 Pet 2:4; Jude 1:6). Collectively, those angels who fell from grace are termed, with **Satan**, the fallen angels (2 Pet 2.4). They are variously called demons (1 Cor 10:20), unclean spirits (Mark 5:13), angels of the devil (Matt 25:41), and angels of the dragon (Rev 12:7). Other references to fallen angels can be found in Rev 9:11 and 2 Cor 12:7. (*See also* **Demon**.)

ANGEL OF THE LORD *See under* **Angel**.

ANGER One of the human passions; it is not in itself wrong, but it needs to be controlled by reason. When not curbed or controlled, anger can advance into resentment and hate and become one of the seven capital sins.

The Old Testament often speaks of the anger of God, an **anthropomorphism** that is used to express not an uncontrollable emotion within God, but the fixed response of divine holiness to sin. God's anger is often directed at Israel because of its infidelity, unbelief, and idolatry. This is a common theme in the history of Israel (Exod 32; Num 11:1, 12:9, 13:25–14:35, 18:5, 32:10–14; Deut 1:34, 9:80; Judg 2:14, 3:8, 10:7; 1 Kgs 14:15; 2 Kgs 17:17). Especially deserving of God's wrath are the idolators who betray him for other gods (Jer 4:4, 7:20, 17:4, 32:31, 36:7; Ezek 6:12, 8:18, 14:19; Hos 5:10, 8:5, 13:11). God's anger was not limited exclusively to Israel: it could also be expressed toward foreign nations (Isa 10:5–15, 13:5, 30:27, 59:18; Ezek 25:15–17).

The anger of God is described variously as a consuming fire (Isa 65:5, 30:27; Jer 17:4; Ezek 21:36), a storm (Ps 83:16; Isa 30:30), and a scalding liquid poured out on the wicked (Ps 69:25; Jer 6:11; Ezek 7:8, 14:19). Such anger can be placated by repentance, supplication, prayer, and humiliation (Ps 6:2; 38:2) and especially through the zealous intervention of God's chosen prophets (Exod 32:11; Num 16:46–50, 25:1–8; Deut 9:19; Jer 7:6, 14:11, 15:1, 18:20; Ezek 9:8, 13:4; Amos 7:3).

In the New Testament, Christ taught clearly that uncontrolled human anger is an offense against the fifth commandment and damages relationships (Matt 5:22), and the anger of God so manifest in the OT was expressed in terms of righteous justice against sin (Matt 24:51; Rom 3:5, 12:19). Similarly, there are references to fire as a means of punishment (Matt 3:12, 18:6, 25:41; Mark 9:43–48; Luke 3:17). God's anger is also eschatological, seen in visions of the last judgment (Matt 24:51; Rom 2:4–5, 3:5, 12:19; Rev 11:18, 14:19, 16:1, 19:15) (CCC 1765, 1866, 2262).

ANNA The name of two women in the Bible.

1. The wife of Tobit and mother of Tobias (Tob 1:9). When Tobit lost his sight, she went to work to support the family (Tob 2:11).

2. A prophetess and member of the tribe of Asher who recognized the infant Jesus as the Messiah (Luke 2:36–38).

3. According to apocryphal writings (e.g., the Protevangelium of James), Anna was the name of the mother of Mary, mother of Jesus.

ANNAS (Greek *Hannas*) The father-in-law of the high priest Caiaphas and former high priest in his own right; Annas took part in the trial of Jesus and wielded considerable influence in the Sanhedrin. According to Josephus

(*Ant.* 18.12), Annas received appointment as high priest in A.D. 6 by Quirinius, the Roman governor of Syria. He served until A.D. 15, when he was deposed by Governor Valerius Gratus. Yet even after his deposition Annas enjoyed wide influence, as evidenced by the fact that five of his sons and one son-in-law, Caiaphas, all served as high priest in ensuing years.

Annas is described as high priest along with Caiaphas in Luke 3:2, a reference to his earlier office. It is clear that he was a prime mover in the legal effort to arrest and condemn Jesus. Thus in John 18:13–14, Annas first interrogates Jesus. He is also mentioned in Acts 4:6.

ANNUNCIATION

ANNUNCIATION The announcement made to **Mary** by the angel **Gabriel** that she was "full of grace" and would become the Mother of the Messiah (Luke 1:26–38). The Church's calendar marks the feast of the Annunciation on March 25.

ANOINTING

ANOINTING The ritual act of pouring oil on a person or thing with the intention of making the anointed one sacred. In a practical, daily sense, anointing was part of the preparations for celebrations or festivals (Deut 28:40; Ruth 3:3; Jdt 16:10). In its deeper religious meaning, anointing served the function of consecration. Hence, altars were anointed (Exod 29:35), as were the Tabernacle (Lev 8:10) and the ark of the covenant (Exod 30:26). Above all, anointing was used for the consecration of kings (1 Sam 10:1), priests (Exod 28:41), and prophets (1 Kgs 19:16). Anointing is a sign of the Spirit pouring his graces upon the recipient.

The anointing of priests is described in detail in Exod 29:4–7 and Lev 8:6–12. It began with the anointing of Aaron and his sons by Moses (Lev 8:12), initiating a custom that would be followed by Aaron's successors in the priesthood.

In the anointing of kings, the ruler was made a sacred representative of God (1 Sam 24:7, 26:9, 11; 2 Sam 1:14, 16). The rite itself dated from the very beginning of the monarchy, with the anointing of Saul by Samuel (1 Sam 9:16; 10:1). David was later anointed king of Judah at Hebron (2 Sam 2:4) and then of Israel (2 Sam 5:3; cf. 2 Kgs 9:3; 2 Sam 19:11). The king was therefore known as the Lord's Anointed (see, e.g., 1 Sam 24:6; 2 Sam 22:51; Ps 2:2; and cf. Isa 45:1): **Messiah** (*māšîaḥ*) in Hebrew, which was translated into Greek as Christ (*christos*).

In the New Testament, Jesus Christ was "anointed" by the Spirit (Luke 4:18; Acts 10:38).

ANOINTING OF THE SICK, SACRAMENT OF

ANOINTING OF THE SICK, SACRAMENT OF A sacrament of the new law instituted by Christ to strengthen the sick and dying to face the challenges that come with illness, to intercede for the restoration of health, and to remit the sins of the infirm. Once known as "extreme unction," this sacrament consists of the anointing of a sick or infirm person's forehead and hands with olive oil that has normally been blessed by a bishop. The scriptural basis for the sacrament is found in the New Testament. First, in Mark 6:13, after Christ sent out the disciples, "They cast out many demons, and anointed with oil many who were sick and cured them." Even more explicit is Jas 5:14: "Are any among you sick?

They should call for the elders of the church and have them pray over them, anointing them with oil in the name of the LORD." Thus in this sacrament the whole Church, through the prayer of the priest, commends the sick and suffering to the Lord (CCC 1499–1525).

ANTHROPOMORPHISM A kind of literary representation by which God is presented with human passions, emotions, and feelings. In Scripture, anthropomorphic language is a form of divine condescension, in which God bends low and accommodates himself to the weakness of our minds.

Scripture affirms that God is spirit rather than flesh, and more unlike mortals than like them. But to make the mystery of God more accessible to human minds, the Old Testament also uses language that gives God the emotions and actions of a mortal being: anger (Exod 32:10), sorrow (Gen 6:6), and jealousy (Exod 20:5), for example. Sometimes God is given physical characteristics: he has a face, arms, eyes, lips, ears, and so forth.

Such anthropomorphic language reminded Israel that God is "personal," capable of entering into a deep and genuine relationship with human persons. God was not a remote, emotionless power, but rather a being whose love for his Chosen People was expressed in actions they could see and remember.

ANTICHRIST (Greek *antichristos*, "against Christ") The name given to the chief enemy of Christ, who will lead the forces opposing God just before the Second Coming of Christ; also anyone who denies that Jesus is the Christ. The word itself appears in the New Testament only in this latter sense: in 1 John 2:18, 22; 4:3; and 2 John 7, the Antichrist is any false prophet who denies that Jesus is "the Christ" (1 John 2:22), fosters a spirit of denial (1 John 4:3), and leads others into apostasy (2 John 7).

The idea of the Antichrist goes back to apocalyptic Jewish literature. In the NT we see clear allusions in the false messiahs and false prophets in the apocalyptic discourse in the Gospels (Matt 24:5; Mark 13:21), and the "man of lawlessness" whose coming is "apparent in the working of Satan, who uses all power, signs, lying wonders, and every kind of wicked deception for those who are perishing, because they refused to love the truth and so be saved" (2 Thess 2:3–12).

The Antichrist will unleash the "mystery of iniquity" (2 Thess 2:7) that will seduce people away from the truth to a false messianism and persecution of the faithful. The deception from the truth will offer humanity a solution to all problems, but at the price of apostasy and through the glorification of humanity itself.

In Revelation a strikingly similar figure is found in the beast (Rev 13:11–18). His famous mark is 666, and the beasts are allied with the "great harlot" (Rev 17:9). Efforts to identify this beast with a historical person have centered in Rome, the great persecutor of the Church. The number of the beast, 666 (Rev 13:18), is likely a cryptogram for the title Caesar **Nero**, which in Hebrew adds up to 666 (KSR NRWN; a few ancient manuscripts use the number 616, based on the value of Nero's name according to its Latin spelling). The number 666 also appears in 1 Kgs 10:14, where it is the number of talents of gold that came in to Solomon in one year. (*See* CCC 675–77.)

The Antichrist is also named in early Jewish-Christian texts such as the Greek *Apocalypse of Ezra* 4:31, the *Apocalypse of Shedrach* 15:3, and Saint Irenaeus's *Against Heresies* 3.7.2 and 5.30.5.

ANTI-LEBANON A mountain range extending parallel to the Lebanon Mountains and separated by the Beqaʿ Valley. The highest peak in the range—as well as its terminal ridge—is Mount Hermon. The name Anti-Lebanon appears in the Bible only in Jdt 1:7.

ANTIOCH One of the most prominent cities in the Roman Empire, first built in 300 B.C. by Seleucus I Nicator on the Orontes River in Syria and named after his father Antiochus (*see* **Seleucids**). Located some seventeen miles from the sea, the city was supported by the port city of **Seleucia** Pieria.

Antioch was situated in a fertile region that provided grain, olives, grapes, and fish in great abundance, and was well-positioned for access to the trade routes from the East and West. Growing swiftly after its founding, Antioch eventually became one of the three chief cities of the Roman Empire, with Rome and Alexandria. By the second century B.C., there were perhaps as many as 600,000 people there, according to Pliny the Elder (*Nat.* 6.122). The city had a reputation for beautiful buildings and opportunities for luxury.

Following the collapse of the Seleucid Empire in the first century B.C., and its final de-

feat by Pompey the Great in 64 B.C., Antioch passed into Roman control and became the chief city of what became the Roman province of Syria. As such, it was a key strategic post for the empire and a leading center of learning that endured well into the Christian era.

Antioch is mentioned in the Old Testament only in 1 and 2 Maccabees as the capital of the Seleucids (1 Macc 3:37, 4:35, 6:63, 11:13, 56; 2 Macc 4:33). In the New Testament, the city became home to a Christian community that fled Jerusalem after the martyrdom of Stephen. The church at Antioch was the first to reach out to the Gentiles in a systematic way, and it was at Antioch that the followers of Christ were first called Christians (Acts 11:19–26). Such was the success of the church in Antioch that Barnabas was sent there from the church in Jerusalem (Acts 11:22). Barnabas then summoned Paul to the city, and Antioch thus became the place of Paul's first apostolic labors (Acts 11:26). It was also in Antioch that Paul and Peter had a major disagreement over the issue of circumcision of new Gentile converts (Gal 2:11–14).

ANTIOCH OF PISIDIA A city in the Roman province of Galatia, in modern central Turkey. (It should not be confused with the city of Antioch in Syria, which, confusingly, is also in modern Turkey.) Pisidian Antioch was founded by the Seleucids in the early third century B.C. By the time of Paul's arrival, the city was a prominent Roman colony.

Antioch of Pisidia was visited by Paul and Barnabas during the first missionary journey (Acts 13:13–14) and perhaps during Paul's next two missionary journeys (Acts 16:6 and 18:23). The first visit was noteworthy for the poor reception Paul and Barnabas met with among the Jews of the city, whereupon Paul preached with considerable success to the Gentiles. He and Barnabas were ejected from the city by officials under the influence of local Jewish leaders (Acts 13:13–51). The persecutors then pursued Paul to Lystra, where a mob was encouraged to stone him (Acts 14:8–20). Paul and Barnabas soon returned, however, to Antioch of Pisidia (Acts 14:21).

ANTIOCHUS For kings under this name, *see under* **Seleucids**.

ANTIPAS

1. Herod Antipas; *see* **Herod Antipas**.

2. A Christian of the community in **Pergamum**. He was martyred for the faith (Rev 2:13).

ANTIPAS, HEROD See under **Herod Antipas**.

ANTIPATER (Greek *Antipatros*, "in place of the father")

1. The father of King Herod the Great and the son of Antipas, an Idumean governor appointed by Jannaeus Alexander. Antipater was much disliked by most of the Jews of Palestine but managed to remain a leading political figure during the early Roman occupation until his death around 43 B.C. In particular, he perceived that the Roman domination of Palestine would not be a fleeting one so he worked to ingratiate himself with the Romans politically. Antipater thereby secured the client status for his line, a position strengthened further by his son. The city of Aphek was rebuilt by Herod the Great and named Antipatris in his honor around 9 B.C.

2. The son of Jason and one of the representatives sent to Rome and Sparta by Jonathan to attempt a renewed treaty with the Judeans (1 Macc 12:16; 14:22).

ANTIPATRIS *See* **Aphek**.

ANTONIA, TOWER OF Also called the Fortress of Antonia, a Hasmonean fort reconstructed by King Herod the Great at the northwest corner of the Temple of Jerusalem. There had been an earlier fortress on the site in Nehemiah's time (Neh 2:8; 7:2). Herod, however, completely transformed the structure and named the impressive bastion in honor of his political patron, the Roman general Mark Antony. Based on this naming, it has been concluded that the fortress was constructed before 31 B.C. and the defeat of Antony and Cleopatra at the battle of Actium. While Herod's palace was under construction, he used the tower as his residence.

The Antonia had a commanding view of the city and Temple, and the Romans made use of it. According to Acts 21:31–36 and 22:24, there was at least a cohort (between three hundred and six hundred soldiers) stationed there in a barracks. Josephus (*B.J.* 5.238–47) described the fort as having four towers and four turrets; there were also baths, various courtyards, and the usual requirements for garrisoned troops, as well as quarters for visitors. The fortress was destroyed during the Jewish rebellion against Rome in A.D. 70.

The trial of Jesus before Pontius Pilate may have taken place on the stone pavement in the courtyard of the fortress. It is also possible that the trial occurred in a palace serving as the procurator's residence, such as Herod's palace in the upper city. (*See also* **Gabbatha**; **Trial of Jesus**.)

ANTONIUS FELIX *See* **Felix, Marcus Antonius**.

APELLES A Christian in the community of Rome who received greeting from Paul (Rom 16:10).

APHEK The name of four places in the Old Testament.

1. A Canaanite city identified with the modern site of Ras el 'Ain, approximately ten miles east of the Mediterranean, near Joppa. It was noted for the abundance of its springs (the source for the river Yarkon). Aphek was included in the list of cities captured by Joshua (Josh 12:18). It was also used by the Philistines for two of their campaigns (1 Sam 4:1; 29:1). King Herod the Great built the city of Antipatris on the site of the old Aphek in 9 B.C., renaming it after his father, Antipater. Paul stayed in Antipatris for one night during his journey from Jerusalem to Caesarea (Acts 23:31).

2. A town belonging to the tribe of Asher (Josh 19:30; Judg 1:31), located south of Akko. It is identified today as Tell Kurdaneh.

3. A town on the border of the Amorites, north of Israel (Josh 13:4); it is probably modern Afqa in Lebanon, east of the ancient city of Byblos.

4. A town in Golan east of the Sea of Gal-ilee, modern Fiq (or Afiq), where **Ahab** defeated **Ben-hadad** of Syria (1 Kgs 20:26–30). It was also probably here that **Joash** defeated the Arameans according to the instructions of **Elisha** (2 Kgs 13:14–25).

APOCALYPSE *See* **Revelation, book of**.

APOCALYPTIC LITERATURE Writing preoccupied with the eschatological future, e.g., the end of world history, when the powers of evil launch their terminal struggle against God, only to be defeated in a terrible struggle. The name is derived from the Greek *apokalypsis* ("disclosure," "unveiling," or "revelation"), and hence the literary genre was used for revelations of the future, the unveiling of God's future plan (cf. Rev 1:1).

Apocalyptic literature claims to make known what was previously hidden or unknown. The revelation is always in the form of a vision of coming events.

Persecution under foreign empires was the backdrop for most apocalyptic literature in Jewish and Christian history. The apocalypse gives assurance to the present audience of future hope in the light of God's proven fidelity in the past. God will triumph in the future, just as he has triumphed throughout human history, and God's divine plan will prevail. The oppressors of the covenant people will be overthrown, and the righteous will reign victorious with God. Thus regardless of the severity of present circumstances and suffering, there is eschatological hope—even if the details of the future fulfillment are beyond our present capacity to understand fully. (*See also* **Revelation, book of**.)

There are several examples of apocalyptic literature in the Bible: the books of Daniel and Zechariah, parts of Isaiah (Isa 13), Ezekiel (Ezek 38–39), and Zephaniah (Zeph 1), and the book of Revelation. Outside the Bible, many apocalypses were written under the names of great figures of history (e.g., Adam, Baruch, Elijah, Ezra, or Enoch), and some of those books had wide circulation. The apocalypse of Enoch is quoted in Jude 14–15.

APOCRYPHAL BOOKS (Greek *apokrypha*, "hidden things") The name used for various Jewish and Christian writings that are often similar to the inspired works in the Bible, but that were judged by the Church not to possess canonical authority.

Catholics and Protestants disagree over the precise use of the term "apocryphal." Protestants apply that name to the **deuterocanonical** books—works that are found in the Catholic canon but that were omitted from the Protestant canon when it was formulated in the sixteenth century. Protestants reject Tobit, Judith, Wisdom, Sirach, Baruch, 1 and 2 Maccabees, and parts of Esther and Daniel, terming these "apocryphal" books. The Protestant "apocrypha" also include 1 and 2 Esdras and the Prayer of Manasseh, books that often appeared as noncanonical appendices to the Vulgate (*see* **Versions of the Bible**). For the books called apocryphal by the Catholic Church, Protestants use the term **pseudepigrapha**.

The apocryphal writings are of considerable value as works of religious literature and religious history, preserving important details of the development of Judaism and early Christianity, as well as offering scholars the means of tracing the emergence of heretical doctrines in the nascent Christian community (e.g., Gnosticism). Old Testament apocrypha offer a means of appreciating the different currents in formative Judaism, the influence of Hellenism on Jewish culture, and the impact of the destruction of the Herodian Temple in A.D. 70 on the culture, religious outlook, and political institutions of the period.

Old Testament apocrypha include writings of Messianic expectations, private revelations, visions, and proverbial and didactic passages. New Testament apocrypha include gospels, acts, epistles, and apocalypses.

I. OLD TESTAMENT APOCRYPHA

The term "Old Testament Apocrypha" is used to denote various Jewish writings that were composed from 250 B.C. to A.D. 200. The earliest Jewish documents in this large collection date from about the third century B.C., while others are placed to the tumultuous period from A.D. 70 to 200, between the destruction of Jerusalem and the compilation of the Mishnah. The final and latest elements of the collection date to a period around or after the fourth or fifth century A.D.

These sources give us significant information on Jewish culture and religious sensibility, both in Palestine and in the **Dispersion**. They also preserve valuable elements of folklore and legends, such as the extensive teachings on angels in Enoch and Esdras.

The works that are classified apocryphal were generally compiled by members of the Jewish community; some of them may have been later reworked by Christian writers. The

OLD TESTAMENT APOCRYPHA

Apocalyptic Literature and Related Works

2 Baruch
3 Baruch
1 Enoch
2 Enoch
3 Enoch
Apocalypse of Abraham
Apocalypse of Adam
Apocalypse of Daniel
Apocalypse of Elijah
Apocalypse of Sedrach
Apocalypse of Zephaniah
Apocryphon of Ezekiel
The Fourth Book of Ezra
Greek Apocalypse of Ezra
Questions of Ezra
Revelation of Ezra
Sibylline Oracles
Treatise of Shem
Vision of Ezra

Testaments

Testament of Adam
Testament of Job
Testament of Moses
Testament of Solomon
Testaments of the Three Patriarchs
    (Abraham, Isaac, and Jacob)
Testaments of the Twelve Patriarchs

Expansions of the Old Testament and Legends

Letter of Aristeas
Jubilees
Martyrdom and Ascension of Isaiah
Joseph and Aseneth
Ladder of Jacob
4 Baruch

Life of Adam and Eve
Jannes and Jambres
History of the Rechabites
Eldad and Modad
History of Joseph
Pseudo-Philo
Lives of the Prophets

Wisdom and Philosophical Literature

3 Maccabees
4 Maccabees
Ahiqar
Pseudo-Phocylides
Syriac-Menander

Prayers, Psalms, and Odes

More Psalms of David
Odes of Solomon
Prayer of Jacob
Prayer of Joseph
Prayer of Manasseh
Psalms of Solomon
Synagogal Prayers

Fragments of Judeo-Hellenistic Works

Philo the Epic Poet
Orphica
Fragments of Pseudo-Greek Poets
Demetrius the Chronographer
Theodotus
Ezekiel the Tragedian
Eupolemus
Aristobulus
Aristeas the Exegete
Cleodemus Malchus
Pseudo-Eupolemus
Artapanus
Pseudo-Hecataeus
(*See* **Canon**; *see also* **Deuterocanonical**.)

titles and subject matter of the writings deliberately imitated the books of the OT, demonstrating the influence of such literary forms as **wisdom literature**. Many were attributed to famous figures of the OT: Moses, Enoch, Solomon, Ezra, and Isaiah. Works like these are called "pseudepigrapha," after the pseudepigraphical (or false) attribution of authorship.

There is no standard, agreed-on list of OT apocryphal writings. It is possible, nevertheless, to assign certain writings to specific categories, such as Apocalyptic Literature, Testaments, Expansions, Wisdom Literature, Prayers and Psalms, and Fragments of Judeo-Hellenistic Works.

II. NEW TESTAMENT APOCRYPHA

The use of the term "apocryphal" for the New Testament apocrypha does not necessarily imply that all the writings are inaccurate or unorthodox (although some certainly were). These books were not included in the canon of Scripture either because they were of doubtful authenticity or because they were not in common use among the early Christian churches.

Some of these writings abound in fantastic details and easily prove themselves non-scriptural. Others were held in high regard and still are today. For example, the Codex Sinaiticus, the oldest extant codex of NT writings, includes both the Shepherd of Hermas and the Epistle of Barnabas. Tertullian, however, thought little of the Shepherd of Hermas, referring to it disparagingly as both secret and false (*Pud.* 10.6). There is evidence as well that some of the NT apocrypha were read within the context of early liturgies. The translations of these writings into many languages—Greek, Latin, Syriac, Armenian, Arabic, Coptic, and Ethiopic—demonstrate the degree of popularity and regard.

Dating the NT apocrypha is a challenge to scholars, owing to the absence of a closing date for their composition. Apocryphal writings continued to be compiled into the fifth century. Some of the writings may date to the first century; most were written in the second and third centuries.

Our knowledge of the NT apocrypha increased significantly in 1945 when a large cache of Coptic Gnostic texts was found at Nag Hammadi in Upper Egypt. The Nag Hammadi discovery gave the world fifty-two texts previously unknown or known only in fragmentary form.

The writings that fall under the classification of NT apocrypha are, like the OT apocrypha, widely diverse in their theology and genres, ranging from gospels and acts to epistles and apocalypses. Collectively, the NT apocrypha offer a significant source of information on the early Christian communities, in particular heretical sects such as Manicheanism and Gnosticism that broke away from the mainstream of Christianity.

The most common system of classification puts the NT apocrypha in four genres:

1. *Gospels*, which purport to give us more information about the life and sayings of Jesus,
2. *Acts*, which narrate fictional or traditional events in the lives of the apostles,

New Testament Apocrypha

Gospels

The Gospel of the Ebionites

The Gospel of the Egyptians

The Gospel of the Hebrews

The Gospel of Mary

The Gospel of the Nazoreans

The Gospel of Nicodemus (The Acts
of Pilate)

The Gospel of Peter

The Gospel of Philip

The Gospel of Thomas

The Infancy Gospel of Thomas

The Protoevangelium of James

Acts

The Acts of Andrew

The Acts of Andrew and Matthias

The Acts of John

The Acts of Paul

The Acts of Paul and Thecla

The Acts of Peter and Andrew

The Acts of Peter and Paul

The (Coptic) Acts of Peter

The (Greek) Acts of Peter

The Acts of Peter and the Twelve
Apostles

The Acts of Philip

The Acts of Thaddaeus

The Acts of Thomas

Epistles

The Abgar Legend

The Correspondence Between Paul
and Seneca

The Epistle of Pseudo-Titus

Letters of Lentulus

Paul's Letter to the Laodiceans

Third Corinthians

Apocalypses

The (First) Apocalypse of James

The (Second) Apocalypse of James

The (Coptic) Apocalypse of Paul

The (Arabic) Apocalypse of Peter

The (Coptic) Apocalypse of Peter

The (Greek/Ethiopic) Apocalypse
of Peter

The (Latin) Apocalypse of Paul

The Apocalypse of Sophonias

The Apocalypse of Thomas

The Apocryphon of James

The Apocryphon of John

The Book of Elchasai

The Book of Thomas the Contender

The Christian Sibyllines

The Letter of Peter to Philip

The Mysteries of St. John the Apostle
and the Holy Virgin

The Sophia of Jesus Christ

(*See* **Canon**; *see also* **Apocalyptic
Literature**, **Gospel**, and **Nag Hammadi**.)

3. *Epistles*, which—like the epistles in the NT—are letters from prominent early Christians, and

4. *Apocalypses*, which purport to reveal future events.

APOLLONIA A city in Macedonia, positioned on the Via Egnatia between **Thessalonica** and **Amphipolis**. Paul and Silas passed through Apollonia as they traveled to Thessalonica from Philippi (Acts 17:1).

APOLLOS A Jewish Christian from Alexandria described in Acts 18:24–28 as being eloquent, well versed in Scripture, and possessed of considerable oratorical talent.

Apollos knew only the baptism of John the Baptist, but he preached the "Way of the Lord" with both fervor and skill. He preached in the synagogue of Ephesus and attracted the support of **Priscilla** and **Aquila**, who gave him a fuller understanding of the Gospel. He then journeyed to Corinth with letters of introduction and there preached among the local Jewish population, using the Scriptures to proclaim Jesus as the Messiah (Acts 18:24ff.).

The success of Apollos in establishing the faith was noted by **Paul** (1 Cor 3:6), who said that Apollos had watered what Paul had planted. A group of Christians, however, formed a separatist faction in the Corinthian community in Apollos's name. Paul did not consider Apollos at all responsible for the formation of the faction (1 Cor 3:3–9; 4:6), as Paul clearly respected Apollos as a fellow laborer. Instead Paul tries in 1 Corinthians to break down the divisions among the Corinthian Christians. For his part, Apollos apparently left Corinth voluntarily and refused to return, despite Paul's invitation for him to do so (1 Cor 16:12). Apollos is also mentioned in Titus 3:13.

APOLLYON (Greek, "destroyer") The Greek name for the Hebrew **Abaddon**, the "angel of the bottomless pit" (Rev 9:11).

APOSTLE The title commonly used in the New Testament to denote the twelve closest disciples of Christ. Aside from the Twelve chosen by Christ (Acts 14:4; 2 Cor 8:23; Phil 2:25), the title was also used for Christ himself as the One sent by the Father (Heb 3:1), and for those sent by churches (Acts 1:21–22; 2 Cor 12:12; cf. Rom 15:19; Acts 5:12; 2 Pet 3:2). The existence of other apostles, however, in no way denigrated or compromised the unique place of the Twelve as the disciples whom Christ chose to be witnesses of the Resurrection, and who were solemnly commissioned by the risen Jesus to proclaim the Gospel and to organize the Kingdom of God on earth (CCC 765).

In the NT, Jesus himself is called an apostle, in Heb 3:1: "Jesus, the apostle and high priest of our confession." The use of the term reflects Christ's own self-identification as one sent by God (cf. Matt 15:24; Mark 9:37; Luke 9:48; John 3:17). Christ's apostleship is part of the whole mystery of the Incarnation in John's Gospel (John 3:16–17, 34; 5:36–38; 6:29, 57; 7:29; 10:36; 11:42; 17:3, 8, 18, 21, 23, 25; 20:21; cf. 1 John 4:9, 10, 14). All other apostleship derives from and imitates the apostleship of Christ.

I. Who Is an Apostle?
II. The Twelve Apostles

I. WHO IS AN APOSTLE?

The Greek title *apostolos* comes from the verb *apostellō*, "send," implying that an apostle is one who is sent. There is no certain background to the term, but scholars have suggested a connection with the Hebrew concept of *šālîaḥ*, one officially delegated by a rightful authority and sent out on a mission (compare 2 Chr 17:7–9, where Jehoshaphat delegated certain men to go forth and teach the book of the Law, with Acts 9:2).

Origen provided a starting definition of "apostle" (*In Johannem* 32.17): "Everyone who is sent by someone is an apostle of the one who sent him" (cf. John 13:16; Matt 10:40–42; Gal 4:14). In the NT, the word "apostle" is used eighty times; it always implies that the apostle is sent in the service of Jesus Christ (with the exception of the reference in John 13:16). Acts 1:21–22 defines an apostle more narrowly as "one of the men who have accompanied us during all the time that the Lord Jesus went in and out among us, beginning from the baptism of John until the day when he was taken up from us."

II. THE TWELVE APOSTLES

A. *The Institution of the Twelve*

The disciples or Twelve (after the death of Judas, the Eleven) were understood at an early time in the Church to be a distinct and separate institution (1 Cor 15:5), representing the twelve tribes of Israel (Matt 19:28). The Twelve were Peter, Andrew, James the Great, John, Thomas, James the Less, Jude, Philip, Bartholomew, Matthew, Simon Zealot, and Judas (Matt 10:1–4; Mark 3:13–19; Luke 6:12–16); the precise enumeration varies slightly (Acts 1:13, 23, 26), probably because some of the apostles were known by more than one name (as Simon Peter was, for example).

After the death of Judas, the apostles were divinely inspired to select Matthias as his successor (Acts 1:21–26) in order to restore the number to twelve, reasserting the Old Testament association of the twelve tribes (Acts 6:2). Thus, by the definition in Acts 1:15–26, the Twelve were a symbolic unit that typified the restoration of Israel around the Messiah. The mission divinely given to Paul and Barnabas (Acts 9:15; 13:2–4) qualifies them as apostles in a second sense, and the Bible twice identifies them as apostles (Acts 14:4, 13). Thus Acts uses the term "apostle" in two senses, one restricted to the Twelve and one more general that includes others sent in the service of Christ. (*See also* **James, brother of the Lord.**)

The appointment of the Twelve is given by the three Synoptic Gospels (Mark 3:13–19; Matt 10:1–4; Luke 6:12–16). The appointment is considered a historical event in which "Christ the Lord chose a select group of disciples who followed Him from the very beginning. They saw His works and heard His words. Thus they were in a good position to be witnesses to His life and teaching" (*Sancta Mater Ecclesia*, 2. "Elaboration of the Gospel"; cf. LG §§20–23). The apostles took part in the key moments of Jesus's public ministry and life, including feeding the five thousand (Mark 6:30–44), the Last Supper (Luke 22:14), and Gethsemane (Mark 14:32–33). Although they dispersed at the arrest of Jesus (Mark 14:27; John 20:19), they later all became witnesses to the resurrected Jesus (Matt 26:32, 28:16; Mark 14:28, 16:7; Luke 24:36–53; John 20:19–29, 21:1–14; Acts 1:1–3; 1 Cor 15:5) (CCC 641–42).

B. The Mission of the Twelve

In addition to the calling of the Twelve, two of the Synoptic Gospels provide an account of the appointment of the Twelve to their office. Mark 3:14–15 tells us, "He appointed twelve to be with him and to send them to herald, and to have power to heal the illnesses and to cast out demons"; Matthew 10:1 says that "He gave them power over unclean spirits so as to expel them, and to heal every disease and every illness."

Jesus subsequently sent the Twelve on their missionary labors and provided specific instructions (Matt 10:5–15; Mark 6:7–13; Luke 9:1–5). The postresurrection sayings of Christ give more instructions (Matt 28:19–20; Luke 24:46–49; Acts 1:8, 21–22), including the charge to "make disciples of all the nations, baptizing them in the name of the Father, and the Son, and the Holy Spirit, teaching them to observe all I have commanded you" (Matt 28:19–20).

The apostles received from Christ the authority of teaching, ruling, and sanctifying, and the power to found churches (Mark 16:16; Luke 24:49; Acts 2:37, 15:29; 1 Cor 7:12ff.; 1 Thess 2:13; cf. Saint Clement of Rome, *Ad. Cor.*, 42; Pontifical Biblical Commission, *Sancta Mater Ecclesia*, 2. "Elaboration of the Gospel")

(CCC 880–96). To assist them in their mission the apostles were endowed with certain extraordinary gifts that are characterized as fourfold: the immediate commissioning by Christ; the power to preach to all peoples; personal infallibility when teaching doctrines of faith or morals; and a universal episcopal jurisdiction.

C. The Primacy of Peter

Peter held a special place among the apostles. He alone was given individual primacy and universal headship over the pilgrim Church on earth (Matt 16:18–19). The bishops (*episkopoi* in Greek) succeeded the apostles in order, not in universal jurisdiction, but the bishops conjointly have universal jurisdiction, and so collectively represent the Apostolic college. Such a jurisdiction is exercised in subordination to the pope, as the apostles exercised theirs in subjection to Peter (CCC 857–65; LG §§19–23).

III. PAUL AS AN APOSTLE

Paul, too, was an apostle, on an equal footing with the Twelve. He too had seen the risen Jesus (1 Cor 9:1) and was commissioned by Jesus to lay the foundations of the Church in the world (Acts 9:15; 1 Cor 3:10). Paul pointed out that he had performed "the signs of a true apostle" (2 Cor 12:12; cf. Acts 5:12; Rom 15:19).

Paul repeatedly describes himself as an apostle (e.g., 1 Cor 2:7, 15:3–10; 2 Cor 1:1; Rom 1:1; Col 1:1; Eph 1:1; 1 Tim 1:1; 2 Tim 1:1, 11; Titus 1:1), and he points out that the other apostles accepted him as a fellow minister of the gospel (Gal 2:9). The basis for his apostleship is his encounter with the risen Jesus (1 Cor 9:1–5;

15:1–10) and the claim that he had been called by Christ to preach the gospel to the Gentiles (Gal 1:15–16; in Rom 1:1 and 1 Cor 1:1, where he says he is "called to be an apostle"), and thus was Christ's representative (1 Thess 1:6, 11:1; Phil 3:17; cf. 1 Cor 1:8; 2 Cor 1:14, 11:2; Phil 2:15; Col 1:22; Eph 5:27).

IV. OTHER APOSTLES

A. Apostles Sent by the Churches

Aside from Paul and the Twelve, who were directly chosen by Christ, there were other types of apostles in the first period of the Church. They preached the Gospel under the direction of the apostles. Barnabas was one of these (Acts 14:4, 14), perhaps Andronicus and Junias (Rom 16:7), and Epaphroditus (Phil 2:25; cf. Acts 1:21–22, 5:12, 6:2–6, 11:30, 13:1; 2 Cor 12:12; Rom 15:19; 1 Thess 5:12–13; 2 Pet 3:2; LG §20). Paul called them *apostoloi ekklēsiōn*, "apostles" or "messengers of the churches" (2 Cor 8:23; cf. Phil 2:25). The details of their activities are limited, but the apostles sent by the churches emulated the Twelve in their commitment to itinerant evangelization (see 1 Cor 9:5, 12:28; Eph 2:20, 3:5, 4:11; Rev 18:20; *Did.*, 11:3–6). Acts 13:1 also notes the presence of prophets and teachers (cf. 1 Cor 12:28). They too traveled, and the *Didache* provided the ideals for their behavior, including the admonition that they should not stay more than a day or two at a guesthouse (*Did.*, 11–13).

B. False "Apostles"

Paul was also careful to distinguish between the true and false apostles (2 Cor 11:13). He attacked such false claimants as "false apostles" (2 Cor 11:13) and (sarcastically) "superlative apostles" (2 Cor 11:5; 12:11).

APOSTOLIC COUNCIL See **Jerusalem, Council of**.

APOSTOLIC FATHERS Important churchmen, mostly bishops, who immediately succeeded the apostles. These Fathers were responsible for many important writings that have survived completely or in part and that have long been held in great esteem. Among the Apostolic Fathers are Saint Clement of Rome (Pope Clement I), Papias, Hermas, Saint Polycarp of Smyrna, and Saint Ignatius of Antioch. The term "Apostolic Fathers" has been used since the 1600s.

APPHIA A woman to whom the Letter to Philemon is partly addressed (Phlm 2). She may have been the wife of Philemon.

APPIAN WAY The Via Appia, one of the most famous of the major roads in the Roman Empire, stretching across southern Italy, from Rome to Brundisium on the Adriatic Coast. The road was constructed in 312 B.C. by Appius Claudius Caecus; it originally connected Rome to Capua but was later extended and by the end of the second century B.C. had been paved. It is likely that Paul traveled along the Appian Way on his journey to Rome, since he was met by admirers from the Forum of Appius (Acts 28:15), a site on the road from Rome to Capua.

APPLE (Hebrew *tappûaḥ*) A fruit that was cultivated in some parts of the Middle East during biblical times, in particular in Egypt and Syria. It is not certain which fruit is meant in the scriptural references to "apples." For example, the "apples of gold" in Prov 25:11 may be apricots. Other references are likewise debatable, such as in Josh 1:12, and Song 2:5, 7:8, and 8:5. The fruit of the tree of the knowledge of good and evil is often called an "apple" in tradition, but the narrative in Gen 2–3 does not make that identification.

AQUILA (Latin, "eagle") A Jewish Christian, the husband of **Priscilla**, and a friend of Paul. Aquila was a native of Pontus and later lived in Rome until Emperor **Claudius** expelled the Jews from that city (Acts 18:2–3). Aquila and Priscilla then went to Corinth, where they met Paul and were possibly his first converts in the city. Both Paul and Aquila shared the trade of tent-making. Aquila and Priscilla welcomed Paul into their home, then accompanied him to Ephesus. There Aquila used his house as a place of worship (Acts 18:26; 1 Cor 16:19) and encountered the impressive preacher **Apollos**, to whom he and his wife provided additional instruction in the Gospels (Acts 18; also 1 Cor 16:19; 2 Tim 4:19).

Aquila and Prisicilla returned to Rome, using their home again as a church (Rom 16:3–5). Paul sent them greetings from Corinth, referring to them as fellow workers and also thanking them for their courage in risking their lives to save his; no other details on the episode are preserved.

ARAB A town in Judah southwest of Hebron (Josh 15:52; also 2 Sam 23:35).

ARABAH (Hebrew, "arid") A Hebrew word that is used variously to describe a desert or wilderness. When written with a definite article, the word means a particular place, probably the region of the Great Rift Valley, including the Jordan Valley and the Dead Sea area stretching to Elath and the Gulf of Aqaba (Josh 11:16, 18:18; Deut 1:7, 2:8, 3:17; Num 33:49; 2 Sam 4:7; Ezek 47:8).

ARABIA The Hebrew noun 'ărāb was used in the Old Testament both for "Arabs" as a people and for the region in which they lived. The term was understood to mean various desert tribes beyond the frontiers of Israel (2 Chr 17:11, 21:16, 22:1, 26:7; Ezra 27:21; Isa 21:13; Jer 25:24). They are also called "sons of the East" (Gen 29:1; Judg 6:3; 1 Kgs 4:30, 5:10), "East" in this context meaning northern Arabia; the region itself was called "land of the East," or simply "East" (Gen 25:6; Isa 2:6). "Arab" might also denote simply a nomad (Isa 13:20) or a bandit (Jer 3:2). Solomon had commercial dealings with Arabia (1 Kgs 10:15; 2 Chr 9:14), and Arab raiders sometimes struck Judah (2 Chr 21:16; 22:1; 26:7). According to the Jewish historian Josephus, the Arabs are descendants of Abraham's son Ishmael (*Ant.* 1.220–221). The only mentions of Arabia in the New Testament are Galatians 1:17, where **Paul** says he went to Arabia after his conversion, and in Gal 4:25, where Paul locates Mount Sinai.

ARAD A Canaanite city in the **Negeb** in southern Palestine, identified as modern Tel Arad, south of Hebron. The ruler of the city launched an attack upon the Israelites as they made their way into the Promised Land (Num 21:1–3). The Israelites vowed revenge and later sacked the city (Num 33:40; Josh 12:14).

ARAM, ARAMEANS A Semitic people concentrated in ancient Syria who had close relations with the Israelites. According to the **Table of Nations** (Gen 10:22), Aram is listed as a son of Shem and a grandson of Noah.

The Arameans held a number of small but commercially active city-states that did not unite sufficiently to create an empire. They often had dealings with the Israelites, especially the northern kingdom. Chief among the Aramean kingdoms was that centered at **Damascus**; it fell under the sway of the Davidic kingdom (2 Sam 8:5) but was later independent (1 Kgs 11:23–25). **Ben-hadad**, king of Damascus, attacked Israel at the behest of **Asa** of Judah, dominated **Omri** of Israel, and was twice defeated by **Ahab** (1 Kgs 20). In 732 B.C. the kingdom of Damascus finally fell to the Assyrians under Tiglath-pileser III, who added the area to Assyria's rapidly expanding empire. The fall of the Aramean states thus removed a buffer between Israel and the advancing Assyrians. (*See also* **Aramaic**.)

ARAMAIC A northwest Semitic language (other members of the same subfamily include Ammonite, Canaanite, Edomite, Hebrew, Moabite, Phoenician, and Ugaritic) that served as the primary language of business and communication across the Near East from around 600 B.C. to around A.D. 700. Aramaic was also a commonly spoken language throughout Pal-estine, Syria, and Mesopotamia in the first period of Christian history.

By the time of **Hezekiah**, Aramaic was the recognized language of diplomacy (2 Kgs 18:26). The language was spread further by the forced resettlements of conquered peoples throughout the Assyrian Empire. Thus by the sixth century it had become the common language of the Semitic peoples. In the Persian Empire, Aramaic was the language of government and its subjects. After the arrival of Alexander the Great in the fourth century B.C., Greek took over as the language of government, literature, and commerce, but Aramaic remained the language of the common people in Palestine until the Arab Muslim conquest.

Although Hebrew is the principal language of the Old Testament, a few OT texts are written in Aramaic: Ezra 4:8–6:18, 7:12–26; Dan 2:4–7:28; Jer 10:11. Jews living outside of Palestine also translated the Hebrew Bible into Aramaic versions, known as the Targums; another major Aramaic translation of the Hebrew Bible was the Peshitta, a Syriac (that is, late Aramaic) version still used by some eastern Christians.

As Aramaic was spoken commonly in Palestine during the New Testament times, Jesus and his disciples spoke Aramaic (Matt 26:73). Fragments of Aramaic appear, for example, in Matt 16:17; Mark 5:41, 7:34, 14:36, 15:34; John 1:42; and Acts 1:19. The Gospel stories were probably first transmitted orally in Aramaic, although only the Gospel of Matthew is reported to have been written originally in Hebrew or Aramaic (*see* **Matthew, Gospel of**, for other details). The influence of Aramaic is seen also in late biblical and rabbinic Hebrew, rabbinic literature, and the writings of Syriac Christianity.

A modern version of Aramaic is still spoken in some areas in the Middle and Near East and is used as a liturgical language in the Syrian Catholic Church, whose members are found in Iraq, Lebanon, Egypt, Turkey, Kuwait, and North America.

ARARAT A region identified with Urartu in the mountains of Armenia and centered near Lake Van; it also encompassed parts of modern Turkey, Iraq, Iran, and Armenia. It is best known as the place where the ark of Noah came to rest after the Flood (Gen 8:4). The sons of the Assyrian king Sennacherib also fled to Ararat after they had murdered their father (2 Kgs 19:37; Isa 37:38). It is also mentioned in Jer 51:27 as one of the nations summoned to war against Babylon.

ARATUS A Greek poet (ca. 315–240 B.C.) from Soli in Cilicia, author of an astronomical poem, *Phaenomena*. **Paul** quoted from the work in his preaching on the Areopagus of **Athens** (Acts 17:28).

ARAUNAH A Jebusite citizen of Jerusalem (2 Sam 24:5–25), also known as Ornan (1 Chr 21:5). When David offended the Lord by taking a census of the people, the Lord sent a plague to Israel. David saw the destroying angel by Araunah's threshing floor and was told by Gad the prophet to build an altar there. Araunah offered the floor as a gift, but David was careful to purchase the floor for the price

of 50 shekels of silver (2 Sam 24:24; 1 Chr 21:25 reports 600 shekels of gold "for the site," which may be the price for the whole property rather than just the threshing floor). David made offerings and holocausts, and the plague ended. Solomon would later build the **Temple** on the same site (2 Chr 3:1).

ARBA The father of Anak (Josh 15:13; 21:11). He was considered the greatest of the **Anakim** (Josh 14:15).

ARCHAEOLOGY The science that excavates and studies sites of ancient human habitation.

Archaeology is a fairly recent science. Before the nineteenth century, written records were the source of most historical information, along with what few artifacts and remains immediately presented themselves to historians. Gradually, however, scholars discovered that excavating below the surface of an ancient site brought much more information to light. The more care that was taken to probe beneath the most modern layers of a site, the deeper into the past the archaeologist was able to penetrate. Effective archaeology throws vital light on the history of a place or people, yielding information that might otherwise be unknown if written documents alone are studied.

Archaeology, of course, does not exist in isolation from other methods of scientific inquiry. For example, archaeologists dig up large numbers of inscriptions, seals, ostraca, and assorted texts, and these remains are then interpreted by specialists in ancient writings. It may take a battery of specialists—geologists, zoologists, cultural anthropologists, climatologists, paleo-ethnobotanists, and so on—to interpret the results of one excavation.

I. BIBLICAL ARCHAEOLOGY

Biblical archaeology—sometimes described as Syro-Palestinian archaeology—studies Palestine and adjacent regions of the Near East to find out more about the times and cultures of the biblical period. Biblical archaeologists are interested in the customs and cultural traditions of the Hebrews; the influence of civilizations such as Assyria, Canaan, Egypt, Phoenicia, and Babylonia on Hebrew life; and the impact on cities, towns, and villages of such biblically reported events as war, famine, drought, and disease. For example, archaeologists have worked to determine the dates when the walls of Jericho were built, and they have devoted immense resources to the careful study of Jerusalem to establish a broad picture of its antiquity, its expansion and catastrophes, and the many eras of habitation that have marked its life.

The problems in biblical archaeology are the same as in any other kind of archaeology. Experts often disagree on the location of a biblical site, and excavations will frequently fail to provide enough details for the final determination. Furthermore, the exact methods of excavation, stratification, and preservation are still being perfected. The unstable politics of the Middle East are a special challenge, and progress is often held up for years by political conditions.

We need to remember, too, that much of archaeology depends on subjective interpretation. Archaeologists often disagree about what they have found, and the same evidence can be interpreted many different ways by many different scholars.

II. HISTORY AND DEVELOPMENT

The history of modern biblical archaeology in Palestine began in 1838, when the Americans Edward Robinson and Eli Smith made the first surveys and surface explorations of several sites that were named in the Bible. The first excavation was made by the Frenchman Saulcy in 1863 near Jerusalem, followed two years later by the start of surveys under the auspices of the Palestinian Exploration Fund that continued until 1914. The fund's efforts led to the Palestine Ordnance Map, which gave the first accurate map of the region.

Early excavations were haphazard by modern standards, but gradually methods improved. The famed English archaeologist Sir Flinders Petrie, who laid much of the foundation of modern archaeology, excavated Tell el-Hesi in 1890 and established the first ceramic or **pottery** index and stratigraphical chronology. This work provided archaeologists with a clear chronological pattern based on the various styles of pottery used in different periods. This information was then cross-dated with remains found in Egyptian tombs. Further progress in this area was made by later archaeologists, in particular the American William F. Albright at Tell Beit Mirsim from 1926 to 1932. He established an absolute chronology that was used with only minor modifications by generations of later archaeologists. (*See also* **Tell**.)

Albright was followed by several post–World War II archaeologists such as Kathleen Kenyon of England and G. Ernest Wright of the United States.

Kenyon was one of the greatest of the twentieth-century archaeologists and one of the most influential through her stratigraphical methodology and her discoveries, such as her excavations at Jericho from 1952 to 1957 and the City of David in the 1960s. Wright, a student of Albright, undertook famed excavations at Tell Balatah, ancient Shechem (1956–1969), which became the basis for the training of many later American archaeologists.

III. CAUTIONS

From the standpoint of biblical studies, archaeology is immensely valuable in understanding the setting and context of the biblical times and happenings. It can often identify the exact locations of ancient cities discussed in the Old Testament and widens our knowledge of the places mentioned in the New Testament. Archaeology was of irreplaceable importance in the understanding of the **Dead Sea Scrolls**, first discovered in 1947, which added greatly to our understanding of Judaism in the time of Christ. Gaps in our knowledge of the NT period and early Christianity (ca. A.D. 200–500) are constantly being filled in by biblical archaeologists. Names mentioned in the Gospels have been confirmed by assorted discoveries. For example, Lysanias, the tetrarch of Abilene, was unknown outside Luke 3:1 until an inscription with his name was discovered near Damascus.

Nevertheless, archaeological results must be applied with care. Despite many decades of research, biblical archaeologists still disagree on a number of basic issues, including the time periods of the **patriarchs** and the conquest of Canaan.

Biblical archaeology can provide data and materials for improving our understanding of the material aspects of the Bible and biblical history, but it cannot prove the word of God or establish scientific tests for the proof of God's saving plan in history. Fundamentalists sometimes abuse archaeology to "prove" the literal truth of the Bible; anti-Christians sometimes abuse it to "disprove" the Bible. Neither will succeed. Archaeology often confirms the historical accuracy of the Bible, but it cannot prove or disprove the more important theological truths of salvation history. When we properly understand its limits, however, archaeology can give us an immeasurably richer understanding of the Bible and deepen our faith by bringing us closer to the lives of its greatest figures.

ARCHANGEL (Greek, "chief angel") A member of one of the choirs, or orders, of angels, generally counted as the eighth of nine. The word appears only twice in the Bible: once in 1 Thess 4:16 and once in Jude 1:9.

Michael, who led the angelic hosts in the struggle against Lucifer and his fellow fallen angels, is the one angel who is explicitly called an "archangel" (Dan 10:13–21; Jude 1:9; Rev 12:7). Two other angels named in Scripture are called archangels in Christian tradition: **Raphael**, who assisted Tobias (Tob 3:25); and **Gabriel**, who was sent to Daniel, Zechariah, and Mary (Dan 8:16, 9:21; Luke 1:19–26). (*See* **Angel** for other details.)

ARCHELAUS The son of King **Herod the Great** and Malthace, mentioned only briefly in Matt 2:22, in which it is declared that the Holy Family was reluctant to live in Judea because Archelaus was ruler there. Archelaus, like his brothers Philip and Herod Antipas, had a share in the inheritance of the kingdom upon their father's death in 4 B.C. Archelaus's share included Judea, Samaria, and Idumea, but his holdings were reduced by Emperor **Augustus** (r. 27 B.C.–A.D. 14) in order to decentralize the Jewish state, and Archelaus was not granted the title of king but ethnarch. Archelaus was much disliked by his Jewish subjects, both because of his cruelty and incompetence and because of his marriage to the ex-wife of his brother Alexander, who had already borne her husband children. In A.D. 6, Jewish and Samaritan groups petitioned Rome to remove him. Augustus deposed Archelaus and sent him into exile in Gaul; Judea then became part of the imperial province of Syria. Archelaus died in A.D. 18.

ARCHIPPUS One of the individuals to whom the Letter to Philemon was addressed (Phlm 2); he is called a "fellow soldier." Archippus is also mentioned in Col 4:17, with the admonition that he remain mindful of his duties.

ARELI The son of Gad and grandson of Jacob (Gen 46:16; Num 26:17).

AREOPAGITE *See* **Areopagus**.

AREOPAGUS (Greek, "hill of Ares") A hill in **Athens** northwest of the Acropolis upon which the Athenian supreme council held its deliberations; the name was also used for the council itself. According to Acts 17:19, Paul was brought before the Areopagus by Epicurean and Stoic philosophers, although it is unclear whether this is a reference to his appearance before the council or upon the hill. Parties in Athens were interested in hearing Paul's preaching after he had addressed them in the synagogue and marketplace. Paul's speech is preserved in Acts 17:22–31.

ARETAS The name of four kings of **Nabatea**, two of which are mentioned in the Bible.

1. Aretas I (second century B.C.) was mentioned in 2 Maccabees (5:8) in relation to the flight of the high priest Jason in 168 B.C. Aretas expelled Jason, who then went to Egypt.

2. Aretas IV (r. 9 B.C.–A.D. 39) enjoyed the favor of Emperor Gaius Caligula (r. 37–41), who apparently gave him temporary authority over Damascus. Aretas installed a governor there who sealed off the city in order to capture **Paul**, but Paul escaped in a basket lowered from a window (2 Cor 11:32–33).

ARGOB A region in **Bashan** in the northern Transjordan (Deut 3:4, 13–14). Originally a Canaanite region, Argob was conquered by the Israelites under Jair, son of Manasseh, given to the tribe of Manasseh, and renamed Havvoth-jair. Argob was a region of sixty fortified cities that formed one of the administrative districts of Solomon (1 Kgs 4:13).

ARIEL (Hebrew, "lion of God," also "heroes" or "champions")

1. One of the men handpicked by **Ezra** to

recruit twelve Levites to serve as ministers for the house of God when the Jews returned to Israel from exile in Babylon (Ezra 8:16).

2. The name Ezekiel gives to the "altar hearth" in the **Temple** of Jerusalem (Ezek 43:15–16).

3. A symbolic name for Jerusalem (Isa 29:1–2).

ARIMATHEA *See* **Ramah**; *see also* **Joseph of Arimathea**.

ARIOCH The name of two men in the Old Testament.

1. The king of Ellasar (Gen 14:1, 9) and one of the four kings (with Amraphel, Tidal, and Chedorlaomer) who waged war upon the five kings of the plain. They captured Lot and his family but were soon routed by Abraham and his allies.

2. The captain of the guard in the service of Nebuchadnezzar of Babylon (Dan 2:14–15, 24–25). He was given the task of executing the wise men of Babylon after they failed to relate the contents of the king's dream and provide an interpretation of it.

ARISTARCHUS (Greek, "excellent ruler") A Macedonian of Thessalonica and companion of Paul at Ephesus on his third missionary journey (Acts 19:29). He also met Paul in Troas (Acts 20:4–5) and joined the apostle when he sailed to Italy and Rome (Acts 20:4; 27:2). Paul mentioned him as a fellow prisoner in his epistle to the Colossians (Col 4:10) and as a fellow laborer in his letter to Philemon (Phlm 24).

ARISTOBULUS (Greek, "excellent counselor") A man in Rome to whom Paul sends greeting in Romans (16:10). Aristobulus was probably head of the household; it is also possible that he was a relative of King Herod Agrippa I.

ARK The vessel **Noah** constructed at the command of God and in which he and his family with animals escaped the **Flood**. God commanded Noah to build the ark according to precise measurements: 300 cubits long, 50 cubits wide, and 30 cubits high (Gen 6:15; approximately 450 feet long, 75 feet wide, and 45 feet high), with a roof or window and three decks (Gen 6:17). After the deluge, on the twenty-seventh day of the seventh month, the ark came to rest on the mountains of Ararat. Outside of Genesis, reference is made to the ark in Wisdom (10:4; 14:6) and in the New Testament (Matt 24:38; 1 Pet 3:20–21; 2 Pet 2:5).

The specific word for ark (Hebrew *tēbâ*) appears only once outside of Genesis, in Exod 2:3, to describe the way that Moses is saved in the ark (or basket). Such a use stresses the connection of Moses with Noah: both escape the waters of judgment in an ark sealed with pitch, and both survive to found a new world—in the case of Moses, the nation of Israel (CCC 56–58).

ARK OF THE COVENANT A chest, two and a half cubits (3.75 feet, 1.1 meters) in length and one and one half cubits (1.5 feet, 0.5 meter) in height and width, that contained the two stone tablets on which the Ten Commandments were inscribed (Exod 25:10–16).

(*See also* **Cubit**.) It was made of acacia wood and covered both on the inside and the outside with gold plating (Exod 25:10–26). At the four corners of the ark were placed golden rings that permitted gilded acacia poles to be inserted, so that the ark could be carried without being touched. The ark had a lid made from a solid slab of gold that formed the propitiatory or mercy seat, the *kappōret* (perhaps meaning "place of atonement"), surmounted by two **cherubim** of beaten gold facing each other (Exod 25:17–22).

Also called the ark of testimony, the ark of God, the ark of Yahweh, and the ark of the Lord, the ark was built by the command of God to Moses on Mount Sinai. Moses commanded that a golden vessel of manna (Exod 16:34) and the rod of Aaron that had blossomed (Num 17:10) be kept "before the testimony" (Exod 16:34; Num 17:10). According to Heb 9:4, the vessel and the rod were in the ark.

The ark was the mark of the Lord's intimate presence among his people. The two golden cherubim form the throne, so that the ark served as the footstool for the feet of the Lord (cf. 1 Chr 28:2; Ps 99:5; Num 10:33–35). When the Israelites camped, the ark was kept in the **holy of holies** of the Tabernacle (Exod 26:33; 40:21), and there Moses conversed with the Lord (Num 7:89).

The ark was carried before the army in battle, although it was not present when the Israelites were defeated by the Canaanites (Num 14:44). At the siege of **Jericho**, the ark was used as an instrument of holy war: it was carried in the middle of the procession around the city for seven days straight, with warriors in front and behind (Josh 6:9–15).

After the Israelites had entered the Promised Land, the ark was placed at Gilgal (Josh 4:19; 7:6). It was probably then moved with the Tabernacle to Shiloh (Josh 18), then to Bethel (Judg 20:27), and then back to Shiloh (1 Sam 3:3). During the struggle with the Philistines, the ark was captured during the battle of Aphek (1 Sam 4:11) and was carried to Ashdod, Gath, and Ekron (1 Sam 5:3–6). The Philistines suffered seven months of earthquakes (1 Sam 5:3) and plague (1 Sam 5:6, 9) as divine punishment, and they finally returned the ark to the Israelites, along with a guilt offering. After that the ark was kept for a time at Kiriath-jearim in the home of Abinadab. After the ark had stayed at Kiriath-jearim for twenty years, **David** placed it prominently in a Tabernacle (2 Sam 6; Ps 132) in his established capital at Jerusalem.

The task of enshrining the ark in the **Temple** was left to David's son Solomon (2 Chr 5:2–9). The ark remained in the Temple for approximately four hundred years, until the fall of Jerusalem to the Babylonians in 586 B.C. (cf. Jer 3:16). The ark was not accounted among the spoils claimed by the Babylonians (2 Kgs 25:13–17); 2 Macc 2:5 says that it was saved from destruction by Jeremiah and hidden on Mount Nebo. There it would stay, Jeremiah said, "until God gathers his people together again and shows his mercy" (2 Macc 2:7).

In Rev 11:19 the ark appears in the heavenly temple, fulfilling the prophecy of Jeremiah. This vision of the ark leads immediately into the vision of the "woman clothed with the sun" (Rev 12:1).

In Church tradition, the ark was seen by the Church Fathers and Saint Thomas Aquinas as a symbol of Christ, the bearer of the New Law. Saint Bonaventure described the ark as a representation of the Holy Eucharist.

Finally, the ark has been seen as a prefiguring of the Blessed Virgin **Mary**, called by the Church the "ark of the covenant." Where the ark in the Old Testament carried the Old Covenant, Mary, as the ark of God's New Covenant, carried the Messiah. The Blessed Mother was thus a sacred vessel wherein God's presence dwelled intimately with his people. The connection is most apparent in the visitation narrative in Luke, which exhibits several parallels with 2 Samuel and the bringing of the ark to Jerusalem under King David (cf. Luke 1:39 and 2 Sam 6:2; Luke 1:43 and 2 Sam 6:9; and Luke 1:41 and 2 Sam 6:16) (CCC 2058, 2130, 2578, 2594). The vision of the ark in Rev 11:19–12:1 hints at this identification: the "woman clothed with the sun" is the mother of the Messiah. (*See also* **Covenant**; **Tabernacle**.)

ARMAGEDDON (Greek, from the Hebrew for "mountain of Megiddo") The site, southeast of Mount **Carmel**, of the final battle at the end of history when all the kings of the earth are mustered. The name appears only once in Scripture (Rev 16:16). (*See* **Megiddo**.)

ARMENIA *See* **Ararat**.

ARMONI A son of King Saul and his concubine Rizpah. He was hanged by the Gibeonites (2 Sam 21:8–9).

ARMY *See* **Warfare**.

ARNI (Hebrew *Arni*) An ancestor of Jesus (Luke 3:33).

ARNON A river that flows into the midpoint of the Dead Sea from the east; today it is called Wadi Mojib. In the time of Moses, the river marked the northern boundary of Moab and the southern boundary of the Amorite kingdom (Num 21:13; Deut 2:24, 3:8, 12, 16; Josh 12:1–2, 13:9; 2 Kgs 10:33). (*See also* **Aroer**.)

AROER The name of three places mentioned in the Old Testament.

1. A city on the northern edge of the Arnon Valley in the region of the Amorite kingdom (Deut 2:36; Josh 12:2; Judg 11:26). After the Israelite conquest, the city was allotted to the Reubenites (Josh 13:16; 1 Chr 5:8). It remained an Israelite possession (Judg 11:26) and was part of the Davidic kingdom (2 Sam 24:5) until it fell to King Mesha of Moab (Jer 48:19; cf. 2 Kings 10:33).

2. A city in Gilead east of Rabbah (Josh 13:25).

3. A town in Judah mentioned in 1 Samuel (30:28).

ARPAD A town always mentioned with **Hamath** and located in northern Syria. It is identified with the modern site of Tell-Rifaat about nineteen miles north of Aleppo. The city was ruled by the Syro-Hittites and was besieged and captured several times by the Assyrian kings (Jer 49:23), in particular **Sennacherib** (2 Kgs 18:34; Isa 10:9, 36:19) and Tiglath-pileser III.

ARPHAXAD Also Arpachshad. One of the sons of Shem and a grandson of Noah appearing in the **Table of Nations** in Genesis (Gen 10:22, as Arpachshad; also Gen 11:10–13; 1 Chr 1:17–18). His name also appears in Luke's genealogy of Jesus (Luke 3:36). In Judith (1:1–6), an Arphaxad is named as an otherwise unknown king of the Medes who built Ecbatana and was defeated by Nebuchadnezzar.

ARTEMAS A disciple and companion of Paul. Paul expected to send Artemas to the island of Crete, to replace **Titus** (Titus 3:12); Titus was to meet Paul at Nicopolis.

ARTEMIS A Greek goddess, identified with the Roman deity Diana and one of the most widely worshipped goddesses of the ancient Mediterranean world. In Greek mythology Artemis was the goddess of hunters, the forest, and fertility. She was also the patron of women in childbirth, in keeping with her origins as a fertility goddess of Asia Minor: her chief image was a goddess with a multitude of breasts. Artemis was especially revered in **Ephesus**, which claimed to be the place of her birth. A rock believed to resemble her image was kept in Ephesus; it was said to have fallen from heaven (Acts 19:35) and was revered in all Asia Minor (Acts 19:27). She was honored with two major festivals each year, and her great temple in Ephesus, the Artemision (or Artemisium), was one of the seven wonders of the ancient world.

Artemis is mentioned only once in Scripture (Acts 19). Paul's preaching in Ephesus attracted so many listeners that Demetrius, a silversmith who made "silver shrines of Artemis," feared a loss of trade and profit for the wealthy silver guild and instigated a riot (Acts 19:23–40). The riots placed the lives of Paul, **Gaius**, and **Aristarchus** in danger.

ARVAD A Phoenician city occupying a small island just off the Syrian coast, north of Beirut, identified with modern Ruad. According to the **Table of Nations**, the people of Arvad were considered Canaanites (Gen 10:18; 1 Chr 1:16). Arvad was known as a commercial center, and its people were reputed to be superb sailors (Ezek 27:8, 11).

ARZA A prime minister of the northern kingdom of Israel under King **Elah**. Elah was murdered by Zimri in Arza's house after the king became drunk (1 Kgs 16:9).

ASA The third king of Judah (r. ca. 911–870 B.C.) and the son and successor of **Abijam** (1 Kgs 15:9–24; 2 Chr 13:23–16:14). He ruled for forty-one years and launched a crusade to rid Judah of idols, including the sacred prostitutes and also the fertility cults that had been protected by his grandmother, **Macaah**. When **Baasha** of Israel attacked him, Asa convinced **Ben-hadad** of Damascus to make a covenant with Judah and break his covenant with Israel, offering to Ben-hadad the Temple treasure as a gift. The scheme succeeded in wrecking Baasha's plan against Judah, and Asa then dismantled Baasha's fortifications at Ramah and used the materials to fortify Geba and Mizpeh (1 Kgs 15:9–24). He is also credited with the defeat of Zerah the Ethiopian (2 Chr 14:8–14), although he was criticized by the prophet Hanani for his alliance with Ben-hadad (2 Chr

16:7). His final years were marked by his suffering from an ailment of the foot (2 Chr 16:12).

ASAHEL (Hebrew, "God has done") The son of Zeruiah, sister of David, and the brother of **Joab** and **Abishai**. Asahel's death was one of the most notorious in the reign of David. Asahel was counted among the thirty "mighty men" in the service of David during his struggle against the house of Saul (2 Sam 23:24; 1 Chr 2:15, 11:26, 27:7). At the battle of Gibeon, Asahel chose to pursue **Abner** despite the warning of the latter; Asahel refused to retreat, and Abner killed him (2 Sam 2:18–23), thereby setting off a blood feud that ended with the murder of Abner by Joab in Hebron (2 Sam 3:26–30).

ASAIAH A servant of King **Josiah** (2 Kgs 22:12–14; 2 Chr 34:20). He was among those sent to the prophetess **Huldah** to inquire about the "book of the Law" that had been found in the Temple. The name Asaiah was also borne by several other individuals, including one of the heads of the tribe of Simeon (1 Chr 4:36) and the head of a Merarite family of Levites (1 Chr 6:30; 15:6, 11).

ASAPH The eponymous ancestor of the "sons of Asaph," the Levitical guild of singers. A member of the clan of Gershom and the son of Berechiah, Asaph was named with Heman and Jeduthun by David to be the ones "who should prophesy with lyres, with harps, and with cymbals" (1 Chr 25:2); they were thus in charge of the liturgical music of the sanctuary. The musical guild of the "sons of Asaph" was mentioned in the list of those who returned from exile with Zerubbabel (Ezra 2:41; Neh 7:44). A number of Psalms are called Psalms "of Asaph" (Ps 50, 73–83); this designation may mean that they were in the repertoire or collection of the guild of Asaph, rather than that they were composed by Asaph himself.

ASCENSION OF CHRIST The elevation of Christ into heaven forty days after his Resurrection. Christ's Ascension took place in his glorified body, in the presence of his disciples. The event was recounted in Mark (16:19), Luke (24:51), and Acts (1:1–11) (CCC 659–64).

The location of the Ascension was Mount Olivet, based on the return of the disciples "to Jerusalem from the mount called Olivet, which is near Jerusalem, a sabbath day's journey away" (Acts 1:12).

The Ascension was anticipated in the Old Testament by the bodily assumptions of **Enoch** (Gen 5:24) and **Elijah** (2 Kgs 2:11). The description of Christ as sitting "at the right hand" of the Father comes from Psalm 110. The Greek verb used in the Septuagint to describe the ascension of Elijah, *analambanō*, "take up" (2 Kgs 2:11), is used for the Ascension of Christ in Mark 16:19; Acts 1:2, 11, 22; and 1 Tim 3:16.

The image of sitting at the right hand of the Father in Ps 110:1 is prominent in Mark 16:19 and Acts 2:33. It means that the Ascension culminates in the enthronement of the Messiah, which marks the historical beginning of the Messianic kingdom that was described in Dan 7:14: "And to him was given dominion and glory and kingdom, that all peoples, nations, and languages should serve him; his dominion is an everlasting dominion, which shall not pass away, and his kingdom one that shall not be destroyed." Finding the literal fulfillment of Psalm 110 in Jesus Christ (not David), Acts 2:33–35 stresses the link between the Ascension of Christ and the descent of the Holy Spirit: "Being therefore exalted at the right hand of God, and having received from the Father the promise of the Holy Spirit, he has poured out this which you see and hear. For David did not ascend into the heavens; but he himself says, 'The Lord said to my Lord, Sit at my right hand, till I make thy enemies a stool for thy feet.'"

The Gospel of John highlights the connection between the Ascension and the Incarnation: "No one has ascended into heaven but he who descended from heaven, the Son of man" (John 3:13, 6:62, 20:17; cf. Eph 4:8–10). Christ forecasts his return to the Father in John's Gospel (John 6:62, when Christ asks the Jews: "Then what if you were to see the Son of man ascending where he was before?") and declares it as a coming event (John 20:17, when the risen Christ speaks to Mary Magdalene: "Do not hold me, for I have not yet ascended to the Father; but go to my brethren and say to them, I am ascending to my Father and your Father, to my God and your God.") The Gospel of John also refers to the Ascension elsewhere to emphasize the heavenly origins of Christ and the heavenly place to which he returned (John 7:33; 8:14; 13:3; 14:2–3; 16:5, 10). (*See also* **Parousia**; **Resurrection**.)

Another description of the Ascension of Christ alludes to the Danielic imagery of a cloud, as in Acts 1:9, which calls to mind Dan 7:13: "and behold, with the clouds of heaven there came one like a son of man, and he came to the Ancient of Days and was presented before him." The next time Christ appears in the narrative of Acts, he appears in glory as the "Son of man" (Acts 7:55–56).

The Ascension of Christ elsewhere in the New Testament affirms the place of Christ in glory, enthroned in power at the side of God the Father (Eph 1:20–21; Phil 2:9; Rev 1:12–20, 3:21), speaking of the event both as fact (Eph 4:8–10; 1 Tim 3:16; Heb 4:14) and as having been achieved by Christ's own will (Eph 4:10; cf. John 3:13, 6:62). Where a formal description is not given, the event is still assumed (Rom 8:34; Eph 1:20–21, 4:8–11; Heb 6:20).

Hebrews refers to the Ascension when it says that Jesus "passed through the heavens" (Heb 4:14) and "entered . . . into heaven itself" (Heb 9:24). In Hebrews the Ascension of Christ brings him into the heavenly phase of his priesthood, now that the earthly ministry has been accomplished. "Now the point in what we are saying is this: we have such a high priest, one who is seated at the right hand of the throne of the Majesty in heaven, a minister in the sanctuary and the true tent" (Heb 8:1–2). Returning to Psalm 110, Hebrews underlines the *royal* dignity of the Messiah (Ps 110:1) as well as the *priestly* dignity (Ps 110:4). Christ is enthroned as the Anointed One at the right hand of God in heaven and ordained as an eternal priest. From there "he is able for all time to save those who draw near to God through him, since he always lives to make intercession for them" (cf. Heb 7:25, 8:1–2) (CCC 519, 662).

Like Christ himself, the righteous will also be taken up "in the clouds" to be in heaven forever (1 Thess 4:17). The Ascension of Christ is thus the model for the assumption of all the saints destined for glory. The Feast of Ascension is celebrated forty days after Easter Sunday.

ASCENTS, SONG OF *See under* **Psalms**.

ASENATH The daughter of Potiphera, the Egyptian priest of On (Heliopolis), who was given in marriage to Joseph by Pharaoh (Gen 41:45). Asenath was the mother of Joseph's two sons, Manasseh and Ephraim (Gen 41:50–52; 46:20). The "nath" in Asenath is a reference to the Egyptian goddess Neith.

ASHAN A city within the territory of Judah (Josh 15:42) that was given for the tribe of Simeon (Josh 19:7–9).

ASHBEL The third son of **Benjamin** (Gen 46:21; Num 26:38; cf. 1 Chr 8:1).

ASHDOD One of the cities of the Philistines in southwest Canaan. It is identified with modern Tel Ashdod near the coast of the Mediterranean Sea. The city was included among the five cities of the Philistines (Josh 13:3) and was assigned to the tribe of Judah in the distribution of the Promised Land (Josh 15:47). It remained, however, in the power of the Philistines; Israel conquered it only in the reign of Uzziah of Judah (r. 792–740 B.C.). During the Philistine occupation, the **ark of the covenant** was brought to Ashdod after its capture in battle. The ark was placed in the temple of **Dagon** (1 Sam 5:1–2), but so severe were the disasters inflicted on the city that it

was moved to **Gath** (1 Sam 5:1–8; 6:17–18) and later returned to the Israelites. In the period of the Divided Kingdom, from 930 to 722 B.C.— when the tribes split apart and formed two rival states, Israel (north) and Judah (south)— Ashdod revolted against Sargon II of Assyria in 711 B.C. But the revolt was put down, and Ashdod remained an Assyrian possession until the fall of the empire in about 612 B.C. During the period of Persian occupation, Ashdod was opposed to the rebuilding of the walls of Jerusalem (Neh 4:7). By Maccabean times, the city was known as "Azotus" and was sacked by Judas Maccabeus (1 Macc 5:68), Jonathan Maccabeus (1 Macc 10:77–85), and John Hyrcanus (1 Macc 16:10). Philip evangelized in Ashdod (Acts 8:40).

ASHER (Hebrew, "happiness") The eighth son of Jacob, by Zilpah (the handmaid of his wife Leah), and the eponymous ancestor of the Israelite tribe of Asher. He was named for the happiness Leah felt at the time of her son's birth (Gen 30:13). Asher in turn had four sons and a daughter (Gen 46:17). The tribe of Asher was described as prosperous in the blessings of Jacob (Gen 49:20) and Moses (Deut 33:24– 25); nevertheless the tribe was not a significant one in Israelite history. Throughout the journey in the desert the tribe remained near the tribes of Dan and Naphtali (Num 2:27; 10:25–26). Their allotted territory was along the Mediterranean coast, north of Mount Carmel, and they lived among the Canaanites (Josh 19:24–31; Judg 1:31–32). The members of Asher declined the summons from Deborah to fight the Canaanites (Judg 5:17), but they did answer the call from Gideon (Judg 6:35;

7:23). Apparently a remnant of the Asherites survived into New Testament times, for the infant Jesus was hailed by the devout prophetess **Anna** "of the tribe of Asher" (Luke 2:36).

ASHERAH (Hebrew *'ăšērâ*)

1. A Canaanite goddess and the wife of El, the supreme god in Ugaritic mythology. Called "Lady," "Mother of the Gods," and "Lady of the Sea," Asherah is sometimes also described as the consort of Baal.

2. A cult object—normally of wood—erected in honor of the goddess and used in Canaanite fertility rites. The cult object appears at times in conjunction with an altar to Baal (Judg 6:25; cf. 1 Kgs 14:23, 15:13, 16:33, 18:19; 2 Kgs 13:6, 21:7, 23:6). (*See also* **Ashtoreth**.)

ASHIMA A Semitic deity worshipped by the Aramite peoples who were settled in Samaria by the Assyrians (2 Kgs 17:30); possibly one of the prominent goddesses (e.g., Anath, Asherah, or Astarte) revered by northwestern Semites. There may be a connection between this god and the one worshipped on Elephantine Island in Egypt, as well as a possible mention in Amos 8:14, which refers to those who swear allegiance to "Ashimah of Samaria."

ASHKELON One of the five major cities of the Philistines (Josh 13:3), located to the north of Gaza; it is today a major seaport on the Mediterranean coast. The city was an ancient one and figured in the expansion of Egypt, Assyria, and Babylon. According to Judg 1:18, Ashkelon was captured for a time by the tribe of Judah. The Philistines held it, however, for most of the period of the Judges (Judg 14:19; cf. 1 Sam 6:17). David mentioned the city in his lamentation over Saul (2 Sam 1:20). Ashkelon was denounced frequently by the prophets (Jer 25:20, 47:5, 7; Zeph 2:4, 7; Zech 9:5). The city was also famous for the quality of its onions.

ASHKENAZ The grandson of Japheth and one of the three sons of Gomer (Gen 10:3; 1 Chr 1:6), according to the **Table of Nations**. The name is also used for a kingdom (Jer 51:27) associated with Ararat and Minni (some scholars consider Ashkenaz to be the Scythian kingdom).

ASHPENAZ The chief eunuch in the court of Nebuchadnezzar (Dan 1:3–4). He had the duty of recruiting for the royal service from among the Jewish nobility exiled in Babylon.

ASHTAROTH The plural form of **Ashtoreth**.

ASHTAROTH A city in the region of Bashan in the upper **Transjordan**. It was the home of the Amorite king Og, who attempted to halt the Israelite invasion of Canaan (Deut 1:4; Josh 12:4). Following the defeat of Og, Ashtaroth was given to the tribe of Manasseh (Josh 13:31) and was later a Levitical city of the family of Gershom (1 Chr 6:71). The location of the site is uncertain, although it may be modern Tell Ashtara. (*See also* **Ashteroth-karnaim**.)

ASHTEROTH-KARNAIM A city located east of the Sea of Galilee, it belonged to the Rephaim, pre-Israelite inhabitants of Canaan. The Rephaim were defeated at Ashteroth-karnaim by the army of Chedorlaomer (Gen 14:5). As the Amorite ruler Og was one of the final heads of the Rephaim, Ashteroth-karnaim may be the city of Ashtaroth (Josh 9:10; 13:31).

ASHTORETH One of the three chief fertility goddesses revered by the Canaanites, with Anath and **Asherah**. The real name was Astarte; Ashtoreth (or Ashtaroth in the plural) is derived from the same Semitic word, but with the addition of the vowels of the Hebrew word *bōšet*, "shame" or "abomination." She was a consort of Baal, the Canaanite storm and fertility god. She was worshipped especially at Sidon (1 Kgs 11:5, 33; 2 Kgs 23:13). The cult was introduced into Jerusalem under Solomon (1 Kgs 11:5), who established high places east of Jerusalem in her honor. Josiah (2 Kgs 23:13) defiled those high places. Often the plural "Ashtaroth" is used to refer to the idols of Canaan in general, especially in the formula "the Baals and the Ashtaroth" (Judg 2:13, 10:6; 1 Sam 7:3, 4, 12:10).

ASIA In its broadest sense, Asia was used by the Greeks to describe the continent extending east of Europe and Africa into the Asian Steppe. Asia in 1 and 2 Maccabees refers to the Seleucid kingdom that stretched from the Hellespont to India (1 Macc 8:6; 2 Macc 3:3). In 1 Macc 8:6, Antiochus III, who was king of Syria and a large part of Asia Minor, is described as the great king of Asia. After his defeat by Rome he lost much of his territory to the Romans, although Antiochus and his successors were still called kings of Asia (their territory encompassed only Syria and Cilicia, 2 Macc 3:3).

In the New Testament, Asia refers to the Roman province that occupied an extensive region in Asia Minor (in modern western Turkey) composed of the territories of Mysia, Lydia, and Phrygia (Rhodes was later added). Its chief cities were Ephesus and Pergamum. Paul spent considerable time in the province of Asia (Acts 19:1–41), including over two years in Ephesus (Acts 19:10), and he wrote a letter to the Christians of Ephesus, as he did to those of another Asian city, Colossae. Asia is mentioned in several other letters (1 Cor 16:19; 2 Cor 1:8; 2 Tim 1:15; 1 Pet 1:1). In Revelation, John listed seven major cities of Asia, sending letters to each: Ephesus, Smyrna, Pergamum, Thyatira, Sardis, Philadelphia, and Laodicea (Rev 2:1–3:22).

ASIARCHS (Greek *asiarchēs*) The title used in Acts 19:31 for a group of officials in the province of Asia who met annually at Ephesus; aside from Acts, they are known chiefly through inscriptions, with little else known of their function. They probably belonged to the chief families of the province; perhaps they were part of the imperial cult, with the task of organizing various festivals in honor of the emperor. Paul had friends among the Asiarchs who helped protect him from a riot in Ephesus.

ASMODEUS The name of the demon mentioned in Tob 3:8. According to Tobit, the virgin Sarah, daughter of Raguel, had been married seven times, but "the evil demon Asmodeus had slain each of [her husbands] before he had been with her as his wife." The pious youth Tobias followed the instructions of the angel Raphael, married Sarah, and expelled the demon by burning the heart and liver of a fish upon live ashes of incense. The demon "fled to the remotest parts of Egypt, and the angel bound him" (Tob 8:2–3).

Some scholars find the origin of the name Asmodeus in the Persian demon of wrath and destruction, Aeshma Daeva. Other scholars trace it to a Hebrew root meaning "to destroy." There may thus be some identification of Asmodeus with Abaddon, the Destroyer (Rev 9:11).

ASS An animal belonging to the genus *Equus* found in two varieties, the wild ass and the domesticated ass. The domesticated ass was a very common animal in the ancient Near East, so it is no surprise to find it mentioned in Israelite Law (Exod 20:17; 21:33). It was used as a beast of burden (Gen 44:13; Josh 9:4) as well as an animal for transport (Exod 4:20; 1 Sam 25:20), even for a king. It was an animal of peaceful utility, rather than a beast of war. Hence Zechariah's prophecy of the Messiah riding upon an ass (Zech 9:9) indicates that the Messiah comes in peace; the war horse will be "cut off" from Jerusalem (Zech 9:10). The prophecy is fulfilled in Jesus's entry into Jerusalem (Matt 21:1–7; John 12:12–16). Because of its utility, the ass was seen as a proper gift (Gen 12:16; 32:15) and a blessing (Job 1:3; 42:12). The ass figured prominently in several episodes in the Old Testament, including the famed ass of Balaam (Num 22:21–33); the use

of the jawbone of an ass by Samson to slay a thousand Philistines (Judg 15:14–17); and the role played by asses in Saul's finding of Samuel and Samuel's anointing of Saul as king (1 Sam 9:1–27; 10:1).

The wild ass, or onager, was a symbol of untamed freedom (Gen 16:12; Job 39:5–8) as well as aimless wandering; the latter image was used to describe the exile of Israel (Hos 8:9).

ASSOS A port city on the Gulf of Adramyttium in Mysia in the Roman province of Asia. Paul went to Assos from Troas and embarked from there on his final journey to Jerusalem (Acts 20:13–14).

ASSUMPTION OF THE VIRGIN MARY *See under* **Mary**.

ASSYRIA A region in northern Mesopotamia, bordered by Babylonia and Elam on the south, Armenia to the north, Syria to the west, and the Zagros mountains to the east.

The Assyrians established one of the first great empires of the ancient world, an empire that reached its zenith in the days of the Divided Monarchy of Israel and Judah. They were monumental builders and artisans who forged key elements of Near Eastern trade, commerce, and cultural exchange that endured long after the demise of the empire.

But they were also notorious for their cruelty and ruthless foreign policy. The Assyrian army was the most fearsome military force the ancient Near East had ever seen. Often their campaigns left whole regions depopulated and cities completely destroyed. Surviving populations were forced into slavery and resettled in distant parts of the empire. To their enemies, the Assyrians were a feared and hated scourge. They were a constant threat to the kingdoms of Israel and Judah, which bought their precarious independence at the price of bloody wars or humiliating tribute. The Assyrian capital, **Nineveh**, was a prophetic symbol of all that was evil in the world (Jonah 1:2; Nah 3:7).

Under Shalmaneser III (r. 858–824 B.C.), the Assyrians clashed at Qarqar with a coalition of Arameans that included among its allies King **Ahab** of Israel. Later, in about 842 B.C., **Jehu** of Israel and other Aramean cities paid tribute to Assyria in an effort to bribe the Assyrians not to attack any further. The tribute payment is depicted on an Assyrian monument, the Black Obelisk of Shalmaneser III.

Tiglath-pileser III (r. 745–727 B.C.) pushed into Syria, Phoenicia, and Palestine and captured Damascus (1 Kgs 16:9). He invaded the kingdom of Israel (2 Kgs 15:19–20, where he appears as "Pul"; but cf. 1 Kgs 15:29); half of the kingdom of Israel was assumed into Assyrian territory in about 734 B.C., and Judah paid tribute. He also installed himself as king in Babylon and captured Gaza. As part of his policy of solidification, he engaged in mass deportation, moving the whole population of the region of Galilee to Assyria (2 Kgs 15:29).

Shalmaneser V (r. 727–722 B.C.) brought destruction to Samaria after a revolt of King Hosea of Israel, who vainly appealed for help from Egypt. His successor, **Sargon II** (r. 722–705 B.C.), deported the population of conquered Israel (2 Kgs 17:5; 18:9–10), sending the people to Assyria, and in their place he brought in colonists from Babylonia and elsewhere (2 Kgs 17). Such resettlement was standard Assyrian policy; it was an attempt to destroy any spirit of patriotism in the conquered population that might later stir up revolt. Except for a few remnants (the prophetess **Anna** was an Asherite, for example), the ten northern tribes of Israel disappear from history after the Assyrian conquest.

Sargon's chosen heir, **Sennacherib** (r. 705–681 B.C.), invaded Judah in the reign of Hezekiah. He never captured Jerusalem, owing to a defeat of his army brought about by an angel (2 Kgs 18:13, 19:35; 2 Chr 32:1–21). When he returned to Assyria, he was assassinated by his sons. After his father's death, **Esarhaddon** (r. 681–669 B.C.) waged an effective campaign against Egypt, sacked the capital of Memphis in 671, and set up twenty client kings who were toppled almost immediately after the Assyrians departed. He died on campaign, and his successor, Ashurbanipal (r. 668–627 B.C.), faced new revolts in Egypt, reduced Thebes, and installed vassals to rule in his stead while he warred against Elam.

Even as Assyria reached its greatest territorial extent, however, the empire collapsed with stunning speed. Weakened by bloody revolts, the empire was challenged by the two rising powers of the era, the Medes and the Chaldeans. The two launched a massive offensive in 616 B.C. Nineveh was destroyed in 612 B.C., and the last remnant of the Assyrian Empire fell in 609 B.C. The Babylonian Empire now emerged as the dominant imperial power of the Near East.

The forcible mass movement of peoples

by the late Assyrian rulers, which destroyed (among many other nations) the northern kingdom of Israel, was an intentional effort to create a global empire of "Assyrianized" peoples under the leadership of the Assyrian state. The effort failed partly because of the harshness of Assyrian rule. Still, although their empire collapsed, the Assyrians changed the Near East forever. They passed on to the Babylonians, Persians, and finally Alexander the Great a culturally unified Near Eastern world.

ASTARTE *See* **Ashtoreth**.

ASYNCRITUS A Christian in Rome who received greetings from Paul (Rom 16:14).

ATAD A town in southern Transjordan where the funeral procession bearing the body of Jacob halted for seven days of mourning (Gen 50:10–11). The site was renamed Abel-mizraim ("the mourning of Egypt"). Its exact location is unknown beyond the fact that it was situated east of the Jordan River. (*See also* **Abel-Mizraim**.)

ATARGATIS A fertility goddess worshipped in ancient Syria. Hadad, the Semitic storm god (Greek Adonis), was said to be her consort. Her temple in Carnaim in Transjordan was burned by Judas Maccabeus (1 Macc 5:43–44; 2 Macc 12:26).

ATAROTH The name of several places.

1. A city that was taken from Sihon the Amorite and rebuilt by the tribe of Gad (Num 32:3, 34).

2. A territory in the Jordan Valley on the eastern border of Ephraim (Josh 16:2; cf. 16:5, 16:7, 18:3).

3. A town mentioned in 1 Chr 2:54, otherwise unidentified.

ATHALIAH (perhaps an Akkadian derivative meaning "Yahweh is manifest in glory") The wife of **Jehoram**, king of Judah, and apparently the daughter of King **Ahab** and **Jezebel**; she was also the mother of **Ahaziah**, king of Judah (2 Kgs 8:18, 26). One of the most infamous queens in the Old Testament, she usurped the throne after the death of her son Ahaziah and commanded the murder of the whole royal family, nearly exterminating the line of David (2 Kgs 11:1; 2 Chr 22:10). Only the infant **Joash** was spared, because the priest **Jehoiada** hid the child in the Temple (2 Kgs 11:2–3; 2 Chr 22:11–12). From about 841 to 835 B.C., there was no Davidic king on the throne of Judah. Athaliah appears to have promoted the cult of Baal (2 Kgs 11:18), which adds to her infamy in sacred history. In the sixth year of her reign, Jehoiada secured the support of the palace guard and had Joash proclaimed king, restoring the house of David to the throne (2 Kgs 11:4–20; 2 Chr 23:1–21). Athaliah was taken by surprise and was seized with little trouble. She was then executed in the palace (2 Kgs 11:16, 20), and her temple of Baal in Jerusalem was destroyed (2 Kgs 11:18).

ATHENS The chief city of Greece and one of the foremost centers of learning and culture in the ancient world. By the first century A.D., the once great city had lost virtually all of its political importance, owing to the supremacy of the Roman Empire. Nevertheless it retained its great reputation for philosophy and the arts, still rivaling other eminent centers such as Alexandria and Rome. Athens is mentioned only once in the New Testament, when Paul preached there during his second missionary journey (Acts 17:15–34). While there he met with the Epicurean and Stoic philosophers and was invited to address them at the Areopagus. Some mocked his speech, but others were willing to hear more, and a few believed: **Dionysius the Areopagite** and **Damaris** are named specifically.

ATONEMENT See **Redemption**; **Resurrection**; **Sacrifice**.

ATONEMENT, DAY OF One of the most solemn holy days of the Jewish year, observed on the tenth day of the seventh month (Tishri, September–October), five days before the Feast of **Tabernacles**. On this day in ancient Israel, all work was forbidden for all people (including aliens), and a fast was required to be observed by all of the people. According to Lev 16:30, "on this day atonement shall be made for you, to cleanse you; from all your sins you shall be clean before the Lord."

The day was an annual renewal of the Mosaic covenant ratified at Sinai. It was a reminder that the sins of the people were obstacles to their intimacy with God. Expiation for those sins was necessary for proper reconciliation. For that expiation, the blood of sacrificial victims was offered (Lev 17:11), and on this one day of the year, blood was brought into the **holy of holies** by the high priest, who acted as the representative of the people.

The high priest was dressed in simple robes and, after two ritual baths, offered animals in sacrifice—first for his own sins and then for the people's. Atonement was made first by the priest: he must be purified as mediator between God and the Israelites. The Tabernacle was also purified, as it was also defiled by the sins of the nation. The high priest sacrificed sin offerings—a bull calf (for himself) and a goat (for the people)—and the blood of both victims was then taken into the holy of holies and sprinkled on the mercy seat of the ark (Lev 16:11–15, 18–19). Next the high priest took a second goat and placed his hands upon its head. He then ritually confessed the sins of Israel. The goat, a **scapegoat**, symbolically carried the sins of all and was turned loose in the desert (Lev 16:8–22, 23:26, 32; Num 29:7–11). The remains of the burnt offerings, the bull calf and the goat, were carried outside the camp or city and burned.

The book of Hebrews sees the Day of Atonement as a **type** of the atonement by Christ for the sins of the world (Heb 9–10). Jesus is the perfect high priest who entered once for all into the holy of holies of heaven and obtained eternal redemption, not with the blood of goats and calves, but with his own blood. Unlike the Old Testament high priest, however, Christ had no need to make sacrifice for himself, as he was sinless.

Hebrews infers that the yearly repetition of the ritual points to the insufficiency of the sacrificial cult of Israel to expiate sin in a definitive way. The sacrifice of Christ, on the other hand, was once and for all, so there was no longer need for an annual offering (Heb 9:12; 12:10). As the high priest, Christ has entered into the holy of holies, but the tent he entered is heaven, "the greater and perfect tent (not made with hands, that is, not of this creation)" (Heb 9:11). Finally, just as the bodies of the sacrificed animals were burned outside the camp, "Jesus also suffered outside the city gate in order to sanctify the people by his own blood" (Heb 13:11–12).

ATTALIA A port city of Pamphylia on the southern coast of Asia Minor (modern Turkey). The city was founded by King Attalus II Philadelphus of Pergamum (r. 159–138 B.C.) and was visited by Paul and Barnabas on their return to Antioch (Acts 14:25).

ATTALUS The king of Pergamum (possibly King Attalus II Philadelphus, r. 159–138 B.C., or Attalus III, r. 138–133 B.C.) to whom the Romans sent a letter calling for the protection of Jews (1 Macc 15:22).

AUGUSTUS CAESAR The first Roman emperor (31 B.C.–A.D. 14) and the ruler of the Roman Empire at the time of Jesus's birth at Bethlehem (Luke 2:1). Known originally as Octavian, he was the grand-nephew of Julius Caesar and triumphed in a series of civil wars over his rivals to become undisputed ruler of Rome. His final victory took place at the battle of Actium in 31 B.C., at which he defeated Marc Antony and Queen Cleopatra of Egypt. Once established in Rome, he received the title Augustus in 27 B.C. from the Roman senate in recognition of his place as *princeps* (ruler or chief). The title and position of emperor henceforth became a hereditary one, and the events of the New Testament were influenced by both Augustus and his successors, including Tibe-

rius (A.D. 14–31), Gaius Caligula (A.D. 31–37), and Claudius (A.D. 37–54). (*See also* **Roman Empire**.) The decree that brought Joseph and Mary to Bethlehem just before the birth of Christ was issued by Augustus (Luke 2:1–7).

Under Augustus, the Roman Empire began a long period of general peace and prosperity (known as the *Pax Romana*, "Roman Peace"). Many of the reforms and innovations that were introduced during his reign—including the expansion of trade, commerce, and travel, as well as the vast network of imperial roads—helped establish an atmosphere ideally suited for the spread of the Christian message.

AUTHORIZED VERSION *See* **Versions of the Bible**.

AVENGER OF BLOOD (Hebrew *gôʾēl*, from *gāʾal*, "to redeem") The kinsman of a murder victim whose duty was to hunt down and take the life of the killer. In early tribal societies, a murder could be avenged upon the killer by a relative of the victim. The deterrent to murder was not courts or police but the assurance that the relatives of the dead man or wronged party would seek revenge. Under this system issues of justice were settled without a legal process, but the result was likely a self-perpetuating cycle of violence, as clans sought out vengeance for each subsequent killing.

In biblical law, retaliation for personal harm was restricted to seeking vengeance in strict proportion to the crime: "If any harm follows, then you shall give life for life, eye for eye, tooth for tooth, hand for hand, foot for foot, burn for burn, wound for wound, stripe for stripe" (Exod 21:23–25). Death was not permitted for injury. Subsequent law made distinctions between killings that were accidents (Num 35:11) or without malice (Num 35:22; cf. Deut 19:4; Josh 20:3) and premeditated murder. In cases where a killing took place without malice, the perpetrator could be killed by an avenger unless he was able to reach asylum at an altar (Exod 21:13) or at a city of asylum (Num 35:11–28; Deut 4:41–43, 19:1–13; Josh 20:1–9). At that point, the elders of his home city determined guilt or innocence, and a suitable punishment was imposed. If malice was proven, the killer was removed from the altar and delivered up (Exod 21:14). Israelite law did not accept the payment of a fine for murder, as only God could claim the right of life and death over every man (Gen 9:6; Num 35:31–34). (*See also* **Marriage**.)

AVVA A city in Assyria or Syria (the location is not certain) from which colonists came to Samaria after the Israelite inhabitants were taken away. They were forcibly resettled by the king of Assyria, Sargon II (2 Kgs 17:24).

AVVIM The inhabitants of southwest Palestine in the period before the Philistines, called the Caphtorim, conquered the territory (Deut 2:23; Josh 13:3).

AXA *See* **Achsah**.

AYIN The sixteenth letter of the Hebrew alphabet (ע).

AZARIAH (Hebrew, "Yahweh has helped") The name of a large number of men in the Old Testament.

1. A king of Judah, also known as Uzziah, who reigned from about 792 to 740 B.C. (*See* **Uzziah**).

2. The son of **Nathan** (1 Kgs 4:5) and an official in the government of King Solomon.

3. A prophet, the son of Oded, who was sent by the Lord to **Asa** after his victory over Zerah and the Ethiopians. Azariah declared that Asa would prosper if he remained faithful to God (2 Chr 15:2–7).

4. A son of King **Jehoshaphat** (2 Chr 21:2). He was murdered by **Jehoram** along with his brothers to ensure the succession.

5. The name used by the angel **Raphael** when he presented himself to **Tobias** (Tob 5:12; 6:6; 9:2).

6. One of the three companions of Daniel with whom he was thrown into the fiery furnace (Dan 1:6; 3:49). He is also called **Abednego**.

AZATOS *See* **Ashdod**.

AZAZEL The term used on the Day of Atonement when the high priest imposed his hands upon the scapegoat upon which the sins and transgressions of the people were laid. The goat was then sent into the desert "for Azazel" (Lev 16:8–10, 20–28). The meaning is uncertain. According to one Jewish tradition, Azazel is the name of a fallen angel (*1 Enoch* 8:1; 10:4–6); it may also mean a **demon** of the desert, or the **devil**, or the location to which the goat flees. (*See also* **Atonement, Day of**).

AZEKAH A town in Judah (Josh 15:35) to which five Canaanite kings fled after Joshua defeated them (Josh 10:10–11). The town also figured in the Philistine campaign against Saul (1 Sam 17:1) and was one of the sites fortified by King Rehoboam (2 Chr 11:9). In the Babylonian invasion of 586 B.C., Azekah was listed as one of the last strongholds of Judah to fall (Jer 34:7)—an event also recorded in contemporary Babylonian documents, such as the Lachish Letters, in which a commander noted that the flames of Lachish's signals were still visible, but those of Azekah were not. The site is believed to be the modern Tell Zakariya, first excavated in 1898–99 by Frederick J. Bliss.

AZOTUS *See* **Ashdod**.

B

B The traditional designation for the Codex Vaticanus. (*See under* **Codex** for details.)

BAAL (Hebrew, "Lord" or "Master") The name of the most important Canaanite deity, the god of rain, storms, and fertility. The god was worshipped under a variety of titles and in various ways. In Canaanite mythology, Baal merges with the Semitic storm god Hadad ("Thunderer"). Although **El** was the father of the gods in the Canaanite pantheon, Baal seems to have been the main focus of Canaanite worship.

Frequently mentioned in the Old Testament, Baal is also a prominent figure in Ugaritic texts (*see* **Ugarit**). The myths tell of Baal's struggle against several opponents who are personified dangers, including Mot (death) and Yamm (the sea). Against Mot, Baal enters into the depths of the earth and is mourned by El. Baal's companion, Anath, however, searches for her husband and triumphs over Mot, whereupon Baal returns to life and regains his power over the earth. The tale itself represents the agricultural cycle of death and rebirth, dry season and rainy season. Against Yamm, Baal was a figure of order against the forces of chaos, and thus to be emulated by the Canaanite ruler, who likewise stood as the symbol of order for his people.

Baal was depicted iconographically as a bull (a symbol of fertility) and also as a warrior grasping lightning (a symbol of his power over nature).

The Baal cult was always popular in Canaan, and it was opposed bitterly throughout the OT period by the prophets of Israel. The worship of Baal was attended by Baal's prophets (1 Kgs 18; Jer 2) and was conducted at the so-called high places, where a stone pillar was erected in his honor (2 Kgs 3:2; 10:26). The early Israelites may have used the term "Baal" for Yahweh; it appears in various personal and place names (Baal-perazim in 2 Sam 5:20; Esh-baal in 1 Chr 8:33; Merib-baal in 1 Chr 8:34). Later, because of its direct associations with idolatry, the term "Baal" was clearly separated from, or dissociated with, the worship of Yahweh, and the name was used exclusively for pagan gods (Hos 2:16–17). The worship of Baal was tolerated and even promoted at times in the dark days of the Divided Monarchy (1 Kgs 16:31–33, 18:22; 2 Kgs 17:16; 2 Chr 33:3–6; Jer 19:5, 32:35); it was opposed by the prophets of God, who then faced persecution by its royal patrons. Of particular note was **Elijah**, whom Jezebel hated for his zeal against the cult (1 Kgs 16–18). The other great opponents of Baal included **Gideon** (who destroyed the altar of Baal in Judg 6:25ff.) and the kings **Asa, Jehu, Hezekiah,** and **Josiah**. Josiah's great reforms went far in extirpating the worship of Baal (2 Kgs 23:4–5), but it came back in the next reign (2 Kgs 23:31–32) and persisted until the **Exile**.

Baal was probably the most common of the "abominations of the nations" (2 Chr 36:14) that seduced the people of Israel and Judah away from the worship of God. Their infidelity brought on the curses that Moses had warned them would come if they broke the covenant (Deut 30:15–20). (*See* **Idolatry**; *see also* **Covenant**.)

BAALAH An earlier name used for **Kiriath-jearim** (Josh 15:9; 1 Chr 13:6).

BAALATH A city within the tribal lands assigned to Dan (Josh 19:44). It was later fortified by Solomon (1 Kgs 9:18; 2 Chr 8:6). Joshua 15:9 says that "Baalah" is the same as **Kiriath-jearim**. It is probably the site of modern el-Maghar.

BAAL-BERITH (Hebrew, "Lord of the Covenant") A Canaanite god worshipped in the city of Shechem (Judg 9:4). Baal-berith was venerated by the Israelites after the death of Gideon (Judg 8:33).

BAAL-GAD A Canaanite town near Mount Hermon that marked the farthest extent in the north of the conquests of Joshua (Josh 11:17; 12:7; 13:5).

BAAL-HAMON A site that was used by Solomon as the place for his vineyard (Song 8:11). The location is unknown.

BAAL-HANAN The seventh king of Edom, before the rise of the Israelite monarchy (Gen 36:38; 1 Chr 1:49).

BAAL-HAZOR A mountain, near the town of **Bethel** in cental Canaan, where **Absalom** murdered his half brother **Amnon** (2 Sam 13:23).

BAALIS A king of the Ammonites who sent Ishmael, the son of Nethaniah, and his band to murder **Gedaliah**, the governor of Judah who had been appointed by King Nebuchadnezzar after the destruction of Jerusalem in 586 B.C. (Jer 40:13–16). His intent was to create political instability and thereby profit by expanding his own influence over Judah. Baalis later gave sanctuary to the assassins of Gedaliah.

BAAL-PEOR *See* **Beth-peor**.

BAAL-PERAZIM A site southwest of Jerusalem where David won a major victory over the Philistines (2 Sam 5:20; 1 Chr 14:11). The triumph helped solidify David's position as king.

BAALZEBUB See **Beelzebul**.

BAAL-ZEPHON A town to which the Israelites were directed during their flight from Egypt (Exod 14:1–2), near the third encampment of the Exodus journey (Num 33:7). According to Exodus, Moses was instructed to have the people of Israel "encamp in front of Piha-hiroth, between Migdol and the sea, in front of Baal-zephon." Probably Baal-zephon was a seaport.

BAANAH AND RECHAB Two brothers who served as captains in the army of **Ish-bosheth**, the son of Saul and his sole surviving heir (2 Sam 4:2). They murdered their master and brought his severed head to David in the hopes of receiving a reward. Instead David had them executed; Ish-bosheth was then given a proper burial (2 Sam 4:5–12).

BAASHA King of Israel from around 909 to 886 B.C. (1 Kgs 15–16). The son of **Ahijah**, he was a commoner (1 Kgs 16:2) and ascended to the throne through the assassination of Nadab, son of Jeroboam, thus becoming the northern kingdom's third king and founding its second dynasty. His reign was taken up chiefly with his war against King **Asa** of Judah. Against his effort, Asa secured the support of **Ben-hadad** of Damascus, and Baasha was forced to withdraw from the fortified city of Ramah (1 Kgs 15:16–22). Baasha was rebuked by the prophet Jehu for his impiety (1 Kgs 16:1–4).

BABEL, TOWER OF The tower "with its top in the heavens" begun on the plain of Shinar (Gen 11:1–9). The story tells us that at that time humanity spoke one common language and had settled in the region of Shinar, the central Mesopotamian plain (Gen 11:1–2). There the people decided to construct "a city, and a tower with its top in the heavens" to "make a name [Hebrew *šēm*] for ourselves" (11:4). In their pride, the people rejected dependence upon God (11:6); they also implicitly rejected the leadership of the righteous line of **Shem** (Hebrew *šēm*). God intervened, confused their language, and scattered them across the face of the earth (11:7–8). Thus the name for the tower comes from the Hebrew word *bābel*, which resembles the Hebrew word *bālal*, "confuse."

The account of the Tower of Babel makes the diversity of the world's languages and the scattering of peoples a consequence of divine judgment. Significantly, immediately after the account of Babel, Abraham is introduced, the antithesis of the pride and rebellion that the tower represented. Thus, both historically and literarily, the story of Babel sets the stage for the calling of Abraham, through whom the Lord will regather the divided human race into the unity of the family of God. Some scholars see a connection between the story of Babel and the enormous ziggurats, or step-pyramids, of ancient **Babylon**. The name *bābel* is also the Hebrew name of the city of Babylon (CCC 57).

BABYLON, BABYLONIA The name of an ancient empire centered in Mesopotamia. The empire took its name from its capital city, which was built on the east bank of the Euphrates River; its territory covered modern southern Iraq. Babylon had a significant influence on the history of the Near East and was particularly important in shaping the history of Israel.

I. *Geography*
II. *History*
    A. *Up to the Assyrian Conquest*
    B. *Under the Assyrians*

I. GEOGRAPHY

The city of Babylon was located on the banks of the Euphrates River, approximately 550 miles (885 kilometers) east across the Syrian Desert from Jerusalem. The area of Babylonia was part of Mesopotamia, bordered to the north by Assyria, to the west and south by the Arabian Desert, to the east by Persia, and to the southeast by the Persian Gulf. It is mentioned in Gen 10:10 as "the land of Shinar" and the heart of the kingdom of **Nimrod**.

What became Babylonia was situated on a broad and fertile alluvial plain, with rich soil deposited by the Tigris and Euphrates rivers as they flowed southward from their sources in the highlands of Asia Minor. Apart from the rivers, the region was dry, receiving around four inches of precipitation annually. Irrigation was crucial, therefore, and a system of canals and reservoirs was constructed in prehistoric times.

II. HISTORY

A. Up to the Assyrian Conquest

Babylonia had no natural barriers to invasion, and the flat plain proved an inviting target for migrating peoples. As with **Assyria** and **Per-**sia, Babylonia was subjected to repeated invasions.

The city of Babylon is mentioned for the first time by Sargon of Akkad (c. 2350–2294 B.C.). Its importance began under the first Amorite dynasty in the nineteenth century B.C., especially in the reign of its greatest ruler, Hammurabi, in the mid- to late eighteenth century B.C. Hammurabi made Babylon his center of operations against various neighbors (Elam, Larsa, and Assyria) and developed it into a key administrative and economic center. He and his successors promoted art and culture and did much to make Babylon an enduring symbol of Mesopotamian life and religion. He also codified law, an achievement that had wide-ranging implications for the Near East. Nevertheless, the Amorite Empire collapsed under Hammurabi's successors, and it was eclipsed by the ascendancy of **Assyria** in the early first millennium B.C.

B. Under the Assyrians

The Assyrians respected the cultural influence of Babylon and controlled it as a vassal kingdom. The Neo-Babylonian dynasty began with the arrival of the Chaldeans in the Aramean invasion. While Chaldeans paid tribute to the Assyrians, they came to control Babylon until the Assyrian resurgence under **Tiglath-pileser III**, when they were driven into the south. When the northern kingdom of Israel was overthrown by the Assyrians in 722 B.C. and many of its people carried into captivity, colonists were sent from Babylon to Samaria to replace the exiled population (2 Kgs 17:23–24; 1 Chr 5:26). The Chaldeans returned to Babylon in 721 B.C., when **Merodach-baladan**

(2 Kgs 20:12; Isa 39:1; the name is the Hebrew pronunciation of "Marduk-apallidin") claimed the throne of Babylon and later defeated the Assyrians while in alliance with Elam. The Assyrian ruler **Sennacherib** destroyed the city in 689 B.C.

C. Establishment of the Neo-Babylonian Empire

In 626 B.C. the Chaldean leader Nabopolassar launched a revolt against the Assyrians and seized the Babylonian throne. With their allies, the Medes, the Babylonians crushed the Assyrians and conquered Nineveh in 612 B.C.; the last Assyrian king established himself at Harran, where he was again defeated; after that the Assyrians faded from history. Under **Nebuchadnezzar II** (605–562 B.C.), Babylonian armies defeated the Egyptians and Carchemish in 605 B.C. and posed an immediate threat to Syria and Palestine.

D. The Conquest of Judah

Daniel tells us that Babylonian armies invaded Judah and took numerous captives, including Daniel himself, in 605 B.C. (Dan 1:1–4). Around 604 B.C., King **Jehoiakim** of Judah was compelled to become a political vassal of Babylon (2 Kgs 24:1ff.), and Jerusalem surrendered to the Babylonians in 597 B.C. Nebuchadnezzar installed **Zedekiah**, son of Josiah and uncle of the deported Jehoiakim, on the throne of Judah as a vassal of Babylon. Zedekiah embarked upon an ill-fated revolt in 588 B.C. The army of Babylon stormed and destroyed Jerusalem in 586 B.C. and carried off the inhabitants into exile in Babylonia (2 Kgs 25; 2 Chr 36), as had been foretold (2 Kgs 20:16–18; Jer 15:1–14, 21:8–14; Ezek 4–5; Amos 2:4–5; Mic 3:12). (*See* **Exile**.)

E. Decline and Persian Conquest

The successors to Nebuchadnezzar were unable to maintain the vitality and influence of the Babylonian Empire. King Nabonidus (r. 556–539 B.C.) focused on conquests in Arabia, leaving the royal prince, **Belshazzar**, in charge as regent. Babylon fell to the army of **Cyrus II** (the Great), king of the Medes and Persians, in 539 B.C., as had been foretold (Isa 21:1–9; Jer 51:31–37; Dan 5:28). Cyrus released the Jews from their long Exile and permitted them to return to Palestine (Ezra 1:1; 5:14). Henceforth Babylon was a major center of the Persian Empire. After the conquest of the Persian Empire in 331 B.C. by Alexander the Great (d. 323 B.C.), the city of Babylon declined steadily in importance.

III. CULTURAL SIGNIFICANCE

A. The Cradle of Civilization

The cultural and historical significance of Babylon in the history of the Near East is unquestionable. Justifiably called a cradle of civilization, Babylon was responsible for important advances in arts and crafts, architecture, and social structures. A large body of literature grew up in the Babylonian language; it included the famous epic of Gilgamesh, a vivid creation account, and various wisdom writings.

B. Babylonian Law

Babylonian law was equally influential. The common people enjoyed basic rights, including the ownership of private property. Slavery existed but under specific regulations. The code of Hammurabi included an early version of the *lex talionis*, or law of exact retribution (Exod 21:23–27), and it helped establish the idea of a written law as the supreme legal authority. (*See also* **Law**.)

C. The Fame of the City Itself

Nebuchadnezzar began an ambitious building program in Babylon. Excavations have revealed a grand city that stretched across the Euphrates and that was defended by a double wall and moat. The city was entered through eight gates, and the river was crossed by two bridges. The city was famed especially for the Ishtar Gate that led to the Processional Street, and for the "hanging gardens" that were hailed as one of the seven wonders of the ancient world. Aside from the two massive palace complexes, there were more than fifty temples; the largest temple was the Esagil, the temple of Marduk, where the statue of Marduk stood. To the north of the temple was the ziggurat of Marduk, a seven-tiered tower (*see* **Babel, Tower of**).

IV. BABYLON AS A SYMBOL IN THE NEW TESTAMENT

In the New Testament the name "Babylon" is often used figuratively as the capital of the kingdom of the Antichrist (Rev 14:8) and as the personification of evil forces arrayed against the people of God (Rev 16:19).

The imagery of Babylon in the NT reaches its climax in Revelation, where the empire is called "Babylon the great" (Rev 14:8; 17:5; 18:2, 10, 21), the "great harlot" (Rev 17:1, 15; 19:2), and the "great city" (Rev 16:19; 17:18; 18:10,

16, 18, 19, 21). For early Christians, Babylon could be seen as a **type** of Rome, the world power that oppressed the Christians as Babylon had oppressed the people of Judah (1 Pet 5:13; cf. the apocryphal books *2 Esdras* 3:1, *2 Baruch* 2:1).

But in Revelation Babylon also serves as a symbol of Jerusalem, where Jesus Christ was crucified (Rev 11:8), and where the prophets and martyrs were killed (Rev 18:24). This "Babylon" is destined for destruction by fire (Rev 18:8–9)—which is exactly what happened to Jerusalem at the end of the failed rebellion in A.D. 70.

BABYLONIA *See* **Babylon**.

BABYLONIAN CAPTIVITY The name coined by the writer Petrarch (d. A.D. 1374) for the period of almost seventy years in Church history (1309–1377) during which the popes resided at Avignon in southern France, instead of at Rome. He compared the exile of the papacy to the **Exile** of the Jews in Babylon.

BACCHIDES A Syrian leader of the time of Kings Demetrius I Soter (r. 162–150 B.C.) and Antiochus IV Epiphanes (175–164 B.C.). In 162 B.C. Bacchides was one of the commanders of the army that was sent by Antiochus V into Palestine. He installed **Alcimus** as high priest in Jerusalem and then returned to the royal court. After the triumph of **Judas Maccabeus** over **Nicanor**, Bacchides returned to Palestine and defeated Judas at the battle of Elasa in 161 (1 Macc 7:8–20; 9). Later Bacchides attacked **Jonathan** but lost a thousand men after an unsuccessful siege of Jonathan and **Simon**

in Bethbasi. Bacchides came to terms with the Maccabees and left the country (1 Macc 9:58–73; 2 Macc 8:30).

BAGOAS The eunuch in charge of the personal affairs of Holofernes (Jdt 12:11). He discovered the decapitated body of the general the morning after Judith had killed him (Jdt 14:14–18).

BAHURIM A Benjaminite village near Jerusalem (2 Sam 3:16; 16:5; 17:8). The village was the home of **Shimei**, who cursed David as he fled to the desert after learning about the uprising of Absalom (2 Sam 19:16–23; 1 Kgs 2:8). Bahurim may be either modern Ras et-Tmim or modern Khirbet Ibqe'dan.

BALAAM A seer or prophet from Pethor in upper Mesopotamia, the son of Beor. Balaam was hired by Balak, king of Moab, to curse the Israelites while they were encamped upon the plain of Moab and preparing to enter Canaan (Num 22:5). At first, warned by God, Balaam refused to go, but after repeated pleas from Balak he agreed to go with Balak's representatives. While on the way, he was stopped by an angel, invisible to Balaam but visible to his donkey. When his donkey refused to go on, Balaam struck her with his staff; then "the LORD opened the mouth of the donkey," and Balaam argued with the donkey. When Balaam's eyes were opened to the angel, the angel warned him to speak "only the word which I bid you."

When Balaam finally came to Balak, he pronounced blessings upon Israel instead of curses. The blessings came in four oracles: (1) a short poem honoring Israel as chosen by the Lord from among the nations (Num 23:7–10); (2) an affirmation of God's saving presence among his people and the impossibility of defying God's will (Num 23:18–24); (3) an assurance of the victory of Israel over its enemies (Num 24:3–7); (4) a prophecy of Israel's triumph over its neighbors, the founding of the Israelite monarchy, and the coming of the Messiah (Num 24:15–24; cf. Acts 2:34–36; 1 Cor 15:22–28).

According to a later account in Numbers, Balaam advised the Moabites and Midianites to use their women to seduce the Israelites into idolatry; for this he was put to the sword (Num 31:16). Balaam is seen in the New Testament as a **type** of the false prophets encountered by the early Christians (2 Pet 2:15; Rev 2:14). Scholars believe that the oracles of Balaam are some of the oldest specimens of Hebrew poetry preserved in Scripture.

Balaam, son of Beor, is mentioned as a "seer" in an inscription at Tell Deir Alla (in modern Jordan) that dates back to the eighth century B.C.

BALADAN The father of **Merodach-baladan** of Babylon (2 Kgs 20:12; Isa 39:1). He was king of Babylon from about 721 to 710 B.C., and then again in 704 B.C.

BALAK The king of Moab and son of Zippor; he is best known for his attempt to persuade the prophet **Balaam** to curse the Israelites (Num 22–24). When the Israelites were camped on the plain of Moab in anticipation of moving across Canaan, Balak and his chief advisors sought to defeat them by supernatural means.

Yet when Balaam at last agreed to go with the princes of Moab to visit Balak, he proved capable of speaking only blessings (Num 23–24) and giving assurance of the inevitable victory of the Israelites. Balak is also mentioned in Josh 24:9–10, Judg 11:25, Mic 6:5, and Rev 2:14, each time in reference to the events in Num 22–24.

BALDNESS Lack of hair on the scalp. Baldness was often viewed in the Old Testament as a curse (Isa 3:24; Ezek 7:18; Amos 8:10) and shameful, especially among women (Isa 3:24; 15:2). On the other hand, the prophet **Elisha** was bald, and forty-two boys of Bethel were ripped to pieces by bears for mocking his hairless head (2 Kgs 2:23–24). Priests were prohibited from shaving their heads (Lev 21:5).

BALM Also balsam, a sweet-smelling resin harvested from several trees that grew in Palestine and the Transjordan. Balm was esteemed highly for its soothing and healing properties (Jer 8:22; 46:11; 51:8) and was an important trade item (Gen 37:25, 43:11; Ezek 27:17). (*See* **Gilead**.)

BALSAM *See* **Balm**.

BALTHASAR The name Christian tradition gives to one of the three **magi**, or wise men. The name is not mentioned in the Bible.

BAMOTH One of the sites where the Israelites stopped to make camp while heading to Canaan; it was located in the region of Moab (Num 21:19–20). It is probably the same as

Bamoth Baal (Num 22:41), where Balak took Balaam to curse the Israelites, who were then encamped in the plains of Moab, opposite Jericho.

BAPTISM (Greek, "immersion" or "dipping") The rite of cleansing with water, practiced first by John the Baptist and then by the apostles. John's baptism was a sign of repentance and a foreshadowing of the sacramental baptism established by Jesus. Christian baptism possesses a spiritual power that John did not claim for his own rite (John 1:33; Acts 1:5, 19:4–5). In the sacrament of baptism, a person is cleansed of all sin, reborn, and sanctified in Christ through water and the Holy Spirit. Repentance and baptism are the beginning of the Christian life (cf. Acts 2:37–38) and essential to Christian mission (Matt 28:19). As the Catechism declares, "Through Baptism we are freed from sin and reborn as sons of God; we become members of Christ, are incorporated into the Church and made sharers in her mission" (CCC 1213–74).

I. *Types of Baptism in the Old Testament*
    A. *Creation*
    B. *The Flood*
    C. *Circumcision*
    D. *The Exodus*
    E. *Purification*
II. *Baptism Before Christ*
    A. *Baptism at Qumran*
    B. *John the Baptist*
III. *The Beginning of Christian Baptism*
    A. *The Baptism of Jesus*
    B. *The Commandment to Baptize*
IV. *The Effects of Baptism*

I. TYPES OF BAPTISM IN THE OLD TESTAMENT

A. Creation

Baptism is a "new creation" (2 Cor 5:17; Gal 6:15), and Christians find an image of baptism at the very beginning of the Bible. **Creation** begins with water and the Spirit (Gen 1:2), just as the new creation begins in baptism.

B. The Flood

Another new creation began with the **Flood**, which cleansed the world of sin while "a few, that is, eight persons, were saved" (1 Pet 3:20) to begin life again. Baptism "corresponds to this" (1 Pet 3:21): it likewise washes away sin (cf. Acts 22:16), so that human beings can be created anew. The dove released by Noah returned with an olive-tree branch in its beak as a sign that the floodwaters had truly subsided and that the land was once more habitable; for Christians the dove is a sign of the Holy Spirit (CCC 701, 1219).

C. Circumcision

When God made his covenant with Abraham, he instructed the patriarch to have "every male among you . . . circumcised" (Gen 17:10). In subsequent generations, male children were traditionally circumcised shortly after birth. Paul makes the typological connection between circumcision and baptism: "you were circumcised with a circumcision made without hands, by putting off the body of flesh in the circumcision of Christ; and you were buried with Him in baptism" (Col 2:11–12). The circumcision of infants prefigured the baptism of those who would be "newborn" in Christ. The old rite marked a child's "birth" as a son of Abraham; the new rite marks the still greater birth of a child of God.

D. The Exodus

Paul sees the **Exodus** as a baptism of the entire people of Israel. "I want you to know, brethren, that our fathers were all under the cloud, and all passed through the sea, and all were baptized into Moses in the cloud and in the sea" (1 Cor 10:1–2). The Israelites also had to cross the Jordan River in order to enter the land the Lord had promised them. That promise had been made to **Abraham**, but its complete fulfillment would not come until the New Covenant (CCC 1220–21).

E. Purification

Ritual defilement required ritual washing (see, for example, Num 19:11–22). The purification laws of the ancient Israelites specified washing and sprinkling "water for impurity" to cleanse one who had become ritually unclean. In these rituals we can see an anticipation of baptism, which washes away the impurity of sin.

II. BAPTISM BEFORE CHRIST

A. Baptism at Qumran

Baptism is first mentioned in the Bible with John the Baptist, but John did not invent the practice. From the **Dead Sea Scrolls** we know that a community at **Qumran** practiced a form of baptism (cf. the *Community Rule*, 1QS 3.6–9). The Qumran writings use language similar to John's (cf. Mark 1:8) in insisting that God will send his Spirit on those who are washed. It is possible that John the Baptist knew of the Qumran practices or similar baptisms elsewhere.

B. John the Baptist

John the Baptist preached a baptism for the forgiveness of sins, but he himself declared that his was not the final baptism: he anticipated the baptism of the Spirit that would be brought by Christ (Mark 1:8). John preached repentance and the forgiveness of sins in the tradition of Ezekiel (Ezek 18:31; 36:25–26), even as he proclaimed that the one who would follow him would baptize not only with water but with fire and the Spirit (Matt 3:11; Luke 3:16; John 1:27).

III. THE BEGINNING OF CHRISTIAN BAPTISM

A. The Baptism of Jesus

When Jesus came to be baptized by John the Baptist, he did not come to confess his sinfulness. Rather he signaled his sharing of true union with the sinful humanity he had come to redeem (Phil 2:7). His baptism is a Trinitarian event: the Father's declaration of Christ's sonship, and an anointing with the Spirit. The baptism in the Jordan served also as the prototype of Christian baptism. The Church Fathers interpreted the Gospel narrative in several complementary ways. Some saw him as the representative of all humanity (in his baptism, human flesh is sanctified); others looked to his baptism as the pattern for human sanctification (he demonstrates so that humans will

imitate). Still other Church Fathers held that Christ's descent into the waters purified the waters of the earth and made them holy for use in Christian baptism.

Mark's version emphasizes the divine sonship of Jesus: "You are my beloved Son; with you I am well pleased" (Mark 1:11). Matthew likewise follows the theme of sonship, recording a dialogue between John and Jesus (Matt 3:14–15) stressing that divine sonship entailed a radical obedience to God's will (Matt 4:1–11; 5:9, 45; 26:39; 27:43). Luke's version puts the focus on the public proclamation of Jesus as the Son of God, working under God's Spirit (Luke 3:21–22, 38; 4:1, 14, 18). Finally, John, rather than narrating all the details of Jesus's baptism, relates the testimony of John the Baptist as to what he saw and said to Jesus at the Jordan; John the Baptist says that he saw the Spirit descend upon Jesus like a dove, and that he proclaimed to Israel that Jesus is the Son of God (John 1:32–34; 3:26).

B. The Commandment to Baptize

Jesus, in his own ministry, spoke of baptism as a formal rite ("of water and the Spirit," John 3:5), performed in the name of the Trinity (Matt 28:19), and required for salvation (Mark 16:16).

At the end of his earthly ministry Christ gave this commandment to the disciples: "Go therefore and make disciples of all nations, baptizing them in the name of the Father and of the Son and of the Holy Spirit, teaching them to observe all that I have commanded you" (Matt 28:19–29; Mark 16:15–16).

As soon as they had received the Holy

Spirit at **Pentecost**, the apostles began to carry out that order. On that first day, they baptized about three thousand people (Acts 2:38–41). As Saint Peter declared, "Repent, and be baptized every one of you in the name of Jesus Christ for the forgiveness of your sins; and you shall receive the gift of the Holy Spirit" (Acts 2:38). From then on, every new believer was baptized in the name of Jesus Christ.

IV. THE EFFECTS OF BAPTISM

Jesus told his disciples that his journey to Jerusalem would bring a "baptism" that they might be reluctant to share (Mark 10:38; cf. Luke 12:50). Indeed, through baptism Christians do share in the death of Christ (Rom 6:3), but also in his Resurrection. The early Church often spoke of Christ's Passion and death as the source of baptism's cleansing power: Christians were said to be "washed . . . in the blood of the Lamb" (Rev 7:14).

Through baptism the believer "puts on Christ" (Gal 3:27); and through the Holy Spirit baptism becomes the ordinary means of purification, sanctification, and justification (1 Cor 6:11; 12:13). Based on 1 John 5:8, the Church has traditionally spoken also of extraordinary circumstances that serve the purpose of baptism: "baptism by desire," as in the case of those who have died while preparing for Christian initiation, and "baptism by blood," as in the case of catechumens who died as martyrs.

Paul often spoke of the close communion between the life of the baptized and the life, death, and Resurrection of Jesus Christ: "Do you not know that all of us who have been baptized into Christ Jesus were baptized into his death? We were buried therefore with him by baptism into death, so that as Christ was raised from the dead by the glory of the Father, we too might walk in newness of life" (Rom 6:3–4; cf. Col 2:12). Baptized into Christ, the Christian receives the Holy Spirit (Rom 5:5), is washed in water and the word (Eph 5:26), is granted adoption and sonship, and receives the power to call upon the Father as Abba (Rom 8:15, 17; Gal 3:16, 4:4–7). The baptized are coheirs with Christ, the Son of God (1 Cor 6:15, 12:27; Rom 8:17; *see also* **Inheritance**.)

Baptism also brings incorporation into the body of Christ: "For by one Spirit we were all baptized into one body" (1 Cor 12:13), and "we are members one of another" (Eph 4:25). Baptism means membership in "a chosen race, a royal priesthood, a holy nation, God's own people" (1 Pet 2:9) (CCC 1265–70). (*See also* **Grace**.)

BARABBAS (Aramaic, "son of the father") A notorious robber, revolutionary, and murderer mentioned in all four Gospels. When Pilate, following custom, offered to release one prisoner on the feast of the Passover, the people chose Barabbas, whose name means "son of the father," over Christ, the Son of the Father (Matt 27:15–26; Mark 15:6–15; Luke 23:17–25; John 18:39–40). Barabbas is described as a rebel "who had committed murder in the insurrection" (Mark 15:7; Luke 23:19), a "notorious prisoner" (Matt 27:16), and a "robber" (John 18:40). Pilate had hoped to secure the release of Jesus through the custom, but the chief priests and elders persuaded the crowd to choose Barabbas instead (Matt 27:20; Mark

15:11). The name Barabbas does not appear anywhere else in the New Testament.

BARACHEL The father of **Elihu**; he came from the land of Buz (Job 32:2).

BARAK (Hebrew, "lightning") Son of Abinoam of the tribe of Naphtali and a military commander from Kedesh (Judg 4:6). When the Israelites were oppressed by the Canaanite kings of the north, the prophetess and judge **Deborah** summoned Barak and told him to organize a coalition against Sisera, commander of the forces of King Jabin of Hazor. After some hesitation, Barak gathered together his troops from various tribes (Benjamin, Issachar, Zebulun, and Naphtali) and led them to triumph in battle near Mount Tabor. After the victory Barak and Deborah sang a canticle of praise to God (Judg 5). The account in Judges places the strength of personality on Deborah; Barak is praised more effusively in Hebrews for his faith (Heb 11:32) and in 1 Samuel (12:11) he is named as a savior of Israel.

BAR-JESUS (Aramaic, "son of Jesus") A Jewish magician and false prophet in the court of the proconsul Sergius Paulus in Cyprus (Acts 13:6). Also called Elymas, a name meaning "wise man" or "magician" (Acts 13:8), he opposed the preaching of Paul and Barnabas and was struck blind (Acts 13:6–11). So impressed was Paulus with this exchange that he became a Christian believer (Acts 13:12).

BAR-JONA (Aramaic, "son of Jonah") The surname of Simon Peter (Matt 16:17).

BARLEY A common crop in Palestine (2 Sam 14:30; Job 31:40; Joel 1:11) that was coarser than wheat and was sold at half the price of wheat (2 Kgs 7:1, 16, 18). Bread made from barley was a regular item in the diet of the inhabitants of Palestine (Judg 7:13; 2 Kgs 4:42; Jer 41:8; John 6:9).

BARNABAS (Aramaic, "son of encouragement") An associate of **Paul** described in Acts as "a good man, full of the Holy Spirit and of faith" (Acts 11:24). Barnabas was a Levite from the Mediterranean island of Cyprus. He is first mentioned as a man who sold some land and gave all of the proceeds to the apostles in Jerusalem (Acts 4:36–37); he was also the cousin of **John Mark** (Col 4:10). His birth name was Joseph; he was given the name Barnabas or "son of encouragement" by the apostles, probably because he had the gift of exhortation and the ability to inspire others in the faith. Barnabas introduced Paul, the former persecutor, to the Jerusalem community (Acts 9:27) and assuaged the fears and doubts of the apostles. Barnabas was sent to Antioch to look into the affairs of the growing church there and summoned Paul from Tarsus to assist in spreading the Gospel. They both returned to Jerusalem with alms from the Antioch church (Acts 11:19–30). Together they set out on Paul's first missionary journey, with John Mark. John Mark departed at Perga, and Barnabas and Paul continued on with the journey (Acts 13:13). Returning to Antioch, they found the community divided over the issue of **circumcision** of Gentile converts, and both became opponents of compulsory circumcision. They went to Jerusalem to settle the matter authoritatively at a gathering of the leaders of the Church (Acts 15:2, 22). The decision of Peter and others was in their favor (Acts 15:6–11; Gal 2:1–10).

After laboring together once more at Antioch, Paul and Barnabas planned to revisit the cities of their earlier journey, but they disagreed on whether John Mark should be allowed to come along. Barnabas wished him to take part, but Paul was against it because John Mark had left them once before (Acts 15:37–38). Barnabas sailed for Cyprus with John Mark (Acts 15:39), while Paul set out with Silas.

Nothing else about Barnabas is known with certainty (cf. 1 Cor 9:6). Early Christian tradition names Barnabas as the founder of the Cypriot church, and it is likely that he was martyred. The story has it that he was put to death in A.D. 61 at Salamis. Most scholars believe that the postapostolic work called the Epistle of Barnabas was probably not written by him. His feast day is June 11.

BARSABBAS (Aramaic, "son of the Sabbath") The name of two men in the New Testament.

1. Joseph Barsabbas, called Justus, was a disciple of Christ who was also one of the two candidates (with Matthias) proposed to take the place of Judas Iscariot among the apostles (Acts 1:23). According to a tradition mentioned by Eusebius (*Hist. Eccl.* 3.39), he once swallowed poison but was miraculously unharmed.

2. Judas Barsabbas was a disciple and member of the Jerusalem community who was sent with Paul, Barnabas, and Silas to Antioch to deliver the news of the Council of Jerusalem (Acts 15:22–33).

BARTHOLOMEW (Aramaic, "son of Tholami" or "son of Tholomaeus") One of the twelve apostles, mentioned in the Synoptic Gospels as sixth (Matt 10:3; Mark 3:18; Luke 6:14) and in the Acts of the Apostles (1:13) as seventh. Other than the noted references, Bartholomew is unknown, although scholars often identify him with the figure of Nathanael in the Gospel of John, who was brought to Christ by Philip (John 1:45–51; 21:2). According to a prominent early tradition, Bartholomew journeyed to India, where he preached and spread the Word. He was supposedly flayed alive and beheaded at Albanopolis, in Armenia. The historian Eusebius (*Hist. Eccl.* 5.10) wrote that when the philosopher Pantaenus reached India (ca. A.D. 150–200), he found there a copy of the Gospel of Matthew written in Hebrew, which had been left behind by Bartholomew. His feast day is August 24.

BARTIMAEUS A blind beggar of Jericho who was healed by Jesus (Mark 10:46–52). Upon hearing that Jesus of Nazareth was passing by, he called out, begged for mercy, and refused to be silenced. Matthew (Matt 20:29–34) and Luke (Luke 18:35–43) also note the incident, but only Mark gives the man's name. Matthew says that he was one of two blind men.

BARUCH (Hebrew, "blessed") Son of Neriah and secretary to the prophet **Jeremiah** (Jer 32:12). He is described in the book of Jeremiah as a scribe (Jer 36:32) who wrote down the prophecies of Judah's destruction that came to Jeremiah (Jer 36:4–8). Once he had written the prophecies down, Baruch read the scroll to people in the Temple (Jer 36:10), and then to a group of royal ministers (Jer 36:22). The ministers read the scroll to King **Jehoiakim**, who burned it in the fireplace (Jer 36:23). Jehoiakim then commanded that both Baruch and Jeremiah be seized, but with God's help they escaped (Jer 36:26). Jeremiah dictated a new scroll to Baruch (Jer 36:27–32) containing the same oracles, with some new material. On another occasion Jeremiah bought a piece of land from his cousin Hanamel, the purchase signifying that Judah would be restored after the Exile. Baruch witnessed the purchase, and Jeremiah gave him the deed for safekeeping (Jer 32:6–15). Jeremiah issued an oracle in which Baruch was assured of his own survival wherever he might go after the fall of Jerusalem (Jer 45:1–5). Like Jeremiah, he was permitted by the Babylonians to remain in Palestine. He was accused of encouraging Jeremiah to persuade the survivors not to leave for Egypt (Jer 43:3). In spite of their objections, Baruch and Jeremiah were both carried off to Egypt after the assassination of **Gedaliah**, the Babylonian-appointed governor of Judah (Jer 43:5–7). (*See also* **Baruch, book of.**)

BARUCH, BOOK OF A canonical book of the Old Testament that bears the name of **Baruch**, Jeremiah's personal companion and secretary (Jer 36:1–32; 43:1–7). Although the book of Baruch is not in the Jewish or Protestant canon, it is considered canonical by the Catholic Church (*see* **Deuterocanonical books**). It is placed after Lamentations in the Catholic canon of Scripture. The title is sometimes given as 1 Baruch to differentiate it from two pseudepigraphical writings, the Syriac *Apocalypse of Baruch* (*2 Baruch*) and the Greek *Apocalypse of Baruch* (*3 Baruch*).

I. AUTHORSHIP AND DATE

Tradition names Baruch as the author, but the book has been the subject of much scholarly speculation. Some scholars contend that Baruch is the work not of one person but of several people—a compilation of previously independent writings, linked by the common motif of sin-exile-return. Some scholars see Baruch as a final editor who was possibly author of part of the book.

Although Baruch was probably written in Hebrew, only a Greek version survives. That and the book's varied literary styles make Baruch difficult to date exactly. Dates have been proposed that vary from the sixth century B.C. to as late as the first century A.D. References in Baruch to Nebuchadnezzar and Belshazzar suggest an early date, but the total evidence is not conclusive. The names might refer to those historical rulers, but they might also be used for later rulers such as Antiochus IV and his son. Probably the most common scholarly opinion puts the date early in the second century B.C. The book itself purports to be written in the sixth century B.C., "in the fifth year, on the seventh day of the month, at the time when the Chaldeans took Jerusalem and burned it with fire" (Bar 1:1–2).

II. CONTENTS
I. Introduction (1:1–14)

II. Confessions (1:15–3:8)

III. Wisdom and the Law of Moses (3:9–4:4)

III. THEMES

Although it is much shorter, the book of Baruch bears some resemblance to the book of Jeremiah. Its recurring theme is the righteousness of God and the justice of his judgment on his people. There is also a promise of happier days in the future if the people will turn back to God.

The theme of sin, exile, and return echoes Deuteronomy, where Israel's conduct is connected with the sanctions of the covenant (Deut 29:10–30:10). Sin brings the *curse* of exile, but repentance triggers the *blessing* of national restoration and return from exile.

The last chapter (6) is different in style and content from the rest of the work; it urges the exiles in Babylon to refrain from the sin of idolatry, and marshals multiple arguments to show the utter impotence of false gods.

BARZILLAI A wealthy benefactor from Gilead who gave assistance to David during the rebellion of **Absalom** (2 Sam 17:27–29). When David crossed the Jordan and reached Mahanaim with his loyal followers, Barzillai gave him food and material support, and David's army went on to victory. David offered Barzillai a reward for his loyalty and the right to reside in the royal palace, but Barzillai refused because of his advanced years, and asked instead that his son Chimham be given the honor in his place (2 Sam 19:31–39). David did not forget Barzillai's loyalty; on his deathbed he commended Barzillai's sons to Solomon (1 Kgs 2:7).

BASEMATH The name of two women in the Old Testament.

1. The daughter of Elon the Hittite, and one of the wives of Esau (Gen 26:34; 36:3, 4, 10, 13, 17).

2. A daughter of King Solomon (1 Kgs 4:15); she was married to one of the royal governors.

BASHAN A region of the upper Transjordan, east of the Sea of Galilee and north of the Yarmuk River. It was noted for its lush landscape and its many flocks (Deut 32:14; Jer 50:19; Ezek 39:18). Its abundance supported a group of prosperous cities (Num 32:33). **Og** was king of Bashan in the time before Israel, led by Moses, conquered the Transjordan (Deut 3:1–11). The area was then assigned to the tribe of Manasseh (Josh 13:30; 17:1).

BASKAMA A town in Gilead, east of Jordan. **Jonathan Maccabeus** was executed and buried at Baskama by **Trypho**, general of the Seleucid army (1 Macc 13:23). The exact location of Baskama has not been determined.

BASKET A container made of woven reeds, fiber, or cane. Baskets were very common in biblical times and were made in a variety of sizes depending upon their function, such as storing bread, grapes, fruit, and other items. They could also be large enough to accommodate a man; Paul escaped from Damascus by being lowered from the city wall in a basket (2 Cor 11:33). Baskets of fruit also appear in two prophetic visions (Jer 24:2; Amos 8:2).

BATH *See* **Weights and measures.**

BATHING In Scripture, bathing was, as now, a matter of personal hygiene (Dan 13:15), but it was also a sign of hospitality, especially washing the feet of travelers (Gen 18:4, 19:2, 24:32, Luke 7:44). Above all, bathing was a means of **purification** from ritual defilement from contact with something the Law deemed unclean, including blood, corpses, leprosy, and unkosher foods. Bathing was a preparation for anointing (2 Sam 12:20). Priests bathed as part of the ritual of ordination (Lev 8:6; cf. Exod 40:12–15), and they were required to wash before performing their duties (Exod 30:17; Lev 16:4). Bathing was also essential as a means of being cleansed in the event of any kind of ceremonial uncleanness (Lev 14:8; 2 Sam 11:2, 4). Extensive ablutions were a prescribed part of the daily ritual among the members of the **Qumran** community.

BATHSHEBA (Hebrew, "daughter of seven" or "daughter of an oath") The daughter of Eliam and the wife of Uriah the Hittite (2 Sam 11:3); one of David's wives (2 Sam 11:27); and the mother of Solomon (2 Sam 12:24). (The name appears as "Bath-shua" in 1 Chr 3:5.)

David fell in love with Bathsheba when he saw her taking a bath on a rooftop; he then seduced her and fathered a child by her in adultery. After he tried and failed to have the paternity attributed to Uriah (2 Sam 11:6–13), David ordered Joab to place Uriah in the front line of battle and so ensure his death. When Uriah fell as planned, David wed Bathsheba (2 Sam 11:14–27). As **Nathan** predicted, the child born of the adultery died, but Bathsheba later bore a second son, Solomon, who became David's successor, as well as three other sons

(1 Chr 3:5). The intervention of Bathsheba and Nathan was crucial to Solomon's victory in the struggle with **Adonijah** (1 Kgs 1:11–21). Bathsheba later requested that Solomon secure the marriage of Adonijah with Abishag, but her mediation did not succeed, and Solomon had Adonijah killed (1 Kgs 2:13–25). In the New Testament, Bathsheba is one of four women mentioned (though not by name) in Matthew's genealogy of Christ (Matt 1:6).

Bathsheba is the first **queen mother** of the Davidic kingdom, and her prominent role in history sets the pattern for the other women who held that powerful position. She is also a type of **Mary**, the Queen Mother in the Kingdom of Christ.

BATH-SHUA (Hebrew, "daughter of Shua") The Canaanite wife of **Judah**, Jacob's fourth son (1 Chr 2:3; cf. Gen 38:2). She was the mother of Er, Onan, and Shelah. Bath-shua is also an alternate name of **Bathsheba**.

BDELLIUM A fragrant translucent yellow or brown resinous gum obtained from a tree found in southern Arabia (Gen 2:12). **Manna** was described as looking like bdellium (Num 11:7).

BEALIAH A warrior in the service of David; he belonged to the tribe of Benjamin (1 Chr 12:6).

BEAR No longer found in modern Palestine, the bear was common in biblical times, certainly in the period of the Old Testament. In the New Testament, the only reference to a bear is in Rev 13:2, where a bear appears in a prophetic vision (cf. Dan 7:5). The bear was feared as a dangerous predator (1 Sam 17:34–37; 2 Sam 17:8; 2 Kgs 2:24; Prov 17:12) and was known also by its growl (Isa 59:11). The anger of the Lord was also described as being like the anger of a bear (Lam 3:10; Hos 13:8; Amos 5:19).

BEARD Among Semitic men, beards were almost universal. Their beards set the Semitic peoples apart from neighboring peoples, in particular the Egyptians (Gen 41:14) and later the Greeks and Romans. Trimming the edges of the beard, which seems to have been a pagan mourning rite (Lev 19:27; 21:5), was forbidden among Israelites, and to have one's beard plucked or partially shaved was a great indignity and sign of disrespect (2 Sam 10:4; Isa 50:6). Beards were shaved off or torn out as a sign of great mourning (Isa 7:20; 15:2; Jer 41:5; Bar 6:31).

BEATITUDES Most commonly, the eight blessings in Jesus's Sermon on the Mount (Matt 5:3–10; cf. Luke 6:20–26). In a wider sense, the term can describe a literary form found in ancient Egyptian, Greek, and Jewish literature that expresses praise or congratulation.

The term "beatitudes" comes from *beati* (the plural of "blessed"), the word that starts each of the sayings in the Latin translation of the Sermon on the Mount.

Beatitudes are found in both the Old Testament and the New Testament. Most of the OT beatitudes are found in **wisdom literature**. In the Psalms, for example, we find several well-known beatitudes: all those who walk in the way of the Lord (Ps 1), trust in God (Ps 16:20), meditate upon his words (Ps 29:9), receive forgiveness for their sins (Ps 32:1), and fear the Lord (Ps. 112:1) are called "blessed."

In the New Testament there are thirty-seven beatitudes (Matt 5:3–11, 11:6, 13:16, 16:17, 24:46; Luke 1:45, 6:20–22, 7:23, 10:23, 11:27–28, 12:37, 43, 14:15, 23:29; John 20:29; Rom 4:7, 8, 14:22; Jas 1:12; Rev 1:3, 14:13, 16:15, 19:9, 20:6, 22:7). Of these, seventeen of the Gospel beatitudes are sayings of Jesus. They express the fundamental change of life that faith in Jesus Christ demands (Matt 11:6, 24:46; Luke 7:23, 12:37; John 13:17, 20:29). There are seven beatitudes in Revelation (1:3; 14:13; 16:15; 19:9; 20:6; 22:7, 14), where they express the blessed state of the faithful who are saved.

The Beatitudes of the Sermon on the Mount are a concise summary of the way of Christ (CCC 1697). They are the heart of his preaching and the fulfillment of all the "promises made to the chosen people since Abraham. The Beatitudes fulfill the promises by ordering them no longer merely to the possession of a territory, but to the Kingdom of heaven" (CCC 1716). Indeed, they pronounce "blessed" various circumstances that are, by worldly standards, accursed: poverty, mourning, persecution, and so forth. Yet these are the circumstances of Christ's own life on earth; and they "express the vocation of the faithful associated with the glory of his Passion and Resurrection" (CCC 1717).

Matthew's beatitudes differ from Luke's in several ways. In Matthew's account, Jesus states his blessings in the third person ("Blessed are they . . ."), while in Luke he uses the second person ("Blessed are you . . ."). Also Luke's blessings, unlike Matthew's, are followed by curses, statements that begin, "But woe to you . . ." These different renderings are not necessarily contradictory or conflicting. As an itinerant preacher, Jesus surely addressed the same themes on many occasions, often varying his presentation.

Though Jesus, using the indicative mood, seems to be making observations, Christian tradition has interpreted the Beatitudes as moral imperatives—that is, as divine prescriptions for human behavior. The Beatitudes are often presented as supplementary or complementary to the Ten Commandments. In fact, the "moral" section of the *Catechism of the Catholic Church* begins with a discussion of the Beatitudes: "The Beatitudes reveal the goal of human existence, the ultimate end of human acts: God calls us to his own beatitude. This vocation is addressed to each individual personally, but also to the Church as a whole, the new people made up of those who have accepted the promise and live from it in faith" (CCC 1719).

Christ's Beatitudes are "eschatological." They pronounce blessings that will be fulfilled completely at the end of time; but they proclaim them as "blessings and rewards already secured, however dimly, for Christ's disciples" (CCC 1717). "The beatitudes raise our hope toward heaven as the new Promised Land; they trace the path that leads through the trials that await the disciples of Jesus. But through the merits of Jesus Christ and of his Passion, God keeps us in the 'hope that does not disappoint'" (CCC 1820).

Scholars sometimes distinguish between two types of beatitude, *eulogism* and *macarism*. A eulogism (from the Greek *eulogia*, "blessing") is usually associated with the blessings of a covenant; a macarism (from *makarios*, "happy" or "fortunate") describes the natural happiness enjoyed by someone who possesses a virtuous quality or habit. The distinction is not particularly helpful in interpreting the Beatitudes of the Sermon on the Mount, since they begin with *makarios*, yet describe conditions, such as mourning, that are incompatible with natural happiness. Rather these circumstances lead us to a supernatural blessedness; they "purify our hearts in order to teach us to love God above all things" (CCC 1728). In the biblical worldview, there is no place for fortune or luck; and even adversity can be understood as a blessing when seen in light of God's Providence and his covenant. "The Beatitudes respond to the natural desire for happiness. This desire is of divine origin: God has placed it in the human heart in order to draw man to the One who alone can fulfill it" (CCC 1718).

THE BEATITUDES IN MATTHEW (5:3–10)

Eight beatitudes are listed by Matthew:

1. Blessed are the poor in spirit, for theirs is the kingdom of heaven.

2. Blessed are those who mourn, for they shall be comforted.

3. Blessed are the meek, for they shall inherit the earth.

4. Blessed are those who hunger and thirst for righteousness, for they shall be satisfied.

5. Blessed are the merciful, for they shall obtain mercy.

6. Blessed are the pure in heart, for they shall see God.

7. Blessed are the peacemakers, for they shall be called sons of God.

8. Blessed are those who are persecuted for righteousness' sake, for theirs is the kingdom of heaven.

THE BEATITUDES IN LUKE (6:20–26)

Four beatitudes are listed by Luke:

1. Blessed are you who are poor, for yours is the kingdom of God.

2. Blessed are you that hunger now, for you shall be satisfied.

3. Blessed are you that weep now, for you shall laugh.

4. Blessed are you when men hate you, and when they exclude you and revile you, and cast out your name as evil, on account of the Son of man!

BEAUTIFUL GATE A gate of Herod's Temple in Jerusalem where Peter and John healed a paralytic (Acts 3:2, 10).

BECHER The second son of **Benjamin** (Gen 46:21; 1 Chr 7:6, 8).

BECTILETH An unidentified plain in northern **Cilicia** (Jdt 2:21).

BEELIADA One of the sons of **David**. He was born in Jerusalem (1 Chr 14:3–7; cf. 2 Sam 5:13–16); his mother is not named.

BEELZEBUB (Hebrew, "lord of flies," a disparaging pun on "Baal-zebul," meaning "Prince **Baal**") A deity worshiped by the Philistines at Ekron. **Ahaziah**, king of Israel, sent messengers to consult this god for him when

he was wounded (2 Kgs 1:2). In the New Testament the Greek spelling **Beelzebul** is used as an epithet for the devil (for example, Matt 10:25, 12:24; Mark 3:22; Luke 11:15).

BEELZEBUL (Greek spelling of Baal-zebul; see **Beelzebub**) A term used by the Pharisees for the "prince of demons," the devil. Jesus was accused by the Pharisees of expelling demons by the power of Beelzebul (Matt 10:25, 12:24–27; Mark 3:22–26; Luke 11:15–19). Jesus prefers to call him "Satan" or "the devil."

BEERI The name of two men in the Old Testament.

1. The father of Esau's wife, Judith (Gen 26:34).

2. The father of the prophet Hosea (Hos 1:1).

BEEROTH A town in the territory of Benjamin (Josh 18:25), situated to the north of Jerusalem. It was originally one of four Hivite cities that joined the Gibeonites in forging a covenant of peace with Joshua and the Israelites (Josh 9:17) as a tactical move to avoid destruction. After that the people of those cities were reduced to a servile status under Israel (Josh 9:26–27). Two men from Beeroth, **Baanah and Rechab**, murdered Saul's heir, **Ishbosheth**, and brought his head to David in anticipation of a reward. They were put to death instead (2 Sam 4:2–12).

BEEROTH BENE-JAAKAN (Hebrew, "wells of the sons of Jaakan") A site where the Israelites camped during their journey through the wilderness (Deut 10:6).

BEER-SHEBA (Hebrew, "well of seven" or "well of the oath") A town and oasis in the **Negeb**, in the southern Judean desert. It is known chiefly for its connection with the patriarchs and as the southern limit of Israelite territory. The site is today identified with Tell es-Sheba'. The town was the home for a time to both Abraham (Gen 22:19) and Isaac (Gen 26:23; 28:10) and was the site of Abraham's covenant with **Abimelech** over water rights (Gen 21:31); Isaac made a similar agreement (Gen 26:31–33). Genesis 21:31 derives the name of the place from the oath Abraham swore with Abimelech there, for which he offered seven lambs (the Hebrew word for "oath" comes from the same root as the word for "seven"). Genesis 26:33 adds that Isaac named the place Shibah. Two visions in the night—that is, revelatory dreams—came at Beer-sheba, one to Isaac (Gen 26:23) and the other to Jacob (Gen 46:1–5). After the conquest of Canaan, Beer-sheba became part of the territory of Judah (Josh 15:28). It was then listed repeatedly as the southernmost limit of Israelite lands; the common idiom "from Dan to Beer-sheba" indicated the whole extent of Israelite dominions from north to south (Judg 20:1; 1 Sam 3:20; 2 Sam 17:11, 24:15; 1 Kgs 5:5; 1 Chr 21:2; 2 Chr 30:5; cf. 2 Sam 24:7; 1 Kgs 19:3; 2 Kgs 23:8; 2 Chr 19:4).

BEHEMOTH (Hebrew, plural of "animal") A huge animal described in Job 40:15–24. It is probably the hippopotamus.

BEL (Hebrew *bēl*, which represents Akkadian *belu*, "lord") The name used in the Old Testament for the Babylonian god **Marduk** (Isa 46:1; Jer 50:2, 51:44). **Daniel** exposed the fraud of the Babylonian priests and so was given permission to destroy the idol and its temple (Dan 14:3–22).

BELA The name of two men in the Old Testament.

1. The son of Beor (Gen 36:32; 1 Chr 1:43) and the first king of **Edom**.

2. The firstborn son of **Benjamin** (Gen 46:21; Num 26:38, 40; 1 Chr 7:6, 8:1).

BELIAL (Hebrew, "wickedness" or "worthlessness") In the Old Testament, the term "children of Belial," translated "base fellows" or "worthless men" in the RSV, is used for the exceptionally wicked (Deut 13:14; Judg 19:22; 1 Sam 2:12, 30:22; 2 Sam 20:1). The word "Belial" ("Beliar" in the Greek) is found once in the New Testament (2 Cor 6:15); there it is used as a name for Satan. The name "Belial" also occurs frequently in **apocalyptic literature** outside the Bible as a proper name for the "angel of wickedness." It is a common epithet for the devil in the **Dead Sea Scrolls**.

BELOVED DISCIPLE An unnamed disciple of Jesus who appears in the Gospel of John, one who must have had an especially close relationship with Jesus (John 13:23; 19:26; 21:7, 20). In John 21:24 the writer of the Gospel (identified in early Christian tradition as the apostle **John**, son of Zebedee) states that he is the disciple "whom Jesus loved," the same disciple who reclined upon Jesus's chest at table on the evening of the Last Supper.

BELSHAZZAR (Akkadian, "Bel protect the king") The vice-regent of **Babylon** before the

Persian conquest of the Babylonian Empire in 539 B.C. (Dan 5:1; 8:1). From historical records we know that his father, Nabonidus, was the king, but when he went on an extended campaign in Arabia he left Belshazzar in charge of the government. (That father and son ruled as king and vice-regent is confirmed in Dan 5:7, where the highest honor open to Daniel is to be *third* ruler in the kingdom.) In Dan 5:1–2 Belshazzar is the host of a banquet for a thousand noblemen; **Nebuchadnezzar** is called his "father" or ancestor. At the feast, wine was served to the guests in the sacred vessels that had been looted from the Temple in Jerusalem. During the meal a hand appeared upon the wall and wrote on the plaster. **Daniel** was called to interpret the words: MENE, MENE, TEKEL, PARSIN. He declared them to be a prediction of the imminent ruin of Babylon (Dan 5:26–28). That night the city fell to the Medes and Persians, and Belshazzar was murdered.

BELTESHAZZAR (Akkadian, "Bel guard his life") The name given to **Daniel** by Nebuchadnezzar's chief eunuch, Ashpenaz (Dan 1:7).

BENAIAH (Hebrew, "Yahweh has made") Son of **Jehoiada** and an unshakably loyal soldier in the army of David and Solomon. Benaiah was commander of David's personal bodyguard unit, the Cherethites and Pelethites (2 Sam 8:18, 20:23; 1 Chr 11:25), and was one of the thirty "mighty men" of David (2 Sam 23:23). Benaiah also played a key role in the accession of Solomon (1 Kgs 1:32–49), especially in the struggle over the crown between

Solomon and his older brother **Adonijah**. At Solomon's command, Benaiah later executed Adonijah, Joab, and Shimei the son of Gera (1 Kgs 2:13–46). With Joab removed, Benaiah became head of Solomon's army (1 Kgs 2:35; 4:4). Six other people in the Old Testament bear this name.

BENEDICTUS, THE The canticle sung by Zechariah in Luke 1:68–79 at the birth of his son, John the Baptist. The canticle contains two parts. The first part (Luke 1:68–75) praises God and expresses thanks for the redemption promised to the patriarchs and prophets and now embodied in the Messiah of the house of David. The second part (Luke 1:76–79) is addressed to the child, describing him as a prophet who will prepare the way of the Lord.

BEN-HADAD (Hebrew, "son of [the god] Hadad") The name of at least two kings of Damascus.

1. Ben-hadad, son of Tab-Rimmon, was bribed by **Asa**, king of Judah, to invade the territory of Israel in order to cripple the military ambitions of **Baasha** of Israel with regard to Judah (1 Kgs 15:18–20; 2 Chr 16:1–5). He is probably, but not certainly, the same Ben-hadad who made war on **Ahab**, king of Israel, but was twice defeated and signed a treaty (1 Kgs 20:1–34). The treaty included the promise to return the cities captured in his earlier campaign and to initiate reciprocal trade. The two kings fell out, however, over Ramoth-gilead, and in the war that followed Ahab was killed (1 Kgs 22:1–38; 2 Chr 18). It is possible

that he is also the same Ben-hadad who besieged Samaria (2 Kgs 6:8–8:15). He was perhaps assassinated in 842 B.C. (2 Kgs 8:7–15) by Hazael. Some scholars, however, believe that another Ben-hadad ruled between the son of Tab-Rimmon and the son of Hazael.

2. Ben-hadad, son of Hazael, was defeated three times by **Jehoash**, king of Israel (2 Kgs 13:14–25), and **Jeroboam II** (2 Kgs 14:25–28).

BENJAMIN (Hebrew, "son of the right hand" or "son of the south") The youngest son of Jacob and the second son of Rachel (Gen 35:18) and the founding father of one of the twelve tribes of Israel (Gen 49:27–28). His mother died soon after giving birth to him; before she died she named him Benoni, "son of my sorrow." Jacob called him Benjamin, "son of the south," perhaps because he was the only one of his sons born after Jacob moved south to Canaan (Gen 35:18). When Joseph's brothers were sent to Egypt to purchase grain during the famine, Jacob kept Benjamin at home (Gen 42:4). Pretending not to trust them, Joseph insisted that Benjamin be brought to Egypt (Gen 42:15, 20, 34; 43:7), and Jacob reluctantly allowed Benjamin to go (Gen 43:8–15). Joseph then tested the supposedly reformed nature of his brothers by hiding his silver cup in Benjamin's sack as the brothers were leaving (Gen 44:2, 12). When Judah offered himself in Benjamin's place to become Joseph's slave, Joseph revealed his identity (Gen 44:18–45:15).

In Jacob's final blessing, Benjamin is described as "a ravenous wolf, in the morning devouring the prey, and at evening dividing the spoil" (Gen 49:27). This was a reference to the warlike nature of the tribe. In Moses's blessing it is said of Benjamin, "The beloved of the Lord, he dwells in safety by him; he encompasses him all the day long, and makes his dwelling between his shoulders" (Deut 33:12). During the Exodus, Benjaminites grew from 35,400 (Num 1:37) to 45,600 (Num 26:41); following the conquest of Canaan the territory assigned to Benjamin was south of the territory of Ephraim and north of the territory of Judah (Josh 18:11–28). While the smallest of the tribes (1 Sam 9:21; Ps 68:28), it was renowned for its fighting spirit. The judge **Ehud**, who slew Eglon, king of the Moabites, was a Benjaminite (Judg 3; cf. Judg 19–21). **Saul**, the first king of Israel, was also of the tribe of Benjamin (1 Sam 9:1–2), and the Benjaminites remained loyal to **Ish-bosheth** until Abner convinced them to submit to David (2 Sam 3:19). The territory of Benjamin was included in the kingdom of Judah after the division of the kingdom of Solomon (1 Kgs 12:21–24). **Paul** was also a member of the tribe (Rom 11:1; Phil 3:5).

BENONI *See* **Benjamin**.

BEN SIRA *See* **Sirach**.

BEOR The father of the Mesopotamian seer **Balaam** (Num 13:8, 22:5, 24:3, 15; Deut 23:4; Josh 13:22, 24:9; Mic 6:5).

BERA King of **Sodom** in the time of Abraham (Gen 14:2). With four other kings (of Gomorrah, Admah, Zeboim, and Bela), Bera rebelled against the Elamite overlord, Chedorlaomer (Gen 14:4). The five kings were defeated by

Chedorlaomer and the three other kings allied with him, but Bera escaped (Gen 14:10) and met up with **Abram** after Abram and his retainers had defeated the kings of Mesopotamia and recovered the possessions of Sodom and Gomorrah as well as Abram's nephew Lot (Gen 14:17, 21).

BERIAH The name of three men in the Old Testament.

1. The grandson of Jacob and Zilpah, fourth son of Asher, and father of Heber and Malchiel (Gen 46:17; 1 Chr 7:30–31).

2. A son of Jacob's grandson Ephraim (1 Chr 7:23).

3. The head of a Benjaminite clan, father of Zebadiah, Arad, Eder, Michael, Ishpah, and Joha (1 Chr 8:13, 16).

BERITH *See* **Covenant**.

BERNICE The daughter of King Herod Agrippa I and the sister of Herod Agrippa II. She was present in A.D. 60 when her brother listened to Paul's defense of his evangelization (Acts 25:13–26:32) at the invitation of the procurator Festus. Bernice led a notoriously immoral life. She married Marcus Julius Alexander; when he died, she promptly wed her uncle, Herod of Chalcis (ca. 44 A.D.) and gave birth to two sons, Berenicianus and Hyrcanus (Josephus, *B.J.* 2.221). After Herod of Chalcis died in 48, Bernice lived with her brother, but persistent rumors of an incestuous affair with her brother prompted her to marry Polemo of Cilicia. She quickly left Polemo and returned to her brother. In later years, she was a mistress to Emperor Titus; she died around A.D. 79.

BEROEA A city in the Roman province of Macedonia in northern Greece, located east of **Thessalonica**; it is known today as Verria. Paul and Silas traveled to Beroea (Acts 17:10) after fleeing Thessalonica. They preached to great effect in Beroea, and a number of Jewish and Gentile converts were made. Hostile Jews from Thessalonica, however, learned that Paul and his companions were in Beroea and journeyed to the city to stir up trouble. Once more Paul was forced to leave to avoid riots, but Timothy and Silas remained in Beroea (Acts 17:11–15).

BERYL A precious stone that is found in various colors (the green form, for example, is known as emerald); it was set in the breastplate of the Israelite high priest (Exod 28:20; 39:13).

BETH The second letter of the Hebrew alphabet (ב); it sounds like our letter *B*.

BETHANY The name of two places in Palestine.

1. A town on the eastern slope of the Mount of Olives, roughly two miles east of Jerusalem (John 11:18); it is called El ʿAziriyeh today. It was the residence of **Lazarus** and his sisters, **Mary** and **Martha** (John 11:1; 12:1), and also of **Simon the Leper** (Matt 26:6; Mark 14:3). Jesus set out from the vicinity of Bethany for his triumphant entry into Jerusalem (Mark 11:1; Luke 19:28), and he spent his nights there in the days before the Passion (Mark 11:11; 14:3).

2. A place east of the Jordan where **John the Baptist** preached and baptized (John 1:28). The exact location is not known.

BETH-AVEN

1. A wilderness that bordered the territory of Benjamin at its northwest corner (Josh 18:12).

2. A disparaging term, meaning "house of wickedness," that was used for the city of Bethel owing to the idolatry performed there by the Israelites (Hos 4:15; 10:5).

BETH-BARAH A town near the Jordan River (Judg 7:24). **Gideon** and the Ephraimites "seized the waters as far as Beth-barah" during a battle with the Midianites.

BETH EDEN An Aramean kingdom in upper Mesopotamia (Amos 1:5).

BETHEL A town about fourteen miles north of Jerusalem, identified with the modern Tell Beitin, although el-Bireh has also been suggested. Over time Bethel became a city of religious importance, so the name is mentioned with great frequency in the Old Testament—both positively, as the place where the **patriarchs** worshipped and the Tabernacle was erected for a time, and negatively, as the home of a "golden calf" set up by Jeroboam I. Genesis tells us that the town was originally called Luz, but **Jacob** gave it the name Bethel ("house of God"). He consecrated it twice (Gen 28:18–22 and 35:6–15) and set up both a memorial pillar and a sacrificial altar to commemorate the fact that God spoke to him there. Bethel was also the place where Deborah, the nurse of **Rebekah**, was buried under an oak (Gen 35:8).

Bethel had no natural defenses, so the city was vulnerable to attack. In the campaign in Canaan it fell to the Ephraimites (Judg 1:22–26) and was assigned to their territory (Josh 16:1; 1 Chr 7:28). In the succeeding period of the Judges it hosted the sanctuary where the ark of the covenant was kept for a time (Judg 20:26–27). The judge **Deborah** lived nearby (Judg 4:5), and Samuel judged the people there on a yearly rotation (1 Sam 7:16). When the ten northern tribes rebelled after the death of Solomon, **Jeroboam I** established Bethel as a place of worship to supersede Jerusalem and set up a golden calf there (1 Kgs 12:28–33), earning sharp criticism from the prophets **Amos** and **Hosea** (Hos 4:15, 5:8, 10:5, in all of which the prophet calls it **Beth-aven**; Amos 3:14, 4:4, 5:5). Amos was banned from Bethel by the priest Amaziah (Amos 7:10–12). The city was part of the ongoing rivalry between Judah and Israel and changed hands on several occasions (1 Kgs 12:29; 2 Chr 13:19). **Josiah**, king of Judah, destroyed its altar (2 Kgs 23:15–19), after which Bethel declined in importance.

BETHESDA *See* **Beth-zatha**.

BETH-HORON The name of twin towns, called Upper and Lower, twelve miles northeast of Jerusalem. The towns were ideally positioned strategically and hence were the scene of fighting during the Israelites' conquest of Canaan (Josh 10:10–11). Lower Beth-horon was given to the Ephraimites (Josh 16:3), and Upper Beth-horon was on the border between Ephraim (Josh 16:5) and Benjamin (Josh 18:14). They were fortified by Solomon (1 Kgs 9:17) and served as a military staging point during the time of the Maccabees (1 Macc 3:16; 7:39). Beth-horon was also one of the forty-eight Levitical cities (Josh 21:22; 1 Chr 6:68).

BETHLEHEM (Hebrew, "house of bread") The name of two towns in Palestine.

1. Bethlehem of Judah was a village about five miles south of Jerusalem, on the south-bound road to Hebron (Judg 19:9). It is also identified with Ephrath, the birthplace of **Benjamin** and the burial place of **Rachel** (Gen 35:16–20).

Bethlehem was the hometown of **Boaz** (Ruth 1:2; 2:1) as well as **David** and his family (1 Sam 17:12). It was in Bethlehem that David fed his flocks and was anointed king by the prophet Samuel (1 Sam 16:1–13). Therefore Bethlehem was sometimes called the City of David (Luke 2:4), and it was prophesied that the **Messiah** would come from Bethlehem (Mic 5:2; John 7:42). **Rehoboam** fortified it (2 Chr 11:6), and Bethlehem had a famous cistern (2 Sam 23:15; 1 Chr 11:17). Bethlehem is best known, of course, as the birthplace of Christ (Matt 2:1–16; Luke 2:4–15).

2. Bethlehem of Zebulun (Josh 19:15), located between Nazareth and Mount Carmel, may be the burial place of **Ibzan**, a minor judge (Judg 12:8–10).

BETH-PEOR (Hebrew, "house of Peor" or "temple of Peor") The site of the Canaanite shrine to **Baal**, on the plain of Moab east of the Jordan (Deut 3:29; Josh 13:20). Here the second generation of Israelites wandering in the wilderness fell into idolatry, just as their parents had worshipped the **golden calf**.

Seduced by Moabite women (Num 25:1; the scheme is attributed to the crafty seer **Balaam** in Num 31:16), large numbers of the Israelites took up the worship of the Baal of Peor. A plague killed 24,000 of the Israelites before the ringleaders of the apostasy were executed (Num 25:3–9). Before their invasion of Canaan, the Israelites camped "in the valley opposite Beth-Peor" (Deut 3:29). Moses reminded them of the earlier catastrophe that had occurred there (Deut 4:3–4), related the story of the giving of the **Law** on **Sinai** or Horeb (Deut 4:9–24), and prophesied Israel's faithlessness, Exile, and return (Deut 4:25–31). Here also Moses viewed the Promised Land from "the top of Pisgah," died, and was buried "in the valley in the land of Moab opposite Beth-Peor" (Deut 34:1–6). (See **Covenant** and **Deuteronomy** for other details.)

BETHPHAGE (Aramaic, "house of the unripe figs") The name of a small village on the Mount of Olives, due east of Jerusalem, on the road to Bethany. From here Jesus sent the disciples to find the donkey on which he was to make his triumphal entry into Jerusalem (Matt 21:1; Mark 11:1; Luke 19:29). The exact location is not known with certainty.

BETH REHOB A city in southern Syria. The Arameans of the city sent mercenaries to assist the Ammonites in their war against King David (2 Sam 10:6–8).

BETHSAIDA A city on the northeast shore of the Sea of Galilee. It is mentioned frequently in the New Testament and is best known as the home of **Philip**, **Andrew**, and **Peter** (John 1:44; 12:21). It was visited often by Jesus and was the scene of the cure of a blind man (Mark 8:22). A little way outside of the city Jesus fed the multitude (Luke 9:10). Bethsaida was also cursed by Jesus for unbelief (Matt 11:20–22; Luke 10:13–14).

The tetrarch Philip, son of Herod the Great, was a great patron of Bethsaida. He made it one of his chief cities and named it Julias after Julia, daughter of Emperor Augustus. A large building project was launched, and Philip commanded that he be buried there (Josephus, *Ant.*, 18.4.6).

BETH-SHAN A Canaanite city on the southeastern plain of **Esdraelon** where the Jezreel and Jordan valleys meet; it is probably modern Tell el-Husn. After the Israelites' conquest of Canaan, it was allotted to Manasseh (Josh 17:11), but it remained in Canaanite hands because the Israelites could not overcome the Canaanites' chariots (Josh 17:16; Judg 1:27). It was in Philistine hands at the time of the defeat and death of Saul, and the bodies of Saul and his sons were fastened to the city wall (1 Sam 31:10–12). By Solomon's reign, however, Beth-shan was included as one of twelve royal districts (1 Kgs 4:12). It took part in the Maccabean wars (1 Macc 5:52; 12:40–42). In later eras it became known as Scythopolis or Nysa Scythopolis (2 Macc 12:29–31).

BETH-SHEMESH (Hebrew, "house of the sun") The name of three towns in Palestine.

1. A town on the border between Judah and Dan (Josh 15:10), perhaps the same location as Ir-shemesh (Josh 19:41) in the territory of Dan. It was also a Levitical city (Josh 21:16; 1 Chr 6:59), but its chief fame was as the place to which the **ark of the covenant** was taken when the Philistines restored it to the Israelites (1 Sam 6:9–15). The city was also the site of a battle between **Jehoash** of Israel and **Amaziah** of Judah (2 Kgs 14:11; 2 Chr 25:21).

2. A town in the territory of Issachar (Josh 19:22).

3. A town in the territory of Naphtali (Josh 19:38) that remained a Canaanite settlement even after the Israelites' conquest of Canaan (Judg 1:33).

BETH SHITTAH A place to which the Midianites fled after their defeat by Gideon (Judg 7:22).

BETHUEL Nephew of **Abraham** (Gen 22:20–22) and father of **Rebekah** (Gen 24:15) and **Laban** (Gen 28:5).

BETHULIA The home of **Judith** and the site of the events of the book of Judith. The book makes clear that the city was north of Jerusalem, near Betomesthaim, opposite Esdraelon, and near Dothan (Jdt 4:6). The exact location has not yet been identified. The city was besieged by the Mesopotamian general **Holofernes**, who was then killed by Judith (Jdt 8–15).

BETH-ZATHA A double pool in Jerusalem that was surrounded by four porticoes or porches, with a fifth separating the two pools. At the pool Jesus cured a man who had been disabled for thirty-eight years (John 5:1–15). Some manuscripts of the Gospel of John term the pool Bethesda ("house of mercy"), and the name Bethsaida ("house of the fisherman") is also used. The pool was excavated in modern times; the remains of five colonnades were found, and the pool itself consisted of a double cistern.

BETH-ZUR A fortress town in the territory of Judah, about twenty miles south of Jerusalem (2 Macc 11:5), probably the modern Khirbet et-Tubeiqah. It was occupied by a clan of Caleb (1 Chr 2:45). **Rehoboam** fortified it (2 Chr 11:7) to protect his capital city (Jerusalem) from attacks from the south (Philistines, Edomites, Egyptians, etc.). It was here that **Judas Maccabeus** defeated the Seleucid army of Lysia (1 Macc 4:29; 2 Macc 11:5); afterward Judas fortified it against the Idumeans (1 Macc 4:61). The Seleucids seized control of it temporarily (1 Macc 6:31–49), but it was recaptured by Simon Maccabeus (1 Macc 11:65; 14:7–33).

BEULAH (Hebrew, "just married") A name that appears in some translations of Isa 62:4. It is used to describe Jerusalem in expectation of its restoration after the Exile; the image refers to an impending marriage to the Lord. The RSV translates it as "married."

BEZAE CODEX *See* **Codex**.

BEZALEL (Hebrew, possibly "in the shadow of God") Son of Uri and a member of the tribe of Judah (1 Chr 2:20). He was a craftsman of wood, metal, and stone. He was chosen as the head of the craftsmen in charge of constructing the **Tabernacle** and its furnishings. For this task he was equipped by the "Spirit of God" (Exod 31:1–11; 35:30).

BEZEK A town in southern Palestine that was ruled at the time of the conquest of Canaan by the Canaanite king **Adonibezek**. It was here that the tribes of Judah and Simeon defeated the Canaanite king (Judg 1:4–5). Saul gathered his forces against the Ammonites at a place named Bezek (1 Sam 11:8–11), but this may be a different town from the one mentioned in Judges.

BIBLE (Greek *biblia*, "books") The collection of seventy-three books that the Church believes is the written expression of God's revelation. These books form a single "Book," since God is the divine author of them all, and collectively they bear witness to God's unified plan for salvation.

In its Dogmatic Constitution on Divine Revelation, *Dei Verbum*, the Second Vatican Council taught: "The Church has always venerated the divine Scriptures just as she venerates the body of the Lord. She has always regarded the Scriptures together with Sacred Tradition as the supreme rule of faith, and will ever do so. For, inspired by God and committed once and for all to writing, they impart the word of God himself without change, and make the voice of the Holy Spirit resound in the words of the prophets and apostles. Therefore, like the Christian religion itself, all the preaching of the Church must be nourished and ruled by sacred Scripture" (§21).

Since God is the principal author of the Bible, it is both inspired and inerrant. (*See also* **Inspiration**.) The specific writings, or "books," of the Bible are enumerated according to the authentic list, called the canon, accepted by the Church. These works, written by men under the inspiration of the Holy Spirit, constitute the rule of Catholic faith, in conjunction with the tradition and teaching authority of the Church. Sacred Tradition and Sacred Scripture form one sacred deposit of the word of God, which is committed to the Church (DV §10). That sacred deposit is the basis of all the doctrine of the Church.

There are seventy-three books in the Bible: forty-six in the Old Testament and twenty-seven in the New Testament. Some lists separate or combine certain OT books, so the number might be slightly different, but the contents are the same.

The Bible is divided into the Old and New Testaments, which bear witness to two covenants, old and new, between God and his people as part of the fulfillment of the divine plan of salvation. The Catholic Church, in *Dei Verbum*, declares, "Now the books of the OT, in accordance with the state of mankind before the time of salvation established by Christ, reveal to all men the knowledge of God and of man and the ways in which God deals with men. These books show us true divine pedagogy . . . The books of the OT with all their parts, caught up into the proclamation of the Gospel, acquire and show forth their full meaning in the NT (cf. Matt 5:17; Luke 24:27; Rom 16:25–26; 2 Cor 3:14–16) and in turn shed light on it and explain it" (DV §16). Regarding the NT, *Dei Verbum* states: "The word of God is set forth and shows its power in a most excellent way in the writings of the NT. For when the fullness of time arrived (cf. Gal 4:4), the Word was made flesh and dwelt among us in the fullness of grace and truth (cf. John 12:32). This mystery had not been manifested to other generations as it was now revealed to his holy apostles and prophets in the Holy Spirit (cf. Eph 3:4–6), so that they might preach the Gospel, stir up faith in Jesus, Christ and Lord, and gather the Church together. To these realities, the writings of the NT stand as a perpetual and divine witness" (DV §17). (*See also* **Testament**.)

The chapter and verse divisions of the Bible are not original to the inspired writings; they were devised by later scholars to make it easier to refer to particular passages. The divisions came about gradually. Some early manuscripts, such as the Vaticanus collection from the fourth century (see **Codex**), make certain divisions in the text. The first division of the Bible into chapters was undertaken by Archbishop Stephen Langton of Canterbury (d. 1228) in about 1205; with some refinements his divisions are the ones we use today. The further division of the chapters into verses was made around 1551 by Robert Estienne (d. 1559), also known as Robert Stephanus, a printer in Paris.

BIBLE, ENGLISH VERSIONS AND TRANSLATIONS *See* **Versions of the Bible**.

BIBLICAL COMMISSION, PONTIFICAL *See* **Pontifical Biblical Commission**.

BIBLICAL CRITICISM The application of modern literary and scientific methods to the study of Scripture. The word "criticism" does not imply a negative stance toward the Bible, but comes from the Greek *krinein*, meaning "to judge" or "to discern." Criticism thus refers to informed judgments about the meaning of the biblical texts and about the circumstances that brought them into existence. Though biblical interpretation is something as ancient as the Bible itself, biblical criticism refers more narrowly to scientific methods of study that were developed in modern times.

I. *Principles of Biblical Criticism*
    A. *Theological Basis*
    B. *Methodological Limits*
II. *Methods of Biblical Criticism*
    A. *Diachronic Methods*
    B. *Synchronic Methods*
III. *The Church and Biblical Criticism*
    A. *Early Response*
    B. *Later Response*
IV. *The Critique of Criticism*

I. PRINCIPLES OF BIBLICAL CRITICISM

The validity of biblical criticism must be established before its methods can be applied in the interpretation of Scripture. This is so because biblical interpretation is a theological enterprise, and so the aims and presuppositions of biblical criticism must be compatible, even coordinate, with the aims and presuppositions of theological science. Moreover, modern times have often witnessed faithful believers resisting and occasionally rejecting the use of scientific procedures for the purpose of studying Scripture. To address these important issues, the principles of biblical criticism must be theologically justified and its limits made clear.

A. Theological Basis

The basis of biblical criticism is the reality of the Incarnation. In other words, it responds to the fact that God, who created both history and humanity, has always made use of his creation in revealing himself to the world and bringing about its salvation. This "divine condescension" is preeminently exampled in the person of Jesus Christ, the Son of God who entered the stream of human history as true God and true man. Scripture bears the image of this incarnational mystery in its own unique way: it is the eternal Word of God expressed in the historical words of men. Like Jesus, the Bible is truly divine and yet truly human at the same time. And since it comes to us in the dress of human language, its human dimensions can and must be studied in order to ascertain its intended meaning. Biblical criticism does precisely this by investigating the human activities and circumstances that brought the biblical books into existence. On the one hand, this entails *historical* study in order to understand what religious, political, cultural, and intellectual forces helped to shape the perspective of the biblical authors. On the other hand, it entails *literary* study of such things as the biblical languages, the literary genres and conventions operative in biblical times, and the cognate literatures of neighboring peoples in the biblical world. Without serious attention given to these human facets of Scripture, biblical interpretation would inevitably lack a solid and objective foundation. Just as the Church acknowledges both the humanity and divinity of Christ, without confusing or separating the two, so the Church acknowledges the need to investigate both the human and the divine aspects of Scripture.

B. Methodological Limits

This is not to say that biblical criticism supplies a comprehensive range of methods equipped to interpret every aspect of the Bible. In point of fact, the procedures of modern scholarship are more or less restricted to the human and historical dimensions of the text. Though essential to the task, the critical methods are by no means fully sufficient to discover the full meaning of Scripture. Interpretation must ultimately go beyond the critical disciplines to consider the divine realities of the Word, to listen for the voice of God speaking through its various modes of human speech. Failure to do this often leads to a biblical exegesis that is sterile and lifeless, having nothing to inspire faith or to encourage a deeper commitment to the Lord. It must always be remembered that the Bible, though truly human, is not merely human. The text of Scripture is indeed a rich source of human information, but its ultimate goal is human salvation.

Biblical criticism is thus limited in its ability to grasp the spiritual message of the Bible. Its emphasis on historical matters entails a sustained focus on the past, leading primarily to judgments about what the Bible meant when it was first written. Again, this is a necessary part of a fully informed interpretation. But because the Bible is truly the Word of God, its message not only echoes down the corridors of history, but proceeds from the eternity of God himself, who is contemporary with every moment of history. Scripture, because it ultimately comes forth from God, is able to address the faithful in every age. Its message is thus always relevant to the life of faith and is capable of giving direction and strength to every generation that listens attentively to its divine teaching.

Mother Church has always recognized this fact. Never has she advocated an exclusive reliance upon critical methods in the interpretation of Scripture, for this would betray the uniqueness of the Bible as the written Word of God. Instead, she steers the middle course between *rationalism*—the philosophical stance that interprets reality solely on the basis of reason without regard for faith—and *pietism*—the mind-set that rejects scientific methods of study in favor of spiritual interpretations that stem from religious inspirations or the desire for personal edification. Neither extreme accounts for the reality of Scripture as a book that is both human and divine. On the contrary, the philosophical traditions of the Church insist that faith and reason, though clearly distinct, must always be united. Faith must work together with reason if the Bible's divine and human dimensions are to be fully appreciated and its message adequately understood (see, e.g., John Paul II, encyclical letter *Fides et Ratio*, 1998).

II. METHODS OF BIBLICAL CRITICISM

The methods of biblical criticism can be classified in different ways. In the late eighteenth century a distinction was made between "lower" and "higher" criticism. Lower criticism was essentially textual criticism, the discipline that seeks to establish the original wording of the Bible as the basis for all further interpretation (for details, see **Texts of the Bible**). Higher criticism was then the application of literary-historical criticism that aimed to uncover the sources, traditions, compositional stages, and life settings that underlie the biblical writings. Another distinction, more in vogue today, is made between "diachronic" and "synchronic" methods of study. *Diachronic* methods seek to describe the formation of the biblical books through time, focusing on the historical process of development that resulted in the canonical writings we possess today. The diachronic approach is thus concerned with the prehistory of the scriptural texts insofar as this can be discovered. *Synchronic* methods, by contrast, study the text in its final, canonical form. Their concern is with the meaning of a given text as it now stands in the Bible through a study of its structure, rhetoric, and canonical acceptance.

A. Diachronic Methods

Several methods can be called diachronic insofar as they study the history of how select biblical texts passed through stages of growth and editorial shaping over time. Following is a synopsis of the most popular and influential of the diachronic methods.

1. Source Criticism. Source criticism seeks to isolate and identify what oral and written source materials were incorporated into the texts of the Bible. In general, it theorizes that many of the biblical writings were not fresh compositions produced by a single author; rather it supposes that oral and literary traditions that were already in existence were incorporated into the Bible without formal acknowledgment by the author. As clues to the presence of sources, scholars look for abrupt transitions in style or perspective within a work, perceived inconsistencies or tensions between different parts of a work, and repetitions or doublets of material retained within the same work. Prime examples of source

criticism applied to the Bible include the Documentary Hypothesis, which posits the existence of four sources (labeled J, E, D, and P) incorporated into the Pentateuch, and the Two-Source Hypothesis, which contends that the Gospels of Matthew and Luke drew much of their information about Jesus from the Gospel of Mark as well as a hypothetical sayings source called "Q."

2. Form Criticism. Form criticism seeks to classify the literary genre of the biblical books and of their individual parts. Beyond this, it attempts to trace the evolution of literary units from the initial stage of oral proclamation to the final stage of written composition, and to identify what life situations or social contexts gave rise to such units. One of its working assumptions, at least in the case of certain books like Genesis and the Synoptic Gospels, is that small units of tradition circulated independently of one another and were subject to the shaping influence of the communities that valued them. Early form criticism of Genesis classified its various stories as myths, legends, epics, and so forth. Applying this method to the Synoptic Gospels, scholars defined its component parts as parables, miracle stories, apothegms, controversy dialogues, and so on. One of the main contentions of form criticism applied to the Gospels is that their components are basically homiletic; that is, they were designed to address the spiritual and pastoral needs of the earliest church communities.

3. Redaction Criticism. Redaction criticism builds on the conclusions of source and form criticism and seeks to evaluate the contribution of the final authors of the Bible. Given the assumption that many of the biblical writers pieced together an array of traditions and source materials, the final author is essentially viewed in his role as an editor or redactor. Redaction criticism thus forms judgments about how the editorial process was carried out by the individual(s) responsible for the final edition of the biblical writings. In particular, it looks for the theological interests and tendencies that influenced the final stages of composition. For example, in Old Testament scholarship, efforts have been made to assess how the author(s) responsible for incorporating the "P" or Priestly source handled the earlier materials (J, E, and D) in casting the Pentateuch in its final form. Likewise, in New Testament studies, scholars seek to describe how Matthew and Luke have incorporated materials from Mark while making minor adjustments in the interests of their own theological viewpoints.

B. Synchronic Methods

Since the development of the diachronic methods, more recent scholarship has witnessed the rise of synchronic methods. Synchronic approaches give primary consideration to the text as it stands in the Bible. The driving conviction is that the study of a text's development through time must be followed by the study of a text's meaning once its final form has become fixed for all time. Following is a synopsis of the most valuable of the synchronic methods.

1. Rhetorical Criticism. Rhetorical criticism studies how the texts of Scripture are written to persuade or dissuade their readers in matters of faith and life. That is, it seeks to understand how the biblical writings were designed to impact their original audiences. This involves the study of rhetorical devices and techniques, the order and logic of presentation, and the ability of the author to evoke sentiments or stir the emotions of the readership. Comparative studies look to Semitic models of composition, which show a preference for such things as parallelism, wordplay, and meaningful repetition, as well as Greek and Roman models, which employ a range of oratorical techniques developed in classical times. Conventions of ancient rhetoric, once understood, can help the exegete to ascertain better the intentions and emphases of the biblical author and his work.

2. Narrative Criticism. Narrative criticism studies the features and functions of storytelling in the Bible. Analysis is made of such things as plot, character development, conflict resolution, and the narrator's point of view. Narrative analysts try to appreciate how stories are told to impart convictions and to construct or even deconstruct entire worldviews. By means of well-crafted stories, the reader's beliefs can be strengthened, undermined, or simply adjusted. The theory is that many lessons for faith and life are conveyed by the author through his manner of presentation. Narrative criticism is a particularly important method of study inasmuch as most of the Bible is cast in narrative form.

3. Canonical Criticism. Canonical criticism studies the biblical texts not in isolation but in the context of the biblical canon. Its interpretive frame of reference is thus the entire collection of books grouped together into the Bible and deemed authoritative by the believing Church. Its rationale is that Scripture, despite the diversity of its works, has an underlying unity that coalesces around a common perspective of faith. Interpretation of the sacred books in their canonical form must therefore take account of the total witness of the Bible as a whole. Unlike many of the other methods, canonical criticism does not approach the Bible as it would any other collection of writings. Rather it attempts to take seriously the "sacredness" of Scripture as something authoritative for the community that reveres it and strives to live by its teaching. Canonical criticism presupposes that, quite apart from its historical foundations, the Bible can and does speak directly to our situation today.

III. THE CHURCH AND BIBLICAL CRITICISM

Biblical criticism, being a modern science, was not a concern of the Church until modern times. For most of Christian history, the Bible was interpreted with the use of "precritical" methods and techniques (see, e.g., Saint Augustine's *On Christian Doctrine*). This is not to say that ancient and traditional scholarship lacked intellectual rigor or yielded conclusions that are no longer relevant to a proper understanding of Scripture. Far from it. Still, the fact remains that the development of scientific criticism opened a new era of biblical studies that continues to advance our understanding of the Bible within its historical and literary context. Not all modern developments have proven helpful, however, so the Church has had to respond to the new situation with guidance and occasional correction.

A. Early Response

The Church first addressed the questions and challenges of modern biblical science when Pope Leo XIII promulgated his 1893 encyclical *Providentissimus Deus*, which was offered as authoritative guidance on a range of biblical matters. Much of it was concerned with settling doctrinal questions related to the nature of Scripture, most notably by expounding a Catholic understanding of the divine inspiration and inerrancy of Scripture. Numerous statements, however, were directed to the issue of biblical interpretation in light of recent trends sweeping across the academic world in Europe.

For the most part, Leo XIII assumed a defensive posture toward the historical-critical methods being developed and employed in his day. This is not surprising, since the Church of the late nineteenth century was the target of countless attacks in the name of critical science—not a few of which were launched on biblical grounds. This was hardly the atmosphere in which the pope could encourage Catholic exegetes to climb aboard the bandwagon of critical scholarship. In fact, to the extent that biblical criticism was often misused as a weapon against the claims of historic Christianity, it must have been extremely difficult at the time to see biblical criticism's positive potential for good. Apart from sound conclusions yielded by the critical methods, the soundness of the methods themselves would inevitably be left in doubt.

Nevertheless, the defensive stance of Leo XIII must not be mistaken for a rejection of scientific research. The pope did not condemn the use of biblical criticism—only its misuse and abuse. In fact, it is all the more striking, given the hostile environment of the times, that Leo urged Catholic scholars to excel their opponents in the technical disciplines of exegesis. His concern was not to halt the progress of biblical studies but to steer it in the right direction by exhorting exegetes to master the biblical languages, to expand and improve their knowledge of history, and to study the conventions of ancient literature contemporary with the Bible. His main proviso was that Catholic scholarship must always respect the authority of the Magisterium and never lose sight of the Bible's inspiration and inerrancy as defined by the Church.

Not content with papal directives and encouragement, Leo XIII demonstrated his commitment to biblical science by establishing the Pontifical Biblical Commission (apostolic letter *Vigilantiae studiique*, 1902). At its inception, this was a body of learned cardinals who addressed particular biblical questions submitted for examination. Intermittently, the commission formulated official responses with the endorsement of the pope (the *Responsa* of the Pontifical Biblical Commission, 1905–1933). This initiative was followed up by several interventions on the part of Pope Pius X, which dealt with standards for the teaching and proper understanding of Scripture (e.g., the apostolic letter *Quoniam in re biblica*, 1906; the encyclical letter *Pascendi dominici gregis*, 1907; the apostolic letter *Praestantia Scriptu-*

rae Sacrae, 1907). The last major landmark in this early period was the 1920 encyclical of Pope Benedict XV, *Spiritus Paraclitus*, which commemorated the contribution of Saint Jerome to Catholic biblical studies. Throughout the first decades of the twentieth century these popes basically took their cue from the norms laid down by Leo XIII. In other words, they essentially maintained the Church's guarded position against the methods of biblical criticism so obviously (at the time) susceptible to abuse.

B. Later Response

The Church's stance toward modern biblical studies was decisively altered when Pope Pius XII promulgated his 1943 encyclical *Divino Afflante Spiritu*. A fuller openness to the contribution of scientific criticism, along with fresh encouragement for Catholic scholars working in the field, permeates the encyclical from beginning to end. The doctrinal norms put forward by Leo XIII are reaffirmed in the document, but its pastoral perspective on biblical criticism is much more positive and accepting.

Historically, it is known that Pius XII was responding in part to the circulation of a pamphlet in Italy that attacked the principles of biblical criticism as essentially incompatible with a Catholic view of Scripture. Instead, the pseudonymous pamphleteer (now identified as one Dolindo Ruotolo) advocated a purely mystical approach to the Bible that aimed at spiritual edification to the exclusion of historical understanding. The pope's response was forceful and clear: scientific criticism, be it historical, textual, linguistic, or archaeological, is indeed a proper means of biblical interpretation, so long as the Catholic exegete remains faithful to the Church and her doctrinal Tradition. Spiritual exegesis was by no means ruled out, but guidelines were given to ensure that it had a solid and objective basis in the text of Scripture.

Probably the two most important norms established by Pius XII are the priority of the literal sense and the propriety of studying literary forms. The first responsibility of biblical scholars, according to the encyclical, is the determination of the literal sense, that is, the meaning of the words intended by the human authors of Scripture. Deeper, spiritual readings of the Bible can certainly be legitimate and fruitful, but they must be built on the foundation of the literal sense. Ascertaining the literal sense is greatly helped by the study of the literary forms and genres that were once current in the ancient world. To know, for example, whether a text is a parable, a poem, a proverb, or a prophecy is to know something about how the sacred author intended readers to understand his words. Prudent use of biblical criticism is thus endorsed by the pope as an important (but not all-sufficient) tool for modern Scripture study.

The same positive assessment of biblical criticism was offered by Vatican II in its 1965 dogmatic constitution *Dei Verbum*. This document, which dealt with the whole question of divine revelation and its transmission, gives most of its attention to the importance of Sacred Scripture. Doctrinal matters concerning its inspiration and inerrancy are summarized (DV §11), and pastoral encouragement is given for the use of Scripture in the lives of the Christian faithful (DV §§21–26). On the issue of biblical interpretation, the council Fathers reaffirmed the perspective of Pius XII by giving the following instruction:

> Seeing that, in sacred Scripture, God speaks through men in human fashion, it follows that the interpreter of sacred Scripture, if he is to ascertain what God has wished to communicate to us, should carefully search out the meaning which the sacred writers really had in mind, that meaning which God had thought well to manifest through the medium of their words.
>
> In determining the intention of the sacred writers, attention must be paid, inter alia, to literary forms, for the fact is that truth is differently presented and expressed in the various types of historical writing, in prophetical and poetical texts, and in other forms of literary expression. Hence the exegete must look for that meaning which the sacred writer, in a determined situation and given the circumstances of his time and culture, intended to express and did in fact express, through the medium of a contemporary form. Rightly to understand what the sacred author wanted to affirm in his work, due attention must be paid both to the customary and characteristic patterns of perception, speech and narrative which prevailed at the age of the sacred writer, and to the conventions which the people of his time followed in their dealings with one another. (DV §12)

Such is the current perspective of the Church on the value of biblical criticism. The Council, following in the footsteps of Pius XII, stresses both the importance of the literal sense and the necessity of studying ancient models of literary expression as a means of interpreting its literal meaning.

More detail about the procedures of biblical criticism and their application to the texts of Scripture has been offered by the Pontifical Biblical Commission in the latter half of the twentieth century. In the midst of Vatican Council II, the Commission issued a document that affirmed the historicity of the Gospels and established basic guidelines for employing contemporary methods of Gospel scholarship while cautioning against some of its pitfalls (Instruction on the Historical Truth of the Gospels, 1964). Almost three decades later the Pontifical Biblical Commission released a major document examining the principles and methods of biblical criticism, assessing their strengths and weaknesses, and insisting on their importance for a modern understanding of the Bible (Document on the Interpretation of the Bible in the Church, 1993).

IV. THE CRITIQUE OF CRITICISM

At the close of the twentieth century, Cardinal Joseph Ratzinger (later Pope Benedict XVI) called for a "critique of criticism"—a sober examination of historical criticism's practical limitations and its sometime tendency to theoretical hubris. Pope Benedict's most basic criticism of criticism is that it is far from what it purports to be—a value-neutral science akin to the natural sciences, the findings of which are objective and rendered with a high degree of certitude. In 1988, he lectured in New York on "Biblical Interpretation in Crisis: Foundations and Approaches of Biblical Exegesis"

(a.k.a. the "Erasmus Lecture"), during which he noted that many critical scholars employing the same critical methods have arrived at "reconstructions" that are "incompatible with one another." Rather than "uncovering an icon that has become obscured over time, they are much more like photographs of their authors and the ideals they hold." Pope Benedict did not seek to invalidate the historical-critical method, but rather to "purify" it through self-examination, so that it can truly serve its proper function in the search for the truth. Why, after all, should scholarship itself be exempt from the methods it applies to the sacred texts?

According to Pope Benedict XVI, the proper use of critical methods calls for the Catholic exegete to subordinate them to "a hermeneutic of faith" (versus a "hermeneutic of suspicion"). Accordingly, such an adaptation of critical methods would require exegetes to recognize: (1) the limitations of the scientific methods; (2) the possibility and "knowability" of divine activity in human history; (3) the consistent application of the same criteria for studying natural and supernatural occurrences; (4) the potential authenticity and historicity of the various biblical materials; and (5) the positive role played by the Church and its Tradition.

BIGTHAN One of the eunuchs who guarded the entrance to King **Ahasuerus**'s private chambers (Esth 2:21; 6:2).

BILDAD One of **Job**'s three friends who arrived to give him consolation and comfort (Job 2:11). He became a participant in the book's dialogue, usually speaking second (Job 8:1; 18:5–6).

BILHAH The handmaid given to **Rachel** by **Laban** at the time of her marriage to **Jacob** (Gen 29:29). She became the mother of Dan and Naphtali (Gen 30:3–8; 1 Chr 7:13). **Reuben**, Jacob's firstborn by Leah, later lay with Bilhah (Gen 35:22), and for that Reuben lost his father's blessing (Gen 49:3–4).

BIRSHA King of **Gomorrah** at the time of **Abraham** (Gen 14:2). In alliance with four other kings (of Sodom, Admah, Zeboiim, and Bela), Birsha rebelled against their Mesopotamian overlord **Chedorlaomer** and was defeated and forced to flee the battlefield.

BIRTH OF JESUS *See under* **Jesus Christ**.

BIRTHRIGHT *See* **Firstborn**.

BISHOP (Greek *episkopos*, "overseer") A successor to the apostles (*see* **Apostle**, and cf. Acts 1:20–22) who has received the fullness of Christ's priesthood and is responsible for the oversight of a diocese or ecclesiastical territory (cf. 1 Thess 5:12; Heb 13:17; 1 Pet 5:14).

In traditional Greek usage, the word *episkopos* originally meant an overseer or guardian; the word was used for officials in charge of temples (cf. 1 Pet 2:25). The word appears often in the Septuagint Greek Old Testament, which uses it metaphorically in the oracle of Isaiah: "I will make your overseers peace and your taskmasters righteousness" (Isa 60:17).

The New Testament uses the word to describe a position of leadership in the Church,

specifically the role of apostles and their chosen delegates. Some translations render *episkopos* as "office" (RSV, NAB), others as "bishopric" (Douai, KJV). In Acts 1:20 Peter cites Ps 109:8 as he initiated the process of replacing Judas in the band of apostles: "His office (Greek *episkopēn*, "bishopric") let another take."

The office of bishop is divinely instituted and was clearly in place during the first generation of the Church. The apostles were chosen and sent by Christ with the task of proclaiming the Gospel, that is, of giving personal testimony of the divinity of Christ to those who had not seen the Savior (Matt 10:2, 28:16–20; Mark 16:14–18; Luke 24:47–49; John 20:19–23; cf. 1 Cor 9:1). The bishops were responsible for "the care of all the churches" (2 Cor 11:28).

Christ had appointed the twelve apostles as a unique college, with connected authority and duties (Matt 10:1–4, 16:18; Mark 3:13–19; Luke 6:12–16, 24:34; 1 Cor 15:5; cf. LG §§19–23). The apostles in turn ordained bishops by the sacramental rite of the laying on of hands. Thus they passed on to their successors the gift of the Spirit, which has been transmitted down to the bishops of today (Acts 1:8; 2:4; John 20:22–23; 1 Tim 4:14; 2 Tim 1:6–7; LG §21).

In the NT the distinction between "elders" (Greek *presbyteroi*) and "overseers" (Greek *episkopoi*) is not always clear. Paul named elders in Asia Minor (Acts 14:23; cf. Acts 20:17), describing them later (Acts 20:28) as overseers of the local church (cf. Titus 1:5). The qualities of the bishop were stressed in the NT (1 Tim 3:1–8; Titus 1:6–9). The two terms *presbyteros* and *episkopos* seem to have been interchangeable, as we see in other Epistles (Jas 5:14; 1 Pet

5:1, 5). As Christian communities grew, resident bishops began to replace the first generation of itinerant apostles and their immediate successors—a pattern that had already begun to emerge in Jerusalem, where James was head of the church, and in Rome, where Peter settled. Eusebius (*Hist. Eccl.* 4.22) thus could provide unbroken lists of bishops back to the apostles for the sees of Rome, Alexandria, Antioch, and Jerusalem.

By the early second century in Asia Minor, Smyrna, Magnesia, Philippi, Ephesus, Tralles, and Philadelphia all had resident bishops, as we see from the letters of Saint Ignatius of Antioch. Ignatius refers to bishops being present "in the farthest parts of the earth" (Ign. *Eph.* 3) and admonishes the Smyrnaeans, "let no one do anything that pertains to the church apart from the bishop" (Ign. *Smyrn.* 8). "Where the bishop is," Ignatius says, "there is the Catholic Church."

The early Christians saw the orders of Christian clergy as a fulfillment of the OT hierarchy of high priest, priest, and levite. These offices corresponded, respectively, to bishop, priest, and deacon (see, e.g., the Didascalia Apostolorum). The Qumran community, too, seems to have had an office similar to that of bishop, called the *mebaqqer*.

Having received the fullness of Christ's priesthood, bishops are empowered to ordain other bishops and priests (cf. Acts 20:28; 1 Tim 1:3, 3:1–7, 4:11–14, 5:1ff.; Titus 1:5–14). While responsible to the pope, bishops govern their flocks in the name of God as representatives of Christ; in this sense, they are not delegates of the Holy See, although they are subject to its authority. Their powers are executed by virtue of their office. A bishop does not enjoy personal infallibility, but the college of bishops, when acting collectively and in union with the pope, is infallible.

BITHYNIA A part of northwestern Asia Minor; by New Testament times it was a province in the Roman Empire. Bithynia was part of the wider province of Bithynia et Pontus, with the provincial capital at Nicomedia.

On his second missionary journey Paul, accompanied by Timothy, hoped to visit Bithynia but he was prevented by the "Spirit of Jesus" (Acts 16:7). Nevertheless a Christian community was established there in the first century, as Peter addressed his First Letter to the Christians of Bithynia, among others (1 Pet 1:1).

BITUMEN A black mineral pitch found especially in the region of the Dead Sea (Gen 14:10). It was used to seal Noah's ark (Gen 6:14), as mortar for the bricks in the construction of the Tower of Babel (Gen 11:3), and for waterproofing the basket that carried the infant Moses on the Nile (Exod 2:3).

BLASPHEMY (Greek, "reviling" or "speaking ill of") Speech, thought, or action that entails contempt for God. Blasphemy may also involve the contemptuous ridicule of saints, sacred objects, or the Church; it is directly opposed to the second commandment (CCC 1031, 2148, 2162). The gravity of the sin is made manifest in biblical law, where blaspheming the divine Name is a capital crime punished by stoning (Lev 24:10–16; John 10:33).

In his public ministry, Jesus was accused

of blasphemy and false prophecy—religious crimes that would have made him subject to execution by stoning (Mark 2:7; John 5:18; 7:12, 52; 8:59; 10:31, 33). The accusations stemmed from his deeds, including the expulsion of demons, the forgiving of sins, healing on the Sabbath, and his interpretation of the Law regarding purity (e.g., Matt 9:3; Mark 2:7; Luke 5:21), as well as his Messianic claims (Matt 26:65; Mark 14:64; cf. John 5:17, 10:33).

At his trial before the Sanhedrin, Jesus was charged with the crime of blasphemy. As the Sanhedrin did not have jurisdiction in capital cases, the case was sent to the Roman authorities, who alone had the legal power to execute criminals (John 18:31). In Acts, **Stephen** was condemned as a blasphemer and stoned to death by an act of mob violence (Acts 6:11). **Paul**, looking back on his days as a persecutor of the Church, referred to himself as a former blasphemer (1 Tim 1:13).

When Jesus cured a mute demoniac, the admiring crowds wondered if he might be the Son of David. The Pharisees responded by saying, "This man drives out demons only by the power of Beelzebul, the prince of demons" (Matt 12:24). Jesus countered that "if it is by the Spirit of God that I drive out demons, then the kingdom of God has come upon you . . . Whoever is not with me is against me, and whoever does not gather with me scatters. Therefore, I say to you, every sin and blasphemy will be forgiven people, but blasphemy against the Spirit will not be forgiven" (Matt 12:28, 30–32). Not every commentator agrees on exactly what sort of sin Jesus meant. One interpretation is that the sin is in obstinately refusing to accept Jesus for who he is,

thus rejecting the very one through whom forgiveness is granted. A more likely meaning of "blasphemy against the Spirit" is the very sin the Pharisees had just committed in attributing Jesus's work, which was the work of the Spirit, to Satan.

BLASTUS The chamberlain of **Herod Agrippa I** (Acts 12:20).

BLESSING God's bestowing of good things on his creatures, or the invocation of God's goodness upon another. In Scripture all goodness, all blessings, come from God. Indeed, the whole of Scripture attests to the truth that God's work is a blessing, from the first account of creation in Genesis to the final hymn of glory in the heavenly Jerusalem. Our human blessings are a kind of praise to God for the blessings of his creation.

The blessing is fundamental to prayer: it is our gratitude for God's heavenly gifts. Prayer is a thanksgiving for the blessings from God and a recognition of God's love. We bless God for having blessed us.

At creation, God blessed all living things (Gen 1:22, 28; 2:3; 5:2) and commanded that his creatures be fruitful—granting us a share in the creative ability of God. In spite of our sin, God renewed the covenant with Noah and with all living things after the **Flood**, repeating the commandment to "be fruitful and multiply" (Gen 9:1). In the covenant with Abraham, God promised that through the line of Abraham the blessing would extend to all the peoples of the world (Gen 12:2–3; 18:18; 22:18; 26:3–4; 28:14). Blessings were thus connected intimately to the covenants made between the

Lord and his Chosen People; fidelity to the covenant would bring blessings, while infidelity would trigger the corresponding covenant curses (cf. Deut 11:26ff.; 15:4, 18; 28:1). (*See* **Covenant**.)

Blessings often come through a human mediator—usually a father or a priest—who acts with authority to utter the blessing. Abram received a blessing from Melchizedek (Gen 14:19); Jacob received a blessing from Isaac (Gen 27: 27–29; 28:3–4); Joseph's sons received a blessing from Jacob (Gen 48:15–16); the Israelites were blessed by Aaron (Lev 9:22), by Balaam (Num 23:8–10), by Moses (Deut 33:1–29), and by Joshua (Josh 8:33). David blessed the people after installing the ark in Jerusalem (2 Sam 6:18), and Solomon blessed the people after the dedication of the Temple (1 Kgs 8:14, 55).

In the New Testament, blessings follow the same form as in the Old Testament. God blesses; in return, his creatures bless God, although not in the same way (cf. Luke 1:68). Thus, Jesus blessed the loaves and fishes (Matt 14:19; Mark 6:41; Luke 9:16), the bread and wine before instituting the Eucharist (Matt 26:26; Mark 14:22), and the meal at Emmaus (Luke 24:30). Christ's last act on earth before the Ascension was to bless the disciples (Luke 24:50–51).

Mary, the Mother of God, was blessed by God more than any other created person, for she was chosen from all eternity by God to be the mother of his Son and so was redeemed from the moment of her conception (Pope Pius IX, *Ineffabilis Deus*; LG §56; Eph 1:3–4). Elizabeth called Mary "blessed among women" (Luke 1:42), and all the generations to come would acknowledge her blessedness (Luke 1:48) (CCC 491–93, 1077–82, 2627). (*See also* **Liturgy**.)

BLINDNESS A common affliction in the biblical world. The Mosaic Law gave it special protection, prohibiting people from placing stumbling blocks in the way of the blind (Lev 19:14) or leading the blind astray (Deut 27:18). **Isaac** went blind in his old age (Gen 27:1), as did the prophet **Ahijah** (1 Kgs 14:4). **Tobit** was blinded by bird droppings (Tob 2:11), but the gall of fish was prescribed as a medicinal eye ointment (Tob 6:9). Sometimes blindness in the Old Testament is a punishment for wickedness, as seen in **Sodom** (Gen 19:11; Wis 19:17) and with the enemies of the Maccabees (2 Macc 10:30). The Philistines blinded **Samson** (Judg 16:21), and Nebuchadnezzar blinded King **Zedekiah** (2 Kgs 25:7).

Jesus miraculously cured many who were blind (Matt 9:29–30; 20:30–34; Mark 8:22–25; John 9:1–12). Blindness was also used in the New Testament as a metaphor for the spiritual darkness of unbelief or lack of spiritual perception (Matt 23:16–19; John 9:41; Rom 2:19; 2 Cor 4:4). **Paul** was struck blind at his first vision of Christ (Acts 9:8), and later he blinded the magician Elymas, also called **Bar-Jesus** (Acts 13:11).

BLOOD The word for "blood" (or related words) occurs more than four hundred times in the Bible. In the **Law**, blood is "the life of the flesh," and the blood of sacrifices is what makes atonement, "by reason of the life" (Lev 17:11). Because of its sacredness, the Old Testament prohibited consuming blood (Gen 9:4; Lev 7:26; Deut 12:16; cf. Acts 15:20, 29). This prohibition is expressed in Deut 12:23 (cf. Lev 17:11): "for the blood is the life, and you shall not eat the life with the flesh." This prohibition was so fundamental that even foreigners staying in Israelite territory were required to obey it (Lev 17:12–13). Blood of slaughtered animals was thus not to be eaten and had to be poured out into the ground (Deut 12:16). To murder someone was to "shed blood," and the **avenger of blood** sought to do the same (Gen 6:9; Num 35:19).

The great importance of blood is visible in its role in the sacrificial ritual (Lev 3:2–4, 8–10, 13–15). In ritual sacrifice, blood was sprinkled on the sides of the altar (Lev 1:5) or sprinkled before the sanctuary (Lev 4:6), or smeared on the horns of the altar (Lev 4:7, 25). On the Day of Atonement (*see* **Atonement, Day of**), blood was sprinkled on the mercy seat of the ark. The **covenant** of the Law was sealed in blood (Exod 24:6) to signify the kinship bond that the covenant established between the Lord and Israel.

In the New Testament, the blood of Jesus Christ takes the role of the blood of the sacrificial victim in the OT. Like the blood of the sacrifices, the blood of Christ was shed for the remission of sins (Matt 26:28). In the **Eucharist**, the sacrament of Christ's divine life (John 6:53–58), Christ continues to offer his blood for the sins of the world (1 Cor 10:16) and to communicate his saving life to us through the sacrifice of the Mass. Thus Jesus proclaimed, "Drink of it, all of you; for this is my blood of the covenant, which is poured out for many for the forgiveness of sins" (Matt 26:28)—"blood of the covenant" being the very phrase Moses used in the ceremonial ratification of the Law

(Exod 24:8). The sacrificial nature of the Eucharist is thus revealed in the very words of institution.

The Epistles also insist on the atoning power of Jesus's blood. Romans tells us that sins are expiated by his blood (Rom 3:25) and that sinners are justified by his blood (Rom 5:9); Ephesians tells us that we are redeemed by his blood (Eph 1:7). In Hebrews, we learn that Jesus's blood is far superior to that of animals and, unlike the blood of animals (which cannot remove sin, Heb 10:4), Jesus's blood can remove sin and effect eternal redemption (Heb 9:12) and purify the conscience from sin (Heb 9:14, 22) (CCC 610, 1365). (*See also* **Purification** and **Sacrifice**.)

BLOOD, AVENGER OF See **Avenger of blood**.

BLOOD, FIELD OF See **Akeldama**.

BLOODY SWEAT See **Passion**.

BOANERGES ("sons of thunder") The name given by Christ to **James** and **John**, the sons of Zebedee (Mark 3:17).

BOAZ (Hebrew, perhaps "in him is strength")

1. An ancestor of David, of the tribe of Judah (Ruth 4:13, 18–22). He married **Ruth** the Moabitess and was the father of Obed. He was also a wealthy landowner in Bethlehem.

2. The name of one of the two bronze columns in front of the **Temple** of Solomon. Boaz was on the left; **Jachin**, the other column, was on the right (1 Kgs 7:17, 19, 21; 2 Chr 3:17; Jer 52:21–22).

BODY OF CHRIST See **Church**; *see also* **Jesus Christ**.

BOOK In the ancient world, a book was commonly a scroll of papyrus about 9 to 12 inches high and 35 feet long, made by gluing sheets of papyrus end to end. Aside from papyrus, leather and parchment, among other materials, were also used for writing. Usually only one side of the scroll was used for writing (but see Ezek 2:9–10). A rod was sometimes used to roll and unroll the scroll, and libraries consisted chiefly of rolled scrolls marked and stacked. Such a book form was in common use throughout the world of the Bible.

The modern book, with individual pages bound together on one side, developed in the second century A.D. A book of this sort is called a **codex**. The most ancient codices that have been discovered are almost entirely biblical or Christian in content, so that the conclusion is often drawn that the codex was an invention of the early Christian Church. (*See also* **Codex**.)

BOOK OF LIFE, THE A registry of the saints destined for glory, written by God himself and hidden away in heaven. Those not found in the book of life will be cast into the fire (Rev 3:5; 13:8; 20:15). The title is used variously in both the Old Testament and New Testament (Exod 32:32–33; Ps 68:29, 138:16; Phil 4:3). In Revelation, it is said that God entered the names of the faithful in the book of life before the foundation of the world (Rev 13:8).

BOOTHS, FEAST OF Also known as the festival of Tabernacles and the festival of Ingathering, a harvest festival listed in Deut 16:13–15 and Lev 23:43 (cf. Ezra 3:4; Zech 14:16). In Exod 23:16 and 34:22, the festival is celebrated at the end of the year, when the fruits of their labors are gathered. According to Deuteronomy, the festival was to be kept for seven days and was celebrated after the people had gathered in the produce from the "threshing floor and the wine press." The celebration was held from the fifteenth to the twenty-second day of the seventh month (September–October) and was one of the three annual festivals that every male was required to celebrate (Exod 23:14–17, 34:23; Deut 16:16). The name was derived from the booths or tabernacles in which every Israelite was commanded to reside for the period of the festival; the booths were made of branches of palm trees and the boughs of trees (Lev 23:42). Num 29:12–38 specified the sacrifices that were to be offered on each of the days of the festival, starting with thirteen bullocks and other animals on the first day and then decreasing in the number of bullocks each day until seven bullocks were sacrificed on the seventh day. On the eighth day, a solemn assembly was held at which one bullock, one ram, and seven lambs were offered (Num 29:36; cf. John 7:37). Lev 23:40–41 commanded the celebration with "the fruit of goodly trees, branches of palm trees, and boughs of leafy trees, and willows of the brook" (cf. 2 Macc 10:6–8).

The feast was celebrated under **Solomon** (2 Chr 8:13), under **Hezekiah** (2 Chr 31:3), and after the **Exile** (Ezra 3:4; Zech 14:16–19). At its heart the festival was not just an agricultural celebration but a recognition of salvation and dependence on the Lord. It was a memorial of the deliverance from bondage in Egypt: "You shall dwell in booths for seven days; all that are native in Israel shall dwell in booths, that your generations may know that I made the people of Israel dwell in booths when I brought them out of the land of Egypt: I am the LORD your God" (Lev 23:42–43).

BOW One of the chief weapons of the ancient world, along with the sword, spear, and sling. In biblical imagery, the bow (and arrow) was a symbol of war and dread.

It is likely that the bow and arrow first appeared in the Near East with the Akkadians and spread to the different peoples of Mesopotamia and Palestine. Art of the biblical period suggests that the bow was the weapon of the noble classes and royalty; it was used for both war and hunting. It was prized for its range and power and gradually became a favorite weapon for cavalry and chariot in the development of battlefield tactics (1 Chr 5:18; 2 Chr 35:23; Jdt 2:15). The bow is mentioned frequently in the Old Testament (Gen 48:22; Josh 24:12; 1 Sam 20:20; 2 Sam 1:22; 2 Kgs 6:22, 9:24, 13:15; 1 Chr 8:40, 12:2; 2 Chr 14:7, 17:17, 26:14; Hos 1:7, 2:20).

The rainbow (the same Hebrew word is used for "rainbow" as for the weapon) that appears in the sky after the **Flood** signals God's promise that there will never again be a worldwide flood (Gen 9:13–16). It is a "sign of the covenant," and commentators have interpreted it in two ways. Some see it as a sign that God will no longer make war against humanity: God hangs up his war bow and retires it from service. Others see it as a bow drawn and aimed at heaven, a symbolic threat that rep-

resents God's covenant oath. (For more about such symbolic threats, see **Covenant**.)

BOZRAH A city in **Edom**, first mentioned as the home of an Edomite king; it was the residence of **Jobab** the son of Zerah (Gen 36:33; 1 Chr 1:44). The city was mentioned in various oracles by the prophets (Isa 34:6; Jer 48:24, 49:13, 22; Amos 1:12); it was destroyed by **Judas Maccabeus** (1 Macc 5:28). The location is probably modern Buseira, south of Amman, Jordan.

BRASS *See* **Bronze**.

BRAZEN SERPENT *See* **Bronze serpent**.

BREAD *See* **Eucharist**.

BREAD OF THE PRESENCE (Hebrew, literally "bread of the face") The name given to twelve loaves of unleavened bread that were displayed in the **Temple** sanctuary. They symbolized the covenant between God and the twelve tribes of Israel (Lev 24:5–9). The name came from the bread's nearness to the presence of the Lord: the bread was placed on a golden table in the Holy Place, just outside the **holy of holies**. Every Sabbath, the loaves were replaced with fresh bread; the old loaves were eaten by the priests (Lev 25:8–9).

BREASTPIECE The outermost vestment of the high priest; it is described in detail in Exod 28:5–30 and 39:8–21 (cf. Lev 8:8). The breastpiece was made of linen with gold, blue, purple, and scarlet woolen threads embroidered into it; the fabric formed a 10-inch

(25–centimeter) square that covered the chest and held the sacred lots, the **Urim and Thummim**. The breastpiece was set with twelve precious stones, in four rows of three stones, each inscribed with the name of one of the tribes. (*See also* **Ephod**.)

BREASTPLATE Armor worn by soldiers to protect the chest, and thus the heart (1 Kgs 22:34; 2 Chr 18:33). The breastplate was also used metaphorically to describe righteousness (Isa 39:17; cf. Eph 6:14; 1 Thess 5:8).

BRETHREN OF THE LORD *See* **Brothers of the Lord**.

BRICK A molded block used in construction throughout the ancient Near East. Bricks were commonly made by mixing clay with some kind of binding agent (such as straw), molding it into rectangular blocks, and then baking the blocks in the sun or in ovens. The tower of Babel was made of bricks (Gen 11:3). The Hebrews in Egypt were also forced to make bricks, for which they had to gather their own straw (Exod 1:14; 5:7).

BRIDE *See* **Marriage**; *see also* **Covenant**.

BRIDEGROOM *See* **Marriage**.

BRIMSTONE *See* **Sodom and Gomorrah**.

BRONZE An alloy of copper and tin. Bronze was commonly used in the manufacture of vessels, musical instruments, and weapons (Exod 26:11, 37; 27:2–19; 38:2–20, 31; Lev 6:28; Josh 6:19; 1 Sam 17:5; 1 Kgs 7:14–47; 1 Chr 15:19; 2 Chr 4:1–18). When used figuratively, "bronze" could signify strength or courage (Jer 1:18, 15:20; Mic 4:13), but also corruption (Jer 6:28; Ezek 22:18) and unproductivity (Lev 26:19). Some versions translate the word as "brass," which refers to an alloy of copper and zinc.

BRONZE SERPENT A bronze image, made to look like a serpent, constructed by Moses at the command of God. According to Num 21:4–9, the bronze image was hoisted up on a tree, and when those who were bitten by fiery serpents in the desert looked at the bronze serpent they were cured. The serpent became a figure for salvation (Wis 16:6–7) and was seen as a type of Jesus's Crucifixion (John 3:14). It later became the object of idolatry and was broken apart by King Hezekiah (2 Kgs 18:4).

BROTHER (Hebrew *ʾāḥ*; Greek *adelphos*) In modern English, "brother" usually means a male sibling born of the same father and mother. In the Bible, however, the term has a wide range of meanings. Broadly, it means a male "kinsman." It often means a son of the same mother and father, but the word is also used for half brothers (Gen 42:15), nephews, uncles, and cousins (Gen 13:8; Lev 10:4; 1 Chr 9:6). Because of the close relationship in marriage, "brother" is also a term of endearment used by a wife for her husband (Tob 7:12). In Semitic custom, "brother" can also mean a member of the same clan or tribe, as tribal affiliations used familial language. The ancient tribal societies dated back to the days of the nomads, when covenant, marriage, or adoption extended kinship to all members of the tribe, with the head of the clan in the role of father (cf. Num 8:23–26; 2 Sam 1:26; 1 Kgs 9:13; 2 Kgs 19:12; 1 Chr 12:2). More broadly, "brothers" can mean fellow members of the family of Israel (Josh 14:8; 1 Sam 30:23) or parties to a relationship established by **covenant** (2 Sam 1:26; Amos 1:9), members of the same nation (Gen 16:12; Exod 2:11), or even members of different nations who trace their lineage to a common—even if distant—ancestor (for example, in Deut 2:4, the Edomites and Israelites are "brothers" because both come from the line of **Isaac**). Finally, because all are descended from Adam and Eve, all are "brothers" (Gen 9:5; cf. Heb 2:11).

Although the New Testament was written in Greek, the Jewish writers who composed most of the text used "brother" in all these senses. Paul, for instance, refers to fellow Israelites as "brethren" (Rom 9:3–4). The common fatherhood of God, coupled with the divine adoption of believers, is the basis for calling all Christians brothers (cf. Acts 1:16; Rom 1:13; 1 Cor 15:58). "Brother" can *also* simply mean "fellow man" (Matt 5:22; 7:3).

BROTHERS OF THE LORD Relatives of Jesus mentioned several times in the New Testament (Matt 12:46, 13:55; Mark 3:31, 6:3; Luke 8:19; John 2:12, 7:3, 20:17; Acts 1:14; 1 Cor 9:5; Gal 1:19), of whom four are named: James, Joses or Joseph, Simon, and Judas (Matt 13:55; Mark 6:3). The word "brothers" is used here in the extended sense of "**brother**" found throughout the Bible. The NT witness makes clear that the four brothers mentioned are not sons of Mary. Jesus commends Mary into the keeping, not of any brothers of his own, but of the disciple John (John 19:26), which would be unlikely if she had other sons to take care of her. No NT writer ever calls the "brothers" the "sons" of Mary. The most ancient tradition suggested that these "brothers" were sons of Joseph by a previous marriage. More likely Saint Jerome is right in arguing that the "brothers" are Jesus's cousins; by comparing the different Gospels that mention the "brothers," we can make a good argument for that interpretation. James and Joses are sons of another Mary who stood with the Mother of Jesus at the foot of the Cross (Matt 27:56; Mark 15:40).

BRUCHUS *See* **Locust**.

BUL The eighth month of the ancient Canaanite calendar. The month corresponded approximately to October–November (1 Kgs 6:38).

BULL A traditional symbol of strength and fertility in the religious cults of the ancient Near East. The bull was used to represent various pagan deities, including Sin, Marduk, and El. In Israelite ritual, bulls were common sacrifices, and a bull was sacrificed on the **Passover** (Num 28:16–25), the feast of Weeks (Num 28:26–31), the feast of Booths (Num 7), and at the consecration of priests (Exod 29:1–37). Some ancient writers saw these sacrifices as a symbolical slaying of the pagan gods of Israel's neighbors: Apis in Egypt, El in Canaan, and Marduk in Babylon were all represented as bulls. (*See also* **Ox**.)

BURIAL The ritual interment of the dead, either in the ground or in a cave or a tomb hollowed out of rock.

I. THE NECESSITY OF BURIAL

Since a corpse was seen as ritually impure (*see* **Purification**), it was necessary to bury the dead as soon as possible (Deut 21:23; Acts 5:5–6). Not to be buried was considered a truly great misfortune (2 Kgs 9:10; Jer 16:4, 22:19; Ezek 29:5) and a terrible dishonor (1 Kgs 14:10–14; 2 Kgs 9:34–37). For example, Ahijah the prophet predicted to the wife of Jeroboam that her husband would be punished for his faithlessness: "Any one belonging to Jeroboam who dies in the city the dogs shall eat; and any one who dies in the open country the birds of the air shall eat; for the Lord has spoken it" (1 Kgs 14:11). Such was the severity of concern that such a calamity should not take place that anyone who found a body on the roadside was compelled to bury it as soon as possible (Tob 1:18; 2:2–7).

The respect and care of the dead was displayed especially by Tobit in his burial of the dead (Tob 1:16–19). The Church continues this tradition, calling upon the faithful to treat the dead with respect and charity, in faith and hope of the Resurrection. The burial of the dead is considered a corporal work of mercy (CCC 2300).

II. BURIAL, CREMATION, AND EMBALMING

Throughout the ancient world, including among the Canaanites, the Greeks, and the Romans, cremation was a common means of disposing of a corpse. Among the Israelites, however, the only attested instance of cremation was that of Saul and his sons (1 Sam 31:12), and that was only because the bodies were found in a state of mutilation and decomposition. Even in this case, however, cremation was a preparation for the burial of their bones. It was also permitted to burn the dead in cases where doing so might prevent the spread of plague or disease (Amos 6:10). Jacob and Joseph died in Egypt, where embalming was the norm, so they were embalmed and mummified in a process that took forty days to complete (Gen 50:2–3, 26); but embalming did not become the practice among the Israelites.

III. MOURNING CUSTOMS

The body was carried on a wooden bier by friends, servants, and relatives (Luke 7:14). Mourning entailed public displays of grief (2 Sam 3:31, 32; Job 21:33; Amos 5:16; Matt 9:23); the old Canaanite ritual of slashing oneself with a sharp blade or instrument was forbidden under Jewish law (Lev 19:27–28, 21:5; Deut 14:1). "Mourning for the dead lasts seven days," Sir 22:12 declares (cf. Gen 50:10, Jdt 16:24), but exceptionally important figures were mourned longer. Aaron (Num 20:29) and Moses (Deut 34:5–8) were mourned for thirty days after burial; the period for Jacob in Egypt was seventy days, including forty days of embalming (Gen 50:3).

IV. PREPARING THE BODY

Much of our knowledge of burial customs goes back no further than the early first century A.D., but from passing references elsewhere we can see that the customs changed very little over time. The normal practice in preparing the dead for burial was first to close the eyes (Gen 46:4) and tie the mouth shut (John 11:44), wash the body (Acts 9:37), anoint it (Mark 16:1; Luke 24:1), and wrap it in a white linen sheet (Matt 27:59; Mark 15:46; John 11:44). The face was covered with a handkerchief (John 20:7). Assorted spices and other aromatics were buried with the corpse or as part of the wrappings (Mark 16:1). It was also common practice in the New Testament period for the bones to be exhumed and placed in a small limestone box called an ossuary.

The body was not usually placed in a coffin. Instead, whenever possible, the body was buried in a family burial ground, as is apparent from the many references to a man being buried "among his fathers," thereby stressing the continuity of a family line (Gen 47:30; 1 Kgs 13:22; 2 Macc 12:39). All the **patriarchs** and their wives, for example, were buried at Machpelah in the cave that Abraham had bought for Sarah, even when the burial involved a long journey from Egypt (Gen 49:29–32).

The wealthy and members of royalty were buried with jewelry, pottery, furniture, and weapons, as well as with ornate robes and other fine garments (Ezek 32:27).

V. TOMBS

Early forms of Israelite burial included the use of caves as tombs. The first burial mentioned in the Old Testament is that of Sarah in the cave at Machpelah at Hebron (Gen 23:4–19). There were also vaults excavated out of rock; the bodies were placed on slabs or benches carved out of the interior rock walls. Family tombs were common, such as those of Gideon (Judg 8:32), Samson (Judg 16:31), Asahel (2 Sam 2:32), and Ahithophel (2 Sam 17:23).

Burial in the ground was common for those of limited financial resources. A tree might mark the spot (Gen 35:8), while those who died condemned had their burial mounds marked by a pile of rocks (2 Sam 18:17). For example, in the case of Achan and his family, who were stoned to death for plundering spoils from Jericho, "a great heap of stones" was raised over their graves (Josh 7:24–26). Outside Jerusalem, in the Valley of **Hinnom**, there was a specific plot set aside for burial of the condemned who had been executed (Jer 19:11; 26:23) and for strangers who had died while in the territory. (See also **Akeldama**.)

The wealthy had tombs prepared for themselves in gardens (2 Kgs 21:18, 26; Matt 27:57–60; John 19:41–42) and included pillars (Gen 35:20; 2 Sam 18:18) or other monuments (2 Kgs 23:17; 1 Macc 13:27). Typical tombs hewn from rock were enclosed by a large rounded stone, similar to a millstone, which was rolled into place along a channel, so that the tomb was difficult to open once shut (cf. Isa 22:16). The tombs of Lazarus (John 11:38) and Jesus (Mark 16:1–4) were of this type. The tombs of the kings of Judah were located in the old City of David (1 Kgs 2:10, 11:43, 14:31; 2 Kgs 16:20).

The tomb of Jesus was an expensive one, and the Gospels describe it in detail. It had been recently constructed by Joseph of Arimathea and had not yet been used (Matt 27:60; Luke 23:53; John 19:41). It was located in a garden (John 19:41) near the city of Jerusalem (John 19:42). The entryway was small (John 20:5–11), and the tomb was closed up with a large stone (Mark 16:1–4). The Roman guard sealed the stone so that no one could tamper with it (Matt 27:66). The fact that Jesus had been buried in a tomb was part of the earliest Christian preaching (1 Cor 15:4).

BURNING BUSH *See* **Theophany**.

BURNT OFFERINGS *See* **Sacrifice**.

BUZI (Hebrew, "from the land, or tribe, of Buz") The father of the prophet Ezekiel (Ezek 1:3).

BYBLOS *See* **Gebal**.

ℭ

CAESAR A title used by the Roman emperors. Originally it was the family name of the famed Roman general and dictator Gaius Julius Caesar. After his assassination in 44 B.C., his heir and adopted son Octavian (later Emperor Augustus) took Caesar's names, according to accepted Roman custom (cf. Dio Cassius, 46.47.6). After that, Caesar became a title of all the Roman emperors. Three Caesars are mentioned by name in the New Testament: **Augustus** (Luke 2:1), **Tiberius** (Luke 3:1), and **Claudius** (Acts 18:2). (*See also* **Census**.)

CAESAREA The foremost seaport on the Mediterranean coast of Palestine, south of Mount Carmel and around 60 miles (97 kilometers) northwest of Jerusalem. The city was also known as Caesarea Maritima or Caesarea Palestinae; the modern name is Kaisariyeh. Caesarea was founded by **Herod the Great** and constructed between 25 and 13 B.C. From the start, Caesarea was considered a great cultural, economic, and political success for Herod, and later the Roman procurator of Judea would make his headquarters there. The city was also the administrative center for Herodian government. As a largely Hellenistic settlement, it had a majority Gentile population and a Jewish minority.

Caesarea was the home of **Philip** the evangelist (Acts 21:8), who preached in the city (Acts 8:40), as did **Peter** (Acts 10:24–43). Philip gave welcome there to **Paul** and his companions (Acts 21:8) while Paul was engaged on his missionary journeys. Paul was taken there from Jerusalem (Acts 23:23–24) and spent two years there in custody; his hearing was conducted in Caesarea (Acts 24–26) before **Felix** and **Festus**. Caesarea was also notable as the site where Peter baptized the first Gentile convert, **Cornelius** the centurion (Acts 10:3–48).

In the First Jewish War (A.D. 66–70) the city was the site of the terrible slaughter of some twenty thousand Jews by the Romans. Several thousand more were forced to fight to the death as gladiators during the victory celebration of General (later Emperor) Titus held in the city's amphitheater. Emperor Vespasian then reestablished the city as a Roman colony, Colonia Prima Flavia Augusta Caesarea.

CAESAREA PHILIPPI A town, also called Paneas, on the northern frontier of Palestine at the base of Mount Hermon, near one of the sources of the Jordan River. Originally a small town and known for a time as Panion (or Paneas) after the temple of Pan, the city was largely rebuilt by **Philip**, tetrarch of Iturea and son of King Herod the Great, and renamed Caesarea in honor of Emperor Tiberius. To distinguish it from other cities by the name of Caesarea, Philip added his own name.

It was at Caesarea Philippi that Jesus asked of his disciples, "Who do you say that I am?" Peter responded by affirming Jesus as the Messiah, and thus Caesarea Philippi was where Jesus made Peter the foundation of his Church (Matt 16:13–20; Mark 8:27–30; Luke 9:18–22).

CAIAPHAS (Greek *Kaïaphas*) The high priest at the time of Jesus's trial and death. The name Caiaphas is the surname of Joseph; Caiaphas was the son-in-law of the powerful **Annas**. The Roman governor Valerius Gratus appointed him to the post of high priest in A.D. 18. He was deposed by Governor Vitellius in A.D. 36.

Caiaphas apparently was the first religious authority to suggest that Jesus needed to die (John 11:49–52; 18:14). He then hosted a conspiratorial meeting of priests and elders at his palace residence, at which the plans to arrest Jesus were discussed (Matt 26:3–5, marking the start of Matthew's Passion narrative). His house was again used for the hearing of Jesus before the **Sanhedrin** after his arrest in the Garden (Matt 26:57–58; Mark 14:53–54; Luke 22:54), and Caiaphas interrogated Jesus about his Messianic claims. On the basis of his questioning, Caiaphas accused Jesus of blasphemy (Matt 27:62; Mark 14:61). Caiaphas later took

part in the trial of Peter and John (Acts 4:6), although in this text Annas is called the high priest. As the house of Annas long enjoyed control of the office of high priest, this last reference may refer to the wider influence enjoyed by Annas (five of his sons were to serve as high priest, according to Josephus, *Ant.* 20.9.1). It may also be that Annas, deposed by the Roman government, was still seen as the "real" high priest by most of the Jewish people.

CAIN First son of **Adam** and **Eve** and father of Enoch (Gen 4:1, 17). Cain, the first man born of a woman, appears in Genesis 4:1, when Eve gives birth, declaring, "I have produced a man with the help of the Lord"; a Hebrew wordplay relates the name "Cain" (*Qayin*) to the verb "to get" (*qānāh*). Genesis then reports that Eve bore his brother **Abel**. Abel became a keeper of sheep, while Cain was a tiller of the ground. Cain brought to the Lord an offering of the fruit of the ground, while Abel offered him the firstlings of his flock. The Lord rejected Cain's offering and accepted Abel's. When Cain was disappointed, the Lord declared, "Why are you angry, and why has your countenance fallen? If you do well, will you not be accepted? And if you do not do well, sin is lurking at the door; its desire is for you, but you must master it" (Gen 4:7). The response suggests that it was Cain's sinful disposition, not the things he offered, that made his sacrifice unacceptable (cf. Heb 11:4).

Cain plunged into envy and anger and murdered his brother. The actions of Cain were a consequence of original sin, and his envy propelled him to murder (Wis 2:24; John 8:44)

(CCC 2259, 2538–39). Notably, Cain was presented with an opportunity for confession and repentance and declined, asking, "Am I my brother's keeper?" (Gen 4:9). Cain thus followed his father in refusing to beg for mercy (Gen 3:9–12). He is branded a murderer (cf. 1 John 3:12 and the apocryphal 4 Macc 18:11). In consequence of his crime, Cain was marked with a sign, banished from the soil, and henceforth forced to live in the land of "Nod" or wandering—in other words, as a nomad (Gen 4:16).

Cain's descendants were responsible for cultural advances like the development of music (Gen 4:21) and metalworking (Gen 4:22). They were also infamously depraved, however, as sin spread through the world (4:17–24). Genesis establishes a contrast between the wicked line of Cain and the righteous line of **Seth** (Gen 5:1–32). Cain sought to build a "name" for himself by establishing a city, named after his son, Enoch (Gen 4:17); Seth and his son, Enosh, devoted themselves to proper worship of the Lord (4:25–26). The contrast is especially stark with Cain's descendant of the seventh generation, the vengeful **Lamech**, who was the first polygamist and the author of a song boasting of the murders he had committed (Gen 4:18–24). Seth's descendant of the same generation, **Enoch**, walked with the Lord (Gen 5:21–24). The two lines were clearly divergent, climaxing in the Deluge, in which the line of Seth (through Noah and his family) was spared and the line of Cain was drowned in the waters of judgment (Gen 5:32; 6:9). (*See also* **Covenant**; **Tubal-Cain**.)

CALEB (Hebrew, possibly derived from "dog") Son of Jephunneh (Num 32:12) and one of the twelve spies sent out by Moses to scout the land of Canaan (Num 13–14). Caleb, who represented Judah, differed from his fellow spies in his assessment of the feasibility of the conquest. His colleagues spoke of Canaan as a land filled with fortified cities and imposing warriors, but Caleb and **Joshua** encouraged the attack, urging faith in the Lord's protection (Num 13:30; 14:6–9). The people, however, shared the hesitation of the other spies; they allowed fear to extinguish their faith, and threatened to go back to Egypt. As a punishment for their faithlessness, God doomed the people of that generation, except for Joshua and Caleb, to wander and die in the wilderness, cut off from the good things of the **Promised Land**.

Caleb was noted by God as "my servant" and was promised that he would enter Canaan, and that a plot of territory would be given to his descendants (Num 14:24; cf. Num 26:65; 32:12; Deut 1:36). He was one of the twelve tribal representatives who helped divide the land (Num 34:19); he received Hebron for himself (Josh 14:6–15). He defeated and expelled the sons of Anak (Josh 15:14); his nephew Othniel, son of Kenaz, captured Kirjath-sepher (Josh 15:17; cf. Judg 1:10–11).

Another Caleb, this one the son of Hezron, is listed in the genealogies in 1 Chronicles (1 Chr 2:18); his name is also given in the form "Chelubai" (1 Chr 2:9).

CALVARY *See* **Golgotha**.

CAMEL Frequently mentioned in the Old Testament, chiefly as a beast of burden (2 Kgs 8:9) but also as a symbol of prosperity and wealth (Gen 12:16; 24; 31:17; Exod 9:3; 1 Kgs 10:2). It is not certain when the camel was first domesticated in the Near East. Camels appear in the Bible as early as the patriarchal era, including with **Abraham** in Egypt (Gen 12:16) and in Canaan (Gen 24:10), and with **Jacob** (Gen 30:43; 31:17; 32:7, 15). Midianites and other desert raiders rode against Israel on camels (Judg 6:5; 7:12; 8:21), and camels were later confiscated by **David** (1 Sam 27:9), and they were a common possession of nomadic tribes of the Sinai Peninsula (1 Sam 15:3, 30:17; 2 Kgs 8:9). The camel was considered an unclean animal, and therefore could not be eaten (Lev 11:4; Deut 14:7).

In the New Testament, the camel appears exclusively in metaphorical language, most famously in the passage about the camel passing through the eye of a needle (Matt 19:24; Mark 10:25; Luke 18:25); likewise, a swallowed camel figured in the critique of the Pharisees (Matt 23:24).

CANA A village in lower Galilee mentioned in the Gospel of John (2:1–11). Jesus performed his first miracle at Cana, turning water into wine at a wedding feast. Jesus was in Cana a second time when, from a distance, he healed the son of a royal official in Capernaum (John 4:46–54). The town was the home of **Nathaniel**, one of the Twelve (John 21:2). The exact location of Cana remains uncertain; several sites have been suggested, including Ain Qana, Kafr Kanna, and Khirbet Qana. (*See* **Marriage**.)

CANAAN The strip of land at the eastern end of the Mediterranean Sea; it runs from the southern border of Syria in the north to the Sinai Peninsula in the south, and from the sea in the west to the Jordan River in the east. The Israelites settled here after the **Exodus** and the conquest of Canaan. The understanding of the boundaries of the "land of Canaan" changed through history (cf. Gen 15:18–20; Num 34:3–12; Josh 15:2–4; Ezek 47:15–19).

The Canaanites, Hamites (Gen 10:6) who spoke a West Semitic language related to Hebrew, may have settled in the region sometime in the third millennium B.C. Canaan was subsequently invaded by the **Philistines**, the **Arameans**, and finally the Israelites.

As narrated in Genesis, **Ham**, the second son of Noah and the brother of Shem and Japheth (Gen 5:32; 6:10; 7:13; 9:18, 22; 10:1, 6, 20; 14:5; 1 Chr 1:4, 8; 4:40; Ps 78:51; 105:23, 27; 106:22), "saw the nakedness of his father" when Noah became drunk and lay naked in his tent (Gen 9:22). The expression "saw the nakedness of his father" is likely a euphemism; the meaning would be that Ham had incestuous relations with his mother (cf. Lev 18:7–8; 20:17). As a result, Noah cursed Ham's son, Canaan (Gen 9:25–27), who would have been the offspring of that incestuous union; that would explain why the curse fell with such severity on one of Ham's four sons.

In the **Table of Nations** of Gen 10, Ham is listed as the father of Cush (Ethiopians), Misraim (Egypt), Put, and Canaan (Gen 10:6; 1 Chr 1:8). From the line of Ham emerged the Canaanites, Egyptians, Philistines, Assyrians, and Babylonians. By Noah's curse, Canaan would be a slave to Ham's brothers, Shem and Japheth—a curse that was realized when the Israelites conquered Canaan.

At the time of the conquest of Canaan, the Canaanites lived along the coastal regions and in the Jordan Valley (Num 13:29; Deut 1:7, 11:30; Josh 11:3).

The book of Joshua documents the military conquest of Canaan by the forces of Israel (Josh 1–12) and the subsequent division of Canaan's territories and cities among the tribes (Josh 13–22). The conquest of Canaan was launched 40 years after the **Exodus** from Egypt, which is placed 480 years before Solomon began to build the Temple. If this chronology is reliable, the date of the conquest of Canaan is around 1406 B.C., although many scholars prefer a date around 1200 B.C. for the events of the campaign.

For the Israelites, the conquest marked the fulfillment of the oath that the Lord swore to Abraham in which the patriarch's descendants were promised that one day they would come into possession of the land of Canaan at the expense of the nations already situated there (Gen 15:18–21; 17:8). The promise is threaded throughout the accounts of the patriarchs (Gen 26:3; 28:4, 13; 35:12) and the Exodus from Egypt (Exod 3:8; 6:8; 13:5; 23:23–33). The Lord led his people and aided them in the campaign (Josh 3:11–13; 5:13–15; 10:11–14; 23:10; 24:11–12). The conquest of Canaan began with the capture of the fortress of **Jericho**, followed in swift succession by the fall of Ai and the seizure of the central highlands. There then followed the defeat of the Amorite kings and then the cities of Galilee. Noah's curse had come to rest on the Canaanites (Josh 16:10, 17:13; Judg 1:28, 33; 1 Kgs 9:20–21).

In spite of the revulsion for Canaanite culture that Moses and the prophets tried to teach, much of Canaanite culture endured even after the conquest of Canaan: the Israelites failed to conquer the land completely and left Canaanite pockets throughout the land (Josh 13:1–7, 15:63, 16:10, 17:11–13; Judg 1:27–33; cf. Deut 20:17). Canaanite influences in religion, in particular **idolatry**, were felt for centuries and played a role in the collapse of the monarchy.

After the book of Judges, references to "Canaan" are rare (Isa 19:18, 23:11; Zeph 2:5; Hos 12:7; Zeph 1:11). The Psalms stress the place of Canaan as the gift of the Lord (Ps 105:11; 135:11) and a place of idolatry (106:38). In the New Testament, Canaan is referred to in connection with Old Testament events featuring the patriarch Joseph (Acts 7:11) and the conquest of Canaan (Acts 13:19) (CCC 117).

CANAANITE, SIMON THE *See* **Simon the Cananean**.

CANON OF THE BIBLE (Greek *kanōn*, "rule" or "standard," from the Hebrew *qāneh*, "reed") The authentic list of inspired writings that are recognized and received by the Church and that make up the Old and New Testaments.

I. *The Idea of a Canon*
   A. *The Origin of the Idea*
   B. *The Canon and the Liturgy*
II. *The Old Testament Canon*
   A. *The Jewish Canon*
   B. *The Christian Canon*
III. *The New Testament Canon*
   A. *Many Choices*
   B. *How Choices Were Made*

I. THE IDEA OF A CANON

A. *The Origin of the Idea*

The word "canon" comes from the word for a reed. A reed was used as a measuring rod, so the word came to mean a measure and then a rule or standard (translated "rule" in Gal 6:16; "limit" in 2 Cor 10:13, 15–16).

Origen (d. 254) was the first person to use the term in reference to Scripture, but Saint Athanasius (d. 373) first gave the phrase "canonized books" common currency among subsequent writers by listing the twenty-seven books of the NT in his *Epistola Festalis* of 367. In the same century, the Council of Laodicea spoke of the *kanonika biblia* (biblical canon). Thus the idea of a *canon* as a defined collection came into use in the early Church and remained in acceptance throughout the subsequent history of ecclesiastical literature.

B. *The Canon and the Liturgy*

The canon is determined by the authoritative tradition of the Church. A book is canonical because it is divinely inspired; a book is not inspired because it is judged to be canonical (*see* **Inspiration**).

The **liturgy** is the natural environment, so to speak, of the canon. The primary purpose of the canon is to distinguish those books that, because they are inspired, are suitable for public reading in the liturgy, and thus for public instruction in the teachings of the Church.

II. THE OLD TESTAMENT CANON

A. *The Jewish Canon*

There was no fixed Jewish canon of the Bible in the period before the Christian Church. There was certainly a collection of sacred books, but the extent and makeup of the collection was still in question. Modern Jewish scholars rely upon the list of twenty-four books in the Masoretic Hebrew text, divided into the Law (Genesis, Exodus, Leviticus, Numbers, and Deuteronomy); the Prophets, divided into the former prophets (Joshua, Judges, 1 and 2 Samuel, 1 and 2 Kings), the latter prophets (Isaiah, Jeremiah, Ezekiel), and the twelve prophets counted as one book (Hosea, Joel, Amos, Obadiah, Micah, Jonah, Nahum, Habakkuk, Zephaniah, Haggai, Zechariah, and Malachi); and the Writings (1 and 2 Chronicles, Ezra-Nehemiah, Esther, Ruth, Psalms, Proverbs, Job, Lamentations, Ecclesiastes, Song of Songs, and Daniel). The Alexandrian collection, translated into Greek as the **Septuagint**, also included 1 and 2 Maccabees, Tobit, Judith, Sirach, Wisdom, Baruch, and some additions to Esther and Daniel (*see* **Deuterocanonical**).

The Septuagint was the Bible for most early Christians, and in general they accepted all the books in it as Scripture. The deuterocanonical books were not accepted in Palestinian Judaism, however, although they were apparently accepted among the Greek-speaking Jews of the **Dispersion**.

In the late first century A.D., the Jewish historian Flavius Josephus wrote that there were twenty-two inspired books, a list that corresponds to the current Hebrew canon of twenty-four books (Josephus unites Judges with Ruth and Jeremiah with Lamentations). Thus Josephus excluded the more recent writings in the Septuagint, and he seems to have been following an intellectual trend in certain Jewish circles. Around the same time that Josephus was writing, a rabbinical synod at Jamnia (A.D. 90) supposedly formalized the Hebrew canon of twenty-four books, although its exact proceedings remain uncertain and some scholars are skeptical as to the existence of the synod.

B. The Christian Canon

Christians, on the other hand, embraced the Septuagint rather than the shorter Palestinian collection, perhaps because of the dominance of Greek as the common language of the Roman Empire in the East. Christ and the apostles did not provide any kind of authoritative statement as to what books might be consulted, but throughout the NT there are some 350 quotations from the OT writings, the majority of them in agreement with the Greek of the Septuagint. All of the books of what became the Hebrew canon are quoted expressly except for Ezra, Nehemiah, Esther, Ruth, Ecclesiastes, Song of Songs, Obadiah, and Nahum; there are also allusions to Maccabees, Sirach, and Wisdom.

Christian writings and canons of the first centuries assume the canon of the Septuagint, including the Cheltenham Canon (mid-fourth century), the decree of Pope Saint Damasus I (382), and the Councils of Hippo (393) and Carthage (397 and 419). Part of the Greek canon (Tobit and Judith) was also translated by Saint Jerome and was approved by Pope Saint Innocent I (r. 401–417). Later the Council of Florence (1441) affirmed the Greek canon, and

likewise the Council of Trent issued an official decree supporting it in the mid-1500s, against the founders of Protestantism, who rejected the deuterocanonical books and accepted only the books of the Hebrew canon. (*See also* **Dead Sea Scrolls**; **Qumran, Khirbet**.)

III. THE NEW TESTAMENT CANON

A. Many Choices

The question of the NT canon was very different for the early Christians; here there was no ancient tradition to rely on. The Gospel message that Jesus had entrusted to the apostles was carefully preserved and transmitted, and it was not long before it was written down. But which of those written versions truly reflected the message Jesus had intended? Luke tells us that "many have undertaken to compile a narrative" of the Gospel story (Luke 1:1), and we know from the remains of apocryphal gospels that still more were written after Luke (*see* **Apocrypha**).

In addition to the Gospels, there were apostolic letters and other writings to sort out. Which ones were authentically apostolic? Which were inspired and suitable for public proclamation in the context of Christian worship?

B. How Choices Were Made

The process of determining the canon began while the events of Christ's ministry were still living memory, and the four evangelists "used every possible means to ensure that their readers would come to know the validity of the things they had been taught" (*Sancta Mater Ecclesia*, 2.3). It was still relatively easy to verify what was true and reject what was false by appealing to eyewitnesses, including the apostles themselves (tradition says that John, for example, lived until about the year 100).

The formation of the NT canon probably began very early. Already 2 Pet 3:15–16 assumes that the audience was familiar with Paul's letters and counts them with "the other scriptures." Quotations of the canonical books were also used in the writings of Saint Clement of Rome, Saint Ignatius of Antioch, Saint Polycarp of Smyrna, and the *Didache* in the late first century and early second century A.D., and in the *Shepherd of Hermas* in the second century A.D.

Thus the beginnings of a canon of the NT appear already in the first century, and a nucleus of four Gospels and over a dozen Pauline letters is in evidence in the second century.

C. Disputed Books

Not every book in the NT canon was accepted at once. Seven books—Hebrews, James, Jude, 2 Peter, 2 and 3 John, and Revelation—have been doubted at times, but all were ultimately accepted. Some passages in the Gospels also do not appear in some old manuscripts: Mark 16:9–20; Luke 22:43; John 5:4, 8:1–11. These likewise, however, were accepted by the authoritative tradition of the Church.

The first formal list of a NT canon appears during the time of Marcion, the second-century heretical leader who rejected the OT and approved only portions of the NT writings; the others he rejected because of their Jewishness. He was opposed by Saint Irenaeus (d. 200) and others, and the orthodox Church had to respond with its own list of canonical books. The Muratorian Fragment, dating from around A.D. 200, listed most of the books recognized as canonical in later decrees. Saint Clement of Alexandria (d. ca. 215) was the first to use the title "Testament" for the books of the NT.

D. The Final Form of the Canon

Various lists appeared in succeeding years, and by A.D. 350 the canon in the West was set in the form we know today. Saint Jerome included all twenty-seven books in the **Vulgate**. In the East, there was still some doubt as to the canonicity of 2 Peter, 2 and 3 John, Jude, and Revelation. These doubts led the Syrian churches initially to adopt a canon of only twenty-two books.

In the 1500s Martin Luther questioned Hebrews, James, Jude, and Revelation, but he kept them in his German translation of the Bible. Other reformers also questioned various books of the NT, but ultimately all Protestants embraced the traditional NT canon.

IV. THE CATHOLIC CANON OF THE BIBLE

The early Protestants raised questions about the deuterocanonical books of the OT and soon rejected them. At the Council of Trent in 1546, therefore, the Council Fathers gave a formal definition of the "Canon of the Bible," accepting the list that had always made up the Christian Bible until the questions raised by the Reformation. According to the dogmatic decree *De Canonicis Scripturis*, April 8, 1546, the OT has forty-six books; the NT has twenty-seven books. In issuing the decree, the Fathers added: "The council follows the example of the orthodox Fathers; and with the same sense of devotion and reverence with which it accepts and venerates all the books of both the Old and New Testaments, since one God is the author of both, it also accepts and venerates traditions concerned with faith and morals as having been received orally from Christ or inspired by the Holy Spirit and continuously preserved in the Catholic Church."

The Canon of the Bible, then, includes the following books:

The **Old Testament Canon** of forty-six books:

- **The Pentateuch**, the first five books: Genesis, Exodus, Leviticus, Numbers, Deuteronomy
- **Historical Books**: Joshua, Judges, Ruth, 1 and 2 Samuel, 1 and 2 Kings, 1 and 2 Chronicles, Ezra, Nehemiah, Tobit, Judith, Esther, 1 and 2 Maccabees
- **Wisdom Books**: Job, Psalms, Proverbs, Ecclesiastes, Song of Songs, Wisdom, Sirach
- **The Prophets**: Isaiah, Jeremiah, Lamentations, Baruch, Ezekiel, Daniel, Hosea, Joel, Amos, Obadiah, Jonah, Micah, Nahum, Habakkuk, Zephaniah, Haggai, Zechariah, Malachi

The **New Testament Canon** of twenty-seven books:

- **The Gospels**: Matthew, Mark, Luke, John
- **The Acts of the Apostles**
- **The Pauline Letters**: Romans, 1 and 2 Corinthians, Galatians, Ephesians, Philippians, Colossians, 1 and 2 Thessalonians, 1 and 2 Timothy, Titus, Philemon, Hebrews
- **The Catholic Letters**: James; 1 and 2 Peter; 1, 2, and 3 John; Jude
- **Revelation**

CANONICITY *See* **Canon**.

CANTICLES *See* **Song of Solomon**.

CAPERNAUM A city on the northwest shore of the Sea of Galilee, probably modern Tell Ḥum. It was Jesus's chief residence during his Galilean ministry (Matt 4:13; Mark 2:1). Here he made his home, performed several healings (Matt 8:5; Mark 1:21–28, 2:1–12; Luke 7:1–10; cf. John 4:46–54), and taught in the synagogue (Luke 4:31–38; John 6:22–59). The city was also the scene of the discussion of who was the greatest (Mark 9:33–37). In John, Jesus traveled there from Cana (John 2:12) and taught in the synagogue (John 6:59). While in Cana, Jesus healed the ruler's son in Capernaum (John 4:46–54).

CAPHTOR The traditional place of origin for the Philistines (Jer 47:4; Amos 9:7). The Caphtorim are described as the descendants of Egypt (Gen 10:13–14) and were said to reside in the land of Awwim, the coastal strip of southwest Canaan, after expelling the inhabitants (Deut 2:23). The Septuagint connects Caphtor with **Cappadocia**; most associate Caphtor with the island of Crete. Regardless, the term was also applied to the broader Aegean region.

CAPPADOCIA A region in Asia Minor that in New Testament times formed a province in the Roman Empire. The Christians of Cappadocia were mentioned in 1 Peter (1 Pet 1:1; cf. Acts 2:9). (See also **Caphtor**.)

CAPTIVITY *See* **Exile**.

CARAVAN *See* **Travel**; *see also* **Camel**; **Inn**.

CARCHEMISH A major city in the Hittite Empire that was later (ca. 717 B.C.) conquered by Sargon and the Assyrians (cf. Isa 10:9). The city was the site of a titanic battle between the armies of Nebuchadnezzar of Babylon and Pharaoh Neco II of Egypt in 605 B.C. (2 Chr 35:20).

CARMEL (Hebrew, "orchard") A town in Judah (Josh 15:55) situated to the southeast of Hebron. There Saul erected a monument (1 Sam 15:12) following the defeat of the Amalekites. Carmel was also the home of Nabal (1 Sam 25) and **Abigail** (1 Sam 27:3, 30:5; 2 Sam 23:35; 1 Chr 11:37).

CARMEL, MOUNT A prominent mountain in Palestine, extending almost from the shore of the Mediterranean to a bluff some 12 miles (19 kilometers) inland. It is covered with lush vegetation (Isa 33:9), and in Old Testament times was proverbial for its beauty (Song 7:5). Mount Carmel is most famous as the site of **Elijah**'s contest with the prophets of **Baal** (1 Kgs 18:20–40). It was also where **Elisha** was staying when he set out to restore the wealthy woman's son to life (2 Kgs 4:8–37).

CARMI The name of two men in the Old Testament.

1. The fourth son of Reuben (Gen 46:9; Exod 6:14; 1 Chr 5:3).

2. The son of Zabdi (Josh 7:1, 18) and father of **Achan**, who violated the ban of Joshua upon the city of Jericho (Josh 6:17–19).

CARPENTER A worker in wood. Carpentry was not a well-developed trade among the early Israelites, a deficiency that required Solomon to seek out competent carpenters from King Hiram of Tyre (1 Kgs 5:1–6). The craft was much more common in the later monarchy period. In the New Testament, "carpenter" is used to describe the trade of Joseph (Matt 13:55) and also of Jesus (Mark 6:3); the term itself denoted not just a worker with wood but a general contractor, skilled in various forms of wood and stone construction.

CARPUS A man from Troas, perhaps a Christian, with whom Paul left some of his clothes (2 Tim 4:13).

CARSHENA One of the seven princes of Persia and Media who served as counselors to King **Ahasuerus** (Esth 1:14).

CATHOLIC EPISTLES The name given to seven letters of the New Testament: James; 1 and 2 Peter; 1, 2, and 3 John; and Jude. They are called "catholic" because they appear to be addressed to the universal Church rather than to particular communities.

CAVE Caves served several purposes in biblical times, providing shelter, refuge, and also a place for the burial of the dead. Natural formations of limestone and sandstone in Palestine provided a wide variety of caves. Caves used as shelter or a hideout are mentioned frequently in the Old Testament (Gen 19:30; Josh 10:16; Judg 6:2; 1 Sam 13:6, 22:1, 24:3; 2 Sam 23:13; 2 Macc 6:11). The **patriarchs** and their wives were all buried in a cave (Gen 49:29–32). (*See* **Burial**; *see also* **Lazarus**.)

CEDAR Cedar was used as a building material by the Egyptians, the Babylonians, and the Israelites. The Cedar of Lebanon was one of the most precious of all woods in the ancient world. It was strong and straight, and therefore was much sought after for temples and palaces, as well as the masts of ships. Cedar trees were used especially in royal construction projects. David's royal residence used cedar given by Hiram of Tyre (2 Sam 5:11); Solomon used cedar extensively for his palaces, his administrative complex, and the Temple (1 Kgs 5–7). It was a symbol of wealth and luxury (Jer 22:14), but above all the tree itself symbolized pride (Isa 2:13; Ezek 31:3; Zech 11:2), strength (2 Kgs 14:9; Ps 29:5; Amos 2:9), and security (Num 24:6).

CEDAR OF LEBANON *See* **Cedar**.

CENDEBAEUS Chief military commander of the Phoenician coast under the Seleucid king Antiochus VII Sidetes. He attacked Judea with a series of raids until he was defeated by Judas Maccabeus and John Hyrcanus (1 Macc 15:37–16:10).

CENSER A metal receptacle or container used to carry coals for the burning of incense (Lev 10:1; 16:12). It had a handle and may have resembled a short shovel. The censers of the **Tabernacle** were made of bronze (Exod 27:3);

those of Solomon's **Temple** were made of gold (1 Kgs 7:50; 2 Kgs 25:15; 2 Chr 4:22).

CENSUS A registration of the population in a given area. In the Old Testament, censuses are taken to assess taxation (Exod 30:13–16; Num 3:40–51) and to count able bodies for military service (Num 1:3, 26:2; 2 Sam 24:9). The census ordered by David (2 Sam 24; 1 Chr 21) was taken for motives of pride, and it brought down the Lord's judgment on David's kingdom.

Most scholars believe that the empirewide census mentioned in Luke 2:1–3 was taken to assess taxation in the Roman provinces. But that interpretation has long posed problems for scholars. Luke is an uncommonly careful historian (*see* **Acts of the Apostles** and **Luke**), but Luke's narrative is hard to reconcile with other known censuses taken during the reign of Emperor Augustus (27 B.C.–A.D. 14). Luke says that the census was ordered by a decree of Caesar Augustus "that all the world should be enrolled" (Luke 2:1), adding the detail that it took place "when Quirinius was governor of Syria" (Luke 2:2).

Three recorded censuses were held during the reign of Augustus: in 28 B.C., 8 B.C., and A.D. 14. While the second census comes closest to fitting the time frame of the census in Luke, the political situation in Palestine is against this possibility. Herod the Great at the time was then not subject to direct Roman oversight and hence would not have participated, especially as he collected his own taxes. And the census under Quirinius, as Roman governor of Syria, was not held, according to Josephus, until A.D. 6, a date generally considered too late to match the events in Luke.

Recent scholarship has called some of the long-standing assumptions into question. For example, Josephus reports that the residents of **Judea** were required to give proof of their loyalty to Rome, and the same was required of the other regions of the empire around 3 B.C. It is thus possible that the census in Luke was not for taxation but for the purpose of gathering a loyalty oath from every subject.

As for Quirinius's role, as mentioned explicitly by Luke, it is possible that he was a government official in Syria at this time and not the provincial legate (as he was in A.D. 6).

CENTURION A Roman military officer in charge of a hundred soldiers. The Roman centurion was one of the most important soldiers in the entire legion, and most were legionnaires of long service and experience; the modern equivalent would be the sergeant or sergeant major. The legions of Rome would not have functioned without them. Several centurions are singled out for attention in the New Testament (Matt 8:5–13, 27:54; Luke 7:2–10, 23:47; Acts 10:1–8, 27:43).

CEPHAS *See* **Peter**.

CHALDEA Southern Mesopotamia, around the lower Euphrates. In the Bible, "Chaldea" chiefly refers to the Babylonian Empire that rose to prominence in the sixth century B.C. (*see* **Babylon, Babylonia**).

CHARIOT The horse-drawn chariot was first introduced into the Near East by the Hyksos around 1700 B.C. It made a considerable impression on the peoples of Egypt, Canaan, Mesopotamia, and Syria: the chariot was adopted almost immediately as a weapon of war, although its use was limited to the aristocracy and royalty. Kings also used the vehicle for hunting and transportation (Gen 41:47, 46:29; Exod 14:6–7). Chariots were typically open vehicles with two spoked wheels, drawn by horses, and able to accommodate a driver and one or more other riders. They were armored and highly mobile, making them a devastating tactical weapon in open-field battles. The Israelites did not adopt the chariot until the time of the monarchy (2 Sam 8:4). It was a key element in Solomon's military buildup, so that he could boast of forty thousand "stalls for horses and chariots" (1 Kgs 4:26; cf. 1 Kgs 10:26; 2 Chr 9:25). Succeeding kings of Israel and Judah continued to rely on chariots for war. **Ahab** died in battle while being driven in a chariot (1 Kgs 22:34–35). The continued use of chariots after Solomon's time is attested by Isa 2:7: the prophet complains that confidence is placed not in the Lord but in chariots (Isa 30:16; 31:1; cf. 36:8–9).

Nations boasted of their chariots, but the prophets reminded Israel that God was more powerful than chariots (Ps 20:7; Jer 51:21). Chariots were also an image of the power and swiftness of heavenly beings (Zech 6:1). The **ark of the covenant** was the Lord's chariot throne (1 Chr 28:18); he rides the clouds of heaven as his chariot (Ps 104:3); he appears to Ezekiel in glory on a chariot of cherubim (Sir 49:8; cf. Ezek 1). (*See* **Warfare**.)

CHARISMA *See* **Grace**; **Spirit**.

CHARITY *See* **Love**.

CHEBAR A canal (translated "river" in the RSV) in Mesopotamia at which the prophet **Ezekiel** had his visions (Ezek 1:1, 3; 3:15, 23; 10:15, 20, 22; 43:3). Its watercourse began north of Babylon, and it rejoined the Euphrates about 60 miles downstream near Erech.

CHEDORLAOMER King of Elam (Gen 14:1, 4, 5, 9, 17) who led a coalition of four Mesopotamian kings (of Elam, Shinar, Ellasar, and Goiim) against a rebellion by the kings of Sodom, Gomorrah, Admah, Zeboiim, and Zoar (Gen 14:1–12). Sodom and Gomorrah were plundered, and among the captives taken away was Abraham's nephew Lot; Lot was then rescued by Abraham, who defeated the returning kings in a sudden raid by night (Gen 14:13–16).

CHEMOSH The national deity of the Moabites (Num 21:29; Jer 48:46). Led astray by his pagan wives, Solomon permitted the worship of Chemosh (1 Kgs 11:7, 33) and sponsored the construction of a cultic shrine or high place in the god's honor. It survived for some three hundred years until destroyed by King **Josiah** in his effort to purge the kingdom of Judah of idolatry (2 Kgs 23:13). (*See* **Moab**; *see also* **Mesha**.)

CHERETHITES AND PELETHITES King David's personal bodyguards under the command of Benaiah, distinct from the regular army (2 Sam 8:18). Both units of the guard were noted for their fierce loyalty to the king (2 Sam 20:23; 1 Chr 18:17). They took part in protecting David during his flight in the rebellion of Absalom (2 Sam 15:18) and pursued the political rebel Sheba (2 Sam 20:7). They also played a part in court politics by assisting in the succession of Solomon as king (1 Kgs 1:38, 44). They cease to be mentioned after the death of David (although cf. Ezek 25:16; Zeph 2:5). The Cherethites and Pelethites were probably mercenaries from among the Philistines.

CHERITH A stream east of the Jordan River; here **Elijah** lived while hiding from Ahab and Jezebel (1 Kgs 17:2–7).

CHERUB, CHERUBIM A rank of **angel**, usually grouped with Seraphim and Thrones as one of the highest ranks (or orders) of angels. In the Old Testament, the cherubim ("cherubim," Hebrew *kĕrûbîm*, is the plural of "cherub," Hebrew *kĕrûb*) are mentioned over ninety times, if we include references to artistic images of cherubim (see, for example, Exod 25:18).

We first hear of cherubim in Genesis, when the Lord stationed cherubim at the entrance to the Garden of Eden to prevent the return of Adam and Eve (Gen 3:24). Visions and poetic depictions of God often included cherubim (2 Sam 22:11; Ps 18:10; Ezek 10:1–22).

Cherubim appear variously in the OT with faces that are human or animal-like, with varying numbers of legs. All cherubim are described with wings, however, to express their freedom of movement. In some ways the poetic descriptions of them resemble the winged hybrid creatures so popular in ancient Near Eastern iconography, such as the sphinx and the carved guardian spirits in front of Mesopotamian temples. The most vivid description of the cherubim is the one given by Ezekiel, although he does not specifically identify the creatures as cherubim: "Each had four faces, and each of them had four wings. Their legs were straight, and the soles of their feet were like the sole of a calf's foot; and they sparkled like burnished bronze . . . the four had the face of a human being, the face of a lion on the right side, the face of an ox on the left side, and the face of an eagle" (Ezek 1:6–9).

In art, cherubim were used extensively as symbols of the divine and were stationed in sacred precincts. Two golden cherubim with wings extended were placed on the **ark of the covenant** as part of the mercy seat, where the presence of the Lord was enthroned (Exod 25:18–22, 37:7–9; 1 Sam 4:4; 2 Sam 6:2). Images of cherubim also decorated the sanctuary veil (Exod 26:31). Two olivewood cherubim, overlaid with gold, towered as guardians over the ark in the holy of holies of Solomon's **Temple** (1 Kgs 6:23; 8:6–7).

CHIDON The name of the threshing floor where **Uzzah** was struck dead after touching the ark of the covenant (1 Chr 13:9).

CHILEAB David's second son, and his first son with Abigail; Chileab was born at Hebron (2 Sam 3:3). In 1 Chronicles 3:1 he is called Daniel.

CHILION Son of Elimelech and Naomi and the husband of **Orpah**, and thus the brother-in-law of **Ruth** (Ruth 1:2, 5; 4:9). Chilion, who came from Bethlehem, wed Orpah in her native Moab (Ruth 4:9–10).

CHIMHAM The son of **Barzillai** of Gilead. When Barzillai assisted David during the re-volt of Absalom (2 Sam 17:27–29), David decreed that Barzillai should reside in the palace (2 Sam 19:31–33). Barzillai declined the royal offer but asked instead that his son be permitted to do so (2 Sam 19:38–39). On his deathbed, David asked that Solomon continue to show royal favor to the sons of Barzillai (1 Kgs 2:7).

CHINNERETH, CHINNEROTH A fort town located on the northwest corner of the Sea of Galilee (Josh 19:35). In ancient Israel, the Sea of Galilee was called the Sea of Chinnereth (Num 34:11; Josh 12:3, 13:27). The town was abandoned in the eighth century B.C., and it was not until Roman times that it was rebuilt and resettled as Gennesaret (Matt 14:13). The Sea of Galilee was therefore sometimes called the Sea of Gennesaret in New Testament times.

CHISLEV The ninth month of the Hebrew calendar; it corresponds approximately to November and December.

CHLOE A woman whose people had informed Paul about divisions and strife within the Corinthian community (1 Cor 1:11). Nothing more is known about her.

CHORAZIN A town in Galilee that was cursed by Jesus for rejecting the Gospel message, even though its people had witnessed miracles (Matt 11:21; Luke 10:13). The town is probably modern Khirbet Karazeh, situated to the northwest of Capernaum.

CHRIST See **Messiah**; see also **Jesus Christ**.

CHRISTIAN A follower of Christ. The title "Christian" was first used for the followers of Christ at **Antioch** around A.D. 40–44, according to Acts 11:26. The word appears in only two other places in the New Testament. First, in Acts 26:28, it is used by King Herod Agrippa when speaking to Saint Paul. Second, in 1 Pet 4:15–16 it may be an insulting name applied by those persecuting the Church, but Peter urges the faithful to be proud of it: "But let none of you suffer as a murderer, or a thief, or a wrongdoer, or a mischief-maker; yet if one suffers as a Christian, let him not be ashamed, but under the name let him glorify God." Roman writers quickly adopted the name for the new sect. For example, in his *Annals* (15:44), Tacitus notes the use of the word among the Romans at the time of Nero's persecution in the 60s A.D. Pliny the Younger, who was governor of Bithynia, spoke of "Christians" early in the second century. The name was not generally used among the earliest Christian authors except in reference to persecutions and the struggle against paganism. Nevertheless, though it may have been a term of derision at first, the Christians proudly accepted the name. In the generation after the apostles, Saint Ignatius of Antioch wrote: "Let me not merely be called 'Christian'; let me be one" (*Rom.* 3:2).

CHRONICLES, BOOKS OF Two of the Historical Books of the Old Testament that together summarize biblical history from Creation to the end of the Babylonian Exile. The account, which gives its primary attention to the Israelite monarchy, is a collection of historical traditions interpreted to present an ideal picture of all Israel governed by divine law and united in Temple worship of the one true God. The two books originally formed one work in Hebrew, and the division into two books occurred first in the Greek **Septuagint**, from which it was carried over into the Latin **Vulgate**; the division was not adopted in Hebrew Bibles until the fifteenth century A.D.

The books of Chronicles are counted among the Writings in the Hebrew canon and among the Historical Books in the Christian Bible. The title in the Hebrew Bible is *dibrê hayyāmîm*, "The Events of the Days," while the Septuagint termed it *Paraleipomena*, meaning "Things Omitted," because the books were considered to be a kind of supplement to the books of Samuel and Kings. Saint Jerome, in his *Prologus Galeatus* (a preface to the books of Samuel and Kings), called them a *chronicon totius divinae historiae*, or "chronicle of the entire divine history," and the name Chronicles has been adopted in most English versions of the Bible.

I. Authorship and Date

II. Contents

III. Purpose and Themes

    A. Sources

    B. The Messiah, Priest and King

I. AUTHORSHIP AND DATE

Jewish tradition names Ezra as the author of Chronicles. The tradition can be neither proved nor disproved with absolute certainty, so most scholars consider the actual writer to be unknown, calling him simply "the Chronicler." There are some signs that the author may have been a Levite. One popular theory has it that the two books were written by the same author as the books of Nehemiah and Ezra. The last verses of 2 Chronicles (2 Chr 36:22–23) are repeated as the first verses of Ezra (Ezra 1:1–3), but that might be the work of a later writer using earlier material to make a literary bridge between the two works.

The date of Chronicles is equally difficult to determine, and several possible dates have been proposed over the years. As the final event mentioned is the return from the **Exile** (2 Chr 36:22–23), the books must have been written after 538 B.C., when **Cyrus** allowed the Jews to return home. But how long after? The Davidic genealogy in 1 Chr 3:10–24 extends beyond the return from the Exile, but scholars disagree over just how far it extends. Some count six generations beyond Zerubbabel, in which case the last generation would have lived after Rephaiah as contemporaries of Zerubbabel's grandsons; in that case, the genealogy ends at about 460 B.C. Still others, on the basis of the Septuagint version, count eleven generations, which could bring the line down to as late as 250 B.C. It is also possible, of course, that a later editor updated the genealogy, in which case the original books could have been written earlier than the time of the last few names listed.

II. CONTENTS

III. PURPOSE AND THEMES

A. Sources

The obvious parallels between Chronicles and Samuel-Kings would suggest that the Chronicler used the books of Samuel and Kings as key sources for his own narrative. He adapts and supplements the material, however, to suit his own purposes. Chronicles is not only a historical recounting; clearly the author also meant it to be a grand interpretation of Israelite history, culminating in King David, the establishment of Jerusalem as the center of worship, and the dedication of the Temple.

The author also relied extensively upon earlier canonical writings, including Genesis, Exodus, Numbers, Joshua, and Ruth, especially for his genealogies. In addition, he cites a number of now-lost sources outside the Bible, such as "the Book of the Kings of Israel and Judah" (2 Chr 27:7), a work called "The Commentary on the Books of the Kings," and "the acts of King David, from first to last, written in the records of the seer Samuel, and in the records of the prophet Nathan, and in the records of the seer Gad" (1 Chr 29:29).

B. The Messiah, Priest and King

The Chronicler takes a great interest in David and Solomon, and comparing Chronicles and Samuel–Kings reveals that Chronicles has less interest in political events and more in the liturgical events that had a lasting impact on Israel's worship. In 1 Kings, for example, we read the whole story of the intrigues and infighting that surrounded the accession of Solomon (1 Kgs 1:5–53). The first book of Chronicles gives us none of that story, but it does give us minutely detailed information on David's organization of the priesthood (1 Chr 23–26) and emphasizes that David himself gave Solomon the plan for the Temple (1 Chr 28:11–19). Throughout the story of David in Chronicles, we see David as a religious leader: as the Lord's Anointed, David becomes the ideal figure pointing toward the future Messiah who would be even greater than David, uniting fully in himself the royal and priestly offices.

Thus the account of David's reign in 1 Chronicles is built around the accounts of the bringing of the ark of the covenant to Jerusalem (1 Chr 15), the Levitical families and their offices, and the liturgical functions of the Levites (1 Chr 23–26). Solomon appears mostly in the building and the dedication of the Temple, with no mention made of the decline that characterized his last years.

The rest of Chronicles concentrates almost exclusively on Judah, whose kings were the true inheritors of the Davidic line. The kings of the northern kingdom are mentioned only when they have dealings with the southern kings. The kings of Judah are judged according to the rigid standards established by David and Solomon: Were they faithful to the legacy of David? Did they promote the proper worship of God? Appropriately, the whole work ends with the decree of Cyrus the Great permitting the rebuilding of the Temple, the center of the religious life of God's people.

Where Kings sought to show the historical reasons for the Exile that were rooted in the sinfulness of Israel, Chronicles exhorts the people to the faithful worship of God in the restored Temple and the recognition that survival for the community depends upon worship in that sanctuary. Following the example of David brings prosperity and divine blessings. Apostasy brings disaster. For the Chronicler, this is the lesson to be learned from the history of Judah.

CHRONOLOGY, OLD TESTAMENT See **Appendix**.

CHURCH The community of baptized believers in Jesus Christ, founded by Christ himself and still ruled by Christ as King. Also any local part of that community: a local congregation or group of congregations that share the same faith as the universal Church.

I. NAMES OF THE CHURCH

The English word "church" is ultimately derived from the Greek *kyriakon* ("belonging to the Lord"); the Scots and northern English form "kirk" shows the derivation more clearly. The Greek term used in Scripture, however, is *ekklēsia* ("assembly"). In classical Greek, *ekklēsia* meant a civic assembly, but the word was used in the **Septuagint** for the religious assembly of the Israelites (cf. Deut 23:2–3; 1 Kgs 8:5, 14, 22; Ps 22:26).

Ekklēsia is used extensively in the New Testament, including over sixty times in the Pauline writings. The word is used in much the same way we use the English word "church": it can mean the whole Church ("on this rock I will build my church," Matt 16:18) or a local part of it ("the seven churches that are in Asia," Rev 1:4). Since the earliest Christians had not yet put up buildings for their assemblies, however, the word never refers to a building but always to an assembly of people.

II. THE CHURCH AND THE OLD TESTAMENT

A. Salvation History Prepares for the Church

Salvation history in the OT is a record of how God prepared the world for his Church. In a series of covenants (*see* **Covenant**), the scope of God's covenant widened from a couple to a household, a tribe, a nation, a kingdom, and finally a worldwide Church. In the Church, the promise God made to **Abraham** is fulfilled: "by you all the families of the earth shall bless themselves" (Gen 12:3).

B. Israel, a Type of the Church

Israel, God's covenant people, was a **type** of the universal Church. Israel professed the same creed, worshipped by the same cult, and lived by the same commandments. This union of the twelve tribes into a single family of faith prefigured the union of all nations in the belief that Jesus Christ is Lord. Through the covenant with **Moses**, Israel was bound to live by God's Law and made the custodian of the worship of the True God. The sacrifices (*see* **Sacrifice**) offered under the Law prefigured the sacrifice of Christ on the Cross (Heb 9:22–28), which is present to us in the **Eucharist**, the covenant meal of the Church.

C. The Promised Restoration of the Kingdom

The covenant with **David** promised an everlasting kingdom to the son of David (1 Sam 7:13), with "the ends of the earth" as its boundary (Ps 2:8). David left a small empire with several tributary nations to his son Solomon, but after Solomon the empire broke up, and the long-lasting Davidic dynasty in **Judah** came to an end with the Babylonian conquest of Jerusalem.

In spite of the violent end of the Davidic kingship in Israel, prophets promised a restored kingdom far more glorious than the original: "nations shall come to your light, and kings to the brightness of your rising" (Isa 60:3). There would be a time when the covenant would expand to include all the nations, not just Israel: "And many nations shall join themselves to the LORD in that day, and shall be my people" (Zech 2:11).

III. THE CHURCH IN THE NEW TESTAMENT

A. The Founding of the Christian Church

This promise of the restored Davidic empire was fulfilled with the coming of the Son of David, Jesus Christ, who reigns as king with the Church as the earthly and historical manifestation of his kingdom. Christ's throne is established forever in heaven, and "the ends of the earth" are indeed the kingdom's boundaries. Thus the chief message of the apostles at the beginning of the Church was that the kingdom had been restored (Acts 1:6; 2:30–31; 8:12; 19:8; 28:23). Through **baptism**, anyone who

believes can now enter the kingdom (John 3:5; Acts 2:38).

Christ himself proclaimed that the "kingdom" was at hand (Matt 4:17; Mark 1:15), and he often used the phrase "**Kingdom of God**" or "kingdom of heaven" to describe his Church (see, for example, Mark 4:26; 4:30; 10:15). His words were taken at first by his contemporaries, including the apostles, to be a promise of the restored kingdom of David that would bring an end to the Roman occupation. But Jesus insisted that "My kingship is not of this world" (John 18:36). He had come to establish a greater kingdom than the Roman Empire, a kingdom that would span the world and last to the end of time. His kingdom touches down in history, but its authority comes from heaven.

The Holy Spirit—the soul of the living body of believers united in Christ—was given by Jesus to the Church at Pentecost (Acts 1:2; 2:23). With the coming of the Spirit, the apostles began to preach and to baptize and so to enlarge the membership of the Church (Acts 2:4–41; 4:2).

B. The Structure of the New Testament Church

Jesus gave his kingdom a structure and authority (Matt 16:16–18, 18:15–18; Mark 6:7; Luke 10:1–2). He chose twelve apostles, with Peter as their leader (Matt 16:18; John 21:15–17), to provide a firm foundation for this Church and to represent the twelve tribes of Israel (Eph 2:20; Rev 21:12–14). This kingdom, founded upon Peter, will endure even the attacks of Satan. Thus the Church had a hierarchy from the beginning, in which the apostles were placed over the laity (1 Thess 5:12). Some are shepherds, some sheep (John 21:15–17; Acts 20:17, 28; 1 Pet 5:1–2) (CCC 553, 642, 771, 874–87, 894–95).

The apostles, in turn, chose successors for themselves (Acts 1:15–26) and appointed other ministers to help spread the message and to tend to the affairs of the growing Church (Acts 6:1–3).

Already in the time of the apostles we see a hierarchy of **deacon**, presbyter (or **priest**), and **bishop** (Acts 14:23; Phil 1:1; 1 Tim 5:17; Titus 1:5–9; 1 Pet 5:1; "presbyters" is translated "elders" in the RSV). The difference between a bishop and a priest may not have been sharply defined yet, but the basic organization of the Church was already established in the generation that had known Jesus on earth.

C. The Body of Christ

Paul provides an expansive theological explication of the Church, using the word *ekklēsia* some sixty-five times. For Paul, the Church is the body of Christ, who is its head (Col 1:18; Eph 5:22–24, 29–30) and from whom the Church receives her fullness (Eph 1:22–23; Col 1:18). The members of the body have different functions, as a hand differs from a foot or an eye; but they all belong to the same body, and each has its particular function (Rom 12:4–8; 1 Cor 12:4–26; cf. 1 Cor 12:27–31; Eph 4:11–14).

The Church as the body of Christ also gives Paul the means to stress the unity among all believers (1 Cor 12:12; Rom 12:4). This unity finds its sacramental reality first in baptism (1 Cor 12:13), then in the Eucharist: "Because there is one bread, we who are many are one body" (1 Cor 10:17).

D. The Bride of Christ

The Church is also the Bride of Christ (2 Cor 11:2–3; Eph 5:22–33; Rev 19:7–8). Christ loves his bride as a husband loves his wife: "Christ loved the church and gave himself up for her, in order to make her holy by cleansing her with the washing of water by the word, so as to present the church to himself in splendor, without a spot or wrinkle or anything of the kind—yes, so that she may be holy and without blemish" (Eph 5:25–27). This relationship between Christ and the Church is a mystery (Eph 5:22–32), but it develops from the OT's imagery of Yahweh as the divine husband of Israel (Hos 2:2, 14–23; Jer 2:2), and it is also consistent with Jesus's reference to himself as a bridegroom (Matt 9:15; Mark 2:19; Luke 5:34).

E. The Living Temple

For Paul, the Church is also a living temple, indwelt by the Spirit (1 Cor 3:16–17; Eph 2:19–22; cf. Matt 16:18). Christ himself is the cornerstone, the "living stone" that was rejected by the builders (1 Pet 2:4), and all Christians, like living stones, are built on that foundation into "a spiritual house" where the true sacrifices are offered (1 Pet 2:5). The Holy Spirit makes the Church one united people (Gal 3:24–29), the children of God (Eph 4:1–6), who are equal members of the kingdom and who are reconciled through the love of Jesus Christ (Eph 2:11–22; 1 Cor 12:13; Col 3:11).

F. The Church Perfected in Glory

Finally, the Church is the bearer of divine life and eschatological hope. The progress of the Church in the world will culminate on the day when Jesus Christ returns, when the Church will be perfected in the glory of heaven. Until then, the Church continues her pilgrimage in the face of persecutions, living in confident expectation of the full coming of the Kingdom, when "all of us must appear before the judgment seat of Christ, so that each may receive recompense for what has been done in the body, whether good or evil" (2 Cor 5:10).

G. The Marks of the Church

The Nicene Creed calls the Church *one*, *holy*, *catholic*, and *apostolic*, and these four distinctive marks define the Church and distinguish it as the guardian of true faith:

One, because its members are united in faith
    and doctrine, under the pope;
Holy, because it offers the means of receiv-
    ing sanctifying grace and because it was
    founded by Christ and is animated by the
    Holy Spirit;
Catholic, because it is universal, meaning that
    its blessings are intended for all peoples
    of the world;
Apostolic, because the leadership of the
    Church goes back in an unbroken line
    through the bishops to the apostles,
    who were appointed by Christ (CCC
    811–65).

CHUZA A steward of **Herod Antipas**. His wife, Joanna, was a financial supporter and follower of Jesus (Luke 8:3). He might be the same royal official whose son was healed by Jesus (John 4:46–53). The name Chuza is preserved in both Nabatean and Syrian inscriptions.

CILICIA A Roman province in southeastern Asia Minor, to the south of the Taurus Mountains and west of Mount Amanus. It was known for its fertile plains. The region once belonged to the Hittites, and before Roman times it was part of the Seleucid (1 Macc 11:14; 2 Macc 4:36) Empire. Paul was born in Cilicia's chief city, Tarsus (Acts 21:39; 22:3; 23:34); he spent some time there after his conversion to Christianity (Acts 9:30) and was active in evangelizing his native country (Gal 1:21–23; cf. Acts 15:23, 40–41; 18:23).

CINNAMON A spice that was harvested in Ceylon, India, and the East Indies. It was an expensive luxury item in the biblical period. Cinnamon was used in food and the preparation of holy oils (Exod 30:23); it was also used as a perfume (Prov 7:17; Song 4:14).

CIRCUMCISION The rite of cutting away the foreskin from the male generative organ, performed on Jewish boys on their eighth day of life. In Israel, circumcision was not just a surgical procedure; it was primarily a religious rite. It was a sign of God's **covenant** with **Abraham** (Gen 17:10), and no man could belong to God's covenant people without being circumcised (Gen 17:14).

I. *Circumcision in the Old Testament*
    A. *A Sign of the Abrahamic Covenant*
    B. *A Rite of Initiation into the Worship Life*
       of Israel
    C. *An Outward Sign of Inward Faith*
II. *Circumcision in the New Testament*
    A. *Must Christians Be Circumcised?*

B. *"No Distinction" Between Circumcised and Uncircumcised*

I. CIRCUMCISION IN THE OLD TESTAMENT

A. A Sign of the Abrahamic Covenant

Circumcision was not unique to the Israelites: Jeremiah lists Egypt, Edom, Ammon, Moab, and other desert states as nations in which circumcision was practiced, and an Egyptian tomb painting from the Sixth Dynasty depicts the circumcision of two boys. But in these other nations, circumcision was performed on a male child at the time of puberty; it was likely seen as a rite of passage, although many details of its purposes remain elusive.

For Israelites, however, circumcision was not a rite of passage but a fundamental part of their identity as the Chosen People of God. The rite of circumcision was the sacrament of initiation into the covenant, the means by which entry into the covenant family of Abraham was granted: "He that is eight days old among you shall be circumcised; every male throughout your generations, whether born in your house, or bought with your money from any foreigner who is not of your offspring, both he that is born in your house and he that is bought with your money, shall be circumcised. So shall my covenant be in your flesh an everlasting covenant. Any uncircumcised male who is not circumcised in the flesh of his foreskin shall be cut off from his people; he has broken my covenant" (Gen 17:12–14).

The terms of the covenant were clear, and any violation of it could bring God's judgment. Moses, for example, might have died for neglecting it if his quick-thinking wife had not circumcised their son (Exod 4:24–26).

B. A Rite of Initiation into the Worship Life of Israel

Only the circumcised were permitted to participate in the liturgy and worship of Israel (Lev 12:3). Circumcision was mandatory for the celebration of Passover, and slaves and sojourners residing in Israel were not eligible to participate unless they were first circumcised (Exod 12:43–49). Circumcision was also necessary for marital unions (Gen 34:15), a requirement that was used with great cunning by Jacob's sons in exacting bloody vengeance upon the men of Shechem (Gen 34:24–25).

C. An Outward Sign of Inward Faith

Circumcision was so important because it was an outward sign of something deeper: the obedience of Israel to God's covenant. It was a permanent reminder that Israel had a unique responsibility. "Circumcise therefore the foreskin of your heart," Moses told the people (Deut 10:16); and near the end of his long life he promised, "And the Lord your God will circumcise your heart and the heart of your offspring, so that you will love the Lord your God with all your heart and with all your soul, that you may live" (Deut 30:6). Circumcision of the flesh symbolized the spiritual circumcision of the heart: the cutting away of the heart's stubborn resistance to the Lord and his commandments (cf. Deut 10:16). It was this inward disposition that was truly important, and without it even a circumcised Israelite was "circumcised but yet uncircumcised," in the words of Jeremiah (Jer 9:25).

II. CIRCUMCISION IN THE NEW TESTAMENT

A. Must Christians Be Circumcised?

The spiritual significance of circumcision was the key to the Christian understanding of the rite. As soon as Gentiles began to enter the Church, the question could not be avoided: Must a Christian be circumcised?

Most Gentiles at that time were not circumcised; in most of the Roman world, circumcision was an exclusively Jewish practice. Some Jewish Christians insisted that "Unless you are circumcised according to the custom of Moses, you cannot be saved" (Acts 15:1). Paul, who had begun his mission to the Gentiles, "had no small dissension and debate with them" (Acts 15:2).

B. "No Distinction" Between Circumcised and Uncircumcised

The matter was settled by a meeting of all the apostles at Jerusalem circa A.D. 49 (see **Jerusalem, Council of**). Here Peter decisively took Paul's side. They had seen, Peter said, how the Holy Spirit had come equally to the Gentiles, "and he made no distinction between us and them, but cleansed their hearts by faith" (Acts 15:9). This is a decisive point: since the Gentiles had received the Spirit without circumcision, circumcision is not a sacrament of our new life in Christ. There is no reason, then, to place a "yoke" on the Gentile converts that even the Israelites found hard to bear (Acts 15:10). Requiring circumcision would be an al-

most insurmountable barrier to the Church's missionary efforts among the Gentiles.

The prophecy of Moses was fulfilled: the time had come when "the Lord your God will circumcise your heart" (Deut 30:6).

By this decision, the apostles clearly defined the Church as an entity distinct from Judaism. For Paul, the coming of Christ meant that we no longer need the rituals of the Mosaic **Law**, including circumcision (Gal 3:24–25). Before Christ, circumcision was indeed the means of entering into God's covenant with Abraham and the sacrament of initiation into the family of Israel (Lev 12:3). But by the Crucifixion of Jesus Christ, circumcision has been set aside. Outward circumcision is no longer the sign of membership in the covenant (1 Cor 7:19; Gal 5:6, 6:15). In its place comes the inward circumcision of the heart (Rom 2:28–29), which Christ himself performs in **baptism** (Col 2:11–12; cf. Acts 22:16; Titus 3:5; 1 Pet 3:21; cf. Saint Thomas Aquinas, *Summa theologiae* III, Q. 70, a. 1.) (CCC 1226–27). "For in Christ Jesus neither circumcision nor uncircumcision counts for anything; the only thing that counts is faith working through love" (Gal 5:3) (CCC 162, 1814, 1972).

CISTERN An artificial reservoir designed to collect rainwater. Cisterns were carved or excavated out of the rock and lined with lime. There were also courtyard cisterns designed to capture the water falling from roofs. Palestinian cities required cisterns to supplement the water supply, as local resources were rarely adequate for an entire population, and it was common for both municipal authorities and private citizens (who could afford them) to have them dug. **Jeremiah** uses a broken cistern as a metaphor for Israel's idols: the Lord is the fountain of living water, but the idols are broken cisterns that hold no water (Jer 2:13). Jeremiah himself was thrown into an old courtyard cistern where there was only mud; he survived and was later pulled out by order of the wavering king **Zedekiah** (Jer 38:6–13). (*See also* **Siloam**.)

CITIES, LEVITICAL *See* **Levitical cities**.

CITIES OF REFUGE *See* **Refuge, cities of**.

CITY OF DAVID *See* **Jerusalem**.

CLAUDIUS LYSIAS The Roman tribune whose soldiers took Paul into custody in Jerusalem (Acts 21:31–36; 23:26; some versions call him a "chilearch," the Greek word translated "tribune" in the RSV). Claudius and his troops were stationed in the **Antonia Tower** next to the Temple. When Paul was attacked by a group of rioters protesting his supposed entry into the Temple with an uncircumcised companion, Claudius intervened with his soldiers and brought Paul into the barracks of the tower. He then permitted Paul to address the crowd, but the apostle so agitated the angry mob that Claudius commanded Paul to be brought into the barracks. Claudius then ordered Paul to be scourged to find out why the Jews wanted him dead. As the troops were preparing to scourge him, Paul revealed his Roman citizenship (Acts 22:24–29). No Roman citizen could be scourged, so Claudius immediately stopped the proceedings. But he still desired to know more about the riot, so he brought Paul before

the **Sanhedrin**, where again Paul provoked an uproar (Acts 22:30–23:10). Once more, Claudius intervened to keep Paul safe, and upon learning of a plot against Paul's life (23:12–22), Claudius arranged for a nighttime military escort to bring Paul to Caesarea and the jurisdiction of the procurator **Felix** (23:23–35).

CLEAN AND UNCLEAN *See* **Purification**.

CLEOPAS One of the two disciples who met Jesus on the road to **Emmaus** (Luke 24:18).

CLOPAS A male relative of the woman Mary who stood at the foot of the Cross of Jesus (John 19:25). The relationship between Clopas and Mary is uncertain, because the Greek text describes her only as "Mary of Clopas"— which probably means the wife of Clopas, but could also mean the daughter or mother of Clopas. (The RSV calls her "Mary, the wife of Clopas.") Some scholars think Clopas might be the same person as **Cleopas**. Early tradition held that Clopas's son, Symeon, was elected the second bishop of Jerusalem (see Eusebius, *Hist. Eccl.* 3.11).

CLOTHING In Genesis, clothing—worn to conceal nakedness—is a consequence of **sin**. Before the **Fall**, man and woman lived in a proper relationship with God and each other, and nakedness was not shameful (Gen 2:25). After the Fall, nakedness was shameful (Gen 3:7), and God himself made clothes for Adam and Eve out of animal skins.

The typical attire for men in Palestine during biblical times was the "loincloth" (ʾēzôr), a short skirt or kilt (2 Kgs 1:8; Isa 5:27; Jer 13:1;

Ezek 23:15). A tunic was also worn, made of wool or linen and with or without sleeves. It reached below the knees but could be folded or tucked into a belt when needed for the performance of work or for travel ("girding up the loins," Exod 12:11; 2 Kgs 4:29, 9:1). An outer cloak or coat could be added when needed; it was used almost exclusively to keep the wearer warm and had little other purpose (Matt 24:18). The moneylender was prohibited from keeping a poor person's cloak as collateral overnight (Exod 22:26; Deut 24:13). A belt of leather was used to bind the clothes to the body, but it also helped to hold various items, including a money bag, weapons, or tools in various small pockets. Finally, an outer robe (*měʿîl*) was worn by persons of authority, such as priests and kings (Exod 28:31; Lev 8:7; 1 Sam 18:4; 24:5, 11). Jesus wore a tunic and a cloak. The Roman soldiers in charge of his Crucifixion divided his other clothes, but they cast lots for his tunic because it was woven in one piece, like the sacred robe of a priest (John 19:23–24; cf. Exod 28:32). In the Sermon on the Mount, Jesus had declared, "if any one would sue you and take your coat, let him have your cloak as well" (Matt 5:40; cf. Luke 6:29).

The clothing of women differed only slightly from that of men, but cross-dressing between men and women was forbidden (Deut 22:5). Important occasions—such as festivals—were proper occasions for clothes made of more expensive fabric and brighter colors (cf. Gen 27:15; Judg 14:12; Matt 22:11; Luke 15:22).

Since nakedness was seen as shameful, priests had to take special care to conceal their nakedness while ministering to the Lord (Exod 20:26; 28:42). Prisoners of war were paraded in disgrace after their defeat and their clothes divided among the conquerors (Isa 20:4, 47:3; Amos 2:16; cf. Ps 22:18; John 19:23–24). Prophets warned that infidelity to God would bring a similar shame (Nah 3:5; Jer 13:26).

CLOUD A cloud in the Bible may be a simple rain cloud (Judg 5:14; Isa 5:6), but it can also be a visible manifestation of the divine Spirit. (See CCC 697.) In the Old Testament, a cloud is almost always mentioned when God makes his glory visible (Exod 19:16; Judg 5:4; Ezek 1:4). The pillar of cloud by day and the pillar of fire by night were manifestations of the Lord's presence and glory on the **Exodus** journey (Exod 13:21; 14:19; 16:10); this glory and presence continued with the cloud that filled the **Tabernacle** of Moses in the desert (Exod 40:36–37) and the **Temple** of Solomon (1 Kgs 8:10). Poetically, clouds are used by God as his chariot (Ps 18:10) and his transport (Isa 19:1); they are also his abode or tent (Ps 18:12; 104:3). In the New Testament, the cloud continues to have theophanic associations, in particular during the Transfiguration (Matt 17:5; Mark 9:9; Luke 9:34) and the expected **Parousia** (Matt 26:64; Mark 14:62; cf. Acts 1:9; 1 Thess 4:17). In rabbinic theology, the glorious fire cloud of God's presence is called the Shekinah (*šěkînâ*). (*See also* **Son of Man**.)

CODE *See* **Law.**

CODEX A book made of separate sheets or "leaves" bound on one edge, like a modern book, in contrast to a papyrus scroll (*see also*

Book). The codex first came into prominence in the first centuries A.D. It was the most common form of book used for Christian literature, and indeed some scholars believe the Christians may have invented it. With the spread of Christianity, the codex was embraced throughout Roman territories, bringing an end to centuries of dominance by the traditional scroll.

Most of the earliest Christian texts are preserved in codices (the plural of "codex"). A text in such a codex is said to be "pure" or "mixed," according to whether the codex contains exclusively Greek texts ("pure") or texts and commentaries in Greek, Latin, and Syriac ("mixed"). The oldest and most important codices are Codex Vaticanus (fourth century), containing most of the Bible from Gen 46:28 to Heb 9:14 (except a section of the Psalms and the books of the Maccabees, which are missing) and most likely of Egyptian origin; Codex Alexandrinus (early fifth century) containing most of the Old and New Testaments (portions are missing from Matthew, John, and 2 Corinthians) and probably from Egypt; Codex Sinaiticus (fourth century), a manuscript of the Greek Bible, discovered in the monastery of Saint Catherine on Mount Sinai; Codex Bezae (fifth century), a manuscript of the Gospels in Greek and Latin, presenting them in the order of Matthew, John, Luke, and Mark, with an expanded version of Acts and a fragment of 3 John; Codex Ephraemi (fifth century), a Greek manuscript of the Old and New Testaments in fragmentary form, so named because its pages were erased and reused in the twelfth century for a collection of sermons by Saint Ephrem of Syria (by using chemical agents and careful observation, scholars have been able to decipher about two-thirds of the original text). (*See also* **Book**.)

COELE-SYRIA (Greek, "hollow Syria") The stretch of land between Lebanon and Anti-Lebanon, the Great Rift Valley, although the extent of the territory under that name varied according to the time period. Under the Seleucids, the province of Coele-Syria included most of southern Syria but not Phoenicia (1 Macc 10:69; 2 Macc 3:5–8, 4:4, 8:8, 10:11). The region in the Roman period was considered to include most of Syria-Palestine between Egypt and the Euphrates.

COLOSSAE A city in Phrygia, in Asia Minor, located near the Lycus River at the base of Mount Cadmus. The city is mentioned in the New Testament only as the destination of Paul's letter to the **Colossians**.

COLOSSIANS, LETTER TO THE A letter of Paul sent to the young church of Colossae in Asia Minor. It includes highly important Christological passages, a warning against false teachings, and instruction on the demands of the Christian life.

I. AUTHORSHIP AND DATE

The letter twice asserts that the apostle Paul is the author of Colossians (Col 1:1; 4:18), and the Fathers of the Church readily accepted the letter as Paul's. In the nineteenth century some German scholars raised doubts about Paul's authorship. Modern scholars are divided; some see differences in literary style, vocabulary, and doctrinal emphasis that suggest a different author, but others point out that the letter addresses a unique situation (see below), which sufficiently accounts for Paul's speaking in a different way. More significantly, there are strong correspondences between this letter and the letter to Philemon, which is almost universally accepted as Paul's: both are sent by Paul and Timothy together (Col 1:1; Phlm 1); both mention Paul's imprisonment (Col 4:3; Phlm 1), surrounded by the same friends (Col 4:10–14; Phlm 23–24); both mention the runaway slave Onesimus (Col 4:9; Phlm 12). Thus accepting Paul as author of Colossians is a critically defensible position, and the weight of tradition makes it a preferable position.

The letter was written during a time in which Paul was in prison (Col 4:3, 10, 18), probably during his first imprisonment in Rome (Acts 28:16, 30–31); it thus figures with the other so-called captivity Epistles (Ephesians, Philippians, and Philemon), which were written from Rome between A.D. 60 and 62. Some scholars suggest other possible locations for its composition, especially Ephesus, in which case the letter would date from the 50s A.D. Scholars who argue against Pauline authorship usually propose a date for the letter toward the end of the first century.

II. CONTENTS

I. *Address (1:1–2)*

II. *Thanksgiving (1:3–14)*

III. *The Role of Christ (1:15–2:23)*

    A. *Christ's Supremacy (1:15–23)*

    B. *The Ministry of Paul (1:24–2:7)*

    C. *Fullness of Life in Christ (2:8–15)*

    D. *False Teachers (2:16–23)*

IV. *Christian Duty (3:1–4:6)*

    A. *A New Life in Christ (3:1–17)*

    B. *The Christian Family (3:18–4:1)*

    C. *Prayer and Conversation in Christ (4:2–6)*

V. *Personal Messages (4:7–18)*

III. PURPOSE AND THEMES

The Letter to the Colossians was sent by Paul to the Christian community in the city of Colossae, in southwest Phrygia, in Asia Minor along the Lycus River. The community had not been founded by Paul, nor had he visited there (Col 2:1). A native Colossian and a follower of Paul named Epaphras had first proclaimed the Gospel sometime before (1:7). Paul's comment in 2:13 suggests that most of the members of the church in Colossae were uncircumcised Gentiles.

The occasion of the letter was a report given to Paul by Epaphras regarding the conditions in the Colossian church (4:12). While the report was generally favorable (1:4–9), Paul also heard of certain false teachers who were ready to "delude you with beguiling speech" (2:4). Exactly what they were teaching is uncertain. Perhaps they preached a syncretist doctrine that blended elements of the Christian faith with aspects of Jewish and Greek thought ("human tradition," 2:8); some scholars consider them forerunners of the Gnostics who troubled the Church in the second century. More likely, Paul was concerned with tensions between the Christians and the local Jewish community in Colossae. This better explains why Paul stresses that Christians are not bound by Jewish ceremonies of the **Law**: circumcision, food prohibitions, festivals, and Sabbaths (2:11–16).

In place of the false doctrines he denounces, Paul stresses both the supremacy of Christ and the completeness of life in Christ. Colossians is of special note for its emphatic references to the divinity of Christ (cf. 1:15–20; 2:9, 15). Christ is both Creator and Redeemer of all things: "in him all the fullness of God was pleased to dwell, and through him God was pleased to reconcile to himself all things, whether on earth or in heaven, by making peace through the blood of his cross" (1:19–20). Creation has its very existence through Christ and finds its meaning in him.

Paul proceeds to bolster the spirits and the moral strength of the Colossians by reminding them of the fullness of life that is theirs in Christ. He urges them to conform their lives to Christ and to set their "minds on things that are above, not on things that are on earth" (3:2). They must clothe themselves with compassion, kindness, humility, meekness, and patience, let the peace of Christ rule in their hearts, and order their entire household in accordance with Christian principles (3:18–4:1).

At the letter's close, the reader is informed that Tychicus, the carrier of the epistle, and Onesimus, a runaway slave, will bring news of Paul's affairs (4:7–9). Reference is also made to two of the Evangelists, Mark (4:10) and Luke (4:13). (*See also* **Ephesians, Letter to the.**)

COMING OF CHRIST, SECOND *See* **Parousia.**

COMMANDMENTS, TEN *See* **Ten Commandments.**

CONFESSION *See* **Repentance.**

CONFIRMATION, SACRAMENT OF The sacrament by which a fuller measure of the Spirit and his grace is conferred upon a baptized Christian, making him or her a soldier of Christ and a witness of his gospel to the world. Along with **baptism** and the **Eucharist,** it is considered one of the three "sacraments of initiation." Confirmation was instituted by Christ in his promise to send the Holy Spirit (John 14:15–21). That promise found fulfillment at Pentecost, when the Holy Spirit descended on the apostles (Acts 2:3–4). The apostles were transformed by the Holy Spirit, receiving the powers of speaking persuasively (Acts 4:33), performing miracles (Acts 2:43), and demonstrating the personal holiness of the Christian life (Acts 2:42–47; 4:32–35). Confirmation perpetuates the grace of Pentecost. In Samaria, we see confirmation as a sacramental action distinct from baptism: Peter and John visit a group of believers who had been baptized in the name of Jesus, but had not yet received the Holy Spirit. The apostles lay their hands on the baptized believers, and the Spirit came to them (Acts 8:14–17). Imposition of hands remains the way the rite of confirmation is administered by the bishops today in the West (CCC, 1285–1321).

CONIAH *See* **Jehoiakim.**

CONQUEST OF CANAAN *See* **Canaan.**

CONSCIENCE The moral awareness that every human person possesses.

In the Old Testament, there is no specific

Hebrew word for conscience, and the Greek word *syneidēsis* appears only in Wis 17:11, and in the **Septuagint** version of Eccl 10:20. Nevertheless, the underlying notion of conscience is found throughout the OT, as we can see in Gen 3 and the actions of conscience following the **Fall**. The closest term that would approximate the Hebrew sense of conscience is the "heart," which was considered the intellectual and emotional center of the person (e.g., Mark 7:21–23). The heart was the place where God could read a person's state of mind or moral condition (1 Sam 16:7; Jer 17:10).

In the New Testament, the Greek word for "conscience" is used thirty-one times in the letters of Paul, three times in 1 Peter, and twice in Acts. In doing what is right without knowing the Law, the Gentiles "show that what the law requires is written on their hearts, while their *conscience* also bears witness" (Rom 2:14–15). Conscience is an interior judge (2 Cor 1:12) that both convicts us of doing wrong and commends us for doing right, and "by the open statement of the truth we commend ourselves to the *conscience* of everyone in the sight of God" (2 Cor 4:2; cf. 2 Cor 5:11). The objective for the Christian is to serve God with a good conscience—meaning that we have listened to its guidance (Acts 24:16; Heb 13:18). There is a close connection between conscience and sin, as baptism provides a fresh start and a cleansed conscience (Heb 10:22; 1 Pet 3:21). Love flows from a pure heart and a good conscience (1 Tim 1:5). Habitual sin, however, dulls the conscience (Titus 1:15), and rejecting conscience makes a "shipwreck" of one's faith (1 Tim 1:19) (CCC, 1776–1802).

Any action is right or wrong because of *objective principles* that should direct the mind, not because of *subjective opinion*. Those objective principles are already present in the mind through the light of reason or through divine faith responding to God's revelation. Conscience accepts the principles and makes decisions based on them; it does not produce the principles. In the words of the Second Vatican Council, "In the depths of his conscience man detects a law which he does not impose on himself, but which holds him to obedience . . . For man has in his heart a law written by God" (GS §16).

Conscience is the link between human freedom and moral truth: it must be formed through experience and critical investigations of the sources of moral wisdom. A person who follows the dictates of conscience can still commit wrong acts if the conscience itself is misinformed.

CONVERSION *See* **Repentance**.

COPPER The most common metal used in Palestine until the beginning of the Iron Age in about 1200 B.C. (see **Iron**). Deut 8:9 notes that among the riches to be found in Canaan are mines full of copper. There were large copper deposits in the Sinai Peninsula, in the Araba, and at Ezion-geber, on the northern coast of the Gulf of Aqaba. At the latter site, Solomon established copper foundries and refining centers.

CORBAN A Hebrew term for a "gift" or "offering" consecrated to God. The word is used extensively in Leviticus and Numbers, where it appears more than sixty times. In the New Testament, the Aramaic term *Corban* was used to denote the Temple treasury (Matt 27:6, translated "treasury" in the RSV). Jesus used the word as an example of the Pharisees' hypocrisy: "but you say, 'If a man tells his father or his mother, What you would have gained from me is Corban' (that is, given to God)— then you no longer permit him to do anything for his father or mother, thus making void the word of God through your tradition which you hand on. And many such things you do" (Mark 7:11–13).

CORIANDER An annual plant (*Coriandrum sativum*) whose seeds are ground and used especially for flavoring foods, and also in perfumes and in medicines as a stimulant and carminative. Manna was described as being similar to coriander in color, namely off-white or yellowish (Exod 16:31; Num 11:7).

CORINTH A city in Greece on the Isthmus of Corinth, which connects the Peloponnesian Peninsula to the European continent. Its position on the isthmus gave Corinth considerable strategic importance as the shortest means to travel from the Adriatic to the Aegean Sea. Corinth was also an infamous place of pleasure and dissolution, and in fact several Greek writers used the name of the city to coin new terms for sexual vices (e.g., *korinthiazomai*, "commit fornication"; *korinthiastēs*, "whoremonger"; and *korinthia korē*, "prostitute").

The city was destroyed in 146 B.C. by the Romans when they defeated the Achaean League. It remained in ruins until 44 B.C., when Julius Caesar decided to rebuild it and establish the Colonia Laus Julia Corinthus as the capital of the new Roman province of Achaea.

By the time of the New Testament, Corinth enjoyed considerable prominence as an economic center and boasted a host of large and beautiful buildings, including temples, an amphitheater, theaters, and baths; the city was also the site of the Isthmian games (cf. 1 Cor 9:24–27). Paul spent eighteen months preaching and teaching in Corinth (Acts 18:1–18) and wrote at least two epistles to the community there (1 Corinthians and 2 Corinthians; cf. 1 Cor 5:9, 11). He arrived there on his second missionary journey and met **Aquila** and **Priscilla**. He lived with them while practicing his trade as a tentmaker and preaching in the local synagogue. He converted Crispus, head of the synagogue, but moved to the house of Titus Justus after a disagreement with the Jews in the city. After eighteen months he was brought before the Roman proconsul Gallio on charges of "persuading men to worship God contrary to the law" (Acts 18:13), but Gallio refused to intervene in what he considered strictly a matter of Jewish religion (Acts 18:14–15). Sometime after this incident, Paul departed for Ephesus (Acts 18:18). After Paul left, **Apollos** ministered in the city (Acts 18:27–19:1).

CORINTHIANS, LETTERS TO THE Two letters by Paul addressed to the local church in Corinth. The first epistle was intended to correct abuses in the community; to curtail disunity that had emerged in the community; and to answer various questions that had been sent to him on morality, marriage and celibacy, the Eucharist, and the resurrection of the body. The second epistle sought to respond to developments since the sending of the first letter, in particular to the charges of some false apostles who had been trying to discredit Paul in Corinth. Both letters are full of Paul's theology, but they also give us a vivid picture of the early Christian community and of Paul's own vibrant personality.

1 CORINTHIANS

I. Authorship and Date

II. Contents

III. Purpose and Themes

    A. Background of the Letter

    B. Internal Divisions

    C. Marriage and Celibacy

    D. Food Offered to Idols

    E. The Body of Christ

    F. Christian Love

2 CORINTHIANS

I. Authorship and Date

II. Contents

III. Purpose and Themes

    A. Background of the Letter

    B. Paul Defends His Ministry

    C. Letter and Spirit

    D. Charity for Palestine

    E. Paul Confronts His Opponents

1 Corinthians

I. AUTHORSHIP AND DATE

Paul's authorship of this epistle has never been seriously questioned. As early as Saint Clement of Rome (A.D. 95), 1 Corinthians is mentioned as an authoritative letter from the apostle, and long tradition has accepted Pauline authorship. Paul states that he wrote the Epistle while at Ephesus (16:8), probably during his third missionary journey (A.D. 53–58). Since Paul was in Ephesus and planned to proceed to Corinth (11:34), the letter was probably written in the spring of A.D. 56.

II. CONTENTS

I. Introduction (1:1–9)

II. Divisions in the Corinthian Church (1:10–4:21)

    A. The Problem of Division and the Need for Unity (1:10–17)

    B. The Wisdom of Christ (1:18–2:16)

    C. Division in the Corinthian Church (3:1–23)

    D. The Apostles (4:1–13)

    E. An Admonition (4:14–21)

III. Sexual Immorality (5:1–6:20)

    A. The Scandal of Incest (5:1–13)

    B. Lawsuits Among Believers (6:1–11)

    C. Sexual Immorality and the Body (6:12–20)

IV. Questions from Corinth (7:1–14:40)

    A. Concerning Marriage and Celibacy (7:1–40)

    B. Food Offered to Idols (8:1–10:33)

    C. Liturgical Assemblies (11:1–34)

    D. Spiritual Gifts (12:1–14:40)

V. The Resurrection of the Dead (15:1–58)

    A. Christ's Resurrection (15:1–11)

    B. The Resurrection of Christians (15:12–58)

VI. Epilogue (16:1–24)

    A. The Church Collection for Jerusalem and Paul's Future Visit (16:1–12)

    B. Final Advice (16:13–24)

III. PURPOSE AND THEMES

A. Background of the Letter

Paul established the Church in Corinth during his stay there in about A.D. 51, as recorded in

Acts 18:1–18. He was gratified by the favorable response to his preaching among the Corinthians after the difficult time he had encountered in **Athens**. The community was made up of both Gentiles (1 Cor 8:7; 12:2) and Jews (7:18–20) coming from all social classes, including the wealthy (11:22), the poor (1:26), and even slaves (7:21).

But in the years after his departure, the new Corinthian church was beset by internal divisions and other crises that were dividing the unity of the faith in that city. Paul heard distressing news of parties forming in the Christian community there. "What I mean is that each of you says, 'I belong to Paul,' or 'I belong to Apollos,' or 'I belong to Cephas,' or 'I belong to Christ'" (1:12). Disquieting reports described not only internal divisions (1:12–15), but also incest (5:1–5), sexual immorality (6:12–20), lawsuits within the community (6:1–8), and even denials of the Resurrection (15:12). At the same time, the Corinthian Christians were permitting various liturgical abuses in the celebration of the Eucharist (11:17–34) and were creating problems by their disruptive exercise of charismatic gifts (14:1–40). A message also arrived from Corinth to ask about marriage and virginity and whether it was permissible to eat food that had been offered to idols.

During his time in Ephesus, Paul wrote to the Corinthians a brief letter that has not survived, which he refers to in 1 Corinthians 5:9–13, and Paul clearly planned to visit Corinth to settle these many issues (11:34). Trying to bring a swift resolution to the troubling situation, Paul wrote what we know as 1 Corinthians.

B. Internal Divisions

This letter gives us our most detailed glimpse into the early Christian community—the world of the early Christians, their local church organization, and the host of challenges they faced. Paul was acutely aware of these difficulties, and he adopts a fatherly and pastoral approach even as he is firm, direct, and willing to chastise and correct. The issues he confronted were not unique to Corinth's Christians, so the epistle has a value for all of the Christian churches. It has just as much meaning today, as the Church confronts similar challenges and pressures.

In the first part of the letter, Paul reminds the Corinthians that neither he nor Apollos nor Cephas (Peter) taught or ministered except through divine authority. He asks, "Has Christ been divided? Was Paul crucified for you? Or were you baptized in the name of Paul?" (1 Cor 1:13). He goes on to confront the serious moral problems that had developed, including the toleration of incest and the tragedy of Christians suing each other in secular courts. In his declaration on sexual morality, he memorably writes, "Every sin that a person commits is outside the body; but the fornicator sins against the body itself. Or do you not know that your body is a temple of the Holy Spirit within you, which you have from God, and that you are not your own? For you were bought with a price; therefore glorify God in your body" (6:18–20).

C. Marriage and Celibacy

Paul answers the questions that were posed to him by the delegation from Corinth regarding marriage (1 Cor 7:1), celibacy (7:25), food offered to idols (8:1), and spiritual gifts (12:1). He has a preference for the unmarried state, as it affords greater freedom for spiritual concerns, but marriage is an honorable state so long as it is respected fully by both husband and wife. However, a lawful and consummated marriage between unbaptized persons can be dissolved when one of them converts to Christianity and the other opposes the faith or desires to be separated from the newly baptized spouse (7:12–15). This exception—known to theologians as the "Pauline privilege"—was promulgated by Paul as a means of protecting the faith of converts.

D. Food Offered to Idols

The question of food offered to idols was a delicate one. Christians could not knowingly participate in idolatry, but food that had been offered to idols was sometimes sold at market. Did Christians need to know where every bit of food they ate came from? Paul responds that the food itself could do no damage: "We are no worse off if we do not eat, and no better off if we do" (1 Cor 8:8). Thus unknowingly consuming food offered to idols would not harm a Christian. But Christians who knowingly ate food offered to idols, though the food was harmless in itself, might do great harm to the weak in faith. "For if any one sees you, a man of knowledge, at table in an idol's temple, might he not be encouraged, if his conscience is weak, to eat food offered to idols? And so by your knowledge this weak man is destroyed, the brother for whom Christ died" (8:10–11). To avoid sending the wrong message, Christians were not to eat food they knew had been offered to idols. Better never to eat meat than to cause a weaker brother to fall (8:13).

E. The Body of Christ

The liturgical irregularities included the dress of women (1 Cor 11:2–16), the celebration of the Eucharist (11:17–34), and the charisms or gifts that had been granted by the Holy Spirit to members of the community (12:1–14:40). Paul's primary concern in the liturgy was proper order. The spiritual gifts, he suggests, come from the same Spirit and so should not be the cause of dispute or rivalry. The Eucharist is likewise a sacrament of unity that joins believers to Christ and one another (10:16–17). "For just as the body is one and has many members, and all the members of the body, though many, are one body, so it is with Christ. For in the one Spirit we were all baptized into one body—Jews or Greeks, slaves or free—and we were all made to drink of one Spirit" (12:12–13).

F. Christian Love

All these spiritual gifts are subordinate to the theological virtues of faith, hope, and love. The greatest of those is love: without it all of the others would be in vain (1 Cor 13:1–13). Paul's teaching on love (Greek *agapē*) in chapter 13 is one of the most beautiful and profound in the whole of the New Testament. He describes its main characteristics (13:4–7): "Love is patient; love is kind; love is not envious or boastful or arrogant or rude. It does not insist on its own way; it is not irritable or resentful; it does not rejoice in wrongdoing, but rejoices in the truth. It bears all things, believes all things, hopes all things, endures all things." Unlike spiritual gifts, such as prophecy and tongues, love lasts forever. He provides love with its eschatological orientation and its primacy by noting that "For now we see in a mirror, dimly, but then we will see face to face. Now I know only in part; then I will know fully, even as I have been fully known. And now faith, hope, and love abide, these three; and the greatest of these is love" (13:12–13). (*See* **Love**.)

In chapter 15 Paul confronts those who challenge the doctrine of the **Resurrection**. He considers the evidence of Christ's Resurrection (15:1–11) and connects it directly to the future resurrection of Christians (15:12–58).

2 Corinthians

I. AUTHORSHIP AND DATE

Almost all scholars accept Paul as the author of 2 Corinthians. A variety of Church Fathers name Paul as the author, and the language and style are unmistakably Paul's. Some scholars have suggested, however, that 2 Corinthians is really a composite of multiple letters from Paul. One common scheme sees two letters, with the second beginning at chapter 10; its proponents suggest that there is a striking change in tone at that juncture, from loving to severe. Another scheme sees three additions attached to the main letter: 2 Cor 6:14–7:1; chapter 9, which repeats the basic content of chapter 8; and chapters 10–13, which return to the subject of chapter 7. Regardless of whether the book is one letter or more, there remains no question that Paul was the author of all of it.

As with 1 Corinthians, Paul wrote 2 Corinthians during his third missionary journey (cf. Acts 18:23–21:16), soon after sending the first letter to Corinth. Whereas 1 Corinthians was penned at Ephesus, the second letter was dispatched from Macedonia in northern Greece, where he had traveled after Ephesus (2 Cor 2:13; 7:5; 9:2). The letter, clearly written after 1 Corinthians, was probably composed in late A.D. 56 or early 57.

II. CONTENTS

I. *Introduction (1:1–11)*
   A. *Salutation (1:1–2)*
   B. *Thanksgiving (1:3–11)*
II. *Paul's Apostolic Labors (1:12–7:16)*
   A. *Paul's Travel (1:12–2:17)*
   B. *Ministry of the New Covenant (3:1–4:18)*
   C. *The Life of Faith (5:1–10)*
   D. *The Ministry of Reconciliation (5:11–6:10)*
   E. *Reconciliation with Corinth (6:11–7:16)*
III. *The Jerusalem Collection (8:1–9:15)*
   A. *The Macedonian Church (8:1–7)*
   B. *Generosity (8:8–15)*
   C. *Titus and Companions (8:16–24)*
   D. *The Collection (9:1–15)*
IV. *Paul Defends His Ministry (10:1–13:10)*
   A. *Obedience (10:1–6)*
   B. *The Challenge to Dividers (10:7–18)*
   C. *Suffering in the Lord's Service (11:1–12:13)*
   D. *Paul's Planned Visit to Corinth (12:14–13:10)*
V. *Farewell and Blessing (13:11–14)*

III. PURPOSE AND THEMES

A. Background of the Letter

Written not long after the first letter to Corinth, 2 Corinthians is striking in its deeply personal and emotional tone. The letter was needed because the Corinthian community was still troubled. The difficulties mentioned in the first letter had largely been corrected, but a new threat had emerged: Judaizing missionaries ("false apostles," 2 Cor 11:13) had arrived and were attacking Paul's authority, credibility, and integrity. As the enemies of Paul succeeded in finding a following, they created tension between Paul and his spiritual children and necessitated a brief emergency visit to Corinth. During the visit, he was attacked viciously by an unnamed enemy (2:5; 7:12), and the apostle was shocked to learn that some in Corinth were unwilling to defend his honor and authority. Later, the majority of the Christians did give a statement of their loyalty (7:9), but there was still a vocal minority against him (12:20–21).

B. Paul Defends His Ministry

Much of the epistle is devoted to a defense of Paul's apostolic vocation. Faced with accusations that his motives were less than pure, Paul appeals to what the Corinthians already know about him: they have seen him at work, and they can judge his sincerity for themselves. He has suffered greatly in his labors (2 Cor 1:3–11), but throughout he has acted with simple sincerity (1:12–14). He regrets the painful confrontations of his earlier visit (1:15–2:4), but he begs the Corinthians to forgive the enemy who caused the ugly scenes (2:5–11). He has confidence that his commission comes from God (1:21; 2:17).

C. Letter and Spirit

Paul is confident, even "very bold" (3:12), because the Gospel he preaches is the message of life. Here he returns to one of his favorite themes: the contrast between the Old Covenant and the New, the "written code" (literally "letter") and the "Spirit." Paul's confidence comes not from his own abilities, but through Christ and the life-giving ministry of the New Covenant: "for the written code kills, but the Spirit gives life" (3:6). The Law was "the dispensation of condemnation," but the New Covenant is "the dispensation of righteousness" (3:9), toward which the Law pointed. As Moses veiled his face from the Israelites, so the meaning of the Old Testament Scriptures is veiled from those who do not approach them through Christ (3:12–18).

In spite of his suffering and persecution, Paul has the strength to go on, because he has learned that divine power is made more effective through his weakness (12:9–10). "For this slight momentary affliction is preparing us for an eternal weight of glory beyond all comparison" (4:17).

Over and over, Paul stresses that his preaching does not come from himself, but from God (1:12, 21; 4:6; 5:20). Keeping the ultimate goal in mind gives Paul the strength to go on, and it should do the same for his readers.

D. Charity for Palestine

Having reconciled himself to the Corinthians, Paul feels confident enough to bring up the subject of monetary donations. In 2 Cor 8–9, Paul appeals to the Corinthians to give generously to a collection being taken up for the needy Christians of Judea. He points out the generosity of the Macedonian church (8:1–5) and urges the Corinthians to give in the same "cheerful" spirit (9:7).

E. Paul Confronts His Opponents

Paul returns to the defense of his ministry in the last four chapters, but now in a very different tone. Here he is speaking directly to his recalcitrant opponents, responding directly to their charges (2 Cor 10:10–11; 11:22–23) and describing his labors and his sufferings in the service of the Lord (11:1–12:13). He must have been hurt by the events in Corinth, and the anguish comes out especially in the final chapters. Paul warns his detractors that he "will not be lenient" (13:2) in dealing with them when he makes another visit to Corinth (13:1; cf. 12:14).

CORNELIUS A Roman centurion in charge of the Italian cohort at Caesarea, and the first Gentile to become a convert to Christianity (Acts 10:1–11:18; cf. 15:6–11). Cornelius was "a devout man who feared God with all his household; he gave alms generously to the people and prayed constantly to God" (Acts 10:2). Being both a non-**Jew** and a religious man, he was one of the so-called God-fearers (Gentiles who worshipped God and accepted Jewish Law but did not become full proselytes to Judaism or receive **circumcision**). Acts reports that while he was at prayer he was visited by an angel who instructed him to summon Peter from Joppa (Acts 10:3–8).

When Peter came to the house of Cornelius, Peter instructed him in the Gospel, and the Holy Spirit came upon Cornelius and his household and conferred upon them the gift of tongues (Acts 10:44–46). Peter then baptized them, even though they were Gentiles.

When conservative Jewish Christians in Jerusalem upbraided him for entering the home of a Gentile and eating with him, Peter related his vision (Acts 10:9–16; 11:4–15) and the coming of the Holy Spirit to the house of Cornelius, asking rhetorically, "who was I that I could withstand God?" (Acts 11:17). At that the believers rejoiced: "Then to the Gentiles also God has granted repentance unto life" (Acts 11:18).

The conversion of Cornelius made it clear that the Church's mission to the Gentiles could begin in earnest. It also showed that the Gentiles could become baptized believers without the need for circumcision, since they too received the Spirit by grace through faith (as Peter later argues in Acts 15:8–11). (*See* **Circumcision**; *see also* **Jerusalem, Council of.**)

CORNERSTONE A foundation stone placed at the bottom corner of a building. The cornerstone was fundamental to the construction of a stable building, and hence it was used metaphorically in Scripture to describe a key person or figure (Isa 19:13; Jer 51:26; Zech 10:4). In Isa 28:16 the Lord proclaims, "See, I am laying in Zion a foundation stone, a tested stone, a precious cornerstone, a sure foundation." Paul, following one strong current of Jewish tradition, interpreted this passage as a prophecy of the Messiah. Psalm 118:22 reads, "The stone that the builders rejected has become the chief cornerstone." In the New Testament, Jesus used this Psalm to declare himself the foundation stone for a new temple (Matt 21:42; Mark 12:10; Luke 20:17), a connection reiterated by Peter (Acts 4:11; 1 Pet 2:7). Christ is the cornerstone for the Church, which is a living temple of the Spirit (Eph 2:20; 1 Pet 2:4).

COS A small island in the Aegean Sea, first settled by the Mycenaeans in the mid-fifteenth century B.C. The island figured in the events of the Maccabean War (1 Macc 15:23) and was mentioned once in the New Testament at Acts 21:1: following Paul's third missionary journey, the apostle journeyed from Miletus to Cos; there he spent the night before setting sail for Rhodes.

COUNCIL *See* **Sanhedrin**; *see also* **Jerusalem, Council of**.

COUNCIL OF JERUSALEM *See* **Jerusalem, Council of**.

COVENANT A kinship bond between two parties, with conditions or obligations, established by an oath or its equivalent. Covenants were ubiquitous in the ancient Near East as well as Greco-Roman culture as a means to forge and maintain relationships between individuals, families, tribes, and even nations. Covenant is also the master-theme of the Bible, which records the various ways throughout history that God has drawn humanity into a familial relationship with himself through divine oaths.

The imperfect rendering of the word "covenant" (Hebrew *běrît*; Greek *diathēkē*) as "Testament" in the Latin tradition has obscured the fact that the Bible is divided into the Scriptures based on two covenants, the Old and the New. Nonetheless, this division of the canon on the basis of covenant distinctions points to the undeniable centrality of the concept of covenant to biblical thought and Christian theology. Moreover, for Catholics, the fact that the source and summit of the Christian life, the **Eucharist**, is identified by Christ as "the New Covenant" (Luke 22:20) should suffice to demonstrate the importance of covenant to the plan of salvation.

I. THE ESSENCE AND DEFINITION OF COVENANT

The definition of "covenant" has been widely debated by biblical scholars. Especially in German scholarship there has been a tendency to reduce the notion of "covenant" to a synonym for "law" or "obligation." Covenants do frequently contain laws or obligations. However, research on ancient Near Eastern covenants in the second half of the twentieth century has established a virtual consensus among Protestant (Frank Moore Cross, Gorden Hugenberger), Catholic (D. J. McCarthy, Paul Kalluveettil), and Jewish (Moshe Weinfeld, David Noel Freedman) scholars that a "covenant" is, in its essence, a legal means to establish kinship between two previously unrelated parties. Harvard scholar Frank Moore Cross explains that a covenant "is . . . a widespread legal means by which the duties and privileges of kinship may be extended to another individual or group, including aliens." This kinship, or familial, relationship was regulated by conditions and obligations specified during the covenant-making ceremony, usually consisting of a liturgical rite culminating in a verbal or ritual oath performed by one or both of the parties to the covenant.

It is incorrect to view a covenant simply

as a contract. Generally, a contract involves the exchange of goods, whereas a covenant involves the exchange of persons. Unlike most contracts, covenants are not merely civil but sacred bonds, in which an oath is employed to call on God (or the gods, in polytheistic societies) to enforce the covenant obligations.

II. THE MEANS OF ESTABLISHING A COVENANT

The Bible and various ancient Near Eastern texts describe a variety of ways that were used to establish or solemnize a covenant between two parties.

In almost every case the central act of covenant-making was the swearing of an oath by one or both of the parties to the covenant (Gen 21:31–32, 22:16, 26:28; Josh 9:15; Ezek 16:59, 17:13–19). The oath generally took the form of a self-curse. The covenant-maker called on God or the gods to inflict death or some other grave penalty upon himself should he fail to keep the obligations of the covenant he was entering. This oath could be verbally pronounced, or it could be expressed by a ritual. Secular covenant texts from the ancient Near East record a wide variety of ritual self-curses, such as this one described in an Assyrian text from 754 B.C.:

> This head is not the head of a lamb, it is the head of Mati'ilu (the covenant-maker). If Mati'ilu sins against this covenant, so may, just as the head of this spring lamb is torn off . . . the head of Mati'ilu be torn off. (ANET 532)

A similar ritual self-curse was performed by cutting animals in two and passing between the carcasses (Gen 15; Jer 34). This ritually represented the intention, "May I be slain like these animals if I do not maintain this covenant" (see Jer 34:18). The Bible records other ritual self-curses as well: the sacrifice of animals and the sprinkling of blood (Exod 24:8; Ps 50:5), expressing, "May my blood be shed like the blood of these animals"; and circumcision (Gen 17:10), expressing, "May I myself be cut off if I do not keep the covenant."

Other rituals associated with covenant solemnization in Scripture do not express a self-curse but exemplify other aspects of the covenant relationship. Often the covenant-making parties shared a common meal to confirm their new familial relationship (Gen 26:30, 31:54; Exod 24:11; Josh 9:14–15; Luke 22:14–23). The use of family terms ("brother," 1 Kgs 20:32–34; "father" and "son," Ps 89:26–28; 2:7; 2 Sam 7:14) and the exchange of clothing (1 Sam 18:3) or other gifts (Gen 21:27) could also express familial intimacy.

The New Covenant is established at the **Last Supper**, a communal meal between the covenant-making parties analogous to Moses and the elders sharing a meal with God on Mount Sinai (cf. Exod 24:11). On the other hand, Jesus's very words, "This is my blood of the covenant" (Matt 26:28), recall Moses's words when sprinkling the shed blood of the sacrificial animals during the ratification of the covenant on Mount Sinai (Exod 24:8). The Eucharist thus is both the family meal and the solemn sacrifice of the New Covenant.

Most of the rituals used in covenant making or covenant renewal were essentially liturgical in nature. They were performed according to sacred customs, in the presence of

God (or the gods), who was called on to witness to and enforce the covenant obligations. Since the divine presence was important to the liturgical rites of covenant making, sacred locations such as temples or holy mountains were preferred places for covenant rituals.

Examining covenant-making ceremonies helps us to see that a covenant had *familial*, *legal*, and *liturgical* dimensions. In brief, a covenant was a *familial bond* established by a *legally binding* oath sworn during a *liturgical* ritual. All these aspects are visible during the covenant ceremony at Mount Sinai (Exod 24:3–11). The *familial bond* is illustrated by the shared meal between God and the elders of Israel on Mount Sinai (Exod 24:9–11). The *legally binding oath* is expressed by the solemn words of the people followed by the sprinkling of blood, a ritual self-curse (Exod 24:7–8) that binds them to obey all the legal obligations enunciated in Exod 20–23. A *liturgical ritual* serves as the context for swearing the oath: sacrifices offered at an altar in a sacred place (Exod 24:4–5) while invoking the name of the Lord (Exod 24:7–8).

III. CATEGORIES OF COVENANT

Covenants may be placed into two categories according to the status of the covenant-making parties: "human" covenants are between two human parties, whereas "divine" covenants include God as one partner.

Covenants may also be categorized according to which party actually swears the oath that establishes the covenant.

When both parties swear the covenant oath, a "kinship" (or "parity") covenant is formed. This covenant type is labeled "kin-ship" because the familial nature of the covenant-bond is at the forefront of the relationship, rather than the subordination of one of the parties to the other. The mutual swearing of the oath indicates that both parties accept responsibility for keeping the covenant obligations, resulting in an equal, or at least reciprocal, relationship between the two. Several kinship-type covenants in Scripture included a family meal in the covenant-making ritual (Gen 26:30, 31:54; Exod 24:11).

When the inferior party alone swears the oath, a "vassal-type" covenant results. In this situation, the superior party imposes a covenant relationship on the inferior, who is often a rebellious servant. Ancient Near Eastern examples of vassal covenants include the well-known Vassal Treaties of Esarhaddon (king of Assyria, r. 681–669 B.C.), which Esarhaddon imposed on untrustworthy vassal kings to ensure their obedience to his heir, Ashurbanipal. Biblical examples include the covenant of circumcision in Gen 17, where only **Abraham** performs the covenant-oath ritual (i.e., circumcision); and the covenant of Deuteronomy, in which only the people of Israel invoke the self-curse (i.e., the oath) to fulfill the terms of the covenant (Deut 27:11–26; Josh 8:30–35).

When the superior party alone swears the oath, he establishes a "grant-type" covenant with the inferior party. These "grant" covenants were frequently employed by ancient Near Eastern kings to reward faithful servants, often by granting them a piece of royal land (hence the term "grant") in perpetuity. In this covenant form, the superior party assumes all responsibility for the maintenance of the covenant, in view of some prior meritorious action by the inferior. Biblical examples include the final form of the Abrahamic covenant (see Gen 22:15–18), and the Davidic covenant, especially as described in Ps 89:3–37.

IV. HUMAN COVENANTS IN ANTIQUITY AND THE BIBLE

Ancient Near Eastern archaeology has brought to light a number of non-Israelite covenant texts. Two of the larger collections of these texts are the Hittite Treaties and the previously mentioned Vassal Treaties of Esarhaddon. The Hittite Treaties date from the second millennium B.C. and consist of covenants established between the king of Hatti-land (modern Turkey) and the kings of the surrounding nations, functioning as the ancient equivalent of an international treaty. The actual texts of these covenants followed a regular structure, which is also evident in the book of Deuteronomy:

1. Preamble (1:1–5)
2. Historical Prologue (1:6–4:49)
3. Stipulations (5:1–26:19)
4. Blessings and Curses (27:1–30:20)
5. Storage and Reading Arrangements (31:1–34:12)

Some scholars have pointed to the similarity of structure between Deuteronomy and the Hittite treaties as an argument for dating Deuteronomy to the second millennium B.C. (consistent with Mosaic authorship), since ancient Near Eastern covenants from the first millennium B.C. did not follow the same structure. The Vassal Treaties of Esarhaddon (eighth century B.C.), for example, omit the historical prologue and the blessings. These harsh treaties, imposed by Esarhaddon on his vassals, are no-

table for their extremely lengthy and colorful lists of covenant curses, some of which sound similar to those of Deut 28:15–68.

A number of covenants between two human parties are recorded in the Bible: between Abraham and **Abimelech** (Gen 21:22–33), **Isaac** and Abimelech (Gen 26:26–33), **Jacob** and **Laban** (Gen 31:43–54), the Israelites and Gibeonites (Josh 9:15), **David** and **Jonathan** (1 Sam 18:1–4; 20:8), **Ahab** and **Ben-hadad** (1 Kgs 20:32–34), **Jehoiada** and the palace guards (2 Kgs 11:4), and others. These numerous human covenants recorded in Scripture testify to the widespread use of covenants in ancient society over an extended period of time. These covenants formed sacred bonds that could not be broken without incurring a curse, even if the covenant was established under false pretenses or duress (Josh 9:19; Ezek 17:11–21).

V. DIVINE COVENANTS IN THE BIBLE

The people of Israel were unique among ancient nations in believing that God had entered into covenants with themselves and their ancestors. The Bible is structured according to a sequence of divine covenants established between God and man, through the mediation of different individuals: **Adam, Noah, Abraham, Moses, David,** and ultimately **Jesus Christ.**

Although the **Creation** narrative (Gen 1–3) does not use the word "covenant" (Hebrew *bĕrît*), there are various implicit or indirect indicators that a covenant is present between God and creation, mediated by Adam: (1) the creation account culminates on the Sabbath, which is the "sign" of the covenant elsewhere in Scripture (Exod 31:12–17); (2) in Gen 6:18, the verb used for the making of the covenant with Noah is not the usual one for covenant initiation (Hebrew *kārat*), but a term indicating the maintenance or renewal of a preexisting covenant (Hebrew *hēqîm*). The similarity in language between Gen 6 and Gen 1 suggests the covenant being "renewed" with Noah is the one present at creation; (3) In Hos 6:7 the prophet compares Israel with Adam in terms of covenant unfaithfulness: "Like Adam they transgressed the covenant."

The creation or Adamic covenant bound God with Adam, whose status was Son of God (cf. Gen 1:26–27, 5:1) and vice-regent of creation (Gen 1:28). The condition of the covenant was to refrain from eating of the tree of the knowledge of good and evil (Gen 2:16–17); the corresponding curse was death (Gen 2:17).

Adam and Eve's subsequent breaking of the covenant introduces death into human history (cf. Gen 4:8) and begins a cycle of sin that ultimately necessitates the cleansing of the earth by the Flood. After the Flood, the original creation covenant is renewed with Noah (Gen 9:1–17), although with modifications: the once-peaceful relationship between man and nature has been marred (cf. Gen 1:29–30; 9:2–6).

God begins the process of the redemption of mankind with Abraham, the covenant recipient par excellence of the Old Testament. God makes at least two covenants with Abraham in Gen 15:1–21 and 17:1–27. In addition, in light of the close relationship between "oath" and "covenant" (see Gen 21:31–32; Ezek 17:13–19), it is likely that the divine oath of Gen 22:15–18 also establishes a covenant with Abraham.

These covenants should be viewed as cumulative, each building on the previous one.

Genesis 15 establishes the initial covenant between Abraham and God, solemnizing the earlier promise that Abraham would become a "great nation" (Gen 12:2). The promises of the Gen 15 covenant include numerous descendants for Abraham and a land to call their own, the ingredients necessary for his people to become a great nation.

Genesis 17 augments the earlier Abrahamic covenant by including a promise of kingship for Abraham's descendants (Gen 17:6), and the expectation that Abraham would become not just one but "many nations" (Gen 17:5–6). Also included for the first time is the covenant obligation of circumcision (Gen 17:9–14).

In Gen 22, after the near sacrifice of Abraham's "only begotten" (Hebrew *yāḥîd*) son, Isaac, which so strongly foreshadows Calvary, God swears a covenant oath to Abraham reiterating earlier covenant promises but also confirming the promise of blessing to all nations through Abraham's seed (Gen 22:18), a promise given earlier in Gen 12:3 but not included as a provision of the covenant in either Gen 15 or Gen 17. In Gen 22:15–18, the Abrahamic covenant reaches its final form.

The remaining divine covenants recorded in Scripture are grounded in the Abrahamic covenant. The book of Exodus records the flight of Abraham's descendants from Egypt and their assembly at the foot of Mount Sinai to receive a covenant from God through Moses. This covenant had within it the potential to fulfill the promises given to Abraham of great nationhood, kingship, and universal blessing. The descendants of Abraham had multiplied remarkably, the land of Canaan lay before them, and they were about to receive a law forming, as it were, their constitution as a political entity, a "great nation." In addition, the promise prior to the giving of this Sinaitic (or Mosaic) covenant stated that obedience to the covenant would result in Israel's attaining the status of a "royal priesthood" (Hebrew *mamleket kōhănîm;* Exod 19:6), that is, a nation of king-priests, fulfilling the promise of Gen 17 ("kings will come from you") and of Gen 22:18 concerning blessing to all the nations, since a major function of a priest is to bring blessings (cf. Num 6:22–27).

This promise of Abrahamic covenant fulfillment was not attained under the Mosaic covenant, however, because of the immediate violation of the covenant with the fashioning of the golden calf (Exod 32). The golden calf incident necessitated a remaking of the Mosaic covenant (Exod 34:1–35) in which the general priesthood of the firstborn of Israel transferred to the Levites (Exod 32:27–29; Num 3:5–51) and a great deal of additional law was added (Exod 35–Lev 27). Additional rebellions in the desert (Num 11; 12; 14; 16; 17), especially the idolatry and promiscuity at Beth-peor (Num 25), set the stage for yet another renewal of the Mosaic covenant described by the book of Deuteronomy. Promulgated at Beth-peor in the Plains of Moab (Deut 1:5; 3:29; 4:44–46) almost forty years after the Sinai event, the Deuteronomy covenant is clearly a distinct covenant augmenting the one made and renewed at Sinai (also called "Horeb"; see Deut 29:1). For the first time laws are given to Israel permitting a human king (Deut 17:14–20), total warfare (Deut 20:16–18), and divorce (Deut 24:1–4). Jesus will later indicate that at least some of these covenant provisions were not the divine ideal but were concessions to the hard-heartedness of Israel (Matt 19:8–9).

Israel's subsequent track record under the Mosaic covenant was checkered at best, but Yahweh's plan for his people reached a high point under David and the early reign of Solomon (2 Sam 5–1; 1 Kgs 10). David united the nation under a strong central government at his capital in Jerusalem (2 Sam 5) and made proper worship of the Lord a national priority (2 Sam 6–7). God granted to David a covenant as recorded in 2 Sam 7:5–16, although the word "covenant" only appears in later references to this event (2 Sam 23:5; Ps 89:19–37, 132:1–18; Isa 55:3; 2 Chr 13:5, 21:7; Jer 33:20–22). The terms of this covenant made David and his heirs sons of God (2 Sam 7:14; Ps 89:26–27) and high kings over the earth (Ps 89:27; 2:6–9) who would enjoy an everlasting reign (2 Sam 7:13, 16) and would build the House of God—that is, the **Temple** (2 Sam 7:13).

After a brief period of glory under Solomon, during which these covenant promises appeared to be visibly fulfilled (1 Kgs 4–10), the Davidic monarchy entered a long period of decline, beginning with the division of Israel into the ten tribes in the north and southern Judah (2 Kgs 12). During the decay of the divided people of God, the prophets spoke of a new covenant to come (Jer 31:31; cf. Isa 55:1–3, 59:20–21, 61:8–9; Ezek 34:25, 37:26) that would be unlike the unsuccessful Mosaic covenant (Jer 31:32; cf. Ezek 20:23–28; Isa 61:3–4). Simultaneously, the Davidic covenant would be restored (Jer 33:14–26; Isa 9, 11, 55:3; Ezek 37:15–28).

The Gospels, particularly Matthew and Luke, clearly depict Jesus as the Son (heir) of David and thus the one to restore the Davidic covenant (Matt 1:1–25; Luke 1:31–33, 69; 2:4). At the Last Supper, Jesus explicitly identifies his body and blood as the New Covenant (Luke 22:20; 1 Cor 11:25) promised by the prophets (Jer 31:31), thus strikingly fulfilling the promise of Isaiah that the servant of the Lord would not simply *make* a covenant but would *become* a covenant (Isa 42:6; 49:8). According to Hebrews, the New Covenant is superior to the old (that is, the Mosaic covenant) because it is established by a better mediator (Christ versus the high priest; Heb 8:6, 9:25), based on better sacrifices (the blood of Christ versus the blood of animals; Heb 9:12, 23), in a better sanctuary (heaven itself versus the earthly tabernacle; Heb 9:11, 24).

If the New Covenant surpasses the Mosaic covenant, it restores and transforms the Davidic covenant. Jesus Christ is the Son of David who rules eternally from the heavenly Zion (Heb 12:22–24) and manifests his rule over Israel and all the nations (Matt 28:18–20) through his royal steward Peter (cf. Matt 16:18–19; Isa 22:15–22, esp. 22) and his other officers, the apostles (Luke 22:32; Matt 19:28; cf. 1 Kgs 4:7). Thus James sees the growth of the Church among Jews and Gentiles as a fulfillment of Amos's promise that God would restore the fallen "tent" (i.e., the kingdom) of David (Acts 15:13–18; cf. Amos 9:11–12).

The New Covenant involves the fulfillment of the other covenants of salvation history, as well. Thus, Jesus is a new Adam (Rom 5:12–19) who makes us into a new creation (2 Cor 5:17; Gal 6:15). He fulfills all the promises of the Abrahamic covenant (Luke 1:68–75, esp. 72–73), including great nationhood (the Church; 1 Pet 2:9), kingship (Rev 19:16), the fatherhood of many nations (Rom 4:16–18), and the "blessing to all nations" experienced in the outpouring of the Spirit on all people (Acts 3:25–26; Gal 3:6–9, 4–18). Even the Mosaic covenant, which to a certain extent is abrogated (Gal 3:19–25), is fulfilled in its essence by the New Covenant, which grants believers the power of the Holy Spirit to fulfill the very heart of the Mosaic Law, the commands of love for God and neighbor (Rom 8:3–4, 13:8–10; Matt 5:17, 22:37–40).

VI. ENGLISH TRANSLATION OF THE TERMS FOR COVENANT

The word employed for "covenant" in the OT is the Hebrew *bĕrît*. The ancient Greek translation of the OT, the Septuagint, consistently rendered this term with the Greek word *diathēkē*. There can be little doubt that the New Testament authors followed the practice of the Septuagint and employed the term *diathēkē* to mean *bĕrît*, "covenant." But, because classical Greek authors used *diathēkē* to refer to a "testament" (i.e., a will), some older English translations, such as the King James Version, rendered *diathēkē* as "testament" in certain passages. More recent translations correct this error, except in a few instances. For example, Heb 9:15–17 reads as follows in the RSV:

Therefore he [Christ] is the mediator of a new covenant [diathēkē], so that those who are called may receive the promised eternal inheritance, since a death has occurred which redeems them from the transgressions under the first covenant [diathēkē]. For where a will [diathēkē] is involved, the death of the one who made it must be established. For a will [diathēkē] takes effect only at death, since it is not in force as long as the one who made it is alive.

The word *diathēkē* is translated as "covenant" in verse 15 but as "will" in verses 16–17. Many think the author switches to the classical meaning of *diathēkē* in these latter verses, where the discussion seems to revolve around executing a will at a person's death. However, it may well be that the author of Hebrews means "covenant" in verses 16–17 as well. The covenant under discussion is the broken covenant at Sinai, which required the death of the Israelites according to the ritual self-curse of Exod 24:8 (see Exod 32:9–10). The Greek of these verses may be translated as follows: "For where a [broken] covenant is involved, it is necessary for the death of the covenant-maker to be borne. For a [broken] covenant is enforced upon dead bodies, since it certainly is not in force while the covenant-maker still lives."

The author of Hebrews is emphasizing that the (broken) Sinai covenant required the death of the Israelites (Exod 32:9–10), because they invoked a curse of death upon themselves during the covenant-making ceremony (Exod 24:8). That curse of death was not paid when the people turned from the Lord and worshiped the golden calf (Exod 32:14) but is ultimately paid by Christ himself on behalf of Israel (Heb 9:15).

A similar issue appears in Gal 3:15: "To give a human example, brethren: no one annuls even a man's will [*diathēkē*], or adds to it, once it has been ratified."

Here there is even less reason to translate *diathēkē* as "will." In the context (Gal 3:15–18), Paul is discussing the inviolability of covenants. Since even a human covenant cannot be changed after the fact (Gal 3:15; cf. Josh 9:18–20), a divine one certainly cannot be (Gal 3:17). God cannot change his covenant with Abraham (Gen 22:15–18) to bless all nations through his seed (Gen 22:18; cf. Gal 3:14) by adding the Mosaic Law as a condition four hundred years later (Gal 3:17–18). Changing covenants after the fact is not allowed by human justice, much less divine.

To summarize, all the occurrences of *diathēkē* in the NT may and should be translated "covenant," following the example of the Septuagint.

CREATION The formation of the universe out of nothing by the action of God.

The creation account in Genesis may use figurative language (see "Truth of the Creation Account" below), but it is very different from the creation myths of Israel's pagan neighbors. In those myths, creation was the result of the triumph of some deity or hero over the pantheon or some god or primordial being, such as Marduk's defeat of Tiamat or Baal's triumph over Yaam. In all these myths, the universe arose out of preexistent matter, the result of an undesired or unforeseen accident.

The Genesis account, on the other hand,

stresses the uniqueness and omnipotence of God. God creates out of nothing by the power of his Word. His creation proceeds according to an orderly plan and has a very definite purpose. All that he creates is good (Gen 1:10).

I. *The Six Days of Creation*
   A. *Creating the Form*
   B. *Filling the Void*
II. *Important Messages of the Creation Account*
   A. *Creation Is Good*
   B. *We Are a Special Creation, Made Like God*
   C. *God Is Our Father*
   D. *The Cosmos Is a Temple*
III. *The Truth of the Creation Account*
IV. *"A New Creation"*

I. THE SIX DAYS OF CREATION

At the beginning of creation, "the earth was without form and void" (Gen 1:2). This is the statement of the problem, so to speak, and the rest of the creation account is the story of how God formed the world and filled the void.

A close look at the first chapter of Genesis shows a careful literary structure. We can look at the six days of creation as two sets of three days. In the first three days, God created *forms*; in the second three days, God filled those forms with inhabitants. Thus there is a close correspondence between days one and four, two and five, three and six.

A. Creating the Form

1. *Time.* On the first day, God separated light from darkness, creating day and night, and thus time.
2. *Space.* On the second day, God created sea and sky, marking divisions of space.

3. *Life.* On the third day, God created dry land and filled it with vegetation, the beginning of life.

B. Filling the Void

4. *Rulers of time.* On the fourth day, God created the stars, the sun, and the moon to "rule" the day and night and to mark the seasons and days and years.
5. *Rulers of space.* On the fifth day, God created sea creatures and birds to fill the sea and sky.
6. *Rulers of life.* On the sixth day, God created animals and humans to fill the dry land.

At the end of creation, God rested and made the seventh day holy. This holy seventh day suggests a **covenant** with creation (*see* **Adam**; CCC 288); it crowns the work of creation the way a pediment crowns a temple.

II. IMPORTANT MESSAGES OF THE CREATION ACCOUNT

In contrast to the almost random creation recorded as part of Near Eastern mythology, the account in Genesis carefully uses the creation to convey important truths about God's relationship with the universe.

A. Creation Is Good

"And God saw that it was good": we read this statement four times in the first chapter of Genesis (Gen 1:12, 18, 21, 25). At the end of creation, "behold, it was very good" (Gen 1:31). The message is clear and simple: creation is good. It is not the work of some evil or incompetent demiurge; the material world was created to be good. And, though it was subsequently wounded and disordered by the sin of Adam, creation is being restored and renewed in Jesus Christ.

B. We Are a Special Creation, Made Like God

Man and woman were made "in the image of God" (Gen 1:27), unlike any other creature. We are not, of course, equal to God, but we have the potential to relate to God and live as part of God's family.

C. God Is Our Father

"Let us make man in our image, after our likeness," God says (Gen 1:26). The next time the words "image" and "likeness" appear together, they refer to Adam's begetting his son Seth "in his own likeness, after his image" (Gen 5:3). The language points out that we are related to God the way Seth was related to Adam.

D. The Cosmos Is a Temple

Genesis describes the pristine creation in sacral terms. According to a Jewish tradition, the Garden of Eden is the holy of holies, the most sacred core of the cosmic temple that is the world (Jubilees 8, 19). The seven days of the creation story parallel the narrative of the building of the Tabernacle, which proceeded according to seven commands (Exod 40:16–33), and the erection of the Temple, built in seven years (1 Kgs 6:38). The world is thus viewed as a cosmic sanctuary filled with God's glory (Isa 6:3), and Adam is portrayed as the first priest. (For more on this sacral view of creation, see **Adam**.)

III. THE TRUTH OF THE CREATION ACCOUNT

The Church does not require Christians to believe either that the universe came to be in six literal days or that it did not; Christians are free to interpret the scientific evidence for themselves. Even the Church Fathers were divided. Many insisted on the literal interpretation: "six days" meant six days as we count them today. But even in early centuries, others took a different view. Saint Clement of Alexandria warned against a literalistic interpretation: "how could creation take place in time, seeing time was born along with things which exist?" (*Miscellanies*, 6.16). Our days are twenty-four hours long, Saint Augustine wrote, but "we must bear in mind that these days indeed recall the days of creation, but without in any way being really similar to them" (*Gen. Litt.*, 4:27).

The truth of Genesis, however, is not at all in doubt. Genesis may use poetic and figurative language, but the important message that language expresses is clear. The universe is God's creation, and that creation is good. It was creation ex nihilo, out of nothing. Moreover, the creation of man—however it may literally have taken place in time—is a special act by God. Man was created good and given stewardship over creation; he brought evil and disorder into the world by his own disobedience. These truths are basic axioms, so to speak, for the rest of Scripture, and they are fundamental to the Christian faith.

The Church has given some guidelines for understanding the scientific data about cosmic and human origins in light of the biblical doctrine. It has ruled out atheistic evolution—the belief in blind progress unguided by God (see Pius XII, *Humani Generis* 35). And the Church has condemned "polygenism," the belief that mankind descended from multiple ancestors (see *Humani Generis* 37).

The Genesis creation narrative establishes a theological worldview. Its purpose is not scientific, but apologetic, countering the many myths of the ancient Near East. The pagan stories speak of multiple gods, which are somehow embodied in nature; these gods have limitations and needs; the world emerged as a result of a struggle between them; and mankind was created to serve the gods in slavery. Genesis counters this worldview, teaching clearly that there is only one God; that he is not limited by space, time, or nature; that he created the entire cosmos by his mere utterance; and that he made the human race in his own image. The relationship between God and creation is the basis for all the rest of biblical revelation (CCC 337–44).

IV. "A NEW CREATION"

The Old Testament prophets looked forward to a renewal of creation, a time when the land would produce abundantly and people would live in peace, faithful to God's covenant (see, e.g., Isa 4:5, 65:17, 66:22; Jer 31:35–36; Ezek 36:8–11). The OT wisdom literature presents a more developed reflection on the created order (see, e.g., Ps 8, 19, 96; Wis 7–8; Sir 17–18). In the fullness of time, the New Testament presents Christ as a "new Adam" (see **Adam**), the focal point of the long-awaited new creation.

The Gospel of John begins with a restatement of the creation account: "In the beginning was the Word, and the Word was with God, and the Word was God" (John 1:1). So far there is nothing startling in John's interpretation. But several lines later, John tells us something astounding: "And the Word became flesh and dwelt among us" (John 1:14). The Word of God, present at creation, became the man Jesus Christ. The power of God the Father created the universe through the love of God the Son.

Creation began with water and the Spirit: "and the Spirit of God was moving over the face of the waters" (Gen 1:2). Christ told us, "Truly, truly, I say to you, unless one is born of water and the Spirit, he cannot enter the kingdom of God" (John 3:5). The striking parallel suggests that baptism initiates a new creation, and Paul makes the suggestion an explicit statement: "Therefore, if any one is in Christ, he is a new creation; the old has passed away, behold, the new has come" (2 Cor 5:17). "For neither circumcision counts for anything, nor uncircumcision, but a new creation" (Gal 6:15).

Paul tells us that creation has been in "bondage" until the coming of Christ (Rom 8:21). Thus the coming of Christ makes all things new, a promise that will be fulfilled perfectly at the end of time, when "a new heaven and a new earth" (Rev 21:1) will replace the old. But Christians already possess the new creation in baptism; though they live in this world, they are already citizens of the heavenly Jerusalem.

CREMATION *See* **Burial**.

CRESCENS A Christian who accompanied Paul during his Roman imprisonment (2 Tim 4:10); he then went to Galatia.

CRETE The largest island in the Aegean Sea, located south of Greece. The island was the center of the Minoan civilization (ca. 1700–1450 B.C.). In the Old Testament, Crete was known as Caphtor, although the term itself was applied to the wider Aegean region (*see* **Caphtor**). From Caphtor came the so-called Sea Peoples, among whom were the **Philistines**.

A Jewish population on Crete was established by the second century B.C. (Tacitus, *Hist.* 5.2) and enjoyed Roman protection from around 141 B.C. (1 Macc 15:23). There were Jews from Crete in Jerusalem at Pentecost (Acts 2:11). Paul was shipwrecked after sailing from Crete (Acts 27:7, 12) and had suggested that his Roman officers spend the winter there (Acts 27:11–12). He conducted a missionary campaign at some time, perhaps in the middle sixties, and appointed **Titus** to serve as bishop on Crete, to appoint presbyters, and to resist various abuses (Titus 1:5–14).

CRISPUS A Jew of Corinth and head of the synagogue in that city. Crispus and his household were converted through the preaching of Paul (Acts 18:8). According to 1 Corinthians (1:14), Crispus was one of the few people baptized by Paul himself.

CRITICISM, BIBLICAL *and* **LITERARY-HISTORICAL** *See* **Biblical criticism**.

CROCODILE *See* **Leviathan**.

CROSS An instrument of torture and execution reserved by the Romans for the worst criminals (see **Crucifixion**), and the symbol of Christian faith in the redeeming death of Jesus Christ. In the Gospels the Cross is the literal instrument of Jesus's death, but it also takes on the metaphorical meaning of the sacrifices required by faith in Christ: "he who does not take his cross and follow me is not worthy of me" (Matt 10:38). For Paul, the Cross shows the "folly" of human wisdom against God's plan of salvation: "For the word of the cross is folly to those who are perishing, but to us who are being saved it is the power of God" (1 Cor 1:18). Here Paul points out that Christ's death and the Cross are central to the Gospel message. The instrument of shameful execution has become the only legitimate source of Christian pride: "But far be it from me to glory except in the cross of our Lord Jesus Christ" (Gal 6:14).

Early Christian preaching, most likely under the influence of Deut 21:22, referred to the Cross as a "tree" (Acts 5:30; Gal 3:13). That the image of the Cross was prevalent throughout the early Church is noted by Paulinus of Nola and Prudentius, who refer to it in the late 300s as the *signum Christi*, the sign of Christ. That it was a focal point of Christian piety by the 200s was confirmed by Tertullian when he described Christians in the *Apologia* as the *crucis religiosi*, the devotees of the Cross. Because of the persecution of Christians, members of the first Christian communities had to disguise the Cross as another symbol. Anchors, for example, are found on stone slabs in the oldest sections of Christian catacombs; the **anchor** not only symbolizes Christian hope, but also resembles a cross. Another common disguise was the Greek letter *tau* (T). As the Church became more established, eventually triumphing across the Roman world in the 300s A.D., it was possible for depictions of the Cross to be more open, and the Cross became the universal symbol of Christian faith.

CROWN OF THORNS *See* **Thorn.**

CRUCIFIXION Execution by hanging on a cross. The Romans generally reserved the gruesome punishment of crucifixion for criminals, brigands, and slaves; it was long forbidden to execute Roman citizens by this means, as attested by Cicero, who thought it improper for a citizen even to speak about the subject in public discourse. Suetonius and other Roman writers tell us that execution by crucifixion was extended to the lower classes (*humiliores*) at least by the end of the first century A.D.

The manner of crucifixion varied from place to place, depending upon the circumstances and era, but by Roman times the practice was fairly uniform. By consulting various writers, such as Plautus, Plutarch, Josephus, Cicero, Tacitus, Seneca, Lucian, and Pliny, we can put together a fairly accurate picture of the process. The condemned was first scourged and then led to the place of death through the crowds, who would inflict various humiliations upon him. The prisoner was forced to carry the cross along the way—at least the transverse beam on which his arms would be nailed (John 19:17). At the execution site, he was stripped naked and tied to the transverse beam with cords. Four nails were then used to hammer the victim to the wood, one for each hand (or wrist) and each foot, and the weight of the body was supported by a kind of peg. In some cases, the victim's hands were nailed to the transverse beam first, then the beam and victim lifted up to the vertical beam. A *titulus* or sign was then affixed above his head, giving his name and sentence (cf. Matt 27:37; Mark 15:26; Luke 23:38; John 19:19–22). In a set of skeletal remains found some years ago near Jerusalem, nails had been driven through the sides of the ankles, but most experts agree that in this case the victim was still placed on the front of the cross and the legs then placed on either side of the central upright (owing to the way the nails were inserted).

A crucified man might linger for days, slowly withering from the pain and finally expiring from thirst. The Romans left a corpse upon the cross to be food for the birds of prey. In Palestine, however, the dead were removed on the evening of their execution to ensure burial according to the Law (Deut 21:22–23). Soldiers were known to hasten the death of the condemned by breaking their legs, thus causing asphyxiation from the collapse of the lungs (John 19:32). In Rome, the place of execution was Sessorium, beyond the Esquiline Gate. Jerusalem, likewise, had an appointed place for executions—**Golgotha**. (On the theology of the Crucifixion, see **Sacrifice**.)

CUBIT The length from the elbow to the tip of the fingers. The measurement was used not only in ancient Israel, but also in Egypt, Babylon, and Sumer. The cubit was the common unit of measurement in the Old Testament

(Deut 3:11; Josh 3:4; 1 Sam 17:4; 2 Kgs 14:13). The variety of measurements in the OT creates some problems in determining the exact length of a cubit, but the average length was probably about 18 inches or 46 centimeters. For measurements longer than the cubit, it was customary to use the reed (approx. 10½ feet or 3.2 meters).

CUMIN A plant whose seeds are used for spice and relish. The seeds were harvested by beating the plant with a rod (Isa 28:27). A **tithe** was required of even such a relatively insignificant crop under Jewish law. Thus Jesus said of the Pharisees: "For you tithe mint and dill, and cumin, and have neglected the weightier matters of the law: justice and mercy and faith" (Matt 23:23).

CUNEIFORM The most widely used form of writing in the ancient Near East. The name is derived from the wedge (Latin *cuneus*) shapes that are characteristic of cuneiform writing. They were produced by pressing a triangular reed into a soft clay tablet. Once inscribed, the clay tablet was dried in the sun or baked in a furnace, creating a very durable form of communication, so much so that vast libraries of cuneiform documents survive today. First developed around 3000 B.C. by the Sumerians, the cuneiform writing system was used as late as the first century A.D. Many different civilizations adopted it to write their own languages, including the Assyrians, Babylonians, Hittites, Canaanites, Persians, Elamites, and Hurrians. Much of our knowledge of these cultures, all of them important to biblical history, comes from cuneiform documents unearthed by archaeologists.

CUP Both cups and chalices were commonly used in the ancient world for drinking and divination (Gen 44:4–5), but the term also bore a significant metaphorical meaning in Scripture, symbolizing the lot imposed by God upon people and nations. The cup might be a blessing or a curse, depending upon what is deserved.

The cup of God's anger was a metaphor for the intense suffering awaiting the wicked: "a scorching wind shall be the portion of their cup" (Ps 11:6; cf. Ps 75:8); "you who have drunk at the hand of the Lord the cup of his wrath, who have drunk to the dregs the bowl of staggering" (Isa 51:17). A similar image is used to denote the suffering that will be the lot of nations, most notably in Jeremiah with his vivid passages on the "cup of God's wrath" (Jer 25:15–29) from which the evil nations will be compelled to drink: "They shall drink and stagger and go out of their minds because of the sword that I am sending among them" (Jer 25:16; cf. Ezek 23:31–33). In the New Testament, Revelation uses a similar image in the pouring forth of the bowls of wrath (Rev 14:10, 16:19, 18:6). The wicked will be compelled to drink from the cup, as a bitter wine, and the whore is described as holding a cup "full of abominations and the impurities of her fornication" (Rev 17:4).

On the other hand, the image of the cup also symbolizes the lot of the faithful, so that "the Lord is my chosen portion and my cup" (Ps 16:5) who makes his blessings overflow (Ps

23:5). The faithful believer is able to proclaim, "I will lift up the cup of salvation and call on the name of the Lord" (Ps 116:13).

The best-known cup in the NT is the cup that Jesus consecrated at the Last Supper. But Jesus also used the image of a cup to describe his Passion and death. For the sake of sinners, Jesus was willing to drink from the cup of misery, even though he was blameless and was obedient to the divine plan of salvation (John 18:11) (CCC 607).

The theme of the cup in the Gospels is used to demonstrate the willingness of Jesus to accept the burden of redemption. It is the cup of the New Covenant that was anticipated at the Last Supper when Christ offered himself. That the cup will entail Jesus's death is seen in a number of key passages, in particular Matt 20:22–23 and Mark 10:38–39. In the Garden of **Gethsemane**, Jesus prays: "My Father, if it be possible, let this cup pass from me" (Matt 26:39; cf. Mark 14:36; Luke 22:42). Jesus remains obedient to the will of the Father and entrusts himself to the Father's will (Phil 2:8; Heb 5:7–8). He consequently accepted his own redemptive death (CCC 475, 612). (On the cup in the Eucharist, see **Eucharist**; CCC 1334–35, 1365, 1396.)

CURSE Punitive suffering inflicted by a god or other spiritual agent; also, any invocation of suffering upon a person, people, or thing. Curses in Scripture can be brought on in at least three ways:

1. Triggered by the violation of a **covenant**;
2. Invoked upon one or more persons by another;

3. Imposed upon a person or nation by a practitioner of magical or occult arts.

I. CURSES TRIGGERED BY THE VIOLATION OF A COVENANT

At the ratification of a covenant, the curses that will befall the parties should they break the covenant are set forth. The covenant parties acknowledge the judgments they face for violating the terms of the covenant, and frequently invoke conditional curses upon themselves (Neh 10:29; Matt 26:74; Acts 23:12). Curses are thus threats to deter the parties from breaking the covenant.

In salvation history, the people's infidelity to the covenant with God brings curses; fidelity to it, on the other hand, brings blessing. Both Lev 26:14–39 and Deut 28:15–68 list the curses that would befall Israel if the people were unfaithful to the covenant oath. Anyone who broke the covenant did so knowing the consequences (Judg 21:18).

II. CURSES INVOKED BY ANOTHER

Cursing was a serious matter, and placing curses upon the innocent or undeserving was always prohibited. Some forms of cursing were punishable by death, such as cursing one's parents (Exod 21:17; Lev 20:9), the handicapped (Lev 19:14), an anointed king (2 Sam 16:9), and especially God (Lev 24:15–16). Curses might, however, be justifiably pronounced on wicked people or places, such as the curse of Joshua on Jericho and the Gibeonites (Josh 6:26, 9:23; cf. Gen 9:25, 49:7; Mal 1:14). The curses of God were always manifestations of his justice: thus God cursed the **serpent** (Gen 3:14), the enemies of Abraham (Gen 12:3), and the ground, owing to man's **Fall** (Gen 3:17; 5:29). (*See also* **Mercy**.)

III. CURSES IMPOSED BY A MAGICIAN OR SORCEROR

Certain practitioners of magic were supposed to possess the ability to impose especially powerful curses. For example, Balak, king of Moab, hired the seer **Balaam** to curse Israel (Num 22:5), but Balaam, following the word of the Lord, blessed the Israelites instead.

IV. CURSES IN THE NEW TESTAMENT

In the New Testament, the curse is seen against the backdrop of the new age brought by Christ. Jesus taught his disciples, "Bless those who curse you" (Luke 6:28; Rom 12:14). Paul tells us that Christ redeemed us from the curse of death by becoming himself a curse on the cross (Gal 3:13), and Rev 22:3 assures us that Christ has brought an end to "the curse"—sin, disease, and death—that had first been imposed on account of Adam and Eve's breaking the first covenant.

CUSH *See* **Ethiopia**.

CUSHAN-RISHATHAIM The king of upper Mesopotamia. He is mentioned only once, in Judg 3:7–11. According to the account, Cushan-Rishathaim oppressed the Israelites for eight years until Othniel, the first of the Judges, delivered Israel from his oppression.

CUSHI The father of the prophet Zephaniah (Zeph 1:1).

CUTH A city in Mesopotamia, north of Babylon (2 Kgs 17:30; appears as "Cuthnah" in 1 Kgs 17:24). Cuth was the cultic center of the Mesopotamian god of the underworld, Nergal. When Assyrians conquered the city, the inhabitants were forcibly deported to Samaria by King Sargon II (2 Kgs 17:24). There they continued to worship Nergal (2 Kgs 17:30).

CYMBAL A percussion instrument that was used for musical accompaniment in Israelite liturgy (2 Sam 6:5; 1 Chr 13:8; 15:16, 28; 16:5; 25:6; 2 Chr 5:12, 29:25; Neh 12:27). The book of Psalms stresses the use of cymbals in praising the Lord: "Praise him with clanging cymbals; praise him with loud clashing cymbals!" (Ps 150:5).

CYPRESS A tree native to the region of Palestine, in particular Lebanon (Isa 41:19; 60:13). Several different Hebrew words seem to refer to this tree, although the RSV normally uses "cypress" for the word *běrôš* (at times, "fir" is also used). Cypress was used by Solomon in the building of the Temple (1 Kgs 5:8, 10; 2 Chr 3:5) and was used elsewhere in the ancient Near East for furniture, shipbuilding, and musical instruments.

CYPRUS An island in the eastern Mediterranean, the third-largest island in the Mediterranean, after Sicily and Sardinia. The name Cyprus was derived from the island's copper mines (Greek *kupros*). In the Old Testament, the Hebrew for the people of Cyprus is *Kittîm* (Ezek 27:6), a word also used for Greeks (Gen 10:4) and Romans (Dan 11:30). The name Cyprus is used in Isa 23:1. From an early time, there was a Jewish community in Cyprus (1 Macc 15:23). The island was under the control of the Ptolemies from 294 to 58 B.C. and then passed into Roman control. The island was attached to the Roman province of Cilicia under the authority of a proconsul (Acts 13:7). The Gospel arrived there through the preaching of Christians from Jerusalem who had fled the city after the martyrdom of Stephen (Acts 11:19–20). Cyprus was Paul's first destination on his first missionary tour, and he and Barnabas preached there at the cities of Salamis and Paphos (Acts 13:4–13). Barnabas then returned with Mark after he parted company from Paul (Acts 15:39).

CYRENE The chief city of the Roman province of Cyrenaica (modern Libya) in North Africa. The city was founded by Greek colonists from the island of Thera around 630 B.C. and took its name from the goddess Kyrana. Cyrene fell to Alexander the Great in 331 B.C., passed to the Ptolemies, and then was claimed by the Romans, who established it as part of the province of Cyrenaica. There was a Jewish community at Cyrene from the time of Ptolemy I (1 Macc 15:23; 2 Macc 2:23), and the Jews of Cyrene had their own synagogue in Jerusalem (Acts 6:9) and were present in Jerusalem on the day of Pentecost (Acts 2:10). Simon of Cyrene, most likely a pilgrim to the Passover in Jerusalem, was forced by the Roman soldiers to help carry Jesus's cross (Matt 27:32; Mark 15:21; Luke 23:26). Lucius of Cyrene (Acts 13:1) was a prophet and teacher in the Christian community of Antioch.

CYRUS THE GREAT (Persian *kurash*, "shepherd") Founder of the Persian Empire (*see* **Persia**) and ruler from 559 to 529 B.C. The son of Cambyses (600–559 B.C.), he inherited the throne of Anshan, which was then a vassal of the more powerful **Medes**, in 559 B.C. He immediately sought to free himself of the domination of the Medes by allying himself with King Nabonidus of Babylon and launching a rebellion against Astyages, king of the Medes. With the help of Astyages's own ministers, Cyrus succeeded in capturing Ecbatana, defeating Astyages, and reducing Media to the position of being a satrapy within the now wider Persian Empire. Alarmed by the sudden emergence of a united Median and Persian state in the Near East, King Croesus of Lydia forged an alliance with Babylon and Egypt. Cyrus set off against the alliance. He captured the capital of Lydia, Sardis, in 547 B.C. along with its king, and then seized the various Greek cities along the coast of Asia Minor. By these campaigns, he extended the Persian Empire westward across Anatolia. In 546 B.C., he turned on Babylon, his conquests culminating in the fall of Babylon in 539 B.C. He was killed in 529 B.C. in battle against Tomyris, queen of the Massagetae.

Cyrus's meteoric ascent was accompanied by an equally striking departure from the customs of the Near Eastern rulers who had preceded him. He preferred an enlightened policy of ingratiation rather than the old tactic of intimidation. Rather than force wholesale migrations of defeated peoples—as the Assyrians and Babylonians had done—Cyrus instead treated vassal states with respect and even permitted the repatriation of deported people. He issued a decree in 538 B.C. permitting the Jews to return to their homeland (*see* **Exile**). His terms were very generous: he sponsored and financed the rebuilding of the Temple and ordered the vessels plundered by Nebuchadnezzar to be returned to Jerusalem (2 Chr 36:22; Ezra 1:1–7). The text of the edict is presented in Ezra 6:3–5. Honored by the Babylonians for allowing them to restore the worship of the god Marduk (they had been forced to worship the god Sin under Nabonidus), Cyrus was even more highly esteemed by the liberated Jews. Isaiah strikingly calls Cyrus the Lord's anointed (Isa 45:1)—that is, the **Messiah** or Christ, a title that previous writers had reserved for the kings of Israel, and that New Testament writers would apply to Jesus. Cyrus, whose name meant "shepherd" in Persian, accomplished the will of God (Isa 44:28), beginning the redemption of God's people from captivity (Isa 41:2–5, 25; 44:24, 28; 45:1–5, 13; 48:14–15). Cyrus was a Solomon figure who commissioned the rebuilding of the Temple that Solomon had built, and when Ezra points out that the new Temple would be built of Lebanon cedar floated down to the port of Joppa (Ezra 3:7), the returned exiles would have remembered that most of the building supplies for Solomon's original Temple were procured in the same way (see 1 Kgs 5:7–12; 2 Chr 2:16).

D The abbreviation for the "Deuteronomic" source in the "documentary hypothesis" postulated in the nineteenth century. In that theory, the letters J, E, D, and P each represent an ancient source document incorporated into the Pentateuch, and D is the primary source for the book of Deuteronomy. (For a discussion of the JEDP division, see **Pentateuch**.)

DAGON A Semitic agricultural god worshipped by the **Philistines** (Judg 16:23; 1 Sam 5:2). Adopted from the Amorites and the Assyrians, Dagon had numerous temples among the Philistines (1 Sam 5:1–7; Judg 16:23; 1 Chr 10:10; 1 Macc 10:83–84, 11:4), including a large and magnificent one at Gaza.

In Judg 16:23–30, the blinded captive **Samson** is brought into the temple of Dagon at Gaza to entertain several thousand worshippers. In a final show of superhuman strength, he brings down the entire temple, killing himself and "all the lords of the Philistines."

After its capture at the battle of Aphek, the **ark of the covenant** was placed by the Philistines in the temple of Dagon at Ashdod. The idol of the god was discovered facedown on the floor the next morning. Restored to its proper place, the idol was again discovered prostrate

the next morning, only this time it was broken (1 Sam 5:4). This temple was eventually destroyed by **Jonathan Maccabeus** (1 Macc 10:83; 11:4).

DALETH The fourth letter (ד) of the Hebrew alphabet. It has the numeric value of four.

DALMANUTHA A town or region on the shore of the Sea of Galilee (Mark 8:10). The name is not known outside the New Testament. Jesus and the disciples visited Dalmanutha after the second miracle of the loaves; as it was reached by boat it must have been on the coast of the Sea of Galilee. Important manuscripts of the parallel verse in Matt 15:39 read "**Magdala**," which suggests a place on the northwest shore.

DALMATIA A Roman province on the eastern shore of the Adriatic Sea, roughly corresponding to modern coastal Croatia and Bosnia-Herzegovina. The region passed into Roman hands in 228 B.C. but local tribes continued to resist the Romans for a long time. The name Dalmatia was derived from the warlike tribes of the area, the Delmatae or Dalmatae. By the first century A.D., Dalmatia was attached to the Roman province of **Illyricum**. Paul preached as far as Illyricum (Rom 15:19) and may have sent **Titus** to Dalmatia (2 Tim 4:10).

DALPHON One of the ten sons of Haman, vizier of King Ahasuerus (Esth 9:7). He was executed for plotting to murder Jewish exiles in Persia.

DAMARIS An Athenian woman converted by Paul (Acts 17:34) during his stay in Athens. According to Saint John Chrysostom, she was the wife of Dionysius the Areopagite, who is mentioned in the same passage.

DAMASCUS One of the chief cities of Syria, located on a fertile plain fed by the Abana (modern Barada) and Pharpar rivers (2 Kgs 5:12) on the frontiers of the Syrian desert. The city is an ancient one whose origins are obscure; its location on the major trade routes made it one of the region's most thriving and important commercial centers. It was the capital of the Aramean kingdom during the tenth to the eighth centuries B.C. and thus had many dealings with the kingdom of Israel, at times hostile (cf. 1 Kgs 15:18–20, 19:15, 20:22; 2 Kgs 5–7, 8:7–15, 10:32–33). With the advance of **Assyria**, however, Damascus entered into alliance with other Near Eastern states, including Israel. The Assyrians were checked temporarily at the battle of Qarqar in 853 B.C. (*see* **Ben-hadad**). Assyria proved unstoppable, however, and Damascus fell to **Tiglath-pileser III** around 732 B.C. and was annexed to the empire (2 Kgs 16:9; Isa 7:8, 8:14, 17; Jer 49:23; Amos 1:5). It passed under the control

of succeeding empires, including **Babylon**, **Persia**, **Alexander the Great**, and the **Seleucids** (1 Macc 11:62; 12:32). After the collapse of the Seleucid Empire, the city came under the control of the Nabateans. When Pompey the Great established the Roman province of Syria in 63 B.C., he allowed the Nabateans to govern Damascus. The city finally passed into direct Roman control only in the middle of the first century A.D.

When **Paul** was in Damascus, the city was subject to King Aretas of Nabatea (2 Cor 11:32). The Christian community had been founded there only a few years after the Crucifixion, and it grew so quickly that Paul (called Saul) was on his way to persecute the Christians of Damascus when he underwent his remarkable conversion. Blinded by the glory of Christ on the road to Damascus, he was led to the Straight Street in Damascus to the home of Judas, where Ananias baptized him and ended his blindness. When he preached the Gospel in the city, his life was threatened, and he escaped over the wall in a basket (Acts 9:1–25).

DAN The fifth son of Jacob, born of Bilhah, Rachel's handmaid (Gen 30:6, 35:25, 46:23; Exod 1:4), the maternal brother of Naphtali, and the ancestor of the tribe of Dan (Gen 49:16). At the time of the Exodus, the Danites numbered 62,700 fighting men (Num 1:12, 38, 39). Dan was blessed by Moses as "a lion's whelp" (Deut 33:22).

Once in the Promised Land, the Danites settled in the area around Zorah and Eshtaol in the **Shephelah** (Josh 19:40–48), along the Palestinian coast. The Amorite inhabitants resisted the movement toward the coast (Judg

1:34), and additional pressures were created by the Philistines. Compelled to relocate, the Danites resettled in northern Israel (Judg 17–18) and took Laish as their chief city, later renamed Dan (Josh 19:40–48)—an event scholars call the "Danite migration." Dan became the northernmost territory of the land of Israel, and "from Dan to Beer-sheba" was a common way of referring to all of Israel from north to south (Judg 20:1; 1 Sam 3:20; 2 Sam 24:2; 2 Chr 30:5). Samson was a member of the tribe of Dan (Judg 13:2–24).

DANCING In the Old Testament, dancing was an expression of joy and worship. It was often accompanied by song and musical instruments (Judg 21:21; 1 Sam 18:6; Eccl 3:4; Jer 31:12–13). Ritual dancing accompanied the Lord's victory at the Red Sea (Exod 15:20) and the celebrations in honor of the **ark of the covenant** (2 Sam 6:12–16; 1 Chr 13:1–14, 15:1–29). Dance was also part of victory marches and triumphs, or the return of heroes (Judg 11:34; 1 Sam 18:6; Jdt 15:12–13).

On the other hand, the dancing performed before the golden calf (Exod 32:18–19) was a perverse expression of festive joy—dancing not to honor God but to worship idols and induce licentious behavior.

In the New Testament, dancing is noted at various celebrations, including birthdays (Matt 14:6; Mark 6:21–22), family gatherings (Luke 15:25), and weddings (Matt 11:17).

DANIEL (Hebrew, "God judges") The name of three men in the Old Testament, of whom the first is by far the best known.

1. The hero of the book of Daniel. Daniel is presented in the account as a youth of a noble Judahite family who was also noted for his intellectual gifts. In 605 B.C., he was deported to Babylonia (Dan 1:1–7). There he was taken into the palace of Nebuchadnezzar and educated in the ways and language of the Chaldeans, along with three other Jews: Abednego, Meshach, and Shadrach.

By correctly recounting and interpreting the dream of **Nebuchadnezzar** (Dan 2:1–45), Daniel earned himself a high position in the court of Babylon (Dan 2:46–48). He continued to interpret the king's dreams (Dan 4:19–27). Like Joseph before him (cf. Gen 40:1–41:38), Daniel revealed to the ruler the meaning of his dreams, and that the dreams revealed the mystery of the Kingdom of God (Dan 3:13–4:34).

Years later, at the end of the reign of **Belshazzar**, Daniel interpreted the mysterious writing that appeared on the walls of a banquet hall during a feast and that proclaimed the impending fall of the Babylonian Empire in 539 B.C. (Dan 5:1–6:1). The deuterocanonical material in the Greek version of Daniel includes an account of Daniel saving Susanna from accusations of adultery by three lecherous men (Dan 13) and his encounter with the priests of the god Bel (Dan 14)—stories that vividly demonstrate his practical intelligence as well as his righteousness. Daniel remained in Babylon until 538 B.C. and the reign of Cyrus.

As a prophet, Daniel received divine wisdom from an angel of God to comprehend the mystery of the divine plan in history (Dan 9:22; 10:12). He was given a series of visions

(Dan 7:1–12:13) that demonstrated a concern not only for the world but for God's providential designs for history (Dan 7:9–27). Daniel's visions thus included vivid depictions of the passing away of the earthly kings and tyrants and the triumph of the Son of Man in receiving an eternal Messianic Kingdom (Dan 7:21–27). Finally, Daniel was granted a vision of the resurrection of the body (Dan 12:2–3). These eschatological hopes made Daniel a key figure among the OT prophets. In proclaiming the Son of Man and the Kingdom of God, Daniel laid important groundwork for understanding the Resurrection and Ascension of Christ (cf. Mark 1:15, 8:27–33, 11:10; John 5:28–29; Acts 1:9, 7:55–56; Col 1:18; 1 Cor 15:1–58; Rom 8:29), and ultimately the **Parousia** (Mark 14:62; Rev 14:14). (*See* **Daniel, book of**.)

2. David's second son (1 Chr 3:1), born to his royal wife Abigail in Hebron. His name is given in 2 Samuel 3:3 as Chileab. As he did not appear in any of the struggles surrounding the royal succession, it is assumed that Daniel died at an early age or was disqualified from future kingship because of some mental or physical handicap.

3. A postexilic figure from the priestly line of **Ithamar** (Ezra 8:2). He was among the leaders in Jerusalem who put their seal on the covenant-renewal document encouraged by **Ezra**.

DANIEL, BOOK OF One of the prophetic books of the Old Testament, the last of the four "major prophets." Daniel recounts the story of **Daniel**, a young Jew who was taken to Babylon in 605 B.C., where he lived for most or all of his life. The stories recount the trials and triumphs of Daniel and his three companions. The book is both apocalyptic and prophetic in the way it envisions the future glory of Israel and conveys the message that people of faith can resist temptation and overcome adversity. In the Hebrew canon, the book is listed among the "Writings" rather than the "Prophets," along with 1 and 2 Chronicles, Ezra, Nehemiah, Job, Psalms, Proverbs, Ecclesiastes, Lamentations, Song of Songs, Ruth, and Esther. Although some of its visions are obscure, the primary themes are understandable: right conduct, divine control of men and events, and the final triumph of the kingdom.

Parts of Daniel come to us in all three languages of the Bible: **Hebrew**, **Aramaic**, and **Greek**. The book begins in Hebrew but changes suddenly to Aramaic at 2:4. A long prayer in Greek comes between 3:23 and 3:24. Then the Aramaic continues through 7:28; after that, Hebrew is used again for 8:1–12:13. Chapters 13 and 14 are entirely in Greek, though it is likely they were translated from Semitic originals. In modern rabbinic Judaism, the Greek sections, referred to as the Additions to Daniel, are considered apocryphal; Protestants generally follow the modern Jewish canon. The Catholic and Orthodox churches, however, accept the Greek sections as **deuterocanonical**, and their canonicity was affirmed by the Council of Trent in 1546.

I. *Authorship and Date*
  A. *The Second-Century Theory*
  B. *The Sixth-Century Theory*
II. *Contents*

I. AUTHORSHIP AND DATE

Ancient Jewish and Christian tradition holds that Daniel was written by the prophet Daniel himself in the sixth century B.C. Many scholars accept this tradition, but many others argue for a more recent date in the second century B.C.

A. The Second-Century Theory

Scholars who accept the second-century theory believe that the author of Daniel was an unknown Jew who probably composed his work around 165 B.C. If that assumption is true, then the work reflects the oppression of the Jewish people under the **Seleucid** Empire, in particular Antiochus IV Epiphanes (r. 175–163 B.C.). The struggle of the **Maccabees**, then, would be the context for the book's composition. The four empires mentioned in the work (chapters 2 and 7) are often identified as **Babylon**, the **Medes**, **Persia**, and the Seleucids (instead of the traditional interpretation, which sees them as Babylon, Persia, Greece, and **Rome**; see "Interpreting the Visions" below). In this view, the author compiled ancient traditions, reworking and adapting them to speak to the events of his own time. It is certainly true that the book gave great encour-agement to the Jews during the period of the Maccabean revolt (cf. 1 Macc 2:59–60).

B. The Sixth-Century Theory

On the other hand, the traditional view of authorship and date is not without support. The narrator identifies himself with Daniel and sometimes speaks in the first person, as in Dan 8:1–4, and Jesus in Matt 24:15 recalls the words spoken "by the prophet Daniel." In addition, in the text there are many details of proven historical value regarding the Babylonians, such as the internal workings of the Babylonian Empire and that Belshazzar was coruler of Babylon during the reign of Nabonidus—a fact that was not otherwise known until relatively modern times. Finally, the Aramaic language in Dan 2:4–7:28 is striking in its similarity to that found in Ezra (4:7–6:18; 7:12–26) and the Elephantine Papyri of the fifth century B.C. All of these indications point, some scholars suggest, to a dating well before the Maccabean period and thus leave open the possibility that Daniel may have been the author, or at least that the book dates from the sixth century B.C.

II. CONTENTS

III. PURPOSE AND THEMES

A. *The Faith of Daniel and His Friends*

The first six chapters, written in the third person, follow the adventures of Daniel. He is introduced as one of the Jewish youths who had been deported to Babylon by King Nebuchadnezzar "in the third year of the reign of Jehoiakim king of Judah" (Dan 1:1). Daniel and his friends Hananiah, Azariah, and Mishael—renamed Shadrach, Meshach, and Abednego—enter the service of the royal household. Daniel distinguishes himself for his ability to interpret dreams and mysterious signs (chaps. 2, 4, and 5), such as Nebuchadnezzar's dream of the statue and the famed writing on the wall (*see* **Mene, Mene, Tekel, Peres**). His three friends are thrown into a furnace for refusing to worship an idol, but escape unharmed (chap. 3). A Greek addition, "The Prayer of Azariah and the Hymn of the Three Young Men," is either distinguished from the rest of the chapter and given a separate versification (vv. 1–68), or it is incorporated into chapter 3, with the first verse of the song being verse 24. This section is preserved in the Greek of the **Septuagint**

(*see* **Deuterocanonical**). Daniel similarly refuses divine worship to Darius, and is thrown into the lions' den; he, too, emerges unharmed (chap. 6).

B. *Apocalyptic Visions*

The second part, chapters 7–12, present a series of revelations that are granted to Daniel; most of this section is written in the first person. Some of the visions are explained by an angel: the four beasts (7:1–28); the ram and the goat (8:1–27); the Seventy Weeks (9:1–27); the conflict of the Nations (10:1–11:45); and the vision of the End (12:1–13).

Daniel 7. In a vision that repeats some of the themes of Nebuchadnezzar's dream (chap. 2), Daniel sees four beasts rising from the sea. They signify four great Gentile empires that will hold dominion over Israel, but that will be judged in time by "the Ancient of days" and replaced by the universal and everlasting kingdom of God.

Daniel 8. The angel Gabriel explains the vision of the ram and the goat: the animals represent earthly empires. The ram with two horns signifies the Medes and the Persians, who advance toward the west, north, and south, until crushed by the goat (the king of Greece) with a great horn (Alexander) between its eyes. The great horn is soon broken, however, and succeeded by four others (suggesting the successor states of Egypt, Syria, Macedonia, and Thrace); from the Syrian kingdom comes the "little horn," Antiochus IV Epiphanes.

Daniel 9. Daniel next "perceived in the books the number of years that, according to the word of the Lord to the prophet Jeremiah, must be fulfilled for the devastation of Jerusalem, namely, seventy years" (9:2). The prophecy of 70 weeks of years is divided into three periods of seven, 62, and one weeks of years, respectively. The first period, one of seven weeks (or 49 years) stretches from the permission to rebuild Jerusalem to the "time of an anointed prince." During the second period, of 62 weeks or 434 years, the Holy City will "be built again with streets and moat, but in a troubled time." After the 62 weeks, an anointed one (Messiah) shall be cut off and the forces of "the prince who is to come shall destroy the city and the sanctuary . . . He shall make a strong covenant with many for one week, and for half of the week he shall make sacrifice and offering cease" until he meets his fate.

Daniel 10–11. The final vision, of the conflict of the nations (10:1–11:45), contains a detailed summary of the events involving the Medes, Persians, and Greeks. Chapter 11 describes the principal events concerning four Persian kings, Alexander and his successors, and the actions of Antiochus Epiphanes.

Daniel 12. The visions climax with a time of great tribulation and the end of all things. The prophecy includes a clear statement of the resurrection of the dead: "Many of those who sleep in the dust of the earth shall awake, some to everlasting life, and some to shame and everlasting contempt" (12:2). Two numbers are given at the very conclusion. For 1,290 days, or three and a half years, daily sacrifices will cease and the abomination of desolation will be established, but "Blessed is he who perseveres and attains the thousand three hundred thirty-five days."

C. The Further Adventures of Daniel

At the end of the book come a few further adventures of Daniel; these chapters, again, are preserved only in the Greek Septuagint. Chapter 13 presents the story of Susanna, a Jewish woman living in Babylon who is falsely accused of adultery by two lechers and is saved by Daniel in a clever legal stratagem. (The story of Susanna is placed as chapter 13 in the **Vulgate** and in versions that follow the Vulgate, but in the Septuagint it comes at the beginning as a sort of preface to the book.) Chapter 14 includes two stories. In the first, Daniel proves to the Persian king Cyrus that the food placed before the image of Bel is secretly eaten by the priests. In the second, Daniel kills a crocodile worshipped at Babylon, which causes him to be thrown into the lions' den again; once again, he is delivered by the LORD unharmed. These stories show Daniel's God-given wisdom at work, and they demonstrate again the folly of idolatry and the providential care of God for his faithful people in adversity.

IV. INTERPRETING THE VISIONS

A. Identifying the Four Empires

The visions of Daniel 2 and 7 depict a succession of four empires having dominion over Israel and the ancient Near East. At the end of this sequence, after the four Gentile powers have come and gone, the prophet envisions the kingdom of God being forever established in history and spreading throughout the world. Identifying the four kingdoms is necessary to ascertain the time of the vision's fulfillment.

Those who date the book of Daniel in the second century B.C. generally list the four empires as (1) Babylonia, (2) Media, (3) Persia, and (4) Greece. On this reading, the climax of the divine plan reveals itself in history with the downfall of the Seleucid Greek ruler, Antiochus IV Epiphanes, and the success of the Maccabean revolt, which liberated Israel from the yoke of Gentile oppression for the first time in centuries. Despite the popularity of this interpretation in modern times, it is difficult to square with the facts of history. For example, Media never really attained the status of an empire, and it did not succeed Babylonia as a ruling power. Media fell to the Persians and essentially became part of the Persian Empire in 550 B.C., more than ten years before Babylon was even conquered (539 B.C.). Beyond this, regaining Israel's temporary independence from foreign rule, made possible by the efforts of the Maccabees, seems like a far cry from the grandiose vision of an everlasting kingdom that stretches throughout the world.

Those who date the book of Daniel in the sixth century B.C. generally configure the list of the four empires as (1) Babylonia, (2) Medo-Persia, (3) Greece, and (4) Rome. This is a traditional scheme that is not only held by some modern scholars but is also attested in several ancient Jewish and Christian sources. According to the Christian interpretation, the four empires are followed not by the Maccabean (Hasmonean) Dynasty in Israel but by the Messianic Kingdom established by Jesus Christ and spread throughout the world by the missionary efforts of the Church. In its favor is the historical fact that Media and Persia were merged into a single entity before the fall of Babylon (reflected in Dan 5:28, 6:12, and 8:20). Likewise, the unparalleled strength of the fourth empire (see, e.g., Dan 7:7) fits better the mighty Roman Empire than the historical kingdom of Greece, which fractured into four parts soon after it was founded and never regained its unity. The traditional scheme is thus adopted in this article.

B. Historical Background

The Kingdom of Judah fell in the early sixth century B.C.; there followed the destruction of the **Temple** and the **Exile**. Under the Persian king **Cyrus the Great**, whose rise brought an end to the Babylonian Empire in 539 B.C., some of the exiles returned to Jerusalem, and work began on restoring the Temple. Nevertheless, Israel would still be dominated, as Daniel foretells, by giant empires—first Babylon during the Exile, and then Persia, Greece, and Rome. Politically subservient, Israel would turn to her faith in the true God as the thing that made her unique among the nations. The long years of servitude would be a time of great spiritual renewal. Daniel sees the subjection of God's people as preparing them for the Kingdom of God.

C. Visions of the Future

In Daniel 2, Nebuchadnezzar dreams of a statue: "The head of that statue was of fine gold, its chest and arms of silver, its middle and thighs of bronze, its legs of iron, its feet partly of iron and partly of clay" (Dan 2:32–33). A stone from a mountain strikes the statue, shatters it into pieces, and grows to a mountain that "filled the whole earth" (2:34–35). In the dream as interpreted by Daniel, the statue's four sections are four great empires, and the stone is the Kingdom of God: it will prevail over the earthly kingdoms, and it will endure forever (2:36–45).

In Daniel 7, Daniel himself has a night vision whose message is the same as Nebuchadnezzar's. He sees four beasts, and again these are the four Gentile empires that dominate Israel—the lion is Babylon, the bear is Persia, the leopard is Greece, and the monster is Rome. Then comes "one like a son of man" whose "dominion is an everlasting dominion, which shall not pass away, and his kingdom one that shall not be destroyed" (7:14; *see* **Son of Man**).

It is apparent that the stone in Nebuchadnezzar's dream is the Son of Man in Daniel's, and that the mountain that fills the whole earth is the eternal kingdom of the Son of Man. With the coming of the Son of Man, the Messianic Kingdom will be established.

Chapter 9 provides the timetable for these events. Time is needed for Israel to atone for her transgressions. The angel Gabriel announces that the time will be 70 weeks of years: in other words, 490 years (70×7) would pass before Israel atoned for her sins. In that time, the four empires would rise and fall one after another, the fourth one seeing the Kingdom of God established on earth. At the end of the period of atonement will come two important events: "An anointed one shall be cut off"; and Jerusalem and its Temple will be destroyed (9:26).

Christians see these two events as the Crucifixion of Christ ("Christ" is the Greek translation of "Anointed One"; *see* **Messiah**) and the destruction of Jerusalem and the Temple in A.D. 70. Jesus Christ is the "Son of Man" whose

kingdom shall have no end; his Church is his kingdom, the stone that toppled the statue and grew to fill the whole earth.

DAPHNE A suburb of Antioch that hosted a temple of Apollo and Artemis with rights of sanctuary, according to Strabo (*Geography* 16.2.6). In 2 Macc 4:33, the deposed high priest Onias III took refuge from his enemy, the high priest Menelaus, in the Daphne sanctuary. He was eventually lured away from the refuge and assassinated by Adronicus at the prompting of Menelaus.

DARDA One of the wise men listed in 1 Kgs 4:31. His wisdom was reputedly surpassed only by that of Solomon. His father was Mahol.

DARIC A gold coin of Persia (Ezra 2:69; Neh 7:70–72) that was first struck by Darius I (r. 522–486 B.C.). (*See* **Money**.)

DARIUS The name of three kings of Persia: Darius I Hystaspes, the Great (r. 522–486 B.C.), Darius II Nothos (r. 423–404 B.C.), and Darius III Codomannus (r. 336–330 B.C.). Only the first of these is mentioned in the Bible (but see also **Darius the Mede**).

Darius I came to the throne in 522 B.C. Once secure in power, he undertook an aggressive reform of the Persian Empire. He organized twenty satrapies (governorships) and placed his own image on the gold coin that came to be called the Daric. Around 520 B.C. Darius started construction of a grand capital at Persepolis.

In secular history, Darius I is best known for his campaigns against Greece. His massive army marched against the Ionian cities and ended the Ionian revolt (499–494 B.C.), during which the Greek cities of Asia Minor fought to regain their independence. His fleet was wrecked by a storm off the Greek coast in 492 B.C. After his bloody triumph at the famed battle of Thermopylae, Darius was defeated by the Athenians at the equally famous battle of Marathon in 480 B.C., an event that curbed for a time Persian ambitions in southern Greece.

Darius renewed the order of **Cyrus** for the Jews to rebuild the Temple at Jerusalem (Ezra 4:25), and the work ended in the sixth year of his reign (Ezra 6:15). He was also mentioned as "Darius the Persian" in Neh 12:22, and during his time both **Zechariah** and **Haggai** were active in the prophetic labors (Hag 1:1, 15; 2:10; Zech 1:1, 7:1).

DARIUS THE MEDE Successor of the slain king Belshazzar as ruler of Babylon after the conquest of the city in 539 B.C. He is mentioned only in the book of Daniel, which states that Darius was a "Mede" by birth who became "king" over the ancient region of Babylonia (Dan 9:1). He came to this office at the advanced age of "sixty-two" (Dan 5:31) and soon appointed "one hundred and twenty satraps" over his kingdom (Dan 6:1).

Darius the Mede is unknown to history outside the book of Daniel. This has given rise to differing perspectives on his identity and his very existence. Critical scholars tend to regard this figure either as a fictional character, representing the kingdom of Media as distinct from Persia, or consider the matter a case of mistaken identity, the author of Daniel having confused him with Darius I Hystaspes,

king of Persia from 522 to 486 B.C. Conservative scholars generally accept the historicity of Darius the Mede based on the witness of the book of Daniel. However, there are difficulties in squaring the information in Daniel with other information about the Persian conquest of Babylon from secular sources. Twentieth-century scholarship proposed several solutions that would align the biblical and nonbiblical data into a coherent historical picture. Three solutions have dominated the discussion, and each involves identifying Darius the Mede with a prominent person known to history under a different name:

1. *The Gubaru solution.* Some scholars identify Darius the Mede with Gubaru, who was the governor of Babylon under King Cyrus the Great of Persia and the satrap of the Persian province called Beyond-the-River. This figure wielded king-like authority under Cyrus, though he was not a monarch in the strict sense. Nevertheless, the Hebrew term for "king" can at times denote a "ruler" of lesser rank. According to advocates, this would make sense of the passive expression used in Dan 9:1, which seems to imply that Darius the Mede was installed by some higher authority (i.e., King Cyrus).

2. *The Cyrus solution.* Other scholars identify Darius the Mede with the Persian king Cyrus himself. This too would fit the description in Daniel, which speaks of Darius in royal terms, and it coheres well with extrabiblical sources, which make Cyrus the successor of Belshazzar as king of Babylon. It is even possible that the Hebrew conjunction translated "and" in Dan 6:28 is explicative ("namely") rather than conjunctive ("and"), thus identify-

ing Darius the Mede and Cyrus the Persian as one and the same person. Interestingly, some evidence suggests that King Cyrus descended from the royal families of both Media (mother's side) and Persia (father's side).

3. *The Ugbaru solution.* Still other scholars identify Darius the Mede with the elderly general Ugbaru, whose tactical genius led the Persians to victory over Babylon. This identification fits nicely with the advanced age of Darius (Dan 5:31). It could also explain why Darius is only mentioned in connection with the "first year" of Cyrus's reign over Babylon (Dan 9:1), since General Ugbaru lived only a short time after the fall of the city. Moreover, evidence indicates that Cyrus never adopted the title "king of Babylon" for himself until near the end of his first year of rule.

None of these solutions has created a consensus opinion among conservative scholars. Each has its strengths, and each has its weaknesses. For the time being, at least, the biblical figure Darius the Mede remains something of a mystery. It is hoped that a future discovery by archaeologists or historians will come forth to shed light on the precious little we know of him from the book of Daniel.

DATE *See* **Palm tree**.

DATHAN Son of Eliab of the tribe of Reuben. With Abiram, Korah, and 250 leaders of Israel, he conspired to rebel against the leadership of Moses and Aaron in the wilderness (Num 16:1–33; 26:9). Korah and his followers rebelled against the religious authority of Aaron and Moses (Num 16:3); Dathan and Abiram seem to have rebelled more against the secular power of Moses (Num 16:13–14). The rebellion was a long-remembered symbol of Israel's continual rebellion against God (cf. Deut 11:6; Ps 106:17; Sir 45:18). The conspirators were swallowed up by the earth for their flagrant insubordination.

DATHEMA A fortress city in Gilead, east of the Jordan; the exact location is uncertain. During the Maccabean revolt, Jews fled to the fortress to escape the persecution and reprisals of the Seleucids (1 Macc 5:9). They were then besieged, and called for aid from Judas Maccabeus. He arrived and broke the siege (1 Macc 5:24–34).

DAUGHTER OF ZION *See* **Zion, daughter of**.

DAVID The second and greatest king of Israel, whose forty-year reign and whose covenant with God made him the supreme model of kingship for all of his successors. In salvation history, David is both God's chosen king and a **type** of the future **Messiah**.

I. *Early Life*
   A. *The Genealogy of David*
   B. *David Is Anointed*
   C. *His Growing Reputation Attracts Saul's Jealousy*
   D. *On the Run from Saul*
II. *King of Israel*
   A. *Civil War for the Succession*
   B. *David Establishes His Rule*
   C. *David as Religious Leader*
   D. *David's Sin*
   E. *His Troubled Later Reign*

I. EARLY LIFE

A. The Genealogy of David

David was the youngest son of **Jesse** of **Bethlehem** (1 Sam 17:12–14), one of eight brothers (he also had at least two sisters, Abigail and Zeruiah; 1 Chr 2:16). The name of his mother is not known. He was the great-grandson of **Ruth** and **Boaz**, and his ancestry is recorded in a number of places (Ruth 4:18–22; 1 Chr 2:1–15; Matt 1:2–6; Luke 3:31–38) that demonstrate his descent from the tribe of **Judah**, a crucial genealogical truth in light of the royal promise given to Judah in Gen 49:8–12.

B. David Is Anointed

David was a shepherd in the countryside around Bethlehem in the last years of the second millennium B.C. (1 Sam 16:11; 17:15). The humble nature of his beginnings and the simple life he led as a shepherd made God's choice of him all the more surprising. When God rejected **Saul** as king of Israel, **Samuel** was told to anoint David at Bethlehem, because David was to succeed Saul (1 Sam 16:1–13), an event that was soon followed by the surprising irony of David's being chosen to soothe the troubled King Saul with his music (1 Sam 16:17–21). The two men—one a king, the other destined to succeed him—became inextricably drawn together.

The choice of David as Saul's court minstrel shows one aspect of David's many talents: as a young man he was already famous as a musician, and later he would compose the most memorable poetry (originally set to music) in Hebrew literature.

C. His Growing Reputation Attracts Saul's Jealousy

David demonstrated his skill not only as a musician but as a warrior and royal armor-bearer. He slew the giant **Goliath** and cut off his head (1 Sam 17:48–51), and he struck down and circumcised two hundred Philistines (1 Sam 18:27). David's success on the battlefield was celebrated by the women of Israel, who chanted, "Saul has killed his thousands, and David his ten thousands" (1 Sam 18:7)—a popular ditty that inflamed Saul's insane jealousy of David (1 Sam 18:8–9). Further, Saul's son, **Jonathan**, formed a unique friendship with David, going so far as to form a covenant of brotherhood with him (1 Sam 18:1–4).

D. On the Run from Saul

The next period of David's life was marked by flight from Saul's envious rage. The increasingly deranged king hunted David with fervor and pettiness. For his part, David accepted his plight with patience and perseverance; when he had the chance to slay Saul he spared his life, because he still revered Saul as "the LORD's anointed" (1 Sam 24:6, 10; 26:9, 11, 16, 23). Eventually, David allied himself with the Philistine king **Achish** of Gath, who gave him sanctuary and control over Ziklag in return for the use of David and his warriors at appropriate times (1 Sam 27:1–7). David, however, did not take part in the terrible events at Gilboa that brought an ignominious end to the reign of Saul (1 Sam 31). David composed a moving elegy for the fallen king and his son Jonathan, whom David had loved as a "brother" (2 Sam 1:19–27).

II. KING OF ISRAEL

A. Civil War for the Succession

With the death of Saul, David was free to return to Judah. In the turmoil following the defeat of Saul, civil war descended upon the tribes of Israel (2 Sam 2–3). The elders of Judah embraced David as their king and anointed him at Hebron, which he took as his royal city. David was thirty years old at the time and reigned at Hebron for more than seven years. The first years were taken up with the civil war against the supporters of Saul's son, **Ish-bosheth**, but victory was achieved through the deaths of Ish-bosheth and Saul's chief courtier **Abner**.

B. David Establishes His Rule

In the face of these events, opposition against David ceased among the tribes, and the elders of all Israel consolidated the kingship under David (2 Sam 4–5). David reigned at Hebron until the time was right to transfer his capital to **Jerusalem**, which until this time was still in the hands of the Jebusites, a Canaanite tribe. David next conquered Jerusalem to use it as his capital (2 Sam 5; cf. 1 Chr 11:4–9, 14:1–7). His success was part of God's plan: "And David became greater and greater, for the LORD, the God of hosts, was with him" (2 Sam 5:10). David reigned for the next thirty-three years in Jerusalem.

David demonstrated his greatness in the years that followed. He defeated the enemies of Israel—the Philistines, Canaanites, Moabites, Ammonites, Edomites, Arameans, and Amalekites. As king, he improved his capital, Jerusalem, constructed a palace, and brought the political stability that had been so badly needed for so long by the people of Israel.

C. David as Religious Leader

The heart of royal policy, though, was more religious than political, and David reigned with a great fervor and love for the Lord. Jerusalem had once been the seat of **Melchizedek**, Priest of God Most High and king of Salem (Gen 14:18). David would once again make Jerusalem the seat of a holy priest-king. In 2 Sam 6, he ordered that the **ark of the covenant** be brought to Jerusalem from Kiriath-jearim, a crucial first step in making the royal city the host city of the central sanctuary demanded by Deut 12:10–11. Significantly, as the ark was carried through the city, David danced before it and wore a linen ephod, meaning that he acted and was dressed like a Levitical priest. He even blessed and offered sacrifices like a priest. He purchased the site where the **Temple** would be built (1 Chr 21:18–22:1) and gathered material for building it (1 Chr 22:3–5), although it would be left for Solomon to accomplish the construction.

We can see, then, that David was not merely establishing his own earthly power: he was very much aware that he was building God's own kingdom on earth. Chronicles twice uses the phrase "the kingdom of the LORD" to describe the Davidic monarchy (1 Chr 28:5; 2 Chr 13:8; cf. 1 Chr 17:14, 29:11–22).

Yet when David decided to build a "house" for the Lord, he got an unexpected response. Through the prophet Nathan, God told David that he was not the one who would build a house for God. Instead, God would build a "house"—that is, a dynasty—for David. Establishing a covenant with David, God made some amazing promises: David would be one of the great kings of the earth, the people of Israel would have peace, and the son of David would reign forever on David's throne (2 Sam 7:4–17). The reign of the House of David would be based on a divine covenant in which the son of David would also be declared to be the son of God (2 Sam 7:14; Ps 2:7, 89:27). The kingdom of David was the manifestation of God's rule on the earth. Faced with this unexpected blessing, David could only fall on his knees and offer a long prayer of thanksgiving (2 Sam 7:18–29).

Blessed by God, David became the greatest of the kings of Israel, a brilliant poet, statesman, warrior, and musician. He made incalculable contributions to the cultural life of Israel: David was honored as the author of seventy-three Psalms; the founder of musical worship in Israel; and the composer of music, compositions, odes, and elegies (2 Sam 1:19–27, 3:33–34, 23:1–7; Neh 12:24, 36, 45–46; Amos 6:5).

D. David's Sin

But in spite of his many virtues, David was not immune to temptation. He was consumed with desire for **Bathsheba**, the wife of Uriah the Hittite, one of David's officers. He committed adultery with her, and then treacherously arranged for Uriah to die in battle. God sent Nathan the prophet to convict David of his sin, which Nathan did with a parable that struck deep into David's conscience (1 Sam 12:1–6). As a result of David's sin, Nathan declared, "the sword shall never depart from your house" (2 Sam 12:10). David repented, and the guilt of his sin was forgiven (1 Sam 12:13), but he still had to pay the temporal price for it.

E. His Troubled Later Reign

Before the adulterous affair, David's reign had been an unmitigated triumph. The rest of the history of his reign, however, consists of a string of rebellions and betrayals. His own son **Absalom** betrayed him (2 Sam 15–18); the story of David's grief at the death of Absalom is one of the most heart-wrenching scenes in all literature (2 Sam 18:28–33). Even as David was near death, his own son **Adonijah** plotted to steal the throne from Solomon, David's son by Bathsheba and his designated successor. Only by the timely intervention of Bathsheba was the plot foiled. David's sin filled the last years of his life with misery.

Yet David remained the pattern for the divinely instituted monarchy. He sinned deeply, but he never turned away from God. That makes him almost unique among the kings of Israel and Judah; almost every one of them, even Solomon, either turned to idols himself or tolerated idolatry. Even the reformer **Josiah** fell far short of the glory of David.

III. THE DAVIDIC COVENANT

The covenant with David was the charter of the Davidic dynasty, which would rule longer than any other dynasty that we know of in the ancient Near East. This covenant was a pure grant, bestowed on David as a reward, and God alone swore the oath.

A. Seven Primary Features

The terms of the covenant with David are expressed in 2 Sam 7, and amplified in Ps 2, 89, and 110. There are seven main features in the covenant:

1. *Kingdom.* David and his descendants would be great kings. "And I will make him the firstborn, the highest of the kings of the earth" (Ps 89:27).

2. *Dynasty.* Unlike Saul's line, which was extinguished as a punishment for his disobedience, the line of David would continue to rule the kingdom: "the LORD will make you a house" (2 Sam 7:11).

3. *Divine sonship.* The son of David, when he was anointed as king, would be adopted as God's own son: "I will be his father, and he shall be my son" (2 Sam 7:14). The image of a royal adoption expresses the especially close relationship God promises to keep with the Davidic kings.

4. *Unlimited duration.* The kingdom of David's sons would be established "for ever" (2 Sam 7:13).

5. *Jerusalem the center.* The capital of the kingdom and the center of worship would be Jerusalem: "I have set my king on Zion, my holy hill" (Ps 2:6).

6. *The Temple.* David's son would build the Lord "a house for my name" (2 Sam 7:13), and that Temple would become the center of wor-

ship for Israel and all the nations drawn to the Lord. The very structure of the Temple would be erected by Gentiles and Israelites working together: **Solomon**'s men worked side by side with the Phoenician artisans sent by King **Hiram** of Tyre (1 Kgs 5).

7. *Wisdom.* The **Law** ruled Israel as a nation apart, but "this is the law for man," says David in 2 Sam 7:19 (see footnote in RSV). Solomon's wisdom lured the kings of the earth to his court (1 Kgs 4:29–34), and the **wisdom literature** traditionally attributed to Solomon reaches out to all mankind, leading all the nations to God by way of universal truths.

B. Three Secondary Features

Besides these seven primary features, there are three characteristics of the Davidic kingdom in Israel and Judah that might be called secondary features:

1. *Queen Mother.* The queen mother would take on an especially important role. Bathsheba set the pattern: she actively advised her son Solomon and sat on a throne next to him (1 Kgs 2:19). Throughout the history of the Davidic kingdom, the queen mother would be an advisor to the king, an advocate for the people, and one of the most important members of the royal administration. Even in the chaotic final days of the Davidic line, we see Jehoiachin giving up "himself, and his mother," to Nebuchadnezzar (2 Kgs 24:12).

2. *Prime Minister.* Each Davidic king had a certain royal official who acted as his prime minister or head of household, as Solomon had Ahishar (1 Kgs 4:6). The sign of the prime

minister's office was the keys of the kingdom, or "key of the house of David" (Isa 22:22).

3. *Sacrifice of Thanksgiving*. The "sacrifice of thanksgiving," or thank offering, emerged as the most important liturgy in Davidic times: "Do I eat the flesh of bulls, or drink the blood of goats? Offer to God a sacrifice of thanksgiving, and pay your vows to the Most High" (Ps 50:13–14). Our word "Eucharist" comes from a Greek word that Jews of the **Dispersion** (such as Philo of Alexandria) used to translate "sacrifice of thanksgiving."

IV. THE KINGDOM RESTORED

These features of the Davidic covenant would take on new meaning in the New Testament, when Jesus Christ, the Son of David, restored the kingdom. The **Church** is that restored kingdom, and in it the promises of the Davidic covenant are perfectly fulfilled. The King, the Son of David and the Son of God, rules forever over a kingdom without boundaries. The queen mother is enthroned with honor (Rev 12:1–2), Peter and his successors function as the King's prime minister, and the Eucharist is the liturgy of thanksgiving of the restored kingdom. Through the sacramental actions of the Church, the heavenly kingdom of Christ extends throughout the world. (*See* **Church**; **Kingdom**; **Acts of the Apostles**.)

DAVID, CITY OF *See* **Jerusalem**.

DAY In Scripture, "day" has roughly the same range of meanings that it has in our language. Primarily, day is the period of daylight from sunrise to sunset, as opposed to night (see, for example, Num 11:32). It may also mean the whole period of night and day from sunset to sunset (see, for example, Lev 23:32). In the Old Testament, the divisions are the obvious natural ones: morning, midday, and evening. In the New Testament period, the Greek system of dividing the daylight between morning and evening into twelve hours was adopted. The night was customarily divided into four "watches" (Matt 14:25; Mark 13:35; Luke 12:38). The "hours" of the day began at sunrise, and the duration varied according to the time of year (Matt 20:3–6; Mark 15:25; John 1:39, 4:6, 52, 11:9; Acts 2:15, 10:9). The six stages in the creation of the world are called "days" in Genesis, each with an "evening" and a "morning" (Gen 1:1–2:3).

The account of creation in Genesis uses the Hebrew word for "day" in different ways (in Gen 2:4, for example, "day" refers to a whole week). For a more detailed discussion of the days of creation, see **Creation**.

DAY OF ATONEMENT *See* **Atonement, Day of**.

DAY OF CHRIST *See* **Parousia**.

DAY OF JUDGMENT *See* **Judgment**.

DAY OF THE LORD A biblical expression for "the time of God's judgment." Related phrases include "the day of the anger of the Lord" or "the Lord has a day." It expresses the eschatological hope that the Lord's overwhelming power and glory would be manifest in history, but also the dread of a divine reckoning. The phrase appears over two dozen times in prophetic books (Isaiah, Joel, Amos, and Zephaniah), and once in Lamentations (Lam 2:22).

The day of the Lord is described in terms of power and majesty, in which the Lord appears in cosmic glory to sit in judgment and to defeat the enemies of righteousness. One of the oldest references to the day of the Lord occurs in Amos 5:18–20, in which Amos asks, "Is not the day of the LORD darkness, and not light, and gloom with no brightness in it?" (Amos 5:20). The notion must already have been popular, because Amos is contradicting "you who desire the day of the LORD": some Israelites hope for it, but Amos sees it as a judgment upon Israel (Amos 3:1–2; 6:3; 8:9), an assessment shared by other preexilic prophets (cf. Isa 2:11–17, 13:9–10; Zeph 1:7–11, 12–18; 2:1–3).

In the postexilic prophets, "the day of the Lord" expresses the hope of eschatological salvation for Israel. The event is still envisioned as being characterized by shattering and cataclysmic power, but now the judgment of the wicked is balanced by the deliverance of the righteous remnant of Israel (cf. Joel 2:2; Zech 14:1; Ezek 38–39), when the enemies of Israel will be defeated and a final judgment passed.

In the New Testament, the "day of the Lord" becomes the "day of our Lord Jesus Christ" (1 Cor 1:8). It is the day when Christ, the Son of Man (cf. Luke 17:24, 30), will return in glory to bring deliverance and judgment (1 Cor 1:8; 2 Cor 1:14; Phil 1:6, 10; 2:16). In a historical sense, the day of the Lord can be seen as referring to the cataclysmic destruction of Jerusalem in A.D. 70; liturgically, the "Lord's day" (Rev 1:10), when Christians gather to worship, fulfills the image of the "day

of the Lord." Both these senses point forward toward the end of time, when the full glory of Jesus will be made manifest for all (1 Thess 5:2, 4). (*See also* **Parousia**.)

DEACON (Greek *diakonos,* "servant" or "minister") An ordained assistant to priests responsible for such ministerial duties as preaching, baptizing, witnessing marriages, distributing Communion, and presiding at funerals (but not saying the funeral Mass). In the modern Church there are two forms of the diaconate: the permanent diaconate (including single and married men) and the transitional diaconate (for those who will eventually be ordained as priests) (CCC 1569–70).

The traditional understanding is that the diaconate was established in Jerusalem through the ordination of seven men (Stephen, Philip, Prochorus, Nicanor, Timon, Parmenas, and Nicolas) for the task of serving the poor and distributing alms (Acts 6:1–6). Deacons were also known as clerical ministers who assisted the bishops (Phil 1:1). Paul establishes high standards for the dedication and service of deacons (1 Tim 3:8).

In the book of Acts, we see deacons performing several functions: serving at the table (Acts 6:2), preaching (Acts 7:2–53), and administering baptism (Acts 8:38). Further testimony is provided by Saint Clement (*1 Clem.* 42:4–5), as well as by Saint Ignatius of Antioch (*Ign. Magn.,* 6:1).

The primitive diaconate was not merely a preparation for the priesthood. Rather, the deacons were understood to be serving in a lifelong ministry, unless a deacon was elected to be a bishop.

Saint Paul mentions the deaconess Phoebe at Cenchreae (Rom 16), the only female "deacon" mentioned by name in the Bible. The "women" mentioned in 1 Tim 3:11 may be deaconesses or wives of the deacons. The Council of Nicaea in 325 A.D. counted deaconesses among the laity, rather than among the ordained clergy (canon 19). After extensive study, the International Theological Commission concluded in 2002 that the appointment of a deaconess, unlike the ordination of a deacon, has no connection with the sacrament of holy orders. Since the permanent diaconate belongs to the sacrament of orders, it is limited to men.

The commission recognized that deaconesses had the responsibility during the early Church of serving as a bridge or connection between women laity and the local church authorities. They did not perform liturgical actions in the strict sense, as did their male counterparts, but they assisted with the baptism of women and with other rites of the Church.

DEACONNESS *See* **Deacon.**

DEAD SEA The large body of water at the termination of the Jordan River; it is some 50 miles (80 kilometers) long and 10 miles (18 kilometers) wide. It is the lowest inland body of water on the face of the earth: the surface is approximately 1,290 feet (290 meters) below sea level, and the water reaches a depth of 1,300 feet (396 meters).

The Dead Sea is fed by the waters of the Jordan and various smaller streams, but owing to evaporation it has an extremely high concentration of salt (some 25 percent), the highest salinity of any body of water in the world. Hence it is known in Scripture as the Salt Sea (Gen 14:3; Num 34:3; Deut 3:17). It is also known as the Eastern Sea (Ezek 47:18; Joel 2:20; Zech 14:8), and the Sea of Arabah (Deut 4:49; Josh 3:16, 12:3). The name Dead Sea was not used in the Bible but was first applied by Pausanias (*Descr.* 5). Josephus (*Ant.* 1.9) referred to it as the Asphalt Lake, owing to the large quantities of asphalt in the region (Gen 14:10 mentions bitumen pits). The name Dead Sea is an appropriate one, since the water supports no animal or plant life because of the salinity. There were, nevertheless, a number of notable settlements in the Dead Sea Valley, including Qumran and Masada. (*See also* **Dead Sea Scrolls**.)

DEAD SEA SCROLLS A collection of some eight hundred biblical and religious manuscripts found between 1947 and 1956 in the caves northwest of the Dead Sea, near the remains of an ancient settlement called Khirbet Qumran. Most scholars believe that the manuscripts were part of the library of the Qumran community; they were likely deposited in the caves for safekeeping during the Jewish rebellion against the Roman Empire (A.D. 66–70). The war ended with the destruction of Jerusalem, and as part of the military operations, the Romans besieged Qumran and occupied it until the fall of Masada in A.D. 74, after which the site was abandoned. The scrolls thus remained forgotten in the caves, as none of the members of the community survived to reclaim them.

In 1947, two shepherds of the Bedawi

Ta'amireh Bedouin tribe happened upon jars of ancient scrolls in what was later called Cave 1. The tribesmen sold the scrolls to a Bethlehem antiquities dealer, and the writings made their way by different paths to the Syrian Patriarch of Jerusalem and to Professor E. L. Sukenik, who purchased them for the Hebrew University of Jerusalem. The new owners confirmed independently of each other their authenticity. Additional scrolls began appearing over the next years, until scholars and authorities launched a formal exploration of the Qumran area caves. The excavations were directed by Father Roland de Vaux of the École Biblique of Jerusalem and G. L. Harding, director of Antiquities for Jordan in 1951, and from 1953 to 1956 the areas under study included the caves and the ruins of a nearby settlement in order to establish their connection. A report on the work was published in *Revue Biblique,* followed by a final report in 1961 in *L'archéologie et les manuscrits de la mer Morte.*

Most of the Dead Sea Scrolls were written in Hebrew; one-fifth were in Aramaic, and a few were in Greek. Most were written on leather, some on papyrus, and one text was hammered on a roll of copper. They were written between roughly 250 B.C. and A.D. 70—about the same period of time during which archaeologists have determined the Qumran community was occupied.

Of the eight hundred manuscripts and fragments that have been discovered, two hundred were copies of biblical books. Every book of the Hebrew canon was included, at least in fragmentary form, with the exception of Esther and Nehemiah. The manuscripts

were a millennium older than any surviving extensive Hebrew manuscript (the oldest previously had been dated to the ninth century A.D.). But although there are some variations from the **Masoretic Text**, which was standardized in early Christian times, in general the differences are very minor. Where there are variations, they often agree with the readings of the **Septuagint**. The most celebrated find among the biblical manuscripts was a complete scroll of the book of Isaiah, which was roughly a thousand years younger than the Masoretic version of the text but contained only the slightest variations.

In addition to the biblical manuscripts and fragments, there were pseudepigraphical and apocalyptic texts, including the *Testament of the Twelve Patriarchs,* the *Book of Jubilees,* and parts of *1 Enoch.*

Finally, there were other writings describing the beliefs and practices of the sect at Qumran. Among these were The Manual of Discipline (also called the Community Rule), the rule of the sect; the Damascus Document (or Zadokite Fragment), which was known from manuscripts found in the synagogue of Old Cairo and published in 1910, thereby permitting a close comparative analysis; and the War Scroll, or the War of the Sons of Light against the Sons of Darkness, describing an eschatological struggle between good and evil.

The relationship of the Dead Sea Scrolls to the New Testament has been a special subject of study by biblical scholars. Although the community of Qumran was exterminated before the emergence of the NT canon, the scrolls do reveal similarities between the sect and some of the practices of the first Christian communities—for example, community property, baptismal washings, and a common meal. There was also a special interest in the books of Deuteronomy, Psalms, and Isaiah, and the NT writings show a similar interest in those books. Both communities viewed themselves as the beneficiaries of a *new* covenant in fulfillment of Old Testament oracles.

DEATH The separation of the soul from the body and the end of earthly life.

As the Church teaches, a person is no longer able to sin after death, nor can one gain a higher place in heaven. By particular judgment, eternal salvation in heaven or eternal damnation in hell depends upon the condition of the soul at the moment of death. A Christian, however, has the hope of sharing in Christ's death and Resurrection: "He who believes in me, even if he die, shall live; and whoever lives and believes in me, shall never die" (John 11:25).

I. THE ORIGIN OF DEATH

Death first appears in the Bible in God's command forbidding Adam and Eve to eat of the tree of the knowledge of good and evil: "in the day that you eat of it you shall die" (Gen 2:17). The expression in Hebrew could be literally rendered, "you shall die the death." Grammatically, it is an infinitive absolute, which is used in Hebrew to intensify the meaning of a verb and to stress the certainty of its occurrence. An idiomatic rendering might be "you shall most certainly die."

God had told Adam that on the very day he ate the fruit, he would die. Yet Adam and Eve did not physically die on that day. Their death was a spiritual death, the inevitable result of "mortal sin" (see CCC 1855–61) and the precursor of the mortality of their bodies. Just as there is natural life and supernatural life, so there is natural death and supernatural death.

The first-century Jewish philosopher Philo of Alexandria interpreted this passage to mean that there are two kinds of death. "The death of the man is the separation of the soul from the body. But the death of the soul is the decay of virtue and the bringing in of wickedness. It is for this reason that God says not only 'die' but 'die the death,' indicating not the death common to us all, but that special death, which is that of the soul becoming entombed in passions and wickedness of all kinds."

Death, then, was not part of the original divine plan, but entered into the human condition as a consequence of sin (Rom 5:12, 6:23; 1 Cor 15:21) and is connected intimately with divine judgment (Rev 2:11; 20:6; 21:8). "For God created man for incorruption, and made him in the image of his own eternity, but through the devil's envy death entered the world, and those who belong to his party experience it" (Wis 2:23–24; see also CCC 1006–9). (*See* **Fall, the**; **Sin**.)

II. DEATH IN THE OLD TESTAMENT

All subsequent history is affected by this dissolution. The rest of the Old Testament treats death as inevitable and final, as the natural end of human life: "We must all die, we are like water spilt on the ground" (2 Sam 14:14).

The ideal for mortals was to lead a long life and thus face a "good" death at an advanced age (Gen 25:8, 46:30; Num 23:10; Judg 8:32; Job 21:23, 29:18–20). There was, however, little joy or happiness associated with any death (Job 3:21; Jonah 4:3).

For the dead, the place of abode was in Sheol, where they dwelt in utter silence and gloom (Ps 94:17; Prov 2:18, 5:5, 7:27). As a place of silence, Sheol was bereft of the worship of God (Ps 6:5, 30; 115:17). God's power extended over Sheol (Ps 139:7–8), but his presence was not felt there (Isa 38:18). Nevertheless, even in the midst of Sheol, there was the hope that the Lord would not abandon his people (Ps 16:9) and that God would bring redemption from that place (Ps 49:16; cf. 1 Sam 2:6).

Just as there was optimism concerning Sheol, so too were there indications in the OT that death did not have the final say. In Isaiah, the promise is made, "He will swallow up death for ever, and the Lord GOD will wipe away tears from all faces, and the reproach of his people he will take away from all the earth; for the LORD has spoken" (Isa 25:8; cf. 26:19). Similarly, in his prophecies of the coming Messianic era (Ezek 33–36), Ezekiel also describes the vision of the dry bones, implying God's power to raise the dead: "And you shall know that I am the LORD, when I open your graves, and raise you from your graves, O my people. And I will put my Spirit within you, and you shall live" (Ezek 37:13–14). The Resurrection is also described in Dan 12:2, and positively asserted in 2 Macc 7:23.

III. DEATH IN THE NEW TESTAMENT

What is different in the New Testament is the proclamation that death has been defeated by the death and Resurrection of Christ. Jesus suffered the same death that is part of the human condition (Mark 14:33–34; Heb 5:7–8),

doing so in a free submission to the Father's will, bringing eternal life (Rom 5:19–21). Christ stands in contrast to Adam, for where Adam's sin brought death into the world, Christ as the new Adam (or the "last Adam," 1 Cor 15:22, 45) has destroyed death (Rom 5:10; 2 Tim 1:10; Heb 2:14; cf. Rev 1:18). The contrast between Adam and Christ is expressed in detail in Romans 5: "If, because of one man's trespass, death reigned through that one man, much more will those who receive the abundance of grace and the free gift of righteousness reign in life through the one man Jesus Christ" (Rom 5:17).

Because of the death and Resurrection of Christ, "to die is gain" (Phil 1:21). The finality of death feared in the OT becomes now for the Christian a sign of hope. In death one might achieve the emulation of Christ in obedience to the divine will (Luke 23:46) and the object of our departure (Phil 1:23; 2 Cor 5:8). Through baptism, one dies sacramentally in Christ and is reborn to a new life (cf. John 3:3–8). Nevertheless, there remains for everyone the danger of spiritual death from mortal sin (see 1 John 5:16–17). (*See also* **Parousia**; **Resurrection**.)

DEATH OF JESUS *See* **Passion**.

DEBIR Known originally as Kiriath-sepher (Josh 15:15; Judg 1:11), a town in southern Judah; probably modern Tell Beit Mirsim. Debir was inhabited by the **Anakim** at the time of the Israelite invasion (Josh 11:21) and was included in the list of cities captured and destroyed by Joshua (Josh 10:38–39). Othniel, the son of Kenaz, captured the city and so won the hand of Achsah, daughter of Caleb, in marriage (Josh 15:15–19; Judg 1:11–15).

DEBORAH The name of two women in the Old Testament.

1. The nurse of Rebekah (Gen 24:59) who was buried at Bethel (Gen 35:8).

2. An important prophetess and judge, the wife of Lappidoth, who was active in the days of the Judges. Deborah was a woman of great courage and was respected as a military advisor (Judg 4:6–7, 14) and local arbitrator (Judg 4:5) during the persecution by Jabin, king of Canaan, and **Sisera**, Jabin's general. Summoning **Barak**, a warrior of the tribe of Naphtali, she speaks with divine authority (Judg 4:6), ordering him to engage in holy warfare against Sisera. Barak will not march into battle without Deborah (Judg 4:8), who fulfills her prophetic role by exhorting Barak forward with a prophecy that credit for the triumph will belong to a woman, not to Barak (Judg 4:9). Her prophecy is proved when Sisera is murdered by **Jael**, but so too is her assurance of victory, as well as her courageous leadership in bringing it about. The Song of Deborah (Judg 5:2–31) is a poem that may be much older than the prose narrative surrounding it. Many believe its composition should be dated near the time of the event it commemorates. Scholars regard the Song of Deborah as one of the earliest specimens of Hebrew verse that survives in the Bible.

DECALOGUE *See* **Ten Commandments**.

DECAPOLIS (Greek, "ten cities") A confederation of ten Hellenistic cities mainly east and south of the Sea of Galilee; it extended from **Damascus** in the north to Philadelphia in the south. The cities were established initially by Greek soldiers following the campaigns and death of Alexander the Great. After the Roman conquest of Palestine in 63 B.C. Pompey organized them into a confederation as a strategic buffer for the frontier. While the members apparently differed at various times (and sometimes included more than ten cities), Pliny the Elder (*Nat.* 5.18.74) listed the members in A.D. 75 as Damascus, Hippo, Gadara, Pella, Scythopolis, Raphana, Canatha, Philadelphia, Dion, and Gerasa. Jesus performed at least two miracles in the Decapolis: he cast out the demons from the Gerasene demoniac (Mark 5:1–20), and he healed "a man who was deaf and had an impediment in his speech" (Mark 7:31–37; see also Matt 4:25).

DEDAN A tribe living in northwest Arabia on the border of Edom (Jer 49:8; Ezek 25:13); it was well known for its caravans (Isa 21:13) and its trade with Tyre (Ezek 27:20). In the Table of Nations, the founder is the grandson of Noah's youngest son, Ham (Gen 10:7; 1 Chr 1:9). Another Dedan is mentioned in the genealogy of Gen 25:3 and 1 Chr 1:32; he is identified as the grandson of Abraham and Keturah through Jokshan.

DEDICATION, FEAST OF (Hebrew *Hanukkah*) Also called the feast of Lights, a feast that celebrates the rededication of the Temple in 164 B.C. after it had been defiled by Antiochus IV Epiphanes (1 Macc 4:56). At its inception, the festival was observed for eight days during the winter months, starting with the twenty-fifth day of the Jewish month Kislev (1 Macc 4:52–59; 2 Macc 10:5–8), although few details were provided as to how it was celebrated. The feast was celebrated by the Jews in the time of the New Testament (John 10:22).

DEEP *See* **Abyss.**

DEI VERBUM The Dogmatic Constitution on Divine Revelation, a document promulgated on November 18, 1965, by Vatican Council II. It summarizes the cumulative teaching of the Church on Sacred Scripture and Sacred Tradition, and it is the most recent and most authoritative teaching on the subject. It is generally considered to be a successor or complementary document to the "Dogmatic Constitution on Catholic Faith," *Dei Filius,* that had been issued by Vatican Council I in 1870.

The 1965 Constitution is divided into the following related categories: Revelation, Transmission of Revelation, Inspiration and Interpretation, the Old Testament, the New Testament, and Scripture in Church Life.

The essence of revelation, according to the Council Fathers, is the fact that God has chosen to make known to the human race both himself and the eternal decrees of his will (§§2 and 6). In examining the transmission of revelation, *Dei Verbum* observes that

Christ the Lord, in whom the full revelation of the supreme God is brought to completion . . . , commissioned the apostles to preach to all men that gospel which is the source of all saving truth and moral teaching . . . But in order to keep the gospel forever whole and alive within the Church,

the apostles left bishops as their successors, "handing over their own teaching role" to them. This sacred tradition, therefore, and sacred Scripture of both the Old and New Testament are like a mirror in which the pilgrim Church on earth looks at God. (DV §7)

Dei Verbum (§§9, 10) then traces the development of doctrine, elaborating upon the "close connection and communication between Sacred Tradition and sacred Scripture," which "form one sacred deposit of the word of God, which is committed to the Church." It adds, however, the important element of the Magisterium, the teaching authority of the Church, declaring that all three—Sacred Scripture, Sacred Tradition, and the Magisterium—"are so linked and joined together that one cannot stand without the others, and that all together and each in its own way under the action of the one Holy Spirit contribute effectively to the salvation of souls" (§10).

In examining both the inspiration and the interpretation of the Bible, *Dei Verbum* states that "Holy Mother Church, relying on the belief of the apostles, holds that the books of both the Old and New Testament in their entirety, with all their parts, are sacred and canonical because, having been written under the inspiration of the Holy Spirit . . . they have God as their author and have been handed on as such to the Church herself" (§11). It then studies the questions of inerrancy, literary forms, and guidelines for interpreting Scripture within the framework of Catholic teaching.

Both the Old and New Testaments are given their place in "planning and preparing the salvation of the whole human race" (§14).

The OT is described as having as its primary purpose "to prepare for the coming both of Christ, the universal Redeemer, and of the Messianic kingdom, . . . the books of the Old Testament with all their parts, caught up into the proclamation of the gospel, acquire and show forth their full meaning in the New Testament" (§§15, 16). The NT, written under the inspiration of the Holy Spirit, gives confirmation of "those matters which concern Christ the Lord" and "His true teaching is more and more fully stated, the saving power of the divine work of Christ is preached, the story is told of the beginnings of the Church and her marvelous growth, and her glorious fulfillment is foretold" (§20).

Finally, the role of Scripture in Church life is emphasized, exhorting that ease of "access to sacred Scripture should be provided for all the Christian faithful" and calling for biblical studies to progress "under the watchful care of the sacred teaching office of the Church," adding that the careful study of Sacred Scripture is "the soul of sacred theology" (§§22–24).

DELILAH A woman of the valley of Sorek best known for her betrayal of **Samson** (Judg 16:4–21) to the Philistines. Samson fell in love with her, and she was then hired by the Philistines to learn the secret of his strength. She lured him into betraying his **Nazirite** vow by cutting his hair (Judg 16:17–20). It is not certain whether Delilah was a Jewess or a Philistine. For her betrayal, she was paid the sum of eleven hundred pieces of silver from each of the five Philistine princes.

DELUGE *See* **Flood**.

DEMAS A resident of Thessalonica and a onetime disciple of Paul. He is listed in Philemon 24, along with Mark, Aristarchus, and Luke, among Paul's associates during his first Roman imprisonment. In Colossians, Demas is named with Luke (Col 4:14), Aristarchus and Mark (4:10), Jesus Justus (4:11), and Epaphras (4:12). According to Tim 4:10, Demas abandoned Paul: "For Demas, in love with this present world, has deserted me and gone to Thessalonica."

DEMETRIUS The name of two men in the New Testament.

1. A silversmith in Ephesus who earned his living by making small silver models of the temple of Artemis at Ephesus (Acts 19:24). As his trade was threatened by the preaching of Paul, who was converting the people to Christianity, he instigated a riot that drove Paul out of Ephesus (Acts 19:25–41).

2. A disciple praised by the apostle John (3 John 12).

DEMETRIUS I SOTER Seleucid king of Syria from 162 to 150 B.C. (1 Macc 7:1; 2 Macc 14:1–2), called Soter or "Savior." He was the son of Seleucus IV Philopator (r. 181–175 B.C.) and the nephew of Antiochus IV Epiphanes (r. 175–164 B.C.). At the death of his father, he was sent to Rome as a hostage, but then escaped and returned to the Seleucid kingdom upon hearing of his uncle's passing. After defeating the rival claimant Antiochus V Eupator, he secured the throne (1 Macc 7:1–49). At the time of his accession, he was faced by threats from Ptolemaic Egypt and Rome as well as a struggle for control of Palestine with the Jews owing to severe resentment over the recent Seleucid attempt to suppress the Jewish religion and way of life, including violations of the sanctuary in Jerusalem.

First Maccabees documents his conflict with the Jews (1 Macc 7:1–10:52). Demetrius sent Bacchides against **Judas Maccabeus** (1 Macc 7; 2 Macc 14), along with Alcimus, a Hellenist who was scheming to become high priest. When Judas and his men proved a formidable force, he sent Nicanor, who was defeated and slain (1 Macc 7; 2 Macc 15). Bacchides was sent back into Judah again. This time, Judas was defeated decisively and died in battle (1 Macc 9:11–18). Judas's brother, **Jonathan**, then assumed leadership and crushed Bacchides (1 Macc 9:23–73). Bacchides returned a third time, only to face yet another defeat.

Demetrius himself died in battle against the claimant Alexander I Balas (1 Macc 10:1–50).

DEMETRIUS II NICANOR

The son of Demetrius I Soter; he was Seleucid king of Syria around 145–140 B.C. After his father was defeated by Alexander I Balas, Demetrius launched his own struggle for the throne (1 Macc 10:67–69) and found an ally in Ptolemy VI Philometor, king of Egypt, who gave him his daughter Cleopatra in marriage. He earned his nickname Nicanor ("Victor") by defeating Alexander.

The relations between Demetrius II and the Hasmoneans in Palestine varied depending upon prevailing political circumstances (1 Macc 10:67–13:30). **Jonathan Maccabeus** had supported Alexander, but Demetrius gave him various favors. When the general Diodotus Trypho installed Alexander's son on the throne in Antioch as Antiochus VI, Jonathan switched sides and used the power struggle in Syria as a means to consolidate his power. For this shift of allegiance, Trypho treacherously captured Jonathan and killed him. Soon after, Trypho murdered Antiochus and declared himself king, whereupon Simon Maccabeus allied himself with Demetrius. In 140 B.C. Demetrius embarked upon a campaign against the Parthians and was captured. He was freed by Antiochus VII in 129 B.C. and reclaimed the throne upon Antiochus's death. After a failed attempt to seize Egypt, he was murdered while on a ship at Tyre.

DEMON

The name applied to all varieties of evil spirits, including the devil or Satan. Demons, like angels, are pure spirits, which means that they do not have bodies and are invisible; nevertheless, they sometimes manipulate or possess a human or animal body (cf. Gen 3:13–15; Isa 34:14).

Stories of demons or evil spirits are found in virtually all ancient civilizations. The Egyptians used magical incantations to protect themselves from foul spirits that brought disease and disaster, and the Greeks believed in various spirits who existed in a state between men and the gods.

In the Old Testament, demonic forces are quite plainly active in the world. There are different words for demons and a number of named demons. The word *šēdîm* is a general term for malevolent spirits. The *śĕ'îrîm* (literally "hairy ones," translated "satyrs" in the RSV) were probably goat idols: that is, demons worshipped in the form of a goat (Lev 17:7). Demons might also be associated with natural disasters such as pestilence (Ps 91:6; Hos 13:14; Hab 3:5) and destruction (Hos 13:14); and *bārād,* a demon of freezing cold (Ps 78:48; Isa 28:2). The specific named demons included Azazel (Lev 16:8), connected to the goat sent forth into the desert in the ritual of atonement and the name of a fallen angel in Jewish tradition (*1 En.* 8:1; 10:4–6); and Asmodeus (Tob 3:8), who figured in the story of Tobit.

Chief among the demons was **Satan**. He is the judicial adversary or accuser in Job (Job 1:6ff., 2:1ff.; cf. Zech 3:1), and the chief evil spirit, the tempter who took the form of the serpent in Gen 3 (Wis 2:24). Books of the centuries just before Christ were filled with details on both demons and angels, showing that demonology expanded and developed in Second Temple Judaism (cf. *Jubilees, 1 Enoch*).

In the New Testament, demons—also called unclean spirits, evil spirits, and similar names—are an assumed reality. They are servants of evil, the angels of Satan, determined to tempt and destroy humanity and to spread evil and suffering in the world. The devil and the other demons are fallen angels who refused definitively to serve God and so work against his plan and seek ever to corrupt men and women (CCC 391–94, 414). Evil spirits sought to impede the establishment of the Kingdom of God and afflicted men and women. They brought infirmity and physical suffering (Matt 8:28, 9:32, 12:22, 17:15; Mark 5:1–17, 9:16–26; Luke 13:11). Sometimes persons possessed by demons showed superhuman strength, making them physically dangerous to those around them (Mark 5:2–4; Acts 19:16). Satan himself even tempted Jesus in the wilderness as he prepared for his public ministry (Matt 4:1–11; Mark 1:12–13; Luke 4:1–13) (CCC 538–40, 566, 2119).

The activity of demons in the NT, especially in the Synoptic Gospels, was manifested especially in their possession of the bodies of the afflicted. These possessions, however, gave opportunity for the demonstration of one of the most important facets of Jesus's earthly ministry, namely the casting out of demons (cf. Matt 12:25–29; Mark 3:23–27; Luke 11:17–22). In his exorcisms, Jesus showed his absolute power over the demonic world of sin, and that the Kingdom of God was in direct conflict with the kingdom of evil (CCC 421, 447, 539, 550, 566, 635–36, 1086, 1708). Jesus gave this power to continue the struggle with the demonic to the disciples, and the Synoptic Gospels stress that Jesus gave them authority and power to cast out demons (Matt 10:1; Mark 3:14–15, 6:7; Luke 9:1–2). Thus Paul also cast out demons (Acts 16:16–18; 19:11–12). The activity of the disciples in doing so is connected intimately with the spread of the Kingdom of God and the call of Jesus to share in his ministry of healing and compassion (Mark 6:12–13) (CCC 1506). (*See also* **Baptism**; **Beelzebul**; **Belial**; **Exorcism**.)

DEMOPHON The Seleucid governor of a district of Palestine during the period of **Judas Maccabeus** (2 Macc 12:2).

DENARIUS A Roman coin of 3.8 grams of silver. In the New Testament, a denarius was considered a fair day's wage for a laborer (Matt 20:2). The denarius was the coin used to pay taxes to the Roman emperor (Matt 22:19;

Mark 12:15; Luke 20:24; see also Mark 6:37, 14:5; Rev 6:6).

DERBE A city in Lycaonia, a region in southern Asia Minor in the province of Galatia. Paul visited Derbe on his first and second missionary journeys (Acts 14:6, 20; 16:1). Gaius, a disciple, was a native of Derbe (Acts 20:4).

DESCENT INTO HELL An article of the Apostles' Creed declares that between his Crucifixion and Resurrection Jesus descended to the realm of the dead (Greek *Hadēs,* the underworld). The purpose of the descent was to bring salvation to the righteous dead who lived before his coming and to usher them into heavenly glory. The power of Christ's redemption reaches not only into the future but also into the past to deliver the saints of the Old Covenant.

Peter clearly states that Jesus "went and made a proclamation to the spirits in prison, who in former times did not obey, when God waited patiently in the days of Noah, during the building of the ark, in which a few, that is, eight persons, were saved through water" (1 Pet 3:18–20). A little later, Peter assures us that "the gospel was preached even to the dead" (1 Pet 4:6). In Heb 11:39–40 the implication is that the just of the Old Testament had to wait for the reward of Jesus (CCC 624, 631, 632–35).

Although "hell" is the common translation, the Greek word "Hades" does not refer to the place of eternal damnation. It is simply the place of the dead—"**Sheol**" in the OT. Sheol was the place to which the dead sank down, and when one rises it is from Sheol. There are clear OT passages that describe Sheol as a joyless place (Eccl 9:10) from which escape is impossible (Job 17:16; Isa 38:10); but God had power to deliver his people from Sheol (1 Sam 2:6; Ps 30:3; Wis 16:13; Hos 13:14). The same idea of Sheol (translated *Hades* in Greek) continues in the New Testament as the conceptual background of Christian preaching about Christ's death and Resurrection (1 Cor 15:3–4; cf. 1 Thess 1:10). In his first sermon, Peter declared that Jesus "was not abandoned to Hades" (Acts 2:31). Jesus had power over the living and the dead (Matt 11:5; Luke 7:22). The great message of Christianity was that God had raised Christ "from the dead" (Acts 3:15; 4:10; 10:41). Bringing up from the dead, for Paul, implies going down "into the abyss" (Rom 10:7). In Phil 2:10, Paul says that "at the name of Jesus every knee should bend, in heaven and on earth and under the earth" (cf. Isa 45:23). Here we see clearly the three theological levels of the world in Jewish tradition: heaven above, the earth in the middle, and the place of the dead beneath. Jesus "descended into the lower depths of the earth" to rescue the "captives there," says Paul, and then "ascended far above the heavens, that he might fill all things" (Eph 4:8–10)—in other words, Jesus is present in all three levels of the world, even in the place of the dead.

DESERT Today, scientists define a desert as a place of arid conditions with annual rainfall of less than 10 inches (25 centimeters). Generally, vegetation, animal life, and water are scarce. The deserts in the Bible are all part of the vast Saharo-Arabian desert chain. The Sinai desert is described aptly in Deut 8:15 as "the great and terrible wilderness, with its fiery serpents and scorpions and thirsty ground where there was no water."

Deserts were a reality of daily life, for they stood menacingly on the southern and eastern borders of the narrow fertile strip that is the Holy Land. To survive in the difficult conditions, people needed to work hard together and remember the lessons of the past. Even today, many desert dwellers are nomadic, since staying in one place too long will exhaust what few resources the desert can offer.

The memory of the desert was especially significant to the Israelites as a result of their **Exodus** experience. It was in the desert that Israel first met the Lord, and the tradition was forever set that it was in the desert that one might meet God.

The desert was notable in the account of the patriarchs (Gen 12–50) and especially in the flight from Egypt and the journey in the wilderness (Exod 15:22, 16:1, 17:1, 18:5, 19:1–2; Num 14:33, 32:13). In the deserts Israel received the loving protection of the Lord, but the time in the desert was also a time of divine testing and discipline. The desert was therefore also a powerful reminder of the need for Israel to live in fidelity to its covenant promises and its love for the Lord (Hos 2:16; Acts 7:41; 1 Cor 10:5; Heb 3:8).

The desert was a place of desolation and also of refuge (Gen 16:7; Exod 2:15–3:1; 1 Sam 23–26; 1 Kgs 19:1–4). It also figured in the New Testament. John the Baptist prepared for his own mission in the desert (Matt 3:1–12, 1:7–10; Mark 1:3–4; Luke 3:1–20; John 1:23). Jesus was also led by the Spirit into the desert to make his final preparation for his earthly ministry and to be tempted by the devil (Matt 4:1–11; Mark 1:12–13). Jesus also retreated to the desert for the peaceful solitude of meditation and prayer (Matt 14:13; Mark 6:30–32; Luke 4:42, 5:16; John 6:15).

DESTINY An idol god of fate worshipped by unrepentant Israelites in Babylon (Isa 65:11). The name of the deity appears in Hebrew as *měnî;* thus some translations have "Meni" in this verse. The prophet refers to this god to make an ominous wordplay: those who forsake the Lord and serve *Destiny* will themselves be *destined* to a violent death (Isa 65:12).

DEUEL The father of Eliasaph of Gad and a commander under **Moses** (Num 1:14; 2:14; 7:42, 47; 10:29).

DEUTEROCANONICAL Those books (and parts of books) of the Old Testament whose inclusion in the Catholic **canon** was disputed at one time: Judith, Tobit, Sirach, Wisdom, 1 and 2 Maccabees, and Baruch; also Dan 3:24–90 and chapters 13 and 14 and Esth 10:4–16 and chapter 24. The term "deuterocanonical" (from the Greek for "second canon") was first used by the Dominican Sixtus of Siena (d. 1569). Books regarded as canonical with little or no debate were called "protocanonical" (from the Greek for "first canon").

The Catholic Church accepts both the protocanonical and deuterocanonical books as divinely inspired and canonical and treats them with the same reverence. The Orthodox churches also accept them, along with additional works found in ancient codices of the Greek **Septuagint:** 1 Esdras (or 3 Ezra), the

Prayer of Manasseh, 3 Maccabees, and Psalm 151, which are not accepted in the Catholic canon. Rabbinic Judaism and the founders of Protestantism rejected the deuterocanonical books; some Protestant Bibles print them in a separate section called "**Apocrypha.**"

The deuterocanonical books were accepted by the Church from the earliest times, and their inclusion in the Canon of Scripture was given formal definition at the Council of Trent on April 8, 1546, in the dogmatic decree *De Canonicis Scripturis.* The Council Fathers declared the **Vulgate** to be the authentic Latin version of the Bible and promulgated the list of the books accepted as entirely canonical. The Canon of the Bible, including the deuterocanonical books, consisted of the forty-six books of the Old Testament and twenty-seven books of the New Testament.

In addition to the OT deuterocanonical books, parts of the NT have also been subject to dispute at times: the Epistle to the Hebrews, the Epistle of James, the Epistle of Jude, 2 Peter; 2 and 3 John, Revelation, and Mark 16:9–20; also Luke 22:43 and John 5:4, 7:53; 8:1–11. Sometimes these sections of the NT are also described as "deuterocanonical," but most modern Christians accept them as Scripture.

DEUTERONOMY (Greek, "second law") The fifth and last book of the Pentateuch. Its title is derived from Deut 17:18 as translated in the **Septuagint:** the king "shall write for himself in a book this law [*to deuteronomion*]."

Deuteronomy records the details of the second **covenant** under **Moses** that was made on the plains of Moab forty years after the cov-

enant ratified at Sinai (Deut 29:1). The Hebrew title for Deuteronomy comes from its opening expression, *ʾēlleh haddĕbārîm* ("these are the words"): "These are *the words* that Moses spoke to all Israel" (Deut 1:1). The Latin title, *Liber Deuteronomii,* like the English title, was taken from the Septuagint *Deuteronomion.*

In form, the book of Deuteronomy is a collection of farewell discourses by Moses recounting the terms of the covenant under which Israel was to live. The discourses were given by Moses on the plains of Moab (Deut 1:1–5) as the Israelites were preparing to enter the land of Canaan. Israel is to live in total fidelity to the Lord and the detailed covenant stipulations: sanctions, blessings, and curses. The book sets forth the rewards and punishments that would come with obedience or disobedience to the covenant law code. In short, it is a national constitution for the state of Israel, by which the tribes were to live as a secular state under the direction of the Levites and administered from a central sanctuary.

I. *Author and Date*

II. *Contents*

III. *Purpose and Themes*

    A. *The Sinai and Moab Covenants*

    B. *The Covenant as Treaty*

    C. *A National Constitution*

    D. *Joshua*

IV. *Deuteronomy in the New Testament*

I. AUTHOR AND DATE

By tradition, Moses wrote the whole **Pentateuch**, and Deuteronomy specifically, with his own pen (cf. Deut 31:9, 22, 24). If Moses was the author, then the book of Deuteronomy would be dated near the end of Moses's life in the 1400s B.C. (or perhaps the 1200s B.C., depending on the date we accept for the Exodus). Indeed, Deuteronomy shows strong resemblances to treaties of the second millennium B.C. (see below), and the setting envisioned in the text is consistent with the period prior to the conquest of Canaan. Moses would be the likely author of such a work: his own background in the Egyptian court not only would have taught him to read and write, but also would have given him an education in the legal formalities of Near Eastern government and foreign policy. He knew the procedures of covenants and treaties, not just the terms (cf. Exod 2:5–10; Acts 7:22).

Biblical criticism in modern times has moved away from the tradition of Mosaic authorship. Many scholars instead support the idea of multiple traditions behind the text that were assembled by editors living in different places at different times. Some scholars have suggested that Deuteronomy is entirely the result of postexilic authors and editors. In the "JEDP" source theory, Deuteronomy is said to come largely from the D source, the substance of which is said to date back to the seventh century B.C. (see **Pentateuch** for more on source theories).

Modern scholarship puts less trust in the JEDP paradigm than previous generations of scholars did, and the best clue to the date of the book may be the format of the covenant treaty itself. Deuteronomy as it stands in the canon corresponds to second-millennium treaties more closely than it does to first-millennium treaties, strongly suggesting an earlier date rather than a later one.

II. CONTENTS

III. PURPOSE AND THEMES

Deuteronomy begins with a historical overview of the Sinai covenant and wilderness wanderings, then gives Israel its national constitution. The book ends with Moses's prophetic visions of the future of the nation. Thus the book gives Israel not only the terms of the covenant by which Israel would live, but also a theology of its history. The fate of Israel, for better or for worse, will be determined by its fidelity or infidelity to the Deuteronomic covenant.

A. *The Sinai and Moab Covenants*

At Sinai, God spoke directly to Israel and called the nation his "firstborn son" (Exod 4:22) and a "kingdom of priests" (Exod 19:6). The covenant at Sinai (see Exod 19–24) was ratified and then broken by the apostasy of the golden calf (Exod 32; Num 12–14, 25:1–18), after which the Israelites were placed under the clerical supervision of priests and Levites (cf. Exod 34–40; Lev 1–26). Owing to obdurate disobedience, the Israelites were forced to spend forty years in the wilderness as punishment and to prevent the entry of the first generation into the Promised Land. Yet the second generation fell into idolatrous apostasy again at Beth-peor in Moab. After that, the covenant of Deuteronomy was instituted.

The book itself makes a clear distinction between the covenant at **Sinai** (or Horeb) and the later covenant in Moab: "These are the words of the covenant which the Lord commanded Moses to make with the people of Israel in the land of Moab, besides the covenant which he had made with them at Horeb" (Deut 29:1).

Several important differences should be noted:

1. *Place.* The first covenant was made at Sinai (Horeb), the second on the plains of Moab, east of the Jordan River.

2. *Time.* The covenant at Sinai was made in the first year of the **Exodus**; the covenant in Moab was made in the fortieth year.

3. *People.* The covenant at Sinai was made with the generation that had left Egypt; the covenant in Moab was made with their children.

4. *Presence of God.* At Sinai, God appeared to his people in fire and cloud; in Moab, Moses spoke to the people with no visible manifestation of the Lord's presence.

The repeated apostasy of Israel made the second covenant very different from the first. The idolatry of the golden calf (Exod 32), and again in Moab (Num 25), showed that Israel was not yet ready to assume the responsibilities of being a priestly kingdom. The laws in Deuteronomy therefore had to make concessions to Israel's unholiness. "I gave them statutes that were not good and ordinances by which they could not have life," God says in Ezek 20:25. This startling declaration comes after a summary of the covenant and rebellion in the wilderness, the point being that some of the laws in Deuteronomy made concessions to Israel's sinful nature. This same idea underlies Jesus's teaching on Deuteronomy's legal provision for divorce: "For your hardness of heart he wrote you this commandment. But from the beginning of creation, 'God made them male and female'" (Mark 10:5–6).

Thus we can see much of Deuteronomy as the fallout from the apostasy in the wilderness. Deuteronomy lowers the bar of moral expectation for a people struggling with weakness. Divorce is "not good," but it must be regulated to prevent even worse abuses (Deut 24:1). The wars of extermination in Canaan were "not good," but were made necessary by Israel's constant attraction to the abominable idols of her neighbors (Deut 20:16–17; cf. Matt 5:43–44). The Lord alone is King (Deut 33:5; 1 Sam 8:4–7), and earthly kings are "not good" (cf. 1 Sam 8:10–18), but the Israelites would demand one anyway (Deut 17:14–20). The principle behind these concessions was to prevent, if possible, the worst excesses of evil by permitting lesser ones.

B. The Covenant as Treaty

The covenant is expressed in Deuteronomy in a form that closely resembles what we know of ancient Near Eastern treaties between suzerain kings and their vassal subjects. Hittite treaties, for example, which date to the second half of the second millennium B.C., began with a *preamble* (cf. 1:1–5). After that, a *historical prologue* gave an overview of the suzerain's relationship to the vassal (cf. 1:6–4:49). Then came *stipulations* that detailed the demands of the covenant on the vassal (cf. 5–26). After these stipulations came *curses and blessings,* or sanctions, that would result from compliance or noncompliance with the covenant's terms (cf. 27–30). Finally, *succession arrangements*

provided for the disposition of the treaty itself and ensured the periodic reading of its terms (cf. 31–34).

In this sort of treaty, a king subjects a vassal people to himself and demands from them an oath of loyalty. He also enumerates the consequences of loyalty and disloyalty in the form of blessings and curses. Conventional language declared the king to be a "father" and the vassal his "son."

We see exactly these patterns in Deuteronomy: the Lord is the divine "king" (33:5) and Israel his vassal (4:15–40; 5:6–7; 26:17). The Lord likewise demands oaths of allegiance from Israel (27:15–26) and lists blessings and curses (28:1–68). God is the Father, Israel the son (1:31; 8:5; 14:1; 32:6, 19–20).

C. A National Constitution

The Jewish historian Josephus (*Ant.* 4) described Deuteronomy as the "constitution" of the Jewish people. Where Exodus and Leviticus gave liturgical and ethical laws, Deuteronomy gave a secular shape to the state. The Law would be in the hands of the priests (Deut 17:18; 31:9). The people might choose a king, but even he would rule under the divine Law (17:14–20). The book gives judges clear procedures for applying the Law (19:15–21; 25:1–3).

Thus much of Deuteronomy is devoted to very specific laws regulating every aspect of secular life: debts (15:1–3), loans (23:19–20; 25:10–13), commerce (25:13–16), divorce and remarriage (24:1–4), inheritance (21:15–17), rebellious children (21:18–21), and sexual immorality (22:22–30). Even war was also carefully regulated (20:1–20). Deuteronomy thus gave the means for Israel to exist as a secular nation-state that would last until the coming of Jesus.

D. Joshua

Deuteronomy also validated the succession of Joshua as Moses's successor and head of the Israelites (cf. Deut 31:7–23; 34:9–12). Deuteronomy is truly Moses's farewell discourse, but he does not simply say good-bye. He provides for the smooth and proper transition of authority by certifying Joshua as his successor.

IV. DEUTERONOMY IN THE NEW TESTAMENT

Deuteronomy was quoted by Jesus Christ more often than any other book of the Old Testament, and seventeen of the twenty-seven books of the New Testament refer to it as well. Christ makes its teaching a foundation for his own, in particular the Deuteronomic commandment to love, which he called the greatest of all commandments (cf. Deut 6:4; Matt 22:37–38). Christ uses Deuteronomy to refute the temptations of the devil in the wilderness (cf. Deut 6:13, 18; 8:3; Matt 4:4, 7, 10). Jesus is also the fulfillment of the Deuteronomic prophecy that God would raise up a prophet like Moses and would put his words in the mouth of the prophet (Deut 18:15–18; Acts 3:22, 7:37).

DEVIL *See* **Satan**.

DIASPORA *See* **Dispersion**.

DIATESSARON (Greek *dia tessarōn*, "through [the] four [Gospels]") The name given by Eusebius in his *Ecclesiastical History* (*Hist. Eccl.* 4.29.6) to the book organized by Tatian around A.D. 170. Tatian combined the four canonical Gospels to create a single narrative of Jesus's life. Although the Church did not accept the Diatessaron as a substitute for the four individual Gospels, it is often cited as confirmation that by the middle of the second century A.D. there were exactly four accepted Gospels (cf. Saint Irenaeus, *Against Heresies* 3.1.1).

DIBLAIM The father of Gomer, wife of the prophet Hosea (Hos 1:3).

DIBON A city of Moabites that was captured by Sihon, king of the Amorites, shortly before the arrival of the Israelites on the plains of Moab (Num 21:26–30). After Israel's conquest of the Transjordan, the city was assigned to the tribe of Gad (Num 32:3, 34; 33:45; cf. Isa 15:1–9; Jer 48:18–22).

DIDRACHMA A Greek coin worth two drachmas. It was equivalent in value to the half shekel that was to be paid each year to the Temple (Exod 30:13; Matt 17:24).

DIDYMUS The Greek name of the apostle **Thomas** (John 11:16; 20:24; 21:2). The name means "twin" in Greek (*Didymos*), as "Thomas" does in Aramaic (*tĕʾômāʾ*).

DINAH The daughter of Jacob and Leah (Gen 30:21; 46:15). She was raped by Shechem, son of Hamor, a Hivite who used the incident as a pretext for negotiating with Jacob for his marriage to Dinah. Jacob consented but demanded that the men of Shechem undergo circumcision. While the male inhabitants were recovering from the procedure, Dinah's brothers Simeon and Levi captured the city and massacred the inhabitants in revenge (Gen 34:1–31), bringing Jacob's curse on them for their violence (Gen 49:5–7).

DINHABAH A city of Edom that served as the residence of the Edomite king Bela, son of Beor (Gen 36:32; 1 Chr 1:43).

DIONYSIUS Called the Areopagite, a prominent Athenian who was converted by Paul (Acts 17:34). Dionysius was a member of the professional council in Athens called the Areopagus, and his conversion was probably a significant event. According to Eusebius in his *Ecclesiastical History* (*Hist. Eccl.* 3.4.11; 4.23.3), Dionysius became the first bishop of Athens. A variety of writings were attributed to him in the first Christian centuries.

DIOSCORINTHIUS The name of the first month of the Macedonian calendar and used to date the letter of Lysias to the Jews (2 Macc 11:21). The name may have come from the *Dioskouroi,* the twin sons of the god Zeus in Greek mythology.

DIOTREPHES A Christian leader who is censured by the apostle John (3 John 9–10) for his pride and stubbornness.

DISCIPLE A student or follower who emulates the example set by a master and seeks to identify with the master's teachings (cf. Matt 10:24–25). In the Old Testament, disciples followed prophets (Isa 8:16). In the New Testament, John the Baptist had disciples (Matt 14:12; John 1:35, 3:25), as did the Pharisees (Matt 22:16; Mark 2:18; Luke 5:33), who called themselves disciples of Moses (John 9:28). Most often, a "disciple" in the NT means a follower of Jesus Christ. It can mean any follower (cf. Acts 6:1; 9:1, 19; 13:52, etc.), but more specifically one of the Twelve **apostles** (Matt 10:2, 28:16–20; Mark 16:14–18; Luke 24:47–49; John 20:19–23; cf. 1 Cor 9:1). There are over 250 references to "disciple" in the NT, most of which are found in the Gospels and Acts, and the majority of those refer to the apostles.

Being a disciple of Jesus implied more than merely being a student or adherent. Jesus was no ordinary **rabbi**. He had not studied a course of instruction under another rabbi, nor did he seek or need permission to teach (Matt 13:54; John 7:15). His teaching was unprecedented (Matt 7:29; Mark 1:22), and his closest disciples did not come to him for instruction; rather, he called them to the life of discipleship by his own authority (Matt 4:18–22; Mark 1:16–20) (CCC 767, 787). Further, discipleship did not entail the ambition of eventual equality with their master, as it did with the disciples of the Pharisees. It was not merely a matter of listening to the teachings and learning wisdom: it was a commitment to a new way of life modeled by Jesus. The disciple must "take up his cross" and follow Jesus (Matt 16:24; Mark 8:34; Luke 14:27). The follower must be willing to leave everything behind—family, friends, and possessions—and be willing to share in his mission, his joy, and his suffering, even to die for the sake of Jesus (Matt 8:19, 10:37; Luke 9:57, 14:26).

DISEASE *See* **Medicine**.

DISPERSION Also Diaspora (from the Greek word for "dispersion"). The name used collectively for the Jewish communities that had settled outside of Palestine. The Dispersion began with the first removal of Israelites from Palestine as a result of deportations by **Assyria** (eighth century B.C.) and then **Babylon** (sixth century B.C.). Following the conquest of Galilee and Samaria by the Assyrians in about 732 and 722 B.C., the Israelite survivors were deported from Palestine. A second deportation occurred under the Babylonians when Nebuchadnezzar conquered Jerusalem in 586 B.C. The Israelites deported from Samaria never returned en masse, but the Jews sent to Babylon did, and they became the nucleus for the restoration of the Temple and the religious traditions of the Jews in Judea once repatriation was permitted under the Persian ruler Cyrus the Great. Many Jews stayed on in Babylon, however, and the Jewish community there remained large and prosperous into the medieval period.

Jewish settlements were established elsewhere in the sixth century B.C., most notably in Egypt. Fleeing the wrath of Nebuchadnezzar, a large group of refugees from Judah fled to Egypt, taking Jeremiah the prophet with them (Jer 43:5–7). The Ptolemaic Dynasty, which ruled Egypt from the fourth to the first centuries B.C., encouraged more Jewish immigration. Indeed, the Jewish population in Egypt—especially in Alexandria, where one entire quarter of the city was Jewish—became the wealthiest and most influential Jewish community outside of Palestine, keeping close ties to Jerusalem. Other Jewish communities were established throughout the Hellenic world and then the Roman Empire, including in Antioch, across the Mediterranean islands, and into Italy and Rome. There were synagogues in most major cities of the Roman world, and Jews from the empire and beyond made pilgrimages to Jerusalem (Acts 2:9–10).

The Jews of the Dispersion were generally prosperous, hardworking, and peaceful, and the Hellenic states and especially the Roman imperial administration showed them great favor. They were respected businesspeople and merchants, and they enjoyed religious toleration and freedom and definite political rights; many, such as Paul, were Roman citizens, with attendant privileges. Further, the Jews were exempt, for religious reasons, from the demands of military service and were also permitted to pay a tax for the Temple in Jerusalem. Each community of the Dispersion had its synagogue, and when they began to spread the Gospel, the apostles made these synagogues the primary forum for their evangelization.

While long accepted as productive participants in the economic and cultural life of the times, the Jews of the Dispersion still encountered various forms of hostility. Riots struck in Alexandria with frequency, driven by the envy of Gentiles who resented the affluence of the Alexandrian Jews. Their success, along with the exclusive nature of Jewish society, sparked hostility in other areas, as we can see in the writings of Cicero, Seneca, and Tacitus. Formal persecution in Alexandria was launched by Emperor Gaius Caligula, who also demanded that his own image be installed in the Temple. Massive riots were prevented in A.D. 41 only by his assassination. In A.D. 49, the Jews were expelled from the city of Rome by Emperor Claudius as part of his wider campaign against foreign religions (Acts 18:2). They soon returned, however, along with most of the people of other religions whom Claudius had tried to root out.

The **Jewish Wars** (A.D. 66–70 and 132–135; *see* **Jerusalem**) made the Jews of the Dispersion more suspect in the eyes of the Roman authorities. After the destruction of Jerusalem in A.D. 70, it was the Jews of the Dispersion who were left to carry on Jewish tradition, and ultimately to reconfigure Judaism, so that the study of the Law replaced the service of the Temple as the center of rabbinic Judaism.

DIVIDED KINGDOM *See* **Israel, kingdom of**; **Judah, kingdom of**.

DIVINATION The effort to learn the future by occult means. Divination was a common practice in the ancient Near East: assorted diviners tried (but failed) to interpret Pharaoh's dream (Gen 41:8), Nebuchadnezzar's dream (Dan 2:10), and the warning given to Balthasar (Dan 5:8). Predicting the future was forbidden under Mosaic Law, and divinatory practices were called "abominations" (Deut 18:9). The punishment for illicit divination was death (Lev 19:31; 20:6), and the Israelites were reminded that they were to heed instead the prophet, who served as an intermediary

between the people and God (Deut 18:13–22). Nevertheless, **Saul** consulted the Witch of Endor to conjure up the spirit of **Samuel** (1 Sam 28:6–25). (*See also* **Magic**.)

DIVINO AFFLANTE SPIRITU An encyclical issued on September 30, 1943, by Pope Pius XII that gave important encouragement and guidance to biblical scholars in their scientific study of the Bible. It was published on the fiftieth anniversary of the encyclical *Providentissimus Deus* by Pope Leo XIII in 1893, which Pius called the "supreme guide in biblical studies" (§2). The encyclicals were commemorated by Pope John Paul II, who observed that while both were concerned with problems in their own era, they nevertheless possessed a validity for continuing studies and translations of Scripture (*Address on the Interpretation of the Bible in the Church,* April 23, 1993).

Divino Afflante Spiritu recognized the immense progress made in the study of ancient languages and the more open environment that prevailed in the field of biblical study, especially when compared with the turbulent era of Leo XIII (r. 1878–1903). Nevertheless, Pius was aware of the dangers of abuse and speculation in biblical studies without proper analysis and the need for a clear sense of direction from the Church for those involved in such scientific endeavors.

The encyclical sanctioned the careful study of ancient languages so as to promote a more precise understanding of the original texts of Scripture. An important part of this study is the scientific application of textual criticism, with its goal of determining the original wording of biblical texts. Pope Pius reaffirmed the doctrinal teaching of Leo XIII. He stressed the need to determine the *literal* sense of Scripture, but he acknowledged that scholars can study literary forms as a way of ascertaining meaning. (*See* **Biblical criticism**.)

DIVORCE *See under* **Marriage**.

DODANIM *See* **Rodanim**.

DODO The name of three men in the Old Testament:

1. The grandfather of Tola, a minor judge (Judg 10:1).

2. The father of Eleazar, a famed warrior in the service of David (2 Sam 23:9; 1 Chr 11:12).

3. The father of Elhanan of Bethlehem, another of David's famed warriors (2 Sam 23:24; 1 Chr 11:26).

DOEG An Edomite who was head of the shepherds in the service of King Saul (1 Sam 21:7; 22:9, 18). Doeg spied on David when he fled to the sanctuary of Nob and received bread from Ahimelech. This was reported to Saul (1 Sam 22:9–10), and the king condemned Ahimelech to death along with the other priests of Nob (1 Sam 22:16–17). When Saul's troops refused to execute the sentence, Doeg executed all the priests of Nob and many of the people who resided in Nob (1 Sam 22:18–19). This incident, according to the traditional superscription, forms the backdrop of Ps 52.

DOG The dog in the Old Testament is a scavenger, equated with impurity. Dogs devoured corpses left unburied (1 Kgs 14:11, 16:4, 21:19, 22:38; 2 Kgs 9:10; Ps 68:23; Jer 15:3). Calling a person a dog was a strong insult (1 Sam 17:43, 24:14; 2 Sam 3:8, 16:9; Ps 22:16), and the word was used specifically for male prostitutes (Deut 23:18). Dogs were not widely domesticated, but occasionally we hear of dogs used in shepherding (Job 30:1) and even as family pets (Tob 5:16).

In the New Testament, the dog similarly represents worthlessness and impurity. Testing a Canaanite woman, Jesus observed, "It is not fair to take the children's food and throw it to the dogs" (Matt 15:26). But she replied, "Yes, Lord, yet even the dogs eat the crumbs that fall from their masters' table" (Matt 15:27), and Jesus praised her faith. In Jesus's parable of the rich man and Lazarus, the fact that dogs licked the wounds of Lazarus was an indication of his pitiful state (Luke 16:21). "Dog" was an insulting epithet for Judaizers (Phil 3:2). Revelation declares that "the dogs and sorcerers and fornicators and murderers and idolators, and everyone who loves and practices falsehood" will be excluded from the heavenly Jerusalem (Rev 22:15).

DOPHKAH The name of the site where the Israelites made their first encampment after departing the wilderness of Sin; the eighth encampment since the beginning of the **Exodus** (Num 33:12).

DOR A coastal city south of Mount Carmel; modern Khirbet el Burj near Tantura. The city joined a Canaanite coalition against Joshua and the advancing Israelites (Josh 11:2; 12:23). While defeated, it apparently remained a Canaanite possession for some time afterward (Judg 1:27). The scheming general Trypho took refuge there and was besieged by Antiochus VII (1 Macc 15:11–14).

DORCAS The Greek name of Tabitha, a Christian woman of Joppa who was famous for her works of charity (Acts 9:36). She died and was restored to life by Peter (Acts 9:37–41).

DOTHAN A town in Ephraimite territory north of Samaria, probably located at modern Tell Dotha. Here Joseph found his brothers with their sheep (Gen 37). It is also mentioned in connection with Elisha (2 Kgs 6:13) and Judith (Jdt 3:9; 4:6; 7:3, 18).

DOUAY-RHEIMS VERSION *See* **Versions of the Bible**.

DOVE The name used for several species of wild pigeons in Palestine, including the ring dove, stock dove, rock dove, and turtledove. The dove was a suitable sacrifice for poor people who could not afford a lamb (Lev 12:8), and Mary and Joseph offered two turtledoves at the Presentation of Jesus in the Temple (Luke 2:22–24). The selling of doves in the Temple courts for sacrifices was condemned by Jesus (Matt 21:12; Mark 11:15; John 2:14–16). The dove served to inform Noah whether the flood had subsided after being released from the ark (Gen 8:6–12). The dove was also used in imagery in both prophetic and wisdom literature (Song 1:12; 2:10, 14; 4:1; 5:12; cf. Isa 38:14, 59:11, 60:8; Ps 55:6). In the New Testament, the dove symbolizes the Holy Spirit. The Holy Spirit descended upon Jesus at his baptism in the form of a dove (Matt 3:16; Mark 1:10; John 1:32). The dove is also a common symbol of innocence (Matt 10:16).

DOWRY *See* **Marriage**.

DRACHMA A Greek silver coin (2 Macc 12:43). It was the equivalent of the Roman **denarius** or a quarter of a Jewish **shekel**, a laborer's wages for a day. Jesus referred to the "silver coin" of the drachma in the parable of the lost coin (Luke 15:8–9).

DREAM The ancient world believed that dreams were full of meaning. There were experts who specialized in dream interpretation, such as those who failed to interpret Pharaoh's dream (Gen 41:8) and Nebuchadnezzar's dream (Dan 2:2).

The Old Testament warns against treating dreams as a form of **divination**, as they are often misleading (Deut 13:1–5; Sir 34:7). The Psalmist saw them as fleeting (Ps 73:20; 90:5). Jeremiah considered them untrustworthy, even though he did acknowledge that they could be a source of revelation (Jer 23:27, 32; 29:8). God's people must beware of false prophets, whose dreams come from their own minds, and who give Israel a false sense of security in spite of the sins of the nation (Jer 23:16).

Still, God did use dreams to communicate with his prophets—in contrast to Moses, with whom God spoke "mouth to mouth, clearly" (Num 12:6–8). Dreams played a positive role in the account of three figures in particular: Jacob (Gen 31:10–13, 24), Joseph (Gen 37–41), and Daniel. Solomon asked for wisdom in a dream (1 Kgs 3:5–15), and God sometimes sent dreams to foreigners (Gen 20, 31; Judg 7:13–14).

In the New Testament, dreams are found only in Matthew and Acts. Joseph is told in a dream that Mary's child is divine (Matt 1:20), is warned in a dream to flee to Egypt (Matt 2:13), and is later told in a dream when to return (Matt 2:19–20). The wise men are also warned in a dream to avoid Herod the Great (Matt 2:12). Later, Pilate's wife has a dream and warns Pilate against pursuing the trial against Jesus (Matt 27:19). In Acts, the word "dream" is not directly used; instead divine revelations that come by night are called "visions" (Acts 16:9, 18:9–10; cf. Acts 23:11, 27:23–24).

DROSS Impurities that are produced in the process of smelting and cleaning ores. The slag is extracted in the process of smelting and purifying metal. In biblical imagery, the dross was used to describe moral and spiritual impurities: namely, evil and sin. Similarly, purified metal was used to describe souls that had been tested and proven worthy (Prov 17:3, 25:4–5, 27:21; Sir 2:5; Isa 1:25, 48:10; Zech 13:9; Mal 3:3; 1 Pet 1:6–7).

DRUNKENNESS Intoxication through an excess of drinking alcohol. The Bible does not prohibit the drinking of wine and other forms of alcohol, as the fruits from which they were made exist for use by man (Ps 104:15; Sir 31:35). Nevertheless, drunkenness was a common social ill in the ancient world, and the Bible does condemn overindulgence and the vice of alcoholism (Prov 23:29–35, 31:4–5; Sir 19:1, 31:29–30; Isa 5:11, 22; Hos 4:11; Amos 6:6; Hab 2:5) as they lead to misery and ruin (Prov 20:1; 23:20–

21). Drunkenness was especially frequent at festivals (Jdt 13:2). In contrast, wine enhances the quality of life if consumed in moderation (Sir 31:27–28). **Nazirites** were forbidden to drink wine, or even to eat fresh grapes or raisins (Num 6:1–3). Priests were forbidden to drink strong drink before entering the tent of meeting (Lev 10:8–9). (*See also* **Cup**.)

Christ's first miracle was changing water into wine for a wedding celebration, which clearly implies that he did not disapprove of alcohol consumption per se (John 2:1–12). Still, Jesus spoke clearly against the vice of drunkenness in the parable of the drunken servant (Matt 24:49; Luke 12:45). Elsewhere in the New Testament, drunkenness is listed as a serious sin that can exclude the sinner from eternal life (Rom 13:13; 1 Cor 5:11, 6:10; Gal 5:21), and potential candidates for the office of bishop are disqualified by this vice (Titus 1:7; 1 Tim 3:3). As in the Old Testament, sobriety is considered a virtue in the NT (1 Thess 5:6–11). On the other hand, Paul does not prohibit ministers from drinking alcohol (cf. 1 Tim 5:23). The sin is not in drinking, but in excessive drinking (Eph 5:18) (CCC 2290).

DRUSILLA The Jewish wife of **Felix**, Roman procurator of Palestine, who heard Paul's case in Caesarea (Acts 24:24). According to Flavius Josephus, she was born around A.D. 38 and was the youngest daughter of Herod Agrippa (*Ant.* 18.132; *B.J.* 2.220). She and Felix had a son who was killed in the eruption of Mount Vesuvius in A.D. 79 (*Ant.* 20.144).

DUMAH The sixth son of Ishmael (Gen 25:14; 1 Chr 1:30).

DUNG GATE One of the gates in the southern wall of Jerusalem; it led out to the **Hinnom Valley** (Neh 2:13; 3:13, 14; 12:31).

DURA (From Akkadian, "city wall, fortress") A site in the province of Babylonia mentioned in Dan 3:1. The account declares that King **Nebuchadnezzar** erected a "golden statue whose height was sixty cubits and whose width was six cubits; he set it up on the plain of Dura in the province of Babylon." Because they refused to bow before the image, Daniel's friends **Shadrach**, **Meshach**, and **Abednego** were hurled into the fiery furnace. The location of the site is uncertain.

DYE, DYEING The process of coloring or staining material. The art of dyeing was a common one in the ancient world, including Palestine, as evidenced by the archaeological remains found of a local dyeing industry at Gezer, Tell en-Nasbeh, Beth-zur, and especially Tell Beit Mirsim. It is known that both the Egyptians and the Mesopotamians were skilled in the craft of dyeing, and dyed fabrics were highly prized possessions. The most important and expensive color was purple or crimson, known in Ugarit as early as 1500 B.C. Among the most important centers of dye was Tyre, with its specialty in purple. This purple dye was made from the murex mollusk that was found in the waters of the Mediterranean off the coast of Phoenicia. The color became associated with royalty and was worn only by the wealthy (Luke 16:19). The soldiers dressed Christ in a purple robe in mockery of his claim to be King (Mark 15:17). Lydia, a convert of Paul, was a seller of purple goods (Acts 16:14). Aside from that mollusk dye, most other colors came from vegetable dyes.

DYSMAS The name tradition gives to the Good Thief who was crucified with Jesus (Luke 23:40–43). His name does not appear in Scripture.

E

E The abbreviation for the so-called Elohist source for the **Pentateuch**.

EAGLE A symbol of divinity in Babylon, the eagle was considered by the Israelites to be an unclean bird (Lev 11:13; Deut 14:12). In prophetic imagery, it was a symbol of the terrible speed of Israel's enemies as they descended upon God's people (Deut 28:49; Prov 23:5; Job 9:26; Jer 48:40; Hos 8:1), as well as a symbol of the Lord bearing the people of Israel upon his wings and his divine providence and care (Exod 19:4; Deut 32:11; Ezek 1:10, 10:14; Rev 12:14).

EARTH *See* **World.**

EARTHQUAKE An active fault at the rift of the Jordan Valley makes Palestine prone to disastrous earthquakes, and various Old Testament allusions point to frequent tectonic activity. One specific earthquake was recorded in the reign of **Uzziah** (Amos 1:1; Zech 14:5). Earthquakes were seen as acts of the Lord in his role as supreme judge (Ps 60:4; Jer 4:24, 51:29, 97:4–5; Joel 2:10), as a **theophany** (Judg 5:4; 2 Sam 22:8; Ps 18:8, 68:9; Joel 4:16), or as part of the **day of the Lord** (Isa 13:13; 24:18–19). In the New Testament, earthquakes were reported at the death of Christ (Matt 27:51) and the Resurrection (Matt 28:2). An earthquake struck while Paul and Silas prayed in prison (Acts 16:26). The earthquake is also seen as a symbol and event of the apocalypse (Matt 24:7; Mark 13:8; Luke 21:25–26; Rev 6:12, 8:5, 11:13, 16:18).

EASTER *See* **Resurrection.**

EASTERN SEA A body of water generally identified with the **Dead Sea.**

EAST WIND *See* **Palestine.**

EBAL A large mountain in central Samaria, opposite Mount Gerizim, to the south of Shechem. One of the highest mountains in central Palestine (2,950 feet or 900 meters), Mount Ebal was the site where Moses was commanded to renew the covenant (Deut 11:29–32; 27:11–26). According to the ritual (Josh 8:30–35; Deut 11:26–32, 27:1–26) the tribes of Reuben, Gad, Asher, Zebulun, Dan, and Naphtali stood upon Mount Ebal and shouted the covenant curses while the other tribes stood upon Mount Gerizim and shouted the covenant blessings. (*See* **Covenant.**)

EBED-MELECH (Hebrew, "servant of the king") An Ethiopian eunuch in the court of King Zedekiah of Judah. He assisted Jeremiah during the time of the prophet's imprisonment (Jer 38:7–13; 39:15–18).

EBENEZER (Hebrew, "stone of help") The battlefield where Israel defeated the Philistines under the leadership of **Samuel** (1 Sam 7:12). On the site Samuel erected a monument for the victory, from which the site received its name in honor of the great help provided by the Lord. The field is also associated with the crushing defeat in which the Philistines captured the ark (1 Sam 4:1; 5:1), although the two places are probably not the same. (*See* **Aphek**.)

EBER The descendant of Shelah and **Shem** in the **Table of Nations** (Gen 11:14), father of Peleg (Gen 11:16) and Joktan (Gen 10:24–25), and eponymous father of the **Hebrews**. His lineage is traced variously through his sons Joktan (Gen 10:21–31) and Peleg (Gen 11:14–17), but the two genealogies are combined in 1 Chr 1:17–27.

ECBATANA (Persian, "gathering place") The capital city of the Medes, situated at the foot of Mount Orontes in the Zagros Mountains; ancient Ecbatana is identified with the modern city of Hamadan, in modern northwestern Iran between the cities of Tehran and Baghdad. The city was captured by **Cyrus the Great** of Persia and became the summer residence of the Persian kings owing to its cool temperatures. According to Ezra 6:2, when King **Darius I** ordered a search for the records to confirm Cyrus's decree authorizing the res-

toration of Jerusalem and the Temple, he found no information in Babylon. The search was extended to Ecbatana, and the decree was found. Mention is also found in Tobit, Judith, and 2 Maccabees. In Tobit (3:7; 6:5, 9; 7:1; 14:12, 14), Ecbatana is named as the home of Raguel, Tobit's brother. In Judith (1:1, 2, 14), it is said to be the headquarters of King **Arphaxad**. According to 2 Macc 9:3, King **Antiochus IV** died near Ecbatana.

ECCE HOMO "Behold the man": the Latin translation of the words of Pontius Pilate when he presented Christ to the mob (John 19:5).

ECCLESIASTES, BOOK OF One of the Wisdom books of the Old Testament, Ecclesiastes is given the Hebrew title of "*Qoheleth*" (or *Koheleth*), from the name used by the writer. The word "Qoheleth" is the active feminine participle of the Hebrew verb meaning "to gather" and thus provides the basis for the Greek *Ekklēsiastēs* and the Latin *Ecclesiastes*. The RSV translates the word "Qoheleth" as "preacher," so the full title is "The words of the Preacher (Qoheleth), the son of David, king in Jerusalem." The author is perhaps to be described as the Teacher or Preacher (Qoheleth) who presides at the gathering or assembly. The book shows us that all things in life are vanity except for fear of the Lord, revering God, and keeping his commandments.

I. *Authorship and Date*
II. *Contents*
III. *Themes*
    A. *The Meaning of Life*
    B. *The Journey of Faith*

I. AUTHORSHIP AND DATE

The writer declares in Eccl 1:1 that he is son of David; later he states that he was king over Israel in Jerusalem (Eccl 1:12). These details suggest that he was Solomon, as tradition claims, although they could also apply to any other king of the Davidic line. The claim is a common literary device by which a teacher or author might assert teachings under the name of a great figure such as Solomon (cf. 1 Kgs 3:12). When the book received its present form is uncertain. Some scholars have suggested that the book was written by an unknown author in the third century B.C.

Some critics have seen the book as a compilation of several authors, the later ones trying to balance the evident pessimism of the original. Many recent scholars, however, accept the book as the work of one author, and the balance between pessimism and faith as intentional.

II. CONTENTS

Ecclesiastes is framed at the beginning and end by two memorable poems on the vanity of human life (Eccl 1:2–11; 11:7–12:7). In between those two poems, the Preacher's repeated investigations demonstrate the futility of trying to understand life and the wisdom of taking God's gifts as they come.

III. THEMES

A. *The Meaning of Life*

Ecclesiastes has one central question: "What is the meaning of life?" In answering, the Preacher ponders life from a remarkable variety of perspectives in the hopes of determining whether any true happiness can be found. The book begins with the famous declaration, "Vanity of vanities, says the Preacher, vanity of vanities! All is vanity. What does man gain by all the toil at which he toils under the sun?" (Eccl 1:2–3) and concludes with the simple admonition: "Fear God, and keep his commandments; for that is the whole duty of man. For God will bring every deed into judgment, with every secret thing, whether good or evil" (12:13–14).

To demonstrate these two basic points, the Preacher relies on a frequent pattern of point and counterpoint: trying to solve the riddles of life by human wisdom is utterly futile, so we should enjoy life within the limits established by God, recognizing that "the righteous and the wise and their deeds are in the hand of God" (9:1). In a sober and realistic analysis of the human condition, the mystery of evil and suffering is discussed in a vivid way, but the presence of wickedness and suffering is insufficient reason for abandoning faith in God.

B. The Journey of Faith

Unlike the true pessimist, the Preacher does not speak against God, but keeps his focus on man: "See, this alone I found, that God made man upright, but they have sought out many devices" (Eccl 7:29). The book's expressions of doubt and even cynicism speak for all who have confronted the anguish and disappointments of life and have come to question their belief. The author has gone through the same anguish and disappointments, and raised the same questions. Early in his quest, he even questions an afterlife (3:21), but later he affirms it (12:7). He holds back nothing of his doubts and speculations.

C. Moderation in All Things

The author recognizes the immutability of the laws of nature and of the created order, but this fatalism is offset by realization that those very laws depend on the divine will (Eccl 3:14; 6:2; 7:14), and the freedom of man resides within these limits, including the choice to act against God (7:29). His apparent fatalism is also equalized by his compassion for those who suffer, arguing that contentment and satisfaction are found only in the quiet enjoyment of God's blessings. He suggests, "I know that there is nothing better for them than to be happy and enjoy themselves as long as they live; also that it is God's gift to man that every one should eat and drink and take pleasure in all his toil" (3:12–13). This is not some recipe for Epicureanism, but an embrace of moderation that comes from accepting God's gift of life and blessing (cf. 7:16–17).

D. Reliance on God's Wisdom

Ultimately, in the face of the riddles of life, the Preacher admits repeatedly the inadequacies of his own wisdom. But as an alternative to the limited grasp of human wisdom, he suggests another way: "When I applied my mind to know wisdom, and to see the business that is done on earth, how neither day nor night one's eyes see sleep; then I saw all the work of God, that man cannot find out the work that is done under the sun. However much man may toil in seeking, he will not find it out; even though a wise man claims to know, he cannot find it out" (Eccl 8:16–17).

ECCLESIASTICUS *See* **Sirach**.

EDEN The son of Joah and a Levite of the Gershonite family. He took part in the cleansing of the Temple during the first year of the reign of King **Hezekiah** (2 Chr 29:12). It is possible that he is to be identified with the person of the same name who helped distribute Temple funds among Levitical towns (2 Chr 31:15, 18).

EDEN, GARDEN OF *See* **Garden of Eden**.

EDNA (Greek *Edna*, "delight") The wife of **Raguel** and mother of Sarah (Tob 7:7).

EDOM, EDOMITES (Hebrew, "red" or "ruddy") A territory stretching south and east of the Dead Sea to the Gulf of Aqaba; the Edomites are its inhabitants. They are described as the descendants of **Esau**, the elder brother of Jacob (Gen 25:30, 32:4, 36:1; 1 Chr 1:35). Archaeologists trace the origins of the Edomites to Semitic settlers who migrated into the region in the thirteenth century B.C. It is likely that the people there were organized into twelve tribes (Gen 36:20–30) under a chieftain, although they had a king before Israel (Gen 36:31).

The Edomites refused to grant passage to the Israelites on their way to the Promised Land (Num 20:14–21), forcing them to go around Edom. On another occasion, the Israelites were permitted passage, and Moses was commanded by God not to attack the Edomites (Deut 2:4–8; Num 21:4). Still, the Edomites were to be excluded from membership in the people of God (Deut 23:8).

The location of Edom on the main trade route, including control of the so-called King's Highway that was a conduit of trade between Arabia and Syria, made it both economically and strategically important (Num 20:17). It was repeatedly conquered by neighboring powers. Saul defeated the Edomites, but the formal conquest came under David (2 Sam 8:14). Edom remained tributary to Judah until the time of **Jehoram** of Judah (849–842 B.C.;

2 Kgs 8:20–22). Under **Amaziah** (r. 800–783 B.C.) and **Uzziah** (r. 783–742 B.C.), Edom was brought back under the sway of Judah (2 Kgs 14:7, 22). Edom won its independence during the time of **Ahaz** of Judah (2 Kgs 16:6), but soon fell under the domination of **Assyria**.

The Edomites supported Nebuchadnezzar's campaign against Jerusalem (587 B.C.) and celebrated the fall of Judah (Ps 137:7; Lam 4:21–22; cf. Amos 1:11–12; Isa 11:14; 21:11, 12; 34:5–17; Jer 49:7–22). Edomite cities were later conquered by **John Hyrcanus I** in 129 B.C., who compelled the non-Jewish population to be circumcised (1 Macc 4:36–59; 2 Macc 10:1–8). By the first century B.C. Idumea (the Greek spelling of Edom) was under the control of the Hasmonean line, and the region by that time extended from the southern Judean hill country, south of Beth-zur, to the frontier of the Negeb.

With the extensive political reorganization of Palestine by Pompey in 63 B.C., Idumea was part of the Roman province of Syria, but it remained in the hands of the Hasmoneans. As such, it served as the political foundation for the rise of **Herod the Great** and the gradual ascendancy of the Herodian line. Upon his death in 4 B.C., Emperor Augustus gave Idumea to the ethnarch Archelaus; it later belonged to Herod Agrippa I from A.D. 41 to 44 and then passed fully into Roman hands as part of the province of Syria.

EDREI A Transjordanian town and one of the residences of Og, the Amorite king of Bashan. Just south of the city, Og fought a battle with the Israelites and was killed. The Israelites then seized Og's land (Num 21:33–35; cf. Deut 1:4, 3:10; Josh 12:4; 13:12, 31).

EGLAH One of David's wives and the mother of Ithream (2 Sam 3:5; 1 Chr 3:3; cf. 2 Sam 3:2–5; 1 Chr 3:1–3).

EGLAIM A town, perhaps near the border of Moab, that was mentioned in Isaiah's oracle against Moab (Isa 15:8).

EGLON

1. The king of the Moabites who was assassinated by **Ehud** (Judg 3:12–22) after persecuting the Israelites for eighteen years. His name is derived apparently from a play on the words for "fat" and "calf" to refer to his obesity. He allied himself with the Ammonites and Amalekites, as a means of conquering and oppressing the Israelites.

2. An old city in Canaan that was attacked and captured by **Joshua** (Josh 10:34–35). It was later added to the **Shephelah** (Josh 15:39). Before its defeat, Eglon had joined a coalition of Canaanite city-states to sack Gibeon for its success in making peace with Joshua and the advancing Israelites (Josh 10:1–5).

EGYPT An ancient civilization along the Nile in northeast Africa, and a persistent symbol of bondage and slavery in Scripture. The history of Egypt goes back five thousand years, and for most of the existence of ancient Israel, Egypt was a looming presence.

Up to the Persian conquest, Egypt was ruled by a pharaoh, a god-king whose power was absolute. Society was tightly controlled and well organized. The Egyptians were especially good at harnessing the power of forced labor, as the pyramids attest.

I. DIVISIONS OF EGYPTIAN HISTORY

A pagan Egyptian priest of the third century B.C. named Manetho wrote a history of Egypt that has survived in fragments and various summaries. His division of Egyptian history, with various additions and modifications, is the basis for the one scholars use today:

Predynastic Period—Prehistory (10,000–3300 B.C.)
Archaic Period—Dynasties 1–2 (2920–2575 B.C.)
Old Kingdom—Dynasties 3–8 (2575–2134 B.C.)
First Intermediate Period—Dynasties 9–10 (2134–2040 B.C.)
Middle Kingdom—Dynasties 11–12 (2040–1640 B.C.)
Second Intermediate Period—Dynasties 13–17 (1640–1550 B.C.)
New Kingdom—Dynasties 18–20 (1550–1070 B.C.)
Third Intermediate Period—Dynasties 21–25 (1070–712 B.C.)
Late Period—Dynasties 26–30 and Persian Period (712–332 B.C.)
Greco-Roman Period—Ptolemaic Dynasty and Roman provincial government (332 B.C.–A.D. 395)

II. IN THE TIME OF THE PATRIARCHS

Egypt was already ancient by the time of **Abraham**, whose visit (Gen 12:10–20) most scholars place at the time of the early Middle Kingdom. **Joseph** rose to prominence in the Egyptian government a few generations later (Gen 41:39–40). He took advantage of the Egyptian government's thorough and efficient organization and stored up enough grain during the seven years of plenty to take the country through seven years of famine (Gen 41:34–36). During the famine, the whole family of Jacob moved to Egypt, where they were welcomed and given some of the best grazing land (Gen 45:16–46:7).

III. IN THE TIME OF THE EXODUS

During the New Kingdom, Egypt built an empire that, for a time, extended from the Sudan to the Euphrates. Most scholars place the **Exodus** and the conquest of Canaan during this time—a time of new pharaohs "who did not know Joseph," and who used the common Egyptian suspicion of foreigners as an excuse to enslave the descendants of Jacob (Exod 1:8–11). The **Exodus** from Egypt was the defining event of Israel's history: the narration of it takes up four books (Exodus, Leviticus, Numbers, and Deuteronomy), and the Israelites were always to remember their God as the one "who brought you out of the land of Egypt, out of the house of bondage" (Exod 20:2; cf. Josh 24:17; Judg 2:12, 6:8; 1 Sam 8:8, 10:18; 1 Kgs 8:16, 9:9; 2 Kgs 17:7; Neh 9:9; Ps 81:10; Jer 16:14).

IV. INFLUENCE ON ISRAEL AND JUDAH

Egypt was not able to keep its hold on the Israelites or on Palestine and the other conquered lands, but it remained a powerful force in the politics of Israel and Judah. The pharaoh Shishak (known to Egyptian historians as Shoshenq I, who reigned from 945 to 924 B.C.) invaded Palestine and sacked Jerusalem (1 Kgs 14:25–28; 2 Chr 12:2–9). The Assyrian siege of Jerusalem during the reign of Hezekiah was part of a larger war between Assyria and Egypt (cf. 2 Kgs 19:9; Isa 37:9). The pharaoh Neco (Necho II) launched a campaign against the rising power of Babylon; King **Josiah** stood in his way and died from wounds at the battle of **Megiddo**. Neco installed Josiah's son Eliakim as king instead of Jehoahaz, changing the name to **Jehoiakim** (cf. 2 Chr 35:20). Neco was defeated at Carchemish in 605 B.C. by **Nebuchadnezzar**, and in the conflict that followed Judah and Jerusalem were both destroyed. Following the conquest of Jerusalem, many of the inhabitants of Judah fled to Egypt, taking **Jeremiah** with them (Jer 41–44). Thus, in the **Exile**, the Exodus was symbolically reversed; Israel was back in bondage (cf. Jer 23:7–8).

V. IN THE TIME OF THE MACCABEES

The Persians controlled Egypt as a satrapy of the empire with varying degrees of effectiveness until Alexander the Great conquered Egypt in 332 B.C. Alexander founded the new city of **Alexandria**, which became the new capital of Egypt. The brief period of Macedonian rule (332–304 B.C.) was ended by the former Macedonian general Ptolemy I Soter, who stole the corpse of Alexander the Great and declared himself ruler of Egypt. The Ptolemaic Dynasty, enduring from 304 to 30 B.C., brought the **Hellenization** of Egyptian government and administration. Alexandria grew to be the leading cultural, intellectual, and commercial center of the ancient world.

In the time of the Maccabees, Judea once again was caught up in rivalry between Egypt (now under the Ptolemies) and a powerful Near Eastern empire (this time the empire of the **Seleucids**).

With the death of Cleopatra VII in 30 B.C. following her defeat (with Marc Antony) at the battle of Actium in 31 B.C., Egypt passed into Roman control and was incorporated into the Roman Empire.

VI. IN NEW TESTAMENT TIMES

By New Testament times, there was a large Jewish community in Egypt (see **Dispersion**). Following the Nativity of the Lord, **Joseph** was told by an angel to go down to Egypt with Mary and the child Jesus to avoid Herod (Matt 2:13). The stay in Egypt may have lasted one or two years. Thus Jesus came out of Egypt, symbolically repeating the Exodus (Matt 2:15). Elsewhere in the NT, Egypt is usually mentioned in the context of the stories in Genesis and Exodus. Revelation expresses the wickedness of Jerusalem by calling it "Sodom and Egypt" (Rev 11:8), once again using Egypt as the symbol of spiritual bondage.

Christianity was established in Alexandria in the first century A.D. Paul did not preach there, but Saint **Mark** is traditionally honored as the first leader of the Christian community of Egypt. By the second century, there was a well-established body of believers.

EHUD (Hebrew ʾēhûd, "where is the glory?") The second of the major judges in the book of Judges (3:12–30; 4:1; cf. 1 Chr 8:6). A member of the tribe of Benjamin, Ehud was best known for assassinating **Eglon**, the obese Moabite king at Jericho who had oppressed the Israelites for eighteen years. Ehud, a master of left-handed combat (Judg 3:15, 20:16; cf. 1 Chr 12:2), was charged with bringing Israel's tribute to Eglon. Ehud used one such occasion to draw a weapon from his left thigh (where guards did not check) and murder the king (Judg 3:20–22). Ehud then rallied Israelite forces and routed the Moabites at the Jordan (Judg 3:26–30).

EKRON A city in the **Shephelah**, in the territory between the Israelites and the Philistines (Josh 3:13). The city was captured by the Israelites in the conquest of Canaan (Josh 15:11, 45, 46; 19:43; Judg 1:18; 1 Sam 7:14) but did not come fully under their control until the time of David. After they captured the ark of the covenant, the Philistines brought the ark to Ekron. The inhabitants were soon afflicted with an epidemic, and the ark was restored into Israelite hands (1 Sam 5–6).

EL *See* **God**.

ELAH King of Israel from 877 to 876 B.C. He was assassinated by one of his officers, Zimri, at a banquet (1 Kgs 16:8). The name is also used by one of the eleven tribal chiefs of Edom (Gen 36:41; 1 Chr 1:52).

ELAM

1. The eldest of the five sons of **Shem** (Gen 10:22; 1 Chr 1:17).

2. The territory that was settled by the descendants of Elam. Known also as Anshan, the country lay east of the Tigris and Euphrates rivers and extended from Media to the Persian

Gulf, with its center in the Zagros Mountains. The chief city was **Susa** (Dan 8:2). According to Genesis, Elam was counted among the descendants of Shem (Gen 10:22). Throughout the history of the Near East, the Elamites enjoyed some influence, although they were mentioned only rarely in the Bible (Gen 14:1; Isa 11:11, 21:2, 22:6; Jer 49:34–39; Ezek 32:24). The destruction of Elam was prophesied by Jeremiah and Ezekiel (Jer 25:25; 49:34; Ezek 32:24). As predicted, Susa was captured by Cyrus the Great of Persia.

ELASA A region near Beth-horon (probably modern Ramallah or Khirbet Il'asa). The site is best known for the final battle of Judas Maccabeus against Bacchides in 160 B.C. (1 Macc 9:5).

ELASAH (Hebrew, "God has made") The son of Shaphan and a messenger who carried the letter of Jeremiah to the exiles in Babylonia (Jer 29:3). He was sent on a mission with Gemariah by King **Zedekiah** to Babylon and brought with him Jeremiah's letter. His family developed close relations with the prophet (Jer 26:24; 36:25).

ELATH A city on the north coast of the Gulf of Aqaba (1 Kgs 9:26). It may be the same place as **Ezion-geber**.

ELDAD One of the seventy elders of Israel. He was reputed to have the gift of prophecy, and Moses refused Joshua's request that he be stopped from making prophecies (Num 11:26–29).

ELDER Also "ancient," the term used for the recognized head or patriarch of a clan, family, or tribe. The elder was the main voice of authority in the tribe, and, over time, groups of elders came to speak for the Israelite people in a collective sense (cf. Exod 17:5; 18:12). Elders appear throughout the **Pentateuch** and most of the remaining Old Testament, and groups of elders were participants in some of the most decisive moments in the long history of the Israelites. They were present during the days of Moses (Exod 3:16; 4:29), at the ratification of the covenant (Exod 24:1–9), and in the time of Joshua (Josh 24:1).

During the settlement period in Canaan, elders continued to provide social and even military stability (Josh 9:11; Judg 8:5, 11:5; 1 Sam 11:3). They were also involved in the establishment of the monarchy (1 Sam 8:4) and in the election of David as king (2 Sam 5:3). In the monarchic period, elders provided a useful consultative body (2 Sam 17:4; 1 Kgs 20:7; 2 Kgs 10:1). Elders formed a judicial body as well (Deut 19:12, 21:3, 22:15, 25:8; Ruth 4:1–11; 1 Kgs 21:8; 2 Kgs 10:1).

Councils or groups of elders remained an integral part of Jewish life, as manifested in the **Sanhedrin**, with its role in the New Testament account of Jesus's trial and Passion (Matt 16:21; 21:23; 26:3, 57; 27:1, 12, 20, 41). The Sanhedrin also played a part in the conflict between the authorities and the early Church in Jerusalem (Acts 4:23; 23:14, 15; 24:1).

ELEALEH A city in Transjordan usually mentioned in the Old Testament with **Heshbon**. After the conquest of Canaan, Elealeh was added to the territory of the Reubenites (Num 32:3, 37). It later passed under the control of the Moabites, and Isaiah (Isa 15:4; 16:9) and Jeremiah (Jer 48:34) spoke of Elealeh in their prophecies against Moab.

ELEAZAR (Hebrew, "God has helped") The name of six men in the Bible.

1. The third son of **Aaron** and Elisheba (Exod 6:23) and father of Phinehas (Exod 6:25); Eleazar was consecrated a priest by Moses (Exod 28:1; Num 3:3–4) and designated Aaron's heir (Num 20:25–28; Deut 10:6). Eleazar was given charge over the holy oils and the incense (Num 4:16; 19:3) and the transportation of the Tabernacle (Num 4:16). After the death of his brothers **Nadab** and **Abihu** (Lev 10:1–3), Eleazar became Aaron's heir, and as successor to Aaron he was clothed by Moses in the robes of the high priest on Mount Hor (Num 20:26). In the period between the deaths of Aaron and Moses, Eleazar was a key figure in the Israelite leadership (Num 27:1–11; 31:12, 13, 25–31), and he supervised the elevation of Joshua as Moses's successor (Num 27:18–23). In the passage into the Promised Land, he oversaw the division of the territories among the tribes (Num 34:17; Josh 14:1; 19:51; 21:1). Eleazar was buried at Gibeah in the hills of Ephraim (Josh 24:33). He was succeeded as high priest by his son Phinehas, and the **Zadokite** priests of Jerusalem claimed their descent from Aaron through Eleazar (Ezra 7:1–5; 1 Chr 5:29–41, 6:35–38, 24:3).

2. The son of **Abinadab**. He was appointed to be one of the guards of the ark of the covenant (1 Sam 7:1).

3. One of the warriors in the service of David (2 Sam 23:9–10).

4. The fourth son of **Mattathias**, also called Avaran. He fought at the victory against Nicanor (2 Macc 8:22) but was later killed in battle against Antiochus V Eupator when an elephant he had slain fell on him (1 Macc 6:43–46).

5. A venerable scribe during the persecution of **Antiochus IV Epiphanes** (2 Macc 6:18–31). He was executed for refusing to eat pork. His friends had encouraged him to pretend to eat the forbidden meat, but he remained committed wholeheartedly to the dietary laws and so served as a model to younger Jews.

6. One of the ancestors mentioned in the genealogy of Jesus (Matt 1:15).

ELECTION The principle of God's deliberate and entirely gratuitous selection of a people, specifically the people of Israel, for the accomplishment of his plan in human history.

I. THE HEBREW AND GREEK TERMS USED

The term used in the Old Testament for election, *bāhar*, had various applications, including basic acts such as choosing or selecting (e.g., Gen 13:11; Deut 23:16; 1 Sam 17:40), but *bāhar* is understood theologically to denote the act of a deliberate and irrevocable choice by God. The deliberate choice of God by man is a rare occurrence in the OT, seen chiefly in Josh 24:15, 22 and Judg 5:8, 10:14. The most common New Testament applications are the words *eklogē* and *eklektos* for elect and electing, with the specific theological intent of implying divine election (except in Rom 16:13). Similar words used less frequently include *eklegomai* ("to choose") and the singular uses of *hairetizō* ("to choose," Matt 12:18), *tassō* ("to ordain," Acts 13:48), *haireō* ("to choose,"

2 Thess 2:13), and *suneklektos* ("also chosen," 1 Pet 5:13).

II. THE GRATUITOUS ELECTION OF ISRAEL

The election of Israel begins in Genesis, where God speaks his promises directly to the patriarchs (Gen 12–50). Chief among these were the promises made to **Abraham** (Gen 12:1–3; cf. Gen 25:19–23; Rom 9:10–12) concerning his progeny. These promises are made entirely unconditionally and gratuitously by God. The election is due entirely to the love of God, not to any special merits of Israel: "It was not because you were more numerous than any other people that the Lord set his heart on you and chose you—for you were the fewest of all peoples. It was because the Lord loved you and kept the oath that he swore to your ancestors" (Deut 7:7–8; cf. Deut 4:37).

III. THE DUTIES OF GOD'S ELECT

As the people chosen by God and with whom God entered into a **covenant** relationship, the Israelites became "a priestly kingdom and a holy nation" (Exod 19:6) and "his own possession" (Ps 135:4; cf. Exod 19:5; Deut 32:9; Mal 3:17). "All the peoples of the earth shall see that you are called by the name of the Lord, and they shall be afraid of you" (Deut 28:9). Because of that election, Israel had obligations and responsibilities that were not placed upon other peoples (cf. Amos 3:2). These included the obligation of recognizing the Lord alone as their God (Deut 4:39), keeping his commandments (Deut 4:40) and laws (Lev 17–26), remaining in fidelity to the covenant oaths

that were made—in short, being a holy people (Lev 19:2; cf. Exod 22:30; Lev 20:26). God's righteous anger falls on those who threaten God's elect (Isa 9:16; Zech 1:14), but especially on God's own holy people who abandon their promises of holiness and fidelity (Deut 4:24; cf. Exod 34:14; Josh 24:19). Failure to remain obedient would invoke the covenant curses and a more severe punishment would be visited upon Israel than that imposed upon other peoples (Amos 3:2), including the demotion to the level of other nations (Amos 9:8).

The prophets often reminded Israel that its election was only the will of God, not what Israel deserved. Also the Israelites must not believe that their election meant they always had the Lord's protection even when they had lost his favor through infidelity: "Will you steal, murder, commit adultery, swear falsely, burn incense to Baal, and go after other gods that you have not known, and then come and stand before me in this house, which is called by my name, and say, 'We are delivered!'— only to go on doing all these abominations?" (Jer 7:9–10; cf. Mic 3:11).

IV. ELECTION EXTENDED TO ALL NATIONS

The election of Israel was not for the purpose of saving the Israelites alone; it was part of the divine plan to save the whole human race. The promise to Abraham would climax in Christ, the son of Abraham (Matt 1:1). Isaiah and other prophets had already taken God's message to the other nations: "Turn to me and be saved, all the ends of the earth! For I am God, and there is no other . . . In the LORD all the offspring of Israel shall triumph and glory" (Isa 45:22, 25). The NT promise of salvation for all through Christ is thus simply the fulfillment of promises already made in the OT. Once again, the sacred writers stress the undeserved grace of God in offering election and salvation to all, both Jew and Gentile (cf. John 6:37; 15:16; 17:2).

Since Christ has come, all believers of all nations are called to the role that Israel filled in the OT: "But you are a chosen race, a royal priesthood, a holy nation, God's own people, in order that you may proclaim the mighty acts of him who called you out of darkness into his marvelous light" (1 Pet 2:9; cf. Exod 19:6). And just as the election of Israel entailed specific demands, so too does the new designation through the New Covenant, including the obligation to proclaim the Gospel (CCC 1268, 1546).

V. ISRAEL IS STILL THE ELECT OF GOD

Has God rejected Israel, then? "By no means!" Paul exclaims (Rom 11:1). "So I ask, have they stumbled so as to fall? By no means! But through their stumbling salvation has come to the Gentiles, so as to make Israel jealous. Now if their stumbling means riches for the world, and if their defeat means riches for Gentiles, how much more will their full inclusion mean!" (Rom 11:11–12). Paul reminds us that "the gifts and the calling of God are irrevocable" (Rom 11:29).

ELECT LADY A woman of Ephesus to whom John addressed his second epistle (2 John 1:1). This is the only reference, and many readers think it refers figuratively to a church founded by John, rather than to a particular person.

ELEUTHERUS A river in Syria flowing from the base of the Lebanon Mountains to the Mediterranean. The river figured in **Jonathan**'s march with the Egyptian king Ptolemy (1 Macc 11:7) and was the site of Jonathan's victory over Demetrius (1 Macc 12:30).

ELHANAN The son of Jair (or Dodo) and one of the great warriors in the army of David. Elhanan is credited with slaying Goliath the Philistine (2 Sam 21:19), creating an obvious discrepancy as he is elsewhere credited with the defeat of Lahmi, Goliath's brother (1 Chr 20:5). The latter citation is considered perhaps an adjustment to the tradition in 1 Sam 17, which hails David for the defeat of Goliath. A similar editorial question emerges regarding the name of Elhanan's father, with two names appearing, Jair (2 Sam 21:19) and Dodo (2 Sam 23:24; 1 Chr 11:26).

ELI The priest at the sanctuary of Shiloh (1 Sam 1:9; 2:11) to whom Hannah entrusted her son **Samuel** after the consecration of her son to the service of the Lord (1 Sam 1–2). Eli's two sons, Hophni and Phinehas, were priests of the Lord (1 Sam 1:3), but they had no regard for the Lord (2:12): they treated with contempt both the offering of the Lord (2:17) and those who came to Shiloh (2:14), and they indulged in liaisons with the women who served at the entrance to the tent of meeting (2:22). In sharp contrast was Samuel, who "ministered before the Lord" (1 Sam 2:11, 18; 3:1), "grew in the presence of the Lord" (2:21), and stood in the Lord's favor (2:26).

Eli chastised his sons for their evil ways, but they refused to listen to him (1 Sam 2:22–25). Eli was therefore warned that his sons' corruption and sins would bring judgment and ruin on the family (2:27–36), a warning that was repeated also by Samuel. Eli accepted what God had in store for his sons (3:11–18). Hophni and Phinehas accompanied the **ark of the covenant** into battle against the Philistines (4:1–4) and apparently were killed in the military disaster that ensued (4:10–11) at **Aphek**. By the time of his sons' deaths, Eli suffered from obesity (4:18), old age (4:15), and increasing blindness (3:2; 4:15). Upon hearing the news of the deaths of his sons, he fell from his chair, snapped his neck, and died. He had served as a judge over Israel for over forty years.

ELI, ELI, LAMA SABACHTHANI The cry of Jesus from the Cross, meaning "My God, my God, why have you forsaken me?" as preserved in Matt 27:46. The same phrase is also presented in Mark 15:36 in an Aramaic version: *Eloi, eloi, lema sabachthani*. The words are the opening of Ps 22, and although the Psalm begins with a cry of extreme distress, it ends by praising God for the deliverance he will bring.

ELIAKIM (Hebrew, "God will establish") The name of three men in the Old Testament.

1. The son of Hilkiah and master of the palace or chamberlain under King **Hezekiah**. He was much respected by Isaiah (2 Kgs 18:18, 26, 37; 19:2; Isa 36:3, 11, 22; 37:2).

2. The second son of King **Josiah**; he was installed as king of Judah by Pharaoh Neco of Egypt in place of his brother Jehoahaz around 609 B.C. (2 Kgs 23:34; 2 Chr 36:4). The pharaoh changed Eliakim's name to Jehoiakim and forced him to pay large amounts of silver and gold to Egypt (2 Kgs 23:34–35).

3. One of the priests who blew a trumpet at the dedication of the restored Temple of Jerusalem under **Nehemiah** (Neh 12:40–41).

ELIAM The father of **Bathsheba** (2 Sam 11:3) and a warrior in the army of David (2 Sam 23:34).

ELIASHIB The high priest of the Temple in Jerusalem during the governorship of **Nehemiah** (Neh 3:1; Ezra 10:6). Eliashib was active in the rebuilding of Jerusalem, and the prosperity of his family was demonstrated by the size of his house (Neh 3:20–21).

ELIEL (Hebrew, "my God is God") The name of several individuals mentioned in First and Second Chronicles (1 Chr 5:18–22, 23–26; 6:18–19; 8:20, 22; 11:46, 47; 12:12; 15:9, 11; 2 Chr 31:13).

ELIEZER (Hebrew, "my God is strength") The name of five men in the Old Testament.

1. **Abraham**'s servant from Damascus (Gen 15:2). He journeyed to Mesopotamia in search of a wife for Isaac (Gen 24). He was also Abraham's heir in the event that the patriarch should die childless (Gen 15:2).

2. The second son of **Moses** and Zipporah (Exod 18:2–4; 1 Chr 23:15, 26:25). He had one son (1 Chr 23:17), although another refer-

ence (1 Chr 26:25) suggests additional descendants.

3. One of the priests who blew trumpets when David arranged for the **ark of the covenant** to enter Jerusalem (1 Chr 15:24).

4. The head of the tribe of Reuben during the reign of Solomon (1 Chr 27:16).

5. A prophet who foretold to **Jehoshaphat**, king of Judah, that his fleet would be wrecked owing to his cooperation with **Ahaziah** of Israel (2 Chr 20:37).

ELIHU (Hebrew, "God it was indeed") The name of three men in the Old Testament.

1. The great-grandfather of **Samuel** (1 Sam 1:1). He is also called Eliab (1 Chr 6:12) and Eliel (1 Chr 6:19).

2. A chief from Manasseh who joined David at Ziklag and so abandoned Saul (1 Chr 12:21).

3. A young man who attempted to confute **Job** (Job 32–38).

ELIJAH (Hebrew, "the Lord is God") A ninth-century B.C. prophet who was active in the northern kingdom of Israel during the reigns of **Ahab** and **Ahaziah**. The account of his prophetic ministry is found in 1 Kgs 17–19, 21 and 2 Kgs 1–2. Elijah was a great and determined defender of the worship of the Lord against the religious syncretism and apostasy that were then plaguing the country under Ahab and his wife, **Jezebel**. He fought against pagan cults, in particular the cult of **Baal**, and was given the power to work miracles as a means of convincing Israel that Yahweh was their true God.

Very little is known of his early life except for a reference in 1 Kgs 17:1 that calls him "the Tishbite, of Tishbe in Gilead." From the start of his ministry, Elijah was involved in the royal affairs of the dynasty of Omri, and he was single-mindedly committed to his appointed role. He cared little for his personal appearance and gave little thought to human comforts. He was fed by ravens, by a widow, and by an angel (1 Kgs 17:6, 15; 19:5).

I. THE ELIJAH CYCLE (1 KINGS 17– 2 KINGS 2)

The account covers six episodes that make up the Elijah cycle: The Prediction of Drought (1 Kgs 17); The Contest on Mount Carmel (1 Kgs 18; Luke 4:25; Jas 5:17); The Flight to Horeb (1 Kgs 19:1–21); The Naboth Affair (1 Kgs 21:1–29); The Oracle on Ahaziah (2 Kgs 1); and Elijah's Translation (2 Kgs 2:1–18).

1. *The Prediction of Drought*

Elijah first appears proclaiming to Ahab a drought that will endure for three years as punishment for idolatry. He is commanded by the Lord to go beyond Ahab's reach to Cherith, east of the Jordan, where he is fed by ravens (1 Kgs 17:2–8). He then goes to Zarephath, where he receives hospitality from a widow and miraculously raises her son to life (1 Kgs 17:9–24). The conflict with Ahab and idolatry is a private one, as Elijah survives in the land dominated by Baal by the assistance of the Lord while the rest of the land suffers under divine judgment.

2. *The Contest on Mount Carmel*

The second episode begins three years later when Elijah challenges Ahab through the royal servant Obadiah (1 Kgs 18:1–17). The private struggle now erupts into open conflict as Elijah takes on the prophets of the pagan god at Mount Carmel to determine who will be able to end the drought. Elijah makes an appeal to Yahweh, and the plea is answered with rain (1 Kgs 18:18–46). Elijah makes manifest the supremacy of Yahweh.

3. *The Flight to Horeb*

To avoid the wrath of Jezebel, Elijah flees to Horeb (another name for **Sinai**) in great sadness over the apparent failure of his mission. In reply to his cry, Elijah receives a vision of God upon the mountain of the covenant. There are awe-inspiring tempests, fire, and earthquakes like the ones that characterized earlier theophanies, but the Lord chooses to reveal himself as a gentle whisper (1 Kgs 19:11–12). Elijah is commanded to anoint **Hazael** the king of Aram, **Jehu** the king of Israel, and **Elisha** as his successor as prophet (1 Kgs 19:15–18). He goes out immediately and throws his mantle over Elisha (1 Kgs 19:19–21).

4. *The Naboth Affair*

Elijah then proclaims the demands of the Mosaic Law by upholding the principle that the land owned by an Israelite is a gift from God and must be recognized as part of fidelity to the covenant. Thus Elijah condemns Jezebel for bringing about the murder of Naboth to seize the vineyard that Ahab coveted. For this crime, Elijah predicts the downfall of the house of Ahab.

5. *The Oracle on Ahaziah*

Elijah resumes his defense of the Lord's supremacy by threatening the death of **Ahaziah** because of his dependence upon Baalzebub, the god of Ekron. Two companies of soldiers are killed by lightning when they are sent to arrest the prophet.

6. *Elijah's Translation*

Elijah is carried up to heaven with Elisha as his witness: "And as they still went on and talked, behold, a chariot of fire and horses of fire separated the two of them. And Elijah went up by a whirlwind into heaven" (2 Kgs 2:11).

II. ELIJAH'S SIGNIFICANCE

The prophet Elijah constantly declared the Lord's unique and utterly supreme divinity. He fought, at times alone, with immense courage against the idolatry of the period, making the powerful pagan queen Jezebel his implacable enemy. Elijah demanded not merely the repudiation but the outright extermination of idolatry. Like Samuel, he changed the dynastic destiny of the Israelites: Samuel anointed Saul as king and David to replace Saul, and Elijah anointed Hazael and Jehu to overthrow their respective rulers. Above all, Elijah stressed fidelity to the Law of Moses and to the covenant.

We see a number of parallels between Elijah and Moses. Elijah meets God at Horeb or Sinai, the place where God gave the Law to Moses. Elijah is succeeded by Elisha, just as Moses was followed by Joshua. At the end of his career, Elijah is taken away under mysterious circumstances, just as Moses was buried in secret.

The translation of Elijah was also the basis for the belief that he would at some point return (Mal 3:23; Sir 48:10). This idea was prevalent in New Testament times (Matt 11:14, 17:10; Mark 9:11; John 1:21, 25). Jesus was thought by some to be Elijah (Matt 16:14; Mark 8:29; Luke 9:19), and John the Baptist was asked also if he was the prophet (John 1:21, 25). Jesus replied that John the Baptist was indeed the new Elijah whose coming was foretold by the prophet Malachi (Matt 11:14, 17:11; Mark 9:12). Jesus also referred to Elijah at Nazareth when he noted that a prophet is rejected in his own country (Luke 4:25).

Elijah was present with Moses at the Transfiguration of Jesus (Matt 17:3; Mark 9:4; Luke 9:30): Elijah representing the Prophets and Moses the Law, the Old Testament Scriptures giving witness to the glorification of Jesus (CCC 2581–84).

ELIKA One of the elite warriors in the army of David, a member of the famed "Thirty" (2 Sam 23:25).

ELIM An oasis of twelve springs and seventy palm trees where the Israelites camped as they made their way through the desert (Exod 15:27–16:1; Num 33:9–10). The Israelites reached Elim approximately four days after crossing the Red Sea.

ELIMELECH A resident of Bethlehem, husband of Naomi, and father-in-law of **Ruth** (Ruth 1:1–4; 2:1). Owing to financial hardship, Elimelech migrated to Moab with his wife and two sons, Mahlon and Chilion, who married Moabite women, Orpah and Ruth. Elimelech died soon after, followed by his sons, and Naomi and Ruth returned to Palestine, where Ruth wed Boaz (Ruth 1–3).

ELIPHAZ (Hebrew, possibly, "God is victor" or "God is gold")

1. The firstborn son of **Esau**, and the father of Theman (Gen 36:12; 1 Chr 1:36).

2. The oldest of the three friends of **Job** (Job 2:11; 22:1; 42:7, 9). A native of Teman in Edom, he became one of the chief antagonists in Job, delivering three speeches (Job 4:1–5:27; 15:1–35; 22:13).

ELIPHELET The name of two men in the Old Testament.

1. A son of David (1 Chr 3:6; 14:5), born by one of David's wives in Jerusalem.

2. The son of Ahasbai and a member of David's famed "Thirty" (2 Sam 23:34).

ELISHA (Hebrew, "God is salvation") A ninth-century B.C. prophet of Israel, the designated successor of **Elijah** (1 Kgs 19:16–21; 2 Kgs 2), whose ministry extended across the reigns of **Ahab**, **Ahaziah**, **Jehoram**, **Jehu**, **Jehoahaz**, and **Jehoash** (1 Kgs 19:19–21; 2 Kgs 2–13). He was the son of Shaphat from Abel-meholah. Little else is known with certainty about his background, except that he was young when Elijah called him from behind his plow. From then on, he accompanied Elijah. He received a "double portion" of Elijah's prophetic spirit— that is, the portion of an heir and successor (2 Kgs 2:1–18). He was a witness to the departure of Elijah.

The prophetic ministry of Elisha is detailed in 1 and 2 Kings (1 Kgs 19; 2 Kgs 2–9;

13) and ends with his death (2 Kgs 13:14–21). Unlike the Elijah cycle, the account of Elisha is more of a collection of anecdotes or events: the purification of the waters (2 Kgs 2:19–22); cursing the small boys (2 Kgs 2:23–25); his participation in the campaign against Moab (2 Kgs 3:1–27); the performance of miracles (2 Kgs 4:1-7); the raising of the son of the Shulamite woman (2 Kgs 4:8–37); the poisonous stew (2 Kgs 4:37–41); the multiplication of the loaves (2 Kgs 4:42–44); the cure of the leprosy of **Naaman** of Damascus (2 Kgs 5:1–20); the theft of Gehazi and his punishment with leprosy (2 Kgs 5:21–27); the miraculous rescue of the ax from the Jordan (2 Kgs 6:1–7); the deception of the Arameans (2 Kgs 6:8–23); the prediction of the siege of Samaria (2 Kgs 6:24–7:26); the prediction of **Hazael**'s ascent to the throne of Damascus (2 Kgs 8:1–15); the anointing of **Jehu** (2 Kgs 9:1–10); the predictions of triumph over Damascus (2 Kgs 13:14–19); and the resurrection of the man placed in Elisha's tomb (2 Kgs 13:20).

Particular focus is placed in the Elisha cycle on the miraculous and wonderful. Many events in the Elisha cycle are obviously similar in miraculous tone to those of the Elijah cycle. Elisha demonstrated a gift for clairvoyance and received ecstatic experiences in a way that was more noteworthy than for any other Old Testament prophet (2 Kgs 3:11–20; 5:21–27; 6:24–7:20; 8:15). Elisha was like Samuel in his gifts of foresight, his wanderings, and his wide appeal to both the common people and the leaders of the country. Like Samuel, he shaped the government of Israel, most so in his encouragement to **Jehu** to exterminate the line of Omri. He was head of a prophetic school and was active in the political and dynastic events of the period. Although immensely influential, he remains in the shadow of his mentor, Elijah, the way Joshua remained in the shadow of Moses.

ELISHAH A son of Javan (Gen 10:4; 1 Chr 1:7), grandson of Japheth, and great-grandson of Noah. On the basis of the Table of Nations (Gen 10), his name was attached to a geographical location, most likely in the Aegean.

ELISHAMA (Hebrew, "God has heard") The name of two men in the Old Testament.

1. The grandfather of Joshua (1 Chr 7:26). Son of Ammihud, he was the leader of the tribe of Ephraim and took part in the census of the Israelites under Moses in the wilderness (Num 1:10; 2:18; 7:48, 53; 10:22).

2. One of the sons of David born in Jerusalem (2 Sam 5:16; 1 Chr 3:8, 14:7).

ELISHEBA (Hebrew, "God makes an oath") The wife of **Aaron**; she was the daughter of Amminadab and the sister of Nahshon (Exod 6:23).

ELISHUA One of the sons of David born in Jerusalem (2 Sam 5:15; 1 Chr 14:5). The identity of his mother is not known.

ELIUD An ancestor of Jesus (Matt 1:14, 15).

ELIZABETH The wife of **Zechariah**, mother of **John the Baptist**, and a relative of Jesus's mother, Mary. She was a descendant of Aaron. For many years she had prayed for a child, and the Angel Gabriel announced to Zechariah the birth of the great precursor of the Lord. Her relationship to Mary is not specified, but during Mary's visit Elizabeth recognized her dignity and praised Mary with great joy (Luke 1:5–66).

ELIZUR (Hebrew, "God is a rock," "my God is a rock") The son of Shedeur and the leader of the tribe of Reuben during the time in the wilderness. He supervised a census of the fighting men of the tribe (Num 1:5; also Num 2:10; 7:30, 35; 10:18).

ELKANAH (Hebrew, "God has created") The father of Samuel and the husband of Hannah (1 Sam 1:1).

ELKOSH (Hebrew, "God gives") The birthplace of the prophet Nahum (Nah 1:1). The location is unknown.

ELLASAR A city in the domain of Arioch (Gen 14:1, 9); the location is not otherwise known.

ELMADAN An ancestor of Jesus (Luke 3:28).

ELOHIM (Hebrew 'ĕlōhîm) One of the names of God, a plural form of "El." (*See* **God**.)

ELOHIST *See* E; *see also* **Pentateuch**.

ELON (Hebrew, "oak") One of the so-called minor judges. A member of the tribe of Zebulun, he served as a judge for ten years (Judg 12:11–12). He was buried at Ayyalon.

ELUL The sixth month of the Hebrew calendar; it corresponded approximately to August and September.

ELYMAIS A region in ancient Persia roughly equivalent to modern Khuzistān, in Iran (1 Macc 6:1; Tob 2:10). Susa was the chief city.

ELYMAS (Greek *Elymas*) A Jewish magician and false prophet (Acts 13:8; in Acts 13:6 he is termed **Bar-Jesus**) who attempted to turn the Roman proconsul of Cyprus, **Sergius Paulus**, away from the faith when he was being evangelized by Paul and Barnabas.

EMBALMING The ancient method of preserving human and animal corpses from decomposition through extensive desiccation and the application of organic preservatives, in particular natron. Embalming is mentioned only twice in the Old Testament, in the burials of Jacob and Joseph (Gen 50:2, 26), both of whom died in Egypt. The Egyptians had developed a complex mummification process: the chief organs were removed and preserved in "canopic jars"; the body was washed with fragrant spices; and the remains were then wrapped in linen strips before being placed in a sarcophagus. (*See also* **Burial**.)

EMIM (Hebrew 'ēmîm, "terrible ones" or "frightful ones") The name used by the Moabites for a race of giants who lived in the Transjordan. They were ejected from their land by the Moabites. In Deut 2:10 they are described as "a large and numerous people, as tall as the **Anakim**," another race of giants; the two are termed Rephaim (Deut 2:11). Nothing else is known about them.

EMMANUEL (Hebrew, "God is with us") A Hebrew name used by Isaiah (in the form "Immanuel," Isa 7:10–17; 8:8) for a child whose birth the prophet announced to King Ahaz. At the time of the prophecy, Rezin of Damascus and Pekah of Israel were attacking Judah to force Judah into their alliance against Tiglath-Pileser III of Assyria (734–733 B.C.); if King **Ahaz** refused to enter the alliance, the attacking kings intended to remove Ahaz and replace him with a more pliant monarch. Isaiah brought Ahaz an oracle telling him to do nothing (Isa 7:1–10) but trust that the two kings would soon be rendered powerless. Such neutrality would prevent Judah's being subjugated by Assyria, and it would only be a matter of time before the Assyrians dealt effectively with the problem of the coalition. Ahaz was not convinced, however, and a second promise was given to him: "Behold, a young woman [or *virgin*, as the **Septuagint** translated it] shall conceive and bear a son, and shall call his name Immanuel," and before the child reached maturity, Ahaz was told, the two enemies would be utterly vanquished.

When Isaiah refers again to Emmanuel (Isa 8:8), he is clearly speaking of Hezekiah. Thus the prophecy is fulfilled first in Hezekiah, and the young woman (Hebrew ʿalmâ) noted in the oracle was the wife of Ahaz. But the prophecy has even more far-reaching import: Jews of the time before Christ expected it to be fulfilled in the eventual birth of the Messiah, who would liberate Israel once and for all. Thus Matthew refers to Isaiah in his infancy narrative (Matt 1:23).

EMMAUS The village in the **Shephelah** where Christ appeared to two disciples following his Resurrection (Luke 24:13–35). The town was also known for the victory of **Judas Maccabeus** over the Seleucids under the general Gorgias (1 Macc 3:40–57; 4:1–15). The exact location of Emmaus is uncertain; some suggest modern Khirbet Imwas, some nineteen miles west of Jerusalem. Such a location is not consistent with the account in Acts, which places the village sixty stadia (seven miles) west of Jerusalem (Luke 24:13). Another possibility is El-Qubeibeh, around eleven miles west of Jerusalem.

ENDOR A town situated in the Esdraelon Plain to the south of Mount Tabor. It was given to the tribe of Manasseh by Joshua, although the inhabitants were not entirely driven out (Josh 17:11–13). **Deborah** and Barak won a great victory over Sisera at Endor (Ps 83:9–10), and the site was especially known as the home of the medium traditionally known as the Witch of Endor (1 Sam 28:7). This necromancer was consulted by Saul in his effort to obtain knowledge from the spirit of Samuel.

EN-EGLAIM A site on the shore of the Dead Sea. It was described in Ezekiel as an oasis (Ezek 47:1–12).

EN-GEDI (Hebrew, "spring of the young goat") An oasis and town located on the western shore of the Dead Sea, southeast of Jerusalem. It was mentioned in the Old Testament both as an oasis and as a military outpost or fortress. Its natural defenses attracted David when he was hiding from Saul (1 Sam 24:1–23), and it was here that David cut off a part of Saul's mantle instead of killing him (1 Sam 24:5–8). The place was also where Moabites, Ammonites, and Meunites attacked Jehoshaphat (2 Chr 20:2).

ENGLISH LANGUAGE VERSIONS *See* **Versions of the Bible**.

EN-HAKKORE (Hebrew, "the spring of the caller") The name of a spring where Samson drank after defeating the Philistines (Judg 15:19). The location is unknown.

EN-MISHPAT *See* **Kadesh**.

ENOCH The name of four men in the Old Testament.

1. The son of Cain and the father of Irad (Gen 4:17–18). Cain also built a city and named it Enoch after his son.

2. The son of Jared and the father of Methuselah, according to the genealogy for Seth in Genesis (5:1–32). Enoch was born when Jared was 162 years old, and Enoch fathered Methuselah at the age of 65 (Gen 5:21). He was a seventh-generation descendant of Adam in the line of **Seth** (contrasting favorably with **Lamech**, Cain's seventh descendant and a man of sin and blood, Gen 4:23–24). Enoch lived for 365 years; such was his character that he "walked with God; and he was not, for God took him" (Gen 5:22–24). These terse words are

interpreted more fully for us by later passages in Scripture: Enoch was taken into heaven without experiencing death, in the same manner as the prophet **Elijah** (2 Kgs 2:3, 9, 10), and hence he was the first person in the OT to be given this unique honor. In Sir 44:16 he is a model of repentance; Heb 11:5 mentions him as a model of faith. Enoch was also revered as a prophet (Jude 14–15). He was a major figure in extra-biblical apocalyptic literature: three influential apocalyptic books are attributed to his authorship (CCC 2569).

3. A nephew of Abraham and the son of Madian (Gen 25:4).

4. The oldest son of Reuben (Gen 46:9; Exod 6:14; 1 Chr 5:3).

ENOSH (Hebrew, "man") The son of Seth (at the age of 105) and the father of Kenan (Gen 4:2; 5:6–11). Enosh lived 905 years, having fathered Kenan at the age of 90. Gen 4:26 notes that the birth of Enosh marked the first time that people began to call on the name of Yahweh.

EN-RIMMON *See* **Rimmon**.

EN-ROGEL (Hebrew, "spring of the cleaner") A spring near Jerusalem along the boundary between Judah and Benjamin (Josh 15:7; 18:16). During the revolt of Absalom, Jonathan and Ahimaaz took up a position at En-Rogel, in order to be able to report news and developments to King David (2 Sam 17:17).

EPAENETUS A Christian residing in Rome who was mentioned by Paul as "my beloved" and as the first convert to the faith in the province of Asia (Rom 16:5).

EPAPHRAS A Christian from Colossae, mentioned by Paul as a "fellow servant" (Col 1:7). He was also a "fellow prisoner in Christ Jesus" (Phlm 23), suggesting that they shared imprisonment. Epaphras is also credited with teaching the Colossians (Col 1:7) and with bringing news of the Colossians' faith (Col 1:4) while Paul was incarcerated. It is apparent that Paul thought highly of Epaphras (Col 1:7; 4:12). There is some question as to whether Epaphras should be considered synonymous with **Epaphroditus**.

EPAPHRODITUS (Greek *Epaphroditos*) A Christian who had come to Paul with the collection from the Philippians and to assist the apostle (Phil 2:25; 4:18). It is possible that he could be identified with Epaphras.

EPHAH A form of dry measurement. The ephah was equivalent to one-tenth of a **homer**. Ezekiel states: "The ephah and the bath shall be of the same measure, the bath containing one-tenth of a homer, and the ephah one-tenth of a homer; the homer shall be the standard measure" (Ezek 45:10–15; cf. Zech 5:6–10; Judg 6:19; Ruth 2:17; 1 Sam 1:24). (*See* **Weights and measures**.)

EPHESIANS, LETTER TO THE A letter sent by Paul to the Christian community of Ephesus. It is especially concerned with the doctrine of the Church as the mystical body of Christ. The letter is one of the "captivity Epistles" (with Colossians, Philippians, and Philemon) that were written by Paul while in prison.

I. AUTHORSHIP AND DATE

Twice in the letter the apostle Paul declares himself to be the author (Eph 1:1; 3:1). This assumed authorship went unchallenged until the end of the eighteenth century. From that time onward some scholars have questioned Pauline authorship, suggesting instead that the letter was by some disciple of Paul writing in his name. They say that the letter is not epistolary in form, that it has significant changes in vocabulary from known Pauline letters, and that the emphasis of the letter on ecclesiology rather than eschatology is not typical of Paul. On the other hand, the absence of controversy could account for the calmer and more sober structure and tone of the epistle, the vocabulary is appropriate to the material and topics for discussion, and the ecclesiological emphasis is consistent with Paul's wider purpose in developing the dogmatic material on the mystery of salvation and of the Church. On the whole, there seems little reason for doubting the unquestioned tradition of seventeen centuries.

The date of the letter depends, of course, on who was the author. If the epistle was truly the work of Paul during the time of his imprisonment (3:1; 4:1; 6:20)—most likely in Rome—then the letter can be dated approximately to the early sixties, the same time as the other captivity Epistles. If Paul was not the author of Ephesians, then the date could be as late as the nineties.

The original destination of the letter is difficult to know with certainty. Many manuscripts begin with a salutation, "To the saints who are in Ephesus" (1:1), but the words "in Ephesus" are missing from some of the earliest manuscripts (they are not translated in the RSV) and so may have been added after the original composition. The title of the epistle, "to the Ephesians," was added in the second century. Even more unusual is the fact that Paul does not apparently know the Christians to whom he addressed the letter (1:15; 4:21) nor is he known to them (3:2–4), despite his having resided in Ephesus for some three years (Acts 19:8, 10, 22; 20:31). Some scholars theorize that Paul wrote a general letter to the Christian communities of Asia Minor, and that the copy that was circulated to Ephesus is the one that has survived. Regardless, Paul certainly had the Ephesians in mind as he penned the epistle.

II. CONTENTS

III. PURPOSE AND THEMES

Paul's Letter to the Ephesians is a treatise or homily in epistolary form. Its tone is more formal and impersonal than the tone of some other letters from Paul, and it lacks much of the personal flavor of Colossians, even though it treats many of the same themes.

The letter itself is divided into two main parts: a dogmatic section (Eph 1:3–3:21) and a moral or practical section (4:1–6:20). In a magnificent theological hymn (1:13–14), Paul praises God for the blessings that he has bestowed upon the faithful in accordance with the eternal plan of his will, "For he has made known to us in all wisdom and insight the mystery of his will, according to his purpose which he set forth in Christ as a plan for the fulness of time, to unite all things in him, things in heaven and things on earth" (1:9–10). The Christian mystery is one that requires divine assistance to be understood (1:9–12), and Paul writes with pride of his own understanding (3:2–4) and implores the faithful to pray that they may comprehend it (1:17–19; 3:16–19).

The mystery of Jesus Christ that was hidden in the Old Covenant is now revealed in the New Covenant (1:9; 3:4, 9). All things in heaven and earth are brought together under Christ's authority (1:20), and through his death upon the Cross, the Savior redeemed Israel and all nations (1:7; 2:16; 5:2) that had been alienated. He has brought the world, alienated and corrupted by sin, back to God and has restored peace between humanity and the Father, "which he accomplished in Christ when he raised him from the dead and made him sit at his right hand in the heavenly places, far above all rule and authority and power and dominion, and above every name that is named, not only in this age but also in that which is to come" (1:20–21).

The teaching on mystery refers as well to the mystery of the Church. As in Colossians, Paul writes of the Church as the body of Christ (Col 1:18; Eph 1:22–23), with Christ as the head. For Paul, the Church is the body and bride of Christ, who is the bridegroom (Eph 5:22–32), a holy temple in the Lord, a dwelling place for God (2:21–22). The unity of the Church is marked by the unity of Jew and Gentile, who have been brought together under Christ, who has reconciled both groups to God in one body through the Cross, into the family of the New Covenant (2:11–22; 3:4–6).

EPHESUS The chief city and seaport and capital of the Roman province of Asia in western Asia Minor (modern Turkey) during the period of the New Testament. Ephesus was situated at the mouth of the Caÿster on the Aegean Sea. Occupied by the Ionians around 1100 B.C., it passed into Roman hands in 133 B.C. and was established as the capital of the province of Asia; under Emperor Augustus (r. 27 B.C.–A.D. 14), it enjoyed the title of "First and Greatest Metropolis of Asia." As such, it was subjected to an extensive architectural aggrandizement and became one of the foremost Roman cities in the eastern Mediterranean with a population in excess of 250,000. Its port facilities were complicated by the accumulation of silt and a receding shoreline, so the city moved westward over the years to maintain its vital access to the sea.

Paul first visited Ephesus toward the end of his second missionary journey (Acts 18:19–21) while journeying from Corinth to Jerusalem. He preached in the synagogue and left after promising to return. Following Paul's departure, Apollos arrived and received instruction from Aquila and Priscilla; although recently baptized by John, Apollos nevertheless proved a gifted preacher and subsequently traveled to Corinth (Acts 18:24–28). Paul returned on his third journey and took up residence for two years in the city (Acts 19). He preached in the synagogue until the hostility of the local Jews forced him to move to the home of Tyrannus (Acts 19:8–12). He then left the city in the wake of a riot started by Demetrius the Silversmith, who believed that Paul was endangering his livelihood—as he made his money making small models of the temple of Diana (Acts 19–20).

Paul was again actively involved in the affairs of the church in Ephesus later when he summoned the Ephesian Christian leaders to meet him at Miletus. There he gave them a farewell discourse that moved them to tears (Acts 20:17–38). It is considered likely that Paul composed First Corinthians and Galatians while in Ephesus (*see* **Ephesians, Letter to the**, for other details).

John addressed the first of the seven letters in Revelation to the angel of Ephesus. In that letter John gives praise to the Ephesians, but he notes also that the fervor of their charity has cooled (Rev 2:1–5). There was a longstanding tradition that John lived in Ephesus, and this was affirmed by Saint Irenaeus of Lyons. There was also a tradition that Mary lived in Ephesus, since she lived with John until the end of her earthly life.

EPHOD A special garment worn only by the high priest, although the exact nature of the ephod remains uncertain. The ephod worn by

Aaron is described in detail in Exod 28:6–9 and 39:2–4; it was similar in shape to the chasuble and made of gold, violet, purple, and scarlet, with two onyxes on the shoulders and ornamented with twelve precious stones. Two stones bore the names of the twelve tribes of Israel, so that "Aaron shall bear their names before the LORD on his two shoulders for remembrance" (Exod 28:12). Over the ephod was a pouch or burse containing the **Urim and Thummim** (Exod 28:15–30; 39:8–21). Only the high priest was permitted to wear the ephod (1 Sam 14:3).

The "linen ephod" was the identifying uniform of ordinary priests (1 Sam 2:18; 22:18). It was not ornamented like the ephod worn by the high priest. David wore an ephod when he danced before the ark (2 Sam 6:14), signifying that he was taking on a priestly role in his kingdom. The ephod that Gideon made (Judg 8:27; 1 Sam 23:6–10, 30:7) was apparently a cultic object or image that was misused in false worship after his death (cf. the ephod of Micah in Judg 17:5; 18:14).

EPHPHATHA A Greek transliteration of the Aramaic word meaning "open." Christ used the word (Mark 7:34) in his cure of a man who was deaf and had a speech impediment.

EPHRAIM The second son of Joseph by Asenath and the ancestor of the tribe of Ephraim. Ephraim was born in Egypt (Gen 41:52; 46:20). In giving his blessing to the sons of Joseph, Jacob adopted both Ephraim and Manasseh as his own, but he preferred the younger Ephraim to his older brother (Gen 48:14–16). The tribe of Ephraim became the most powerful and influential after the tribe of Judah and was essential to the unity of the Israelites prior to the monarchy. Joshua was an Ephraimite (Josh 19:49, 50; 24:30), as was Samuel (1 Sam 1:1). During the time in the desert, the tribe marched just behind the ark of the covenant (Num 2:18–19).

After the conquest, the tribe received a large tract in the central hill country of Palestine (Josh 16:4–10; 1 Chr 7:28). The members of the tribe fought frequently with enemies (Josh 16–17), and the Ephraimites took part in the effort against the Midianites (Judg 3:27; 5:14). In the campaign, however, they upbraided Gideon for neglecting to summon them earlier.

Ephraimites spoke a distinctive dialect, as we learn from Judges 12. A conflict arose between the Ephraimites and Jephthah and the Gileadites, which ended with the Ephraimites defeated and trapped along the Jordan. Fleeing survivors were recognized by their distinctive dialect: the victors made everyone who passed pronounce the word "Shibboleth." The Ephraimites were unable to say it properly, pronouncing it *Sibboleth*, and so were recognized and executed (Judg 12:1–6). The Ephraimites later played a central role in the northern kingdom, of which they were the most prominent tribe (1 Kgs 11–12).

Nevertheless, Ephraim became by far the largest and most powerful tribe in the northern kingdom of Israel—so much so that "Ephraim" was a poetic name for the whole northern kingdom (see Ezek 37:15–19; cf. Hos 4:17, 5:3; Isa 9:9; Jer 7:15; 31:9).

EPHRATH, EPHRATHAH

1. The wife of Hezron and later his son Caleb (1 Chr 2:19; 4:4) and hence the mother of

Hur and Ashbur (1 Chr 2:24). On the basis of the genealogical lists in 1 Chronicles, the families of David and Elimelech were called Ephrathites (cf. Ruth 1:2; 1 Sam 17:12), and the clan was considered part of the tribe of Judah.

2. An alternate name of **Bethlehem** (Gen 35:19; Mic 5:2).

EPHRON A Hittite in Hebron from whom Abraham purchased, for four hundred shekels of silver, the field containing the double cave of Machpelah, in which Sarah was buried (Gen 23:8–17; 25:9; 49:29–30; 50:13). The name is used also for a mountain (Josh 15:9) and a town belonging to the tribe of Benjamin (2 Sam 13:23; 1 Sam 13:17; 2 Chr 13:19).

EPISTLE (Greek, "a letter") Any of the twenty-one books of the New Testament titled "letters" or "epistles." They were addressed to individuals or churches, and they covered all the topics important to the Christian life: doctrine and morals, disciplinary action, practical advice, and exhortation to true Christian living.

The Epistles are divided into two main groups.

The Pauline letters, consisting of approximately one-fourth of the NT, are Romans, 1 and 2 Corinthians, Galatians, Ephesians, Philippians, Colossians, 1 and 2 Thessalonians, 1 and 2 Timothy, Titus, Philemon, and Hebrews. (On the question of authorship, see under individual titles.) Of those, Colossians, Philippians, Ephesians, and Philemon are often called the "captivity Epistles" because they were written while Paul was under house arrest or another form of detention. 1 and 2 Timothy and Titus are termed the "pastoral Epistles" because their chief concern is with effective pastoral ministry.

The **Catholic Epistles**, so called because it was long thought that they were not addressed to particular communities, are James, 1 and 2 Peter, 1, 2, and 3 John, and Jude.

EPISTLES, CATHOLIC *See* **Catholic Epistles**.

ERASTUS A name mentioned several times in the New Testament. An Erastus was an assistant to Paul and journeyed with Paul and Timothy to Ephesus (Acts 19:22). In 2 Timothy, Erastus "remained at Corinth" (2 Tim 4:20), suggesting that he had been traveling with Paul and then chose to remain in Corinth. It is likely or at least distinctly possible that this Erastus is the same man mentioned in Acts. A third Erastus was the city treasurer of Corinth (Rom 16:23).

ERECH A Mesopotamian city, mentioned only once (Gen 10:10) with Babel (Babylon) and Akkad as one of the cities of the kingdom of Nimrod. The modern site of the city is Warka, the ancient Sumerian city of Uruk.

ERI A son of Gad and the grandson of Zilpah and Jacob. He is considered the ancestral head of the Erites (Gen 46:16).

ESARHADDON (Assyrian, "the god Ashur has given a brother") The son of the Assyrian king **Sennacherib** and ruler of Assyria from ca. 681 to 669 B.C. He came to the throne after his father's assassination (2 Kgs 19:37; Isa 37:38). As his name denotes, he had several other brothers, and it is believed that he overcame rival claimants. He moved settlers into the former kingdom of Israel (Ezek 4:2).

ESAU The twin brother of **Jacob** and the oldest son of **Isaac** and **Rebecca** (Gen 25:25). Esau struggled with his brother even in the womb for the right of being the firstborn. Esau was the first to be born, but he would lose the rights of the firstborn to his brother, Jacob. Esau was a hunter, whereas his brother was a herdsman (Gen 25:27). Esau was Isaac's favorite, but Esau thoughtlessly sold his birthright to Jacob for a mere plate of lentils after returning home hungry from a hunt (Gen 25:29–34; Heb 12:16). He then displeased his parents by marrying two Hittite women (Gen 26:34) and took a third wife from the daughters of Ishmael, the son of Abraham (Gen 28:6–9).

Jacob secured the blessing from Isaac through a deception (Gen 27), and Esau threatened Jacob's life in anger once the stratagem had been discovered (Gen 27:39–40). The rivalry between the brothers was then severe, and Jacob left for Mesopotamia, while Esau prospered in the highlands of Seir (Gen 36:6–8). The two later met again on friendlier terms, and Esau was present at Isaac's funeral (Gen 35:29). The conflict between the brothers nevertheless continued in the conflict between Israel, the descendants of Jacob, and Edom, the descendants of Esau (Gen 25:30, 32:4, 36:1, 1 Chr 1:35). (See **Edomites** for other details.)

The prophet Malachi interpreted the struggle in terms of Yahweh's deliberate election of the line of Jacob to be the means of realizing the **Messiah** (Mal 1:2). Building on Malachi, Paul argued God's freedom of election prior to any merit or demerit ("Even before they had been born or had done anything good or bad"; Rom 9:11–13). Hebrews 12:16 emphasizes the sinfulness of Esau in his willingness to sell "his birthright for a single meal."

ESDRAELON *See* **Jezreel**.

ESDRAS *See* **Ezra**; *see also* **Apocryphal books**.

ESDRIS A Jewish military officer mentioned in 2 Macc 12:36.

ESEK (Hebrew, "strife") The name of a well dug by the servants of Isaac (Gen 26:20). The site derived its name from the struggle that ensued between Isaac's herdsmen and those of Gerar over access to the water.

ESSENES A religious Jewish sect that flourished from around the middle of the second century B.C. to the second half of the first century A.D. Although they are not mentioned in the New Testament, they were discussed by several Greek and Latin authors, including the Jewish writers Philo and Josephus, as well as the Roman writers Pliny the Younger, Dio, and Hippolytus. Their name was written in the Greek as *Essaioi* or *Essēnoi* and in the Latin as *Esseni*, and according to Philo the word was derived from the Greek *hosiotēs*, meaning "holiness." The Hebrew equivalent for the name was *ḥasîd,* suggesting "pious ones," although scholarly opinion differs, and a host of etymological origins have been proposed.

The variety of ancient sources on the Essenes permits a relatively detailed picture to be painted on their lives and activities. According to Pliny, they were situated along the Dead Sea, and the famed site of Khirbet **Qumran** is now generally accepted to have served as the center of an Essene settlement, meaning that the **Dead Sea Scrolls** were almost certainly used by them as their library. Other communities of Essenes lived in Jerusalem and in the area around Damascus. Their daily lives were monastic in structure, taken up with a wide variety of rituals, including especially complex purification rites and ablutions. Their austerity was marked by the practice of celibacy, communal life, and holding possessions in common. Initiation was according to strict rules, and offenses against the laws could lead to expulsion.

The exact relationship of the Essenes with the Temple is still a matter of debate. While Jewish, they did not participate in the Temple sacrifices, in large part because they rejected the priesthood of the time. They adhered to the Torah but gave it their own interpretation. They accepted principles such as predestination and the resurrection (but probably not the resurrection of the body), as well as an expectation of the Messiah, the activity of angels, and an overall apocalyptic worldview akin to that found in Daniel. The degree to which the Essenes influenced first-century rabbinical Judaism and especially early Christianity is a source of much discussion among scholars.

The Essene communities died out after the rebellion against Rome that ended with the destruction of Jerusalem in A.D. 70. The Qumran community was probably wiped out during the fighting.

ESTHER *See* **Esther, book of.**

ESTHER, BOOK OF A canonical book of the Old Testament that tells how the Jews in the Persian Empire were spared from annihilation through the central role played by Esther, the Jewish wife of Ahasuerus; the event is commemorated by the Jewish feast of Purim. In the Catholic canon, Esther is placed among the Historical Books, between Judith and 1 and 2 Maccabees.

The Greek **Septuagint** version of Esther includes the so-called Additions to Esther, 107 **deuterocanonical** verses that are not found in the Hebrew text. In the **Vulgate**, Jerome separated the passages unique to the Septuagint (where they were scattered throughout the text) and placed them immediately after the protocanonical text as chapters 11–16, which accounts for the confusing arrangement of the narrative in some Bibles. The acceptance of the additions as inspired was affirmed by the Council of Trent in 1546. The additions include Mordecai's dream and the discovery of a plot against the king; the royal edict against the Jews dictated by Haman; the prayers of Mordecai and Esther; the royal edict dictated by Mordecai; Esther's appeal to Ahasuerus; and the interpretation of Mordecai's dream. The Greek additions emphasize the name of God, which does not appear in the Hebrew text.

I. AUTHORSHIP AND DATE

On the basis of Esth 9:20, 32, the authorship of the book is attributed to Esther's uncle, Mordecai. Another tradition attributes it to **Ezra**. The date of the work is uncertain. If Ahasuerus is to be identified with Xerxes (r. 485–465 B.C.), then the book was written sometime after 465 B.C. According to the additions, the Greek text was brought to Egypt by Dositheus, a priest and Levite, in the fourth year of the reign of Ptolemy and Cleopatra. The translation was made by Lysimachus, son of Ptolemy, one of the residents of Jerusalem. Five Ptolemies had wives named Cleopatra; the most likely candidates are Ptolemy VII Euergetes II (r. 146–116 B.C.), Ptolemy VIII Soter II (r. 116–107 B.C.), and Ptolemy XII Auletes (r. 80–58 B.C. and 55–51 B.C.). The book was accepted late into the **canon**; it is not quoted in the New Testament nor was it included among the texts at Qumran. As the theme of the book is the Jewish people under threat, some suggest a period of composition corresponding to the Maccabean period in the second century B.C. when **Antiochus Epiphanes** was trying to force the Hellenization of the Jews of Palestine. The Greek addition gives in Esth 11:1 the date of 114 B.C., suggesting perhaps that was the time when the Greek translation was made.

II. CONTENTS

I. *Prologue (11:2–12:6)*

II. *Esther, Persia's New Queen (1:1–2:23)*

  A. *Queen Vashti Expelled (1:1–22)*

  B. *Queen Esther Installed (2:1–18)*

  C. *Plot Discovered by Mordecai (2:19–23)*

III. *Plot to Exterminate the Jews (3:1–5:14, includes chaps. 13, 14, 15)*

  A. *Extermination Decreed (3:1–13; 13:1–7; 3:14–15)*

  B. *Esther Pressed to Intercede (4:1–14)*

  C. *Prayers for Deliverance (13:8–14:19)*

  D. *Esther Before the King (15:1–16; 5:3–8)*

  E. *Haman Plots Against Mordecai (5:9–14)*

IV. *Salvation of the Jews (6:1–9:32, includes chap. 16)*

  A. *Promotion and Execution (6:1–8:2)*

  B. *Esther Intercedes (8:3–12)*

  C. *Decree of Deliverance for the Jews (16:1–24; 8:13–17)*

  D. *Jews Destroy Their Enemies (9:1–15)*

  E. *Feast of Purim (9:16–32)*

V. *Epilogue (10:1–11:1)*

III. PURPOSE AND THEMES

Esther relates, in the literary form of a historical novel or romance, the courage of a Jewish maiden in saving her people from destruction. Esther was the daughter of Abihail of Benjamin and lived in exile with her uncle and foster father Mordecai. Her Persian name, Esther, means "star" (Esth 2:7; Persian *stareh*; Akkadian *Ishtar*), and her Jewish name, Hadassah, means "myrtle." The events took place in Susa, Persia, during the fifth century B.C. When Ahasuerus (Xerxes) deposed Queen Vashti, Esther was chosen as queen. Haman, a royal courtier and minister, was angered by Mordecai because the latter refused to give him homage that belonged to God alone and so conspired to win a royal decree to massacre the Jews of the empire. Esther appealed to the king, brought about the destruction of Haman, and saved her people from annihilation.

Like **Judith**, Esther emphasizes absolute trust in Divine Providence and indicates that God's saving will is sometimes realized by persons acting in unlikely ways. God's protection of his people is stressed as a reward for their fidelity. God's plan may not be recognized during times of struggle and suffering, but in the end he will always prove the victor. This theological emphasis is heightened especially in the Greek text.

The book of Esther also provided the foundation for the feast of Purim, which was established to celebrate the deliverance of the Jews on this occasion (Esth 9:17–10:3). Purim means "lots," and the book describes the lots cast by Haman to determine the day on which the Jews of the Persian Empire were to be exterminated (Esth 3:7). When the king changed the decree, the day of death was transformed into a time of celebration. Purim is also called "the day of Mordecai" (2 Macc 15:37).

For Christians, Esther is also a **type** of the Blessed Virgin Mary. Esther saved her people from death by making appeal to the great king, Ahasuerus. Mary also saved humankind from death by making appeal to the King of Kings, her divine Son. Like Esther, Mary has constant access to the King and brings comfort and aid to the oppressed and the suffering.

ETHAM The site or station visited by the Israelites during the Exodus (Exod 13:20; Num 33:6–7) following their departure from **Succoth**.

ETHAN The name of two men in the Old Testament.

1. The son of Zerah (1 Chr 2:6; Gen 38:30). He was the father of **Azariah** (1 Chr 2:8).

2. Called the Ezrahite, a wise man whose wisdom was so great that it was surpassed only by Solomon's (1 Kgs 5:11).

ETHANIM The seventh month of the Canaanite calendar, corresponding to September–October. It was later called Tishri (1 Kgs 8:2).

ETHBAAL (Hebrew, possibly "man of Baal") King of the Sidonians and father of **Jezebel**, wife of Ahab (1 Kgs 16:31). Ethbaal was king of Tyre, although the biblical text refers to him as ruler of the Sidonians (i.e., Phoenicians).

ETHIOPIA *also* Cush. A country to the south of Egypt, corresponding to ancient Nubia and modern Sudan, with its territories stretching to modern Saudi Arabia and Yemen and all the way south to modern Ethiopia and Eritrea. The name Ethiopia appears only once in Scripture, in Acts 8:27, although the **Septuagint** uses it frequently to translate the Hebrew name Cush.

Cush, or Ethiopia, played a notable role in the history of ancient Egypt, and various Old Testament references to it are in close connection with the land of the Nile (Ps 68:3; Isa 20:3–5; Ezek 30:4; Dan 11:43; Nah 3:9). According to Gen 10:6, Ham was the father of Cush, who became the ancestor of the Ethiopians. Long under Egyptian dominion (see **Egypt**), Cush gained its independence in the Second Intermediate Period (ca. 1780–1550 B.C.), lost it during the New Kingdom (1500–1070 B.C.), and then exacted revenge when the Ethiopian leaders Piankhy and Shabako seized power in Egypt and established the Twenty-fifth Dynasty, which endured from around 715 to 663 B.C. Taharqa, a king of the dynasty, was an ally of King Hezekiah of Judah against the advance of Sennacherib of Assyria in 701 (2 Kgs 19:9; Isa 37:9). The alliance proved a failure, for the Ethiopian Dynasty in Egypt fell in 664 to the Assyrian army. The Ethiopian rulers thereafter maintained themselves at Meroe, and the dynasty survived into the fourth century A.D. By New Testament times, the Ethiopians were ruled by various queens bearing the title Candace. **Philip** the deacon baptized the **Ethiopian Eunuch**, a minister of one of the Candaces (Acts 8:27). Cush also figured in several prophecies (Isa 18:1–7, 20:3–4, 30:4–5, 38:5, 43:3; Zeph 2:12; Amos 9:7).

ETHIOPIAN EUNUCH An Ethiopian mentioned in Acts 8:26–40 who converted to the Christian faith through the efforts of **Philip**. He is described in some detail by Luke, with particular attention paid to his Ethiopian descent and the fact that he was a eunuch. According to Luke, he was a court official of **Candace**, queen of the Ethiopians, and was in charge of her entire treasury. He had journeyed to Jerusalem to worship and was returning home when he encountered Philip. Their ensuing conversation led to the baptism of the eunuch, an event of double significance for the readers of Acts. According to Deut 23:2, eunuchs were excluded from being followers of the Lord; in Isa 56:3 (cf. Isa 11:11) foreigners were excluded. Luke was thus making a clear statement on the universality of the Gospel. (*See also* **Ethiopia**.)

EUBULUS A Christian and disciple of Paul (2 Tim 4:21).

EUCHARIST (Greek *eucharistia*, "thanksgiving") "The source and summit of the Christian Life" (LG §11); the sacrament in which Christ is really and truly present under the appearances of bread and wine. Other names for the Eucharist are Holy Communion, the Lord's Supper, the table of the Lord, the breaking of the bread, the unbloody sacrifice, our daily bread, the most blessed sacrament, the sacrifice of praise, and agape. The Sacrament of the Eucharist was described as follows by the Second Vatican Council:

> At the Last Supper, on the night when he was betrayed, our Savior instituted the Eucharistic Sacrifice of his Body and Blood. He did this in order to perpetuate the Sacrifice of the Cross throughout the centuries until he should come again, and so to entrust to his beloved spouse, the Church, a memorial of his death and resurrection: a sacrament of love, a sign of unity, a bond of charity, a paschal banquet in which Christ is consumed, the mind is filled with grace, and a pledge of future glory is given to us (Sacrosanctum Concilium, *Constitution on the Sacred Liturgy*, §47) (CCC 1322–1419).

I. *The Last Supper*

    A. *Where the Meal Took Place*

    B. *Accounts of the Institution*

II. *The Real Presence*

    A. *The Bread of Life*

    B. *Transubstantiation*

III. *Eucharist as Sacrifice*

I. THE LAST SUPPER

A. Where the Meal Took Place

The setting of the Last Supper was a large up-stairs room, traditionally called the Cenacle (Latin *cenaculum*, "supper room"), in a house in Jerusalem (Mark 14:15; Luke 22:12), probably the same upper room where the apostles stayed and prayed after the Ascension and before Pentecost (Acts 1:13). There are accounts of the Last Supper in all four Gospels (Matt 26:20–29; Mark 14:17–25; Luke 22:14–38; John 13), but they provide few details about the physical circumstances of the meal. Jesus sent Peter and John to Jerusalem to make arrangements for the meal (Matt 26:17–19; Mark 14:12–16; Luke 22:7–13). The participants likely ate reclining at the table (John 13:25). (For the question of whether the Last Supper was a Paschal meal, *see* **Passion of Christ**; *see also* **Passover**.)

B. Accounts of the Institution

The Eucharist was instituted by Christ at the Last Supper. In doing so, the Savior fulfilled his own promise made earlier in his public ministry, to give himself as the "bread of life" (John 6:26–59).

The accounts of the institution are found in Matt 26:26–28, Mark 14:22–24, Luke 22:19–20, and 1 Cor 11:23–25. In John, the institution is omitted, although Jesus leaves no doubt that he is referring to the Eucharist in the "Bread of Life" discourse (John 6:35–65).

The accounts agree in their essentials: Jesus gave thanks, consecrated the bread and wine, and gave his body and blood as spiritual nourishment to his apostles and for the salvation of all. In this ritual, Christ anticipated the bloody sacrifice to take place on the Cross at Golgotha on the next day. The Eucharist instituted by Christ is both the commemoration of Christ's sacrifice on the Cross and the sacrament of the Real Presence (CCC 1333–35).

II. THE REAL PRESENCE

A. The Bread of Life

In telling his apostles, "This is my body" (Luke 22:19), Jesus reveals that he is the High Priest offering the Eucharist, but he is also commanding his followers, "Take and eat" (Matt 26:26), an invitation to participate in his offering and partake of its benefits. The reception of the Eucharist—the reception of himself—is a source of salvation (cf. 1 Cor 11:27–29). The Bread of Life discourse in John is especially significant in attesting to the real presence:

"Truly, truly, I say to you, unless you eat the flesh of the Son of man and drink his blood, you have no life in you; he who eats my flesh and drinks my blood has eternal life, and I will

raise him up at the last day. For my flesh is food indeed, and my blood is drink indeed. He who eats my flesh and drinks my blood abides in me, and I in him. As the living Father sent me, and I live because of the Father, so he who eats me will live because of me. This is the bread which came down from heaven, not such as the fathers ate and died; he who eats this bread will live for ever" (John 6:53–58).

B. Transubstantiation

The Catholic doctrine on the Eucharist was officially stated by the Fourth Lateran Council in 1215, and the Real Presence was examined in great detail by Saint Thomas Aquinas (*Summa theologiae* III, 75–77). The doctrine was then reaffirmed fully by the Council of Trent to counter the Protestant Reformers. The Council declared:

> *Because Christ our Redeemer said that it was truly his body that he was offering under the species of bread, it has always been the conviction of the Church of God, and this holy Council now declares again, that by the consecration of the bread and wine there takes place a change of the whole substance of the bread into the substance of the body of Christ our Lord and of the whole substance of the wine into the substance of his blood. This change the holy Catholic Church has fittingly and properly called transubstantiation. (DS 1642; cf.* Sacrosanctum Concilium, *§7)*

III. EUCHARIST AS SACRIFICE

A. A Renewal of the One Perfect Sacrifice

By the actions of the priest's consecration of the bread and wine at Mass, Christ becomes really and truly present under the two elements; thus the Eucharist renews the same sacrifice that Christ made upon the Cross. Moreover, Christ joins to this offering the prayers and good works of the entire Church, especially the faithful who take part in the Mass and join with the priest in offering the sacrifice to God.

B. The Eucharist Perfects Old Testament Sacrifices

Ritual sacrifice under the Old Law was the sign of the covenant between God and his people. In the New Testament, the sacrifice achieves perfection through Christ. Jesus's sacrifice is the new Passover that is carried forward in the Eucharistic meal and replaces all of the sacrifices of the past. In the Mass, Christ is at once the High Priest and the victim who offers himself, through the ministry of his priest, with the same offering he made upon Calvary. The Eucharistic Sacrifice is thus the most perfect act of worship that can be offered to God.

When, thereafter, the disciples renewed the ceremonial action of Christ in their Eucharistic celebrations, they recalled the sacrifice of Christ that sealed the New Covenant. In his death upon the Cross and his Resurrection, Jesus established the New Covenant just as Moses ratified the Old Covenant at Sinai with the sacrifice of the blood of bulls (cf. Exod 24:5–8; Matt 26:28; Mark 14:24; Luke 22:20; 1 Cor 11:25).

C. The Eucharist as Memorial

Christ's intention, however, was that the Eucharist should be more than a mere ritual action or ceremony that recalled his death. Jesus commanded the apostles that when they celebrated the Eucharist they should do so in remembrance of him, but this order had a very important meaning to the Jewish mind of the time. A memorial ritual in Old Testament terms was more than remembrance; it involved a real presence of God's saving action, as was evident in the Passover, the commemoration of the deliverance from Egypt that was instituted by God (Exod 12:14). The feast celebrated not just God's saving action in bringing Israel to freedom, but also God's continuing protection of his people and his ongoing saving action.

D. The Nature of the Eucharistic Sacrifice

The sacrificial nature of the Mass was affirmed by the Council of Trent. The Council declared that the basis of the sacrifice of the Mass is the eternal priesthood of Christ and that it was instituted at the Last Supper. The instruments of the transmission of the sacrifice are the apostles and their successors. The sacrifice is guarded and offered by the Church through the priesthood; it is a commemorative and representative sacrifice of the Cross; it consists in the offering of the body and blood of Christ under the species of bread and wine.

The conciliar decree went on to declare that the OT sacrifices serve as the type of the Eucharist and that Melchizedek, the priest and king of Salem, was the OT's most profound type of the priesthood of Christ. In his words, "Do this in remembrance of me," Christ established the priesthood of the New Covenant and commanded that the apostles and their successors should offer his body and blood. The decree further affirmed that the Mass contains the unbloody immolation of the Cross and is distinct from the sacrifice on the Cross

only in the manner of the offering. On the Cross, the sacrifice was bloody and was made by Christ alone; in the Mass, the offering is unbloody and is made by Christ through the ministry of the priest. In addition, the Mass contains a propitiatory sacrifice that is efficacious for the living and the dead, and that is offered for the satisfaction of sin and the temporal punishment for sins (CCC 1362–72).

Through the actions of the priest, the Church repeats the Last Supper and thereby is united by Christ to his sacrifice. The Mass, then, is the sacrifice of the whole Church, but it would be a mistake to think that *two* sacrifices are being offered. The Church offers the sacrifice of the Cross, and Christ, being sacramentally present, offers his sacrifice in union with the Church; for this reason we call the Eucharist the sacrifice of the Church. But the Church does not add anything to the sacrifice except for what is derived from Christ.

IV. EUCHARIST AS SACRAMENT

The Eucharist is a **sacrament** in that it is an efficacious sign of the sacrifice offered by Christ on the Cross. Christ offers himself to the Father in the Mass just as he did on the Cross, but the offering is made through the consecratory action of the priest. This is possible because when he instituted the Eucharist at the Last Supper, Christ established at the same time the sacramental priesthood. The apostles, their successors, and the priests they appoint repeat Christ's actions at the Last Supper; their actions are as efficacious as Christ's, because Christ is using the priests as his appointed instruments.

The sacrament of the Eucharist is thus a

sign that actually gives grace to the communicant who is worthy to receive it. In that way it is similar to the other sacraments that are celebrated by the Church. But the Eucharist is unique because of the real presence of Christ under the appearance of bread and wine (CCC 1373–75).

V. THE EFFECTS OF THE EUCHARIST

A. Unites the Recipient to Christ

The Church proclaims that each of the seven sacraments produces its effects in the recipient that also are symbolized by the sacrament. The first effect of the Eucharist is to *unite the recipient to Christ*, for the Eucharist contains Christ himself. This union was what Christ promised in the Bread of Life Discourse (John 6:56).

B. Gives Life

The Eucharist also *gives life*, for just as material food and drink assist in maintaining, improving, and building up our life, so too does the Eucharist—the "true food" and "true drink"—bestow life (John 6:54). It increases habitual grace in the recipient and has the power to remit venial sins and to fortify against mortal sins; it also brings joy to the souls of the devout.

C. Gives a Share in the Life of Christ and the Trinity

The life that is nourished by the Eucharist is a *share in the life of Christ*. The life bestowed extends to the spiritual life, to eternal life that will culminate in the future resurrection of the body (John 6:55). This life is also a *share in the communion of the Holy Trinity* (John 6:58; cf. Matt 5:23–24; 1 John 3:19–24).

D. Unites the Church

The social or communitarian aspect to the Eucharist *builds up the mystical body of Christ*: "The cup of blessing that we bless, is it not a sharing in the blood of Christ? The bread that we break, is it not a sharing in the body of Christ? Because there is one bread, we who are many are one body, for we all partake of the one bread" (1 Cor 10:16–17). Jesus prayed at the Last Supper, "I do not pray for them alone. I pray also for those who will believe in me through their word, that all may be one as you, Father, are in me, and I in you" (John 17:20–21). Just as the Christian faithful are united to each other in faith and baptism, so too are they united in Christ through the Eucharist. The Eucharist brings the union of the individual with Christ and through him brings as well the union of Christians among themselves (CCC 790, 1003, 1074, 1212, 1275, 1322, 1370, 1391, 1398, 1436, 2837).

VI. THE HEAVENLY BANQUET

The Church has long been faithful to Christ's command "Do this in remembrance of me" and will continue to celebrate the Eucharist as the center of her life. The fidelity to Christ's command will continue as the Pilgrim People "proclaim the Lord's death until he comes" (1 Cor 11:26) and move forward toward the heavenly banquet (CCC 1000, 1326, 1402–5, 1419).

Jesus taught of the future Kingdom of God in terms of a meal or banquet, saying to his apostles, "I tell you I shall not drink again of this fruit of the vine until that day when I drink it new with you in my Father's kingdom" (Matt 26:29; cf. Matt 22:2; Luke 14:16, 22:18; Mark 14:25). The prophets had already cast the Messianic hopes of Israel in terms of a banquet (Isa 65:13; Ps 23:5). The Last Supper was a prophetic announcement of the Messianic meal and its fulfillment: first in the Eucharist, celebrated by the Church, and then in its complete realization at the time of Jesus's return at the end of all things. The Eucharist is the pledge of future glory, and in the celebration of the sacrament the Church remembers Christ's promise (Rev 1:4, 22:20; 1 Cor 16:22; cf. *Didache* 10.6). The Eucharist is the pledge of the Christian hope in the new heaven and the new earth (2 Pet 3:13). The Second Vatican Council expressed this in *Sacrosanctum Concilium*:

> *At the Last Supper, on the night he was betrayed, our Savior instituted the eucharistic sacrifice of his Body and Blood. This he did in order to perpetuate the sacrifice of the cross through the ages until he should come again, and so to entrust to his beloved Spouse, the Church, a memorial of his death and resurrection: a sacrament of love, a bond of charity, a paschal banquet in which Christ is consumed, the mind is filled with grace, and a pledge of future glory is given to us. (§§47–48)*

(*See also* **Liturgy**; **Priesthood**; **Redemption**; **Sacrament**; **Sacrifice**.)

EUMENES Specifically, Eumenes II Soter, the son of Attalus I, the brother of Attalus II, and the king of **Pergamum** from 197 to 159 B.C. (1 Macc 8:8). He entered into alliance with Rome against the Seleucid **Antiochus III** and was granted extensive territories in return.

EUNICE A Jewish-Christian woman of the city of Lystra in Lycaonia. She was a convert from Judaism and was the mother of **Timothy** (2 Tim 1:5; Acts 16:1).

EUNUCH A man who has been castrated or who is otherwise incapable of fathering children. Eunuchs in the Near East were customarily in charge of the women's quarters in palaces and households. Maintaining eunuchs was not customary in ancient Egypt, nor was it common in ancient Greece and Rome. It was largely an eastern development, with eunuchs trusted especially to administer the harem, and so forth. The very name "eunuch" later was associated with various court officials or chamberlains (Gen 37:36, 39:1, 40:2; cf. 2 Kgs 24:12–15, 25:19).

According to the Old Law (Deut 23:2; Lev 22:24), the eunuch was outlawed, and the eunuch was considered excluded from the community of faith. Anticipating the New Law, Isa 56:3 announced that both foreigners and eunuchs would share in the redeemed community. Wisdom 3:14 promised an honored place in the Temple of the Lord for virtuous eunuchs. In the New Testament, the **Ethiopian Eunuch** was a court official of the queen of Ethiopia (Acts 8:27). His baptism confirmed Isaiah's prophecy. Jesus called those who chose not to marry out of love of God "eunuchs" (Matt 19:12).

EUPHRATES The chief river of Mesopotamia. The Euphrates emerges from its source in the mountains of Armenia, through the union of the two rivers, Kara Su and Murad Nehri; it then flows into the great plain of Mesopotamia, uniting with the Tigris River and emptying into the Persian Gulf. The river is prominent in the Old Testament. It was the fourth of the rivers in Eden (Gen 2:14). Elsewhere, it is called the "great river" (Gen 15:18; Deut 1:7). The might of the river became a recurring image of the majesty and power of the Assyrian armies and succeeding empires (Isa 8:7; Jer 13:4). The territory promised to Abraham extended as far as the Euphrates (Gen 15:18), so the river was also a target of Israelite ambitions during the monarchy (2 Sam 8:3, 10:16; 1 Kgs 5:4). (*See also* **Babylon**.)

EUTYCHUS A young man of Troas who fell from an upstairs window while listening to Paul (Acts 20:9–10). He was "taken up dead," but Paul bent over him, took him in his arms, and said, "Do not be alarmed, for his life is in him." The young man was indeed alive, and his friends "were not a little comforted" (Acts 20:12).

EVANGELIST (Greek, "one who proclaims the good news") Broadly, anyone who announces or proclaims good news. More specifically, the four writers of the Gospels: Matthew, Mark, Luke, and John. In the New Testament, the word is used for the preachers in the early Church, including those blessed with charismatic gifts. In Eph 4:11, "evangelists" are counted among the officeholders in the community, after the apostles and prophets, implying that evangelist was a recognized office. Philip the deacon (Acts 21:8) and Timothy

(2 Tim 4:5) are both described as evangelists, but the context suggests that they were more preachers of the Gospel than officeholders.

EVE The name of the first woman, the wife of **Adam**, the mother of Cain, Abel, and Seth, and the mother of all of the living (Gen 3:20). Eve is mentioned by name only five times in Scripture, appearing chiefly in Genesis 2–4. The origins of the name (Hebrew *ḥawwâ*) are uncertain, although it is possible that it is derived etymologically from the verb "to live"; Gen 3:20 thus declares: "And Adam called the name of his wife Eve, because she was the mother of all the living." The **Septuagint** translated the name into Greek as *Zōē* ("life"; cf. Gen 4:1, 25). In Gen 2:23, she is referred to in Hebrew as *'iššâ*, "woman."

The Genesis narrative (Gen 2:20) states that Eve was created by God to be "a helper fit for" Adam, as it was not good for him to be alone (Gen 2:18; cf. Tob 8:8). She was made from the side of Adam (Gen 2:21–22), signifying that, unlike the animals, she was of the same kind as Adam. They were directed to increase and multiply and to fill the earth (Gen 1:28). The Genesis account emphasizes the sinless condition of the first couple before the **Fall**, noting that "the man and his wife were both naked, and were not ashamed" (Gen 2:24–25). The account likewise offers a picture of the equal dignity of women and men, the original institution of monogamous marriage ("a man leaves his father and his mother and cleaves to his wife, and they become one flesh"), and the natural orientation of man toward woman through the intimate union between husband and wife.

This condition was altered with the first

sin. Eve, deceived by the serpent, disobeyed God's command, and Adam did likewise (Gen 3:1–7; cf. Sir 25:33; Wis 2:24). The sin wounded the peaceful relationship between Adam and Eve, and among the punishments faced by Eve were the pains of childbirth and subjection to her husband (Gen 3:16; cf. 2 Cor 11:3; 1 Tim 2:13). Adam and Eve lost the grace of original holiness and the harmony that existed because of original justice. The ruptured harmony affected the union of man and woman, a relationship now marked by lust and domination (CCC 399–400).

While sin entered into the world through Adam and Eve, there is as well the hope of a redeemer in posterity who will bring victory over sin and death. As seen in the Genesis narrative, enmity was established between Eve and the serpent, between his seed and her seed, but from her will come the Redeemer who will crush the serpent's head. Through this progeny, she will be victorious. In Eve, then, is seen the first preparation for and the Old Covenant anticipation of Mary, the New Eve, in the plan of salvation. Saint Irenaeus wrote, "The knot of Eve's disobedience was untied by Mary's obedience; what the virgin Eve bound through her unbelief, the Virgin Mary loosened by her faith" (Saint Irenaeus, *Haer.* 3.22.4; cf. LG §56) (CCC 489, 726). (*See also* **Mary, Mother of God**.)

Scripture tells us little of the subsequent history of Eve. Genesis 4:1 states that she bore a son whom she named **Cain** and later gave birth to **Abel**. After the murder of Abel by Cain, she bore a son and called his name **Seth** (Gen 4:1–2, 25). Adam and Eve also had other children (Gen 5:4).

EVI (Hebrew, "to seek shelter") A Midianite king (Num 31:8; Josh 13:21).

EVIL-MERODACH (Hebrew, "man of Marduk") The son and successor to Nebuchadnezzar and king of Babylonia from 562 to 559 B.C. At the time of his accession, he freed King **Jehoiachin** of Judah and granted him various honors, including permission to dine at his royal table (2 Kgs 25:27; Jer 52:31). The purpose of this treatment may have been to restore Judah as a political buffer between Babylon and Egypt. If that was the scheme, however, it was cut short by Evil-merodach's assassination by his successor, Neriglissar.

EVODIA A Christian woman in **Philippi** (Phil 4:2).

EXEGESIS *See* **Interpretation of the Bible**.

EXILE The period from around 587/586 B.C. to around 537 B.C. during which much of the population of **Judah** was deported and forced to live in captivity in Babylonia.

I. *The Policy of Deportation*
II. *The Babylonian Conquest of Judah*
    A. *Obeisance and Rebellion*
    B. *The Destruction of the Temple and the First Exile*
    C. *The Assassination of Gedaliah and the Final Exile*
III. *Life in Exile*
    A. *Prosperity in Babylon*
    B. *Religious Renewal*
    C. *Expected Redemption*

I. THE POLICY OF DEPORTATION

Deporting conquered or subjugated peoples was common in the ancient Near East. In about 732 B.C., the Assyrian king **Tiglath-pileser** III seized the territories of Naphtali, Gilead, and Galilee as part of the Assyrian expansion at the expense of the kingdom of Israel (2 Kgs 15:29); the captured inhabitants were then sent to **Assyria**. There remained the capital, **Samaria**. It was then besieged by the Assyrians under Shalmaneser V and Sargon II and finally fell in 722 B.C. (2 Kgs 17:1–6). Sargon ordered the deportation of the population to Assyria. In place of the Israelites, the Assyrians settled the inhabitants from other regions: "And the king of Assyria brought people from Babylon, Cuthah, Avva, Hamath, and Sepharvaim, and placed them in the cities of Samaria instead of the people of Israel; and they took possession of Samaria, and dwelt in its cities" (2 Kgs 17:24; cf. Ezra 4:2, 10). The object of the deportations and enforced resettlements was simple: to destroy the cultural, ethnic, and political identity of the vanquished people and territory. By doing so, the Assyrians hoped to make a homogeneous empire with no local centers of rebellion.

II. THE BABYLONIAN CONQUEST OF JUDAH

A. Obeisance and Rebellion

In 605 B.C., the Babylonians under King Nebuchadnezzar defeated the Egyptians at the battle of Carchemish. Now **Babylon** dominated the Near East. King **Jehoiakim** of Judah recognized the dangerous political situation and initially gave obeisance to the Babylonian king. Four years later, he ill-advisedly rebelled (2 Kgs 25:1–2), and Nebuchadnezzar marched against Jerusalem in 598 B.C. Jehoiakim died at the start of the siege (2 Kgs 25:6; cf. Jer 22:18–19, 36:30; 2 Chr 36:6) and was succeeded by Jehoiachin (*see under* **Eliakim**). The new king surrendered to Nebuchadnezzar after three months, and Jehoiachin, his mother, the royal family, many prominent figures in the city, and the artisans and the smiths were taken to Babylonia as prisoners (2 Kgs 24:10–17).

B. The Destruction of the Temple and the First Exile

Nebuchadnezzar permitted Judah to keep a degree of autonomy. As king of Judah, the Babylonians named Mattaniah, Josiah's third son; he was given the throne-name **Zedekiah** (2 Kgs 25:17). Under constant pressure to assert independence, in the face of those who favored a conciliatory position, Zedekiah finally chose the course of rebellion after receiving assurances of support from Pharaoh Psammetichus II in 591 B.C. (Ezek 17). The uprising began when Zedekiah withheld his tribute from Nebuchadnezzar at the time when Egypt invaded Phoenicia as the first stage in their operations against Babylon.

The Babylonian reaction was devastating, and Zedekiah fled from Jerusalem when it was apparent the rebellion had no chance of success. Zedekiah was captured near Jericho and sent into exile (2 Kgs 25:5–7). Babylonian troops stormed Jerusalem, destroyed the Temple and royal palace, and reaped massive destruction on the rest of the city. A large number of executions followed, and the survivors were deported to Babylon (2 Kgs 25:8–21) to the area below the Tigris and Euphrates rivers. The biblical testimony as to the number of exiles varies (cf. 1 Kgs 24:16; 2 Kgs 24:14; Jer 52:28–30), and it is a challenge to estimate how many Jews were killed or slaughtered in 597 B.C. and the retributive campaign by the Babylonians in 587/586 B.C. or how many people were left in Jerusalem in the aftermath. The archaeological evidence in Jerusalem suggests widespread devastation extending even into the outlying towns.

C. The Assassination of Gedaliah and the Final Exile

Nebuchadnezzar chose an administrator, **Gedaliah**, from the surviving population (2 Kgs 25:22–24). He was assassinated by a onetime officer from the Davidic family, along with his family and Babylonian guards (2 Kgs 25:25–26; Jer 40:13–41:3). To escape the inevitable Babylonian reprisal, many in Jerusalem fled to Egypt; they dragged **Jeremiah** with them (Jer 41:17–43:7). As anticipated, the murder of Gedaliah caused another round of exiles in 581 B.C. (Jer 52:30).

III. LIFE IN EXILE

A. Prosperity in Babylon

The exiles were settled in several locations in Mesopotamia and were permitted to establish their own communities with a certain degree of autonomy. Jewish settlements were found near the river (or canal) **Chebar** at Tel-abib (Ezek 3:15) and in other locations (Ezra 2:50). The Jews earned positions as traders, bankers, and landowners. Within the obvious limitations of the Exile, they were thus able to make lives for themselves, and the period was a rich one for literary activity. The events of the destruction of Jerusalem and the Exile gave obvious shape to their literary endeavors. Scholars think that the works of Ezekiel, for example, were written during this era.

B. Religious Renewal

Above all, the Exile changed the hearts of the exiles, and with that change of heart came an abiding theological and religious change. The exiles understood that the destruction of Jerusalem and their deportation was a defeat that exposed their pride and false confidence in the inviolability of the Temple and the protection of the Lord. This catastrophe was not the failure of God. It was, instead, the failure of his people to remain faithful to their covenant promises. Jeremiah understood this and encouraged them to see the Exile for what it was: a process of purification (Jer 7). The prophet thus called upon the Jews to live as a community in exile. He urged them to settle into their lives there and accept the purification as a means of being shaped for the future (Jer 24).

C. Expected Redemption

Since God was cleansing them for their future redemption, the exiles were therefore determined to live up to the religious demands of their faith, including circumcision and the Sabbath. The years in Babylonia also witnessed the start of the synagogue as the place for common prayer and hence the heart of the community in banishment.

The Exile was thus marked by the reinvigoration of Messianic expectations. The exiled People of God looked forward to a new **Exodus**, remembering the renewal by captivity foretold in Deuteronomy (Deut 28–30; cf. Lev 26; Jer 13–16).

IV. THE END OF EXILE

The Exile ended when Babylon fell to the Persians under **Cyrus** II the Great of Persia (r. 559–529 B.C.). Cyrus conquered Babylonia in 539 B.C. and instituted a change in the long-standing policy of repopulation. He ordered the repatriation of all exiles and captives in Babylonia, including the Jews. The royal order included permission to rebuild the Temple and to return to Jerusalem the sacred vessels that had been looted and carried off by the forces of Nebuchadnezzar (2 Chr 36:22; Ezra 1:1–7). The Jews honored Cyrus as a great and magnanimous conqueror whom God had chosen to liberate his people; Isaiah even calls him the Lord's Anointed (Isa 41:2–5, 25; 44:24; 45:1–5; 48:14–15).

V. THE EXILE IN CHRISTIAN THOUGHT

The early Church Fathers saw the Exile as symbolizing the life of penance and redemptive suffering and pointing toward the Exodus wrought by Christ. Only in the captivity of Israel could God work authentic renewal. The new Exodus brought by Christ is greater than the old. It will bring Israel back to Zion, and the restored renewed Davidic kingdom will be inclusive rather than exclusive, always looking forward to the eschatological fulfillment achieved by Christ. (*See also* **Servant of the Lord**.)

EXODUS (Greek, "going out") The departure of the Israelites from **Egypt**. The narrative encompasses the suffering of the Israelites, the emergence and activities of Moses, the ten plagues, and the final passage from Egypt.

I.   The Story of the Exodus
    A. Bondage in Egypt
    B. Escape from Egypt
    C. Crossing the Sea
    D. To Sinai
II. Date of the Exodus
III. Theology of the Exodus
IV. The Exodus in the New Testament

I. THE STORY OF THE EXODUS

A. Bondage in Egypt

The descendants of Jacob flourished in Egypt, and "the Israelites were fruitful and prolific; they multiplied and grew exceedingly strong, so that the land was filled with them" (Exod 1:7). But their lot changed dramatically under the regime of a new pharaoh, who forgot all the good things Joseph had done for Egypt, and who oppressed the Israelites and placed them into servitude (for the background on this, see **Joseph**) and forced them to build (or rebuild) the cities of Pithom and Raamses.

Some of the details in the account of the Egyptian bondage fit together with what we know from Egyptian sources. For example, mandatory work quotas (Exod 5:8, 13–14) were commonly imposed on foreign captives. Likewise, Egyptian records sometimes express the Egyptians' frustration at workers' demands for time off or away from labor, as Pharaoh did when Moses asked in Exodus 5 that his people be permitted to worship their God.

B. Escape from Egypt

Moses was chosen by God to lead his people out of their bondage. He applied his divinely established authority to break the stubbornness of Pharaoh, assured by God that Israel would be set free (Exod 6:1–5). There follows in the account the struggle between Moses and the Egyptian priests (Exod 7:11, 22; 8:7, 18) and then the ten **plagues of Egypt** (Exod 7:14–12:30; Ps 78:42–51, 105:28–36) that culminated in the **Passover**.

The Hebrews lived in the area of Pithom-Raamses (Exod 1:11). Pithom is located at Tell el Ratabeh, near the Wadi Tumilat and to the southeast of Raamses. Raamses was probably located at Qantir. After departing these two cities, the Israelites journeyed to Succoth (Exod 12:37; identified with the Egyptian city of Theku at Tell el Mashkhuta, east of Pithom). The distance from Pithom-Raamses would have been approximately twenty-two miles, although many Israelites would have traveled less than that depending upon their initial location.

C. Crossing the Sea

From Succoth the caravans of Israel went to Etham (Exod 13:20) and then to Pi-hahiroth near the sea (Exod 14:2). It was from this location that Israel, trapped between the water and the pursuing army of Egypt, was given a path of escape through the sea by a miracle of God (Exod 14:21–31).

Scholars have long debated the identity of this body of water. In Hebrew, it is called *yām sûp*, meaning "Sea of Reeds." The Greek **Septuagint** took this to mean the Red Sea, i.e., the Gulf of Suez, which reaches up between Egypt and the Sinai Peninsula. This is consistent with 1 Kgs 9:26, which informs us that Solomon docked his fleet of merchant ships in *yām sûp*, there referring to the Gulf of Aqabah, a second inlet of the Red Sea along the east side of the Sinai Peninsula. Interestingly, a variety of saltwater reeds continue to grow alongside the banks of the Suez Canal even today.

Other possible sites for the sea crossing include the smaller lakes that lined the border between Egypt and Sinai in ancient times. So far as the research indicates, the Bitter Lakes, Lake Timsah, and Lake El-Ballah all supported salt-tolerant reeds and were once more sizable bodies of water than what remains of them today.

D. To Sinai

Once across the sea of reeds, the Israelites sang songs of praise to the Lord for their deliverance (Exod 15) and set out through the desert of Shur for three days (15:22), eventually reaching Elim (15:27). From there, they went across the desert of Sin. "On the fifteenth day of the second month after they had departed from the land of Egypt" (16:1), they reached the **Sinai**. The route taken across the Sinai was determined chiefly by geography. Three routes were available to them. The northern route was not feasible because of the presence of Egyptian fortresses. The line across central

Sinai was not possible because of the arid conditions of the central plain. That left only the southern course as practicable, the one that would take them eventually toward **Kadesh-barnea**.

II. DATE OF THE EXODUS

Modern scholarship is divided on the date of the Exodus event. Some, following a strict reading of biblical chronology, put it in the fifteenth century B.C. Others, based on a reading of the archaeological data, place the Exodus in the thirteenth century B.C. The issue is not easily settled, because the pharaoh whose stubbornness is showcased in the biblical account is never named.

1. *Fifteenth-Century Exodus.* The biblical timeline is based on 1 Kgs 6:1, which indicates that Solomon began construction on the Jerusalem Temple in the fourth year of his reign, some 480 years after the Exodus took place. Counting back from 966 B.C., the year the Temple foundations were laid, we arrive at a date for the Exodus of around 1446 B.C. This date is indirectly corroborated by Judg 11:26, where Jephthah insists that Israel had occupied the tribal lands east of the Jordan River for a full three hundred years—something impossible if the Exodus took place in the thirteenth century.

On this model, the pharaoh of the Exodus was most likely Thutmose III (ca. 1479–1425 B.C.), or possibly Amenhotep II (ca. 1427–1400 B.C.). The subject of Egyptian chronology is itself in dispute, so it is difficult to be certain. In any case, archaeologists have discovered large storage facilities in the eastern Delta—in the same area as the cities of Pithom and Raamses

mentioned in Exod 1:11—that date back to the fifteenth century B.C. and probably served as military supply depots for the western campaigns of Thutmose III. Scarabs bearing the name of this pharaoh were found at one of the sites. Likewise, the tomb of Rekhmire, vizier of Thutmose III, shows Semitic and Nubian slaves making bricks under the supervision of armed taskmasters to build a temple at Karnak (cf. Exod 5:6–21). None of this proves a fifteenth-century date for the Exodus, but it creates a historical picture that is consistent with the biblical timeline.

2. *Thirteenth-Century Exodus.* Modern scholars generally date the Exodus roughly two centuries later than a literal reading of biblical chronology would suggest. Texts such as 1 Kgs 6:1 are often read symbolically (e.g., 480 years = 12 generations), and the notation at Exodus 1:11 is taken to mean that the storage city of Raamses was constructed by one of Egypt's most celebrated builder-kings, Pharaoh Ramesses II (ca. 1279–1213 B.C.). Ramesses II is thus identified as the pharaoh of the Exodus.

On the archaeological front, it is said that a thirteenth-century Exodus fits the situation in Palestine around this time. For example, some archaeologists judge that the city of Jericho, which figured prominently in Israel's conquest of Canaan (Josh 6), was uninhabited in the fifteenth century B.C. but not in the thirteenth century. Unfortunately, massive erosion at the site of ancient Jericho (Tell es-Sultan) makes it extremely difficult to reconstruct the history of occupation there. Also, numerous excavated towns in Palestine show destruction levels dating back to the thirteenth century B.C., suggesting widespread conflict in Canaan at this time. It is said that this too fits the picture of an Israelite invasion and conquest in the thirteenth century.

On balance, it is preferable to date the Exodus to the fifteenth century B.C. Biblical chronology points unambiguously in this direction, and the archaeological record can be interpreted to support both alternatives. In point of fact, the findings of modern archaeology are evaluated differently by different scholars, so it seems unwise to make such data the primary foundation for a drastic revision of the biblical timeline.

III. THEOLOGY OF THE EXODUS

The central theme of the Exodus is proclaimed by God to Moses: "'I will take you as my people, and I will be your God. You shall know that I am the LORD your God, who has freed you from the burdens of the Egyptians. I will bring you into the land that I swore to give to Abraham, Isaac, and Jacob; I will give it to you for a possession. I am the LORD'" (Exod 6:7–8).

The Exodus was an extension of the promise to Abraham that Israel would be granted the land of Canaan (Exod 3:8; 6:8). The event was a cause for eternal celebration and commemoration as a great victory for the Israelite people through the power of God (cf. Ps 78:12–14; 106:8–10; 135:8–11). But the memory of the Exodus was more than merely a celebration of past events; it was the continuing proclamation of God's mighty works for his people. By the people's commemorating God's saving deeds through celebrating the holiday, God's works could be made real and present to each new generation (CCC 1363).

In the story of the Exodus, the very foundation of Israel as a nation was traced back, not to a conquest, but to God's direct intervention in favor of his people. References to the Exodus were thus frequent among the prophets, who saw hope in the saving power of God even as they lamented the infidelity of the Jewish people (Isa 10:26, 51:10, 63:11; Jer 31:32; Ezek 20:5; Mic 6:4). The deliverance was a **type** for future salvation (cf. Isa 41:18; 43:19; 48:21; 49:10).

IV. THE EXODUS IN THE NEW TESTAMENT

The Exodus was the decisive pattern on which Israel based their expectations for salvation and liberation. It provided historical precedent for a belief in Yahweh's power to save. The Exodus underlies Isaiah's anticipation of the return to Judah after the Babylonian Exile (Isa 40–66), but most important is the lasting significance of Exodus for the New Testament and the deliverance brought by the Messiah. The Exodus is a **type** of Christian redemption. The ultimate fulfillment of God's saving plan was Christ, so that Paul could write: "all were baptized into Moses in the cloud and in the sea, and all ate the same spiritual food, and all drank the same spiritual drink. For they drank from the spiritual rock that followed them, and the rock was Christ" (1 Cor 10:2–4).

The deliverance of Israel from Egypt prefigures our own deliverance from the slavery to sin (Rom 6:6–7; cf. 1 Cor. 10:1–2); the feast of Passover anticipates Christ, the Lamb of

God, by whom came deliverance from death and whose flesh became food in the Eucharist (1 Cor 5:7–8; 1 Pet 1:18–19); the Eucharist is also seen in the manna provided by God in the wilderness (John 6:31–35; 1 Cor. 10:1–4); finally, the Tabernacle is a type of the humanity of Christ, who chose to dwell in the midst of his people through the Incarnation (John 1:14).

EXODUS, BOOK OF The second book of the Old Testament and the second book of the Pentateuch. The Hebrew title for Exodus is *wě'lleh šěmôt*, meaning "and these are the names" (Exod 1:1), which restates Gen 46:8: "Now these are the names of the Israelites, Jacob and his offspring, who came to Egypt." The title thereby suggests that the book is a continuation of the Genesis account, which ends with the family of Jacob living in Egypt. The Greek **Septuagint** uses the title *Exodos*, meaning "departure" or "a going out," describing the contents of the work: the departure of Israel out of Egypt. The Latin Vulgate adopted this title for the book, *Liber Exodus*; the English title is derived from the Vulgate.

The book of Exodus is taken up with two of the most important events in the long history of the OT—the departure of the Israelites out of Egypt under the leadership of Moses and the covenant of Sinai. In Exodus, the history of the patriarchs is carried forward to the formation of the nation of Israel through the Sinai covenant and its renewal after the idolatry of God's people.

I. *Authorship and Date*
II. *Contents*

III. *Purpose and Themes*
   A. *Demonstration of God's Power*
   B. *Covenant for a Priestly Kingdom*
   C. *The Renewal of the Covenant*

I. AUTHORSHIP AND DATE

According to tradition, the author of the whole Pentateuch was Moses. Modern scholars have often preferred to see Exodus as a collection of narrative and legal traditions that were transmitted first in oral form and then as written accounts through the long history of Israel (see **Pentateuch** for a detailed discussion of the various source hypotheses), receiving their final form much later.

On the other hand, the claims of Moses's authorship of Exodus are supported not only by both Jewish and Christian tradition but also by the book itself. In the New Testament, Jesus describes Exodus as the "book of Moses" (Mark 12:26). The text of Exodus displays a number of characteristics that remind us of the literature, law codes, and treaties of the Near East during the fifteenth century B.C., such as the Code of **Hammurabi** (cf. Exod 21–23). The description of the tabernacle is similar to those involving tent sanctuaries in Egypt and Ugarit in the second millennium B.C. These features strongly suggest that Exodus was written at least near the time of Moses.

II. CONTENTS

I. *The Exodus from Egypt (1:1–18:27)*
   A. *Israel's Slavery in Egypt (1:1–22)*
   B. *The Birth and Call of Moses (2:1–4:31)*
   C. *Moses and Aaron Demand Freedom for Israel (5:1–7:13)*

III. PURPOSE AND THEMES

Exodus continues the history of Israel's beginnings where Genesis left off. Exodus is considered the pivotal work of the Torah because of the event of the covenant at Sinai. The Sinai covenant was only possible because of the direct intervention of God in securing the liberation of Israel out of Egypt. To accomplish these mighty deeds, God chose Moses. The book is thus dominated by two figures—Moses, the covenant mediator and the lawgiver; and God, the loving Creator by whom the covenant was bestowed.

A. Demonstration of God's Power

The Exodus from Egypt (Exod 1:1–18:27) begins with a description of the plight of Jacob's descendants (cf. Gen 37:2–50:26) who had settled in Egypt and were enslaved. Faithful to his promises to Abraham, God raised up the extraordinary figure of Moses. God revealed himself to Moses and proclaimed the name of Yahweh, the God of the patriarchs (Exod 3:13–15). Commissioned but accepting reluc-

tantly, Moses proved equal to the enormous task given to him: he challenged the pharaoh and ultimately succeeded in freeing Israel. The triumph came about through the Lord's demonstration of his power, not only over the false gods of Egypt, but also over the whole created order, as manifested in the plagues visited upon Egypt. The climax of the first half of the book is the Passover (Exod 12:1–27).

Having won the freedom of the Israelites, Moses led his people out of Egypt to the base of Mount Sinai across the wilderness (Exod 13:17–18:27). The journey was an eventful one, marked again by God's intervention in parting the waters of the Red Sea and destroying the army of the pharaoh (14:1–29).

B. Covenant for a Priestly Kingdom

The second half of the book (Exod 19:1–40:38) is taken up with the covenant (chaps. 19–24), the enumeration of its terms through the Sinai laws beginning with the Ten Commandments and a code of social and religious ethics (chaps. 20–23).

The purpose of the Exodus and the covenant is declared by Yahweh to Moses: "Now therefore, if you obey my voice and keep my covenant, you shall be my treasured possession out of all the peoples. Indeed, the whole earth is mine, but you shall be for me a priestly kingdom and a holy nation" (Exod 19:5–6). Israel was meant to be sent forth by its father as his firstborn son (4:22) to all of the nations of the world, fulfilling a royal-priestly role as elder brother to the nations. The laws by which the covenant was configured were intended to transform the loose confederation of tribes into God's national family. The covenant was solemnly sealed between God and Moses, Aaron, Nadab, Abihu, and the seventy elders of Israel with a covenant meal upon the mountain (24:10).

C. The Renewal of the Covenant

The covenant was soon broken by the idolatry involving the golden calf. The renewal of the covenant takes up the remainder of the book (Exod 33–40). Through the intervention of Moses, the Sinai covenant is renewed, but the Sinai law code is expanded. Indeed, the enumeration and promulgation of laws takes up the final part of Exodus, particularly the host of laws guiding the fabrication and furnishings of the moveable sanctuary, the Tabernacle. Here the Lord dwells with his people, although he is hidden from them (chaps. 25–31, 35–40). The laws continue through Leviticus and the first ten chapters of Numbers.

Moses serves as the covenant mediator, and after the golden calf his mediation becomes almost Christlike. The Levites then assume the priesthood that has been forfeited by Israel, replacing the firstborn sons from the tribes. From now on, the Levites will offer animal sacrifices in the Tabernacle on behalf of Israel.

Throughout the narrative, Israel encounters the God who renders the other supposed deities powerless, who has chosen the descendants of Abraham and Jacob for his divine purposes and called them to become a nation of priests. God has consecrated Israel as his firstborn son and has revealed himself and his divine purposes and glory (cf. 3:14; 19:18; 33:18–23) as well as his mercy, love, and faithfulness (3:16–17; 6:3–8; 34:5–9).

EXORCISM See **Demon**; *see also* **Miracles**; **Tobit**.

EYE The organ of sight. The eye in Scripture has several metaphorical meanings. The eye is considered a gift from God (Prov 20:12) and a mirror of the soul (Sir 14:8–9). Figuratively, the eye is a means of expressing the entire person or the will. Hence, to turn one's eyes toward God is to be obedient entirely to his will (Ps 25:15; 123:2). Conversely, the eyes betray vices such as pride (Prov 6:17), covetousness (Sir 14:9; Jer 22:17), and greed—as with the blindness of judges (Exod 23:8) in accepting bribes. As death can enter the soul through the eyes, one should keep watch over his eyes (Prov 4:25, 23:26; Sir 9:5–9; cf. 2 Sam 11). "The eyes of God" imply God's omniscience (2 Chr 16:9; Prov 15:3), power to judge, as with David (2 Sam 11:27), and lasting care for his creatures (1 Kgs 8:29; Isa 37:17).

EZEKIEL (Hebrew, "God makes strong," or "may God strengthen," Ezek 1:3; 3:8). A prophet living during the Babylonian Exile and active from 593 to 571 B.C., author of the third book of the major prophets. Little biographical information is contained in the book, although it is declared that Ezekiel was the son of Buzi (Ezek 1:3), "in the land of the Chaldeans by the river Chebar." A priest, Ezekiel shared in the Exile of his people when he was deported from Jerusalem in 598 B.C. with Joachim (2 Kgs 24:12–16; cf. Ezek 33:21, 40:1).

With the other exiles he settled in Tel-abib, on the Chebar (Ezek 1:1; 3:15) in Babylonia, and apparently spent the rest of his life there. In 593 B.C., the fifth year following his exile, Ezekiel received his call as a prophet in a vision described at the beginning of his prophecy (Ezek 1:4; 3:15).

Based on the testimony of Ezek 29:17, he prophesied for around twenty-two years. Since he was a priest, we can presume that he was well educated. Little else is known, except that he was married (Ezek 24:18) and likely performed all of his preaching in Babylonia (Ezek 3:15). According to legend, he was buried in a tomb at al-Kifl, near modern Hilla, Iraq.

The legitimacy of Ezekiel as a prophet was recognized both in the Old Testament (Sir 49:8) and the New Testament. Although Ezekiel is not mentioned by name in the NT, his prophecies are often referred to (e.g., Matt 22:32 with Ezek 17:23 and John 10 with Ezek 34:11). Ezekiel is quoted especially in Revelation (cf. Rev 18–21 with Ezek 27, 38, 47). (*See* **Ezekiel, book of**; *see also* **Prophet**.)

EZEKIEL, BOOK OF A prophetic book of the Old Testament that takes its name from the priest-prophet who prophesied in Babylon during the first phase of the **Exile**, from 593 to 571 B.C. The book was intended to prepare his fellow early exiles for the impending fall of Jerusalem and to teach his fellow Israelites that divine judgment was coming for their past sins, but also to assure them that after that judgment would come salvation.

The prophet **Ezekiel** lived as an exile in Babylon, probably in the Jewish settlement of Tel-abib on the **Chebar** canal near Nippur (Ezek 3:15). As he was already in Babylon before the fall of Jerusalem, he was most likely among the first citizens deported after Nebuchadnezzar seized Jerusalem in 598–597 B.C. (2 Kgs 24:10–17).

I. *Authorship and Date*

II. *Contents*

III. *Purpose and Themes*

    A. *Exile as Punishment for Infidelity*

    B. *Prophecies Against Judah's Neighbors*

    C. *The Coming Restoration*

I. AUTHORSHIP AND DATE

The book is named for the prophet who is mentioned at the very beginning of the work and features first-person narrative throughout. The authorship of Ezekiel was unquestioned until the twentieth century, when some scholars suggested that the book was written perhaps as late as the latter half of the third century B.C. The theories did not find a wide following, and the general opinion is that, at the very least, Ezekiel is a work of the Exile. It was almost certainly written by Ezekiel himself, or possibly assembled from Ezekiel's prophecies just after his death by a group of editors who were also disciples of the prophet. Thus the book would date around 592–570 B.C.

There was some debate about Ezekiel's place in the **canon**. Sirach 49:8 clearly names the book as authentic, but in the first century A.D. there was an effort to have the book suppressed. Through the efforts of Hananiah ben Hezekiah, however, Ezekiel was given its rightful place in the Hebrew canon. It is counted third among the latter prophets.

II. CONTENTS

III. PURPOSE AND THEMES

A. Exile as Punishment for Infidelity

Ezekiel wrote as one of the many Israelites who had been carried off and forced to endure exile at the hands of the Babylonians. With the other exiles, he found himself in Tel-abib, on the river Chebar (Ezek 1:1; 3:15), and in the fifth year he received his call as a prophet in one of the most memorable visions of the OT. He told his fellow Israelites that their terrible plight was not because of the failings or infidelity of God but because of their own sins and their own infidelity.

He foretold the destruction of the kingdom of Judah, the capture of Jerusalem, and the destruction of the Temple (3:22–24). These events could not be prevented and the prophecies were readily fulfilled. The fall was just punishment for the failings of the people, including idolatry in the Temple, as a result of which God chose to depart from the Temple's precincts (chap. 9): "The guilt of the house of Israel and Judah is exceedingly great; the land is full of bloodshed and the city full of perversity; for they say, 'The Lord has forsaken the land, and the Lord does not see'" (9:9).

The prophet then compared Jerusalem to the dead wood of the vine, doomed for the fire (chap. 15) and denounced Judah as a harlot, more wicked and malicious than Samaria and Sodom (chap. 16). As the horror of the conquest descended, Ezekiel's wife died, but God did not permit the prophet to mourn publicly. Rather, Ezekiel's loss would be transformed into a lesson for his people: the exiles should be strong enough to lose everything without grief (24:15–27).

B. Prophecies Against Judah's Neighbors

Ezekiel also offered prophecies concerning the Gentiles (Ezek 25–37), starting with those peoples who profited from the downfall of

Judah: the Ammonites, the Moabites, the Edomites, and the Philistines. Their fate is declared in chapter 25, while he speaks in greater detail about the fate that will befall Tyre and its prince (chaps. 26–28), Sidon (28:20–26), and Egypt (chaps. 29–32).

C. The Coming Restoration

Ezekiel then proclaimed the eventual return of the people from their exile, assuring them of the eventual triumph of the Kingdom of the Messiah, the second David. Promise of this was made in Ezek 11:19–21: "I will give them one heart, and put a new spirit within them; I will remove the heart of stone from their flesh and give them a heart of flesh, so that they may follow my statutes and keep my ordinances and obey them. Then they shall be my people, and I will be their God. But as for those whose heart goes after their detestable things and their abominations, I will bring their deeds upon their own heads, says the Lord God."

The Messiah, however, would not be a militant warrior king but a shepherd through whom God promises to purify his people and reestablish its former splendor (35–37). Israel, though dead, should rise again, dry bones covered with flesh and given life before the eyes of the prophet. Central to this restoration is the second David. In the new temple (40–43), God will dwell among his people and be served in the tabernacle by priests of his choice, "And the name of the city from that time on shall be, The Lord is There" (48:35). The restoration envisioned by Ezekiel involved the restoration of the Davidic covenant and would encompass the twelve tribes of Israel (47:13; 48); hence it would include both the house of Israel and the house of Judah (37). (*See also* **Restoration**; **Resurrection**.)

EZION-GEBER A port city on the northern edge of the Gulf of Aqaba, near modern Aqaba and identified today with modern Tell-el-Khelefeih; it was, according to the Old Testament, "near Eloth on the shore of the Red Sea, in the land of Edom" (1 Kgs 9:26). Archaeological excavations indicate that Eloth and Ezion-geber are essentially synonymous. The site was used as an encampment by the Israelites during the journey to Canaan (Deut 2:8; Num 33:35). In the time of Solomon, it was an active seaport used for commerce with Arabia (1 Kgs 22:49; 2 Chr 20:36), and archaeology shows that it was an important manufacturing site for copper and iron goods.

EZRA A Zadokite priest and scribe, an expert in the Mosaic Law, and a member of the Jewish community in Babylon (Ezra 7) who was sent on a mission to Jerusalem. Ezra probably held a position in the Persian court, and in the seventh year of the reign of Artaxerxes he was dispatched to Jerusalem with the authority to bring with him as many Babylonian Jews as desired to return home, along with a gift of silver and gold offered to the God of Israel (Ezra 7:14). In addition, he was empowered to use royal treasury funds as needed for the cost of refurbishing the Temple (Ezra 7:15–24) and to instruct his fellow Jews in the Law of God, making that Law the binding one on the Jews of the Persian Empire (Ezra 7:14, 25–26).

Ezra proceeded with his mission; the exercise of his duties is recounted in Neh 8–9.

He gathered together the community of Jerusalem and proclaimed to them the Law of Moses. Scribes then gave an explanation of the Law, so that all could understand (Neh 8:1–9). (Some scholars take this explanation as evidence that the people were already used to speaking **Aramaic**, and thus needed to have the Hebrew interpreted to them.) The discourse took two days to complete and that was followed by the celebration of the feasts of tabernacles (Neh 8:13–18) (*see under* **Booths, Feast of**) and a ceremony of penance. Ezra expressed deep sorrow that many Jewish men had married foreign wives, and the Jews swore that from then on they would end the practice (Ezra 10:5); they went even further by forcing those with foreign wives to divorce them and even abandon the children born of the unions (Ezra 10:44).

The mission of Ezra was consistent with the general policy of toleration practiced by the Persian Empire, and it marked a truly significant moment in Jewish history. Having been permitted to return home after the Exile, the Jewish population not only gave thanks for their restoration; they also pledged themselves to rigid and faithful adherence to the Law. Indeed, thanks to Ezra, the Law stood with the Temple and ritual as one of the pillars of postexilic Judaism.

The relations between Ezra and Nehemiah pose a long-standing challenge for biblical scholars regarding the dates for the activities of each man. The issue hinges on the exact identity of Artaxerxes. The mission of Ezra took place in the seventh year of the reign (Ezra 7:7), but the difficulty emerges in whether the king in question was Artaxerxes I (r. 465–425 B.C.) or Artaxerxes II (r. 404–359 B.C.). If the mission of Ezra was under the first Artaxerxes, then it came before the mission of Nehemiah (which took place in the twentieth year of that reign); if it was in the reign of Artaxerxes II, then it followed the labors of Nehemiah. On balance, the traditional sequence of Ezra followed by Nehemiah is the least problematic.

EZRA, BOOK OF Also called 1 Esdras, one of the Historical Books of the Old Testament; it recounts the return of the people to their homeland after the Exile.

Ezra and **Nehemiah** were originally one book in Hebrew. In the **Vulgate**, Ezra and Nehemiah are separated and called 1 and 2 Esdras. There are also two apocryphal books (*see* **Apocrypha**) attributed to Ezra: one a retelling of the history in Ezra and Nehemiah, and the other an apocalypse (*see* **Apocalyptic literature**). Although they are not among the **deuterocanonical** books of the Catholic canon, they are included in the Protestant Apocrypha, where they are called 1 Esdras and either 2 Esdras or 4 Ezra.

I. AUTHORSHIP AND DATE

According to Jewish tradition, the author of this book was Ezra himself. Some scholars are of the view that Ezra and Nehemiah formed a continuation of the Chronicler's history covered by 1 and 2 Chronicles, perhaps written by the same author. Notable sources for the work included the "memoirs" of Ezra (cf. Ezra 7–10), official records, correspondence to the Persian court, decrees, and genealogies, and therefore little of the books were probably by the Chronicler's own hand, except for such sections as Ezra 7–9.

The book was probably composed within living memory of the events it records. If one accepts that Ezra himself is its author, and that he came to Palestine during the reign of Artaxerxes I, then a date may be assigned of around 420 B.C. Otherwise, attempts to date the book have ranged between 400 and 300 B.C.

II. CONTENTS

III. PURPOSE AND THEMES

The book begins as 2 Chronicles ended, with the decree of **Cyrus** the Great that permitted the Jews of the empire—who had long lived as exiles under the Babylonians—to return home and restore the Temple. The account details the efforts at the restoration of national and religious life, and the institution of a reformed and faithful community.

The renewed Jewish community was a chastened one that has taken the spiritual and moral lessons of the Exile to heart. The fledgling community of the faithful was aware of the dangers posed to it by a pagan world, but also of the moral threats of infidelity to the covenant. Thus intermarriage with Gentile neighbors appeared as a grave danger to the tiny community of returned exiles: it might lead them back to the sins of their ancestors, and the small colony of the faithful might once again be overwhelmed by paganism.

Hope is not in the rebirth of the grand Davidic and Solomonic kingdom. Indeed, there can be no question of that; the book shows how completely the little community depended on the pleasure of the Persian emperor (see Ezra 4–6). Instead, hope was placed in the proper worship of God in the Temple, in the fulfillment of the liturgical demands, and in faithful observance of God's Law.

F

FACE The word "face" (Hebrew *pānîm*) occurs over twenty-one hundred times in the Old Testament. The Hebrew word is always in the plural, as it is understood to represent the multiple features that make up the human face. The face not only represented the actual visage of a person, but also served to express the interior disposition and attitude. Thus it was a figurative term for the self or even the entire person or presence.

Resolve or stubbornness might be described as hardening of the face (Deut 28:50; Prov 7:13, 21:29; Isa 50:7; Jer 5:3; Ezek 3:8). Anger, most notably because of failure or rejection, was seen in a fallen face (Gen 4:5; Jer 5:3), while to fall on one's face suggested giving homage or obeisance. Similarly, to hide one's face denoted disgust or aversion (Isa 53:3), especially when speaking of God (Ps 13:2, 27:9, 102:3; Isa 54:8; Jer 33:5). To placate or appease God was to sweeten his face (Exod 32:11; 1 Kgs 13:6; 2 Kgs 13:4; 2 Chr 33:12; Jer 26:19). Joy and happiness were seen in the shining face (Job 29:24), again as seen with God (Num 6:25; Ps 4:7, 31:17, 44:4, 67:2, 80:4). To lift or raise one's face was to give acceptance or approval, and when applied to the Lord it meant a sign of blessing (Deut 10:17; Job 34:19).

Exodus (33:20) says that no man can see the Lord or the Lord's face and live. From this, references to seeing the face of Yahweh (Gen 33:10; Job 33:26) and being in his presence (Exod 23:15, 34:20; Ps 42:3) imply the attendance of a mortal in the sanctuary that was the place in which Yahweh dwelt. Jacob (Gen 32:31) and Moses (Exod 33:11) saw God face-to-face, and tradition held that **Moses** alone beheld God (Deut 34:10; cf. Deut 5:4; Judg 6:22, 13:22).

FAIR HAVENS (Greek *Kaloi Limenes*) A harbor or bay on the southern coast of Crete near the town of Lasea. The ship carrying Paul to Rome stopped here (Acts 27:8). Choosing to ignore the advice of Paul that they should remain for the winter, the centurion in charge of the ship set sail from the harbor. The ship was wrecked at sea, but with no loss of life (Acts 27:9ff.).

FAITH Hebrews 11:1 gives a simple and elegant definition of faith: "Now faith is the assurance of things hoped for, the conviction of things not seen." Saint Thomas Aquinas in the *Summa theologiae* gave us the classic theological definition of faith: "Faith is the act of the intellect when it assents to divine truth under the influence of the will moved by God through grace" (*Summa theologiae* II.II. q2.a.9).

I. *Faith in the Old Testament*
    A. *God's Saving Acts Are the Basis for Faith*
    B. *The Faith of Abraham*
    C. *Strength in Trust, Not in Ourselves*
II. *Faith in the New Testament*
    A. *Faith in the Gospels*
    B. *Paul's Theology of Faith*
    C. *The History of Faith in Hebrews*

I. FAITH IN THE OLD TESTAMENT

A. God's Saving Acts Are the Basis for Faith

In the Old Testament there is both the faith of God toward man (Deut 32:4) and the faith of man toward God (Ps 119:30). God's people had seen the evidence: God always proved steadfast and absolutely trustworthy. For that reason it was the duty of his people to accept his word and his commandments, trusting that they were right and good (Exod 14:31, 19:9; Num 14:11; Deut 1:30–33). Throughout the OT, we see the same persuasive argument for faith: "Only fear the LORD, and serve him faithfully with all your heart; for consider what great things he has done for you" (1 Sam 12:24).

B. The Faith of Abraham

Abraham is the best-known example of biblical faith in God. He believed God's promise concerning his descendants: "And he believed the Lord; and the Lord reckoned it to him as righteousness" (Gen 15:6). Abraham responded to God's call with the obedience of faith (Rom 1:5; 16:26). He submitted his will and intellect to God and committed himself without reservation to God's will and saving power (cf. Jer 17:5–6; Ps 40:5, 146:3–4) (CCC 142–43). When God tested him by commanding him to sacrifice **Isaac**, Abraham demonstrated his own worthiness to be a participant in a relationship with God by readying Isaac for sacrifice.

C. Strength in Trust, Not in Ourselves

Isaiah delivered a stern demand for faith to **Ahaz** when Israel and Aram made an alliance to attack Judah: "If you will not believe, surely you shall not be established" (Isa 7:9). Only trust and confidence in the Lord will bring the sure hope of safety and salvation: "in quietness and in trust shall be your strength" (Isa 30:15). God will deliver Judah from danger and annihilation, but the way lies not in military alliances and action; hope lies in trusting absolutely in God.

II. FAITH IN THE NEW TESTAMENT

A. Faith in the Gospels

Jesus demands faith from those who hear him (Matt 9:28; Mark 4:36; Luke 8:25), making faith a precondition for eternal life and salvation (Matt 9:22; Luke 8:48). In the OT, faith had been a response to the saving acts of God; in the New Testament faith is a response to the signs and miracles given by Christ (Matt 11:1–5; 12:27). All things are possible for those who believe (Matt 17:20; 21:21). Against this response is the hardness of heart and pride that prevent belief (Matt 18:1–7).

John declares the purpose of his Gospel:

"that you may come to believe that Jesus is the Messiah, the Son of God, and that through believing you may have life in his name" (John 20:31). Faith is freely given, but it is also a gift from God (John 6:37, 44, 65). The one who believes accepts Christ's word (John 2:22; 5:47; 8:45) and receives eternal life and so passes from death to life (John 11). (Cf. *Dignitatis Humanae*, §§10–11; John 18:37, 12:32.) Those who reject this faith are condemned (John 3:18–19): "Those who believe in him are not condemned; but those who do not believe are condemned already, because they have not believed in the name of the only Son of God. And this is the judgment, that the light has come into the world, and people loved darkness rather than light because their deeds were evil" (CCC 160).

Acts makes it clear that for the early Christian community, belief is the basic requirement of membership (Acts 4:4; 13:12; 15:7): faith in Jesus Christ as Lord (Acts 5:14; 9:42), by whose grace one is saved (Acts 15:11).

B. Paul's Theology of Faith

Paul rejects the Law of Moses in favor of faith in Jesus Christ, for the Law does not lead the believer to righteousness (Rom 3:20). The contrast between faith and the Law is a major theme in Romans, with Abraham held up as an example of faith. Paul argues forcefully that Abraham's faith was conversion, which he underwent before the Law, before his **circumcision**, "a seal of the righteousness that he had by faith while he was still uncircumcised" (Rom 4:11; cf. Gen 15:6; Eph 2:8–10; Gal 2:16). For Paul, those who consider themselves saved merely by the works of the law without faith cannot obtain the promised righteousness that is possible by faith.

We are made righteous by the union of faith with baptism (Rom 1:17; 3:22; 26; 4:5, 9:30; Gal 2:16, 3:8). The Christian is saved by grace (Eph 2:8), and henceforth the Christian, a son of God through Christ (Gal 3:26), makes his life an expression of faith in Jesus Christ (Gal 2:20). "We know that our old self was crucified with him so that the sinful body might be destroyed, and we might no longer be enslaved to sin. For he who has died is freed from sin. But if we have died with Christ, we believe that we shall also live with him" (Rom 6:6–8). (*See also* **Justification**.) Hence, "we walk by faith, not by sight" (2 Cor 5:7).

C. The History of Faith in Hebrews

Hebrews 11 traces the legacy of faith in the OT, citing examples from Abel to the Maccabees. Yet the faith of these OT heroes had to point toward the future: "though well attested by their faith, [they] did not receive what was promised, since God had foreseen something better for us, that apart from us they should not be made perfect" (Heb 11:39–40). The perfection of faith did not come until the coming of the Messiah, "the pioneer and perfecter of our faith" (Heb 12:2) (CCC 147, 163).

FALL, THE The original sin freely committed by the first human beings. Narrated in figurative language in Gen 2–3, the Fall describes a primeval event that caused man's break with God's friendship and grace, which the first humans had received from God not only for themselves but for the whole human race. The whole of human history is stained by the original fault freely committed by our first parents: "Behold, I was brought forth in iniquity, and in sin did my mother conceive me" (Ps 51:7). Humanity, said Cardinal Newman, "is out of joint with the purposes of its Creator" (*Apologia pro vita sua;* cf. GS §13.1).

I. The Story in Genesis
  A. The Sin of Adam and Eve
  B. The Curse
  C. The First Gospel
II. Christ Reverses the Fall

I. THE STORY IN GENESIS

While acknowledging that the story of **Adam** and **Eve** in Genesis may use figurative language, the Church stresses that the drama of the first sin is part of the revealed truths of creation (CCC 289, 390).

A. The Sin of Adam and Eve

As recounted in Genesis, Adam and Eve freely broke their **covenant** with God. They were free to choose moral evil, even though they were recipients of grace.

The account of the Fall is notable for the actions of both Adam and Eve. Traditionally, the first sin was attributed to both pride and rebellion on the part of Adam and Eve who desired to be like God. Tempted and deceived by the serpent, Eve tasted of the fruit from the tree of the knowledge of good and evil and gave some to Adam, whereupon "the eyes of both were opened, and they knew that they were naked" (Gen 2:7). Although Eve eventually offered the fruit to Adam, she resisted the temptation with some strength before giving in, showing greater determination than Adam,

who seems to have been present at the time of the initial exchange between the serpent and Eve. (The serpent addresses both of them in Gen 3:4–5, using plural forms translated with "ye" in some older English versions.) Adam, on the other hand, did not resist her efforts to involve him in her sin. Adam thus not only freely partook in the sin (when Eve was overcome), but also failed to defend Eve and the garden from the serpent. He brought upon himself greater culpability because he had received the commandment directly from God (Gen 2:16–17).

B. The Curse

The effects of the first sin were manifest immediately. When questioned by the Lord, Adam blamed not himself but Eve (Gen 3:12); Eve then blamed the serpent (3:13). It is thus apparent that sin had broken the unity of their relationship with God and with each other (CCC 1607). God pronounced the covenant curses: Adam lost for himself and all succeeding generations the supernatural gift of sanctifying grace and the preternatural gifts of integrity, bodily immortality, and impassibility (CCC 390, 400). Adam and Eve were cursed with physical death, the separation of body and soul (Gen 3:19; Rom 5:14; 1 Cor 15:22): "you are dust, and to dust you shall return" (Gen 19; cf. Eccl 12:7) (CCC 400). In addition, there were the pains of shame (Gen 3:7), division (3:12), toil for food (3:16–19), and above all eviction from the Garden and losing friendship with the Lord (3:23–24) (CCC 1609). Eve would face the trial of pain in childbirth, subjection to her husband, and permanent struggle with the serpent.

C. The First Gospel

But future victory is assured to the "seed" of the woman, a proclamation made to the serpent as well (Gen 3:15). In that prediction, Genesis anticipates the triumph of the Messiah (Rom 16:20; Heb 2:14) (CCC 410–11). The disobedience of Eve will be replaced by the obedience of **Mary**, so that where Eve brought death into the world, Mary will bring life (Saint Irenaeus, *Haer.* 3.22; Saint Jerome, *Epist.* 22.21). For those reasons, Gen 3:15 has been called the Protevangelium ("first gospel").

Man was not abandoned by God after the Fall. *Dei Verbum* expressed the wider plan of salvation revealed by the Genesis account: "After the fall, [God] buoyed them up with the hope of salvation, by promising redemption; and he has never ceased to show his solicitude for the human race. For he wishes to give eternal life to all those who seek salvation by patience in well-doing" (DV §3; cf. Gen 3:15; Rom 2:6–7). Genesis announces the future promise of the Messiah, the Redeemer, the "new Adam" (cf. 1 Cor 15:21–22, 45; Phil 2:8; Rom 5:19–20) (CCC 410–11).

II. CHRIST REVERSES THE FALL

The covenant curses imposed upon Adam and Eve and their progeny were thus remedial, but the assumption and bearing of the curse by Christ, through his sacrifice upon the Cross, became ultimately redemptive. This becomes especially prominent in the theology of Paul, who shows us how the rebellion of Adam was canceled by the righteous obedience of Christ. Adam made us sinners subject to death, but Christ, by a superabundance of grace, makes us righteous heirs of eternal life (Rom 5:12–21; 1 Cor 15:20–22).

In Rom 5:12–21 Paul stresses the ultimate meaning of the Genesis account by contrasting the old Adam and the New Adam, Christ. Through Adam sin and death entered into the world, while through Christ eternal life is offered to all. Christ as the second Adam brings grace and righteousness, which defeat the sin and death brought by the first Adam. Similarly, in 1 Corinthians, Paul continues to see Adam and Christ as the two figures who have most shaped the whole of the human race: "For since death came through a human being, the resurrection of the dead has also come through a human being; for as all die in Adam, so all will be made alive in Christ" (1 Cor 15:21–22). Likewise, "Just as we have borne the image of the man of dust, we will also bear the image of the man of heaven" (1 Cor 15:49; cf. Rom 8:11). (*See also* **Garden of Eden**; **Justification**; **Sin**.)

FAMILY The most fundamental unit of human society. In its most basic form, the family consists of mother, father, and children; more broadly, "family" can mean grandparents, aunts and uncles, cousins, and every degree of relation.

Christians call the family the "domestic church": it forms a community of faith, and the love of the human family is an image of the communion of the Father, Son, and Holy Spirit in the Holy Trinity.

I. The Family of God
  A. The Trinity as Family
  B. Family Bound by Covenant

I. THE FAMILY OF GOD

A. The Trinity as Family

God Himself is a family—Father, Son, and Spirit. From eternity, God is a mystery of interpersonal and life-giving love. Earthly households mirror this mystery in varying degrees, but always imperfectly. The life of the Trinity is "the central mystery of Christian faith and life," says the *Catechism* (234): "It is the mystery of God in Himself. It is therefore the source of all the other mysteries of faith, the light that enlightens them."

B. Family Bound by Covenant

The Trinity, then, is the essential context for approaching the question of the family in the history of salvation. The family in Israelite society dictated where its members would live, how they would work, and whom they might marry. A nation in the ancient Near East was largely a network of such families, as Israel was made up of the twelve tribes named for Jacob's sons. Unifying each family was the bond of **covenant**. When a family welcomed new members, through marriage or some other alliance, both parties—the new members and the established tribe—would seal the covenant bond, usually by solemnly swearing a sacred oath, sharing a common meal, and offering a sacrifice.

C. The Faithful Become God's Family by Covenant

God's relationship with Israel was similarly defined by a covenant, as were his relationships with **Adam**, **Noah**, **Abraham**, **Moses**, and **David**. With each succeeding covenant, God opened membership in his covenant family to more people: first to a married couple, then to a household, then to a tribe, then to a nation, then to a kingdom—until, finally, the invitation was made universal with Jesus. Christ's "true family" consists of those who receive new birth as children of God through baptism (John 3:3–8), and who do the will of the Father in heaven (see Matt 12:49). They become His younger brothers (see Rom 8:14–15, 29).

II. FAMILY IN THE OLD TESTAMENT

A. The Extended Family

In ancient Israel, the family was usually spoken of as the "father's house," a term that stresses the patriarchal nature of the family. Such a family was not only the immediate nuclear family of husband, wife, and children, but consisted of the extended family, including those of the same blood (except those daughters who had married and thus entered their husband's families), male and female slaves and their families, workers, and concubines. A typical family would consequently consist of several generations living under the same roof and could number dozens of people (cf. Josh 7:17; Judg 6:11, 27, 30; 8:20; 18:14).

The extended family was the most important unit in the nation of Israel, for it assured the continuation of the tribes of Israel and also served as the place where new generations were taught the faith, history, law, and traditions of Israel. The father had the obligation to teach his children about the Law of the Lord (Deut 6:7; 11:19; 32:46) as well as the traditions, feasts, and rites of Israel (Exod 12:26, 13:14; Deut 6:20–24; Josh 4:6, 21–23).

B. Consecration of the Firstborn Son

The family was patrilineal: descent was reckoned through the male line. Having sons was thus vital to carrying on the family line. The **firstborn** son was consecrated by the sacrifice or redemption of all firstborn animals (Exod 13:2, 12–15; 22:28; 34:1–20; Num 3:11–13; 8:16–18; 18:15). In the sacrifice, the firstborn son was a representation of the fact that Israel belonged entirely to the Lord, as well as a reminder of the way that the firstborn of Israel had been saved by the blood of the lamb in the **Passover**. In addition, the sacrifice was a way for God to declare his continuing fidelity to the covenant and to claim each new successive generation as his own.

C. Mutual Responsibilities in the Family

The bonds of the family were very tight, and fellow family members were always there to provide mutual support and defense. The family provided legal protection and also maintained rudimentary justice (*see* **Avenger of blood**). The family also answered for crimes and was responsible collectively for the misdeeds of its members. Punishment might extend, then, to the entire family, and sin could be punished over several generations (Exod 20:5; Deut 5:9; Josh 7:24; cf. Deut 24:16; 2 Kgs 14:6).

III. FAMILY IN THE NEW TESTAMENT

A. Family, the Center of Christian Life

The family household, not surprisingly, was a major feature of the early Christian community. Just as the Israelite family was the center of teaching, prayer, and the celebration of the Passover, so too was the early Christian family the center of worship and education in the faith. Luke writes, "And day by day, attending the temple together and breaking bread in their homes, they partook of food with glad and generous hearts, praising God and having favor with all the people" (Acts 2:46; cf. Acts 5:42; 12:12). When Gentiles became Christians, often the entire household converted to the Christian faith, starting with the significant conversion of the entire household of **Cornelius** (Acts 10).

B. Household Churches

Households were also the starting point for new churches in the cities where Paul's preaching took hold, and a large number of households can be mentioned: Philemon's at Colossae (Phlm 1); Nympha's at Laodicea (Col 4:15); Lydia's and the jailer's at Philippi (Acts 16:15, 31–34); the households of Stephanas, Crispus, and Gaius at Corinth (Acts 18:8; 1 Cor 1:14–16, 16:15; Rom 16:23); of Priscilla and Aquila, and

Onesiphorus at Ephesus (1 Cor 16:19; 2 Tim 1:16, 4:19); and of Aristobolus, Narcissus, and others at Rome (Rom 16).

IV. THE CHURCH AS FAMILY

A. The Christian's Extended Family: God and the Church

The Christian family itself was a powerful image of the wider membership in the Family of God that was offered by baptism and the new life in Jesus Christ: "So then you are no longer strangers and sojourners, but you are fellow citizens with the saints and members of the household of God" (Eph 2:19). God is a family, and Christians are his. Christ founded one Church—his mystical body—as an extension of his Incarnation. By taking on flesh, Christ divinized flesh, and he extended the Trinity's life to all humanity, through the Church, his mystical body. Incorporated into the body of Christ, Christians become "sons in the Son." They become children in the eternal household of God. They share in the very life of the Trinity, becoming part of God's own family (CCC 1655).

The Church and the family are also more than "communities"; each is, like the Trinity, a communion of persons. And so they also bear a family resemblance to one another. As the Church is a universal family, the family constitutes a "domestic Church" (CCC 1656).

B. Christians Enter the Divine Family by Covenant

Baptism and the **Eucharist** are now the means by which men and women are incorporated into God's covenant family. They are the Christian's covenant oath, common meal, and sacrifice.

Receiving these sacraments makes a profound difference in a Christian's life; for now he can call God "Abba! Father!" (Gal 4:4–6). Christians are truly children of God (John 1:12; 1 John 3:1–2), brothers and sisters and mothers of Christ (Mark 3:35), who is the "firstborn among many brethren" (Rom 8:29). Christians are "members of the household of God" (Eph 2:19). The primary revelation of Jesus Christ is God's fatherhood (see John 15). Jesus reveals God first as Father to himself, and then by extension to Christians, as "sons in the Son."

The book of Revelation makes clear that this New Covenant is the closest and most intimate of family bonds. John's vision concludes with the marriage supper of the Lamb (Jesus) and the Lamb's bride (the Church). With this event—which tradition has understood as the Eucharist—Christians seal and renew their family relationship with God. With this sacrament they call God himself their true Brother, Father, and Spouse.

C. Family, the Image of the Divine Life

A household becomes an image of the divine life through marriage, itself a sacrament of the New Covenant. Saint Paul wrote: "For this reason I bow my knees before the Father, from whom every family in heaven and on earth is named" (Eph 3:14–15). Earthly families, then, receive their "name," their identity, from God himself.

Thus, as an image of God, who is faithful and One, the family bond between husband

and wife must be permanent and indissoluble. Thus, too, as God is fecund and generous, a married couple must be open to life, willing to cooperate with the Father in the conception of children. In this context, it should be clear why the Church forbids acts of contraception, abortion, homosexuality, and adultery—all acts that distort the sanctity of marriage and the divine image in the family. As the domestic church, the family must be holy and ordered to the worship of God. (*See* **Church**; *see also* **Covenant**; **Elder**; **Firstborn**; **Marriage**.)

FAMINE Famines often happened in Palestine and surrounding countries. Common causes were droughts, plagues of locusts, unusually extreme flooding along the Nile in Egypt, and war. Periods of starvation were sometimes seen as a consequence of sin (Deut 28:20, 48; 32:24; Isa 51:19; Jer 5:12; Ezek 6:11), an image especially used by Jeremiah. Specific famines are mentioned in the time of Abraham (Gen 12:10), Isaac (Gen 26:1), and Jacob (Gen 47:1); Joseph accurately predicted the seven-year famine in Egypt (Gen 41:27). In later times, famines were mentioned during the time of David (2 Sam 21:1) and Ahab (2 Kgs 18:2). Metaphorically, Amos speaks of a famine, not of bread and water, but "of hearing the words of the LORD" (Amos 8:11).

FASTING Abstention from food, either wholly or partially, as an act of mourning or penance.

According to the Law of Moses, there was only one day in the year appointed as a fast day, namely the tenth day of the seventh month, the Day of Atonement (Lev 16:29; 23:27, 32; Num 29:7). Nevertheless, fasting was also practiced in the Old Testament times in recognition of some great disaster (Judg 20:26; 1 Sam 7:6, 14:24; 2 Sam 12:16; 1 Kgs 21:12, 27; 2 Chr 20:3; Ezra 8:21; Tob 12:8; Jer 14:12, 36:9; Joel 1:14, 2:15; 1 Macc 3:47; 2 Macc 13:12), and in times of mourning (Num 30:13; 1 Kgs 21:27; 1 Sam 31:13; 2 Sam 1:12, 3:25, 36). Likewise, private fasts were permitted, although a wife could fast only with her husband's consent (Num 30:14–16). The prophets spoke of the proper spirit in which fasting should be done to make it acceptable to God: it must be an outward sign of real penance and amendment (Isa 58:1–6; Jer 14:12; Zech 7:5).

In the New Testament, the Pharisees fasted, as did the disciples of John the Baptist (Matt 9:14; Mark 2:18; Luke 5:33, 18:12). Like the OT prophets before him, Jesus condemned the hypocritical fasting of the Pharisees (Matt 6:16). On the other hand, Jesus himself fasted for forty days before beginning his public ministry (Matt 4:2), as Moses did before he received the Law (Exod 34:28; Deut 9:9). While he was with them on earth, Jesus's disciples did not fast. When questioned on this, Jesus replied that one does not fast while with the Bridegroom, but when the Bridegroom is taken the time of fasting will come (Matt 9:14; Mark 2:18; Luke 5:33). Christ also stressed the proper spirit in which we should fast (Matt 6:17–18) and declared the need for prayer and fasting by his disciples in order to be able to expel evil spirits (Matt 17:20). The apostles did fast before making important decisions and recommended fasting for the spiritual betterment of the Christian (Acts 13:2, 14:22–23; 2 Cor 6:5, 11:27) (CCC 1434, 2043).

FAT The portion of animals that was considered the most highly prized. The Israelites were prohibited from consuming the fat of certain animals (Lev 7:23, 25) because the fat of these animals was burned as part of some prescribed sacrifices (Lev 3:3–5; 9:11, 14–16, 18).

FATHER See **God**; see also **Family**.

FATHER OF LIES The title given to the devil by Christ (John 8:44).

FATHOM (Greek *orguia*) A measure of depth that was calculated roughly by the length of both arms outstretched, from fingertip to fingertip (Acts 27:28). The fathom was estimated to be 4 cubits (around 6 feet or 1.8 meters).

FELIX, MARCUS ANTONIUS The procurator of Palestine from A.D. 52 to 59. A freed slave in the service of Emperor Claudius, he was the brother of the powerful imperial freedman Pallas and enjoyed the favor of Claudius. This esteem was likely part of the reason for Claudius's decision to appoint Felix procurator, an unusual assignment for a freedman (Suetonius, *Claud.* 28). As a governor, he proved so harsh and generally incompetent that he earned the enduring enmity of the Jews. He was a key figure in fostering the rebellion that brought massive destruction to Palestine from A.D. 66 to 70. During his tenure there were several uprisings, including one mentioned in Acts 21:38. Succeeded by Porcius Festus in A.D. 60 (Acts 24:27; Josephus,

B.J. 2.271; *Ant.* 20.182), Felix escaped punishment through his brother's influence. While procurator, Felix granted an interview to Paul, who had been arrested and imprisoned (Acts 23:24–24:27).

Felix was noted for his three marriages: to a granddaughter of Mark Antony and Cleopatra; to the Jewish princess Drusilla; and to an otherwise unknown Roman woman. Drusilla was lured away from her husband, Azizus, king of Emesa, and bore Felix a son, Agrippa, who was killed during the eruption of Mount Vesuvius in A.D. 79.

FESTUS, PORCIUS Procurator of Judea from around A.D. 60 to 62, although the exact dates are uncertain. Successor to Marcus Felix, he is best known for presiding over Paul's case. Virtually nothing is known about him outside of what was recorded by Josephus and in the Acts of the Apostles. Josephus had a far more favorable opinion of Festus than of his predecessor and noted his determined efforts to curb unrest and brigand activity in the region.

Almost immediately after his arrival as procurator, Festus became involved in Paul's trial. He attempted to move the trial from Caesarea to Jerusalem but agreed to expedite Paul's appeal to Caesar on the grounds of his Roman citizenship and sent him to Rome (Acts 24:27–26:32). "I found that he had done nothing deserving death," Festus explained to Herod Agrippa II (Acts 25:25). During the trial, Festus consulted with Agrippa II and the king's sister **Bernice**. Festus died after barely two years as governor.

FIELD OF BLOOD See **Akeldama**.

FIG The oblong or pear-shaped fruit of a tree found very commonly throughout Palestine. The fig tree is mentioned often in the Bible. Its fruit was eaten in a variety of forms, including fresh, dried, or cooked (1 Sam 25:18, 30:12; 1 Chr 12:41). The spies who were sent by Moses into the Promised Land returned with figs to demonstrate the richness of the land (Num 13:24). Figs were thus a symbol of prosperity (Song 2:13; Joel 2:22) and peace (1 Kgs 4:25; Mic 4:4; Zech 3:10; 1 Macc 14:12). Similarly, the barren fig tree was seen as a symbol of Israel's infidelity (Matt 21:18–22; Mark 11:12–25).

FIRE Flame and fire served a useful purpose in biblical symbolism, as well as having obvious value in cultic rituals and for the practical necessities of everyday life. Fire in the Old Testament was a common symbol of purification and cleansing. Thus sacred articles that were no longer to be used, such as the remains of the Passover lamb, were ritually burned to prevent any use of them for sacrilegious purposes (Exod 12:10). Fire was understood to be a representation of suffering and calamity (1 Kgs 8:51; Jer 11:4), but it could still have a purifying quality; much as metals are smelted and purified by fire, so could the just be made pure by their ordeals (Ps 66:12; Mal 3:2; Isa 43:2; Jer 6:29; Ezek 22:20, 24:12) and tested in their virtue (Zech 13:9; 1 Cor 3:13).

God appeared at times accompanied by fire (Gen 15:17), the best-known example being the burning bush (Exod 3:2). The presence of God was seen in fire, such as the pillar of fire (Exod 13:21, 14:24; Num 14:14) and the perpetual flame on the altar of burnt offerings (Lev 6:12). The fire surrounding God's manifesta-

tions made it impossible for man to draw near (Deut 4:24; Isa 33:14). God's anger was also like a fire (Ps 79:5, 89:47; Jer 4:4; Ezek 21:36, 22:21), and flames and fire were a means of expressing the terrible judgment of the Lord upon the wicked (Gen 19:24; Lev 10:2; Num 11:1; Amos 1:4, 2:5; Jer 5:14, 11:16, 17:27, 21:14; Ezek 38:22). Fire, however, was also an expression of God's pleasure (Gen 15:7; Lev 9:24; Judg 6:21).

In the New Testament, fire is frequently associated with the Holy Spirit (Matt 3:11; Luke 3:16; Acts 2:3). The NT also retains and develops further the OT theme of fire as a symbol of divine judgment, with mention made of the fire of hell (Matt 5:22, 13:50, 18:8; Mark 9:48; Jude 7; Rev 19:20).

FIRMAMENT The word used in most English translations of the Bible to express the Hebrew word *rāqîa'*. The Hebrew term, while meaning something like "a beaten metal plate," was used to describe the sky, which was imagined poetically as an inverted bowl that divided the waters of the upper abyss and those of the lower abyss (Gen 1:6; cf. Gen 17:20; Ps 19:2, 150:1; Dan 12:3; Ezek 1:22, 23, 25).

FIRSTBORN The oldest or firstborn son in an Israelite family was entitled to important privileges. By custom, the firstborn was entitled to claim the main share of his father's inheritance (Deut 21:15–17; 2 Chron 21:3), and the law stipulated that a father in a polygamous family should favor his firstborn over the firstborn of any of his other wives. The firstborn son also traditionally received a special blessing from his father (Gen 27:33–36). Upon his inheritance, the firstborn son received the place of patriarch, or head of the family, with all due authority and rights over his brothers and sisters and the other relatives and members of the household (Gen 27:29, 37). There are, nevertheless, many instances in the Old Testament in which the rights were passed to a younger brother. Jacob secured primogeniture from Esau by a ruse, but once the deception was discovered, he did not lose this status. In turn, Jacob reversed the rights between Ephraim and Manasseh.

The birth of the first son was an event of great significance for a family, as a son guaranteed the perpetuation of the family line (Gen 49:3). The firstborn son was thus to be consecrated as the first fruits, so that he belonged to God in the same way as the firstborn of animals (Exod 13:2, 12–15; 22:28; 34:1–20; Num 3:11–13; 8:16–18; 13:2, 12; 18:15; Deut 15:19). Whereas ordinarily firstborn animals were sacrificed to God, the firstborn son was redeemed by making an offering to God (Exod 34:19–20); the fixed amount was five shekels of silver (Num 18:15–17). The claim of God upon the firstborn was rooted in the experience of the Passover (Exod 13:9). At the first Passover God had spared the firstborn of Israel but had claimed the firstborn of Egypt (Num 3:13). The consecration of the firstborn son was a potent reminder of God's right to claim every generation as his own, and thus every Israelite family was reminded of the wider relationship between Israel and the Lord: Israel was God's and was chosen by him as his firstborn. The firstborn of every family reminded the entire nation of this truth and its attendant obligations (cf. Jer 2:3).

Israel was consecrated as God's firstborn in the Mosaic **covenant** (Exod 4:22; 19:6; *see* **Moses**). Through the Davidic covenant, the Lord declared **David** and his royal heir, Solomon, to be his firstborn sons (Ps 89:26). They were to serve both as kings and as priests (2 Sam 6:12–19; 1 Kgs 3:15, 8:62–63) and so prepare for the Incarnation, through which God would send his firstborn Son to inaugurate the New Covenant. In this covenant, the Son entered fully into his inheritance as the firstborn, priest, and king (Heb 1:2–13; 5:5–6). In Romans (8:29) Christ is "firstborn within a large family"; he is the "firstborn of all creation" (Col 1:15), "firstborn from the dead" (Col 1:18; Rev 1:5), and "firstborn of God" (Heb 1:6). Through the life of grace that is mediated by the Son, all members of the family of faith are invited to share in the inheritance (Heb 12:23) and become coheirs with Christ (Rom 8:17). Such an inheritance entails participation as a royal and priestly people (1 Pet 2:9; Rev 1:6).

FIRST FRUITS The first fruits were considered the rightful and sacred property of God, including produce, grain, wine, oil, wool, and honey (Deut 18:4; 2 Chr 31:5; Exod 23:19, 34:26) in recognition of God's dominion over all creation, and in a manner perhaps analogous to the place of the **firstborn** son. By extension also Israel is called "the first-fruits of his [God's] harvest" (Jer 2:3), and Paul refers to some of his early converts in Greece as first fruits (1 Cor 16:15; 2 Thess 2:12). Likewise, he declares that Christ is "the first fruits of those who have died" (1 Cor 15:20).

FISH Fish were commonly available in the waters of the Mediterranean, the Jordan, and the Sea of Galilee, but the Old Testament makes little mention of fishing and fish. It is clear that the skill of fishing was known (Isa 19:8; Amos 4:2; Job 40:25; Hab 1:15), and there were fish markets after the exile (Neh 13:16) and a Fish Gate in Jerusalem both before and after the Exile (2 Chr 33:14; Neh 3:3, 12:39; Zeph 1:10). There were specific dietary laws governing their consumption: fish with scales and fins could be eaten, but those without fins and scales were considered unclean and were forbidden (Lev 11:9–12). The identity of the "great fish" in Jonah 2:1 is not known.

In the New Testament, fish are more commonly mentioned (Matt 7:10, 14:17, 15:36; Mark 6:38; Luke 9:13, 11:11, 24:42; John 21:9–13). Several of Jesus's apostles were fishermen on the Sea of Galilee. Jesus performed two miracles involving fish (Luke 5:1–11; John 21:1–23), and there was the miraculous multiplication of the bread and fish (Matt 14:15–21, 15:32–39; Mark 8:1–9). The apostles were also told to be fishers of men (Matt 4:19; Mark 1:17; Luke 5:10; cf. Matt 13:47).

FLESH Specifically, the muscular or soft portions of the human body (Gen 2:23; Exod 4:7). More generally, the entire body (Exod 30:32; 1 Kgs 21:27). Thus the union of man and woman forms them into "one flesh" (Gen 2:24). Most broadly, the expression "all flesh" means all living beings (cf. Gen 6:17, 19; 7:21; Lev 17:14; Num 18:15; Ps 136:25).

I. FLESH IN THE OLD TESTAMENT

In its broadest sense, "flesh" was used to drive home the contrast between the weak and transitory nature of humanity and the eter-

nal strength of God (Ps 78:39; Isa 40:5–8; 2 Chr 32:8). The flesh is mortal and corruptible. When the depravity of humanity became severe, "God saw that the earth was corrupt; for all flesh had corrupted its ways upon the earth" (Gen 6:12; cf. Deut 5:23; Ps 65:3).

The Lord is the judge and lord of all flesh, a theme especially discernible in Isaiah (Isa 40:6–8; 49:26; 66:16) and Jeremiah (Jer 12:12; 25:31; 32:27; 45:5). Isaiah (Isa 40:5–7) compares all flesh ("all people" in the NRSV) to grass that withers and fades; against this, "The grass withers, the flower fades; but the word of our God will stand forever" (Isa 40:8). Jeremiah also stresses the right of God to stand in judgment of all flesh: "The clamor will resound to the ends of the earth, for the Lord has an indictment against the nations; he is entering into judgment with all flesh, and the guilty he will put to the sword, says the Lord" (Jer 25:31). A similar pronouncement is found in Ezek 21:4, with its reference to the sword of the Lord cutting all flesh from south to north.

Job 12:10 declares the utter dependency of all living things upon the Lord and the inherent obligation to offer praise, worship, and thanksgiving (cf. Ps 145:21). The purpose of all flesh is to glorify God: "From new moon to new moon, and from sabbath to sabbath, all flesh shall come to worship before me, says the LORD" (Isa 66:23).

II. FLESH IN THE NEW TESTAMENT

As in the Old Testament, Paul closely associates flesh and sin. "Flesh" might imply human nature or the human body (Gal 2:20), an element of human existence (1 John 4:2), and, in the collective sense, humankind (Matt 24:22).

The flesh is thus still transitory, in sharp contrast to God, and its weakness—in particular the tendency toward temptation—is again placed in distinction with the new life of grace brought by Jesus Christ.

Jesus summed up the weakness of the flesh in one statement: "The spirit indeed is willing, but the flesh is weak" (Matt 26:41). "Now the works of the flesh are plain," Paul says: "fornication, impurity, licentiousness, idolatry, sorcery, enmity, strife, jealousy, anger, selfishness, dissension, party spirit, envy, drunkenness, carousing, and the like" (Gal 5:19–21). The struggle or rebellion is part of the heritage of sin (Rom 7:5–25, 13:14; 2 Cor 7:1; Gal 5:13, 19; Eph 2:13–23) and is both a consequence and also a confirmation of the power of sin (Eph 2:3; 2 Pet 2:18; 2 Cor 10:2).

We have, therefore, an obligation to engage in a spiritual struggle, lest the power of sin increase (1 John 2:16), culminating in spiritual bondage to sin (Rom 6:19, 8:5–7; Eph 2:3). Against this, the New Testament exhorts the believer to live in the **spirit** and not the flesh (Rom 8:4; cf. Rom 8:6, 13). The believer will willingly engage in the struggle against the weaknesses of the flesh, to crucify the flesh (Gal 5:24; Col 2:23). "By contrast, the fruit of the Spirit is love, joy, peace, patience, kindness, generosity, faithfulness, gentleness, and self-control" (Gal 5:22–23). Those who sow in the flesh will reap corruption, whereas those who sow in the Spirit will reap eternal life (Gal 6:8; John 3:6). Through their baptism, Christians put off their body of flesh and receive immersion in the death and Resurrection of Christ (Rom 7:5, 8:9; Gal 5:24; Col 2:11) (CCC 2514–16).

The flesh is not naturally sinful. Christ, who was without sin, assumed human flesh (John 1:14)—meaning that he assumed fully the human condition without sin (Heb 4:15)—so that he might redeem those in the flesh (Rom 8:1–4; Gal 2:20; Eph 2:14–16; Col 1:22). The Incarnation is proclaimed in John 1:14 in clear terms: "And the Word became flesh and lived among us." The historical and corporeal reality of the Incarnation is made manifest in the physical reality of Christ, who was the culmination of salvation history. It is possible, consequently, to trace the direct, physical lineage of Jesus (Rom 8:3; 9:5) from the Jews who claim descent from the flesh of Abraham (Rom 4:1; Heb 12:9).

The physical reality of the Incarnation is attested elsewhere throughout the NT (Phil 2:5–8; 1 Tim 3:16). It was in the flesh that Jesus suffered and died to redeem man (1 Pet 3:18; 4:1); it was in the flesh that Jesus "has abolished the law with its commandments and ordinances, that he might create in himself one new humanity in place of the two, thus making peace, and might reconcile both groups to God in one body through the cross" (Eph 2:15; cf. Heb 10:20). (*See also* **Death**; **Eucharist**; **Fall, the**; **Man**.)

FLOOD, THE Also Deluge, the devastating flood recounted in Gen 6–9 that covered the whole land. The Flood was sent by God to destroy every living thing because of the wickedness of man (Gen 6:5). **Noah** and his family alone were spared as Noah had "found favor in the eyes of the Lord, for he was a righteous man, blameless in his generation" (Gen 6:9). Noah was thus chosen to become the mediator of a second covenant and to participate in the new creation.

I. THE FLOOD NARRATIVE IN GENESIS

At the command of the Lord, Noah constructed an **ark** 300 by 50 by 30 cubits in size, made of gopher wood (Gen 6:14) and covered with pitch inside and out. (*See also* **Ark**.) Two of every type of animal were led into the ark; Noah included seven pairs (Gen 7:2) of clean animals. Once all were aboard—Noah, his family, the animals, and appropriate supplies—a period of seven days passed, after which the rains began and the flood was unleashed upon the earth (Gen 6:11; cf. 2 Kgs 7:2, 19). The rain continued for forty days and forty nights, during which time every living thing died except for the passengers on the ark. God, however, finally ended the deluge and remembered Noah (Gen 8:1), and the waters subsided. The water remained on the earth for 150 days, finally abating enough that on the seventeenth day of the seventh month the ark came to rest on the "mountains of Ararat" (Gen 8:4; cf. 2 Kgs 19:37; Jer 51:27). After forty days, Noah released a raven to fly across the land. He then also released a dove, which returned to the ark. Seven days later, he sent the dove out one more time; this time it returned with an olive leaf. Once more, Noah sent it out, but after seven days it did not return.

Finally, the earth had dried, and Noah was ordered to leave the ark with his family and the animals. After leaving the ark, Noah constructed an altar and offered a burnt offering of every clean animal and bird. The Lord was pleased (Gen 8:21) and made a **covenant** with Noah (*see* **Noah**), promising never again to destroy every living creature by flood. Just as he had done with **Adam**, God commanded Noah to be fruitful and multiply, and to fill the earth, and he gave him dominion over the animals, birds, and fish (Gen 9:2).

II. LITERARY ARTISTRY

In the nineteenth century, many scholars began to analyze the Flood story in terms of the hypothetical sources that supposedly went into the **Pentateuch**. According to source-critical methods, the Flood account fused together "J" and "P" versions of the same event, which had differing insights and purposes, with the added work of a final editor.

Recent scholarship, however, has focused more on the remarkable literary artistry of the Genesis account as we have it now. Several exegetes have argued convincingly that the second half of the Flood story is a mirror of the first:

GENESIS 6:10–9:19

A Noah (6:10a)

B Shem, Ham, and Japheth (6:10b)

C The ark is ordered to be built (6:14–16)

D The Flood is announced (6:17)

E A covenant is made between God and Noah (6:18–20)

F Food is brought to the ark (6:21)

G The command is given to enter the Ark (7:1–3)

H Seven days of waiting for flood (7:4)

I Seven days of waiting for flood (7:10)

J Entry into the ark (7:11–15)

K Yahweh shuts in Noah (7:16)

L Forty days of flood (7:17a)

M   The waters increase (7:17–18)

N   The water covers the mountains (7:19–20)

O   The waters prevail for 150 days (7:21–24)

P   God remembers Noah (8:1)

O′ The water wanes for 150 days (8:3)

N′ Mountaintops are visible (8:4–5)

M′ The water declines (8:5)

L′ Forty days of waiting (8:6)

K′ Noah opens the windows of the ark (8:6b)

J′ The raven and the dove leave the ark (8:7–9)

I′ Seven days of waiting for the waters to subside (8:10–11)

H′ Seven days of waiting for the waters to subside (8:12)

G′ Command to leave the ark (8:13–17)

F′ Food outside of the ark (9:1–4)

E′ Covenant with every living creature (9:8–10)

D′ God promises no future flood (9:11–17)

C′ The ark is emptied (9:18a)

B′ Shem, Ham, and Japheth (9:18b)

A′ Noah

III. THE FLOOD IN THE NEW TESTAMENT

The Flood is also considered to have a typological correspondence to the sacrament of baptism, for through the deluge the earth was cleansed of sin while "a few, that is, eight persons, were saved" (1 Pet 3:20, 21), representing the entire faithful family of God (cf. Rom 6:4; Heb 11:7). Water represented both the judgment of God and his saving power (cf. Acts 22:16). At the same time, the presence of the dove at the close of the Flood was a symbol of baptism; the Holy Spirit appeared as a dove at the baptism of Jesus (Mark 1:10) (CCC 701, 1219).

IV. THE TRUTH OF THE FLOOD ACCOUNT

Obviously, the most important truths of the Flood account are theological. From a Christian point of view, the story of the Flood shows us God's grace in saving his faithful people from the world of sin and death. Thus the Flood is, in a sense, a type of every Christian life.

Whether the Flood account is literal history is another question. For much of Christian history, it was accepted unquestioningly as historical truth.

In the nineteenth century, **cuneiform** tablets were discovered that narrated a Babylonian flood legend obviously based on the same tradition as the story of Noah. Since the cuneiform tablets were much older than the book of Genesis as we have it now, many scholars jumped to the conclusion that the Hebrew story was based on the Babylonian story—an unjustified conclusion, since both written versions were almost certainly based on already ancient oral traditions. Anthropologists point out that a story of a great flood, with one family surviving it in a boat, is found in cultures throughout the Near East and Europe, suggesting that the tradition goes back to some real cataclysmic event. One intriguing study has speculated recently that the flood stories could be based on the catastrophic flooding of the Black Sea, which archaeology shows was a much smaller freshwater lake ringed by human settlements until the Mediterranean suddenly burst in on it.

FLY Flies are a common annoyance in the Near East. The fourth plague of Egypt was a swarm of insects, probably horseflies or gadflies (Exod 8:21–29; Ps 78:45). Ecclesiastes 10:1 compares a small dose of folly to the few dead flies it takes to spoil perfume.

FOLLY Folly in **wisdom literature** does not suggest a low intelligence, but is seen always in contrast to wisdom. Much of wisdom literature is taken up with the contrast between the fool and the wise man. The wise man listens to the counsel of wisdom and so is prudent and just and fears the Lord; the fool obdurately refuses to listen to the counsel of wisdom and is imprudent, unjust, and does not fear the Lord (Prov 12:11, 15, 16; 15:5; 18:13; 24:30–31; Eccl 4:5; Sir 20:13, 21:16, 27:13). Wisdom is a gift of the Lord, but the fool considers only himself wise (Prov 12:15) and does not do the will of God (1 Sam 13:13, 22:21; 2 Sam 13:11–14). The fool is always self-defeating and brings his own ruin upon himself (Prov 11:29; 21:20). The fool persists in sin and vice (Eccl 5:1; Prov 10:18, 23).

In the New Testament, it is folly not to obey the teachings of Christ (Matt 7:24–27) and Jesus speaks against the one who would call his fellow man a fool (Matt 5:22), pointing out the importance of the interior disposition of the heart. Jesus likewise rebukes the Pharisees as blind fools (Matt 23:17, 19; Luke 11:40). He refers to the disciples as fools (Matt 15:16; Mark 7:18; Luke 24:25), suggesting that they are spiritually witless. (*See also* **Wisdom literature**.)

FORGIVENESS *See* **Repentance**.

FORM CRITICISM *See under* **Biblical criticism**.

FORTUNATUS (Latin, "blessed, well off") A Corinthian Christian who was sent with Stephanas and Achaicus to see Paul at Ephesus (1 Cor 16:17).

FORUM OF APPIUS A market town in Latium, in Italy, situated on the Appian Way south of Rome. Christians from Rome journeyed there to meet Paul soon after he arrived at the harbor city of Puteoli (Acts 28:15).

FOUNDATION GATE One of the inner gates of Jerusalem. In the preparations for the accession of **Josiah**, **Jehoiada** stationed troops at this gate as a part of his security plans (2 Kgs 11:6; 2 Chr 23:5). There were several names used for the gate, including the Sur Gate and Middle Gate.

FOUNTAIN GATE A gate in the southeastern wall of Jerusalem. It was rebuilt in the days of **Nehemiah** (Neh 3:15; 12:37).

FOURFOLD SENSE *See* **Interpretation of the Bible**.

FOWL Domesticated fowl made their first appearance in the ancient Near East around the second millennium B.C., and chickens first appeared in Israelite art in seals dating from around the late eighth century B.C. Nevertheless, domestic fowl as food was not common in Palestine and was not mentioned specifically in the Old Testament. By the Greco-Roman period, domesticated fowl became more numerous in Palestine, and they were mentioned in the New Testament (Matt 23:37; Luke 11:12). The crowing of the cock marked the confirmation of Jesus's prediction that Peter would betray him three times (Matt 26:34, 74; Mark 14:20, 72; Luke 22:34, 60; John 13:38, 18:27).

FOX The Hebrew word for fox was probably used to denote both the fox and the jackal. The fox was said to ravage vineyards and crops (Song 2:15; Ezek 13:4; Lam 5:18). **Samson** captured three hundred foxes, tied torches to their tails, and set them loose in the fields of the Philistines (Judg 15:4–5). Tobiah the Ammonite complained that the walls **Nehemiah** was rebuilding could be breached by a fox (Neh 4:3). Jesus referred to Herod Antipas as a fox (Luke 13:32) and contrasted his own wandering life with that of the fox, noting that, unlike Jesus, even "foxes have holes" (Matt 8:20).

FRANKINCENSE *See* **Incense**.

FREEDMEN, SYNAGOGUE OF THE A synagogue in Jerusalem so named because its members were Greek-speaking Jews who had been freed from slavery. It was mentioned in Acts 6:9; its congregation included Cyrenians, Alexandrians, Cilicians, and Asians. The synagogue adherents argued with **Stephen**, and the agitation led to legal proceedings against Stephen and then to his martyrdom (Acts 6:10–15).

FREEDOM The power to choose good or evil. Human freedom is expressed eloquently in the Old Testament by Sirach: "It was he [the Lord] who created man in the beginning, and he left

him in the power of his own inclination" (Sir 15:14). The *Catechism of the Catholic Church* states: "Freedom is the power, rooted in reason and will, to act or not to act, to do this or that, and so to perform deliberate actions on one's own responsibility. By free will one shapes one's own life. Human freedom is a force for growth and maturity in truth and goodness; it attains its perfection when directed toward God, our beatitude" (CCC 1731).

I. IN THE OLD TESTAMENT

In the OT, freedom is usually opposed to **slavery** or domination by another person or country (cf. Exod 21:2, 5; 26–27; Lev 19:20; Deut 15:12–18; Jer 34:8–17; Ezek 46:17; Job 3:19). Freedom is usually seen as having come after a period of slavery or bondage, hence a condition of release. The concept of freedom is especially important in the redemption of Israel from slavery in Egypt (Deut 15:15). The OT, however, does not suggest a complete emancipation for Israel. Freedom was granted so that the Israelites could be God's covenant people (Exod 19:3; Lev 25:42, 55; Deut 6:20–25; Isa 43:21), and the people are redeemed rather than freed. God was responsible for the redemption of the Israelites from their bondage in Egypt; their release was a gracious gift that was entirely unmerited by its recipients. God was responsible for the subsequent progress of the Israelites into Canaan (Exod 3:8; Deut 8:7). Therefore the Israelites were required to adhere faithfully to their covenant oaths, and their continued freedom was maintained only by this fidelity. In the event of their infidelity, they would suffer the loss of their freedom (Deut 28:25; Judg 2:14, 3:7, 4:1, 6:1) and enslavement by foreign powers (Deut 28:64; Amos 5; 2 Kgs 17:6–23; Ps 137:1–4).

II. IN THE NEW TESTAMENT

The New Testament keeps the OT sense of the meaning of freedom as release from bondage but deepens the theological understanding of bondage. By his glorious Cross, Christ has broken the chains of **sin** to which all men are bound and has won salvation for all. By his redemptive act, he has set man free (John 8:32–36; Rom 8:21; Gal 5:1). The Christian is free from sin (John 8:31–36; Rom 6:18–23), from the Law (Rom 7:3; 1 Cor 10:29), and from death (Rom 6:21; 8:21).

God's grace, by which we receive this freedom, is in no way a challenge or a threat to authentic freedom. Quite the opposite: the more we strive to be faithful to the promptings of grace, the greater will be our growth in freedom. We have our true freedom in obedience to the Truth, so that any claim to freedom or liberty that suggests license or a departure from fidelity to the moral law is false (Rom 6:15; cf. 2 Pet 2:19). Thus, freedom is oriented toward God, who is the ultimate good, and entails a choice between good and evil, between striving toward perfection and falling into error and sin. The more eagerly the ultimate good is pursued, the freer the person becomes (CCC 1732–34).

FRINGES Also tassels. The Jewish people were commanded by God to fasten tassels with violet cords to each of the four corners of their cloaks to serve as a reminder to keep the commandments of the Lord (Num 15:37–41; Deut 22:12). Such a cloak was worn by Jesus (Matt 9:20; cf. Matt 14:36; Mark 6:56; Luke 8:44). The fringe became a symbol of Jewish obedience to the Law, and the Pharisees in Christ's time wore especially large ones (Matt 23:5), earning them Jesus's condemnation as hypocrites who display the tokens of piety but are too often impious in their hearts (Matt 23:5).

FROG The only reference to frogs in the Old Testament is in connection with the plagues that afflicted Egypt (Exod 8:1–15; Ps 78:45, 105:30). In Rev 16:13, three foul spirits are described as frogs.

FUNERAL *See* **Burial**.

GAAL The son of Obed, from the city of **Shechem**. He led a rebellion of the city against King **Abimelech** and its governor Zebul (Judg 9:26–41). He was defeated and expelled.

GAASH A mountain in the district of Mount Ephraim (Josh 19:50, 24:30; Judg 2:9). The exact location of the mountain is uncertain, but it was probably to the south of Shechem. One of David's bravest warriors, Hiddai or Hurai, came from "the torrents of Gaash" (2 Sam 23:30; 1 Chr 11:32).

GABBATHA (Aramaic, "elevated") The Aramaic word for the place where Jesus stood before Pilate in Jerusalem during the trial (John 19:13); the meaning of the word is still uncertain, probably "elevated" or "height." The term is used in the New Testament only here, and John notes that the place was known both by the Aramaic and the Greek word *lithostrōton*, meaning "stone pavement." The trial took place in the **Praetorium** (Matt 27:27; Mark 15:16), and it was there that Pilate had his judgment seat or tribunal (Matt 27:19) before which Jesus appeared.

The location of the Gabbatha is uncer-
tain. Several sites are considered possibilities. The first is in the upper forum near the palace of Herod, south a little ways from the modern Jaffa Gate. This is a likely spot, as the Praetorium was probably located in the Herodian palace. A second site once proposed was the stone pavement discovered beneath the modern Sisters of Zion Convent, but archaeologists now believe that the pavement was not built before A.D. 70. A more recent candidate is a podium discovered in the Armenian quarter of Jerusalem.

GABRIAS The father (Tob 4:20) or brother of Gabael (Tob 1:14).

GABRIEL (Hebrew, "God is my warrior," or "God is strong") One of three angels, with **Michael** and **Raphael**, named in the Old Testament; he is also called the "Angel of the Annunciation" for his appearance in the New Testament. Gabriel appeared as a man to the prophet Daniel (Dan 8:16; 9:21), having been sent to interpret several visions (Dan 8:15–26; 9:20–27); Gabriel is also assumed to be the angel in Dan 10–12. In the NT, the angel was sent to Zechariah to announce the impending birth of John the Baptist (Luke 1:11–19) and to the Blessed Virgin Mary to announce the birth of Jesus (Luke 1:26–38; cf. Luke 2:9; Acts 5:19, 8:26, 12:7). Gabriel also figured prominently in apocalyptic writings, in particular *1 Enoch*. In the War Scroll of Qumran (see **Dead Sea Scrolls**), he is named with Michael and Sariel.

GAD The son of Jacob and Zilpah, Leah's handmaiden (Gen 30:11); the ancestor of the tribe of Gad. The etymological origins of his name are not known with certainty. The warriors of Gad were distinguished for their military skill and their courage, as predicted by Jacob (Gen 49:19; cf. Deut 33:20–21). Their allotted territory was east of the Jordan, west of Ammonite land, and stretched from the southern edge of the Sea of Galilee to the Arnon (Num 32; Josh 13:24–28). This location placed them in frequent conflict with the Moabites to the south and the Arameans to the north (2 Kgs 10:33). Following the Exile, the territory of Gad was taken by the Ammonites (Jer 49:1).

GADARA A city in the **Decapolis** in Transjordan identified with modern Umm Qeis, south of the Sea of Galilee. According to Matt 8:28, Jesus cast out demons from two men and sent the demons into a herd of swine. This event takes place at Gerasa in Mark 5:1 and Luke 8:26.

GAHAM (Hebrew, "flame") The second son of **Nahor**, Abraham's brother, by his concubine Reumah (Gen 22:24).

GAIUS The name of four men in the New Testament.

1. A Christian in Corinth who was one of two people baptized by Paul during his stay in Corinth (1 Cor 1:14). He is probably the same Gaius with whom Paul stayed while in Corinth (Rom 16:23).

2. A Macedonian Christian who traveled with Paul, along with **Aristarchus**. Gaius was with Paul in Ephesus during the riot begun by **Demetrius** the silversmith (Acts 19:29). Gaius and Aristarchus were set upon by the mob and questioned about Paul's activities. They were freed soon after (Acts 19:35–41).

3. A man from Derbe, probably a Christian, who journeyed with Paul from Corinth to Troas (Acts 20:4).

4. The person to whom John wrote his third epistle (1:1).

GALAAD *See* **Gilead**.

GALATIA (Greek *Galatia*) A Roman province in central Asia Minor. It had long been the territory of a Celtic people known as the Galatians who had invaded the region in the third century B.C. Around 25 B.C., the Romans seized their kingdom and annexed it to the Roman Empire as the province of Galatia, with its provincial capital at Ancyra. The precise boundaries of the province subsequently varied, including the southern regions of **Pamphylia** and **Pisidia**. The varying boundaries have complicated determining who exactly were the intended recipients of Paul's Letter to the Galatians, which is addressed "to the churches of Galatia" (Gal 1:2; 1 Cor 16:1).

It is known that Paul preached in southern Galatia (Acts 16:6; 18:23), and Peter seems to have sent his first letter to an audience that included north Galatia (1 Pet 1:1).

GALATIANS, LETTER TO THE A letter written by the apostle Paul to the Galatians to counteract Judaizing opinions and efforts to undermine his authority; the letter asserts the divine origin of Paul's authority and doctrine, states that justification is not through Mosaic **Law** but through faith in Christ, and insists on the practice of evangelical virtues, especially charity.

I. AUTHORSHIP AND DATE

The first line of the letter attests to the authorship of the apostle Paul (1:1); the closing claims the letter was written in his own hand (Gal 6:11). This attribution has never been seriously questioned.

The dating of the epistle is more complex. Paul salutes the "churches of Galatia" (1:2) and mentions "Galatians," but which Galatians were the intended recipients of the letter? The province of **Galatia** in Paul's time was a large territory in Asia Minor. The word "Galatians" may refer to the ethnic Galatians in northern Galatia, but the word might also designate those who lived within the territorial boundary of the province, both in the north and the south.

Acts records that Paul preached in the cities of southern Galatia during his first missionary journey (Acts 13:13–14:24) and may have ventured into the cities of northern Galatia during his second missionary journey (Acts 16:6). In any case, the date of the letter depends mainly on the date of Paul's visit to Jerusalem mentioned in Gal 2:1–10. Scholars who prefer the earlier date for the letter argue that Paul is referring to the visit mentioned in Acts 11:29–30, while those who favor a later date argue that Paul is remembering the Jerusalem Council in Acts 15:1–29 that was held in A.D. 49. The latter argument seems more compelling, so it is safest to date the letter sometime in the early 50s A.D.

II. CONTENTS

I. *Salutation (1:1–5)*
II. *The False Gospel (1:6–9)*
III. *Paul's Apostolic Authority (1:10–2:21)*
    A. *Paul's Vindication (1:10–24)*
    B. *Paul and the Apostles (2:1–11)*
    C. *Paul and Peter at Antioch (2:12–14)*
    D. *Jews and Gentiles (2:15–21)*
IV. *Law and Faith (3:1–4:31)*
    A. *Appeal to Galatian Experience (3:1–5)*
    B. *The Covenant with Abraham (3:6–18)*
    C. *The Purpose of the Law (3:19–28)*
    D. *Christian Maturity (4:1–20)*
    E. *The Allegory of Sarah and Hagar (4:21–31)*
V. *Christian Freedom (5:1–6:10)*
    A. *The Nature of Christian Freedom (5:1–15)*
    B. *Life in the Spirit (5:16–26)*
    C. *Bearing Burdens (6:1–10)*
VI. *Final Admonitions and Benediction (6:11–18)*

III. PURPOSE AND THEMES

The community in Galatia was plagued by tension. Opponents of Paul were challenging his apostolic authority. These rivals, called Judaizers, demanded that Gentile Christians adhere to ritual observance of Mosaic Law, especially **circumcision**, which the Judaizers considered a requirement for full Christian status (Gal 4:10; 5:2–12; 6:13). In effect, they rejected that "in Christ Jesus neither circumcision nor uncircumcision counts for anything; the only thing that counts is faith working through love" (5:6) and held to the demands of the Old Covenant. The success of the Judaizers among the Galatians compelled Paul to write to defend his own authority and to assist the Galatians in avoiding apostasy (3:1–4).

Paul is vigorous in his defense of himself and the Gospel. He begins by expressing astonishment that the false teachings of the Judaizers had gained such ground among the Galatians (1:6–10), and he moves to a defense of his claim that his apostleship came directly from Christ (1:11–17) and was undertaken with the recognition of the Church's leaders (2:1–10).

Paul then progresses to the heart of his argument: man is saved by faith in Jesus Christ and not by observance of Jewish Law (3:15–20). He notes that from the beginning the Galatians had acknowledged receiving the Spirit from faith (3:1–5). No one is justified before God by the Law; rather, the Law convicts man of sin (3:10–14). The Law was a preparation for salvation, and that salvation has now come through Christ (3:19–21). The Law was our temporary custodian during our spiritual minority; now we are heirs with Christ, and we no longer need a custodian (3:23–29). Christ redeemed us from the curse of the Law and freed us from its slavery (4:1–11).

What Paul seeks to clarify is the contrast between the New Covenant and the Old Covenant from which it came, and the foremost example of the requirements of the Old Covenant is circumcision. Circumcision was held up by the Judaizers as the means of entering into God's covenant with Abraham (Gen 17:9–14) and the family of Israel (Lev 12:3). But Paul insists that the New Covenant has set aside the requirements of the Mosaic Law, including circumcision. Christ, Paul writes, "redeemed us from the curse of the law by becoming a curse for us" (Gal 3:13). By his death upon the Cross, Christ lifted the curses of the Old Covenant. Christ has ratified the New Covenant, and in so doing he has fulfilled the Abrahamic covenant of blessing for all nations and has terminated the Mosaic covenant. Hence Paul cites the example of Abraham as a classic example of justification by faith for believers (3:6–9). Through Christ, "those who believe are the descendants of Abraham" (3:7). As Paul writes, "God sent his Son, born of a woman, born under the law, in order to redeem those who were under the law, so that we might receive adoption as children" (4:4–5).

GALBANUM A resinous and aromatic gum derived from a herbaceous plant that grew in Persia, Afghanistan, and Syria. It was an ingredient in incense (Exod 30:34; cf. Sir 24:15).

GALEED (Hebrew, "heap of witness") The name used by **Jacob** for the pile of stones that he made with **Laban** as a commemoration of the covenant (Gen 31:44–54). Laban named the heap Jegar-Sahadutha, an Aramaic term that meant the same as the Hebrew, "heap of witness."

GALGALA See **Gilgal**.

GALILEE (Hebrew, possibly "district") A region of northern Palestine bounded by the Mediterranean to the west, the Jordan and the Sea of Galilee to the east, the plain of Esdraelon to the south, and the Nahr-el-Qasimiyeh to the north. The region is geographically diverse: the Lebanon Range extends into northern Galilee, giving it a rugged, mountainous terrain, whereas southern Galilee is a land of rolling hills and fertile plains.

At the time of the conquest of **Canaan**, Galilee was dominated by a number of Canaanite cities. Following the conquest of Canaan (Josh 11), the region was divided among the tribes of Zebulun, Naphtali, Asher, and Issachar (Josh 19:10–39). By the time of Solomon, it was a territory of relative unimportance, so much so that Solomon gave **Hiram** of Tyre twenty of its cities in payment for the materials used to build the Temple and palace in Jerusalem (1 Kgs 9:10–13). It was seized by Tiglath-Pileser III of **Assyria** around 732 B.C. and attached to the Assyrian provinces (2 Kgs 15:29). Galilee's association with Gentiles was noted by Isaiah (Isa 9:1), but there were Israelites living there throughout the biblical period (1 Macc 5:14–23). Galilee was later part of the kingdom of **Herod the Great** and then part of the tetrarchy of **Herod Antipas** (Luke 3:1; 13:31).

Galilee is best remembered as the setting for much of Jesus's public ministry. Jesus grew up in **Nazareth**, a town of Galilee, and the apostles (except **Judas Iscariot**) were Galileans. A number of Galilean cities are mentioned in the New Testament, including **Cana**, **Capernaum**, **Nazareth**, and **Tiberias**. In NT times, Galilean Jews were not held in high regard by their countrymen in Jerusalem and Judea (John 1:46; 7:52), probably because of the foreign populations who had long lived in Galilee (cf. Matt 4:15) and the distance between Galilee and Jerusalem. Galilee is mentioned outside of the Gospels only in Acts 9:31.

GALILEE, SEA OF The largest freshwater lake in Palestine (Matt 4:18; Mark 7:31; John 5:1), part of the Jordan River system in the Great Rift Valley that separated Galilee from the Gaulan and **Decapolis**. Many names have been used for it. In the Old Testament, the lake was called "the sea of Chinnereth" (Num 34:11; Josh 12:3, 13:27; derived from the Hebrew for "lyre"). Josephus called it "the lake of Gennesar(itis)" (*B.J.* 2.573; 3.463, 506, 515–16; *Ant.* 5.84; 13.158; 18.28, 36). In the New Testament, Luke uses the Lake of Gennesaret (Luke 5:1; cf. 1 Macc 11:67) or simply "the lake" (Luke 5:2; 8:22, 23, 33). Mark and Matthew also use the word "lake," but they sometimes use "sea" and "sea of Galilee" (Mark 1:16, 7:31; Matt 4:18, 15:34). John calls it "the Sea of Galilee, which is the Sea of Tiberias" (John 6:1).

The Sea of Galilee is about 9 miles long (14.5 kilometers) and 5 miles wide (8 kilometers), with a depth reaching over 800 feet (245 meters) below sea level. It is famous for its abundant supply of fish, so there was a vital and active fish trade there that included several of the apostles (see, e.g., Matt 4:18–22; Luke 5:1–11). The Sea of Galilee was noted also for its sudden and violent storms (Matt 8:24). Much of Christ's public life was spent near the Sea of Galilee, and several miracles took place there, including his walking upon water (Matt 14:21–33; Mark 6:45–52) and quieting the storm (Matt 5:23–27; Mark 4:35–41; Luke 8:22–25).

GALL The word commonly used for both the gallbladder and bile. The word was used in the Old Testament to describe the hardships or bitterness of life (Deut 32:32), as well as for anything that is bitter (Job 20:14; Jer 8:14). Gall also refers variously to poison or bitterness when denoting a bitter fluid (Matt 27:34; cf. Mark 15:23), such as that mixed with wine and offered to Christ before his Crucifixion. The purpose of this concoction was to ease suffering (cf. Tob 6:9; 11:4, 8, 13). It is likely, however, that the reference is to myrrh mixed with wine.

GALLIO, MARCUS ANNAEUS NOVATUS (later L. Junius Gallio Annaeus after he was adopted by Lucius Junius Gallio) The oldest son of L. Annaeus Seneca and a brother of Seneca, the famous orator and tutor to Emperor Nero. Born in Roman Spain (Hispania), he was part of a very prominent family in Rome and was named proconsul of **Achaia** under Emperor Claudius. He died in A.D. 65 probably from suicide after being caught up in the Pisonian plot to assassinate Nero; virtually the entire family was forced to commit suicide (Dio Cassius, *Historia Romana* 62.65.3; Tacitus, *Ann.* 15.73.3).

When Gallio was proconsul of Achaia, the Jews brought Paul before him on the accusation of preaching an illegal cult. Gallio, however, expressed little interest in the case; he declared it a matter of Jewish Law and threw the case out of court (Acts 18:12–17). Roman sources indicate that he was proconsul al-

most certainly in A.D. 52; based on this date it is possible to estimate the arrival of Paul in **Corinth** at A.D. 50.

GAMALIEL (Hebrew, "God has repaid me") A famed Jewish teacher who was respected for his learning and was a member of the **Sanhedrin** in Jerusalem (Acts 5:34). In tradition, he is honored as the first of the seven rabbans, or great rabbis. He was an adherent of the school of Hillel in the interpretation of the Torah and was apparently the teacher of **Paul** (Acts 22:3). While serving as a member of the council that passed judgment on Peter and the apostles, he warned the Sanhedrin against taking action: "for if this plan or this undertaking is of men, it will fail; but if it is of God, you will not be able to overthrow them. You might even be found opposing God!" (Acts 5:38–39). According to later tradition, he became a Christian, perhaps under the influence of Paul. He should not be confused with Gamaliel of Jamnia, who was a prominent leader of the Sanhedrin at Jamnia in the period following the destruction of Jerusalem in A.D. 70.

GARDEN Gardens as cultivated plots of land for growing trees and plants were found in Ancient Egypt and Mesopotamia. In the Old Testament, a "garden" is usually an orchard (Jer 29:5; Amos 9:14; cf. Deut 11:10; 1 Kgs 21:2; Song 4:12ff.; Jer 39:4, 5:1, 6:10; Amos 4:9), normally supplied with water from a cistern (Isa 58:11; Jer 31:12). A cultivated garden was a highly prized symbol of prosperity, as it implied control of water resources (Isa 58:11; Jer 31:12; cf. Isa 1:30). It also signified leisure, for it provided beauty as well as produce (Dan

13:17), so that the rest found in the embrace of a lover was equated with spending time in the garden (Song 4:16; 5:1; 6:2; 18:13).

The royal garden was probably attached to the palace (2 Kgs 25:4; Jer 39:4, 52:7), although reference is also made to the garden of Uzzah where Manasseh (2 Kgs 21:18) and Amon (2 Kgs 21:26) were buried. Gardens or groves were also used for idolatrous activities (1 Kgs 14:23; 2 Kgs 16:4, 17:10; Isa 1:29, 65:3, 66:17). As with Manasseh and Amon, the dead were sometimes buried in gardens; Christ was buried in a garden tomb owned by Joseph of Arimathea (Matt 27:60; John 19:41). (*See also* **Garden of Eden; Gethsemane**.)

GARDEN OF EDEN A place of abundance and natural beauty where the first humans were installed before the Fall. Genesis 2:8 refers specifically to the Garden of Eden, "in the East," describing the garden as abundant with trees, "pleasant to the sight and good for food, the tree of life also in the midst of the garden, and the tree of the knowledge of good and evil" (Gen 2:9). In Isaiah (51:3) and elsewhere, it is portrayed as the garden of the Lord (cf. Ezek 31:8–9; Joel 2:3), the eternal dwelling place of God (CCC 374–79).

Where was the Garden of Eden? Since ancient times, Bible readers have been debating what location was meant. Genesis 2:8 places the garden "in the east" (cf. Gen 3:24; 4:16; cf. Ps 77:6, 12; 78:12; 143:5; Prov 8:22–23), which many have taken to mean somewhere in Mesopotamia. The Garden is described as the source of the great rivers of the world, the Pishon, Gihon, Tigris, and Euphrates (Gen 2:10–14). At any rate, the most useful way to read the account of Eden is to seek not where it fits in the terrestrial landscape, but rather where it fits in the biblical view of the universe.

The creation account in Gen 1–3 progresses from the whole universe to the earth and finally to the Garden of Eden, the place chosen by the Lord for the first humans. Here God dwelt with his creatures in a blessed and intimate way.

In fact, God is present in the Garden as in a temple (Gen 3:8; Lev 26:12; 2 Sam 7:6). Notice how cherubim guard the Garden and just they are seen in the later Temple (Gen 3:24; 1 Kgs 6:23–28). The Tree of Life stands at the center of the Garden just as the oak, and later carved palm trees, decorated the interior of the sanctuary (Gen 2:9; Josh 24:26; 1 Kgs 6:29–32); the Garden was the source of sacred flowing waters much as prophets envision the Temple giving forth streams of living water (Gen 2:10; cf. Ezek 47:1–12; Joel 3:18; Ps 46:4); and the Garden was entered from the east, as was the Tabernacle and Temple (Gen 3:24; Exod 27:13; Ezek 47:1).

Adam is installed in this tabernacle as the royal high priest. He is told in Gen 2:15 to till and keep the garden—the same words the Law uses to describe the duties of the priests and Levites of Israel (Num 8:26, translated "minister" and "keep" in the RSV). That he was to "keep" (a better translation might be "guard") the Garden suggests that he should be ready to defend it from the intrusion of an enemy—such as the serpent, which enters in Gen 3:1.

Elsewhere in the Old Testament, references to Eden appear most frequently in Ezekiel (28:13; 31:9, 16, 18; 36:35); there are also references in Isa 51:3 and Joel 2:3. Isaiah 51:3 and

Ezek 36:35 promise the Israelites in Exile that the land of Israel will be restored to abundance and fertility, like Eden: "This land that was desolate has become like the garden of Eden; and the waste and desolate and ruined cities are now inhabited and fortified" (Ezek 36:35). In other passages in Ezekiel, Eden is similarly stressed as the model for abundance and fecundity. Joel 2:3 uses the image of Eden to contrast the fertility of the land before a devastating plague of locusts with its grim condition afterward: "The land is like the garden of Eden before them, but after them a desolate wilderness, and nothing escapes them."

In Ezekiel, we see how the Garden of Eden possessed a deeper sense beyond merely the abode of the first humans in the time before the first sin. Ezekiel 28:13 makes a direct connection between Eden and the Garden of God ("You were in Eden, the garden of God"), suggesting that Eden was not only a paradise for human habitation, but also a divine dwelling.

In the New Testament, the term "paradise" is used three times (Luke 23:43; 2 Cor 12:3; Rev 2:7), with the application tied closely to the Garden of Eden, although the emphasis has shifted from the imagery of a place of terrestrial bliss to one of eschatological expectation. As Isa 51:3 and Ezek 36:35 had foretold, the bliss of Eden will reappear in the future. But it will be more than Eden: the heavenly bliss of Paradise is the "Kingdom of heaven," to which the Father's adopted children are called through grace (CCC 736; cf. Saint Basil the Great, *De Spiritu Sancto*, 15.36). Thus Jesus, dying on the Cross, promises paradise to the good thief (Luke 23:43) (CCC 1721; cf. LG §49).

In 2 Cor 12:3, Paul writes of being "caught up into paradise," an account that indicates a heavenly dwelling place. A heavenly paradise is equally apparent in Rev 2:7: "the tree of life that is in the paradise of God," which uses the typological imagery of Genesis to describe the coming joy of heaven.

GARDEN OF GETHSEMANE *See* **Gethsemane**.

GAREB (Hebrew *gārēb*) One of David's elite warriors and a member of the famed "Thirty" (2 Sam 23:38; 1 Chr 11:40).

GASPAR In Christian tradition, the name of one of the Three Wise Men (or **Magi**), who are not named in the Bible.

GATE An opening in a city wall. When cities were walled, the city gate was normally the only means of entering a city. Thus it was the most vulnerable and most heavily fortified part of the defenses. By custom, commercial and even political activities were held at the city gates, including the formal receiving of ambassadors, concluding business deals, and issuing of judgments (cf. Gen 23:10, 18; Deut 21:19; 25:7; 1 Kgs 22:10; 2 Kgs 7:1, 18; 2 Chr 32:6; Ps 69:13; 127:5; Job 31:21; Prov 22:22, 31:23; Isa 29:21; Amos 5:10, 15). Ruth 4 shows the gate as the place where important legal business could be transacted in front of witnesses. Since controlling the gate meant having the power to admit or to deny entry, the gate was also a symbol of power. Mention is made of the gates of death (Ps 107:16; Isa 38:10), the gates of Sheol (Matt 16:18), and the gate of heaven (Gen 28:17).

GATH One of the five main cities of the **Phi-listines** (Josh 13:3; 1 Sam 5:7–10). The city was located in the **Shephelah** and was the closest to Judah, although its modern location is uncertain. It was first occupied by the **Anakim** (Josh 11:22; 2 Sam 2:22; 1 Chr 20:8), a race of giants. David served King Achis of Gath during his flight from Saul (1 Sam 17:52). David later conquered the city (2 Sam 21:11; 27:2).

GATH-HEPHER A town on the border of the territory of Zebulun (Josh 19:13). It was the birthplace of the prophet **Jonah**, son of Amittai (2 Kgs 14:25).

GATH-RIMMON A **Levitical city** given to the tribe of Dan (Josh 21:24; 1 Chr 6:54).

GAZA One of the five principal cities of the **Philistines**, on the southern boundary of Palestine and situated near the main road between Egypt and Asia. That road is called in Exodus "the way of the land of the Philistines" (Exod 13:17) and was known later as the "Way of the Sea" (Isa 8:23). Gaza therefore occupied a strategic position of immense significance, and the area was frequently involved in military campaigns from the time of Pharaoh Thutmose III of Egypt in the fifteenth century B.C. Originally a Canaanite city, it was inhabited by the Avvim (Deut 2:23) and later became a Philistine stronghold. It was allocated to the tribe of Judah by Joshua, but it is considered likely to have been conquered only in the time of Solomon (Josh 15:47; 1 Kgs 4:24). Samson was held captive there, and it was there that he brought down the temple of Dagon (Judg 16).

Listed as the southern edge of Solomon's kingdom, Gaza was captured by **Tiglath-pileser III** of **Assyria** in 734 B.C. (cf. Amos 1:6). It subsequently fell to the forces of Cambyses of Persia in 529 B.C. and Alexander the Great of Macedon in 332 B.C. It then became a key strategic point in the conflict between the Ptolemaic and Seleucid Empires until it was captured by the latter in 198 B.C. and rebuilt by Antiochus III. The city then figured in the Maccabean wars (1 Macc 11:61 and following). It is mentioned in the New Testament only in Acts 8:26. The modern city of Gaza rests upon the same site as the ancient one.

GEBA A Benjaminite and Levitical town (Josh 18:24, 21:17; 1 Chr 6:60), identified with the modern town of Jaba (or Jeba), northeast of Jerusalem. The site figured prominently in the struggles against the Philistines (Judg 20:10, 33; 1 Sam 13:3, 16; 14:5; 2 Sam 5:25; Isa 10:29), but textual studies indicate that the references may actually suggest Gibeah. Asa later fortified the town (1 Kgs 15:22; 2 Chr 16:6; cf. Ezra 2:26; Neh 7:30, 11:31, 12:29).

GEBAL A famous ancient Phoenician seaport city, known to the Greeks as Byblos, on the Mediterranean coast north of Beirut. The modern name is Jubail. Gebal was one of the most important of the Phoenician cities; it was noted as a trading center among the peoples of Egypt, Mesopotamia, and Palestine. The Gebalites were known to the Hebrews as shipbuilders (Ezek 27:9) and superb stone cutters and masons (1 Kgs 5:18) who assisted in the building of the great Temple (1 Kgs 6:32). The Greeks gave the city the name Byblos, from "book," because the inhabitants made paper from the imported papyrus reeds from Egypt. The paper (papyrus) was exported and used for official documents, state correspondence, and various other texts. The word "Bible" is derived ultimately from Byblos.

GEDALIAH (Hebrew, "Yahweh is great") The name of two men in the Old Testament.

1. The son of Ahikam and the grandson of Shaphan, who was appointed by **Nebuchadnezzar** as governor of conquered Judah (2 Kgs 25:22–26; Jer 40:5–41:18) in 586 B.C. Given the devastation in Jerusalem, Gedaliah took up residence at Mizpah and set about trying to establish some semblance of organization. Despite being warned of the threat (Jer 40:13–16), Gedaliah was assassinated by a group of fugitives led by Ishmael, son of Nethaniah, a royal prince. The surviving Judahites, fearing for their lives as reprisal for Gedaliah's death, fled to Egypt, taking **Jeremiah** with them (Jer 42:1–43:7; 2 Kgs 25:26).

2. The son of Pashur and a high-ranking courtier during the reign of Zedekiah (Jer 38:1–6). He was a leading voice in the efforts to have Jeremiah arrested and imprisoned.

GEDEON *See* **Gideon**.

GEDEROTH A town in the **Shephelah** that was given to the tribe of Judah (Josh 15:41). It fell to the Philistines (2 Chr 26:6–7; 28:18) during the time of **Ahaz**.

GEHAZI The servant of the prophet **Elisha** (2 Kgs 4:12–36; 5:20–27; 8:4–6). In the account of the wealthy Shunammite woman (2 Kgs 4:8–37), Gehazi was given the prophet's rod to restore her son, but the effort failed. Later, after Elisha cured Naaman the Syrian of leprosy, Gehazi took two talents from Naaman, though Elisha had refused Naaman's gifts. For his greed, Gehazi and his descendants were struck with leprosy (2 Kgs 5:19–27).

GEHENNA (Hebrew, "Valley of Hinnom" or "Valley of the son of Hinnom") The valley of the son of Hinnom, south of Jerusalem, identified with the modern Wadi er-Rababeh. It became synonymous with a place of eternal torment and suffering for the damned. The name itself is taken perhaps from the original owner of the land, and in the Old Testament the valley separated ancient Jerusalem from the surrounding valleys (cf. Josh 15:8, 18:16; Neh 11:30). The valley earned an evil reputation from an early time as the location of an idolatrous cult that performed human sacrifices (2 Kgs 23:10; 2 Chr 28:3, 33:6). Because of this reputation, Jeremiah cursed it (Jer 7:31–32; 19:2–13; 32:35). Notably, Isaiah described it as a place where the rebels against the Lord will be strewn, "for their worm shall not die, their fire shall not be quenched, and they shall be an abhorrence to all flesh" (Isa 66:24). In apocalyptic writings the valley subsequently assumed the character of a place of suffering and damnation.

In the New Testament, Gehenna is mentioned twelve times (seven times in Matthew, three times in Mark, once in Luke, and once in James), where it is the equivalent of hell, with unquenchable and perpetual fires; many English translations render the word as "hell" (Matt 5:22; 18:9; Mark 9:43; Jas 3:6; cf.

Matt 3:10, 12; 18:8; 7:19; Luke 3:9, 17). It is a pit (Matt 5:29; 18:9; Mark 9:45, 47; Luke 12:5) and a place of unspeakable misery (Matt 5:25–26; 8:12; 13:42, 50; 22:13; 24:51).

GELBOE *See* **Gilboa**.

GEMARIAH The name of two men in the Old Testament.

1. The son of Shaphan and an official in the court of King **Jehoiakim** (r. 609–598 B.C.). His father enjoyed a position of great prominence, and Gemariah was able to secure a post that included his own chambers. It was in his office that **Baruch** read for the first time publicly the scroll of Jeremiah (Jer 36:10). He then attempted unsuccessfully to dissuade the king from destroying it.

2. The emissary of King **Zedekiah** to **Nebuchadnezzar**, who took part in carrying a letter from Jeremiah to the exiles (Jer 29:3).

GENEALOGY A tracing of the ancestry or descent of a person. The Old Testament is replete with genealogies (e.g., in Genesis, Numbers, 1 Chronicles, Ezra, Nehemiah, and Ruth). Genesis is concerned especially with tracing the ancestry of Israel through history back to Adam, in particular the line from Adam to Abraham. In all, Genesis includes ten major genealogical tables and several minor tables.

In Israelite culture, the genealogy documented membership in a particular clan, tribe, or family. Genealogical records were thus crucial after the Exile when membership in the priesthood was restricted to those of rightful priestly descent (Ezra 2:59–63; Neh 7:61–65).

The genealogies in Genesis also gave roots to the tribes and people of Israel. The stress upon the descent of Adam to Abraham also served to underscore the shared heritage of all humanity as God's creatures and the fact that man's sinful nature is passed from one generation to the next. (*See* **Sin**.)

Two genealogies for Christ are given in the New Testament (Matt 1:1–17; Luke 3:23–38). Both are selective and incomplete, and both serve a distinct purpose. Matthew's genealogy extends from Abraham to Jesus in descending order, with forty-two generations broken into three groups. Luke's genealogy reaches from Jesus to Adam in an ascending order, covering a span of seventy-seven generations. According to Matthew (1:16), Joseph was the son of Jacob, while Luke (3:23) names him as the son of Heli. Two plausible explanations have been proposed for the discrepancy. It may be that Matthew's genealogy was the biological one, and that Luke's list was drawn up according to the **levirate** law; or it may be that Matthew's was a paternal genealogy through Joseph, and Luke's was a maternal genealogy through Mary.

GENEALOGY OF JESUS CHRIST *See* **Genealogy**.

GENESIS, BOOK OF The first book of the Bible. Genesis is known in the Hebrew as *bĕrē'šît*, meaning "in the beginning." The Greek **Septuagint** version calls the book *genesis*, meaning "origin" or "birth"; the Latin **Vulgate** and English versions follow the Septuagint. The title is apt: the book deals with origins—the origins of the Cosmos, of life, of man, of sin, and of the Chosen People. Throughout, Genesis demonstrates the providential love of God as he guides human history according to his own salvific purposes. The intent of Genesis, then, is to describe the most distant origins of the people of Israel; the covenants between God and creation, Adam, Noah, and Abraham; and the first events of salvation history pointing toward the Sinai covenant in the books to come.

I. AUTHORSHIP AND DATE

A. Moses, the Traditional Author

Genesis does not name its author. Both Jewish and Christian tradition, however, attribute the whole Pentateuch to Moses. By the eighteenth and nineteenth centuries, many scholars began to deny that Moses wrote the Pentateuch, seeing the book as a compilation of different and even conflicting traditions attributed to different authors writing at different times and places. (See **Pentateuch** for a more detailed discussion.) Both then and now, a minority of scholars question that theory, and the traditional view of Moses as author still has much to recommend it.

The long-standing tradition of Moses as the author of Genesis does not insist that he wrote every word of the book. Rather, the essence of Genesis is dated to the time of Moses in the fifteenth century B.C. (or perhaps the thirteenth century B.C.). He would have been responsible for compiling, editing, and organizing assorted family records and archives as well as handing on oral traditions.

B. The External Evidence Is Consistent with Moses Being the Author

Comparisons with other Near Eastern literature show that the theory of Moses as author fits well with what we know about his time. The early chapters of Genesis, for example, show many similarities to creation and flood stories found in ancient Mesopotamia in the early second millennium B.C., such as the Sumerian King List, Sumerian Flood Story, Atrahasis Epic, Enuma Elish, and the Gilgamesh Epic. Likewise, the patriarchal narratives found in Gen 12–50 show us a world consistent with what we know about the Near East in the second millennium B.C. (cf. Gen 11:31; 12:4–5, 10; 13:1; 24:10; 28:6–7; 37:28) as well as the often complex political situation found in Mesopotamia before 1700 B.C. (cf. Gen 14:1–4). Such aspects of the text do not prove decisively that Moses was the author of Genesis, but they do make it seem likely that the original book came from Moses's time.

II. CONTENTS

III. STRUCTURE AND THEMES

A. The Covenants in Genesis

Genesis is divided into two uneven parts. The first, chapters 1–11, covers the primeval history of the world and the origins of man and the first people. The second, chapters 12–50, covers the history of the patriarchs. The key theme in the transition from the first to the second is divine providence. God has a plan for the salvation of humanity—a plan that begins to be revealed through a series of expanding covenants: with creation (Gen 1:1–2:4), with Adam and Eve (2:15–17), with Noah and the world (9:8–17), and with Abraham and his descendants (15:18–21; 17:1–21; 22:16–18, etc.). The covenants of Genesis are preparation for the later covenant that will bring the entire human race into the family of God.

Genesis is thus both historical and eschatological. It reflects upon the earliest days of creation, but it also focuses its gaze ahead to the fulfillment of the divine promise of salvation through Abraham's offspring and the substitution of the covenant curses triggered by Adam's first sin with the covenant blessings brought by Jesus Christ.

B. Important Truths of Primeval History

The Pontifical Biblical Commission enumerated nine "narrated facts" in Genesis whose "literal and historical meaning" should not be questioned: (1) the creation of all things by God at the beginning of time; (2) the special creation of man; (3) the formation of the first woman from man; (4) the unity of the human race; (5) the original happiness of our first parents in a state of justice, integrity, and immortality; (6) the divine command laid upon man to prove his obedience; (7) the transgression of that divine command at the instigation of the devil under the form of a serpent; (8) the fall of our first parents from their primitive state of innocence; (9) the promise of a future redeemer. The *Catechism of the Catholic Church* added, "The account of the fall in Genesis 3 uses figurative language, but affirms a primeval event, a deed that took place at the beginning of the history of man" (CCC 390).

C. Patriarchal History

The patriarchal history is made up of family traditions that were handed down across generations. Archaeology has shed much light on the cultural, religious, and social customs of the period, and has confirmed many of the essential details of the narrative. It is clear that the patriarchs lived and were not merely legendary figures invented to pass along moral lessons.

Genealogies appear throughout as signposts for the progress of the story, each beginning with the formula "these are the generations" (Gen 2:4; 5:1; 6:9; 10:1; 11:10, 27; 25:12, 19; 36:1, 9; 37:2). These genealogies help us follow the progress of divine providence from one generation to the next.

D. Types Fulfilled in Christ

For Christian readers, the threads of salvation history begun in Genesis find their fulfillment in Jesus Christ. **Adam** is a type of the perfect man, Jesus Christ, who heals the damage done by Adam's rebellion (Gen 2–3; Rom 5:12–21). The **Flood** prefigured the saving waters of baptism (Gen 6–8; 1 Pet 3:20–21). **Melchizedek**, the king and priest of Salem, offers bread and wine as a type of Christ, the king and priest who offers the Eucharist (Gen 14:17–20; Matt 26:26–29; Heb 7:1–19). **Abraham** is the great model for the believer whose faith is emulated by the Christian (Gen 15:1–6; Rom 4:1–12; Gal 3:6–9). **Isaac** is a type of Christ: offered in willing sacrifice by his father, he prefigured the death and Resurrection of Jesus, who was not spared by his Father but died as a willing sacrifice for the redemption of all (Rev 22:1–14; Rom 8:32; Heb 11:17–19).

GENNESARET, LAKE OF See **Galilee, Sea of**.

GENTILE

Any member of a non-Jewish nation. The Hebrew word *gôyîm* means "nations" or "peoples" (cf. Gen 10:5, 12:2, 15:14, 17:20, 18:18; Josh 3:17; 10:13; etc.); the people of Israel, as God's Chosen People, were distinct from the rest of the nations. Thus the term (often translated "nations" in the RSV) is sometimes used in a derogatory sense (Ps 2:1, 8; 9:6, 12, 21; Ezek 36:6, 7, 23). When Judaism encountered the Hellenic world—in particular the Seleucids, who were oppressive and enforcers of a competing pan-Hellenic religious sensibility—the distinction between God's people and Gentiles became all the more important. Gentiles were viewed contemptuously as idolators, worshippers of demons, and perpetrators of vice and immorality. They stood in contrast to those who adhered to the Law. By New Testament times, the word was grouped with "tax collector" or "publican" to designate one who should be despised or pitied (Matt 5:47; 6:7, 32; 10:5; 18:17; 20:19; Mark 10:33; Luke 12:30, 18:32; 1 Cor 5:1; 1 Thess 4:5).

While the Gentiles were viewed with contempt and hostility, there was at the same time in the Old Testament a clear message that the call to salvation was universal (Gen 49:10; Num 24:17; Deut 32:43; Ps 2:8, 22:28, 68:32, 80:1, 97:4; Isa 2:2, 11:10; Jer 9:26; Hos 2:1; Mic 4:2; Zeph 3:9; Zech 2:11). By the third century B.C., Jewish missionaries were reaching out to the Gentiles, but the converts from the Gentiles had to embrace the Jewish life in all senses of the word, including a strict adherence to the Mosaic Law.

The conversion of the Gentiles to Christianity, on the other hand, involved an entirely different approach. The Gospel was deliberately universal in scope, especially once the issue of the obligations to the Law had been resolved (Acts 15; Gal 1–2; see **Jerusalem, Council of**). Paul called himself the "Apostle of the Gentiles" (Rom 11:13; Gal 1:15, 16).

GENTILES, COURT OF

A courtyard in the **Temple** of Herod in Jerusalem to which entry was permitted to both Jews and Gentiles. It was forbidden, however, for Gentiles to go beyond this point (Mark 11:15).

GERA A name used for members of the tribe of Benjamin (Gen 46:21; 1 Chr 8:3, 5). It was also the name of the father of **Ehud** (Judg 3:15).

GERAR A city in the western **Negeb** identified by modern scholars with Tel Haror, west of Beer-sheba. Gerar marked the southern boundary of Canaan, near Gaza (Gen 10:19). Its king, **Abimelech**, had dealings with Abraham (Gen 20:2) and Isaac (Gen 26:6). It was also listed as a Philistine city (Gen 26:1) and was captured by **Asa** of Judah (2 Chr 14:12).

GERASA (Greek *Gerasa*) A Hellenistic city in the **Decapolis**, identified with the modern city of Jerash, in **Transjordan**, to the north of Amman, Jordan. The city was supposedly founded by Alexander the Great, but its origins can be definitely traced only to the time of Antiochus Epiphanes in the second century B.C. Jesus cured two demoniacs there (Mark 5:1; Luke 8:26; in Matt 8:28, the cure is placed in Gadara). The people of Gerasa asked Jesus to leave the city out of fear of his powers (Luke 8:37). The city attained its prominence in the second century A.D., and the archaeological remains of the city have been studied with great interest. (*See* **Gadarenes**.)

GERGESENES A variant for the Gadarenes and Gerasenes in some of the manuscripts of Matthew (8:28), Mark (5:1), and Luke (8:26). (*See* **Gadara**; **Gerasa**.)

GERSHOM The son of Moses and Zipporah (Exod 2:22) who was born during Moses's stay in Midian. His mention by name does not oc-

cur again in the Pentateuch. He is honored as the ancestor of the priesthood of Dan (Judg 18:30) and as the father of a Levite family (1 Chr 23:15; 26:24). A second Gershom was a descendant of **Phinehas** (Ezra 2:2). (*See also* **Gershon**.)

GERSHON The eldest son of Levi (Gen 46:11; Exod 6:16; Num 3:17; cf. 1 Chr 6:1, 2, 5, 28, 47, 56; 15:7, where he is called Gershom) and ancestor of the Levite clan of Gershon (Josh 21:27; 1 Chr 6:56–61).

GESHUR A small kingdom in **Transjordan**, east of the Sea of Galilee and north of Bashan. Although it was claimed by the Israelites, it was never fully occupied (Deut 3:14; Josh 12:5, 13:11). David enjoyed good relations with Geshur and married Maacah, daughter of King Talmai of Geshur. By Maacah, David had **Absalom** (2 Sam 3:3; 1 Chr 3:2). After murdering Amnon, Absalom fled to Geshur (2 Sam 13:37). A different region by the same name is mentioned in Josh 13:2 and 1 Sam 27:8.

GESTAS The name in Christian tradition of the "bad thief" who was crucified with Christ and the "good thief" (Luke 23:39–43). His name does not appear in Scripture. (*See* **Dysmas**.)

GETHSEMANE (Aramaic, "oil press") An orchard located just to the east of the Kidron Valley from Jerusalem (John 18:1), on the lower slopes of the Mount of Olives (Matt 26:30; Luke 22:39), also called the Garden of Gethsemane. Jesus often used the place to rest, pray, and spend time with the disciples (Luke 21:37, 22:39; John 18:2). After the Last Supper,

Jesus went to pray in Gethsemane. He prayed in agony in the face of the impending completion of his task (Matt 26:42; Mark 14:36; Luke 22:40, 44, 46; John 18:1–11; cf. Heb 5:7–8). There he was betrayed by Judas Iscariot and arrested (Matt 26:36–56; Mark 14:32–52; *see* Luke 22:39–53). Only John's account describes the place as a garden (Greek *kēpos*), and the traditional name of the "Garden of Gethsemane" is taken from John (18:1). The garden was probably a large enclosed grove (Matt 26:36–39; Mark 14:32–35).

GEZER A city in Canaan in the Judean range, around 18 miles northwest of Jerusalem and identified with Tell Jezer. The king of Gezer joined in the coalition of five cities against Joshua and the Israelites (Josh 10:33), and Joshua slew the ruler (Josh 10:33; 12:12). Nevertheless, the Israelites failed to capture the city, and it remained under Canaanite control (Josh 16:10; Judg 1:29). The city later came into the possession of the **Philistines**, and so figured in the struggle between the Philistines and the Israelites (2 Sam 5:25; 1 Chr 14:16, 20:4). It was listed as a **Levitical city** of Ephraim (1 Chr 6:52). Gezer at last passed into Israelite hands when it was taken by an Egyptian pharaoh and given to Solomon as a dowry for his daughter (1 Kgs 9:16). Solomon made Gezer one of his chariot cities (1 Kgs 9:15–17). It later figured in the Maccabean Wars (1 Macc 4:15, 9:50, 13:43–48, 14:7, 15:28; 2 Macc 10:32–38).

GHOST, HOLY *See* **Spirit, Holy**.

GIANT *See* **Anakim; Nephilim; Rephaim**.

GIBBETHON (Hebrew, possibly "little hill") A **Levitical city** (Josh 21:23) and a possession of the tribe of Dan (Josh 19:44). The city also figured in the struggles with the Philistines and was besieged unsuccessfully by **Nadab** (1 Kgs 15:27) and Omri (1 Kgs 16:15–18).

GIBEAH (Hebrew *gib'ah*, "hill") A Benjaminite city (Judg 19:13, 14; 1 Sam 10:5; 13:2, 3; 2 Sam 23:9; Isa 10:29), located to the north of Jerusalem (Judg 19:12). The city was the scene of a terrible outrage committed against the concubine of a Levite who was spending the night as a guest. The death of the concubine sparked the conflict described in Judg 19–21. The city was the birthplace of **Saul** (1 Sam 10:10–26, 11:4, 15:34; Isa 10:29) and served as his royal residence (1 Sam 22:6; 23:19; 26:1).

The location of Gibeah is not known with certainty. **Geba** may also refer to Gibeah in some passages.

GIBEATH-ELOHIM (Hebrew, "hill of God") A hill in the country of the Benjamin tribe to which Samuel sent Saul to meet a band of prophets, and where the Spirit would come upon Saul and he would "be turned into another man" (1 Sam 10:5).

GIBEON A Benjaminite (Josh 18:25) and **Levitical city** (Josh 21:17), probably modern el-Jib, some eight miles northwest of Jerusalem. A Horite city at the time of the arrival of the Israelites, the people of Gibeon used trickery to make a covenant or peace treaty with Joshua (Josh 9–10). Joshua adhered to the covenant but made the Gibeonites manual laborers. Later, Saul violated the rights of Gibeon by killing a number of Gibeonites; as penance, David delivered seven of Saul's sons and grandsons to be put to death (2 Sam 21:1–14). The city was also the site of a victory of David over the Philistines (1 Chr 14:16). Around the great pool of Gibeon the contest between the adherents of **Abner** and Joab took place (2 Sam 2:12ff.; 20:8). **Ishmael**, the assassin of **Gedaliah**, was killed at Gibeon (Jer 41:12).

GIDEON (Hebrew, "warrior" or "hewer") The son of Joash, member of the tribe of Manasseh from Ephra (Judg 6:11), and a judge in Israel (Judg 6–8); also called Jerubbaal (meaning "Let Baal prosecute"; Judg 7:1, 8:29–35, 9:1; 2 Sam 11:21) after he destroyed the altar of Baal (Judg 6:25–32). His chief accomplishment was organizing the Israelites against the Midianites, who were then raiding during the harvests (Judg 6:1–10). Told by an angel that the Lord would be with him (Judg 6:11–16), Gideon surprised the Midianite camp with a small force and drove them in chaos to the Jordan, where their escape was cut off by Gideon's allies (Judg 7:9–25). Gideon then pursued the defeated enemy over the Jordan, captured two kings, executed them, and then punished the Midianite cities (Judg 8:10–21). While in pursuit of the Midianites, Gideon was refused hospitality by the towns of Succoth and Penuel; on his return home, he exacted a fearsome reprisal, massacring the townsmen and tearing down the tower of Penuel (Judg 8:4–9; 14–17). In recognition of his triumph, Gideon was offered the crown but refused (Judg 8:22–27). He was buried at Ephra.

GIHON

1. One of the four rivers of Paradise (Gen 2:13); it flowed around the land of **Cush**. Although attempts have been made to identify the river with a specific geographic location, such as the Nile River, in particular the Nubian or Sudanese part of the Nile, no definite identification may ever be made.

2. A fountain or spring on the eastern slope of the hill of Zion in Jerusalem, probably modern Ain Sitti Maryam (Ain Umm ed-Daraj). Solomon was anointed king at Gihon (1 Kgs 1:33). King **Hezekiah** ordered an aqueduct or conduit constructed to bring the water of Gihon into Jerusalem in the event of a siege (2 Kgs 20:20; 2 Chr 32:30; Sir 48:17).

GILBOA One of two mountains (with Moreh) on the eastern side of the valley of Jezreel, identified with modern Jebel Fuqu'ah. It was at Gilboa that Saul fought his last disastrous battle with the Philistines at which he was killed (1 Sam 28:4; 31:1, 8; 2 Sam 1:6; 21:12; 1 Chr 10:1, 8).

GILEAD (Hebrew, "pile of testimony") A mountainous region in **Transjordan** with varying geographical boundaries depending on changing political realities. At its broadest extent, it covered most of the area between the east bank of the Jordan and the territory of Ammon to the west (Num 32:26, 29; Josh 22:9, 13, 15, 32; Judg 10:8; 20:1; 2 Sam 2:9; Hos 6:8). The region is named after Gilead, the son of Machir of the tribe of Manasseh (Num 26:29; 36:1; 2 Chr 2:21).

Gilead was the birthplace of the judge **Jeph-**

thah (Judg 11:1) and also of the prophet **Elijah** (1 Kgs 17:1). The Israelite inhabitants proved stern and capable fighters during the period of the Judges (Judg 10:3; 12:7), and the Gileadites were important participants in the struggle against the Philistines. Hence, **Ish-bosheth** established his seat in Gilead after the death of Saul at Gilboa (2 Sam 2:9). The balm of Gilead was well known and compared to the healing power of the Lord (Jer 8:22; 46:11).

GILGAL (Hebrew, "circle of stones") A name used in the Old Testament for several locations. The best known was east of Jericho, although its exact location remains elusive. The king of Gilgal was defeated by Joshua (Josh 12:23), and the site became the place at which the Israelites established their first encampment after crossing the Jordan River (Josh 4:19). Here the men were circumcised (Josh 4:19–20; 5:2), and the name for Gilgal was derived from the "circle of stones," twelve stones from the Jordan River that were set up as a memorial of the twelve tribes (Josh 4:20). From here, Joshua attacked Jericho, negotiated with the Gibeonites (Josh 9:6), and came back in triumph from the campaign in Canaan (Josh 10:43). After declining in importance (Judg 2:1), Gilgal returned to prominence: it was one of the places where Samuel judged Israel (1 Sam 7:16; 10:8), and it is likely that Saul was affirmed as king at Gilgal (1 Sam 10:8); he was later rebuked for offering sacrifices there (1 Sam 13:9–14), suggesting that it was by that time a sanctuary (cf. Hos 4:15; Amos 4:4) of some importance. Various sites have been proposed for the site of Gilgal, including Tell en-Nitla and Khirbet Mefjir, but no consensus has been reached.

A second Gilgal was located in the southern hill country of Samaria, in the mountains of Ephraim, near Bethel, although some commentators think this is the same Gilgal as the first one. Elijah and Elisha started their final journey to **Transjordan** from here (2 Kgs 2:1–2; 4:38).

GIMEL The third letter of the Hebrew alphabet (‫ג‬).

GINATH The father of Tibni. He disputed **Omri**'s claim to the Israelite kingship (1 Kgs 16:21–22).

GIRGASHITES One of the peoples who inhabited Canaan at the time of the Israelite entry into Canaanite lands (Deut 7:1; Josh 3:10, 24:11; Neh 9:8). They were named as descendants of Canaan in the Table of Nations (Gen 10:15–16; 1 Chr 1:13–14). Nothing else is known about them.

GIRZITES A tribe of Bedouins (residing in the area between the Philistines and Egypt) who were attacked by David from his base at Ziklag (1 Sam 27:8).

GLEANING Gathering food from a harvested field. The Torah commanded that a farmer not reap his field to the absolute furthest extent up to the corners (Lev 19:9–10, 23:22; Deut 24:19–22). That way the poor, widows, orphans, and foreigners could glean the fields for food, as we see in Ruth 2, where Ruth gleaned the fields of Boaz to provide for her mother-in-law Naomi and herself.

GLORY The manifestation of power or might. "Glory" might be attributed to earthly power (2 Kgs 14:10), wisdom (Prov 25:2), or wealth (Esth 1:4), but it chiefly describes the majesty and sovereignty of God.

I. Old Testament
    A. Physical Phenomena
    B. Prophetic Images
    C. Creation Shows God's Glory
II. New Testament
    A. Manifestations of Christ's Glory
    B. We Share the Glory of God
    C. Christ's Death and Resurrection Are the
        Sign of His Glory
    D. Glory in Revelation

I. OLD TESTAMENT

A. Physical Phenomena

In the **Pentateuch**, God's glory is often manifested in physical phenomena: a cloud (Exod 16:10; 24:16; Lev 9:6, 23; Num 14:22; 16:19; 17:7) and as fire and smoke (Deut 5:21), and of course the pillar of cloud and pillar of fire, especially on Mount Sinai (Exod 24:16–17). When he asks to see God's glory, Moses is told: "I will make all my goodness pass before you, and will proclaim before you my name 'the LORD'" (Exod 33:18–19). God's glory traveled with the Israelites through the wilderness (Exod 13:21) and filled the tabernacle: "Then the cloud covered the tent of meeting, and the glory of the LORD filled the tabernacle. And Moses was not able to enter the tent of meeting, because the cloud abode upon it, and the glory of the LORD filled the tabernacle" (Exod

40:34–35). Later God's glory filled the Temple (1 Kgs 8:10–11; 2 Chr 7:1–3).

B. Prophetic Images

In Isaiah, God's glory is described as a cloud (Isa 4:5; cf. Isa 58:8) and also as a brilliant light (Isa 24:23; 60:1). Ezekiel associates God's glory with a cloud, a chariot, and especially a luminous cloud (Ezek 1:28; 3:12; 3:23; 8:4; 10:18; 44:4). In the same way, Ezekiel describes the earth as being filled with the light of the Lord's glory (Ezek 43:2; cf. Num 14:21).

C. Creation Shows God's Glory

Even without unusual and spectacular phenomena, the world itself displays the glory and goodness of God. The Psalms celebrate the glory of God in creation (Ps 19, 29, 97, 104). The anticipatory quality of God's glory in creation is advanced further by Isaiah (60:1–3; cf. Hab 2:14), who ties that glory with the coming of the Messianic age.

II. NEW TESTAMENT

A. Manifestations of Christ's Glory

The New Testament thus develops the prophets' Messianic expectations in the light of their fulfillment in Christ. The glory of Christ is revealed in his death and Resurrection (Luke 24:26), and his glory will be seen when he comes again (Matt 16:27, 24:30; Mark 8:38, 13:26; Luke 21:27). He shares in the glory of God, and the throne of glory in which he shares becomes the object of emulation for the disciples who wish to sit on thrones of glory (Mark 10:37).

The theophanic quality of divine glory is also seen in the accounts of the birth of Christ (Luke 2:9), the witness by Stephen of the glory of God before his martyrdom (Acts 7:55), and in Paul's dazzling vision on the road to Damascus (Acts 22:11). Christ becomes the means of salvation and the glorification of God through his suffering and death (Phil 2:11), and the theme of glory returns consistently in references to the sufferings of the Savior (Heb 2:9; 1 Pet 1:11), his Resurrection (Rom 6:4; 1 Pet 1:21), and the expectation of his return (1 Pet 4:13).

B. We Share the Glory of God

Paul points out that the old Law came with visible glory, which he compares to the greater glory of the New Law (2 Cor 3:7). Through Christ, Paul says, we shall share in the glory of God (Rom 5:2). We share in the glorious suffering of Christ: "we suffer with him in order that we may also be glorified with him. I consider that the sufferings of this present time are not worth comparing with the glory that is to be revealed to us" (Rom 8:17–18). Joining Christ in his glorious suffering is the road to personal glorification (Phil 3:21; Col 3:4; 2 Thess 2:14).

C. Christ's Death and Resurrection Are the Sign of His Glory

John's Gospel emphasizes the Passion, death, and Resurrection as the sign of Jesus's glorification (John 12:23; 13:31–32). God's glory is revealed in Jesus (John 1:14); it has existed in the Son since before the beginning (John 17:24). The Son, therefore, is the sign of glory (John 2:11), and, in turn, Jesus is glorified by God through the work of the Spirit (John 16:14). The signs worked by Jesus reveal his divinity and permit his disciples to behold his glory (John 2:11). In seeing this sign of glory, all are called to believe. The signs, however, point to the glorification of Jesus only through his suffering, death, and exaltation (John 12:23). Jesus promises the disciples that they will see his glory and that he will send the Spirit to them so that they will understand fully his words (John 7:39; 12:16).

D. Glory in Revelation

Revelation returns to the vivid images of the Old Testament: the cloud of glory (Rev 15:8) and a brilliant light (Rev 18:1). "Glory" is also a praise given to God in recognition of his perfection and majesty (Rev 4:11; cf. Ps 105).

GLORY, BOOK OF *See* **John, Gospel of**.

GLOSSOLALIA *See* **Tongues, gift of**.

GNOSTICISM (Greek *gnōsis,* "knowledge") A system of religious thought that emphasized secret knowledge. Christian Gnosticism first evolved out of pre-Christian pagan religious currents, influenced by Neoplatonists and pagan philosophers. It was found initially in numerous Christian schools, became increasingly established in various shapes, and by the late second century had split from the Christian Church. The sects of Gnosticism varied considerably in their particular doctrines, but they shared certain common characteristics.

Central to Gnostic teachings was the

idea of gnosis, knowledge of salvation made known to a select few, namely, initiates of the Gnostic sect. The source of the gnosis was usually a supposed secret oral transmission of the knowledge by Christ, either to the twelve apostles or to the leader of the sect. The universe was sharply divided between spiritual and material worlds, the first representing perfection and goodness, the second imperfection and evil. For Gnostics, the world and everything in it—including humanity—is imperfect and opposed to the spiritual world. God is a transcendent and spiritual being, so he could not have created the material world. Instead, the material world was created in some manner by a lesser god, the Demiurge, a creator god derived from the Divine Being through a series of emanations, or aeons.

Certain humans, however, contain within them a gift of spirituality, described by some as a spark of the Divine Being. They will be able to achieve salvation and become reunited with the Divine Being through the gnosis. Christ, to the Christian Gnostics, was a representative of the Divine Being, sent to deliver the gnosis to the elect. Gnosticism thus divided all of humanity into two main groups, the select (the saved—a small group) and those of the flesh (the damned—most of humanity).

It is obvious at once that the Gnostic message was completely opposite of the message of orthodox Christianity. Orthodox Christians insist that Christ had openly taught the truth of salvation for everyone; Gnostics preached that a tiny minority might be qualified to possess the secret of salvation.

It is not certain when the Gnostics first began to trouble the Church. Some suggest that Saint Paul was already confronting them at Corinth and Colossae (cf. Col. 1:9; 2:2), and 1 John might refer to Gnostics when it speaks of "those who would deceive you" (1 John 2:26). Specific sects can be identified by the second century in the leading centers of the Church—Alexandria and Rome—and to this period belong the best-known Gnostic teachers: Basilides, Valentinus, and Marcion.

The Gnostics were challenged by a number of orthodox writers, in particular Saint Clement of Rome, Saint Irenaeus, Saint Hippolytus, and Tertullian. These anti-Gnostic spokesmen helped mark out the important theological differences between the Gnostics and the Church.

Until the last century, most of what we knew about the Gnostics came from the writings of their orthodox opponents, but the discovery of the collection of Coptic texts at **Nag Hammadi** in Upper Egypt gave us a large number of the Gnostics' own writings.

GOAD A wooden stick, sometimes tipped with iron and reaching six to seven feet long, that was used by plowmen to drive oxen (1 Sam 13:21). The goad could also be used as a weapon; Shamgar slew six hundred Philistines with one (Judg 3:31). In metaphorical or figurative language, a goad is anything that drives us into the right path: "the sayings of the wise are like goads" (Eccl 12:11; cf. Acts 26:14).

GOAH A part of Jerusalem mentioned in the vision of a resanctified city by Jeremiah (Jer 31:39). Its location is uncertain.

GOAT A cloven-hoofed and hollow-horned ruminant. The goat was one of the first animals to be domesticated, and raising goats was practiced in Palestine from an early time (Gen 15:9; 30:32; 31:38). Goats provided milk (Deut 32:14; Prov 27:27), meat (Gen 27:9; Deut 14:5; Judg 6:19, 13:15), and skins (Gen 21:14; Num 31:20; Josh 9:4). As they were ritually clean, goats were used as sacrificial victims (Lev 10), most notably in the annual ritual of the "scapegoat," in which a goat was symbolically burdened with the sins of the community and driven out of the camp or city (Lev 16:8–10, 21–26). Goats were also used to lead flocks of sheep (Jer 50:8); hence, leaders of people are sometimes called goats (Ezek 34:17, 39:18; Zech 10:3; Dan 8:5). In his parable of the judgment (Matt 25:31–46), Jesus notes that while goats and sheep share the same pasture, they are separated when taken to the market. (*See also* **Kid**.)

GOD In SMALL CAPS, a translation of the Name of God in the RSV and many other English versions (*see* "Yahweh" *under* **God**). The Name is normally translated "LORD," but "GOD" is used when the Hebrew word for "Lord" precedes the Name.

GOD The Creator of all things. God is perfect and all-powerful, one in being yet three Persons (Father, Son, and Holy Spirit). In English, "God" is used as the proper name of the Supreme Deity while "god" is a common noun for other deities mentioned in the Bible.

Christians derive their knowledge of God from two sources: Sacred Scripture and reason. Each finds support in and is reaffirmed by the other. Reason tells us that there must be a God; Scripture shows us who God is as he reveals himself to humanity.

In Scripture, God is described in a host of different ways. The unbelievers meet him in creation; the Chosen People encounter him in creation and history; and then the whole world beholds him in creation, in history, and in the very person of Jesus Christ.

Our encounter with God is always a meeting between two *persons*. God is a Person who acts, and the human being is a witness to that activity. What we know about God, therefore, is incomplete and is entirely subject to his will and activity of self-revelation. Our knowledge will be made complete only when we see him face-to-face at the final revelation of the beatific vision.

I. *Knowing God Through Reason*
   A. *God Revealed in Creation*
   B. *Saint Thomas's Proofs of the Existence of God*
   C. *The Limitations of Reason*
II. *The Old and New Covenants*
   A. *The Plan of Revelation*
   B. *God's Revelation in the Old Testament*
   C. *The Perfection of God's Revelation in the New Testament*
III. *The Divine Nature and Attributes*
   A. *Knowing God Through His Revelation*
   B. *The Perfection of God*
   C. *The Eternity of God*
   D. *The Omnipotence of God*
   E. *The Holiness of God*
   F. *The Love of God*

I. KNOWING GOD THROUGH REASON

A. God Revealed in Creation

As Saint Paul wrote, "Ever since the creation of the world his [God's] eternal power and divine nature, invisible though they are, have been understood and seen through the things he has made" (Rom 1:20; cf. Acts 14:15, 17:27–28; Wis 13:1–9).

God has shown to all—the believer and the unbeliever alike—his majesty and creative power in the movement of the heavens, the surety of the seasons, and the beauty and abundance of the world. From the earliest times of human existence, mankind has seen this truth and has tried to be united with the Creator through worship.

B. Saint Thomas's Proofs of the Existence of God

The pagan philosophers encountered God through reason as the Supreme Being who remains transcendent and is outside the world. Saint Thomas Aquinas taught that reason alone can prove the existence of God in five ways:

1. The argument from motion: since everything that moves must have been set in motion by something else, there must be a First Mover.

2. The argument from "efficient causes": everything that is caused is caused by something else, and therefore there must be a First Cause.

3. The argument from possibility: since everything in nature is generated, decays, and ceases to be, it is possible for anything to be or not to be; therefore there could at one time have been nothing that existed. But if nothing existed, it would have been impossible for anything to come into being, unless there was some Being who already existed by necessity.

4. The argument from gradation: since things are more or less good or true, there must be one Being who is *most* good and true.

5. The argument from design: since things that are not intelligent in themselves act according to intelligent laws, there must be an Intelligence that designs and directs the universe.

C. The Limitations of Reason

Such a revelation is incomplete, however. Paul laments the folly of the pagan philosophers: "Claiming to be wise, they became fools, and they exchanged the glory of the immortal God for images resembling a mortal human being or birds or four-footed animals or reptiles" (Rom 1:22–23).

There are obstacles in coming to know God by the light of reason alone. Pope Pius XII wrote:

> *For the truths that concern the relations between God and man wholly transcend the visible order of things, and, if they are translated into human action and influence it, they call for self-surrender and abnegation. The human mind, in its turn, is hampered in the attaining of such truths, not only by the impact of the senses and the imagination, but also by disordered appetites which are the consequence of original sin. So it happens*

that men in such matters easily persuade themselves that what they would not like to be true is false or at least doubtful. (Humani Generis, §561; DS 3875)

Mankind, therefore, is in need of enlightenment by divine revelation. God has chosen freely to reveal himself by "revealing the mystery, his plan of loving goodness, formed from all eternity in Christ, for the benefit of all men. God has fully revealed this plan by sending us his beloved Son, our Lord Jesus Christ, and the Holy Spirit" (CCC 50).

This is not to say that reason is useless. On the contrary, reason can help lead us to faith. The Catechism teaches two ways of seeing God's existence: "Man's faculties make him capable of coming to a knowledge of the existence of a personal God. But for man to be able to enter into real intimacy with him, God willed both to reveal himself to man and to give him the grace of being able to welcome this revelation in faith. The proofs of God's existence, however, can predispose one to faith and help one to see that faith is not opposed to reason" (CCC 35; Vatican Council I, *Dei Filius* 2; DS 3004).

II. THE OLD AND NEW COVENANTS

A. The Plan of Revelation

Because reason alone is insufficient, especially for our sinful natures, God also willed to reveal himself and so make known eternal salvation. God reveals himself to us directly in Scripture and in the person of Jesus Christ, the Word made flesh.

Dei Verbum proclaimed:

In His goodness and wisdom God chose to reveal Himself and to make known to us the hidden purpose of His will (see Eph 1:9) by which through Christ, the Word made flesh, man might in the Holy Spirit have access to the Father and come to share in the divine nature (see Eph 2:18; 2 Peter 1:4). Through this revelation, therefore, the invisible God (see Col 1:15; 1 Tim 1:17) out of the abundance of His love speaks to men as friends (see Exod 33:11; John 15:14–15) and lives among them (see Bar 3:38), so that He may invite and take them into fellowship with Himself. This plan of revelation is realized by deeds and words having an inner unity: the deeds wrought by God in the history of salvation manifest and confirm the teaching and realities signified by the words, while the words proclaim the deeds and clarify the mystery contained in them. By this revelation then, the deepest truth about God and the salvation of man shines out for our sake in Christ, who is both the mediator and the fullness of all revelation. (DV §2.)

B. God's Revelation in the Old Testament

God made himself known to the first humans, the parents of the human family. But God's revelation did not cease with the sin of Adam and Eve. Indeed, he gave them a promise of future salvation and never abandoned his beloved creatures (cf. Gen 3:15; Rom 2:6–7).

God's revelation continued through the covenants with Noah and then with Abraham. Abraham and his descendants worshipped the one true God—a worship founded on God's steadfast love and fidelity to his people. God commissioned Moses to lead his people out of Egypt and to establish the covenant of Mount

Sinai. The covenant called upon Israel to be a nation of holy priests, elder brethren to the nations, and to "recognize him and serve him as the one living and true God, the provident Father and just judge, and so that they would look for the promised Savior" (CCC 62; cf. DV §3).

C. The Perfection of God's Revelation in the New Testament

After speaking through the prophets, and so continuing to prepare the expectations and hope of salvation, God made his final and definitive self-revelation in Jesus Christ (cf. Heb 1:1–2; John 1:1–18). Jesus, the Word made flesh, perfected revelation and "confirmed with divine testimony what revelation proclaimed, that God is with us to free us from the darkness of sin and death, and to raise us up to life eternal. The Christian dispensation, therefore, as the New and definitive Covenant, will never pass away and we now await no further new public revelation before the glorious manifestation of our Lord Jesus Christ (see 1 Tim 6:14 and Titus 2:13)" (DV §4). (*See* **Revelation, Divine** *for other details; see also* **Covenant**; **Jesus Christ**; **Holy Spirit**; **Trinity**.)

III. THE DIVINE NATURE AND ATTRIBUTES

A. Knowing God Through His Revelation

Because God reveals himself in creation and in Scripture, we can understand something of his nature and divine attributes.

God is pure spirit in his nature (Gen 1:2–3), as Christ declared to the Samaritan woman at the well: "God is spirit, and those who wor-ship him must worship in spirit and truth" (John 4:24). God, then, has no body or physical presence (cf. Rom 1–20; John 1:18). When Scripture speaks of God in human terms (as having emotions such as anger or possessing eyes and ears), it does so in anthropomorphic language that expresses the immediacy of God and his engagement in human history while acknowledging his complete divine transcendence.

B. The Perfection of God

God's nature is absolute perfection and is beyond our ability to comprehend. As our knowledge of God is limited, our language concerning him must likewise be imperfect.

But because we are made in the image and likeness of God, we can seek to understand him by reflecting on ourselves, our experiences, and our spiritual capacities. The perfections in truth, goodness, and beauty that we understand reflect the supreme and infinite perfection of God (CCC 39–43). God's perfections can be seen in a variety of ways, such as in his transcendence, immanence, immutability, eternity, omniscience, holiness, and love. Vatican Council I (1869–1870) declared God to be the "one, true, living God, Creator and Lord of heaven and earth, omnipotent, eternal, immense, incomprehensible, infinite in intellect and will and in every perfection . . . one unique spiritual substance, wholly simple and unchanging . . . really and essentially distinct from the world, totally blessed in himself and of himself and ineffably elevated above all things which are and can be thought of apart from him."

God's infinite existence likewise extends

to his omniscience (he possesses unlimited knowledge), his omnipresence (he is not limited by considerations of space), and his omnipotence (he possesses absolute power). Further, he is transcendent, meaning that he is set above nature and guides and directs it (cf. Isa 40:12–17), and immanent, being omnipresent in his creation. He does not stand removed from the world, however, for he holds his creation in existence and is eternally present to it.

C. The Eternity of God

God's eternal presence is expressed in his own statement to Moses, "I AM WHO I AM . . . Say this to the people of Israel, 'I AM has sent me to you'" (Exod 3:14). God was present in the beginning of the world, at the time of Abraham, when Israel was led out of Egypt, and as salvation history progressed across the ages. As the Psalms declare, "Before the mountains were brought forth, or ever you had formed the earth and the world, from everlasting to everlasting you are God" (Ps 90:2). Thus Jesus said, "Truly, truly, I say to you, before Abraham was, I am" (John 8:58), and Paul taught the philosophers of Athens: "The God who made the world and everything in it, being Lord of heaven and earth, does not live in shrines made by man, nor is he served by human hands, as though he needed anything, since he himself gives to all men life and breath and everything" (Acts 17:24–25).

D. The Omnipotence of God

God's eternal presence testifies as well to his universal power. He is revered in Scripture as the "Lord of hosts," the Lord of the universe, and the master of history (cf. Gen 49:24; Isa 1:24; Ps 24:8–10, 135:6; Jer 27:5, 32:17; Luke 1:37). The book of Wisdom proclaims: "It is always in your power to show great strength, and who can withstand the strength of your arm?" (Wis 11:21; cf. Esth 4:17; Prov 21:1; Tob 13:2).

E. The Holiness of God

In the majesty of his power, God is also supremely holy, merciful, and loving. All that is holy pertains to God, for only he is truly holy (Isa 6:3). Wherever he appears or whatever he touches is deemed holy (cf. Gen 28:16; Exod 3:4; Lev 16:12), as is wherever he chooses to dwell; thus the Tabernacle where God chose to dwell included what was called the "holy of holies" (Exod 26:33–34), and the Temple was deemed holy (1 Chr 29:3; Isa 64:10). The altar and the ministers of God's worship were termed holy (Exod 40; Lev 8–9), as were all aspects of worship and liturgy (cf. Lev 22:10–16; 1 Sam 21:5–7; Neh 10:32). God's holiness is revealed throughout the whole of Scripture, from the first Creation account in Genesis to the final verses of the book of Revelation. As God announced in Ezekiel: "And I will vindicate the holiness of my great name, which has been profaned among the nations, and which you have profaned among them; and the nations will know that I am the LORD, says the Lord GOD, when through you I vindicate my holiness before their eyes" (Ezek 36:23; cf. Ezek 20:41, 39:27; Isa 40:25–26, 41:13–16).

Confronting God's infinite holiness, his creatures are brought face-to-face with their own sinfulness (cf. Exod 34:30–35; Mark 9:1–7) at the same time as God's infinite mercy and his infinite love are brought into the foreground. By his mercy, God brings the promise of hope to sinners: In speaking to God about his mercy, the author of the book of Wisdom says, "You are merciful to all, for you can do all things" (Wis 11:23). (*See* **Mercy**.)

F. The Love of God

God's love is revealed completely by Jesus Christ. Love rests at the very foundation of creation, and God's love has never wavered, even in the face of Israel's infidelity (cf. Deut 4:37; Isa 43:4, 48:14; Ps 33:5, 37:28, 146:8). Because of his love, God willingly gave his own Son to bring salvation for all (Rom 5:8–9; John 3:16; 1 John 4:10–11). Christ revealed that God is love (1 John 4:8), and through Christ the believer is invited to participate in that holiness and to enjoy a profound intimacy with God. By his love, God brings the Christian into the very life of the Holy Trinity and accomplishes adoption of the believer as a father adopts a son (Rom 8:14–17) (CCC 26–141, 198–324, 2807–27).

IV. THE FATHERHOOD OF GOD

A. Israel as God's Son

God called Israel to be his son, his firstborn (Exod 4:22), and in the Sinai covenant, the Lord expected Israel to be "a kingdom of priests and a holy nation" (Exod 19:6) sent forth by its Father to all of the nations of the world, fulfilling the role of royal priest and elder brother (cf. Matt 28:20; Luke 4:25–27, 24:47; John 10:16, 17:11, 20:21). God remained faithful to his promises to be a Father (cf. Hos 11:1; Mal 1:6, 63:16), and the Israelites were to be his children, as members of a nation that had been granted sonship (Deut 14:1). The Israelites were expected to be faithful sons, but their status did not change even when they demonstrated infidelity (Isa 30:9). Membership in the wider people of Israel was also seen as providing individual sonship and an intimate relationship with God (cf. Wis 2:13–16).

B. Christians Share Christ's Sonship

The New Testament brings to completion the recognition of God as Father, presenting him as the Father not only of Israel but of all men and women. Christ spoke of God as "my Father" and said to the disciples that God was "your Father." He taught them to pray to "Our Father" (Matt 6:9). Jesus addressed his Father as **Abba** (Mark 14:36), a term that expresses the deep intimacy between them. In inviting his followers to call God "Father," Jesus permits Christians to share in that intimacy.

In revealing the Father, Jesus teaches God's transcendent authority and also God's goodness and loving care for all of his children. God transcends all human terminology, analogy, and imagery, and he also transcends human fatherhood and motherhood, even as he is their origin and model: for no one is father as God is Father (cf. Ps 27:10; Eph 3:14; Isa 49:15; Matt 6:32, 7:7–11, 10:29; Luke 15:1–32, 7:50). As the *Catechism* teaches: "Jesus revealed that God is Father in an unheard-of sense: he is Father not only in being Creator; he is eternally Father in relation to his only Son, who is eternally Son only in relation to his Father: 'No one knows the Son except the Father, and no one knows the Father except the Son and any one to whom the Son chooses to reveal him' (Matt 11:27)" (CCC 240).

Paul addressed God's fatherhood when he taught on the sonship of Christians. He wrote to the Galatians, "in Christ Jesus you are all sons of God, through faith. For as many of you as were baptized into Christ have put on Christ" (Gal 3:26–27). Christians become sons of God by virtue of their baptism, the sacrament that brings a new life and adoption as God's children. The close, intimate union between Christ and God makes God, therefore, the Father of Christians in a real sense and not merely in the metaphorical sense of the Old Law. This adoption gives the Christian the freedom and the privilege to refer to God as "Father" in the same way as Our Lord calls him Father: "but you have received the spirit of sonship. When we cry, 'Abba! Father!' it is the Spirit himself bearing witness with our spirit that we are children of God, and if children, then heirs, heirs of God and fellow heirs with Christ, provided we suffer with him in order that we may also be glorified with him" (Rom 8:15; Gal 4:6) (CCC 238–42).

V. THE NAMES OF GOD

Three principal names—El, Elohim, and Yahweh—are used for God in the Old Testament. There are also several other particular names.

• **El** ("god" or "divinity") was used for a god in a broad sense. The name was also used for the supreme deity of the Canaanite pantheon; his son was **Baal**. In Scripture, it appeared as an adjective or a predicate and in titles such as El-Shaddai ("Almighty God"), El Elyon ("God Most High), and El Bethel ("God of Bethel," Gen 31:13). In the plural, the name is Elohim. El Elyon, "God Most High," was the title of God as worshipped by **Melchizedek** (Gen 14:19–20). Another version of El was Eloah, a singular form of Elohim that is found chiefly in biblical poetry (cf. Deut 32:15).

• **Elohim** is the plural of El, but it was also a name for the supreme deity in the singular. When used as a plural, it was often preceded by a definite article to express "the gods" (see, for example, Exod 18:11). When referring to the supreme deity, it denoted in the OT the one God of Israel as the summit of divinity, the God of gods. The breadth of the divinity suggested by the name stood in comparison to the limited nature of man (cf. Num 23:19) and spoke to the relationship between the supreme deity, who is all-powerful and yet a person, and the created order (cf. Gen 1:1).

• **Yahweh** (*YHWH*, LORD) The personal name of God in the OT. Because of the supreme sanctity and respect attached to the name of God, the title Adonai was uttered in place of Yahweh in spoken Hebrew, and in written texts, the vowel points (see **Hebrew language**) of Adonai were combined with the consonants YHWH, so that readers would know to speak the word Adonai instead of Yahweh. The name Jehovah comes from pronouncing the word as written. The divine name YHWH appears more than six thousand times in the OT, and was most likely pronounced *Yahweh*.

In Genesis 1 and 2, we see a good example of how the names Elohim ("God") and Yahweh ("the LORD") are used differently in the OT. In Genesis 1, Elohim calls the cosmos into existence; in Genesis 2, Yahweh forms Adam from the ground and places him in the Garden of Eden. The two names show two different forms of divine activity. Elohim depicts the infinite power of the Creator, while Yahweh suggests God's covenant love. Something similar is seen in the change between the broad or generic term of "God" and the more intimate use of "Abba, Father," as was spoken by Jesus. The interpretive key for the difference is the Sabbath, the sign of God's covenant with creation. In the movement from Elohim to Yahweh, Genesis teaches that in the creation of the world and of Adam—the establishment of God's covenant with creation—God has become more than the Creator. He is a loving Father, and humanity has become his covenant family.

• The name **Adonai** (Hebrew *'ădōnāy,* "Lord") is derived from *'ādôn* ("lord") and used as a name for the deity. It is similar to the term *ba'al* (also "lord"). Adonai is used extensively in the prophetic books, especially in the book of Ezekiel, where the prophet applied it to distinguish the God of Israel from the gods of Babylon. (*See also* **Yahweh**.)

• **Yahweh Sabaoth** ("Lord of Hosts"; Greek *kyrios pantokratōr,* "Lord Almighty") is a title used some three hundred times in the OT and twice in the New Testament (Rom 9:29; Jas 5:4) to give expression to the majesty and power of Yahweh. (See **Sabaoth** for other details.)

GOD, KINGDOM OF *See* **Kingdom**.

GOG Also Gog and Magog. The leader of Meshech and Tubal, from the land of Magog (Ezek 38:2). The word "Magog" is most likely derived from the Akkadian for "the land of Gyges (or Gog)," seen in the Table of Nations (Gen 10:2) and appearing (as in Ezekiel) with Meshech and Tubal. According to Ezek 38–39, Gog will lead an invading army upon Israel at some future time (Ezek 38:8–15) and so incur God's wrath and suffer utter defeat and annihilation (Ezek 38:18–22; 39:4–5, 11–15). The defeat will serve to proclaim God's holiness and power (Ezek 38:16, 21; 39:6, 22, 25–29). Meshech and Tubal are in Asia Minor along the Black Sea, and some scholars have suggested that Gog refers to Gyges, king of Lydia. But such identification is entirely conjectural; Gog is an eschatological or apocalyptic figure, and his location is in the north, the direction from which invaders traditionally arose. Gog is thus connected with the evil opposition to God that will emerge prior to the end of the world and the last judgment. In Rev 20:7–11, Gog and Magog are evil nations joined in alliance who march at the urging of Satan against the Church following the millennial reign of Christ (Rev 20:8).

GOIIM (Hebrew, "nations") The kingdom of Tidal, an ally of Chedorlaomer of Elam (Gen 14:1, 9).

GOLAN A city in the territory of Manasseh in Bashan in **Transjordan**. It was a **Levitical city** allotted to the sons of Gershon (Josh 21:27; 1 Chr 6:71) and a city of refuge (Deut 4:43; Josh 20:8).

GOLD A precious metal that is not found naturally in Palestine; nevertheless, it was known, used, and prized by the Israelites from an early time. As it was not found naturally, it was obtained from other sources such as Havilah (Gen 2:12), Sheba (1 Kgs 10:1; Isa 60:6; Ezek 27:22), and Ophir (1 Kgs 9:28; 10:11). Gold was used in a wide variety of applications, including personal ornamentation (Gen 24:22; 41:42), the ritual items in the Tabernacle and Temple (Exod 25:11, 37:1; 1 Kgs 6:22, 7:48), and as a medium of exchange (1 Chr 21:25), but not as coinage. The Temple's interior was decorated richly with gold (1 Kgs 6:15ff.), as were the vestments of the high priest (Exod 28:5) and the altar of incense (Exod 30:1; 1 Kgs 6:20).

GOLGOTHA (Greek *Golgotha,* probably from the Aramaic, *gulgultā',* meaning "skull") The place located just outside of Jerusalem used by the Romans for executions (Matt 27:32; Mark 15:21; Luke 23:33). Christ was crucified there and then placed in a new tomb in a nearby garden (John 19:17–42). The three Gospels use also the Greek translation *kranion,* "skull" (Luke does not use the Aramaic word but refers to it only as "skull"). The name may have been a description of the site as a place of death, or it may have come from the skull-like appearance of the hill. The name Calvary, often used in Christian writings for the same place, comes from the **Vulgate**, which uses a Latin translation of Golgotha (*calvariae locus,* "place of the skull").

According to John, Golgotha was near the city (John 19:20; cf. Heb 13:12), and the traditional Christian identification of the location is the Church of the Holy Sepulcher. The location was originally within the city walls of Jerusalem, but after Jerusalem was rebuilt by the Romans as Colonia Aelia Capitolina, the city limits were moved farther to the north, and so Golgotha rested at the city center beneath the Temple of Aphrodite. That building was replaced by the Constantinian basilica in the fourth century. The church was destroyed by the Muslims in the eleventh century and rebuilt and consecrated by the Crusaders in 1149.

GOLIATH (Hebrew *golyāt*) The famous Philistine giant of Gath who was killed in combat by David (1 Sam 17). The account of the combat is one of the most famous in all of Scripture. Goliath challenged the Israelite army at Elah each day for forty days until the challenge was met by David, a youth armed only with a shepherd's staff and slingshot. After slaying the giant warrior with his slingshot, David cut off Goliath's head with the giant's own sword and brought it to Jerusalem. The incident catapulted David to fame. Goliath was described as being six cubits and a span (1 Sam 17:4), meaning he was over eight feet tall. (*See also* **Elhanan**; **Lahmi**.)

GOMER (Hebrew *gōmer*) The name of two people in the Old Testament.

1. The son of Japheth, grandson of Noah, and the father of Ashkenaz, Riphath, and Togarmah (Gen 10:2; 1 Chr 1:6) and the Cimmerians, an Indo-European people from the Black Sea region in the eighth century B.C. who settled in Asia Minor. They were defeated by the Assyrians in the mid-seventh century B.C., became intermingled with surrounding peoples, and faded from history.

2. The daughter of Diblaim and the wife

of the prophet **Hosea**, who was commanded by God to marry her (Hos 1:2–9) even though she was a woman of loose morals. She continued to be an adulteress; in the book of Hosea, her infidelity is a symbol of the infidelity of Israel to the Lord.

GOMORRAH *See* **Sodom and Gomorrah**.

GOOD SHEPHERD A title given to Christ, who compared himself with a good shepherd (John 10:11). In the parable of the shepherd, Jesus describes the shepherd who leaves the flock of ninety-nine sheep to search for one that is lost (Matt 18:12–13; Luke 15:1–7).

GORGIAS A general in the Seleucid army under Antiochus IV Epiphanes in the campaign against **Judas Maccabeus** (1 Macc 3:38; 2 Macc 8:9). He suffered a defeat at the battle of Emmaus (1 Macc 4:1–22) but defeated an attack by Joseph and Azarias, who acted against the orders of Judas (1 Macc 5:18–19). He was subsequently named governor of Idumea (2 Macc 10:14) but continued to fail in his efforts against Judas (2 Macc 12:32–37).

GOSHEN A region in the eastern Nile Delta where the Israelites settled under Jacob and Joseph (Gen 46:28; 47:1, 4, 6, 27; 50:8). The move to Egypt had been forced by a famine in Canaan, and the Hebrews settled in "the land of Goshen," which featured excellent pastures for their flocks (Gen 46:28–34; 47:1–10). The Egyptian pharaoh gave permission for them to remain and went so far as to permit the Israelite flocks to be pastured with his own (Gen 46:33–34; 47:6). Jacob's family prospered in

Goshen, and his descendants were still there at the time of the **Exodus** (Exod 8:18; 9:26). The exact location of Goshen is not known. It was probably in the eastern part of the Nile Delta, and the location most often proposed is the Wadi Tumilat.

GOSPEL (from the Anglo-Saxon *gōd-spell*, "good tidings" or "good news") The name generally given to the four divinely inspired accounts of the life, death, and Resurrection of Our Lord Jesus Christ in the Bible. More broadly, "the gospel of the Kingdom" (Matt 4:23; Mark 1:15; Luke 4:43, 8:1, 16:16), the good tidings of salvation for all men through Jesus; or, most broadly, the whole revelation of salvation by Christ (cf. Matt 9:35, 24:14; Mark 1:14, 13:10, 16:15; Acts 5:42, 11:20, 14:7, 20:24; Rom 1:9, 10:16, 15:20; 1 Cor 15:1; 2 Cor 4:3). Paul provides a useful definition:

Paul, a servant of Jesus Christ, called to be an apostle, set apart for the gospel of God which he promised beforehand through his prophets in the holy scriptures, the gospel concerning his Son, who was descended from David according to the flesh and designated Son of God in power according to the Spirit of holiness by his resurrection from the dead, Jesus Christ our Lord, through whom we have received grace and apostleship to bring about the obedience of faith for the sake of his name among all the nations, including yourselves who are called to belong to Jesus Christ. (Rom 1:1–6)

Clear direction and teaching on the Catholic understanding of the Gospels are provided by two essential documents: the Dogmatic Constitution on Divine Revelation, *Dei Ver-*

bum, of the Second Vatican Council; and the document of the Pontifical Biblical Commission, *Sancta Mater Ecclesia*, "On the Historicity of the Gospels."

I. ORIGINS

The New Testament understanding of Gospel is traced in part to the Old Testament prophetic writings, in particular Isaiah's predictions of the Good News of salvation of Zion (Isa 40:9; 41:27; 52:7; 61:1). Isaiah 61:1 says that the "good news" is "to bring good tidings to the afflicted . . . to bind up the brokenhearted, to proclaim liberty to the captives, and the opening of the prison to those who are bound." The traditional understanding of the Greek word *euangelion* was the "reward of good tidings" that was given to the one bearing the news, in particular word of victory. By the first century A.D., the word *euangelion* was understood by the Romans to denote the "good tidings" surrounding the birth of an imperial heir to the emperor (Caesar) or the accession of a new emperor to the throne. That Luke uses the word in the latter sense is apparent in the proclamation of the births of John the Baptist (Luke 1:19) and Jesus (Luke 2:10). Likewise, John the Baptist announces the Good News (Luke 3:19), as does Jesus (Matt 4:23; Mark 1:35–39; Luke 4:43–44).

II. STAGES OF DEVELOPMENT

As we saw, the Gospel proclamation in the NT did not imply the four Gospels as we have them today in written form. Rather, *euangelion* meant the Good News of the Kingdom. This difference forms a key element in understanding the place of the written Gospels in the process of handing on the Gospel proclamation.

As long as there was no formal and authentic written record of the Good News, the NT sense of "Gospel" was the only meaning. Significantly, the understanding of the Gospel as representing the proclamation of the Kingdom of God and the salvation wrought by Jesus Christ did not change even after the evangelists committed the Gospel to the written form. There was, after all, only one Gospel, and the appearance of four records of it did not represent four different Gospels, but rather individual accounts of the same Gospel. But fairly early, the word "Gospel" was also attached to the written accounts. This is already apparent in Saint Justin's first *Apology* (46), when he writes of the "Memoirs of the Apostles which are called *Euangelia*," manifestly pointing not to the one Gospel proclamation, but to the four books (CCC 2763).

Before the original inspired Gospels there was an oral tradition on which the narratives were based (DV §§7–10, 18; *Sancta Mater Ecclesia*, II, "Elaboration of the Gospel Message") (CCC 76–79). *Dei Verbum* notes:

> *Indeed, after the Ascension of the Lord the Apostles handed on to their hearers what He had said and done. This they did with that clearer understanding which they enjoyed after they had been instructed by the glorious events of Christ's life and taught by the light of the Spirit of truth. The sacred authors wrote the four Gospels, selecting some things from the many which had been handed on by word of mouth or in writing, reducing some of them to a synthesis, explaining some things in view of the situation of their churches and*

preserving the form of proclamation but always in such fashion that they told us the honest truth about Jesus. For their intention in writing was that either from their own memory and recollections, or from the witness of those who "themselves from the beginning were eyewitnesses and ministers of the word" we might know 'the truth'" concerning those matters about which we have been instructed (see Luke 1:2–4). (DV §§18–19)

Sancta Mater Ecclesia cautions interpreters of Scripture to note three stages in the tradition, "through which the life and teaching of Jesus have come down to us." First, there was Christ's teaching, and when he gave his teaching orally, he "used the forms of thought and expression prevailing at that time" and "adapted Himself to the mentality of his audience so that His teaching would be firmly impressed on their minds and easily remembered by His disciples."

Second, there was the apostles' teaching, by which the apostles gave testimony to Jesus and proclaimed his death and Resurrection. In telling the story of Jesus's life and setting forth his words, the apostles used words and phrases that were ideally suited to their audience, including such forms of speech as "catechetical formulas, narrative reports, eyewitness accounts, hymns, doxologies, prayers, and similar literary genres commonly found in Sacred Scripture and the speech of that period."

Third, the four Evangelists set down in written form the apostolic teaching, applying the methods that were best suited to their specific audiences and above all for the churches:

Of the many elements at hand they reported some, summarized others, and developed still others in accordance with the needs of the various churches. They used every possible means to ensure that their readers would come to know the validity of the things they had been taught. From the material available to them the Evangelists selected those items most suited to their specific purpose and to the condition of a particular audience. And they narrated these events in the manner most suited to satisfy their purpose and their audience's condition. (Sancta Mater Ecclesia, II)

On the basis of this threefold pattern of tradition, we can see also how and why there are certain differences among the four Gospels. Such apparent discrepancies are in keeping with the intentions of the Evangelists. Our task as readers is to understand all the relevant factors involved in the origin and composition of the Gospels, in light of the intentions of the Evangelists. We must also remember that the teachings of Jesus were not merely preserved or passed on to be remembered; they were preached: "Thus the exegete, by scrutinizing the testimony of the Evangelists over and over again, will be able to illustrate more clearly the perennial theological value of the Gospels as well as the importance and necessity of the Church's interpretation" (*Sancta Mater Ecclesia*, II) (CCC 109–19). (*See also* **Inspiration**.)

III. NONCANONICAL GOSPELS

Aside from the four inspired Gospels, there were also many apocryphal gospels that found distribution in the first centuries of the Church (cf. Luke 1:1–4). These noncanonical gospels were notable for their frequently flamboyant literary style; their diverse heretical, Jewish, or Gnostic teachings that placed them in stark contrast to the authentic teachings of the four Gospels; and the different periods in which they were produced, from the first to the fourth centuries A.D. Four Gospels were recognized early for their apostolic origins; while many of the apocryphal gospels made claim to apostolic authorship, their claims were rejected by the early Church. Modern scholarship confirms the spurious origin of most of these documents. Among the more famous of the apocryphal gospels are

The Gospel of Basilides
The Gospel According to the Egyptians
The Gospel of Eve
The Gospel According to the Hebrews
The Gospel of Judas
The Gospel of Marcion
The Gospel of Matthia
The Gospel of Nicodemus (Acts of Pilate)
The Gospel of Peter
The Gospel of Philip
The Gospel Teleioseos
The Gospel of Thomas
The Gospel of the Twelve Apostles
The Gospel of Valentinus
The Protoevangelium of James
Genna Marias

(See **Apocryphal books**; see also **Canon of the Bible**.)

GOSPELS, THE FOUR *See under individual titles:* **Matthew**; **Mark**; **Luke**; **John**.

GOURD The word used in some translations for the plant that gave shelter to Jonah and that was suddenly destroyed (Jonah 4:6–10). It might have been a castor bean, which has very large leaves. The RSV calls it "a plant."

GOYIM *See* **Goiim**.

GOZAN (Hebrew *gôzān*) A region or district in Mesopotamia that was conquered by the Assyrians. Tiglath-pileser III transferred part of the population of Israel to Gozan (2 Kgs 17:6; 18:11). There is also a river in the district called Gozan (2 Kgs 17:6, 18:11; 1 Chr 5:26).

GRACE The supernatural gift that God bestows entirely of his own benevolence upon men and women for their eternal salvation. Justification comes through grace, and through the free gift of grace the ability is bestowed to respond to the divine call of adoptive sonship, participation in the divine nature, and eternal life.

Grace is more than the gifts of nature; it is a supernatural gift surpassing the attributes of created nature. The gifts of grace—sanctifying grace, infused virtues, actual grace, and the gifts of the Holy Spirit—are the indispensable means necessary to achieve the beatific vision. Grace also depends entirely on the initiative of God, surpassing the human intellect and will (cf. 1 Cor 2:7–9). "The grace of Christ is the gratuitous gift that God makes to us of his own life, infused by the Holy Spirit into our soul to heal it of sin and to sanctify it. It is the sanctifying or deifying grace received in Baptism. It is in us the source of the work of sanctification" (CCC 1999; cf. 2 Cor 5:17–18) (CCC 1996–2005, 2023–24). (For a full treatment of other topics related to grace, see **Baptism**; **Eucharist**; **Justification**; **Mercy**.)

The chief terms used in Scripture for grace were the Hebrew noun *ḥēn*, meaning "favor," the Hebrew verb *ḥānan*, meaning "to show favor," and the Greek noun *charis* for "grace."

I. GRACE IN THE OLD TESTAMENT

In the Old Testament, the words "favor," "grace," and "gracious" are all closely related.

"Gracious" (the same word as "favor" in Hebrew) may characterize physical appearance: "A gracious woman gets honor" (Prov 11:16). It may also refer to politeness or polish in speech: "He who loves purity of heart, and whose speech is gracious, will have the king as his friend" (Prov 22:11).

"Favor" appears most commonly in the phrase "find favor in the eyes of," meaning that the one showing the favor is disposed positively toward the one finding the favor. Often the proof of the favor is the granting of a request to one in an inferior position (Gen 47:29; Exod 33:13; 1 Sam 20:29; 1 Kgs 11:19). The superior party acts in a personally gracious manner, and the petitioner asserts no claim or right. This is especially important when "favor" is used to express the favorable disposition of God.

The word "gracious" is often used in petitions, as in Ps 27:7: "Hear, O Lord, when I cry aloud, be gracious to me and answer me!" The favor that is being sought is the willingness of a superior to accept a petition and to respond favorably. There is an implicit inequality between the petitioner and the one being petitioned and with that an assumption of the gratuity of the favor. Similar is the prayer, "Turn to me and be gracious to me, for I am lonely and afflicted" (Ps 25:16; cf. Ps 86:16; 119:132).

The verb *ḥānan* has a similar range of meanings. The verb appears seventy-eight times in the OT; it can mean "to be gracious" or "to show favor to," but it can also mean "to seek favor" when understood reflexively. It can mean the appropriate behavior demonstrated toward those in need, such as orphans or those in dire circumstances. When the word is applied to God, it might be understood broadly, as in Gen 43:29: "God be gracious to you" (cf. Num 6:25). It might also denote some kind of blessing, such as children (Gen 33:5). Above all, the verb expresses the powerful favor or concern of God in bringing deliverance and succor in times of trouble and danger, a theme especially prevalent in the Psalms (Ps 4:2; 6:3; 9:14; 25:16; 26:11; 27:7; 30:11; 31:10; 56:2; 77:10; 86:3). God shows great favor to Israel by delivering it from enemies (2 Kgs 13:23; Isa 30:18, 33:2).

Closely connected to the concept of grace as gratuitous favor is mercy (*ḥesed*), a term also used to signify God's steadfast love and his commitment to the covenant. That the terms are to be differentiated is made clear in Exodus: "I will be gracious to whom I will be gracious, and will show mercy on whom I will show mercy" (Exod 33:19; cf. Exod 34:6–7). This mercy is a gift and not a right, but it requires a relationship between God and the one who receives it—a relationship in which God is plainly the superior party. Both terms, however, imply that God's actions are entirely gratuitous. He is under no compulsion to show mercy and favor. (*See also* **Covenant**; **Mercy**.)

II. GRACE IN THE NEW TESTAMENT

In the New Testament, grace (*charis*) is understood in the light of salvation brought by Jesus Christ. The word "grace" itself appears most often in Acts and the Epistles. In the Synoptic Gospels it appears only in Luke (translated as "favor": Luke 1:30; 2:20, 52); it is also used in John 1:14, 16, 17.

Grace was seen as a general blessing of God toward people (Acts 14:26, 15:40; 2 Cor 8:1) and also as his goodwill toward Jesus (Luke 2:40). Such favor is given to those who ask (Jas 4:6; 1 Pet 5:5): as in the OT (compare Prov 3:34), God comes to the assistance of those in need. God's grace is itself sufficient (2 Cor 12:9; cf. Heb 4:16; 1 Pet 5:10).

"Grace" is part of many greetings and closings. New Testament epistles customarily begin and end with salutations of grace to their audiences, such as Paul's typical greeting "Grace to you and peace" (Rom 1:7, 16:20; 1 Cor 1:3, 16:23; 2 Cor 1:2, 13:13; Gal 1:3, 6:18; Phil 1:2, 4:23; cf. Eph 1:2, 6:24; Col 1:2, 4:18; 1 Thess 1:1, 5:28; 2 Thess 1:2, 3:18; Phlm lines 3 and 25; 1 Tim 1:2, 6:21; 2 Tim 1:2, 4:22; Heb 13:25; Titus 1:4, 3:15; 1 Pet 1:2; 2 Pet 1:2; 2 John 3; Rev 1:4, 22:21), a practice followed also in Revelation (Rev 1:4) and that summed up the saving work of Christ (Eph 2:8, 14). Grace is thus God's giving of himself in Christ in order to bring salvation, so much so that it became a central word for the whole of the Gospel (Eph 2:4; 1 Tim 1:14; Titus 2:11; Heb 2:9, 10:29). Acts sees a direct equivalence between the "word of grace" and the Gospel of Christ (Acts 14:3, 20:32, 11:23; cf. Gal 1:6; Col 1:6).

Ephesians 2 offers a useful teaching on grace, expressing the two categories of meaning attached to *charis*: "But God, who is rich in mercy, out of the great love with which he loved us even when we were dead through our trespasses, made us alive together with Christ—by grace you have been saved—and raised us up with him and seated us with him in the heavenly places in Christ Jesus . . . For by grace you have been saved through faith, and this is not your own doing; it is the gift of God" (Eph 2:4–6, 8).

First, there is the adverbial sense, by which is explained the way or conditions under which salvation has been achieved, that is by the gratuitous and entirely unmerited favor of God. The initiative was undertaken by God (cf. Rom 3:24; Eph 1:6; Titus 5:15–21). In Rom 3:24, Paul writes that sinners "are now justified by his grace as a gift, through the redemption that is in Christ Jesus."

Second, there is the grace that speaks of the content of salvation, the supernatural life offered by God that first comes to us in baptism (Acts 2:38–41; 1 Pet 3:21; John 4:14, 7:38–39; 2 Cor 5:17–18). Paul wrote: "For if the many died through the one man's trespass, much more surely have the grace of God and the free gift in the grace of the one man, Jesus Christ, abounded for the many" (Rom 5:14). Salvation is a free gift from God that is given gratuitously that we might partake in the divine nature and attain eternal life (John 1:12–18; Rom 8:14–17) and receive divine adoption

(CCC 1996–2001). We have no strict right to salvation on our own merits, for salvation comes from God's initiative (Rom 6:23; Titus 3:5) and demands man's free response.

As Paul notes, salvation "is the gift of God—not the result of works, so that no one may boast" (Eph 2:9; 1 Cor 4:7). Paul positions himself against those who would claim that salvation can be achieved through one's own work, on one's own merits (Gal 5:4; Rom 4:4, 6:14); "I do not nullify the grace of God; for if justification comes through the law, then Christ died for nothing" (Gal 2:21). Once grace is established in a person, good works proceed in Christ—from the predispositions provided by the Holy Spirit—and man's merit "before God in the Christian life arises from the fact that God has freely chosen to associate man with the work of his grace" (CCC 2008): "For we are what he has made us, created in Christ Jesus for good works, which God prepared beforehand to be our way of life" (Eph 2:10; Phil 2:13; cf. Heb 13:20–21). In this way, the life of the Christian becomes perfected and the very love for God becomes the impetus for the performance of works of mercy (Matt 25:34–40; Titus 2:14; Jas 2:14–26). Merit is thus to be attributed first to the grace of God and then to the willing collaboration on the part of man (CCC 2006–11).

GRAF-WELLHAUSEN THEORY *See* **Pentateuch**.

GRAPE *See* **Wine**.

GRAVE *See* **Burial**.

GRAVEN IMAGE *See* **Idol, idolatry**.

GREAT SEA The Mediterranean Sea (Num 34:6–7; Josh 1:4; 9:1; 15:47; 23:4; Ezek 47:15, 19, 20; 48:20).

GREEK LANGUAGE The language of the New Testament, as well as of certain **deuterocanonical** books of the Old Testament (see also **Septuagint**).

The language in which the entire NT was composed was common Greek (but see **Matthew, Gospel of**), known as koine (Greek *koinē*). Koine Greek served as the lingua franca of much of the Mediterranean world for nearly a millennium, from the fourth century B.C. to the sixth century A.D. In the wake of Alexander the Great's sweeping conquests, Greek emerged as the language of government and commerce. It was spoken by non-Greeks across the wide cultural arc under the influence of Hellenism, and its impact is visible in the vocabularies of Jewish Aramaic, rabbinical Hebrew, Syriac, and Coptic.

Koine Greek is a genetic descendant of the classical Greek dialects, mainly Attic, but with elements of Ionic and Doric as well. Gradually they intermingled into a unified language throughout the Hellenistic world.

The study of the language has been assisted in modern times by the discovery of thousands of papyrus documents (mostly in Egypt) and ostraca (shards of pottery used for short notes) in archaeological excavations. Such a body of writings permits a direct comparison between the Koine Greek that was commonly used for commerce and the Greek

THE GREEK ALPHABET

Greek Letters

Capital	Small	Name
A	α	alpha
B	β	beta
Γ	γ	gamma
Δ	δ	delta
E	ε	epsilon
Z	ζ	zeta
H	η	eta
Θ	θ	theta
I	ι	iota
K	κ	kappa
Λ	λ	lambda
M	μ	mu
N	ν	nu
Ξ	ξ	xi
O	o	omicron
Π	π	pi
P	ρ	rho
Σ	σ, ς	sigma
T	τ	tau
Υ	υ	upsilon
Φ	φ	phi
X	χ	chi
Ψ	ψ	psi
Ω	ω	omega

of the NT, and scholars have found that NT Greek is more closely related to Koine Greek than to the traditional Attic Greek preferred by many writers of the same period, such as Dionysius of Halicarnassus, Dio Chrysostom, and Lucian.

New Testament Greek shows still other influences, such as occasional Latinisms and an abundance of Hebraisms and Aramaisms. The language also changes subtly from book to book in the NT, as we would expect from different authors who varied in their own levels of education and possessed distinctive styles.

GRIESBACH HYPOTHESIS *See* **Synoptic problem**.

GUILT OFFERING *See* **Sacrifice**.

GUM A resin produced from various plants. Gum was a prized commodity in the ancient world (Gen 37:25; 43:11).

H

HABAKKUK, BOOK OF The eighth book of the minor prophets. The dramatic focus of the book turns around the Babylonian conquest of Judah, soon to take place, and the prophet's struggle to understand this imminent tragedy as a form of divine punishment. A note of confidence also sounds as the Lord declares that the just will not perish.

I. AUTHORSHIP AND DATE

Nothing is known of the prophet Habakkuk or his background. The name is related to the Hebrew root *ḥbq*, "to embrace," and many scholars suggest that it is taken from the Akkadian *ḥabbaqūqū*, a type of garden plant. On the basis of internal evidence, in particular the reference to the Chaldeans in 1:6, the estimated date for the composition of Habakkuk is put at sometime in the late seventh century B.C., between the battle of Carchemish in 605 B.C. and the invasion of Judah by the Babylonians in 597 B.C.

II. CONTENTS

III. PURPOSE AND THEMES

The main purpose of Habakkuk is to explain the great crisis that Judah was facing after the Babylonians had emerged as a world power and were threatening the very survival of the kingdom. Some theological explanation was necessary: it might easily appear to the bewildered people of Judah that the power of the Lord was unable to deliver his people from peril.

Apart from its short title (Hab 1:1), the book is divided into two parts. The first two chapters form a kind of dialogue between the Lord and the prophet. The prophet complains and protests, but he is taken up with great themes including the sovereignty of God and divine justice, and he questions the very ways of the Lord. God's first reply (1:5–11) is that divine justice is already unfolding in the form of the Chaldeans, a harsh and rapacious people who will deliver divine judgment. As Habakkuk then complains that cruelties are being permitted, the Lord replies (2:2–4) that judgment will come but that one must wait to see it. The Lord adds (2:4) that the just man lives in his faith while the arrogant carries with him the seeds of his own destruction. This idea was used in the New Testament epistles (Rom 1:17; Gal 3:11; Heb 10:38).

In the second part of Habakkuk (chap. 3), satisfied with God's responses to his complaints, Habakkuk writes of the woes to be suffered by the wicked and then delivers a magnificent lyric poem.

HABIRU *See* **Hebrew.**

HABOR A tributary of the Euphrates River; it is known today as al-Khābûr. The Assyrians settled a number of deported Israelites along the river following the conquest of Samaria in 721 B.C. (2 Kgs 17:6, 18:11; cf. 1 Chr 5:26).

HACALIAH The father of Nehemiah (Neh 1:1; 10:1).

HACHILAH A hill in the Judean hill country, near **Ziph**. David took refuge there when Saul was pursuing him (1 Sam 23:19; 26:1, 3).

HADAD

1. The god of storms, rain, and thunder among the Canaanites and Akkadians. (*See* **Baal**.)

2. The name of two kings of Edom before the establishment of the Israelite monarchy (Gen 36:31–39).

HADADEZER (Hebrew, "Hadad is help") The Aramean king of Zobah who was defeated twice by David (2 Sam 8:3, 5; 10:16; 1 Chr 18:3, 5; 19:16).

HADADRIMMON An ancient Canaanite deity connected with mourning "in the plain of Megiddo" (Zech 12:11). He is identified with the god **Baal** and with fertility cults.

HADASSAH (Hebrew, "myrtle") The name used for Esther when she is first introduced in the book of Esther (Esth 2:7).

HADES *See* **Sheol.**

HADRACH A district or place located north of Damascus, on the Orontes River, probably identified with modern Tell Afis. In Zechariah (9:1), it is named in connection with a prophecy concerning "the cities of Aram."

HAGAR An Egyptian handmaid, servant, or slave of **Sarah**, the wife of Abraham (Gen 16). When Sarah proved sterile, she suggested that Abraham take Hagar as his wife and so bear children (Gen 16:2). Abraham then had a son, Ishmael, by Hagar. When, however, Hagar became excessively proud of her son and held Sarah's sterility over her, Abraham permitted Sarah to treat Hagar with great cruelty and so caused Hagar to flee. An angel of the Lord instructed Hagar to return to Sarah (Gen 16:1–16). The place where the vision took place was named Beer-Lahai-roi (Gen 16:14).

After Sarah bore her son, **Isaac**, she insisted that Abraham cast out Hagar and **Ishmael** from the camp. Abraham was reluctant, but on God's instruction he sent them into the desert. When Hagar and Ishmael were in danger of death from lack of water, they received God's protection in the desert of Beer-sheba (Gen 21:9–21). When Ishmael grew up, Hagar found him a wife from Egypt (Gen 21:1–21).

Saint Paul declared the relationship of

Hagar and Sarah to be an allegorical one (Gal 4:24) that revealed the difference between the old and the new Law. Paul makes the two women represent the two covenants: representing the old Law, Hagar corresponds to the present Jerusalem, living in slavery with her children; representing the new Law, the Jerusalem above, Sarah is free and our mother through Isaac's line. Ishmael, the child of a slave, was born according to the flesh; Isaac, the child of a free woman, was born through the promise made to Abraham. Paul writes: "Now you, my friends, are children of the promise, like Isaac. But just as at that time the child who was born according to the flesh persecuted the child who was born according to the Spirit, so it is now also. But what does the scripture say? 'Drive out the slave and her child; for the child of the slave will not share the inheritance with the child of the free woman.' So then, friends, we are children, not of the slave but of the free woman" (Gal 4:28–31).

HAGGADAH (based on the Hebrew root *ngd,* "to announce" or "to tell"; also spelled *aggadah*). One of the two chief divisions of rabbinic Midrash; it encompassed most forms of exegesis that did not belong to the **Halakah**, or legal discourse, which was legally binding.

HAGGAI, BOOK OF One of the twelve minor prophets. It presents a message delivered between August and December 520 B.C. that encouraged the returning exiles to reestablish their community and to complete the second Temple (dedicated in 515 B.C.), for which the prophet envisioned greater glory, in a Messianic sense, than that enjoyed by the original Temple of Solomon. In his labors, Haggai was assisted by the prophet **Zechariah** (Ezra 5:1).

I. AUTHORSHIP AND DATE

Haggai was one of the first of the postexilic prophets. He carried out his prophetic ministry in the years following the return of the Jews from the Babylonian Exile (537 B.C.). The book itself indicates that Haggai composed his oracles in 520 B.C., the year work on rebuilding the Jerusalem Temple was resumed.

II. CONTENTS

The book of Haggai is made up of four prophetic declarations, each one headed by the date on which it was delivered:

1. The First Oracle (Hag 1:1–13) is dated on the first day of the sixth month (August) of the second year of Darius's reign (520 B.C.) and is delivered to **Zerubbabel** and **Joshua**. It urges them to resume the work of rebuilding and restoring the Temple. The result of this call was that work resumed within weeks (1:12–14).

2. The Second Oracle (2:1–9) was delivered on the twentieth day of the same month and was addressed to the same people. It foresees the future splendor and glory of the Temple, which will be more wonderful than the former Temple of Solomon.

3. The Third Oracle (2:10–19) was given on the twenty-fourth of the ninth month (November–December) and declares that as long as God's House is not restored, the Jewish people will suffer. The people must be purified, and their repentance must be genuine

repentance, not mere ritual. God will reward their change of heart.

4. The Fourth Oracle (2:20–23) is given on the same day as the third and is addressed again to Zerubbabel and Joshua. The oracle promises the Lord's blessings, including the promise, "I am about to shake the heavens and the earth, and to overthrow the throne of kingdoms; I am about to destroy the strength of the kingdoms of the nations, and overthrow the chariots and their riders; and the horses and their riders shall fall, every one by the sword of a comrade" (2:20).

III. PURPOSE AND THEMES

Haggai's chief purpose is to prod and encourage the Jews who had returned from the Exile to begin work once more on the Temple. After returning from Babylonia, the Jews had laid the foundations for a restored Temple, but political troubles caused by the Samarians prevented any further progress. The interruption lasted for well over a decade, a time that saw poor harvests, self-indulgence displayed among wealthy members of the Jerusalem community, and a decline in religious fervor. As the Persian Empire was troubled by internal difficulties that ended all possible obstacles to the project, Haggai spoke out that the time had come for work to resume.

Haggai begins with a review of the recent past and then proceeds into the future. The oracles are blunt, and the literary style is distinctly unadorned. Its practical purpose is plain—rebuilding the Temple. There is, as well, a deeper point at work, for several passages (Hag 2:7–8, 9, 21–24) are Messianic in their imagery and point to the glory of a Temple that will surpass any of the wonders of Solomon's Temple. The book's final passages make note of the promise of the Davidic dynasty as it is represented in Zerubbabel—the Messianic dynasty will endure despite tumultuous events that will eclipse the nations.

HAGGI (Hebrew *ḥaggî*) A son of Gad, grandson of Zilpah and Jacob (Gen 46:16; cf. Num 26:15).

HAGGITH (Hebrew *ḥaggît*) A wife of David and the mother of Adonijah (2 Sam 3:4; 1 Kgs 1:5, 11; 2:13; 1 Chr 3:2). She supported her son in his royal ambitions.

HAGIOGRAPHA The third part of the Hebrew canon of the Old Testament, after the Law and the Prophets. Also called the Writings, it is made up of Psalms, Proverbs, Job, Song of Songs, Ruth, 1 and 2 Samuel, Ecclesiastes, Esther, Daniel, Ezra, Nehemiah, and 1 and 2 Chronicles.

HAGRITES (Hebrew *hagrî*) A nomadic tribe that resided east of Palestine, in **Transjordan** (Ps 83:6). During the reign of Saul, the land of the Hagrites was occupied by the tribes of Reuben, with the help of the tribes of Gad and Manasseh (1 Chr 5:10, 19–22). Jaziz the Hagrite served as head of the royal flocks under David (1 Chr 27:30).

HAIL With thunder and lightning, hail strikes frequently in Palestine during the rainy season. Hail causes damage to crops and brings injury to both man and beast (Exod 9:18–34;

Hag 2:17). Hail was commonly mentioned in relation to God's punishments of his enemies (Isa 28:2, 17; 30:30; Ps 18:13; 148:8; cf. Ezek 38:22) and was used against the Canaanites (Josh 10:11).

HAIR Among the Israelites of the Old Testament, long, luxuriant hair was considered to be a mark of beauty (Song 4:1; 5:11), and both men and women wore their hair long. Men might braid their hair, like Samson (Judg 16:17), and some took great pride in their hair, as did **Absalom** (2 Sam 14:26), whose vanity cost him his life when his hair became entangled in tree branches and he was easily killed. It was also common for men to keep their hair trimmed (Ezek 44:20). Shorter hair—under the influence of the Greeks and Romans—was more fashionable by New Testament times (1 Cor 11:7–15). Women typically wore their hair long and were concerned with its appearance and care (Song 4:1; 1 Cor 11:15).

Nazirites were forbidden from cutting their hair until the fulfillment of their vow (see Num 6). Upon completion of the vow, the hair was cut off and burned (Num 6:1–21; Judg 13:5, 16:17; 1 Sam 1:11). Similarly, men or women might shave their heads as an act of mourning (Jer 7:29, 41:5, 7:29; Amos 8:10; Isa 15:2; Mic 1:16). **Baldness** was considered a kind of curse (2 Kgs 2:23; Isa 3:24; Ezek 7:18; Amos 8:10) and was shameful, especially among women (Isa 3:17, 24; 15:2; Jer 47:5). The use of hair as a symbol of supplication and honor was visible in the way that the woman washed Jesus's feet with tears and wiped them with her hair (Luke 7:38, 44), and Mary, sister of Lazarus and Martha, did likewise (John 11:2; 12:3).

HALAH A region in Mesopotamia to which Shalmaneser V or Sargon II brought some of the Israelites after the Assyrian conquest of Israel (2 Kgs 17:6, 18:11; 1 Chr 5:26). (*See also* **Habor**.)

HALAKAH One of the two chief divisions of the **Midrash**, with **Haggadah**. Halakah usually signifies that portion of rabbinic literature that focuses on legal matters. It was especially common to use Halakah to clarify or discuss legal matters arising from new or changing circumstances facing the community. (*See* **Midrash**.)

HALF-SHEKEL The amount of Temple tax that was to be paid by every Jewish male age twenty or older. It was the equivalent of two Greek drachmas, or a didrachma (Matt 17:24).

HALLEL (Hebrew from the verb *hālal,* "to praise") The name used for a group of Psalms that contain the phrase "Praise the Lord!" The listing includes several groupings: Psalms 104–106, 111–118, 120–136, and 146–150. Several of the Hallel Psalms were used during the three great feasts of the year: Passover, Pentecost, and Tabernacles.

HALLELUJAH A transliteration of two Hebrew words meaning "Praise the Lord!" or "Praise Yahweh!" a liturgical exclamation that is found at the beginning or the end of several Psalms (104–106, 111–113, 115–117, 135, 146–150). In the New Testament, the phrase occurs only four times, each time in Rev 19:1–6, where allusion is made to the use of **Hallel** Psalms in the Passover liturgy. In Rev 19, they are part of the victory hymn sung by the choirs of Heaven. The Hallelujah was adopted extensively into the Christian liturgy (CCC 1340).

HAM (Hebrew *ḥām*) The second son of **Noah** and the brother of Shem and Japheth (Gen 5:32; 6:10; 7:13; 9:18, 22; 10:1, 6, 20; 14:5; 1 Chr 1:4, 8; 4:40; Ps 78:51; 105:23, 27; 106:22). Ham entered the ark and so survived the Flood (Gen 7:13). After the deluge, Ham sinned against his father, Noah, when the latter lay drunk and unclothed in his tent, most likely by committing maternal incest (compare Gen 9:2 with the idioms in Lev 18:7–8 and 20:17). As a result, Noah cursed Ham's son, **Canaan**, who was probably conceived by Ham's sinful union with his mother (Gen 9:25–27). In the Table of Nations of Gen 10, Ham is listed as the father of Cush (Ethiopians), Misraim (Egypt), Put, and Canaan (Gen 10:6; 1 Chr 1:8). In effect, from the line of Ham emerged the notorious archenemies of Israel: Canaanites, Egyptians, Philistines, Assyrians, and Babylonians. (*See also* **Nimrod**.)

HAMAN A courtier who was promoted to the rank of vizier by King Ahasuerus (**Xerxes** of Persia) in Esth 3:1. He became a bitter enemy of the Jews when Mordecai refused to give him what Haman considered proper homage (Esth 3:2–5). Not content with ordering the death of Mordecai, Haman schemed to launch a pogrom against all of the Jews in Persia (Esth 3:6) by convincing the king that the Jews were disobedient to his rule and so deserved to be eradicated (Esth 3:7–11). Mordecai, meanwhile, appealed to the queen, Esther,

to intervene. With Mordecai, she maneuvered adroitly against Haman and foiled his plans. Not only was the pogrom prevented, but Haman was utterly destroyed. The king turned against him and became convinced that Haman had designs on the queen. Haman was thus hanged from the same gallows that he had intended to use to kill Mordecai (Esth 7:5–10). (*See* **Esther**.)

HAMATH (Hebrew *ḥămāt*) A city in Syria, identified with modern Hama on the Orontes River. The site was on the list of Asiatic cities conquered by Thutmose III of Egypt in the fifteenth century B.C. and was later occupied by the Hittites and Arameans (2 Sam 8:9). It subsequently emerged as a prosperous kingdom that opposed the Assyrians, although it eventually fell to **Tiglath-Pileser III** (r. 745–727 B.C.; 2 Kgs 17:24; 18:34; Isa 36:19), who forced the city to pay tribute. Under **Sargon** the city was destroyed, and many of its people were deported to Samaria (2 Kgs 17:24).

The "Entrance of Hamath" marked the northern boundary of Israel (Num 34:7–9; Josh 13:5; 1 Kgs 8:65; 1 Chr 13:5; Ezek 47:15, 16, 20). But the boundary was a political reality only under David, Solomon, and Jeroboam II of Israel (Num 13:21; 1 Kgs 8:65; 2 Kgs 14:25; 2 Chr 7:8; Amos 6:14). The exact location is uncertain. It may refer to the Orontes Valley or to the area at the entry of the valley between the Lebanon and the Anti-Lebanon (cf. Josh 13:5; Judg 3:3; Num 13:21).

HAMMURABI The sixth king of the First Amorite Dynasty of Babylon (r. 1728–1686 B.C.), best known for a collection of laws that were found on a stele at Susa in Elam in 1902. The Laws of Hammurabi were not the first such collection—the Laws of Ur-Nammu, Lipit-Ishtar, and Bilalama were older by at least a century—but Hammurabi's collection was more detailed, with 282 clauses. From them we learn much about the common legal traditions of the ancient Near East. (*See* **Law**.)

HAMON GOG, VALLEY OF (Hebrew, "the multitude of Gog") The name of a valley in Ezek 39:11, 15, where the armies of Gog will be buried after their final struggle with the people of God. (*See* **Gog**.)

HAMONAH (Hebrew, "multitude") The place in the **Valley of Hamon Gog** where the armies of Gog will be buried after their annihilation (Ezek 39:16). The location is uncertain, and this is the only reference to it.

HAMOR The father of **Shechem** (Gen 33:19). When Shechem raped Jacob's daughter, **Dinah**, Hamor arranged the marriage of Shechem with Dinah. But when Simeon and Levi exacted their revenge for the outrage upon their sister, Hamor was killed in the reprisal (Gen 34). (*See* **Dinah**.)

HAMUTAL Daughter of Jeremiah of Libnah, the wife of King **Josiah**, and the mother of **Jehoahaz** and **Zedekiah**, kings of Judah (2 Kgs 23:31, 24:18; Jer 52:1).

HANAMEL (Hebrew, "God is gracious") The cousin of **Jeremiah** (Jer 32:6, 8, 9) who sold his field at Anathoth to the prophet. The sale occurred during the Babylonian siege of Jerusalem (587 B.C.) while Jeremiah was in prison; it represented the hope for the eventual restoration of Judah following the Exile.

HANANEL, TOWER OF A tower in the north wall of Jerusalem (Neh 3:1, 12:38–39; Jer 31:38; Zech 14:10). The exact location and date of construction of the tower is uncertain, although it is known to have stood on the spot later occupied by the fortress of Antonia, which was placed at the northwestern corner of the Temple quarter during Herod's era.

HANANI (Hebrew, "Yahweh has taken pity"; a shorter version of Hananiah) The name of several men in the Old Testament.

1. The father of the prophet **Jehu** (1 Kgs 16:1, 7; 2 Chr 19:2; 20:34). He was also a seer (2 Chr 16:7).

2. **Nehemiah**'s brother, who carried to Nehemiah word of the sad state of Jerusalem (Neh 1:2; 7:2).

Other men named Hanani appear in Ezra 10:20; 1 Chr 25:4, 25; and Neh 12:36.

HANANIAH (Hebrew, "Yahweh is gracious") The name of three men in the Old Testament.

1. The son of Azzur and a false prophet from Gibeon who opposed **Jeremiah**. Hananiah spoke against Jeremiah's advice that Judah should continue to accept subjugation under Nebuchadnezzar, king of Babylon (Jer 28). He even went so far as to proclaim the impending defeat of Babylon and the return within two years of the exiles who had been deported to Babylon in 597 B.C., including King **Je-**

hoiachin (Jer 28:1–4). Jeremiah denounced Hananiah as a false prophet and prophesied Hananiah's impending death; the false prophet died that same year (Jer 28:12–17; cf. Ezek 11:1–13). The Babylonian destruction of Jerusalem soon proved Hananiah's prophecy false.

2. A son of **Zerubbabel**; he was also a descendant of David (1 Chr 3:19, 21).

3. A young friend of the prophet Daniel in the Babylonian Exile (Dan 1:6). Along with other intelligent nobles from Judah, he was selected to receive a Babylonian education en route to a position of civil service (Dan 1:3–5). The eunuch in charge of his formation renamed him Shadrach (Dan 1:7). Shadrach was one of the three young men who were thrown into the fiery furnace (Dan 3:23) and miraculously delivered by the Lord (Dan 3:24–30).

HAND The hand is often used in figurative language to describe the power or authority of a person. For example, the phrase "the hand of the Lord" expresses the power of God both to smite and to deliver (Num 11:23; Isa 9:7–10:4, 59:1), and similarly Jesus "stretched out" his healing hand (Mark 1:41; cf. Matt 3:12) to demonstrate his saving power. To be delivered into someone's hands means to be surrendered into that person's power (Gen 9:2). Metaphorically, the prophets spoke because the hand of the Lord was upon them (2 Kgs 3:15; Ezek 1:3; 3:14, 22; 37:1; 40:1).

Hands were laid on another person to impart a blessing, such as that of Jacob (Gen 48:14). Jesus placed his hands upon the recipient of his blessing (Matt 19:15; Mark 10:13). Notably, the imposition of hands was also part of the act of commissioning or ordaining, as when Moses appointed Joshua to succeed him (Num 27:18–21) and when the seven deacons were ordained by the laying on of hands (Acts 6:1–6). (*See also* **Orders, Holy, Sacrament of.**)

HANNAH (possibly a shortened version of **Hananiah**) The mother of **Samuel** (1 Sam 1:20) and the first and favorite wife of Elkanah the Ephraimite from Ramathaim. While Elkanah's favorite, Hannah was barren and suffered at the hands of Elkanah's second wife, Peninnah, who was the mother of Elkanah's children (1 Sam 1:6–8). Finally, Hannah went to Shiloh and made the vow that if God would grant her a son, she would devote him to the service of God. Soon she was pregnant and gave birth to Samuel (1 Sam 1:19–20); she also bore Elkanah three other sons and two daughters. Faithful to her promise, Hannah returned to Shiloh and gave her son Samuel into the keeping of the priests. Each year she returned with clothing for her son (1 Sam 2:19–20). The Song of Hannah (1 Sam 2:1–10), celebrating the power and security of the Lord, is one of several eloquent prayers by women in the Old Testament (*see also* **Deborah**). The **Magnificat** of Mary uses imagery from the Song of Hannah (Luke 1:46–55).

HANOCH The name of two men in Genesis.

1. The third son of Midian (Gen 25:4) and a grandson of Abraham and Keturah.

2. The first son of Reuben (Gen 46:9) and the ancestor of the Hanochites (Num 26:5).

HANUKKAH *See* **Dedication, feast of.**

HANUN The son and successor of **Nahash** (2 Sam 10:1–4; 1 Chr 19:1–4) as king of the Ammonites; he was also the brother of Shobi (2 Sam 17:27). Hanun received condolences from David upon his father's passing, but as the new king Hanun heeded the advice of his own nobles, who suspected that David's emissaries were actually spies intent on preparing the way for an attack (2 Sam 10:2–4; 1 Chr 19:2–4). Hanun thus humiliated the ambassadors, an act that led to war and the defeat of the Ammonites (2 Sam 10:6–12:31; 2 Chr 19:6–20:3).

HAPIRU *See* **Hebrew**.

HARAN The son of **Terah**, brother of Abraham and Nahor, and father of Lot, Milcah, and Iscah (Gen 11:27–32).

HARAN A city or region in northwestern Mesopotamia on the Balikh River. The city was an important commercial center owing to its location on the major trade routes in the Near East, in particular between Nineveh and the cities of Syria. Haran was also a major cultic center for the worship of the moon god Sin and for various astral cults. The city fell to the Assyrians in the thirteenth century B.C. (cf. 2 Kgs 19:12). **Terah** and his family, including Abram, migrated from Ur to Haran. Terah died there (Gen 11:31, 32; 12:4–5), and it was at Haran that Abraham received his call from God (Gen 11:31–32; 12). Abraham later sent his servant to Haran to find a wife for Isaac (Gen 24), and Jacob fled to Haran to escape the anger of his brother, Esau. Jacob married the two sisters Rachel and Leah, daughters of his uncle Laban (Gen 28–29), at Haran.

HARE There are several species of hare in Palestine, but the animal is mentioned only rarely in the Old Testament (Lev 11:6; Deut 14:7). It was considered an unclean animal.

HARIM (Hebrew *ḥārim*)

1. The name of the third of the twenty-four priestly families during the time of David (1 Chr 24:8).

2. A family of priests during the postexilic period; they returned from Babylon under Zerubbabel (Ezra 2:39; Neh 7:42).

HARLOT *See* **Prostitution**.

HAROSHETH The home of **Sisera**, commander of Jabin of Hazor's army; Sisera was defeated by Deborah and Barak (Judg 4:2, 13, 16). The exact location has never been determined with certainty.

HARP *See* **Music**.

HART The Hebrew word translated "hart," "hind," or "gazelle" signified any kind of deer, including the hind or buck. Although harts were found in Palestine in biblical times, they are not found in Palestine today. It was considered a clean animal (Deut 12:15; 14:5; 15:22) and was mentioned often as a symbol of grace and swiftness (Gen 49:21; 2 Sam 22:34; Song 2:9, 17; 3:5; 8:14; Isa 35:6; Hab 3:19).

HARVEST The harvesting or gathering of crops traditionally marked the beginning of the year for the Israelites, a tradition that changed only with the subjection of the kingdom by the Babylonians at the end of the seventh century B.C. After this, the calendar was maintained according to Babylonian custom, with the spring marking the beginning of the year. Indeed, the entire Israelite year was characterized by different aspects of agricultural activity. The year began with several months of ingathering, followed by four months of planting, the seedtime. The next month was devoted to flax gathering, followed by a month each for barley and wheat, and then two months for pruning and a month for harvesting the fruits of the summer.

The feast of Weeks, also called the harvest festival or the feast of Pentecost, was celebrated "seven weeks from the time you first put the sickle to the standing grain" (Deut 16:9) and was celebrated at the time of the wheat harvest (Gen 30:14; Exod 34:22; 1 Sam 6:13; 12:17). The feast of Weeks was the second of the year (following Passover). Israelites were forbidden to harvest their fields to their fullest extents in order to ensure that the poor might be able to glean some grain from them (Lev 19:9–10, 23:22; Deut 24:19–22). The preaching of the Gospel was also equated with the harvest (Matt 9:37).

HASADIAH (Hebrew, "God is kind") The name of two men in the Old Testament.

1. The sixth son of **Zerubbabel** (1 Chr 3:20).
2. The son of Hilkiah and the ancestor of **Baruch** (Bar 1:1).

HASHMONAH One of the encampments during Israel's journey to Canaan (Num 33:29–30).

HASHUBAH The third son of **Zerubbabel** (1 Chr 3:20).

HASIDEANS (derived from Hebrew, "pious ones") The name of a group of pious Jews at the time of the **Maccabees** who were noted for their fidelity to the Law and their support of the priest **Mattathias** and his sons in resisting the activities of the Seleucid overlords in Judah (1 Macc 2:42). Sixty of their number were massacred by Alcimus in one day (1 Macc 6:12). The event that precipitated their joining Mattathias was the slaughter of a thousand Jews who had hidden in caves outside Jerusalem so they could practice their faith and who refused to fight on the Sabbath (even when attacked) for fear of breaking the Law (1 Macc 2:29–38). Mattathias offered them a new principle, namely, that defensive action in the face of death was allowable, even on the Sabbath (1 Macc 2:41).

HASMONEAN DYNASTY (Greek *Asamōnaios*) The name of a family of high priests and kings who ruled Judea from around 135 to 63 B.C.; the family also wielded great influence in Judea from 165 until 37 B.C. The name of the Hasmoneans was derived from Asamonaeos, the father of **Mattathias** (according to Josephus, *Ant.* 12.263), although it does not appear in the books of the Maccabees.

In ruling Judea, the Hasmoneans filled the power vacuum politically between the collapse of the Seleucid Dynasty and the rise of Roman influence in Palestine. The dynasty first came to prominence as a result of Mattathias's rebellion against the anti-Jewish decrees of Antiochus IV Epiphanes in 167 B.C. His sons carried on the uprising as leaders, organizing resistance throughout Judea and achieving remarkable military success through **Judas**

Maccabeus. Judas defeated several Syrian armies before facing defeat. His capture of Jerusalem and rededication of the Temple in 165 B.C. solidified the family's position. Generally, the name **Maccabees** is used for Mattathias and his sons, and the name Hasmoneans for the descendants who ruled Judea. The rulers of the dynasty between 135 and 63 B.C. were:

• **John Hyrcanus** (r. 135–105 B.C.) The son of Simon who enjoyed the rule of Judea under the titles of priest and ethnarch. He proved an aggressive ruler, extending Jewish influence over Edom and compelling the Idumeans to accept circumcision. He then attacked the Samaritans and destroyed their temple on Mount Gerizim.

• **Aristobulus I** (r. 105–104 B.C.) The son of John Hyrcanus, he claimed the title of king. He came to the throne by imprisoning his mother—who had been named heir to John—along with his brothers. He was assassinated after ruling for only a year.

• **Alexander Jannaeus** (r. 104–76 B.C.) The brother of Aristobulus I, he was released from imprisonment by his sister-in-law, the royal widow Salome (whom he then married), and was given the throne. He devoted himself to the expansion of Hasmonean influence and ultimately during his reign the kingdom reached its greatest expanse, approximately the dimensions of the Davidic realm. This program of expansion entailed conflicts with Ptolemaic Egypt and the Nabateans. By the time of his death, he had very poor relations with the Pharisees, and he left instructions to his widow for her to improve the situation.

• **Salome** (r. 75–67 B.C.) The widow of Alexander Jannaeus, she presided over the gradual decline of the dynasty, although she did appoint Alexander's son, Hyrcanus II, to the post of high priest.

After Salome's death, a civil war erupted between Hyrcanus and his brother Aristobulus. To resolve the matter, both brothers sought the help of Pompey the Great, then engaged in his campaigns in the East. But when Aristobulus rejected Pompey's mediation, the Roman general used the crisis as a pretext to seize Jerusalem in 63 B.C. The Hasmonean Dynasty was effectively ended when Judea was attached to the Roman province of Syria. Aristobulus was taken to Rome, and Hyrcanus was appointed high priest and ethnarch.

HATE "Hate" in the Bible has a broad range of meanings. It sometimes means "love less" or "not love," as we see when the Lord loves Jacob but "hates" Esau (Mal 1:3) or when a husband "hates" his wife because he no longer loves her (Deut 21:15, 22:13, 24:3; Judg 11:7; cf. Gen 29:31; Mal 2:16). In other places, "hate" may imply genuine loathing (Gen 26:27; Lev 19:17; Deut 19:11; Judg 11:7; 2 Sam 13:22; 1 Kgs 22:8). Hatred of a family member was forbidden by the Law (Lev 19:17).

When speaking of God, "hate" was used in anthropomorphic descriptions, as we see in his love of Jacob and hatred for Esau. The image of God "hating" describes the insuperable gulf between God and idolatry (Deut 12:31, 16:22; Jer 44:4), injustice (Isa 61:8; Jdt 5:17), and especially sin and sinners (Num 10:35; Deut 7:15, 33:11; Ps 5:6; Hos 9:15; Sir 27:24).

In the New Testament, acceptance of the Gospel entails a conflict between love and hate in a way largely unknown in the Old Testament, as seen especially in 1 John. Christians must hate the life of sin and love Jesus more than everything and everyone else (Matt 10:37; Luke 14:26). Christians must love those who hate them (Luke 6:27), and must understand that the world will hate them (Matt 10:22; 24:9; Mark 13:13; Luke 6:22, 27; 21:17) because the world hates Jesus (John 7:7; 15:18).

HATHACH (Hebrew *hătāk*) A eunuch named by King Ahasuerus to care for Esther (Esth 4:5–12). (*See* **Haman.**)

HAURAN (Hebrew *hawrān*) The name of a region in the **Transjordan**, north of the Yarmuk. Hauran appears only in Ezek 47:16, 18. In the New Testament period, Hauran was part of the tetrarchy of Herod Philip (Luke 3:1). (*See* **Bashan.**)

HAVILAH (Hebrew *hăwîlâ*) A region mentioned in Gen 2:11–12 as being rich in gold, resin, and onyx and surrounded by the river Pishon. In the **Table of Nations**, Havilah appears as a descendant of **Ham** through Cush (Gen 10:7) and a descendant of **Shem** through Joktan (Gen 10:29; 1 Chr 1:9, 23). Ishmael lived in the region (Gen 25:18; 1 Sam 15:7). On the basis of its natural resources, some scholars place Havilah in southern Arabia (cf. Pliny, *Nat.* 12.23).

HAVVOTH JAIR *See* **Jair.**

HAZAEL The Aramean king of Damascus from around 844 to 804 B.C., or 842 to 800 B.C. A royal official in the Aramean court, Hazael was anointed by the prophet **Elijah** (1 Kgs 19:15–16), and his reign was predicted by Elisha. Hazael used the prediction to overthrow and kill **Ben-hadad**, his predecessor, and claim the throne. His reign was contemporaneous with **Jehoram** (849–842 B.C.), **Jehu** (842–815 B.C.), and **Jehoahaz** of Israel; he was filled with ambitions for expansion, in particular against Israel (2 Kgs 8:13, 28–29; 10:32–33; 13:22). He took part in the effort against the advancing Assyrians—he was dismissively described as "son of a nobody" by **Shalmaneser III**—and suffered defeat at Mount Senir. Damascus was then besieged but not taken, and Hazael was able to survive the Assyrian onslaught in 837–836 B.C., after which Shalmaneser ceased to campaign against him. Hazael's campaigns against Israel were marked by advances into eastern Palestine, and his capture of Jerusalem was prevented by a bribe offered to him by **Jehoash** of Judah (2 Kgs 12:17–18).

HAZARMAVETH An Arabian tribe that derived its name from Hazarmaveth, son of Joktan (Gen 10:26, 36; 1 Chr 1:20); the name was subsequently applied to a region in southern Arabia.

HAZAZON TAMAR An Amorite city located in southern Palestine in Abrahamic times. The inhabitants were defeated by Chedorlaomer (Gen 14:7). According to 2 Chr 20:2, it is the same as **En-gedi** on the western edge of the Dead Sea.

HAZEROTH A site where the Israelites halted during their Exodus from Egypt. At Hazeroth,

Miriam and Aaron spoke against Moses (Num 11:35–12:16; 23:17).

HAZOR

1. A Canaanite town in Galilee, north of the Sea of Galilee and identified with the modern Tell el-Qedah. Because the city was situated on a strategically important position along the main trade route from Damascus, it figured prominently in the conquest of Canaan (Josh 11). It was the seat of Jabin, king of Hazor, who headed a coalition against the Israelites (Josh 11:10) and was defeated. The city was destroyed by Joshua; it was the only one of the northern cities to be so treated (Josh 11:13). Hazor was then given to the tribe of Naphtali (Josh 19:36). In Judg 4, Hazor appears again as the city of Jabin, who was an enemy of the Israelites and who sent against them an army led by **Sisera** (Judg 4:2, 17). Once more, Jabin was defeated, this time by **Deborah** and **Barak** (cf. 1 Sam 12:9). The city was later fortified by Solomon (1 Kgs 9:15) and was captured and devastated by Tiglath-pileser III of Assyria (2 Kgs 15:29). The plains of Hazor (1 Macc 11:67) figured in the Maccabean War.

2. Several towns by the name Hazor were mentioned in Joshua (15:23–25) as being located in the Negeb, although nothing is known of them.

HE The fifth letter of the Hebrew alphabet (ה).

HEAD The chief member of the body, understood in the Bible as the ruler of the other members, and used metaphorically for the place or person first in rank. In a tribe or a community, the "head" was the chief person (e.g., Exod 6:14). For Paul, Christ is the head of humanity, the Church, and "every ruler and authority" (Col 2:10; 1 Cor 11:2–4). This image is given even more forceful proclamation in Ephesians (1:10; 1:20), in which stress is placed upon Christ's exalted status, "far above all rule and authority and power and dominion, and above every name that is named, not only in this age but also in the age to come" (Eph 1:21). Christ is the head of the Church, which is his body (Eph 5:23; Col 1:18); from the head life is given to the community and "the whole body, nourished and held together by its ligaments and sinews, grows with a growth that is from God" (Col 2:19). Christ is thus both the principle of unity and governance in the Church and its principle of life (Eph 4:6; 1:22). (*See also* **Body**.)

HEART The vital center of life in the body, mentioned over a thousand times in Scripture. Sometimes it refers to the literal bodily organ (e.g., 2 Sam 18:14; 2 Kgs 9:24; Tob 6:5; Ps 45:6), but far more often "heart" is used metaphorically to mean the emotional center or the seat of life (e.g., Jer 7:31; Mark 7:21–23; Luke 6:45; 1 Cor 2:9). Thus the condition of the "heart" describes the state of mind or moral condition of the person (Ps 24:4, 73:1; Mark 7:21; 2 Cor 5:12). The heart displays happiness and joy (Prov 15:13; John 16:22; Acts 2:26), sadness and grief (Ps 13:3; Prov 14:10, 13; 15:13; John 14:1; Acts 2:37), and fear (Ps 27:3).

God can scrutinize the human heart and discern all that lies within (Ps 17:3; Jer 12:3; Luke 16:15; Rom 8:27): "I the LORD search the mind and try the heart, to give to every man according to his ways, according to the fruit of his doings" (Jer 17:10). But God can also transform the human heart and cleanse it (Jer 4:4; 24:7; 31:33, 34; 32:39; Ezek 36:24–26).

In the New Testament, a change of heart is also stressed in light of the power of the Gospel (Rom 2:13, 5:5; 2 Cor 3:3 [cf. Jer 31:31–34]; Heb 8:8–13). God sends the Spirit into the heart (Gal 4:6; Rom 5:5; 2 Cor 1:22). Dwelling in the heart is Christ (Eph 3:17).

HEATHEN *See* **Gentile.**

HEAVEN The physical sky with its stars and planets, and the abode of God and the blessed, often imagined metaphorically as being in the sky.

I. *Heaven as a Part of Creation*
II. *Heaven as the Abode of God and the Blessed*
   A. *In the Old Testament*
   B. *In the New Testament*

I. HEAVEN AS A PART OF CREATION

The physical heaven was described by Old Testament writers as a "firmament," a vault or solid dome that arched over the earth and that separated the heavenly waters and the earthly waters (Gen 1:6–8; Ps 148:4). The waters of heaven fell upon the earth as rain (Gen 7:11, 8:2; Isa 24:18) through holes or windows that were also the means by which God sent down his blessings (Mal 3:10). In this heavenly place were stored rain, snow, thunder, and hail (Exod 9:22–35; Isa 55:10; Josh 10:11; Ps 135:7; Jer 10:13; Job 37:9, 38:22; Rev 11:19).

In a broader sense, "heaven and earth" were used together to signify the entire universe (Gen 1:1; Deut 4:26; Ps 121:2, 146:6; Mark 13:31; Acts 17:24). The heavens manifested God's glory; they were also the place where he displayed his anger (2 Sam 22:8) and gave sign of his power and judgment (Dan 6:27; Joel 2:30–31; Isa 64:1; Matt 24:30; Luke 21:11; Acts 2:19; Rev 15:1). Thus heaven, understood as the visible sky, was where he gave the sign to Noah of the covenant (Gen 9:12–17) and had an eschatological aspect, most so in the areas of final judgment, hope, and promise (Amos 8:9; Jer 4:23; Isa 51:6; Matt 24:35; Mark 13:24–26; Luke 16:17; 2 Pet 3:10; Rev 8:12; 21:1). In the final consummation, there will be a renewal of heaven and earth: that is, of the whole creation (Isa 65:17, 66:22; 2 Pet 3:13; Rev 21:1).

II. HEAVEN AS THE ABODE OF GOD AND THE BLESSED

A. *In the Old Testament*

Heaven was the place where God dwelt and maintained his throne (Gen 11:5, 19:24; Deut 10:14; 1 Kgs 22:19; Isa 6:1, 40:22, 66:1; Ps 11:4, 102:19, 148:4), an image carried forward into the New Testament (Matt 5:16, 6:9; Mark 11:25; Rev 3:12, 4:2). As the abode of God, heaven was also where the blessed were taken—Elijah went to heaven (2 Kgs 2:11)—especially as conceived in the NT (John 14:2; 2 Cor 5:1–10; Phil 3:20; Heb 11:16; Rev 11:12).

The OT also describes God as coming down from heaven (Gen 11:5, 7; Exod 19:18; Isa 64:3), even as he remains transcendent. Salvation history is revealed in God's activity in the world and his concern for the people of Israel (Exod 29:45–46; 1 Kgs 6:13; Zech 2:10–11). This was also seen in the image of the heavens opening up. (*See also* **Theophany.**)

B. In the New Testament

In the NT, the descent of God reaches its climax in the coming of Jesus Christ into the world through the Incarnation and birth (Matt 3:16; Mark 1:10; Luke 3:21; John 1:32, 3:13, 6:38). The kingdom proclaimed by Jesus is called the "kingdom of heaven" in Matthew (e.g., Matt 3:2; 4:17; 5:3, 10). Jesus ascended into heaven (Mark 16:19; Acts 1:9, 2:33) and was seated at the right hand of the Father (Matt 26:64; Mark 14:62, 22:69; Acts 7:55; Rom 8:34; Eph 1:20). He will return from heaven in the Second Coming (Matt 24:30, 26:64; Mark 14:62).

For the Christian, heaven is the reward and the true dwelling place (Matt 5:12, 6:20; Col 1:5; 2 Cor 5:2; Phil 3:20; Heb 13:14), where Christian citizenship is realized (Phil 3:20), the inheritance is received (1 Pet 1:4), the mansion is built (John 14:1–3), and a true home is found (2 Cor 5:1–5). Heaven is also the end of exile caused by sin (Gen 3) and the result of true conversion (Luke 15:18–21). Christian discipleship entails a share in Christ's Cross, Resurrection, and Ascension (John 3:13, 12:32, 14:2–3, 16:28, 20:17; Heb 1:3, 2:13). For those who die in God's grace, heaven is the perfect life with the Holy Trinity, where one sees God as he is, "face to face" (1 John 3:2; cf. 1 Cor 13:12; Rev 22:4). Being in heaven means being with Christ forever (Phil 1:23; cf. John 14:3; 1 Thess 4:17) (CCC 1023–29, 2794–96).

HEAVE OFFERING See **Sacrifice**.

HEBER (Hebrew ḥeber, "companion") A Kenite and the husband of Jael (Judg 4:11). Heber lived apart from the other Kenites in Galilee. He was an ally of Jabin of Hazor (Judg 4:17), although his wife murdered Sisera, Jabin's general, in Heber's tent when the general fled there after suffering defeat by Deborah and Barak (Judg 4:11, 17–23). (See also **Eber**.)

HEBREW (Hebrew 'ibrî) The popular understanding of the word "Hebrew" is as a designation of a member of the Israelites, or simply, a Jew. In Scripture, the word 'ibrî has a much more specific meaning; namely it was a term used for the Israelites by foreigners (Gen 39:14, 17; 41:12; Exod 1:16–19; 2:6, 9; 3:18; 5:3; 7:16; 9:1; Jonah 1:9) and by Israelites when speaking to foreigners and referring to themselves (1 Sam 13:19; 14:11; 29:3). The origin of the name is traced to Abraham's ancestor, Eber (sometimes transliterated "Heber"; Gen 10:24–25, 11:14–26; 1 Chr 1:18–19) and the genealogical references related to Abraham (Gen 14:13, 39:14, 40:15, 43:32; Exod 2:6; Deut 15:12; 1 Sam 4:9). The word "Hebrew" is first applied to the language of biblical Israel in the prologue to Sirach. (See **Hebrew language**.)

In the New Testament, "Hebrew" refers to an **Aramaic**-speaking Jew as distinct from a Greek-speaking Jew (Acts 6:1; 2 Cor 11:22; Phil 3:5). As a language, Hebrew is called in the Greek Hebraïs, or Hebraïsti ("language of the Hebrews"), and so was identified as the language of the Jews (John 5:2; 19:13, 17, 20; 20:16; Acts 21:40; 22:2; 26:14; Rev 9:11; 16:16). It is likely, therefore, that many references to "Hebrew" in the NT refer to what modern scholars would call Aramaic rather than Hebrew.

HEBREW CANON See under **Canon of the Bible**.

HEBREW LANGUAGE The language spoken by the ancient Israelites and the language in which most of the books of the Old Testament were composed. Hebrew is a dialect belonging to the Canaanite family of languages that were part of the northwestern Semitic language group (which included Aramaic, Ugaritic, and Amorite). Other dialects in the Canaanite family include Phoenician, Moabite, and Edomite. Canaanite is known from the second millennium B.C. and was spoken throughout Palestine and Syria. Hebrew is known in the OT as "the language of Judah" (2 Kgs 18:26, 28; Isa 36:11, 13; 2 Chr 32:18; Neh 13:24), or as "the language of Canaan" (Isa 19:18). Over time variations in dialect and pronunciation developed; in Judg 12:6, the variant pronunciation of "Shibboleth" distinguishes the tribe of Ephraim.

Hebrew remained the principal language of Israel until the end of the Babylonian Exile in the sixth century B.C. After the Exile, **Aramaic**, the common language of international affairs throughout the Middle East, became the spoken tongue. Hebrew subsequently declined and finally disappeared as the spoken language of the Jews, although it remained the language of literature and the sacred texts in rabbinical schools into the first millennium A.D., and developed into the language of the Mishnah and much of the Talmud. More developed than biblical Hebrew, this later Hebrew was influenced primarily by Aramaic. When the NT refers to the Hebrew language (cf. John 5:2; 19:13, 17, 20; 20:16; Acts 21:40; 22:2; 26:14), it is sometimes speaking of Aramaic, except in Rev 9:11.

The OT is written largely in Hebrew, with

THE HEBREW ALPHABET	
Letter	Name
א	'alef
ב	bet
ג	gimel
ד	dalet
ה	he
ו	waw
ז	zayin
ח	ḥet
ט	ṭet
י	yod
כ	kaf
ל	lamed
מ	mem
נ	nun
ס	samek
ע	ʿayin
פ	pe
צ	ṣade
ק	qof
ר	resh
שׂ	śin/šin
ת	taw

a few exceptions. Daniel 2:4–7:28, Ezra 2:8–6:18 and 7:12–26, and Jer 10:11 are preserved in Aramaic; Wisdom and 2 Maccabees were composed in Greek; 1 Maccabees, Judith, and perhaps the **deuterocanonical** portions of Daniel and Esther are available only in Greek translation, but they may derive from Semitic originals; Sirach and Tobit are preserved in complete form only in Greek, although most of the original Hebrew of Sirach and some of the Aramaic of Tobit have been found.

HEBREWS, LETTER TO THE One of the most profound sources of Christian teaching, the Letter to the Hebrews presents a complex study on Christology. The book stresses the superiority of the New Covenant over the Old, expresses the pattern for Christian living, and above all focuses on the priesthood and sacrifice of Christ. The work is more of a theological discourse or homily than a traditional epistle. The author himself terms it a "word of exhortation" (Heb 13:22).

I. Audience

II. Authorship and Date

III. Contents

IV. Purpose and Themes

    A. Christ as King and Redeemer

    B. Christ the Superior High Priest

    C. The Superiority of the New Covenant

    D. Our Response to Christ

I. AUDIENCE

The first verses provide no clue as to who the intended audience of the letter might have been, let alone where its readers might have been located. The title of the letter, "to the Hebrews," is the traditional one assigned to it, the consequence of the ancient belief that it was composed for Jewish converts to Christianity. Some modern scholars, however, have advanced the theory that the book was addressed to Gentiles of Hellenistic backgrounds. In favor of this opinion is Hebrews' use of the **Septuagint** for citations instead of the Hebrew Old Testament, the use of Greek rhetoric, and the possible influence of Philo of Alexandria. On the other hand, supporting the traditional notion of a Jewish Christian audience is the clear assumption that the audience is at risk of lapsing back into traditional Judaism (cf. Heb 6:4–6; 10:29), the many references to the OT, and the overall argument that the New Covenant is superior to the Old, which would not have been nearly so important to a Gentile audience.

The location of the recipients is also disputed. Various ancient and modern scholars and commentators have suggested an audience in Jerusalem, while others have proposed Rome, Corinth, or some location in Asia Minor. Because the book examines issues relevant to priestly activities and sacrifices, some have suggested that the book was intended for Levitical priests who had recently been converted (Acts 6:7). Another possibility is an audience of Jewish Christians in Italy.

II. AUTHORSHIP AND DATE

The authorship of Hebrews has likewise long been a matter of considerable question. The letter is anonymous, although the original readers apparently knew the writer (Heb 13:18–19). The very old tradition in the Eastern Church declared Saint Paul to be the author, a view not immediately shared in the Western Church. By the fourth and fifth centuries, however, the Eastern tradition had largely been accepted through the influence of Saint Jerome and Saint Augustine. The view of Pauline authorship was not disputed until the sixteenth century. Since that time, many scholars have rejected Paul as the author on the basis of the work's sharply different literary style as compared to recognized Pauline writings, its unique subject matter, and the absence of a Pauline signature and greetings.

As to who the author might have been if

it was not Paul, a number of possibilities have been advanced, including Barnabas, Luke, Apollos, Silas, and Clement of Rome. Origen reflected the lack of a consensus view when he declared, "God only knows" who wrote the epistle. In support of Pauline authorship are some notable similarities between the theology of Hebrews and Paul's theology. Certainly, the writer was at least influenced by Paul. The author mentions Timothy (Heb 13:23), suggesting also that he knew or was familiar with Paul and his missionary helpers (cf. Acts 16:1–3; Phil 2:19–24). The weight of evidence against Pauline authorship is ultimately not decisive.

Dating the letter is also difficult, but since it does not mention the destruction of Jerusalem in A.D. 70, Hebrews was probably written before that time (see, e.g., Heb 10:1–3, in which sacrifices are apparently still being performed in the Temple). Had the letter been penned after A.D. 70, the end of the Temple would have been a powerful piece of evidence for providing that the New Covenant had superseded the Old. The most likely date of composition, then, is in the sixties A.D.

III. CONTENTS

IV. PURPOSE AND THEMES

The Letter to the Hebrews develops masterfully a number of themes, but the most significant are the high priesthood of Christ, the superiority of the New Covenant over the Old, the progress of divine revelation in history, and the progress of the Christian people.

A. Christ as King and Redeemer

The Christological stress of the letter is established from the very start with a prologue that asserts the unique status of the Son. The author then develops the place of Christ as both King and Redeemer (Heb 1:5–3:1) seen through various OT references (1:5–14, arranged according to the triple coronation rite of ancient Near Eastern kings),

Christ's reign over the universe (2:5–10), and Christ's redemptive action that was achieved because of his Incarnation and willingness to assume our human nature (2:11–3:1).

B. Christ the Superior High Priest

The Priesthood of Christ is superior to that of Moses and Aaron and can, ultimately, be seen only in comparison to the priestly example of Melchizedek, the King of Salem who appears mysteriously in Genesis (Heb 3:2–5:10). As Christ is the "great high priest who has passed through the heavens, Jesus, the Son of God, let us hold fast to our confession" (4:14). This exhortation includes an important lesson in the covenant oath (5:11–6:20), that when God made a promise to Abraham, he swore by himself "since he had no one greater by whom to swear," while humans "swear by a greater than themselves, and in all their disputes an oath is final for confirmation" (6:13, 16), a truth that is the source of "hope that enters into the inner shrine behind the curtain, where Jesus has gone as a forerunner on our behalf, having become a high priest for ever after the order of Melchizedek" (6:19–20).

The letter proceeds to an explication of Christ's priesthood (7:1–10:18) and begins with the figure of Melchizedek as the type of Christ (7:1–28). The author declares that the priesthood of Christ is entirely superior to the priesthood of the OT. The Aaronic priests exercised a purely earthly ministry (8:4), were plagued by sin (5:3), were succeeded by others because of death and infirmity (7:23), and were unable to take away sin (7:27; 10:1–4). Christ, however, enjoys a heavenly ministry (8:1–6) through his Resurrection (7:16) and Ascension (9:24), is

free from the stain of sin (4:15), reigns forever as high priest (7:24), and removes sin by offering his life as an eternal act of redemption (9:11–14; 10:5–18).

C. The Superiority of the New Covenant

Christ also is more excellent by virtue of the covenant he inaugurated: "Christ has obtained a ministry which is as much more excellent than the old as the covenant he mediates is better, since it is enacted on better promises. For if that first covenant had been faultless, there would have been no occasion for a second" (Heb 8:6). Moreover, his sacrifice is immeasurably superior because it is the sacrifice of himself, made in the heavenly sanctuary of which the tent established by Moses was merely a type (9:1–10:18).

From this, the letter develops the preeminence of the New Covenant over the Old and underpins the argument in salvation history as it unfolded in the OT. Christ accepted the burden of the covenant curses triggered by the sin of Adam (2:5–15) and the broken covenants of Israel (9:15–17). In their place, Christ liberated the blessings that were promised by God in his covenants with Abraham (Heb 2:16–18, 6:12–18; cf. Gen 22:16–18) and David (Heb 1:5, 3:1–6, 5:5–6, 7:11–28; cf. Ps 110:4).

D. Our Response to Christ

The final chapters of the Letter to the Hebrews take up the author's concern with the response of the Christian to Christ (Heb 10:19–13:21). Christ's priesthood is the key to that life, for he opened the heavenly sanctuary, "and since we have a great priest over the house of God, let us draw near with a true heart in full assurance of faith, with our hearts sprinkled clean from an evil conscience and our bodies washed with pure water" (10:21–22). Giving added encouragement is the example of the faith of the great OT figures: Abel, Enoch, and Noah, Abraham, Moses, and the heroes of Israel. But the supreme model of faith is that of Christ "the pioneer and perfecter of our faith, who for the joy that was set before him endured the cross, despising the shame, and is seated at the right hand of the throne of God" (12:2).

HEBRON An important city in the mountains of Judah, to the southeast of Jerusalem; the modern city of Hebron is almost certainly on the same site. According to Num 13:22, Hebron was built seven years before the foundation of Zoan (Greek Tanis) in Egypt, the capital of the Hyksos. Therefore it was not in existence during the period of Abraham, who is more closely identified with nearby Mamre (Gen 13:18; 14:13). Also called Kiriath-arba ("city of four"; Gen 23:2; 35:27; Josh 14:15; 15:13, 54; 20:7; 21:11; Judg 1:10), Hebron was associated with various peoples before the conquest of Canaan, including the Amorites (Gen 14:3), Hittites (Gen 23), Anakim (Num 13:22), and Canaanites (Judg 1:10). The city was scouted by Israelite spies before the conquest (Num 13:22) and was eventually captured (Josh 10:36–37). It was then given to Caleb (Josh 14:13) and later assigned to the Kohathites; it is also listed as a Levitical city (Josh 21:11–13) and a city of refuge (Josh 20:7; 21:13).

The inhabitants of Hebron were supporters of **David** (1 Sam 30:26–31), and David reigned as king of Judah from Hebron for more than seven years (2 Sam 2:4, 11; 5:5).

When the leaders of the northern tribes offered David their kingship, he received them at Hebron and there was anointed king of a united people (2 Sam 5:1–4; 1 Chr 11:1–3). After that, he moved his capital to Jerusalem (2 Sam 5:7–12; 1 Chr 11:4–9). Nevertheless, Hebron was the place where six of David's sons were born (2 Sam 3:5; 1 Chr 3:1, 4), including **Absalom**, who revolted against his father and used Hebron as his chief center (2 Sam 15:7–12). Hebron was later fortified by **Rehoboam** (2 Chr 11:5–12). Finally, the city fell under the control of the Edomites (or Idumeans) following the destruction of Jerusalem (1 Macc 24:33), although it was recaptured during the Maccabean War (1 Macc 5:65). After the return from the Exile Hebron was inhabited by the tribe of Judah (Neh 11:25).

HEGAI A eunuch in the court of King **Ahasuerus** (Esth 2:3, 8, 15). His chief duty was to serve as overseer of a royal harem.

HEGEMONIDES Governor of Judea and its surrounding regions under Antiochus V Eupator (2 Macc 13:24).

HEIFER, RED See **Red heifer**.

HEIR See **Inheritance**; *see also* **Family**.

HELAM A city in **Transjordan**, east of the Sea of Galilee. Here David defeated an Aramean army under **Hadadezer**, king of Zobah (2 Sam 8:3; 10:16–17). (*See* **Hanun** for details.)

HELI *See* **Eli**.

HELIODORUS Minister of Seleucus IV Philopator, king of Syria (r. 187–175 B.C.). According to 2 Maccabees 3, he was sent by Seleucus to plunder the Temple treasury in Jerusalem and bring it to Antioch. While in the Temple treasury, however, Heliodorus was prevented from his crime by a mysterious rider in golden armor and two youths who delivered so many blows that he fell unconscious. Saved and healed by the prayers of the high priest Onias III, Heliodorus was chastised by the same mysterious beings and instructed to show proper gratitude for his life. Heliodorus then offered sacrifice to God and returned to Seleucus determined to put an end to the scheme against the Temple treasury.

HELIOPOLIS *See* **On**.

HELKATH-HAZZURIM A site near the pool of **Gibeon** where a skirmish was fought between the soldiers of David and Ishbaal, twelve on each side (2 Sam 2:14–16).

HELL *See* **Gehenna**.

HELLENISM, HELLENISTS "Hellenism" was the pervasive Greek influence that dominated the Near East after the time of Alexander the Great's conquests in 333–323 B.C. In the time of the **Maccabees**, a "Hellenist" was one who adopted the fashionable Greek culture, as opposed to the faithful Jews who kept to the Law and the traditional Jewish way of life.

Historians speak of the period from Alexander the Great (356–323 B.C.) to the advent of the Roman Empire (ca. 31 B.C.) as the Hellenistic era. In that time Greek culture, mixed with important Asiatic influences, flourished throughout the eastern Mediterranean and penetrated as far as India.

Long before the conquests of Alexander, Greeks had had contact with various cultures in the Mediterranean, but their cultural influence was limited. After Alexander, however, Hellenism was adopted as an element of statecraft, so that the Greek-Macedonian regime established Greek-speaking cities across Asia Minor and throughout Syria, Palestine, Mesopotamia, and Egypt. The populations were made up initially of Greek veterans, soldiers of the campaigns who became the most socially prominent leaders of the towns and cities. They ensured that Greek was the language of government and commerce and designed their cities along Greek models. The program of Hellenization was hastened by the Greek-Macedonian dynasties that were created following Alexander's death and the breakup of his far-flung empire (e.g., the Seleucids and Ptolemies).

For those peoples who were henceforth subject to these governments, social advancement depended on embracing Greek language and customs. Greek served as the common language of the towns and cities (*see* **Greek language**). Greek philosophy and literature served as models for intellectual thought, and Greek forms were adopted in art as far east as India. At the same time, the influences of the East were felt among the colonial Greeks. Local art forms and motifs were gradually assimilated, and Oriental cults began to spread westward.

For Jews living in the Diaspora, the influence of Hellenism was ultimately irresistible.

Greek language, customs, and culture were adopted to varying degrees, until the chief things that separated Jews from their fellow citizens were the Jews' adherence to the Law and their worship in the synagogue. Even synagogues were built in Greek style, however, and the Scriptures had to be translated into Greek (*see* **Septuagint**).

But there were some, notably among the Jews, who rejected Greek ways and saw Hellenism as a threat to their cultural identity and traditions. In Scripture, "Hellenism" or "Hellenization" was used to express "the Greek way of life" (2 Macc 4:13); the use of this term was in deliberate and pejorative contrast to "Judaism," or "the Jewish way of life" (cf. 2 Macc 2:21; 8:1; 14:38). Hellenism in this context was perceived as a danger and a threat to proper Jewish living. Indeed, the imposition of Hellenism by the Jews' Greek overlords sparked the Jewish rebellion of the Maccabees.

On the other hand, when Acts 6:1 (cf. 9:29; 11:20) refers to Hellenists, it means simply Greek-speaking Jews of the Diaspora. Unlike 2 Macc 4:13, the use of the term in Acts does not seem to imply that the Jews in question had lost touch with the Jewish way.

Hellenism was a powerful universalizing tendency across the ancient world, and that tendency was one key element in preparing for the spread of Christianity. The Panhellenic culture cultivated throughout the Mediterranean world and the common language spoken throughout prepared the world for a universal religion that spoke to the hearts of all peoples.

HEMAN The name of two men in the Old Testament.

1. One of the four sons of Mahol (1 Kgs 5:11), with his brothers Ethan, Calcol, and Darda. The vast wisdom of Solomon was said to be superior to that of Heman. According to 1 Chr 2:6, Heman was a member of the tribe of Judah, and the four are listed, along with Zimri, as the sons of Zerah.

2. A son of Joel listed in the genealogical list of 1 Chr 6:18–32. He was a member of the Levites, of the clan of Kohath, and was appointed head of one of the choirs in Jerusalem (1 Chr 15:16–17, 25:1; 2 Chr 5:12). In 1 Chr 16:41-42, Heman and Jeduthun were said to have sounded trumpets and cymbals (cf. 2 Chr 5:12).

HEPHER

1. The head of a clan in the tribe of Manasseh (Num 26:32, 33; 27:1; 17:2, 3).

2. One of the warriors in the service of David (1 Chr 11:36; 2 Sam 23).

3. A defeated Canaanite town, next to Tappuah (Josh 12:17). It was in the territory of Manasseh.

HEPHZIBAH (Hebrew, "my delight is in her") The wife of King **Hezekiah** and the mother of **Manasseh**, king of Judah (2 Kgs 21:1). There is no information on her origins.

HERESY (Greek, "sect" or "party") Knowing denial of the truths of faith. In the New Testament, the Greek term is commonly translated as "party," and does not have the force of the later Christian usage; it applied to the Sadducees and Pharisees (Acts 5:17; 15:5; 26:5), and the term was also used for the so-called Nazarenes (Acts 24:5). Paul begins the development of the term: "factions" and "party spirit" are vices (1 Cor 11:19; Gal 5:20). Similarly, in 2 Pet 2:1, "heresies" are the work of "false prophets."

HERMENEUTICS *See* **Interpretation of the Bible**.

HERMES

1. A Christian in Rome who received greetings from Paul (Rom 16:14).

2. A Greek god, known to the Romans as Mercury, the messenger of the gods. Paul was mistaken for Hermes by the people of Lystra (Acts 14:12).

HERMOGENES A Christian who, with Phygelus and "all who are in Asia," turned away from Paul (2 Tim 1:15).

HERMON, MOUNT A mountain (Josh 11:17) in the **Anti-Lebanon**, reaching a height of 9,232 feet (2,814 meters); its snows are a source for the Jordan River. Also known as Sirion (Deut 3:9; Ps 29:6), Senir (Deut 3:9; 1 Chr 5:23; Ezek 27:5), and Sion (Deut 4:48), the mountain was described as the land of **Og**, king of Bashan (Josh 12:4, 5) and the Amorite king **Sihon** (Josh 13:10, 11). After the conquest of Canaan (Josh 11:17; 12:1; 13:5), Mount Hermon was part of the land of Manasseh (1 Chr 5:23). Mount Hermon often appears in poetry (Ps 29:6, 42:7, 89:12, 133:3; Ezek 27:5).

HEROD AGRIPPA I The son of **Aristobulus** and **Bernice** and grandson of King **Herod the Great**. He was called Agrippa in honor of Marcus Agrippa, a key Roman official and pa-

tron of his grandfather. Herod Agrippa was born around 10 B.C. and spent most of his youth in Rome, where he ingratiated himself with Gaius Caligula, the future emperor (r. A.D. 37–41). Imprisoned by the aged emperor Tiberius after remarking that he hoped Caligula would one day succeed him, he was released immediately upon Caligula's accession and rewarded with much imperial favor. The emperor granted him a royal territory that had once belonged to the Tetrarch **Philip**, who died in A.D. 34, and the lands of **Herod Antipas** after his fall from favor. Upon the assassination of Caligula in A.D. 41, Herod managed to gain the favor of Emperor Claudius (r. A.D. 41–54), who confirmed his royal title and added to his lands Samaria and Judea.

Herod carefully promoted good relations with his Jewish subjects, especially in the enforcement of the Law. He thus persecuted the Christians, putting James the Apostle to death, and imprisoning Peter (who was miraculously delivered from prison, Acts 12). Herod died suddenly but horribly at Caesarea in A.D. 44 at the age of fifty-four (Acts 12:1–23).

HEROD AGRIPPA II The son of Herod Agrippa I. He was about seventeen years old when his father died, and thus the Roman emperor Claudius considered him too young to succeed his father. Over time, however, he managed to accumulate extensive lands, although these did not equal his father's. Like his father, he cultivated good relations with his subjects. He also attempted without success to convince the Jews to abandon their revolt against the Romans in A.D. 66; he failed to prevent the bloody conflict that followed, but his commitment to the Romans secured his safety and control over his lands. He died around A.D. 100.

Herod Agrippa II engaged in what is generally recognized as an incestuous relationship with his famous sister, Bernice, the widow of his uncle, Herod of Chalcis. With Bernice, he attended the trial of Paul before the Roman procurator of Judea, Festus (Acts 25:13–26:32). His comment that Paul had nearly convinced him to become a Christian was probably not a sincere one.

HEROD ANTIPAS A son of **Herod the Great** and Malthace, and the tetrarch of Galilee and Perea from 4 B.C. to A.D. 39. Antipas was one of the fortunate children of Herod the Great, as he managed to survive his childhood. Upon his father's passing, he harbored ambitions toward Judea, but he was named by Emperor Augustus (r. 27 B.C.–A.D. 14) to the throne of Galilee and Perea. Like his father, Antipas embarked upon a building program; he founded Tiberias and improved Sepphoris. Also like his father, he succeeded in winning the favor of the emperors, especially Tiberius (r. A.D. 14–37), who relied upon him as his eyes and ears among Roman officials in the East. He was wedded originally to the daughter of the Nabatean ruler Aretas IV, but he divorced her after becoming enamored of his brother's wife and Antipas's own niece, **Herodias**. In reply, Aretas attacked Antipas's territories, but Rome did not respond to the assault. Herodias also pushed him to his building projects and was the driving force behind his ill-considered request that Emperor Gaius Caligula give him the right to rule as an independent king. The paranoid Caligula deposed Antipas in favor of Herod Agrippa I. Antipas and Herodias were exiled to Lugdunum (modern Lyons, France).

Of all the members of the House of Herod, Antipas was the most frequently mentioned in the Gospels. He imprisoned and executed John because the Baptist denounced Antipas for marrying his brother Philip's wife while Philip was still alive (*contra* Lev 18:16). The execution was achieved by Herodias after Herod became intoxicated at his own birthday party and promised any reward to Herodias's daughter after her enchanting dance before him. By prearrangement, she demanded the head of the Baptist on a platter (Matt 14; Mark 6). Pontius Pilate later sent Jesus to Herod in an effort to free himself of the troublesome case on the pretext that Jesus was from Galilee and hence one of Herod's subjects. After Jesus refused to answer his questions, Herod sent him back to Pilate (Luke 23:7–15).

HEROD THE GREAT King of Judea from 37 to 4 B.C., and founder of the Herodian Dynasty. His father, Antipater, was an Idumean and minister of state to the family of Jannaeus Alexander. Through his father's influence, Herod and his brother Phasael attained considerable influence in the government, and in 47 B.C., Herod was named governor of Galilee. In 43 B.C., when Herod was about twenty-five, Antipater was assassinated, and Herod proved instrumental to Hyrcanus, ethnarch of Judea, in eradicating the party of Malichus and thus guaranteeing the political stability of the region. Such was his position in the kingdom that Hyrcanus was compelled by political reality to give his daughter, Mariame, to Herod as his wife, entailing a claim to the royal power. In 40 B.C., however, the Parthians invaded Palestine. Hyrcanus was captured, Phasael killed himself, and Herod fled to gather support from the Romans. Once at Rome, Herod won the backing of Marc Antony, including the claim to the throne of Hyrcanus as ethnarch, against the claim of Hyrcanus's brother Antigonus, who had been installed at Jerusalem. With Roman troops, Herod finally won his way into Jerusalem after three years of war. He spent the next several years as king, maintaining the patronage of Marc Antony and preventing the seizure of his lands by Queen Cleopatra VII of Egypt, whose ambitions encompassed most of the East. But when Antony and Cleopatra were defeated at the battle of Actium in 31 B.C., Herod was forced to contend with the emergence of Octavian (later Emperor Augustus) as the master of the Roman Empire. With considerable energy, Herod convinced Augustus of his worthiness to remain as Rome's chief Palestinian client ruler. The emperor confirmed his status and added to his holdings, and Herod used flattery and patient cunning to acquire Idumea, Samaria, Judea, Galilee, and Transjordan.

Suspicious of all enemies, especially those within his kingdom, Herod presided over a tyrannical and at times paranoid regime. His foreign origins made him unpopular with his Jewish subjects, and their dislike was compounded by his religious indifference and his tolerance of Hellenic cults in the Hellenized parts of the kingdom. Consumed by fears of conspiracies, he had many in the royal household executed, including his wife, Mariame,

and three sons, as well as many subjects who were accused of conspiring against him. Emperor Augustus was said to have joked—in a Greek pun—that it was safer to be one of Herod's pigs (*hus*) than his son (*huios*), because, as a Jew, he could not eat pork.

Herod was one of the most ambitious builders in Jewish history. He established various cities along Greek lines (e.g., Caesarea, Sebaste, Antipatris, and Jericho) and erected or strengthened a host of public buildings and fortresses, such as Masada, Herodium, and Alexandrium. To gain public favor, he launched a massive rebuilding of the Temple at Jerusalem in 19 B.C., although work was not completed until A.D. 64.

He is mentioned in the New Testament directly only in connection with the birth of Jesus (Matt 2:1; Luke 1:5) and the visit of the Magi and the resulting slaughter of the Holy Innocents (Matt 2). The narrative of the slaughter is consistent with his cruel and despotic tendencies. This penchant for murder and tyranny eventually undermined his ambitions to establish a permanent Hasmonean domination of Palestine, and he ultimately divided the kingdom among his surviving sons, Archelaus, Herod Antipas, and Philip. Herod finally died of a terminal disease in Jericho in 4 B.C.

HERODIANS A faction or party whose exact identity has been the source of much discussion among scholars. They are mentioned twice in the New Testament, both times with the Pharisees (cf. Matt 22:16–22; Mark 3:6, 12:13–17). In Mark 3:6, the Herodians plot with the Pharisees to achieve the death of Jesus; in

Matt 22:16–22 and Mark 12:13–17, they pose with the Pharisees the question to Jesus concerning tribute to Caesar. Scholars have suggested over the years that the Herodians were a religious faction, but today most believe that they were not connected to the religious establishment; they are more likely to have been supporters of the House of Herod. It is also possible that the term refers simply to members of the retinue or palace establishment of the Herods.

HERODIAS The daughter of **Aristobulus** (son of Herod the Great and Mariamne) and **Bernice** (daughter of Herod the Great's sister, Salome). Herodias figured prominently in the death of John the Baptist (Mark 6:17–29; Matt 14:3–12; Luke 3:19–20). She was born between 9 and 7 B.C. and was later married to Herod the Great's son **Philip**, to whom she bore a daughter, Salome (Josephus, *Ant.* 18.136). She divorced Philip to marry **Herod Antipas** after the two developed a deep attachment. Their relationship and subsequent marriage were incestuous by the laws of the Old Testament (Lev 18:13, 16; 20:21; cf. Matt 19:1–9; Mark 10:12) and were much hated by the Jews of Galilee. John the Baptist spoke out firmly against their union, and Herod had him imprisoned. Still, Antipas refused to have the Baptist put to death. Herodias, however, plotted his death (Mark 6:19) and finally brought about John's execution (cf. Josephus, *Ant.* 18.116–19) through a scheme launched during Antipas's birthday dinner (see also Salome).

She continued to scheme for her husband's benefit, but her efforts to improve his position with Emperor Gaius Caligula resulted in an order that he be exiled to Lugdunum (modern Lyons) in Gaul. Herodias was not included in the order—as she was the sister of Herod Agrippa I, at the time a favorite of the emperor—but she voluntarily accompanied Antipas into exile. Her decision was perhaps the only unselfish act she ever performed (Josephus, *Ant.* 18.252–53; *B.J.* 2.183).

HERODION A Jewish Christian in Rome who was greeted by Paul (Rom 16:11).

HESHBON A Moabite town east of the Jordan River, identified with Tell Hesban. Heshbon was the chief city of the Amorite king **Sihon**. It was captured by the Israelites under Moses (Num 21:25; Deut 1:4, 2:26; Judg 11:12–28) and later given to Reuben and designated a Levitical city and a city of refuge (Josh 13:17, 26; 21:37; 1 Chr 6:66). It was later in the possession of the Moabites (Isa 15:4, 16:8–9; Jer 48:2).

HETH The eighth letter of the Hebrew alphabet, usually transliterated *ḥ* (ח).

HETH *See* **Hittite.**

HEXATEUCH (Greek, "six books") A term used by modern scholars for the first six books of the Old Testament: Genesis, Exodus, Leviticus, Numbers, Deuteronomy, and Joshua. These scholars believe that the style and content of Joshua are closely related to those of the **Pentateuch.**

HEZEKIAH The king of Judah from around 715 to 687 B.C., and the son and successor of

Ahaz. His reign was marked by the great religious reform that placed Jerusalem at the heart of religious life, and by his foreign policy centered on gaining independence from Assyria. The judgment of 2 Kgs 18:5–6 (cf. 2 Chr 29:30) on him was clear: "He trusted in the LORD the God of Israel; so that there was none like him among all the kings of Judah after him, nor among those who were before him. For he held fast to the LORD; he did not depart from following him, but kept the commandments which the LORD commanded Moses."

Hezekiah acceded to the throne at the age of twenty-five and ruled for twenty-nine years (2 Kgs 18:2; 2 Chr 29:1). His mother was Abi (2 Chr 29:1), daughter of Zechariah. He was honored for his piety (2 Chr 32:20; Isa 38:10–20) and was determined to reverse his father's religious policies and launch a genuine religious reform. He decreed the destruction of the high places (2 Kgs 18:4) to eradicate the places of **Baal** worship; destroyed the **Nehushtan**, the bronze serpent made by Moses in the desert (Num 21:9); cleansed the Temple (2 Chr 29:3–36); renewed the celebration of the Passover (2 Chr 30:1–27); and reorganized the priesthood (2 Chr 31:2–19). All of these reforms had as their chief aim centralizing the worship of the kingdom in the Temple cult. He received guidance from **Isaiah** (2 Kgs 19:2–7, 20–34; Isa 37:2–7, 21–35) but met opposition from the prophet over alliances and rebellions against Assyria (Isa 30:1–17, 31:1–5, 37:33–35; cf. 2 Kgs 19:32–34).

The second key to Hezekiah's reign was his effort to address the problem of Judah's subjugation by the Assyrians. This question had direct ramifications for the religious life of the country, as the Assyrian influence promoted a loss of fidelity on the part of the Jewish people and a proliferation of idolatry. The events of his reign are attested both in Scripture and in a large number of ancient Near Eastern sources, although the exact dates of many events have been subject to scholarly debate, in particular the chronology presented in 2 Kgs 18:13–20:19 and Isa 38–39. What is likely is that Hezekiah waited patiently for the best moment to rebel against the Assyrians, and when **Sennacherib** succeeded as heir to Sargon II in 705 B.C., under difficult political circumstances, Hezekiah took his opportunity. Having formed alliances and made contact with Tyre, Egypt, and even Babylon (2 Kgs 18:21, 20:12–15; Isa 1–2, 31:1), Hezekiah withheld tribute and cast his lot with the rebellions against Assyria. Sennacherib, however, recovered, suppressed various revolts, and marched on Judah. According to 2 Kings (18:13–16), Hezekiah was forced to sue for peace and paid tribute. What followed is uncertain chronologically; Scripture describes the slaughter of 185,000 Assyrians by an angel of God (2 Kgs 19:35; Isa 37:36; 2 Chr 32:21) while Assyrian sources claim victory over Judah. Sennacherib returned to Nineveh and was later assassinated (2 Kgs 19:36–37; Isa 37:37–38; 2 Chr 32:21). Some scholars suggest that the events present two campaigns—one in 701 B.C. and another some ten years later—although there is no agreement on this supposition. Notably, Hezekiah forecast the eventual siege of Jerusalem and took steps to improve the city's defenses (2 Chr 32:5). Among his plans was the construction of an underground aqueduct excavated in the rock to carry water from the spring of Gihon to Jerusalem to keep the city supplied even in distress (2 Chr 32:30; 2 Kgs 20:20; Isa 22:9–11). This aqueduct still exists, and archaeologists have confirmed that it was commissioned by Hezekiah.

HIDDEKEL The Hebrew name for the river Tigris. It is mentioned as one of the four rivers that flowed out of the Garden of Eden (Gen 2:14; Dan 10:4).

HIEL (Hebrew, "my brother is God") A man of Bethel who rebuilt Jericho during the time of Ahab, king of Israel (1 Kgs 16:34), despite the curse upon the city (Josh 6:26). He established a new city "at the cost of" his eldest son, Abiram, and the city gates "at the cost of" his youngest son, Segub. The precise meaning of this expression is still uncertain; Abiram and Segub either died or were offered in sacrifice.

HIERAPOLIS A city in Phrygia, in the Lycus Valley of Asia Minor. The Christian community in Hierapolis was established by **Epaphras** (Col 1:7; 4:12) around A.D. 60 (Col 4:13), probably as a consequence of Paul's missionary labors (Acts 19:10).

HIGH PLACES Open-air cultic sites. The term "high place" is the usual translation of these worship sites. Although these sites were often located on hills, they were not all so placed (cf. 1 Kgs 11:7; 2 Kgs 16:4, 17:9–10; Jer 7:31, 32:35). They could be sited on mountaintops (Deut 32:13; Isa 58:14; Amos 4:13; Mic 1:3) or even by the sea (Job 9:8). The high places were dedicated to God or to Canaanite deities, and in the period before the establishment

of the permanent Temple at Jerusalem, such worship centers could be considered legitimate (Exod 20:24; Judg 6:26; 2 Kgs 14:4; 1 Chr 21:15). The first mention of them is in 1 Sam 9–10, likely a reference to Ramah.

After the foundation of the Temple, however, the high places had no part in orthodox worship of the Lord. A frequent complaint about wicked or insufficiently zealous kings was that they built or failed to suppress high places that were in competition with the Temple (1 Kgs 12:31–32; 13:33). Jerusalem was now the only legitimate center of worship.

High places were also dedicated to Canaanite and other foreign idols throughout the full span of the Israelite monarchy (1 Kgs 3:3; 15:14; 22:44; 2 Kgs 12:3; 14:4; 15:4, 35; 16:4) until the reign of Hezekiah. The destruction of the high places was a key element in his religious reform because of their role in pagan worship and infidelity to the covenant (Deut 12:13–14; 2 Kgs 18:4, 22; Isa 57:5–7; 65:7; Jer 2:20; 3:6; 7:31; 17:2–3; 19:5; Ezek 6:13; 16:6, 31; Hos 10:8; Mic 1:5). Although high places were restored briefly by Hezekiah's successor, Manasseh (2 Kgs 21:3), they were outlawed anew by Josiah (2 Kgs 23:5). Typically, these pagan worship sites featured an Asherah, a wooden stake or tree that symbolized the goddess of fertility; the *maṣṣēbâ*, the stone pillar that symbolized the fertility god; and altars for the sacrifices.

HIGH PRIEST *See* **Priest.**

HILKIAH The son of Shallum, father of **Azariah**, and high priest during the reign of **Hezekiah** (2 Kgs 22:4; 1 Chr 5:39–40; 2 Chr 34:9; Ezra 7:1–2). Hilkiah is best known for finding "the book of the Law" in the Temple during the repairs undertaken by King **Josiah**, which spurred on Josiah's ambitious reform movement (2 Kgs 22:8, 10, 12, 14; 23:4, 24; 2 Chr 34:14, 15, 18, 20, 22).

The name Hilkiah was borne by a number of other individuals in the Old Testament, including a Levitical gatekeeper (1 Chr 26:11); the father of **Eliakim** (2 Kgs 18:18; Isa 36:3); and the father of the prophet **Jeremiah** (Jer 1:1).

HILLEL A Pharisee, head and perhaps founder of one of the two leading Pharisaic schools in the late first century B.C. He was the counterpart of Shammai, leader of the other school. (*See* **Midrash**.)

HIND *See* **Hart**.

HINNOM, VALLEY OF *See* **Gehenna**.

HIPPOPOTAMUS *See* **Behemoth**.

HIRAM The king of Tyre from around 969 to 936 B.C. He was a friend and ally of both David and Solomon (2 Sam 5:11; 1 Kgs 5:15). Hiram provided Solomon and David with timber, raw materials, ships, and labor for their ambitious building programs (1 Kgs 5:15–32; 2 Chr 1:18–2:15), in particular David's palace and Solomon's Temple (2 Sam 5:7, 11; 1 Kgs 5:1, 10; 7:13). He also assisted Solomon's efforts to build a fleet of merchant ships at Ezion-geber (1 Kgs 9:26–28; 10:11, 22; 2 Chr 8:17–18; 9:10, 21). (*See also* **Ophir**.) In payment for these services, Hiram was initially granted food, but as

this was hardly adequate, Solomon gave him twenty cities in Galilee (1 Kgs 9:11ff.). A second Hiram was sent by King Hiram of Tyre to perform the bronze work needed for the Temple (1 Kgs 7:13–47; 2 Chr 2:12–15).

HISTORICAL BOOKS A group of books in the Old Testament that present a long history of Israel and Judah, interpreted in light of the **covenant**. This is not to say that the other books do not contain history, but only that the emphasis of these books is primarily historical.

The Historical Books are Samuel 1 and 2, from the end of Judges to the end of David's reign (ca. 961 B.C.); 1 and 2 Kings, from the last days of David to the start of the Babylonian Exile and the destruction of the Temple (587 B.C.); 1 and 2 Chronicles, from the reign of Saul (ca. 1020–1000 B.C.) to the return of the people from the Exile (538 B.C.); Ezra and Nehemiah, covering the reorganization of the Jewish community after the Exile (458–397 B.C.); 1 and 2 Maccabees, recounting the struggle against attempted suppression of Judaism (168–142 B.C.). The books of Esther, Tobit, and Judith are also considered part of the historical writings.

In the New Testament, the four Gospels and Acts are often called "historical" to distinguish them from the Epistles and the Revelation.

HISTORICAL CRITICISM *See* **Biblical criticism**.

HISTORY OF SALVATION *See* **Salvation history**.

HITTITES A people who pushed into Asia Minor and settled there around 2000 B.C.; they spoke an Indo-European language known from numerous **cuneiform** tablets. The Hittites emerged as a great empire in the ancient Near East. From their capital at Hattusas (identified with modern Boghazköy, Turkey), they pushed into Syria and into Mesopotamia, but the greatest extent of their imperial ambitions was reached under Suppiluliumas at the start of the fourteenth century B.C. The collapse of the Hittite Empire in the thirteenth century B.C. was rapid, and the state was succeeded by a series of smaller Syrian states (Neo-Hittite kingdoms) that were eventually subjugated by the Assyrians in the ninth century B.C.

Heth, the eponymous ancestor of the Hittites, is listed as a son of Canaan (Gen 10:15; 1 Chr 1:13), establishing a link between the Hittites and the Canaanites and thus establishing the Hittites among the pre-Israelite inhabitants of Canaan (Exod 3:8, 17; 13:5; 23:23; Deut 7:1; 20:17; Josh 1:4; 3:10). The Hittites were in Hebron at the time of Abraham, and he purchased the cave at Machpelah from Ephron, a Hittite (Gen 23:10; 25:9; 49:29–30; 50:13). Esau married a Hittite (Gen 26:34; 27:36; 36:2). David also used Hittites in his army, such as Ahimelech (1 Sam 26:6) and Uriah (2 Sam 11:3), and Solomon counted Hittites among his many wives (1 Kgs 11:1). Neo-Hittite states apparently had dealings with Solomon's kingdom (1 Kgs 10:29).

HIVITES *See* **Horites.**

HOBAB *See* **Jethro.**

HOBAH An area north of Damascus (Gen 14:1–15).

HOLINESS *See* **God.**

HOLINESS CODE The code of laws enumerated in Lev 17–26. (*See* **Law.**)

HOLOCAUST *See* **Sacrifice.**

HOLOFERNES A Persian general in the service of **Nebuchadnezzar**, king of Assyria. He was the principal enemy of the Jews in the book of **Judith**. During his siege of Bethulia, Judith beheaded him as he lay drunk in his tent. His head was then taken back to Bethulia and hung upon the city wall.

HOLY GHOST *See* **Spirit, Holy.**

HOLY OF HOLIES The inner sanctuary of the Tabernacle or Temple. (*See* **Ark of the covenant; Tabernacle; Temple.**)

HOLY INNOCENTS *See* **Innocents, Holy.**

HOLY ORDERS, SACRAMENT OF *See* **Priest, priesthood.**

HOLY SPIRIT *See* **Spirit, Holy.**

HOMOSEXUALITY In its general sense, homosexuality refers to sexual relations between men or between women. Moral theology teaches that active homosexual acts are morally indefensible: they are contrary to the natural law, and they close the sexual act to the gift of life. They also do not represent a genuine affective and sexual complementarity. For those reasons, homosexual acts cannot be approved under any circumstances. Moral theology and pastoral practice also recognize, however, that responsibility may be conditioned and diminished by compulsion and related factors. Compassion is due to those who struggle daily with this objectively disordered condition.

Christian teaching has been unequivocal in both Scripture and tradition (cf. CDF, *Persona Humana*, §8) regarding homosexuality. Scripture, especially, reflects this unchanging position, placing homosexuality within the wider biblical call to a high sexual ethic that includes opposition to abortion and the exploitation of children, adultery, rape, and homosexuality (cf. Gen 19:1–29; Rom 1:24–27; 1 Cor 6:10; 1 Tim 1:10). In its description of laws pertaining to sexual relations, Leviticus describes homosexuality as an "abomination" (Lev 18:22) and punishable by death (Lev 20:13) (CCC 2357–58).

HONEY Honey was found in abundance throughout Palestine and was used as the primary sweetener of foods in ancient times, especially as sugar was unknown. Metaphorically, honey described anything sweet or delightful (cf. Ps 19:11, 119:103; Prov 16:24, 24:13; Song 4:11; Sir 24:27, 49:2; Ezek 3:3; Rev 10:9–10). Honey was definitely a delicacy (Gen 43:11; 2 Sam 17:29; Ps 24:13), but it was not acceptable as a sacrifice (Lev 2:11), as it fermented easily. John the Baptist lived on locusts and wild honey (Matt 3:4; Mark 1:6; cf. Luke 24:43). The

place of honey as a prized and treasured commodity is best expressed in Scripture in Exodus (Exod 3:8; cf. Exod 3:17, 13:5, 33:3; Deut 6:3, 8:8, 27:3), when Moses declares, "I have come down to deliver them from the Egyptians, and to bring them up out of that land to a good and broad land, a land flowing with milk and honey."

HOPE The confident expectation of some desired good. Hope entails personal volition, and we must act to bring about what is desired; hope understands that what is desired will not necessarily be attained easily or readily. The opposite of hope is despair, a complete loss of confidence.

In Scripture, hope is intimately tied to **faith**. As a theological virtue, hope is the supernatural confidence that we will attain the kingdom of heaven and eternal life by placing our trust in Christ's promises and relying upon the grace of the Holy Spirit rather than our own strength. As noted in the book of Hebrews, "Let us hold fast the confession of our hope without wavering, for he who promised is faithful" (Heb 10:23). The hope of the Old Testament finds fulfillment in the New Testament.

I. *Hope in the Old Testament*

  A. *Abraham, the Model of Hope*

  B. *The Hope of a New Covenant*

II. *Hope in the New Testament*

  A. *Christ Fulfills the Hope of the Old Testament*

  B. *Hope in Struggle*

  C. *Hope, Faith, and Love*

I. HOPE IN THE OLD TESTAMENT

A. Abraham, the Model of Hope

The whole of the OT is suffused with the atmosphere of hope, for the OT is a history of God's promise to Abraham (Gen 12:3; 22:18), a promise to which God remained faithful even in the face of the manifest infidelity of the Israelites to their own covenant oaths (2 Sam 7:9, 16). Abraham is the model for hope in the rest of the OT, for "Hoping against hope, he believed, and thus became the father of many nations" (Rom 4:18).

B. The Hope of a New Covenant

The Lord was the hope of Israel (Jer 14:8; 17:13) and of all Israelites (Jer 17:7; Isa 8:17, 26:8; Ps 71:5). The Lord's fidelity to his people in the past (Gen 15:7; Ps 13:6, 33:18) points to the sure fulfillment of his promises for the future (Gen 17:8; Exod 3:8, 17; 6:4; Deut 1:8).

God's promise continued even as the unity of the kingdom was shattered and the kingdoms of Judah and Israel were formed. Hope was tested as the kingdom of Israel fell before the Assyrians in 721 B.C. and the kingdom of Judah fell before the Babylonians in 587 B.C. But through the prophets, such as Elijah, Elisha, Amos, Hosea, and Isaiah, God formed his people in the hope of salvation with a clear expectation of a new and everlasting covenant. Hope of this radical redemption and purification can come only from placing trust in the Lord, for only he can give true hope (Jer 29:11; 31:17). Whoever hopes in men is cursed (Jer 17:5), but whoever hopes in the Lord is blessed (Jer 17:7).

Jeremiah spoke of hope even as the threat of the Babylonians approached the kingdom of Judah and as Jerusalem was soon to be destroyed and the people deported to Babylon: "But this is the covenant that I will make with the house of Israel after those days, says the LORD: I will put my law within them, and I will write it upon their hearts; and I will be their God, and they shall be my people" (Jer 31:33; cf. Jer 31:31; 32:38). This hoped-for salvation is promised to all nations (Ezek 36; Isa 49:5–6, 53:11).

II. HOPE IN THE NEW TESTAMENT

A. Christ Fulfills the Hope of the Old Testament

In the NT, the hope of the OT finds its fulfillment in Christ.

The fidelity of God to his covenant promises throughout the OT was preparation for the Incarnation and the saving work of the Son of God. Jesus pointed toward the promise to Abraham and its final fulfillment when he declared, "Abraham rejoiced that he was to see my day; he saw it and was glad . . . Truly, truly, I say to you, before Abraham was, I am" (John 8:56–58). In the **Beatitudes**, Christ gave his followers the confident hope of heaven as the new Promised Land. He assured his disciples that they need not worry about the future; instead, they should have their eyes always set on the heavenly kingdom.

B. Hope in Struggle

The epistles develop this Christian idea of hope. The hope of the Christian is the glory of God (Rom 5:2) and the freedom from sin (Rom 8:20). "Let us hold fast the confession of our hope without wavering, for he who promised is faithful" (Heb 10:23). Hope is the "sure and steadfast anchor of the soul . . . that enters . . . where Jesus has gone as a forerunner on our behalf" (Heb 6:19–20). It is a helmet that protects us in our struggle for hope in salvation with the breastplate of faith and charity (1 Thess 5:8). The Christian is saved through hope, but it is hope in what is not seen: "Now hope that is seen is not hope. For who hopes for what he sees? But if we hope for what we do not see, we wait for it with patience" (Rom 8:24).

Hope for Saint Paul is not something easily obtained. Rather, it is found in suffering and difficulties and is sustained and nourished in prayer: "Rejoice in your hope, be patient in tribulation, be constant in prayer" (Rom 12:12). In the pilgrimage of the Christian life (1 Cor 13:13), we should "boast in our sufferings, knowing that suffering produces endurance, and endurance produces character, and character produces hope, and hope does not disappoint us, because God's love has been poured into our hearts through the Holy Spirit that has been given to us" (Rom 5:4–5).

C. Hope, Faith, and Love

Hope is also connected intimately with faith and love, the other theological virtues. The object of hope is rendered real through faith (Heb 11:1), which permits the perception of unseen realities, and love, which is faith in action. "For through the Spirit, by faith, we eagerly wait for the hope of righteousness" (Gal 5:5). The Holy Spirit is the wellspring of hope, and the Chris-

tian is called to demonstrate the same faith as that of Abraham, who "hoped against hope" (Rom 4:18–19). Confidence is found in hope because of our trust in God, who is the God of hope (Rom 15:13; cf. 2 Cor 3:12), and "the sufferings of this present time are not worth comparing with the glory about to be revealed to us" (Rom 8:18) (CCC 1817–21, 2090).

HOPHNI (from the Egyptian for "tadpole") One of the sons of the priest **Eli** and the brother of Phinehas. Hophni and Phinehas were priests like their father at the temple of Shiloh (1 Sam 1:3, 7, 9, 24). But they were utterly corrupt and abused the power of their ministry, stealing from the sacrifices and sinning with the women of the tent door (1 Sam 2:12–22). Though Eli warned them about their behavior and ordered them to reform (1 Sam 2:22–25), they refused to do so. Samuel, therefore, prophesied that because of their sins, Eli's family would be exterminated (1 Sam 3:13–14). Both brothers were killed at Aphek when they carried the ark of the covenant into a disastrous battle against the Philistines; the ark was then captured (1 Sam 4:4, 10, 11). Eli died upon hearing the news (1 Sam 4:12–22).

HOPHRA A pharaoh of Egypt, the fourth king of the Twenty-sixth Dynasty, who succeeded Psamtik II (Psammetichos) in 589 B.C. He sought to oppose the advance of Nebuchadnezzar, king of Babylon, and so supported King **Zedekiah**. He compelled the Babylonians briefly to lift their siege of Jerusalem (Jer 37:5–11), but he could not save the city from its eventual destruction. Hophra then gave permission for the Jewish survivors to settle in Egypt after 587 B.C. Jeremiah prophesied Hophra's end: "into the hands of his enemies, those who seek his life, just as I gave King Zedekiah of Judah into the hand of King Nebuchadnezzar of Babylon, his enemy who sought his life" (Jer 44:30). This came to pass when Hophra was overthrown by Amasis and later executed.

HOR (Hebrew *hōr*) A mountain on the borders of Edom where Aaron died (Num 20:22–29, 33:37; Deut 32:50; cf. Deut 10:6, which lists Aaron's place of death as Moserah). The exact location of Hor is uncertain.

A site where the Israelites encamped during the journey through the desert (Num 21:4; 33:37).

HOREB See **Sinai**; *see also* **Theophany**.

HORITES Also the Horim, Hivites, Hurrians, and Mitanni, a people of western Asia who settled in the Near East in the third millennium B.C. and invaded Mesopotamia and Palestine in the second millennium B.C. Their activities were well attested in ancient sources, especially as a result of their dealings with the civilizations in Mesopotamia, Syria, Egypt, and Asia Minor. The Horites exercised a considerable influence in the ancient Near East, especially after the sixteenth century B.C., especially through the Mitanni state in northern Syria and Mesopotamia. The Mitanni had contact with Egypt and took part in commerce and trade until their collapse in the fourteenth century B.C. Their territory was then a battleground between the Assyrians and Hittites until the time of **Shalmaneser I** of Assyria,

who annexed Mitanni in the mid-thirteenth century.

The Horite people were mentioned among the peoples who lived in Seir in the time of Abraham (Gen 14:6), prior to the Edomites (Deut 2:12, 22), and they were listed in the genealogy of Esau (Gen 36:20–22, 29–30; 1 Chr 1:39). If scholars are correct that the name Hivite should be taken to mean Horite, then the Horites lived in Shechem (Gen 34:2) and later in Gibeon, Chephirah, Beeroth, Kiriath-jearim (Josh 9:17; 11:19), and elsewhere (Josh 11:3; Judg 3:3). A portion of the population survived in Canaan into the eras of David and Solomon (1 Sam 24:7; 1 Kgs 10:20–21).

HORMAH (Hebrew, "destruction") A city in the **Negeb** region in southern Palestine. The city figured in several different events in the Israelites' conquest of Canaan. In one instance (Num 14:15; Deut 1:44), the Israelites were repelled in their invasion into southern Canaan and pursued as far as Hormah. In the second episode (Num 21:1–3), the name of Hormah ("destruction") was given to the city once called Zephthah after the Israelites captured the city and defeated the king of Arad. Hormah was listed as part of the territory of Simeon (Josh 19:4) and Judah (Josh 15:30; 1 Chr 4:30; cf. Judg 1:17; 1 Sam 30:30). The location is not known with certainty. Proposed sites include Tell el-Milh, Tell esh-Sheriah, and Tell Masos.

HORN The horn of an animal, such as a goat, ram, or ox, was used in Scripture as a symbol of power or strength (e.g., 1 Sam 2:10), especially in Psalms (Ps 75:5; 92:11; 112:9; 148:14). A horn could refer to the power of God (Ps 18:2; cf. 2 Sam 22:3; Luke 1:69). Conversely, the loss of a horn was a symbol of defeat or humiliation (Job 16:15; Ps 75:11; Lam 2:3; Jer 48:25). In apocalyptic literature, the horn represented the strength of kings (Dan 7:7–8; 8:3–22; Rev 12:3; 13:1, 11; 17:12).

HORSE First introduced into the Near East in abundance with the arrival of various Indo-European peoples in the early second millennium B.C., the horse had been known in Mesopotamia at least a thousand years before that. The Indo-Europeans, in particular the Hittite and Hyksos, used horses in the development of the **chariot** as an instrument of war. The chariot was subsequently used by the Egyptians (Exod 14:9, 23; 15:1, 19, 21) and by the armies of David and especially Solomon (2 Sam 8:4; 1 Kgs 5:6, 10:26). To judge by what we read in Scripture, the horse was mainly an animal of war and was seldom used in agriculture.

For Solomon, the possession of horses for war was one of his symbols of power and prestige; he claimed to have forty thousand stalls for horses (1 Kgs 4:26) and twelve thousand horsemen, and chariot cities such as Megiddo had extensive facilities for horses (1 Kgs 10:26). After Solomon, the kingdom declined, and by Hezekiah's time the cavalry was minimal: the **Rabshakeh** of Assyria sneeringly offered to give Judah two thousand horses—if King Hezekiah could find enough riders for them (2 Kgs 18:23; Isa 36:8).

Cavalry did play a role on the battlefield, especially from the time of the Assyrians, but massed cavalry was not given a priority in tactics until the Greek and Roman periods (cf. Hos 1:7; Ps 20:8, 31:1–3, 33:17). Alexander the Great's use of cavalry—in particular his companions, or *hetaroi*—became legendary in classical warfare. The Romans utilized auxiliary cavalry units but focused tactical practice on the legions in battle with remarkable success.

In prophetic writings, the horse was a symbol of speed (Isa 63:13) and strength (Job 39:19–25), while in apocalyptic literature the horse usually indicated war or conquest (Zech 6:2–36; Rev 6:2–8; 19:11, 19–21).

HOSANNA (Greek, "save, we ask") A liturgical invocation that occurs five times in the Gospels (Matt 21:9, 15; Mark 9:11; 11:10; John 12:13) and was chanted by the crowds as Jesus made his triumphant entry into Jerusalem at the start of the week that climaxed with the Passion. The term had liturgical origins as an invocation of the Lord; it occurs only once in the Hebrew Bible: "Save us, we beseech you, O Lord! O Lord, we beseech you, give us success!" (Ps 118:25).

HOSEA *See* **Hosea, book of.**

HOSEA, BOOK OF The first of the so-called minor prophets: The book bearing Hosea's name consists of a prophetic parallel between the author's marriage and the Lord's relations with his people. Just as the prophet was married to a faithless wife whom he would not give up, God was bound in covenant with an idolatrous and unjust Israel whom he would not desert but would chastise for purification. The tradition that Hosea inaugurated—of describing Yahweh's relation to Israel in terms of a marriage—found its completion in the New Testament.

I. AUTHORSHIP AND DATE

Hosea belonged to the northern kingdom of Israel; he began his career about the middle of the eighth century B.C., in the final days of the reign of **Jeroboam II**. He performed his prophetic ministry around the same time as the prophet **Amos**, and both challenged the same basic evils in Israel. Hosea continued to labor as a prophet until the fall of Samaria in 722 B.C. Little is known of Hosea beyond what is revealed in the book. He was a sensitive man who possessed a deep understanding of the covenant with the Lord and his temperament was very different from that of the prophet Amos.

While it is apparent that the text of Hosea underwent editing over the centuries, there is generally little question that the book of Hosea contains the prophecies of the prophet Hosea and that it was written in the second half of the eighth century B.C. It is likely, moreover, that the biographical details contained in the work originated with Hosea himself.

II. CONTENTS

III. PURPOSE AND THEMES

Hosea's purpose was to pronounce the divine judgment against Israel for its sin, comparing Israel's apostasy vividly to the adultery of a faithless wife. Where Amos, with his pastoral wisdom, spoke against the corruption of wealth and the perversion of justice that would bring the day of the Lord, Hosea was taken up chiefly with Israel's idolatry. What was apparent to Hosea, however, was that this apostasy was a symptom of deeper spiritual infidelity to the covenant and a damning alienation from God. As a consequence of its sin, Israel had moved away from God and sunk into moral decline. Such a grim state of affairs stood in appalling contrast to Israel's historical election. The life of the nation was to be measured by its fidelity to God and obedience to his covenant.

Hosea's own marriage serves as the perfect representation of God's relationship with Israel. The prophet relates that he was called by God to marry a certain Gomer, the daughter of Diblaim. She is described as "a wife of harlotry" and was utterly unfaithful, despite Hosea's efforts to nurture his relationship with her. She bore Hosea three children, all of whom he gave allegorical names: a son, Jezreel ("God will sow"), named for the sinful royal capital of Israel; a daughter, Lo-ruhamah ("Not pitied"); and another son, Lo-ammi ("Not my people").

The tragedy of Hosea's marriage is a

powerful allegory for God's relationship with his Chosen People. Hosea will not abandon his marriage and refuses to give up his wife, no matter how unfaithful she is. Likewise, God refuses to give up on Israel. She has been betrothed to him after her deliverance from Egypt and the forging of the covenant at Sinai, and she will be chastised for her infidelity. But God will permit the punishment only in the hope that Israel will see the error of her ways and return to the love that is proper to the marriage vows.

The adultery of Israel consists of idolatry, corruption, and injustice. Poisoned by sin, Israel is estranged from its spouse, and all the sacrifices in the world will do nothing to restore her relationship with God. Until there is a change of heart, sacrifices are empty gestures: "For I desire steadfast love and not sacrifice, the knowledge of God, rather than burnt offerings" (Hos 6:6). Only chastisement will bring that true restoration of spiritual well-being and true healing in Israel's right relationship with the Lord. But the love of God for Israel is true, just as is the love of a spouse for his bride, and his mercy will be shown when she returns: "And I will betroth you to me for ever; I will betroth you to me in righteousness and in justice, in steadfast love, and in mercy. I will betroth you to me in faithfulness; and you shall know the LORD" (2:19–20).

HOSHEA (Hebrew *hôśēaʿ*)

1. The first name of Joshua, son of Nun (Num 13:8, 16; Deut 32:44) before it was changed by Moses.

2. The son of **Elah** and the last king of Israel (ca. 732–724 B.C.; 2 Kgs 15:30). Hoshea as-sassinated his predecessor, **Pekah**, following the latter's defeat at the hands of the Assyrians under **Tiglath-Pileser III** in 732 B.C. The deed was done with the support of the Assyrians, and Hoshea proved a reliable vassal for some years. But in 724 B.C. he entered into an alliance with So of Egypt (2 Kgs 17:3–4) and conspired against the Assyrians. **Shalmaneser V**, king of Assyria, invaded Israel and took Hoshea captive. Samaria was besieged and taken, and the inhabitants were deported.

HOSPITALITY (Greek *philoxenia*, "love of strangers")

The practice of hospitality—meaning giving welcome to guests or strangers—was considered a great virtue and duty in biblical times throughout the Near East (Exod 22:21; Lev 25:4; Job 31:32). The custom derived in large part from the necessities of desert survival: travelers could survive only if they could rely on food, water, and shelter in the regions through which they traveled. As the practice developed, any guest or stranger was entitled to hospitality, and the person of the guest was sacred. Even an enemy could not be killed under such circumstances, at least not for three days. Special protection was due to guests even at great personal or tribal cost (cf. Gen 19:8). Food, water, and rest were expected, and no payment or return gift was to be accepted. The guest, meanwhile, was to behave appropriately and give no offense to his host.

The Hebrew books of the Old Testament do not use a specific word for hospitality, unlike the New Testament and the Greek books of the OT (cf. Sir 29:25; Acts 10:23; Heb 13:2; 1 Tim 3:2; 1 Pet 4:9; Rom 12:13), but the general principle is more than evident. The best-known example in the OT is Abraham, who hastened to give welcome to the three strangers (Gen 18:1–8) and prepared a feast for them (cf. Gen 24:1–49). Similarly, Lot showed hospitality in inviting two angels into his house (Gen 19:1–8), and when the townsmen of Sodom came seeking "intimacies" with Lot's guests, he pleaded with them to spare his guests, offering his own daughters as a means of satisfying their lust (Gen 19:6–11).

In the NT, Jesus stressed the importance of hospitality and considered it a way of distinguishing the just from the unjust (Matt 25:35, 43). As Jesus declared, "Foxes have holes, and birds of the air have nests; but the Son of Man has nowhere to lay his head" (Matt 8:20; cf. Luke 9:58); he thus relied upon others to welcome him into their homes (e.g., Mark 1:29; Luke 7:36, 9:51). Likewise, Paul's missionary journeys depended upon the hospitality of strangers across much of the Roman Empire, and he considered the welcome he received to be a Christian duty (Rom 12:13; 1 Tim 3:2; Titus 1:8; Heb 13:2). Commonly, Paul stayed with Jews, accepting the welcome of Gentiles only when he was refused it first by the Jews (Acts 14:28; 15:33; 16:15; 18:3; 21:6).

HOSTS OF HEAVEN God is called "LORD of hosts" ("Yahweh Sabaoth") some three hundred times in the Old Testament and twice in the New Testament (Rom 9:29; Jas 5:4). The name expresses the majesty and power of God (cf. 1 Sam 4:4, 8; Ps 24:7–10); it is used especially in apocalyptic contexts in reference to the "hosts of heaven." The title in the OT appears especially in the prophets (Isaiah, Jeremiah, Hosea, Amos, Micah, Nahum, Ha-

bakkuk, Zephaniah, Haggai, Zechariah, Malachi) and far less frequently in other books (e.g., 1 and 2 Samuel, 1 and 2 Kings, 1 Chronicles, and Psalms). God created the hosts of heaven (Gen 2:1; Ps 33:6; Isa 40:26; Neh 9:6), but readers still disagree as to exactly which hosts are meant. Some suggest angelic armies; others suggest creation itself (cf. Judg 5:11–21; Josh 10:12–14). In some uses, the armies of Israel are also termed the hosts of the Lord (Exod 7:4; 12:41).

HOUR The division of time into hours and minutes was unknown to the people of the Old Testament, so there was no Hebrew expression for this period of time. The day was divided typically into rough periods of dawn (Josh 6:15), the morning (Exod 18:13), noon (1 Kgs 18:29), afternoon (1 Sam 11:11), sunset (Gen 15:12), and night, which was itself divided up into watches. By the New Testament era, Jews had adopted the Greek and Roman division of the day into twelve hours, with the length varying according to the season (Matt 27:45; Mark 15:33; Luke 23:44; Acts 3:1); the night was broken up according to Roman custom into four watches (Matt 14:25; Mark 13:35).

Notably, the NT also uses "hour" to denote an event or the time at which some event takes place, in particular the "hour of Jesus." This "hour" is mentioned in all four Gospels, but is especially notable in John (John 7:30; 8:20; 12:23; 13:1; 17:1; cf. Matt 26:34; Mark 14:35, 41; Luke 22:35). In this hour, the Son of Man was glorified, meaning it was the time when Jesus was handed over to sinners and darkness: it was the hour of the Passion. The use of the term underscores the Passion as the fulfillment of Christ's life and ministry, and the completion of the divine plan of salvation at one particular point in time (cf. John 2:4; 7:30; 8:20).

HULDAH The wife of Shallum and a prophetess of Jerusalem during the reign of King **Josiah** (2 Kgs 22:14–20; 2 Chr 34:22–28). Little is known about her. Her husband was "keeper of the wardrobe" for the king, and she was consulted by Josiah after the book of the Law was discovered in the Temple. Her response was to deliver a prophetic oracle (in two parts, 2 Kgs 22:16–17 and 22:18–20) that included a judgment against Judah and a promise of comfort to the king. She is unique as the only female prophet named in 1 and 2 Kings.

HUNTING While hunting was a pastime in the ancient world, it is not mentioned frequently in the Old Testament. Nevertheless, the Israelites engaged in hunting for food (Deut 14:5; Jer 16:16; Lev 17:13; 1 Sam 17:35; 2 Sam 23:20; Job 10:16). Deuteronomy 14:3 lists the game that was acceptable: deer, the gazelle, the roebuck, the wild goat, the ibex, the antelope, and the mountain sheep. Such animals were, of course, subject to the same dietary laws as other animals (cf. Lev 17:14). Predators were also hunted (1 Sam 17:35; 2 Sam 23:20; Job 10:16).

Nimrod is called "a mighty hunter before the LORD" (Gen 10:9), and his name became a byword for a great hunter. Esau delighted in hunting (Gen 25:27), although he compares poorly with Jacob and was seen as a frivolous person who could be tricked out of his inheritance (Gen 27). Samson tore a lion to pieces with his bare hands (Judg 14:6). David was an adept hunter (1 Sam 17:34–37).

HUR A close companion and collaborator of Moses and Aaron. He and Aaron held Moses's arms up when Joshua led the Israelites to defeat **Amalek** (Exod 17:10, 12). He shared leadership of the Israelites with Aaron when Moses was on Mount Sinai (Exod 24:14). After that, he is not mentioned. Another Hur is named in several genealogies of the tribe of Judah (1 Chr 2:50; 4:1, 4); it is not certain whether this is the same Hur as in the Exodus account.

HURRIANS *See* **Horites**.

HUSHAI A trusted advisor—the "king's friend"—to King David and a member of the tribe of Benjamin (2 Sam 15:32). He is best known for his role during the rebellion of Absalom. On instructions from David, Hushai remained in Jerusalem after David's flight and gave his allegiance to Absalom in order to win his confidence. Hushai worked against Absalom's interests and kept David informed of developments through Zadok and Abiathar (2 Sam 15:33–37). Hushai won Absalom's full trust, going so far as to convince Absalom not to finish off David in favor of a strategy to gather stronger forces—against the wishes of Ahithophel, who urged faster action (2 Sam 17:5–14). David used this delay to recover his position and ultimately destroy Absalom's uprising.

HYKSOS An Asiatic people who invaded Egypt toward the end of the eighteenth century B.C., during Egypt's Second Intermediate Period (between the Middle Kingdom and the New Kingdom), and ruled Egypt for more than a century (ca. 1640–1532 B.C.) before the Egyptians drove them out. Although they were expelled from Egypt, the Hyksos nevertheless introduced horses into Egypt and broadened the sphere of the Egyptians' political and cultural involvement in Palestine and Syria. Israel's presence in Egypt both preceded and stretched beyond the Hyksos period.

HYMENAEUS (Greek *Hymenaios*) A Christian who was among those who lost faith and were excommunicated ("delivered to Satan so that they may learn not to blaspheme," 1 Tim 1:20). He lived apparently in Ephesus (1 Tim 1:3) and was associated in his loss of faith with Alexander (1 Tim 1:20) and Philetus (2 Tim 2:17). Paul condemned him for "rejecting conscience" and hence making "a shipwreck" of his faith (1 Tim 1:19).

HYMN A song of praise to God. The Psalms were the chief source of hymns in the Old Testament (e.g., Ps 8, 19, 29, 33, 65, 100, 103–105, 135–136, 145–150), although they are found in many other places (Exod 15:1–18; Judg 5:9–16, 12:13–25; 1 Sam 2:1–10; Isa 42:10–12, 44:23, 52:9–10; Sir 39:14–35, 42:15–43:33). The structure of these hymns may be loose, but generally hymns in the Psalms begin with an introduction that is an invitation to praise God, followed by an enumeration of the reasons for such praise, including God's titles, attributes, and glorious works. The conclusion often reiterates the invitation to praise or returns to the theme established in the introduction. Some hymns might be entirely an invitation to

praise, such as Ps 150, with its recurring refrain of "Praise him . . ."

In the New Testament, a hymn was likewise a song of praise to God (Matt 26:30; Mark 14:26; Acts 16:25), and some of Scripture's most cherished hymns were contained in the Gospel of Luke, the Magnificat (Luke 1:46–55), Benedictus (Luke 1:68–79), and Nunc Dimittis (Luke 2:29–32). It is likely that the early Christian communities included hymns in their liturgies (cf. Acts 16:25; 1 Cor 14:26; Eph 5:19). Paul used the term "hymn" (Eph 5:19; Col 3:16) and included some notable hymn elements (Phil 2:5–11; Col 1:13–20; 1 Tim 3:16), as did Revelation (4:8; 5:9–10; 7:10–8:1; 11:17; 15:3; 19:1–8).

HYPOSTATIC UNION *See* **Jesus Christ**.

HYRCANUS, JOHN I *See* **Hasmonean Dynasty**.

HYSSOP A plant noted for its dense leaves and its habit of growing on walls (1 Kgs 4:33; cf. Lev 14:6; Num 19:6; Heb 9:19). Scholars believe that the hyssop in Scripture was the herb we call marjoram. Hyssop was used especially in liturgical rites for sprinkling the blood of the Passover on the doorposts in Egypt (Exod 12:21–22; cf. Num 19:18; Heb 9:19). Hyssop was used also in the purification of lepers (Lev 14:4–6) and the house of a leper (Lev 14:49–52). John (John 19:29; cf. Matt 27:48; Mark 15:36) makes mention of a branch of hyssop used to offer Jesus a sponge soaked in vinegar. This is probably an allusion to the use of hyssop in the Passover, dipped in the blood of the Paschal lamb.

J

IBHAR One of the sons of David, born in Jerusalem (2 Sam 5:15; 1 Chr 3:6; 14:5). The name of his mother is not known.

IBLEAM A city in the territory of Issachar; it was later given to Manasseh, although the Israelites were unable to oust the Canaanite inhabitants (Josh 17:11–12; Judg 1:27). It was also a **Levitical city** (1 Chr 6:55).

IBZAN (Hebrew, "swift") One of the minor judges (Judg 12:8–10). A native of Bethlehem, he fathered thirty sons and thirty daughters, for all of whom he arranged marriages outside his clan.

ICHABOD (Hebrew, "no glory") The son of Phinehas and the grandson of Eli (1 Sam 4:19–21; 14:3). His birth occurred prematurely when his mother was shocked to learn that the ark of the covenant had been captured by the Philistines and that her husband and father-in-law were dead. His name thus reflected the great disaster.

ICONIUM A city in Lycaonia in central Asia Minor, in the Roman province of **Galatia**.

Paul visited the city on his missionary journeys (Acts 13:51; 14:1, 19, 21; 16:2).

IDDO A prophet whose writings were used by the Chronicler in the account of the reigns of Jereboam (2 Chr 9:29), Rehoboam (2 Chr 12:15), and Abijah (2 Chr 13:22).

IDOL, IDOLATRY (Greek *eidōlon*, "image") An idol is a representation of a deity created for the purpose of receiving worship and divine honors. Idolatry is the sacred worship given to the idols themselves. Among the Israelites all forms of idolatry and idol worship were viewed negatively and firmly prohibited, especially in the **Ten Commandments**: "I am the Lord your God . . . You shall have no other gods before me. You shall not make for yourself a graven image, or any likeness of anything that is in heaven above, or that is in the earth beneath, or that is in the water under the earth; you shall not bow down to them or serve them" (Exod 20:2–5; cf. Lev 26:1; Deut 4:16). The struggle against idolatry was a major concern in the Old Testament writings and was of particular concern to the prophets.

Idols were more to ancient cultures than

mere representations of their deities. The idol was the means by which the god could be appeased, worshipped, mollified, and communicated with. Thus the idol was treated with the same reverence and awe as the god itself. It was common for the idol to be given food offerings, to be washed and dressed, to be offered songs and sacrifices—in effect to receive all that might be given to the god.

The Israelites prohibited idol worship and enforced that prohibition with determination—a practice that was without parallel in the ancient world. No image was sufficient to represent the Lord, whose transcendence defied all possible depiction. To make an idol of God was to reduce him or place limitations on his supremacy over nature and all of creation; idols would bring him to the level of the "abominations" of Egypt and Canaan.

For that reason, idolatry was also considered a form of treason against God's majesty and a violation of the covenant oaths made with the Lord. Hence, idolatry is often described in terms of infidelity or adultery (cf. Exod 20:4; Isa 57:8; Jer 2:2, 3:14, 13:27, 31:32; Hos 2:16; 3:1).

Nevertheless, idolatry was a chronic challenge in the history of Israel, and the use of the high places for idol worship was a problem throughout the period of the Israelite monarchy. Hezekiah made the destruction of these cultic sites a priority in his policy of religious reform (Deut 12:13–14; 2 Kgs 18:4, 22; Isa 57:5–7; 65:7; Jer 2:20; 3:6; 7:31; 17:2–3; 19:5; Ezek 6:13; 16:6, 31; Hos 10:8; Mic 1:5).

Old Testament writers often mock the weakness of idols, as is summed up in the following: "Our God is in the heavens; he does whatever he pleases. Their idols are silver and gold, the work of men's hands. They have mouths, but do not speak; eyes, but do not see. They have ears, but do not hear; noses, but do not smell. They have hands, but do not feel; feet, but do not walk; and they do not make a sound in their throat" (Ps 115:3–7). Similarly, Isa 45:20 dismisses those "who carry about their wooden idols, and keep on praying to a god that cannot save."

Often the writers target in particular the manufacture of idols (Wis 13:10; Isa 40:19, 41:6, 44:9–20; Jer 10:2–9; Hab 2:18). By New Testament times, the idol trade was an important industry. Gods such as Diana (Acts 19:35) and Mercury and Jupiter (Acts 14:10–11; 19:35) were immensely popular in the cities of Asia Minor; the silversmiths of Ephesus sparked a riot when they feared that Paul's preaching threatened their livelihood (Acts 19–20). There was a bewildering array of pagan temples and altars in Athens (Acts 17:16) and they were a key element in the state religion of the Roman Empire, so much so that Christians were charged with treason for refusing to take part and to make sacrifices to the emperor.

In spite of the warnings against idolatry, Scripture makes clear that the use of images, including icons, statues, paintings, and medals, is not itself prohibited as idolatry. The objects in question are not idols: no form of adoration, sacrifice, or divine worship is given to them. They merely represent those whom they depict, to whom the real honor is given. Using images of the Blessed Virgin Mary and the saints does not suggest divine worship;

such veneration is secondary to the proper worship reserved for God alone. These teachings have been affirmed throughout Church history, most notably by the Council of Nicaea in 787, the Council of Trent (DS 1821–1825) in 1546, and the Second Vatican Council's *Sacrosanctum Concilium* (§126) and *Lumen Gentium* (§67) (CCC 2129–32).

IDUMEA *See* **Edom**.

IGDALIAH (Hebrew, "great is the Lord") The father of **Hanan** (Jer 35:4). Jeremiah calls him "the man of God," which may mean that he was a prophet.

ILAI One of the famed "Thirty" warriors of David (1 Chr 11:29).

ILLYRICUM A Roman province that was evangelized by Paul (Rom 15:19). Located along the east coast of the Adriatic Sea, Illyricum was attached to the Roman provincial system in A.D. 9, along with the other regional provinces of Moesia, Dacia, and Pannonia.

IMAGE OF GOD A term that signifies the unique position of man and woman in creation (Gen 1:26–28; 5:1–3; 9:6). As the narrative of creation makes clear, man and woman received a special place over creation, with kingship over the created order (Gen 1:26–28). A second vital clue to the meaning is provided in Gen 5:1–3 in the list of Adam's descendants, where Adam becomes the father of Seth "in his own likeness, after his image"; thus the relationship of God to humans is parallel to the

relationship of father to son. Finally, in Gen 9:6, the human life is inviolable because humans are God's image.

We are made in the "image of God" because our souls, with their intellect and free will, reflect the intelligence and freedom of God in a limited and imperfect way. Through sanctifying grace and the infused virtues, this imperfect human nature can be elevated to a supernatural plane of being and acting. Saying that we are made in the "image of God" affirms the dignity of creation and our unique place as beings who are called to know and love God and to share in God's own life. Hence, while all of creation was for man, it brings with it the responsibility for man to make a free response of faith and love that is likewise unique among creatures. The mystery of that creation is made clear only in Christ.

The idea of the "image of God" was developed in the New Testament through the writings of Saint Paul, who taught that Christ is the perfect image of God (2 Cor 4:4), the firstborn of all creation (Col 1:15). By the Spirit, the Christians are transformed, and "with unveiled face, beholding the glory of the Lord, are being changed into his likeness from one degree of glory to another" (2 Cor 3:18; cf. Rom 8:29). Reflecting on the image of the two Adams, Paul stresses that the first man was "from the earth, a man of dust" and the second man "from heaven": "Just as we have borne the image of the man of dust, we shall also bear the image of the man of heaven" (1 Cor 15:47–49; cf. Saint Peter Chrysologus, *Sermo* 117) (CCC 343, 355–58).

IMAGE WORSHIP *See* **Idol, idolatry**.

IMALKUE (Greek *Imalkoue*) An Arab chieftain to whom Antiochus VI Epiphanes was entrusted by his father, the Seleucid king Alexander Balas (1 Macc 11:39) during Balas's war against Demetrius II Nicator in 146 B.C.

IMLAH (Hebrew *yimlâ*) The father of the prophet **Micaiah** (1 Kgs 22:8–9).

IMMACULATE CONCEPTION *See* **Mary, the Mother of Jesus**.

IMMANUEL *See* **Emmanuel**.

IMMUTABILITY *See* **God**.

IMPALEMENT A form of execution in the ancient world in which the condemned was stuck or forced upon a spike or stake. In his decree concerning the rebuilding of the Temple, Darius decreed, "Furthermore I decree that if anyone alters this edict, a beam shall be pulled out of the house of the perpetrator, who then shall be impaled on it" (Ezra 6:11). Other references to impaling as a form of capital punishment include Num 25:4; Deut 21:22–23; Josh 8:29; and 2 Sam 21:6, 9.

IMPOSITION OF HANDS *See* **Hand**; *see also* **Priest**.

INCARNATION The assumption of human nature by the second Person of the Blessed Trinity: "And the Word was made flesh, and dwelt among us" (John 1:14). According to Church teaching, God Incarnate had two natures—divine and human—united in one person. He had a true human body, a true human soul, and a true human will united to his divine nature. The union of the two natures is called the hypostatic union. (*See* **Jesus Christ**.)

INCENSE A mixture of gum and resin used for various aromatic purposes. Incense was common in the ancient world. In the Old Testament, it is connected intimately with worship. It was a specific ingredient mentioned in Exod 30:1–10, with rites attached to its burning on a gold-covered altar in the holy of holies before the ark. The incense was to be burned every morning and evening. Similar requirements were established for the burning of incense in the Temple of Solomon (1 Kgs 6:20–21; 7:48). A supply of frankincense was therefore maintained in the Temple (1 Chr 9:29; Neh 13:9). Incense was also prescribed for various other sacrifices (Lev 2:1, 15; 6:15; 24:7).

In the New Testament, the most famous reference to incense is found in Matt 2:11, where the Magi brought frankincense and myrrh as gifts for the newborn King (cf. 1 Kgs 10:2, 10; Isa 60:6). The incense in the Temple is mentioned in Luke 1:8–13.

Symbolically, incense represents the zeal with which the faithful should be consumed, just as the incense is consumed by the embers. Equally, it is a physical symbol of the so-called good odor of Christian virtue (hence it is said in the accounts of saints that they died in the odor of sanctity). Finally, the burning of incense represents the ascent of our prayers to God. The smoke rises to the heavens just as our praises and supplications fly upward to God.

INCEST Incestuous relations are condemned unambiguously in Leviticus (18:6–18) with its list of forbidden activities that are termed "abominations." The penalty for incest—along with various other sexual crimes and perversions (e.g., bestiality and homosexuality)—was death. Leviticus regulates the permitted degrees of relation between husband and wife in great detail.

Throughout the Old Testament, incestuous relations are recorded and condemned. Reuben had intercourse with Bilhah (Gen 35:22; Jacob curses him for it in Gen 48:4). Lot's daughters had children by Lot (Gen 19:30–38). Absalom seized his father's harem as a means of claiming the crown (2 Sam 16:22). There are also references to marriage with a paternal half sister (Gen 20:12; Deut 27:22; Lev 18:9; 2 Sam 13:13) and sisters (Lev 18:18).

In the New Testament, Paul complained vociferously to the Corinthian church about the permitted marriage of a man to his father's wife. He states that the man should be expelled from the community (1 Cor 5:1–5).

INDIA (Hebrew *hōddû;* Greek *Indikēs*) The Hebrew name for India, *hōddû,* was likely derived from the Sanskrit word *sindhu,* which meant "stream," and was also used to describe the Indus River. India is mentioned twice in Esther (Esth 1:1; 8:9; cf. 1 Macc 6:37) as the farthest extent of the eastern boundary of King **Ahasuerus's** lands, which extended as far as the Indus River Valley. Trade from India found its way to Palestine, especially through caravans that brought such goods as ivory, ebony, exotic animals, and assorted luxury goods (cf. Ezek 27:15, 19, 24).

INERRANCY The principle that the Bible cannot teach error. *See* **Inspiration.**

INHERITANCE The Bible speaks of inheritance in two senses. The first is the traditional legal claim to property and rights as a consequence of family or other ties. The second, arising from the first, is a theological concept that is found in both the Old Testament and the New Testament, and sharply focused in the hands of NT writers to designate the kingdom and salvation.

I. *Legal Inheritance in the Old Testament*
II. *Theological Inheritance*
   A. *The Election of Israel*
   B. *Adoption*
   C. *The Future Inheritance*

I. LEGAL INHERITANCE IN THE OLD TESTAMENT

No specific Hebrew code existed to specify the laws pertaining to the passing on of property. Hebrew custom must, therefore, be deduced by examining practice, with the understanding that the practice was neither uniform nor consistent throughout the whole of ancient Jewish history. Common practice dictated that the sons shared in the inheritance with a strong emphasis placed on the rights of the firstborn (cf. Gen 21:15–17). The oldest son received a double share of all that was owned by the father (cf. 2 Kgs 2:9), even if the father had a second son by a favored second wife. The oldest son also succeeded as head of the family. There are, however, numerous examples of older sons being rejected as heirs in favor of younger ones: Ishmael was rejected in favor of Isaac, Jacob in favor of Esau, Reuben in favor of Joseph. But each of these rejections was a special case, with special circumstances explaining it; succession of the firstborn was still the rule.

Widows did not share in the inheritance. If the wife returned to her father's house, the property passed to the closest male relative outside the immediate family. Normally, the widow remained with the oldest son, or returned to the family of her father if she had no sons (Gen 38:11; Lev 22:13; Ruth 1:8). The exact disposition of property in a **levirate marriage** is not known.

In cases where a man died without any male heirs, the Law decreed that the property should pass to a daughter (Num 27:1–11); if there was no daughter, it went to the dead man's brothers, then to the most closely related members of the clan (Num 27:8–11). There was a supplementary requirement that daughters who inherited had to marry within the tribe of their father to ensure that the inheritance remained within the tribe (Num 36:6–9).

If a man had sons by slaves, those sons could still share in the inheritance. The sons of Bilhah, the slave girl of Rachel, and of Leah's slave girl Zilpah were counted equal with the rest of Jacob's sons (Gen 30:1–13), in both cases by the express intention of Jacob's wives.

II. THEOLOGICAL INHERITANCE

A. The Election of Israel

The customs of inheritance in the legal sense provided a certain foundation for understanding the **election** of Israel and the inheritance of the Kingdom of God that Christ promised.

God promised Abraham that his descendants would inherit **Canaan**, a territory that would be conquered and settled by the Israelites following the Exodus. In numerous passages, Canaan is referred to as an inheritance (e.g., Exod 32:13; Num 16:14, 34:2; Deut 4:21, 12:10, 15:4, 19:10, 20:16; Ezek 35:15) (CCC 2570–74).

In spite of the long war of conquest, the "inheritance" of Israel was not achieved by force of arms (Deut 8:17–20). Rather, it is the fulfillment of God's promise, a free gift that was entirely unmerited.

B. Adoption

The NT continues the theological theme of promise, election, and inheritance, extending it to all people. Through Christ, we receive a "spirit of adoption" (Greek *huiothesia,* "adoption as sons": Rom 8:15, 23; Eph 1:5; Gal 3:26–27; 4:5–6) (CCC 2009).

Thus we as Christians are heirs of the covenant with Abraham (Gal 3:18, 4:30; Rom 4:13–14). The inheritance of Abraham is no longer the land of Canaan but adoption as children of God (Gal 3:29, 4:5, 4:7; Rom 8:15). While Christ alone is the natural Son of God, we are all adopted children who can claim God as our Father, "and if children, then heirs, heirs of God and fellow heirs with Christ" (Rom 8:17). "So you are no longer a slave but a child, and if a child then also an heir, through God" (Gal 4:7).

Christ makes possible this entry into inheritance, just as he is the inheritance in which we share (Gal 3:26–29). The theological theme of inheritance through adoption is carried forward extensively throughout the rest of the NT, especially in the **Synoptic Gospels** (Matt 21:38; Mark 12:7; Luke 20:14).

C. The Future Inheritance

The Synoptic Gospels speak of an inheritance of eternal life as something to be received in the future (Matt 19:29; Mark 10:17; Luke 18:18). This is most so in Matthew (cf. Matt 5:5; 25:34), who also associated the future inheritance with the coming of the Son of Man (Matt 19:28; cf. Dan 7:13). Paul takes up the same notion of future inheritance (1 Cor 6:9–10; Gal 5:21), and elsewhere throughout the NT future language is applied (Col 3:24; Eph 1:14, 18; 5:5; Titus 3:7), while the future is accentuated in the terms of kingdom (1 Cor 6:9; Gal 5:21) and salvation (Heb 1:14).

The Acts of the Apostles deals with the Abrahamic inheritance in three passages (Acts 7:5; 13:19; 20:32), acknowledging the promise of land and its association with Canaan but proclaiming "the inheritance among all who are sanctified" (Acts 20:32).

Hebrews also develops the Abrahamic theme, underscoring the patriarch's faith that permitted him to look forward "to the city that has foundations, whose architect and builder is God" (Heb 11:8–10). In effect, the promise is one of an eternal inheritance (Heb 9:15). Hebrews notes early on (Heb 1:2) that Christ is "heir of all things" even as he is the High Priest and mediator of the New Covenant.

Finally, the First Letter of Peter rounds out the theme of a future inheritance by assuring us that it is "imperishable, undefiled, and unfading, kept in heaven for you" (1 Pet 1:4). This inheritance, however, comes to us because "we have been born anew to a living hope through the resurrection of Jesus Christ from the dead" (1 Pet 1:3), connecting the promise of future life as an inheritance with the Resurrection.

INK Ancient forms of ink were made from wood, ivory, or other materials burned to create carbon that was then suspended in a gum or glue solution. Ink is mentioned specifically only in Jer 36:18; 2 Cor 3:3; 2 John 12; and 3 John 13.

INN A place of hospitality and lodging for the traveler, where caravans might rest for the night or where a traveler might find shelter (Gen 42:27, 43:21; Exod 4:24; cf. 2 Kgs 19:23; Josh 4:3).

In early Old Testament times, inns were scarce. They were not necessary, since Middle Eastern ideas of **hospitality** dictated that the occasional traveler could expect a welcome in any private home.

But in later centuries, as trade increased and travelers became more numerous, inns developed to accommodate strangers, especially in large towns or in isolated areas. The inns in rustic settings were typically well guarded because of the constant threat of bandits. The typical inn in a city offered lodging for guests, including their animals (1 Kgs 18:27; Luke 2:7, 10:34). The Persian Empire maintained a well-run road system with caravansaries or inns for travelers. The Roman Empire likewise had a massive network of rest stops, used chiefly for purposes of communication among the far-flung provinces of the empire. They were often dangerous places, where a traveler would have to be on constant guard against robbers; as Saint Paul tells us, travel was a dangerous business (2 Cor 11:25–26). In the New Testament, an inn (Greek *kataluma*) is mentioned specifically at Bethlehem (Luke 2:7); the same word was used for the room used by Jesus and the disciples for the Last Supper (Mark 14:14; Luke 22:11). The Samaritan left the wounded traveler in an inn on the road between Jericho and Jerusalem (Luke 10:34; the Greek word here is *pandocheion*).

INNOCENTS, HOLY The male infants of Bethlehem and the surrounding area who were put to death by the command of King Herod the Great following the birth of Christ (Matt 2:16–18). The Magi had told **Herod the Great** of the birth of a king of the Jews, as indicated by the star in the East. When Herod asked where this child would be born, the Magi answered that the place would be Bethlehem of Judea. Thus, Herod ordered all male infants two years and under living in and around Bethlehem to be put to death. The exact number of children killed is impossible to know with certainty, and the event is not reported in any extra-biblical sources. Nevertheless, such an act was hardly out of character for a king who murdered his wife and three of his own sons.

I.N.R.I. The initials of the Latin superscription Iesus Nazarenus Rex Iudaeorum, "Jesus of Nazareth, King of the Jews," placed above Jesus on the Cross. According to John's Gospel (John 19:19–20; see also Matt 27:37; Mark 15:26; Luke 23:38), the inscription was written in Hebrew (meaning probably Aramaic), in Latin, and in Greek.

INSPIRATION A theological term to describe the divine authorship of the Bible. It means that the Holy Spirit acted in and through the Bible's human authors, moving them to write what God wished to communicate in written form. The result is that Scripture, in both content and expression, is truly the word of God.

I. *The Biblical View of Inspiration*
  A. *The Old Testament*
  B. *The New Testament*
II. *The Doctrine of Inspiration*
  A. *Divine Authorship*
  B. *Human Authorship*
  C. *Scope and Extent*
III. *The Effects of Inspiration*
  A. *Inerrancy in History*
  B. *Inerrancy in Papal Teaching*
  C. *Inerrancy at Vatican II*
  D. *Inerrancy in Practical Terms*

I. THE BIBLICAL VIEW OF INSPIRATION

A. *The Old Testament*

The Old Testament has no explicit teaching on the inspiration of Scripture. There is not a term in biblical Hebrew to describe it, nor do we find an examination of God's role in producing the scriptural texts. Nevertheless, the OT lays the foundation for such a doctrine to emerge in later Judaism and the writings of the New Testament. For example, portions of Scripture such as the Law of Moses were venerated as sacred and authoritative because they were held to express the will of God for Israel. Likewise, it is clear that Yahweh often employed prophets as his human mouthpiece to speak the word of God with binding authority (e.g., Deut 18:18–19; 2 Sam 23:2; Jer 1:9; Ezek 3:4; Hos 1:1). When this involved insight into the future or a revelation of truths previously unknown, one can speak of God illuminating the mind of the prophet in a supernatural way. Strictly speaking, prophetic inspiration is not exactly the same as biblical inspiration, but the two are related. The former is a grace to *speak* the word of God, the latter a grace to *write* the word of God. Only rarely are we told that Yahweh instructed his prophets to put their message into writing (e.g., Isa 30:8; Jer 36:1–2; Hab 2:2), and not until the first century A.D. do we have Jewish writers speaking of the divine "inspiration" (Greek, *epipnoia*) of the OT writings (e.g., Josephus, *C.Ap.* 1.7).

B. The New Testament

The New Testament makes reference to the divine origin of the Bible and to the divine action of the Spirit on its human authors. Two passages are prominent in this regard. The first is 2 Tim 3:16–17, which reads: "All scripture is inspired by God and profitable for teaching, for reproof, for correction, and for training in righteousness, that the man of God may be complete, equipped for every good work." The key expression in this passage is the Greek adjective *theopneustos,* translated as "inspired by God" but more precisely meaning "breathed forth by God" (rendered *divinitus inspirata,* "divinely breathed into/upon," in the Latin Vulgate). Having proceeded from the mouth of God, the biblical books are uniquely suited for the moral and spiritual formation of God's people. Hence Paul insists that they are "sacred writings" whose purpose is to instruct the reader "for salvation" (2 Tim 3:15). The focus here is on the divine origin of the Bible without consideration of the human contribution. The second passage addresses more directly the process of inspiration as the action of God affected the sacred writer. The statement is found in 2 Pet 1:20–21, which reads: "First of all you must understand this, that no prophecy of scripture is a matter of one's own interpretation, because no prophecy ever came by the impulse of man, but men moved by the Holy Spirit spoke from God." Here the operative word is the Greek verb *pherō*, which means "move" or "carry along." It can describe, as in the book of Acts, how rushing wind is borne along (Acts 2:2) and how it can drive sailing ships out to sea (Acts 27:15). Thus, prophetic speech, whether spoken or written down as part of Scripture, is divine speech that originates with God and comes to expression as the Spirit moves the human recipient to communicate it to others.

Among other verses of the NT relevant to inspiration, we are told that the Lord spoke through the biblical prophets (Matt 1:22; Luke 1:70) and that David spoke in or by the Spirit when composing the Psalms (Mark 12:36; Acts 1:16). The authors of the NT view the OT writings as nothing less than the "oracles of God" (Rom 3:2), which explains why an equation is sometimes made between what God says and what Scripture says (Matt 19:4–5; Acts 4:24–26; Heb 3:7). The word that God speaks in the Scriptures is the standard by which we must live (Matt 4:4). So, too, the word that comes from God is always true (John 17:17), for he can never lie (Titus 1:2) and his Scriptures can never be annulled (John 10:35).

Though most of these passages are statements about the OT books, the divine origin of the NT was also accepted in earliest Christianity. In 1 Tim 5:18, for instance, a quotation from Deut 25:4 is coupled with a quotation from Luke 10:7, and both are cited to tell us what "scripture says." Similarly, in 2 Pet 3:16, the "letters" of the apostle Paul are placed on a par with the OT writings, called "the other scriptures." In a unique way, the book of Revelation claims to give us heavenly mysteries and prophecies that John wrote down in the book (Rev 1:1–3; 22:7, 10, 18–19).

II. THE DOCTRINE OF INSPIRATION

For the most part, the Catholic Church's doctrine of inspiration was formulated within the one hundred years between Vatican I (1870) and Vatican II (1965). Now it is true that the Church Fathers held an extremely high view of Scripture as inspired revelation, but inspiration as such was not the subject of extensive theological analysis. So, too, the same exalted view of the Bible reigned throughout the Middle Ages, and although an effort was made among the medieval schoolmen to explain Scripture's divine origin with the help of philosophical principles, a thoroughgoing study of inspiration still had not been undertaken. It was not until the 1800s, with the rise of modern historical criticism and the growing climate of intellectual skepticism, that the doctrine of inspiration was subjected to serious examination. Modern times have since witnessed a stream of ecclesiastical statements issued to clarify the Church's belief on inspiration and to condemn errors that are incompatible with it.

A. Divine Authorship

Faced with a diminishing reverence for the Bible among academics, as well as with recent theories of inspiration that departed from traditional notions, Vatican Council I set forth a definition of inspiration that would serve as an enduring benchmark of Catholic orthodoxy. The Council Fathers, echoing a similar formulation made at the Council of Trent, defined inspiration in this way:

> These [books of the Bible] the Church holds to be sacred and canonical, not because, having been composed by simple human industry, they were later approved by her own authority, nor merely because they contain revelation without error, but because, having been written by the inspiration of the Holy Spirit, they have God for their author and were delivered as such to the Church. (Dei Filius 2)

Inspiration thus means that God is the divine author of the books of Scripture, and this is why the Church reveres them as sacred and canonical. Such is the positive content of the doctrine. But one notices that this definition is set in opposition to two incorrect notions of inspiration. The mistaken views in question are those of the nineteenth-century theologians D. Haneburg and J. Jahn. Haneburg maintained a theory of subsequent approval whereby the Bible was written by human authors, and in a fully human way, but was later approved by the Church. This theory, which the Council rejects, would mean that inspiration was not intrinsic to the text of Scripture but was something conferred upon it by the Church. Jahn maintained a theory of *negative assistance,* meaning that God prevented the biblical authors from stating anything in their writings that was untrue. This theory is also rejected by the Council, not because the Bible is brimming with misinformation, but because the Church's belief that Scripture is the word of God is left unaccounted for. Human writings that contain no misstatements of fact are still human writings, and one could hardly say that God speaks or expresses his will in them for that reason alone.

The definition of inspiration as divine authorship was reaffirmed by the Church several times since Vatican I. The point was made, for instance, in 1893 (Leo XIII, *Providentissimus Deus* §41), in 1920 (Benedict XV, *Spiritus Paraclitus* §3), in 1943 (Pius XII, *Divino Afflante Spiritu* §1), and again in 1965 (Vatican II, DV §11).

B. Human Authorship

The question of inspiration is not settled by the assertion that God is the author of the Bible. The fact is that Scripture was actually penned by human authors under the influence of the Spirit. Inspiration, then, is more fully described as a mystery of dual authorship—of God and man working in tandem to compose the biblical texts.

Historically, emphasis was always placed on God's role as the Bible's divine author. Modern studies, however, have given increased attention to the human contribution. This is true not only of biblical and theological schol-arship but of ecclesiastical statements on the nature of inspiration, which maintain that the human authors wrote as instruments guided by the Holy Spirit. All now agree that the inspiring grace of the Spirit did not suppress the freedom or consciousness or personality of the sacred writers, nor were they merely passive, acting like stenographers taking dictation. Rather, the human authors of Scripture were genuine authors actively involved in all stages of the composition of the work. This aspect of inspiration was succinctly stated by Vatican II:

> To compose the sacred books, God chose certain men who, all the while he employed them in this task, made full use of their powers and faculties so that, though he acted in and by them, it was as true authors that they consigned to writing whatever he wanted written and no more. (DV §11)

The truth of this observation is borne out by the distinct styles and temperaments of the biblical authors. No one doubts, for instance, that the stamp of Paul's personality is pressed deeply into his letters, and that it differs quite noticeably from that of other authors such as Matthew or John or Peter or Jude.

Finally, Catholic tradition often speaks of God as the *principal author* of Scripture and the human writers as the *instrumental authors* of Scripture. This distinction has its roots in patristic theology but was given classic expression in medieval times by Saint Thomas Aquinas. The Church considers it a suitable (though not exhaustive) way of expressing the mystery of the Bible's dual authorship (see *Divino Afflante Spiritu* §19).

C. Scope and Extent

Following the divine and human authorship of the Bible, it remains to consider the extent of inspiration. The question is whether the totality of Scripture is inspired or whether inspiration applies only to select statements within it. Vatican I, again echoing words used by the Council of Trent, declared that inspiration extends to "the books of the Old and New Testaments, whole and entire, with all their parts" (*Dei Filius* 2). In other words, the Bible is fully inspired from beginning to end, embracing everything in between. This includes the deuterocanonical books that are part of the Catholic canon as well as the deuterocanonical portions of books that the Church likewise accepts as Scripture (e.g., the additions to Esther and Daniel).

Despite this conciliar definition, and most likely under pressure to deal with difficulties in the Bible, theologians writing in the aftermath of Vatican I still proposed a narrowing of the scope of inspiration. Theories to this effect were proposed by A. Rohling (1872), who would restrict inspiration to statements dealing with faith and morals; by F. Lenormant (1880), who would restrict it to revealed teachings unknowable by reason; and by Cardinal J. H. Newman (1884), who held that inspiration did not apply to passing comments (*obiter dicta*) made in Scripture insofar as these had no bearing on doctrinal or moral matters.

Still, the Church rejected all such attempts to restrict inspiration to select parts of Scripture. Pope Leo XIII led the way in 1893 by making this clarification:

> But it is absolutely wrong and forbidden either to narrow inspiration to certain parts only of Holy Scripture or to admit that the sacred writer has erred. For the system of those who, in order to rid themselves of these difficulties, do not hesitate to concede that divine inspiration regards the things of faith and morals and nothing beyond, because (as they wrongly think) in a question of the truth or falsehood of a passage, we should consider not so much what God has said as the reason and purpose that he had in mind in saying it—this system cannot be tolerated. (Providentissimus Deus §40)

Instead of endorsing a notion of partial inspiration, the pope affirmed a doctrine of plenary inspiration. This is the belief that the entire contents of the Bible are inspired—the whole as well as every part, no matter the subject each part may be said to deal with. Subsequent popes would reaffirm this in 1920 (Benedict XV, *Spiritus Paraclitus* §5) and again in 1943 (Pius XII, *Divino Afflante Spiritu* §1).

Lastly, there is the question whether plenary inspiration amounts to plenary *verbal* inspiration. In other words, did the Spirit guide the biblical authors in their selection of the individual words of Scripture? A negative answer was returned at the end of the nineteenth century by the cardinal theologian J. B. Franzelin. He promoted a theory sometimes called "content inspiration," according to which the Spirit supplied the sacred writers with the *ideas* to be communicated in the Bible but left it to the writers' discretion to express those ideas in suitable *words*. On this view, Scripture conveys an inspired message in noninspired language. Now, the cardinal did maintain that the Spirit protected the human authors in a negative way from using unsuitable words, but the positive choice of words was still a fundamentally human choice.

Franzelin's theory of nonverbal inspiration quickly faced a barrage of criticism at the beginning of the twentieth century, and so it found few adherents. And although the Church never officially rejected or even addressed his views explicitly, most have thought it a deficient theory of inspiration, one that simplistically and artificially separates words and ideas.

From the standpoint of Church teaching, there has never been a solemn definition to specify that God inspired every individual word of the Bible. Nevertheless, there are several pointers that suggest plenary verbal inspiration is an authentically Catholic view. Consider the following: (1) Both Jesus and the apostle Paul make arguments about the saving plan of God that hinge on the importance and meaning of individual words expressed in the Bible (see, e.g., John 10:34–35 and Gal 3:16). (2) The Council of Trent, Vatican I, and Pope Leo XIII have all described the inspiration of Sacred Scripture in terms of "dictation." Since it is otherwise clear that the human authors were fully and freely engaged in the processes of writing the Bible, and every indication suggests that the influence of inspiration was imperceptible to their human consciousness, it appears certain that a mechanical or stenographic dictation is not envisioned. Rather, the word "dictation" indicates that God played a decisive role in selecting the words and phrases that would be used to communicate his message. (3) Catholic tradition often refers to the Bible as the inspired "word of God." However, in a few Church pronouncements, Scripture is said to express the very *words* of God. For example, Pope Leo XIII says that the promises of the Bible are uttered *ipsius Dei nomine et verbis,* "in God's name and in his own words" (*Providentissimus Deus* §6). Likewise, Pius XII says that Scripture gives us *Dei verba humanis linguis expressa,* "the words of God expressed in human language" (*Divino Afflante Spiritu* §20). This latter statement was reused in the Vatican II document on divine revelation (see DV §13). Given these pronouncements, it is fully in line with Catholic teaching to say that Scripture is the word of God in both content and expression.

III. THE EFFECTS OF INSPIRATION

There are numerous effects of inspiration that are open to theological investigation. One is the *canonicity* of Scripture. Because the Bible is the written word of God, composed under the influence of the Holy Spirit, its books are likewise holy, set apart from other written documents and uniquely suited for liturgical proclamation and prayer. Thus, when the Church canonized the books of the OT and NT, she simply recognized the divine holiness that is inherent in them. Another effect is the *sacramentality* of Scripture. That is to say, the Bible not only reveals the will of God for his people, but God reveals himself to his people in such a way that reading and contemplation of Scripture can bring about a transforming encounter with the Lord. Likewise, the *authority* of the Bible is a consequence of its inspiration. Being the word of God expressed in the very words of God, it is the primary source of the Church's teachings on faith and life. Vatican II thus urges that Scripture should be "the very soul" of sacred theology (DV §24).

A. Inerrancy in History

The most debated effect of inspiration is *inerrancy*, the belief that Scripture is trustworthy and true, untainted by anything false, erroneous, or deceptive. This follows logically from the divine authorship of the Bible—if God is its primary author, and God himself is the perfection of truth, then all that Scripture claims to be true must necessarily be true. The ancient Church believed this in no uncertain terms. As early as the second century, theologians declared that Scripture is entirely perfect (Saint Irenaeus, *Against Heresies* 2.28.2) and true (Saint Clement of Rome, *1 Clem.* 45.2). Despite apparent tensions within, it never contradicts itself (Saint Justin Martyr, *Dial.* 65). Similar sentiments were expressed throughout the patristic and medieval periods, all the way up to the European Enlightenment, when the sweeping consensus of Christian tradition was first seriously challenged.

The occasion for this confrontation was the birth of historical criticism, which turned a spotlight on numerous difficulties in the Bible touching on historical, geographical, scientific, and moral matters. Historically, these had always been viewed as "apparent discrepancies," difficulties that God wished to reside in Scripture as a way of inducing humility in the reader. Of course, much effort was spent on solving the riddles posed by problematic passages, but no one in ancient Christian times concluded that the Bible was in error. In the seventeenth and eighteenth centuries, however, scholars of various stripes and persuasions began to disparage the Bible for containing "real discrepancies" of both fact and perspective.

B. Inerrancy in Papal Teaching

In the midst of this emerging crisis, Pope Leo XIII issued a strong and decisive statement on biblical inerrancy that reaffirmed the Church's long-standing tradition. Beginning with the premise that God is the author of Scripture, he stated:

> For all the books that the Church receives as sacred and canonical are written wholly and entirely, with all their parts, at the dictation of the Holy Spirit. And so far is it from being possible that any error can coexist with inspiration, that inspiration not only is essentially incompatible with error but excludes and rejects it as absolutely and necessarily as it is impossible that God himself, the Supreme Truth, can utter that which is not true. (Providentissimus Deus §40)

This is the Church's first official declaration of Scripture's unlimited inerrancy. And yet, because some scholars felt the pope's teaching was inadequate, there arose a number of theories of limited inerrancy that said, for instance, that errors could be attributed to the human authors of Scripture rather than its divine author, or else they restricted the scope of inerrancy to the Bible's religious truths and excluded from its realm statements that made reference to profane matters. For this reason,

Pope Benedict XV strongly reaffirmed Pope Leo's teaching regarding the Bible's "absolute immunity from error" and added, "We can never conclude that there is any error in Sacred Scripture" (*Spiritus Paraclitus* §5). Likewise, Pope Pius XII reaffirmed Leo's doctrinal stance that the Bible was free "from any error whatsoever" and reiterated that its truth could not be restricted "to matters of faith and morals" (*Divino Afflante Spiritu* §1). In fact, due to an ongoing resistance to this teaching, Pius was forced to address the issue again less than a decade later, when he lamented, "Some go so far as to . . . put forward again the opinion, already often condemned, that asserts that immunity from error extends only to those parts of the Bible that treat of God or of moral and religious matters" (*Humani Generis* §22). Such is the clear and constant teaching of the modern popes on biblical inerrancy.

C. Inerrancy at Vatican II

The most recent statement on inerrancy was issued at Vatican II in its Dogmatic Constitution on Divine Revelation, *Dei Verbum,* issued in 1965. Oddly, the wording of this key document, which basically summarizes the Church's teaching on Sacred Scripture and Sacred Tradition, is claimed by many to represent a move away from the classical doctrine of inerrancy advanced by the popes. The relevant statement reads as follows:

> *Therefore, since everything asserted by the inspired authors or sacred writers should be regarded as asserted by the Holy Spirit, it follows that we must acknowledge the Books of Scripture as teaching firmly, faithfully, and*

without error the truth that God wished to be recorded in the sacred writings for the sake of our salvation. (DV §11)

The question is whether Vatican II is expounding a doctrine of unlimited inerrancy, in continuity with previous magisterial teaching, or a position of limited inerrancy, which would constitute a departure from the doctrinal tradition of virtually all preceding centuries. Many who argue for the latter detect an innovative change in magisterial perspective in the phrase "for the sake of our salvation." The claim is that truth is given "without error" only insofar as it directly concerns "our salvation." It is said on the basis of this statement that the Church no longer commits herself to insisting on the truthfulness of nonsalvific matters contained in the Bible. By implication, statements made about history, geography, and similar nonreligious subjects are now said to fall outside the scope of inerrancy.

Though numerous scholars maintain this interpretation and have come to embrace a limited inerrancy view, there is reason to think this is a misunderstanding of the Council's intention. Indeed, there are several indicators that Vatican II's formulation stands in historical continuity with earlier papal teachings on unlimited inerrancy. Consider the following points.

1. The disputed expression "for the sake of our salvation" (Latin, *nostrae salutis causa*) is a prepositional phrase used as an adverbial phrase modifying "recorded" (Latin, *consignari*). In other words, it tells us *why* God wished truth to be recorded in the Bible, namely, to facilitate our salvation. It is not

an adjectival phrase that modifies the noun "truth." In fact, it should be noted that the penultimate schema of *Dei Verbum* did refer to "saving truth" (Latin, *veritatem salutarem*), but at the request of numerous Council Fathers and the urging of Pope Paul VI, it was amended to read "truth" (Latin, *veritatem*) alone, so that its scope would not be restricted by the adjective "saving" to matters of faith and morals and nothing beyond. The final and official wording of the Constitution thus tells us the purpose of inerrancy, not its extent.

2. Attached to *Dei Verbum*'s statement on the truth of Sacred Scripture is a footnote citing earlier Church teachings—the single longest footnote in the entire Constitution. Included are statements from Saint Augustine, Saint Thomas Aquinas, the Council of Trent, Pope Leo XIII, and Pope Pius XII, all of which affirm the Bible's divine inspiration and complete freedom from error. Since virtually all the footnotes running throughout the Constitution highlight the continuity of the document with earlier ecclesiastical teaching, it is highly improbable that the expression "for the sake of salvation" represents a departure from the Church's constant belief in unlimited inerrancy.

3. Pope Leo XIII called the doctrine of unlimited inerrancy "the ancient and unchanging faith of the Church" (*Providentissimus Deus* §41). This was the view of patristic and medieval theologians, and it was taught authoritatively by popes Leo XIII, Benedict XV, and Pius XII. There is thus an unbroken line of continuity from earliest Christianity to the middle of the twentieth century on what it

means to say that the Bible is free from error. Surely the Council Fathers at Vatican II had a grave obligation to alert the faithful if in fact a new understanding of inerrancy was being advanced in 1965. That they did not is a telling indication that they intended no real change of position from classical Catholic teaching on this subject.

In all probability, then, given the history of the doctrine and the points considered above, the official Catholic teaching remains one of unlimited inerrancy. Vatican II has issued no repeal of this teaching, neither has it given us signs of a real departure from the solemn decrees of the modern popes. One can legitimately speak of a new emphasis introduced by the Council, but not a new understanding of the doctrine. Only in this limited sense has doctrinal development taken place regarding inerrancy.

D. Inerrancy in Practical Terms

Unlimited inerrancy is the belief that the Scripture is completely and comprehensively true in all that it intentionally affirms. Nothing within its pages is factually erroneous, nor will one find there anything to deceive or mislead. With respect to its content, the Bible is a reflection of the mind of God, who is the perfection of Truth.

What this means on a practical level requires explanation, lest the Catholic position be confused with the similar teaching of Protestant fundamentalism. Fundamentalists believe in the full inerrancy of the Bible but without regard for the literary genres employed in Scripture or the intention of its original human authors. That is, they tend to interpret the words of the Bible at face value—literalistically rather than literarily according to the type of writing used to express the author's intent. This often leads to grave misunderstandings, especially when the Bible is said to teach elements of science that are at variance with modern findings.

According to Catholic teaching on inspiration and inerrancy, the Bible does not make strictly scientific statements. Rather, when the writers of Scripture talk of the natural world, they speak either "figuratively" or "phenomenologically," that is, according to the way things appear to the senses. References to the rising of the sun, for example, are not actual scientific assertions that insist the earth is stationary and the sun follows an ascending and descending course of motion. Such expressions are based on sense perception and common experience, and many are still in use today. Saint Augustine, whose view on this was endorsed in modern papal teaching, holds that Scripture was not written to tell us about "the essential nature of the things of the visible universe" (*Gen. Litt.* 9.20, quoted in both *Providentissimus Deus* §39 and *Divino Afflante Spiritu* §3). Thus, since the Bible makes no properly scientific assertions, it cannot be charged with teaching error on scientific matters.

The situation is different, though, when it comes to historical matters. The Bible makes countless assertions about events that transpired in ancient times, and these do indeed come under the mantle of inerrancy. In part, this is because the words and deeds of God in history are inextricably bound together in Scripture; that is, God reveals himself and accomplishes our salvation through historical actions as well as through written and spoken words (see DV §2). The record of these events must necessarily be trustworthy and true or else the revelation of God would not be successfully communicated. Likewise, one cannot attempt to separate saving history from profane history in the Bible, for all events that appear in Scripture are providentially ordered to the goal of our salvation. For this reason, magisterial teachings have consistently taught that the Bible is inerrant in its presentation of historical events. Pope Benedict XV, for example, censures those who deny that "the historical portions of Scripture do not rest on the absolute truth of the facts," since those who hold this position are "out of harmony with the Church's teaching" (*Spiritus Paraclitus* §6). The idea is that inspiration guarantees the factual accuracy of the historical statements of the Bible so long as a historiographical intent on the part of the author can be demonstrated.

Finally, the doctrine of unlimited inerrancy is not a denial that difficulties remain in our interpretation of the Bible. There are many passages that seem to contradict one another, many that appear to be at variance with non-biblical sources, and even a few that strike us as unworthy of the character of God. Yet, these problematic verses are not misstatements shot wide of the truth. They are rather an invitation to humility. Saint Augustine wisely observed that when one stumbles across an apparent discrepancy in the Bible, he should assume that either the text was miscopied, the original language was mistranslated, or the interpreter has simply failed to understand its meaning (see *Letters* 82). Under no circumstances is it correct to claim that the Bible is in error.

INTERPRETATION OF THE BIBLE The effort to ascertain the meaning of the Bible intended by its divine and human authors. At one level, biblical interpretation makes use of historical and literary tools, for attention must be given to the historical context in which the biblical books were written as well as the literary conventions employed at the time of their composition. At another, biblical interpretation is a theological endeavor, which means the interpreter must be aware that God is speaking through the medium of human words and that often he intends a spiritual level of meaning that stretches beyond the horizon of the human writer's intention. On both levels, authentic interpretation can take place only within the framework of the Church's faith.

I. *The Senses of Scripture*
  A. *The Literal Sense*
  B. *The Spiritual Sense*
II. *Principles of Scriptural Interpretation*
  A. *Criteria for Authentic Interpretation*
  B. *The Church as Final Interpreter*

I. THE SENSES OF SCRIPTURE

Catholic exegesis recognizes both a literal and a spiritual sense of Scripture. The literal sense is the meaning conveyed by the words of the Bible in accordance with the literary genre in which they were written. The spiritual sense is the meaning that God has invested, not in the words of the Bible per se, but in the historical realities that the words of the Bible describe. This spiritual meaning is subdivided into the allegorical sense, the moral or tropological sense, and the anagogical sense. A medieval couplet originating with Augustine of Dacia (d. 1282) offers a summary description of the four senses of Scripture and their respective spheres of reference:

> *Littera gesta docet, quid credas allegoria,*
> *Moralis quid agas, quo tendas anagogia.*

> The letter teaches events, allegory what you
>   should believe,
> the moral meaning what you should do,
>   anagogy what you should aim for.

A. *The Literal Sense*

The literal sense is the foundational sense of Scripture; the spiritual senses presuppose it and are built upon it. It follows that the first priority of biblical interpretation must be to ascertain the literal meaning of its words. Theological scholarship has long maintained this perspective (e.g., Saint Thomas Aquinas, *Summa theologiae* Ia.1.10), and in modern times the point was authoritatively restated by Pius XII: "Let the interpreters bear in mind that their foremost and greatest endeavor should be to discern and define clearly that sense of the biblical words which is called literal" (*Divino Afflante Spiritu* §23; cf. CCC 115–16).

That said, it is crucial to understand what this first step entails. It means interpreting the literal words of the text, but not necessarily in a literal way. In point of fact, the *literal* sense of Scripture is the *literary* sense of Scripture—the meaning of the author's words as expressed through the literary form or device he chose to employ. Thus, careful study must be made of the literary genre in which the individual books of Scripture were written. Poetry must be read with the awareness that poetic language is largely figurative language. Parables must be read in accord with the purpose and techniques of parabolic teaching employed in ancient times. Apocalyptic texts must be read with a knowledge of how their graphic and sometimes bizarre symbolism is intended to be read. Historical narrative must be read according to the aim of the genre, namely, to relay historical information from the point of view of the historian. So, too, on a smaller scale, the interpreter must be familiar with the literary devices and idioms employed by the biblical writers. Metaphors should be read as metaphors, similes as similes, hyperboles as hyperboles, and so forth. This approach to a discovery of the literal sense is summarized in the Vatican II document on divine revelation:

> For truth is differently presented and expressed in various types of historical writings, in prophetic or poetic texts, or in other modes of speech. Furthermore, the interpreter must search for what meaning the sacred writer, in his own historical situation and in accordance with the condition of his time and culture, intended to express and did in fact express with the help of literary forms that were in use during that time. Thus, to understand correctly what the sacred author wanted to assert, one must pay suitable attention both to the customary and character-

> istic modes of perception, speech, and narrative that prevailed at the time of the sacred writer, and to the customs that people of that time generally followed in their dealings with one another. (DV §12)

B. The Spiritual Sense

The spiritual sense is that meaning which God, who is the author of history as well as the biblical texts, expresses through the historical realities and events spoken about in the Bible. Classically understood, the spiritual sense is not an additional layer of meaning that is hidden within the words of Scripture. It consists rather of the mysteries of faith, life, and eternity that are symbolized by the historical persons, actions, and institutions showcased in the Bible. If literal exegesis deals with the written texts of Scripture, spiritual exegesis deals with all that is described by those texts.

From the earliest days of the Church, as seen in the New Testament itself, Christians have discerned a spiritual meaning in biblical history that goes beyond (but not against) the literal meaning of the biblical writings. Various expressions were used by ancient theologians to describe this nonliteral meaning, including allegorical, typological, or mystical meaning. In the Middle Ages, when spiritual interpretation was subjected to more systematic reflection, theologians came to delineate three spiritual senses (CCC 117–19). These were generally defined as follows:

1. The *allegorical sense* reveals the mystery of Christ and the New Covenant foreshadowed in the historical realities and institutions of the Old Covenant. This is discovered by reading the Old Testament in the light of the New

Testament, aware that all of Scripture has its fulfillment in Jesus Christ and the religion he established. The Trinity, the Church, the Mother of God, the sacraments—all such mysteries are seen in prefigurative form through allegorical reflection on biblical history. The allegorical sense promotes the theological virtue of faith.

2. The *moral* or *tropological sense* reveals the pattern of Christian living foreshadowed in the OT and exemplified in the lives of Jesus and his disciples in the NT. The claim is that Scripture encourages virtue and discourages vice, not only by commandments and laws, but through tropological reflection on the experiences of its many saints and sinners. The moral sense promotes the theological virtue of charity.

3. The *anagogical sense* reveals the heavenly and eschatological realities that await us beyond this life. Key aspects of biblical history are seen as earthly reflections of the greater realities of heaven for which we strive. Inasmuch as the anagogical sense leads us to contemplate eternal glory as our destiny, it promotes the theological virtue of hope.

Underlying the spiritual senses is the belief that Scripture is a unified book that presents God's unified plan of salvation. Despite its numerous authors, its many phases of development, its variety of perspectives, and its division into two distinct Testaments, the texts of the Bible are held together around the saving purpose of God in history. Jesus Christ is the cornerstone that supports and unites the entire message of Scripture; for he is its whole exegesis, the final and definitive revelation of God's salvation to the world (CCC 128–30).

II. PRINCIPLES OF SCRIPTURAL INTERPRETATION

The Bible is unlike any other book, and so the principles that govern its interpretation must likewise be unique. Of course, being a monument of human history and industry, it is rightly studied as other human documents are studied. This means that interpreters can bring to the biblical text an array of tools and methodologies that are used in the study of ancient literature in general. Whether historical, linguistic, sociological, archaeological, or otherwise, the human dimension of Scripture is intrinsically open to this level of analysis.

But this is not what makes the Bible unique. Scripture stands in a class apart because it is a collection of writings inspired by God. Interpretation falls short of this divine dignity of Scripture when it fails to produce a properly theological exegesis that considers its message in relation to Christian faith and life. Scripture, as the Church has often told us, was written for our salvation and not merely for our information (see, e.g., DV §§2–6). Hence, the Bible has its natural habitat not in the study or the library or the university, but in the life and liturgy of the pilgrim Church on earth. It is here that its message is received in faith, actualized in the disciplines of Christian living, and proclaimed to the world with zeal and conviction.

A. Criteria for Authentic Interpretation

The Bible thus has its home in the heart of the Church. It is primarily a gift from God above and only secondarily a monument of religious or cultural history. As such, we must bring to its sacred pages more than a collection of scientific tools and methods that can give us insight into the human circumstances that had an impact on the content and composition of the biblical texts. If its divine message is to be heard and received as God intends, we must bring our faith to the Bible along with the tools of reason. The one who reads or listens with faith opens himself to the voice of the Spirit who inspired and infused the Scriptures with its saving message. The Church encourages this when it declares: "Sacred Scripture must be read and interpreted in the light of the same Spirit by whom it was written" (DV §12).

What this means in practice is spelled out in the same sentence of the same Vatican II document. In addition to reading the Bible in light of the literary conventions in use in the biblical world, we are told that no less attention must be given to three interpretive criteria that place the Bible within the context of the Church's living faith (see DV §12 and CCC 112–14). These are delineated as follows:

1. The *content and unity* of the whole of Scripture. By this we are called to interpret the Bible as a unified book that reveals God's unified plan of salvation. The OT must not be isolated from the NT or set in opposition to the NT. Likewise, the NT must not be interpreted without reference to the OT upon which it builds. Thus, the context in which any passage of Scripture should be interpreted is the full canon of biblical books.

2. The *living Tradition* of the whole Church. By this we are called to interpret the Bible with reference to the Church's ongoing efforts, stretching across centuries, to discern its authentic meaning. Account must be taken of liturgical tradition, of the theology and exegesis of the Church's doctors and saints, and of the authoritative pronouncements of popes and Church councils. Here the context of interpretation widens beyond the literary confines of the Bible and encompasses the Church's entire historical experience of reading and responding to the word of God.

3. The *analogy of faith.* By this we are called to interpret the Bible with reference to the Church's doctrines and creeds. Insofar as these communicate truths divinely revealed and definitively known, they establish limits on the interpretation of Scripture and thus serve as a safeguard against misinterpretation. More positively, the harmony and inner unity of the faith allows what is known to throw light on what is unknown or obscure. Here the context of interpretation is the sphere of all that the Church infallibly proclaims to be true.

B. The Church as Final Interpreter

At the end of the day, all efforts at interpreting the Bible should be placed at the service of the Church. The individual, whether a clergyman, a trained exegete, or simply a lay reader, is not endowed with a gift of infallible interpretation (cf. 2 Pet 1:20–21). The charism of infallibility belongs to the Magisterium of the Church, who is guided by the Spirit into the full truth of the gospel (cf. John 16:13) and stands as the unshakable pillar of truth in the world (cf. 1 Tim 3:15). The Church, then, is final judge on the correct meaning of the Bible.

The point is not that the Church stands above the written Word of God. Rather, the Church is herself subject to the Scriptures and is entrusted with the task of safeguarding and proclaiming their message. Biblical scholarship contributes to this mission by helping the Church to make firmer and more informed judgments about the meaning of the biblical texts. The Church's role in biblical interpretation is succinctly expressed, once again, in the Vatican II document on divine revelation:

But the task of giving an authentic interpretation of the Word of God, whether in its written form or in the form of Tradition, has been entrusted to the living teaching office of the Church alone. Its authority in this matter is exercised in the name of Jesus Christ. Yet this Magisterium is not superior to the Word of God, but is its servant. It teaches only what has been handed on to it. At the divine command and with the help of the Holy Spirit, it listens to this devoutly, guards it with dedication and expounds it faithfully. (DV §10)

See also **Biblical criticism**; **Typology**.

IOTA The ninth letter of the Greek alphabet (ι), corresponding to the English letter *i*. It is the smallest mark in the Greek alphabet; in Matthew 5:18, Jesus says that "not an iota, not a dot, will pass from the law," meaning that not even the smallest letter of the Torah would pass away until its fulfillment by the **Messiah**.

IRA The name of two men in the Old Testament.

1. One of the priests during the reign of David (2 Sam 20:23–26).

2. One of David's famed "Thirty" warriors (2 Sam 23:8–39; 1 Chr 11:10–47).

IRAD The son of **Enoch** and the father of Mehujael, and hence a descendant of **Cain** (Gen 4:18). In Gen 5:18, 19, an Irad is listed as a descendant of Seth.

IRIJAH (Hebrew, "the Lord sees") A sentry at the Benjamin Gate of Jerusalem. He arrested Jeremiah on suspicion that he was planning to desert to the Chaldeans (Jer 37:13–14). He refused to listen to Jeremiah's pleas of innocence, partly because Jeremiah advocated surrender (Jer 21:9).

IRON A metal that came into widespread use in the late second millennium B.C. when the so-called Iron Age began, although rudimentary forms of iron technology were known long before this. The first mention of ironmaking in Scripture is the reference to Tubalcain, a descendant of **Cain**: "he was the forger of all instruments of bronze and iron" (Gen 4:22). Iron was in use at the time of the conquest of Canaan, as attested in Josh 6:24 and 22:8. Later on, the Philistines protected the secrets of iron work and refused to permit the Israelites any ironsmiths on the assumption that thereby they would prevent them from forging iron weapons. Indeed, the Israelites were forced to bring their tools to the Philistines to be sharpened (1 Sam 13:19–20). The Canaanites likewise had iron-plated chariots, but despite their obvious tactical disadvantages, the Israelites defeated the chariots of Jabin (Judg 1:19; 4:3). After the defeat of the Philistines, David made sure that iron was made available to the Israelites (1 Chr 22:3; 29:7). Metaphorically, iron in Scripture is an image of stubbornness (Lev 26:19), strength (Deut 33:25), and especially cruel oppression and war (Deut 4:20; 1 Kgs 8:51; Jer 11:4; Dan 2:40). (*See also* **Ezion-geber**.)

ISAAC (Hebrew, "he laughs") The second great patriarch, the son of **Abraham** and **Sarah** (Gen 17:18; 21:3) and the father of **Jacob** (Gen 25:26) and **Esau**. He is ranked as a forefather of Israel with Abraham and Jacob and was a key participant in the promise of God to bless all nations through Abraham's seed (Gen 22:15–22). Nevertheless, he is only rarely mentioned on his own in the Old Testament outside of Genesis and is most often seen in relation to Abraham and Jacob as the link between those two important figures (e.g., Deut 1:8; 6:10; 9:5, 27; 29:12; 30:20; 34:4; cf. Exod 3:6, 15, 16; 4:5; 1 Kgs 18:36).

The name Isaac ("he laughs") comes from the reaction of Abraham (Gen 17:17) and Sarah (Gen 18:10–15) to the news that despite their old age and Sarah's barrenness, they would give birth to a son (cf. Gen 21:6). The significance of Isaac's birth was thus immediate: he was the fulfillment of God's promise and was to be the bearer of the covenant unto future generations (Gen 17:19–21; 18:14): "I will establish my covenant with him as an everlasting covenant for his descendants after him" (Gen 17:19).

Isaac was circumcised eight days after his birth (Gen 17:12; 21:4), and to guarantee his position as Abraham's primary heir, Sarah secured the expulsion of Hagar and her son, Ishmael (Gen 21). Isaac was then the object of the profound test of Abraham's faith when God commanded him to slay Isaac as a sacrifice; when the Lord found Abraham willing to sacrifice even his own son in submission to God's will, Isaac was spared (Gen 22:1–19). In this, Isaac displayed essential attributes of obedience in his own right and was thus a type of Christ. Just as Christ offered his own life to his Father, so too was Isaac—who Jewish tradition believed to be an adult in his twenties or thirties at the time of testing—prepared to die out of obedience to his own father, Abraham. The ultimate act of sacrifice, however, was asked only of Jesus, as Isaac was spared and returned to his faithful and obedient father to fulfill his role in salvation history (CCC 145, 257).

At the age of forty Isaac married **Rebekah**, the daughter of Abraham's nephew Bathuel, after she was brought from Haran to Canaan (Gen 24). Rebekah later gave birth to twin sons, Esau and Jacob. Isaac showed favor to his firstborn twin, Esau (Gen 25), but the clever Jacob—with his mother's help—secured the birthright and also the crucial blessing of his father (Gen 27).

After settling in Beer-sheba, Isaac received a promise from God similar to that given to Abraham (Gen 26:3–5): "I will make your offspring as numerous as the stars of heaven, and will give to your offspring all these lands; and all the nations of the earth shall gain blessing for themselves through your offspring" (Gen 26:4). Isaac died at Hebron and was buried beside Esau and Jacob in the family tomb (Gen 35:27–30).

ISAIAH (Hebrew, "the Lord is salvation") The first of the four major prophets, to whom the book of Isaiah is attributed (see **Isaiah, book of**). Sirach 48:23–25 is an eloquent tribute to the prophet Isaiah:

> In his days the sun went backward,
>   and he lengthened the life of the king.
> By the spirit of might he saw the last things,
>   and comforted those who mourned in Zion.
> He revealed what was to occur to the end
>   of time,
>   and the hidden things before they came
>   to pass.

According to the book of Isaiah, Isaiah was the son of Amoz (Isa 1:1; 2:1); some Fathers of the Church believe that Isaiah's father was the prophet **Amos**. This association, however, was disputed by Saint Jerome in the preface to his *Commentary on Amos*. In any case, he must have belonged to a leading family in Jerusalem (Isa 3:1–17, 24; 4:1; 8:2; 31:16), since he had easy access to the aristocracy. He probably began his public ministry at the age of twenty and prophesied from around 742 to 701 B.C. in Jerusalem. He held the post of royal advisor to the kings of Judah. He was also married and had two sons, Shear-jashub and Maher-shalal-hash-baz. Shear-jashub's name meant "a remnant will return," in recognition that a faithful portion of God's people would survive the impending Assyrian conquest and come back home (Isa 7:3–4). Maher-shalal-hash-baz meant "speedy-spoil-quick-booty": "for before the child knows how to call 'My father' or 'My mother,' the wealth of Damascus and the spoil of Samaria will be carried away before the king of Assyria" (Isa 8:3–4).

As a prophet, Isaiah was given a mission to proclaim the fall of Israel and chastisement of Judah due to their flagrant violations of the Lord's covenant. When he began his ministry, however, the kingdoms of Judah and Israel were enjoying peace and prosperity. His call to prophetic ministry (Isa 6:1–13) came in Solomon's Temple: "Make the mind of this people dull, and stop their ears, and shut their eyes, so that they may not look with their eyes, and listen with their ears, and comprehend with their minds, and turn and be healed" (Isa 6:10). As dark as the promise appeared, Isaiah was also given the promise of the survival of a remnant (the "holy seed") in the coming destruction (Isa 6:13).

A contemporary of **Micah**, he labored as prophet during a time of immense political and social upheaval, and his prophetic ministry stretched across the reigns of three Judean kings: **Jotham**, **Ahaz**, and **Hezekiah**. In his time, the Assyrians conquered most of western Asia—including the kingdom of Israel in northern Palestine along with its capital city, Samaria.

Isaiah advised King Ahaz of Judah not to ally himself with Assyria against the anti-Assyrian alliance of Syria and Israel around 735 B.C. To bring pressure on Ahaz, the allies laid siege to Jerusalem, threatening to supplant the king with a more pliant vassal. This "Syro-Ephraimite conflict" was the occasion of Isaiah's famous **Immanuel** prophecies (Isa 7:9–14; cf. Matt 1:20–23). Isaiah's call for neutrality went unheeded: Ahaz became a vassal to Assyria (2 Kgs 16:7–9), and as a result foreign religious cults were introduced (2 Kgs 16:10–18).

The Assyrians advanced rapidly, as predicted by Isaiah, and Assyrian forces razed Damascus in 732 B.C. and conquered Samaria in 722 B.C. Isaiah worked with King **Hezekiah** to restore peace and order to the nation and gave him key support when **Sennacherib** besieged Jerusalem in 701 B.C. in retaliation for Hezekiah's anti-Assyrian policies (Isa 36–38; cf. 2 Kgs 18:13–20:19). The siege was broken, as prophesied, when "the angel of the LORD went forth, and slew a hundred and eighty-five thousand in the camp of the Assyrians; and when men arose early in the morning, behold, these were all dead bodies" (Isa 37:36; cf. 2 Kgs 18:13–19:37). Under **Manasseh**, relations with Assyria were repaired (2 Kgs 20:21; 2 Chr 32:33) with a resulting increase in Assyrian influences, including Assyrian cults and religious practices. Isaiah condemned the revival of idolatrous practices (cf. 2 Kgs 21:1–7; 2 Chr 33:1–10). The apocryphal *Martyrdom of Isaiah* says that Manasseh had Isaiah sawed in two around the year 668 B.C.

ISAIAH, BOOK OF The first among the latter prophets in the Hebrew canon, named for the prophet **Isaiah**. The book is renowned for its brilliant literary style and imagery as well as its profound spiritual insights. Of the prophets, Isaiah offers the most significant teaching on the Messiah. He is also more frequently cited in the New Testament than any other prophet.

I. *Authorship and Date*
   A. *The Multiple-Author Theory*
   B. *Arguments for Isaiah as Author of the*
      Whole Book
II. *Contents*

III. *Purpose and Themes*
   A. *The Moral Decline of Israel and Judah*
   B. *The Hope of the Messiah*
   C. *Vindication of the Remnant*
   D. *A Plea for Faith in the Lord*
   E. *The Promise of Salvation*
   F. *The Servant of the Lord*
   G. *The New Creation*
IV. *Isaiah in the New Testament*

I. AUTHORSHIP AND DATE

A. The Multiple-Author Theory

The unanimous view of tradition holds that Isaiah was the author of the entire book of prophecies that bears his name. Many scholars in the modern era, on the other hand, suggest that multiple authors are responsible for the book. In their view, chapters 1–39 are the writings of Isaiah himself; chapters 40–55, called Deutero-Isaiah (Second Isaiah), are attributed to an anonymous prophet who wrote toward the end of the Exile; and chapters 56–66 are oracles written in the postexilic period either by the author of Deutero-Isaiah or by a later disciple (called Trito-Isaiah, or Third Isaiah). In support of this theory, these scholars point out, for example, that the subject matter of Deutero-Isaiah is decidedly exilic, such as the references to Babylon rather than Assyria (the dominant power in Isaiah's time) and to the Persian king Cyrus the Great by name (Isa 44:28; 45:1).

If Isaiah was written by multiple authors, then the different parts were written at different times. Chapters 1–39 are placed at the time of the prophet Isaiah, that is to say around 700 B.C. There is less agreement about the rest of the book. Chapters 40–55 are usually dated to the middle of the sixth century B.C., during the rise of Cyrus the Great and the defeat of the Babylonians. Chapters 56–66 are dated either at the time of Haggai and Zechariah in the late sixth century B.C. or the middle of the fifth century B.C. Still other scholars consider the disputed chapters to date in part to periods earlier than the sixth century or as late as the second century B.C.

B. Arguments for Isaiah as Author of the Whole Book

On the other hand, tradition has been consistent in accepting Isaiah as author of the whole book. NT writers always treat Isaiah as one complete book. When the NT writers quote from chapters 40–66, they always ascribe them to Isaiah (cf. Matt 3:3, Isa 40:3; Matt 12:17–21, Isa 42:1–4; John 12:38, Rom 10:16, Isa 53:1). In point of fact, there are literary and stylistic features in Isaiah 1–39 that continue on into Isaiah 40–66. There is certainly a shift in tone and emphasis when one crosses the threshold of chapter 40, but the transition to a different selection of themes need not imply a different author is responsible for either the content or its expression. So long as one is open to the possibility of true prophecy, chapters 40–66 need not be disassociated from the eighth-century B.C. prophet, even if his oracles look forward to significant events destined to take place in the fifth century and later.

II. CONTENTS

III. PURPOSE AND THEMES

A. The Moral Decline of Israel and Judah

Isaiah speaks out against the moral conditions of his time in the kingdom of Judah, to promise hope and salvation for those who remain faithful to the covenant with the Lord, and to bring comfort and consolation in the face of the mounting threats to the kingdom and God's Chosen People. During Isaiah's early prophetic ministry, the relative peace of Judah had encouraged a decline in the religious life of the people. Idolatry, corruption, indifference to the suffering of the poor, and growing oppression flourished in this lax atmosphere. On the eastern horizon, however, the threat of the Assyrian Empire was looming ominously. Soon the Assyrians would engulf much of Syria and Palestine. The prophetic call of Isaiah in 6:10 comes during the lamentable decline of the kingdom of Judah, and the punishment of wickedness is assured. Nevertheless, Isaiah is also given the promise that a remnant will survive the coming destruction (Isa 6:13).

B. The Hope of the Messiah

The promise of future hope leads to one of the most famous of Isaiah's prophecies, that of **Immanuel** (Isa 7:14). The prophecy had immediate meaning to King Ahaz and his question about whether to enter into a foreign alliance. The prophecy of Immanuel also forecast the later scriptural revelation in Matt 1:20–23 and the Incarnation.

The Immanuel prophecy was only one of Isaiah's many prophecies relating to the Messiah. Other texts fill out the picture by highlighting the kingly qualities of the coming Messiah (Isa 9:1–6; 11:1–12:6). These characteristics make a direct connection between the expected deliverer and the promise given to David that from his royal line would come the Messiah (2 Sam 7:11–16) in a way that echoes the royal Psalms (Ps 2; 20; 21; 45; 72; 89; 101; 110).

In prophesying the birth of the **Messiah** (Immanuel), Isaiah gives assurance of the promise of God that he would be with his people. Isaiah 9:1–7 offers a portrait of the promised

victory inaugurating a kingdom "with justice and with righteousness from this time forth and for evermore" (9:7) (CCC 1502). Four key titles describe the Messiah in spectacular terms: "Wonderful Counselor, Mighty God, Everlasting Father, Prince of Peace" (9:6).

C. Vindication of the Remnant

In chapter 14, Isaiah predicts the defeat of the Assyrians (Isa 14:24–27) and their eventual judgment for arrogance (Isa 10:12). The prediction of the defeat came to pass (37:36) when the "angel of the Lord" wiped out an Assyrian army. The arrogance of the Assyrians is matched by the grim spiritual situation in Judah: the people's disobedience of the laws of God, their poorly considered foreign alliances, and their entirely perverted assumption that God would protect the kingdom in spite of their sins. In the terrible events to come, God would cleanse the people and vindicate the faithful remnant (29:24; 30:8). The promise of deliverance is eloquently proclaimed in Isa 33:1–35:10, and the theme of a cosmic or universal judgment has prompted some scholars to call chapters 34–35 a "little apocalypse."

D. A Plea for Faith in the Lord

Throughout chapters 1–39, Isaiah makes a plea for monotheism, because the kingdom was plagued with idolatry. For Isaiah, the Lord is the king and the holy one who will demonstrate his mastery over the pagan nations of the world. Isaiah calls as well for Judah's people to cease their infidelity or face the chastisement of divine wrath. Assyria is chosen to be the rod of God's punishment upon sinful Israel. Isaiah encouraged those who still had faith to remain firm in their resolve and to know that the survival of a remnant was promised.

E. The Promise of Salvation

Chapters 40–55 begin with an unmistakable statement of the author's purpose: "Comfort, comfort my people, says your God. Speak tenderly to Jerusalem, and cry to her that her warfare is ended, that her iniquity is pardoned, that she has received from the LORD's hand double for all her sins" (Isa 40:1–2). Instead of prophecies of doom, which dominate the first thirty-nine chapters, the prophet declares a promise of the Lord's salvation for his people. Israel is expected to announce to the world the uniqueness and the greatness of its Lord: "Who is like me? Let him proclaim it, let him declare and set it forth before me" (44:7). In contrast to the consolation given to Israel, these chapters announce that the Lord judges the nations and their idolatry and finds them to be in error (41:21–29; 44:9–20; 45:20–46:13). Babylon is singled out for destruction (chapters 46–47).

F. The Servant of the Lord

Chapters 40–55 are also marked by the four celebrated Servant Songs: 42:1–4; 49:1–6; 50:4–9; 52:13–53:12. The most significant of these is 52:13–53:12, which describes the Suffering Servant: "Surely he has borne our griefs and carried our sorrows"; "he was wounded for our transgressions, he was bruised for our iniquities"; "he was oppressed, and he was afflicted." The passage reveals a surprising part of God's plan of salvation: "Yet it was the will of the LORD to bruise him; he has put him to grief; when he makes himself an offering for

sin, he shall see his offspring, he shall prolong his days; the will of the LORD shall prosper in his hand" (53:10). For obvious reasons, Christians see the Servant Songs as a prediction of the redemptive suffering of Jesus Christ. (*See* **Servant of the Lord**.)

G. The New Creation

Chapters 55–66 then continue the general theme of hope and restoration. In language reminiscent of the prophet **Haggai** (Hag 2:1–9), Isa 55–66 anticipates the rise of the holy city, to which will gather the nations of the world (cf. Isa 60:10; 61:14). The prophet announces a new heaven and a new earth exemplified by the New Jerusalem to come: "But be glad and rejoice for ever in that which I create; for behold, I create Jerusalem a rejoicing, and her people a joy. I will rejoice in Jerusalem, and be glad in my people; no more shall be heard in it the sound of weeping and the cry of distress" (65:18–19).

IV. ISAIAH IN THE NEW TESTAMENT

In the NT, Christ and the apostles quote the book of Isaiah more frequently than they do any other prophet: some fifty direct quotations and more than forty paraphrases (e.g., Matt 3:3, 8:17, 12:18; Mark 1:7; Luke 3:4; John 1:12; Acts 8:28; Rom 9:20). Only the book of Psalms is referenced more frequently. The influence of Isaiah on NT theology is likewise extensive.

The Church also derives the list of the seven gifts of the Holy Spirit from the Greek Septuagint version of Isa 11:2–3. "And the Spirit of GOD shall rest upon him, a spirit of wisdom and understanding, a spirit of counsel and strength, a spirit of knowledge and piety; a spirit of the fear of God shall fill him." The seven gifts—permanent dispositions that help us to follow the promptings of the Holy Spirit—are *wisdom, understanding, knowledge, counsel, piety, fortitude,* and *fear of the Lord.* They complete and perfect the virtues of those who receive them (CCC 1830–31).

ISCARIOT *See* **Judas Iscariot.**

ISHBAAL *See* **Ish-bosheth.**

ISHBAK (Hebrew *yišbāq*) The fifth son of **Abraham** and Keturah (Gen 25:2; 1 Chr 1:32).

ISH-BOSHETH (Hebrew, "man of the shameful thing") The son of **Saul** who was established as king by **Abner** after the defeat and death of Saul at Mount Gilboa (2 Sam 2:8–11). He was proclaimed "king over Gilead, the Ashurites, Jezreel, Ephraim, Benjamin, and over all Israel." He was forty years old at the time he took the throne and reigned for only two years. **David,** who was ruler of Judah, soon entered into war with Ish-bosheth (2 Sam 2:12ff.). Ish-bosheth and Abner fell out over a concubine, and Abner entered into negotiations with David to deliver the kingdom. Abner was then murdered by **Joab** (2 Sam 22–39), and his death deprived Ish-bosheth of his last hope of resisting David. Ish-bosheth was assassinated by two officers, Baanah and Rechab, who were themselves executed by David for treachery (2 Sam 4). Upon Ish-bosheth's death, the kingdom of the north passed into David's hands.

The name Ish-bosheth was a deliberate corruption of his true name, Ishbaal (meaning "man of Baal"). At one time, **Baal** (meaning "Lord" or "Master") had been used as a legitimate title for the Lord; but in later times, the title became exclusively associated with the popular Canaanite god. As scribes were unwilling to write the name of the Canaanite god Baal, they altered the original name of Saul's son.

ISHMAEL The son of **Abraham** and **Hagar,** **Sarah**'s slave (Gen 16; 17:18–26; 21:8–21; 25:9, 12–17; 28:9; 36:3; 1 Chr 1:28–31) and the ancestor of the Ishmaelites. Sarah, who was barren, had encouraged Abraham to father a son by Hagar. But when Hagar was with child, she began to taunt Sarah, and subsequently Sarah treated Hagar so badly that she fled Abraham's camp (Gen 16). Hagar returned after encountering an angel. After the birth of Isaac, Ishmael was expelled from the camp with his mother (Gen 21). In the desert, he and Hagar faced death until an angel of God helped them find water and then assured them that Ishmael's descendants would prosper. Ishmael grew up into a capable archer and nomad. He took a wife from Egypt, resided in the wilderness of Paran, and was the father of twelve sons and a daughter who married **Esau** (Gen 28:9; 36:3). He died at the age of 137 (Gen 16:15; 21:9–21; 25:13–17).

The descendants of Ishmael formed several tribes in northwest Arabia and were called the Ishmaelites (Gen 25:12–18). Occasionally, they are closely associated with Midianites, perhaps because the area of Ishmaelite occupation (Havilah to Shur) encompasses the land traditionally called Midian. Ishmaelite traders purchased Joseph and then sold him into slavery in Egypt (Gen 37:25–28; they are called Midianites in Gen 37:28). Midianites were captured by Gideon (Judg 6–8; they are referred to as Ishmaelites in Judg 8:24). The territory of the Ishmaelites extended from Havila to Shur in Arabia (Gen 25:12–18).

In Gal 4:21–31, Paul discusses the allegorical meaning of the story of Ishmael and Isaac: "Now this is an allegory: these women are two covenants. One is from Mount Sinai, bearing children for slavery; she is Hagar. Now Hagar is Mount Sinai in Arabia; she corresponds to the present Jerusalem, for she is in slavery with her children. But the Jerusalem above is free, and she is our mother" (Gal 4:24–26). For Paul, Christians are the sons (like Isaac) of the free woman (Sarah).

Another Ishmael, the son of Nethaniah, was a member of the royal house of Judah (Jer 41:11; 2 Kgs 25:25) and an officer in the Judean army (Jer 41:1). Following the destruction of Jerusalem in 586 B.C., he refused to accept the yoke of Babylonian rule and assassinated Gedaliah, the appointed ruler of Judah, at Mizpah (Jer 41:2; 2 Kgs 25:23). The women and children were then carried off. Johanan recovered the captives, but Ishmael escaped to the Ammonites, whose patronage he enjoyed (Jer 41:11–18).

ISHTAR *See* **Ashtoreth**.

ISHVI *See* **Ish-bosheth**.

ISRAEL (Hebrew, possibly "one who strives with God") The name given to **Jacob** after a night of wrestling at Peniel: "You shall no longer be called Jacob, but Israel, for you have striven [from the Hebrew *śārâ,* "strive"] with God and with humans, and have prevailed" (Gen 32:28). The renaming of Jacob is reiterated in Gen 35:10, and throughout the Old Testament the name can refer to Jacob or, more frequently, to the descendants of Jacob.

The nation of Israel thus traced itself to the twelve sons of Jacob, and was termed the people of Israel (Exod 1:8), the tribes of Israel (Gen 49:16, 28), the Israelites (Gen 32:32), or simply Israel (Gen 34:7). This was the people with whom God entered into a covenant relationship for the fulfillment of the divine plan of universal salvation. The Israelites were chosen to become "a priestly kingdom and a holy nation" (Exod 19:6) and "his own possession" (Ps 135:4; cf. Exod 19:5; Deut 32:8–10; Mal 3:17).

I. THE NAME "ISRAEL"

The earliest known use of the name "Israel" outside the Bible appears in the Egyptian victory stele of Pharaoh Merneptah in the late thirteenth century B.C. The inscription states that following an Egyptian campaign in Palestine "Israel is laid waste, his seed is not." The next non-Israelite reference is in an Assyrian inscription of King Shalmaneser III in the middle of the ninth century B.C. Around the same time, a Moabite inscription pompously asserts that "Israel perished utterly and forever."

II. THE HISTORICAL ISRAEL

The nation of Israel began as a multitribal family descended from Jacob that lived in the eastern Delta of Egypt (*see* **Goshen**). The Egyptians eventually compelled them to serve as laborers, but they were galvanized into a cohesive people through the efforts of **Moses**.

Under the leadership of Moses, the Israelites passed out of Egypt and, at the base of Mount Sinai, entered into a covenant relationship with God, by which they were called to be a priestly nation set aside for the Lord.

The Israelites went on to seize control of Canaan, partitioning the land among the tribes. The tribes enjoyed a high degree of autonomy in their respective territories, but the common danger posed by the Philistines encouraged a greater sense of unity and common resolve against a determined enemy (cf. Judg 5:14–18, 19–21). The Philistines were the most feared enemies of Israel, and often they were far superior in military strength (1 Sam 13). They even captured the ark of the covenant at Aphek (1 Sam 4). The Philistine domination encouraged the Israelites to demand a king: "we will have a king over us, that we also may be like all the nations, and that our king may govern us and go out before us and fight our battles" (1 Sam 8:19–20).

Saul was anointed the first king of Israel, but his reign ended with defeat and disaster after he lost the divine mandate (1 Sam 31). Saul was succeeded by the divinely chosen heir, **David**. The new king succeeded in uniting the northern tribes with Judah in the south into a unified monarchy that became the subsequent ideal of kingship in the history of Israel. The stability of the monarchy was passed on to David's son, **Solomon**. During his reign, the Temple was built in Jerusalem, and the power and glory of the kingdom reached their zenith.

The unity of the kingdom did not long endure. Under Rehoboam, son of Solomon, the northern tribes seceded. Henceforth, there were two kingdoms: Israel in the north and Judah in the south. (For the subsequent histories of these two kingdoms, see **Israel, Kingdom of**, and **Judah**.) Both of the kingdoms were swept up in the greater events engulfing Palestine and the Near East. Israel fell in 722 B.C. to the armies of **Assyria**, and Judah fell in 586 B.C. to the forces of Nebuchadnezzar of **Babylon**.

The demise of Judah brought to an end as well Israel as a formal political and geographical entity. The Israel that returned from the Exile in Babylon was a people set apart for the Lord, living in fidelity to the covenants and in expectation of the Messiah. But the people were not a nation; Palestine was part of a province in the great Persian Empire. Nevertheless, the people continued to use the name "Israel" for themselves in the period after the Exile; to outsiders, however, they were "Jews," a name derived from the dominant surviving tribe of Judah (cf. 1–2 Macc) (CCC 529, 673–74).

III. ISRAEL AND SALVATION HISTORY

The Israelites were a Chosen People, a nation elected by God to fulfill a divine purpose in human history. God spoke to the patriarchs (Gen 12–50) and made promises to **Abraham** (Gen 12:1–3; cf. Gen 25:19–23; Rom 9:10–12) concerning his descendants. God promised Abraham that he would have innumerable descendants through the single son born of Sarah, and that his descendants would become a source of blessing for all the nations (Gen 12:3; 22:18). That promise would climax in Christ, the son of Abraham (Matt 1:1), and the plan of salvation would expand to encompass the entire human race (cf. Matt 8:11–12; Luke 13:28–29) (CCC 59–61, 2570–74).

After the period of the patriarchs, God formed Israel as his people through the labors of Moses when God established with them the covenant of Mount Sinai. Israel was to be a priestly people and the elder brother to the nations of the world. Its failure to remain obedient, however, destroyed the kingdoms of Israel and Judah.

For its part, Israel was expected to recognize the Lord alone as its God (Deut 4:39), keep his commandments (Deut 4:40) and laws (Lev 17–26), and remain in fidelity to the covenant oaths they had made. Israel was above all to be a holy people (Lev 19:2; cf. Exod 22:30; Lev 20:26), ever faithful to the recognition of God's sovereignty and call. God's righteous anger is assured toward those who threaten God's elect (Isa 9:16; Zech. 1:14), but especially toward God's own holy people who abandon their promises of holiness and fidelity (Deut 4:24; cf. Exod 34:14; Josh 24:19).

The prophets accused Israel of breaking the covenant, but they also proclaimed the coming of a new and eternal covenant. This was instituted by Christ, who restored the faithful of Israel in the Church. Christ also fulfilled the Father's plan of salvation for all nations. By his preaching and his death and Resurrection, he founded the Kingdom of God that "shines out before men in the word, in the works and in the presence of Christ" (LG §5). "But you are a chosen race, a royal priesthood, a holy nation, God's own people, in order that you may proclaim the mighty acts of him who called you out of darkness into his marvelous light" (1 Pet 2:9). The First Letter of Pe-

ter incorporates the central covenant theme of Exod 19:6—the consecration of Israel as a holy and priestly nation—but asserts plainly that the election of Israel that had been lost has been restored by Christ in the New Covenant (CCC 1268, 1546).

The new Israel, the Church, is the "Israel of God" (Gal 6:16), the heir to the covenant promises made by God. Jesus appointed the twelve apostles to be the new heads of the twelve tribes of the restored Israel (Matt 19:28; Luke 22:30). They are to sit on twelve thrones in judgment of the twelve tribes. Paul sees the "Israel of God" in contrast to "Israel according to the flesh" (1 Cor 10:18).

The supreme ideal of the new Israel is expressed in the book of Revelation. The number of those who are sealed with a mark of protection equals 12,000 from each of the tribes, 144,000 in total (Rev 7:4–8), a number that symbolizes utter completeness. The new heavenly city of Jerusalem has twelve gates, each named after one of the twelve tribes (Rev 21:12) (CCC 759–62, 1093).

ISRAEL, KINGDOM OF The northern kingdom of Israel that was established around 930 B.C. after the collapse of the unified monarchy. It endured until 722 B.C. In the increasingly despotic final years of **Solomon**'s reign, the king created twelve administrative districts for securing revenue and supplying food for the royal household. When Solomon's successor, **Rehoboam**, chose on the advice of his advisors to continue this oppressive royal policy, the northern tribes complained bitterly. When the king attempted to assert his royal prerogative at the gathering at Shechem, he so infuriated the tribes that open rebellion soon followed.

After seceding from the Davidic kingdom, the ten northern tribes set themselves up as an independent kingdom under the rule of **Jeroboam** (1 Kgs 12:1–20; 2 Chr 10:1–19). As king, Jeroboam tried to end the hegemony of the Davidic kingdom of Judah in religious affairs by establishing two centers of worship at Bethel and Dan, where he set up golden calves (1 Kgs 12:25–33). As a result Jeroboam was severely criticized as the king who brought Israel into a state of sin and doomed the kingdom to inevitable destruction. The death of Jeroboam's son, Abijah, was seen as punishment for this sinful deed (1 Kgs 14:1–18), and it was common for his successors to be named followers of Jeroboam who "made Israel sin."

The kingdom of Israel was plagued by two permanent political problems: the constant threat from foreign enemies and the severe dynastic instability of the kingdom. The kingdom of Judah didn't face these challenges but instead enjoyed general political constancy and relatively limited strategic exposure to the attacks of the various empires of the period. The chief early enemy of the kingdom of Israel in its first period was the Aramean kingdom of Damascus.

The political chaos that troubled Israel was epitomized by the ability of only two dynasties (those of **Omri** and **Jehu**) to survive for more than a few generations. Jeroboam's son, Abijah, was assassinated in the very year of his succession by one of his generals, Baasha. Baasha himself was murdered twenty years later, and the kingdom sank into civil war, from which Omri emerged triumphant. Omri created a

new capital at **Samaria** (1 Kgs 16:24). The capital was expanded by King **Ahab**, who added an ivory palace (1 Kgs 22:39; Amos 6:4); but his marriage to a Phoenician princess, the infamous **Jezebel**, led to the promotion of **Baal** worship. The prophet Elijah promised the imminent doom of the royal house.

Jehu exterminated the line of Ahab (ca. 841 B.C.); Samaria was damaged in the struggle (2 Kgs 10). Jehu reversed the idolatry of the Ahab dynasty, but the civil strife left the kingdom vulnerable to attack by the Arameans. The northern kingdom was on the verge of genuine disaster at the hands of the Syrians when the new menace of the Assyrians emerged suddenly. Damascus was attacked and the Arameans were compelled to give tribute, but for the kingdom of Israel the events also marked an opportunity for recovery. The armies of Israel then succeeded in recapturing a number of cities that had fallen to the Arameans in the previous years. A period of prosperity ensued, especially under **Jeroboam II** of the Jehu Dynasty. Nevertheless, the voices of the prophets—such as **Amos** and **Hosea**—continued to warn that the people of Israel needed to be faithful to the promises of the covenant and give proper worship to God.

The Jehu Dynasty was brought to an end by violence. **Menahem** (2 Kgs 15:13–22), the son of Gadi, came to the throne around 745 B.C. by assassinating Shallum, the son of Jabesh, a usurper who had already murdered Zechariah, the last king of the Jehu Dynasty. Menahem's chief act was to pay tribute to the Assyrian ruler **Tiglath-pileser** III, and to use Assyrian backing to strengthen his own hold on power. An anti-Assyrian policy was then pursued by **Pekah**, who embarked on a foolish alliance with Syria against the Assyrians. Tiglath-pileser stormed Damascus and punished Israel by seizing portions of the kingdom and deporting the inhabitants to regions of the Assyrian Empire.

The last ruler of the northern kingdom, **Hoshea** (ca. 732–722 B.C.; 2 Kgs 15:30), assassinated his predecessor, Pekah, following the latter's defeat at the hands of the Assyrians in 732 B.C. The murder was instigated by the Assyrians, and Hoshea proved a reliable vassal for some years. In 724 B.C., however, he entered into an alliance with the Egyptians (1 Kgs 17:3–4). In response, **Shalmaneser V**, king of Assyria, invaded Israel and took Hoshea captive. Samaria fell to the army of Shalmaneser V and Sargon II (2 Kgs 17:1–6) after an extended siege lasting from 724 to 722 B.C. The inhabitants of the kingdom of Israel were deported and the northern kingdom was brought to an end. In its place the Assyrians established the province of Samaria. In keeping with Assyrian policy, other conquered peoples were forcibly resettled in the region.

Underlying the political and military events that led to the death of the kingdom was a deeper and more troubling religious aspect. Rehoboam had squandered the covenant, and the result was the shattering of the unity of the kingdom. The northern kingdom never fully recovered from the religious policies of Jeroboam I. The prophets warned against setting up an alternative to the sacred ecclesial order in the south, but Jeroboam persisted in doing precisely that. He expelled the Levite priests and established worship centers at Dan and Bethel. As idolatry persisted and even flourished under the kings of Israel, such as Ahab, messengers of the covenant rose up—Elijah and Elisha, for example—to give warning and threats and to announce impending catastrophe if their words were not heeded.

ISSACHAR (Hebrew, "there is a reward") The ninth son of Jacob, the fifth son born to Leah, and the ancestor of the Israelite tribe of Issachar (Gen 30:17–18). The origins of his name are traced to Gen 30:1–18 and the efforts of Leah to conceive a child. Following the conquest of Canaan, the tribe of Issachar established itself on the plain of Esdraelon in lower Galilee (Deut 33:18–19; Josh 19:17–23, 21:28; 1 Chr 6:57), and its towns were listed in Josh 19:17–23 (cf. Josh 21:28; 1 Chr 6:57 lists the Levitical cities). While the region was still heavily populated by Canaanites, Issachar nevertheless took part in the campaign against Sisera (Judg 5:15). Thereafter, the tribe of Issachar appears rarely in biblical history. Among its most famous members were Tola, son of Puah, a minor judge (Judg 10:1), and Baasha, king of Israel (1 Kgs 15:27).

ITALIAN COHORT A Roman cohort (a unit in the Roman legions) that was stationed in Caesarea. It is likely that the unit was the Cohors II Italica Civium Romanorum (Second Italian Cohort of Roman Citizens). One of its centurions, **Cornelius**, was the first Gentile to be baptized in the name of Jesus (Acts 10:1–48).

ITALY The Italian peninsula is mentioned only rarely in Scripture. The first reference to Jews in Italy occurs in 1 Macc 8, where mention is made of a delegation sent to Rome by Judas Maccabeus (cf. 1 Macc 12:1–4; 14:16–19, 24). The first New Testament reference is in Acts 18:2, when **Aquila** and **Priscilla** were forced out of Italy because of the expulsion of Jews from Rome by Emperor Claudius in A.D. 49. The second reference occurs in Acts 27:1, where Paul begins his journey to Italy to stand trial before Caesar. Other references include Acts 28:13–16 and Heb 13:24. (*See also* **Rome**.)

ITHAMAR The fourth son of **Aaron** and **Elisheba** (Exod 6:23; Num 26:60; 1 Chr 6:3, 24:1). Ithamar was recognized as the father of eight of the twenty-four priestly classes (1 Chr 24:4); the rest claimed descent from **Eleazar**. Neither Ithamar nor Eleazar took part in the worship of **Nadab** and **Abihu**, and Ithamar was spared with Eleazar from the plague (Lev 10; Num 3). Ithamar was given the duty of directing the construction (Exod 38:21) and the transportation (Num 4:28, 33; 7:8) of the Tabernacle.

ITHRA Father of **Amasa**, the commander of the Israelite army during Absalom's revolt against David (2 Sam 17:25; 1 Kgs 2:5, 32; 1 Chr 2:17).

ITHREAM The sixth son of **David** (2 Sam 3:5; 1 Chr 3:3). He was born at Hebron, and his mother was Eglah.

ITTAI A Philistine from Gath and the captain of David's mercenary troops. During the re-volt of **Absalom**, Ittai proved utterly loyal to King David (2 Sam 15:19, 21, 22). He later took part as a commander in the battle against the forces of Absalom during which Absalom was slain (2 Sam 15:19–22; 18:2, 5, 12).

ITURAEA The Greek name for the region of **Bashan**.

IVORY A precious commodity in the ancient world, as today, that was used throughout Palestine and the ancient Near East for sculpture and ornamentation. Its applications were as varied as the imaginations of craftsmen; it was used in chairs, tables, and beds, as well as smaller personal items such as combs and knives. Imported into Palestine from Arabia, Africa, and the East (1 Kgs 10:22), ivory was a symbol of luxury and wealth. It was used for Solomon's throne (1 Kgs 10:18; 2 Chr 9:17) and for the famous ivory house of Ahab (1 Kgs 22:39; cf. Amos 3:15; Ps 45:9). Tyre was a chief ivory center in Palestine (Ezek 27:15).

IYE ABARIM (Hebrew, "ruins of Abarim") The location of an Israelite encampment during their Exodus journey through the wilderness (Num 21:11–12), it was situated south of Moab (cf. Num 33:44–45).

IYYAR The second month of the Hebrew calendar. It corresponds to April–May.

J

J The letter used to designate the so-called Yahwist source in the four-source theory of the composition of the **Pentateuch**. The letter itself is an abbreviation of the German word *Jahvist*.

JAAZANIAH The name of three men in the Old Testament.

1. An officer who served under **Gedaliah**, the Babylonian-appointed ruler of Judah, following the destruction of Jerusalem in 586 B.C. (2 Kgs 25:23; cf. Jer 40:8).

2. The son of Shaphan and one of the seventy elders whom Ezekiel beheld in a vision committing idolatry (Ezek 8:11). Jaazaniah was probably a leader among them, as he is the only one of them actually mentioned by name.

3. The son of Azzur and one of the twenty-five men beheld in another vision by Ezekiel. (Ezek 11:1). Jaazaniah must have been an important figure in the government of Judah: he is described as one of the "princes of the people" (cf. Jer 26:10).

JABAL Son of **Lamech** and Adah, brother of Jubal, and a descendant of **Cain** (Gen 4:20). He is named the father of tent dwellers and herdsmen (Gen 4:20).

JABBOK An eastern tributary of the **Jordan** and one of the major waterways of **Transjordan**. (The modern name is Nahr ez-Zerqa.) The Jabbok begins near Amman, Jordan (the biblical Rabbath-ammon), and flows into the Jordan north of the Dead Sea. It was the site of **Jacob**'s struggle with the angel of God (Gen 32:22). Before Israel's conquest of Canaan, the Jabbok served as a natural border between the Amorites and the Ammonites (cf. Num 21:24; Josh 12:2).

JABESH The father of King **Shallum** of Israel (2 Kgs 15:10, 13–14).

JABESH-GILEAD (Hebrew, "well-draining soil of Gilead") A city in **Transjordan**, probably near modern Wadi el-Yabis, a tributary that feeds into the Jordan. Suggested locations for Jabesh-gilead have been ed-Deir (Deir el-Halawe), Miryamim, Tell Maqlub, and Meqbereh-Tell abu Kharaz. In the days of the Judges, Jabesh-gilead's inhabitants failed to participate in the war of retribution against the tribe of Benjamin and so were subjected to severe attack by the Israelites. All of the men and married women were massacred and the surviving virgins, some four hundred of them, were given to the Benjaminites as wives (Judg 21:8–15). The result was a close relationship between the city and Benjamin.

Saul rescued the city from an Ammonite assault (1 Sam 11), and in return the people of Jabesh-gilead retrieved the bodies of Saul and his sons after they had been hanged from the wall of Beth-shan by the Philistines (1 Sam 31:11). David was grateful for their concern and was later able to give Saul a proper burial (2 Sam 2:4–7; 21:12–14).

JABIN The king of **Hazor** who headed a coalition that was defeated by **Joshua** and Israel (Josh 11:1–14). Jabin was responsible for organizing other kings of northern Canaan in an alliance. In the struggle, Jabin was killed, and Hazor was burned to the ground. A second Jabin was a king of Canaan, in Hazor, during the time of **Deborah** (Judg 4). The commander of Jabin's army was Sisera, who was defeated by Deborah and Barak; the second Jabin was likewise killed.

JABNEEL (Hebrew, "God will build") Also called Jabneh and later Jamnia, a town in the northwest corner of Judah (Josh 15:11), located to the south of Joppa and four miles from the Mediterranean; the town is probably the modern Yavneh. Jabneel was captured from the Philistines by King **Uzziah** of Judah (2 Chr 26:6) and later was used as a strategic center by the Syrians during the revolt of the Maccabees (1 Macc 4:15; 5:58; 10:69; 15:40). Taken by Judas Maccabeus, it was burned (2 Macc 12:8–9). Jamnia was a rendezvous point for Jewish rabbis after the Roman conquest of Jerusalem in A.D. 70, until the Second Jewish Revolt under Simon Bar Kokhba (132–135). Between these dates, the city was a center of Jewish learning: rabbinic legend even made it the site of a gathering in about A.D. 100 that addressed various religious issues such as the Old Testament canon. A second Jabneel was located in northern Israel in the territory of Naphtali (Josh 19:33).

JACHIN The name of one of the two bronze pillars (the other was **Boaz**) that were installed by King Solomon at the vestibule of the Temple. Boaz was on the right of the sanctuary doors; Jachin was on the left (1 Kgs 7:17, 19, 21; 2 Chr 3:17; Jer 52:21–22). The pillars were eighteen cubits (about 27 feet or 8 meters) high and twelve cubits (about 18 feet or 5.5 meters) in circumference.

JACINTH, HYACINTH A precious stone, noted for its rich orange color (Exod 28:19, 39:12; Rev 21:20).

JACKAL A scavenging and omnivorous animal found throughout Palestine. In Scripture, the jackal is typically associated with desolate or forgotten regions and cities (Ps 44:19; Isa 13:22, 34:13; Jer 9:11, 10:22, 49:33, 51:37; Lam 5:18; Mal 1:3).

JACOB The younger of twin sons born to **Isaac** and **Rebekah**, the third great patriarch, and the ancestor of the twelve tribes of Israel (Gen 25:19–34; 35:22–26). The name of Jacob in Hebrew, *ya'ăqōb*, is associated with the Hebrew *'āqēb*, "heel," as Jacob was born grasping the heel of his brother Esau (Gen 25:26), and with the verb *'āqab*, "cheat," as Esau claimed that Jacob cheated him of his birthright and his father's blessing (Gen 27:36). Jacob also received the name "Israel" as a symbol of his struggle with an unidentified angel (Gen 32:28); his twelve sons gave their names to the twelve tribes of Israel and were called the "children of Israel."

I. BIOGRAPHY

A. Winning the Birthright

Jacob was concerned from an early time with acquiring the birthright from his brother Esau. Even in the womb he struggled against his brother (Gen 25:22–23). His mother, Rebekah, favored Jacob, whereas Isaac favored Esau. Jacob bought the rights of the firstborn from Esau for a bowl of stew (Gen 25:29–33), and later Rebekah counseled Jacob how to fool his blind father, Isaac, into giving him the blessing due the firstborn (Gen 27:1–37).

B. Jacob's Ladder

To escape the anger and vengeance of Esau and also to obtain a wife from his parents' lineage (rather than a Canaanite), Jacob heeded his mother's counsel and set out for Haran (Paddan-Aram), the dwelling place of **Laban**, his maternal uncle (Gen 27:41–45). On his journey to Haran, Jacob stopped at Luz and saw a vision of a ladder (or stairway) that reached from earth to heaven and that was used by angels to ascend and descend. At its summit was the Lord, who renewed for Jacob the promises that had been made to Abraham and to Isaac (Gen 28:10–22). When Jacob awoke, he erected a pillar, named the place of the vision Beth-El, "the house of God," and made a vow to the Lord.

C. Jacob's Wives and Children

Upon reaching Haran, Jacob encountered **Rachel**, Laban's daughter, at a well, and offered to work for his uncle Laban for seven years in return for Rachel's hand in marriage. When seven years had passed, however, Laban substituted his elder daughter, **Leah**, as Jacob's bride. She was veiled both at the wedding ceremony and at the consummation of the marriage, and Jacob did not recognize her until the morning. Now Jacob the deceiver had become the deceived. Laban then promised Rachel to Jacob if he agreed to another seven years of labor (Gen 29:1–25).

Jacob was blessed with children through Leah (Reuben, Simeon, Levi, Judah, Issachar, and Zebulun, and a daughter, Dinah), as well as through his concubines Bilhah (Dan and Naphtali) and Zilpah (Gad and Asher). Although initially barren, his beloved Rachel eventually gave birth to Joseph and later Benjamin (Gen 29:26–30:24). Jacob's cleverness brought him material prosperity, especially in comparison to Laban (see Gen 30:41–43). Jacob desired to return to Canaan, but Laban wished to prevent his departure. After his first request to return home met with resistance (Gen 30:25–28), Jacob was instructed by

God to depart, and, with his household and flocks, Jacob left in secret (Gen 31:1–21). Rachel secretly stole the teraphim, the household idols that gave Laban authority as head of the family. When Laban angrily pursued Jacob's caravan, Rachel concealed the idols beneath the camel saddle and sat upon them as Laban searched the camp (Gen 31:22–42). Jacob appeased his angry father-in-law and established a covenant with him by which he agreed not to mistreat Laban's daughters or to marry other wives. Both parties also agreed to respect the boundaries established by the pile of stones that marked the covenant (Gen 30:25–31:54).

D. Wrestling with God

While returning to Canaan, spent a night wrestling with an unidentified angel (Hos 12:4) until dawn. After the night's labors, Jacob received a new blessing and the name Israel, "for you have striven with God and with men, and have prevailed." Jacob renamed the place Peniel because "I have seen God face to face, and yet my life is preserved" (Gen 32:30).

Continuing on, Jacob encountered Esau. As with Laban, he appeased his brother Esau, who had come to meet him with four hundred men (Gen 33:1–17). The meeting proved amicable, and the brothers were reconciled. Jacob then made stops at Shechem (Gen 33:18) and Bethel, where God confirmed Jacob's new name of Israel and renewed his promises (Gen 35:6–15). Going farther south, Jacob arrived at Ephrath, where he buried Rachel, who died giving birth to Benjamin, and erected a monument in her honor (Gen 35:16–20). Settling at Hebron, Jacob lived quietly as the head of his large family (Gen 35:27).

E. Moving to Egypt

The rest of his life was caught up with the events surrounding his son **Joseph** (including the agony of his son's apparent death), severe famines, and finally the discovery that Joseph was both alive and the vizier of Egypt. Joseph invited his father and extended family to move to Egypt (Gen 46:1–47:12), and there Jacob died. Before his death, Jacob gave his blessing to Joseph and his brothers (see **Jacob, blessing of**). Joseph and his brothers carried Jacob's remains to Machpelah for burial (Gen 49:29–50:14).

II. JACOB IN SALVATION HISTORY

Jacob's place in salvation history is summarized in Exodus: "I am the God of your father, the God of Abraham, the God of Isaac, and the God of Jacob" (Exod 3:6; CCC 205). Jacob was chosen by God to become the father of the twelve tribes of Israel, and with him God renews the covenant oaths that were made to Abraham and Isaac. In guiding his people, God chose to pass over the proud firstborn (Esau) in favor of the younger son, a pattern already established in Genesis (cf. Cain and Abel, Ishmael and Isaac) and that would recur again soon after (cf. Reuben and Joseph, Manasseh and Ephraim).

Jacob is also considered a model for Christian prayer. At Peniel, he prepared to meet his brother Esau by spending the night wrestling a mysterious figure who refused to reveal his name. At the end of the struggle, Jacob received a blessing, an event interpreted by the Church as a symbol that prayer is a battle of faith that brings blessings for perseverance (CCC 2573; cf. Gen 32:24–30; Luke 18:1–8).

JACOB, BLESSING OF The words delivered by Jacob to his sons in Gen 49:2–27. Judah receives a blessing of royal dignity (Gen 49:8–12), and Joseph receives his father's firstborn blessing (Gen 49:22–26; cf. 1 Chr 5:1–2). There are stern words as well as blessings: Reuben, Simeon, and Levi are all rebuked for wicked behavior that had so far gone unpunished (Gen 49:3–7). The words are also a prophecy or promise of the future increase of the tribes of Israel.

JACOB'S WELL The site where Jesus spoke with the Samaritan woman (John 4:6). The well—the only one mentioned specifically in the New Testament—was said to have been used by Jacob's family and flocks (John 4:12). It is not named in the Old Testament, but traditionally, the site is said to be near Shechem, and John's narrative probably connects it with this location as well (John 4:5; cf. Gen 18:33). In the sixth century, a Byzantine church was built over what was believed to be the well; a restored church was never finished.

JAEL (Hebrew, "mountain goat") The wife of **Heber** the Kenite (Judg 4:17). She gave shelter to **Sisera**, the fleeing general in charge of the Canaanite armies of Jabin, king of Hazor, following his defeat by Barak and **Deborah** (Judg 4:16). When Sisera fell asleep, Jael pounded a tent stake through his skull (Judg 4:17; 5:6).

The story is told in prose form (Judg 4:17–22) and then celebrated poetically in the Song of Deborah (Judg 5:24–27).

JAHVEH, JAHWEH *See* "Yahweh" *under* **God.**

JAIR The name of four men in the Old Testament.

1. The son of **Manasseh** (Num 32:41; Deut 3:14; 1 Kgs 4:13). He seized several villages in **Gilead** belonging to the Amorites, probably in the region of lower Bashan. The villages eventually received his name.

2. One of the so-called minor judges (Judg 10:3–5), who judged Israel for twenty-two years. He is said to have been a Gileadite and had thirty sons who rode on thirty donkeys and controlled thirty towns in Gilead. His tomb was at Kamon (probably modern Qamm).

3. A Benjaminite and the father of **Mordecai**, the guardian of **Esther** (Esth 2:5).

4. The father of **Elhanan**, who slew Lahmi, brother of **Goliath** (1 Chr 20:5). In 2 Sam 21:19, we read that an Elhanan, son of Jaareoregim—apparently an expanded version of the name "Jair"—slew Goliath himself.

JAIRUS The "ruler of the synagogue" who implored Jesus to heal his dying daughter (Mark 5:21–24, 35–43; Luke 8:40–42, 49–56). Before Jesus reached the girl, she died, but Jesus said that she was merely sleeping, stressing that her death was only temporary, and raised her. Mark relates Jesus's command in Aramaic: "'*Talitha cumi*'; which means, 'Little girl . . . , arise'" (Mark 5:41). Jairus is a Greek form of the Hebrew proper name **Jair**.

JAMES (Greek *Iakōbos,* a Hellenized form of the Hebrew name "Jacob") The name of several men in the New Testament.

1. James the son of Zebedee (d. 44), brother of John, and one of the twelve apostles. Tradition sometimes calls him James the Great to distinguish him from James the Less, perhaps because he was older or taller than James the Less (Mark 15:40). James was originally a Galilean fisherman, along with his father and brother. Jesus called him while he and his brother were in a fishing boat with their father (Matt 4:21; Mark 1:19). The two brothers displayed tremendous zeal (Mark 10:37; Luke 9:49, 54), and Christ gave them the name "Boanerges," which means "sons of thunder" (Mark 3:17). James was a member of the trio of disciples, with John and Peter, who witnessed the raising of **Jairus**'s daughter (Mark 5:37; Luke 8:51), the **Transfiguration** (Matt 17:1; Mark 9:2), and the Agony in the Garden of **Gethsemane** (Matt 26:37; Mark 14:32–33).

He was the first apostle to suffer martyrdom—he was beheaded at the command of King Agrippa I of Judea in A.D. 44. His death, recorded in Acts 12:2, is the only martyrdom among the twelve apostles reported in the NT. According to long Spanish tradition, James preached in Spain before his death, and thus he became one of the most popular Spanish saints. It was generally accepted in Spain that his body was moved to Santiago de Compostela, one of the foremost of all pilgrim sites. His feast day is July 25.

2. James, "Brother of the Lord" (Matt 13:55; Mark 6:3; Gal 1:19), the leader of the Christians of Jerusalem, and an important figure in the early Church. He was the brother of Joseph (or Joses), Simon, and Judas (Matt 13:55; Mark 6:3). According to Paul, this James had a unique and personal encounter with the risen Christ (1 Cor 15:7) and subsequently became a leader among the Christian community of Jerusalem. Paul mentions him in Gal 1:19, and James and Peter played prominent roles at the Council of Jerusalem that decided whether Gentiles must be circumcised (Acts 15). His authority grew after Peter fled the city to escape execution at the hands of Herod Agrippa (Acts 12:2). James was also visited by Paul (Acts 21:18) on his last trip to Jerusalem.

James is traditionally considered the first bishop of Jerusalem. Clement of Alexandria, as recorded by Eusebius of Caesarea in the *Ecclesiastical History*, calls him the Just, because of his zealous adherence to the Jewish Law. Eusebius, quoting the second-century historian Hegesippus, says James was put to death by the Sanhedrin in A.D. 62. According to this account, James was thrown off a tower in the Temple of Jerusalem, then stoned, and finally clubbed to death (Eusebius, *Hist. Eccl.* 2.23). The Jewish historian Josephus (*Ant.* 20.200) notes only that James was condemned to be stoned. His symbol in art is a club or heavy staff.

James's name was attached to a number of postbiblical writings and traditions (*see* **Apocryphal books**). Among these are the Apocalypses of James, two works found in the Nag

Hammadi Library; an epistle of James, also found at Nag Hammadi; the Liturgy of Saint James, traditionally ascribed to him; and the so-called Infancy Gospel or the book of James, also known as the *Protoevangelium*, which was based on the Gospels of Mark and Luke.

Many scholars favor James "the brother of the Lord" as the author of the NT epistle of James. Tradition also connects him with the Liturgy of Saint James.

James is sometimes considered to be the same person as James the Less (son of Alphaeus; see below) and shares with that James and Saint Philip the feast day May 3.

3. James the Less, called "the Less" or "the Lesser" to distinguish him from James the Greater, who was older or taller; almost certainly this is the same James as the James discussed above as James, "the brother of Jesus." He is always identified in relation to his mother. Mark 15:40 describes "James the younger" as the son of Mary, a woman who, with Mary Magdalene, stood and witnessed the Crucifixion, and calls this Mary "the mother of James" a little later (Mark 16:1). In Matt 27:56, this James is again called the son of the woman Mary. He shares the same feast day as Saint Philip: May 3. (*See also* **Brothers of the Lord**.)

4. James, the son of Alphaeus, one of the twelve apostles (Luke 6:15; Acts 1:13).

JAMES, LETTER OF The first of the seven Catholic Epistles of the New Testament (the others are 1 and 2 **Peter**; 1, 2, and 3 **John**; and **Jude**), so called because they appear to be addressed to the whole Church. An exhortation to practical Christian living, the letter is noteworthy for it stress on the value of good works and its reference to the anointing of the sick.

I. AUTHORSHIP AND DATE

The author of the epistle is identified simply as "James, a servant of God and of the Lord Jesus Christ" (Jas 1:1). The identity of this James is technically uncertain, but many scholars agree that he was James, the brother of the Lord (Gal 1:19) who governed the Jerusalem community of Christians after Peter (Acts 12:17; 15:13–21) and who was martyred in Jerusalem in A.D. 62 by order of the Jewish high priest. A few modern scholars suggest that the author wrote pseudonymously—that is, in the name of James. The arguments for that assertion are not strong, and, regardless, the author clearly was a Jewish Christian and wrote with authority.

Determining the date of the letter's composition is difficult, as it depends in large measure on the assumed authorship. If the epistle was written by James, the brother of the Lord, then it had to be composed before his death in A.D. 62. The exact date is impossible to know, but a tentative time period might extend from around A.D. 49 to the early sixties. Some scholars who maintain that the letter was written by an anonymous Christian suggest a later date, between A.D. 80 and 100.

II. CONTENTS

I. Opening Address (1:1)
II. Statement of Themes (1:2–27)
    A. The Value of Suffering and Trials (1:2–18)
    B. Hearing and Doing the Word (1:19–27)

III. PURPOSE AND THEMES

James wrote his epistle to "the twelve tribes in the Dispersion" (Jas 1:1), which may indicate an audience of Christian converts from Israel spread out across the Mediterranean world. The letter uses a variety of literary forms, and in particular it models itself after the wisdom literature of the Old Testament. It is written in excellent Greek, but also uses Jewish terms and OT allusions that give it a Semitic flavor (2:21–26; 5:10, 11, 17).

James shows himself familiar with the Synoptic Gospel traditions (especially Matthew) when he alludes to many elements of the Lord's teachings, such as joy in suffering (1:2), the place of the Father (1:17), the poor and the kingdom (2:5), love of neighbor (2:8), the tree and its fruit (3:12), humility and exaltation (4:10), the prohibition against oath swearing (5:12), and confidence in our prayer life (5:17).

The letter is an elegant teaching on Christian spirituality, justification by faith and works, confession, and anointing of the sick. James focuses on the pressures and challenges faced by Christians as they spend their lives in a pagan world, and so writes as a spiritual father giving direction and encouragement in the faith. The discourse is concerned, then,

with practical Christian living, admonitions, and encouragement and is less preoccupied with matters of doctrine. Echoing the **Sermon on the Mount**, James urges Christians to find joy in suffering (1:2–12). God, James reminds his readers, is not the cause of temptations—they spring from our wounded nature: "but each person is tempted when he is lured and enticed by his own desire" (1:14). God is the source only of good, and he "brought us forth by the word of truth that we should be a kind of first fruits of his creatures" (1:18).

Exhorting Christians to "be doers of the word, and not hearers only" (1:22), James urges them to be impartial in viewing rich and poor equally (2:1–3) and exhibiting charity toward others (2:14–26) because "a man is justified by works and not by faith alone" (2:24). James goes on to command control of the tongue (3:1–12), which must be trained to serve and bless the Father. Authentic Christian wisdom pursues peace and humility: "the wisdom from above is first pure, then peaceable, gentle, open to reason, full of mercy and good fruits, without uncertainty or insincerity" (3:17).

Against this wisdom is discord, which must be avoided (4:1–12). Rather, all Christians should readily submit themselves to God's care and providence (4:13–17) and live in awareness of God's coming judgment (5:1–12). Prayer is the means of overcoming suffering and the mark of the true Christian: "The prayer of a righteous man has great power" (5:16).

Finally, James writes, "Is any among you sick? Let him call for the elders of the church, and let them pray over him, anointing him with oil in the name of the Lord; and the prayer of faith will save the sick man, and the Lord will raise him up; and if he has committed sins, he will be forgiven" (5:14–15). This passage is a witness to the sacrament of the anointing of the sick as it was administered in the earliest days of the Church; according to the Council of Trent (Session 14, November 25, 1551), Catholic teaching on that sacrament is grounded on this passage. (*See also* **Anointing of the Sick**; **Repentance**.)

JAMNIA *See* **Jabneel**.

JANNES AND JAMBRES The two magicians who challenged Moses and Aaron before Pharaoh (Exod 7:11–12, 22). Their names are not given in the Exodus narrative but have come down through Jewish tradition in the **Dead Sea Scrolls** and an apocryphal work called *Jannes and Jambres*. They represent obstinate opposition to God (2 Tim 3:8–9).

JANNEUS *See under* **Hasmonean Dynasty**.

JAPHETH The second son of Noah (Gen 5:32, 6:10, 7:13, 9:18, 10:1; 1 Chr 1:4). In the Genesis narrative, only one deed of Japheth is mentioned: he covered the nakedness of his father, for which he received a blessing (Gen 9:27). He is listed in the Table of Nations as the ancestor of the Japhethites, various non-Semitic peoples, including Gomer, Magog, Tubal, and Tiras, all of whom settled in Asia Minor and several Mediterranean islands.

JARED Son of Mahalalel and the father of the patriarch **Enoch** (Gen 5:15–20; cf. 1 Chr 1:2). He was born when Mahalalel was 65 years old, and at the age of 162 Jared fathered Enoch. Jared lived to the age of 962.

JARMUTH A town in southern Canaan that joined a military alliance against Israel but was overthrown by Joshua (Josh 10:3, 5, 23; 12:11). It was later listed among the cities of Judah (Josh 15:35; Neh 11:29). It is identified with modern Khirbet Yarmuk.

JASHAR, BOOK OF (Hebrew *sēper hayyāšār,* "book of the upright," or "book of the valiant") A lost collection of early Israelite poetry that is twice quoted in the Old Testament. The first excerpt, quoted in Josh 10:12–13, commemorates Joshua's triumph at the battle of Gibeon over the Canaanites. The second, in 2 Sam 1:19–27, is David's elegy for Saul and Jonathan after their fall in battle. Some scholars believe that a third excerpt appears in 1 Kgs 8:12–13, in the form of a couplet in Solomon's prayer at the dedication of the Temple.

JASON The name of four men in the Bible, three of them in the time of the Maccabees.

1. High priest from 174 to 171 B.C. and the brother of the high priest Onias. Jason secured the position of high priest by buying it from **Antiochus IV Epiphanes** for the prodigious sum of 590 talents—more than 48,000 pounds (almost 22,000 kilograms) of silver (2 Macc 4:7–9). As a chief figure in the Hellenizing party of the period, he changed his name from Jesus to Jason, and after his installation he worked to Hellenize practices in Jerusalem (2 Macc 4:6–17), including the introduction of Greek games, clothing, and the construction of a gymnasium. His program eventually counte-

nanced even idolatry (2 Macc 4:18–20). When he sent his brother **Menelaus** on a mission to Antiochus, Menelaus used the opportunity to offer a bigger bribe to Antiochus. Jason was ejected and fled to the Ammonites (2 Macc 4:23–26). He then raised an army and marched on Jerusalem. The city fell, but Jason proved unable to hold it; he again sought refuge with the Ammonites. Incarcerated by **Aretas**, ruler of Nabatea, he managed to flee to Egypt and later died in Sparta (2 Macc 5:5–10).

2. Jason of Cyrene, a historian. His history of the Maccabees, in five volumes, was used as a source for 2 Maccabees (2 Macc 2:19–23).

3. Son of Eleazar. He was sent as an ambassador to Rome and Sparta by **Judas Maccabeus** (1 Macc 8:17; 12:16–17; 14:22).

4. A Christian in Thessalonica who hosted Paul and his missionary team on the apostle's second missionary journey (Acts 17:5–9).

JAVAN One of the seven sons of **Japheth** and a grandson of **Noah** (Gen 10:2; 1 Chr 1:5). He is the father of Elishah, Tarshish, Kittim, and Rodanim. The name "Javan" was used for the Ionian cities that developed along the coast of Asia Minor, a region that included Smyrna and Ephesus (Isa 66:19; Ezek 27:13). The name was also applied to Greece proper (Dan 8:21, 10:20, 11:2; Joel 3:6; Zech 9:13).

JAWBONE *See* **Samson**.

JEALOUSY A feeling of intense possessiveness. Jealousy in Scripture can be either positive or negative, depending on whether it is directed toward a worthy object, such as God, or represents personal selfishness expressed in disordered desire or anger. The term "jealousy" is often used to translate the Hebrew word *qin'â* (Num 5:14; Prov 6:34; Ezek 16:42) in certain passages. The related verb *qānā'* is sometimes translated "to be jealous of": two notable examples are in Genesis: the jealousy of Joseph's brothers over the favor showed him by their father (Gen 37:11) and the jealousy of Rachel for the motherhood of Leah (Gen 30:11; cf. Gen 26:14; Prov 3:31; Ezek 31:9). In the New Testament, jealousy (Greek *zēlos*) is counted among the sins and the works of the flesh, and "those who do such things shall not inherit the Kingdom of God" (Gal 5:19–21) (CCC 1852).

On the other hand, jealousy may mean zeal and single-minded concern—in particular, an all-encompassing love for God, especially to the exclusion of false gods. Thus, Jesus expelled the merchants from the Temple out of a jealous love for the Father: " 'Take these things away; you shall not make my Father's house a house of trade.' His disciples remembered that it was written, 'Zeal for your house will consume me' " (John 2:16–17; cf. Ps 69:10) (CCC 584).

This is the kind of "jealousy" we see in the anthropomorphic descriptions of God's jealous love. God is jealous in his love and possession of his Chosen People and will defend them against enemies (Ezek 36:5, 38:19; Isa 26:11, 37:32, 42:13; Zeph 1:18, 3:8). Equally, God is jealous in demanding from his Chosen People the exclusive allegiance due to him as their Lord and Creator (cf. Exod 20:5, 34:14; Deut 4:24, 5:9, 6:15; Josh 24:19; Nah 1:2). They must worship him as the only true God and not fall into idolatry (Exod 20:2). Denying the absoluteness, uniqueness, and exclusivity of his divinity will inflame his jealous wrath. "So be careful not to forget the covenant that the Lord your God made with you, and not to make for yourselves an idol in the form of anything that the Lord your God has forbidden you. For the Lord your God is a devouring fire, a jealous God" (Deut 4:23–24). In the face of their infidelity, he will exhibit anger and fire toward those who transgress against the covenant (Deut 29:19) and those who sink into idolatry (1 Kgs 14:22; 2 Kgs 2:17; Ezek 8:3).

JEBUSITES A people who occupied part of Palestine before the Israelites conquered Canaan (Gen 15:21; Exod 3:8, 23:23, 34:11; Deut 7:1). They are listed in the Table of Nations as descendants of **Canaan** (Gen 10:16). The Jebusites lived in the hill country of Canaan (Num 13:29; Josh 11:3). The phrase "shoulder of the Jebusite" was used to designate the elevation on which pre-Israelite Jerusalem was built (Josh 15:8; 18:16). Although the Israelites conquered several parts of Canaan, the Jebusites kept control of what became **Jerusalem** (Josh 15:63; Judg 1:21; 2 Sam 5:6; 1 Chr 11:4) until it was captured by David (2 Sam 5:6–9; 1 Chr 11:4–7).

JECONIAH *See* **Jehoiachin**.

JEDIDIAH (Hebrew, "beloved of the Lord") The name David gave **Solomon** when he heard through the prophet Nathan that the Lord loved the boy (2 Sam 12:25).

JEDUTHUN A Levitical singer during the reign of David and Solomon, and the head or founder of a family of liturgical musicians and gatekeepers (1 Chr 16:41, 42; 25:1–6; 2 Chr 5:12; 29:14; 35:15). According to some scholars, the name Ethan refers to Jeduthun. (*See also* **Asaph** *and* **Heman**.)

JEHOAHAZ (Hebrew, "the Lord grasps") The name of the eleventh king of Israel (2 Kgs 13:1–9) and the sixteenth king of Judah (2 Kgs 23:31–34).

1. The king of Israel from around 814 to 798 B.C. and the son and successor of **Jehu** (2 Kgs 10:35; 13:1–9). His reign was marked by the domination of the kingdom by the rulers of Damascus, **Hazael** and **Ben-hadad**. He was also accused of failing to oppose idolatry.

2. The king of Judah in 609 B.C. and a successor to King **Josiah**. He reigned for only three months and was deposed by Pharaoh Neco of Egypt, who had already defeated Josiah at Megiddo. Jehoahaz was taken as a captive to Egypt, where he died (2 Kgs 23:30–35). He is also called Shallum (Jer 22:11).

JEHOASH *See* **Joash**.

JEHOIACHIN (Hebrew, "may the Lord establish") The eighteenth king of Judah in 598–97 B.C., the son and successor to King **Jehoiakim**. His reign began when he was eighteen years old and endured for a mere three months, after which he surrendered without struggle to **Nebuchadnezzar** and the Babylonians who were besieging Jerusalem. The Babylonian ruler then deported Jehoiachin along with his family and ten thousand of his people to Babylon (2 Kgs 24:6–16; 2 Chr 36:9, 10; Jer 22:24–30). In 561 B.C. he was freed from prison and permitted to reside in Babylon with honor equal to that of other captive kings, including a seat at the royal table, along with a daily food allowance for him and his sons (2 Kgs 25:27–30; Jer 52:31–34)—a fact also attested to in Babylonian records.

JEHOIADA (Hebrew, "the Lord knows") The name of two men in the Old Testament.

1. The father of Benaiah, commander of the personal bodyguard of King David (2 Sam 8:18, 20:23, 23:20; 1 Kgs 1:8).

2. A priest in Jerusalem who was the prime mover in the coup against Queen **Athaliah** and the installation of **Joash**, son of Ahaziah, on the throne of Judah (2 Kgs 11:4–20). The plot succeeded only because Athaliah had executed all of the other members of the royal family but had failed to find Joash, the infant son of Ahaziah; he had been hidden by his aunt Jehosheba. With the help of the palace guard, Jehoiada toppled Athaliah and revealed the existence of Joash. Athaliah was then executed (2 Kgs 11:16). Jehoiada also renewed the covenant (2 Kgs 11:17) and so sparked a sharp rejection of the worship of Baal that had been promoted by Athaliah. Jehoiada then held the position of royal tutor to the boy king, so that he did "what is right in the eyes of the Lord" (2 Kgs 12:2). Joash, however, later complained that Jehoiada had failed to complete the needed repairs on the Temple. To ensure the proper use of funds, he commanded that all money collected for the repairs actually be used for that purpose (2 Kgs 12:4–16).

JEHOIAKIM (Hebrew, "the Lord raises up") The seventeenth king of Judah from 609

to 598 B.C., the son of **Josiah** and Zebidah, daughter of Pedaiah of Rumah (2 Kgs 23:36). Known originally as Eliakim, he succeeded his brother **Jehoahaz** after the latter was deposed by Pharaoh Neco of Egypt. In order to demonstrate his state of vassalage, Eliakim was renamed Jehoiakim, and he was forced to pay to the Egyptian ruler a large tribute that was raised by the imposition of severe taxes on the subjects of the kingdom of Judah (2 Kgs 23:34–35). In 605 B.C., he was forced to become a vassal to the Babylonian king, **Nebuchadnezzar** (2 Kgs 24:1). He rebelled in 602 B.C., and Judah suffered a punitive invasion (ca. 601 B.C.).

The king had a well-known dislike of **Jeremiah**, an antipathy that was entirely mutual (Jer 22:13–19). He tried twice to dispose of Jeremiah. Jeremiah criticized Jehoiakim sharply for his corruption and obsessive self-interest. Jehoiakim especially hated the prophet for his prediction of the city's ruin and for the oracles that he dictated to Baruch. These prophecies were read to the king by his court officer Jehudi, and Jehoiakim sliced them from the scroll as each was recited and tossed them into the fire (Jer 36:1–27).

JEHONADAB *See* **Jonadab**.

JEHORAM (Hebrew, "the Lord is exalted"; *see also* **Joram**) The fifth king of Judah from 848 to 841 B.C., the son and successor of **Jehoshaphat** (1 Kgs 22:50; 2 Kgs 8:16–24; 2 Chr 21). Jehoram married **Athaliah**, daughter of King **Ahab** of Israel and the sister of King **Joram** of Israel. As Judah was itself a vassal of Israel, he was compelled to take part with Joram of Israel in a campaign against the Moabites. Through the influence of Athaliah, Jehoram was induced to abandon his father's faith in God and follow in the tradition of Ahab and **Jezebel** in the pernicious toleration of idolatry. The Chronicler adds that Jehoram murdered his brothers (2 Chr 21:4). His reign was also marked by several disasters: Edom and Libnah were successful in throwing off their vassal status to Judah, and both the Philistines and the Arabians invaded the kingdom of Judah and brought great hardship. Jehoram died of a terrible illness of the bowels, and he passed with no regret by his subjects (2 Chr 21:18–20).

The name "**Joram**" is a shortened form of Jehoram; the king of Israel and the king of Judah bore the same name. Scripture most often calls the king of Israel "Joram" and the king of Judah "Jehoram," but both names are used for both kings.

JEHOSHAPHAT (Hebrew "the Lord is Judge") The name of two men in the Old Testament.

1. The son of Ahilud and a royal scribe during the reigns of David (2 Sam 8:16, 20:24; 1 Chr 18:15) and Solomon (1 Kgs 4:3).

2. The fourth king of Judah from around 873 to 849 B.C., the son and successor of **Asa** (1 Kgs 15:24) by Azubah, daughter of Shilhi (1 Kgs 22:42; 2 Chr 20:31). He came to the throne at the age of thirty-five and was a contemporary of King **Ahab** of Israel, as well as Kings **Ahaziah** and **Jehoram** of Israel; he fought as an ally with them against common enemies in times of war (1 Kgs 22; 2 Kgs 3). Generally, his long reign was marked by its comparative tranquillity, troubled chiefly by the king's failed effort to rebuild the Red Sea trade with **Ophir** that had developed under Solomon. His outfitting of a fleet of merchant ships was a disaster; it was wrecked near Ezion-geber (1 Kgs 22:48). Ahaziah urged him to enter a renewed economic alliance, but Jehoshaphat declined (1 Kgs 22:49). He was pious and "did what was right in the eyes of the Lord" (1 Kgs 22:43), but it is noted that he failed to abolish worship in the high places.

JEHOSHAPHAT, VALLEY OF The location mentioned in Joel 3:2, 12 (cf. Joel 3:14, "The Valley of Decision") where the Lord will gather the nations and render apocalyptic judgment. The exact location of the valley is unknown.

JEHOSHEBA (Hebrew, "the Lord has sworn") Also Jehoshabeath. The daughter of **Jehoram** and sister of **Ahaziah**, kings of Judah (2 Kgs 11:1–2; 2 Chr 22:11), and the wife of the priest Jehoiada. When **Athaliah** staged a violent takeover of Judah and massacred the members of the royal family, Jehosheba played a crucial role in hiding the infant **Joash**, son of **Ahaziah**, who was the sole surviving male of the Davidic royal line. Six years later, Jehoiada revealed the existence of **Joash** as part of the coup that toppled Athaliah (2 Kgs 11:4–16).

JEHOVAH See "Yahweh" *under* **God.**

JEHU (Hebrew, "the Lord is God") The tenth king of Israel from 841 to 814 B.C., the son of Jehoshaphat, son of Nimshi (1 Kgs 19:16; 2 Chr 22:7). An officer in the army, Jehu was anointed at Ramoth-gilead at the command of **Elisha** (1 Kgs 19:15–18; 2 Kgs 9:1–10). He began to conspire against **Joram**, and eventually defeated the Omride Dynasty, slaying Joram at Jezreel. He had **Jezebel** killed (2 Kgs 9:11–37) and then slaughtered the rest of the royal family (2 Kgs 10:1–11) and various kinsmen of **Ahaziah** of Judah (2 Kgs 10:12–14). In these actions, Jehu fulfilled the prophecy of **Elijah** against the Omride Dynasty (1 Kgs 21:21–24), and the change of rule marked as well a significant change in religious policy. Having installed himself, Jehu set out to eradicate the **Baal** worship that had flourished through the patronage of Jezebel (2 Kgs 10:15–27). His zeal in stamping out Baal worship won him a four-generation dynasty (2 Kgs 10:30). But his violence went too far (2 Kgs 10:11), and the prophet Hosea condemned him for spilling too much blood in Jezreel (Hos 1:4).

JEHUDI An officer in the court of King **Jehoiakim** (Jer 36:14, 21, 23). He is best known as the scribe who read the oracle scroll of **Jeremiah** to the king. As Jehudi read the oracle, Jehoiakim tore off and burned each of the columns and threw it into the fire. (*See also* **Baruch**; **Jeremiah**.)

JEMIMAH The first daughter born to **Job** after the end of his immense sufferings (Job 42:14). He had three older daughters who perished (Job 1:2, 19).

JEPHTHAH (Hebrew, "may he [the Lord] open [the womb]") One of the major judges of Israel whose career is detailed in Judges (Judg 10:6–12:7). Jephthah was the son of a prostitute in Gilead; he was expelled from the family by his father's legitimate sons and took up a living as an outlaw and a bandit (Judg 11:1–3). But when the Ammonites attacked, the elders of Gilead recognized that only Jephthah was capable of saving them. He agreed to get involved on condition that he be accepted as the Israelites' leader. He then defeated the Ammonites (Judg 11:4–33) but made the foolhardy vow to sacrifice the first person he met upon his return should he prove to be victorious. When he came home, the first person he met was his daughter and only child (Judg 11:34–40). From this tragic incident began a custom: once a year Israelite daughters left their families and went into the mountains to mourn Jephthah's daughter. Jephthah later slaughtered the Ephraimites over a tribal dispute (Judg 12:1–6). He died after six years of judging Israel (Judg 12:7). Jephthah is named among the heroes of faith in Hebrews (Heb 11:32).

JEREMIAH (Hebrew, "the Lord will restore") One of the major prophets of the Old Testament. We know more about Jeremiah than about any of the other prophets, because the book of Jeremiah—the longest in the Bible—includes many biographical details. As with the book, the life of Jeremiah is filled with sadness and tragedy. The prophetic ministry of Jeremiah from 627 to 586 B.C. witnessed the drama of sweeping international events in the Near East that ended with the capture and destruction of Jerusalem in 586 B.C. by the Babylonians under King **Nebuchadnezzar**, an event that Jeremiah had long foretold.

I. EARLY LIFE

Few details are extant concerning Jeremiah's early life except for the statement made in the opening line of his book. He was the "son of Hilkiah, of the priests who were in Anathoth in the land of Benjamin" (Jer 1:1), and it is stated that his father was delighted the day he was born (Jer 20:15). Anathoth was a village situated a few miles north of Jerusalem; it was one of the forty-eight Levitical cities set apart for the descendants of Aaron (Josh 21:18). Hilkiah may have been a descendant of the priest **Abiathar** (1 Kgs 2:26–27).

Jeremiah was called by God to become a prophet in the thirteenth year of **Josiah** (Jer 1:2, 4), or 627 B.C. In his account, Jeremiah emphasizes that he was a youth (Jer 1:2–10), and it is deduced that he was born around the year 650–645 B.C. (or perhaps as late as 640 B.C.). We can see some similarities between Jeremiah and Samuel, such as the young age at which both were called (cf. 1 Sam 2:11, 18, 21, 26; 31:1, 8). There are also key similarities to Moses, including Jeremiah's excuse that he is not a good speaker (Jer 1:6; cf. Exod 4:10) and the assurance that God would place words in Jeremiah's mouth (Jer 1:9), as he did with Moses (Deut 18:18).

Little is known of his early career as a prophet during the reign of Josiah (640–609 B.C.) with its determined effort to bring about a true reform in the kingdom of Judah (2 Kgs 22–23; 2 Chr 34–35). Jeremiah would certainly have approved of Josiah's reform, with its goal of purging Judah of the contamination of idolatry. In 2 Chr 35:25, we read that Jeremiah composed a lamentation for Josiah: "Jeremiah also uttered a lament for Josiah; and all the singing men and singing women have spoken of Josiah in their laments to this day. They made these an ordinance in Israel; behold, they are written in the Laments." (*See also* **Lamentations, book of**.) With the passing of Josiah, however, international events overtook the kingdom of Judah. The conquest of Jerusalem loomed, and Jeremiah entered his period of greatest activity.

II. THE INTERNATIONAL SITUATION

The prophetic ministry of Jeremiah came at a crucial moment in the history of the Near East and Palestine. The moribund Assyrian Empire, already in a state of decline, was hastened toward its death by the revolt of the Babylonians under Nabopolassar, a conflict that ended with the conquest of Nineveh around 612 B.C. The rapid decline of Assyria induced Pharaoh Neco II of Egypt to march in support of the Assyrians to prevent the rising star of Babylon from becoming the next Near Eastern superpower. Palestine stood along the line of march, and Josiah unwisely chose to embark upon a campaign to stop the Egyptian advance. He was slain (or later died of his wounds) after engaging in battle at Megiddo in 609 B.C. (2 Chr 35:20–24). Four years later, Neco II was himself defeated and killed by **Nebuchadnezzar** at the battle of Carchemish on the Euphrates. Babylon then emerged as the direct successor of the Assyrian Empire, and the eyes of the Babylonians looked at Palestine as territory ripe for annexation.

In the years following the death of Josiah,

the throne of David passed to his three unworthy sons: **Jehoahaz, Jehoiakim**, and **Zedekiah**. Jehoahaz was deposed by Pharaoh Neco II in favor of Jehoiakim, but the latter swiftly submitted to Nebuchadnezzar (2 Kgs 24:1). Soon, however, Jehoiakim entered into revolt against Babylon, an act that brought Nebuchadnezzar marching toward Jerusalem (2 Kgs 24:10). Jehoiakim died as the Babylonians approached, and his successor, Jehoiachin, surrendered in 596 B.C. The Babylonians sent more than ten thousand Israelites, including the royal family, artisans, and warriors, into exile in Mesopotamia, with Zedekiah left to rule the remnant kingdom of Judah. Once more, ignoring the dire warnings of Jeremiah, the king of Judah heeded the anti-Babylonian party and entered into open rebellion. Nebuchadnezzar captured Jerusalem in 586 B.C. after a siege of eighteen months. The city was utterly destroyed, Judah was decimated, and a large number of surviving Judahites were taken to Babylon (2 Kgs 25:8–12).

III. PROPHETIC MINISTRY

As these events were unfolding, Jeremiah stood as a voice in Judah calling for repentance and reform in the face of impending destruction. He proclaimed the Lord's judgment and assured the execution of the divine decree (Jer 1:12). To drive home his point that he beheld the imminence of slavery and bondage, he stood before the people with a yoke upon his shoulders (cf. Jer 27, 28). The reality of the approaching ruin was so palpable to Jeremiah that he did not marry, as he would not father children who would be killed (Jer 16:1–4), nor did he participate in festivals, as he saw the day when no one would be left alive to celebrate festivities or to mourn for the dead (Jer 16:5–9).

His ceaseless teaching incurred the wrath of many in the kingdom, including the extreme nationalist party, who believed that the presence of the Temple was enough to guarantee God's protection, despite the people's corruption (Jer 7:4). Similarly, those who favored an alliance between Judah and Egypt opposed Jeremiah because he condemned the proposed coalition with Egypt against Babylon (Jer 25:17–19). The Judean nationalists despised him for his pessimism (cf. Jer 27, 28). He was thus the target of conspiracies in his own town (Jer 11:18–23) and spent a night locked up in the Temple for prophesying its destruction and that of the city (Jer 19:14–20:6). Charged with blasphemy, he escaped condemnation through the assistance of the royal official Ahikam, son of Shaphan (Jer 26:1–24).

Given the foolhardy policies of the kings, Jeremiah had poor relations with the royal court. He rebuked Jehoiakim (Jer 22:13–19), receiving a flogging and brief incarceration for his unflinching criticism (Jer 20:1). In 605 B.C., he gathered together his prophetic discourses and had **Baruch** the scribe write down a collection of oracles that the prophet dictated (Jer 36:1–10) and read them in the Temple. The scroll, understood immediately by royal officials for its critical attitude toward the king, was brought before the king, but not before Jeremiah and Baruch were encouraged to hide themselves. Jehoiakim burned the scroll column by column as it was read aloud. Jeremiah and Baruch were already in hiding, and the prophet dictated another scroll (Jer 36:27–32).

With Zedekiah, a slight change in relations was effected. The king consulted with Jeremiah (Jer 21; 37; 38), but in the end Zedekiah heeded the counsel of the politicians instead of the prophet, and Judah rushed headlong to destruction. In a brief intermission in the siege that followed, Jeremiah was arrested for attempting to leave the city to attend to personal affairs at Anathoth and was imprisoned for desertion (Jer 37:11–16). He was released from prison but not from captivity by Zedekiah (Jer 37:17–21). As he continued to predict doom, the prophet was placed in a cistern to starve to death, only to be released by Ebed-melech the Ethiopian (Jer 38:1–13).

Jerusalem fell, as Jeremiah predicted, but Jeremiah survived the carnage. In 2 Maccabees, we read that he hid the **ark of the covenant** in the mountains so that the Babylonians could not capture it (2 Macc 2:4–8); that was the last time the ark was seen (Jer 3:16) until John saw an image of it in heaven (Rev 11:19).

Unquestionably, Jeremiah loved his country, but once Jerusalem had fallen he was viewed by the Babylonians as a sympathizer. In the aftermath, he was spared exile to Mesopotamia and given a choice between Babylon and Judah. He chose Judah and called on the survivors to live in peace (Jer 39:1–40:12). His Lamentations, written at this time, expressed his overwhelming sorrow over the destruction of Jerusalem (Lam 1:1).

Jeremiah and Baruch were later forced to settle in Tahpanhes (Jer 43:7), in Egypt, by emigrating Judeans (Jer 40–43). There, Jeremiah prophesied the fall of Egypt to the Babylonians (Jer 43:8–13). According to a tradition first noted by Tertullian (*Scorp.*, 8; cf. Heb 11:37), Jeremiah was stoned to death in Egypt by his own countrymen. In the years and centuries after his death, he was revered by the Jewish people, and the memory of Jeremiah was revered during the **Exile** and after (Dan 9:2; cf. Eccl 49:8; 2 Macc 2:1–8, 15:12–16; Matt 16:14).

There were a number of other persons named Jeremiah in the OT.

2. Jeremiah of Libnah, the father of Hamutal, and grandfather of **Jehoahaz** (2 Kgs 23:31) and **Zedekiah** (2 Kgs 24:18), kings of Judah.

3. A warrior of the tribe of Benjamin; he joined David at Ziklag (1 Chr 12:4) during the persecution by King Saul.

4. A Gadite warrior who also served under David at Ziklag (1 Chr 12:13).

5. Another Gadite warrior who joined David at Ziklag (1 Chr 12:10).

6. The father of Jaazaniah, a Rechabite, and a contemporary of Jeremiah the prophet (Jer 35:3).

7. A priest who returned from Babylon with **Zerubbabel** (Neh 12:1) to Jerusalem. The name also denotes a priestly family in the time of the high priest Joiakim (Neh 12:12).

8. The head of a priestly family and one of the priests who signed the covenant of Ezra (Neh 10:2).

JEREMIAH, BOOK OF A book by the second of the major prophets and the longest book of the Bible. It contains the oracles of

Jeremiah, who foretold the destruction of Jerusalem and the Temple, as well as the founding of a New Covenant in Messianic times.

I. AUTHORSHIP AND DATE

Many scholars accept the book as made up of the authentic teachings of Jeremiah, although they may have been written down by his disciples, such as his scribe **Baruch** (Jer 36). A later editor may have compiled the book in its present form. In the **Septuagint**, the book is shorter and follows a different sequence; although there is much debate, some scholars suggest that this version may translate an older form of the book than the standard Hebrew text.

The core of the work is a collection of judgment oracles against Judah and Jerusalem and the nations. These were proclaimed by Jeremiah in the years leading up to 586 B.C. and were dictated to **Baruch** (36:2, 29, 32). Chapters 1–20 are oracles at the time of **Josiah** and **Jehoiakim**; chapters 21–39 come from the time of Jehoiakim and **Zedekiah**; chapters 40–45 are oracles of the fall of Jerusalem; chapters 46–51 are oracles against the nations; and chapter 52 is a historical epilogue.

A second edition of the prophecies was created after the destruction of the first collection at the command of King Jehoiakim (36:1–32). Baruch may at this time have added biographical details about Jeremiah, including precise dates for the reigns of Jehoiakim and Zedekiah and the departure of surviving Judahites to Egypt after the fall of Jerusalem. An appendix also was added (chapter 52) that is derived in large part from 2 Kgs 24:18–25, 34. Scholars suggest that the final form of the book crystallized during the **Exile** or shortly after.

II. CONTENTS

I. *Prophecies and Visions of Judgment (chaps. 1–24)*

   A. *Introduction and Jeremiah's Call (1:1–19)*

   B. *Call to Israel to Repent (2:1–4:4)*

   C. *Threats of Invasion (4:5–6:30)*

   D. *Jeremiah Proclaims God's Judgment (7:1–11:17)*

   E. *Jeremiah Is Threatened (11:18–12:17)*

   F. *Various Visions, Prophecies, and Complaints (13:1–24:10)*

      1. *Oracles on the Kings of Judah (21:11–23:8)*

      2. *Jeremiah and the Jerusalem Prophets (23:9–40)*

      3. *Vision of the Good and Bad Figs (24:1–10)*

II. *Speeches of Jeremiah and Stories (chaps. 25–44)*

   A. *God's Wrath (25:1–38)*

   B. *Prophecies (26:1–27:22)*

   C. *Hananiah (28:1–17)*

   D. *Various Prophecies (29:1–32)*

   E. *Book of Consolation (30:1–33:26)*

   F. *Zedekiah (34:1–22)*

   G. *The Rechabites (35:1–19)*

   H. *The Scroll in the Temple (36:1–32)*

   I. *Zedekiah and Jeremiah (37:1–38:28)*

   J. *The Fall of Jerusalem and the Aftermath (39:1–44:30)*

III. *Prophecies Against the Nations (chaps. 45–51)*

   A. *Comfort to Baruch (45:1–5)*

   B. *Judgment on Egypt, the Philistines, Moab, the Ammonites, Edom, Damascus,*

III. PURPOSE AND THEMES

Honored as one of the Messianic prophets, not only did Jeremiah forecast—to his own anguish—the destruction of Judah, Jerusalem, and the Temple, but he also had the task of proclaiming why the cataclysm was a moral and spiritual necessity. His prophecies of judgment were a response to moral ruin and decay in Judah beginning in the time of **Manasseh** (2 Kgs 21:10–15). The Chosen People had forsaken their covenant with God, throwing off the yoke of the Lord in moral obduracy (Jer 2:20), and so earned the more severe Babylonian yoke. Jeremiah repeatedly preached the direct link between moral decline and political degeneration with the aim of sparking a real moral reformation.

Although he failed to prevent the doom of Judah, Jeremiah nevertheless began a process of spiritual renewal by fulfilling his appointed task: "to pluck up and to break down, to destroy and to overthrow, to build and to plant" (Jer 1:10). Jeremiah was a potent preacher against sin. He saw that his people would not change (13:23) and he foretold that in the end God "will scatter you like chaff driven by the wind from the desert" (13:24). Still the prophet prayed for his people and suffered severe torments of the soul as the Lord's discipline approached (cf. 14:7–9, 19–22). Even in the face of the fall of Jerusalem, Jeremiah remembered God's promises and assured God's people that those promises would come to pass:

For I know the plans I have for you, says the LORD, plans for welfare and not for evil, to give you a future and a hope. Then you will call upon me and come and pray to me, and I will hear you. You will seek me and find me; when you seek me with all your heart, I will be found by you, says the LORD, and I will restore your fortunes and gather you from all the nations and all the places where I have driven you, says the LORD, and I will bring you back to the place from which I sent you into exile. (29:11–14; cf. 23:5–8; 31:23–40; 33:1–13)

Jeremiah paid a high price for his prophetic mission. He cursed the day of his birth (15:10; 20:14–18). Yet he never lost sight of his Messianic hope. He made a few directly Messianic prophecies (e.g., his discourse on the Good Shepherd of the House of David, 23:1–5; and the deliverance from the Babylonian Captivity as a type of Messianic salvation, chapters 30–33). But even more, in a Christlike manner, he made his life a Messianic prophecy, enduring for his people the very sufferings that were predicted and proclaimed. Where Isaiah spoke of the Suffering Servant as a lamb led to the slaughter (Isa 53:7), Jeremiah saw himself as "a gentle lamb led to the slaughter" (Jer 11:19). Like Christ, he wept for his people and called upon them to turn aside at the last hour, only to receive from his people rejection and anger.

JERICHO (related to Hebrew *yārēaḥ*, "moon") Also called the "city of palms" (Deut 34:3), Jericho is a city to the northwest of the Dead Sea at the southern end of the Jordan Valley. It was the first major site conquered by the Israelites when they entered Canaan. The city rested in a fertile oasis and is today identified with Tell es-Sultan, a site explored by Ernst Sellin and Carl Watzinger from 1907 to 1909, John Garstang from 1930 to 1936, and the British School of Archaeology under Dr. Kathleen Kenyon from 1952 to 1958. Archaeological work has noted that human occupation around the site can be traced back to around 9000 B.C., with various periods of abandonment. Much of what we know about early urbanization comes from excavations at Jericho.

According to Num 22:1 and 26:3, the Israelites camped across the Jordan from Jericho, preparing to invade from the east. To scout the dispositions of the city, **Joshua** sent two spies to the city (Josh 2). He then captured the city by a memorable combination of liturgical and military actions recounted in Joshua (Josh 5:13–6:23). Following the conquest of Canaan, the city was given to the tribe of Benjamin (Josh 16:7; 18:21). It was later seized by Eglon of Moab (Judg 3:13), despite the prohibitions placed upon rebuilding the city at the time of the conquest of Canaan (Josh 6:26). Hence, the building undertaken by Hiel of Bethel came at the cost of his two sons (1 Kgs 16:34). Nevertheless, during the time of Elijah and Elisha, there existed a school of prophets at Jericho (2 Kgs 2:4–5, 15). King Zedekiah was captured at Jericho while attempting to flee the Babylonians (2 Kgs 25:5; Jer 39:5–7), after which he was blinded.

From Maccabean times onward, "Jericho" refers not to the Old Testament site, but to a nearby settlement southwest of the original city. Simon Maccabeus was betrayed and killed there (1 Macc 16:11).

In the New Testament, Jericho was the home of **Zacchaeus** the tax collector, who gave Jesus hospitality (Luke 19:1–3). Jericho was also the site of Jesus's healing of the blind man **Bartimaeus** (Matt 20:29–31; Mark 10:46–48; Luke 18:35–37). Finally, the parable of the Good Samaritan is set on the road from Jerusalem to Jericho (Luke 10:29–37).

JEROBOAM (Hebrew, "may the people be great") The name of two kings of Israel.

1. Jeroboam I, the son of Nebat and the first king of the northern kingdom of Israel (ca. 930–910 B.C.). Jeroboam had held a position of trust under Solomon as a builder and was named head of all of Solomon's forced labor. The prophet **Ahijah** had predicted the division of the kingdom and that Jeroboam would one day claim ten parts of Solomon's kingdom, signifying the event by tearing his own cloak into twelve pieces and giving Jeroboam ten of them. Because of that prophecy, Solomon sought to kill Jeroboam, who was forced to flee to Egypt until Solomon's death (1 Kgs 11:26–40).

Jeroboam returned home and at Shechem was elevated to the kingship by the tribes of northern Israel after **Rehoboam** failed to secure their allegiance in the wake of Solomon's harsh rule. Only Judah and Benjamin remained loyal to Rehoboam. As predicted, the kingdom had been torn apart and Jeroboam named king of the new kingdom of Israel (1 Kgs 12:1–24).

The large number of his subjects going to Jerusalem, and thus the continued superiority of Judah in religious affairs, led Jeroboam to establish two centers of worship at Bethel and Dan, where he set up golden calves (1 Kgs

12:25–33). For this deed Jeroboam was reproached as the king who brought Israel into a state of sin and thus doomed the kingdom to inevitable destruction. The death of Jeroboam's son, **Abijah**, was seen as punishment for this sinful deed (1 Kgs 14:1–18), and it was common for every succeeding king to be described as a successor to Jeroboam who "made Israel sin."

2. Jeroboam II, king of Israel from 793 to 753 B.C., the son and successor to **Jehoash** (2 Kgs 14:23–28).

JEROME, SAINT See **Vulgate**.

JERUBBAAL See **Gideon**.

JERUSALEM Revered as a "holy city" by the world's three great monotheistic religions: Christianity, Judaism, and Islam. Jerusalem is one of the world's oldest cities. The importance of Jerusalem can scarcely be overestimated: it is central in many of the events related in the Old Testament, and it takes on new theological importance in the New Testament.

Aside from serving as the political capital of Israel, Jerusalem was the heart of Israelite religion, for it contained the central sanctuary of the Lord, the **Temple**. The destruction of the city in 586 B.C. by the Babylonians was thus the greatest possible calamity. The city was likewise beloved as a symbol of Jewish religious and national aspirations. In the NT, the city is seen as a **type** of the new or heavenly Jerusalem (Rev 21:2, 10).

I. Names
II. Geography
III. History
IV. Theological Importance
    A. Jerusalem in the Old Testament
    B. Jerusalem in the New Testament

I. NAMES

The city's name is certainly pre-Israelite. The earliest identifiable literary reference is to Rushalimum in the Egyptian Execration Texts of the eighteenth century B.C.; the Amarna Letters of the fourteenth century B.C. mention Urushalim. The Hebrew name, *yĕrûšālaim*, was probably the original pronunciation (sometimes modified to *yĕrûšālayim*). Some understand the name to mean "foundation of Shalem," Shalem being the name of a Semitic god in Ugaritic mythology. Eventually, however, the name was connected with the Hebrew *šālôm*, "peace" (cf. Heb 7:2). Gen 14:18 mentions Melchizedek, king of Salem (a shorter form of Jerusalem), the first reference to Jerusalem in Scripture. Ps 76:2 associates Salem with **Zion** as the dwelling place of God; Jerusalem was called "Zion" when David first seized possession of the city (2 Sam 5:6–7).

Since the city was occupied by Jebusites until David conquered it, Jerusalem is sometimes called Jebus in histories of the conquest of Canaan (Josh 15:8, 18:28; Judg 19:10; 1 Chr 11:4–5).

II. GEOGRAPHY

Jerusalem is located on a limestone plateau roughly 20 miles (32 kilometers) west of the Dead Sea and 30 miles (48 kilometers) east of the Mediterranean on parallel ridges in the central mountain range of Palestine. The average height of the surrounding Judean hills is 2,300 feet, or about 700 meters, above sea level. The city is flanked by steep valleys on three sides—the Valley of Kidron to the east, dividing the city from the Mount of Olives, and the Valley of Hinnom to the south and west—that served as powerful natural defenses. Thus Jerusalem was extremely difficult to conquer, as it was assailable only from the north.

III. HISTORY

The earliest history of Jerusalem remains unknown. The Egyptian Execration Texts go back at least as far as the eighteenth century B.C., so we know that the city was in existence early in the second millennium B.C. Archaeology has confirmed that the earliest settlement was on the eastern hill. There is a strong likelihood that the Salem mentioned in Gen 14:18 is none other than the "hill of Moriah," the place where God commanded Abraham to sacrifice his son, Isaac (Gen 22:2–4), and the site where Solomon built the Temple (2 Chr 3:1).

In Genesis, Salem was the city of Melchizedek (Gen 14:18; cf. Heb 7:1, 8) and is identified with Jerusalem through the parallel used with Zion (Ps 76:3). Josephus (*Ant.* 1.180) insists that Jerusalem is identical with the ancient city Salem (see also **Salem**).

By the time of the conquest of Canaan, Jerusalem was an Amorite city under the rule of King Adonizedek. The king organized an alliance against Joshua, but the coalition was defeated (Josh 10:1–11). Nevertheless, the Israelites did not capture the city of Jerusalem, probably because of its imposing natural defenses. The Jebusites remained in control of the area over the first years of the settlement of Canaan, but according to Judg 1:8, at least

a portion of the city fell to the tribe of Judah. The tribe of Benjamin also attempted to oust the Jebusites permanently but had to settle for living alongside them (Judg 1:21).

The Jebusites were still in control at the time of David's accession to the throne of Israel, but David resolved to capture the city. This was accomplished, apparently by a surprise attack led by Joab that went "up the water shaft" (2 Sam 5:6–9; 1 Chr 11:4–6). Having conquered the city, David made it his capital. It was an astute choice. Not only was it an easily defended site, but it was also right on the border between the lands of Benjamin and Judah. This made it a politically neutral site as well as central enough for the northern tribes to access the city as their capital.

David improved the defenses of Jerusalem and made it his seat of government. He also brought the **ark of the covenant** there and so established Jerusalem as the spiritual capital of Israel. Solomon completed this development by constructing the Temple.

When the northern tribes seceded (*see* **Israel, kingdom of**), Jerusalem became the capital of Judah. The city henceforth suffered from the poor decisions and the infidelity of the Judahite kings. The Temple and palace were plundered by the forces of Egypt (1 Kgs 14:25–28), and the city suffered attacks by the Syrians and Israel (2 Kgs 14:11–14; 2 Chr 25:21–24), Assyria (2 Kgs 18:13–19; 2 Chr 32:1–22; Isa 36–37), and finally the Babylonians (2 Kgs 24:1–25:21). Some kings, such as **Uzziah** and **Hezekiah**, tried to strengthen the defenses and improve the city's water supply. Jerusalem miraculously escaped the colossal destruction that engulfed the northern kingdom, but with the collapse of the Assyrian Empire, the rise of Babylon posed a new and even more dire threat.

Jerusalem underwent a first siege by **Nebuchadnezzar** in 597 B.C. (2 Kgs 24:10–17). Then in 586 B.C. the Babylonians took the city after a siege of eighteen months. The city was utterly destroyed in the conflict, and Nebuchadnezzar deported the survivors, leaving behind only a small population of poor peasant farmers (2 Kgs 25:1–17).

After the Persians conquered Babylon in 539 B.C., **Cyrus the Great** gave the Jews permission to return to Jerusalem and build a new Temple in 538 B.C. (Ezra 1–7; Neh 1–4). The city walls were repaired under Nehemiah in 445 B.C.

Jerusalem came under the control of the Ptolemies of Egypt after the death of Alexander the Great in the fourth century B.C., and Palestine passed to the Seleucids under Antiochus II Theos in 198 B.C. The Seleucids under Antiochus IV Epiphanes entered Jerusalem, desecrated the Temple, and tore down its walls; a Syrian garrison was left behind. The aggressive effort to Hellenize the Jewish population sparked the rebellion of the **Maccabees** that led to the rededication of the Temple in 164 B.C. (1 Macc 4:36–59).

After the Maccabees won independence for the Jews, the Hasmonean Dynasty ruled over Jerusalem until the arrival of the Roman legions in 63 B.C. In that year, Pompey the Great captured the city, beginning the Roman rule that was to endure for centuries. **Herod the Great**, Rome's client king, was responsible for several major construction projects in the city, including a military fortress (the Antonia; Acts 21:34) and above all the new Temple (John 2:20).

The Jewish Revolt of A.D. 66 ended with the fall of Jerusalem in A.D. 70 to the Roman armies under the command of Titus, the son of Emperor Vespasian. In a bloody and staggeringly destructive campaign, the Roman legions laid the city in ruins. The Temple was destroyed and to this day has never been rebuilt.

Jerusalem was again a battlefield in the revolt of Simon Bar Kokhba (A.D. 132–135) against Rome. In the aftermath, a new city was constructed on the ruins, Aelia Capitolina, a pagan metropolis dedicated to the pagan god Jupiter Capitolinus. Jews were banned from the city until the time of Emperor Constantine the Great (d. A.D. 337). Beginning in the time of Constantine, the city was a center of Christian pilgrimage, revered as the place of Christ's Passion and Resurrection.

IV. THEOLOGICAL IMPORTANCE

A. Jerusalem in the Old Testament

Jerusalem is centrally important, not simply because it was the political seat of the Davidic Dynasty, but because it was the home of the Temple, the central sanctuary of Israelite worship. Jerusalem was a holy city, the place where God had chosen to dwell among his people: "In Jerusalem will I put my name" (2 Kgs 21:4; cf. 1 Kgs 11:13; 2 Kgs 23:27). So when the prophets cried that the city would be destroyed because of Israel's infidelity, they saw more than a human disaster: they saw a catastrophic end of the worship of the Lord (Jer 9:11; Ezek 4–5; Mic 3:12).

These prophecies came to pass, but Jerusalem still remained in the hearts of the Israelites. Prophets during and after the **Exile** proclaimed the hope of a Jerusalem restored. God would return and once more dwell in the Temple. The city would be the capital of the Messianic Kingdom, and all the nations would be drawn to God (Isa 2:1–5, 49:14–18, 52:1–10, chaps. 60–62, 65:17–25; Jer 31:38–40; Mic 4:1–4; Hag 2:7).

B. Jerusalem in the New Testament

How important Jerusalem was to Jesus is apparent in the Gospels, and all four Evangelists record that Jesus's ministry moved toward the holy city as the place of his Passion and Resurrection. Jesus announced his death in the city with the words, "it cannot be that a prophet should perish away from Jerusalem. O Jerusalem, Jerusalem, killing the prophets and stoning those who are sent to you! How often would I have gathered your children together as a hen gathers her brood under her wings, and you would not!" (Luke 13:33–24; cf. Mark 10:32–34). Jesus noted the prophets who had been put to death in the city and envisioned the city surrounded by armies (Luke 21:20) and assaulted by enemy soldiers (Luke 19:41–44).

Jesus, however, entered Jerusalem in triumph as the Messiah, the son of David (Matt 21:1–11; Mark 11:1–11; cf. Zech 9:9), the promised King (Luke 19:38; John 12:13). The holy city was the heart from which the proclamation of the Gospel to the entire world began (Luke 24:47; Acts 1:18). It was the place where the Holy Spirit came at **Pentecost** and the site of the first Christian community (Acts 2:1–13).

The prophetic visions of a glorified Jerusalem in the OT far exceeded the reality of the restored Jerusalem after the **Exile**. Thus we are led to contemplate a greater reality: a heavenly Jerusalem—the true holy city and the capital of God's new creation—that is *symbolized* by the earthly city but not identified with it. The earthly Zion is the model of the celestial height on which the New Jerusalem is built (Gal 4:26; Heb 12:22), and together with the city it is a place of glory where the redeemed will gather before the Lord (Isa 4:2–6; Joel 3:17; Obad 21; Mic 4:1–7; Rev 14:1). The New Jerusalem is described in Rev 3:12 and 21:1–22:5. In Rev 3:12, the new city is promised to the faithful of the community of Philadelphia if they remain faithful to the word of Christ (cf. Rev 21:7). In Rev 21:1–22:5, Jerusalem represents the Church, the Bride of the Lamb, with whom Jesus unites himself (Rev 21:9–21; cf. Eph 5:25–26; Rev 19:7–9). The heavenly city, built by God (cf. Heb 11:10), permits the worshipping Church to join the heavenly liturgy in the praise of the Lord and the Lamb (CCC 757, 865).

JERUSALEM, COUNCIL OF The apostolic council that gathered in Jerusalem around A.D. 49 to discuss the status of Gentile converts. The question was whether Gentiles needed to follow the Jewish ceremonial law in order to be saved. The council was attended by representatives from the Church in Antioch, including **Paul** and **Barnabas**, as well as other apostles and the elders of the Church in Jerusalem. The account of the council is recorded in Acts 15:1–35.

"After there had been much debate," **Peter** rose to speak (Acts 15:7–11). He recalled his experience with Cornelius, a Gentile who was baptized with his household and received the Holy Spirit quite apart from **circumcision** (see Acts 10:1–11:18). This was enough to convince him that circumcision was no longer a badge of covenant membership for the people of God; it could be set aside with the whole "yoke" of liturgical rites as something no longer binding or operative in the Messianic Church (Acts 15:8–9). Paul then followed, giving testimony to the wonders he had seen achieved by God as the Gospel was preached among the Gentiles.

The apostles were convinced by their testimony, and **James**, the head of the Church in Jerusalem, followed Peter's doctrinal announcement with a pastoral directive. Gentiles were not to be asked to undergo circumcision to be saved; they were asked, however, to respect those aspects of Jewish custom necessary to maintain harmony within the congregation of Jews and Gentiles. The decision was embraced by the Antioch community (Acts 15:31). The decision of the council, after an invocation of the Holy Spirit, gave a strong push to the Church's Gentile mission.

JERUSALEM, NEW *See* **Jerusalem**.

JESHUA *See* **Joshua**.

JESHURUN (Hebrew *yĕšûrûn*) A poetic name for Israel in Deuteronomy (Deut 32:15; 33:5, 26) and Isaiah (Isa 44:2). The meaning of the name is uncertain, although it has been suggested by scholars that the root *yšr* ("be straight, right") may refer to being "upright." Another possibility is "bull" (Hebrew *šôr*).

JESSE The father of **David**, a member of the tribe of Judah from Bethlehem (1 Sam 17:12). Jesse was the son of Obed and the grandson of **Boaz** (Ruth 4:17, 22; 1 Chr 2:12; Matt 1:5–6; Luke 3:32), so the family line was descended in part from **Ruth** the Moabite. Jesse had eight sons, of whom David was the youngest (1 Sam 16:1–13). In the rise of his son as king, Jesse is a largely passive figure. When David fled the wrath of Saul, Jesse and his family moved to Moab for safety (1 Sam 22:3). Isaiah called the Messiah "a shoot from the stump of Jesse" (Isa 11:1, 10), meaning that he would come from the family of David, even though the family's kingly rule had been cut off for a time. Jesus, as the Davidic Messiah, is thus the "root of Jesse" (Rom 15:12; cf. Rev 22:16).

JESUS CHRIST The divine Son of God who "became flesh and dwelt among us" (John 1:14) as a man; "Jesus of Nazareth," the son of Mary (Mark 1:24, 6:3; Luke 24:19). The name "Jesus" is derived from the Greek version of the name Joshua (Hebrew *Yĕhôšūaʿ; Yēšūaʿ*), which means "Yahweh saves." "Christ" was not Jesus's second name but the Greek translation of the Hebrew word "Messiah" (Hebrew *māšîaḥ*; Greek *christos*). Both Jesus's name and his title reveal his identity as the anointed Savior of the world and the long-awaited Redeemer who came to fulfill the prophecies of the Scriptures of Israel. As both Messiah and Savior, fully human and fully divine, Jesus Christ reveals the hidden face of the God of Israel (John 1:17–18; 14:9), redeems all of humanity from sin and death (Mark 10:45; Matt 26:28; John 3:16), and fulfills all of human history and creation in himself (Matt 5:17–18; Eph 1:7–10).

I. JESUS AND HISTORY

A. *The Four Gospels*

The principal historical sources of the life of Jesus are the Gospels of Matthew, Mark, Luke, and John, found in the New Testament. These four Gospels provide us with the most substantive and detailed ancient records of Jesus's birth, infancy, public ministry, Passion, death, Resurrection, and Ascension. Hence, they hold a unique preeminence in the NT and the life of the Church. Although the designation of these books as "Gospels" or "Good News" (Greek *euangelion*) is distinctive, their

literary genre is actually closest to ancient Greco-Roman biographies known as "lives" (Gk. *bioi*), which recorded the personal histories of philosophers, kings, and other important public figures (e.g., Suetonius, *Lives of the Caesars;* Philo, *Life of Moses*). Because they are ancient biographies, the goal of the Gospels is different from that of the letters of the NT, which were often written to address specific issues in a local community. While the Gospels reflect to some extent the context in which the authors wrote them, their principal intention is historical and evangelical: to provide an "accurate" account of the "truth" regarding the words and deeds of Jesus (Luke 1:1–4), so that readers might come to faith in him as the Messiah, the Son of God (John 20:30–31). The fact that none of the Gospels is addressed to a particular community suggests that they were intended for widespread circulation and use in the early Church.

According to both internal evidence (the titles and manuscripts) and external evidence (the ancient Church Fathers), the Gospels of Matthew and John were written by members of the twelve apostles and eyewitnesses to the ministry of Jesus. By contrast, the Gospels of Mark and Luke were written by men who were probably not eyewitnesses but who knew and consulted eyewitnesses. Although modern scholars often claim that the original manuscripts of the Gospels did not include the titles that attribute them to Matthew, Mark, Luke, and John, the manuscript evidence contradicts this theory. All existing manuscripts contain the titles that attribute the Gospels to these men. Moreover, the Gospel of John explicitly describes itself as the eyewitness testimony of the beloved disciple (John 21:23–24); the Gospel of Matthew highlights the conversion of Matthew himself (Matt 9:9); and the Gospel of Mark may contain a fleeting allusion to the author, John Mark of Jerusalem (cf Mark 14:51; Acts 12:12). In addition, the apostolic Fathers—the disciples of the apostles themselves or of men who knew the apostles—unanimously attribute the Gospels to Matthew, Mark, Luke, and John (see Eusebius, *Hist. Eccl.* 3.24, 39; 6.14.5–7; Saint Justin Martyr, *Dial.* 103; Saint Irenaeus, *Against Heresies* 3.1.1). There is no solid historical evidence that would suggest that the Gospels should be attributed to any other authors. Although scholars continue to debate the exact dating of the individual Gospels, the actual evidence suggests that the Gospels were written close to the time of the events of Jesus's life, within the living memory of eyewitnesses.

B. Other New Testament Writings

Although the four Gospels are the principal sources of the life of Jesus, they are not the only ones. There are the other writings of the NT, some of which also contain pieces of biographical information about Jesus. Significantly, this information agrees with the outline of Jesus's life contained in the Gospels: he was of Davidic descent; born of a Jewish mother; lived under the Mosaic Law; performed miracles and wonders; preached the coming of the Kingdom of God to the people of Israel; taught against divorce and remarriage; celebrated the Last Supper with his disciples; was a man or prayer; suffered Crucifixion, died, and was buried; and rose again on the third day (see Acts 10:38–43; Rom 1:3, 15:8; Gal 4:4; 1 Cor 7:10–11, 11:23–26, 15:3; Heb 5:7–8).

C. Non-Christian Sources

Jesus is also mentioned in several non-Christian historical sources. In the first century A.D., Jesus is mentioned twice by the Jewish historian Josephus, who tells us that Jesus worked wonders, was crucified under Pontius Pilate, and was believed to be the "Messiah" (*Ant.* 18.63–64; 20.200). Although many scholars question whether elements of one of these passages were added by a later Christian scribe, there is no doubt that Josephus knew and spoke of Jesus of Nazareth. In the second century A.D., Jesus is also mentioned by Pliny the Elder and the Roman historians Suetonius and Tacitus, the latter of whom records that Jesus suffered "the extreme penalty"—Crucifixion—at the hands of Pontius Pilate (Tacitus, *Ann.* 15.44). Thus, early non-Christian sources agree with the NT on the existence of Jesus as a historical figure and on details of his life and death.

D. Apocryphal "Gospels"

Finally, Jesus is also mentioned in the heretical writings of various Christian sects from the second century A.D. and later, writings often referred to as the "apocryphal" (or "hidden") gospels. The most famous of these is the so-called *Gospel of Thomas*, a collection of 114 sayings attributed to Jesus, written in Coptic sometime between the second and fourth centuries A.D. Another recent discovery is the so-called *Gospel of Judas*, which alleges that

Jesus collaborated with Judas to bring about the Crucifixion. Although such writings are frequently referred to as "gospels," they are very different from the four Gospels. Most important, none of them was written during the first century by eyewitnesses or disciples of the apostles. They were all composed much later, sometimes centuries after the time of Jesus. Moreover, none of the apocryphal "gospels" is a complete biography or "life" (Greek *bios*) like the four Gospels; most are brief accounts of visions, collections of random sayings, or are preserved only in fragments. Finally, many of these texts—such as the Gnostic account of the Crucifixion and Resurrection known as the *Gospel of Peter*—were quickly rejected by the orthodox Church Fathers, who identified them as the forgeries of heretics (Saint Irenaeus, *Against Heresies* 1.20; Eusebius, *Hist. Eccl.* 6.12.3). Hence, from a historical perspective, the noncanonical gospels have no value as sources on the life and teaching of Jesus.

E. The Quest for the "Historical Jesus"

From the very beginnings of the Church, the Gospels have been the object of intense study and fruitful exegesis. One thinks here of the detailed textual criticism of Origen or the work of Saint Augustine in which the author analyzes and provides solutions to the apparent discrepancies between the Gospel records of various events in Jesus's life (see Saint Augustine, *Harmony of the Gospels*). During the patristic age and medieval periods, numerous commentaries were produced on the various Gospels, with the Gospels of Matthew and John being the perennial favorites.

However, for the last two hundred years or more, since the time of the Enlightenment, Gospel study has intensified and focused in particular on understanding the life and teachings of Jesus in their historical context. Such research is commonly referred to as "the Quest for the Historical Jesus." Significantly, this quest had its original genesis among scholars who were either not Christians or who were outwardly opposed to Christianity. Historically, the quest has been largely dominated by secular scholars and Protestants, although in the twentieth century both Catholic and Jewish scholars have made significant contributions to the historical study of the life of Jesus.

Scholars commonly divide the modern quest up into three phases of research:

1. *The First Quest (1770s–1900).* This stage was highly influenced by English Deism and German Rationalism and was led by critics of Christianity such as Hermann Samuel Reimarus and David Friedrich Strauss. It came to an end with the famous work of Albert Schweitzer, *The Quest of the Historical Jesus* (1906), which depicted Jesus as a failed apocalyptic prophet. The results of the First Quest were largely negative, rejecting the miracles of Jesus and casting doubt upon his divinity and Messianic identity.

2. *The "New Quest" (1953–1980s).* This stage of the quest was heavily influenced by the philosophy of existentialism and the skepticism of the German exegete Rudolf Bultmann. It sought primarily to adapt Jesus's message and mission to the modern world, in particular by distancing him from ancient Judaism. Its work is represented by figures such as Ernst Käsemann and Günther Borkamm.

3. *The Third Quest (1970s–Present).* This stage of the quest, which most regard as still ongoing, is characterized by the participation of a greater diversity of scholars, with major figures emerging from England and America, as well as Europe. One of its key characteristics is an emphasis on Jesus's Jewishness and an attempt to understand him in the historical context of ancient Judaism. Some of its prominent authors are E. P. Sanders, John P. Meier, and N. T. Wright. In general, this stage of the quest is less skeptical toward the historical reliability of the Synoptic Gospels, though it continues to treat the Gospel of John as basically unreliable.

In principle, Christian faith is in no way opposed to the historical investigation of the life of Jesus. Indeed, the reality of the Incarnation demands that Christian scholars devote as much energy as possible to understanding Jesus as a real figure of history. Unfortunately, however, because of its origins in the Enlightenment, the modern quest has been dominated by the philosophical outlook known as Rationalism, which denies a priori the possibility of miracles and divine revelation. Because the Gospels are filled with accounts of both Jesus's miracles and his message of divine revelation, Enlightenment scholars and their intellectual heirs have tended to approach the Gospels from the perspective of methodological skepticism. The Gospels are often treated as historically "guilty" until proven "innocent." This approach has led to a false dichotomy between what such scholars refer to as "the Jesus of history" and "the Christ of faith." According to this view, "the historical Jesus" neither performed miracles nor claimed to be divine. This Jesus has supposedly been "obscured" behind the theological portraits of the Evangelists, who have altered history to suit their own ideological and theological interests. The Gospel of John in particular has been treated with skepticism by the quest, because John emphasizes Jesus's explicit teaching about his messiahship and divinity. For many scholars of the quest, the "real Jesus" has been lost behind the haze of dogma and early Church belief in "the Christ of faith." Hence, these scholars believe that the historian's task is to recover or "reconstruct" Jesus's life by selecting certain pieces of the Gospel records and separating the historical words and deeds from those episodes that have supposedly been created or altered by the Church.

The inherent problems of such an approach from a Christian perspective should be obvious. Not only are the philosophical assumptions of rationalism contradicted by the omnipotence of God, but, as we have already seen, the historical evidence strongly supports the authenticity and reliability of the four Gospels. This evidence must be approached without prejudice against the possibility of miracles and divine revelation. In light of the historical evidence, a proper approach to the study of Jesus is to treat the Gospels as credible historical accounts of his words and deeds. This is particularly true for Catholics, who affirm that "the Gospels were written under the inspiration of the Holy Spirit, who preserved their authors from every error" (PBC, *The Historicity of the Gospels,* 12 [1964]). Indeed, the official teaching of the Catholic Church on the historicity of the

Gospels was promulgated at the Second Vatican Council, which unhesitatingly affirmed "the historicity" of all four Gospels and declared that they "faithfully hand on what Jesus, the Son of God, while he lived among men, really did and taught for their eternal salvation, until the day when he was taken up" (see DV §19; CCC 126–27). The Council taught that although the Evangelists selected certain events from Jesus's life and synthesized them with an eye toward their audiences, they did so "always in such a fashion that they have told us the honest truth about Jesus" (ibid). Hence, for Catholics there is no dichotomy between the "historical Jesus" and the "Christ of faith." As Pope Benedict XVI has recently reaffirmed, the "real Jesus"—the Jesus of history—is the Jesus of the Gospels (see Pope Benedict XVI, *Jesus of Nazareth*, 2007).

II. THE LIFE OF JESUS

A. Birth, Infancy, and Hidden Years

Although the coming of Jesus is foretold in the Messianic prophecies of the Old Testament (*see* **Messiah**), his earthly life properly begins with the angel Gabriel's Annunciation to Mary that she would bear a son, and that the child's name would be "Jesus" (Luke 2:26–31; Matt 1:21). Through a miracle of the Holy Spirit, Jesus was virginally conceived in the womb of Mary (Matt 1:20; Luke 1:34–35); hence, he is the adopted (rather than biological) "son of Joseph" (Luke 4:22; John 1:45). After his humble birth in a stable in Bethlehem, Jesus was proclaimed Messiah by angelic messengers (Luke 2:8–15) and recognized as the long-awaited

king of Israel by pagan astrologers (Greek *magoi*) from the East (Matt 2:1–12). Nevertheless, from the beginning, Jesus's life was filled with suffering and opposition, manifested very early on in King Herod's massacre of the infants in Bethlehem in an effort to kill the Messiah, and Joseph and Mary's being forced to flee to Egypt and remain there in exile until the death of Herod (Matt 2:13–23). All these events took place during the reigns of the Roman emperor Caesar Augustus and the tyrannical King Herod of Judea, probably around 4–6 B.C. (cf. Luke 2:1–20).

In contrast to the events surrounding his birth, not much is known about Jesus's "hidden years," the period between his infancy and the beginning of his public ministry, when he was growing up in the town of Nazareth, in Galilee (cf. Luke 2:51). We know that his family was apparently poor, as is indicated by Mary's offering of two turtledoves at Jesus's circumcision and dedication, instead of the more expensive sacrifices (Luke 2:22–24; Lev 12:2–8). We also know that Joseph was a "carpenter" or "builder" of some sort (Matt 13:55), and that Jesus learned this trade from him as a young man and continued in it into adulthood (cf. Mark 6:3). Finally, the Gospels make clear that Joseph and his family were practicing Jews who kept the Law of Moses and worshipped at the Jerusalem Temple (Luke 2:21, 41). The one window into Jesus's youth is the account of his being found by Mary and Joseph in the Temple after having been missing for three days, which reveals that Jesus already knew at age twelve about his divine Sonship and filial mission (Luke 2:42–51).

B. Public Ministry

Jesus's public ministry began with his baptism by John in the river Jordan (Matt 3:1–16; Mark 1:2–11; Luke 3:21–22). John the Baptist called people to repentance from sin in order to "prepare the way" for the coming of the Messiah and the new Exodus spoken of by the prophet Isaiah (Isa 40:1–11). At his baptism, Jesus was revealed to be the one anointed with the Spirit of God, and God's own "beloved Son." Though sinless himself (Heb 4:15), Jesus accepted John's baptism in order to enter into solidarity with sinners, to "fulfill" in himself the whole history of salvation (Matt 3:15), and to point forward to the "baptism" of suffering he would undergo on the Cross (Mark 10:38–45; Luke 12:50).

Immediately after his baptism, Jesus was driven into the desert and tempted by the devil for forty days (Matt 4:1–17; Mark 1:12–13; Luke 4:1–13). In these temptations, he began redeeming humanity from the Fall of Adam by resisting the threefold temptation to which Adam and Eve had succumbed in the Garden (Gen 3:6; cf. 1 John 2:16). He also recapitulated the forty-day fasts of Moses and Elijah (Exod 24:8; 1 Kgs 19:8), as well as Israel's forty years of testing in the wilderness in the Exodus from Egypt (Ps 95:10–11), thus succeeding where both Adam and Israel had failed.

After passing the trial in the desert, Jesus began his ministry proper by beginning to preach about the coming of "the Kingdom of God" throughout the region of Galilee, the very place where the Exile and dispersion of the kingdom of Israel had begun (Matt 4:12–17; Isa 9:1–2). His public ministry was distinctively marked by his frequent performance of "mighty works and wonders and signs" (Acts 2:22)—in particular his great miracles of healing and forgiveness, as well as his exorcisms. Early on in his ministry, Jesus changed water into wine at the Wedding at Cana, providing a sign of the eschatological banquet that the prophets had foretold would be celebrated during the Messianic age (John 2:1–12; Isa 25:6–8) and at the "hour" of the Last Supper (John 13:1–2). He performed a similar sign when he fed the crowds of five thousand and four thousand with just a few loaves and fishes, miracles revealing that he would gather to himself the tribes of Israel (the twelve baskets) and the Gentile nations (the seven baskets) (Mark 6:30–44; 8:1–10, 14–21). He was particularly well known for his "power" (Greek *exousia*) as an exorcist for casting out demons and unclean spirits (Mark 1:27; 5:1–20; 9:14–29). A large bulk of his ministry was spent giving sight to the blind, cleansing the lepers, causing the lame to walk, allowing the deaf to hear, and even raising the dead. The most famous of the latter miracles he performed for his own friend Lazarus, whom he raised from the dead four days after his burial (John 11:1–44). In addition to these wonders, some of Jesus's most powerful miracles were not visible; these consisted of his healing of the souls of those whose sins he declared "forgiven" (Mark 2:1–12; Luke 7:36–50). Jesus himself declared that all of his miracles were indicators of his identity as Messiah (Matt 11:2–6; Luke 7:18–23; cf. Isa 35:5–6, 61:1–2). In particular, his exorcisms signaled the overthrow of the "kingdom" of

Satan (Matt 12:25–28), his true enemy, whom Jesus referred to as "the ruler of this world" (John 12:31). All of Jesus's mighty works together functioned as "signs" of the coming Kingdom of God, in which all mankind will be delivered from the power of sin, Satan, and even death itself, and God's creation will be renewed and restored through the power of the Holy Spirit.

In order to perpetuate his public ministry of preaching and healing, Jesus called to himself disciples who would carry on his work among Israel and the Gentiles. Chief among the various circles of disciples were the twelve apostles, who were a visible sign of the long-awaited restoration of the twelve tribes of Israel (Matt 10:1–4, 19:28; cf. Ezek 37). After receiving "authority" (Greek *exousia*) from him, the twelve were commissioned by Jesus to go out and proclaim the coming of the Kingdom, and to perform many of the same miracles and healings that Christ himself performed (Matt 10:5–23). In addition to the twelve, Jesus also called a wider circle of seventy disciples, modeled on the seventy elders of Israel and the seventy members of the Jewish Sanhedrin (Luke 10:1–20; cf. Exod 24:1). These disciples together represented the visible beginnings of the Kingdom of God present on earth in mystery. They were the firstlings of the "flock" of which Jesus is the "Good Shepherd," whose mission is to gather into his fold many sheep (John 10:1–16). One of the most important moments in the life of the disciples took place at Caesarea Philippi, when Jesus declared his intention to found his "Church" or "assembly" (Greek *ekklēsia*) upon Simon Peter (Matt 16:13–18). This declaration flowed from Peter's profession of faith in Jesus as "the Christ, the Son of the Living God" (Matt 16:16). Immediately following this, Jesus began teaching the apostles that he would have to suffer and die, but that on the third day he would be raised from the dead (Matt 16:21–23). In order to prepare them for his Passion and death, he took Peter, James, and John up a mountain and revealed his glory to them in the Transfiguration (Matt 17:1–8). This mystery not only reaffirmed Jesus's divine Sonship but also pointed forward to the new "Exodus" that he would accomplish in Jerusalem in his Passion, death, and Resurrection (Luke 9:31).

C. Teaching

Jesus was not only a great healer and worker of miracles; he was also the greatest of teachers. He gathered around him "disciples" or "students" (Greek *mathētēs*), who often referred to him as "Rabbi," a Jewish title for teachers (Mark 9:5; John 1:49; Matt 23:7). The bulk of the Gospels consists of the teachings of Jesus.

The central theme of Jesus's teaching was his proclamation of the coming of "the Kingdom of God," or "the Kingdom of heaven." There are over ninety references to the Kingdom in the Gospels. Based on OT prophecies of the Kingdom (Mic 4:1–8; Dan 2:44, 7:13–14), numerous Jews of Jesus's day, such as Joseph of Arimathea, were waiting for the coming of the Messianic Kingdom of God (Mark 15:43). On the one hand, the Messianic Kingdom was modeled on the earthly kingdom of David, "the kingdom of the Lord" (1 Chr 28:5) that had existed under David and Solomon. On the other hand, the kingdom was essentially heavenly, like the "Kingdom of God," which was revealed to Jacob during his vision at Bethel (Wis 10:10; Gen 28:10–16). Jesus inaugurated his public ministry by proclaiming that "the Kingdom of God" was "at hand" and calling people to repent (Mark 1:14). He also explicitly connected the advent of the Kingdom to his own work of exorcisms and healings (Matt 4:23; 12:28). He taught his followers to pray for its coming (Matt 6:13; Luke 11:2), and warned that the impenitent and those who rejected his message could expect eternal exclusion from the Kingdom (Matt 7:21–22; 21:31–32). He primarily taught about the Kingdom through his parables, which used the realities of this world as a window into the "mysteries" of the Kingdom (Matt 13; Luke 14–16). Jesus taught that the Kingdom was present in his own person and ministry (Matt 12:28; Luke 11:20), inaugurated on earth in his disciples and the Church (Matt 13:24–30, 36–43; 16:19), yet still awaiting its future consummation at the Parousia and Last Judgment (Matt 25:31–46). He celebrated the banquet of the Kingdom at the Last Supper (Luke 22:29–30). He made clear that the Kingdom is "not of this world" (John 18:36); it is first and foremost a heavenly reality, which one can either "enter" or be excluded from. The opposite of the Kingdom is the realm of fiery Gehenna (Mark 9:42–48). Humility, repentance, following Jesus, and being born of "water and spirit" are some of the essential prerequisites for entering the Kingdom (Matt 18:1–4; John 3:3–5), which is the ultimate end and beatitude of the children of God (Matt 5:3, 10; 6:33).

In addition to the Kingdom of God, in his teaching Jesus also emphasized the Fatherhood of God. Although there are a few exceptions, God is called "Father" relatively infrequently in the OT (Deut 32:6; Jer 3:4; Sir 23:1; Mal 2:10). By contrast, Jesus calls God "Father" seventeen times in the Sermon on the Mount (Matt 5–7), and addressed God as "Father" throughout his teaching ministry. Indeed, the revelation of God as Father and Jesus as his Son is a distinctive element of his message (Matt 11:25–27; Luke 10:21). He emphasized the love of God the Father for his children (Luke 12:22–32; Matt 10:29–31; John 16:27) and prayer to God as Father (Matt 6:8, 7:7–11; Luke 11:9–13). God is not simply "Lord," or "Master," or even "King"; he is the Father who sends his Son to seek and save the lost (Luke 15:11–32; 19:10). Jesus is the one who reveals "the bosom of the Father," whom no one has seen (John 1:18). He himself prayed to God as "*Abba*, Father" (Mark 14:36).

Jesus also taught in lengthy discourses, like the prophets of the OT, on many other topics. Compendiums of his teaching can be found in his parables of the Kingdom (Matt 13) and his discourses on the mission of the disciples (Matt 10), the nature and mission of the Church (Matt 18), and the destruction of Jerusalem and the final coming of the Son of Man, known as the Olivet Discourse (Matt 24–25; Mark 13; Luke 21). The Olivet Discourse is particularly noteworthy because it contains Jesus's teachings about the Great Tribulation, the destruction of Jerusalem, and his own final "coming" in glory (Greek *parousia*) at the time of the Last Judgment (Matt 24:3, 27). The Gospel of John is particularly full of lengthy teaching discourses, such as the Bread of Life Discourse (John 6), the Good Shepherd and his Flock (John 10), and Jesus's extended discourses at the Last Supper (John 13–17). The most famous of his discourses is the Sermon on the Mount, in which Jesus, like a new Moses, gave his disciples the New Law from atop a mountain (Matt 5–7). Just as God had called the people of Israel to be a "kingdom of priests" (Exod 19:6) by being "holy," as God is holy (Lev 11:44), so Jesus calls his audience to be "sons of God," who are "perfect" as God is perfect (Matt 5:48). This is the essence of Jesus's call: to repent and turn away from sin, and to seek that happiness ("beatitude") that can only be found in the kingdom of heaven (Matt 6:33). Although Jesus did not "abolish" the Decalogue or the Laws of Moses, he called his disciples to go beyond them and to write the twofold law of love of God and love of neighbor on their hearts (Matt 22:36–40; Mark 12:28–31; Luke 10:25–27; cf. Jer 31:31–33; Deut 6:4–9). Indeed, he called his disciples to a "righteousness" that surpasses that of even the most faithful of Law keepers, the Pharisees (Matt 5:20). For Jesus, sin has its origin in the human heart, not in the things "outside" of a person (Mark 7:18–23). These spiritual principles are embodied in the disciplines of prayer, fasting, and almsgiving (Matt 6:1–18).

Although it is sometimes said that Jesus preached the Kingdom of God while the Church preached Jesus, a great deal of Jesus's teaching also revolved around his own identity as Messiah and Son of God (for more detail, *see* **Messiah**). At his inaugural sermon in Nazareth, he identified himself as the "anointed" one spoken of by the prophet Isaiah (Luke 4:16–21; Isa 61:1–2). Although he frequently silenced demons and others who wished to proclaim him Messiah before the opportune time had arrived (Mark 1:24–25; 3:11–12), he never denied that their professions were true. In fact, on one occasion he explicitly identified himself as "the Messiah" while speaking to the Samaritan woman at the well (John 4:25). As Messiah, he taught that belief in him, discipleship to him, and obedience to his teachings would serve as the criteria for one's eternal salvation (Matt 7:21–23; Mark 8:38; John 3:14–15, 8:24, 12:48). Over and over again he taught his disciples about and identified himself as the "Son of Man" who would bring about the redemption of the world (Mark 10:35–45) and who would usher in the glory of the Messianic Kingdom (Matt 10:23, 19:28; Mark 9:1, 13:24–27). Positively, these teachings culminated in Simon Peter's profession of faith in Jesus as "the Christ, the Son of the Living God" at Caesarea Philippi (Matt 16:13–18). Negatively, they led to his being put to death under the false charges of being a blasphemer and a Messianic pretender (Mark 14:53–64; John 19:7).

D. Passion and Death

Over the course of his public ministry, and especially during his last days in Jerusalem, Jesus encountered opposition from various groups (Matt 21:45–46). This opposition ultimately led to his being executed as a common criminal by means of crucifixion. After Peter's profession of faith at Caesarea Philippi, Jesus had begun predicting that he would suffer, die, and be resurrected on the third day (Matt 16:16–23). With these predictions, he revealed that the Messianic Son of Man would also become the Suffering Servant, who would offer his life "as a ransom for many" (Matt 20:28; Mark 10:45; cf. Isa 53).

Jesus was a Jew who kept the Torah of Moses faithfully. He was not executed because he sought to "abolish" the Law and the Prophets (cf. Matt 5:17), but because he came into conflict with Jewish leaders over at least three key issues of authority. First, he claimed authority over the Law by healing on the Sabbath (Matt 12:1–8). Second, he claimed authority over the Temple when he stopped its sacrificial services and prohibited anyone from buying or selling, thereby signaling the Temple's imminent destruction (John 2:13–22; Mark 11:15–17). Third and finally, Jesus was executed because of his self-claims. He was accused of sedition by those who saw his Messianic claim as a threat to the political power of Caesar and the Roman Empire (John 19:12–15). He was also accused of making himself "God" by those who rejected his claims of divine Sonship (John 10:30–33). This conflict came to a head at his trial before the Jewish Sanhedrin, at which he was accused of "blasphemy" and handed over to the Romans to be put to death (Mark 14:53–64).

Shortly before his death, Jesus celebrated a final Passover meal with his disciples and identified himself as the new Passover lamb whose blood would be shed "for the forgiveness of sins" (Matt 26:17–30; Luke 22:7–39; John 13–17). He spent his final evening before his arrest with Peter, James, and John in the Garden of Gethsemane, praying to the Father to take the "cup" of suffering from him if possible (Mark 14:32–42). After being put on trial before the Sanhedrin and Pontius Pilate, the Roman governor, Jesus was scourged, mocked, and made to carry his Cross up the hill of Golgotha, where he was crucified. He died on a Friday afternoon, during the Jewish feast of Passover. Over his head was hung a title written in three languages: "Jesus of Nazareth, King of the Jews" (John 19:17–22). At the foot of the Cross were his mother, the disciple John, and several of his female followers (John 19:25–27). After his death, Jesus was buried by two members of the Sanhedrin, Joseph of Arimathea and Nicodemus, one of whom was secretly his disciple (John 19:38–42). Despite his ignominious death, the Gospels make it clear that Jesus was "innocent" and condemned on false charges (Luke 23:13–16, 47).

E. Descent, Resurrection, and Ascension

The last stages of Jesus's earthly life consisted of the historical and transcendent events of his Descent into Hell, his Resurrection from the dead, and his Ascension into heaven. Although there is no record of the Descent in the Gospels, the NT bears witness to the fact that while Jesus was dead in the tomb, his soul descended into Hades, the realm of the dead, in order to deliver the spirits of the just (1 Pet 2:18–22, 4:6; Eph 4:9). After this, on the Sunday immediately following his Crucifixion, the four Gospels bear unanimous witness that his tomb was empty and that Jesus had risen from the dead (Matt 28; Mark 16; Luke 24; John 20–21). With his Resurrection from the dead, Jesus inaugurated the beginning of the new creation that had been foretold by the prophets (Isa 65:17; 66:22) and which he himself had spoken of (Matt 19:28). Hence, his return to life was no mere bodily resuscitation, nor was it the appearance of a "ghost" or "spirit" (Luke 24:36–39). Jesus's resurrected body was real and authentic, as revealed by the presence of his wounds and his "flesh and bones"; yet it was now in a glorified state, and no longer limited by space and time (Luke 24:40–43; John 20:19). On the octave of Easter Sunday, the fullness of Jesus's divinity is revealed to his disciples, such that the apostle Thomas could say to him: "My Lord and my God!" (John 20:28). After his Resurrection, Jesus spent forty days with the disciples, instructing them about the Kingdom of God, before ascending into heaven and entering into the glory of his heavenly Kingdom (Acts 1:1–11).

III. BIBLICAL CHRISTOLOGY

A. *The Humanity of Jesus*

According to the New Testament, Jesus was fully human, but "without sin" (Heb 4:15; 1 Pet 2:22; 2 Cor 5:21; 1 John 3:5).

Although the Latin term "Incarnation" does not occur in the NT (which was written in Greek), the Scripture nevertheless teaches that the central "mystery" of Christianity is that in Jesus, God was "manifested in the flesh" (1 Tim 3:16; the Latin word for "flesh" is *caro*). As John puts it, "the Word"—who "was God"—"became flesh and dwelt among us" (John 1:14). Hence, he was able to be heard, seen, and touched, like any man (cf. 1 John 1:1–4). Likewise, Paul's famous "christological hymn" proclaims that the divine Son of God "emptied himself" (Greek *kenōsis*) and was born "in human form" (Phil 2:5–8). All these texts point to the true humanity of the "man Jesus Christ" (Rom 5:15; 1 Tim 2:5), who was "born of a woman" (Gal 3:16) and truly suffered and died on the Cross (1 Cor 15:1–3). Indeed, an important litmus test for authentic Christianity in the early Church was whether someone affirmed that Christ had come "in the flesh" or, like the early heretics known as Docetists, denied that Jesus was truly human (1 John 4:2; 2 John 7).

The Gospels in particular are filled with testimony to the true humanity of Jesus. Not only was he born of a human mother, Mary (Matt 1:16; Luke 1:31; Gal 4:4), but his human lineage from David, Abraham, and Adam is emphasized (Matt 1:1–17; Luke 3:23–38; Rom 1:3). During his youth, he is said to have grown like any man "in wisdom and in stature" (Luke 2:52). During his public ministry, Jesus's full humanity was repeatedly manifested: he was subject to human conditions such as hunger and thirst (Matt 4:2; John 19:28), weariness and sleep (John 4:6; Matt 8:24). He displayed human passions and emotions such as joy (Luke 10:21; John 11:15), anger (Mark 3:5), indignation (John 2:13–17), love (Mark 10:21; John 11:36), and sadness (Matt 26:37; John 11:36). He wept over the death of Lazarus and the coming destruction of Jerusalem (John 11:33–35; Luke 19:41). He also possessed a human will, which was distinct from God the Father's will (John 6:38; Luke 22:42). In the face of his own death, he experienced "fear" (Mark 14:33), and was sorrowful and stricken to the heart (Matt 26:37–38). Finally, he suffered the agony of death itself (Matt 27:50; John 19:30; Mark 15:37; Luke 23:46).

B. *The Divinity of Jesus*

According to the NT, Jesus Christ is truly the eternal and divine Son of God. Although some people apparently had difficulty understanding that Jesus was greater than the highest created beings, the angels (Heb 1:5–2:9), Scripture clearly teaches that Jesus is the eternal Son of God. He is "the Word" (Greek *logos*), who existed before the world was made (John 1:1–3; something that theologians refer to as "preexistence"). The ancient Jewish belief in the Messiah's preexistence appears to be rooted in prophecies that speak of his existing "from of old" and being "begotten" before creation (Mic 5:2; Ps 110:1–4; cf. *1 Enoch* 62; *b. Pesahim* 54a). As the eternal Son of God, Jesus not only existed with the Father "before the world was made" (John 17:5, 24), but the entire universe was created through him and by means of his power (John 1:3; Heb 1:1–3; Col 1:15–16), and he was sent "from heaven" by God (John 3:13; 6:38). When John refers to Jesus as "the only-begotten [Greek *monogenē*] Son of God" (John 3:16), he is asserting Jesus's eternal origin and nature and implying that he was "begotten, not made," as clarified later by the Nicene Creed. Outside the Gospels, the divinity of Jesus is indicated by the early Christian application of the title "Lord" (Greek *kyrios*) to him (1 Cor 8:6; cf. Deut 6:4). This title was used in the Greek translation of the OT for the sacred name, "the Lord" (Hebrew *YHWH*; Phil 2:10–11; cf. Isa 45:23). Paul explicitly affirms that "in him the whole fullness of deity dwells bodily" (Col 2:9). Even with regard to his death, Jesus was proclaimed as divine: it was "the Author of Life" and the "Lord of Glory" who was crucified on Golgotha (Acts 3:15; 1 Cor 2:8).

Through his public ministry, Jesus revealed his divinity through both implicit and explicit claims. He implied his divinity when he declared himself "greater than" the greatest men of the Old Covenant, such as Jonah and Solomon (Matt 12:41), and even "greater than" the Temple, the dwelling place of God on earth (Matt 12:6). To his contemporary Jewish audience, the only thing that could be greater than the Temple would be God himself. Christ also used OT images of God to refer to himself, such as the "Bridegroom" of the covenant and the "Lord of the Sabbath" (Mark 2:19–20; Matt 12:8; Isa 54:1–7; Exod 20:10). Moreover, he made demands that only God can make, such as calling his disciples to have "faith" in him (John 14:1; Mark 8:38) and demanding of them an absolute love that transcends all other relationships (Matt 10:37; Luke 14:25). In the Old Covenant, such love was given to God alone (Deut 6:4–8). In addition, Jesus allowed "worship" (Greek *proskynesis*) to be given him (Matt 14:33; John 9:35–39)—the same kind of worship that both Peter and an anonymous angel refused to be given as they believed such worship was due to God alone (Acts 10:25; Rev 19:10). It is hard to believe that Jesus would have accepted such worship if he knew himself to be merely a man. Moreover, Jesus's many miracles reveal his omnipotence (Matt 11:4; John 10:37); through them he demonstrated his divine power over illness, demonic spirits, sin, the natural world, and death itself. Strikingly, Jesus also claimed the divine prerogative to forgive sins, something that "God alone" could accomplish (Mark 2:7), and that his death would have the power to redeem humanity (Matt 20:28; 26:26–28). Significantly, Jesus hinted at the fact that the Messiah was much more than David's "son"; he was David's "Lord" (Greek *kyrios*)—

again, an OT title for God (Mark 11:35–37). Finally, Jesus declared himself to be Judge of the world (John 5:22–25; Luke 12:1–9). Not only does this presuppose omniscience, but in the OT God alone is the universal "judge" (Ps 49:1–6).

In addition to these implicit claims, Jesus also made explicit claims to divinity. The latter are less frequently recorded, perhaps because he sought to gradually reveal himself to his disciples and quite probably because such claims would have led to his being imprisoned and put to death before his hour had come (cf. John 7:4–9). For example, when Jesus paralleled his knowledge as Son with the knowledge of the Father, he thereby equated his knowledge with that of God (Matt 11:25–27; Luke 10:21–22). Moreover, he identified himself with God the Father, claiming that anyone who had seen him had "seen the Father" (John 14:9). Remarkably, he declared, "I and the Father are one" (John 10:30). For this, he was almost stoned, because his Jewish listeners correctly interpreted him as declaring himself to be "God" (John 10:33). Perhaps most revealing of all, Jesus laid claim on several occasions to the divine name that God had revealed to Moses, "I AM" (Greek *egō eimi;* Exod 3:14; see Mark 6:50; John 8:24–38, 58). In a Jewish context, this assertion would have meant laying claim to the divine nature, since a person's name was believed to reveal his or her nature and mission (cf. Matt 16:13–18). Shockingly, Jesus even made belief in his divinity necessary for salvation: "you will die in your sins, unless you believe that I AM" (John 8:24). Finally, at his trial before the Sanhedrin, Jesus solemnly testified to his identity as the heavenly Son of Man (Dan 7:13–14); because of this, he was accused of blasphemy and sentenced to death (Mark 14:61–65; John 19:7). After the Resurrection, the most explicit testimony of Jesus's divinity in all the Gospels occurred when the apostle Thomas, before the face of the Risen Christ, exclaimed "My Lord and my God!" (John 20:28).

C. Redemption

In light of the fullness of Jesus's humanity and divinity, the NT also teaches that Jesus's entire life, and especially his death and Resurrection, are a mystery of "redemption"—that is, liberation or release from sin and death.

This redemptive work begins with the Incarnation, by which the divine Son "becomes poor" in order to bestow the riches of his heavenly inheritance upon humanity (2 Cor 8:9). He does this in order to save mankind from sin (1 Tim 1:15; 1 John 3:5), to reveal the love of God (John 3:15–16; 1 John 4:9–14), to show us the way of holiness and sacrificial love (John 14:6; Matt 11:29; John 15:12–13), and, ultimately, to enable humanity to become "partakers of the divine nature" (cf. 2 Pet 1:4). This redemptive work was being carried out during Jesus's youth and hidden years, when he substituted his obedience for humanity's disobedience (cf. Luke 2:51). He continued redeeming humanity during his temptation in the desert, when he overcame the threefold temptations of Adam, which hold power over fallen man (Luke 4:1–13; cf. Gen 3:6). He also redeemed mankind through his teaching, which liberates humanity by revealing "the truth" that frees us from slavery to sin and falsehood (John 8:31–33; 14:6). Through his miracles of healing and deliverance, he delivered man from suffering, illness, and slavery to demonic spirits (Matt 8:16–17). This redemptive work reached its apex in the mystery of his Passion, death, Resurrection, and Ascension. By means of the Cross, humanity is set free from the power of sin and death, securing "redemption through his blood" (Eph 1:17) and the "forgiveness of sins" (Col 1:13), while the Resurrection ushers in the new life of "righteousness" or "justification" in the Spirit (Rom 4:25). These events signify not only the redemption of humanity from sin and death (Rom 3:24; Eph 1:7; Heb 9:15), but the restoration of mankind's communion with God (Rom 5:10; Col 1:20), that we might become a "new creation" in Christ (2 Cor 5:17–19).

Because of the unique nature of the work of redemption, the NT proclaims that Jesus alone is Savior: there is "no other name" by which men may be saved (Acts 4:12). Through his atoning death, God "reconciled" the world to himself (2 Cor 5:19). This act of redemption was also an act of divine love for every human being, such that every person can say, with Paul: "The Son of God . . . loved me and gave himself for me" (Gal 2:20).

JESUS CHRIST, TITLES OF *See* **Jesus Christ**; *see also* **King**; **Lamb**; **Messiah**; **Priest, priesthood**; **Servant of the Lord**; **Prophet**; **Son of God**; **Son of Man**.

JETHER The name of two men in the Old Testament.

1. The firstborn son of **Gideon**. Gideon asked Jether to execute the Midianite kings, Zebah and Zalmunna, after Gideon had captured them (Judg 8:20). Although the act was to be in revenge for the killing of Gideon's brothers, Jether refused to perform the executions.

2. The Ishmaelite father of **Amasa**, commander of David's army (2 Sam 19:13; 1 Chr 2:17).

JETHRO Priest of Midian and father-in-law of Moses through his marriage with Zipporah (Exod 3:1; 4:18). Also called Reuel (Exod 2:18), he gave asylum to Moses after the flight from Egypt and consented to Moses's marriage to his daughter (Exod 2:21). When Moses returned to Egypt, Zipporah and Moses's sons remained with Jethro and then went with Moses and the Israelites after the departure from Egypt. He met Moses in the desert and offered sacrifices to God near Mount Sinai (Exod 18:1–12). Jethro advised Moses to organize a judicial system to handle domestic disputes among the people (Exod 18:13–27).

JEW The term "Jew" has had different meanings at different times. In early Israel, it meant a member of the tribe of Judah; later, after the division of the tribes, it meant someone from the southern kingdom of Judah (2 Kgs 16:6, translated "men of Judah"; 25:25; Neh 1:2; Jer 32:12, 38:19, 52:28–30). After the **Exile**, "Jew" was used in two ways, one geographic and the other religious: it could mean a resident of Judea, but it could also mean a follower of Judaism or one of those who remained dispersed throughout the Persian and later empires (cf. Esth 9:15; Dan 3:8; Zech 8:23).

In the **Synoptic Gospels**, "Jew" is heard most often on the lips of Gentiles. Jesus, for example, is called "King of the Jews" by the Romans (cf. Matt 27:37; Mark 15:26; Luke 23:36–37).

John's Gospel also uses "Jew" to mean a resident of Palestine (cf. John 2:6; 5:1; 6:4; 18:33, 39; 19:3, 19, 21; see **John, Gospel of**). But more often in John, "the Jews" means the enemies or adversaries of Jesus, whom the Synoptic Gospels would describe as "scribes and Pharisees" (cf. John 2:18; 7:1, 13; 8:48, 52, 57; 9:18, 22; 10:24, 31, 33; 11:8; 19:38; 20:19). The two meanings frequently overlap, since Jesus encountered his stiffest resistance in Judea, where the Jewish leadership was based in Jerusalem. Thus "the Jews" in John most often means the unbelieving leadership in or from Jerusalem.

The **Acts of the Apostles** uses "Jew" in all of these senses. It can be an ethnic term or a religious one (cf., for example, Acts 2:5; 22:3), and possibly even a "hostile Judean leader" (Acts 23:12).

In current usage, of course, "Jew" refers to someone who is either ethnically Jewish or follows the Jewish religion. This is very different from John's use of the term. Ethnically, Jesus and all his disciples were Jewish, but John distinguishes them from "the Jews" who were in authority.

JEZANIAH Son of the Maacathite and an officer who chose to stay at Mizpah with **Gedaliah**, the appointed ruler of Judah, following the destruction of Jerusalem (2 Kgs 25:23; Jer 40:8).

JEZEBEL Daughter of Ethbaal, king of the Sidonians, and wife of King **Ahab** of Israel (1 Kgs 16:29–31). Scripture portrays her as a woman of corrupting influence and power in the court of Ahab. After marrying Ahab she promoted the worship of the Canaanite storm and fertility god **Baal** and was patron of the 450 prophets of that god, who ate "at Jezebel's table" (1 Kgs 18:19). She also persecuted the prophets of Yahweh with such venom that the survivors went into hiding (1 Kgs 18:3–4). She thereby roused the indignation of the prophet **Elijah**, who challenged the Baal prophets directly. In the confrontation on Mount Carmel, Elijah humiliated the Baal prophets and then led them to the brook Kishon, where he slaughtered them (1 Kgs 18:20–40).

Jezebel swore vengeance upon Elijah, who took flight into the wilderness (1 Kgs 19:1–18). She also contrived the death of **Naboth** the Jezreelite, so that her husband could seize his vineyard (1 Kgs 21:5–16).

Elijah foretold a horrible death for Jezebel (1 Kgs 21:23), and his prediction came to pass. When Jehu rose up against the house of Ahab, Jezebel adorned herself and appeared at her window to ridicule the general as a mere pretender. Her eunuchs, however, threw her from the window, whereupon she was trampled under the hooves of horses and then devoured by dogs—as Elijah had prophesied (2 Kgs 9:30–37). In the end, all that remained of her body was her skull, feet, and hands.

Jezebel became infamous as a **type** of

moral and religious apostasy. Revelation calls a false prophetess "Jezebel" (Rev 2:20) because the name was instantly recognizable as a reference to a woman who stood against the worship of the Lord.

JEZREEL (Hebrew, "God sows") The fertile plain located between Galilee and Samaria, and the name of a city on the plain, in the territory of Issachar (Josh 19:18), probably modern Zerʻin (Tel Yizraʼal). Jezreel figured in several Old Testament events. The plain of Jezreel (Esdraelon) was the site of several major battles: it was there that **Deborah** and Barak defeated the forces of Jabin, king of Hazor (Judg 4:4–24); **Gideon** defeated the Midianites (Judg 7:1–25); Saul and Jonathan and his brothers died on nearby Mount Gilboa (1 Sam 31); **Josiah** attempted to halt the advance of Neco II of Egypt but was killed in the fighting on the plain (2 Kgs 23:29). Wounded in battle against the Syrians, King **Joram** of Israel was brought to Jezreel to be healed (2 Kgs 8:29). **Ahab** made Jezreel one of his royal residences, and the city was the scene of the violent and cruel death of **Jezebel** (2 Kgs 9:30–37). On the basis of that account, it is presumed that the city served as Ahab's winter capital and had a royal palace of some dimensions, including a tower or upper floors with windows (2 Kgs 9:32). **Naboth** was from Jezreel (1 Kgs 21:1), and his murder through the connivance of Jezebel led **Elijah** to curse Ahab and his entire house (1 Kgs 21:23–24). Jezreel came to symbolize the guilt of the kingdom of Israel and the inevitable destruction that its failings would bring (Hos 1:4). When the Assyrians destroyed the kingdom of Israel, Jezreel ceased to have any political importance.

JOAB (Hebrew, "the Lord is father") The commander of David's army. Joab was the son of David's sister Zeruiah, and the brother of **Abishai** and **Asahel** (2 Sam 8:16, 20:23; 1 Chr 2:16). Joab was probably involved in David's earlier career before David was made king of Judah, but his name does not appear except as the brother of Abishai (1 Sam 26:6). He distinguished himself in David's campaigns against Ishbaal, son of Saul (2 Sam 2:12–32), whose own army was commanded by **Abner**. Joab took bloody revenge upon Abner for the death of his brother Asahel in combat (2 Sam 2:24–25). This act was not approved by David, and the king censured his general (2 Sam 3:29) and gave Abner a proper burial (2 Sam 3:31–37). Joab, however, led the successful conquest of Jerusalem (1 Chr 11:6), and after that he served as David's commander-in-chief.

Joab was general during a number of notable campaigns, including that against the Arameans and the Ammonites (2 Sam 10:6–19; 12:26–31). During the military effort against the Arameans, Joab assisted David in his plot to secure the death of **Uriah** to permit the king to marry **Bathsheba** (2 Sam 11:14–25). The general subsequently encouraged David to permit **Absalom** to return after he arranged the murder of Amnon (2 Sam 14:1–24), but he was determined to suppress the rebellion of Absalom, and when Absalom caught his hair in the branches of a tree, Joab killed Absalom against David's specific command that Absalom be spared (2 Sam 18:9–15; cf. 2 Sam 18:5).

In the campaign against **Sheba**, Joab was demoted and command was given to **Amasa**. Disagreeing with Amasa's apparent reluctance to summon the Judahites to counter Sheba's rebellion, Joab treacherously murdered him and took command of the army (2 Sam 20). He later opposed David's plan for a census but carried out the royal commandment (2 Sam 24:3–9) and was a supporter of **Adonijah** against **Solomon** in the struggle for the royal succession (1 Kgs 1:7).

Joab was one of the most important military figures in the life and reign of David. Through his martial genius, he helped David attain the throne. The general's forceful and commanding personality gave him such influence over the king that David could not bring himself to put Joab to death or remove him from his post despite Joab's excesses and crimes. Before his passing, however, David urged Solomon to put Joab to death for the murders of Abner and Amasa, and Solomon had Joab executed (1 Kgs 2:5; 28–35).

JOANNA The wife of Chuza and a follower of Jesus. Joanna was one of the women who was healed by Jesus and who then became part of Jesus's devoted group of followers, along with **Mary Magdalene** and Susanna (Luke 8:2–3). A woman of some wealth, Joanna was one of the financial sponsors whose generosity enabled Jesus and his closest disciples to engage in full-time ministry (Luke 24:10).

JOASH (Hebrew, "the Lord has given") The name of eight men in the Old Testament.

1. The father of **Gideon** and a member of the family of Abiezer of Manasseh at Ophrah (Judg 6:11, 25–32). Joash was associated with the altar to **Baal** and an **Asherah** (Judg 6:25) that were replaced by Gideon with an altar to the Lord. When Gideon was threatened by townspeople, Joash urged them not to act, declaring that Baal could take care of himself (Judg 6:30–31).

2. A Judahite, the son of Shelah (1 Chr 4:22).

3. A Benjaminite, the son of Becher (1 Chr 7:8).

4. A Benjaminite, the son of Shemaah of Gibeah, who was reputed to be a mighty ambidextrous warrior (1 Chr 12:3). He sided with David in the war against Saul (1 Chr 12:1).

5. An official in the royal administration of David. He was the overseer of David's oil supply (1 Chr 27:28).

6. Either a son or a servant of **Ahab** (1 Kgs 22:26; 2 Chr 18:25). When the prophet **Micaiah** angered King Ahab by prophesying failure for Ahab's campaign against Syria at Ramothgilead (1 Kgs 22; 2 Chr 18), the prophet was to be taken before "Joash the king's son." It is uncertain, however, whether the title "king's son" refers to an actual son of the king or to some kind of official, especially as the latter meaning pertains in other passages (cf. 2 Chr 28:7; Jer 36:26; 38:6).

7. The son of King **Ahaziah** and Zibiah of Beer-sheba (2 Kgs 11–12; 2 Chr 22:10–24:27) and the king of Judah from around 835 to 796 B.C. The succession of Joash was a difficult one. After the death of his father, **Athaliah** massacred the royal family and assumed rule herself. Unbeknownst to her, Joash had survived through the efforts of the priest **Jehoiada** and Jehosheba, his aunt, who hid

the infant child in the Temple for six years. Finally, at age seven, Joash was revealed as part of a coup that toppled Athaliah and installed him as king of Judah (2 Kgs 11; 2 Chr 22:10–23:21). His reign was taken up with repairing the Temple with the help of Jehoiada (2 Kgs 12:5–16; 2 Chr 24:4–14), but after the latter's passing Joash permitted a resurgence of idol worship in Judah (2 Chr 24:17–18) and killed **Zechariah** for condemning his actions (2 Chr 24:20–22). He also attempted to prevent an invasion by **Hazael** of Syria by paying him off with money from the Temple treasury (2 Kgs 12:17–18). He was assassinated through a plot within the palace (2 Kgs 12:20–21; 2 Chr 24:25–26).

8. The son and successor of King **Jehoahaz** and the king of Israel from around 798 to 782 B.C. His reign was much taken up with disputes and warfare. He waged successful campaigns against **Ben-hadad** of Damascus (2 Kgs 13:24–25) and marched on Jerusalem against **Amaziah** of Judah. He captured the city, destroyed part of the walls, and left with booty and hostages (2 Kgs 14:8–14; 2 Chr 25:17–24). His name is sometimes given as Jehoash.

JOB, BOOK OF One of the Wisdom Books of the Old Testament; a dramatic, didactic poem consisting mainly of several dialogues between Job and his friends. It describes an innocent man's experience of suffering and asks the difficult question: How can the just suffer if God is just? In the end, only faith in God and submission to his will, rather than complete understanding (which is impossible), must satisfy as man's proper response to the mystery of suffering.

I. AUTHORSHIP AND DATE

The author is not known. According to one Jewish tradition in the Talmud, Moses was the author, and this view is shared by some early Christian writers. But the absence of any reliable evidence makes it impossible to name any author with confidence. Scholars have suggested a date from the time of Solomon to the middle of the third century B.C.; the most common estimate is between 600 and 400 B.C.

II. CONTENTS

I.   *Prologue (1:1–2:13)*
II. *First Cycle of Speeches (chaps. 3–14)*
    A. *Job's Lament (3:1–26)*
    B. *Eliphaz: Job Has Sinned (4:1–5:27)*
    C. *Job Replies (6:1–7:21)*
    D. *Bildad: Job Should Repent (8:1–22)*
    E. *Job Replies (9:1–10:22)*
    F. *Zophar: Job Is Being Punished (11:1–20)*
    G. *Job Replies (12:1–14:22)*
III. *Second Cycle of Speeches (chaps. 15–21)*
    A. *Eliphaz Speaks (15:1–35)*
    B. *Job Replies (16:1–17:16)*
    C. *Bildad: God Punishes the Wicked (18:1–21)*
    D. *Job Replies (19:1–29)*
    E. *Zophar: Wickedness Is Punished (20:1–29)*
    F. *Job Replies (21:1–34)*
IV. *Third Cycle of Speeches (chaps. 22–28)*
    A. *Eliphaz: Job Is Wicked (22:1–30)*
    B. *Job Replies (23:1–24:25)*
    C. *Bildad: Righteousness (25:1–6)*
    D. *Job Replies (26:1–27:23)*
    E. *The Inaccessibility of Wisdom (28:1–28)*

III. PURPOSE AND THEMES

The story and purpose of Job are established by the framework of the prologue (Job 1:1–2:13) and the epilogue to the book (42:7–17). In the prologue, Job is described as a wealthy and influential man of the land of Uz, one who "was blameless and upright, one who feared God, and turned away from evil" (1:1). The scene then moves to the heavenly court, where the Lord expresses his satisfaction with Job. Satan, who appears in the Lord's court, proposes that Job is faithful only out of self-interest. If God destroys Job's happiness and takes away his blessings, Satan says, the supposedly righteous servant will turn against God and blaspheme. Satan is allowed to test Job's virtue, and Job is afflicted with a host of miseries, including poverty, disease, and bereavement. Even his friends and wife turn against him because he will not admit that this affliction is the result of sin. Yet Job remains a faithful servant of God, giving praise and saying that God gives and he takes away: "blessed be the name of the Lord" (1:21). In the epilogue, Job's innocence is vindicated, and God gives him "twice as much as he had before" (42:10).

The conventional wisdom of the day was that God rewards the just and punishes the wicked. But Job is just, yet he suffers. The dialogue that explores this mystery is presented in three cycles, as Job converses with each of his friends, Eliphaz, Bildad, and Zophar. His friends speak for the traditional view, con-tending that Job must be suffering because he has sinned. Job, however, rebukes his friends for their faulty reasoning and places the blame for his suffering upon God. His complaint and lament are some of the most powerful and moving in the OT. He assails the Lord for being seemingly indifferent (9:2) but he also pleads for mercy and help. He confronts the Lord and demands, "Let the Almighty answer me!" (31:35); but he also remains faithful to God and confident that God will ultimately vindicate him, "For I know that my Redeemer lives, and that at the last he will stand upon the earth; and after my skin has been thus destroyed, then from my flesh I shall see God, whom I shall see on my side, and my eyes shall behold, and not another" (19:25–27).

Having defeated the arguments of his friends, Job must contend with another challenger: Elihu, a young observer who enters the discussion and who repeats largely the same arguments as Eliphaz, Bildad, and Zophar.

Finally, the Lord himself appears and answers Job. He speaks out of a whirlwind (chaps. 38–42), overwhelming Job with a series of rhetorical questions that demonstrate the infinite gulf that exists between God and his creatures. Humbled by the experience, Job acknowledges his error in questioning God. But his demand has been fulfilled: the Almighty has answered him.

God's reply does not bring false comfort or easy answers. God's overwhelming presence, his omnipotence, his wisdom, his glory, and his Providence are beyond all human understanding. Job submits not out of fear, but out of a new humility made possible only by the experience of God: "I have uttered what I did not understand, things too wonderful for me, which I did not know. 'Hear, and I will speak; I will question you, and you declare to me.' I had heard of you by the hearing of the ear, but now my eye sees you; therefore I despise myself, and repent in dust and ashes" (42:3–6). The answer to the question and the mystery of human suffering, the book of Job declares, lies hidden in the mystery of God, who sends us trials and sufferings to prove our commitment and to bring us to the Lord on our knees.

As Pope John Paul II declared in 1988:

We can say that the ancient figure of Job, of this righteous man afflicted by terrible suffering which, humanly speaking, he does not deserve, represents a great question for man of all times. Man constantly asks about the reasons for suffering and seeks its meaning in the context of all earthly existence. His is a question addressed directly to God. The Gospel provides the answer. Christ is ever near to those who suffer; Christ, who in the end takes upon his shoulders the Cross, sign of disgrace, only to die upon it—he himself is the answer. In him God responds to the Job of the Old Testament and to all the Jobs down through the centuries and the generations. This answer is subtle, but at the same time powerful and definitive. (Homily, February 7, 1988)

JOCHEBED (Hebrew, possibly "the Lord is glory") The wife of Amram the Levite, and the mother of **Aaron**, **Moses**, and **Miriam** (Exod 6:20). She, like her husband, was also a descendant of **Levi** (Num 26:59).

JOEL The second of the twelve minor prophets. *See* **Joel, book of**.

JOEL, BOOK OF A prophetic book whose principal purpose is to call the nation to public repentance in the face of the coming **Day of the Lord**.

I. AUTHOR AND DATE

Nothing is known of the prophet Joel, except that he was the son of Pethuel. The date of composition is a source of disagreement among scholars. Some prefer an early date in the eighth century B.C., while others suggest a date of composition as late as 200 B.C. Possible allusions to the Babylonian **Exile** and the stress on Temple sacrifices point to a time of composition in the period after the Exile, perhaps around 400 B.C.

II. CONTENTS

In the Hebrew **Masoretic** text, the book is divided into four chapters, and many modern versions of the Bible follow that division. In the Greek **Septuagint** and Latin **Vulgate**, the book has three chapters, the second and third chapters of the Masoretic text forming one chapter, and some modern versions, such as the RSV, follow this tradition. The oracles are divided into two long poems, each with its own theme: chapters 1–2 are concerned with a plague of locusts and the call to repentance; and chapters 3–4 predict the outpouring of the Spirit on Israel, the judgment of the nations, and a restoration of Israel after an apocalyptic war.

I. The Plague of Locusts (1:1–12)

II. The Fruits of Repentance (1:13–2:27)

III. The Gift of the Spirit (2:28–32)

IV. God's Judgment (3:1–21)

III. PURPOSE AND THEMES

The book of Joel uses rich and vivid imagery to warn the people of the impending judgment upon Jerusalem and Judah. The book opens with the devastation caused by an invasion of locusts, and some interpreters have suggested that the locusts are a metaphor for an invading army. It is also possible that Joel describes a historical event, since plagues of locusts were common in Palestine. Either way, he uses this catastrophe to point to the supernatural coming of the day of the Lord (cf. Joel 1:15; 2:1, 11, 31; 3:14). Blending historical disaster with divine judgment, Joel moves to the central theme of his prophecy: the nation is called to repentance, fasting, and the summoning of a solemn assembly for liturgical lamentation. The great misfortunes are a purification to prepare the people to receive their salvation.

The Lord is moved by these acts of penance and has pity upon his people (2:18). The rest of the book is taken up with consolation. The renewal of the land is described as colorfully as is the desolation (2:21–27), and the restoration gives testimony that God dwells among his people. The Lord will pour out his Spirit upon all mankind (2:28–29). In Acts 2:16–21, Peter shows that the coming of the Spirit at **Pentecost** is the fulfillment of this prophecy of Joel.

There is also the promise of the judgment against the nations (3:1–21) in the Valley of **Jehoshaphat**, where the Lord will take vengeance upon those who have afflicted his people. The Lord will be "a refuge for his people, a stronghold to the people of Israel" (3:16). At last the Lord will dwell "in Zion, my holy mountain. And Jerusalem shall be holy and strangers shall never again pass through it" (3:17).

JOHANAN (Hebrew, "The Lord is gracious") The name of several men in the Old Testament, including a Benjaminite who joined David at Ziklag during the flight from Saul (1 Chr 12:4) and the eldest son of King Josiah, who did not succeed his father; he probably died young (1 Chr 3:15).

JOHANNINE LITERATURE See **John**; see also **John, Gospel of**; **John, Letters of**; **Revelation, book of**.

JOHN (Greek from Hebrew, "The Lord is gracious") Apostle and Evangelist, one of the Twelve, the son of Zebedee, and the brother of **James** the Greater (Matt 10:2; Mark 3:17; Luke 6:14; Acts 1:13). John is mentioned thirty times in the **Synoptic Gospels**, Acts, and Galatians. Tradition calls him "the beloved disciple" because it identifies him with this unnamed figure mentioned several times in the Gospel of John (e.g., John 13:23; 21:20, 24).

I. LIFE

John and his brother James were sons of Zebedee. Christ gave them the nickname Boanerges ("sons of thunder"; Mark 3:17), most likely because of their zeal. James is twice identified as Zebedee's son, whereas John is identified with James, presumably as his younger brother (Matt 4:21; 10:2; Mark 1:19; 3:17; cf. Matt 17:1).

John and James were originally fishermen with their father in the Sea of Galilee (Matt 4:21, 22; Mark 1:19, 20; Luke 5:10; cf. John 21:3). It is likely that the family lived near **Capernaum**, on the north shore of the Sea of Galilee (Mark 1:21). John and James were at work mending their nets when Christ called them; they were among the first of the apostles to be called (Mark 1:19–20; Matt 4:21–22; cf. Luke 5:1–11).

In the lists of the Twelve, John is placed second (Acts 1:13), third (Mark 3:17), and fourth (Matt 10:3; Luke 6:14). In the fourth Gospel, he appears as "the disciple whom Jesus loved" (John 13:23; 20:2; 21:20, 24). With Peter and James, he was a witness to the raising of **Jairus**'s daughter (Mark 5:37; Luke 8:51), the **Transfiguration** (Matt 17:2–3; Mark 9:2–4; Luke 9:28, 31), and the Agony in **Gethsemane** (Matt 26:37; Mark 14:33). Only John and Peter were delegated by Christ to make preparations for the Last Supper (Luke 22:8; cf. Mark 14:13). At the Last Supper, John sat in the place of honor next to Christ (John 13:23, 25).

Matthew (20:20–28) and Mark (10:35–45) record a key moment when James and John asked to receive seats at the right and left of the Lord in his Kingdom (Matt 20:20–21 attributes the question to their mother, but it is implied that the brothers were in agreement about making the request). Jesus's reply is to offer them the chance to drink from his cup, a chance that they both accept. It is clear that they did not yet understand the nature of the Messianic Kingdom: Jesus's "cup" would not be a share in earthly glory, but a share in Jesus's suffering and sacrifice.

In the **Passion** narratives, John was probably the "other disciple" who followed Christ with Peter after the arrest into the palace of the high priest (John 18:15). John alone among the Twelve stood at the foot of the Cross at Calvary with **Mary** and the pious women, and received Mary into his care at the behest of Christ on the Cross (John 19:25–27).

After the Resurrection John is frequently associated with **Peter**. He and Peter were the first of the apostles to witness the empty tomb (John 20:2–10). John was also the first of the seven disciples present who recognized Christ at the Sea of Galilee (John 21:7). Following **Pentecost**, he held a place of some prominence in the early Church. Paul describes John, along with James (the brother of the Lord) and Peter, as one of the pillars of the Jerusalem community of Christians (Gal 2:9–10). He was with Peter when Peter healed the lame man at the Temple gate (Acts 3:1), both he and Peter were imprisoned shortly thereafter (Acts 4:3), and he accompanied Peter on the visit to Samaria (Acts 8:14).

II. TRADITION

Little else is known with certainty about his missionary labors in Palestine, but his absence in Acts 18:22 and 21:17 during the return of Paul has been taken by some to imply that he left the region between A.D. 52 and 55. The mainline tradition of the Church declared that John moved to Asia Minor and settled in **Ephesus**, where he died at an advanced age from natural causes (cf. Tertullian, *An.* 50). The apocryphal *Acts of John* also placed John in Ephesus. There is also a lesser-known tradition that

John died as a martyr (e.g., see Heracleon in Saint Clement of Alexandria, *Strom.* 4.9 and Philip of Side in the fifth century, as well as the Syriac Martyrology on December 27 and Aphrahat, *On Persecution*).

A chief source on John outside the New Testament is Eusebius (in his *Hist. Eccl.* 3.18.1; 23.3–4; 39.3–4; 4.18.6–8; 5.8.4; 18.14; 20.6). Eusebius based his work on other sources, including Saint Clement of Alexandria (3.39.3–4), Saint Irenaeus (3.1.1; 39, 3–4; cf. *Adv. Her.* 2.22.3.5; 3.1.2; 3.4), Saint Justin (4.18.6–8; cf. *Dial.* 81.4), Polycrates (5.24.3), and Apollonius (5.18.14).

Eusebius was thus responsible for preserving a number of stories about John, such as his raising a man from the dead at Ephesus (*Hist. Eccl.* 5.18.14; see also Saint Irenaeus, *Adv. Her.* 3.3.4, and Saint Jerome, *Comm. Gal.* 6,10). It is also held in tradition that John was banished to the island of Patmos, near Ephesus, during the reign of Domitian (A.D. 81–96; cf. Eusebius, *Hist. Eccl.* 3.13.1), and that he wrote the book of **Revelation** there (Rev 1:9). Eventually, the tradition says, he returned to Ephesus and lived into the reign of Emperor Trajan (r. A.D. 98–117; Saint Irenaeus, *Adv. Her.* 2.22.5).

III. JOHN AS AUTHOR

According to tradition, John was the author of five works of the NT canon (the Gospel of John; 1, 2, and 3 John; and the book of Revelation), the so-called Johannine corpus.

Modern historical criticism has called into question John's authorship of either part or the whole of the Johannine corpus. In the case of the three Epistles of John, some scholars reject the long tradition of apostolic authorship and attribute them instead to another ancient churchman named John "the elder" (2 John 1) or to an otherwise unknown writer who was very familiar with the fourth Gospel.

The long-standing tradition that John was the author of Revelation dates back at least as far as Saint Justin Martyr in the second century. This was likewise the belief of Saint Irenaeus, Origen, Saint Clement of Alexandria, and many others. On the other hand, some in the East held that John was not the author; this was the opinion of Dionysius of Alexandria (mid-third century) and Eusebius of Caesarea (early fourth century), and its basis is the many literary differences between Revelation and John. This argument has been adopted by many modern scholars, although no consensus has been reached as to the author. Proposed authors include John Mark, the figure John "the elder," an otherwise unknown John, or even an anonymous writer who adopted John's name.

Ultimately, the evidence can satisfactorily explain the tradition of apostolic authorship. It is not hard to find explanations for the differences between Revelation and the other Johannine books on the supposition of a single author. For example, they cover three different literary genres (an apocalyptic genre for Revelation, narrative for the Gospel, and epistolary form for the three letters). In 1907, the Pontifical Biblical Commission found the arguments against the authorship of John for the Johannine corpus insufficient to overturn the near consensus of tradition. (For other details on Johannine authorship, see under individual titles.)

JOHN THE BAPTIST (the name "John" is from the Hebrew, "The Lord is gracious") The immediate precursor of Jesus, called "the Baptist" (*ho baptistēs*) and "the Baptizer" (*ho baptizōn*). John was a prophet and ascetic who prepared the way for Jesus as the Messiah and baptized him in the Jordan River. The role of the Baptist in salvation history was expressed eloquently in the Gospel of John: "He was not the light, but came to bear witness to the light" (John 1:8).

I. LIFE

Called the "man sent from God," John was the son of **Zechariah**, a priest of the priestly division of Abijah (Luke 1:5), and **Elizabeth**, also a descendant of the Aaronic line of Levites (Luke 1:5) and a relative of Mary (Luke 1:36). The angel Gabriel appeared to Zechariah and foretold the birth (Luke 1:11–20), assuring Zechariah that the child would be "great before the Lord . . . he will be filled with the Holy Spirit, even from his mother's womb. And he will turn many of the sons of Israel to the Lord their God" (Luke 1:15–16). John's parents were well beyond normal childbearing age (Luke 1:7), and the child's name was divinely appointed (Luke 1:13). These details place John in a line of great Old Testament figures (e.g., Isaac, Samson, and Samuel) chosen to fulfill a role in salvation history.

Luke records that Elizabeth had a visit from Mary when both women were pregnant, and that John "leaped in her womb" in the presence of the Messiah and his mother (Luke 1:41). Even before his birth, John was fulfilling his mission of announcing the coming of the Messiah.

After he was born, he was given the name John, and "the child grew and became strong in spirit, and he was in the wilderness till the day of his manifestation to Israel" (Luke 1:80). Some thirty years passed before John appeared in the wilderness of Judah to announce the kingdom of heaven (Matt 3:1–12; Luke 3:1–20; John 1:19–28), an event that was connected in Mark with Isaiah: "As it is written in Isaiah the prophet, 'Behold, I send my messenger before thy face, who shall prepare thy way; the voice of one crying in the wilderness: Prepare the way of the Lord, make his paths straight'" (Mark 1:2–3). John the Baptist "was clothed in camel's hair, with a leather belt around his waist, and ate locusts and wild honey" (Mark 1:6). In other words, he wore the same clothing as Elijah (2 Kgs 1:8) (CCC 718).

John administered a baptism for the forgiveness of sins and called for repentance because the coming of the Judge was imminent, and the kingdom of heaven was at hand (Matt 3:2). His powerful preaching and his rigorous austerity gained him wide influence, and people came from across the whole Judean countryside and Jerusalem to be baptized by him in the river Jordan, confessing their sins (Matt 3:5; Mark 1:5). They recognized him as a prophet (Matt 11:9; cf. Luke 1:76, 77). Luke preserves a few details of his moral teachings (Luke 3:10–14).

John baptized those who came to him at the Jordan as a sign of repentance (unlike the **baptism** of Jesus, which is a sacrament of regeneration). This baptism was the characteristic mark of his ministry: even Christ called him "the Baptist" (Matt 11:11). The Pharisees asked why he was baptizing "if you are neither the Christ, nor Elijah, nor the prophet" (John 1:25). John dismissed any identification with the Messiah by declaring, "After me comes he who is mightier than I, the thong of whose sandals I am not worthy to stoop down and untie. I have baptized you with water; but he will baptize you with the Holy Spirit" (Mark 1:7–8; cf. Thomas Aquinas, *Summa theologiae*, III, Q. 38, art. 1–6) (CCC 720).

Jesus journeyed from Galilee and presented himself to John for baptism in the Jordan (Matt 3:13–17; Luke 3:21–22; John 1:29–34). Mark tells the story: "In those days Jesus came from Nazareth of Galilee and was baptized by John in the Jordan. And when he came up out of the water, immediately he saw the heavens opened and the Spirit descending upon him like a dove; and a voice came from heaven, 'You are my beloved Son; with you I am well pleased'" (Mark 1:9–10). After the baptism of Jesus, John continued his ministry in the Jordan Valley.

In his ministry, John attracted a group of followers who chose to remain with him. He demanded that they fast (Mark 2:18), and ultimately directed them to Christ, declaring, "Behold the Lamb of God" (John 1:29; cf. Matt 11:2–6; Luke 7:18–23; John 3:25–30). John's disciples once asked why they were required to fast while the disciples of Jesus were not (Matt 9:14; Mark 2:18; Luke 5:33). Similarly, Jesus himself pointed out the contrast between the austerity of John and the apparent ordinariness of Jesus's own daily life (Matt 11:18; Luke 7:33). John himself understood that his mission was complete with the coming of the Christ: "He must increase, but I must decrease" (John 3:30).

When John publicly rebuked **Herod Antipas**'s unlawful marriage to **Herodias**, his brother Philip's wife (Matt 14:1–12; Mark 6:17–18; Luke 3:19–20), Herod threw him in prison. While he was in prison, John sent his followers to visit Jesus and to confirm that Jesus was the Messiah (Matt 11:2–6; Luke 7:18–23). Herod was afraid of John and would have kept him alive, but his wife Herodias had other ideas. When Herodias's daughter, Salome, danced for guests at a banquet, Herod was so enchanted by her performance that he promised her anything she might demand. On her mother's advice, she asked for John the Baptist's head on a platter (Matt 14:6–8; Mark 6:21–25; cf. Josephus, *Ant.* 18.5.2). John's disciples claimed the body and placed it in a tomb (Mark 6:29); they also informed Jesus of the event (Matt 14:12). Rumors later circulated that Jesus was John returned from the dead (Matt 16:14; Mark 8:28; Luke 9:19), which shows how great an impression John had made during his brief ministry.

II. PRECURSOR TO CHRIST

John the Baptist is honored in tradition as the precursor of the Messiah. Jesus himself honored John, saying, "among those born of women there has risen no one greater than John the Baptist; yet he who is least in the kingdom of heaven is greater than he" (Matt 11:11; cf. Luke 7:24–30). Jesus also made explicit what had already been suggested by John's appearance and had been prophesied by the angel (Luke 1:17): John fulfilled the mission of Elijah (Matt 11:13–14, 17:10–13; Mark 9:13).

Through the Spirit, John brought to completion the quest of the prophets: whereas they saw Christ from a distance, John saw him in the flesh (cf. 1 Pet 1:10–12). His baptism of repentance prefigured the new birth by baptism in water and the Spirit (cf. John 3:5) and what the Spirit achieved "in and with Christ" (CCC 717–20). (*See also* **Baptism**.)

JOHN, GOSPEL OF The fourth Gospel of the New Testament, traditionally ascribed to the apostle **John**, the son of Zebedee. Its structure, style, and contents are oftentimes different from those of the three **Synoptic Gospels**. The most theologically rich and complex of the Gospels, John gives us a clear and simple statement of its purpose: "that you may believe that Jesus is the Christ, the Son of God, and that believing you may have life in his name" (John 20:31).

I. AUTHORSHIP AND DATE

The Evangelist does not give us his name, but he does refer to himself indirectly as "the disciple whom Jesus loved" (John 21:20, 24), the "beloved disciple" (13:23; 19:26; 21:7), and "another disciple" (18:15). Tradition identifies the figure as John, son of Zebedee, an attribution supported by the prominent place enjoyed by that apostle in the Gospel narrative. The "beloved disciple" was present at the Last Supper (John 13:23; Mark 14:17–25), was at the tomb after the Resurrection (John 20:4–10), and was presumably with the disciples at the appearance of Jesus (20:19–23). He was also part of Jesus's inner circle (with James and Peter), and in the Gospel he is matched only by Peter in prominence (cf. 1:35, 40–42; 6:8, 67–69; 13:5–11, 23–26, 36–38; 18:15–16; 19:25–27). John may also be the unnamed disciple of the Baptist who, with Andrew, followed Jesus (1:37–40).

Saint Irenaeus (ca. A.D. 180) tells us that the fourth Gospel was written by John, a claim with some authority because Irenaeus had known Saint Polycarp, bishop of Smyrna, who had been a disciple of Saint John.

Although John is most likely the author of the Gospel, there is some internal indication that it may have been edited or given a final form by the hand of some other disciple or disciples. For instance, the Last Supper discourse appears to end twice (14:31 and 18:1), suggesting that the second part was an addition, either by an editor or by the author himself at a later time. The story of the adulteress (7:53–8:11) is also out of sequence in the Gospel narrative and is actually missing in a number of Greek manuscripts of the Gospel. These fingerprints may suggest the existence of more than one *edition* of the Gospel, but not necessarily more than one *author*. Regardless, there is no question that all these passages are inspired and belong in the **canon** of the Bible.

Tradition suggests that the Gospel was written sometime before the end of the first century. Some scholars once held that the Gospel was composed in the middle of the second century, but that view had to be abandoned in 1935 when a papyrus fragment of the Gospel that dated to around A.D. 120 was discovered in Egypt. In addition, Saint Ignatius of Antioch referred to the Gospel's teachings in a letter written around A.D. 107. As it would have taken time for the Gospel to gain circulation and widespread acceptance, there is a strong likelihood that it was composed before A.D. 100.

But how long before A.D. 100? Most scholars believe that the Gospel was written toward the end of the first century, but some argue for a much earlier date. In John 5:2, the Evangelist writes, "Now there is in Jerusalem by the Sheep Gate a pool, in Hebrew called Bethzatha, which has five porticoes." Jerusalem was destroyed in A.D. 70, yet here the author speaks in the present tense, as though the city was still intact at the time of writing. Perhaps it is safest to say that the date of composition is an open question.

II. CONTENTS

Modern scholarship has come up with a convenient division of the book of John into two main parts, the "Book of Signs" and the "Book of Glory":

I. *Prologue (1:1–18)*
II. *Book of Signs (chaps. 1–12)*
  A. *John the Baptist (1:19–34)*
  B. *The First Disciples (1:35–51)*
  C. *The Wedding at Cana (2:1–12)*
  D. *The Cleansing of the Temple (2:13–25)*
  E. *Nicodemus (3:1–21)*
  F. *Jesus and John the Baptist (3:22–36)*
  G. *The Samaritan Woman (4:1–54)*
  H. *Jesus's Ministry on the Sabbath (5:1–47)*
  I. *The Bread of Life (6:1–71)*
  J. *The Feast of Tabernacles and the Unbelief of the Authorities (7:1–53)*
  K. *The Light of the World (8:1–59)*
  L. *The Man Born Blind (9:1–41)*
  M. *The Good Shepherd (10:1–42)*
  N. *The Raising of Lazarus (11:1–57)*
  O. *Jesus's Entry into Jerusalem and the Plot to Kill Him (12:1–50)*
III. *Book of Glory (chaps. 13–20)*
  A. *Jesus Washes the Disciples' Feet (13:1–21)*
  B. *The Last Supper Discourse (13:22–16:33)*
  C. *Prayer of Jesus the High Priest (17:1–26)*
  D. *The Passion Narrative (18:1–19:42)*
  E. *The Resurrection and Jesus's Appearances (20:1–31)*
IV. *Epilogue (21:1–25)*

III. LITERARY FEATURES

The Gospel of John is renowned for its mystical and theological depth, so much so that it was known in the early Church as the "spiritual" Gospel. On the one hand, its treasures are easily appreciated by simply reading or listening to the text. On the other, it is a work of tremendous richness that a lifetime of study and contemplation could never exhaust.

The fourth Gospel is notably different from the Synoptic Gospels. Rarely does it restate the tradition shared by the Gospels of Matthew, Mark, and Luke. It does show a familiarity with the Synoptics, in particular the Gospels of Mark and Luke, but it is clearly not based on them. It is an independent literary witness to Jesus Christ.

John differs from the other Gospel writers mostly in what he chooses to emphasize. The Synoptics mention only one visit by Jesus to Jerusalem, at the climax of his earthly ministry, culminating with his Passion and Resurrection. John mentions visits to Jerusalem three times (John 2:13; 6:4; 12:1). The Synoptics pay attention to Jesus's ministry in Galilee, while John supplements their account by telling us of Jesus's ministry in Judea (1:43; 4:3–4; 11:54; 21:1). The Synoptics relate the events of the Last Supper; John places his emphasis on the Bread of Life Discourse, through which Jesus promises to give himself to the world through the Eucharist (6:35–58).

The Evangelist has a keen ear for dramatic dialogue, using verbal confrontations to deepen our understanding of Jesus. Jesus's dialogues with the Samaritan woman (4:4–38), with Martha (11:20–27), and before Pilate (18:33–38; 19:8–11), reveal Jesus's identity bit by bit. As the characters in the dialogue learn more about Jesus, we the readers learn, too. The fourth Gospel pays special attention to those times when a misunderstanding gave Jesus an opportunity to explain his meaning more thoroughly, leading us to a deeper understanding of his words and teachings. One famous example is the dialogue with **Nicodemus**, who cannot understand how a grown man could be "born again" (3:4–8).

IV. MAJOR THEMES

The Gospel of John begins with a declaration of both the divinity and the humanity of Jesus Christ (John 1:1–18). Its opening line proclaims the deity of Jesus: "The Word was God" (1:1). The Gospel comes to a climax in John 20:28 with the confession of **Thomas**: "My Lord and my God." Between these declarations is the proclamation of Jesus's divine Sonship and mission. Here John is unique as compared to the Synoptic Gospels because he does not concentrate on parables, healings, and exorcisms; there are only four healing miracles (4:43–54; 5:1–15; chap. 9; chap. 11). Each of these miracles, however, has a specific theological purpose in describing Jesus's ministry; thus they serve, as John says, as "signs" that show who Jesus is for those with the faith to see and believe.

In John's accounts, those who encounter Christ begin a journey—either toward understanding and discipleship or away from the saving truth Jesus offers. In episode after episode, Jesus proclaims his identity, and those who hear him either begin a journey of faith or reject him.

John's prologue starts with a deliberate echo of the creation account in Genesis: "In the beginning" (1:1), the "Word" of God as instrument of creation (1:1–3), "all things were made" (1:3), "the light shines in the darkness" (1:5). The important addition is that Christ, the Word, was present from the beginning.

In the rest of the first chapter, a number of titles are applied to Christ, including Son of God, Son of Man, Messiah, and King of Israel. The first title, proclaimed by John the Baptist, is "Lamb of God" (1:29, 36) and is further specified with the words "who takes away the sins of the world" (1:29). The Servant Songs in Isaiah (Isa 42:1–4; 49:1–6; 50:4–9; 52:13–53:12), with their explicit imagery of the lamb in Isa 53:7, show the pattern of Jesus's obedience to the Father. The imagery of the lamb also echoes the **Passover** lamb, slain for the salvation of God's people. Jesus is the Suffering Servant who allows himself to be led to the slaughter without complaint and who bears the sins of the multitude. He is the obedient agent of God whose life and death result in liberation and who is the liberating revealer of God. "I came down from heaven not to do my own will but the will of the one who sent me" (John 6:38).

The "Book of Signs" begins with the call of the first disciples and the miracle at **Cana**. This is immediately followed by the cleansing of the Temple, the central sanctuary of Jewish faith that would be destroyed and replaced by Jesus, the new Temple (2:19–21). This part of the Gospel also charts the reaction of those who encounter Jesus, from Nicodemus (3:1–21) to the Samaritan woman (4:1–42), to the royal official (4:43–54), to the Pharisees and the authorities (e.g., 5:17–47; 6:25–59; 7:14–36; 8:12–59). Jesus gives signs of his identity and power throughout, culminating in the most dramatic of his demonstrations: raising Lazarus from the dead (chapter 11). By this act, Jesus shows the world that he possesses the supernatural power to give life (11:25), but it also propels Jesus's enemies into the final plot to bring about his death.

The "Book of Glory" (chaps. 13–20) includes some of the most beautiful discourses in the whole NT, including the metaphor of the vine and the branches (15:1–8) and the high priestly prayer (chap. 17), which is a kind of preface to the Passion narrative that follows.

The Passion of Jesus is the completion of the tasks given the Son by the Father (cf. 4:34; 5:36; 17:4; 19:30), and Jesus's exaltation and glory are revealed in mystery upon the Cross. These truths are then revealed in history by his Resurrection: the Paschal mystery includes both the dying and the rising of the Son.

The drama of John's Gospel reaches a peak with Thomas's confession of faith—"My Lord and my God" (20:28). At last the truth of Christ is fully and explicitly revealed. Thomas's Christological confession is the faith of the Church for all times.

JOHN, LETTERS OF Three letters traditionally attributed to John, the son of Zebedee, although none of the letters mention his name. The letters are included among the seven **Catholic Epistles** (with James, 1 and 2 Peter, and Jude).

1 John

A letter addressed to unnamed churches; tradition puts them near Ephesus in Asia Minor. The letter's message is that God is made known to us in the Son, and that fellowship with the Father is attained by living in the light, justice, and love of the Son. It also corrects the error of those who were claiming that they were sinless and not bound by the Ten Commandments.

I. AUTHORSHIP AND DATE

The author of the letter is not identified. Twelve times the letter suggests that it was written by an individual (e.g., "I am writing," 2:1, 7, 8, 12, etc.); but he also speaks with authority on behalf of others (e.g., "we are writing," 1:4).

The earliest traditions identify the author as John the apostle, the son of Zebedee (Mark 3:17). The attribution remained uncontested in Christian antiquity. The doctrine and vocabulary of the letter are very similar to those of the fourth Gospel, also attributed to the apostle John in early Christian times (*see* **John, Gospel of**). Some scholars prefer to attribute authorship to a different John, "the elder" (2 John 1), or to an otherwise unknown individual who was deeply familiar with the teachings of the fourth Gospel. Nevertheless there is insufficient evidence to reject the longstanding Christian tradition of authorship by the apostle.

The date of the letter is uncertain beyond the general boundaries of A.D. 50 to 100. Many scholars date the First Letter of John to a period after the publication of the Gospel of John. If that Gospel was composed in the 90s A.D., then the letter may have been composed around A.D. 100. If the Gospel was composed at an earlier time, then the letter might also have been composed earlier. It is also possible, however, that the date of composition is earlier than the Gospel. In short, an exact date is impossible, but on balance it is most likely that the letter was written between A.D. 90 and 100.

II. CONTENTS

III. PURPOSE AND THEMES

The First Letter of John was written to confront a dangerous situation: a breakaway group of false teachers (John calls them Antichrists, liars, and deceivers) were leading the Christian believers into error. John was probably writing to members of the community in Ephesus, and he was probably acquainted personally with the recipients of the letter (1 John 2:1, 12–14; 3:11). Unlike the second and third letters of John, the First Letter of John is more like an address than a letter.

False teachers have broken away from the community (2:19) and denied that Jesus was "the Christ" (2:22; 5:1) and "the Son of God" (2:23; 5:5), although the exact identity of the heretics is difficult to determine. Perhaps they were Cerinthians, who claimed that the divine Christ had descended on the ordinary man Jesus but then left him just before the Passion. Or perhaps they were Docetists, who believed that Jesus only seemed to suffer and die on the Cross. Or maybe they were Gnostics, who believed that the true knowledge of Christ was hidden from all but the chosen few. The false teachers believed themselves to be free from sin, so they were free from the obligations of keeping the Ten Commandments, including the commandment to love other Christians.

The First Letter of John refutes these false doctrines with several key points. No one loves God who does not keep his commandments (2:3, 4; 3:24; 5:3) or who sins freely (3:6–8; 5:18). No one is able to declare himself free of sin (1:10), and the only way to overcome sin is to admit it and seek forgiveness through Christ (1:7–9; 2:1, 12). One does not honor God who does not accept that Jesus Christ comes from God (3:23; 4:2, 3, 14; 5:1), and anyone who refuses to believe the Son refuses to believe the Father (2:22, 23).

The letter also stresses authentic fellowship with God, who is love (4:16). Jesus had shown God's love by giving his life, so we have an obligation to show our love to others (3:16–18; 4:9–12). Therefore the great commandment of the Christian is love of one's brother (3:23;

4:21); conversely, one who hates a brother does not love God (2:7–11; 3:10; 4:7, 8, 20; 5:2).

A sharp contrast is thus drawn between the children of God and the false teachers who belong to the Antichrist (2:18) and to the devil (3:7–10; 5:19). The children of God are anointed (2:20) and need no instruction; they are urged to adhere to what they were taught from the beginning (2:24). If they do, they will be victorious (5:4, 5).

2 John

Addressed to "the elect lady and her children," which probably refers to a church in Asia Minor. The letter praises its recipients for standing firm in the faith and urges them to continue their perseverance.

I. AUTHORSHIP AND DATE

The author does not give his name but refers to himself as "the elder" (v. 1), the same title used in 3 John. Christian tradition attributes authorship of all three Johannine letters to the same person, the apostle John, but this view is not unanimous. Even in the ancient Church, some (such as Papias in the second century) held that 2 and 3 John were written by someone other than the apostle, such as a presbyter named "John the Elder" who may have been a contemporary of the apostle in Asia Minor. On the other hand, the tradition that the apostle John was the author is very ancient, and there are strong literary similarities between the first two letters (cf., 1 John 2:27 and 2 John 5; 1 John 2:18–22 and 2 John 7; 1 John 1:4 and 2 John 12). Given the similarities, it seems safe to conclude that 2 and 3 John

were composed by the same hand that had written 1 John and probably around the same time.

II. CONTENTS

I. *Salutation (chaps. 1–3)*

II. *Truth and Love (chaps. 4–12)*

III. *Closing Greeting (chap. 13)*

III. PURPOSE AND THEMES

The Second Letter of John is much briefer than 1 John and is in the form of a letter (where 1 John is more of an address). Its chief purpose is to encourage the faithful to practice perseverance in the face of false teachers. Such teachers are "men who will not acknowledge the coming of Jesus Christ in the flesh; such a one is the deceiver and the antichrist" (2 John 1:7). Such is the author's concern that he looks forward to visiting the recipients in person to discuss the problem. While short, the letter offers a threefold program of fraternal love, devotion to the faith, and rejection of false teachers and their doctrines.

3 John

A letter addressed to "the beloved Gaius, whom I love in the truth," concerned with settling a jurisdictional dispute in a local church (probably near Ephesus).

I. AUTHORSHIP AND DATE

The Third Letter of John is remarkably similar in literary style, structure, and length to 2 John. Long-standing Christian tradition makes John the apostle the author. Some scholars consider 3 John to be the first of the three Johannine letters, but such a claim cannot be confirmed with certainty.

II. CONTENTS

I. *Salutation (v. 1)*
II. *Commendation of Gaius (vv. 2–8)*
III. *Diotrephes and Demetrius (vv. 9–12)*
IV. *Final Greeting (vv. 13–15)*

III. PURPOSE AND THEMES

The Third Letter of John is directed to Gaius, who serves as a host to traveling Christian missionaries (vv. 5–8). The author praises him as one who "follows the truth" (3), and he is encouraged to continue in his valuable work of Christian charity. The letter is concerned also with one named Diotrephes, who has proven himself a poor leader in the community (9–11), and with Demetrius, a faithful brother (12).

The letter is the shortest in the New Testament, but it gives us important information about certain features of the early Church. It shows especially how the Church addressed questions of jurisdiction and rivalry among its leaders, as demonstrated by the dispute between John, the shepherd and leader of communities in Asia Minor, and the local leader Diotrephes, who exercised his authority in a ruthless and reckless way. In the middle was Gaius, who is asked by the author to support true authority, stand firm in the faith, and give welcome to Demetrius. The elder is hopeful of coming himself to settle the matter (14) and to "call attention to what he is doing in spreading false charges against us" (10).

JOHN MARK *See* **Mark**.

JOKTAN The son of Eber, the brother of Peleg, and the father of thirteen descendants who lived in Arabia (Gen 10:25–30).

JONADAB (Hebrew, "the Lord is noble") The name of two men in the Old Testament.

1 The son of David's brother Shimeah. He was a friend of **Amnon** and gave him advice on how to seduce and rape his half sister **Tamar** (2 Sam 13:3–5).

2. The son of Rechab and the leader of the Rechabites in the ninth century B.C. (2 Kgs 10:15–28; Jer 35:6–7; 1 Chr 2:55). His name is sometimes given the longer spelling "Jehonadab."

JONAH (Hebrew, "dove") The fifth of the minor prophets and the chief figure of the book of Jonah (*see* **Jonah, book of.**) The prophet was from Gath-hepher in Galilee, the son of Amittai (2 Kgs 14:25). He lived in the reigns of **Joash** (r. 798–782 B.C.) and **Jeroboam** II (r. 793–753 B.C.), kings of Israel. Little else is known about him before he was commissioned by God as recounted in Jonah; 2 Kgs 14:25 is the only mention of him in the Old Testament outside the book of Jonah. The book of Jonah tells how the prophet received a commission from God to go to the Assyrian city of **Nineveh** and announce its destruction for its wickedness. He was called to prophesy and preach repentance. Jonah, however, was a patriotic Israelite who hated **Assyria**, Israel's mortal enemy. He fled as far as he could in the opposite direction, sailing from **Joppa** (Jaffa) for **Tarshish**. At sea, a storm arose, and the sailors, sensing that someone on board had brought a curse upon them, drew lots to find the source of their peril. The lot fell on Jonah, who confessed and told the sailors to cast him into the sea to lift the curse (Jonah 1:1–16).

God sent a great fish to swallow Jonah and preserve him from drowning (Jonah 1:17). In this unusual and extreme moment of crisis, Jonah cried out to the Lord and sang a psalm (Jonah 2:2–9). His cry was heard, and after three days he was vomited onto the shore by the fish (Jonah 2:10). Having delivered Jonah from the sea, God repeated his command to Jonah to go to Nineveh.

Obedient this time, Jonah traveled to Nineveh and warned the people of their impending destruction. Jonah was shocked when the people and the king actually believed his message and did penance in sackcloth and ashes. Because of their earnest repentance, God revoked the sentence of doom against them (Jonah 3).

Angry that Nineveh, the hated enemy of Israel, had been spared, Jonah complained to the Lord. Building a booth east of the city, he waited "till he should see what would become of the city" (Jonah 4:5).

Here the Lord prepared a practical demonstration for Jonah. God sent a plant (perhaps a castor oil plant, which is known for its rapid growth and large leaves) whose shade was delightful to Jonah. Soon after, though, God sent a worm to attack the plant, and the plant died. Jonah was furious at losing his shade and once again complained to the Lord. Then the Lord rebuked Jonah for his selfishness: he grieved over the withering of a plant, while at the same time desiring that God should be unmoved by the repentance of thousands and thousands of people in the city (Jonah 4).

Jonah is mentioned several times in the New Testament (Matt 12:41; Luke 11:32). Jesus refers to Jonah's time in the belly of the fish as a **type** of his own burial and Resurrection (Matt 12:39–40, 16:4; Luke 11:29–31). Jonah was frequently pictured in this setting in the catacombs as a type of Christ. One tradition, preserved through Saint Jerome (*Comm Jon.* Prol.) holds that Jonah was the son of the widow of Zarephath, who had been brought back to life by the prophet **Elijah** (1 Kgs 17:17–24).

JONAH, BOOK OF The fifth book of the minor prophets, a story of divine mercy whose message is that the Lord wills the repentance of all nations. Its protagonist, **Jonah**, was a reluctant prophet; called by God to warn the pagan Assyrians of God's judgment, he was highly successful in his mission, but he was also angry at God's concern for those who did not belong to the Chosen People.

I. AUTHORSHIP AND DATE

The book of Jonah provides no indication as to its author. It is possible that Jonah was the author or at least the source of the story, but the book does not use the first person (I, me, my, etc.), and scholars are generally disinclined to accept this attribution. Many scholars believe the book was written after the **Exile**, although some prefer an earlier date, perhaps in the eighth century B.C.; others less plausibly argue for the possibility of composition as late as the third century B.C. In Jonah 3:3, the author speaks of **Nineveh** in the past tense, which suggests a date of composition after Nineveh was destroyed in 612 B.C. The message of the book—a strong plea against the radical forms of Jewish nationalism that caused Jews to look upon Gentile nations as unworthy of God's blessings—would be appropriate to the time just after the **Exile**, perhaps the fifth century B.C.

II. CONTENTS

III. PURPOSE AND THEMES

The purpose of the book is to proclaim that God calls all the nations to repentance, not just Israel. The mercy, love, and forgiveness of the Lord are not limited exclusively to the Israelites; they are intended for all, including the hated inhabitants of Nineveh. Against the exclusivist tendencies of the Israelites in the period after the Exile, the book of Jonah shows how foreign peoples can be open to the saving love and mercy of God, contrasting that openness to the stubbornness and disobedience of Jonah the Israelite. God's pardon and forgiveness are contingent upon repentance and conversion, but his mercy is offered universally, to everyone. This does not minimize, however, the status of Israel as God's special people. Rather, Jonah exemplifies Israel's mission: to serve the Lord as a light for the world in proclaiming the saving mercy of God.

In all these ways, Jonah anticipated Christianity's message of salvation for all men in Jesus Christ. Jesus refers to the preaching of Jonah to contrast the repentance of the Ninevites with the unbelief of many Israelites (Matt 12:41; Luke 11:32), and he refers to Jonah's time in the belly of the fish as a type of his own burial and Resurrection (cf. Matt 12:39–40, 16:4; Luke 11:29–31).

Is the book historical? Scholars vigorously debate that question. Some say that the book is a factual account of events that took place in the eighth century B.C. Others say that the book is a parable, the same sort of parable that Jesus himself often used to teach about God and his ways. Either way, the lesson is the same: God's mercy is for all—even our worst enemies—and our mission is to bring that message to the world.

JONATHAN (Hebrew, "the Lord has given") The name of three men in the Old Testament.

1. The grandson of **Moses** who settled in the town of Bethlehem in Judah (Judg 17:7). He was born of Moses's firstborn, Gershom (Exod 2:22), and established a line of priests that served the Danites (Judg 18:30–31).

2. The eldest son of **Saul** (1 Sam 14:49). Jonathan distinguished himself as a most capable warrior by leading an attack—alone except for his armor bearer—against the **Philistines** at Michmash. As word spread of the confusion in the Philistine ranks, the Israelites became emboldened and pushed forward to a great victory (1 Sam 14:1–23). Saul then declared a

most ill-advised curse upon anyone who ate before evening, before he could avenge himself upon his enemies. Unaware of this prohibition, Jonathan ate some wild honey. The next day, after no answer was given by the **Urim and Thummim**, the sacred lots, as to whether they should push forward in pursuit of the Philistines, Saul determined that the ban had been violated and sought out the transgressor. It was soon learned that Jonathan had violated the curse, so Saul determined that he should be put to death. The soldiers, however, intervened and protested that the victory was itself achieved only because of Jonathan (1 Sam 14:45–46).

Jonathan subsequently became a beloved friend of **David** at the royal court (1 Sam 18:1–4). The two bound themselves together in a covenant oath of brotherhood; and ever after, as relations between Saul and David deteriorated, Jonathan remained steadfast in his devotion and loyalty to his friend. Jonathan was able to arrange for the return of David to the court (1 Sam 19:1–7), although the return was short-lived. In the struggle between David and Saul, Jonathan attempted to serve as a mediator, ultimately failing in this objective. He met David in the desert at Ziph (1 Sam 23:15–18) and then went with his father to war against the Philistines. Jonathan died at the battle of Mount Gilboa, where Saul also died, as well as Saul's other sons **Abinadab** and Malchishua (1 Sam 31:1–2). Upon hearing the news of the deaths of Saul and Jonathan (2 Sam 1:1–10), David composed an elegy for the fallen king (2 Sam 1:17–27) with some particularly moving words about Jonathan (2 Sam 1:26).

3. The son of the priest **Mattathias**, the brother of John, **Judas**, **Simon**, and Eleazar (1 Macc 2:1–5), and a leader during the Maccabean War. After the death of Judas Maccabeus (ca. 160 B.C.), Jonathan assumed the leadership of the Jews against Syrian leader Bacchides (1 Macc 9:28–31), but he was forced to retreat to the desert of Tekoa and soon encountered troubles with the Nabateans, who killed his brother John. He subsequently fought an indecisive engagement with **Bacchides** and was forced with his men to swim to safety across the Jordan (1 Macc 9:32–49). With the death of **Alcimus**, there was a period of peace (1 Macc 9:57), but this ended with the scheming of the Hellenizing party to bring back Bacchides and seize Jonathan. He learned of the scheme, however, and fled. Soon after, Simon defeated Bacchides; Bacchides withdrew and Jonathan emerged as unquestioned ruler of the Jews in 157 B.C. (1 Macc 9:58–73).

Jonathan solidified his political position through his alliance with Seleucid king **Demetrius I** (1 Macc 10:1–14) but then changed sides to support **Alexander Balas**, Demetrius's rival, who offered Jonathan the post of high priest in 152 B.C. (1 Macc 10:18–20). Demetrius increased his own offers to Jonathan, but so extravagant were his promises that Jonathan discounted them and remained true to Alexander. It proved to be a wise decision, for Alexander defeated and killed Demetrius (1 Macc 10:48–50). Jonathan then defeated Demetrius I's son, **Demetrius II Nicator**, and thus won greater favor with Alexander (1 Macc 10:67–89). Nevertheless, Demetrius managed to secure the Seleucid throne, but he opted to deal diplomatically with Jonathan, given the latter's strong military position, and so confirmed Jonathan as high priest (1 Macc 11:20–37). Jonathan gave him assistance against **Trypho**, a Seleucid general who was acting in the name of Alexander Balas's son, Antiochus VI Epiphanes Dionysus, but Demetrius failed to honor his own promises. Jonathan thus joined Trypho and defeated a force sent against him by Demetrius (1 Macc 11:63–74). Jonathan then renewed his alliances with both Rome and Sparta. Sensing Jonathan's strength, Trypho lured Jonathan to Ptolemais with only a small force, slaughtered the troops that were with him, and took Jonathan hostage (1 Macc 12:39–53). Even though Jonathan's brother Simon made the ransom payment, Trypho had Jonathan put to death in about 143 B.C. (1 Macc 13:12–23).

JOPPA A port city on the Mediterranean coast to the northwest of Jerusalem (modern Jaffa). Joppa was originally part of the territory assigned to Dan (Josh 19:46). The port was used to import timber from Lebanon for the building of the **Temple** by Solomon (2 Chr 2:15) and then for the rebuilding of the Temple by Zerubbabel (Ezra 3:7). **Jonah** also sailed from Joppa on the ship to Tarshish "away from the presence of the LORD" (Jonah 1:3). Conquered by **Sennacherib** of Assyria in 701 B.C., the city was later fought over by the Jews and their Syrian neighbors and changed hands several times during the Maccabean Wars (1 Macc 12:33; 13:11; 14:5). Simon Maccabeus fortified it, and it remained in Jewish hands until the advance of Pompey the Great into Palestine around 63 B.C. Julius Caesar returned Joppa to the Jews in 47 B.C., although the Romans captured it again in A.D.

67 at the start of the First Jewish Revolt. In the New Testament, Joppa was where **Peter** raised **Tabitha** from the dead (Acts 9:36–42).

JORAM (Hebrew, "the Lord is exalted"; *see also* **Jehoram**) The king of Israel from 852 to 841 B.C., successor of **Ahaziah** (2 Kgs 1:17; 3:1–3), and the last ruler of the Omride Dynasty (1 Kgs 16–2 Kgs 9). The son of King **Ahab** and his infamous wife, **Jezebel** (2 Kgs 1:17; 3:1–3), he generally followed their religious policy in tolerating idolatry, though to a lesser extent. Early on, he was confronted by a rebellion of the Moabites and waged a campaign against them with the assistance of **Jehoshaphat** of Judah. The prophet **Elisha** assured them of victory, but in the succeeding siege of Kir-hareseth, King Mesha of Moab sacrificed his firstborn son on the walls of the city. At this Joram withdrew, and Mesha was able to claim a victory over Israel (2 Kgs 3:4–27). Years later, Joram embarked on another campaign, this time against **Hazael** of Damascus. In an engagement at Ramoth-gilead, Joram was wounded. While recovering from his wounds at Jezreel, Joram was assassinated by **Jehu**, the next king of Israel, in the field of Naboth. An arrow plunged into his chest and pierced his heart, and his body was thrown in the field, thus fulfilling the prophecy of the end of the dynasty (2 Kgs 9:21–26).

The name Joram is a shortened form of "Jehoram," which is also the name of Joram's brother-in-law, **Jehoram** the fifth king of Judah (848–841 B.C.). Scripture most often calls the king of Israel "Joram" and the king of Judah "Jehoram," but both names are used for both kings.

JORDAN RIVER (Hebrew, possibly "the descender") The most important river in Palestine. Its headwaters begin with melting snows from the slopes of Mount Hermon, which form several main streams that converge in the Jordan; from there the river flows southward into Lake Huleh, then into the Sea of Galilee (*see* **Galilee, Sea of**), and finally empties into the Dead Sea. The part north of the Sea of Galilee is called the Upper Jordan; the portion south of the Sea of Galilee is the Lower Jordan. The Jordan River is the world's lowest river, reaching a depth of almost 700 feet (213 meters) below sea level at the Sea of Galilee and a depth of 1,286 feet (392 meters) where it reaches the **Dead Sea**. In all, the river extends some 80 miles north to south, but the sharply winding course covers over 200 miles, and the river has an average width of 90–100 feet (27–30 meters). The river is also lined on both sides for much of its extent by steep mountains, especially on the eastern side, except for the area just north of the Sea of Galilee.

The most significant river in Scripture, the Jordan divided the territory of Israel into western and eastern parts. The Lower Jordan served as the dividing boundary between the Transjordanian tribes of Reuben, Gad, and half of Manasseh and the rest of the tribes who settled west of the river in Canaan proper. It also touched the borders of Issachar (Josh 19:22), Ephraim (Josh 16:7), Benjamin (Josh 18:12), and Judah (Josh 15:5). The Upper Jordan established the eastern boundary of Naphtali (Josh 19:33–34). (*See also* **Bethsaida**; **Capernaum**; **Dead Sea**; **Galilee, Sea of**; **Tiberias**.)

JOSAPHAT *See* **Jehoshaphat**.

JOSEPH The name of several important men in Scripture. See individual entries.

    1. **Joseph**.
    2. **Joseph, the husband of Mary**.
    3. **Joseph, brother of Jesus**.
    4. **Joseph of Arimathea**.
    5. **Joseph Barsabbas**.

JOSEPH (Hebrew, "may he [the Lord] add") The eleventh son of the patriarch **Jacob** and the first son of Rachel (Gen 30:24, 35:24; 1 Chr 2:2), the ancestor of the tribes of Manasseh and Ephraim, sometimes called the "tribe of Joseph" (Josh 17:14) or the "house of Joseph" (Judg 1:22; Amos 5:6). His life is the main focus of Gen 37–50.

I. LIFE

Born in Haran, Joseph was shown favor by his father throughout his youth; his father gave him the gift of "a long robe with sleeves" (Gen 37:3; translated in the **Septuagint** as a "coat of many colors"). His status as favorite son sparked the jealousy and hatred of his brothers, animosity only furthered when Joseph related two dreams he'd had in which his brothers bowed down to him (Gen 37:5–11). They conspired to kill him, but at the intervention of Reuben and Judah, he was sold into slavery instead for twenty shekels of silver (Gen 37:21–26) to Midianite merchants who were traveling to Egypt. The merchants took Joseph to **Egypt** and sold him to **Potiphar**, the chief of the royal guard (Gen 37:36; cf. Gen

39:1). Joseph's brothers, meanwhile, dipped Joseph's fine garment in the blood of a kid and sent it to Jacob as proof that Joseph had been killed by a wild beast. Jacob was overcome with grief (Gen 37:31–35).

Potiphar treated Joseph with respect, and his slave soon earned his master's trust and confidence. Joseph became steward over Potiphar's entire household, a position of some social prominence but one that also brought him into constant contact with Potiphar's flirtatious wife. Angered by his steady resistance to her advances, she accused him of trying to rape her. Joseph was thrown into prison (Gen 39:7–20).

In prison, the unjustly accused Joseph was not abandoned by God. He earned the trust of the warden (Gen 39:21–23) and came to the attention of the household of the pharaoh. By interpreting Pharaoh's dream (Gen 41:25–36), Joseph came into favor with Pharaoh, who made him the vizier or prime minister of Egypt (Gen 41:37–44; Ps 105:16–22; Wis 10:13). Pharaoh bestowed on him the Egyptian name of Zaphenath-paneah (which may mean "God spoke, and he came into life"). The ruler also gave Joseph as a wife Asenath, the daughter of Potiphera, a priest of the sanctuary at On (Heliopolis; Gen 41). Asenath bore him two sons, both of whose names resemble Hebrew expressions: Manasseh (whose name sounds like the Hebrew for "to make forget") and Ephraim (whose name sounds like the Hebrew for "to be fruitful"). (See Gen 41:51–52.)

As Joseph had foretold from Pharaoh's dream, seven years of plenty were followed by seven years of famine. But Joseph had prepared the country by storing up grain through the years of plenty.

The famine spread to surrounding countries, including Canaan. Hearing that grain was still abundant in Egypt, Jacob sent his sons—except Benjamin—down to Egypt to buy some. When they were brought before Joseph, they did not recognize their brother. Joseph tested them to determine the extent of their sorrow and repentance for their past deeds. Joseph's tests were harsh, but he determined their sincerity and finally revealed himself to them (Gen 42–44). Joseph calmed their fears that he might seek revenge, and sent them back with an invitation to Jacob to come and settle in Egypt, in **Goshen** (Gen 45:9–10).

The venerable Jacob journeyed to Egypt, and the pharaoh gave land to Joseph and his brothers. Jacob adopted Joseph's two sons, Manasseh and Ephraim (Gen 48:1–22), and made them coheirs with his own sons. Through the blessing given to Joseph by Jacob on his deathbed (Gen 49:22–26), Ephraim and Manasseh became, like the other sons of Jacob, fathers of Israelite tribes. Just before Jacob's passing, Joseph swore to his father that he would bury him in Canaan (Gen 47:29–31). Following Jacob's death, Joseph and his brothers carried Jacob's remains to Machpelah for burial (Gen 49:29–50:14). Joseph also renewed his assurance to his brothers that he had no plans for revenge upon them once Jacob had died.

Joseph died at the age of 110, and his body was embalmed and placed in a coffin in Egypt (Gen 50:36). The remains of Joseph were carried out of Egypt later by Moses and eventually buried in Shechem (Exod 13:19; Josh 24:32).

Joseph in Genesis is one of Scripture's most attractive, faithful, and virtuous figures. In the face of severe adversities, he demonstrated unflagging fidelity to God. Sold by his brothers into slavery, he relied on God to deliver him from his predicament. He became a model both of the "wise man" and of the "righteous sufferer." His fortitude and temperance were displayed further in the face of the adulterous advances of Potiphar's wife and after being hurled into prison. When elevated to a place of honor and power in Egypt, he served with skill and energy, taking as his chief concern the well-being of those in his charge.

Christian tradition sees Joseph as a **type** of Christ. He was a beloved son, rejected by his brothers and cast out, but achieving salvation through suffering and by overcoming severe humiliations. Once exalted, Joseph invited his brothers to share in his blessings, offering not revenge but forgiveness and welcome (cf. Acts 7:9–16).

II. HISTORICAL BACKGROUND

Is the story of Joseph history? Much circumstantial evidence supports the authenticity of the Genesis account. The treatment in Genesis shows notable familiarity with Egyptian social and funerary customs, as well as a working knowledge of Egyptian administrative protocol. Egyptian terms and names are also preserved. History tells of Semites migrating to Egypt in the second millennium B.C., some working as slaves of the state, others holding government positions. These observations suggest that the account of Joseph in Genesis is based on genuine historical tradition.

III. HIS MEANING IN SALVATION HISTORY

Joseph is a heroic figure, but the emphasis in Genesis is clearly on the action of God in history. God used the rejection of Joseph to bring about the salvation of Israel. Joseph himself proclaimed to his brothers that God had been in control throughout his life: "Fear not, for am I in the place of God? As for you, you meant evil against me; but God meant it for good, to bring it about that many people should be kept alive, as they are today. So do not fear, I will provide for you and your little ones" (Gen 50:19–21). God chose not only to protect the worthy Joseph, but through him to advance the larger plan of salvation.

By telling how the family of Jacob came to Egypt, the narrative sets the background for the Exodus. Without losing any of his freedom of will, Joseph played a part in fulfilling the promise that God had made to Abraham (Gen 15:12–16). Joseph saw this himself on his deathbed: "I am about to die; but God will surely come to you, and bring you up out of this land to the land that he swore to Abraham, to Isaac, and to Jacob" (Gen 50:24).

JOSEPH, BROTHER OF JESUS One of the "**brothers of the Lord**" (Matt 13:55; 27:56; Mark 15:40, 47). Also called Joses, a Greek equivalent of the Hebrew "Joseph," he had a brother, **James**, called the "brother of the Lord" (Gal 1:19). His mother, Mary, is probably "Mary the wife of Clopas" (John 19:25).

JOSEPH, THE HUSBAND OF MARY (Hebrew, "may he [the Lord] add") The husband of **Mary** and the legal father of **Jesus**. He was a member of the tribe of Judah who stood in the royal line of **David** (Matt 1:2–16). Characterized as a just or righteous man (Matt 1:19), he was a "carpenter" by trade (Matt 13:55; Mark 6:3); the Greek word describes a craftsman skilled in all kinds of woodwork and probably some masonry as well.

Matthew does not mention Joseph's hometown, but Luke writes, "And Joseph also went up from Galilee, from the city of Nazareth, to Judea, to the city of David, which is called Bethlehem, because he was of the house and lineage of David" (Luke 2:4). Matthew notes that Jesus was born in Bethlehem, but that Joseph settled his family in Nazareth of Galilee (where he and Mary had lived before the census that caused them to travel to Bethlehem) after their sojourn in Egypt. It is thus possible that Joseph was originally from Bethlehem, though he had been living in Nazareth.

Joseph is mentioned in Matthew, Luke, and John, but does not appear by name in Mark (some manuscripts add the phrase "the son of the carpenter" in Mark 6:3). Jesus is called "son of Joseph" (Luke 4:22; John 1:45, 6:42).

Joseph is a silent figure in the Gospel narratives: he thinks and acts but never speaks. The story of Joseph begins with him betrothed to Mary, who "was found" with child (Matt 1:18). When an angel told him in a dream not to fear to take Mary as his wife (Matt 1:20), Joseph promptly obeyed (Matt 1:24) (CCC 497, 1846).

When a census required him to return to his ancestral home, Joseph journeyed with Mary from Galilee to Bethlehem (Luke 2:4–6). There the child Jesus was born. After the visit of the **Magi**, Joseph was warned in a dream that Herod sought to kill the child. He fled with his family to Egypt (Matt 2:13). There the parents and child remained until after Herod's death (Matt 2:19).

The Holy Family returned to Palestine from Egypt and settled once more at Nazareth. After that, the only incident of Joseph's life that is recorded in the Gospels is the time when Jesus at twelve years old was found in the Temple in Jerusalem (Luke 2:41–50). The last mention of Joseph in the Gospel is when Jesus went back to Nazareth and was obedient to Joseph and Mary (Luke 2:51) (CCC 532).

Jesus's mother and brothers (see **Brothers of the Lord**) are mentioned during his public ministry (Matt 12:46; Mark 3:31; Luke 8:19; John 7:3), but Joseph is not present. It may be that Joseph died at some point before Jesus began his public ministry.

Joseph figured prominently in apocryphal literature, such as the *Story of Joseph the Carpenter*, which claimed that Joseph lived to be 111. This is unlikely, and the ages asserted by such later writers as Epiphanius are not clearly reliable. A host of other traditions pertaining to Joseph were preserved in the apocryphal New Testament writings, including the *Protoevangelium of James*, the *Gospel of the Nativity of the Virgin Mary*, and the *Life of the Virgin and Death of Joseph*.

Joseph demonstrates a pattern of virtue and obedience to the will of God. When he learned of Mary's pregnancy, he made sure not to expose her situation; when he was told in a dream who the child was, he accepted his commission from God to care for Mary and Jesus (CCC 437) "as the angel of the Lord commanded him" (Matt 1:24). Pope John Paul II called this obedience "the beginning of 'Joseph's way'" (*Redemptoris Custos*, §17).

At the same time, Joseph, as head of the Holy Family, gave the Church "an example and model for human families, in the order of salvation and holiness" (*Redemptoris Custos*, §22). Joseph is also honored as the patron of a happy death (CCC 1014) as well as the patron of the universal Church. Pope Leo XIII declared in his encyclical *Quamquam Pluries* (1889):

> [T]he Church in turn draws exceeding hope from his care and patronage, chiefly arising from his having been the husband of Mary and the presumed father of Jesus . . . Joseph was in his day the lawful and natural guardian, head and defender of the Holy Family . . . It is thus fitting and most worthy of Joseph's dignity that, in the same way that he once kept unceasing holy watch over the family of Nazareth, so now does he protect and defend with his heavenly patronage the Church of Christ.

Matthew gives us the royal genealogy of Joseph as it extends from David through Solomon, while Luke gives us a nonroyal genealogy that extends from David through Nathan. One possible explanation for the difference is that Matthew gives us the ancestry of Joseph, whereas Luke gives us the ancestry of Mary. Another possibility is that Joseph actually had two genealogies, one biological and one a legal genealogy based on the levirate law (cf. Deut 25:5–6).

JOSEPH OF ARIMATHEA A wealthy member of the **Sanhedrin** and a disciple of Christ (John 19:38); he was called a "good and righteous man" (Luke 23:50) and a man "who was also himself looking for the kingdom of God" (Mark 15:43). Joseph refused to consent to the condemnation of Christ by the Sanhedrin (Luke 23:51), and following the Crucifixion, he obtained permission from **Pilate** to bury the crucified body of Jesus (Mark 15:43–45; John 19:38). He wrapped the body in fine linen and placed it in a tomb that had been prepared for himself (Matt 27:59–60; John 19:40–41).

Joseph figured in New Testament apocryphal writings (e.g., the apocryphal *Acts of Pilate* and *Gospel of Nicodemus*) and was later given a preeminent place in medieval legend as the first keeper of the Holy Grail. His feast day is March 17.

JOSEPH BARSABBAS Also called Justus, an early disciple of Christ and a witness to his public life and Resurrection. He was a candidate to fill the apostolic office left vacant by Judas Iscariot (Acts 1:23). Although he was not chosen to be an apostle, he was considered a saintly man (Acts 1:21–26).

JOSEPHUS, FLAVIUS Jewish historian, politician, and soldier of the first century A.D. His writings are of great value as a primary source for events that took place in Palestine during the first centuries B.C. and A.D. Born the son of one Mattathias in A.D. 37, he came from a priestly family and was proud of his family's connections to the Hasmonean Dynasty. Educated in Jerusalem, he was chosen to head a Jewish delegation sent to Emperor **Nero** in A.D. 64. In A.D. 66, however, he became a soldier in the First Jewish Revolt against Rome. Surrendering to Roman forces, he served the Romans for the rest of the war and tried to convince his fellow countrymen that the rebellion was doomed to fail. After the war, he became a Roman citizen and enjoyed the patronage of the Flavian emperors Vespasian, Titus, and Domitian. In their honor, he adopted the name Flavius Josephus. His writings include the *Jewish War* (ca. 75), a history of the rebellion written in Aramaic and translated into Greek; *Jewish Antiquities* (ca. 85), an account of Jewish history from the Creation to the Jewish War; a *Life,* written just before his death; and *Against Apion,* a defense of Judaism against the prevailing anti-Semitism of the period. He died around A.D. 100.

JOSES *See* **Joseph, brother of Jesus**.

JOSHUA (Hebrew, "the Lord is salvation")

1. The son of Nun (Num 13:16), the servant (Exod 33:11) and minister to Moses during the period of the wilderness, and the warrior (Exod 17:9) chosen by Moses (Deut 31:3) as his successor and approved and commanded by the Lord (Deut 31:23) to lead the people into the land beyond the Jordan. Under Joshua's leadership, Israel seized possession of the Promised Land. He was the central figure of the biblical book of Joshua, which recounts the conquest of Canaan by the Israelites under Joshua's command (*see* **Joshua, book of**).

I. LEADER OF THE ISRAELITES

Originally named Hosea (Heb., "salvation"; Num 13:8, 16), he belonged to the tribe of Ephraim (Josh 24:30; 1 Chr 7:27). Moses changed his servant's name from Hosea to Joshua (Num 13:16)—from "salvation" to "The Lord is salvation"—in recognition of his loyalty to the Lord. Joshua first appears in the Pentateuch as a warrior in the army of God who fought against the Amalekites (Exod 17:9–13). He was then chosen by Moses to ascend the slopes of Mount Sinai (Exod 24:13) and, like Moses, he experienced the intimate presence of the Lord in the tent of meeting (Exod 33:11). Joshua was then named one of the twelve spies sent to scout Canaan (Num 13–14); only Joshua and Caleb spoke with confidence that victory was possible. Their views placed them at odds with the people, who were filled with such fear and doubt that they wished to stone Joshua and Caleb (Num 14:10). Before Moses died, Joshua was named the leader of the Israelites (Num 27:18–23; Deut 31:23), with the task of guiding his people into Canaan. Before the gathered assembly of the people, Moses laid his hands on Joshua (Num 27:18; Deut 34:9). After the death of Moses, Joshua "was full of the spirit of wisdom, for Moses had laid his hands upon him; so the people of Israel obeyed him, and did as the LORD had commanded Moses" (Deut 34:9).

The book of Joshua documents the ensuing conquest of the Promised Land and the subsequent division of Canaan into separate tribal territories. Joshua served as a pivotal figure throughout, launching the conquest after receiving military intelligence about Jericho from spies, and requiring that all the males born in the wilderness period (Josh 5:5) should be circumcised to permit Israel to celebrate Passover. As during the **Exodus**, the Lord intervened directly in favor of his people. First, there was the crossing of the Jordan, which miraculously parted to let the Israelites pass (Josh 3:14–17). Then there was the capture of Jericho—the key city deep in the Jordan Valley that was a gateway into the central hill country of Canaan—a feat once again achieved by the power of God (Josh 5–6). When Joshua set about conquering the fortifications of Ai, a strategic center for the advance into Canaan (Josh 7–8), the victory came only after Joshua had discovered and punished the disobedience of one of the Israelites. Yet again, God alone was responsible for the success.

At Ai, Joshua established an altar, after which he launched campaigns that gave Israel a decisive foothold in Canaan (Josh 9–12). (For details on the chronology of the conquest of Canaan, *see* **Joshua, book of.**)

With the initial phase of the conquest behind them, Joshua supervised the division of the land among the tribes of Israel (Josh 13–22). The epilogue of the book of Joshua contains the last message and death of Joshua (Josh 23–24). According to Josh 24:29–30, he died at 110 years old and was buried at Timnath-serah, in the hill country of Ephraim in central Canaan.

Joshua's final achievement was organizing a national ceremony at **Shechem** to renew the Mosaic covenant. He recognized that the hearts of the Israelites might still stray from honoring the covenant and loving the Lord. Joshua wrote the ordinances in "the book of the law of God," using a stone set up "under the oak in the sanctuary of the LORD" as a standing witness to the renewal of the covenant (Josh 24:26–28).

II. A SECOND MOSES

The whole story of Joshua stresses his similarities to Moses, and there are obvious typological parallels between Moses and Joshua. Like Moses, Joshua was mediator for his people with the Lord (cf. Josh 7:6–9). Like Moses, he received his instructions directly from God (Josh 1:1; 3:7; 4:1, 15; 5:13–6:5; 8:18; 20:1). Joshua received a vision of God and the promise that God would be with him (Josh 1:5; 3:7), sent out spies (as he had been sent by Moses; Josh 2), crossed a body of water miraculously parted by God (Josh 3:14–17), and purified the people for their appointed task.

Above all, Joshua mirrored Moses in functioning as a covenant mediator at Shechem (Josh 8:30–35; 24:1–28), as Moses had been at Sinai (Exod 20–24). Shechem was in the valley between Ebal and Gerizim where the Deuteronomic covenant had first been ratified (cf. Deut 27:12–13; Josh 8:30–35). Chapters 22–24 of Joshua describe Joshua's prophetic place as covenant mediator, specifically his renewal of the Deuteronomic covenant, thereby fulfilling his appointed role as a second Moses. Joshua renews the covenant with the third generation (as Moses had made the covenant with the second generation at Beth-peor; Deut 3:29).

As with Moses on the Plains of Moab (Deut 30–33), Joshua gives a farewell speech in Josh 23–24 that is strikingly parallel with Moses's addresses to the assembly of Israel at the end of Deuteronomy (Deut 29–32). Both men cite their age (Deut 32:1–43; Josh 23:2), promise the future victory of Israel over the inhabitants of the Promised Land (Deut 31:3–5; Josh 23:4–5), and call upon the people to remain obedient to the Deuteronomic covenant (Deut 31:12–13; Josh 23:6). Both present the people with the option of remaining in obedience or sinking into idolatry, with the choice bringing respective blessings and curses (Deut 30:15–20; Josh 23:6–16).

In all these parallels, Moses has a superior place of honor. Moses was the lawgiver, while Joshua recognized that the Law given by Moses was binding for himself and for the Israelites. Moses's unique authority could not be completely transferred to a successor, and his singular greatness is noted in Deut 34:10–12. Although Joshua's intercessory authority (Josh 7:6–9) helped to secure for him a place in later Jewish traditions as a prophet (e.g., Sir 46:1), his power of intercession again is secondary when compared to Moses's (cf. Exod 32:11–13; Num 14:13–19), and Joshua is also notably in need of priestly mediation (Num 27:15–23; Josh 14:1, 19:51). Finally, whereas Joshua receives three mentions in the New Testament, Moses receives over eighty (CCC 707).

Some scholars see parallels between Joshua and **Josiah** as well as between Joshua and Moses. Both Joshua and Josiah required the people to hear the reading of the book of the Law; both insisted upon a renewal of the covenant (Josh 8:30–35; 2 Kgs 23:2–3); and both launched a program of spiritual renewal. Joshua insisted upon celebrating Passover (Josh 5:10–12), an act of fidelity that served later as the model for Josiah's own emphasis on celebrating Passover as key to renewal (2 Kgs 23:21–23). Josiah may well have looked to Joshua as his example for leading the people of God.

There were other men named Joshua in the Bible.

2. A man of Beth-shemesh in whose field the ark stood as it was being conveyed back from the Philistines to Judah (1 Sam 6:14).

3. The governor of Jerusalem during the reign of King **Josiah** (2 Kgs 23:8).

4. The high priest and son of Jehozadak who returned with **Zerubbabel**, governor of Judah, from the Babylonian Captivity to Jerusalem (Hag 1:1, 12–14; Zech 3:1–8).

5. An otherwise unknown man mentioned in Luke's genealogy of Jesus (Luke 3:29).

JOSHUA, BOOK OF The sixth book of the Old Testament and the first of the Historical Books. Joshua records the fulfillment of God's covenant oath to grant the land of Canaan to the descendants of **Abraham** (Gen 15:18–21; 17:8). In the Hebrew canon, Joshua is the first of the former prophets (Josh–2 Kings, minus Ruth) and comes after the Law (Torah). The title of the book is taken from its main character, **Joshua**, the successor to Moses as spiritual leader of the Israelites. Under his leadership, the Israelites took possession of Canaan by military invasion and conquest.

I. AUTHORSHIP AND DATE

The author of the book of Joshua is anonymous, although, according to the Jewish traditions of the Talmud, Joshua himself was responsible for its authorship; the note concerning his death (Josh 24:29–31), according to this tradition, would have been written by the high priest Eleazar.

Some scholars in the twentieth century saw Joshua as a compilation derived from the same hypothetical documents that were supposedly used to compile the **Pentateuch** (labeled "JEDP"), thus promoting the idea of a Hexateuch (six books, from Genesis to Joshua) instead of the Pentateuch (the traditional five books, from Genesis to Deuteronomy). Others see Joshua as a compilation of various local traditions put together by one or more editors. The narrative clearly preserves ancient traditions of the occupation of Canaan—older place names and other archaic features, for example—and it is certainly possible that Joshua was the author of some parts. On the other hand, the use of such phrases as "until this day" (4:9; 5:9; 6:25; 7:26; etc.) shows the work of a later scribe, who compiled the earlier sources into a tight and consistent narrative. Some scholars suggest that the initial form of Joshua took shape around 1000 B.C., or before the rise of Israel's monarchy, and that its final form appeared during the Babylonian **Exile**.

II. CONTENTS

I. *The Conquest of Canaan (chaps. 1–12)*
 A. *Preparations for Invasion (1:1–2:24)*
 B. *Israel Enters Canaan (3:1–4:24)*
 C. *Circumcision and Passover (5:1–12)*
 D. *The Capture of Jericho (5:13–7:26)*
 E. *The Capture of Ai (8:1–29)*
 F. *The Renewal of the Covenant (8:30–35)*
 G. *The Campaign in the South (9:1–10:43)*
 H. *The Campaign in the North (11:1–23)*
 I. *The Kings Are Defeated by Moses and Joshua (12:1–24)*
II. *The Division of Canaan (chaps. 13–21)*
 A. *The Lands Are Still Unconquered (13:1–7)*
 B. *Territories East of the Jordan, of Reuben, Gad, and the Half-Tribe of Manasseh (13:8–33)*

 C. *Territories West of the Jordan and the Lands Given to Judah, Ephraim, and Half-Manasseh (14:1–17:18)*
 D. *The Distribution of the Remaining Lands Among the Tribes (18:1–19:51)*
 E. *The Cities of Refuge (20:1–9)*
 F. *The Levitical Cities (21:1–45)*
 G. *Dispute with the Eastern Tribes and the Altar East of the Jordan (22:1–34)*
III. *Joshua's Farewell Speeches (chaps. 23–24)*
 A. *Joshua's Farewell Address (23:1–16)*
 B. *The Renewal of the Covenant at Shechem (24:1–33)*

III. PURPOSE AND THEMES

The book of Joshua is a theological history of the conquest of the Promised Land and its subsequent division. The account includes the detailed preparations for the campaign, the actual conquest, the division of the land according to tribal allotments, and the final farewell of Joshua after he had fulfilled his divinely appointed task of leadership. The conquest of Canaan itself is waged in three principal phases. The first (chaps. 1–8) had as its target establishing a bridgehead into Canaan and then reducing key Canaanite strongholds—starting with the impregnable fortress of **Jericho**, followed by **Ai**, and then the central highlands. The second phase of the war was in the southern regions of Canaan (chap. 10), and the third phase was in the north (chap. 11). The book piles up these military victories in swift succession, although the narrative points out that the conquest of Canaan was far from complete in the days of Joshua (cf. Josh 13:1–7; 15:63; 16:10; 17:11–13). The division of the land among the tribes of

Israel is documented with great care in chapters 13–21.

The conquest of Canaan was begun 40 years after the Exodus from Egypt. If the Exodus occurred 480 years before construction began on Solomon's Temple (1 Kgs 6:1) in 966 B.C., the conquest of Canaan began in 1406 B.C. Many scholars, however, suggest that such a date is too early and prefer a later time, around 1250 B.C., one of the chief reasons being the archaeological findings in various Palestinian towns that give evidence of widespread destruction in the thirteenth century B.C. The difficulty with this assertion is the inability to connect the destruction specifically to the Israelite invasion of Canaan. Another obstacle is that Joshua itself intimates that the number of towns that were burned and destroyed was limited to Jericho, Ai, and Hazor (6:24; 8:19; 11:11–13), and that care was taken to preserve existing structures (24:13), in keeping with the divine promise that the Israelites would inhabit the towns of the dispossessed Canaanites (Deut 6:10–11; 19:1–2).

The narrative is not meant to be a complete record of the conquest of Canaan; rather, it emphasizes the initial victories that gave Israel a decisive foothold in the land.

Joshua makes it clear that the conquest of Canaan was the fulfillment of God's oath to Abraham that Abraham's descendants would wrest the land of Canaan from the inhabitants who dwelt there (Josh 21:43; cf. Gen 15:18–21; 17:8). The promise was the foundation of Israel's hope for a new homeland at the time of the **Exodus** (cf. Gen 26:3; 28:4, 13; 35:12; Exod 3:8; 6:8; 13:5; 23:23–33). God himself played a crucial role in the campaign by guiding his people to victory and intervening on their behalf at key moments (Josh 3:11–13; 10:11, 14; 5:13–15; 23:10; 24:11–12). Especially notable was the sun standing still during Joshua's battle at Gibeon (10:12–14). God showed himself faithful to his covenant promises, and through the conquest of Canaan he brought Israel closer to realizing the divine plan of redemption. But the Israelites would prove obdurately unfaithful to their covenant promises: they lapsed into the indigenous idolatry of the Canaanites, and the result was the repeated cycle of apostasy, punishment, and repentance in the time of the **Judges**.

JOSIAH (Hebrew *yōʾšîyāhû*, "may the Lord give") King of Judah from around 640 to 609 B.C., the son of Amon and Jedidah (2 Kgs 22:1, 2), and the grandson of **Manasseh**. Josiah brought about a major reform of the kingdom of Judah and a renewal of the covenant (2 Kgs 23:1–3). He ascended to the throne of Judah at the age of eight, following the murder of Amon and the execution of the conspirators (2 Kgs 21:23–26; 2 Chr 33:25). He ruled for the next thirty-one years (2 Kgs 22:1; 2 Chr 34:1). The young king reigned with great ability and piety (2 Kgs 22:2; 23:25). He made his initial efforts to purify the religious life of the people sometime around the eighth year of his reign (2 Chr 34:3), but he is most noted for the thoroughgoing reform he launched in the eighteenth year of his reign (ca. 622 B.C.). It began when the king gave orders to repair the Temple. During the repairs, **Hilkiah**, the high priest, discovered the book of the **Law**, probably a lost or hidden scroll of the book of Deuteronomy (2 Kgs 22:3–7). When the book was read to the king, Josiah was deeply troubled by the call to adhere to the Law, and the covenant curses that were to be imposed upon those who committed transgressions. Josiah then commanded the book to be read to the people and made the people swear their obedience to the Law. Because he heeded the call of the book, Josiah was told by the prophetess **Huldah** that he would be spared the anguish of seeing the destruction of Jerusalem; he would die "in peace" (2 Chr 34:28).

The reform of Josiah demanded nothing less than undivided allegiance to the Lord in both liturgy and life. Josiah made the demands of the covenant the heart of his reform, taking as his chief objective a true fulfillment of the Law of Moses (2 Kgs 23:25). This commitment made him unique among the kings (2 Kgs 22:2), going far beyond the other reforms of his predecessors.

Josiah also purged the Temple and its precincts of all cultic objects associated with Canaanite religion. These were gathered up and burned outside Jerusalem (2 Kgs 23:4). He then removed the priests who took part in the worship of idols that was forbidden by the Law (2 Kgs 23:5–7). The eradication of the high places of idol worship was then extended beyond Jerusalem and Judah into the old northern kingdom (2 Kgs 23:15–20). The expansion of the reform into northern territory was made possible by the decline of Assyrian influence, owing to its internal political troubles. All forms of idolatry and illegitimate cults were thus eradicated from the life of the covenant people (2 Kgs 8–27), permitting a centralization of worship in accord with Deut 12:10–11.

The reform culminated with the celebration of the Passover (2 Kgs 23:21–23) that sealed the renewal of the covenant and was conducted according to correct prescriptions of the Law. The narrative in Chronicles describes the feast at length (2 Chr 35:1–19), noting in particular that Josiah's Passover celebration was greater than any other in the days of the kings (2 Chr 35:18).

Meanwhile, Assyria was rapidly collapsing. The new Egyptian pharaoh, **Neco** II (r. ca. 610–595 B.C.), had gathered an army to help the Assyrians; both Assyria and Egypt hoped to keep Babylon from becoming the next Near Eastern superpower. Desiring to prevent Egyptian assistance from reaching the Assyrians, Josiah marched to war against Neco at Megiddo. Josiah was mortally wounded in battle and died of his wounds in Jerusalem (2 Kgs 23:29–30; 2 Chr 35:23). His untimely death is presented in Chronicles as being a result of foolish interference in foreign affairs. Josiah set out to fight Neco in an act of disobedience to the word of God that had been declared to Josiah by Neco: "I am not coming against you this day, but against the house with which I am at war; and God has commanded me to make haste. Cease opposing God, who is with me, lest he destroy you" (2 Chr 35:21).

Although he died as a result of his foolish action, Josiah was still ranked as one of Judah's greatest kings because of his remarkable zeal for religious reform (2 Kgs 23:25). The prophets **Jeremiah** and **Zephaniah** were both contemporaries of Josiah (Jer 1:2, 3:6; Zeph 1:1), and Jeremiah composed a lamentation on the king's death (2 Chr 35:25; cf. Jer 22:13–16).

JOT An archaic English transliteration of the Greek **iota** in Matt 5:18, used in the Douay and King James versions (see **Versions of the Bible**). The RSV renders it more literally as "iota": "For truly, I say to you, till heaven and earth pass away, not an iota, not a dot, will pass from the law until all is accomplished." The iota is the smallest letter in the Greek alphabet. When the saying was originally delivered, Jesus probably referred to the smallest letter of the Hebrew and Aramaic alphabets, *yod* (ˈ). The meaning is that not even the smallest part of the **Law** will pass away.

JOTHAM (Hebrew, "the Lord is perfect") The name of three men in the Old Testament.

1. The youngest of the seventy legitimate sons of **Gideon** (Judg 9:5). He escaped the massacre of his sixty-nine brothers at the hands of his half brother **Abimelech**, who was subsequently chosen by the people of Shechem to be their king (Judg 9:6). Jotham climbed to the top of Mount Gerizim overlooking Shechem and proclaimed the parable of the trees choosing the bramble as their king (after the cedar, the fig, the olive, and the vine declined), with disaster as the result (Judg 9:8–20). He then finished by cursing Shechem, a malediction that was fulfilled three years later when the city was destroyed (Judg 9:53–57).

2. Son of **Uzziah** (2 Kgs 15:32; 1 Chr 3:12) and king of Judah from around 750 to 731 B.C. His mother was Jerusha, "the daughter of Zadok" (2 Kgs 15:33). Jotham began his reign as co-regent around 750 B.C. after his father contracted leprosy (2 Kgs 15:5), and he succeeded to the throne after Uzziah's death. Little is recorded of his reign in 2 Kgs 15 and 2 Chr 27.

He initiated several building projects in Jerusalem, including the upper gate of the Temple, and made Ammon a vassal state that paid tribute to Judah (2 Chr 27:3–6).

3. A son of Jahdai and a descendant of **Caleb** (1 Chr 2:47).

JUBAL Son of **Lamech** and Adah, and the brother of Jabal (Gen 4:21). He is named as the father of lyre and pipe players; his name—*yûbāl* in Hebrew—may be a variation on the Hebrew word for the ram's horn, *yôbēl*.

JUBILEE The "year of liberty" for Israel that was to occur every fiftieth year according to Lev 25:8–10.

I. THE JUBILEE IN LEVITICUS 25

In the fiftieth year, on the Day of Atonement, the Jubilee arrived with a trumpet blast, which released all Israelite debt-slaves to return to their families and to reclaim their ancestral land (Lev 25:9–10). As in the Sabbath year (Lev 25:1–7), Israelites were to rest from agricultural labor during the Jubilee (Lev 25:11–12; chaps. 18–24). The Jubilee prevented the permanent sale of land, so the price of land was based on the number of harvests it would yield before the Jubilee (Lev 25:13–17). The Jubilee did not apply to urban property (Lev 25:29–34).

The Jubilee was meant to ensure that the Israelites, newly freed in the Exodus, would never again be reduced to the slavery they had endured in Egypt (Lev 25:42–43; 25:55). It was also the capstone of a liturgical structure for the consecration of time based on patterns of seven. At the end of a seven-day week, the

Israelites rested and worshipped (Lev 23:3). At the end of seven weeks after Passover, they observed an extra, fiftieth-day celebration, later called Pentecost (Lev 23:15–21; Acts 2:1). Likewise, at the end of a "week" of years, the Israelites rested (Lev 25:1–7), and after seven weeks of years, they celebrated the fiftieth year, the Jubilee (Lev 25:8–10). The number seven was sacred and associated with oath-swearing (cf. Gen 21:27–32). To swear an oath in Hebrew is literally "to seven oneself" (Hebrew *nišbaʿ*). Since oath-swearing often established a covenant (cf. Gen 26:28; 2 Kgs 11:4; Ezek 16:59), the number seven also acquired covenant connotations. The sevenfold structures of the Israelite calendar gave a covenant shape to sacred time, culminating in the Jubilee, the ultimate celebration of the covenant blessings of freedom and restoration.

There is a long-standing debate in both the Christian and Jewish traditions concerning whether the Jubilee was the forty-ninth or the fiftieth year. The wording of Lev 25:8–10 is ambiguous. Perhaps the Jubilee was the fiftieth year of the previous Jubilee cycle but simultaneously the first year of the next. This yields Jubilee cycles forty-nine years in length, as in the *Book of Jubilees* and some biblical texts (see below on Dan 9:24).

The Jubilee year should not be confused with three Israelite observances that occurred on a seven-year cycle: the Sabbath year, when the land rested (Exod 23:10–11; Lev 25:1–7); the "Year of Release" (Hebrew *šĕmiṭṭâ*), when monetary debts were forgiven (Deut 15:1–11); and the seventh year of service of a Hebrew slave, when he was released (Deut 15:12–18; cf. Exod 21:2–6). Scholars debate the relationship between the Jubilee and these last two observances. Technically, they do not conflict with one another: the Jubilee did not actually forgive debt like the "Year of Release" (cf. Deut 15:1–6), and unlike the manumission law for the landless "Hebrew" (Deut 15:12–18), the Jubilee applied to landed Israelites (Lev 25:10, 13, 28, 41). "Hebrew" and "Israelite" are not always synonymous (cf. 1 Sam 14:21; *see* **Hebrew**).

Because the Historical Books of the Bible do not record a clear observance of the Jubilee, some scholars consider Lev 25 a fictitious legislation composed in the postexilic period. However, several allusions to the Jubilee in Isaiah, Jeremiah, and Ezekiel (see below) indicate that the Jubilee was certainly known in ancient (i.e., preexilic) Israel, even if—like much of the Mosaic Law—the observance was frequently ignored by the people (cf. 2 Chr 36:21; Jer 34:8–22).

II. THE JUBILEE IN THE BIBLE AND ANCIENT JEWISH LITERATURE

The Jubilee is mentioned elsewhere in the Law (e.g., Lev 27:16–25; Num 36:1–12), and the prophets allude to it. Isaiah commanded Hezekiah to observe two years without sowing or reaping (Isa 37:30; 2 Kgs 19:29), two years that may have marked the seventh sabbatical year and the Jubilee, since such would be the only occasion when a two-year fallow period was required by biblical Law (cf. Lev 25:20–22). Isaiah also predicted the coming of an "anointed" one who would "proclaim liberty" and "the year of the LORD's favor" (Isa 61:1–2), that is, the Jubilee year. This "year of favor" would entail a profound renewal of God's people and even the Gentiles (Isa 61:3–11). For his part, Jeremiah condemned Zedekiah, king of Judah, and his nobles for abandoning their commitment to implement the Jubilee laws (Jer 34:8–22). Ezekiel augmented the Jubilee legislation to regulate the administration of royal property (Ezek 46:16–18). Daniel's prophecy of seventy weeks of years (i.e., 490 years) of penitential exile for Israel and Jerusalem (Dan 9:24) probably reflects ten Jubilee cycles of forty-nine years each.

Several ancient (pre-Christian) Jewish writings, including the Dead Sea Scrolls, reflect a fascination with the Jubilee cycle as a way to measure sacred time, whether past (*The Book of Jubilees*), present (4QOtot), or future (*1 En.* 91:12–93:10, *Testament of Levi* 17–18; 4Q383-91; 11QMelch).

III. THE JUBILEE IN THE NEW TESTAMENT

In the synagogue of Nazareth, Jesus reads the Jubilee prophecy of Isa 61:1–2 and proclaims it fulfilled (Luke 4:16–21). Christians should understand Christ as the true Jubilee. The ancient Jubilee freed servants from their bondage, restoring them to their true families and homeland. In Christ, we are freed from all that holds us in bondage: sin (John 8:34–36; Rom 6:18; 1 Pet 2:16), death (Rom 8:2; Heb 2:15), and the devil (Luke 11:20). He restores us to our true family, the family of God (Luke 15:11–24); and our true homeland, heaven (Heb 11:14–16).

Another New Testament reference to the Jubilee may be found in Matt 18:22, where Jesus commands Peter to forgive "not seven times, but seventy times seven," that is, 490 times, or ten Jubilee cycles, a symbolic number indicating complete forgiveness.

JUDAH (the name resembles the Hebrew verb "to praise") The fourth son of Jacob and the father of the tribe of Judah. The tribe of Judah was destined to be the royal tribe in Israel and to give hope of a Messianic ruler, a hope realized in Christ, the Lion of the tribe of Judah (Gen 49:9–11; Rev 5:5). The name was also used for the southern kingdom that was left to **Rehoboam** after the revolt of the northern tribes in 930 B.C. and that survived until 586 B.C.

I. JUDAH, SON OF JACOB

Judah was the fourth son of **Jacob**; he was born of **Leah** (Gen 29:35, 35:23, 46:12; Exod 1:2). He shares the spotlight with **Joseph** in Gen 37–50. Influential among his brothers, he was able to prevent the murder of **Joseph** by suggesting to his brothers that they sell him to Arab merchants headed for Egypt (Gen 37:26–27). Later when his brothers met up with him in Egypt, Joseph demanded that **Benjamin**—who had remained behind in Canaan with Jacob—should come to him. Judah pleaded with Jacob to allow Benjamin to return to Egypt with him; Judah even offered his own life as "surety" for Benjamin's safe return (Gen 43:8–9). Soon after, he took responsibility as substitute for Benjamin's apparent theft of the cup (Gen 44:18–34).

In spite of his heroism elsewhere, the description of Judah in Gen 38 is less than flattering. Judah married Bathshua, a Canaanite, and had three sons by her: Er, **Onan**, and **Shelah** (Gen 38:2, 12; 1 Chr 2:3). Er wed **Tamar**, but died before fathering any children by her. Onan then was obligated to fulfill the levirate custom and accept his sister-in-law as his wife, but he refused to consummate the union and died for his sin. Fearing for the fate of his remaining son, Judah withheld Tamar's just rights under custom, refusing to give her Shelah as her husband. Tamar, however, outwitted Judah. She dressed as a harlot and drew him into having intercourse with her. She conceived and gave birth to twins, Perez and Zerah; both were finally acknowledged by Judah to be his. Despite this immoral scenario, the Messianic line of Judah was continued and prevented from dying out (Matt 1:2–3).

II. THE TRIBE OF JUDAH

The importance of Perez is revealed in his descendants: King **David** (Ruth 4:18–22) and ultimately **Jesus Christ** (Matt 1:3–16). The line of Judah was to be the royal dynasty that stemmed from Abraham and Sarah (Gen 17:16) through their great-grandson Judah (Gen 49:8–10) and then forward to David and Jesus. This exalted place for his line is expressed powerfully in the blessing given to Judah by Jacob (Gen 49:8–12, 22–26) when he declares that the tribe of Judah is destined to be the royal tribe in Israel. Judah is depicted as a lion wielding a scepter and ruling over the nations (cf. Gen 37:7, 9; 42:6; Num 24:9, 17; 2 Sam 5:1–3; Ezek 21:27).

The name of the tribe of Judah was taken from the patriarch, and its future glory was assured in Jacob's blessing. The tribe played only a minor role in the Exodus and settled in southern Canaan (Josh 15:1–12, 20–62).

The land of Judah extended across a large part of southern Palestine. It was bounded on the north by Dan and Benjamin, on the east by the **Dead Sea**, on the south by the arid lands of the **Negeb**, and on the west by the Mediterranean. Its chief cities were listed in Joshua (Josh 15:20–63). The tribe failed to drive out the Jebusites, the inhabitants of **Jerusalem**, so they failed to seize and control the city for any significant length of time before the city was conquered by **David** (cf. Josh 15:63; Judg 1:8, 21), and there existed a degree of separation between Judah and the remaining tribes. Judah's isolated position created a psychological division of Israel into north and south; Judah, for example, did not take part in the tribal war against northern Canaanites in the time of the Judges (Judg 4–5). This disengagement continued into the early monarchy (cf. 1 Sam 11:8; 15:4; 17:52; 18:16).

III. THE KINGDOM OF JUDAH

With the acceptance of David as king over "all Israel" (2 Sam 5:1–5), Judah became part of the united kingdom and remained so during the reigns of David and Solomon. Yet when the northern tribes rebelled against Solomon's successor **Rehoboam**, Judah became the name of the southern kingdom, while the northern tribes formed the kingdom of Israel (see **Israel, kingdom of**).

From the start, the kingdom of Judah benefited from the wealth of Solomon, and despite its smaller population it was far more stable than the northern kingdom. God had sworn in the Davidic **covenant** to uphold the Davidic line of kings. Judah also had Jerusalem, the center of the proper worship of the Lord. As a result, Judah did not suffer from the severe dynastic difficulties that attended the kingdom of Israel and that hastened the demise of that realm.

But several Judahite kings were unfaithful to the proper worship of the Lord, tolerating or even encouraging pagan cults and idolatry. These tendencies were reversed by other kings who instituted various reforms and promoted the worship of the Lord in keeping with the Davidic covenant. The cycle began with Solomon and continued with Rehoboam, Judah's first king (1 Kgs 14:21–24), who allowed Canaanite forms of idolatry to flourish in Judah, a policy reversed by his grandson **Asa** (1 Kgs 15:9–13).

Another setback took place under Queen **Athaliah**, the wife of **Jehoram**, king of Judah, who was the daughter of King **Ahab** and **Jezebel** and the mother of **Ahaziah**, king of Judah (2 Kgs 8:18, 26). She seized the throne after the death of her son Ahaziah and commanded the murder of the whole royal family (2 Kgs 11:1; 2 Chr 22:10); only the infant **Joash** was spared because the priest **Jehoiada** hid the child in the temple (2 Kgs 11:2–3; 2 Chr 22:11–12). Athaliah promoted the worship of Baal and ruled for six years until she was toppled by a revolt. She was then executed in the palace (2 Kgs 11:16), and her temple of Baal in Jerusalem was destroyed (2 Kgs 11:18). The line of David was back on the throne with the accession of Joash.

For much of its history, the kingdom of Judah was spared the threats of foreign enemies from Mesopotamia and Syria. Luckily, the northern kingdom of Israel acted as a buffer between Judah and such growing regional dangers as **Assyria**. Israel's own insuperable

internal crises led to its final conquest in 722 B.C. by the Assyrians and the destruction of Samaria. After that, Judah was left vulnerable to the ambitions of powerful nations from the east.

The kings of Judah, unable to resist the might of the gigantic empires around them, involved themselves in the dangerous game of political alliances. At first they made Judah a vassal state of Assyria, but then **Hezekiah** revolted against Assyria after the death of Sargon II in 705 B.C. The Assyrians responded under **Sennacherib** with an invasion of Judah. Jerusalem was besieged and a number of cities were captured. Jerusalem was spared only by the miraculous defeat of the Assyrians (2 Kgs 19). Nevertheless, the invasion brought massive suffering to the kingdom, and many of its people were carried away as captives or massacred.

At the low point of Judah's religious life, Hezekiah's son and successor **Manasseh** completely reversed his father's reforms (2 Kgs 21:1–18; 2 Chr 33:1–20). He submitted to the Assyrians and promoted idolatry, including the sacrifice of children. His grandson **Josiah**, the great reformer, once again began a thorough religious reform, a centralization of worship, and a program of religious nationalism that profited from the decline of Assyria (2 Kgs 23:4–25). Josiah maintained nominal vassalage to Assyria, but he acted with a high degree of independence. Hoping that the rising empire of Babylon would take out Assyria once and for all, thus lifting the yoke of political vassalage from the neck of Judah, in 609 B.C. he embarked on a campaign to block Pharaoh **Neco** II from marching to the aid of Assyria against Babylon. At the battle of **Megiddo**, Josiah lost his life against the Egyptians (2 Kgs 23:29).

Only months later, the Egyptians installed **Jehoiakim** on the Judean throne, but he was quickly forced to accept Babylonian suzerainty after the victory of **Babylon** at Carchemish in 605 B.C. Babylon was now the supreme state in the Near East, and Judah fell increasingly under its domination. Jerusalem fell to Babylon in 597 B.C., and much of its population was carried off into exile (2 Kgs 24:10–14). **Zedekiah** was installed as king as a Babylonian puppet (2 Kgs 24:17). The last embers of national spirit inspired the king and his advisors to disregard the prophetic warnings of **Jeremiah** and to launch a highly ill-advised revolt. **Nebuchadnezzar** marched on Judah, besieged Jerusalem, and captured the city in 586 B.C. Zedekiah was captured and put to death, more of the population was dragged away to captivity in Babylon, and the city walls were torn down in a rampage of destruction that climaxed with the demolition of the Temple (2 Kgs 25:8-12). The kingdom of Judah had survived the fall of Israel by more than 130 years, but it too inevitably fell prey to the wider political struggles that eclipsed Palestine.

IV. JUDAH AFTER THE EXILE

The Babylonians carried most of the prominent families of Judah into exile. But when the Persian king Cyrus the Great conquered Babylon in 539 B.C., he granted permission for the restoration of the Temple and the repopulation of Jerusalem and the rest of Judah (Ezra 1:1–4). Exiles from Judah returned home with much enthusiasm and apparently

in large numbers (Ezra 2:1–70). But the Davidic monarchy could not be restored. Judah remained a vassal province of the Persian empire for roughly two hundred years after the Israelites' initial return. The relative political peace did, however, encourage the development of Jewish religious life in the postrestoration period. The rebuilding of Judah created a Temple-state with the religious authority in charge rather than Davidic kings.

The colossal campaigns of Alexander the Great (d. 323 B.C.) and the subsequent division of his empire among his generals placed Palestine once more in a difficult position as a battleground between the Ptolemaic and Seleucid Empires. (For the later history of the territory of Judah, see under **Judea**.)

JUDAS (Greek form of *Judah*) The name of several men in the Bible.

1. Son of Chalphi. He was a commander in the army of **Jonathan Maccabeus** (1 Macc 11:70).

2. The son of **Simon Maccabeus** (1 Macc 16:2). He was murdered with his father and brother **Mattathias** at a banquet at Dok hosted by Ptolemy, the governor of the Jericho region (1 Macc 16:11–17).

3. The Galilean leader of a revolt against the Romans around A.D. 6 at the time of a census taken for the purpose of taxation. He was considered a false Messiah by **Gamaliel** (Acts 5:37).

JUDAS ISCARIOT One of the twelve apostles, the one who betrayed Jesus to the authorities. He may have been from Judea; if so, Judas was the only non-Galilean among the apostles. He served as treasurer of the group that journeyed with Jesus, and the Gospels tell us that he embezzled money from the common fund (John 12:6). He appears in every list of the apostles given in the **Synoptic Gospels** (Matt 10:4; Mark 3:19; Luke 6:16); John describes him as a devil, a thief, and a son of destruction (John 6:70–71; 12:6; 17:12). Judas opposed the anointing of Jesus at Bethany for reasons of avarice: "But Judas Iscariot, one of his disciples (he who was to betray him), said, 'Why was this ointment not sold for three hundred denarii and given to the poor?' This he said, not that he cared for the poor but because he was a thief, and as he had the money box he used to take what was put into it" (John 12:4–6).

In his betrayal of Jesus, Judas—acting under the influence of Satan, according to Luke 22:3 (cf. John 13:2)—negotiated with Jewish authorities to arrest the Master in a nonpublic setting (Matt 26:14–16; Mark 14:10; Luke 22:3–6). He received money for the act, and Matthew details the amount: thirty pieces of silver (Matt 26:15; cf. Zech 11:12). Judas willingly led the authorities to **Gethsemane** and went so far as to point out Jesus to them by giving him a kiss (Matt 27:47–56; Mark 14:43–52; Luke 22:47–52). Jesus knew beforehand what Judas intended to do (Matt 26:20–25; Mark 14:17–21; Luke 22:21–23; John 13:21–26).

After the betrayal, Judas confessed to the chief priests and elders that he had delivered up an innocent man. Matthew 27:5 reports that afterward he hanged himself; Acts 1:18 says he fell and burst open. Although it is difficult to reconstruct the exact manner of death from these two accounts, both agree that he committed suicide; both seem to involve some sort of height (hanging and falling), and both give a partial explanation for the name of the "Field of Blood."

Why did Judas betray Jesus? Luke says that Satan entered into Judas (Luke 22:3; John 13:27), but there were doubtless psychological reasons as well. He never seemed to have developed a particularly strong belief in Jesus as the Christ; he referred to Jesus only as "Rabbi" (Matt 26:25) and never embraced a discipleship beyond that shallow level of belief. Some modern psychologists have suggested that Judas wanted to force Jesus to prove himself as the true Messiah. Whatever his reason, Judas made the conscious decision to betray Jesus to the authorities, and no psychological explanation can mitigate this act of betrayal.

JUDAS MACCABEUS The third of five sons of **Mattathias** (1 Macc 2:2) and the leader of the Jewish revolt against the Hellenizing efforts and religious persecutions of the Seleucid ruler **Antiochus IV Epiphanes**. "Judas" is the Greek form of the name Judah; because of his military success he was given the name Maccabeus, "Hammer."

Judas assumed leadership of the rebellion against the Seleucids after the death of his father (1 Macc 2:66) around 166 B.C. and proved an immensely capable soldier and strategist. A master of guerrilla warfare, he not only survived against numerically superior Seleucid forces but inflicted defeats upon **Apollonius** (1 Macc 3:10–12), **Seron** at Beth-horon (1 Macc 3:13–26), **Gorgias** at Emmaus, and **Lysias** at Beth-zur (1 Macc 3:38–4:35).

Having defeated the Seleucids, Judas organized the purification of the Temple after its profanation by Antiochus IV. The dedication of the Temple on the twenty-fifth day of the ninth month in 164 B.C. was thenceforth celebrated as the feast of Dedication, or Hanukkah. The next year, Judas launched expeditions into Galilee and Transjordan to assist the Jews of those regions when they were threatened by enemies.

The Seleucids finally began a counterattack under Lysias, the regent of the new young king Antiochus V in 162 B.C. Lysias had at his disposal a sizeable army, including elephants, and inflicted defeats on Judas at Bethzur and Beth-zechariah, followed by the siege of Jerusalem (1 Macc 6:18–54). But Judas and the rebellion were saved by internal Seleucid political problems that compelled Lysias to retreat (1 Macc 6:55–63). The accession of a new Seleucid king, **Demetrius** (1 Macc 7:1–4), was followed by the arrival of the general **Bacchides**, who installed **Alcimus** as high priest (1 Macc 7:8–20) and then sent **Nicanor** with the task of inflicting great hardship upon the population. Nicanor was defeated and killed in battle (1 Macc 7:26, 39–50). Judas then sought to consolidate his position by establishing diplomatic relations with Rome (1 Macc 8:1–32). Demetrius then sent Bacchides with another army, and in the battle that ensued Judas was killed. Judas's brothers **Jonathan** and **Simon** buried him in the family tomb at Modein (1 Macc 9:11–22). He was then succeeded by Jonathan (1 Macc 9:23–31).

JUDAS THADDAEUS One of the twelve apostles. He is listed as a disciple of Christ in several books of the New Testament. In Luke 6:16 and Acts 1:13, he is called Judas, son of James; in John 14:22 he is "Judas (not Iscariot)"; and in Matt 10:3 and Mark 3:18 his name is given as "Thaddaeus." His only words preserved in the Gospel accounts are presented in John 14:22. He is often considered the brother of Saint James the Less and the author of the Letter of Jude. One tradition, expressed in the *Passion of Simon and Jude,* declares that Jude went to Persia with Simon, where they were martyred. Jude is one of the most popular saints in the Church and is venerated as the patron saint of lost causes. Feast day: October 28.

JUDE, LETTER OF The twenty-sixth book of the New Testament. It is a brief treatise against erroneous teachings and practices opposed to law, authority, and true Christian freedom. Canonically, Jude is the last of the seven "Catholic Epistles" and comes before the book of Revelation.

I. AUTHORSHIP AND DATE

The author of the letter calls himself "Judas, a servant of Jesus Christ and brother of James" (v. 1). The early Church identified him as the Judas who is named among the relatives of Jesus (Matt 13:55; Mark 6:3). If this is the case, then his brother was James, the head of the Jerusalem community who was also called "the brother of the Lord" (Gal 1:19). Another possibility is that Judas is **Judas Thaddaeus**, one of the Twelve (literally called "Judas of James" in Luke 6:16 and Acts 1:13). Some modern critics suggest that the author is the Judas Barsabbas of Acts 15:22, or an anonymous Christian who wrote much later in the name of Judas.

Assigning a date to the book has proved extremely difficult for several reasons. Verse 17 (and also v. 3) can be read as suggesting that the apostles are dead, although that is not necessarily implied. Some scholars see the errors addressed in the letter as heresies of the second century. However, the "false teachers" mentioned appear less as heretics than as immoral deceivers who, like the people of Sodom and Gomorrah, "indulged in sexual immorality and pursued unnatural lust" (v. 7). Furthermore, the author assumes that his readers are familiar with Palestinian Jewish traditions, which suggests an earlier date for the letter. A conservative estimate, therefore, places the date of composition in the second half of the first century, possibly between A.D. 50 and 70.

II. CONTENTS

I. Salutation (vv. 1–2)

II. The Occasion and Purpose of the Epistle (vv. 3–4)

III. The Condemnation of False Teachers (vv. 5–16)

IV. An Exhortation to the Faithful (vv. 17–23)

V. Doxology (vv. 24–25)

III. PURPOSE AND THEMES

The Letter of Jude is addressed to communities suffering from the plague of false teachers. He had intended to write a discourse on salvation, but the crisis of the false teachers forced him to change his plans. The letter does not designate its recipients precisely, but Jude views the members of the communities with great affection (vv. 3, 17, 20) and has been well-informed as to their problems (8,

12, 16). As the epistle relies heavily upon the Hebrew Scriptures and displays a familiarity with apocryphal Jewish literature (9, 14–15), it is possible that the recipients were Palestinian Jewish Christians.

The false teachings that Jude rejects pervert the Christian message and promote licentiousness; the false teachers "pervert the grace of our God into licentiousness and deny our only Master and Lord, Jesus Christ" (4). Jude considers the refutation of error to be essential to sound discipleship. He urges believers to defend themselves, to pray, to be committed to the faith, and to reach out to those who have been deluded by deception (20–23).

The heart of the letter is the condemnation of the wicked and the assurance that their downfall is inevitable. To drive home his point, the author relies upon biblical history (5–7, 11), apocryphal writings (9, 14–15), and apostolic teachings (17–18). Judgments upon wayward Israel in the past foreshadowed the ultimate destruction of the wicked.

Jude's use of apocryphal sources such as *1 Enoch* and the *Assumption of Moses* was for illustrative purposes; it does not, of course, give the apocryphal books any theological authority. Partly because of these apocryphal citations, some of the Eastern churches did not initially admit Jude to the canon. It was listed among the books of the NT in the **Muratorian Fragment**, suggesting that it was accepted as canonical by the Roman Church in the late second century. It received universal recognition in the Western Church by the fifth century and was decreed a fully inspired book of the canon by the Council of Trent in 1546.

JUDEA (Also "Judaea" in some versions.) The Roman name for the territory of Judah in southern Palestine. Its geographic boundaries varied over the years. In Ezra and Nehemiah, it is the area inhabited by the Jews who had returned from the **Exile** in the sixth century B.C., at which time it was technically a Persian province known in Aramaic as *Yehud*. The extent of Judah in this period was little more than Jerusalem and its surrounding districts. Its size increased considerably under the Maccabees and the Hasmoneans to encompass the coastal plain, Idumea, and the Jordan Valley. After the Roman occupation in 63 B.C., the name Judea was sometimes used for the whole of Palestine, including both Samaria and Galilee, but in a narrower sense it denoted the smaller district of Judea separate from Galilee and Samaria.

King Herod ruled over Judea from 37 to 4 B.C.; his kingdom extended across Palestine as well as into some districts east of the Jordan. His son Archelaus ruled as ethnarch over a truncated territory that reached over Judea, Samaria, and Idumea, but not Perea and Galilee. After Archelaus was banished in A.D. 6, Judea was attached to the Roman province of Syria and subject to more direct Roman rule in the form of procurators (Luke 3:1). The extent of Judea under Roman rule was the same as under Archelaus, although the seat of government was Caesarea; during the time of Herod Agrippa I, Galilee was added to the jurisdiction. The broader sense of Judea is referred to by Josephus (*Ant.* 17.13; 18.1) as well as in the New Testament (Luke 1:5; 7:17; Acts 1:8, 26:20). (*See also* **Procurator** *and under individual rulers.*)

JUDGES, THE *See* **Judges, book of**.

JUDGES, BOOK OF The seventh book of the Old Testament and the second of the Historical Books. Judges records the actions of charismatic leaders, called Judges, of the tribes of Israel between the death of Joshua and the time of Samuel—a time of spiritual and political instability, when God allowed foreign powers to oppress Israel because of the recurrent idolatry among the people. The central theme of Judges is the cycle of sin and punishment, repentance and deliverance.

The title "Judge" does not suggest that the chief figures were legal experts or juridical officials; for the most part, they were military heroes commissioned by God to act as saviors and deliverers (Judg 11:27), and so guarantee the survival of Israel in times of national crisis (6:34).

I. AUTHORSHIP AND DATE

The author of Judges is not named. A Jewish tradition named Samuel as the author, but the evidence is too meager to draw any firm conclusions. The phrase "In those days there was no king in Israel," which occurs three times (Judg 17:6; 18:1; 21:25), implies that the book was written when there was a king in Israel. A strong contrast between the infidelity of Benjamin and the fidelity of Judah might be an allusion to the political tension between the house of **Saul** and the house of **David**—an inference reinforced by the marked contrast between the hospitality of Bethlehem (19:1–9), the home of David, and the extremely inhospitable conduct of Gibeah (19:1–26), the home of Saul. This allusion might point to a time in the early monarchy. The statement that "the Jebusites have dwelt with the people of Benjamin in Jerusalem to this day" (1:21) might point to a time before David's conquest of Jerusalem (2 Sam 5:6–9).

II. CONTENTS

III. PURPOSE AND THEMES

The purpose of Judges is to demonstrate that the fortunes of Israel were related directly to whether the people served the Lord exclusively and observed his **covenant** faithfully. The account covers over three hundred years between Joshua and Samuel, a time of testing but also of transition for the Israelites. The people's previous nomadic existence as shepherds was giving way to a more settled form of life with its focus on agriculture. Complicating this development was tribal discord, political disorganization, geographic provincialism, and the danger of idolatry from contact with the Canaanite people. Because of their infidelity to the Lord, the Israelites were punished, "and he gave them over to plunderers, who plundered them; and he sold them into the power of their enemies round about, so that they could no longer withstand their enemies" (Judg 2:14). When the Israelites cried out, the Lord raised up Judges who saved them (2:16), but the Israelites continually proved faithless and behaved "worse than their fathers, going after other gods, serving them and bowing down to them; they did not drop any of their practices or their stubborn ways" (2:19), and the pattern repeated. Altogether Judges lays out seven cycles of this pattern of sin, subjugation, and salvation.

The Judges displayed a wide variety of personality and skills. Some were violent and even barbaric, such as **Ehud**, who treacherously stabbed to death the king of Moab, and **Jephthah**, a hard warrior who wiped out his Ammonite opponents but made a vow that led to the sacrifice of his own daughter. **Samson** was a powerful fighter whose incredible exploits against the Philistines were offset by his own weakness for women. Some of the Judges, such as Samson, **Deborah**, **Gideon**, and Jephthah, are described in great detail, while others, such as the six minor judges, are given only a brief accounting. Flawed and far from perfect, the Judges were still God's useful instruments for the achievement of his plan of salvation.

The lesson of the book of Judges is clear.

Over and over, the Israelites failed in their promise of fidelity to the Lord, were delivered into the hands of their enemies, and were then rescued by a loving and merciful God. To accomplish his deliverance, God sent them the Judges, who served as types of the true Savior and the perfect Judge who was to come: Christ. The book shows the dynamics of the Deuteronomic covenant at work: Israel's prosperity or adversity is a direct result of the people's fidelity or infidelity to the covenant. Divine retribution is brought about, not by a capricious God, but because of the failings of his people, who trigger the curses of the covenant by sin. Through it all, God remains faithful and continually offers forgiveness and the promise of hope for a better and more stable future.

Hebrews 11:32–34 praises the Judges as heroes of faith. In patristic exegesis, the Judges were seen as **types** of the Messianic savior, who frees us from our subjugation to sin.

JUDGMENT God's just governance, by which he rewards or chastises his people according to their deserts.

From the beginning, the Bible makes clear that human beings stand accountable for their actions. As God issues his first command to Adam, he spells out consequences: "for in the day that you eat of it you shall die" (Gen 2:17). Throughout the Scriptures, whether in narrative or in law, there is a fundamental principle at work: "whatever a man sows, that he will also reap" (Gal 6:7). Since God is by nature righteous, his judgments are always just (Gen 18:25; Deut 1:9–10, Jer 11:20). All human actions are subject to divine justice: our thoughts

(1 Cor 4:5), words (Matt 12:36), and deeds (2 Cor 5:10).

But God's judgments are not simply condemnatory. They are above all disciplinary. Their goal is to reform the human person. In Lev 26, for example, God begins by stating the positive consequences of fulfilling his commandments (26:3–12). If the people fail, they will face a "sevenfold vengeance"—a series of punishments gradually increasing in severity. The first are mild chastisements (26:14–17) that serve as a summons to repentance. If the sinners persist in their offense, however, they will face graver consequences (26:18–20), with the same goal: repentance. If they remain obstinate, the punishments grow more severe (26:21–22), and still more severe (26:23–26). Yet God still awaits their conversion. Only with the curses of Lev 26:27–39 does he resort to banishment. Nevertheless, *even then* he holds out hope: "Yet for all that, when they are in the land of their enemies, I will not spurn them, neither will I abhor them so as to destroy them utterly and break my covenant with them; for I am the LORD their God" (26:44).

Thus, the "sevenfold vengeance" is actually a sevenfold mercy. The just judge is very patient, his judgment corrective, aimed at improvement rather than harm.

God does indeed visit punishment upon people, but always with merciful forewarning. The prophets often announce the arrival of such a "day of the Lord" (e.g., Amos 5:18–20; Zeph 1:14–16)—God's decisive interventions in history. Moreover, the prophets often plead the cause of sinners, hoping to stay the hand of the Lord (e.g., Gen 18). And when such a day does arrive, God punishes the wicked, but not the just, from whom a "remnant" is often preserved.

In the New Testament this divine prerogative, judgment, is assumed by Jesus. In Matt 24–25, Jesus presents himself first as judge of Jerusalem and then as judge of the world. In John, he states plainly: "For judgment I came into this world" (John 9:39), and, "The Father . . . has given all judgment to the Son" (John 5:22). In Acts, Paul, too, identifies Christ as the "man" by whom God "will judge the world in righteousness" (Acts 17:31). Christ himself will judge individuals according to their works: "For we must all appear before the judgment seat of Christ, so that each one may receive good or evil, according to what he has done in the body" (2 Cor 5:10; see also Rom 2:6).

God's judgments are meted out in history and at the consummation of history. They are historical (as in the prophesied doom of Jerusalem); liturgical (e.g., 1 Cor 11:28–32); and eschatological (e.g., Matt 25; Rev 20:11–12). In history, Jesus shares the power of judgment with the hierarchy of the Church: "when the Son of man shall sit on his glorious throne, you who have followed me will also sit on twelve thrones, judging the twelve tribes of Israel" (Matt 19:28; see also Luke 22:30).

John illustrates God's judgment with a series of apparent paradoxes or contradictions. He declares: "God sent the Son into the world, not to condemn the world, but that the world might be saved through him" (John 3:17; cf. John 12:47). At the same time, Jesus states: "For judgment I came into this world,

that those who do not see may see, and that those who see may become blind" (John 9:39). Likewise, God does not judge (John 5:22), but God is unmistakably a judge (John 8:50); Jesus states that he does not judge (John 8:15; 12:47) and yet he stipulates that the Father does not judge for he has granted the authority to his Son (John 5:22).

The contradictions are only apparent; John is showing us that each individual decides the outcome of his own judgment. The key passage is John 3:16–21, which tells us that Christ came not to judge the world but to save it (cf. John 8:15; 12:47). At the same time, however, Jesus's coming into the world brought with it judgment. Sin, "the ruler of this world," has been judged (John 16:11). The unbeliever—the one who rejects the salvation offered by Jesus—imposes his own judgment upon himself (John 3:18). Faith is a gift from God (John 6:37, 44) that is freely accepted or rejected (John 6:66–70). The world is judged in the present, in the rejection of Jesus, and Jesus is the focal point of the choice, the basis and object of judgment. Thus we can say truly that God does not judge, yet the unbeliever is still judged by his very act of unbelief (John 3:18; 5:24).

Judgment is also a major theme in Revelation. The judgments of Revelation are often terrifying, rich with symbolism, especially the judgment of the beasts, the devil, and the dead (Rev 19:11–20:15). Judgment of the earth is launched with the breaking of the seven seals (Rev 6:1–8:5), containing the vivid image of the four horsemen, symbolizing the divine judgments of war (a white horse), bloodshed (a red horse), famine (a black horse), and death (a pale horse) (Rev 6:1–8). The cycle of judgments is concluded with the seven bowls of wrath (Rev 15:1–16:21), culminating with the Last Judgment (Rev 20:11–15; cf. Matt 25:31–46) (CCC 633–35, 677, 1038–41).

Finally, while the NT speaks clearly of the Last Judgment, it also speaks clearly of a particular judgment: immediately after death, the eternal destiny of each separated soul is decided by the judgment of God. The parable of the poor man Lazarus and the words of Christ to the good thief on the Cross clearly refer to the particular judgment (Luke 16:22; 23:43; Matt 16:26; 2 Cor 5:8; Phil 1:23; Heb 9:27; 12:23; cf. Acts 1:25; Rev 20:4–6, 12–14) (CCC 1021–22).

JUDGMENT, LAST *See* **Judgment**; *see also* **Parousia**.

JUDITH (Hebrew, "Jewess") The name of two women in the Old Testament.

1. One of the Hittite wives of Esau and the daughter of Beeri (Gen 26:34).

2. The heroine of the book of Judith. (*See* **Judith, book of**.)

JUDITH, BOOK OF A book listed among the Historical Books in the Catholic Old Testament. The book recounts the preservation of the Israelites from conquest and ruin through the action of the heroine Judith. Its essential theme is how trust in God brings deliverance to Israel. Judith is one of the **deuterocanonical** books, accepted as Scripture by the Catholic Church but not included in Jewish and Protestant canons of the OT.

I. AUTHORSHIP AND DATE

The author of the book is unknown, and the place where it was written is uncertain. The book may have been written in the second century B.C., around the time of the Maccabean revolt (see **Maccabees**). The book's emphasis on faith in the Providence of God, the defense of the Temple and Jerusalem, and the struggle to safeguard the Jewish way of life all point to that time. The book was originally written in Hebrew or Aramaic, but the most ancient version now extant is the translation in the Greek **Septuagint**.

II. CONTENTS

I. *The Historical Background (chaps. 1–7)*
   A. *Nebuchadnezzar's Revenge and Holofernes's Campaign (1:1–3:10)*
   B. *Judea's Refusal to Surrender (4:1–15)*
   C. *Achior's Advice to Holofernes (5:1–6:20)*
   D. *Holofernes's Campaign Against Bethulia (7:1–32)*
II. *The Story of Judith (chaps. 8–16)*
   A. *Introducing Judith (8:1–9:14)*
   B. *Judith's Plot Against Holofernes (10:1–13:10)*
   C. *The Flight of the Enemy (13:11–15:13)*
   D. *The Song of Judith (15:14–16:20)*
   E. *Judith's Death (16:21–25)*

III. PURPOSE AND THEMES

A dramatic and suspenseful story, the book of Judith presents a lesson in the triumph of God within the context of the strife between his people and their enemies. Judith, a pious Jewess, deceives and beheads **Holofernes**, general of **Nebuchadnezzar**, and so represents the victory of good over evil with the help of God.

Her victory over her enemy is total, and especially shameful (from an ancient Near Eastern point of view) is the death of the general at the hands of a woman.

Judith is described as a tribeswoman of Simeon and the widow of Manasseh, whose death by sunstroke took place before the narrative begins (Jdt 8:1–3). Her genealogy is extensive and gives the reader a sense of the key role she will play for her people. According to the account, she lived in Bethulia as a widow. When the city was besieged by Holofernes and the Assyrians, she pledged herself to saving the people. Using her enticing beauty, she ventured out into the camp of the Assyrians and won the affection of Holofernes. One night, as he lay drunk from wine, she beheaded him with his own sword and brought the head back to the city. The Israelites attacked the Assyrians, who—with no general to lead them—fled before the onslaught. Judith gave a canticle of praise after the victory. The book ends by speaking of her renown and revealing that she died at the age of 105.

The story names historical people and alludes to historical events to recall the unsuccessful efforts of foreign nations to annihilate the Jewish faith. The author wanders freely across the history of Israel and chooses different figures to construct the narrative: Nebuchadnezzar, king of Babylon, is here the ruler of Assyria, the names of Holofernes and Bagoas are Persian, and Judith herself, whose name means "Jewess," is perhaps intended to embody the Jewish people. This may well suggest a strategy on the part of the author to invest historical events with symbolic and theological meaning.

Judith is a national hero (13:18) in the tradition of the Judges, especially **Deborah** (Judg 4). She rises up and with the help of the Lord defeats the enemies of Israel. She reminds the Jewish people that their deliverance is promised, but only if they remain faithful to their Lord and trust in his divine protection. Judith proclaims, "for you are God of the lowly, helper of the oppressed, upholder of the weak, protector of the forlorn, savior of those without hope. Hear, O hear me, God of my father, God of the inheritance of Israel, Lord of heaven and earth, Creator of the waters, King of all thy creation, hear my prayer!" (Jdt 9:11).

Judith has been seen as a type of the Blessed Virgin **Mary**. She is called "blessed by the Most High God above all women on earth" (Jdt 13:18; cf. Luke 1:42), and of her it is said, "You are the exaltation of Jerusalem, you are the great glory of Israel, you are the great pride of our nation! You have done all this singlehanded; you have done great good to Israel, and God is well pleased with it" (Jdt 15:9–10). This passage is applied to Mary in Catholic liturgy. Like Judith, Mary defeated evil, and like Judith, Mary is a powerful symbol of opposition to the works of evil and the enemy of God's people, the devil.

JULIA A Roman Christian mentioned by Paul in Romans (Rom 16:15).

JULIUS A centurion who was given the task of watching over Paul during the sea voyage from Caesarea to Rome (Acts 27:1–44). He was noted for his courtesy—even kindness—to Paul during the trip, allowing him to visit friends during a brief stop at the port of Sidon

(Acts 27:3). He ill-advisedly followed the advice of the ship's captain that they continue on to the Cretan port of Phoenix after the sailing season had ended despite the obvious risks to their safety (Acts 27:11). As Paul had feared, they suffered a shipwreck, but Julius prevented the sailors from abandoning the ship and his own men from killing Paul to prevent his possible escape in the confusion (Acts 27).

JUSTICE *See* **Justification**.

JUSTIFICATION One means of expressing the doctrine of salvation in the New Testament. It can refer to a divine action as well as a spiritual process. As an action, justification is the moment when God makes righteous the one who believes in Christ and establishes him or her in a covenant relationship with himself. As a process, justification is the growth in righteousness and grace that takes place in the believer who embraces the demands of the gospel and yields himself or herself to the leading of the Spirit.

I. Terminology
II. In the Old Testament
III. In the New Testament
    A. The Gospels
    B. The Pauline Epistles
    C. The Letter of James
IV. Doctrinal Importance

I. TERMINOLOGY

The vocabulary of justification is interconnected in Hebrew and Greek in a way that is sometimes obscured in translation. In the biblical languages, there is a close relationship between the verb "to justify" (Hebrew *hiṣdîq;* Greek *dikaioō*), the noun "justice, righteousness" (Hebrew *ṣĕdāqâ;* Greek *dikaiosynē*), and the adjective "just, righteous" (Hebrew *ṣaddîq;* Greek *dikaios*). These terms, which are used to describe the action and result of justification, share a common root in both languages. English is partly capable of expressing this with the triad "justify, justice, just," but translators often avoid the latter two terms because of associations derived from classical philosophy and jurisprudence. They tend to prefer the terms "righteousness" and "righteous" as more suitable equivalents. However, modern English lacks a corresponding verb of the "right-" stem. Translational challenges aside, it is important to be aware of the conceptual unity that underlies the biblical vocabulary of justification.

II. IN THE OLD TESTAMENT

Justification is given theological prominence in the New Testament, yet its doctrinal foundations are laid in the Old Testament. Its beginnings can be traced to the administration of law and justice in ancient Israel, where the verb "to justify" meant "to vindicate" or "to acquit someone of charges" by declaring him to be in the right. In this sense, justification is a formal pronouncement of righteousness or innocence by God in heaven (Exod 23:7; 1 Kgs 8:32; Isa 50:8) or by a qualified judge on earth (Deut 25:1; Prov 17:15; Isa 5:23).

The standard of judgment is the covenant between God and his people. Righteousness in the Bible is not strictly equivalent to the notion of "justice" in classical antiquity, where it refers to giving each person in society his due, though the two ideas are not totally unrelated.

Righteousness is a state of conformity to the covenant, and to act in righteousness means to fulfill one's obligations by keeping the commandments of the covenant (Deut 6:25, 24:13; Isa 48:18; Luke 1:6). When the Lord is said to be righteous, it means he is acting in faithfulness to the covenant that he administers—fulfilling its promises, blessing the righteous, and cursing the wicked (Neh 9:8, 33; Ps 119:137; Dan 9:14; Zech 8:8). This is why the Psalmist, pained by his own sins, admits that God is justified in condemning the wrongdoer (Ps 51:4).

The primary and original context of justification is thus the historical covenant between Yahweh and Israel. However, in one key passage, it is projected into the eschatological future. Isaiah's fourth Servant Song is a disturbing vision of a man who is rejected and abused by his own people (Isa 52:13–53:12). Despite his innocence, he will submit to their violence as a way of making himself a sacrifice for the iniquity of all. The prophet then announces that not only will the servant bear "the sin of many" (Isa 53:12), but he will also justify the many; that is, he will "make many to be accounted righteous" (Isa 53:11). It would not go unnoticed by Christian readers that here the notion of justification is linked with a suffering Messiah who offers his life in atonement for sinners, the result of which is a new standing in righteousness for many.

III. IN THE NEW TESTAMENT

A. The Gospels

Justification is not frequently discussed by Jesus in the Gospels, at least not explicitly. There are two passages, however, where the topic is forthrightly addressed. In the first, Jesus says: "I tell you, on the day of judgment, men will render account for every careless word they utter; for by your words you will be justified, and by your words you will be condemned" (Matt 12:36–37). Here he speaks of the final justification of the saints, the verdict rendered at the Last Judgment that acquits the righteous of sinful speech and secures their entry into the Kingdom. In the second instance, the Parable of the Publican, Jesus tells the story of two men praying in the temple: one a Pharisee who reckons himself righteous and parades his credentials before God (Luke 18:9–12), and the other a tax collector who declares himself a sinner and throws himself on the mercy of God (Luke 18:13). In reference to the latter, Jesus declares: "I tell you, this man went down to his house justified rather than the other" (Luke 18:14). The lesson is that justification consists in the mercy of God that is given graciously to sinners who acknowledge their guilt but is withheld from those who consider themselves righteous because of their outward piety.

B. The Pauline Epistles

Justification is discussed in depth and in detail in several of Paul's letters. It is essentially his way of speaking about salvation. For Paul, justification is made possible by the "blood" of Christ (Rom 5:9), and it means that believers are "made righteous" (Rom 5:19) by the gift of "his grace" (Rom 3:24). Those who are justified are at "peace" with God (Rom 5:1) because they have been "freed from sin" (Rom 6:7). More than that, those who are justified have become "heirs in hope of eternal life" (Titus 3:7). This is precisely because Christ has given them "the spirit of sonship" (Rom 8:15) and thus made them "children of God" (Rom 8:16). Such was God's master plan from the beginning, for the apostle contends that God "sent forth his Son . . . so that we might receive adoption as sons" (Gal 4:4–5; cf. Eph 1:5).

For various reasons, Paul was pressed to clarify the means of justification against possible misunderstandings. On the one hand, he identifies faith as the essential basis: "For we hold that a man is justified by faith apart from works of law" (Rom 3:28). The indispensability of faith is something that he often stresses in his teaching (Rom 3:21–26, 4:5, 5:1; Gal 2:16, 3:25–26; Eph 2:8; Phil 3:9). Still, he never claims that faith alone is the means of justification. In fact, Paul is adamant that faith without love amounts to nothing (1 Cor 13:2); what truly avails is "faith working through love" (Gal 5:6). Thus, the Pauline notion of faith cannot be reduced to an intellectual assent or trust, but represents the total response of the believer to Christ, and this includes "obedience" to Christ (Rom 1:5; 16:26). Moreover, justification by faith is effected in the liturgical context of baptism. Paul indicates as much when he tells the Corinthians: "But you were washed, you were sanctified, you were justified in the name of the Lord Jesus Christ and in the Spirit of our God" (1 Cor 6:11). Baptism, being the sacrament of faith, is therefore the sacrament of justification (Titus 3:5–7).

Likewise, because the grace that justifies is a "free gift of righteousness" (Rom 5:17), Paul insists that man cannot be the author of his own justification, either by the performance of good works in general (Titus 3:5) or by the observance of specific works of the Law (Rom

3:28). Were this possible, man would have an occasion for boasting in himself (Rom 4:2; Eph 2:8–9) rather than in the Lord (1 Cor 1:30–31).

C. The Letter of James

Important clarification on the doctrine of justification is found in the Letter of James (Jas 2:14–26). Many scholars hold that James addressed the issue because of misunderstandings circulating about Paul's emphasis on justification by faith. James highlights the ongoing aspect of justification as a process—an idea that is also found in Paul, but with less prominence than the idea of the initial justification of the believer.

Apparently some Christians in the early Church mistook Paul's stress on "faith" to mean that "faith alone" justifies. This is incorrect and potentially dangerous, especially as it led some to depreciate the importance of pursuing works of mercy and charity (Jas 2:14–17). James therefore asserts that believers are also "justified by works" (Jas 2:21). To demonstrate the point, he shows that not only was Abraham righteous by faith, and thus established in a state of friendship with God (Jas 2:23), but Abraham also put that faith into action when the Lord called him to sacrifice Isaac (Jas 2:21). This act too became an occasion for Abraham's justification; only it was not the initial declaration of his righteousness, but a further advancement in righteousness made possible by his faith made active in works. James thus concludes from this scriptural example: "You see that a man is justified by works and not by faith alone" (Jas 2:24).

Paul would hardly agree with this assessment. For he too maintains the importance of works, not as a means of establishing one in a righteous covenant relation with God, but as a means of fulfilling the obligations of the covenant and thereby growing in righteousness (Rom 6:13, 16). For him, saving faith must be a working faith, for "it is not the hearers of the law who are righteous before God, but the doers of the law who will be justified" (Rom 2:13). Moreover, the only way to follow the commandments and live as God's children is to submit ourselves to the grace of the Spirit (Rom 8:1–17). It is the Spirit that pours God's love into the heart of the believer (Rom 5:5), enabling him to love as the Law commands (Rom 13:8–10).

IV. DOCTRINAL IMPORTANCE

The doctrine of justification was not always as central in the debates of later centuries as it was in the apostolic age. One exception is the early fifth century, for at that time Saint Augustine of Hippo expended tremendous energy wrestling with the doctrine and articulating an orthodox understanding of its meaning. He did this in opposition to the heretic Pelagius, who both overestimated the strength of the human will to do good and underestimated man's desperate need for grace to transform and empower him to live the Christian life.

A second major exception is the sixteenth century, which saw the rise of Protestantism and the spread of a new and novel understanding of the doctrine. In the writings of the first reformers, justification was reduced to an imputation of Christ's righteousness to the sinner that made him "right with God" but in no sense transformed him within. In addition, the reformers taught that man is justified by faith alone, and no human action—religious, moral, or otherwise—could alter his justification or lessen the certainty of his salvation.

The Catholic Church responded to this new theology with the *Decree on Justification* issued by the Council of Trent in 1547. Justification was therein defined as "a translation from that state in which a person is born a son of the first Adam into a state of grace and adoption as sons of God through the second Adam, Jesus Christ." The doctrine is thus to be understood in terms of divine sonship, and this by an inward infusion of grace and not merely an external imputation of legal righteousness to the believer. The Council likewise delineated the causes of justification as follows: the *final* cause is the glory of God, and secondarily the eternal salvation of man; the *efficient* cause is the mercy of God; the *meritorious* cause is Jesus Christ, who made atonement for sin and merited the grace of justification for us; the *instrumental* cause is the sacrament of baptism, along with faith for those who are capable of exercising it; and the *formal* cause is the righteousness of God, that is, the grace by which he makes us righteous (CCC 654, 1987–95).

JUSTUS

1. The surname of **Joseph Barsabbas** (Acts 1:23).

2. Titius Justus, a Corinthian proselyte. His house stood next to the synagogue in Corinth (Acts 18:7).

3. A Jewish Christian whose birth name was "Jesus" or "Joshua," who was with the imprisoned Paul when he wrote Colossians (Col 4:11).

KADESH Also Kadesh-barnea, an oasis in northern Sinai, probably near modern 'Ain el-Qudeirat. It is remembered primarily as a place where both Moses and the wilderness generation of Israel rebelled against God and disqualified themselves from entering the Promised Land. Kadesh-barnea was the site of the Mesopotamian king **Chedorlaomer**'s defeat of the Amalekites (Gen 14:7) and is mentioned in the story of **Abraham** (Gen 16:14; 20:1). In the time of the **Exodus**, Kadesh was supposed to be the staging point for Israel's entrance into Canaan from the south (Num 13:26; Deut 1:19–21). Moses sent twelve spies into Canaan. Owing to the Israelites' doubt in God's ability to deliver them the Promised Land, they were condemned to wander for the next forty years in the wilderness until another generation should be established (Num 14:21–35; cf. Deut 2:14). After years of wandering, the Israelites returned to Kadesh, where **Miriam** (sister of Moses and Aaron) died and was buried (Num 20:1). It was also near Kadesh that Moses disobeyed God's command when he struck a rock to bring water rather than speaking to achieve the same feat (Num 20:2–13). The exact site was called Meribah after that (Num 20:13). For this act of disobedience, Mo-

ses was forbidden to enter the Promised Land (Num 34:1–5). After the conquest of Canaan, Kadesh marked the southernmost border of Judah (Josh 15:1–3).

KADMIEL A Levite who returned with **Zerubbabel** from the **Exile** (Ezra 2:40; Neh 7:43, 12:8) and assisted with the rebuilding of the Temple (Ezra 3:9) and the renewal of the covenant (Neh 10:9); his son Jeshua was a leader among the Levitical musicians (Neh 12:24).

KAPH The eleventh letter of the Hebrew alphabet (כ).

KARNAIM *See* **Ashteroth-karnaim**.

KEDESH The chief city in the territory of Naphtali in northern Galilee (Josh 19:37); probably the modern site of Tell Qades. Kedesh had been a Canaanite royal city, and the king of Kedesh was defeated by Joshua (Josh 12:22). After the conquest of Canaan, Kedesh was designated one of the forty-eight Levitical cities (Josh 21:32; 1 Chr 6:76). Kedesh was the residence of Barak (Judg 4:6) and the site where Deborah and Barak began to amass their forces before the battle with Sisera (Judg

4:10). Centuries later, the city was captured by **Tiglath-pileser III** of Assyria (2 Kgs 15:29) and its inhabitants deported. **Jonathan Maccabeus** defeated the army of the Seleucid king Demetrius (1 Macc 11:63–74) at Kedesh.

KEILAH A fortified town in the western hills of Judah (Josh 15:44), probably modern Khirbet Qila. David saved the town from a Philistine attack, but he soon fled to avoid being handed over to Saul by the townspeople (1 Sam 23:1–5). Keilah also figured in the reconstruction after the **Exile** (Neh 3:17–18). It is also mentioned in Egyptian sources.

KENAZ *See* **Kenizzites**.

KENITES A Midianite clan, relatives of Moses on the Midianite side of his family, that settled in southeast Canaan alongside the tribe of Judah (Judg 1:16; 4:11). They resided in Canaan and had dealings with the Israelites in the period before the conquest of Canaan (Gen 15:9). **Jethro**, a priest of Midian, became the father-in-law of Moses when Moses married his daughter Zipporah (Exod 3:1; 4:18), and the Kenites subsequently joined Israel in taking possession of the Promised Land. **Jael**, wife of Heber, was part of a Kenite family that moved into northern Israel. She killed the general Sisera after receiving him in her tent during his flight from battle (Judg 4:11). When **Saul** was about to make war on the Amalekites, he gave advance warning to some of the Kenites who lived among them, so that they would have time to move out of harm's way (1 Sam 15:6). David sought their friendship (1 Sam 30:29).

KENIZZITES An Edomite tribe that derived its name from Kenaz, a grandson of **Esau** (Gen 36:11, 15, 42; 1 Chr 1:36, 53). The tribe was closely connected with the clan of **Caleb** (Num 32:12; Josh 14:6, 14) and had a long-standing association with Judah. They are mentioned in Gen 15:19 as one of the ten peoples occupying Canaan whose lands would be delivered to Abraham's descendants.

KERYGMA (Greek, "proclamation" or "preaching") The announcement of the message of the **Gospel** as preached in the New Testament. The core of this message is the **Kingdom** of God and the redemption of man by Christ. When biblical scholars speak of the "early Christian *kerygma*," they mean a basic summary of the Gospel message as preached by the earliest Christian evangelists.

In the Gospels, the Greek noun *kērygma* is used only in reference to the "preaching" of **Jonah** (Matt 12:41; Luke 11:32), but the verbal form *kēryssō* is used often in reference to the preaching of John the Baptist (Matt 3:2) and Jesus (Matt 4:17).

The preaching of Jesus was centered on heralding the Kingdom of God. For Mark, Jesus's preaching is summed up succinctly by the declaration, "Now after John was arrested, Jesus came to Galilee, proclaiming the good news of God, and saying 'The time is fulfilled, and the kingdom of God is at hand; repent, and believe in the gospel' " (Mark 1:15). Luke (4:16–21) stresses that Jesus's ministry is the fulfillment of Isa 61:1–4: the bringing of the Good News of deliverance to the oppressed, the brokenhearted, the captives, and the prisoners.

The *kerygma* of the early Church continued with enormous fervor, focusing on Jesus Christ as the central content of the message (cf. Acts 8:5, 9:20, 19:13; 1 Cor 1:23, 15:12; 2 Cor 1:19, 4:5). The book of Acts shows that the presentation of the message varied depending upon the recipients of the Good News. For a Jewish audience, the apostles preached Jesus as the fulfillment of the Messianic promises of the Old Testament (Acts 2:14–36; 3:18–26; 13:16–41); for the Gentile audience, the stress was on the movement away from the errors of idolatry and paganism to the recognition of the one true and living God (Acts 14:15–17, 17:18–31; 1 Thess 1:9).

KETURAH The second wife of **Abraham**, after the death of **Sarah** (Gen 25:1–4; 1 Chr 1:32–33; cf. **Hagar**). She bore Abraham six sons: Zimran, Jokshan, Medan, Midian, Isbak, and Shuah, each of whom was the ancestor of one of the Arabian or Aramean tribes.

KEY Mentioned in its literal sense in the Old Testament only in Judg 3:25 (cf. 1 Chr 9:27). Far more commonly, a "key" or "keys" are a symbol of power and authority (Isa 22:22, where the "key" may be a literal key, but is also a symbol of authority). In the New Testament, the key serves a similar purpose. The star that had fallen from heaven to earth was granted the key to the shaft of the bottomless pit (Rev 9:1); likewise, the angel from heaven held the key to the bottomless pit that was used to lock away the dragon for a thousand years (Rev 20:1). Christ holds the "keys" of death and Hades—that is, he has power over them (Rev 1:18). Jesus also gave Peter the keys of the kingdom of heaven: "I will give you the keys of the king-

dom of heaven, and whatever you bind on earth shall be bound in heaven, and whatever you loose on earth shall be loosed in heaven" (Matt 16:19). By giving him the "keys," Jesus made Peter a prime minister over the Church, with heaven's authority to make binding decisions in matters of Christian faith and life.

KIBROTH-HATAAVAH (Hebrew, "graves of craving") An encampment of the Israelites after their departure from the wilderness of Sinai (Num 33:16–17). The place was named for the "strong craving" the Israelites expressed there. After reaching the camp, the Israelites complained to Moses that they lacked meat (Num 11:4–6). Their cry was taken by Moses to God, and the Lord sent a flock of quails. Even as they feasted, however, a great plague struck the camp and many died (Num 11:31–35, Deut 9:22).

KID The young of a goat, highly prized for its tender meat (Gen 27:9; Judg 13:15) and offered in sacrifice (Exod 12:5; Num 15:11–16; Judg 13:19). The elder brother in the Parable of the Prodigal Son complained that his father had never given him a kid (Luke 15:29). The Israelites were commanded not to boil the flesh of the kid in the milk of the mother, perhaps because certain rites among the Canaanites included that ritual (cf. Exod 23:19, 34:26; Deut 14:21).

KIDRON The deep ravine directly east of Jerusalem between the city and the Mount of Olives. Apparently the valley was called "dark" or "murky" because sediment was stirred up by the flow of water in its streambed. In the time of the monarchy, the valley was home to the King's Garden (2 Kgs 25:4; Neh 3:15), where the kings owned land that was watered by the flow down the western slope of the Mount of Olives and that was perhaps supplemented by water from the Gihon spring. The result was a truly lush garden (2 Kgs 21:18). **Asa** (1 Kgs 15:13; 2 Chr 15:16) and **Josiah** (2 Kgs 23:4, 6, 12; 2 Chr 30:14; cf. 2 Chr 29:16) destroyed idols and other cultic objects in this valley. Jesus crossed the Kidron on his way to the Garden of **Gethsemane** (John 18:1).

KIN *See* **Family**; *see also* **Covenant**.

KING The absolute ruler of a city or state. In the ancient Near East, "sacral kingship" was the norm: the monarch was both a political and a religious leader. In **Egypt**, for example, the **pharaoh** was honored as a god, while in Mesopotamia, **Assyria** in particular, the king was the divine representative.

I. *No King but God*
    A. *The Ideal Priestly Kingdom*
    B. *Accommodations to Israel's Sinful Nature*
II. *"We Will Have a King over Us"*
    A. *Chaos Brings the Desire for a King*
    B. *Covenant Restrictions on the King*
III. *The Kings of Israel and Judah*
    A. *Saul*
    B. *David, the Ideal King*
    C. *Decline from the Ideal*
    D. *The End of the Kingdoms*
IV. *The Messiah*

I. NO KING BUT GOD

A. *The Ideal Priestly Kingdom*

The tribes of Israel originally had no king but God. The covenant made with **Abraham** made possible the foundation of the Kingdom of God on earth. Israel's first conception of kingship was in terms of theocracy (God is king) rather than monarchy (an earthly king rules as God's representative). By the covenant made at **Sinai**, God spoke directly to Israel, which he called his "firstborn son" (Exod 4:22), proclaiming that "you shall be for me a priestly kingdom and a holy nation" (Exod 19:6). In the **Law** given at Sinai, there is no provision for a king other than the Lord.

Scripture is clear that God himself was king over Israel (Exod 15:1–18; Num 23:21; Judg 8:23; 1 Sam 8:7, 10:19, 12:12), and even into the time of the monarchy the Psalms still portray God as Israel's true King (cf. Ps 8, 15, 24, 29, 33, 46, 47, 48, 50, 75, 76, 81, 82, 84, 87, 93, 95, 96–99, 114, 118, 132, 149).

B. *Accommodations to Israel's Sinful Nature*

The first covenant at Sinai (see Exod 19–24) was broken, however, by the apostasy of the golden calf (Exod 32). After that, the Israelites were placed on probation under the legal supervision of the Levitical priests (cf. Exod 34–40; Lev 1–26). **Deuteronomy** makes many accommodations to the Israelites' sinful nature, among them the permission for the Israelites to have a king: "you may indeed set as king over you him whom the Lord your God will choose" (Deut 17:14–15).

II. "WE WILL HAVE A KING OVER US"

A. *Chaos Brings the Desire for a King*

After the conquest of Canaan, hostility from foreign nations brought the need for the tribes to depend upon the leadership of certain charismatic figures to help them survive. This was the period of the Judges, military heroes who received authority from God to act as divine judges (Judg 11:27), deliverers, and heroes to ensure the survival of the Israelites (Judg 6:34).

But the Judges unified Israel only for the duration of the threats from outsiders. As soon as there was momentary peace, the unity was broken, the nation began its descent into chaos, and the enemies of Israel saw their opportunity. The people began to demand a king, hoping that a centralized government would bring stability to their chronically unstable world. God allowed Samuel to anoint a king as an accommodation—a departure from the true Kingship of God in which the Israelites were to participate (1 Sam 8).

B. Covenant Restrictions on the King

The Deuteronomic covenant, as we saw, had permitted the institution of a monarchy. Moreover, God promised kings to **Abraham** and **Sarah** (Gen 17:16), and **Jacob** promised royal honors for the line of his son **Judah** (Gen 49:8–10). But by the terms of the Deuteronomic covenant, the king had to live under three restrictions: he must not acquire many horses for himself; he must not acquire many wives for himself; and he must not acquire gold and silver in great quantity for himself. In addition, he must make a copy of the Deuteronomic law code, which he was to read all the days of his life (Deut 17:16–20). The chief purpose of these regulations was to prevent the kings from sinking into the same kind of idolatrous kingship that Israel's Near Eastern neighbors practiced, in which the monarch claimed divinity.

Nevertheless, the Lord's granting permission for the Israelites to have a king was a concession to their sinful nature. Their demand for a king implied a rejection of the Lord as their king and a lack of trust in his leadership. Thus Samuel gave the people a chance to reconsider their demand: "These will be the ways of the king who will reign over you," he said, introducing a list of abuses of power that kings would inevitably commit (1 Sam 8:11–18). But the people demanded a king anyway: "No! but we will have a king over us, that we also may be like all the nations, and that our king may govern us and go out before us and fight our battles" (1 Sam 8:19–20).

III. THE KINGS OF ISRAEL AND JUDAH

A. Saul

God directed Samuel to anoint **Saul** (1 Sam 9:16). At first Saul's reign seemed successful, with victories in battle and an apparent unity of the tribes. Saul, however, irretrievably erred by refusing to wait for Samuel and offering sacrifices himself. For that sin he lost his hope of a dynastic succession (1 Sam 13). When he further sinned by disobeying God's commandments in a war against the Amalekites, he lost his right to the kingdom itself (1 Sam 15). Saul died under shameful circumstances (1 Sam 31), and **David** was installed as God's chosen king.

B. David, the Ideal King

Future generations remembered David as the ideal king of Israel, and his dynasty endured for three and a half centuries. The importance of his kingship was derived from the Davidic covenant as spelled out in 2 Sam 7. When David had been established as king, had defeated the enemies of Israel, and had conquered Jerusalem, he was able to fulfill the terms of the Deuteronomic covenant and create a central sanctuary at Jerusalem, the place where God chooses for his name to dwell, fulfilling Deut 12. The **ark of the covenant** was brought to Jerusalem (2 Sam 6), and David dressed like a Levite and danced before it as it was carried into the city. He acted and was dressed like a priest, he blessed and offered sacrifices like a priest; we can see him as a new **Melchizedek**, both priest and king, and thus as a **type** of the Messiah, the perfect union of priest and king.

David was a model king, not because he was sinless, but because he never dabbled in idolatry. He was guilty of moral transgressions, but he never abandoned the right worship of God. His kingship focused on the Lord and the proper worship that is due to him. In that way, he pointed the way toward the true universal kingdom intended by God. If the priest-king was faithful, the blessings would follow. Further, David's son and successor, **Solomon**, had the gift of divine wisdom, and with it he built the **Temple** in Jerusalem. Solomon, the son of David, also achieved the divine "rest" from Israel's enemies that God had promised to David (2 Sam 7:10)—a rest that was a type of heaven. Both kings put the Lord at the center of Israel's national life: they made Jerusalem both a political and a spiritual capital for the people of God.

C. Decline from the Ideal

The fidelity of the kings did not endure, however. David's sin with Bathsheba (2 Sam 11–12) began a decline of his reign, and the moral slide continued in the reign of his son. Solomon violated all three of the Deuteronomic limitations upon the king: he accumulated wealth, weapons, and wives, and his rule grew tyrannical. The unity of the kingdom, pushed to its limits under Solomon, was finally shattered under **Rehoboam**. With his reign, the united kingdom broke apart into the northern kingdom of Israel (made up of ten tribes that rebelled under Jeroboam) and the southern kingdom of Judah.

Many of the kings of Judah and Israel were weak and wicked, often lapsing into idolatry. Prophets warned the two kingdoms that their infidelity would bring their destruction. Occasional attempts at reform were launched, such as the serious effort under King **Josiah** (2 Kgs 22–23), but the next reign always brought a relapse.

D. The End of the Kingdoms

The failings, corruption, violence, and idolatry of many kings of Israel led to the conquest and collapse of the northern kingdom in 722 B.C. at the hands of the Assyrians. The kingdom of Judah followed in 586 B.C. at the hands of the Babylonians, at which time Jerusalem fell and the Temple was destroyed.

IV. THE MESSIAH

The words of the prophets had assured the Israelites of their impending doom, but they had also expressed hope for the future. **Isaiah**, **Jeremiah**, **Haggai**, **Zechariah**, and **Malachi** spoke of hope rising from the ruin through a purified people returning home from exile. These future hopes would be realized in the **Messiah**, the ideal king who would come forth from the line of David and restore his kingdom. The Messianic hope of Israel found its fulfillment in **Jesus Christ** (Rom 1:1–4) (CCC 440, 453, 547).

Christ proclaimed, "The time is fulfilled, and the kingdom of God is at hand" (Mark 1:15). Christ lays claim to a heavenly kingship in his dialogue with **Pilate** (John 18:33–38). As the fulfillment of the divine plan of salvation, Christ was anointed by the Father with the Holy Spirit and established as priest, prophet, and king (Acts 10:38). He advanced toward his kingship through his death and Resurrection, until he ascended to his throne at the right hand of God in heaven (Mark 16:19; Acts 2:29–36). From here he reigns for all time as sovereign Lord of the universe (1 Cor 15:25–28; Eph 1:16–23) and invites all to enter his Kingdom through **baptism** (John 3:5), to receive his Messianic anointing (1 John 2:20, 27), and to share in his three offices of prophet, priest, and king (CCC 783, 786, 908, 2105). (*See also* **Kingdom**; **Son of God**.)

KING JAMES VERSION *See* **Versions of the Bible**.

KINGDOM A society subject to a monarchical form of government, headed by a king or queen. In the New Testament, "the kingdom" is generally a reference to the "Kingdom of God." This term and concept has a rich background, since "kingdom" is an important theme and image throughout Scripture. Adam exercises a kingly role over creation. Later, God promises to Abraham that kings will arise among his descendants. Israel, the people of God, is first organized into a kingdom by Saul, who is quickly replaced by David and his descen-

dants. The Israelite kingdom under David and his heirs foreshadows the Kingdom of God in the NT—in fact, the Kingdom of God can be understood, in one sense, as the transfiguration of the Davidic kingdom. It can also be identified with (1) Christ himself, or (2) Christ's rule in the hearts of his faithful, or (3) the Church, the assembly of the faithful, and the mystical body of Christ.

I. *The Kingdom in Scripture, Genesis to Revelation*
II. *The Kingdom of God in the New Testament*
   A. *Terms for the Kingdom of God*
   B. *The Three Theological Dimensions of the Kingdom of God*
   C. *The Kingdom of God as Fulfillment of the Old Testament Types of Kingdom*

I. THE KINGDOM IN SCRIPTURE, GENESIS TO REVELATION

A kingdom motif is already present in the creation account of Genesis. God makes man "in his image and likeness." The first word, "image" (Hebrew *ṣelem*), is particularly rich in kingdom connotations. It was commonplace for ancient Near Eastern monarchs to place carved images (Hebrew *ṣĕlāmîm*) of themselves throughout the geographical bounds of their empires, as a representation of their political authority in those regions. Thus, Gen 1–2 suggests that all of creation is the realm or kingdom of God, and mankind is placed in that realm as vice-regent to represent the authority of God. This is further confirmed by the creational mandate to Adam and Eve to "have dominion" (Hebrew *rādâ*) over the earth, a term that is elsewhere used to describe the exercise of royal power (1 Kgs 4:24; Ps 72:8, 110:2). Adam is at the pinnacle of the hierarchy of creation and de facto king among all creatures. Thus, the creation narrative presents an ideal or paradigmatic situation in which the entire created order is a kingdom ruled by humanity on behalf of God.

Later in salvation history, Noah is a "new Adam" figure who once again finds himself as de facto human king of creation (cf. Gen 9:2). Royal motifs are also to be found associated with Abraham. In Gen 14, Abraham's defeat of the coalition of Near Eastern kings leaves him as military ruler of the Levant and therefore in a position to declare himself king. Instead, he recognizes the royal authority of the mysterious priest-king Melchizedek of Salem (i.e., Jerusalem). However, Abraham's own descendants will later be kings of Jerusalem—an intimation of this is given in Gen 17:6, which promises kings among Abraham's descendants as part of God's covenant with him.

The promise narrows to one line of Abraham's descendants in Gen 49:8–10, which promises the "scepter" and "ruler's staff" to Judah, who will receive obeisance not only from the rest of the tribes of Israel but also from the "peoples"—that is, the Gentiles.

Through Moses, the Lord offered a form of corporate kingship and priesthood to the people of Israel, on the condition that they be faithful to the Sinai covenant: "if you will obey my voice and keep my covenant, you shall be . . . to me a royal priesthood" (Hebrew *mamleket kōhănîm*; Greek *basileion hierateuma;* Exod 19:5). But the people did not keep the covenant, beginning with the golden calf incident and continuing in rebellion through-

out the wilderness wandering. The promise of kingship to Abraham's descendants would have to be realized in a different manner.

After the ill-fated reign of Saul the Benjaminite, Jacob's prophecy of the scepter to Judah found fulfillment in the Judahite royal dynasty established by David (2 Sam 5:3).

The kingdom of David is the clearest Old Testament type or prefiguration of the Church and her structure. For that reason, its characteristic features are worth enumerating:

1. The Davidic monarchy was *underwritten by a divine covenant* (Hebrew *bĕrît,* Greek *diathēkē*), the only human kingdom of the OT to enjoy such a privilege (2 Sam 7:8–16, 23:5; 1 Kgs 8:23–24; Ps 89:3; 2 Chr 13:5, 21:7; Sir 45:25; Isa 55:3; Jer 33:14–26).

2. The Davidic monarch was adopted as *the Son of God.* The filial relationship of the Davidide to God is expressed already in the foundational text of the Davidic covenant (2 Sam 7:14), but is also found in other Davidic texts (Ps 2:7, 89:26; 1 Chr 17:13, 28:6).

3. The Davidic monarch was the *"Christ"*— that is, *the "Messiah" or "Anointed One."* The anointed status of the Davidic king was so integral to his identity that he is frequently referred to simply as "the anointed one" or "the Lord's anointed" (1 Sam 16:13; 2 Sam 19:21; 22:51; 23:1; 1 Kgs 1:38–39; 2 Kgs 11:12; 23:30; 2 Chr 6:42; 23:11; Ps 2:2; 18:50; 20:6; 28:8; 84:9; 89:20, 38, 51; 132:10, 17).

4. One of the chief responsibilities of the Davidic monarch was to *build the Temple of God.* David prepared for it (1 Chr 22:1–19), Solomon completed it (1 Kgs 8:12–13), and subsequent

kings maintained it (2 Kgs 12:4–16; 22:3–7). The building of the Temple was central to the terms of the Davidic covenant from the very beginning, as can be seen from the wordplay on "house" ("temple" or "dynasty") in 2 Sam 7:11–13. Even after the Temple was destroyed, the prophets remained firm in their conviction that YHWH would restore his Temple to its former glory as an international place of worship (Isa 2:1–4, 56:6–8, 60:3–16, 66:18–21; Jer 33:11; Ezek 40–44; Dan 9:24–27; Joel 3:18; Hag 2:1–9; Mic 4:1–4; Zech 6:12–14, 8:20–23, 14:16).

5. The Davidic monarchy was inextricably bound to *Jerusalem, particularly Mount Zion*, which was the personal possession of David and his heirs (2 Sam 5:9), and would have had no significant role in Israelite history had not David made it his capital (cf. Josh 15:63; Judg 1:21, 19:10–12; 2 Sam 5:6–12).

6. The Davidic monarch ruled over an *international empire*. David and Solomon ruled over not only Israel but also the surrounding (Gentile) nations (2 Sam 8:11–12; 10:19, 12:30; 1 Kgs 3:1, 4:20–21, 10:15). The Psalms theologically justify and celebrate this state of affairs (Ps 2:8; 18:43, 47; 22:27; 47:1, 9; 72:8, 11; 66:8; 67:2–5; 86:9; 89:27; 96:7; 99:1) and the prophets envision the restoration of this empire (Isa 2:3–4; 42:1–6; 49:1–7, 22–26; 51:4–6; 55:3–5; 56:3–8; 60:1–16; 66:18–19; Amos 9:11–12; Mic 4:2–3; Zech 14:16–19).

7. The Davidic monarchy was to be *everlasting*. One of the most prevalent emphases in the Psalms and Deuteronomic history is that the Davidic Dynasty will be eternal (2 Sam 7:16, 23:5; Ps 89:35–36). Not only the dynasty but the life span of the reigning monarch himself was described as everlasting (Ps 21:4; 72:5; 110:4).

8. The administration of the Davidic monarchy had roles for the Queen Mother (1 Kgs 2:19–20; 15:13; 2 Kgs 24:12, 14; Jer 13:18; 22:26; 29:2), the royal steward (Hebrew *ʾăšer ʿal-habbayit*, "the one over the house/palace": 1 Kgs 4:6; 18:3; 2 Kgs 15:5; 18:18, 37; 19:2; Isa 22:15–24), and twelve officers over all Israel (1 Kgs 4:7).

The Davidic monarchy was understood to be much more than a political arrangement. For the authors of Scripture, it was a sacral kingdom that expressed God's rule on earth. This perspective is evident in several Psalms (Ps 2; 110) but especially in 2 Chr 28:15, where David asserts that God "has chosen Solomon my son to sit upon the throne of *the kingdom of the LORD* over Israel," and 2 Chr 13:8, which speaks of "*the kingdom of the LORD* in the hands of the Sons of David." This phrase "kingdom of the LORD" is the closest OT parallel to the NT phrase "kingdom of God."

Although the Davidic kingdom was the longest-lived dynasty of any in the ancient Near East, it came to an end at the hands of Nebuchadnezzar of Babylon in 586 B.C. (2 Kgs 25:1–26). After the return of the Judean exiles to Jerusalem under Cyrus the Great of Persia, hope for a restored kingdom was kindled when Zerubbabel, a Davidic descendant, was appointed governor of Judah (cf. Hag 2:20–23), but nothing materialized. Much later, hopes were kindled again, first by the Hasmonean Dynasty (134–67 B.C.), and then—to a lesser extent—by the Herodian Dynasty

(37 B.C.–66 A.D.), both of which controlled the throne of Jerusalem and expanded the borders of the kingdom almost to the extent of David and Solomon. However, neither dynasty was Davidic: the Hasmoneans (i.e., the Maccabees) were Levites, whereas Herod the Great and his descendants were Edomites (descendants of Esau).

Given this context of frustrated hopes for a restored Davidic kingdom in Israel, it is not surprising that both Matthew and Luke begin their Gospels by stressing Jesus's Davidic lineage (Matt 1:1; Luke 1:27, 32). Both Gospel writers are at pains to present Jesus as the royal Son of David, who will restore the Davidic kingdom and covenant. Thus Matthew relates that already at birth wise men came from the East to seek out the Christ child (Matt 2), whereas David's greatest heir, Solomon, only received this honor at the height of his career (1 Kgs 4:34). Likewise, when in Luke 1:31–33 Gabriel announces the conception of Christ to Mary, his words are taken almost verbatim from the key Davidic covenant text, 2 Sam 7:8–17, especially verses 13–16.

Jesus began his career by traversing Galilee, proclaiming "the kingdom of God is at hand" (Mark 1:14), and his preaching up to his Ascension focused on announcing and describing this kingdom (Acts 1:3). His emphasis on Kingdom is born out by statistics: the word "kingdom" (Greek *basileia*) is employed 137 times in the NT to refer to the Kingdom of God. Of these, 107 instances (78 percent) occur in the Gospels, of which 94 (68 percent) are found on the lips of Jesus himself.

Jesus began his ministry by proclaiming the Kingdom (Matt 3:2; Mark 1:15; Luke 4:43).

His longest recorded sermons focus on the Kingdom (Matt 5–7; Luke 6:20–49), and the majority of his parables teach about aspects of the Kingdom (Matt 13:1–51). Jesus's miracles, particularly the exorcisms, are signs that the Kingdom is near or even at hand (cf. Matt 12:28). At the Last Supper, he shares the Kingdom with the apostles, appointing them to positions of authority within it (Luke 22:29–30). After the Resurrection, the Kingdom is the main subject of Jesus's discourse with the disciples in the forty days prior to his Ascension (Acts 1:3).

Although references to the Kingdom of God predominate in Jesus's teaching, the Kingdom theme remains important in other parts of the NT. Teaching on the Kingdom introduces (Acts 1:3) and concludes (Acts 28:31) the book of Acts. The point of this literary "inclusion" is to show that the apostles, particularly Paul (cf. Acts 14:22; 19:8; 20:25; 28:23), continued Jesus's ministry of proclaiming the Kingdom. For his part, Paul mentions the Kingdom of God fourteen times in his Epistles (Romans–Philemon), often to warn that those who practice depraved behavior will not inherit it (1 Cor 6:9–10; Gal 5:21; Eph 5:5). Although the book of Hebrews seldom mentions the Kingdom explicitly, it clearly portrays Jesus as a Priest-King after the order of Melchizedek (Heb 7:1–9, 15–17), applies to him royal Davidic Psalms and prophecies (Heb 1:5–9), and describes his heavenly enthronement (Heb 1:3; 2:7–9). All this implies that Christ is reigning over his Kingdom even now. Near the end of Hebrews, approaching Jesus is described in language and images characteristic of the Davidic monarchy: "You have come to *Mount Zion* and the city of the living God, the heavenly *Jerusalem*, and to innumerable angels in festal gathering, and to the *church* of the firstborn who are enrolled in heaven . . . and to Jesus, the mediator of a new covenant" (Heb 12:22–24). This privilege to approach Christ the Priest-King enthroned in the heavenly Jerusalem evokes gratitude: "Let us be grateful for receiving a *kingdom* that cannot be shaken" (Heb 12:28).

In the book of Revelation, there are several key, explicit references to the Kingdom that indicate that the followers of Christ already participate in the Kingdom: "To him who loves us . . . and *made us a kingdom*, priests to his God and Father, to him be glory" (Rev 1:6; cf. Rev 1:9; 5:10). The Kingdom theme of the book is bolstered by the copious application to Christ of descriptive details drawing explicitly and implicitly on the traditions of the Davidic monarchy (Rev 1:5; cf. Ps 89:27; Rev 2:27; cf. Ps 2:9; Rev 3:7, 21; 5:5; 12:5; 22:16). The main setting for the action of the book is the heavenly palace-temple of God, where God sits enthroned (Rev 4:2) with his co-regent, the Lamb, near him (Rev 5:5–6, 13), surrounded by his vice-regents, the enthroned and crown-bearing elders (Rev 4:4). A climactic point is reached in Rev 11:15: "The kingdom of the world has become the kingdom of our Lord and of his Christ, and he shall reign for ever and ever." This concept of the heavenly Kingdom being definitively established over the earth is further developed in Rev 21–22, where the heavenly Jerusalem (David's capital city) descends to earth, from which God and the Christ-Lamb rule the cosmos. The continued emphasis on the royal Davidic identity of the Christ even to the end of the book—"I am the root and offspring of David" (Rev 22:16)—indicates that the Davidic kingdom has been joined to the Kingdom of God, in a way analogous to the joining of the human and divine natures in Christ.

II. THE KINGDOM OF GOD IN THE NEW TESTAMENT

A. Terms for the Kingdom of God

Although "Kingdom of God" is the most frequent term, the NT writers employ several other essentially synonymous phrases to describe the same reality. "Kingdom of heaven" is a variant entirely unique to Matthew, who employs it thirty-two times in instances in which the other Synoptics would have used "Kingdom of God." Variants used by other NT authors include "the kingdom of Christ and of God" (Eph 5:5), "the kingdom of his beloved Son" (Col 1:13), "the eternal kingdom of our Lord and Savior Jesus Christ" (2 Pet 1:11), and "the kingdom of our Lord and of his Christ" (Rev 11:15). In addition, Jesus speaks of "my kingdom" (John 18:36; Luke 22:30) and "my Father's kingdom" (Matt 26:29); others speak to Jesus of "your kingdom" (Matt 20:21; Luke 23:42), and there are many references simply to "the kingdom" without any modifier (Matt 24:14, 25:34; Luke 12:32; Acts 20:25). All of these variants may have slightly different connotations, but nonetheless they denote the same reality as the phrase "Kingdom of God." Some of them indicate clearly that there is no distinction between God's Kingdom and Christ's Kingdom (cf. 2 Pet 1:11; Rev 11:15).

B. The Three Theological Dimensions of the Kingdom of God

The Church Fathers identified three dimensions of the Kingdom of God, and all three remain perennially valid.

First, there is the Christological dimension, in which the Kingdom is Christ himself (Greek *autobasileia*). Jesus is the Incarnation of God's Kingdom. As King, he embodies the Kingdom and makes it present: where the King is, there is the Kingdom. Thus, in certain passages, Jesus indicates the Kingdom is already present in himself: "If it is by the finger of God that I cast out demons, then the Kingdom of God has come upon you" (Luke 11:20); or "Behold, the kingdom of God is in the midst of you" (Luke 17:21). This dimension may also be seen in the parables of the kingdom as a pearl of great price (Matt 13:45–46) or as a treasure hidden in a field (Matt 13:44). Christ is the pearl and the treasure, which one will give everything to possess.

Second, there is the idealistic or mystical dimension, in which the Kingdom is understood as being present in the heart (i.e., the inner person) of the believer. This is related to the previous view inasmuch as Christ the King dwells, through the Spirit, in the heart of each of his disciples (Eph 3:16–17). Origen, who first developed this view theologically, remarked that those who pray the Our Father "pray for the coming of the Kingdom which is already present in themselves." He added, "in every holy man it is God who reigns." This mystical sense may be seen if Jesus's statement "the kingdom of God is in the midst of you"

(Luke 17:21) is understood in the sense of "the kingdom of God is within each of you." Pope Benedict XVI summarizes this perspective by saying, "The kingdom of God is not to be found on any map . . . it is located in man's inner being."

Third, there is the ecclesiological dimension: the Kingdom is the Church. This dimension relates to the previous two because, on the one hand, the Church is in its essence the mystical body of Christ, who is himself the King and the Kingdom; on the other hand, the Church is the assembly of those within whom Christ the King dwells.

The ecclesiological dimension is clearest in some of the Kingdom parables of Matt 13. The Kingdom is compared to a field planted with both weeds and wheat, to be sorted only at the end of the age. Likewise, the Kingdom is like a net that catches fish both good and bad, and the latter are only removed by the angels at the end of the age. Both these parables indicate that the Kingdom is a present, although mixed, reality, that will be perfectly realized at the end of history. The present, mixed state of the Kingdom may be understood as the Church on earth, the Church Militant; whereas the future perfect realization of the Kingdom is the Church in heaven, the Church Triumphant, toward which the Church Militant is making her pilgrimage.

Other Kingdom teaching in the NT corroborates the ecclesiological perspective. Speaking to Nicodemus, Jesus says, "unless one is born of water and the spirit, he cannot enter the kingdom of God" (John 3:5). His words may be understood as a reference to baptism, through which one enters the Church. In this case, the Church is, in some sense, the Kingdom one enters by water and the spirit.

Paul explains to the Church in Colossae that God has already "delivered us from the dominion of darkness and transferred us to the kingdom of his beloved Son" (Col 1:13). Therefore, the members of the Church already participate in the kingdom (cf. Rev 1:6, 9; 5:10).

One of the clearest identifications of the Church with the Kingdom is found in Heb 12:22–28. The author first informs his readers that they have come "to Mount Zion and . . . the heavenly Jerusalem, and to innumerable angels in festal gathering, and to the *church* of the firstborn who are enrolled in heaven, and to a judge who is God . . . and to Jesus" (Heb 12:22–24; cf. Rev 21–22). After having so described the heavenly essence of the Church, in which his earthly readers even now participate, the author of Hebrews continues, "Let us be grateful for receiving a *kingdom* that cannot be shaken" (Heb 12:28). Thus, arriving at the "church of the firstborn" (Heb 12:23) is correlated with "receiving the kingdom" (Heb 12:28).

Finally, as was discussed previously, the book of Revelation is a sustained vision of the Church Triumphant gathered around God. Yet, simultaneously, the thrones, crowns, and other royal images make clear that the angels, saints, elders, and others gathered around the throne of God and the Lamb also constitute a kingdom.

In order to sustain the identification of the Church with the Kingdom, one must fully grasp the implicit teaching of Revelation that the Church in its essence is a *heavenly reality*. The Church in heaven, the Church Triumphant, is the fullest realization of the Kingdom. At the end of time, when all the members of the Church Militant have entered into the Church Triumphant, and therefore the Church Militant has ceased to exist—then the Church will be coextensive and identical with the Kingdom. In the meantime, however, it would be a mistake to deny that the Church Militant manifests the Kingdom and indeed truly is part of the Kingdom, even if imperfectly so. The dogmatic constitution on the Church *Lumen Gentium* states the relationship carefully and beautifully: "To carry out the will of the Father, Christ inaugurated *the kingdom of heaven on earth* and revealed to us the mystery of that kingdom . . . The Church, or, in other words, *the kingdom of Christ now present in mystery*, grows visibly through the power of God in the world" (LG §3). "The Church . . . receives the mission to proclaim and to spread among all peoples the kingdom of Christ and of God and to be, on earth, *the initial budding forth of that kingdom*. While it slowly grows, *the Church strains toward the completed kingdom* and, with all its strength, hopes and desires to be united in glory with its King (LG §1.5).

C. The Kingdom of God as Fulfillment of the Old Testament Types of Kingdom

Once the Kingdom of God is seen to be the Church, the fulfillment of the OT types of the kingdom in the Kingdom of God may also be recognized.

First and foremost, the Church is the fulfillment of the Davidic kingdom. It may be described as the restoration and transformation, or possibly as the transfiguration, of the kingdom of David. As the late Catholic biblical scholar Raymond Brown remarked, "The kingdom established by David . . . is the closest Old Testament parallel to the New Testament church." Thus, the characteristics of the Davidic kingdom (see above) are found both recapitulated and transformed by Christ. As David's kingdom was *underwritten by a divine covenant*, so Jesus's Kingdom is grounded on a New Covenant, established by the offering of his body and blood (Luke 22:20). Jesus is able to establish this covenant because he is *the Son of God* and *the Anointed One* in an even more profound sense than the Davidic kings of old: Son of God by nature, not adoption (cf. Luke 1:35), anointed not with oil but with the Holy Spirit (Luke 3:22; 4:1). This Kingdom is still *centered on Jerusalem*, but here an element of transformation or even translocation comes into play: the "capital" of the Kingdom is no longer the earthly, but the heavenly Zion/Jerusalem, as both Hebrews and Revelation stress (Heb 12:22–24; Rev 21:1–27). Similarly, the Son of David continues *to build the temple in this kingdom*, but the temple has been transformed. No longer a temple of stone, it is the temple of his body, both physical (John 2:21) and mystical (Matt 16:18; 1 Cor 12:27; Eph 4:15–16, 20–22). This temple-kingdom is truly *international*, as Christ extends his reign over Israel and all the nations (Matt 22:19; Luke 24:47; Rev 7:1–12). Christ's Kingdom retains *the royal administration* of David, including place of honor for the Queen Mother (Luke 1:42, 48–49; Rev 12:1), a role for the royal steward (Matt 16:18–19; cf. Isa 22:22), and the twelve officers over Israel (cf. 1 Kgs 4:7), the apostles, to whom Jesus literally "covenants" (Greek *diatithēmi*) the Kingdom, entrusting them with vice-royal authority (Luke 22:29–30).

Acts 15:1–21 shows the degree to which the apostles understood the Church to be the fulfillment of the Davidic monarchy. At the conclusion of the Jerusalem council, James endorses Peter's decision to admit Gentiles into the Church, in part because he understands it as a fulfillment of Amos 9:10–11: "After this . . . I will rebuild the tent of David which has fallen . . . that the rest of men may seek the Lord, and all the Gentiles who are called by my name." Yet Amos's phrase "the tent of David which has fallen" is, in context, a reference to the Davidic dynasty and kingdom—which was defunct in Amos's day. Amos's vision of the Davidic kingdom restored and the nations flocking into it, James sees fulfilled in the Gentile influx to the *Church*. Thus, James sees the Church as the transformed kingdom of David. The same concepts underlie Peter's sermon in Acts 2:29–36 and Paul's in Acts 13:22–23, 32–37).

Revelation 21–22 draws together in a striking way the themes of the Kingdom of God, the kingdom of David, and the Church in its vision of the New Jerusalem descending from God. First, one can identify the New Jerusalem as the Church, because it is described as "the Bride, the wife of the Lamb" (Rev 21:9; cf. Rev 21:2), a metaphor for the Church, as other Scriptures make clear (Eph 5:23–32; but ponder also Matt 22:1–14; 25:1–13). It is also built on "twelve foundations, and on them the twelve names of the twelve apostles" (Rev 21:14), which calls to mind the description of the Church "built on the foundation of the apostles" (Eph 2:20).

Second, one can identify the New Jerusalem as the Kingdom of God, or at least as its very heart and center, because it is the location of the throne of God and of the Lamb (Rev 22:1), from which they rule and guide the nations (Rev 21:24–26).

Third, one can identify the New Jerusalem as the kingdom of David, or at least as its heart and center. It is, after all, the New *Jerusalem*, the City of David (1 Kgs 8:1), his ancient capital (2 Sam 5:9), and there the Son of David, the Lamb who is "Lion of the tribe of Judah" (Rev 5:5), the "Root and Offspring of David" (Rev 22:16), rules from a throne shared with God.

Thus, the last two chapters of Revelation are a compressed metaphor showing, among other things, the fulfillment of the kingdom of David in the Kingdom of God, which is the heavenly Church.

In the Church-as-Kingdom, one sees the fulfillment of other OT kingdom types as well. Peter assures Christians that they constitute "a chosen race, a *royal priesthood*, a holy nation" (1 Pet 2:9). In other words, God's promise of a nation of priest-kings offered to Israel under Moses at Sinai (Exod 19:6) is realized in the Christian community.

The promise to Abraham that "kings shall come forth from you" (Gen 17:6) is most fully realized in Christ the King, through whom Abraham has become a "father of many nations" through faith (Rom 4:16–17).

Finally, the paradigmatic role of Adam as vice-regent over all creation is recapitulated in Christ, the New Adam (Rom 5:14), who makes the Church his body also into "one new man" (Eph 2:15), and together with his body exercises dominion over all things, which have been placed beneath his feet (cf. Gen 1:26, 28; Ps 8:3–9; Eph 1:20–23; Heb 2:6–9). For this reason, Revelation portrays the New Jerusalem, throne-city of the Lamb, also as a new Eden, whence the river of life flows (cf. Gen 2:10–14; Ezek 47:1–12; Rev 22:1–2), and where the Tree of Life grows (cf. Gen 3:22–24; Rev 22:2), the curse of the fall in Eden (Gen 3:14–19) having been removed (Rev 22:3).

KING'S GARDEN *See* **Kidron**.

KINGS, BOOKS OF Two of the Historical Books of the Old Testament; they continue the history begun in 1 and 2 Samuel. Like the books of Samuel, the books of Kings were originally a single work, divided only because the work was too long to fit on one scroll. Together they present a history of the kingdoms of Israel and Judah from the end of David's reign to the **Exile**.

In the Hebrew canon, 1 and 2 Kings come after Samuel as the fourth of the former prophets: Joshua, Judges, Samuel, and Kings. In the **Septuagint**, 1 and 2 Kings were known as 3 and 4 Kingdoms (our 1 and 2 Samuel being known as 1 and 2 Kingdoms), and the **Vulgate** adopted that numbering, calling them 3 and 4 Kings.

I. *Authorship and Date*

II. *Contents*

III. *Purpose and Themes*

    A. *The Scope of the History*

    B. *David, the Ideal King*

    C. *The Importance of the Temple*

    D. *Sin Brings Judgment*

    E. *Hope for the Future*

I. AUTHORSHIP AND DATE

Jewish tradition makes the prophet **Jeremiah** the author of the books of Kings (the same tradition claims Samuel as the author of the books of Samuel). Modern scholarship is disinclined to accept this judgment of the rabbis and is content to regard the author as unknown.

Many modern scholars contend that the books were edited by the so-called Deuteronomists, the writers responsible for the Deuteronomistic history—that is, the books from Joshua to 2 Kings, the connected history that traces the history of Israel from the conquest of Canaan to the Exile. All these books share a common interpretation of history: Israel prospers when faithful to the **covenant** with God, and disaster comes when Israel is unfaithful. The ultimate punishment is the Exile, which ends the whole cycle. The book of **Deuteronomy**, in this view, serves as the theological key to the history that follows.

The date of composition is uncertain. The author or authors wrote at a time after the start of the Exile. The last event mentioned (2 Kgs 25:27) is the release of **Jehoiachin** from captivity in Babylon (561 B.C.), so it is possible that the books were put in their final form at about that time; if so, the place of composition was probably Babylon.

On the other hand, the books preserve much older material. They rely on a variety of documents from the period before the Exile, some perhaps dating back to the time of Solomon: a history of the reign of Solomon (1 Kgs 11:41); annals of the kings of Judah (1 Kgs 14:29); and annals of the kings of Israel (1 Kgs 14:19).

Some suggest that a first edition of Kings appeared before the Exile, and that a second edition was crafted during the Exile.

II. CONTENTS

First and Second Kings are divided into three main parts, focusing on the reign of Solomon, the divided kingdom, and the fate of the kingdom of Judah.

I. *The Reign of Solomon (1 Kgs chaps. 1–11)*
   A. *The Death of David and the Accession of Solomon (1:1–3:15)*
   B. *The Wisdom and Government of Solomon (3:16–4:34)*
   C. *Solomon's Temple and Palaces (5:1–9:14)*
   D. *Solomon's Other Acts (9:15–10:29)*
   E. *Solomon's Last Years (11:1–43)*
II. *The Kingdoms of Judah and Israel (1 Kgs 12– 2 Kgs 17)*
   A. *The Division of the Kingdom (1 Kgs 12:1–19)*
   B. *Jeroboam of Israel (1 Kgs 12:20–14:20)*
   C. *Rehoboam of Judah (1 Kgs 14:21–31)*
   D. *Succeeding Kings of Judah and Israel (1 Kgs 15:1–16:28)*
   E. *Elijah (1 Kgs 17:1–21:26)*
   F. *The Destruction of Ahab (1 Kgs 22:1–40)*
   G. *Succeeding Kings of Israel and Judah (1 Kgs 22:41–53)*
   H. *Elijah (2 Kgs 1:1–2:12)*
   I. *Elisha (2 Kgs 2:13–6:7)*
   J. *The Struggle with the Arameans (2 Kgs 6:8–7:20)*
   K. *Elisha (2 Kgs 8:1–15)*
   L. *Succeeding Kings of Judah and Israel (2 Kgs 8:16–13:13)*
   M. *The Death of Elisha (2 Kgs 13:14–21)*

III. PURPOSE AND THEMES

A. *The Scope of the History*

The books of Kings offer a history of the kings of Israel and Judah from the end of the reign of David to the conquest of Jerusalem and the collapse of the Davidic monarchy in 586 B.C. The narrative concludes with a grim description of events after the fall of Judah, including the sad demolition of the Temple's bronze pillars, the appointment of **Gedaliah** as governor of Judah, and the release of Jehoiachin. The individual reigns are examined in a general chronological order, with the kings of both Israel and Judah connected in an alternating fashion that permits the reader to evaluate contemporary events and personalities.

B. *David, the Ideal King*

The narrative is worked out as an explanation of how and why the Exile came about—how it was inevitable, in fact, because the kingdoms were unfaithful to the covenants. The narrative begins with the transition from David to Solomon at the height of the monarchy and moves to the succeeding kings, who were unable to maintain the unity of the kingdom and who were feeble in comparison to the greatest of the kings in an earlier, more faithful time. David is depicted as the ideal king of Israel, the standard against which all others are measured (1 Kgs 9:4; 2 Kgs 22:2). The reign of David was followed by the long and largely glorious age of Solomon, under whom the Temple—Solomon's greatest achievement—was built, in accordance with the Davidic covenant (1 Kgs 8:14–21; cf. 2 Sam 7:8–17, and *see* **David**).

C. *The Importance of the Temple*

Worship of the Lord in the Temple is another standard by which all the succeeding kings are judged. **Jeroboam**, for example, is severely criticized for establishing other places of worship in the northern kingdom (1 Kgs 12–13). **Josiah**, on the other hand, is hailed for his efforts to bring authentic reform and a return to Temple worship; his reign was a final fleeting moment of fidelity to the Lord (2 Kgs chaps. 22–23).

D. *Sin Brings Judgment*

On the other hand, the reign of Solomon also began the slide into sin and apostasy that would ultimately lead to divine judgment. Solomon allowed his multiple wives (in defiance of Deut 17:17) to lead him into promoting the worship of false gods and turning away from the covenant. Indeed, the "high places" he established for the worship of foreign gods were still in existence during the reign of Josiah (2 Kgs 23:13). The king bore the moral responsibility for the kingdom. It was strengthened or weakened by the king's faithfulness to the laws in Deuteronomy.

In the time after Solomon, the kingdoms of Judah and Israel lapsed into sin, and their apostasy was exemplified by their kings. Chief among the godless kings was **Manasseh**, whose long list of sins can be compared directly to the violations of the covenant warned against in Deuteronomy (cf. 2 Kgs 21:2–9; Deut 17:2–4, 18:9–12). The seeds of Judah's final destruction were planted through his apostasy (2 Kgs 23:26–27). Indeed, the author of Kings does not even report what we learn from 2 Chronicles: that Manasseh repented when he was in distress and returned to the worship of the true God (2 Chr 33:10–17). Josiah tried to bring penance and reform, but it proved to be too late, for the fate of Judah had already been sealed.

E. Hope for the Future

The books of Kings conclude with the two kingdoms of Israel and Judah in ruins. Nevertheless, the narrative makes clear that God is merciful as well as just. God will remain faithful to his people and to the successors of David (1 Kgs 6:12; 11:12–13, 36; 2 Kgs 8:19; 19:34), so there is an implicit hope of a future restoration. Such promise is achieved only by returning to the love of the Lord expressed by embracing the covenant. Since the fate of the nation rode on the shoulders of the king, the concluding scene, with Jeconiah shown favor in exile, would give hope to the people as a whole (2 Kgs 25:27–30).

KIR An unidentified place in Mesopotamia to which the inhabitants of Damascus were exiled by the Assyrians after the city fell to **Tiglath-pileser III** in 732 B.C. (2 Kgs 16:9; cf. Amos 1:5). The name is used in Amos 9:7 as the original home of the Syrians.

KIR-HARESETH The capital of **Moab**, identified with the modern Kerak to the east of the Dead Sea. The strength of this strategic position was demonstrated when **Joram** of Israel, **Jehoshaphat** of Judah, and the king of Edom invaded Moab. **Mesha**, king of Moab, unable to withstand the combined attack, took refuge in Kir-hareseth and survived the siege. He stunned his attackers by sacrificing his firstborn son upon the walls of the city. His enemies retreated, either outraged or superstitiously terrified by the act (2 Kgs 3:25–27). Kir-hareseth is mentioned in various prophetic oracles, where it is sometimes spelled Lir-heres (Isa 16:7, 11; Jer 48:31, 36).

KIRIATHAIM The name of two places in the Old Testament.

1. A town in Moabite territory that belonged to the tribe of Reuben (Num 32:37; Josh 13:19). The city was later in the control of the Moabites, for the Mesha Stele declares that King Mesha rebuilt Kiriathaim and the city was under Moabite control in the time of **Jeremiah** (Jer 48:1, 23) and Ezekiel (Ezek 25:9). It is possible that the city was on the modern site of el-Qereiyat or Qaryat el-Mekhaiyet.

2. A Levitical city in Naphtali (1 Chr 6:76), possibly the same as Kartan in Josh 21:32; and the modern Khirbet el-Qureiyeh.

KIRIATH-ARBA See **Hebron**.

KIRIATH-JEARIM (Hebrew, "town of forests") Originally a Gibeonite city on the border between Judah (Josh 15:9) and Benjamin (Josh 18:14). Its older name, Kiriath-baal (Josh 15:60), suggests that it was probably the location of a shrine to the Canaanite god **Baal**. The city was also called Baalah (Josh 15:9). Kiriath-jearim was prominent in two major events in the Old Testament. First, Joshua made a covenant there with the inhabitants (Josh 9:17). Second, the **ark of the covenant** rested at Kiriath-jearim for twenty years after being brought there from Beth-shemesh following its return by the Philistines (1 Sam 7:1–2; cf. 2 Chr 1:4). Finally, Kiriath-jearim was the home of the prophet **Uriah** (Jer 26:20).

KIRIATH-SEPHER *See* **Debir.**

KISH The name of two men in the Old Testament.

1. The father of **Saul** and a member of the tribe of Benjamin (1 Sam 9:1; 10:21; 14:51).

2. The third son of Jeiel and Maacah and an ancestor of Saul and his father (1 Chr 8:30).

KISHON A river originating in the hills of Samaria that flowed into the Mediterranean to the north of Mount Carmel; it is probably the modern Wadi al-Muqatta. It figured in the victory of **Deborah** and Barak over Sisera (Judg 4:7, 13; 5:21; Ps 83:10): a heavy downpour caused its banks to overflow and flood the battlefield, paralyzing Sisera's chariots. The Kishon was also the place where **Elijah** put the prophets of Baal to the sword (1 Kgs 18:40).

KISS Kissing in biblical times had many related purposes. It was an act of greeting (Rom 16:16; 1 Thess 5:26; cf. Luke 7:45; 1 Pet 5:14); and the "holy kiss" was a common form of greeting in the early Church (cf. Acts 20:37; 1 Cor 16:20; 2 Cor 13:12). Kissing was a sign of family affection (Gen 27:27, 29:11, 33:4; Exod 4:27), a token of romantic love (Song 1:2), and

an act of religious dedication to an idol (Hos 13:2). It could also be a sign of identification (1 Sam 10:1), as when **Judas Iscariot** used a kiss to point Jesus out to the authorities (Matt 26:48).

KITTIM The descendants of **Javan**, according to the **Table of Nations** (Gen 10:4; cf. 1 Chr 1:7). They settled on the Mediterranean island of **Cyprus** and gave their name to the town of Kition (modern Larnaca). They developed a prosperous trade in marine commerce (Num 24:24; Isa 23:1, 12; cf. Jer 2:10; Ezek 27:6). After the **Exile**, the Kittim were identified broadly with other Mediterranean peoples such as the Greeks (1 Macc 1:1) and the Romans (Dan 11:30, and also in the **Dead Sea Scrolls**).

KNOWLEDGE In the Bible, "knowledge" is either the possession of reliable information acquired *intellectually* or a personal acquaintance with another acquired *experientially*. Knowledge of God is our ultimate aim, and giving us that knowledge is the purpose of Scripture. Through the use of reason, it is possible for us to come to know that God exists on the basis of his works (Wis 13:5; DV §6; *Dei Filius* 2). Nevertheless, there are obstacles to reaching that knowledge solely by the use of human reason (Pius XII, *Humani Generis* §561). Therefore, God chose to reveal himself, to communicate his divine life so that "men should have access to the Father, through Christ, the Word made flesh, in the Holy Spirit, and thus become sharers in the divine nature" (DV §2; cf. Eph 1:9, 2:18) (CCC 31–38, 40, 50–64).

I. KNOWLEDGE IN THE OLD TESTAMENT

Knowledge in the Old Testament is very often grounded in experience. It is also intensely relational. To "know" someone might describe sexual intimacy between a man and a woman (Gen 4:1, 17, 25; Num 31:18, 35; Judg 21:12; 1 Kgs 1:4); this is the extreme case of a general principle. Some sort of personal encounter was central to knowing a person. Thus, in describing the changed circumstances in Egypt, Exodus says that "a new king arose over Egypt, who did not know Joseph" (Exod 1:8); the new ruler, that is, did not recognize a relationship with the descendants of Joseph and was not bound by any previous obligations of his predecessors.

Knowledge can be passed on to another, but the knowledge is still passed on as an experience rather than as an argument (cf. Ps 98:2; 106:8). There must also be a conscious *decision* to know—to enter into the relationship that knowledge necessitates. This may be a moral decision. A person who resists evil must make the decision not to know evil: "Perverseness of heart shall be far from me; I will know nothing of evil" (Ps 101:4). Adam and Eve faced that moral decision in its starkest form: whether to eat the fruit from the tree of the knowledge of good and evil. Their wrong choice brought them self-consciousness of sinfulness: the Psalmist can say, "For I know my transgressions, and my sin is ever before me" (Ps 51:3).

Conversely, one enters into knowledge of the good through wise moral choices. Such decisions are reached by knowing the ways of the Lord and adhering to his commandments (Ps 119:79). Knowledge of the good is therefore knowledge of God. Such knowledge, again, is not simply accepting God's existence as an intellectual principle. It is entering into a relationship with him, surrendering entirely to his will and invitation, and fulfilling that surrender with prayer, praise, and adoration (cf. Deut 4:39, 8:5, 29:5; Jer 2:8, 9:2–5; Ps 9:11, 36:11, 87:4; Isa 43:10). The whole faith of Israel in the OT pointed toward knowing God in this way. Indeed, knowing God was the whole point of the Law: "For I desire steadfast love and not sacrifice, the knowledge of God rather than burnt offerings" (Hos 6:6).

II. KNOWLEDGE IN THE NEW TESTAMENT

The New Testament picks up the OT understanding of knowledge, with the crucial added teaching that God "desires all men [not just Israel] to be saved and to come to the knowledge of the truth" (1 Tim 2:4). Eternal life consists in knowing God *and* Jesus Christ, whom God sent (John 17:3).

In the NT, as in the OT, religious knowledge is both *personal* (John 17:3; Eph 3:19) and *propositional* (Mark 10:17–19; 2 Tim 2:25): that is, it involves knowing Christ and his love as well as knowing the truths and demands of the Gospel that Christ gave us.

Paul discusses the question of the intellectual or philosophical knowledge of unbelievers in Romans and First Corinthians. In Rom 1:18–23, Paul observes that the Greeks can know of God through natural reason: "For what can be known about God is plain to them, because God has shown it to them" (Rom 1:19). Philosophers therefore have no excuse for their unbelief. Yet the true knowledge of God revealed in Christ far surpasses the merely human wisdom of ancient sages and thinkers: "For the foolishness of God is wiser than men, and the weakness of God is stronger than men" (1 Cor 1:25).

Paul also describes knowledge as a divine gift or charism (1 Cor 12:8; 14:6)—a gift distinct from the knowledge of faith given to all believers. Faith and love are the foundations of the knowledge of faith (Eph 3:17–18), and its object is Jesus Christ and "the riches of his glorious inheritance in the saints" (Eph 1:18). Paul prays for an increase of such knowledge for the churches to whom he writes (1 Cor 1:5; 2 Cor 8:7; Eph 1:8, 17).

In John 14:6, Jesus tells us that knowledge of him is knowledge of the truth: "I am the way, and the truth, and the life; no one comes to the Father, but by me. If you had known me, you would have known my Father also; henceforth you know him and have seen him." The relationship that we have with Jesus mirrors the relationship between the Father and his Son (John 8:55). Love is the essential means of knowing God, for God is love (1 John 1:5; 4:8), and one who does not know love does not know God (1 John 4:16, 19–21). Equally, the one who knows God keeps his commandments (1 John 2:3–5), and to know the Son is to know the Father (John 10:37–38, 14:7; cf. Matt 11:27; Luke 10:22) (CCC 218–21).

KNOWLEDGE OF GOOD AND EVIL, TREE OF *See* **Eden**; *see also* **Fall, the**; **Sin**.

KOHATH The second son of **Levi** (Gen 46:11; Exod 6:16) and the ancestor of the Levitical clan of the Kohathites. He was the father of Amram (Exod 6:18; Num 3:19) and the grandfather of **Moses** and **Aaron** (Exod 6:20; Num 26:59). The Kohathites had the task of carrying the **Tabernacle** furniture and vessels (Num 3:31; 4:15–20; 7:9). During the wandering in the wilderness, they camped on the south side of the Tabernacle (Num 3:29). The clan at that time numbered some 8,600 males more than one month old (Num 3:28). At the time of the conquest of Canaan, the Kohathites were allotted twenty-three Levitical cities (Josh 21:4–5, 20–26), and in the days of the monarchy in Israel, their duties changed from carrying the Tabernacle furniture to providing music and security for the **ark of the covenant** and the **Temple** built by Solomon (1 Chr 6:31–38; 15:16–23).

KOHELETH *See* **Ecclesiastes**.

KOINE *See* **Hellenism**.

KORAH The name of two men in the Old Testament.

1. The third son of **Esau** and his Hivite wife, Oholibamah (Gen 36:5, 14, 18; 1 Chr 1:35).

2. The first cousin of Moses and Aaron, born to their uncle Izhar (Exod 6:18–21). A Levite and descendant of **Kohath** (Exod 6:21–24), Korah instigated a revolt against **Aaron** and the priesthood (Num 16:1–40).

KYRIOS *See* **Jesus Christ**.

LABAN The son of Bethuel (Gen 28:5), the brother of **Rebekah** (Gen 22:23; 24:29), and the father of **Jacob**'s wives **Leah** and **Rachel** (Gen 29:16). He lived in the city of Haran (Gen 27:43; 29:4) and is called an Aramean (Gen 25:20; 31:20). He is first mentioned in Gen 24:29 when Abraham decided to find a wife for his son **Isaac** (Gen 24:1–9). Abraham's servant **Eliezer** traveled to upper Mesopotamia (Gen 24:10) and made his way to Bethuel's house to ask for his daughter Rebekah as a wife for Isaac. Laban met Eliezer and invited him to his house (Gen 24:28–32) and was involved in the subsequent agreement (Gen 24:31, 53). Laban appears again in the account of Jacob (Gen 29–31). Jacob found safety from **Esau** in the house of Laban (Gen 31:38, 41), and his work for Laban led to his marriage to Leah and Rachel. After twenty years of service, Jacob left Laban's camp, and Laban followed him to recover his household gods (Gen 31:19–35). God then appeared to Laban in a dream (Gen 31:24) and warned him not to harm Jacob, so Laban entered into a covenant with Jacob (Gen 31:44–54).

LACHISH A city southwest of Jerusalem, identified as the modern Tell ed-Duweir. The ruler of Lachish took part in the coalition against the Israelites, and Lachish was soon captured by Joshua after a siege (Josh 10:31–32). After the conquest of Canaan, the city was allotted to Judah (Josh 15:39). **Rehoboam** fortified the city (2 Chr 11:9), and **Amaziah** was assassinated there after fleeing Jerusalem to escape a plot against him (2 Kgs 14:19; 2 Chr 25:27). In the campaign of **Sennacherib** of Assyria against Judah in 701 B.C., Lachish was captured and used as a base for the subsequent march against Jerusalem (2 Kgs 18:14–17; 19:8). The capture of Lachish was commemorated by Sennacherib with a panel in his palace at Nineveh. Later, during the campaign of **Nebuchadnezzar**, Lachish, with Azekah, held out for as long as possible (Jer 34:7) as the rest of Judah fell to the Babylonians. The city was eventually destroyed and later resettled by Judeans returning from the **Exile** (Neh 11:30).

LADAN The name of two men in the Old Testament.

1. Son of Tahan, of the tribe of Ephraim (1 Chr 7:26).

2. A Levite of the clan of Gershon (1 Chr 23:7–8; 26:21).

LADDER *See* **Jacob.**

LAHMAM A town in Judah, in the **Shephelah** (Josh 15:40), close to Lachish.

LAHMI The brother of the Philistine giant **Goliath**. He is mentioned only once, in 1 Chronicles 20:5, in which he is reported slain by Elhanan. In 2 Sam 21:19, Elhanan is said to be the slayer of Goliath, but this is most likely a scribal error, as **David** is the one who felled Goliath (1 Sam 17:1–51).

LAISH A city in northern Canaan, also called Leshem, that was captured by the Danites and renamed **Dan** in honor of the tribe (Josh 19:47–48; Judg 18:1–29).

LAKE OF GENNESARET *See* **Galilee, Sea of**.

LAMB The young of a sheep. The common sheep (*Ovis aries*) was domesticated thousands of years ago, starting almost certainly in Asia. Sheep provided both wool and food (Deut 32:14; Amos 6:4). Sheep are notorious for their mild manner and their utter dependence upon man for survival. Likewise, they are entirely docile and can be led to the slaughter without resistance. According to the **Law**, the lamb was to be used in many sacrifices: during the feast of Weeks (*see* **Pentecost**; Num 28:26–27), the feast of Tabernacles (Num 29:12–15), the **Day of Atonement** (Num 29:7–8), and the **Passover** (Exod 12:3–11).

The lamb was used as a metaphor for humans in their relationship with God, most notably in Ps 23, "The Lord is my shepherd." In 2 Sam 12:1–4, in **Nathan**'s parable indicting King David, a stolen ewe lamb is used as an image of Bathsheba, whom David stole from Uriah.

Jesus Christ is called Lamb of God because he offered himself as an expiatory sacrifice for the sins of the world (John 1:29).

The Suffering Servant in Isaiah is portrayed as a lamb (Isa 53:7), pointing toward Jesus's obedience to the Father (cf. Acts 8:32; 1 Pet 18, 19). Jesus is the Suffering Servant who goes to the slaughter without complaint, and who bears the sins of the multitudes. The whole of Jesus's mission from the Father leads to this: "I came down from heaven not to do my own will but the will of the one who sent me" (John 6:38), like the obedient lamb who goes willingly to his own slaughter.

In John's Gospel, Jesus is crucified at precisely the time the Passover lambs were being slain in preparation for the meal (John 19:14). None of Jesus's bones were broken, just as no bone of the Passover lamb was to be broken (John 19:36; cf. Exod 12:46). The recurrence of the Exodus theme in the New Testament shows that Jesus shed his blood as the spotless Lamb of a new and greater Passover (John 1:29, 19:36; 1 Cor 5:7; 1 Pet 1:18–19; Rev 5:6–10).

Thus we can see the sacrificial lambs of the Old Testament as types fulfilled in Christ the Lamb of God. Christ is the unblemished Lamb (Exod 12:5) provided by God, just as God provided a ram for Abraham to sacrifice instead of Isaac (Gen 22:9–14). Christ is the Lamb who takes away sin (John 1:29; cf. Isa 53). In the Eucharist, Christ is the Lamb of a sacrificial meal (1 Cor 5:7; cf. Exod 12:6–10). When the NT writers spoke of Christ as the Lamb, they had all the rich imagery of OT sacrifice in mind (CCC 613–14, 757, 796, 1328–29, 1602, 1612, 1642, 2618).

LAMB OF GOD *See* **Lamb**.

LAMECH The name of two men in Genesis.

1. Son of Methusael of the line of **Cain** (Gen 4:18–24). Lamech was also the husband of Adah and Zillah and the father of Jabal, Jubal, Tubal-cain, and Naamah. He is remembered as the first bigamist and the second murderer mentioned in Scripture. His song to his wives (Gen 4:23–25) boasts of his disproportionate revenge: "I have slain a man for wounding me, a young man for striking me. If Cain is avenged sevenfold, truly Lamech seventy-sevenfold"— also translated "seventy times seven." Jesus would turn Lamech's ethic of limitless revenge on its head, commanding that we forgive seventy times seven times (Matt 18:21–22).

2. The son of **Methuselah**, and the father of **Noah**, of the line of **Seth** (Gen 5:25, 28–30).

LAMED The twelfth letter of the Hebrew alphabet (ל).

LAMENTATION A song of sadness for misfortune, or a dirge for the dead. One-third of the Psalms are lamentations, and other similar lamentations are scattered throughout the Old Testament, both personal (e.g., Jer 11:18–23; 12:1–4; 17:14–18; 18:19–23) and communal (Neh 1:5–11; Isa 63:7–64:12; Jer 14:7–9, 17–22). The lamentation typically included an invocation to God, a lament concerning some disaster that has befallen a person or a people, a plea for divine intervention, and a statement of reasons that God should intervene, men-

tioning especially God's long history of coming to the aid of his people.

Along with the communal and personal lament was the dirge, a song of lamentation for the dead. These songs were sung by private mourners, such as the deceased's family and friends (e.g., 2 Sam 1:17–27; 3:33–34) and also by professional mourners (Jer 9:16). Such a dirge might be applied to an individual or to an entire kingdom or nation (cf. Amos 5:2; Ezek 26:17–18, 27:32–36, 28:12–19). (*See also* **Lamentations, book of.**)

LAMENTATIONS, BOOK OF A collection of five laments or elegies over the destruction of Jerusalem in 586 B.C. and the **Exile** of the people of **Judah**. Lamentations was included in the Hebrew Bible among the Writings; it is placed after Jeremiah in the Greek **Septuagint** and the Latin Vulgate. In the Catholic canon of Scripture, it is placed with the prophetic writings. The title is derived from the Hebrew title *qînôth*, "laments," which appeared in the Babylonian Talmud and in early rabbinic writings; the Greek title (*Thrēnoi*) was a translation of the Hebrew, and the heading in Latin versions was either *Threni* or *Lamentationes*. In the current Hebrew Bible, the book is known as *'ekâ*, which means "How!," taken from the first word of the book. Some manuscripts of ancient translations use the title "Lamentations of Jeremiah" or "Lamentations of Jeremiah the Prophet."

I. AUTHORSHIP AND DATE

The only certain date associated with Lamentations is the destruction of Jerusalem in 586 B.C. The traditional opinion has been that

Lamentations was composed a short time after the fall of the city. Indeed, the account of the siege and its horrors is so vivid and realistic that it is likely that the work was written by an eyewitness while the events were still fresh in his mind. The date estimated for composition is thus sometime during the Exile between 586 and 538 B.C.

Both Jewish and Christian tradition name **Jeremiah** as the author. Jeremiah was described as a prophet who weeps (Jer 9:1; 2 Chr 35:25), and there are stylistic similarities between the books of Jeremiah and Lamentations. The repeated stress on God's divine judgment in bringing about the destruction of the city also echoes the main theme of Jeremiah's prophecies. The attribution of the book to Jeremiah is not found in the Hebrew Bible, however, and many modern scholars reject it.

II. CONTENTS

Each chapter is a separate **lamentation**, complete in itself:

A. The desolation of Zion, the holy city.
B. The judgment of God and the fulfillment of his warnings, focusing on the way that "The Lord has become like an enemy; he has destroyed Israel" (2:5).
C. The cry of "the man who has seen affliction under the rod of his wrath" (3:1) and who endures divine wrath with patience. The chapter includes a plea for mercy and for relief: "I called on your name, O LORD, from the depths of the pit" (3:55).
D. The terrible state of Jerusalem and a contrast between its dark present and its glorious past. There is also the promise of restoration: "The punishment of your iniquity, O daughter Zion, is accomplished, he will keep you in exile no longer" (4:22).
E. A final petition for mercy and relief: "Restore us to yourself, O LORD, that we may be restored! Renew our days as of old! Or have you utterly rejected us? Are you exceedingly angry with us?" (5:21–22).

III. LITERARY STRUCTURE AND THEMES

The first four chapters of Lamentations are acrostic poems, thirty-six lines each (except for chapter 4, which uses forty-four lines). In chapters 1, 2, and 4, each couplet starts with successive letters of the Hebrew alphabet; chapter 3 uses each of the Hebrew letters for three successive one-line verses. Chapter 5 does not use an acrostic but has twenty-two verses, the number of letters in the Hebrew alphabet.

All five chapters are dirges that describe the emotional devastation that accompanied the violent conquest of Jerusalem and its people. The message is clear that God's wrath was divine justice exercised over the people because of their sin, but the author is also hopeful that God's love and mercy will bring relief and restoration. Part of chapter 3 is a personal lamentation, while the others are communal lamentations similar to those found in the Psalms (cf. Ps 44; 60; 74; 79; 80; 83; 89).

Theologically, Lamentations stresses that the cataclysm that struck Judah and the city of Jerusalem was brought about by the sinfulness of the people and their lack of fidelity to the Lord. The doom that came upon Jerusalem was forecast by the prophets, who warned against sin and foretold the righteous judgment of

God (Lam 1:8; 2:14). But the people abandoned their covenant with the Lord, leaving him no choice but to put the curses of the covenant into effect (cf. 1:5, 8–9; 3:40–42; 4:13; 5:7).

But there is still hope even amid the desolation. "The steadfast love of the LORD never ceases, his mercies never come to an end; they are new every morning; great is your faithfulness" (3:22–23). God is faithful to his covenant promises, and there is hope for those who have sinned and failed in their love for him (cf. Deut 30:1–10). Repentance and renewal are possible, "For the LORD will not cast off for ever, but, though he cause grief, he will have compassion according to the abundance of his steadfast love; for he does not willingly afflict or grieve the sons of men" (Lam 3:31–33).

LAMP A principal source of light in the biblical world other than daylight. The typical lamp in ancient times was a clay pot with oil in it, into which a wick was inserted to absorb and burn the oil gradually. The wick was made of flax or other materials, and the oil used in the lamp was normally olive oil, which was found in great abundance throughout the Mediterranean. Many examples have been found in excavations dating back to the third millennium B.C., so the development of the lamp has been well documented. Early versions were crude clay pots. In the fifth century B.C., the first metal lamps came into use. By Hellenistic and Roman times, lamps were a mass-produced commodity, available in all varieties from cheap little clay pots to large and elaborate bronze lamp stands. Some sort of lamp was found in virtually every home, and was usually kept burning because of the absence of natural light and because of the difficulty of relighting a lamp that had gone out.

The lamp stand was a common piece of furniture and has also been found in excavations. The lamp stand was mentioned as part of a wealthy household's furniture in 2 Kgs 4:10, but it is mentioned most frequently in a cultic context. About half the references to lamp stands in the Old Testament refer to the Tabernacle lamp stand (e.g., Exod 25:31–40; 37:17–24). Otherwise known as the menorah, the lamp stand had six branches extending out from a central shaft and a total of seven burning wicks (e.g., Exod 26:35, 40:4; Num 8:2–3).

The lamp's practical value in providing light made it an obvious symbol throughout Scripture. David was hailed as the "lamp of Israel" (2 Sam 21:17), an image that was also used for the perpetuation of his dynasty (1 Kgs 11:36; 15:4). The Lord was compared to a lamp (2 Sam 22:29; Ps 18:28; cf. Ps 119:105; Job 29:3). The extinguishing of a lamp signified destruction, such as that of Judah (Jer 25:10) or the wicked (Job 21:17).

In the New Testament, the lamp signifies the eye of the body (Matt 6:22; Luke 11:34) and the witness of Christian disciples in the world (Matt 5:14–16). John the Baptist was called a lamp (John 5:35). The bridal party was ready with lamps (Matt 25:1), as was the master's servant in charge of his house (Luke 12:35). Christ the glorious Lamb is also the lamp of the heavenly Jerusalem (Rev 21:23).

LANGUAGES OF THE BIBLE *See* **Aramaic**; **Hebrew**; **Greek**; *see also* **Versions of the Bible**.

525

LAODICEA A city in the Lycus Valley of Phrygia, in Asia Minor (Col 2:1; 4:13, 15). Laodicea was founded by the Seleucid ruler Antiochus II in the third century B.C. and named after his wife, Laodice. From the beginning, the city's position on the main trade route between the eastern and western Roman Empire made it a leading commercial center in Asia Minor. Its importance continued after it became part of the Roman province of Asia, when it became a banking center. Such was its wealth that after a severe earthquake in A.D. 60, it had no need of relief funds from Emperor Nero (Tacitus, *Ann.* 14.27). The city was also noted for its medical academy, its eye ointment, and its black wool textiles.

Laodicea probably first received the Gospel while **Paul** resided at Ephesus (Acts 19:10). Most likely, Paul did not establish the Church there; the credit for that goes to **Epaphras** (Col 4:13). Still, Paul assumed responsibility for the members of the Church in Laodicea and mentioned the community in his Letter to the Colossians (Col 2:1; 4:13–16). Paul commands that the Colossians read "the letter from Laodicea" (Col 4:16). The "letter from Laodicea" has not survived. It need not have been a letter that Paul wrote to the Laodicean Church, though it could have been. It is equally possible that it was a known letter of Paul's, such as Ephesians, that was then being circulated in the area.

The Church at Laodicea was one of the seven churches of Asia addressed in Revelation (3:14–22). Its spiritual state is described as "wretched, pitiable, poor, blind, and naked" (Rev 3:17). "I know your works: you are neither cold nor hot" (Rev 3:15). This may be a reference to Laodicea's two well-known neighbors: Colossae, which had cold drinking water, and Hierapolis, which had hot medicinal springs. Thus, Laodicea offered neither cool water to refresh nor hot water to heal. In Revelation, Jesus summons the city to wake up: "Behold, I stand at the door and knock; if any one hears my voice and opens the door, I will come in to him and eat with him, and he with me" (Rev 3:20; Song 5:2).

LAODICEANS, LETTER TO THE *See* **Laodicea**.

LAPPIDOTH The husband of the prophetess **Deborah**, presumably of the tribe of Ephraim (Judg 4:4). His name in Hebrew means "torches."

LASEA A city on the southern coast of Crete that is mentioned in the journey of Paul to Rome (Acts 27:8). It is possible that Lasea is the same place as the Lasos mentioned by Pliny (*Nat.* 4.12.59).

LASHA A city at the southern extreme of Canaan. Genesis 10:19 describes the territory of the Canaanites as extending "from Sidon, in the direction of Gerar, as far as Gaza, and in the direction of Sodom, Gomorrah, Admah, and Zeboiim, as far as Lasha." The exact location of Lasha has not been determined.

LAST JUDGMENT *See* **Judgment**; *see also* **Parousia**.

LAST SUPPER *See* **Eucharist**.

LASTHENES A Cretan who was an official under the Seleucid king **Demetrius II Nicator** during the time of **Jonathan** the high priest (1 Macc 11:20–37).

LATIN An Indo-European language that was the chief language of Rome and was commonly spoken throughout the western regions of the Roman Empire. Latin was one of the two main languages of the empire by the second century B.C., the other being **Greek** (the standard language in most of the East). Classical Latin (such as that of Cicero and Virgil), spoken chiefly by the educated, was called *sermo cotidianus*, or everyday Latin. The lower classes spoke the colloquial language of the streets, called Vulgar Latin—that is, the language of the *vulgus*, or common people. It was more adaptable and less formal than classical Latin. Vulgar Latin is the ancestor of the modern Romance languages: Portuguese, Spanish, Catalan, French, Italian, Romanian, and a number of others. Christian Latin—liturgical, canonical, and biblical—is basically a development of Vulgar Latin put to the service of the Gospel.

Latin is mentioned directly only once in the New Testament, in John 19:20, where Pilate places an inscription on the Cross of Christ in three languages: Hebrew (meaning **Aramaic**), Latin, and Greek. A number of Latin words and phrases appear in the NT, including *census, centurio, denarius, flagellum, legio, libertinus, praetorium, sicarius, taberna, titulus*.

LAW A pervasive concept in the biblical texts. For the most part, law was not a topic of abstract or philosophical reflection but was the concrete manifestation of God's will made known to his people. "Law" almost invariably means the Mosaic Law or *Torah*, which came to Israel through the mediation of **Moses**. The totality of life in biblical Israel was governed by the Law of the Lord, for it defined the obligations and expectations inherent in the covenant that bound Israel to the Lord and made it a nation set apart from other nations.

I. The Law in the Ancient Near East

II. Terms for the Law

III. The Codes of Israel

IV. The Law After the Exile

  A. Spiritual Renewal

  B. The Descent into Legalism

V. The Old Law

  A. The Old Law and the Natural Law

  B. The Old Law Was Temporary

  C. The Old Law Points to the New

VI. The New Law

  A. Not to Abolish, but to Fulfill

  B. The Old Law Was Perfected in the New

  C. "The Law of Christ"

I. THE LAW IN THE ANCIENT NEAR EAST

Legal codes in the ancient Near East have been found from as far back as the third millennium B.C. Codes such as those of Ur-Nammu of Ur (late third millennium B.C.), Lipit-Ishtar of Sumer (nineteenth century B.C.), Eshnunna (ca. nineteenth century B.C.), **Hammurabi** (late eighteenth century B.C.), and the laws of the Hittites, Assyrians, and the Neo-Babylonians show that there were already ancient legal traditions in Mesopotamia and Asia Minor when the laws of Israel were written down.

Not surprisingly, the Law that was given to Israel shows some similarities to other ancient legal codes. We can see a similarity between the covenant stipulations found in Exodus and Deuteronomy and the treaty stipulations used, for example, by the Assyrians and Hittites (*see* **Covenant**). Preambles and epilogues similar to what we find in the Old Testament can be seen in the law codes of Mesopotamian kingdoms. Curiously, no law codes have ever been found from ancient Egypt despite the flurry of archaeological investigation that has taken place there for more than a century.

II. TERMS FOR THE LAW

Jewish tradition divides the books of the Hebrew Bible into the Law, the Prophets, and the Writings. The Law, or Torah, was the most important of the three divisions. It was made up of the first five books: Genesis, Exodus, Leviticus, Numbers, and Deuteronomy—the **Pentateuch**.

The Hebrew *tôrâ* is the term most commonly translated "law" in the OT. It basically means "teaching" or "instruction" (Prov 1:8). In time, it also came to mean established legal precedents—judgments or decisions that were respected by later priests and adopted as legal precedent. When they received divine approbation, the legal decisions were given full binding force.

Other legal terms used in the OT include *miṣwâ*, "commandment," a rule or precept handed down from a higher authority; *mišpāṭ*, "judgment," used for a judicial decision and found especially in criminal law as a type of casuistic formulation (*see* **Judgment**); *ʿēdôt*, "testimonies," the revealed stipulations of God expressed through the covenant; *ḥōq*, "statute," something engraved and hence established as written law; *dābār*, "word," denoting a divine utterance and used especially for the laws enumerated in the **Ten Commandments** (cf. Exod 20:1; 24:3).

III. THE CODES OF ISRAEL

For the people of Israel, all laws, both civil and religious, had their origins in God. Obeying the law was part of being faithful to the covenant, for the commandments of the Torah were the stipulations of the covenant that defined Israel's responsibilities in relation to God and neighbor.

Israel's observance of the law assumed a greater urgency because violating God's law meant violating the covenant itself and rupturing our relationship with him.

The Pentateuchal laws are customarily divided into six main collections or codes:

1. **The Ten Commandments** (Exod 20:2–17): The precepts that guided the conduct of all people, expressing in substance the natural law engraved on the heart (cf. Gen 26:5; Rom 2:14–15) (CCC 2056–63, 2070–72).

2. **The Covenant Code** (Exod 20:23–23:19): A body of case law that regulated the social relationships, both civil and domestic, in the life of Israel. In particular, it envisioned the future life of the Israelites in Canaan. The statutes were to be enforced by the judicial system established by Moses in Exod 18:13–27.

3. **The Covenant Renewal** (Exod 34:10–26): The renewal of the Sinai covenant that was made necessary by the transgression of the

golden calf (Exod 32:1–6). The terms restate various laws already stipulated in the Ten Commandments and the Covenant Code. The most significant revision was that the firstborn sons of Israel had forfeited their priestly consecration (Exod 22:29) and therefore had to be purchased from the Lord by a redemption price (Exod 34:20). The tribes were detained at Sinai for a year while the process of covenant renewal was undertaken. The renewal also reiterates the prohibitions against idolatry.

4. The Priestly Code (Lev 1–16): Laws related to sacrifice in the **Tabernacle** (Lev 1–10) and laws related to ritual purification (Lev 11–16), the most important of which is the annual liturgy for the Day of Atonement (Lev 16; see **Atonement, Day of**).

5. The Holiness Code (Lev 17–27): The set of rules that stressed holiness as being essential for all of God's people: "You shall be holy; for I the LORD your God am holy" (Lev 19:2). The Holiness Code was intended to show the Israelites how to live in God's blessing. There were so many new laws because Israel's apostasy had proved that minute regulation was necessary. In particular, the statutes were to assist the Israelites in turning away decisively from idolatry and striving to be holy as Yahweh is holy (cf. Lev 11:44–45; 19:2; 20:7; 21:8). The code included moral laws (chaps. 18–20) that set Israel apart from the pagan practices of their Gentile neighbors and formed God's people in justice and charity; and liturgical laws (chaps. 17, 21–25) that defined sacred spaces (the Tabernacle), ministers and servants, and the proper liturgical feast days and

years dedicated to the Lord. A final chapter (Lev 27) stipulates vows and tithes.

6. The Deuteronomic Code (Deut 12–26): The terms of the Deuteronomic covenant made at Moab, with Moses as covenant mediator. The code serves as a kind of charter or constitution that governs Israel's life as a nation-state established in Canaan. One purpose of the code is to control unfaithful Israel through a permanent state of strict discipline. The code thus includes laws for worship and piety (Deut 12:1–16:17); civil and sacred leaders (Deut 16:18–18:22); criminal and judicial laws (Deut 19:1–21:9); social and domestic laws (Deut 21:10–25:19); offerings, tithes, and exhortations (Deut 26:1–19). Moral and legal concessions were also made by Moses to permit lesser evils in the hope of preventing even more severe ones by regulating them (Exod 24:1–4). For example, Israelites were permitted to divorce and remarry (Exod 24:1), to wed foreign slave wives (Deut 21:10–14), to wage savage warfare in Canaan (Deut 20:16–17), and to establish a monarchy in Israel (Deut 17:14–20). As Jesus taught, "For your hardness of heart Moses allowed you to divorce your wives, but from the beginning it was not so" (Matt 19:8).

IV. THE LAW AFTER THE EXILE

A. Spiritual Renewal

When **Cyrus** the Great permitted the restoration of Jerusalem and the Temple in 538 B.C., it was not just the Temple that had to be rebuilt. The renewal focused on the Torah as well as the Temple. The whole religious life of the nation had to be reconstructed, and the

Exile had taught the remnant of Israel what the consequences of failure could be. Under **Ezra**, a renewal of faith and liturgy swept the whole community. The Law was respected as it never had been before the Exile.

B. The Descent into Legalism

But the newfound respect for the Law could easily lapse into legalism. Too easily, the Law could become a series of outward acts without inward commitment. The prophets warned against the danger of thinking the substance of the Law had been fulfilled by mere ritual: "Oh, that there were one among you who would shut the doors, that you might not kindle fire upon my altar in vain! I have no pleasure in you, says the LORD of hosts, and I will not accept an offering from your hand" (Mal 1:10).

The **Pharisees** exemplified both sides of the revival of the Law. They taught respect for the Law and earned great popular respect for their sincere attempts to follow every letter of it. On the other hand, they were also known for their excessive scrupulosity in observing the smallest details of the Law. They built up a body of ever more detailed interpretations and found clever loopholes in the wording of the Law to avoid observance (Matt 15:1–6; Mark 7:1–13; Luke 11:37–42).

This excessive legalism was what brought so many sharp rebukes from Jesus. "You have a fine way of rejecting the commandment of God, in order to keep your tradition!" Jesus said (Mark 7:9–13).

> For Moses said, "Honor your father and your mother"; and, "He who speaks evil of father or mother, let him surely die"; but you say, "If a man tells his father or his mother, What you would have gained from me is Corban" (that is, given to God)—then you no longer permit him to do anything for his father or mother, thus making void the word of God through your tradition which you hand on. And many such things you do. (Mark 7:10–13)

Yet Jesus still respected the role of the Pharisees as teachers. "The scribes and the Pharisees sit on Moses' seat; so practice and observe whatever they tell you, but not what they do; for they preach, but do not practice" (Matt 23:2–3).

V. THE OLD LAW

A. The Old Law and the Natural Law

Christians speak of the Law of Moses as the "Old Law." The Old Law is the first stage of revealed law. When God chose Israel as his people and prepared the world for the coming of Christ through them, he gave them the Law to form them in holiness and goodness. The Law of Moses expressed many truths of natural law. The Ten Commandments prohibit what is contrary to the love of God and neighbor and instruct us to avoid evil. They train our conscience to recognize the fundamentals of natural law. Christ confirmed the enduring validity of the Ten Commandments and said they are summed up by the double commandment of love (Matt 22:34–40). He also taught that we must keep the commandments in order to inherit eternal life (Luke 18:18–23).

B. The Old Law Was Temporary

But the Old Law contained much that was transient and temporary, regulations pertaining to the diet and ceremony that were imposed as probationary measures upon a rebellious son (Deut 9:7) who must be controlled by a permanent state of strict discipline under the terms of the covenant. These temporary laws were fulfilled with the coming of Jesus Christ, who brought everything that the Old Law could not: the Spirit, the forgiveness of sin, and true freedom to live in love, charity, and fidelity to God.

C. The Old Law Points to the New

The Old Law is holy, spiritual, and good, and it serves to give direction and to disclose sin, but it is still imperfect (Rom 7:12, 14, 16; Gal 3:24). It revealed sin and even restrained sin to a point. It was also an education in humility: it exposed our inability to live according to God's high standards relying on our own strength. But it was unable to redeem Israel from sin through forgiveness and the interior help of the Spirit. Instead, "the law was our custodian until Christ came" (Gal 3:24). It guarded God's people, saving them from their worst tendencies, until the time was right for the Gospel. It prepared them to appreciate the greatest commandment. As Jesus taught: "You shall love the Lord your God with all your heart, and with all your soul, and with all your mind. This is the great and first commandment. And a second is like it, You shall love your neighbor as yourself. On these two commandments depend all the law and the prophets" (Matt 22:37–40).

The Old Law remained the first step on the path to the New Law, the preparation for the Gospel that will inscribe the Law on the human heart. The Old Law anticipated the Law that would bring liberation from sin and would be fulfilled in Christ. (CCC 1961–64, 2059).

VI. THE NEW LAW

A. Not to Abolish, but to Fulfill

Jesus addressed the Old Law in the **Sermon on the Mount**: "Think not that I have come to abolish the law and the prophets; I have come not to abolish them but to fulfill them. For truly, I say to you, till heaven and earth pass away, not an iota, not a dot, will pass from the law until all is accomplished" (Matt 5:17–18). Jesus alone was capable of keeping the Law perfectly (1 Pet 3:22–23). The people under the Old Law were incapable of observing the Law in its entirety without violating some of its precepts. "Whoever keeps the whole law but fails in one point has become guilty of all of it" (Jas 2:10; cf. John 7:19; Acts 13:38–41, 15:10; Rom 10:2; Gal 3:10, 5:3) (CCC 577–78).

B. The Old Law Was Perfected in the New

Christ revealed that in him the Old Law reached its fulfillment, its perfection, and its chief purpose. Jesus, as teacher of the Law, actually raised the standard of observance of the Law by applying its demands, not only to outward acts, but also to the thoughts and intentions of the heart. He calls for "righteousness" that surpasses that of the Pharisees (Matt 5:20).

Whereas the Law of Moses was meant to form and guide Israel in the proper worship of God and so prepare for the coming of the Messiah, the New Law—the Law of the New Covenant and the Kingdom of God—encompasses all the nations of the earth. Consequently, many of the Old Laws of Israel, such as those regarding diet (Mark 7:18–21; Gal 3:24) and divorce and remarriage (cf. Deut 24:1–4; Isa 50:1; Jer 3:8; Matt 19:6, 8; 1 Cor 7:10–11), were no longer necessary, as they had fulfilled their function. The ceremonial laws of Moses had fulfilled their role of being types and figures of the ideal and perfect sacrifice and sacraments of the New Law. Through his death on the Cross, Jesus took upon himself the curses of the Law and sealed the New Covenant (cf. Jer 31:33; Isa 42:3; Gal 3:13; Heb 9:15).

C. "The Law of Christ"

"Bear one another's burdens, and so fulfill the law of Christ" (Gal 6:2). We are children of God and heirs with Christ, and our faith prompts us to imitate Christ (Matt 11:29; 1 John 2:6)—not out of duty, but out of joy. We also must follow his instructions to love one another (Matt 22:35–40; John 13:34) and to keep the commandments (Matt 19:17–18).

In early Christian catechesis, the standard of the *moral life* is still defined by the precepts of the Decalogue (Rom 13:8–10; 1 Cor 7:19; Gal 5:13–14; Eph 6:2; Jas 2:8–12). The new reality is that the Spirit enables us to fulfill the righteous demands of the Law (Rom 8:2–4).

Christian moral life is also rooted in Christ's love: "A new commandment I give to you, that you love one another; even as I have loved you, that you also love one another" (John 13:34). Every Christian is called to share in the grace and the love of Jesus who came "not to be served but to serve, and to give his life as a ransom for many" (Matt 20:28). Pope John Paul II tied grace and love together when he wrote,

Following Christ is not an outward imitation, since it touches man at the very depths of his being. Being a follower of Christ means becoming conformed to him who became a servant even to giving himself on the Cross (cf. Phil 2:5–8). Christ dwells by faith in the heart of the believer (cf. Eph 3:17), and thus the disciple is conformed to the Lord. This is the effect of grace, of the active presence of the Holy Spirit in us. (VS §21)

Following Christ is the very foundation of Christian morality. Following Christ is not a matter of simply following a commandment. Christian morality evokes a more radical response: "holding fast to the very person of Jesus, partaking of his life and his destiny, sharing in his free and loving obedience to the will of the Father" (VS §19). In so doing, the disciple of Jesus becomes a disciple of God (CCC 1691–96, 1716–24, 1730–42, 1914–74, 1987–2005, 2052–74). (*See* **Covenant**; *see also* **Freedom**; **Love**.)

LAWYER The title is used once in Matthew (22:35) and six times in Luke (7:30; 11:45–46; 14:3; 10:25) to refer to a legal scholar or scribe.

LAZARUS (Hebrew, "God helps") The name of two men in the New Testament, one a character in a parable and the other a friend of Jesus. It is possible that the two are really the same person, though decisive evidence is lacking to confirm the identification.

1. The name of a poor man who appears in a parable of Jesus in Luke 16:19–31; Lazarus is the only proper name to appear in one of Jesus's parables. In the parable, Lazarus dies and is carried by the angels to **Abraham's bosom**, while a rich man who made no effort to relieve the afflictions of the poor man dies

and is carried to the flames of Hades (CCC, 633, 1021, 2463, 2831). Jesus may have had his friend Lazarus of Bethany in mind when he told this parable.

2. A resident of the village of Bethany and the brother of **Martha** and **Mary**. This Lazarus was raised from the dead by Jesus (John 11–12). Lazarus was loved by Jesus (John 11:3, 5, 36) as a friend (John 11:11); in the narrative, he does not speak. His death, which caused Jesus to weep, is vividly described and confirmed in the fourth Gospel: John points out the four days Lazarus spent in the tomb (John 11:6, 17, 39; cf. John 11:13–14), Martha's fear of the stench of death (John 11:39), and Lazarus's state in the tomb wrapped in cloths (John 11:44).

The resurrection of Lazarus is the sixth of the seven "signs" performed by Jesus in John's Gospel. Similar resurrection miracles are recorded elsewhere in the Synoptic Gospels (cf. Mark 5:21–43; Luke 7:11–17). Jesus used the death of Lazarus as a means of glorifying God (John 9:3) that would also promote the faith of the disciples (John 11:15, 42) and manifest with great clarity the truth of Jesus's authority (CCC 994). (*See also* **Resurrection**.)

The resurrection of Lazarus was also the last of Jesus's signs before the Passion, and it spurred the enemies of Jesus into action against him. Thus the resurrection of Lazarus was a sign of Jesus's own Resurrection and triumph over death and the grave, which itself was the final sign of Jesus's power (John 11:45–53, 12:10–11; cf. Mark 11:18; Luke 19:47–48) (CCC 640, 2604).

LEAH (Hebrew, "cow") **Jacob**'s first wife, the firstborn daughter of **Laban**, and the sister of **Rachel**. Leah was given to Jacob as his wife through deception after Jacob had toiled for seven years in anticipation of marrying Rachel. Although Jacob was allowed to take Rachel as his wife a week later, Laban demanded seven more years of work in payment (Gen 29:15–28). Leah gave Jacob six sons and a daughter: **Reuben**, **Simeon**, **Levi**, **Judah**, **Issachar**, **Zebulun** (Gen 35:23), and **Dinah** (Gen 30:14–21). Zilpah, Leah's maid, gave birth to two sons by Jacob, **Gad** and **Asher** (Gen 30:9–13).

Leah, the older sister and the first wife, is described in Genesis as being unloved (Gen 29:31) by Jacob and unattractive (Gen 29:17). Rachel, on the other hand, was the younger sister and Jacob's second wife, but she was loved, even though she was barren until the birth of **Joseph** (Gen 30:1–2, 22–24). The two thus competed for Joseph's attention and struggled for prominence in the household—a struggle that was epitomized by the conflict over the mandrakes (Gen 30:14–20), herbal roots thought to enhance fertility. Despite her supposed superior position as Jacob's fertile wife, Leah bargained away the mandrakes for a night with Jacob, during which she conceived her fifth son (Gen 30:17). Leah journeyed to Canaan with Jacob and was buried with him in the cave of Machpelah (Gen 49:29–31), the same cave in which Abraham was buried with Sarah and Isaac with Rebekah (cf. Gen 23:1–20). With Rachel, Leah is honored as a matriarch and founder of the house of Israel (Ruth 4:11).

LEAVEN An agent added to bread dough that causes fermentation. Bread that was leavened contained yeast or a similar substance; it was kneaded and allowed to rise before baking. Leavened bread was forbidden during the feasts of Passover and Unleavened Bread (Exod 23:18; 34:25) to remind the Israelites of their hurried flight from Egypt (Exod 12:33–34).

Leavened bread could not be used for most sacrifices burned on the altar (Lev 2:11). The reason for this is not specified, but in time leaven came to symbolize corruptive influences in religion. Leaven was thus used as a symbol for the hypocrisy of the Pharisees (Mark 8:15; Luke 12:1). Paul uses the image of leaven to contrast between "the old yeast, the yeast of malice and evil," with "the unleavened bread of sincerity and truth" (1 Cor 5:8; cf. Gal 5:9). On the other hand, Christ used the image in a positive way in his Parable of the Yeast, emphasizing how a little leaven works to rise a whole batch of dough (Matt 13:33; Luke 13:20).

LEBANON A mountain range that extends north to south from lower Syria into upper Galilee. The name is derived from the Semitic root *lbn*, "to be white," and refers most likely to the whiteness of the snow-covered mountaintops (Jer 18:14). The range reaches heights of nearly 10,000 feet (over 3,000 meters). The Lebanon Mountains are divided from the Anti-Lebanon Mountains by a deep valley along the eastern side, the Beqa', approximately five to eight miles (8 to 13 kilometers) wide. The region encompassed by ancient Lebanon roughly corresponds to the modern republic of Lebanon.

Lebanon is mentioned nearly seventy times in the Old Testament. It was renowned for its lush landscape (Jer 22:6), its abundant fruits (Ps 72:6), and its pleasing fragrances (Song 4:11; Hos 14:6–7). Not surprisingly, it was marked out as the northern frontier of the Promised Land (Deut 11:24; Josh 1:4), although Israel was unable to gain possession of Lebanon until the time of the United Monarchy (1 Kgs 9:19; 2 Chr 8:6). Occasionally, the tall trees of Lebanon were used to symbolize the pride of peoples that the Lord threatened to bring low (Isa 2:12–13, 10:33–34; cf. Ps 29:5). More often, the great cedars of Lebanon are celebrated as a magnificent building material sought out by many nations of the ancient Near East. Israel was no exception, and indeed large quantities of timber from Lebanon were used to build such monuments and structures as David's royal residence (2 Sam 5:11) and Solomon's great **Temple** (1 Kgs 5:6; 6:9, 15–18) and armory (1 Kgs 7:2–5).

LEBBAEUS *See* **Thaddeus**.

LEGION The principal division of the Roman army, equaling approximately four thousand to six thousand soldiers, along with cavalry support and auxiliary units. The typical legion was subdivided into ten cohorts, which in turn were broken down into five or six centuries, each under the command of a centurion. The Roman legion was one of the most successful and feared forces in the ancient world.

The word "legion" does not appear in the New Testament in reference to the Roman army, although there were at the time of Christ three or four legions stationed in the Roman imperial province of Syria. Detachments of Roman units in Palestine were likely Roman *auxilia* (or auxiliary cohorts), until the Jewish War (A.D. 66–70) brought the full weight of the legions into the area. Roman troops nevertheless would have passed through Palestine on their way to different postings and theaters of operation.

There are four occurrences of the word "legion" (Greek *legiōn*) in the NT, all in reference to a large number of spirits, whether angels or demons. In Matt 26:53, "legion" implies a host of angels. In Mark 5:9, 15 and Luke 8:30, the word "legion" is used for the name of a group of demons ("for we are many") that was then possessing the man of Gerasa.

LEHABIM An otherwise unknown people, described as the descendants of Egypt, the grandson of Noah (Gen 10:13; 1 Chr 1:11).

LEHI (Hebrew, "jawbone") An unknown location in Judah where **Samson** slew a thousand Philistines with the jawbone of a donkey (Judg 15:14–17).

LEMUEL The king of Massa, who wrote down a collection of wise sayings that were taught to him by his mother and preserved in Prov 31:1–31.

LENTIL A plant of the pea family that is abundant in the Middle East. Lentil seeds were made into bread (Ezek 4:9) and stew (Gen 25:34). **Esau** sold his birthright as firstborn for boiled lentils (Gen 25:34), and **David** received lentils as a gift (2 Sam 17:28).

LEOPARD A carnivorous cat, *Felis pardus*, found in Asia and Africa. It was not common in ancient Palestine but was known to inhabit the mountains of Lebanon (Song 4:8). The leopard appears in the Old Testament in figurative language to express stealth and ferocity (Jer 5:6; Hab 1:8). Jeremiah declared that Judah could no more change its wicked ways than a leopard could change its spots (Jer 13:23). The Lord is compared to a leopard ready to pounce on the wicked of Israel (Hos 13:7), and in eschatological times it was said that the leopard would lie down with the kid (Isa 11:6).

LEPROSY Known today as Hansen's disease and caused by the bacillus *Mycobacterium leprae*. In Scripture, the term "leprosy" is used for a wide variety of skin diseases or conditions as well as lesions or infections that might occur on the skin, on fabrics, and even on the walls of houses (Lev 13:47–59; 14:33–53). The diagnosis and purification rites in Lev 13–14 were not for leprosy in the modern medical sense but for skin infections. Anyone diagnosed with such an infection had to be quarantined to determine whether the disease would spread. A person who was healed had to present himself to the priest, who would provide confirmation that he was clean (Lev 13:3, 9–10; Mark 1:40–45). As "leprosy" rendered the victim unclean, purification was necessary.

Several specific cases of leprosy are mentioned in the Old Testament: **Moses** (Exod 4:6) and **Miriam** (Num 12:10); **Naaman** (2 Kgs 5:1); Geahzi (2 Kgs 5:25); King **Uzziah** (2 Kgs 15:5); and the four lepers at the siege of Samaria (2 Kgs 7:3). In the New Testament, Jesus cured lepers (Matt 8:1–4; Luke 5:12–16, 17:11–19) and gave that power to his disciples (Matt 10:8). Jesus was also given welcome by Simon "the Leper" of Bethany (Matt 26:6; Mark 14:3).

LETTER *See* **Epistle.**

LEVI, LEVITES Levi was the third son of Jacob and Leah (Gen 29:34) and the ancestor of the tribe of Levi (Exod 6:16–25; Deut 33:8–11; 1 Chr 6:1–81). For most of biblical history, the tribe of Levi is set apart as the clerical tribe in Israel, entrusted with all matters related to worship and religious instruction.

I. LEVI AND HIS DESCENDANTS

The patriarch Levi himself participated with Simeon in the massacre of Shechem (Gen 34:25–26). For this act, Jacob cursed the violence of Levi and Simeon and foresaw their being scattered among the other tribes (Gen 34:30).

The descendants of Levi included **Gershon**, **Kohath**, and **Merari** (Gen 46:11; Num 3:17), **Moses** (Exod 6:16–20), **Aaron** (Exod 4:14), and **Zadok** (1 Chr 6:1–8). Thus Levi was the ancestor of all of the religious leaders and ministers of worship of Israel: Levites, Aaronites, and Zadokites. Prominent Levites in the New Testament include **John the Baptist** (Luke 1:5, 57–63) and **Barnabas** (Acts 4:36).

II. THE LEVITES BECOME MEDIATORS

After the Exodus journey to Mount Sinai, the tribe of Levi was chosen for ministerial service as a reward for their zeal. When Moses descended from the mountain and discovered the Israelites worshipping the golden calf, Moses stood in the gate of the camp and called out, "Who is on the LORD's side? Come to me." The Levites came to his call, and Moses commanded them to exact terrible punishment upon the idolators: "Put every man his sword on his side, and go to and fro from gate to gate throughout the camp, and slay every man his brother, and every man his companion, and every man his neighbor" (Exod 32:27). In all, the Levites killed three thousand of their kinsmen, and at the end Moses declared, "Today you have ordained yourselves for the service of the LORD, each one at the cost of his son and of his brother, that he may bestow a blessing upon you this day" (Exod 32:29).

III. THE DUTIES AND PRIVILEGES OF THE LEVITES

The Levitical priesthood was first instituted as part of the covenant renewal necessitated by Israel's apostasy with the golden calf (Exod 28–29). Whereas before all the firstborn sons of Israel were consecrated for the priesthood (Exod 13:2; 22:29), now there would be a separate class of clerics confined solely to the tribe of Levi (Num 3:41, 45). To this tribe alone belonged the ministry of word and sacrifice in Israel (Deut 33:8–10).

The structure of this clerical leadership was threefold. Within the tribe of Levi, Aaron and his line of descendants received the priesthood (Exod 40:12–15), with Aaron himself acting as the high priest and his sons as priests of lesser rank (Lev 8:5–13; 21:10). Men of the tribe of Levi who were not descendants of Aaron made up the corps of the Levites and were given the responsibility of guarding and transporting the Tabernacle and serving as assistants to the priests (Num 1:47–54; 18:1–6). The three Levitical clans of Kohath, Gershon, and Merari were each entrusted with maintaining and moving specific parts of the sanctuary (Num 3:21–37). Because the Levites were sacred ministers, they were exempt from military duty, which is why the Levites were numbered separately from the lay tribes (Num 1–3).

When the **Temple** of Solomon was built, the portable Tabernacle was no longer used as a sanctuary. The duties of the Levites thus changed at the time of the United Monarchy, when they first began to serve as liturgical cantors and musicians (1 Chr 25), gatekeepers (1 Chr 26:1–19), and stewards of the Temple treasuries (1 Chr 26:20–28). Others were assigned to be judges and tax officers who would be distributed throughout the tribal territories (1 Chr 26:29–32).

For all these duties, the Levites were to receive tithes (Num 18:21–24), along with forty-eight designated cities in the territories of the twelve tribes (Josh 21:1–42).

IV. THE LEVITICAL COVENANT

At least three times Scripture refers to this new configuration of priestly ministry as a "covenant" made with the tribe of Levi (Sir 45:7; Jer 33:21; Mal 2:4), part of the renewal of the Sinai covenant that was made necessary after the apostasy of the golden calf. The Levitical covenant included all laws related to priestly ordination and vestments (Exod 28–29), precepts governing the liturgical rites of sacrifice (Lev 1–7), and festival times (Lev 16, 23), and all that pertained to ceremonial purity (Lev 11–15). The covenant with Levi, in other words, finds its literary expression primarily in the book of **Leviticus**, although it also includes

some of the cultic prescriptions found in **Exodus** (Exod 25–31) and **Numbers** (Num 3–6; 15; 18–19; etc.). The Levitical covenant, which regulates the religious leadership of Israel under the leadership of the Levites, thus differs from the Deuteronomic covenant, which primarily regulates the civil life of Israel as a nation established in the land of Canaan.

LEVIATHAN A reptilian sea monster in ancient Semitic mythology. It is believed to represent the "chaos" that threatens the divine order established by God or the gods. In Ugaritic texts, it appears under the name Lotan, a creature with seven heads, and is defeated by the warrior god **Baal**. The Psalms use a similar image of Leviathan defeated by the Lord to describe the power of creation: "You crushed the heads of Leviathan; you gave him as food for the creatures of the wilderness" (Ps 74:14). Some interpreters see Leviathan in this verse as a symbol of the **pharaoh**, crushed during the **Exodus**. In Isa 27:1, the Lord will punish "Leviathan the fleeing serpent, Leviathan the twisting serpent" on the day when Israel is delivered. The "great red dragon" in Rev 12:3 is similarly defeated by the forces of heaven; its seven heads recall the Leviathan of Canaanite mythology, and this time the creature is positively identified as "that ancient serpent, who is called the Devil and Satan" (Rev 12:9).

The book of Job gives us a detailed description of Leviathan (Job 41:1–34); many interpreters think this passage refers to a Nile crocodile, which is still common in Egypt today. On the other hand, the description of

Leviathan breathing fire and smoke (Job 41:19–21) may suggest a mythological creature is in view. In any case, the Lord humbles Job by making it known that the Lord alone can master the cosmic forces that are hostile to his lordship over the world.

LEVIRATE LAW *See under* **Marriage**.

LEVITES *See* **Levi, Levites**.

LEVITICAL CITIES The forty-eight cities given to the Levites after the conquest of Canaan. As the Lord had commanded Moses (Num 35:1–8), the Levites were not given their own tribal territory in the land of Canaan (Josh 13–19); instead they were given forty-eight cities, called "Levitical cities," located throughout the territory of the tribes, along with adjacent pasturelands (Josh 21:1–42; 1 Chr 6:54–81). Six of those cities were "cities of refuge." (*See* **Levi** for other details.)

LEVITICUS, BOOK OF The third book of the Pentateuch. It contains laws regarding sacrifices, legal purity, holiness, atonement, the redemption of offerings, and other subjects. Levitical laws provided directives for all aspects of religious observance and for the manner in which the Israelites were to conduct themselves with respect to God and each other.

The Hebrew title of Leviticus is *wayyiqrā'* ("And he called"), the first word of the book in Hebrew. The title in the **Septuagint** was *Leuitikon,* meaning "pertaining to the Levites," a title that described the use of the book by the Levitical priests to educate the people about the requirements of the covenant. The **Vulgate** adopted the Greek title as *Liber Leviticus,* and the English title is derived from that tradition. In rabbinic tradition, the book is titled *tôrat kôhănîm* ("law of the priests"), since much of it enumerates the responsibilities of the priests as mediators of the Mosaic covenant.

I. *Authorship and Date*

II. *Contents*

III. *Purpose and Themes*

    A. *The Renewal of the Covenant*

    B. *The Purpose of the Regulations*

    C. *Leviticus for Christians*

I. AUTHORSHIP AND DATE

The book of Leviticus tells us that its contents were dictated to Moses and his brother Aaron at Mount Sinai (cf. Lev 1:1; 4:1; 7:37; 10:8; 11:1; 26:46; 27:34, 34:27). Both Jewish and Christian traditions name Moses as the author of this book, along with the whole Pentateuch. If this is true, that would mean that Moses either wrote the book himself (cf. Exod 17:14; 24:4; 34:27) or entrusted its composition to scribes. And if Moses was the author, then the book dates from the fifteenth century B.C. (or the thirteenth century B.C., depending on the date of the **Exodus**).

According to the modern Documentary Hypothesis (*see* **Pentateuch**), Leviticus came from the Priestly (or P-source) traditions; its current form dates from a time during and after the Babylonian Exile in the sixth century B.C. Other modern scholars argue that the book is the product of a long period of development, and that its traditions extend back to the beginning of the first millennium B.C. or even into the second millennium B.C.

II. CONTENTS

III. PURPOSE AND THEMES

A. *The Renewal of the Covenant*

Leviticus is mainly a collection of laws, and it divides into two major sections, the Priestly Code (chaps. 1–16) and the Holiness Code (chaps. 17–27). (*See under* **Law.**)

The incident of the golden calf and Israel's apostasy were such serious breaches of the **covenant** that a complete renewal was required (Exod 34). The renewal was mediated through Moses and it spelled out the responsibilities of the Aaronic priests (Lev 1–7), the Levites (Num 3–4), and the lay tribes (Lev 17–27). Instead of speaking directly to the Israelites, in the renewed covenant God dealt directly with Moses (Exod 34:10), Moses spoke to Aaron and the Levites, and they passed the instruction on to the tribes of Israel (Lev 10:11). God's presence in Israel was concealed in the **Tabernacle** as the sign of the renewed covenant, and the priests and Levites served as mediators and guardians of the Tabernacle's precincts, following the instructions laid out in Leviticus. The book spells out sacrifices and purity rites and the priestly hierarchy that made it possible for the rebellious people to make atonement to the Lord.

B. *The Purpose of the Regulations*

The first part of Leviticus, the Priestly Code (1–16), served as a guidebook to teach and prepare the mediators of the covenant in the fulfillment of their priestly duties. The Holiness Code (17–26), on the other hand, was mainly addressed to the twelve lay tribes of Israel and stressed holiness as being essential for all God's people.

In a sense, the whole purpose of Leviticus is summed up by the following:

Say to the people of Israel, I am the LORD your God. You shall not do as they do in the land of Egypt, where you dwelt, and you shall not do as they do in the land of Canaan, to which I am bringing you. You shall not walk in their statutes. You shall do my ordinances and keep my statutes and walk in them. I am the LORD your God. You shall therefore keep my statutes and my ordinances, by doing which a man shall live: I am the LORD. (Lev 18:2–5)

The Lord is separated from all sin and all sinners, so the Israelites must also separate themselves from sin and sinners (Lev 15:31; 20:26). Since they had not been able to keep the covenant in its original and much simpler form (Exod 20–23), their lives must be minutely regulated.

C. Leviticus for Christians

Christians living in the age of the **Messiah** have seen all the institutions and sacrifices of Leviticus perfectly fulfilled in Jesus Christ. Of particular note is the stress on the Day of Atonement (Lev 16), which forecast Christ's sacrifice upon the Cross. At the same time, Leviticus points to the sanctification of daily life through its call for perfect charity: "you shall love your neighbor as yourself" (19:18). Leviticus, with its many scenes of animal sacrifice, reminds us of the need to put to death our animal urges and to consecrate our lives to God. We are thus urged to confront sin in ourselves and our community of faith and to separate ourselves from everything that might defile us and rupture our proper relationship with the Lord.

LIBERTY *See* **Freedom**.

LIBNAH The name of two places mentioned in the Old Testament.

1. A place in the desert used as an encampment by the Israelites (Num 33:20).

2. A Levitical city in Judah (Josh 21:13). It was conquered by Joshua (Josh 10:29) and allotted to Judah (Josh 15:42). During the reign of Jehoram, the city revolted against his authority (2 Kgs 8:22) because of the king's impiety (2 Chr 21:10), but Libnah seems to have been restored to the control of Judah (2 Kgs 19:8; Isa 37:8). It was also the home of Hamutal, mother of the Judahite kings Jehoahaz and Zedekiah (2 Kgs 23:31, 24:18; Jer 52:1).

LIBNI Son of **Gershon** of the tribe of Levi (Exod 6:17; Num 3:18, 21; 1 Chr 17, 20).

LIBYA A region in North Africa west of **Egypt**. The history of ancient Libya was tied to that of ancient Egypt (Ezek 30:5), and a Libyan, **Shishak** (or Sheshonq), came to power as pharaoh in the tenth century B.C. (2 Chr 12:2). He invaded Palestine with twelve hundred chariots, sixty thousand cavalry, and a vast host of Libyan, Egyptian, and Ethiopian foot soldiers, capturing Jerusalem and looting the Temple (1 Kgs 14:25–28; 2 Chr 12:1–12). Jews from Libya were in Jerusalem at the first Christian **Pentecost** (Acts 2:10).

LIFE The various words that have been translated as "life" in the Bible have about the same broad range of meanings as the word "life" does in English. Life can be simply the principle that separates animate from inanimate matter, or the lifetime of a person, or the way in which a person lives, or the eternal life that resides in the believer even now, and to which he is called as a future hope (CCC 609–10, 994–96).

I. LIFE IN THE OLD TESTAMENT

A. God, the Source of Life

All life owes its existence and continuation to **God** the Creator; this is a fundamental assumption in the Old Testament (Gen 2:7). God lives forever, but his creatures are mortal (2 Sam 14:14; Ps 90:1–6). Unlike the idols of the nations, the Lord is the "living God" (Jer 10:6–10; cf. 1 Thess 1:9). He created life by breathing life into man (Gen 2:7), and life persists only as long as God sustains the spirit in man (Gen 6:3; Job 34:14–15). The book of Psalms stresses both the living principle of God and the degree to which he perpetuates all life (Ps 16:11; 133:3). He is the "fountain of life" (Ps 36:10) and the "light of life" (Ps 56:14). As life is a gift, we have the obligation to express gratitude, just as one should express thanks for deliverance from death or danger and even the loss of dignity (Ps 30:3–4; 71:20; 80:18).

B. The Good Life

That death is the inevitable end of life for mortals encouraged speculation on what would constitute a good "life." A good life was often seen as a long one, ending with a "good" death at an advanced age (Gen 25:8; Deut 5:16; Judg 8:32; Job 21:23). In many ways, the family was the center of a good life: begetting children was a sign of blessing (Ps 128:1–6) and ensured that the family line would be carried on (Gen 35:29, 50:7–8; Job 42:16). Wisdom writings stress that wisdom brings a good life, often seen as a long and prosperous one (Prov 3:16; 8:18). The "good life," then, is one in which we can enjoy peace, happiness, family, friends, and the good things life has to offer. On the other hand, Wisdom Books like **Job** and Ecclesiastes recognized that wisdom alone was not necessarily sufficient to bring all those good things: "For in much wisdom is much vexation, and he who increases knowledge increases sorrow" (Eccl 1:18). Job spent part of his life in misery: was he not therefore leading a good life? Ultimately, utter dependence on God was the only sure course. "The end of the matter; all has been heard. Fear God, and keep his commandments; for this is the whole duty of man" (Eccl 12:13).

Life, then, had an essential moral dimension that entailed keeping the commandments and above all maintaining fidelity to the covenants. Life was a blessing, and the good life was to love God with all your heart and to follow his Law (Sir 24:22–23; cf. Deut 4:1, 6:24, 16:20).

See, I have set before you this day life and good, death and evil. If you obey the commandments of the LORD your God which I command you this day, by loving the LORD your God, by walking in his ways, and by

*keeping his commandments and his statutes
and his ordinances, then you shall live and
multiply, and the LORD your God will bless
you in the land which you are entering to
take possession of it. But if your heart turns
away, and you will not hear, but are drawn
away to worship other gods and serve them, I
declare to you this day, that you shall perish;
you shall not live long in the land which you
are going over the Jordan to enter and possess. (Deut 30:15–18)*

C. Eternal Life

By the time of the Babylonian **Exile**, the outlook turned more eschatological, pointing toward a **resurrection** to everlasting life (Dan
12:2). This eschatological outlook was only intensified as time went on (2 Macc 7:9). Life after death lies beyond our earthly existence: "for
God created man for incorruption, and made
him in the image of his own eternity" (Wis
2:23). Thus there is a deeper purpose for the
trials that come even to the good: "For though
in the sight of men they were punished, their
hope is full of immortality" (Wis 3:4).

II. LIFE IN THE NEW TESTAMENT

A. Eternal Life, the Focus

Eternal life through Jesus Christ is the central
teaching of the New Testament. Consequently,
"life" often means divine life or eternal life. As
Creator, Christ gave "earthly life" to the human race (John 1:1–4), and as Redeemer he
came to give us the abundance of "divine life"
(John 10:10).

This is a continuation of the OT view of
life, but with an even stronger orientation to-

ward eternity. Life consists of more than possessions (Luke 12:15); paradoxically, in order
to have eternal life, one must give up one's life
for Jesus (Luke 14:26) as he gave up his life for
many (Mark 10:45). "Whoever seeks to gain
his life will lose it, but whoever loses his life
will preserve it" (Luke 17:33).

B. Faith in Jesus Christ as the Means to
Eternal Life

John tells us that he wrote his Gospel "that you
may believe that Jesus is the Christ, the Son of
God, and that believing you may have life in
his name" (John 20:31). Faith in the Crucifixion and Resurrection of Jesus Christ form the
basis of our life (John 3:16), and in baptism, we
become partakers in that new life that comes
"from above" (John 3:3–5). Eternal life is the
gift of God for all who believe (Rom 6:23) and
live according to the Spirit (Rom 8:11–13).

In the New Covenant, the ideal life is pred-
icated upon a personal relationship with Jesus
Christ. The way of this life is summed up in
Galatians: "For I through the law died to the
law, that I might live to God. I have been crucified with Christ; it is no longer I who live,
but Christ who lives in me; and the life I now
live in the flesh I live by faith in the Son of
God, who loved me and gave himself for me"
(Gal 2:19–20). Likewise, Paul writes, "So you
also must consider yourselves dead to sin and
alive to God in Christ Jesus" (Rom 6:11; cf.
1 Cor 15:22; Phil 1:21). John especially emphasizes that our eternal life depends on Christ:
"God gave us eternal life, and this life is in
his Son. He who has the Son has life; he who
has not the Son of God has not life" (1 John
5:11–12).

C. Eternal Life Begins in the Present

Eternal life comes to those who worship God, keep his commandments, and follow Christ, "the Author of life" (Acts 3:15; cf. Acts 5:20; 13:48; 17:25). Eternal life is thus a foretaste of the life to come. It is begun at baptism, which brings us new life in Christ (Rom 6:4). The old life has passed away for the sinner, the life of the flesh (Rom 8:12), and a resurrection has occurred in the soul (Rom 6:13) that anticipates the resurrection of the body (Rom 8:11).

The fullness of everlasting life will be possessed in heaven, which Scripture calls "the life which is life indeed" (1 Tim 6:19), but we already have a share in that eternal life through the sacramental actions of the Church: "Very truly, I tell you, unless you eat the flesh of the Son of Man and drink his blood, you have no life in you" (John 6:53). (*See also* **Parousia**.)

LIFE, THE BOOK OF *See* **Book of life, the**.

LIGHT
The first thing created when God brought the world into being (Gen 1:3), and a common symbol in Scripture for everything good. "God is light and in him is no darkness at all. If we say we have fellowship with him while we walk in darkness, we lie and do not live according to the truth; but if we walk in the light, as he is in the light, we have fellowship with one another, and the blood of Jesus his Son cleanses us from all sin" (1 John 1:5–7).

The Old Testament uses light as a symbol of the glory of God as well as the life-giving power of God (Ps 13:3; Prov 29:13). Thanks to God's light, we are able to escape the darkness, which is the symbol of death, sorrow, and sadness (cf. Ps 56:14; 88:7, 11–13; Job 33:30; 38:17). God's favorable countenance is described as light (Num 6:25; Ps 4:6, 31:16, 44:3, 67:3, 80:5) as is his promised deliverance (Ps 43:3; Isa 9:2; 60:1, 19–20; Mic 7:9). God is light when he saves (Ps 27:1; Isa 60:19), and his Servant (Messiah) is a light to the nations (Isa 42:6; 49:6). The Lord is the source of light (Ps 36:9) and so the wise man walks in the light of God's **Law** (Ps 119:105).

Light remains in the New Testament a powerful image for God. God is light (1 John 1:5) and dwells in unapproachable light (1 Tim 6:16) (CCC 157, 214, 234, 242, 257). His light is seen in the Bethlehem sky at Christmas (Matt 2:9; Luke 2:9), at the **Transfiguration** (Matt 17:5), and in the conversion of Paul (Acts 9:3; 22:6). Jesus is the light of the world (John 8:12; 9:5; 12:35–36) who enlightens all (John 1:9), both Israel and the Gentiles (Luke 2:32) (CCC 280, 529, 748, 1202, 2466, 2665, 2715). Those who believe in him are challenged to walk in the light (1 John 1:7) and are called sons of light (Luke 16:8; John 12:36; 1 Thess 5:5). Christians thus emulate Christ in being a light to the world (Matt 5:14–16; Acts 13:47) (CCC 736, 1216, 1695).

Although light is often contrasted with darkness, there is never a sense that good and evil are equal powers (CCC 285). Light always prevails: "The light shines in the darkness, and the darkness has not overcome it" (John 1:5). Light and darkness serve as powerful metaphors for the struggle between good and evil that plays out in our lives. As the Second Vatican Council document *Gaudium et Spes* stresses, "Man is divided in himself. As a result, the whole life of men, both individual and social, shows itself to be a struggle, and a dramatic one, between good and evil, between light and darkness" (GS §13.2).

LIGHTNING A natural phenomenon that symbolically represents the power and presence of God. Thus it is usually one of the elements in a divine theophany or vision of God (Exod 19:16; Ezek 1:13; Rev 4:5, 11:19). It can also represent divine judgment (Ps 144:6; Zech 9:14; Luke 10:18). Lightning is sometimes called "the fire of the Lord" that flares down from heaven (1 Kgs 18:38; 2 Kgs 1:12; Job 1:16).

LIGHTS, FEAST OF *See* **Dedication, feast of**.

LILITH *see* **Night hag**.

LILY A flower, proverbial for its beauty, mentioned in several passages of the Old Testament, especially in the Song of Solomon (Song 2:1–2, 16; 4:5; 6:3). Several of the Psalms are marked "According to Lilies," which may refer to a musical melody to which the Psalm was sung (Ps 45; 69; 80). In Hos 14:5, the lily is seen as a promise of the future restoration of Israel. In the New Testament, the splendor of the lily points to the generous Providence of God (Matt 6:28; Luke 12:27).

LINEN A fine cloth made from flax and manufactured especially in Egypt. It was a luxury item in the ancient world. Hebrew has several different words for linen, including *šēš*, *bad*, *pištâ*, and *bûṣ* (the last is likely a loan word from the Greek *byssos*); the exact difference among them is not always clear. The priests'

vestments were made of linen (Exod 28:6, 39, 42; Lev 6:10; 16:4; 1 Sam 22:18; Ezek 44:17), and it was used for the curtains of the Tabernacle (Exod 26:1), the veil (Exod 26:31), and the screen of the tent (Exod 26:36). Samuel wore a linen ephod like a priest (1 Sam 2:18), as did David when he danced before the ark (2 Sam 6:14). Linen was also a valued and expensive item (Isa 3:23) and made a very fine gift from a husband to his wife (Ezek 16:10, 13). In the New Testament, linen was worn by the rich man in the parable of Lazarus (Luke 16:19) and by the young man in the Garden of Gethsemane (Mark 14:51). The body of Jesus was wrapped in a linen shroud (Matt 27:59; Mark 15:46; Luke 23:53; John 19:40). In Revelation, the Bride of the Lamb is dressed in linen (Rev 19:8), as are the armies of heaven that follow the victorious Christ into battle (Rev 19:14).

LINUS A Roman Christian mentioned in 2 Timothy; he sent greetings to Timothy (2 Tim 4:21). According to Saint Irenaeus (*Against Heresies* 3.3.3), Linus was the first successor to Peter as Bishop of Rome. His episcopate was attested by Eusebius (*Hist. Eccl.* 3.2; 5.6), who noted also that it lasted for twelve years, after which Linus was succeeded by Anacletus (*Hist. Eccl.* 3.13).

LION A feared predator in biblical Palestine, though now extinct in the region, having been hunted out of existence by the twelfth century A.D. The lion preyed upon flocks (Amos 3:12) and its roar was well known (Ps 104:21; Ezek 22:25). Lions were found in forests (Amos 3:4; Jer 49:19), desolate regions (2 Kgs 17:25), and caves (Song 4:8; Amos 3:4). They were also captured as game (Ezek 19:1–9), and both Samson (Judg 14:5–6) and David (1 Sam 17:34) slew them with their bare hands.

The lion's power and majesty were used as symbols of personal courage and strength (Gen 49:9; 1 Macc 3:4), so that Solomon's throne was decorated with two lions by his side and twelve lions on the steps leading up to the throne, six on each side (1 Kgs 10:18–20). In biblical symbolism, the lion can represent the Lord, roaring in anger against sinners (Amos 1:2) or calling them back home from exile (Hos 11:10). Likewise, it is sometimes a symbol of the oppressor or the enemy who devours God's people (Isa 5:29; Jer 2:15; Ps 7:1–2). The devil himself is thus described as a hungry lion stalking his prey (1 Pet 5:8).

In Revelation, Jesus was given the Messianic title "Lion of the tribe of Judah" (Rev 5:5). The title comes from Gen 49:9, where Jacob describes Judah as a "lion's whelp," courageous and destined for kingship. The title was later embraced by the hereditary rulers of Ethiopia, who claimed descent from Judah through Solomon.

LITERAL SENSE *See* "Senses of Scripture" *under* **Interpretation of the Bible**.

LITURGY The public worship of the people of God. In biblical religion, this involves various cultic acts such as the offering of sacrifice and incense, the proclamation of sacred texts, the recitation of prayers, the singing of sacred music, and the administration of sacraments. The shape and substance of liturgy is connected with the succession of covenants that span from primeval to Messianic times. Indeed, liturgy is the principal means of ratifying, renewing, and maintaining the covenants between God and his people in the history of salvation.

I. TERMINOLOGY

The word "liturgy" comes from the Greek *leitourgia*, which means "public service." In ancient Greece, this meant performing civic duties for the state as well as fulfilling religious duties to the gods. The word appears only six times in the Greek New Testament but is used over forty times in the Greek Old Testament, where it most often translates the Hebrew *ʿăbōdâ*, meaning "service" or "worship." In early Christian writings, the term "liturgy" referred to the sacramental worship of the Church with all of its actions and dimensions. Related terms in Greek include *leitourgeō*, "to serve, worship," and *leitourgos*, "servant, minister."

II. OLD TESTAMENT

Liturgy, it must be stated, is as old as creation itself. This can be seen in Genesis where God laid responsibilities on the first man by placing him in the Garden of Eden "to till it and keep it" (Gen 2:15). The verbs employed in the Hebrew text of this verse (*ʿābad* and *šāmar*) are used together elsewhere in the Pentateuch to describe the religious service of Levites and priests who minister to the Lord in the Tabernacle (Num 3:7–8; 8:26; 18:5–6). Combined with hints that the garden is a primordial sanctuary (*see* **Eden**), Genesis implies that man, from the very beginning, was created for the sacred service of worship.

It is no surprise, then, that public acts of worship appear in Scripture as early as primeval times. The instinct to serve God by the sacrifice of animals and the fruits of the ground is visible in the account of Cain and Abel (Gen 4:1–7). Part of the lesson of this episode is that worship has not only an exterior dimension, represented by the physical elements offered on the altar, but also an interior dimension that requires that the heart and intentions of the worshipper be rightly ordered to God. In the patriarch period, additional liturgical rites appeared such as prayer in the name of the Lord (Gen 12:8), altar construction (Gen 12:7; 13:18), libation offerings (Gen 35:14), and the consecration of natural landmarks (Gen 21:33; 28:18–22).

Liturgy underwent significant development in the time of Moses. Whereas the worship of patriarchal religion was discretionary as to times and places, and the responsibilities of the cult rested with the head of the family, the worship of Mosaic religion became much more formalized and regulated. In place of temporal discretion, the Torah specified an elaborate calendar of festivals and holy days that were set aside for worship and rest (Lev 23:1–44; Deut 16:1–17). In place of altars erected wherever the patriarch deemed appropriate, all sacrificial actions were now confined to the precincts of the sanctuary (Lev 17:1–7; Deut 12:5–14). And in place of a natural priesthood, wherein fathers officiated on behalf of their families, a clerical priesthood was instituted and entrusted to the one family of Aaron and his descendants (Exod 40:12–15), and they in turn were assisted by nonpriestly Levites (Num 8:5–22). Moreover, the liturgical rites themselves, namely, the animal and food sacrifices, were the subject of detailed instructions regarding form, matter, and execution (Lev 1–7; Num 28–29). The Tabernacle (and later the Temple) was an elaborately constructed sanctuary with sacred furnishings and zones of holiness (outer court, holy place, most holy place) that curtained off and restricted access to the presence of Yahweh within (Exod 25–27, 30). Other props and elements of Mosaic worship included incense, sacred vestments, tithes and first fruits, and anointing and purification rites.

Liturgy underwent more development in the time of David. For the first time in Israel's history, the ministry of sacrifice was supplemented with the ministry of song. Music as a form of religious expression and worship was not part of the Tabernacle liturgies; presumably these ancient rites were conducted in silence. But David, in preparation for Solomon's construction of the Temple, organized a Levitical guild of singers and musicians to offer continual thanks and praise to the Lord in his sanctuary (1 Chr 15:16–25; 16:4–6; 25:1–8). Instruments used for liturgy included horns, cymbals, harps, lyres, and flutes (1 Chr 15:28; superscription of Ps 5). Numerous songs chanted in the Temple services are canonized in the book of Psalms. It is because of Moses that Israel learned to esteem order, rubric, and holiness; it is because of David that Israel learned to make melody to the Lord with joy and gladness of heart.

III. NEW TESTAMENT

Explicit references to "liturgy" appear only infrequently in the NT, but the reality of Christian liturgy is very much present, even where the word is not used to describe it. In a few instances, the term is employed with reference to OT worship, such as the liturgy at Mount Sinai (Heb 9:21) and the services conducted in the Temple (Luke 1:23; Heb 10:11). In another instance, Paul describes the offering of his life as a sacrificial service on behalf of his readers (Phil 2:17). The sole reference to liturgy as public Christian worship (Greek *leitourgeō*) is in reference to the church at Antioch, which was "worshipping" the Lord with prayer and fasting just before Paul and Barnabas were called to missionary work (Acts 13:2).

It can hardly be deduced from the dearth of references to liturgy that liturgy is relatively unimportant to Christianity. Quite the contrary. Worship itself is brought to perfection in the New Covenant. Jesus made this point when he promised the Samaritan woman, "the hour is coming when neither on this mountain nor in Jerusalem will you worship the Father . . . But the hour is coming and now is when the true worshippers will worship the Father in Spirit and truth" (John 4:21–23). The point here is not that worship will be spiritual as opposed to physical or liturgical, but that worship, taking place "in the Spirit" (Rev 1:10), will no longer be confined to the mountain sanctuaries of Samaritanism and Judaism. Likewise, it will be done according to the truth, untainted by the idolatrous elements that historically plagued Samaritan religion (2 Kgs 17:29–34).

The concrete form of this new worship is sacramental, and its centerpiece is the Eucharistic liturgy, sometimes called the "breaking of bread" (Luke 24:35; Acts 2:42), which became the principal expression of public worship among Christians from earliest times.

And little wonder, for Jesus instituted the Eucharist as the memorial rite of the New Covenant (Luke 22:14–20). Scholars have also suggested that the Christian Eucharist was intended by Jesus to replace the sacrificial rites of Mosaic religion. This is implied in the saying that Christ's blood, which is poured out at table, brings about a true remission of sins (Matt 26:28).

The book of Hebrews has much to say on this subject, although it makes only occasional reference to actions and elements associated with Christian liturgy (Heb 6:2, 4; 10:22; 13:10). The main focus is on Jesus Christ, the high priest and mediator of the New Covenant. Having ascended to the right hand of the Father, he acts as a liturgical minister (Greek, *leitourgos*) in the heavenly sanctuary (Heb 8:2). There he intercedes for the saints (Heb 7:25) by the priestly offering of his body (Heb 10:10) and blood (Heb 9:11–12). It is precisely this celestial ministry of Christ that makes the sacramental worship of Christians more perfect than the sacrificial worship of the Temple. For the blood of animals was incapable of achieving a true expiation of sin (Heb 10:1–4), but the blood of Christ is powerful in doing just that (Heb 9:14). Believers benefit from this, first, when they are washed in the "pure water" of baptism, which cleanses the conscience of guilt (Heb 10:22), and then, when they enter the Lord's presence through the veil of Jesus's "flesh" and "blood," presumably in the Eucharist (Heb 10:19–20). Not surprisingly, the author of Hebrews insists that Christians should not neglect "to meet together" for worship (Heb 10:25), for then they would deprive themselves of the blessings of the Lord's "altar" (Heb 10:13).

Finally, it must be noted that the book of Revelation is dominated by the sights and sounds of the eternal liturgy. The setting is God's temple in heaven (Rev 7:15; 11:19; 15:5–8; 16:17). There, hymns of praise to God and the Lamb are sung without ceasing (Rev 4:8, 11; 5:9–10; 7:10) and the music of harps is played (Rev 5:8). All creatures in heaven bow and prostrate themselves in adoration before the Lord (Rev 4:10; 5:8). Angels clad in priestly vestments offer incense, which are the prayers of the saints (Rev 5:8; 8:3–4). On the one hand, these scenes of celestial liturgy unveil the endless worship of God that takes place beyond the cosmic sphere of space and time. On the other, studies have revealed that ancient Christian liturgies often drew from the book of Revelation in canonizing the words and actions of the Eucharistic service. The underlying belief is that liturgical worship in the Church is not merely an imitation of the celestial liturgy, but a sacramental participation in the eternal praise of the Trinity in heaven.

LOAN In Old Testament money lending, both sides in the arrangement had certain obligations, but (as Deut 28:12, 44 taught), it was far better to be a creditor than a debtor. Loans were not to be made with a charge of interest (Exod 22:24; Ps 15:5; Prov 28:8; Ezek 18:13, 17; 22:12) except to Gentiles (Deut 23:20), although it is apparent that such a rule was not always honored in practice. Likewise, the creditor was encouraged to display mercy and forbearance toward those who were unable to pay back a loan (Ezek 18:16; cf. Neh 5:1–13). For their part, debtors were placed in a difficult position of pledging virtually all of their possessions in return for a loan, including clothing (Exod 22:25; Amos 2:8), animals such as the ox and ass (Job 24:3), and even their children (Job 24:9). A debtor might even pledge himself (Lev 25:39; Amos 2:6) or his family. But if a cloak was seized, it had to be returned each evening to permit the debtor to stay warm overnight (Exod 22:24); similarly, the creditor could not enter the home to seize the pledge (Deut 24:10), nor could the millstone be taken (Deut 24:6). A man and his family were not to be deprived, even under the worst conditions, of their ability to eat, to have a roof over their heads, and to have at least a cloak to cover themselves in the night.

Other writings in the OT testify to the unpleasant consequences of the loan, debts, and the charging of interest (cf. Sir 29:1–10). The debtor is considered a slave (Prov 22:7) and is wicked if the loans are not paid back (Ps 37:21). The good creditor shows mercy and kindness (Ps 112:5) and does not lend to the powerful, as doing so is a sure way to lose the money (Sir 8:12).

In the New Testament, the forgiveness of one's debtors is considered essential for earning the forgiveness of God (Matt 6:12; Luke 11:4), although the meaning of "debtor" can be interpreted broadly. Interest is mentioned plainly in the Parable of the Talents (Matt 25:27; Luke 19:23).

LOAVES AND FISHES *See* **Miracle**.

LOCUST An insect infamous for its ability to wreak disaster on crops. The destructive power of locust swarms is noted in the Old

Testament (Joel 1:4–7; 2:2–11; Nah 3:15, 17). One of the Exodus **plagues** on Egypt was locusts (Exod 10:12–20; cf. Ps 78:46, 105:34–35), and Israel itself was threatened with a curse of ravenous locusts if it failed to keep the covenant (Deut 28:38; 2 Chr 7:13). Vast armies were often compared to the numberless hordes of locusts that were known to ravage the forests and fields (Judg 6:5, 7:12; Jer 46:23). On the other hand, locusts were also listed among the pure animals in Leviticus and therefore could be eaten (Lev 11:22). John the Baptist lived on them (Matt 3:4; Mark 1:6).

LOD Also Lydda, a town in the western lowlands of Palestine that was built by the tribe of Benjamin (1 Chr 8:12; Ezra 2:33; Neh 7:37, 11:35). It is probably the modern el-Ludd.

LOGOS *See* **Word**.

LOIS The mother of **Eunice** and the grandmother of **Timothy** (2 Tim 1:5). She may have been converted by **Paul** and **Barnabas** when they passed through Lystra of Lycaonia (Acts 16:1).

LORD In SMALL CAPITALS, the common English translation of the divine name Yahweh in the Old Testament. (*See* "Yahweh" *and* "The Names of God" *under* **God**.)

LORD A title often used for **Jesus Christ** in the New Testament; the same title is used in the Greek Old Testament to translate the Name of God (*see* "Yahweh" *under* **God**).

LORD OF HOSTS *See* **Hosts of heaven**.

LORD'S DAY An early Christian name for Sunday, the day of Christian worship and rest. Sunday, the day after the Jewish **Sabbath**, is commemorated as the day Jesus Christ rose from the dead (Luke 24:1–5). John's vision in **Revelation** came on the Lord's Day (Rev 1:10). (*See also* **Day of the Lord**).

LORD'S PRAYER The prayer Jesus taught his disciples in Matt 6:9–15 and Luke 11:2–4. It is the only preformulated prayer attributed to him in the New Testament. It is also called the Our Father, from its first two words.

Matthew's version of the prayer (which is followed in the **Didache**, 8:2) is part of the Sermon on the Mount. In Luke, the prayer is Jesus's reply to the apostles' request: "Lord, teach us to pray, as John taught his disciples" (Luke 11:2). Matthew's version contains an invocation and seven petitions, while Luke uses five petitions, omitting petitions three ("Your will be done on earth, as it is in heaven") and seven ("Deliver us from evil"). Some ancient manuscripts of the Gospel of Matthew include the line "for yours is the kingdom, and the power and the glory." Most likely, this was added later through the influence of 1 Chr 29:11 as well as liturgical use (*Did.*, 8.2). It is commonly used by Protestants.

The Lord's Prayer is the fundamental Christian prayer. Tertullian called it "truly the summary of the whole gospel" (*Or.* 1). It is a testament to Christian participation in the life of the Trinity: we are permitted to invoke God as "Father" because the Son of God has revealed the Father to us, and because through baptism, we have become sons of God. The wording "Our Father" stresses participation in the Church, as the family of believers united around the heavenly Father.

The first three petitions have as their aim the glorification of the Father. "Hallowed be your name" is our prayer to sanctify God's name so that it is held sacred in every heart. "Your kingdom come" pleads both for the growth of the Kingdom of God in our daily lives and for the final coming of the reign of God. "Your will be done on earth, as it is in heaven" calls upon the Father to fulfill his plan of salvation in the world.

The final four petitions ask for what is needed from the Father. "Give us this day our daily bread" is a request for the daily nourishment we need for body and soul. "Forgive us our debts, as we also have forgiven our debtors," implores God's mercy for our sins even as we forgive those of others. "Lead us not into temptation, but deliver us from evil" asks God to lead us away from sin and to grant us the strength needed to resist its attraction. It is probable, in fact, that deliverance from evil is a plea to rescue us from the "Evil One" and his efforts to drag us away from the kingdom of heaven.

According to Saint Thomas Aquinas, when we recite the Lord's Prayer "we ask, not only for all the things we can rightly desire, but also in the sequence that they should be desired. This prayer not only teaches us to ask for things, but also in what order we should desire them" (*Summa theologiae* II-II, q. 83, a. 9) (CCC 2759–2865).

Versions of the Lord's Prayer
Matthew 6:9–13

Our Father in heaven,
hallowed be your name.
Your kingdom come.
Your will be done on earth, as it is in heaven.
Give us this day our daily bread,
and forgive us our debts, as we also have
    forgiven our debtors,
and lead us not into temptation,
but deliver us from evil.

Luke 11:2–4

Father, hallowed be your name.
Your kingdom come.
Give us each day our daily bread;
and forgive us our sins, for we ourselves forgive
    every one who is indebted to us;
and lead us not into temptation.

LORD'S SUPPER *See* **Eucharist.**

LOT The nephew of **Abraham** and the son of Haran, Abraham's youngest brother (Gen 11:27–31). After the death of his father, Lot accompanied his uncle, his grandfather **Terah,** and Abraham's wife Sarah on the long journey to Canaan (Gen 12:4–5). Owing to disagreements between their herdsmen, Lot and Abraham separated, with Lot settling in the area of the Dead Sea, near **Sodom** and Gomorrah (Gen 13:1–13). He was captured during the campaign of the Mesopotamian kings against the five cities, and Abraham had to rescue him (Gen 14:1–16).

Lot once again found himself and his family in danger among the inhabitants of Sodom. This time angels rescued him, so that he was spared the destruction of Sodom and Gomorrah (Gen 19:1–29). Lot's wife, however, looked back in defiance of God's command and was turned into a pillar of salt (Gen 19:17, 26).

Genesis then goes on to claim that Lot

became the founder of the Moabites and the Ammonites. The story has it that Lot's two daughters, despairing of finding husbands, engaged in sexual relations with their drunken father and each conceived a son by him, one named Moab and the other Ammon (Gen 19:30–38). The Moabites and Ammonites would later become hostile neighbors and enemies of Israel (Judg 3:12–14, 10:7; Ps 83:5–7). The New Testament describes Lot as "a righteous man greatly distressed by the licentiousness of the lawless" (2 Pet 2:6–8).

LOTAN The son of Seir the Horite (Gen 36:20, 22, 29; 1 Chr 1:38–39), the father of Hori and Heman, and the brother of Timna (Gen 36:22).

LOTS Marked objects cast like dice to make choices in a seemingly random way. The casting of lots was a common means of deciding a question or resolving some dispute in ancient times. Casting lots was accepted by Israelites as a means of determining the will of the Lord, an outlook summed up by Prov 16:33: "The lot is cast into the lap, but the decision is wholly from the LORD." Nevertheless, the casting of lots was seen as distinct from any form of divination (*see also* **Divination**).

Lots were cast after the conquest of Canaan to divide up the territory of Canaan among the tribes (Num 26:55; Josh 14:2, 18:6), and later in history to determine those who might settle in Jerusalem after the end of the **Exile** (Neh 11:1). Similarly, lots were used to select the scapegoat on the Day of Atonement (Lev 16:7–10), to assess the guilt or innocence of a person (Josh 7:14), to divide up spoils (Ps

22:19), and even to establish some divine wish or election (1 Sam 10:20–21). Hence, the phrase "one's lot" came into use to refer to the destiny or fate of a person (Ps 16:5, 6; Jer 13:25).

In the New Testament, lots were used to choose Judas Iscariot's successor (Acts 1:26). At the Crucifixion, the Roman soldiers cast lots for Jesus's tunic, according to the custom that granted the execution squad the right to divide among themselves the possessions of a condemned man that were brought with him to the place of death (Matt 27:35; Mark 15:24; Luke 23:34; John 19:24; cf. Ps 22:18).

LOVE Biblically portrayed as goodwill in action, and thus manifested in specific acts toward others. According to 1 John 4:8, the very nature of God is Love, and love is present in Scripture as one of the central themes in describing the relationship between God and humanity. Indeed, love is the basis of creation as well as the basis of the divine plan of redemption. Because of his superabundant love, God willingly gave his own Son to bring salvation to the fallen world (John 3:16; Rom 5:8–9; 1 John 4:9). The task for us, then, is above all to love God with our entire heart (Deut 6:5; Matt 22:37). We are also to love our neighbors (Lev 19:18; 1 John 4:11–21). Jesus commanded that a special sign of his followers would be such love (John 13:34–35; cf. Luke 10:25–37). Love is the greatest of the three "theological" virtues (faith, hope, and love), the one that will endure even after death (1 Cor 13:13).

I. *Love in the Old Testament*
  A. *The Range of Meanings*
  B. *God's Unmerited Love*

I. LOVE IN THE OLD TESTAMENT

A. The Range of Meanings

In the Old Testament, a number of words are used for love, but the most common is the verb *'āhab*, appearing with its cognate nouns over two hundred times in the Hebrew Scriptures. It can have both a religious and a non-religious meaning, denoting the love between human beings, the love of things or objects, the human love for God, and the divine love that God shows to his people.

When referring to the love between humans, *'āhab* describes the entire spectrum of human affections (Gen 29:18, 34:3; Judg 16:4; Isa 57:8), including passionate love and sexual attraction (Song 1:7, 2:4, 3:1, 5:8, 8:6–7; Prov 5:19). Such attraction might entail the eventuality of marriage (1 Sam 18:20) or simple sexual desire (2 Sam 13:1–2; Jer 2:25). Likewise, *'āhab* might refer to the mutual devotion or attachment expressed in relationships, such as a husband for a wife (1 Sam 1:5), parents for a child (Gen 22:2; 25:28), or even a friendship, such as **David**'s for **Jonathan** (1 Sam 18:1; 2 Sam 1:26).

B. God's Unmerited Love

The greatest commandment of the **Law**, and indeed of the entire OT, is "You shall love the Lord your God with all your heart, and with all your soul, and with all your might" (Deut 6:5; cf. Deut 10:12; 11:1, 13, 22; 13:4; 19:9; 30:6, 16, 20). This commandment formed the basis of Israel's relationship with God. The Lord's love for Israel was freely given, and the history of the election of Israel, including the promises made to **Abraham**, **Isaac**, and **Jacob** (Gen 12–50), and the release of Israel from the bondage in Egypt testified to that love. God's love was unmerited and freely given; it was to be an integral part in the accomplishment of salvation history (Ps 47:5, 87:2; Isa 43:4) and the bringing forth of God's blessings upon the whole of humanity. (*See also* **Mercy**.)

In response to God's love, Israel was called to reciprocate. Hosea expressed the relationship in terms of marriage (Hos 2): "I will take you for my wife forever; I will take you for my wife in righteousness and in justice, in steadfast love, and in mercy. I will take you for my wife in faithfulness; and you shall know the Lord" (Hos 2:19–20). God reached out to Israel as a suitor reaches out to a woman, and Israel was asked to respond (cf. Hos 11:1–4).

God's love never wavered (Deut 4:37; Isa 43:4; Ps 33:5; Jer 21:3), but the fidelity of Israel was tested and proved weak; it failed in its chief obligation to love God with all of its heart, mind, and strength. Israel was called upon to return in faithfulness to God's electing love by keeping his commandments (Deut 10:12; 11:1, 22; 30:16). In its essence, that relationship was rooted in the **covenant** made between God and Israel. In fact, the covenant explains how love can be commanded in the stipulations of Deuteronomy. Treaty covenants in the ancient Near East—that is, those that are forged between a suzerain and his vassal—commonly employ the language of "love" to delineate the obligations of loyalty that bind the covenant partners. In this and many other respects, Deuteronomy and the covenant it establishes between the Lord and Israel mirror these international treaties between kings and their vassal subjects.

II. LOVE IN THE NEW TESTAMENT

At the very heart of the history of salvation resides the perfect communion of love: the Holy Trinity. In this perfect divine family, God the Father loves the Son, the Son loves the Father (John 14:31), and the Holy Spirit is the bond of love (cf. Rom 5:5) between the Father and the Son. From the love of this divine family God's entire plan of creation and salvation flowed, for it was his intention that his creation, humanity, should share in the divine life as sons in the Son (CCC 218–21).

A. Words for "Love"

The Greek words for love, *agapaō* and *agapē* (which describe willing or committed love), occur well over three hundred times in the New Testament. Similar words, such as *phileō* and *philia* (which may also mean willing love but sometimes friendly love), also occur with some frequency, but *agapē* remains the chief expression for love in the NT. Its general rarity in secular Greek may account for its use in the NT writings, as it was a helpful word to denote the unique perspective on love that Christianity was proclaiming. The Greek word *erōs,* meaning passionate or sexual love, does not appear in the NT.

B. Love in the Synoptic Gospels

The Synoptic Gospels showcase the commandments to love the Lord Our God with our whole being and to love our neighbors as ourselves (Matt 22:34–40; Mark 12:28–34; Luke 10:25–28). The two commandments are taken from Deut 6:5 and Lev 19:18. Jesus declares that both commandments are to be followed. In Luke he answers the question "Who is my neighbor?" with the Parable of the Good Samaritan (Luke 10:29–37). By making the good neighbor a Samaritan (Jews had a long-standing hostility to **Samaritans**), Jesus made it evident that he was asking more from us than merely loving our friends and family; he was asking for the commitment to love even strangers and enemies (Luke 6:27, 32–36; Matt 5:43–48).

By following Jesus's commandment to love our neighbor as ourself and to love our enemies, we demonstrate that we are willing to live in imitation of the Father. God's love is manifested in and through Christ and his works, including healing the sick and embracing the sinner. God thus bestows his love, mercy, and forgiveness on those who are undeserving of it (Matt 18:23–35; Luke 15:11–32). God takes the initiative—as in the OT—and it is entirely unmerited (Matt 10:6; 18:12–14; Luke 19:10).

C. Love in the Writings of John

John prefers the term "love" to describe the free and unmerited concern of God for us. It was God's love for us that caused him to send his own Son into the world that he might bring us eternal life (1 John 4:9; John 3:16, 13:34–35), and the life of God in us is displayed in how we love each other: "No man has ever seen God; if we love one another, God abides in us and his love is perfected in us" (1 John 4:12; 3:24; 4:10). Jesus is God's only begotten Son (John 1:13) and is loved by the Father (John 3:35; 10:17; 15:9; 17:24). In return, the Son loves the Father and does what God commands of him (John 14:31; 15:10). Jesus also loved his friends so deeply that he was willing to lay down his life for them (John 13:1; 1 John 3:16) in order to make it possible for them and us to be adopted sons of the Father (1 John 3:1).

In return, the disciples were required to show their own love by imitating the unifying love of the Son and the Father (John 17:21–23). Such a love had to be more than mere words; it had to be manifested by deeds (1 John 3:18), including keeping the commandments of Jesus (John 14:15, 21, 23; 1 John 5:3). Christians should also love one another (John 13:34; 15:17) with the same love that Christ showed to them (John 15:12). In loving Christ, we are loved by God, and God and Christ will abide in us (John 17:23–26).

D. Love in the Writings of Paul

Much as with John, Paul takes a three-part approach to love—the love of God, the love of Christ, and the love of man for Christ and God. Our redemption through Christ is the great sign of God's love for each one of us: "and the life I now live in the flesh I live by faith in the Son of God, who loved me and gave himself for me" (Gal 2:20). It was love that sent Jesus Christ into the world and love that sent him to a sac-

rificial death on the Cross (Rom 5:8; Eph 5:2). The sacrifice of Christ for humanity forms the basis of the Christian life. We embrace the benefits of that loving sacrifice in our total surrender to Christ through faith.

Paul offers the NT's most profound exposition on the Christian concept of love in 1 Cor 13, where he teaches that the greatest attribute of the Christian community must be love. The gifts of speaking in tongues and prophecy are nothing without love; generosity gains us nothing without love (1 Cor 13:1–3). He then describes the key characteristics of love: "Love is patient and kind; love is not jealous or boastful; it is not arrogant or rude. Love does not insist on its own way; it is not irritable or resentful; it does not rejoice at wrong, but rejoices in the right. Love bears all things, believes all things, hopes all things, endures all things" (1 Cor 13:4–7). Love never ends, unlike prophecy and tongues; it will survive to the end of time, when it will be perfected. "For now we see in a mirror dimly, but then face to face. Now I know in part; then I shall understand fully, even as I have been fully understood. So faith, hope, love abide, these three; but the greatest of these is love" (1 Cor 13:12–13).

LOW COUNTRY *See* **Shephelah**.

LUBIM *See* **Libya**.

LUCIFER (Latin, "light-bearer"; Hebrew *hêlēl*, "shining one"; Greek *heōsphoros*, "light-bearer") The Latin name for Venus, the brightest celestial object in the heavens, except for the sun and the moon. Venus was also described as the daystar, or the morning star.

In Isa 14:12, the name was used as a satirical reference to the king of Babylon: "How you are fallen from heaven, O Day Star, son of Dawn!" Among the Fathers of the Church, Lucifer was a name commonly given to Satan, leader of the fallen angels who were expelled from heaven (cf. Luke 10:18; Rev 12:9). The idea is that, before his rebellion against God, Lucifer was the angel of light. The true morning star and light-bearer is Christ (2 Pet 1:19; Rev 22:16).

LUCIUS The name of two men in the New Testament.

1. A Jewish Christian prophet from **Cyrene** who taught at Antioch (Acts 13:1; cf. Acts 11:19–21).

2. A companion of Paul who is called his kinsman and who sent greetings from Corinth to the community in Rome (Rom 16:21). Origen identifies this individual with the evangelist **Luke** (*Comm. Rom.* 10.39).

LUD A name belonging to two people in the **Table of Nations** in Genesis (and its parallel in 1 Chronicles). According to Gen 10:13 and 1 Chr 1:11, the Ludim are descendants of **Ham**, son of **Noah**. In Gen 10:22 and 1 Chr 1:17, Lud is named as the fourth son of **Shem** and a grandson of Noah. Based on these listings, we must distinguish the Hamitic people (Ludim) from the Semitic descendant of Shem (Lud). According to Josephus (*Ant.* 1.144), descendants of Shem through Lud were known in the Hellenistic world as the Lydians. Isa 66:19 and Jer 46:9 describe Lud as a nation adroit with the bow, and Ezek 27:10 and 30:5 refer to Lud as an ally of Tyre.

LUKE A companion of Paul (2 Tim 4:11; Phlm 24). Luke was a Gentile Christian (Col 4:11) hailed by Christian tradition as the author of the third Gospel and its sequel, the Acts of the Apostles. He may have been born in Antioch (cf. Eusebius, *Hist. Eccl.* 3.4); Paul speaks of him as "Luke the beloved physician" (Col 4:14). His training as a physician may be reflected in the New Testament books attributed to him, where we find examples of medical language and an excellent command of Greek style and word choice, the product of the classical education that was customarily provided for the student of medicine.

Paul notes Luke's presence as a companion on three different occasions, in Col 4:14, 2 Tim 4:11, and Phlm 24. In 2 Timothy, Paul writes that "Luke alone is with me." That Luke was with Paul in Rome and elsewhere appears to be confirmed by passages in Acts in which he, as the author, writes the first person plural ("we") (Acts 16:10–17; 20:5–21:18; 27:1–28:16). The second-century Anti-Marcionite Prologues (attached to the Gospels of Mark, Luke, and John, and possibly Matthew, although it was lost) declared that Luke wrote his Gospel in Greece.

Luke's authorship of the third Gospel is affirmed by tradition as expressed by the Muratorian Canon, Tertullian, Origen, and Saint Irenaeus (in the second century), and Saint Jerome and Eusebius (in the fourth century). Luke is considered the author of the Acts of the Apostles, based on its narrative style (Acts 16:10) and its reference to his Gospel (Acts 1:1). Acts was written, according to the Anti-Marcionite Prologues, in the region of Achaea, a Roman province in southern Greece. (See also **Luke, Gospel of** and **Acts of the Apostles** for his theological outlook.)

Luke's writings make up about one-quarter of the NT. Luke and Acts together are as long as the thirteen Pauline Epistles, and Acts itself is longer than the seven Catholic Epistles and Revelation. Luke was also the most literary of the four Evangelists, and his elegant Greek style is considered superior to any found in the NT except for that of Hebrews.

According to one ancient tradition, Luke was said to have died in Boeotia in Greece, unmarried, at the age of eighty-four, and "full of the Holy Spirit." This tradition differs from various unreliable *Acta* (legends that circulated in some quarters of early Christianity) that report his martyrdom. His relics were supposedly transferred to Constantinople by Emperor Constantius II in A.D. 356–357 (Saint Jerome, *Vir. Ill.* 3:7). Luke is honored as the patron saint of doctors and also of painters, from the belief in medieval times that he had painted a picture of the Virgin Mary that was preserved in the Santa Maria Maggiore, Rome. He was called a painter in the tenth-century Menologion of Basil II and by Nicephorus Callistus in the fourteenth century. Most historians date the painting of the Virgin to a later period; it is probably a copy of the painting mentioned by Theodore Lector in the sixth century. Luke's traditional symbol is a bull and his feast day is October 18.

LUKE, GOSPEL OF The third book of the New Testament and counted as one of the three **Synoptic Gospels**. The Gospel of Luke was written for Gentile Christians and is noted for its theme of universality, stressing that the Gospel is for all people, especially the poor and sinners. Luke dedicated the Gospel to **Theophilus**, a convert to Christianity to whom Luke also dedicated the Acts of the Apostles (Acts 1:1). Luke takes as his stated purpose:

> *Inasmuch as many have undertaken to compile a narrative of the things which have been accomplished among us, just as they were delivered to us by those who from the beginning were eyewitnesses and ministers of the word, it seemed good to me also, having followed all things closely for some time past, to write an orderly account for you, most excellent Theophilus, that you may know the truth concerning the things of which you have been informed. (Luke 1:1–4)*

The Gospel is unique in two ways. First, it was the only one written by a Gentile, as all of the other Evangelists (as well as the other NT writers) were Jewish. Second, it is the only NT book to be the first of two parts, with its companion found in Acts. Luke thus should be studied in conjunction with this other work, and together they document the steady progress of the Gospel from Nazareth to Jerusalem, where the saving mission of Jesus reached its culmination and where the Church was established; and from Jerusalem to Rome.

I. AUTHORSHIP AND DATE

Both tradition and the opinion of many scholars identify Luke as the author of both the Gospel and Acts. His authorship is attested in the first four centuries by Saint Irenaeus and Tertullian, as well as the Muratorian Canon, Origen, Eusebius of Caesarea, and Saint Jerome.

The date the Gospel was written is unclear. Conservative estimates place the time of its composition before the Roman conquest of Jerusalem in A.D. 70. More specifically, the date is often pushed back into the early 60s A.D., mainly because the historical narrative of Acts breaks off around A.D. 62, the year that Paul's detainment in Rome ended (Acts 28:14, 30). Nothing in the text of Luke or Acts requires a date later than this. Nevertheless, critical scholars tend to date the Gospel in the 80s A.D., not least because the majority of Gospel scholarship maintains that Luke used the Gospel of Mark in the composition of his story. Since Mark is usually dated shortly before or shortly after A.D. 70, it is judged that time should be allowed for the Gospel of Mark to be published and circulated before Luke took up his task. (*See also* **Synoptic problem**.)

II. CONTENTS

I. Prologue (1:1–4)

II. Infancy Narrative (1:5–2:52)

III. Preparation for Public Ministry (3:1–38)

IV. The Temptation of Jesus (4:1–13)

V. Jesus's Galilean Ministry (4:14–9:50)

VI. Jesus's Jerusalem Ministry (9:51–19:44)

VII. Jesus's Rejection in Jerusalem (19:45–21:38)

VIII. The Passion and Death (22:1–23:56)

IX. Resurrection (24:1–53)

III. LITERARY FEATURES

Luke's background as a Greek, a scholar, and a physician was excellent preparation for composing a Gospel, especially one intended for a Gentile audience. His education is displayed in his skill as a research historian and writer. Unquestionably, the Gospel of Luke is the most literary of the four. The writer chose his words and phrases with great care in order to impart the Good News clearly and eloquently. Aside from their spiritual and exegetical importance, his narratives are excellent literary creations.

Luke was a careful historian, "having followed all things closely for some time past" (Luke 1:3). He studied the life and words of Jesus with utmost care, and he knew and relied upon witnesses to the actual events. As a traveling companion of Paul, Luke came under the influence of his teachings. He seems to have been with Paul during the Caesarean and Roman imprisonments.

Luke followed both Mark and Matthew in their Gospel form, applying a general fourfold outline: John the Baptist's preaching, the ministry of Jesus in Galilee, the ministry of Jesus in Jerusalem, and the Passion and Resurrection. Luke's research enabled him to incorporate unique material not found in the other Gospels, including the Annunciation (Luke 1:26–38), the episode in the Temple when Jesus was a child (2:41–51), the Parables of the Good Samaritan (10:25–37) and the Prodigal Son (15:11–32), and the Ascension (24:50–53). Luke also preserves stunningly beautiful hymns: the Magnificat (1:46–55), the Benedictus (1:68–79), the Gloria (2:14), and the Nunc Dimittis (2:29–35). (*See also* **Synoptic problem**.)

IV. PURPOSE AND THEMES

The central theme of Luke's Gospel is the universality of the Good News. The Gospel proclaims God's unbounded offer of salvation, which is the fulfillment, in the life of Jesus and his Church, of the promises made by God to

Israel. Jesus is first presented by Luke as the Messianic redeemer of Israel, the figure foretold by the prophets (Luke 1:32–33, 68–79). Luke then expands Jesus's saving mission to the Gentiles (2:29–32; 3:4–6), culminating in the command to the apostles "that repentance and forgiveness of sins should be preached in his name to all nations, beginning from Jerusalem" (24:47).

Luke thus stresses the mercy of God, documenting the merciful acts of Christ, including the pardon of the sinful woman (7:36–50), Zacchaeus (19:1–10), the executioners (23:34), and the good thief (23:39–43). Jesus also shows mercy and concern for the poor and oppressed (1:52–53; 4:18; 6:20–26; 14:7–11), and especially shows care and respect for women.

Luke, possibly through personal contact, was able to give a powerful and unique portrayal of Jesus's mother (1:26–56; 2:19, 51). Other women are given prominent parts: Elizabeth (1:39–45), Anna (2:36–38), the widow of Nain (7:11–17), the sinful woman (7:36–50), Mary Magdalene (8:2), Joanna (8:3), Susanna (8:3), Mary and Martha (10:38–42), and the infirm woman (13:10–17). Women are also featured in Jesus's parables, such as the Lost Coin (15:8–10) and the Unrighteous Judge (18:1–8).

Luke's central chapters, 9:51–19:28, trace Jesus's journey from Galilee to Jerusalem, and thereafter also his journey to the Cross and his Resurrection. For Luke, Jerusalem was more than a mere destination. It was the holy city, the site of the **Temple**, the place of divine promises. Luke's Gospel points continually toward Jerusalem, especially as the climactic scene for the Gospel. The infancy account moves toward the Presentation of Jesus in the Temple (2:22) and later Mary and Joseph's discovery of Jesus in the Temple (2:41–51). Similarly, Luke's temptation account reverses the order of the last two temptations as presented in Matthew so that the climax is reached in Jerusalem (4:9). Jesus's entire ministry is hence one of progress toward the city. All who claim to be Christians must take up the Cross and follow Jesus on their own passage to Jerusalem.

Finally, Luke also devotes much attention to the interior life of prayer. Jesus is constantly seen in prayer, seeking the Father's will at numerous critical moments of his ministry (5:16; 6:12; 23:34, 46).

LUZ *See* **Bethel**.

LYCAONIA A territory in central Asia Minor that derived its name from its inhabitants, the Lykaones. The area was divided up among several surrounding regions by Pompey the Great in 64 B.C.: the west was attached to Cilicia; the east to Cappadocia; and the north to Galatia. Nevertheless, the Lykaones retained their own language and cultural identity (Acts 14:11). The Lycaonia of the New Testament was part of the Roman province of **Galatia**, and Paul and Barnabas visited the chief cities—Derbe, Lystra, and Iconium—during their first missionary journey (Acts 14:1–6).

LYCIA A mountainous region on the southwestern coast of Asia Minor. The Lycians, along with several other peoples, received a letter from the Roman consul, Lucius, warning them against all forms of hostility toward the Jews of Palestine, with whom the Romans had made an alliance (1 Macc 15:23). Lycia figured in Paul's journey to Rome (Acts 21:1; 27:5).

LYDIA

1. A Jewish woman, a dealer in purple cloth from Thyatira, who became a Christian when Paul was in Philippi (Acts 16:11–15).

2. A region in western Asia Minor.

LYRE A stringed instrument played with a plectrum (1 Sam 10:5; 1 Kgs 10:12; 1 Chr 13:8; Neh 12:27; Ps 57:8, 81:2, 98:5). The lyre was generally used to accompany singing (Gen 31:27; 2 Sam 6:5; Isa 23:16). With the harp and the lute, it was a popular instrument in the ancient Near East.

LYSANIUS The tetrarch of Abilene, a district situated approximately twenty miles northwest of Damascus, at the time John the Baptist embarked upon his ministry (Luke 3:1).

LYSIAS A Syrian nobleman and member of the royal family who served as temporary regent under **Antiochus IV Epiphanes** over a territory extending from the Euphrates to the Egyptian border at the time that Antiochus invaded Persia (1 Macc 3:32–34). He was also appointed guardian to **Antiochus V Eupator** and given half of Antiochus's army. His chief order was to wage war upon the Maccabees and capture Jerusalem (1 Macc 3:35–36). The troops he dispatched were defeated by **Judas Maccabeus** at Emmaus (1 Macc 3:38–4:25). Lysias then set out for Idumea but was personally defeated by Judas at Beth-zur and compelled to withdraw to await reinforcements (1 Macc 4:26–35; cf. 2 Macc 11:6–15).

Disappointed in Lysias and knowing that he did not have long to live, Antiochus IV Epiphanes named his friend **Philip** to be regent for his son, Antiochus V (1 Macc 6:14–15). This situation proved intolerable to Lysias, so he installed Antiochus V as king and marched against Jerusalem (1 Macc 6:18–20). This time, Lysias was successful, and Judas was killed in battle. Lysias's siege operations against the citadel at Jerusalem were called off, however, when word arrived that Philip was making a bid for the throne in Antioch (1 Macc 6:48–57). After making a hasty peace with the Jews, Lysias headed for Syria and captured Antioch. In 162–161 b.c., he was captured by **Demetrius I Soter**; both Lysias and Antiochus V were put to death (1 Macc 7:1–4).

LYSIMACHUS The name of two men in late Old Testament times.

1. The translator of the "Letter of Purim" in **Esther** (Esth 11:1); he is described as the son of Ptolemy and a resident of Jerusalem.

2. The brother of the high priest **Menelaus** (2 Macc 4:29) who was established by Menelaus in the post of deputy while the latter was summoned to the Seleucid court. In Menelaus's absence, Lysimachus stole from the Temple. Much hated, he was killed in a riot provoked by his acts of sacrilege (2 Macc 4:39–42).

LYSTRA A city in **Lycaonia**, in central Asia Minor. **Paul** and **Barnabas** visited Lystra after they fled from Iconium (Acts 14:6). The inhabitants of Lystra revered the two men as gods after Paul healed a lame man (Acts 14:8–18). But when Paul's enemies arrived from Iconium, they persuaded the inhabitants of Lystra that Paul was a charlatan; the Lystrans then stoned Paul into unconsciousness (Acts 14:19). Still, Paul returned to Lystra to give support and encouragement to the converts (Acts 14:20–23). Lystra was also the home of **Timothy** (Acts 16:1–2).

M

MAACAH The name of several people and a kingdom in the Old Testament.

1. The daughter of Talmai, the king of Gessur. The princess Maacah married **David** and became the mother of **Absalom** and Tamar (2 Sam 3:3; 1 Chr 3:2).

2. The father of **Achish**, the king of Gath (1 Kgs 2:39).

3. One of the wives of King **Rehoboam** of Judah, the mother of King **Abijam** (1 Kgs 15:2), and the grandmother of **Asa** (1 Kgs 15:10). Eventually she was deposed from her position as Queen Mother for the crime of sponsoring idolatry in Israel (1 Kgs 15:13).

4. An Aramean kingdom south of Mount Hermon. Its capital was Abel Beth-maacah (Josh 12:5, 13:11; 2 Sam 20:14). Maacah allied itself with the Ammonites against David (2 Sam 10:6–8).

MAADIAH A priest who returned from the **Exile** (Neh 12:5).

MAARATH A town in central Judah (Josh 15:59).

MAASAI A priest who returned from the **Exile** (1 Chr 9:12).

MAASEIAH A common name in the Old Testament. Among the more notable bearers of the name are the following.

1. A Levitical musician in the time of David (1 Chr 15:18, 20).

2. A commander who took part in the coup that deposed **Athaliah** and enthroned **Josiah** (2 Chr 23:1).

3. The governor of Jerusalem during the reign of Josiah (2 Chr 34:8).

4. The father of the false **Zedekiah** (Jer 29:21).

MAATH An ancestor of Jesus in the genealogy given by Luke (Luke 3:26).

MACCABEES, FIRST AND SECOND BOOKS OF The last of the Historical Books of the Old Testament. They narrate the struggle led by **Judas Maccabeus** and his brothers against the Seleucid kings in the second century B.C. Although related to some extent because of common subject matter, the two books are independent of each other. Both books are among the **deuterocanonical** books, accepted as Scripture by Catholic and Orthodox Christians.

I. AUTHORSHIP AND DATE

In all probability, 1 Maccabees was originally written in Hebrew. Testimony to this effect comes from Saint Jerome, who wrote that he saw the book in Hebrew. Internal evidence also suggests that the books were translated into Greek from a Semitic original. The author is unknown, although the language indicates that the work was composed in Palestine by a writer who was familiar with Palestinian geography and who was deliberately trying to imitate the historical style of an earlier period (e.g., 1 and 2 Samuel and 1 and 2 Kings). The date of its composition is uncertain, but it was probably written after 134 B.C., following the death of Simon and during the period of John Hyrcanus (134–104 B.C.).

The Second book of Maccabees was written in Greek as an abridgment of a five-volume history of the Maccabees written by Jason of Cyrene (2 Macc 2:19–31). The larger work is now lost, and nothing further is known of Jason, except that he probably lived in Palestine, as his work shows considerable geographical knowledge. As for the author of 2 Maccabees, he may have lived in Alexandria, Egypt, and his mention of the resurrection of the dead (7:14) raises the possibility that he may have been a Pharisee. The book was probably composed in Greek, given its limited number of Hebraisms and the presence of native Greek idioms and constructions. The date for its composition has been estimated at a time after 124 B.C. and perhaps as late as 80 B.C.

II. CONTENTS

1 MACCABEES

I. *Introduction (chaps. 1–2)*

    A. *Alexander the Great and the Seleucid Persecution (1:1–63)*

    B. *Mattathias and His Sons (2:1–70)*

II. *The Leadership of Judas Maccabeus (3:1–9:22)*

III. *The Leadership of Jonathan (9:23–12:53)*

IV. *The Leadership of Simon (13:1–16:17)*

V. *The Reign of John Hyrcanus (16:18–24)*

2 MACCABEES

I. *Introduction (chaps. 1–2)*

    A. *A Letter to the Jews in Egypt (1:1–9)*

    B. *A Letter to Aristobulus (1:10–2:18)*

    C. *Preface (2:19–32)*

II. *Heliodorus and the Temple Treasury (3:1–40)*

III. *The High Priesthood—Simon, Jason, and Menelaus (4:1–5:27)*

IV. *Persecution of the Jews (6:1–7:42)*

V. *The Rebellion of Judas Maccabeus (8:1–15:38)*

III. PURPOSE AND THEMES

The First and Second books of Maccabees recount the background and events of the forty-year (175–135 B.C.) struggle against the invasion of paganism and Hellenization into Jewish Palestine. Hellenization was a government policy of Alexander the Great and his successors. It brought especially difficult challenges to Judaism when the Seleucids promoted the pagan Greek cults in opposition to monotheism. Complicating the situation in Palestine was the emergence of a pro-Hellenizing party among the Jewish leadership. In 167 B.C., Antiochus IV Epiphanes (*see* **Seleucids**) of

Syria brought the cult of Zeus into the sacred precincts of the Jerusalem Temple. A revolt ensued, sparked by the zeal of **Mattathias** (1 Macc 2:23–33) and carried forward by his sons Judas Maccabeus (1 Macc 3–9; 2 Macc 8–15), Jonathan (1 Macc 9:23–12:53), and Simon (1 Macc 13:1–16:17). The victory of the Jewish cause was symbolized by the recapture of Jerusalem and the rededication of the Temple (1 Macc 4:36–61; 2 Macc 10:1–8).

The author of 1 Maccabees equates the survival of Jewish monotheism with the survival of Israel, thus forging a close link between religion and patriotism. "Israel" means the faithful people of God, and those who forsake the Law no longer belong to Israel: "Many of the people, every one who forsook the law, joined the Syrians, and they did evil in the land; they drove Israel into hiding in every place of refuge they had" (1 Macc 1:52–53).

The narrative of 1 Maccabees presents the Maccabean line as the custodians of the Mosaic Law. They are raised up by the Lord to fight the forces of Hellenism that were threatening the purity of the Jewish faith. The style of the work emulates that of the earlier Historical Books, but with an even greater emphasis on the Law as the manifestation of God's will. The revolt is seen in terms of the Law's triumph over the enemies of the Lord.

The Second book of Maccabees covers much the same ground as 1 Maccabees 1–7, but it is more explicit in giving a theological interpretation of the events of the period. It explains the feast of the dedication of the Temple, a key event in the survival of Judaism (commemorated in the feast of Hanukkah; see **Dedication, feast of**); it also stresses the primacy of God's action in the struggle for survival and gives witness to a firmly held belief in an afterlife and the resurrection of the body (2 Macc 7:14; 12:43–46). Thus, the religious interpretation of the Maccabean struggle is more important here, and because of the writer's theology of history he sees the war given support by divine will even as he recognizes that the persecution of the Jewish people and the very desecration of the Temple were consequences of the people's sinfulness (5:17–20; 6:12–17). The author exalts the Temple of Jerusalem as the center of Jewish worship and several times reminds the reader of its greatness (cf. 2:19, 22; 5:15; 14:31). He calls upon the Jews to be faithful to the Law, and reminds them of God's fidelity to the covenant. The Lord will not abandon his people if they repent and are faithful to him. The power of God is manifested in miraculous and supernatural deeds that prove God's presence among his people (3:24–27; 5:2–3; 10:29–30). Martyrdom is extolled as a noble sacrifice (6:18–7:42).

Two similar books, 3 and 4 Maccabees, are also extant. The Third book of Maccabees, which is not in the Catholic canon but is accepted by Eastern Orthodox churches, tells the story of the Jewish persecution in Egypt under Ptolemy IV Philopator (r. 221–205 B.C.); it is thus unrelated to the events of 1 and 2 Maccabees. The Fourth book of Maccabees, which is an appendix in some Orthodox Bibles, is a Jewish philosophical treatise on "whether devout reason is sovereign over the emotions"; it uses stories like the martyrdom of Eleazar and of the seven brothers as illustrations (cf. 2 Macc 6–7).

MACCABEUS (Hebrew, "hammer") The nickname of **Judas**, son of **Mattathias** (1 Macc 2:4; cf. 2 Macc 5:27; Josephus, *Ant.* 12.266), the valiant leader of the rebellion against Antiochus IV Epiphanes and his Hellenizing persecutions of the Jews. The nickname was a reference to his hard-hitting guerrilla war; later, the name came to be applied to his brothers who followed him in leading the rebellion.

MACEDONIA A region in northern Greece that emerged into prominence in the fourth century B.C. through its two rulers, Philip II and especially his son, **Alexander the Great**. The Greeks once considered Macedon to be a barbarian region, but the cities of Greece fell under the dominion of Philip, while Alexander built upon these triumphs and conquered the Persian Empire and beyond. The campaigns of Alexander had a lasting influence on the Near East and set in motion a process of Hellenization that continued in the centuries after his death in 323 B.C. (1 Macc 1:1; 6:2). By the first century A.D., Macedonia was a province of the Roman Empire, with its capital at Thessalonica. Paul visited there as a result of a dream of "a man of Macedonia" (Acts 16:9) and revisited Macedonia during his third missionary journey (Acts 20:1–2). He established churches at Philippi and Thessalonica and remembered his time in Macedonia with great affection (Phil 4:1; 1 Thess 1:3). The churches in Macedonia gave generously to Paul's collection of funds in support of the churches in Judea (2 Cor 8:1–4).

MACHAERUS A site east of the Dead Sea where Alexander Jannaeus constructed a fortress around 90 B.C. The fortress was destroyed by the Romans in 57 B.C. but was rebuilt by Herod the Great. According to Josephus, **Herod Antipas** imprisoned **John the Baptist** at Machaerus; he was also beheaded there (*Ant.* 18.116–19). The fortress was again destroyed by the Romans around A.D. 71. The remains are identified with the modern site of Khirbet el Mukawer.

MACHBANAI A warrior of the tribe of Gad who served David as one of his army officers (1 Chr 12:13–14).

MACHIR The son of **Manasseh**, the grandson of the patriarch **Joseph**, and the father of **Gilead**—hence he is ancestor of the Gileadites (Gen 50:23; Num 26:29). His role as father of the Gileadites stems from the conquest of Gilead, which lies directly east of the **Jordan**, and the expulsion of the Amorites (Num 32:39–40). The clan of Machir thus settled the northern **Transjordan** (cf. Josh 13:31, 17:1; Judg 5:14).

MACHPELAH A cave and surrounding field near Hebron that **Abraham** purchased from Ephron the Hittite to serve as the burial site for his family (Gen 23:1–20). Intended originally for the burial of **Sarah**, Machpelah was used for other family members, including Abraham himself (Gen 25:9), as well as **Isaac**, **Rebekah**, **Leah**, and **Jacob** (Gen 49:31; 50:13). A mosque in Hebron built over a cave is reputed to cover the site, the Haram el-Khalil, the Enclosure of Abraham. Local tradition has pointed to that location as the cave of Machpelah at least since the fourth century A.D.

MADMANNAH A village in the **Negeb**, in southern Judah (Josh 15:30).

MADMENAH A town north of Jerusalem mentioned by the prophet Isaiah (Isa 10:31).

MADON A city in northern Canaan ruled by Jobab (Josh 11:1). Madon joined the coalition of **Jabin**, king of Hazor, that attempted to halt the Israelite conquest of Canaan under **Joshua**, but the alliance was defeated (Josh 12:19).

MAGADAN A region into which Jesus traveled after feeding the four thousand (Matt 15:39). In Mark 8:10, the district is called Dalmanutha. It is probably along the western shore of the Sea of Galilee, but its location is unknown. (*See also* **Dalmanutha**.)

MAGDALA (Hebrew, "tower") A town on the western shore of the Sea of Galilee, just north of Tiberias, and identified with the modern site of el-Mejdel. This may have been the home of Mary Magdalene (Matt 27:56, 61; Mark 15:40; 16:1; Luke 8:2; 24:10; John 19:25; 20:1).

MAGDALENE, MARY *See* **Mary Magdalene**.

MAGI Ancient wise men who were specialists in dream interpretation, astrology, and sometimes magic. In the **Septuagint**, the Greek term *magoi* is given to the Babylonian court magicians called in to interpret King Nebu-chadnezzar's dreams (Dan 1:20; 2:2, 10, 27). In the New Testament, a "magi" once refers to a practitioner of occult magic (Acts 13:6). More significantly, the name "magi" was given to the foreign dignitaries who traveled to Palestine from the east to pay homage to the infant Jesus. These are often identified with members of a priestly caste from Persia who specialized in dream analysis and astrology (see, e.g., the description in Herodotus, *Hist.* 1.101). Their occupation explains their interest in unusual astral phenomena (the star of Bethlehem), and their origin makes them the first Gentiles to recognize and give reverence to the Kingship of Christ.

On the basis of the Old Testament (cf. Ps 72:10; Isa 49:7; 60:3, 6) the tradition arose that the Magi were three kings, even though Matthew does not state their number. The idea that there were three of them is inferred from the three gifts, and the idea that they were kings arises from OT prophetic texts (Ps 72:10–111; Isa 60:3, 6). Christian legend names them Balthasar, Gaspar, and Melchior. Later interpreters attached a symbolic meaning to the three gifts: gold, because Jesus was a King; frankincense, because he was God; and myrrh, because he became a mortal man.

Supposed relics of the magi are preserved in the Cologne Cathedral. They were brought there in 1163 from Milan (where they had been transferred to in the fifth century).

MAGIC AND SORCERY The occult art of manipulating natural and spiritual forces. The Church, in harmony with Scripture, teaches that all forms of magic and sorcery are contrary to revealed religion. They are especially reprehensible when practiced with the intention of doing harm and when they involve the invocation of demons (CCC 2117).

Magic was commonplace in the cultures of the ancient Near East. Among the Mesopotamians, magic was understood to be a pervasive force in daily life, and many ordinary troubles of life were attributed to the activities of demons and the casting of spells and curses by sorcerers and witches. Magic was thus essential for personal protection and purification. In Egypt, magic was equally widespread; it was used to prevent illness, cure ailments, and achieve one's desires.

In the Old Testament, all forms of magic and witchcraft are prohibited (Lev 19:31; Deut 18:9–14), with punishments including the death penalty. The fundamental understanding of the Israelites was that God was indisputably superior to any kind of magic, as demonstrated by the superior abilities of Moses and Aaron over the Egyptian magicians (Exod 7:10–23; 8:1–7; 9:8–12) and the inability of Balaam to place curses upon the Israelites (Num 22–24). The magic of foreign nations was viewed derisively (Nah 3:4; Isa 47:12), and Israelites targeted eradicating magic and superstition in much the same way that they sought to suppress idolatry (2 Kgs 9:22, 17:17, 21:6; 2 Chr 33:6; Isa 3:3, 57:3; Jer 27:9; Ezek 13:18; Mic 5:12; Mal 3:5).

In the New Testament, the superiority of God over the power of magic is reiterated, as, for example, when Peter and Paul confounded magicians in Acts (8:9–24; 13:6–11; 19:13–18). Christian converts in Ephesus burned books of magic (Acts 19:19). In Revelation, magic and sorcery were performed by the great harlot (Rev 18:23; cf. Rev 9:21; 21:8). (*See also* **Divination**.)

MAGNIFICAT The first word in the **Vulgate** version of Luke 1:46–55, a hymn of Mary that begins in the Latin, "*Magnificat anima mea Dominum*" ("My soul does magnify the Lord"). The canticle was recited by Mary during her visit to Elizabeth. It borrows images and expressions from the Old Testament Psalms and bears a striking similarity to the Song of **Hannah** (1 Sam 2:1–10). It extols God's merciful deliverance of the lowly and expresses Mary's joy at being chosen by God to be an instrument of his love and mercy. (*See* **Mary**.)

MAGOG *See* **Gog**.

MAGUS, SIMON *See* **Simon Magus**.

MAHALAB A town listed in the tribal territory of Asher (Josh 19:29).

MAHALALEL The son of Kenan, the father of **Jared**, and a patriarch who lived before the **Flood**. Mahalalel was born when Kenan was 70 years old (Gen 5:12), and he fathered Jared at the age of 65; he lived to the age of 895 (Gen 5:15–17). He is counted among the ancestors of Jesus (Luke 3:37).

MAHANAIM (Hebrew, "two camps") A town in Gilead, along the Jabbok River, where **Jacob** had a vision of angels before his meeting with **Esau** (Gen 32:1–2). The name has its origin in this event, when Jacob realized that a heavenly camp of angels was there beside his own camp of family members and livestock. Named a **Levitical city** (Josh 21:38; 1 Chr 6:80), it was used by **Ish-bosheth** (2 Sam 2:12) and by David during the revolt of **Absalom** (2 Sam 17:24–27).

MAHANEH-DAN (Hebrew, "camp of Dan") Located roughly fifteen miles west of Jerusalem in the tribal territory of Judah. It was used as a camp by Danite scouts in search of a new tribal territory (Judg 18:12). Here, too, the Danite judge Samson first felt the stirrings of the Spirit (Judg 13:25).

MAHARAI One of the mighty warriors in the service of David (2 Sam 23:28; 1 Chr 11:30).

MAHER-SHALAL-HASH-BAZ (Hebrew, "speedy spoil, hasty plunder") The name given by **Isaiah** to his son (Isa 8:1–4). It was intended to assure King **Ahaz** that the danger then posed to Judah by Syria and Israel would soon pass because the Assyrians would soon conquer and despoil them.

MAKHELOTH The tenth encampment of the Israelites after their departure from the Sinai wilderness (Num 33:25).

MAKKEDAH A royal city of the Amorites located in southwestern Canaan. The Amorite kings of Jerusalem—Hebron, Jarmuth, Lachish, and Eglon—who had formed a southern alliance against the Israelites fled to a cave near the city, but they were caught and put to death (Josh 10:16–27; 12:16). Following the conquest of Canaan, Makkedah became part of the territory of Judah (Josh 15:41).

MALACHI, BOOK OF The last of the twelve minor prophets of the Old Testament. Its target is the crisis of faith that set in among the Temple priesthood in the period after the **Exile**. The oracles of Malachi are a summons to repentance and renewed commitment to the Lord's "covenant with Levi" (Mal 2:4). The predictions of Malachi look ahead to a "pure offering" that will rise to heaven among the nations (1:11), and to the coming of a "messenger" (3:1) resembling the prophet Elijah who will announce the dreadful "day of the LORD" (4:5).

I. AUTHORSHIP AND DATE

The author of the book is identified simply as "Malachi" (Mal 1:1), which in Hebrew means "my messenger" (cf. 3:1). Nothing further is known of this figure, except that he fulfills the classical role of a prophet who confronts Israel with the Lord's will and calls for a return to the obligations of the covenant.

Scholars generally date the work to the fifth century B.C., and some consider the prophet to have been a contemporary of Ezra and Nehemiah. Support for this judgment is found in the observation that Malachi paid attention to many of the same themes as both of those important reformers.

II. CONTENTS

I. Superscription (1:1)

II. The Love of the Lord (1:2–5)

III. The Iniquity of the Priests (1:6–14)

III. PURPOSE AND THEMES

Malachi's primary purpose was to correct abuses among the priests and people at a time when disappointment and disillusionment weighed heavy on the Jewish community. Frustration was expressed as a general disinterest in the proper rubrics of Temple worship and the demands of spiritual leadership. Whereas Haggai and Zechariah devoted themselves to overcoming low morale among the returnees from exile, Malachi gave his ministry to correcting the abuses that had arisen after the reconstruction of the **Temple** and the resumption of the sacrificial cult.

The book is a literary ensemble of several discourses. The prophet was especially critical of the state of the priesthood and sacrifices (cf. Mal 1:6–13; 2:1–4, 8–9; 3:3–4, 6–11). The priests, Malachi complains, offered blemished animals for sacrifice (1:6; 2:9) and so discharged their duties in violation of the **Law** (cf. Lev 22:17–25; Deut 17:1). In the face of this, the prophet proclaims: "For from the rising of the sun to its setting my name is great among the nations, and in every place incense is offered to my name, and a pure offering; for my name is great among the nations, says the LORD of hosts" (Mal 1:11). Christians see this vision as a prophecy of the **Eucharist** sacrifice of Messianic times, an interpretation affirmed by the Council of Trent.

Malachi was also concerned with perennial challenges to the fidelity of Israel: idolatry (2:10–12), social injustice (3:5), and mixed marriages and divorce (2:10–16). His statements against the practice of divorce and mixed marriage remind us of the reforms of **Ezra** and **Nehemiah**.

In his final oracles, Malachi turns to the subject of eschatological judgment. He speaks of the **day of the Lord** (3:1–5) when "I send my messenger to prepare the way before me, and the LORD whom you seek will suddenly come to his temple" (3:1). This messenger in Jewish tradition was **Elijah** (cf. 4:5). Jesus spoke of the coming of this messenger in **John the Baptist** (11:10–14), who came in the spirit and power of Elijah (Luke 1:17). On the day of the Lord, Malachi tells us, "all the arrogant and all evildoers will be stubble; the day that comes shall burn them up, says the LORD of hosts, so that it will leave them neither root nor branch" (Mal 3:19). In this day, the righteous will rejoice in the defeat of the wicked.

MALCHUS A slave of the high priest **Caiaphas**. At the time of Jesus's arrest in the Garden of **Gethsemane**, Peter cut off Malchus's right ear with a sword (Matt 26:51; Mark 14:47; Luke 22:50; John 18:10). Although all four Gospels record the event, only John mentions the high priest's servant by name. John adds the detail that a relative of Malchus, also a servant of the high priest, recognized Peter as having been with Jesus while the disciple stood outside the gate of the high priest's house (John 18:26). Luke, however, is the only Gospel writer to note that Jesus healed Malchus's ear (Luke 22:51). The name Malchus was a common one in and around the first century, as attested by Nabatean and Palmyrene inscriptions.

MALTA An island in the central Mediterranean Sea that was first occupied in the early fourth millennium B.C. The island came under the control of the Romans in 218 B.C. and was governed as part of the province of Sicily. Paul washed up on the shores of Malta after a shipwreck caused by the severe winds blowing from Crete (Acts 27:13–28:10).

MAMMON (Aramaic, "wealth") A word used by Jesus to refer to wealth in the Sermon on the Mount (Matt 6:24) and in the explanation of the Parable of the Dishonest Steward (Luke 16:9, 11, 13): "No one can serve two masters; for either he will hate the one and love the other, or he will be devoted to the one and despise the other. You cannot serve God and mammon" (Matt 6:24). "Mammon" is used to mean that which is pursued and valued to the point of idolatry and so separates the possessor from God. That use is paralleled in rabbinical writings.

MAMRE An Amorite chieftain who owned a wooded plot of oak trees near **Hebron** in southern Canaan (Gen 14:13). **Abraham** lived near the oaks of Mamre for a time during his travels in Palestine (Gen 13:18; 18:1) and forged a covenant alliance with Mamre and his brothers, Eshcol and Aner (Gen 14:13). In time, the location itself became known as Mamre and was said to lie just west of the patriarchs' family tomb, the cave of **Machpelah** (Gen 23:17; 25:9; 49:30; 50:13). **Isaac** and **Jacob**, like Abraham before them, sojourned for a time at Mamre

(Gen 35:27). One ancient tradition identifies it with the modern site of Ramet-el-Khalil.

MAN (Hebrew *ʾādām*, "man" or "mankind") The word used to describe the human being or the human race, as distinct from the animals. Man, or the human person, is a living being composed of a material body that is mortal and a soul that is immortal. Man is thus both corporeal and spiritual (Gen 2:7); the union of spirit and matter does not result in the presence of two united natures but instead forms the single nature that is the human person (cf. GS §14).

The Genesis account teaches that man is the special creation of God. Man was created in the image of God with the intention that he should live in friendship with God and join him in having dominion over the world. Being a creature, man has the obligation to know, love, and serve God. For this task he is equipped with a rational intellect and a free will capable of responding to God's truth and love. In the biblical vision, man's primary mission in life is to glorify God by his every word and action; having come forth from God, he is called to give himself back to God.

I. MAN IN THE OLD TESTAMENT

Scripture speaks of man in different ways. When viewing the human person as a whole, it can speak of man as "flesh" (Gen 6:2), insofar as he is a bodily creature, or he can be called a "soul" or "person" (Gen 46:27), insofar as his flesh lives and breathes. At other times, however, man is described in terms of his component parts. Genesis offers the figurative description of man's *body* being formed from the dust of the ground and his *soul*, or vital principle, being breathed into him directly by God (Gen 2:7). **Death**, as defined in the Bible, is the separation of these two elements once united (Job 34:14–15; Ps 104:29; Eccl 12:7).

II. MAN IN THE NEW TESTAMENT

The New Testament assumes throughout the fundamental notions of Old Testament anthropology: the union of body and soul, the division into male and female, the commandment to be fruitful and multiply, and death as the separation of the soul from the body. But the NT is more concerned with the *spiritual condition* than with the physical constitution of man.

There is more emphasis on the sinfulness of man through Adam, the reign of sin in the world (Rom 1:18–32), and concupiscence (Rom 7:7–23). Man is a slave to sin (Rom 6:6) and is liberated by Christ (John 8:34–36). The old man must be cast off and the new man put on (Eph 4:22). This new man is a renovation of the image and likeness of God in man (Rom 8:29; Eph 4:24; Col 3:10).

Saint Paul speaks directly of the spiritual situation of man when he contrasts two men: Adam and Christ. Christ is the New Adam (1 Cor 15:49), the new man, who is the beginning of a new humanity through his redemptive death and Resurrection. Man is born into sin and death through Adam, but a new life is possible through Christ. This newness of humanity is the likeness of Christ and begins in baptism (2 Cor 5:17; Gal 3:27).

MAN, SON OF *See* **Son of Man**.

MANAEN One of the leaders of the Christian community in Antioch (Acts 13:1). He is described as a *syntrophos* of Herod Antipas, a title that has been interpreted variously to mean that he was "brought up together" with Herod or was a "foster-brother" or a "companion" from their youth. Regardless of the specific meaning, it is clear that Manaen stood in some close relationship to Herod; the RSV translates *syntrophos* as "a member of the court."

MANASSEH Two important figures bear this name in the Old Testament.

1. The son of **Joseph**, the grandson of **Jacob**, and the ancestor of one of the twelve tribes of Israel. Manasseh was born to Joseph and Asenath, the daughter of Potiphera the priest of On (Gen 41:50–51; 46:20). With his younger brother **Ephraim**, Manasseh was adopted by Jacob and received his blessing, although Jacob preferred Ephraim as firstborn (Gen 48:8–20). The tribe of Manasseh was counted as being 32,200 strong in one census (Num 1:35) and 52,700 strong in a second census (Num 26:34). Half of the tribe settled in the **Transjordan** (Num 32:39–42; Josh 13:29–31), and the other half settled north of Ephraim to the west of the Jordan (Josh 17:7–12). Memorable figures from the tribe of Manasseh include **Gideon** (Judg 6:15) and **Jephthah** (Judg 11:1).

2. The king of Judah from 696 to 642 B.C. and the son and successor of King **Hezekiah** (2 Kgs 20:21; 2 Chr 32:33). He is remembered as one of the worst kings of Judah. He acceded to the throne at the age of twelve (2 Kgs 21:1; 2 Chr 33:1) and had a very long reign. The dominant political force during the period

was Assyria, and Manasseh embraced a pro-Assyrian policy that sought to buy time for his much weaker kingdom. Manasseh supported the installation of foreign cults with an enthusiasm not seen even among the apostate kings of Judah before him. He sacrificed his own son to pagan idols, and he was addicted to every kind of superstition (2 Kgs 21:1–9; 2 Chr 33:1–10). In 2 Chr 33:11–20, we read that Manasseh was taken captive to Assyria, repented, and upon his return suppressed the idolatrous worship. This reformation of the king's character formed the basis of a Jewish apocryphal work called the *Prayer of Manasseh*.

MANASSEH, TRIBE OF *See* **Manasseh**.

MANDRAKE An herb, *Mandragora officinarum*, that is found in Palestine and is noted for its distinctive roots that are shaped like a human body. Probably because of that resemblance, it was especially valued as an aphrodisiac (Gen 30:14; Song 7:13). The Hebrew name of the herb is derived from a root meaning "love."

MANGER A feeding trough for livestock (Luke 13:15). Jesus was placed in a manger soon after his birth (Luke 2:7, 12, 16). Some scholars have suggested that the Greek *phatnē* should be translated "stall" rather than "manger," but this is uncertain.

MANNA The bread from heaven that fed the Israelites on their **Exodus** journey from Egypt to Canaan (Exod 16:4, 35). Each morning the manna spread like wafers over the ground so that each family could gather a daily supply,

and a double supply was collected every Friday in preparation for the Sabbath rest (Exod 16:16–30). According to various descriptions, the manna had a flaky texture (Exod 16:14), it was white but translucent like bdellium (Num 11:7), and its taste resembled wafers made with honey (Exod 16:31). Not until Israel finally arrived in Canaan and began to eat of the produce of the Promised Land did the manna cease to fall (Josh 5:12).

Manna takes its name from the question asked when it first appeared in the wilderness: "What is it?" (Exod 16:14). In Hebrew, this is "*mān hû*?" Manna was also known in biblical tradition by such poetical names as "the grain of heaven" (Ps 78:24), "the bread of the angels" (Ps 78:25), and "bread from heaven" (Ps 105:40).

In the New Testament, manna is considered a type of the **Eucharist**. We see this first in Jesus's Bread of Life Discourse (John 6:31–59). When asked what sign Jesus would give to match that of manna in the wilderness, Jesus replied,

Truly, truly, I say to you, it was not Moses who gave you the bread from heaven; my Father gives you the true bread from heaven . . . I am the bread of life; he who comes to me shall not hunger, and he who believes in me shall never thirst . . . Your fathers ate the manna in the wilderness, and they died. This is the bread which comes down from heaven, that a man may eat of it and not die. I am the living bread which came down from heaven; if any one eats of this bread, he will live for ever; and the bread which I shall give for the life of the world is my flesh.

The "daily bread" of the Lord's Prayer (Matt 6:11; Luke 11:3) may also be an allusion to the manna that fell daily as a sign of God's providential care for his children.

We also see the Eucharistic typology in Paul, who implicitly links the "spiritual food" of the manna with the Eucharist that sustains us in the Christian life (1 Cor 10:3).

MANOAH The father of **Samson** (Judg 13:2).

MANUAL OF DISCIPLINE *See* **Qumran, Khirbet**.

MANUSCRIPTS OF THE BIBLE *See* **Texts of the Bible**.

MARAH (Hebrew, "bitter") The first camp of the Israelites after they crossed the Red Sea (Num 33:8). They journeyed for three days without finding water, and when they arrived at the site they found water, but it was bitter to the point of being undrinkable (Exod 15:22–26). A wordplay is thus made in Hebrew between the "bitter" waters (*mar*) and the place where they were located (*mārāh*). Marah is often identified with the modern site of Ain Hawarah.

MARANATHA An Aramaic expression that appears in 1 Cor 16:22. It may have been pronounced "*marana tha*," meaning "Come, Lord," or as "*maran atha*," meaning "Our Lord has come," or possibly "Our Lord is coming." The first configuration is more likely than the second, in part because the expression appears in the context of prayer rather than catechesis or prophecy. The same can be said for Rev 22:20, where it is believed to underlie the concluding prayer, "Come, Lord Jesus!" Outside the New Testament, the invocation appears at the end of an ancient Eucharistic liturgy: "Let grace come and this world pass away. Hosanna to the God of David. If anyone is holy, let him come; if he is not, let him repent. Maranatha. Amen" (*Did.* 10, 6) (CCC 951, 671).

MARDUK The patron deity of the ancient city of **Babylon**. With the rise of the Old Babylonian kingdom, and especially under the cultural and political leadership of Hammurabi, Marduk himself rose to become the supreme deity of the Babylonian pantheon. His name appears once in the Bible as "Merodach" (Jer 50:2), and several times he is mentioned under the title "Bel" (Jer 50:2; Dan 14:3, 5–6, 9; etc.).

MARE ADRIATICUM *See* **Adria**.

MARE INTERNUM *See* **Mediterranean Sea**.

MARI An ancient city located along the Euphrates River, probably the modern Tell Hariri, in Syria. Although it is not mentioned in the Bible, Mari is important to biblical historians because more than twenty thousand tablets were found there that have provided enormously useful glimpses into the ancient Near East from the third millennium B.C.—the time of the city's founding—to the second millennium B.C., when it flourished as a trade center. Owing to its commercial prominence, it was the target of ambitious regional powers. It fell to Hammurabi, the sixth king of the

First Amorite Dynasty of Babylon (ca. 1792–1750 B.C.), and was destroyed utterly as a result of an unsuccessful rebellion. Abandoned after that, Mari was forgotten until it was discovered in the twentieth century. The site continues to yield tablet fragments and is thus an ongoing source of enlightenment for archaeologists.

MARK Also known as John Mark, he was the son of Mary of Jerusalem (Acts 12:12), a cousin of **Barnabas** (Col 4:10), and regarded by tradition as the author of the second Gospel. An early convert and member of the Christian community of Jerusalem, he might have been the young man who fled naked when Jesus was arrested (Mark 14:51–52)—a peculiar detail that appears in none of the other Gospels. He accompanied Barnabas and **Paul** on the first missionary journey, but, for reasons that are unclear, he left them in Pamphylia (Acts 13:13). This caused a breach between Barnabas and Paul, and the former took Mark with him on a mission to Cyprus (Acts 15:39). Mark was subsequently with Paul when the apostle was imprisoned in Rome, as mentioned in Colossians (4:10), 2 Timothy (4:11), and Philemon (24). He was also with Peter in Rome (1 Pet 5:13). According to Papias, a bishop of the early second century, Mark was an interpreter for Peter and wrote down the substance of the apostle's teaching in the Gospel of Mark (see Eusebius, *Hist. Eccl.* 2.15 and 3.39). Eusebius, in the *Ecclesiastical History*, wrote that Mark later went to Alexandria in Egypt after the death of Peter. He preached there and was the first bishop of the Alexandrian Church (*Hist.*

Eccl. 2.16, 24). The story that he was martyred in Alexandria during the reign of Emperor Trajan is considered unreliable by some scholars. Mark is also connected with Venice, where his relics were brought in A.D. 829 and placed in the original church of Saint Mark's (San Marco). His symbol, the winged lion, subsequently became that of the city and the onetime Venetian Republic. It has graced the coats of arms of three popes in modern times: Saint Pius X (r. 1903–1914), Blessed John XXIII (r. 1958–1963), and John Paul I (1978); each had served as patriarch of Venice before his election. Mark's feast day is April 25. (*See* **Mark, Gospel of.**)

MARK, GOSPEL OF The second book of the New Testament and the second of the **Synoptic Gospels**. Written chiefly for Gentile Christians, the Gospel strives to demonstrate that Jesus is truly the Son of God. The narrative is steeped in realism and detail, focusing more on Jesus's labors and miracles than on his discourses.

I. *Authorship and Date*
II. *Contents*
III. *Literary Features*
IV. *Purpose and Themes*
   A. *Jesus the Messiah and Son*
   B. *Jesus the Son of Man*
   C. *The Cost of Discipleship*
   D. *The Good News*

I. AUTHORSHIP AND DATE

According to tradition, the Gospel was written by John Mark of Jerusalem. Early manuscripts thus bear the title "According to Mark." He was known to be a disciple of Peter, although he was not one of the apostles. Mark is mentioned several times in the Acts of the Apostles and Paul's letters, where he is identified as Mark, John Mark, or John (Acts 12:25; 13:5, 13; 15:37; Col 4:10; 2 Tim 4:11; Phlm 24). He is described in 1 Pet 5:13 as "my son Mark," perhaps suggesting that he was baptized by Peter. Tradition also holds that Peter is the Gospel's principal source, providing the eyewitness testimony that underlies the account of Jesus's life.

The earliest extant reference to Mark as the author of the second Gospel is found in the writings of Papias of Hierapolis (early second century), who calls him the "Interpreter of Peter" and was quoted by Eusebius of Caesarea in his *Ecclesiastical History* (3.39). Additional attestation was made by Saint Irenaeus (ca. 180), Saint Clement of Alexandria (ca. 200), and Tertullian (ca. 200).

Scholars generally date the Gospel to not long before the destruction of Jerusalem in A.D. 70, possibly during the persecution of the Church in Rome under Emperor Nero. In Mark 13:1–37, Jesus predicts that Jerusalem and the Temple will be destroyed, but Mark does not refer to these terrible events as already having happened.

A date before A.D. 70 is supported by Church tradition. At least one strand of tradition implies that the Gospel was written after the martyrdom of Peter in Rome (between A.D. 65 and 67); the Anti-Marcionite Prologue and Saint Irenaeus, both in the second century, state that Mark wrote his Gospel soon after Peter's death, although Saint Clement of Alexandria declared that the Gospel was written before Peter's martyrdom. Finally, Eusebius of Caesarea placed the date for the Gospel even earlier, during the reign of Emperor Claudius (between A.D. 41 and 54).

II. CONTENTS

I. *The Ministry of John (1:1–8)*

II. *The Baptism and Temptation of Jesus (1:9–13)*

III. *Jesus's Ministry and Teaching (1:14–8:30)*
   A. *Jesus's Ministry in Galilee (1:14–3:12)*
   B. *Jesus Teaches (3:13–7:23)*
   C. *The Messianic Secret (7:24–8:30)*

IV. *Jesus the Messiah (8:31–13:37)*
   A. *Jesus's Teaching and Journey to Jerusalem (8:31–10:52)*
   B. *Jesus's Teaching in Jerusalem (11:1–13:37)*

V. *The Passion and Resurrection (14:1–16:20)*

III. LITERARY FEATURES

The Gospel was probably written for Christians living in Rome. Mark takes the time to explain Jewish customs and to translate Aramaic expressions that would have been unfamiliar to a largely Gentile readership, and he uses Latinisms and references to Roman imperial coinage.

On the one hand, Mark's determination to report even the foibles of the apostles with such candor testifies to his dedication as a historical writer. On the other, Mark's style is not literary, and the Gospel is noted for its limited vocabulary and loose narrative construction. It is written in Koine Greek, the common Greek tongue that was the lingua franca of the eastern Mediterranean, and of the four Gospels Mark shows the least influence of traditional literary Greek.

IV. PURPOSE AND THEMES

A. *Jesus the Messiah and Son*

Mark's Gospel follows Peter's preaching closely: the basic outline of the Gospel is strikingly similar to Peter's proclamation in Acts 10:34–43. The chief objective of the Gospel is to reveal the identity of Jesus as Messiah and the Son of God, and the entire Gospel is directed toward Jesus's Passion and death on the Cross as a demonstration and explanation of that identity. The titles of Jesus as the Messiah and the Son of God are discernible in the principal sections of the Gospel: 1:16–8:30 and 8:31–15:47. The prologue makes a connection between **John the Baptist** and Old Testament prophecy; and to inaugurate his Galilean mission, Jesus is baptized by John, an event that includes a voice from heaven announcing that Jesus is the Son and the Servant of God prophesied by Isaiah (Isa 42:1). Jesus is then driven by the Spirit into the desert and there undergoes his temptation.

The narrative of the first section climaxes with the confession of Peter that Jesus is the Messiah (Mark 8:29). From there on, the secret is out, and Jesus labors to show his disciples that suffering is central to his Messianic mission. So prominent is the stress on Jesus's betrayal and execution that some scholars have suggested that the Gospel's core was the Passion account, and that the rest of the Gospel was constructed to provide an extended prologue for that event.

Mark informs the reader at the very start of the Gospel of Jesus's divine Sonship, an identity confirmed periodically by the voice from heaven (1:11; 9:7) and the cry of the demons (1:24; 3:11; 5:7). Yet the crowds and the religious authorities fail to perceive his true identity even after witnessing his teaching and his miracles. Curiously, Jesus himself commands people to be silent about his actions or identity and is reluctant to claim the title of Messiah during his public ministry (see 1:34, 44; 3:12; 5:43; 7:36; 8:26, 30; 9:9).

In this way, the Gospel displays a deliberate pattern of concealment of Jesus's Messianic character, so that the truth was perceived only after the Passion. The narrative must, consequently, always point toward his death and Resurrection, and the Gospel shows that Jesus predicted three times his shameful death as well as his promise to rise again (8:31; 9:31; 10:33–34).

B. *Jesus the Son of Man*

Toward this end, Mark applies another title, the Son of Man, which only Jesus uses for himself.

Whereas the royal titles of Son of God and Christ are applied to Jesus as King, the term "Son of Man" describes what kind of king Jesus will be: a suffering king. This is made evident in Jesus's three predictions of his Passion (Mark 8:31; 9:31; 10:33) in which he uses the title "Son of Man" all three times. Before the **Sanhedrin**, in reply to the question whether he is "the Christ, the Son of the Blessed" (14:61), Jesus says "I am" and then immediately refers to his vindication before God as the glorified Son of Man (14:62) envisioned by the prophet Daniel (7:13). The affirmation of Jesus's kingship is then openly declared in the Passion narrative itself (15:2, 9, 18, 26, 32). This is the climactic confession of Christ's *Sonship*.

C. The Cost of Discipleship

The story of the Passion also throws Mark's idea of discipleship into sharp relief.

The theme of discipleship is introduced in the first chapter with the calling of Simon and Andrew, James and John (Mark 1:16–20), followed by the appointment of the Twelve (3:13–19) and their being sent out on their mission (6:7–13). Much of the Gospel is taken up with teachings on the meaning of discipleship (8:34–38; 9:42–50; 10:23–31, 35–45), but the disciples frequently failed to grasp the deepest implications of what Christ said to them. Peter in particular is often portrayed as quick to act and slow to understand.

For Mark, discipleship is inseparable from suffering and thus from the Cross, so discipleship entails a willingness to share in the suffering of Jesus just as he suffered for many (10:45; 14:24). These teachings resound with even greater significance and urgency if indeed Mark was addressing the persecuted Christians in Rome (cf. 8:34–38; 9:35; 10:29–31, 35–45).

D. The Good News

Nevertheless, Mark is not pessimistic. On the contrary, he uses the word "**gospel**" (or "Good News") more frequently than any other evangelist, and his use makes it apparent that he considers the word to be synonymous, not with a written document per se, but with the message of Christ's victory over sin and death on behalf of the world. The Kingdom of God has been announced and is now present in Jesus Christ; it has been established with his death and Resurrection.

MARK, JOHN *See* **Mark**.

MARKS OF THE CHURCH Four distinctive characteristics of the Church: one, holy, catholic, and apostolic. The marks declare the Church to be the true instrument of salvation in the world, founded by and belonging completely to Christ, and the one Church, as opposed to other rival claimants of Christianity. The Church is

- *one* because her members are united in faith and doctrine, under the pope;

- *holy* because she is sanctified by Christ, the means of sanctifying the world, and the Church has the Holy Spirit dwelling in it;

- *catholic* because she is universal, meaning that the Church is intended for all peoples in all places of the world; and

- *apostolic* because of the unbroken line from the apostles to the bishops whose teaching authority, the Magisterium, holds fast to the apostolic faith, which can be traced to the eternal and unquestionable teachings of Christ.

The Letter to the Ephesians describes each of the marks clearly. The Church is one—"one faith, one baptism" (Eph 4:4); holy—"that she might be holy and without blemish" (Eph 5:27); catholic—"you who were once far off" (that is, all the nations outside Israel) "have been brought near in the blood of Christ" (Eph 2:13); and apostolic—"built upon the foundation of the apostles and prophets" (Eph 2:20).

The marks were proclaimed by the First Council of Constantinople (A.D. 381) in the formalization of the Nicene Creed and were re-affirmed by the Council of Trent (1545–1563). A number of Catholic writers, most notably Saint Robert Bellarmine, described other marks of the Church. Saint Robert declared that there are fifteen; the four marks, however, are of primary significance.

MARRIAGE The union of man and woman was ordained by God from the beginning (Gen 2:23–24). In Israel, marriage came under the protection and administration of the **Law** (Exod 20:14, 17; Lev 20:10; etc.); nevertheless, marriage under the Old Covenant was a natural and legal institution but was not a **sacrament**. As a natural institution, the union of husband and wife is one in which both agree to give and receive rights over one another to foster their mutual love and perform the act of generation. Christ elevated marriage to a sacrament of the Church through which the spouses signify and partake in the mystery of the life-giving love between Christ and his Church. The scriptural account of marriage thus begins with God creating man and woman and bringing them together, and it ends with the account in Revelation of the wedding feast of the Church and the Lamb, of Christ and his Church (cf. Gen 1:26–27, 2:18–25; Rev 19:7) (CCC 1602–20).

I. MARRIAGE IN THE OLD TESTAMENT

A. God Created Marriage

God did not intend man to be alone (Gen 2:18) and therefore created from him a "helpmate," and one who was "flesh of his flesh" (Gen 2:19–25), so that "a man leaves his father and his mother and cleaves to his wife, and they become one flesh" (Gen 2:24). God is thus the real author of marriage (cf. GS §48) and endowed it with laws proper to its nature. Despite its variations across cultures and in history, marriage is not a purely human institution. The union of man and woman is good in the Creator's eyes, and God blessed the man and the woman and gave them specific duties: to be fruitful and to be stewards over the created order (Gen 1:28, 31).

From the beginning, marriage was designed as a monogamous union of one male and one female. Their common bond together, along with the generation of offspring, was to be a foundation for the good ordering and stability of society.

B. Decline from the Primordial Ideal

The union of man and woman in one flesh was meant to be lifelong and indissoluble. But the institution of marriage suffered from the consequences of **the Fall**. Selfishness and distrust strained the relationship between man and woman (Gen 3:12, 16–19). The **Law of Moses** consequently permitted divorce and remarriage in some circumstances as a concession to Israel's hardness of heart (Deut 24:1–4). But it was not so from the beginning (Matt 19:8), and Christ would declare later, "what therefore God has joined together, let no man put asunder" (Matt 19:6; cf. 1 Cor 7:10–11). Polygamy was not encouraged (Lev 18:18; Deut 17:17), and the laws that sought to protect marriages are numerous (Exod 20:17, 21:5; Lev 18:6–20, 20:10, 21:13–14; Num 5:11–31; Deut 5:21, 22:13–30).

C. Polygamy

Nevertheless, the standard of monogamy was soon violated and polygamy appeared in earliest times. Cain's descendant **Lamech** is the first bigamist to appear in the Bible: he took as his wives Adah and Zillah (Gen 4:19–24). **Abraham** was wed to Sarah but had a son by Sarah's slave, Hagar, with the consent of Sarah (Gen 16:1–2; 25:6). Similarly, **Jacob** married the sisters Leah and Rachel (Gen 29:15–30) and later had children by their maids, Bilhah and Zilpah, respectively (Gen 30:1–8, 9–13). **Esau** had three wives (Gen 26:34; 28:9; 36:2–3). **Gideon** fathered seventy sons by his various wives and a concubine (Judg 8:30–31).

Polygamy was recognized by the Law of Moses (Exod 21:10; Lev 18:18), and the Deuteronomic code presupposed polygamy and sought to circumvent the competition that might emerge among the wives and their offspring (Deut 21:15–17).

By the time of the monarchy in Israel, polygamy in excess was the norm among nobles and rulers (2 Sam 3:2–5; 1 Kgs 11:3). **Saul** had several wives and a concubine (2 Sam 12:8); **David** had seven named wives (1 Sam 25:42–44; 2 Sam 3:2–5) and other unnamed ones (2 Sam 5:13); Solomon had seven hundred wives and three hundred concubines (1 Kgs 3:1, 11:3; Song 6:8). **Rehoboam** had eighteen wives and sixty concubines (2 Chr 11:21).

The practical challenges that come with polygamy are proved by the domestic discord that existed in those houses where it was practiced, notably the envy of Sarah for Hagar's fertility (Gen 16:4–6) and that of Rachel for Leah (Gen 30:1); the massacre of Gideon's seventy sons by **Abimelech**, his son by a concubine (Judg 9:1–5); the royal court intrigues in the reign of David (2 Sam 13; 1 Kgs 1–2) and Solomon (1 Kgs 11).

D. Marriage to Foreigners

Deuteronomy 7:3 forbids intermarriage with Canaanite peoples; by implication, it could be said to discourage marriages with Gentiles in general, although exceptions did occur in the history of Israel. Further on, Deuteronomy permitted a warrior to claim a wife from among female captives of war (Deut 21:10–14), and some scholars suggest that there is also permission given (in Deut 23:7, 8) to marry Edomites or Egyptians after three generations (marrying Amalekites was permanently prohibited, Deut 25:17–19). Among his seven hundred royal wives and three hundred concubines, Solomon was married to an Egyptian woman who was the daughter of a pharaoh, as well as to Edomites, Moabites, Hittites, and Sidonians (1 Kgs 11:1–3).

Intermarriage with Gentile women was outlawed by both **Ezra** (Ezra 9–10) and **Nehemiah** (Neh 13:23–30). Polygamy declined in the period after the **Exile**.

E. How Marriages Were Arranged

Marriage in Old Testament times was generally arranged by the families of the bride and groom. Most other cultures of the ancient Near East made similar arrangements. The first arranged marriage recorded in the OT was the one arranged by Hagar for Ishmael (Gen 21:21). Most couples married fairly young, with young women marrying in their early teens. It was still possible for a marriage to be based on love (Gen 29:20), as seen in the match between David and Michal (1 Sam 18:20, 27). The contract between the families was completed or sealed by the payment of a dowry or "betrothal price." The amount is uncertain, but a rough estimate can be made on the basis of Deut 22:28–29, which sets a penalty for a man who violates the virginity of a young woman: "If a man meets a virgin who is not engaged, and seizes her and lies with her, and they are caught in the act, the man who lay with her shall give fifty shekels of silver to the young woman's father, and she shall become his wife. Because he violated her he shall not be permitted to divorce her as long as he lives." It might be concluded that the dowry generally would have been less than this amount, and it is likely that the exact amount was negotiable (cf. Gen 24:53, 34:12; Exod 22:16; 1 Sam 18:25). The dowry could also be paid through service, as seen with Jacob and Laban (Gen 29:18–20, 27–30). The paying of this price did not reduce the wife to the level of a concubine or slave (cf. Exod 21:7–11); there

was always a clear distinction between wives and concubines, even when both (as in the case of Solomon) were multiplied to almost unbelievable excess.

F. Laws Against Adultery

The Law of Moses codifies laws against the infidelity of spouses who were married, and even for couples who were betrothed but did not yet live together as husband and wife. The betrothed were subject to specific laws enumerated in Deut 22:23–27. These laws presupposed that a betrothed couple was already married in a legal sense, so any sexual involvement between a betrothed woman and another man was equivalent to adultery and rendered both parties subject to stoning to death (Deut 22:23–24). By extension of this notion, sexual relations between the betrothed couple, though discouraged before cohabitation, were not condemned as fornication as the two were already pledged to one another by mutual consent. If a woman who was already engaged was raped outside the town—implying that she was beyond help—she was not punished; only the man was condemned to death. But if the betrothed woman lay with a man in a town and did not cry out for help, she was presumed to have consented, and both parties suffered the death penalty (Deut 22:23–27).

Adultery is forbidden by the **Ten Commandments** (Exod 20:14; Deut 5:18) and by later laws of the **Pentateuch** (Lev 18:20). It was a capital crime in ancient Israel (Lev 20:10; Deut 22:22), although in later centuries the death penalty was not often enforced, sometimes due to political restraints (John 18:31).

G. How Marriages Were Celebrated

The marriage ceremony in ancient Israel is not known with certainty, but a few details can be discerned. To signify his intent to marry her, the man might have placed an item of his clothing upon the woman (Ruth 3:9; Ezek 16:18). After a formal proposal of marriage (Gen 24:63–67), and usually after a period of betrothal, there was a marriage procession in which the bridegroom set to claim his bride, who waited for him in her finest clothes and wearing a veil (Song 3:11, 4:11, 6:7; Ps 45:15; Isa 61:10; 1 Macc 9:37; Matt 9:15). The feasting that followed might last for an entire week (Gen 29:27; Judg 14:12), or even as long as two weeks (Tob 8:20; 10:7). The marriage was consummated on the wedding night (Gen 29:21–23; Tob 8:1–8).

H. Levirate Marriage

Marriage was forbidden between close relations (Lev 18:6–18), although the law of *levirate* (from the Latin for "brother-in-law") marriage encouraged a brother to marry the widow of his deceased brother in order to provide him with offspring and to continue his name (Deut 25:5–10). In the event that no brother survived, the nearest relative could assume the responsibility (Ruth 3:12; 4:4–10).

Lev 18:16 and 20:21 prohibited sexual unions between a brother and sister-in-law. This would seem to contradict the levirate law, except that Deuteronomy is confined to situations in which the husband of the sister-in-law had died without fathering a male heir; only then could a man marry his brother's widow. The Sadducees' question to Jesus about the childless woman who was married in succession to six of her dead husband's brothers (Matt 22:23–33; Mark 12:18–23; Luke 20:27–33) does not necessarily attest to the continuation of levirate marriage into the New Testament period. The question was chiefly an academic exercise.

I. Marriage as a Covenant

For the prophets, marriage, itself a covenant in Israel (Mal 2:14), was a common metaphor for the covenant relationship between God and the Chosen People (*see also* **election**). Such a relationship, with the Lord as the bridegroom and Israel as the bride, is implied in the **Pentateuch**, especially where God is described as "jealous" (Exod 20:5; 34:14; Num 5:14, 30). In any case, what is implicit in the Pentateuch is made explicit in the Prophets. Hos 2 and 3, for instance, stresses the love and fidelity of the divine husband Yahweh and his boundless patience in the face of the infidelities of his wife, Israel. Similar imagery is used in other prophetic writings (Isa 54:3, 62:5; Jer 2:2, 3:20; Ezek 16:8–14).

II. MARRIAGE IN THE NEW TESTAMENT

A. Jesus Restores Marriage to the Ideal

At the wedding feast of **Cana**, Jesus performed his first public miracle, at the request of his mother (John 2:1–11). The presence of Jesus at Cana implied his approval of the institution of marriage and established the groundwork for his subsequent teaching. Traditional exegesis often states that Christ sanctified marriage by his presence at the Cana feast and by his contribution to the festivities (i.e., the good wine).

Jesus restored the original meaning of marriage as willed by the Creator in Gen 2:18–25. He preached against adultery in the Sermon on the Mount (Matt 5:27–28), and elsewhere he spoke of the obligations of children to honor their parents (Matt 19:16–22; Mark 10:17–22; Luke 18:18–23). Above all, he redeemed marriage from the sinful distortions that had disfigured it over the centuries, in particular divorce (Matt 19:8). He declared the indissolubility of the matrimonial union: "what therefore God has joined together, let no man put asunder" (Matt 19:6; cf. Matt 5:32; Mark 10:9; Luke 16:18).

The ideal of lifelong monogamy is not an impossible burden. It is, rather, one aspect of discipleship, attainable by following Christ, who came to restore the original order of creation (Matt 11:29–30; 19:11). By living in Christ, and helped by his grace, a married couple can live in fidelity to the new creation (Eph 5:21–33) (CCC 1615–16).

B. The Question of "Unchastity"

In Matt 19:9, Jesus tells the Pharisees, "And I say to you: whoever divorces his wife, except for unchastity, and marries another, commits adultery" (cf. Matt 5:31–32; the text in Mark 10:11 and Luke 16:18 does not contain the exception). Does that mean Jesus is permitting remarriage under certain circumstances?

First, we must understand the background of Jewish teaching on divorce. For there was a great deal of controversy among the Pharisees over the legitimate grounds for divorce authorized in Deut 24:1–4. The debate swirls around the vague expression "some indecency" (Deut 24:1). The school of Hillel maintained that a man could divorce his wife for almost any reason imaginable. The school of Shammai, however, confined the legal basis for divorce to cases of marital infidelity. As it turns out, Jesus not only refused to take sides in this debate, but he went so far as to make the issue irrelevant and outdated. That is, he repealed the Mosaic ordinances that allowed for divorce in the first place (Deut 24:14), declaring divorce to be a temporary concession put in effect to accommodate the hardened hearts of Israel (Matt 19:8).

Second, we must analyze the words of Jesus themselves, for if Jesus revoked the right to divorce and remarry, then an interpretation of his words in Matt 19:9 must be consistent with this fact. The word translated "unchastity" (Greek *porneia*) refers to "sexual misconduct" in a fairly general way. In different contexts, it can mean such things as *fornication* (1 Cor 7:2), *adultery* (Sir 23:23), and even *incest* (1 Cor 5:1). Christian exegesis has thus understood the "exception clause" in Matt 5:32 and 19:9 in different ways.

1. In patristic scholarship, it was believed that Jesus allowed for divorce if one of the spouses had committed adultery, but this did not allow the divorced couple to get remarried so long as both spouses were still living. In other words, an exception was made that allowed for divorce, but no exception was made that allowed for the divorced spouses to embark on a second marriage.

2. In the judgment of Saint Augustine, the exception clause is actually a preterition. The words "except for unchastity" are interpreted to mean "quite apart from the divorce legislation in Deuteronomy and the Pharisaic

debates about its meaning." On this interpretation, Jesus sets the matter aside as outdated and thus irrelevant to his own teaching.

3. Modern scholarship often prefers to interpret Jesus in a very different way. Since the key term "unchastity" can sometimes refer to incestuous unions, it is said that Jesus allows for and even mandates the termination of unlawful marriages—that is, unions between persons too closely related to one another (for the forbidden degrees of consanguinity, see Lev 18:6–18). In these situations, the man and woman are free to find a new spouse because they were never really married in the first place.

So, then, whether a legal divorce takes place or simply the annulment of an invalid union, there is no basis in the NT to claim that Jesus allowed married spouses to divorce and remarry. (CCC 1638–40, 1644–45, 2367; cf. CIC 1141–55).

C. Marriage in Paul's Letters

Paul's pastoral counsel concerning marriage, celibacy, and widowhood appears in concentrated form in 1 Cor 7:1–40. Paul makes it clear that he considers virginity to be a superior state of life to marriage (e.g., 1 Cor 7:32–35), but marriage is normal and is an antidote to immorality (1 Cor 7:2–5; cf. 1 Thess 4:3–8). The matrimonial state is one of mutual surrender between the husband and wife (1 Cor 7:3–4). Paul reiterates Christ's teachings on divorce, confirming that marriage is a lifelong bond that is dissolved only by death (1 Cor 7:10–11, 39; cf. Rom 7:2–3) (CCC 2364, 2382). He also discusses disparity of religion (i.e., marriage between a baptized Christian and a nonbeliever, 1 Cor 7:12) and what became known

as the Pauline Privilege, by which a Christian may be released from a marriage with a nonbeliever under certain circumstances (1 Cor 7:15).

Paul's theology of Christian marriage is articulated mainly in Eph 5:22–33. There he develops the theological theme found in the OT of connecting marriage with the covenant between Israel and the Lord. In the NT, this theme is transformed into the image of the Church and Christ as bride and groom: "As the church is subject to Christ, so let wives also be subject in everything to their husbands. Husbands, love your wives, as Christ loved the church and gave himself up for her" (Eph 5:24–25). Evoking the teaching of Genesis that the two shall become one flesh, Paul adds, "This mystery is a profound one, and I am saying that it refers to Christ and the church" (Eph 5:32) (CCC 1616).

D. The Wedding Feast of the Lamb

The Church as Bride is also found at the high point of the book of Revelation. The wedding of the Lamb appears as the ultimate fulfillment of the everlasting covenant that was prepared for historically by the covenant between God and Israel. The Church, "prepared as a bride adorned for her husband" (Rev 21:2), is presented to her husband at the "marriage of the Lamb" (Rev 19:7).

MARRIAGE, SACRAMENT OF See Marriage.

MARTHA (Aramaic, "lady" or "mistress") The sister of **Mary** (Luke 10:38–42) and **Lazarus** (John 11:1–12:11). The family lived in

Bethany, approximately two miles east of Jerusalem (about 15 stadia, or about 3.2 kilometers; John 11:18). The Gospel accounts suggest that Martha was the elder of the two sisters, as she was the one who gave welcome to Jesus (Luke 10:38), oversaw the practical needs of her guest, and asked for assistance while Mary sat at Jesus's feet and listened to his words. When Martha complains to Jesus that Mary should be helping with the serving, Jesus's reply is one of the more famous passages from the New Testament: "Martha, Martha, you are anxious and troubled about many things; one thing is needful. Mary has chosen the good portion, which shall not be taken away from her" (Luke 10:41–42); Jesus thus ranked contemplative silence over active service as an expression of discipleship. In the Gospel of John, Martha, Mary, and Lazarus are said to be loved by Jesus (John 11:5); they are the only individuals to be so characterized. Interestingly, the personalities of Martha and Mary visible in Luke also show up in John. Again Martha is active—she hurries out to meet Jesus when he arrives in Bethany—while Mary initially sits and waits for the Lord. Likewise, Martha has a memorable exchange with Jesus in which she declares her trust that God will do whatever Jesus asks, and she also confesses faith in Jesus as the **Messiah** and Son of God— one of the clearest Christological confessions in the Gospel of John (John 11:20–27).

MARTYR *See* **Witness**.

MARY The name of several important women in the New Testament; the Greek form is Maria and its Hebrew equivalent is **Miriam**.

1. **Mary, Mother of Jesus**.

2. **Mary Magdalene**.

3. Mary of Bethany, the sister of **Martha** and **Lazarus** of Bethany. In Luke 10:38–42, Mary sat at the feet of the Lord while Martha played the role of the busy hostess; when she complained, Jesus replied, "Martha, Martha, you are anxious and troubled about many things; one thing is needful. Mary has chosen the good portion, which shall not be taken away from her." In John, Mary figured in the story of the resurrection of Lazarus (John 11:1–12:11). She and Martha sent a message to Jesus telling him that Lazarus was ill and imploring him to come to Bethany. As in Luke, she first sat and waited for the Lord; then she went out and met Jesus. On another occasion, Mary anointed Jesus with expensive ointments (John 12:1–3; cf. Matt 26:6–13; Mark 14:3–9, where her name is not given). Tradition sometimes identifies Mary of Bethany with Mary Magdalene (*see discussion under* **Mary Magdalene**).

4. The mother of James (the Less) and Joseph (Matt 27:56; Mark 15:40; Luke 24:10). She was a follower of Jesus during his public ministry, was a witness to his Crucifixion (Mark 15:40–41) and burial (Mark 15:47), and was among the women who visited the tomb on Easter morning (Mark 16:1). She was thus one of the first witnesses to the empty tomb and the angelic announcement of the Resurrection (Matt 28:1–8; Mark 16:1–8; Luke 24:1–12). She is probably the same person as Mary the wife of **Clopas**, who was a witness to the Crucifixion (cf. John 19:25 with Mark 15:40).

5. The mother of John **Mark** of Jerusalem, a fellow missionary of **Paul** and **Barnabas** in

Acts (12:12–16; cf. 12:25, 15:39). Her home was a regular place of meeting for Christians living in the Holy City, and she is noted for her hospitality.

MARY, THE MOTHER OF JESUS The virgin wife of Joseph of Nazareth and the mother of the Davidic Messiah, Jesus Christ. Having accepted this exalted vocation, she became the ideal model of Christian faith and discipleship (Luke 1:38, 45; 8:21; 11:28). More than any other woman in history, Mary is one for whom God has done "great things" (Luke 1:49).

I. *Mary in the Gospels and Acts*
   A. *Her Early Life*
   B. *Wife, Mother, Disciple*
   C. *Later Life*
II. *Mary in Salvation History*
   A. *The Ark of the New Covenant*
   B. *Queen Mother*
   C. *The New Eve*
   D. *A Type of the Church*

I. MARY IN THE GOSPELS AND ACTS

A. Her Early Life

Nothing of Mary's early life is recorded in Scripture. Details about her family background and upbringing are filled in by later traditions and legends. One tradition, which dates back to the second century A.D., identifies Mary as the daughter of a devout Jewish couple named Joachim and Anna. The story has it that Joachim and Anna had long been childless, but after fervent prayer and a promise to devote any future child to the Temple, they were blessed by God with an infant girl whom they named Mary. Mary stayed with her parents until she was three, at which time she was taken to Jerusalem to live with a sorority of Temple virgins until she was twelve. She was then given to the care of Joseph, a building contractor and widower who had fathered several children by a previous marriage (*Protoevangelium of James* 1–9).

B. Wife, Mother, Disciple

Matthew and Luke introduce Mary as a virgin betrothed to Joseph, whose family descended from the royal line of David (Matt 1:18–21; Luke 1:26–27). Before the couple lived together as husband and wife, Mary was approached by the angel Gabriel and invited to become the mother of the Messiah (Luke 1:28–38). Embracing this offer, she conceived the child, not through marital union with Joseph, but by a miracle of the Holy Spirit (Matt 1:18). Joseph was understandably confused by the discovery of Mary's pregnancy, and considered calling off the betrothal until an angel assured him that God wanted him to be the legal father and caretaker of the child (Matt 1:19–25). Soon after this, Mary went to visit her elder kinswoman Elizabeth (Luke 1:39–45), an encounter that prompted her hymn of praise, the Magnificat (Luke 1:46–55).

More traveling was necessary when Caesar Augustus decreed a census that brought Mary to Bethlehem, the ancestral hometown of Joseph (Luke 2:1–5). There Jesus was born (Matt 2:1), possibly in a cave used as a stable (Luke 2:6–7), though the couple was able to procure a house at some point after this (Matt 2:11). Being law-observant Jews, the couple had the infant Jesus circumcised (Luke 2:21) and later presented him in the Temple (Luke 2:22–39). Two things of importance are discovered on this later occasion: one, the reader learns that Mary and Joseph were economically poor, for they offered the Temple sacrifices (Luke 2:24) prescribed for persons unable to afford larger sacrificial animals (Lev 12:6–8); and, two, Mary herself learned that her Son was destined to be a sign of contradiction, and that one day a sword of anguish would be thrust into her own soul (Luke 2:34–35).

When Herod the Great, king of Judea, learned of the birth of the child, he sent a military squad to hunt down and kill the infant Jesus in Bethlehem (Matt 2:16–18). But thanks to angelic intervention, Joseph was able to get Mary and the child out of harm's way by fleeing to Egypt, where they remained until the death of Herod (Matt 2:13–15). Eventually they returned to the couple's original dwelling in Nazareth of Galilee (Matt 2:19–23), from which they made yearly pilgrimages to Jerusalem for sacred festivals such as Passover (Luke 2:41–51).

Though the infancy narratives feature Mary prominently, giving the reader a close-up perspective on her piety, her prayers, her movements, and even the reflections of her heart (Luke 2:19, 51), she is mentioned only infrequently in the narratives of Jesus's ministry (Matt 12:46, 13:55; Mark 3:31, 6:3; Luke 8:19). One notable exception is the wedding of Cana episode in the Gospel of John (John 2:1–11). Here we discover that Mary was instrumental in the performance of Christ's first miracle, the first occasion on which he revealed his divine glory to his disciples (John 2:11). She informed Jesus that the wine of the feast had run out: "They have no wine" (John 2:3). The statement is grammatically indicative but rhetorically imperative. That is, she was asking Jesus to remedy the situation by some miraculous action, to which Jesus responded, "Woman, how does your concern affect me? My hour has not yet come." Despite the abruptness of his response, which sounds to modern ears like a rebuke, it was no such thing, for Mary confidently bid the servants, "Do whatever he tells you" (John 2:5). Christian tradition sees in this episode a type of Mary's ongoing intercession for the saints.

C. Later Life

Mary is last seen in the New Testament in the upper room, where she and the earliest disciples of Jesus devoted themselves to prayer in preparation for Pentecost (Acts 1:14). No mention is made of her movements or activities after this point; it is known only that Jesus, in the final moments of his life, entrusted the care of his mother to the beloved disciple, traditionally identified as the apostle John (John 19:25–27).

Early traditions, historical and liturgical, are divided on the question of Mary's final days. Regarding her whereabouts, one tradition contends that Mary traveled to Ephesus in Asia Minor with the apostle John; another says that she remained in Jerusalem. Regarding the end of her earthly life, one tradition says that Mary died a natural death, while another commemorates her dormition or "falling asleep." Both are agreed, however, that Mary was assumed bodily into heaven. Christian antiquity confirms this by its complete silence regarding relics of Mary and the absence of a venerated burial site. The Assumption of Mary into heaven was defined as a Catholic dogma by Pope Pius XII in the 1950 apostolic constitution *Munificentissimus Deus.*

II. MARY IN SALVATION HISTORY

A. *The Ark of the New Covenant*

Christian tradition addresses Mary as "the ark of the New Covenant," drawing a parallel between the mother of Jesus and the golden ark of the Old Testament where the presence of Yahweh dwelt in the sanctuary (Exod 25:10–22). The basis for this Marian typology is rooted in the NT itself, most clearly in the Gospel of Luke.

In his Visitation narrative, Luke invites the reader to see parallels between the arrival of Mary at the home of Elizabeth and David's transfer of the ark of the covenant to Jerusalem (Luke 1:39–56). Several details echo the version of this story as told in 2 Samuel. The account begins with the notice that Mary "arose and went" into the hill country of Judea (Luke 1:39), just as David "arose and went" into the Judean hills to fetch the ark (2 Sam 6:2). When Mary reaches her destination, Elizabeth is humbled and awed by the presence of Mary (Luke 1:43), much as David was in the presence of the Lord's ark (2 Sam 6:9). Nevertheless, the excitement of the encounter causes John the Baptist, still an infant in his mother Elizabeth's womb, to leap for joy (Luke 1:41), calling to mind how David danced with joy before the ark (2 Sam 6:16). The Evangelist finally notes that Mary stayed as a guest for "three months" (Luke 1:56) in the "house of Zechariah" (Luke 1:40), a detail that recalls how the ark

stayed for "three months" in the "house of Obededom" (2 Sam 6:11).

Luke also makes a subtle link with the ark narratives in 1 and 2 Chronicles. The connection is revealed when Elizabeth, a Levitical descendant of Aaron (Luke 1:5), raises her voice and exclaims the blessedness of her kinswoman (Luke 1:42). The verb "exclaim" (Greek *anaphōneō*) is curiously rare and occurs nowhere else in the NT. This makes it likely that Luke is drawing the term from the Greek OT, where the verb appears five times and is used to describe the musical melodies of the Levites and their instruments before the ark of the covenant (1 Chr 15:28, 16:4–5; 2 Chr 5:13). The typological vision of Mary as the ark of the New Covenant is thus reinforced. For within her womb dwells the divine presence of Israel's God, and the traditional response to this presence is exclamatory praise by the voices and instruments of the Levites.

B. *Queen Mother*

Mary is often hailed as Queen in the spiritual and liturgical traditions of the Church. The basis of this tradition, of course, lies in her relation to Christ the King. But why is the Queen of the New Covenant the mother of the King and not the wife of the King, as so many queens have been through the centuries? The answer lies in the biblical institution of queenship in Israel.

Beginning in the time of Solomon, the Davidic monarchs of Judah imitated their Near Eastern neighbors by reserving the office of queenship to the mother of the king. This, in part, was a practical decision in a world where distinguished and wealthy men commonly possessed multiple wives. This meant that the king's mother was not simply honored in a stately way, but she was a royal court official, an actual government figure who often wielded significant authority in ancient Oriental kingdoms. Things were no different in Israel. The queen not only wore a crown (Jer 13:18) and had a throne at the right hand of the Davidic king (1 Kgs 2:19), but she was revered by the king himself (1 Kgs 2:19), who was accustomed to fulfill her every request (1 Kgs 2:20). Among other things, this made her a powerful advocate on behalf of the people (1 Kgs 2:13–19). This background is important when we read the NT, for Mary is the mother of Jesus, the royal Messiah (Matt 1:1–16) who was destined before his birth to sit on David's throne (Luke 1:32–33; cf. Acts 2:30–36). In other words, it is the Davidic kingship of Jesus that establishes the maternal Queenship of Mary.

Perhaps the clearest indication of Mary's Queenship is in the book of Revelation. In the vision of chapter 12, the mother who gives birth to the Messiah appears with "a crown of twelve stars" (Rev 12:1). Clearly she is a queen and a mother. But just as important, the newborn Messiah is identified as a Davidic king "who is to rule all the nations with a rod of iron" and who is taken up to his "throne" (Rev 12:5, alluding to the anointed king from David's line in Ps 2:8–9). Some might think it odd for a queen to give birth to her king; however, the notion of a Queen Mother is exactly what we find in the Davidic monarchy of biblical Israel. And because Christ is the reigning Davidic Messiah, his Mother too wears the crown of Queenship in the new Kingdom of God.

C. The New Eve

As a corollary to the Pauline vision of Christ as the New Adam (Rom 5:12–21; 1 Cor 15:45–49), theologians from earliest times have called Mary the New Eve. The grounds for this view are both prophetic and typological.

Prophetically, the promise of future redemption in Gen 3:15 is one that pits a "woman" and her "offspring" against the Satanic serpent, who is destined to be trampled down in defeat. If Christ is the promised Redeemer who crushes the Enemy, then his mother can be said to have an instrumental role in bringing this about. Some have detected an allusion to this promise in two episodes of the Gospel of John that feature the person of Mary. In both places she is addressed by Jesus as "woman" (John 2:4; 19:26); and more important, both passages have connections with the "hour" of Jesus, that critical phase of his mission when he overthrows the ruler of this world (John 2:4; 12:27–33). Others have also pointed to the book of Revelation, where the mother of the Messiah is described as a "woman" (Rev 12:1), and the devil is described as the "ancient serpent" and "deceiver" (Rev 12:9) who wages war on the woman's "offspring" (Rev 12:17).

Typologically, the figure of Mary can be seen as the counterimage of Eve. Just as Eve, while still a virgin, was approached by a fallen angel and gave her consent to disobedience (Gen 3:1–6), so Mary, while a virgin, was approached by the angel Gabriel and gave consent to the will of God for her life (Luke 1:26–38). Eve likewise initiated the sin of Adam, who plunged the human race into the darkness of sin and death, whereas Mary brought forth the New Adam, who rescued the human family from bondage to sin and death (Rom 5:12–21).

D. A Type of the Church

Mary is not explicitly called a type of the Church in the NT. But careful study of Mary's role as a model disciple and recipient of the Holy Spirit points in this direction and validates the development of this theme in later Mariology.

First, Mary is clearly depicted as a model disciple, one who illustrates by example the ideal response of the human person to the Word of God. Her acceptance of the mission to be Mother of the divine Messiah indicates as much, for in the words of her *fiat* she says: "Behold, I am the handmaid of the Lord; let it be to me according to your word" (Luke 1:38). The crucial importance of this response, already apparent at some level in the infancy narrative, is heightened still more when we consider the teaching of Jesus. On an occasion when Mary comes to see Jesus, the fact is made known to him, and seizing the opportunity to teach the crowds, he declares: "My mother and my brothers are those who hear the word of God and do it" (Luke 8:21). Some would read this as a depreciation of Mary's biological relation to Jesus as Mother. But this is not the point. In fact, recalling the words of the *fiat*, the reader of Luke comes to see that Mary is blessed to be his Mother precisely because she accepted the Word of God and acted on it. Insofar as this is the essence and standard of true discipleship, Mary models for the Church what it means to be authentically Christian.

Second, it appears in the Greek text of Luke-Acts that the divine motherhood of Mary is actually related to the birth of the Church. This can be seen by comparing the Annunciation, which announces the conception of Jesus by the Spirit, and the final commission of Jesus before his Ascension, which announces the formation of the Church by the Spirit. At the Annunciation, the angel Gabriel tells Mary, "The Holy Spirit will come upon (Greek *eperchomai*) you, and the power (Greek *dynamis*) of the Most High will overshadow you" (Luke 1:35). Likewise, just before his Ascension, Christ tells his apostles, "But you shall receive power (Greek *dynamis*) when the Holy Spirit has come upon (Greek *eperchomai*) you" (Acts 1:8). The parallel is striking, as is the implication. It suggests that Mary experienced a personal Pentecost before the body of Christ's disciples experienced the ecclesial Pentecost that formed the Church. In both cases, by physical conception and missionary witness, Christ is thus brought into the world. The first is an anticipation and type of the second.

MARY MAGDALENE A follower of Christ, probably from **Magdala**, near Tiberias, on the west shore of Galilee. Mary Magdalene is identified as being among the women who accompanied Christ and ministered to him (Luke 8:2–3). Jesus had delivered her from the oppression of seven demons (Mark 16:9; Luke 8:2). She was present at the foot of Christ's Cross (Matt 27:56; Mark 15:40; John 19:25) and witnessed the placing of Christ in the tomb (Matt 27:61; Mark 15:47). Notably, she was the first recorded eyewitness of his Resurrection (Matt 28:1–10; Mark 16:1–8; Luke 24:10). John describes in some detail her remarkable experience at Christ's tomb (John 20:1–18), where she met the risen Lord and carried from him a message to the disciples: "I am ascending to my Father and your Father, to my God and your God" (John 20:17).

Tradition often identifies Mary Magdalene either with the sinful woman who anointed Christ's feet in Luke 7:36–50 or with **Mary** of Bethany, the sister of Lazarus and Martha mentioned in Luke 10:38–42 and John 11–12. By the sixth century A.D., figures such as Gregory the Great had begun to advance the notion that these two women mentioned in Scripture were one and the same person: Mary Magdalene, who hailed from Bethany and who had become a disciple of Jesus after leading a notoriously sinful life. This tradition explains why Mary Magdalene was revered for centuries as the "model penitent." From a biblical standpoint, it is not impossible that Mary Magdalene could be identified with either one or both of these two women, but decisive evidence is lacking and so it must remain uncertain.

Mary Magdalene was the subject of many legends in the early Christian centuries and especially during the Middle Ages. Medieval stories about her were numerous, including a popular one, originating in the ninth century, that had her journeying to France with Martha and Lazarus. Her feast day is July 22.

MASH Great-grandson of **Noah** through **Shem** and Aram, listed in the **Table of Nations** (Gen 10:23).

MASORETIC TEXT The standard text of the Hebrew Bible (often abbreviated MT).

The critical edition in use today represents mainly the text preserved by Jewish traditionalists in medieval Galilee called the Masoretes. The name comes from the Hebrew *massôrâ*, meaning "transmission" or "tradition."

MASSAH (Hebrew, "testing") The wilderness location where Moses brought forth drinking water from a rock to quench the thirst of the complaining Israelites (Exod 17:1–7; Deut 6:16, 9:22). The exact location of the event is not certain. Numbers 20:1–13 records a similar incident at a place called **Meribah**, but there Moses disobeyed the Lord's instructions (cf. Num 27:14; Deut 32:51).

MATTANIAH (Hebrew, "gift of the Lord") The name used for a number of individuals in the Old Testament, including several court officials and priests. The most significant figure to bear this name is King Zedekiah of Judah (597–586 B.C.). (*See under* **Zedekiah**.)

MATTATHIAS The name of two men in the Bible.

1. The son of John and the father of **Judas Maccabeus** and his four brothers (1 Macc 2:1–5). A member of the priestly order of Joarib (or Jehoiarib, 1 Chr 24:7) and a resident of Modein, Mattathias enjoyed some prominence (1 Macc 2:17) and was thus well positioned to become the leader of a rebellion against Antiochus IV Epiphanes (r. 175–164 B.C.; *see under* **Seleucids**) during the severe persecutions of the Jews who remained faithful to the Law. Mattathias sparked this religious revolt when he killed a Jew who made improper sacrifices in accordance with a new decree from

the Seleucid ruler. He then killed the officer in charge, destroyed the altar, and called for the inhabitants to fight the Syrian persecution. Mattathias became leader of the resulting uprising, which was carried forward by his sons after his death in 166 B.C. He was buried in the tomb of his father in Modein (1 Macc 2:70).

2. The father of Maath and the son of Semein in Luke's genealogy of Jesus Christ (Luke 3:26).

MATTHEW (Greek form of the Hebrew *mattanyāh*, "gift of the Lord") One of the twelve apostles selected by Jesus and traditionally identified as the author of the first Gospel. He appears in lists of the apostles (Matt 10:3; Mark 3:18; Luke 6:15; Acts 1:13), but he is called a tax collector only in Matt 9:9 and 10:3. In Mark (2:14) and Luke (5:27–28), he is called Levi; in Mark he is said to be the son of Alphaeus. Matthew (or Levi) hosted a feast for Jesus in his house, and there the exchange between Christ and the Pharisees concerning his eating with tax collectors and sinners occurred (Luke 5:29–32). Aside from the attributed authorship of the Gospel and a collection of Christ's sayings in Hebrew (or Aramaic) credited to him by Papias, the bishop of Hierapolis in the early second century, little is known with certainty about Matthew's life as an apostle. Eusebius of Caesarea in the *Ecclesiastical History* (3.24) states that Matthew preached to his fellow Jews. Other traditions have him suffering martyrdom in Ethiopia, Persia, or Pontus. His feast day is September 21. (*See* **Matthew, Gospel of.**)

MATTHEW, GOSPEL OF The first book of the canon of the New Testament and unani-

mously believed in Christian antiquity to have been the first of the four Gospels to have been written down. This tradition went unchallenged until modern times, and the prevailing opinion among most twentieth-century scholars was that Mark's Gospel should be considered the first. (For details on this issue, *see* **Synoptic problem**.)

Scholars infer that the Gospel was written for Jewish Christians for a number of reasons:

1. It stresses that Christ is the fulfillment of the Old Testament Scriptures.
2. Jewish customs are mentioned without explanation.
3. Tradition holds that it was written to Palestinian believers.
4. The Christology of Matthew is based on a vision of Jesus as a new Moses, and as a new Solomon building a new Temple. Jesus is exalted over the revered figures and institutions of the Old Covenant.

I. *Authorship and Date*
II. *Contents*
III. *Literary Features*
IV. *Purpose and Themes*
   A. *Jesus with Us in the Church*
   B. *The Symbolism of the Genealogy of Christ*
   C. *The Kingdom of Heaven*

I. AUTHORSHIP AND DATE

The Gospel of Matthew does not give the name of its author, but the unanimous testimony of ancient tradition declares that the author was the apostle Matthew. The title "According to Matthew," if not original, was added by the early second century A.D. if not earlier.

The Gospel was well known in the early Church. Excerpts from and allusions to the text appear in the *Didache* and in the writings of Saint Ignatius of Antioch in the early second century A.D. From the time of Bishop Papias of Hierapolis (ca. 120), the authorship was attributed to the apostle Matthew. Doubts about its apostolic authorship emerged only in the nineteenth century.

Assigning a date for the Gospel of Matthew is a difficult matter. The question hinges in part on whether Matthew relied on the Gospel of Mark or not, and whether tradition is correct in its claim that Matthew (or some form of it) was originally written in a Semitic language and only later translated into the Greek text we have today. Suggested dates for the book have thus ranged from A.D. 50 to 100, with most scholars favoring the decade A.D. 80–90. On balance, there is no indisputable evidence that necessitates a date *after* the Roman conquest of Jerusalem in A.D. 70. The Jesus of Matthew certainly prophesied this historical catastrophe (Matt 22:7; 24:1–51), yet there is no indication that the evangelist knew of this event as having already happened. The Pontifical Biblical Commission relied on the strength of this evidence when it addressed the composition of Matthew in the early twentieth century:

> *Support for this position is found within the Gospel itself. Matthew makes no reference confirming the destruction of Jerusalem even though he records Jesus foretelling of the event in the Olivet Discourse (24:2). This marks a departure from Matthew's customary style of noting significant or interesting details that remained relevant to the time of his writing (cf. 27:8; 28:15). Taken together, the evidence would indicate a date of composition prior to the terrible events of 70, although the majority of biblical scholars remain committed to the Marcan primacy.*

II. CONTENTS

III. LITERARY FEATURES

Arguably the best known of the Gospels, Matthew is also the one most suited to catechetical instruction. Matthew groups together alternating sections of narrative and discourse. In the sermons, Matthew captures the voice of Jesus as he taught and spoke (cf. Matt 5:3–7, 27; 10:5–42; 13:3–52; 18:2–35; 23:2–39; 24:4–25:46). The book is organized around these major discourses of Jesus, and the teachings and actions of Jesus work together to reveal the true nature of his identity and mission.

IV. PURPOSE AND THEMES

A. *Jesus with Us in the Church*

Matthew showcases the Good News of Jesus's redemptive work. He writes of Jesus as Emmanuel ("God is with us"), applying the title in the first chapter (Matt 1:23) and the very last words spoken by Jesus (28:20). We might call it the most "ecclesiastical" of the four Gospels: Matthew is alone among the Gospels in using the word "church" (*ekklēsia*, 16:18; 18:17). Matthew shows us that the Kingdom of God has been established on earth in the Church, and that in the Church the risen Christ will always remain with his people.

Matthew goes to some effort to document the governance of the Church and its divinely appointed leadership. The importance of the apostles is proclaimed by Jesus when he declares, "when the Son of man shall sit on his glorious throne, you who have followed me will also sit on twelve thrones, judging the twelve tribes of Israel" (19:28). Headship over the Church is given to Peter as the Rock (16:18) to whom are entrusted the "keys of the kingdom of heaven" (16:19) upon which Jesus will build the Church, the new Temple. Jesus also gives the apostles the power to bind and to loose (18:18).

B. The Symbolism of the Genealogy of Christ

The Gospel begins with a genealogy of Jesus that subtly proclaims him the Davidic **Messiah**. This often goes unnoticed by modern readers of the Gospel who are not equipped to recognize what Matthew is trying to accomplish. He arranges the ancestry in three groups of fourteen generations, judiciously editing the list of names to make it fit the scheme.

Numbers had important symbolic significance to the Jews of Matthew's time. In Hebrew, the letters represented not only sounds but also numerical values. Thus every name has a numerical significance. The name David (*dwd* in Hebrew) adds up to fourteen. David's name is also the fourteenth in the list. Three was a symbol of perfection. Thus three groups of fourteen suggest a perfection of David. Jesus is the perfect Son of David, the anticipated Messiah, and his genealogy itself proclaims this.

C. The Kingdom of Heaven

The "Kingdom of Heaven" is the towering theme of Jesus's discourses. Jesus has come to restore the Davidic kingdom, bringing the fulfillment of God's covenant oath to establish an eternal dynasty through David's line. Thus Matthew's Gospel is full of passages that compare Jesus and the Kingdom he brings to the old Davidic kingdom. Jesus bears the Messianic title "Son of David" (Matt 1:1), born of the Davidic royal line (1:2–16); he is "greater than **Solomon**" (12:42), and greater than Solomon's **Temple** (12:6); he builds a new and greater Temple (16:18); his kingship extends over the twelve tribes (19:28) and all nations (28:19); and he founds his church on a prime minister who holds the "keys" to the Kingdom (16:19), as the kings of David's line governed through their prime ministers (see **Kingdom**).

Thus the Kingdom of Heaven is more than the Davidic kingdom restored: indeed, the Davidic empire, exemplified in the reigns of David and Solomon, was a theatrical preview of the Messianic Kingdom, in which the promises given to David are entirely fulfilled. The Christian life goes beyond the Law and the Old Covenant.

In the Sermon on the Mount, Jesus describes the ideal of the Christian life (Matt 5–7);

in the missionary discourse, he gives direction to the apostles for preaching in Galilee (10:5–15) and forecasts the missionary labors of the Church in the pagan world (10:16–42); in his parables (chap. 13), Jesus reveals the mystery of the Church and gives assurance of the growth and triumph of the Kingdom he has brought forth in the world; in the sermon on the life of the Church (chap. 18), Jesus outlines a procedure for Church discipline, stresses the need for forgiveness of sin, and gives to the Twelve authority to bind and loose in his name (18:15–20); in the Olivet Discourse (chaps. 24–25), he predicts the destruction of Jerusalem and the Temple as the final end of the Old Covenant.

Matthew is always careful to show how the promises of the Old Covenant are fulfilled in the institution of the New Covenant. Jesus brings the blessing promised through Abraham to all nations (cf. 8:10–12; 28:18–20) even as he confirms the transitional and temporary nature of the Mosaic laws. The passing of the Old Covenant is given powerful confirmation when Jesus predicts the destruction of the Temple and when he revokes Moses's permission to divorce and remarry (19:1–9). But Jesus also establishes a New Law—a new standard for living that goes beyond the demands of the Mosaic Law and calls for a deeply interior holiness and brotherly love.

MATTHIAS The disciple who was chosen by lot to fill the vacancy among the Twelve left by the death of Judas Iscariot. Acts indicates that he was a witness to the full scope of Jesus's earthly ministry from his baptism to his Ascension (Acts 1:21–26). Little else is known with certainty about him, although he figured in later legends and apocryphal writings, including a gospel composed in his name. (*See also* **Lots**.)

MAZZOTH, FEAST OF *See* **Passover, feast of**.

MEALS In Old Testament and New Testament times, Israelites customarily ate meals twice a day. The first meal was in the morning and consisted chiefly of bread; the second was in the evening and often included meat. Meals were eaten on the floor, with the diners sitting or squatting on mats. Tables and chairs were used in Egypt and Mesopotamia, but they were used in Israelite lands chiefly by the wealthy who could afford them. By the era of Roman supremacy, the Roman custom of eating while reclining had been adopted (Luke 7:38; John 13:23). A low table was used that could be reached by the guests from the couches or mats. Meals were eaten by hand, as there were no utensils such as knives, forks, and spoons (Prov 26:15; John 13:26). Dishes and various plates and pots were used in considerable variety. The host normally gave the blessing, and the bread was broken by the head of the household before being distributed to the guests (Matt 14:19; 15:36; 26:26). At festive meals, including the **Passover**, weddings, circumcisions, and so forth, the head of the house (or the most honored guest) raised a cup of benediction (a cup of wine), gave a blessing, and was joined by the guests, who replied "Amen." (*See* **Eucharist**.)

The arrival of a guest for a meal was celebrated by custom with a welcome kiss or embrace (Luke 7:45), washing the feet (Gen 18:4,

24:32; Judg 19:21), and even anointing the head with oil (Ps 23:5; Eccl 9:8; Amos 6:6). For their part, the guests dressed in their finest clothes (Isa 61:3; Matt 22:11–12) and sometimes wore garlands (Isa 63:1). To add to the festivities, music was often played (Sir 32:5–6; Matt 14:6). (*See also* **Hospitality**.)

MEASURES, WEIGHTS AND *See* **Weights and measures**.

MEDEBA A Moabite city that was conquered by the Israelites and given to the tribe of Reuben (Num 21:30; Josh 13:16). The town is located in the **Transjordan**, approximately twenty-five miles south of modern Amman, Jordan. According to Isaiah, Medeba was later counted as a Moabite city (Isa 15:2). During the Maccabean revolt, "the Sons of Jambri" from Medeba ambushed and killed **John**, son of **Mattathias** (1 Macc 9:36). Medeba was then captured by the Maccabees but eventually given to the Nabateans by John Hyrcanus II. In the fourth century, Medeba was home to a significant Christian community. Two churches of great historical interest have survived, including one that boasts the remains of a late-sixth-century mosaic floor with a map of Palestine.

MEDES *See* **Media**.

MEDIA A region in northwestern Iran that was the site of an ancient Iranian kingdom. The Medes became key players, in alliance with the Babylonians, in the overthrow of the Neo-Assyrian Empire in 612 B.C. By 550 B.C., the Medes were incorporated into the Achaemenid Empire of Persia.

The Medes first received notice in the mid-ninth century when they were mentioned because of Assyrian campaigns against them. Subject for a time to the Assyrians, the Medes reached their zenith under Cyaxares, who forged an alliance with the Babylonians under Nebuchadnezzar in 625 B.C., and so began the war that culminated in the final defeat of the Assyrians. His successor, Astyages (r. 584–550 B.C.), was defeated by **Cyrus** the Great of Anshan, who united the Medes and Persians into one political entity. Cyrus went on to form the Persian Empire, and the Medes were thenceforth tied to the fortunes of that empire (cf. Isa 21:2; Jer 25:25; 51:11; Esth 1:3, 14, 19; Dan 5:28; 6:9; 8:20). According to the **Table of Nations**, the Medes (called the "Madai") were descendants of Japheth (Gen 10:2; 1 Chr 1:5).

MEDIATION *See* **Mediator**.

MEDIATOR One who brings together or reconciles separate or opposing parties. A situation that requires a mediator is one characterized by estrangement or alienation, and the purpose of the mediator is to effect a full and proper reconciliation. The term itself appears infrequently in Scripture, but the notion of mediation is found throughout the sacred texts. In the Old Testament, **Moses** is the great mediator between God and his people. In the New Testament, **Jesus Christ** is the one mediator between God and the human race.

I. Mediators in the Old Testament

II. The Mediator in the New Testament

    A. Jesus the Mediator

    B. The Object and Nature of Mediation

I. MEDIATORS IN THE OLD TESTAMENT

The idea of mediation is integral to the religion of Israel. God spoke to the ancient Israelites, but in the accomplishment of his divine plan of salvation he communicated through specifically chosen figures—the priests, prophets, and kings—under the terms of the **covenant**. The priests exercised their roles as mediators in a specific context, including the offering of sacrifices and fulfilling of oracular functions (Lev 9:7, 16:15–19; Num 16:40; Deut 33:10; 2 Chr 26:18; Heb 5:1–4). The prophets spoke for God to Israel and acted as God's ambassadors to those who were no longer able or willing to hear God's word (Deut 18:15–22; Isa 43:8–15; 55:6–11). Kings such as David and Solomon also acted as mediators while carrying out priestly functions (2 Sam 6:17–18; 1 Kgs 8:54–61; Ps 110:4), were the means of the people's deliverance, and served as the conduit through which God's blessings were disposed.

Moses was chosen by God to lead Israel out of bondage (Exod 3:10), but it was the people who elected him to be *mediator* because they could not endure the thunderous voice of the Lord at Sinai (Exod 20:18–20; Deut 5:4–5). The same type of mediation continued once the **Tabernacle** was constructed: Moses went in and out of the sanctuary to relay God's instructions to the people (Lev 1:1–2; 4:1; 6:8; etc.). Occasionally the people would bring their questions to Moses to present before the Lord (Num 15:32–35; 27:1–5). When the people sinned, Moses made intercession for them (Exod 32:30–32; Num 14:13–19). He is thus remembered as one of the greatest prophets and mediators of the Old Covenant (Num 12:6–8; Deut 34:10; Acts 7:38; Gal 3:19).

II. THE MEDIATOR IN THE NEW TESTAMENT

A. Jesus the Mediator

The term "mediator" is used six times in the NT, twice for Moses (Gal 3:19–20) and four times for Christ (1 Tim 2:5; Heb 8:6, 9:15, 12:24). But the books of the NT are filled with the idea of Christ's role as supreme mediator. The Son of God reconciles God and the human race. "For there is one God, and there is one mediator between God and men, the man Christ Jesus, who gave himself as a ransom for all" (1 Tim 2:5–6).

Jesus is uniquely qualified to be the mediator of the New Covenant (Heb 9:15; 12:24). His mediation comes through the mystery of the **Incarnation**, for as Redeemer he both reveals the love and mercy of the Father and represents the human family and appeals for mercy with the Father. As the divine and preexistent Son, he was the mediator of creation (John 1:3, 10; Col 1:16; Heb 1:2). As man, Christ is a partaker of our flesh and blood (Heb 2:11–15); he thus represents those who are in need of reconciliation with the Creator.

B. The Object and Nature of Mediation

The object of the mediation of Christ is the salvation of mankind, and Christ as the mediator occupies the central position in the economy of salvation. He destroyed sin and restored grace. The reconciliation of God and man by Christ was achieved by his Passion and death upon the Cross, a suffering that he willingly accepted in obedience to the will of the Father: "For in him all the fullness of God was pleased to dwell, and through him to reconcile to himself all things, whether on earth or in heaven, making peace by the blood of his cross" (Col 1:19–20; cf. John 3:16–17; Acts 20:28; Rom 3:21–26, 5:10–11; 2 Cor 5:18–21; Eph 1:7; 1 John 4:9). Christ has removed the obstacles between God and man and has brought peace between them (cf. Rom 5:1; Eph 2:11–18). He took our sins upon himself and made satisfaction for them to God, and so merited for mankind the friendship of God.

Christ's mediation upon the Cross gave us the means of salvation, yet we still depend on him for his continued role as mediator. Christ continues his work of mediation to communicate the grace that was won by the Cross. Even now he mediates and administers a more excellent covenant than that of Moses, a covenant that reconciles the Father and the human family through eternal redemption from sin (Heb 9:11–14) and perpetual intercession in heaven (Heb 7:25; 1 John 2:1) (CCC 51, 65–67, 257, 294, 2006, 2574, 2634). (*See also* **Grace** and **Justification**.)

MEDICINE The practice of medicine was well established in the ancient Near East. Egyptian surgeons performed basic procedures, and the typical healer was familiar with a wide range of herbs and potions, some of which had real effect. Mesopotamia also had physicians, and the doctor who lost a patient in surgery suffered the loss of a limb according to the Code of Hammurabi. But medicine was not a pure science, as it was often connected with magic and superstition.

Throughout the ancient world, ailments were often blamed upon demons and disgruntled spirits, but in the Old Testament, sickness was more often considered a punishment for sin (Num 12:9–11; Deut 28:21). Healing, therefore, was the prerogative of God (Exod 15:26; Isa 38:9–20), and prayer and penance were sometimes the only reliable means of healing (cf. Ps 32, 38). King **Asa** of Judah was reprimanded in 2 Chronicles for failing to seek the Lord and for putting his faith in physicians (2 Chr 16:12) when he contracted a disease of his feet. **Ahaziah** fell through the lattice of the roof terrace in Samaria and was criticized by **Elijah** for pleading to Baal-zebub, the god of Ekron, instead of the Lord; he subsequently died in sin (2 Kgs 1:2–4).

Nevertheless, physicians are not universally dismissed in the OT. Sirach suggests that the physician should be held in honor: "Honor the physician with the honor due him, according to your need of him, for the Lord created him; for healing comes from the Most High, and he will receive a gift from the king" (Sir 38:1–2); it adds, "There is a time when success lies in the hands of physicians, for they too will pray to the Lord that he should grant them success in diagnosis and in healing, for the sake of preserving life" (Sir 38:13–14). But Sirach also stresses the place of sin in sickness, adding, "My son, when you are sick do not be negligent, but pray to the Lord, and he will heal you. Give up your faults and direct your hands aright, and cleanse your heart from all sin" (Sir 38:9–10).

Leviticus makes reference to medical conditions, and diagnoses are provided, but from the standpoint of ritual purity and participation in Israel's public worship (Lev 12; 13; 15; 21:1–3). Commonly mentioned diseases or ailments were skin diseases and **leprosy**, dropsy, paralysis, dysentery, palsy, weakness of the body, and eye complaints.

In the New Testament, various references are made to physicians and medicine (Mark 2:17, 5:26; Luke 4:23; 1 Tim 5:23). Though it may be said that the OT perspective on physical infirmity is presupposed in the NT writings, Christ repudiates the exaggerated notion that every sickness is brought on by personal sin; thus he says with reference to the man born blind, "It was not that this man sinned, or his parents, but that the works of God might be made manifest in him" (John 9:3). Sickness is considered one of the temporal consequences of sin, so Jesus made healing a major part of his ministry and identified with the sick and the suffering: "I was sick and you visited me" (Matt 25:36). As the supreme physician, Jesus was concerned with healing the entire person, body and soul. His miracles of healing announced his victory over sin and thus over the effects of sin, such as mental and physical illness and even death (cf. Matt 8:14–17; Mark 1:41; 3:10; 5:34, 41; 6:56; 7:32–36; 8:22–25; 9:14–29; Luke 6:19; John 9:6–7; Isa 53:4–6). **Luke** was a physician (Col 4:14), and in fact some scholars have noted that Luke's Gospel takes a particular interest in the sick and even uses medical terminology to describe their symptoms and conditions (Luke 4:38; 5:18; 7:10; 8:43) (CCC 1264, 1501–6).

MEDITERRANEAN SEA

The body of water along the western shore of Palestine; it connects the continents of Asia, Africa, and Europe. In the Old Testament, the Mediterranean is usually called just "the sea" (Isa 24:15; Jer 46:18; Ezek 26:17–18; Jonah 1:11–13, 15).

The Mediterranean Sea figured prominently in the economic growth and the development of communications networks in the ancient world, with port cities like Alexandria, Corinth, Tyre, and Ephesus making up a vast commercial and transportation network. The first wide-ranging colonists were Phoenician; the Greeks soon followed, establishing colonies all around the sea.

By New Testament times, the Roman Empire had taken over all the land around the Mediterranean. Trade throughout the Mediterranean promoted a diverse religious and linguistic culture.

These conditions, with flourishing trade and a stable government all around the Mediterranean, prepared the way for the evangelization of the empire by traveling missionaries such as Paul and Peter (Acts 9:36–49; 10:5–8; 13:13–15; 14:1–2).

MEGIDDO

A fortified settlement that overlooks the fertile plain of Esdraelon between **Mount Carmel** and Mount Gilboa; it is identified with the modern Tell el-Mutesellim. Its location made its people witnesses to various battles in biblical times. Occupation of the site began in the fourth millennium B.C.; it was mentioned as one of the conquests of Pharaoh Thutmosis III in Palestine in the second millennium B.C. Campaigns were also fought by Pharaohs Seti I and Shishak. Joshua reports that the king of Megiddo was killed during the Israelite advance into Canaan (Josh 12:21) and the city was allotted to the tribe of Manasseh

(Josh 17:11), although Manasseh was apparently unable to gain control of it (Judg 1:27). The plain of Megiddo was the place where **Deborah** and the Israelites triumphed over the Canaanites (Judg 5:19), but the city did not become an Israelite possession until the time of **Solomon**, when it was fortified and placed under Solomon's administrative structure (1 Kgs 4:12; cf. 1 Kgs 9:15; 1 Chr 7:29). King **Ahaziah** was wounded by **Jehu** and died at Megiddo (2 Kgs 9:27), and King **Josiah** died on the Megiddo Plain when he ill-advisedly met **Neco** of Egypt in battle (2 Kgs 23:29; 2 Chr 35:20–25). As a place of historical battles—both victories and defeats for Israel—Megiddo became attached in apocalyptic imagery to the place where the final struggle between good and evil would occur (Rev 16:16, 20:7–10; cf. Zech 12:1–11, 14:1–2).

MEGIDDO, PLAIN OF The plain of Esdraelon where it spreads out to the north of Megiddo. It is mentioned twice in the Old Testament as the place where King **Josiah** was cut down in battle (2 Chr 35:22; Zech 12:11).

MELCHIOR *See* **Magi**.

MELCHIZEDEK (Hebrew, "king of righteousness") The king and priest of Salem in the days of **Abraham** (Gen 14:18–20). He is the first person in Scripture to be called a "priest," in Hebrew, a *kōhēn* (Gen 14:18). Abraham encountered Melchizedek following his mission to rescue Lot from a coalition of Mesopotamian invaders (Gen 14:13–17). Bringing out bread and wine, the priest blessed the patriarch with the words: "Blessed be Abram by God Most High, maker of heaven and earth; and blessed be God Most High, who has delivered your enemies into your hand" (Gen 14:19–20). In return, Abraham gave Melchizedek 10 percent of his spoils (Gen 14:20). The only other reference to Melchizedek in the Old Testament occurs in Ps 110:4.

The book of Hebrews considers Melchizedek a foreshadowing of Jesus Christ. First, this is because Jesus, like Melchizedek, is both a king and a priest. For most of biblical history, kings came from the Judahite line of **David**, and priests came from the Levitical line of **Aaron**. But Psalm 110 looks beyond this division to a union of the royal and priestly offices in the person of the Messiah, who would not only be enthroned as a king at Yahweh's right hand (Ps 110:1), but would also be ordained a priest "after the order of Melchizedek" (Ps 110:4). Second, it is significant that Melchizedek ruled over the city of Salem. Beginning with Ps 76:2, a long stretch of Jewish tradition identifies this city with Jerusalem. This too foreshadows Christ insofar as he ministers as a royal priest, not in the earthly Salem, but high above in the "heavenly Jerusalem" (Heb 12:22). Third, Jesus is compared with Melchizedek because both are "without father or mother or genealogy" and neither has a "beginning of days nor end of life" (Heb 7:3). The point here is not that Jesus and Melchizedek were parentless and thus preexistent, but that neither was bound by the requirements laid down for the Levitical priests of the Old Covenant. Eligibility for this priesthood required pure lines of descent on both the father's and the mother's side of the family (Ezra 2:61–62), and the time of priestly service was limited to two decades at the most, beginning at age twenty and ending at age fifty (Num 8:23–26). Jesus and Melchizedek thus belong to an order of priesthood that is not confined within such restrictions (Heb 7:6, 14). Fourth, it is probably implied in Hebrews that Melchizedek also foreshadows Jesus in making bread and wine his signature offering. These very elements are signs of the sacrament that Christians receive as food from the "altar" (Heb 13:10) in the Eucharistic liturgy instituted by Christ (Mark 14:22–25).

Historically, the figure of Melchizedek has been identified in different ways. Several modern scholars consider him a Canaanite priest of the Canaanite supreme god "El" (the name in Hebrew means "God"). Jewish tradition offers a very different perspective. In the **Dead Sea Scrolls**, for instance, Melchizedek appears as an eschatological judge who will descend from heaven in the last times to destroy the devil, called Belial (11Q13). A more common tradition held that Melchizedek was actually the patriarch **Shem**, the firstborn son of Noah (Gen 6:10). This identification rests in part on the fact that Shem, according to his genealogies in Genesis, lived into and beyond the days of Abraham, who was born nine generations after him (Gen 11:10–26). References to Melchizedek as Shem appear in the Aramaic Targums (*Neofiti* and *Fragmentary Targums* at Gen 14:18), in ancient rabbinic commentaries (*Genesis Rabbah* 43.6; *Leviticus Rabbah* 25.6), and in the Babylonian Talmud (*b. Nedarim* 32b). Various strands of Christian tradition came to adopt this identification as well. In patristic times, it was favored by Saint Jerome (*Epist.* 73) and Saint Ephraem the Syrian (*Commentary on Genesis* 11.2). In medieval times, this identification was mentioned by such theologians as Saint Thomas Aquinas, Alcuin, Peter Lombard, and Nicholas of Lyra, and it also found acceptance in the traditional commentary, called the *Glossa Ordinaria*, that ran alongside the text of the Medieval Latin Bible. Martin Luther embraced this ancient perspective as late as the sixteenth century (*Lectures on Genesis* 14.18).

MELITA *See* **Malta**.

MEM The thirteenth letter of the Hebrew alphabet, מ.

MEMMIUS, QUINTUS One of two Roman ambassadors sent to the Jews in 164 B.C. along with Titus Manius (2 Macc 11:34). Exact details relating to the envoys are difficult to ascertain.

MEMPHIS The chief city of ancient **Egypt** beginning in the Early Dynastic Period in the third millennium B.C. Memphis was located on the west bank of the Nile, approximately thirteen miles south of modern Cairo, and was first established as a royal residence under the kings of the Third Dynasty (ca. 2700–2600 B.C.). Its location on the Nile exposed it to constant danger of attack, and it was captured over the centuries by the Assyrians and the Persians. The city returned to some prominence under the Eighteenth and Nineteenth Dynasties (ca. 1550–1186 B.C.), but it declined steadily in importance after the founding of Alexandria in 332 B.C. Memphis was mentioned by several prophets (Isa 19:13; Jer 2:16; 46:14, 19; Ezek 30:13; Hos 9:6). A band of Jewish refugees settled in Memphis to escape the Babylonian invasion of Judah (Jer 44:1).

MENAHEM King of Israel from 752 to 742 B.C. whose troubled reign is documented in 2 Kgs 15:13–22. The son of Gadi, he came to the throne by assassinating Shallum the son of Jabesh; Shallum was a usurper who had already murdered **Zechariah**, the last king of the Jehudite Dynasty. Menahem secured the throne by exterminating all opposition with considerable cruelty. He also paid tribute to the Assyrian ruler **Tiglath-pileser III** ("Pul" in the narrative) in order to strengthen his hold on power. Menahem died and was succeeded by his son, **Pekahiah**.

MENE, MENE, TEKEL, PARSIN The English transcription of the words scrawled on the wall during the banquet of King **Belshazzar** of Babylon (Dan 5:25). The writing, inscribed by a miraculous hand, terrified the king into hysteria (Dan 5:5–6). He summoned his wizards and magicians, but none could explain the meaning of the words. At the queen's urging, Belshazzar called for **Daniel**, who explained that the words refer to three kinds of measurement: *Mene, Mene* suggested a *mina*, *Tekel* referred to a shekel, and *Parsin* referred to a division. The same three terms also resemble the verbs "to number," "to weigh," and "to divide." The words spelled doom for Belshazzar and the Babylonian Empire: "MENE, God has numbered the days of your kingdom and brought it to an end; TEKEL, you have been weighed in the balances and found wanting; PERES [singular of *Parsin*], your kingdom is divided and given to the Medes and Persians"

(Dan 5:27–28). That same night, Belshazzar was overthrown and killed, and **Darius the Mede** became king (Dan 5:30).

MENELAUS High priest in Jerusalem from 172 to 162 B.C. He was named to the office by Antiochus IV Epiphanes (*see* **Seleucids**). Initially a supporter of **Jason**—who obtained the high priesthood by bribing the Seleucid king (2 Macc 4:7–9)—Menelaus was sent by Jason on a mission to deliver the monies promised to the king. Instead, Menelaus undermined Jason's position and secured the office of high priest for himself by outbidding him. Menelaus then set out for Palestine while Jason fled to the Ammonites. But when Menelaus did not produce the money, he was summoned before the king and left his brother, **Lysimachus**, in charge during his absence (2 Macc 4:23–29). As Antiochus was compelled to put down a revolt, Menelaus found himself facing the royal official **Andronicus**. He proved easily bribed—with gold vessels from the Temple—and willing to assist in the assassination of the legitimate claimant to the priesthood, **Onias**, Jason's brother. Upon Antiochus's return, the murder led to the punishment of Andronicus, but Menelaus escaped untouched because he had once again managed to bribe a court official, Ptolemy, who had the king's ear (2 Macc 4:30–50).

Established in Jerusalem, Menelaus was soon attacked by Jason, who returned and laid siege to the city upon hearing the false rumor that Antiochus was dead. Antiochus broke the siege and entered the Temple, and Menelaus gave him everything of value within. Menelaus was then firmly restored to the high priesthood and clung to power for several years. At last, **Lysias**, chancellor to King Antiochus V Eupator, convinced the king that the root of his terrible relations with the Jews was Menelaus. The high priest was then taken to Beroea and put to death (2 Macc 13:1–8).

MENI *See* **Destiny**.

MENORAH *See* **Lamp**.

MEPHIBOSHETH (Hebrew, "from the mouth of shame") The name of two descendants of **Saul**. The name itself was almost certainly Mephibaal, but the sacred authors replaced the name of **Baal** with the word for "shame," so that readers would not have to pronounce the name of the Canaanite god (cf. 1 Chr 8:34).

1. A son of Saul and his concubine Rizpah (2 Sam 21:8). He was executed by the Gibeonites, along with his brother Armoni and five sons of Saul's daughter Merab.

2. Saul's grandson and the son of **Jonathan** (2 Sam 4:4). He was left with crippled legs because of a boyhood accident involving his nurse. David, because of his loyal affection for Jonathan, permitted Mephibosheth to reside in the palace (2 Sam 9:1–18). At the time of Absalom's revolt, Mephibosheth was falsely accused of abandoning David in the hope of seizing power for himself (2 Sam 16:1–4). It was later discovered, however, that he was unable to join up with David because of his handicap, not because of political ambition (2 Sam 19:25–31).

MERAB The eldest daughter of **Saul**, king of Israel (1 Sam 14:49). She was promised initially to **David**, but she was then married to Adriel the Meholathite (1 Sam 18:17–19) as Saul became increasingly threatened by David. Breaking the promise to David was a grievous insult.

MERARI The third son of **Levi** and the eponymous ancestor of the Levitical clan of the Merarites (Gen 46:11; Exod 6:16; Num 3:17; 1 Chr 5:27, 6:1, 23:6).

MERCURY *See* **Hermes**.

MERCY The disposition toward lovingkindness, compassion, and/or forbearance. Mercy impels a person toward concern and a readiness to render assistance. It is also shown to one who offends, in particular the mercy of God to sinners (Neh 9:17; Wis 15:1) (CCC 1422, 1829).

I. OLD TESTAMENT

In the Old Testament, God's "mercy" and "love" are closely related. Two Hebrew terms, *ḥesed* and *raḥămîm*, are both translated either "mercy" or "love." In reference to mercy, God's *ḥesed* is a gift and not a right, but it entails a relationship between God and the one who receives it, who is expected to reciprocate by loving God. Thus the term is applied only to persons and not to inanimate objects or goods. Pope John Paul II expressed the covenantal quality of mercy in his encyclical *Dives in Misericordia* (footnote 52):

When in the Old Testament the word ḥesed *is used of the Lord, this always occurs in connection with the covenant that God es-*

tablished with Israel. This covenant was, on God's part, a gift and a grace for Israel. Nevertheless, since, in harmony with the covenant entered into, God had made a commitment to respect it, ḥesed also acquired in a certain sense a legal content. The juridical commitment on God's part ceased to oblige whenever Israel broke the covenant and did not respect its conditions. But precisely at this point, ḥesed, in ceasing to be a juridical obligation, revealed its deeper aspect: it showed itself as what it was at the beginning, that is, as love that gives, love more powerful than betrayal, grace stronger than sin.

God is faithful to his covenant obligations, and God's mercy is part of that faithfulness. Thus we see the words "love" and "faithfulness" together throughout the OT (e.g., Exod 34:6; 2 Sam 2:6, 15:20; Ps 25:10, 40:11, 85:10, 138:2; Mic 7:20). Israel does not deserve God's mercy when it spurns the Lord's commandments, yet it must seek divine forgiveness when it commits offenses. Pope John Paul II explains, "Therefore Israel, although burdened with guilt for having broken the covenant, cannot lay claim to God's ḥesed on the basis of (legal) justice; yet it can and must go on hoping and trusting to obtain it, since the God of the covenant is really 'responsible for his love.' The fruits of this love are forgiveness and restoration to grace, the reestablishment of the interior covenant" (*Dives in Misericordia* footnote 52).

The Hebrew word *raḥămîm* denotes the kind of love and compassion expressed by a mother for her child (Isa 49:15). In fact, it has the same root as the Hebrew word for "womb" (*reḥem*). It is a love that is not merited but is freely given. This is the love God has for his people: "I will heal their faithlessness; I will love them freely" (Hos 14:4; cf. Neh 9:27–31; Ps 25:6).

The whole history of Israel shows that the mercy of God was unmerited. Even in the face of tragic and repeated apostasy, God's mercy was limitless and unfailing (Sir 18:12–13; Ps 86:15, 103:8, 145:9; Neh 9:17; Jonah 4:2). God saves Israel from its enemies (Ps 40:11, 79:8; Jer 42:12) and assures that restoration will come after the Exile (Ezek 39:25; Isa 54:10, 63:7–9). "O give thanks to the LORD, for he is good, for his steadfast love endures forever" (Ps 136:1). The same Psalm goes on to extol God's enduring love over all of creation (Ps 136:4–9), his bringing Israel out of Egypt (Ps 136:10–16), his victories for Israel during the conquest of Canaan (Ps 136:17–22), and his never-ending care of his people (Ps 136:23–26).

II. NEW TESTAMENT

The mercy of God pours forth to its fullest extent through the person and mission of Jesus Christ. From his coming to his teaching to his healing to his suffering, all is done to restore the broken human family to the grace of the Father, who is "rich in mercy" (Eph 2:4) and who "consigned all men to disobedience, that he may have mercy upon all" (Rom 11:32). As in the OT, so in the New, God reaches out to save us "not because of deeds done by us in righteousness, but in virtue of his own mercy" (Titus 3:5) (CCC 211).

We read in the Gospels that Christ came "not to call the righteous, but sinners" (Mark 2:17; Luke 5:32). Jesus applied in a powerful way the call of Hos 6:6: "For I desire mercy and not sacrifice" (Matt 9:13). This call to sinners is completely consistent with the idea of God's unmerited mercy in the OT, but it is in sharp contrast to the unforgiving "righteousness" of the scribes and Pharisees (cf. Matt 9:10–13; 12:7). In his teachings, Jesus expands the inner connection between love and mercy and reveals in his actions their unimaginable depths.

Jesus's teaching on mercy was a source of scandal when he was willing to dine with sinners and tax collectors (Luke 15:1–2, 22–32). Jesus also forgave sinners, which left the religious authorities of the time asking, "Who can forgive sins but God alone?" (Mark 2:7). Either Jesus was a blasphemer who had the audacity to make himself equal to God, or he truly possessed the divine authority to take away sins (John 5:18; 10:33) (CCC 589).

Jesus taught the nature of God's mercy especially through parables: the Lost Sheep (Luke 15:3–7), the Good Samaritan (Luke 10:30–37), and above all the Parable of the Prodigal Son (Luke 15:11–32). At the heart of this teaching is the mercy of the father toward a son who had abandoned the father's house, who lived in pursuit of a false freedom, and who returned home to a generous and forgiving welcome after experiencing an authentic conversion. The Prodigal Son tells us two important things about God's mercy. First, to receive mercy we must admit our own sins: "If we say we have no sin, we deceive ourselves, and the truth is not in us. If we confess our sins, he is faithful and just, and will forgive our sins and cleanse us from all unrighteousness" (1 John 1:8–9). It is the one who fears God (Luke 1:50) and turns from sin who opens himself to the gift of divine mercy (CCC 1439, 1847).

Second, the love of God does not abide in an unmerciful heart (1 John 3:17), and the mercy of God will not penetrate into the human heart if we fail to forgive those who have trespassed against us (Matt 6:14–15) (CCC 1847, 2840). Thus, according to Pope John Paul II, "mercy constitutes the fundamental content of the messianic message of Christ and the constitutive power of His mission. His disciples and followers understood and practiced mercy in the same way. Mercy never ceased to reveal itself, in their hearts and in their actions, as an especially creative proof of the love which does not allow itself to be 'conquered by evil,' but overcomes 'evil with good.' (Cf. Rom 12:21.)" (*Dives in Misericordia* §6.)

MERCY SEAT *See* **Ark of the covenant**.

MERIBAH Also Meribath-kadesh, a location in the Sinai where the Israelites were tested by the Lord and failed the test (Num 20:2–13, 24; 27:14; Deut 32:51; Ezek 47:19; 48:28). The name Meribah, which means "strife" or "contention" in Hebrew, thus recalls Israel's rebellious discontent in the wilderness (Deut 33:8; Ps 95:8). The account of Meribah is strikingly similar to that of **Massah**, since at both locations Moses made water spring from a rock (Exod 17:1–7; Deut 6:16, 9:22).

MERODACH *See* **Marduk**.

MERODACH-BALADAN (Hebrew, "Marduk has given a son") The ruler of Babylon in the days of King **Hezekiah** (2 Kgs 20:12; Isa 39:1).

He came to power in about 721 B.C., and his reign was marked by a determined opposition to **Assyria**. By 710 B.C. he was forced to become a vassal of the Assyrian king Sargon II, and although he gained independence for Babylon in 704 B.C., the Assyrians unseated him from power in 703 B.C. It is probable that his communications with Hezekiah in 2 Kgs 20:12–19 were meant to achieve a military alliance between Babylon and Judah against Assyria.

MEROM A site in upper Galilee from which a stream, called the "waters of Merom," flows into the northwest side of the Sea of Galilee. Today this is called the Wadii Meron. In the time of **Joshua**, a coalition of northern Canaanite kings gathered their troops at this location in a failed effort to halt the Israelite conquest of Palestine (Josh 11:1–6).

MEROZ A town named in Judg 5:23 and noted for its failure to take part in the campaign of Barak and **Deborah** against Sisera and the Canaanites. The town was cursed for declining to assist in the war effort.

MESHA The king of Moab who led a rebellion against King **Jehoram** of Israel in the ninth century B.C. Jehoram and his allies from Judah and Edom then besieged Mesha at Kirhareseth, but the will of the Israelites was broken when Mesha went so far as to sacrifice his own son atop the walls of the battlements (2 Kgs 3:4–27). A stone monument called the Mesha Stele was discovered in 1868; in it Mesha celebrates how Moab freed itself from vassalage to Israel.

MESHACH The Babylonian name given to Mishael, one of the Jewish companions of **Daniel** taken into exile (Dan 1:7). He was one of the three young men cast in the fiery furnace but delivered by God (Dan 3:23–30).

MESHECH One of the seven sons of **Japheth**, son of Noah (Gen 10:2; 1 Chr 1:5; 1 Chr 1:17 also lists a Meshech who is the son of Shem). Meshech is mentioned variously in the Old Testament as a non-Semitic people connected with **Tubal** and **Javan** (Ezek 27:13; 32:26) and under the rule of **Gog** of the land of Magog (Ezek 38:2–3; 39:1). Some scholars also associate Meshech with the Mushki, a tribe mentioned in Assyrian records and possibly identified with the Phrygians.

MESOPOTAMIA (Greek, "between the rivers") The stretch of land, mostly a plain, that lies between the **Tigris** and **Euphrates** rivers. Mesopotamia was the cradle of several great civilizations of the ancient Near East, including Sumeria, **Assyria**, and **Babylon**.

MESSIAH The "anointed one," the Redeemer who is spoken of by the prophets of the Old Testament and whose mission is to bring salvation to Israel and the whole world. In the OT, the term "anointed one"—from which we get the English words "Messiah" (Hebrew *māšîaḥ*) and "Christ" (Greek *christos*)—was applied to kings, priests, and prophets. Such figures were anointed with oil, water, and/or the Spirit of God, as a means of consecrating them for their particular mission. Alongside these historical figures emerged the hope for a future king, an eschatological "anointed one," who would restore the kingdom of Israel and usher in the Messianic age of deliverance from sin, exile, and death. This hope became particularly pronounced after the death of Solomon and the division of the kingdom of Israel (930 B.C.), the scattering of the ten tribes of Israel in the Assyrian Exile (722 B.C.), and the destruction of Jerusalem and the Temple in the Babylonian Exile (586 B.C.). After this time, there was "none to sit upon the throne of David" (Jer 36:30), and the hope grew that God would one day send a King and Redeemer, the Messiah. Although orthodox Judaism still awaits the coming of the Messiah, Christianity proclaims that he has already come in the person of Jesus Christ, who is the true Priest, Prophet, and King.

I. THE HISTORY OF ISRAEL

A. Prophets

In the OT, prophets are sometimes referred to as "messiahs" or "anointed ones." Anointing was used in order to consecrate them to the task of proclaiming the word of the Lord, although actual accounts of these anointings are rare. For example, the prophet Elijah is commanded by God to anoint Elisha his disciple "to be prophet in your place" (1 Kgs 19:16–21). Moreover, the Psalms identify the patriarchs Abraham, Isaac, and Jacob as both "prophets" and "anointed ones." After describing the hardships of the patriarchs, God says: "Touch not my anointed ones, do my prophets no harm" (Ps 105:15; 1 Chr 16:22), pointing to the fact that the patriarchs were both prophets and "messiahs."

B. Priests

Anointing also played an important role in the consecration of priests. The book of Leviticus repeatedly speaks of "the anointed priest" (Hebrew *hakkōhēn hammāšîaḥ*), which can also be translated "the priest messiah" (Lev 4:3, 5, 16; 6:15). In the rite of priestly ordination, Moses pours "the anointing oil" on Aaron's head in order "to consecrate him" as high priest (Lev 8:12). A similar rite is performed on Aaron's sons after they are washed with water and clothed with the liturgical vestments of the priesthood, suggesting that such anointing was an essential part of their being "ordained" priests (Exod 29:1–8; cf. Exod 28:41; 40:15). Along these lines, it is worth noting that in a few instances, the term "messiah" appears to be used to refer to the whole people of Israel (Ps 84:10; 89:39, 52). This makes sense given that Israel's original vocation was to be "a kingdom of priests" (Exod 19:6).

C. Kings

Above all, it is kings who are the most frequently referred to as "messiahs" or "anointed ones" in the OT (1 Sam 2:10; Ps 2:2, 20:6, 28:8, 84:9). The practice of consecrating kings by means of anointing was known throughout the ancient Near Eastern world and is quite clear in Scripture. For example, the prophet Samuel takes a vial of oil, pours it on Saul's head, and says, "Has not the LORD anointed you to be prince over his people Israel?" (1 Sam 9:16). Through this anointing, not only is Saul ordained king, but he is set apart as Israel's savior (1 Sam 10:1). The significance of this anointing is made clear when David refuses to harm Saul because he is "the LORD's anointed" or "the LORD's messiah" (1 Sam 24:6). The visible sign of the oil is meant to signify the anointing of the king with God's Spirit. When David is consecrated as king, "the Spirit of the LORD" comes "mightily" upon him from that day forward, throughout his royal ministry (1 Sam 16:13; Ps 89:20–21). In similar fashion, Nathan the prophet anoints Solomon with a horn of oil outside Jerusalem in the river Gihon (1 Kgs 1:32–45). Intriguingly, King Cyrus of Persia, who authorizes the return of the Jews from exile in Babylon and the rebuilding of the Temple in Jerusalem, is also referred to as "the LORD's anointed" (Isa 45:1). Although some find it troubling that a pagan king could be referred to as "messiah," the fact is that Cyrus's act of freeing the Jews and restoring the Temple accomplish in a preliminary way what was supposed to be carried out by the true King of Israel, the future Messiah.

II. THE HOPE OF ISRAEL

A. The New Adam

According to many ancient interpreters, the first prophecy of a future Messiah in the Bible occurs immediately after the Fall of Adam and Eve, when God declares that he will put "enmity" between the serpent and the woman, between his "seed" and "her seed," and that the seed of the woman would "crush" the head of the serpent (Gen 3:15). Although this passage is admittedly mysterious, some ancient Jewish rabbis interpreted this oracle as a prophecy of the coming of the Messiah (see *Targum Pseudo-Jonathan*), and Christian tradition has long referred to this passage as the "First Gospel" (Latin *protoevangelium*)—the first announcement of the coming Redeemer. In light of this prophecy, the Messiah is sometimes depicted as a new Adam, who will triumph over the serpent by redeeming humanity from the power of Satan and the curse of death, thereby undoing the effects of the Fall (Rom 5:12–17; 1 Cor 15:20–50). Other texts envision a restoration of Eden during the Messianic age of salvation (Isa 11:1–10; 64:17–25; Ezek 36:33–38).

B. The Seed of Abraham

A second key passage is God's calling of Abraham and his promise to bless "all the families of the earth" through him and his "seed" (Gen 12:1–3; 22:18). Although these texts are not explicitly Messianic, they do point to the fact that the salvation of the world will come through

Abraham's "seed"—that is, through his "descendant." This is significant because this prophecy comes directly after Abraham offers Isaac out of obedience to God, by which "Father" Abraham offers his "only son" whom he "loves" as a sacrifice on Mount Moriah—the same mountain on which the Temple would later be built (cf. 2 Chr 3:1). Again, Christian tradition views Isaac's carrying of "the wood" of his own sacrifice "up the mountain" and willingly offering himself in obedience to the will of his father as a foreshadowing of the Crucifixion of Jesus the Messiah upon the very same mountain in Jerusalem (cf. Heb 11:17–19). Moreover, the OT envisions the promise of universal blessing to be fulfilled in the conversion of the Gentiles during the Messianic age (Isa 66:18–22; Jer 3:15–18; Zech 14:16; Sir 44:21).

C. The Star of Jacob

The figure of Jacob has two key Messianic prophecies associated with him. The first is found in his blessing of his twelve sons, when he declares that the kingdom ("the scepter") would not depart from his son Judah "until he comes"—a reference to a future king (sometimes translated as the proper Hebrew name *Shiloh*) who would come and be obeyed by all "peoples" (Gen 49:10). In other words, this coming king would rule over a universal kingdom. The second prophecy is from the prophet Balaam's oracle that "a star shall come forth out of Jacob" and "a scepter rise out of Israel"—both images of a future king who would destroy the enemies of Israel by "crushing" their heads (Num 24:17). This latter prophecy, which is clearly Messianic, appears to be drawing on the imagery in Genesis

of the "seed" of the woman crushing the head of the serpent (Gen 3:15).

D. The Prophet Like Moses

One of the most important prophecies of a future redeemer is Moses's promise that God would one day "raise up" for Israel "a prophet like me" (Deut 18:1–17)—a new Moses. Israel is commanded to "listen" to this prophet, since God declares: "I will put my words in his mouth, and he shall speak to them all that I command him" (Deut 18:18–19). This text clearly refers to a future figure, since the book of Deuteronomy ends by stating that "there has not arisen a prophet since in Israel like Moses, whom the LORD knew face to face" and who performed such miracles (Deut 34:10–12). So Israel still awaits his coming. Because of this prophecy, it was widely believed in ancient Israel that the future Messiah would be like a "new Moses" who would inaugurate a new and greater Exodus (John 6:14, 25–34; Acts 3:17–26). In fact, biblical scholars have noted striking parallels between the "servant" Moses and Isaiah's suffering "servant" (Hebrew *'ebed*; cf. Exod 14:31; Isa 52:13–53:12).

In light of such connections, later Jewish writings outside the Bible refer to Moses as "the first redeemer" and to the future Messiah as "the latter redeemer" (*Rabbah Ecclesiastes* 1:28). Some rabbis even believed that just as Moses had rained down manna from heaven for Israel, so would the Messiah bring new manna from heaven. And just as Moses had made water flow from the rock in the desert, so would the Messiah make rivers of water flow in the desert (*Rabbah Ecclesiastes* 1:9). According to the first-century Jewish philosopher Philo, Moses held the threefold office of priest, prophet, and king (*Moses* 2:1–7).

E. The Branch of David and the "Son of God"

Of all the biblical prophecies regarding the coming of a future redeemer, those that speak of the coming of a future Davidic king are the most famous and the most explicitly Messianic. The foundational text is the prophet Nathan's oracle to David that his "kingdom" would be established "forever" and that his "seed" would rule over it (2 Sam 7:8–16; 1 Chr 17:7–14; cf. Sir 47:11). After the splitting of the kingdom of David under Solomon's son Rehoboam, the scattering of the ten tribes of Israel in the Assyrian Exile (722 B.C.), and the destruction of Jerusalem and the Temple of Solomon by Babylon (586 B.C.), God's promise that David's kingdom would last "forever" seemed to be in jeopardy. But in the midst of these tragedies, the prophets foretold the coming of a future Davidic king. Sometimes this figure is referred to as a new "David," who would restore the twelve tribes of Israel and the kingdom (Hos 3:4–5; Jer 30:9, 33:15; Ezek 37:24–27). On other occasions, the future king is referred to as "the branch" or "shoot" of David's house, meaning that he would be an heir to David's throne (Isa 11:1–10; Jer 23:5–6; Zech 3:8). It is also prophesied that as a descendant of David, the future king would be born in Bethlehem, the City of David (Mic 5:2–4). His advent is expected in some texts to be accompanied by a period of tribulation or "birth pangs" (Jer 30:4–9; Mic 4:10, 5:1–3).

One of the central hopes of the OT is that the twelve tribes of Israel would be restored and redeemed from exile by this future Davidic king. The age of redemption is first and foremost the restoration of the Davidic kingdom (Amos 9:13–15; Mic 4:1–8; Zech 9:9–10). This age is frequently described as an "ingathering" of the scattered tribes of Israel, which will be inaugurated by the Messiah himself (Isa 11:1–11; Jer 23:5–8, 30:9–31:14; Ezek 37:15–28). Like the shepherd-king David, the future redeemer will be a "shepherd" who will gather the scattered "flock" and bring them home to the Promised Land (Mic 2:12–13; Ezek 34:11–25). This redemption from exile will also be a kind of "new Exodus," which will recapitulate Israel's redemption from the Egyptian Exile at the time of Moses (Hos 2:16–17; Isa 11:10–16, 40:1–11; Ezek 20:36–38; Zech 10:6–12). However, just as David and Solomon opened up their kingdom to the Gentile peoples, this new Exodus would mean not only the salvation of Israel but the conversion and ingathering of the Gentile nations (Isa 2:2–4; Jer 3:14–18; Mic 4:1–5; Zech 8:20–23). Just as David had been shown a "law" for all "mankind" (2 Sam 7:19), so too the prophets foretell that in the Messianic age a new "law" will "go forth" from Jerusalem and be written on the hearts of all peoples (Isa 2:1–4; Mic 4:1–4; Jer 31:31–33). Just as God had made a new "covenant" with David, one that was different from the covenant with Moses, so too the prophets speak of a "new" or "everlasting" covenant that would be made at the time of the coming of the Messiah (Jer 30–31; Ezek 37:24–28; cf. Dan 9:24–27).

Along these lines, it is important to note that the common association between the Davidic Messiah and the "Son of God" has its origins in references to the Davidic king as

God's "son" (2 Sam 7:14; Ps 2:6–7). Although this seems to refer to *adoptive* sonship when it is applied to the historical kings of Israel, there are hints of the *divine* sonship of the future redeemer in other passages. Some appear to speak of a Davidic king whose origin is from eternity, before the beginning of time (Ps 110:1–4; Mic 4:2). The prophet Isaiah goes further and refers to the future "son" who will sit "upon the throne of David" as a "Wonderful Counselor, Mighty God, Everlasting Father, Prince of Peace" (Isa 9:6). Finally, in one of the Dead Sea Scrolls, the "Messiah" appears to be referred to as "God" (Hebrew *'ĕlōhîm*) (*11QMelchizedek*).

F. The Heavenly "Son of Man"

In addition to the prophecies of the Son of God, there is also one key text that refers to the future redeemer as "one like a son of man" (Dan 7:13–14). Although the expression "son of man" (Aramaic *bar 'ĕnāš*) can mean just "man" or "a human being" (Ps 8:4–8), in Daniel's famous vision of the four beasts, it is used to describe a supernatural figure who comes "with the clouds of heaven" and is presented to God in his heavenly throne room (Dan 7:14–15). This figure is clearly Messianic, since he is given an eschatological "kingdom," an "everlasting dominion" that will not pass away (Dan 7:14–27). Arguably, this person is identified as the "anointed one" (Hebrew *māšîaḥ*) elsewhere in the book (Dan 9:25–26), since both figures come during a time of tribulation that precedes a time of salvation. This suggestion is supported by the fact that the most ancient Jewish interpretations of Daniel understood the "son of man" as the Messiah (*4 Ezra* 13; *1 Enoch* 46:1, 48:10, 52:4; *Babylonian Sanhedrin* 98a), as of course did Jesus himself (Mark 13:24–27; Luke 17:22–37).

G. The Suffering Messiah

Alongside the many prophecies of the glorious coming of the Messiah, there are also several important texts that suggest that the Messiah will also suffer and die. The most explicit of these is from the book of Daniel, which explicitly describes the coming of a future "messiah, a prince" (Hebrew *māšîaḥ nāgîd*), who will be "cut off," a Hebrew idiom for being "put to death" (Dan 9:24–27). His death is part of a time of tribulation that will function "to atone for iniquity" and "bring in everlasting righteousness" (Dan 9:24). In addition to this, there is Isaiah's famous prophecy of the Suffering Servant, who suffers and dies (is "cut off") as an atonement for the "sin" and "iniquity" of others (Isa 52:13–53:12). Also important is the prophecy of the people of Jerusalem looking upon "him whom they have pierced" (Zech 12:10), a text that both the New Testament and the ancient rabbis interpreted as a prophecy of the Messiah who would be slain (John 19:37; Rev 1:7; *Babylonian Sukkah* 52a; cf. Zech 3:8–9). Finally, the book of Wisdom contains prophecies of a suffering "righteous man" who would be mocked and suffer a shameful death because he spoke as if he were "God's son" (Wis 2:12–20).

H. The Priestly Messiah

In addition to his royal and prophetic identity, the future redeemer is also sometimes described as a priest. For example, one anonymous prophet speaks of a "faithful priest" whom God will "raise up" and give authority over the Levitical priests and their descendants (1 Sam 2:35–36). In similar fashion, the prophets sometimes depict the future Davidic Messiah as assuming priestly prerogatives of offering sacrifice or going into the Temple (Jer 30:21; Ezek 46:1–16). This intimate connection between Davidic kingship and the priesthood seems to be rooted in the fact that David and his heirs sometimes acted as priests, not according to the order of Levi, but according to the order of Melchizedek (2 Sam 6:13–17, 8:18; 1 Kgs 8:14; Ps 110:1–4). In later Jewish writings, this expectation of a priestly Messiah is even more explicit (*T. Lev.* 17–18), and the Dead Sea Scrolls speak of "the Messiah of Aaron" (1QS 9:10–11) or depict him as a new Melchizedek (*11QMelchizedek* 2).

III. THE COMING OF THE MESSIAH

A. The Birth of the Messiah

The central claim of the early Christian Church is that the Messiah spoken of by the OT prophets has come in the person of Jesus of Nazareth. This is particularly evident in the Gospel accounts of Jesus's birth, which focus on demonstrating his Messianic identity. For example, the Gospel of Matthew begins by providing the genealogy of "Jesus Christ" (or "Jesus the Messiah") and tracing his lineage back to King David and to the patriarch Abraham (Matt 1:1). Luke's Gospel goes even further, tracing Jesus's lineage back to Adam himself, who is called "the son of God" (Luke 3:38). King Herod's interest in the birth of Jesus is specifically tied to Micah's prophecy about the future Davidic king being born

in the city of Bethlehem (Matt 2:4; Mic 5:2). Even the events of Jesus's childhood reveal that he is the new Moses: like Moses, he is saved from a wicked king and later departs from the land of Egypt (Matt 2:13–14; Exod 1–2). At the Annunciation, Jesus is shown to be the awaited Davidic King: Gabriel declares to Mary that her child will sit on "the throne of his father David" and will reign over his everlasting "kingdom." Like King Solomon, the son of David, Jesus will be called "the Son of the Most High"—the Son of God (Luke 2:32–33; cf. 2 Sam 7:14). At Jesus's birth, a "star" rises in the East, signaling the advent of a king from the line of Jacob (Matt 2:1; Num 24:17). Similarly, the angels proclaim to the shepherds that the Davidic "Savior," the "Messiah" has been born (Luke 2:11), and the aged prophet Simeon recognizes the infant Jesus as the "Messiah" whom God had promised he would see before he died (Luke 2:26).

B. The Revelation of the Messiah

Jesus's entire public ministry is characterized by his gradual and deliberate revelation of himself as the prophesied Messiah.

Although his disciples would not fully grasp the nature of Jesus's Messiahship until after the Resurrection (cf. John 20:28), the Gospels report that from very early on disciples such as Andrew suspected that in Jesus they had "found the Messiah" (John 1:41). This declaration follows directly on the heels of Jesus's baptism by John in the Jordan, during which Jesus is revealed to be both the "beloved Son" of God (Matt 3:17; Mark 1:11; Luke 3:22) and the "Lamb of God who takes away the sins of the world" (John 1:29). Some scholars have suggested that John is identifying Jesus as the Suffering Servant, who is sacrificed like "a lamb" for the sins of others and whose coming is tied to the new Exodus (Isa 52:1–15; 53:7–12). After his baptism, Jesus immediately goes into the desert to undergo a threefold temptation that matches that of Adam and Eve; thus he reveals himself to be the New Adam who has come to undo the effects of the Fall (Matt 4:1–11; Luke 4:1–13; Gal 3:6). Jesus also reveals his Messianic identity in his first sermon at Nazareth, when he declares the fulfillment of Isaiah's prophecy that one who is "anointed" will proclaim release to the captives (Luke 4:16–21; Isa 61:1–2).

In addition to these inaugural revelations, Jesus also showed himself to be the Messiah during the course of his ministry in the land of Israel. In response to John the Baptist's question as to whether he was "the one to come," Jesus identified his miracles as signs of the Messianic age of salvation spoken of by the prophets (Matt 11:2–6; Luke 7:18–23; Isa 35:5–6, 61:1; cf. *4QMessianic Apocalypse* 2). In his healings and miracles he also took upon himself the sufferings of the people, showing himself to be the Suffering Servant (Matt 12:15–21; cf. Isa 53). He signaled the restoration of the twelve tribes of Israel in the gathering of his twelve disciples (Matt 10:1–6; 19:28), and he focused his preaching on the coming of "the kingdom of God" (Mark 1:14)—although he stressed that the kingdom he spoke of was "not of this world" (John 18:36). In light of these words and deeds, many of those who witnessed his actions wondered if he might in fact be "the Messiah" (John 7:26–31; 10:24). When the Samaritan woman spoke of the coming of "the

Messiah," Jesus said to her: "I who speak to you am he" (John 4:25). Particularly noteworthy are the numerous passages in which Jesus speaks of himself as "the Son of Man," a reference to the heavenly Messiah from the book of Daniel (e.g., Matt 10:23; 13:41–43; 16:13–20; 25:31–46; Mark 2:10, 28; 10:45; 13:24–27; Luke 17:22–37; John 1:51; 3:13–15; 5:25–28). These revelations climax in Peter's confession that Jesus is "the Christ" or "the Messiah" (Greek *christos*), the "Son of the living God" (Matt 16:16), after which Jesus began instructing his disciples that, as the Messianic Son of Man, he must suffer and die and be raised on the third day (Matt 16:21–23; 17:22–23; 20:17–19).

The ultimate public revelations of Jesus's Messiahship took place during his last days in Jerusalem and in his Passion and death. In his triumphal entry, he deliberately fulfilled the prophecy that the Messiah would enter Jerusalem riding on a "donkey" (Zech 9:9–10). As he taught in the Temple, he revealed that "the Messiah" is more than just the "son of David"; he is both a priestly Messiah and "Lord" (Mark 11:35–37; cf. Ps 110:1–4). At the Last Supper, he revealed himself to be the suffering "Son of Man" whose death would bring the coming of the Kingdom of God, the forgiveness of sins, and the inauguration of a New Covenant (Luke 22:14–30). At the trial before the Sanhedrin, when Jesus was asked by the high priest, "Are you the Messiah?" he responded: "I am" (Mark 14:61–62). Finally, at his Crucifixion, the titulus atop the Cross read: "Jesus of Nazareth, King of the Jews" (Mark 15:2; John 19:19). The ironic truth of this revelation of Jesus's Messiahship is only made clear on Easter morning when "the Christ" is raised from the dead to enter into "his glory" (Luke 24:26). In his glorious Ascension into heaven, Jesus fulfills the ancient hope for the enthronement of the Messiah when he is seated at the "right hand" of God as "Lord and Messiah" over the heavenly Kingdom (Acts 2:33–36; Ps 110:1–4).

C. The Preaching of the Messiah

After the Resurrection, the early Christians referred to and proclaimed Jesus as Messiah on countless occasions. In fact, the word "Messiah" (Greek *christos*) occurs over five hundred times in the NT. From the very beginning, the heart of Christian preaching was proclaiming Jesus of Nazareth to be the Messiah of Israel (cf. Acts 5:42). In Peter's inaugural sermon at Pentecost, he proclaims Jesus as both Lord and "Messiah" (Acts 2:36–37). Later on he teaches that Jesus's sufferings fulfilled God's word, spoken through the prophets, "that his Messiah should suffer" (Acts 3:18). Peter also declares that Jesus was "anointed" with the Holy Spirit and with power and engaged in the ministry of freeing others from the devil (Acts 10:38–39). The preaching of other early Christians, such as Stephen, Apollos, and Paul, also focuses on demonstrating and proclaiming Jesus as Messiah (e.g., Acts 7:52–53, 9:22, 18:24–28; Rom 1:3–4, 9:1–5). Indeed, some Christians suffered excommunication from certain Jewish synagogues because they proclaimed "Jesus is Messiah" (John 9:22).

Particularly noteworthy is the book of Hebrews, which was written to fellow Israelites to show that Jesus is not only royal but also a priestly Messiah, according to the order of Melchizedek (Heb 8:1–10:18). Outside the NT, the early Church's preaching of Jesus as Messiah culminates in Saint Justin Martyr's *Dialogue with Trypho the Jew* (A.D. 150), in which he explains the numerous prophecies of the OT that early Christians saw as fulfilled in Jesus Christ.

METANOIA *See* **Repentance**.

METHUSELAH The son of **Enoch** (Gen 5:21) and the father of Lamech (Gen 5:25). According to Genesis, he is the seventh generation descended from Adam and the grandfather of **Noah** (Gen 5:3–32). He lived to the age of 969, the longest life span mentioned in the Bible.

METHUSHAEL The son of Mehujael and the father of **Lamech** (Gen 4:18).

MEUNIM, MEUNITES A desert people from Arabia or possibly from the village of **Meon** southeast of the Dead Sea. They are remembered in Scripture as enemies vanquished by Israel in the days of **Jehoshaphat** (2 Chr 20:1–23), **Uzziah** (2 Chr 26:7), and **Hezekiah** (1 Chr 4:41). The name also appears in the list of Temple servants returned from the **Exile**, but its meaning in that context is uncertain (Ezra 2:50; Neh 7:52).

MICAH (Hebrew, "Who is like the Lord?") One of the minor prophets. Micah should not be confused with **Micaiah**, son of Imlah, a prophet at the time of Ahab of Israel (1 Kgs 22:8). (See **Micah, book of** for details.)

MICAH, BOOK OF The sixth of the minor prophets in the Old Testament. Micah exercised his prophetic ministry in the eighth century B.C. during the days of Kings **Jotham**, **Ahaz**, and **Hezekiah** of Judah. Micah attacked the injustice and corruption of priests, false prophets, officials, and people. He also announced the judgment and punishment to come upon Samaria and Judah and foretold the restoration of Israel.

I. AUTHORSHIP AND DATE

Little is known of Micah except that he came from Moresheth (Mic 1:1; cf. Jer 26:18), a village identified with Moresheth-gath (Mic 1:14) over 20 miles (32 kilometers) southwest of Jerusalem. A contemporary of **Isaiah**, **Amos**, and **Hosea**, Micah was active in Judah before the fall of Samaria (1:2–7) in 722 B.C. and was a witness to the Assyrian invasion of Judah in 701 B.C. led by **Sennacherib**. The only information about the prophet outside the book of Micah comes from Jeremiah, who tells us that Micah's oracles were fairly well known and influential:

> *Micah of Moresheth prophesied in the days of Hezekiah king of Judah, and said to all the people of Judah: "Thus says the LORD of hosts, Zion shall be plowed as a field; Jerusalem shall become a heap of ruins, and the mountain of the house a wooded height." Did Hezekiah king of Judah and all Judah put him to death? Did he not fear the LORD and entreat the favor of the LORD, and did not the LORD repent of the evil which he had pronounced against them? (Jer 26:18–19)*

There is little reason to doubt that the oracles of the book stem from Micah, although it is possible that his disciples are responsible for transmitting them in written form. Critical scholarship tends to doubt the authenticity of chapters 4–7, but this usually has more to do with a disinclination to accept the possibility of true prophecy than with any literary differences that might point to the text being written at a later time or by a different author.

There is broad agreement that Micah received its final form in the period after the **Exile**. Its individual oracles, however, date to the time of the prophet himself. Some can be dated before 722 B.C. (e.g., 1:2–7), while others appear to reflect events that happened in 701 B.C. (e.g., 1:8–16).

II. CONTENTS

III. PURPOSE AND THEMES

Micah shares with his contemporary Isaiah an abiding concern for the moral and spiritual decline of the kingdom of Judah. The heart of his concern is the Judahites' infidelity to the **covenant** promise that was the basis for the life of Judah. The rise of idolatry and paganism were significant threats to the stability of covenant society. In expressing his prophetic message, Micah uses the traditional pattern of beginning with a message of imminent destruction but adds that the doom can be avoided if the people of Judah repent and return to the Lord of the covenant. Yet even if Jerusalem should fall, there is still hope for a later time, for ultimately a Davidic king will come from the hometown of David himself: "But you, O Bethlehem Ephrathah, who are little to be among the clans of Judah, from you shall come forth for me one who is to be ruler in Israel, whose origin is from of old, from ancient days" (Mic 5:2). Matthew cites this as a prophecy that specifies the birthplace of the **Messiah** (Matt 2:6).

The prophecy itself is divided into three parts. The first part (Mic 1:1–3:12) is concerned with judgment upon a sinful people. The prediction of Samaria's impending doom (1:2–7) was made before 722 B.C., whereas the oracle that follows probably dates from 701 B.C. and the invasion by Sennacherib (1:8–16). Chapters 2 and 3 document the sins committed by the people of Judah. Where Amos and Hosea were preoccupied with the idolatry that plagued and eventually destroyed the northern kingdom, Micah centers his complaints on social injustices that were wreaking havoc in the southern kingdom. He attacks the wealthy who exploit the poor and denounces corrupt merchants, judges, and priests as well as false prophets. Special ire is saved for the priests and prophets because of their failure to fulfill their di-

vinely appointed tasks of leading the people. He accuses them of contributing directly to the moral decline of Samaria and also of Jerusalem. Again, like his contemporary prophets, Micah sees divine judgments being executed upon God's people by a foreign, pagan nation.

The second part of the prophecy (4:1–5:14) begins with words also found in Isa 2:2–4, words that constitute a prophecy of hope for the future. The third part (6:1–7:20) is a trial scene in which God acts as prosecutor presenting a case against his people. When asked how the people should worship and give sacrifice, the answer is a powerful declaration, "He has showed you, O man, what is good; and what does the LORD require of you but to do justice, and to love kindness, and to walk humbly with your God" (6:8).

Micah's prediction of catastrophe for Jerusalem was still known a century later when Jeremiah's similar words were earning him the threat of death (Jer 26:18). For Micah, there was dark inevitability to Jerusalem's fall, owing to the pervasive corruption of idolatry and the moral collapse of the kingdom. His call for repentance and reform touched the heart of King Hezekiah and moved him to repentance (Jer 26:16–19).

MICAIAH An Israelite prophet and the son of Imlah (1 Kgs 22:4–28; 2 Chr 18:3–27). Micaiah labored as a prophet during the reign of **Ahab** (r. 874–853 B.C.) and **Jehoshaphat** of Judah (r. 873–848 B.C.). Ahab formed an alliance with Jehoshaphat with the aim of recapturing Ramoth-gilead from the Syrians. Jehoshaphat agreed to the mission, but he demanded that Ahab first secure the advice of the prophets.

Thus, Ahab summoned four hundred prophets. Not surprisingly, they all supported the war. But Jehoshaphat was not satisfied; he asked whether there were any other prophets left. Ahab was forced to admit that one remained—Micaiah—but he complained that Micaiah never gave favorable prophecies for any venture suggested by Ahab. Still, Jehoshaphat demanded Micaiah be consulted. When Micaiah was brought before Ahab and Jehoshaphat, he initially agreed with the four hundred prophets, but when pressed, he spoke the truth and predicted both the failure of the campaign and the death of Ahab. He then added that the prophets spoke as they did because the Lord had sent a lying spirit to the prophets. For this impudence, Micaiah was struck in the jaw and then hurled into a prison. The prophet was ordered to remain a prisoner fed with bread and water until Ahab returned victoriously from the war. Ahab, however, died in battle as predicted.

MICHAEL (Hebrew, "Who is like God?") The name of an **archangel** who appears in both the Old Testament and the New Testament (Dan 10:13, 21; 12:1; Jude 9; Rev 12:7). He is one of the three angels the Church venerates by name (with **Gabriel** and **Raphael**).

In the book of Daniel, the angel Michael appears as the patron and protector of the nation of Israel. He is given the title "prince" and contends with other angelic princes who look after Gentile nations (Dan 10:13, 21). He is also to play a leading role in Messianic times, when the Lord's faithful will be delivered and raised up to eternal life (Dan 12:1–4). In the NT, reference is made to a dispute between Michael and the devil over the body of **Moses**, a story that probably relies on a Jewish apocryphal work called the *Assumption of Moses* (Jude 9). Finally, the book of Revelation depicts Michael as the leader of the angelic armies who expelled **Satan** and his minions from heaven (Rev 12:7–9).

Michael figures in several nonbiblical texts of early Judaism. There, too, Michael, called the Prince of Light, leads the angelic hosts into battle against the spirits of darkness (*Dead Sea Scrolls* 1QM 13.10; 17:5–9). He is identified as an archangel (*1 Enoch* 71:3) and indeed the greatest archangel (*2 Enoch* 22:6). He is one of four elite angels who stand before God (*1 Enoch* 40:9–10) and who will cast the messengers of Satan into the furnace of God's judgment on the last day (*1 Enoch* 54:6). Angels closely associated with Michael in these traditions include Gabriel, Raphael, Suru'el, Raguel, Saraqa'el, and Phanuel (*1 Enoch* 9:1, 20:1–7, 70:1; 1QM 9.15).

Veneration of Michael dates to a very early time in Christian history, and many stories about his intervention have accumulated over the centuries. He supposedly visited Emperor Constantine the Great (d. A.D. 337), made a dramatic appearance over the mausoleum of Hadrian in Rome during an outbreak of plague (the plague stopped and ever since the mausoleum has been called the Castel Sant'Angelo in his honor), and intervened in various wars and battles. Saint Joan of Arc (d. 1431) credited Michael as one of the holy spirits who aided her and gave her the courage to save France from the English during the Hundred Years' War (1337–1455). Numerous theologians have examined Michael, including Saint Basil the Great and Saint Thomas

Aquinas, who devoted a section of the *Summa theologiae* to angels.

Michael's role as an angel of healing was celebrated by churches in Asia Minor, where he was reputed to have caused healing springs to flow so that churches in his name were visited frequently by the sick and lame. Sailors in Normandy invoke him as their patron, and in 1950 Pope Pius XII named him the patron of policemen. The famous monastery Mont St. Michel is named in his honor. Michael has long been a favorite subject of art, and is usually depicted as a tall, handsome angel holding a sword and shield, lance, banner, or scales; often he is shown doing battle with Satan or a dragon. His feast day is September 29.

MICHAL The younger daughter of **Saul** (1 Sam 14:49), and the wife, first of **David** (1 Sam 18:27) and then of Palti (1 Sam 25:44). She was eventually returned to David after the death of Saul. Knowing that Michal loved David, Saul—hoping to eliminate David by sending him into an impossible combat—told David he could wed her if he produced the foreskins of one hundred Philistines. David set out and returned with two hundred foreskins (1 Sam 18:20–27). Caught in his own scheme, Saul was forced to permit the marriage. Michal proved loyal to her husband, going so far as to help David escape Saul's plan to kill David (1 Sam 19:11–17), lying twice to her father that David was ill (1 Sam 19:14) and that David had threatened her into giving him assistance (1 Sam 19:17).

Michal is last mentioned when the **ark of the covenant** came to Jerusalem (2 Sam 6:16–23). As she looked out the window, she saw David dancing before the ark and "despised" him for it. She criticized David for his behavior, but David rebuked her. As a result, the Lord withheld his blessing from Michal, "the daughter of Saul," and she remained childless for the rest of her days.

MICHMASH A town located between the tribal territories of Benjamin and Ephraim, approximately ten miles north of Jerusalem (1 Sam 13:2; Isa 10:28; Ezra 2:27; Neh 7:31, 11:31; 1 Macc 9:73); probably either modern Mukhmas or Khirbet el-Hara el-Fawqa. The town figured in Saul's conflicts with the Philistines and is the place where Jonathan displayed exceptional courage in battle (1 Sam 13:23–14:23). Centuries later, Michmash was the residence of **Jonathan Maccabeus** (1 Macc 9:73).

MIDIANITES A people of northwest **Arabia** who had an important role in the early history of Israel. Midian was the son of **Abraham** and Keturah, Abraham's second wife (Gen 25:1–2; 1 Chr 1:32). **Moses** fled from Egypt and went to Midian, where he married Zipporah and developed a trusting relationship with his father-in-law, **Jethro**, who was the priest of Midian (Exod 2:15–22; cf. Exod 18:1–24). Another Midianite named Hobab acted as a guide for Israelites during the journey through the desert (Num 10:29–32).

Relations between Israel and Midian were not always cordial, however, because the Midianites entered into an agreement with the Moabites to halt the advance of the Israelites into Canaan. They thus took part in summoning **Balaam** to curse the Israelites before their entrance into the land (Num 22:4–7). Because of Midian's treachery in hiring Balaam, the Lord ordered Moses to wage a punitive war on the Midianites that resulted in heavy casualties for Midian and a treasury of spoils for Israel (Num 31:1–54). **Gideon** defeated the Midianites and was hailed as a savior of Israel; he killed two Midianite chieftains (Judg 6:33–8:28), an event hailed as the "Day of Midian" (cf. Isa 9:3, 10:26; Ps 83:10).

MIDRASH (Hebrew *midrāš*, from the verb *dāraš*, meaning "to seek or inquire") A type of biblical exegesis or homily found in rabbinical literature. Its chief purpose was not to discern the literal meaning of the text but to make a passage of the Bible meaningful to the contemporary generation. No effort was made to examine the text in its precise historical context. Midrash is found in two chief forms, the Haggadah (mainly an exposition of the meaning of biblical narratives) and the Halakah (exposition of legal texts and requirements set forth in Scripture). The noun *midrāš* appears twice in the Old Testament: 2 Chr 13:22 notes that "the rest of the acts of Abijah, his behavior and his deeds, are written in the story of the prophet Iddo"; and 2 Chr 24:27 states, "Accounts of his sons, and of the many oracles against him, and of the rebuilding of the house of God are written in the Commentary on the Book of the Kings."

MIGDOL (Hebrew, "tower" or "fortress") A location in northeast Egypt that is mentioned in various places in Scriptures (Exod 14:2; Num 33:7; Jer 44:1, 46:14; Ezek 29:10). In Exod 14:2 and Num 33:7, Migdol is said to be near Pi-ha-hiroth and Baal-zephon, although its exact location is not certain. Candidates among scholars have included Tell el-Her and Tell el-Maskhuta. The Migdol in Jeremiah is one of the places where Jewish migrants fled and resettled after the destruction of Jerusalem in 586 B.C. In Ezekiel, Migdol seems to refer to a northern site in Egypt. Migdol was also mentioned in the Tell el-Amarna Letters of the Nineteenth Dynasty of Egypt. It is uncertain whether these texts all refer to a single location, or whether there was more than one location bearing the same name.

MILCOM *See* **Molech.**

MILE A unit of measurement. The Roman mile was slightly less than the modern English mile. It was eight **stadia**, and stadia were 220 yards or 200 meters each, although the exact length varied depending on the terrain (cf. Matt 5:41).

MILETUS A city on the western coast of Asia Minor near the mouth of the Meander River, about thirty miles south of Ephesus. Paul paid a visit to Miletus and summoned the elders of Ephesus there (Acts 20:15, 17). His farewell address to the people was so moving that the elders wept and embraced and kissed him (Acts 20:18–38). Trophimus, a companion of Paul, took ill and remained in Miletus (2 Tim 4:20).

MILK One of the staple foods of Palestine, milk was produced from goats and sheep, as well as camels. It was kept in skins (Judg 4:19) and was especially common for drinking where potable water might be scarce. Milk in skins could not be kept for long, obviously, and so curdled milk was made into yogurt and cheese, which were something of a delicacy (Gen 18:8; Judg 5:25). Milk in general was a symbol of wealth and prosperity (Gen 49:12; Deut 32:14; Isa 7:22, 55:1; Joel 3:18). **Canaan** was described as a land flowing with milk and honey (Exod 3:8, 17; 13:5; 33:3).

In the New Testament, Paul compares his simple teachings to the milk given to infants who are not yet ready for solid food (1 Cor 3:1–2; cf. Heb 5:12–14). In 1 Pet 2:2, a similar comparison is used: "Like newborn babes, long for the pure spiritual milk, that by it you may grow up to salvation."

MILL A device for grinding groats, meal, or flour. In the ancient world, almost every household had a mill for preparing the daily food. One of the harshest penalties that could be imposed on families was to take their millstone away, and that was why a creditor could not claim it (Deut 24:6). The simplest method of milling grain was to pound it in a mortar (cf. Num 11:8), but a more efficient method was to use a hand mill (Eccl 12:4; Lam 5:13). In its basic shape, the hand mill consisted of a lower stone that remained stationary, made of basalt (often imported from the Hauran) or limestone, and the upper millstone, made of basalt or sandstone, which was turned on an axis, and the grain was ground between the two stones (cf. Judg 9:53; 2 Sam 11:21). Various improvements in the shape and design of the mill were introduced over the centuries to make the mill tools more efficient (cf. Matt 24:41; Luke 17:35).

Milling was a very difficult and tedious job. It was often performed by slaves in larger homes, but housewives assumed the task in typical families (Exod 11:5; Isa 47:2; Job 31:10; Eccl 12:3; Matt 24:41). Samson was forced by the Philistines to use a hand mill (Judg 16:21), and Judean captives were compelled by the Babylonians to labor in mills (Lam 5:13). The Romans built large mills powered by water, animals, or humans for the mass production of flour.

MILLENNIUM A period of one thousand years. This unit of history appears most notably in the book of Revelation, where it is said that **Satan** will be bound in chains for a span of one thousand years (Rev 20:1–3), during which time the assembly of Christian martyrs will reign with Christ (Rev 20:4–6). At the end of this thousand-year stretch, Satan will be released from his bonds and allowed to make war on the saints of God (Rev 20:7–9). Then follows the general resurrection (Rev 20:5), the final destruction of Satan (Rev 20:10), and the Last Judgment of the living and the dead (Rev 20:1–15).

Catholic exegesis since the time of Saint Augustine and Saint Jerome has preferred to interpret the millennium of Revelation as a symbolic reference to the age of the Church, which spans the distance between the first and second comings of Christ (see, e.g., Saint Augustine's *City of God* 20.7–8). Before this, a number of theologians and churchmen were "chiliasts" (from the Greek *chilioi*, meaning "one thousand"); that is, they believed that Christ would return to inaugurate a literal thousand-year reign on earth, a golden age of human history during which peace and prosperity would reign throughout the world (see, e.g., Saint Justin Martyr, *Dial.* 80; Saint Irenaeus, *Against Heresies* 5.35; Lactantius, *Divine Institutes* 7.21–26).

The Catholic Church has not officially endorsed the view of Saint Augustine, or of anyone else for that matter, but it was decreed by the Holy Office in 1944 that millenarianism, understood as the hope for a coming kingdom on earth, could not safely be taught as authentic Christian doctrine (CCC 676).

MILLO (Hebrew, "filling") Located in the oldest quarter of ancient **Jerusalem** (2 Sam 5:9; 1 Kgs 9:15, 24; 11:27; 1 Chr 11:18), "the Millo" may refer to earthen terraces that supported walls and dwellings around the top of the Ophel ridge where the City of David was built. Or it might also refer to an earthen bridge that filled in the valley between the Ophel and Mount Moriah, which rose beside the city on its north side. After he conquered Jerusalem, **David** decided to build the city "round about from the Millo inward" (2 Sam 5:9), suggesting that the Millo was in existence before David took the city. **Solomon** also undertook work on the Millo, using forced labor (1 Kgs 9:15, 24; 11:27). Similarly, **Hezekiah** repaired the Millo before the attack by **Sennacherib** (2 Chr 32:5).

MINISTER *See* **Deacon**.

MIRACLE (Latin, "marvel"). An extraordinary event or feat that can only be explained by the direct intervention of God. Normally a miracle involves the suspension of the otherwise inflexible laws of nature. The miracles of Jesus are signs of God's power inaugurating the Kingdom through Jesus's ministry (John 9:3; Acts 2:22; *see also* **Signs**) (CCC 547–49).

I. *Miracles in the Old Testament*
  A. *God Ceaselessly Acting*
  B. *Miracles Identify God*
II. *Miracles in the New Testament*
  A. *Miracles Witness to Jesus*
  B. *Healing Miracles*
  C. *Nature Miracles*
  D. *The Miracles Continue*

I. MIRACLES IN THE OLD TESTAMENT

A. *God Ceaselessly Acting*

The Old Testament writers saw God ceaselessly acting in the world. One of his greatest acts was the **Creation** itself, as Job tells us (Job 9:1–10; 26:5–14; chaps. 38–41). Because God is the Creator, he is Lord of nature: all created things are submissive to his mighty will.

God's Lordship over the world is demonstrated by such miraculous feats as flooding of the earth (Gen 6–9), the parting of the Red Sea (Exod 14), water being brought up from a rock (Exod 17), and Israel being given countless military victories over more powerful foes. All these things are humanly and naturally impossible, but they are divinely possible when the God of Israel decides to act.

B. *Miracles Identify God*

These miracles demonstrate the sovereign and saving power of the Lord, as seen in the events of the Exodus (Exod 3:20, 34:10; see also Josh 3:5; Neh 9:17; Mic 7:15) and in the Psalms

(Ps 9:1; 78:11; 96:3–4; 106:7–8). The Psalms also stress the wonders of creation as evidence of God's power: "On the glorious splendor of your majesty, and on your wondrous works, I will meditate. Men shall proclaim the might of your terrible acts, and I will declare your greatness" (Ps 145:5–6).

Sometimes the miracle is described as a "sign"—evidence that what God or his prophet says is true. "'If they will not believe you,' God said to Moses, 'or heed the first sign, they may believe the latter sign'" (Exod 4:8–9; cf. Isa 8:18, 20:3).

The great deeds of God displayed his majesty and called forth the praise of his people (Ps 71:18). God did not just watch over his Chosen People: he actively intervened in the natural order to save, judge, and instruct them. But more than that, God's saving works told Israel who God was. The signs showed the sovereign power of God over all the earth. The wonders of the Exodus, for example, freed Israel from bondage, but, more important, God performed the miracles "that you may tell in the hearing of your son and of your son's son how I have made sport of the Egyptians and what signs I have done among them; that you may know that I am the LORD" (Exod 10:2).

II. MIRACLES IN THE NEW TESTAMENT

A. Miracles Witness to Jesus

The miracles in the New Testament serve the same purposes as those in the OT: to heal God's people and to reveal God's saving power. God has become incarnate in Jesus Christ, and the miracles performed by Jesus show that he has the same power over nature that God had in OT times. Thus the virginal conception (Luke 1:35) and the Incarnation of Christ, the preaching and healings by Christ (Luke 5:17), and the communication of Jesus's divine power to the apostles (Luke 9:1, 10:19; Acts 1:8) all reinforce the message that Jesus Christ was God incarnate.

The "mighty works and wonders and signs" (Acts 2:22; cf. Luke 7:18–23) that Jesus performed revealed that he had divine authority. His words were authenticated by his works: the miracles added credibility to his divine and Messianic claims (Luke 4:17–27; John 5:18–36; 8:58; 9:16; 10:24–37; 14:12).

Nevertheless, the signs and wonders of Christ were rejected by some who witnessed them (Matt 11:6), and some even accused Jesus of being possessed by demons (Mark 3:22; John 11:47–48). That accusation is refuted by Jesus: "if Satan casts out Satan, he is divided against himself; how then will his kingdom stand?" (Matt 12:26; Mark 3:22–26; Luke 11:19).

B. Healing Miracles

The Gospel miracles fall into two basic categories. Jesus's healings bear witness to his saving power to free humanity from evil, suffering, sickness, and even death (Mark 1:32–34; Luke 13:10–17; John 5:2–9). Acts 10:38 declares "how God anointed Jesus of Nazareth with the Holy Spirit and with power; how he went about doing good and healing all that were oppressed by the devil, for God was with him." In Mark we read: "The kingdom of God is at hand" (Mark 1:15), and the proof is in the Son of God's power over Satan (Mark 3:11).

The healing accounts typically follow a set pattern: the seriousness of the situation is described (such as the physical symptoms, the hopelessness of the case, and the failure of treatments; e.g., Mark 5:1–5, 25–26; Luke 13:11); the miracle takes place through physical contact (e.g., Matt 8:3, 15; 9:29) or spoken words (e.g., Mark 2:11, 3:5; Luke 4:39); and the success of the healing is shown by the astonishment of the witnesses (Mark 1:27, 2:12, 7:37; Luke 18:43). Notably, Jesus performed healing miracles in his own name, whereas the apostles healed (Acts 3:6; 4:10, 30) and exorcised demons (Luke 10:17; Acts 16:18; cf. Acts 19:13) always in Jesus's name.

C. Nature Miracles

Jesus's nature miracles are classically represented by his power over the storm (Matt 8:23–27; Mark 4:35–41; Luke 8:22–25), in which Jesus calms a storm on the Sea of Galilee, to the amazement of the disciples. Similar NT nature miracles include the catching of fish (Luke 5:1–11; John 21:4–8) and Jesus's walking on water (Matt 14:22–33; Mark 6:45–52; John 6:16–21). Two nature miracles, both having to do with provision of food, are especially significant: his feeding of the multitude (Matt 14:15–21, 15:32–39; Mark 6:35–44; Luke 9:12–17; John 6:1–14) and his changing water into wine at Cana (John 2:1–11). In these actions, Jesus prefigures the establishment of his **Eucharist** (CCC 1335). Nature miracles demonstrate the Lordship of Jesus over the created world, but they likewise manifest Jesus's saving power. The miracles of Jesus thus attest to divine love: each occurrence is an act of compassion and munificence.

D. The Miracles Continue

The miraculous power of Christ is a sign of a loving and saving God who acts for our salvation (Rom 1:16); the miracles he performed were deeply personal and rooted in love. Thus the miracles did not end when Christ ascended. The apostles were themselves empowered to heal (Acts 6:8; 2 Cor 12:12; Heb 2:3–4), and the power was perpetuated in the Church: miracles both confirm the faith of believers and invite unbelievers to faith (Mark 16:17; 1 Cor 12:10).

The Miracles of Christ

Following is a listing of Jesus's miracles as set forth in the canonical Gospels.

NATURE MIRACLES

Changing the water into wine at Cana (John 2)

The first miracle of the fishes (Luke 5)

The calming of the storm (Matt 8; Mark 4; Luke 8)

The first multiplication of the loaves (Matt 14; Mark 6; Luke 9; John 6)

Walking on the water (Matt 14; Mark 6; John 6)

The second multiplication of the loaves (Matt 15; Mark 8)

Stater in the fish's mouth (Matt 17:24–27)

The cursing of the fig tree (Matt 21; Mark 11)

The second miraculous catch of fishes (John 21)

HEALING MIRACLES

Healing the nobleman's son (John 4)

Healing the leper (Matt 8; Mark 1; Luke 5)

Healing the paralytic (Matt 9; Mark 2; Luke 5)

Healing the sick man at Bethesda (John 5)

Restoring a withered hand (Matt 12; Mark 3; Luke 6)

Healing the centurion's servant (Matt 8; Luke 7)

Healing the blind and dumb (Matt 12; Luke 11)

Healing the woman with a hemorrhage (Matt 9; Mark 5; Luke 8)

Healing two blind men (Matt 9)

Healing the mute man (Matt 9)

Healing the deaf and mute man (Mark 7)

Healing the blind at Bethsaida (Mark 8)

Healing the one born blind (John 9)

Healing the woman with a spirit of infirmity (Luke 13)

Healing the man with the dropsy (Luke 14)

Healing the ten lepers (Luke 17)

Healing the blind man near Jericho (Matt 20; Mark 10; Luke 18)

Restoring Malchus's ear (Luke 22)

EXORCISMS

The demoniac at Capernaum (Mark 1; Luke 4)

The deaf and mute demoniac (Matt 12; Luke 11)

The Gadarene/Gerasene demoniacs (Matt 8; Mark 5; Luke 8)

The mute demoniac (Matt 9)

The daughter of the Syro-Phoenician woman (Matt 15; Mark 7)

The epileptic child (Matt 17; Mark 9; Luke 9)

RESURRECTIONS

Raising the daughter of Jairus (Matt 9; Mark 5; Luke 8)

Raising the son of the widow of Nain (Luke 7)

Raising Lazarus (John 11)

MIRIAM The sister of **Aaron** and **Moses** and the daughter of Amram and Jochebed (Num 26:59; 1 Chr 5:29). "I sent before you Moses, Aaron, and Miriam," the Lord says in Micah 6:4, giving Miriam a place beside the other two great leaders of the **Exodus**. Described as a prophetess, she led the women in a celebration of song and dance after the crossing of the Red Sea (Exod 15:20–21). Later, Miriam and Aaron challenged the authority of Moses, and Miriam was punished with leprosy (Num 12:1–15; cf. Deut 24:9). Moses interceded for her recovery, but she spent seven days outside the camp. She was buried at Kedesh (Num 20:1).

MIRROR The mirror of the ancient world was made of highly polished metal, usually in a circular shape with a handle attached (Exod 38:8; Sir 12:11; cf. Job 37:18). Glass-covered mirrors arrived only with the Romans. Paul uses the image of a mirror to great effect in 1 Cor 13:12 to describe the difference between our current life and the life to come: "For now we see in a mirror dimly, but then face to face" (cf. Jas 1:23).

MISHAEL *See* **Meshach**.

MISHNAH *See* **Talmud**.

MITYLENE The chief city and seaport of the island of Lesbos in the Aegean Sea. During his third missionary journey, Paul spent the night at Mitylene before sailing to Chios and Samos (Acts 20:14).

MIZPAH, MIZPEH (Hebrew, "watchtower") The name of several locations in Scripture, so named because they were positioned to provide a place of observation or a vantage point.

1. The location where **Jacob** sealed a covenant with **Laban** and set up a heap of stones as a perpetual witness to it (Gen 31:44–46).

2. A site in Gilead that was the home of the judge **Jephthah** (Judg 11:11, 29, 34). Some scholars identify this place with Ramath-mizpeh.

3. A place in northern Palestine near the base of Mount Hermon and called "the land of Mizpeh" (Josh 11:3, 8). It was home to an enclave of Hivites before the Israelites conquered Canaan.

4. The location in Moab to which **David** took his family to keep them safe from the envious rage of **Saul** (1 Sam 22:3).

5. A town in the western hills of Judah (Josh 15:38).

6. A town in Benjamin (Josh 18:26) where the tribes met and agreed to punish Benjamin after the outrage committed on a Levite and his concubine by the townspeople at Gibeah (Judg 20:1–48), and where Saul was publicly selected as king of Israel (1 Sam 10:17–24). Later, the city was fortified by King Asa against Baasha of Israel (1 Kgs 15:22; 2 Chr 16:6). After the destruction of Jerusalem in 586 B.C., Mizpah was the residence of **Gedaliah**, the governor appointed by Nebuchadnezzar (2 Kgs 25:23), and was hence the place where Gedaliah was assassinated by Ishmael (2 Kgs 25:25; Jer 41:1–3). After the **Exile**, the city was inhabited by returnees (Neh 3:7, 15).

MNASON A Christian who provided accommodations for Paul and his companions during one of his visits to Jerusalem (Acts 21:16). He was originally from Cyprus.

MOAB, MOABITES The territory directly east of the Dead Sea and bounded by the Arnon and Zered rivers. The Semitic people who inhabited the region were termed Moabites, and they are known mainly through the Hebrew Bible. A culture flourished in this area in the late third millennium B.C., but this ended abruptly around 1900 B.C. Gradually a sedentary Moabite culture was established sometime before the Israelite conquest of Canaan. According to the **Pentateuch**, the Moabites were kinsmen of the Israelites, being descendants of **Lot** through Moab, who was the offspring of Lot's incestuous union with his eldest daughter (Gen 19:37; Deut 2:9).

The Moabite kingdom of the middle second millennium B.C. was distinguished by its prosperity and organization. It extended its influence north of the Arnon, but reverses occurred in the period just before the Exodus when the territories to the north of the Arnon were seized from Moabite control by Sihon, king of the Amorites (Num 21:25–30). After that, the region to the north of the Arnon passed into the hands of Israel and became a source of conflict between the Moabites and Israelites in later years (cf. Judg 11:12–28).

When the Israelites asked permission to cut across a plateau in Moab territory on their way to Canaan, the Moabites refused them permission (Judg 11:17). Although the Lord refused to sanction an attack upon the Moabites (Deut 2:9), they were thereafter excluded from the assembly of Israel (Deut 23:3–6; Neh 13:1–3). The animosity between

Israel and Moab was manifested in the unsuccessful effort by **Balak**, king of Moab, to place a curse upon the Israelites through **Balaam** (Num 22–24). The Israelites camped in the "plains of Moab" (Num 22:1) and fell prey to the idolatrous practices of the inhabitants (Num 25:1–118; Hos 9:10). Moses also died and was buried in Moab (Deut 34:1–8).

During the period of the Judges, the Moabites attacked Israelite lands under Eglon, king of Moab, and oppressed Benjamin for eighteen years until Israel was delivered through **Ehud** (Judg 3:12–30). Over the next years, relations between the Israelites and the Moabites varied. Elimelech of Bethlehem migrated to Moab and his sons wed Moabite women, Orpah and **Ruth**; Ruth later married Boaz and so became an ancestor of **David** (Ruth 4:18–22) and ultimately of Christ (Matt 1:5–16). Saul, however, fought with the Moabites (1 Sam 14:47).

David used Moab as a place of safety for his family during the time that he was a fugitive (1 Sam 22:3–4), but his good relations apparently ended because he waged a brutal war against Moab, made it a vassal, and executed many captives (2 Sam 8:2; 1 Chr 18:2). The Moabites eventually regained their national independence, although **Ahab** of Israel tried and failed to subdue the Moabites, even with the assistance of **Jehoshaphat** of Judah and the king of Edom (2 Kgs 3:4–27). In later years, the Moabites took part in an unsuccessful attack on Judah, along with the Ammonites and Edomites (2 Chr 20:1–30). Moabites also raided Israel (2 Kgs 13:20). The Moabites were often subject to harsh prophetic judgment (Isa 15–16, 25:10; Jer 9:25–26, 25:12, 27:3;

Ezek 25:8–11; Amos 2:1–3; Zeph 2:8–11). (*See also* **Nabatea**.)

Moab was eventually subdued by the Assyrians and forced to pay tribute (Isa 15–16), but Moab regained its freedom after the collapse of the Assyrian Empire. In the wake of the fall of Jerusalem in 586 B.C., Jews fled to Moab for safety but returned after the appointment of Gedaliah by the Babylonians (Jer 40:11). Nebuchadnezzar brought Moab under Babylonian control, and after that Moab passed under the control of the Persians. Intermarriage between Moabites and Jews became a problem in the period after the **Exile** (Ezra 9:1; Neh 13:1, 23).

MODEIN A village north of Jerusalem that was home to **Mattathias**, patriarch of the Maccabees. The town witnessed the start of the Maccabean revolt, when Mattathias refused to obey the demands of Antiochus IV Epiphanes (*see* **Seleucids**) to forsake the **Law**, and then he slew the official sent to carry out the order. Mattathias was buried at Modein, in the family tomb (1 Macc 2:70). **Judas Maccabeus** was also buried there (1 Macc 9:19) along with **Jonathan** (1 Macc 13:25).

MOLECH, MOLOCH A Semitic deity worshipped with child sacrifice. Worshippers offered their sons and daughters to the god by making them "pass through the fire to Molech," a practice that particularly horrified the Old Testament writers (Lev 18:21; 2 Kgs 23:10; cf. Jer 7:31, 19:5). Molech worship, according to the **Law**, was a capital crime punishable by stoning (Lev 20:2–5). Nevertheless, the cult was popular in Israel and Judah, especially under apostate kings. One of the primary places of Molech worship was **Topheth** in the Valley of the Sons of Hinnom, just south of Jerusalem.

MONEY The first minted coins in the Near East appeared around the seventh century B.C. Before that time, bartering was the normal means of exchange, and the medium of exchange might include precious and semiprecious metals (weighed for each transaction), as well as perishable goods (e.g., wheat, dates, and honey) and nonperishable goods (timber, wine, and livestock). Wealth, therefore, was assessed by the extent of a person's holdings in such commodities as cattle and metals (Gen 13:2; Job 1:3). Of the metals used in transactions, the most common was silver. **Abraham** purchased the cave of **Machpelah** with silver shekels (shekels being understood as a unit of weight rather than a currency, Gen 23:15–16), and **Jeremiah** used shekels to purchase the field at Anathoth (Jer 32:9). **Solomon** used silver shekels for military spending on chariots and horses (1 Kgs 10:14, 29). Gold was also used, but usually after silver (cf. 1 Kgs 9:10–14; 2 Kgs 18:14). Barter continued to have a significant role in transactions even after coins came into use (2 Kgs 3:4, 5:23, 20:13; Hos 3:2).

Actual coinage (metals struck with a seal and having a specific weight) appeared for the first time in Asia Minor in the middle of the seventh century B.C.; coins were struck in electrum (a natural alloy of gold and silver). Herodotus (*Hists.* 1.94) credits the first coins to the ingenuity of Croesus of Lydia (r. 561–546 B.C.).

Coinage was adopted by the Persians under **Darius I** (r. 521–486 B.C.) and so was introduced into Palestine in the form of the Persian daric, named after Darius (1 Chr 29:7; Ezra 2:69, 8:27; cf. Neh 7:70–71). The Persian government possessed exclusive rights to mint gold coins, but provinces were allowed to issue coins of baser metal. These coins were followed by the introduction of Greek coinage through the campaigns of Alexander, and the succeeding states of the Ptolemies and Seleucids also minted their own currency, so that various coins were floating around Palestine by the end of the Old Testament period. The Hasmonean Dynasty also minted its own coins (1 Macc 15:6).

The coinage of Palestine in New Testament times was found in three basic types: the Roman denominations that were considered the only valid payment for taxes; the provincial coins minted at Antioch and Tyre; and the local currencies minted by local officials such as the tetrarchs and also the Roman procurator. The latter coins were likely minted at Caesarea. Given the multiplicity of coins in use, there was a need for money changers to convert currency into the Roman standard so that Jews could pay the annual Temple tax (Matt 17:24; 21:12).

Coins were minted typically in gold, silver, and bronze (or brass) (Matt 10:9; Mark 6:8, 12:41; Luke 9:3; Acts 3:6, 8:20, 20:33; 1 Pet 1:18; Jas 5:3). When the Pharisees attempted to trick Jesus by asking him about paying tribute to Caesar, the coin they used was the Roman denarius, which was stamped with the image of the emperor Tiberius (Matt 22:15–22; Mark 12:13–17; Luke 20:20–25). The denarius was the daily wage of the laborer (Matt 20:1–12).

MONEY CHANGERS Those mentioned in the Gospels are **Temple** officials who exchanged various local and imperial coins for the Tyrian standard coin, which was the only coinage that could be deposited in the Temple treasury (Matt 21:12; Mark 11:15). Surcharges of up to 8 percent were sometimes rolled into currency transactions. Money changing could thus be a moneymaking enterprise susceptible to abuse. On one dramatic occasion, Jesus protested the exchange system in the Temple by toppling the tables and spilling out the coins of the money changers (John 2:13–16).

MONOTHEISM *See* **God.**

MONTHS *See* **Calendar.**

MOON Created by God as "the lesser light to rule the night" (Gen 1:16), the moon also ruled the calendar in ancient Israel. The arrival of each new month was celebrated with trumpets (Ps 81:3), sacrifices (Num 28:11–15), and a day of rest (Amos 8:5). In Hebrew, as in English, the name for the "moon" (Hebrew *yārēaḥ*) is related to the word for "month" (Hebrew *yeraḥ*). Especially significant was the new moon of the seventh month (Tishri, or September–October), which was the annual feast of Trumpets (Lev 23:24–25; Num 29:1–6; Neh 8:2). The cycles of the moon represented the stability of the created order guaranteed by the Noahic **covenant** (Gen 8:22; Ps 72:5, 7; 89:38; Jer 33:20). A lunar eclipse could be considered a sign of divine judgment (Isa 13:10; Ezek 32:7; Joel 3:15; Matt 24:29; Mark 13:24). In apocalyptic texts, the moon is said to turn the color of blood (Joel 2:31; Acts 2:20; Rev 6:12).

Israel admired the moon as a wonder of creation (Ps 8:3), in marked contrast to her Mesopotamian neighbors, who revered the moon as the god Sin. Worship of the moon, sun, and stars was prevalent throughout the ancient Near East, which explains why the **Law** explicitly forbids Israel to worship them (Deut 4:19).

MORAL SENSE *See* "Senses of Scripture" *under* **Interpretation of the Bible.**

MORDECAI One of the main figures in the book of Esther, and the cousin and guardian of **Esther.** A Jew living in the royal city of Susa, one of the Persian capitals (Esth 2:5), Mordecai was the son of Jair, a descendant of Kish, and a member of the tribe of Benjamin. Exiled by the Babylonians, he worked in the Persian palace and was responsible for raising his orphaned cousin, **Esther** (Hadassah). Though a prominent figure in the Hebrew version of Esther, Mordecai stands out even more in the Greek version, where his dream about the downfall of the Jews' enemies and his effort to inform the Persian king of a plot against his life introduce the book (Esth 11:2–12; 12:1–6). And his dream eventually led the queen to take bold and courageous action in defense of her people against the plot of Haman. In both versions he is remembered for his wise counsel to Esther (Esth 4:4–17). Through the efforts of Esther, King Ahasuerus was persuaded to allow the Jews to defend themselves. Haman was then arrested and hanged from the same gibbet that had been intended to execute Mordecai, and Mordecai was given the office of vizier. His name is probably derived from

Marduk, the supreme god of the Babylonian pantheon.

MOREH The location of a sacred oak in **Shechem**. It became a place of cultic and religious significance when **Abraham** erected an altar near the oak of Moreh after arriving in Canaan (Gen 12:6–7). It is possible that **Jacob** buried foreign idols under this tree (Gen 35:4) and that **Joshua** later pitched the **Tabernacle** around it (Josh 24:26).

MORESHETH Also Moresheth-gath, the hometown of the prophet **Micah** (Mic 1:1; Jer 26:18) near the village of Gath in the **Shephelah**, identified with the modern site of Tell ej-Judeideh.

MORIAH A place name that appears twice in the Bible. In Gen 22:1, **Abraham** is instructed to sacrifice his son **Isaac** at a site chosen by God in "the land of Moriah." Its whereabouts are not specified in Genesis beyond the detail that it took three days for Abraham to get there from Beer-sheba in southern Canaan (Gen 22:4). In 2 Chr 3:1, we are told that **Solomon** built the Jerusalem **Temple** on the crest of "Mount Moriah." A canonical reading of Scripture thus indicates that Israel's sacrificial worship was conducted at the very site where Abraham made Isaac an offering to the Lord. For the Chronicler, an angel of the Lord had identified this location as a place of sacrifice to **David**, who determined that it should be the place where God's house should stand (1 Chr 21:18–22:1).

MOSERAH One of the forty-two campsites of the Israelites in the wilderness (Num 33:30–31). **Aaron**, the high priest, died and was buried at Moserah, and his son **Eleazar** was installed as high priest there (Deut 10:6). Apparently Moserah was near Mount Hor, which is also connected with Aaron's death (Num 20:22–29; 33:38).

MOSES The founder and first leader of the nation of Israel. The Lord selected him for this task, which involved leading Israel out of Egypt, through the Sinai wilderness, and to the Promised Land of Canaan (Exod 3:1–22).

The name "Moses" is associated with the Hebrew verb *māšâ*, "to draw out." This link is made in Exod 2:10, where Pharaoh's daughter names him Moses because she "drew him out of the water." Others detect a wordplay on the Egyptian verb *msi*, which means "to give birth."

I. *Life and Leadership*
II. *Moses's Attributes and Titles*
   A. *Author*
   B. *Mediator*
   C. *Priest*
   D. *Lawgiver*
   E. *Prophet*
III. *Moses in the New Testament*

I. LIFE AND LEADERSHIP

The only source for information on the life of Moses is Scripture. In the nineteenth century, some scholars doubted the existence of the historical person Moses, but modern scholarship now generally accepts that Moses was a historical figure who lived in the second half of the second millennium B.C.

According to Exod 2:1 and the genealogy of Exod 6:16–27, Moses was a member of the tribe of Levi and the clan of Kohath, and the son of Amram and Jochebed. His older brother was **Aaron** and his sister was **Miriam** (Num 26:59). At the time of his birth, Israel was a nation enslaved in Egypt, and so rapidly did its population grow that newborn Hebrew males were subject to immediate execution in the Nile (Exod 1:22). But Moses escaped this fate when his mother hid him and eventually set him afloat on the Nile in a watertight basket (Exod 2:1–4). He was then discovered by Pharaoh's daughter and adopted into the royal family of Egypt (Exod 2:5–10). There is every reason to assume that Moses was thereafter given all the privileges and education of the Egyptian nobility (Acts 7:22).

After reaching manhood, Moses witnessed firsthand the terrible oppression of the Hebrews, and became so enraged that he killed an Egyptian overseer whom he saw beating a Hebrew worker (Exod 2:11–12). Fearful of the consequences, Moses fled to Midian for safety (Exod 2:15). There he met **Jethro** (Reuel), a priest of Midian who had seven daughters, one of whom, Zipporah, Jethro gave to Moses as a wife; their first son was named Gershom (Exod 2:16–22).

After Moses had spent many years in Midian, God called Moses from a burning bush on Mount Horeb: "I am the God of your father, the God of Abraham, the God of Isaac, and the God of Jacob . . . Come, I will send you to Pharaoh that you may bring forth my people, the sons of Israel, out of Egypt" (Exod 3:6, 10). Moses resisted the mission at first but finally returned to Egypt to demand the liberation of Israel (Exod 5:1). Pharaoh's refusal to free the Jews was finally shattered by the **plagues** sent by the Lord, demonstrating his superior power. The plagues climaxed with the death of every firstborn Egyptian (Exod 7–12). The children of Israel were spared the devastating plague because the Lord instructed each family to smear the blood of a spotless lamb upon the frames of their doors as "the sacrifice of the LORD's **passover**" (Exod 12:27).

Once the tribes of Israel were released from bondage, Moses led them to Mount **Sinai**, where the Lord forged a national covenant with the people and set before them his laws for living (Exod 19–24). Moses himself was elected to be the mediator of the covenant, the go-between who relayed the Lord's instructions to Israel (Exod 20:18–19; Deut 5:5, 22–23).

No sooner was the Sinai covenant established than it was broken when the Israelites worshipped a golden calf (Exod 32:1–29). The covenant, therefore, had to be renewed through the mediation of Moses (Exod 34:10–28), who interceded to spare the lives of his wayward people (Exod 32:30–32). Israel spent most of the next year at Sinai before setting out toward the Promised Land (Num 10:11–13). Throughout the wilderness period, Moses continued in his role as leader and lawgiver, mediator and intercessor (Num 11–36). On one occasion, Moses himself broke faith with the Lord, and for this transgression he was not allowed to enter Canaan (Num 20:2–13; 27:12–14).

Finally, at the end of his life, he delivered a series of powerful farewell sermons on the plains of **Moab**. These constitute the bulk of the book of Deuteronomy. Afterward, Moses died at the age of 120, having passed the reins of leadership to his successor, **Joshua**

(Deut 34:1–9). Deuteronomy ends with an extraordinary tribute: "there has not arisen a prophet since in Israel like Moses, whom the LORD knew face to face, none like him . . . for all the mighty power and all the great and terrible deeds which Moses wrought in the sight of all Israel" (Deut 34:10–12)

II. MOSES'S ATTRIBUTES AND TITLES

It is difficult to overestimate the place of Moses in the history of Israel and in the progress of salvation history. Judaism, Christianity, and Islam all revere him as a man of exceptional holiness, and Christian tradition in particular hails him as a type of Jesus Christ, particularly in his roles as liberator, lawgiver, and mediator between the Lord and his people.

A. Author

Several passages describe Moses as a literate man who kept records of key battles (Exod 17:14), wrote down the Lord's commandments (Exod 24:4), and maintained a travelogue of Israel's encampments in the wilderness (Num 33:2). He is also described as the literary author of the Deuteronomic law code (Deut 31:9) as well as the poetic Song of Moses (Deut 31:19). Jewish and Christian tradition infers from these and similar statements in the New Testament that Moses was the author of the entire **Pentateuch** (cf. John 5:46–47; Rom 10:5).

B. Mediator

The frightened Israelites elected Moses their mediator at Sinai (Exod 20:18–19; Deut 5:5, 22–23). From that time on, Moses spoke to the people for God, and spoke to God for the people. He interceded for them when they deserved destruction for their sins (Exod 32:32–34; Num 14:13–20; Ps 106:23). Of all the prophets, Moses had the most intimate friendship with the Lord (Exod 33:7–11; Num 7:89; 12:3–8).

C. Priest

Moses is called a priest in Ps 99:6. Aaron was the high priest for Israel, but Moses was the head celebrant in the ordination liturgy for Aaron and his sons (Exod 29:1–46; Lev 8:1–36).

D. Lawgiver

Moses gave Israel the **Ten Commandments** (Exod 24:12, 31:18; Deut 5:22), as well as countless additional instructions (Exod 25–31; Lev 1–27; Num 1–10; Deut 5–26). For that reason he was hailed as a teacher of Israel (Sir 45:1–5).

E. Prophet

Moses was revered as the greatest of all the prophets (Deut 34:10) and the model for future prophets (Deut 18:15–18).

III. MOSES IN THE NEW TESTAMENT

Moses is mentioned more often in the NT than any other OT personage. Moses is given a prominent place in the **Transfiguration**, which reveals Jesus to be a new and greater Moses; Moses appears as the representative of the Law, while Elijah represents the Prophets (Matt 17:1–8; Mark 9:2–18; Luke 9:28–36). Together, they point to the transformation of Israel and the revelation of Christ's coming in glory (CCC 554–56). The **Synoptic Gospels** note also Moses's close connection to the Law (cf. Matt 8:4, 19:7–8, 22:24; Mark 1:44, 7:10, 10:3–4, 12:19; Luke 5:14, 20:28).

Moses is also seen in typological terms, as in John: "For the law was given through Moses; grace and truth came through Jesus Christ" (John 1:17). Elsewhere, Paul sees the Exodus as a type of **baptism** (1 Cor 10:2). Paul further develops the contrast between the Law of Moses and the Christian Gospel in 2 Cor 3:7–18. He writes of "the dispensation of condemnation" (cf. Exod 34:29–35) and "the dispensation of righteousness" (2 Cor 3:9) brought by Christ and contrasts the hope of the Christian with the way that Moses hid his shining face behind a veil "so that the Israelites might not see the end of the fading splendor" (2 Cor 3:13). In a similar way, in the long speech of **Stephen** in Acts 7:2–53, Moses's rejection by his own people is implicitly compared to the rejection of Christ by his own fellow Jews (Acts 7:25–29, 39–40, 52).

Hebrews 3:1–6 emphasizes that Christ is superior even to Moses:

[C]onsider Jesus, the apostle and high priest of our confession. He was faithful to him who appointed him, just as Moses also was faithful in God's house. Yet Jesus has been counted worthy of as much more glory than Moses as the builder of a house has more honor than the house. (For every house is built by some one, but the builder of all things is God.) Now Moses was faithful in all God's house as a servant, to testify to the things that were to be spoken later, but Christ was faithful over God's house as a son. And we are his house if we hold fast our confidence and pride in our hope.

MOTH An insect mentioned in Scripture as something that consumes and destroys the things of this world (Isa 50:9; Hos 5:12; Matt 6:19, 20; Luke 12:33).

MOUNT OF OLIVES *See* **Olives, Mount of**.

MOUNT, SERMON ON THE *See* **Sermon on the Mount**.

MOUTH The word "mouth" is used, as in English, in connection with animals and humans as well as inanimate objects or locations, such as the mouth of a cave (e.g., Josh 10:22). Literally, the mouth is used for eating and drinking (Judg 7:6; 1 Sam 14:26) and speaking (Deut 13:15; 23:23). In anthropomorphic metaphor, the Word of God comes from God's "mouth" (Deut 8:3). The notion of "opening one's mouth" means speaking or preparing to speak (Matt 5:2; 13:35). Thus God "opened the mouth" of **Balaam**'s donkey, meaning that God gave the animal the ability to speak (Num 22:28). Jesus taught that "not what goes into the mouth defiles a man, but what comes out of the mouth, this defiles a man" (Matt 15:11), meaning that the words we speak are of far more moral consequence than the food we eat (cf. Matt 12:36–37). We are also instructed to open our mouths so that the Lord can feed us—in a spiritual metaphor using "mouth" (Ps 81:11).

MULE A cross between a horse and a donkey, the mule was used as a beast of burden (2 Kgs 5:17; 1 Chr 12:40; Isa 66:20). The mule was valued for its strength and prudence and was thus considered worthy to carry a king (2 Sam 18:9; 1 Kgs 1:38).

MURATORIAN CANON Possibly the oldest list of books considered canonical by the early Church. It is normally dated to the second half of the second century because of references to Pope Saint Pius I (r. A.D. 140–155), Basilides, and Marcion, all belonging to that era. The list was found by Ludovico Muratori in the Ambrosian Library of Milan and was published in 1740. Some eighty-five lines long, the fragment lists the Gospels of Luke and John (Matthew and Mark are not mentioned explicitly but are assumed to have been mentioned in the beginning of the list, which is missing); the Acts of the Apostles; the thirteen letters of Paul (excluding Hebrews); Jude; 1 and 2 John; the Wisdom of Solomon. Other works such as the Apocalypse of John, the Apocalypse of Peter, and the Shepherd of Hermas are listed as books of private devotions. The canon is composed in poor Latin and is fragmentary, since the beginning is missing, as is probably the ending. Recent scholarship has called the dating of the canon into question, with the theory being advanced that the Muratorian Fragment was composed in the fourth century, in eastern Syria or Palestine. This is unlikely; nevertheless, if it is true, then the Muratorian Canon would no longer be the oldest list of biblical books, because it would be supplanted by that of Eusebius (*Hist. Eccl.* 3.25). (*See* **Canon of the Bible**.)

MURDER Taking the life of the innocent is condemned in the **Ten Commandments**, which mandates without qualification: "You shall not kill" (Exod 20:13; Deut 5:17). Murder is a sin against God and a crime against the dignity of the human person, who is made in God's image (Gen 9:5–6). The **Law** of Moses distinguishes between homicide and involuntary manslaughter (Num 35:9–34). In doing so, it gave legal protection to the accidental manslayer, who would otherwise, on the basis of tribal custom, be hunted down and killed by a kinsman of the deceased called the "**avenger of blood**" (Num 35:19). Still, intentional murder was a capital crime in ancient Israel.

Murder is a sin that "cries to heaven" for the Lord's justice. The first murder in Scripture, Cain's fratricide of Abel, is followed by the divine statement, "The voice of your brother's blood is crying to me from the ground" (Gen 4:10). In the Old Testament, blood was considered a sacred sign of life, and the prohibition against shedding blood by murder is clear in Genesis: "Whoever sheds the blood of man, by man shall his blood be shed; for God made man in his own image" (Gen 9:6). In the New Testament, the commandment against killing is reaffirmed by Jesus in the Sermon on the Mount, but he adds, "But I say to you that every one who is angry with his brother shall be liable to judgment" (Matt 5:21–22; cf. Matt 19:18; Mark 10:19; Luke 18:20; Rom 13:9; Jas 2:11). "Any one who hates his brother is a murderer," 1 John 3:15 adds, "and you know that no murderer has eternal life abiding in him" (CCC 1447, 1867, 2258–69).

MUSIC The traditional founder of music in the Bible was Jubal, "the father of all those who play the lyre and pipe" (Gen 4:21). His name is related to the Hebrew word *yôbēl* (meaning "ram's horn," Exod 19:13). Music, dance, and singing were all important elements in the cultural and liturgical life of Israel. Music remains an integral aspect of the life of the Christian: "be filled with the Spirit, addressing one another in psalms and hymns and spiritual songs, singing and making melody to the Lord with all your heart" (Eph 5:18–19).

Little, unfortunately, is known in detail of the music of the ancient world, especially when it comes to re-creating the actual sound. In any case, music in a variety of forms accompanied festivals (Isa 5:12, 16:10; Amos 6:5) and especially celebrations of victories (Exod 15:20–21; Judg 11:34; 1 Sam 18:6–7) and royal coronations (1 Kgs 1:39–40; 2 Kgs 11:14). Vocal and instrumental music was also used for occasions of mourning and lamentation (2 Sam 1:17–27; 2 Chr 35:25; cf. Matt 9:23).

In the context of worship, music played no part at all in the sacrificial liturgy of the **Tabernacle** established by Moses. Apart from occasional trumpet blasts, there was no singing, no chanting, and no melodies of praise to accompany the offerings of animal flesh and incense (Num 10:8–10). It was not until the reign of King **David** that sacred music became a part of Israelite worship. As one of David's many preparations for the **Temple** to be built by his son **Solomon**, the Levites were appointed to this ministry. The Levitical choir was made up of vocalists and skilled musicians whose responsibility was to offer the Lord continual thanks and praise from the courts of the sanctuary (1 Chr 15:16–24; 16:4–6, 23:30–31; 25:1–8; 2 Chr 7:6). It is no surprise that the Psalter, which has its origin and inspiration in King David, became the hymn book of Israel, and many of its prayers were composed to be sung

with instrumental accompaniment (e.g., Ps 4; 5; 6; 8; etc.).

The Israelites used a wide variety of musical instruments. The first musical instrument mentioned in the Bible (Gen 4:21) is the "lyre," a type of acoustic stringed instrument small enough to be carried in one hand and played with the other. Harps or lyres were used to accompany singing or provide background melodies for various occasions (Gen 31:27; 1 Chr 13:8; 15:16, 21; Ps 33:2; Amos 5:23). Wind instruments included the flute; the pipe, probably a reed instrument, that was used for celebrations (Gen 4:21; 1 Kgs 1:40; Isa 30:29; Matt 9:23); the horn; the trumpet or ram's horn; and the trumpet of silver or metal (Num 10:10; 1 Chr 15:28). Percussion instruments included cymbals and the timbrel, a tambourine-like instrument (Gen 31:27; Exod 15:20; 1 Chr 15:19). (*See also* **Dancing**.)

MUSTARD An herb, *Brassica nigra*, that grows throughout Palestine and is also naturalized as a weed in most of the United States. Mustard can grow up to 8 feet (or 2.4 meters) high in one season, but its seeds are unusually small (Matt 13:31–32; 17:20; Mark 4:30–32; Luke 17:6).

MYRA A city on the southern coast of Asia Minor, probably the modern Dembre. **Paul** changed ships at Myra during his journey to Rome as a prisoner (Acts 27:5).

MYRRH An aromatic and resinous spice produced from the *Commiphora myrrha* bush. In biblical times it was used in a liquid form as an expensive perfume (Esth 2:12; Ps 45:8;

Prov 7:17) and an ingredient in anointing oil (Exod 30:23–25). The infant Jesus was given a gift of myrrh (Matt 2:11), and Jesus's body was anointed with myrrh in preparation for his being placed in the tomb (John 19:39). Myrrh was sometimes mixed with wine and given to a crucified criminal as a means of easing his excruciating pain (Mark 15:23).

MYSIA A region in northwestern Asia Minor (modern Turkey). Its exact boundaries are disputed, but its main cities during the Roman period were Pergamum and the port of **Troas**. **Paul** set foot in Mysia when he made brief stops in Troas on his first and second missionary journeys (Acts 16:7–111; 20:6–12).

MYSTERY In biblical terms, a mystery is a "secret truth" or "secret plan" that is hidden from the common knowledge of men. Mysteries are known to God, and they must be disclosed through revelation in order to be known by his people. The notion of mystery in the Old Testament is confined to the book of Daniel (Aramaic *rāz*) but is found in several books of the New Testament (Greek *mystērion*).

I. MYSTERY IN DANIEL

Nine times the term "mystery" appears in the book of Daniel, and all but one occurrence (Dan 4:9) is found in the second chapter (Dan 2:18–19, 27–30, 47). A mystery was encrypted in a dream of the Babylonian king **Nebuchadnezzar**, who saw in his sleep a giant human image composed of different materials. Its head was gold, its arms and breast were silver, its waist and thighs were bronze, and its legs and feet were iron with a mixture of clay at its base (Dan 2:31–33). Despite the statue's strong and imposing appearance, the king saw a stone mysteriously quarried without human hands smash the statue into pieces and then spread out over the earth in the form of a giant, indestructible mountain (Dan 2:34–35). Daniel received a divine revelation of its meaning (Dan 2:19) and explained to the king that the four metals represented four successive kingdoms, beginning with Nebuchadnezzar's Babylon (Dan 2:36–43). At the end of this historical sequence, God himself would shatter the power of these world empires by hurling a stone that would grow into an everlasting kingdom (Dan 2:44–45). In other words, the Danielic mystery is a vision of the Kingdom of God in history. It will not be the work of human hands or of human genius; it will have no successor; and it will know no geographical limits. It is the plan that God has ordained for the course of history, culminating in the appearance of his Messianic Kingdom in the world.

II. MYSTERY IN THE NEW TESTAMENT

In the **Synoptic Gospels**, Jesus speaks of the "secrets" (or "mysteries") of the Kingdom of God (Matt 13:11; Mark 4:11; Luke 8:10). He reveals divine truths to his apostles, yet he conceals the mystery from the masses by encoding the truths in parables. The likely background for the mysteries of the Kingdom is the book of Daniel, where the mystery of God is the Kingdom of God ushered into the world. Along this line, some scholars suggest that Jesus identified himself with the "stone" that smashed the image in Nebuchadnezzar's dream (Dan 2:34); for not only did Christ see himself as the stone rejected by the builders of Ps 118:22 (Luke 20:17), but he claimed, "Every one who falls on that stone will be broken to pieces; but when it falls on any one it will crush him" (Luke 20:18).

In the writings of Paul, mystery is a theme with considerable depth and dimension. The apostle explains the mystery of God in terms of the divine plan of salvation for the world. This mystery was hidden in former times but has now been made known through the Gospel (Rom 16:25; Eph 1:9, 3:9; Col 1:26). Its essence is the person and work of Christ (Col 1:27; 2:2; 4:4), in whom God is uniting both Jew and Gentile as fellow heirs in the family of faith (Eph 3:4–6). Articulating the mystery in terms of God's providential guidance of history likewise echoes the Danielic mystery of God's Messianic Kingdom in the world. This is the mystery of the Christian faith itself (1 Tim 3:9, 16), which is entrusted to the apostles in order to be made known to all nations (1 Cor 2:7; 4:1; Eph 6:19).

Within this larger framework, Paul can also speak of individual aspects of the mystery of Christ and of history. The mystery entails such things as a temporary hardening of unbelieving Israel (Rom 11:25) as well as a proliferation of iniquity in the world (2 Thess 2:7). More positively, it involves the union of Christ and the Church signified by Christian marriage (Eph 5:32) and includes the bodily resurrection and glorification of believers (1 Cor 15:51).

In the book of Revelation, the word "mystery" is applied to the hidden meaning of apocalyptic symbols (Rev 1:20; 17:5, 7). On one occasion, however, the mystery of God is the Kingdom of God that supersedes all earthly kingdoms at the blast of the seventh trumpet (Rev 10:7; 11:15). Once again, this appears to be an allusion to the mystery-as-kingdom motif from the book of Daniel.

III. MYSTERY IN CHRISTIAN TEACHING

In theological terms, the mysteries of Christianity are the truths of faith that could not be known or discovered by the unaided powers of human reason. The truths made known by God do not contradict reason, for they are logical and intelligible in themselves, yet they are too sublime for the human mind to grasp comprehensively. Mysteries that are revealed thus remain mysteries to the extent that God and his ways can be known and accepted by faith, but they cannot be comprehended in their totality. Defined in this way, the Church's teaching on mystery is simply the teaching of Sacred Scripture, where "mystery" always refers to something revealed by God rather than something discovered by men (Dan 2:27–28; Eph 3:3). The doctrine of the Trinity, which is the hidden life of God himself, is the greatest mystery of the Christian faith. Others include the Incarnation of Christ, the redemption of the world through the dying and rising of Christ, and the sanctification of the world through the Church's worship and sacramental actions. Catechesis proposes these and related mysteries for belief, while theology explores these and related mysteries in order to deepen and enrich our understanding of the Gospel (CCC 50, 234, 1028).

N

NAAM A member of the tribe of Judah, and the son of **Caleb** (1 Chr 4:15).

NAAMAH An Ammonite wife of **Solomon** and the mother of **Rehoboam**, king of Judah (1 Kgs 14:21, 31; 2 Chr 12:13).

NAAMAN The name of two men in the Old Testament.

1. A member of the tribe of Benjamin. He is listed once as the son of **Benjamin** (Gen 46:21) and twice as the son of Bela (1 Chr 8:3), and thus the grandson of Benjamin.

2. The commander of the Aramean army of Syria in the ninth century B.C. He was a leper until he was cured by the prophet **Elisha** (2 Kgs 5:1–27). After hearing of Elisha's extraordinary powers, Naaman found the prophet, who told him he should bathe himself seven times in the Jordan (2 Kgs 5:8–12). His servant convinced him to try it, and he was cured. Naaman was so grateful that he offered Elisha a gift. Elisha refused it, but Naaman returned home with some soil from Israel as a symbol of his gratitude and faith in the Lord. Naaman's leprosy was later transferred to **Gehazi**, Elisha's servant, as a punishment for taking the gift from Naaman that Elisha had refused. In Christian tradition, the healing of Naaman prefigures **baptism** and its ability to wash the soul clean of the sickness of sin. Jesus refers to Naaman's cleansing as an example of God's healing going out to the Gentiles (Luke 4:27).

NAARAH A city near Jericho, in the territory of Ephraim (Josh 16:7).

NABAL (Hebrew, "foolish") A wealthy owner of sheep and goats in Maon, Judah; and the husband of **Abigail** (1 Sam 25:2–3). While David was fleeing from Saul, Nabal refused to provide him any assistance and so earned the bitter enmity of David (1 Sam 25:4–13). Abigail, however, intervened and sent food to David and his men. She then begged mercy by noting that her husband was exactly what his name indicated, a "fool." For this, David chose not to slay Nabal (1 Sam 25:14–35). Nevertheless, ten days later, Nabal died, and David took the widowed Abigail as his wife (1 Sam 25:40–42, 27:3, 30:5; 2 Sam 2:2, 3:3).

NABATEANS A people of northern Arabia who formed the kingdom of Nabatea, with its chief city at Petra. Nabatea flourished from the fourth century B.C. and became a major commercial center that was superbly positioned on the trade routes connecting the Persian Gulf with Palestine, Egypt, and Asia Minor. The Nabateans took possession of the region that had been occupied by Moab and Edom, and their territory eventually stretched across parts of what are today southern Syria, Jordan, the Sinai, and Saudi Arabia. The Nabateans were friends of **Judas** and **Jonathan Maccabeus** (1 Macc 5:24–28; 9:35), although their relations with the later Herodians were poor. They waged a campaign against Alexander Jannaeus and also **Herod Antipas** in revenge for Antipas's divorcing the daughter of King **Aretas** IV of Nabatea in order to marry **Herodias** (*see* **Hasmonean Dynasty**).

NABOTH The innocent victim of court execution contrived by **Jezebel** so that her husband, King **Ahab** of Israel, could take Naboth's land, a vineyard in **Jezreel** that Naboth had inherited from his ancestors (1 Kgs 21:1–16). Naboth refused to sell the land to Ahab, and the king seemed willing to let the matter go; Jezebel, however, orchestrated a conspiracy in which Naboth was falsely accused of cursing God and the king. Convicted on these trumped-up charges, Naboth was stoned to death, and Ahab seized the disputed property (cf. Mic 2:1–2; 6:16). Because of the murder, **Elijah** prophesied doom for Ahab and his dynasty (1 Kgs 21:17–29). As Elijah predicted, the line of Ahab was exterminated by **Jehu** (2 Kgs 9:21–26, 30–37).

NABU *See* **Nebo**.

NABUCHADNEZZAR *See* **Nebuchadnezzar**.

NADAB The name of two men in the Old Testament.

1. The firstborn son of **Aaron** and Elisheba (Num 3:2; Exod 6:23). Nadab was consecrated a priest along with his three brothers, but he and the second-oldest **Abihu** died when they offered an "unholy fire" to God and God had fire consume them (Lev 10:1–3; Num 26:61). The Aaronic priesthood was thus confined to the lines of **Eleazar** and **Ithamar**, since neither Nadab nor Abihu left sons to succeed them.

2. The king of Israel from ca. 910 to 909 B.C., and the son and successor of **Jeroboam** (1 Kgs 14:20). His reign ended when he was assassinated by **Baasha** at Gibbethon (1 Kgs 15:25–31). Baasha then wiped out the royal family.

NAG HAMMADI *See* **Gnosticism**.

NAHALAL A **Levitical city** in the territory of Zebulun (Josh 19:15; 21:35). The location is disputed; it has been identified with modern Tell el Beida and Tell en-Nahl.

NAHALIEL One of the desert encampments during Israel's journey to Canaan (Num 21:19).

NAHARAI The armor bearer of **Joab** and one of the mighty warriors of David (2 Sam 23:37; 1 Chr 11:39). Naharai was from Beeroth.

NAHASH The king of the Ammonites during the reigns of Saul and David. He attacked and laid siege to Jabesh-gilead but then suffered a defeat at the hands of Saul (1 Sam 11:1–2). He enjoyed generally friendly terms with David (2 Sam 10:1–2; 1 Chr 19:1–2). (*See also* **Hanun**; **Shobi**.)

NAHATH The name of two men in the Old Testament.

1. The firstborn son of Reuel and the grandson of **Esau** (Gen 36:13, 17; 1 Chr 1:37).

2. The son of Zophai, a Levite of the clan of Kohath (1 Chr 6:26).

NAHOR The name of two men in the Old Testament.

1. The son of Serug, the father of **Terah**, and the grandfather of **Abraham** (Gen 11:22–26; 1 Chr 1:26). He lived to the age of 148.

2. The son of Terah, the brother of Abraham, and the husband of Milcah (Gen 11:27–29). He had eight sons: Uz, Buz, Kemuel, Chesed, Hazo, Pildash, Jidlaph, and Bethuel, the father of **Rebekah** (Gen 22:20–24). Nahor had four children by his concubine, Reumah: Tebah, Gaham, Tahash, and Maacah. He probably journeyed to Haran with Terah, Abram, and Lot, although he is not named in Gen 11:31. Nevertheless, Haran was later called "the city of Nahor" (Gen 24:10; 27:43).

NAHSHON Chief of the tribe of Judah during the journey in the wilderness (Num 1:7, 2:3, 7:12, 10:14; 1 Chr 2:10). He was the son of Amminadab and the brother-in-law of Aaron (Exod 6:23) through Nahshon's sister, Elisheba. He assisted in taking the census of Israel's fighting men (Num 1:7). He also appears in the Judahite genealogies of David (Ruth 4:20–22) and Jesus (Matt 1:4; Luke 3:32).

NAHUM, BOOK OF The seventh of the twelve minor prophets in the Old Testament. This book is mainly a prophecy of the destruction of **Nineveh** and the overthrow of the Assyrian Empire by the Babylonians. The superscription for the book is: "An oracle concerning Nineveh. The book of the vision of Nahum of Elkosh."

I. AUTHORSHIP AND DATE

Nothing is known of the prophet Nahum outside the book that bears his name, and he is not mentioned anywhere else in the canonical OT. Dating the text is difficult, although scholars generally accept that it must have been composed after the sack of Thebes (Nah 3:8) at the hands of the Assyrian king Ashurbanipal around 663 B.C. Since Nineveh fell in 612 B.C., the historical window for Nahum's composition is between 663 and 612 B.C. If the remark in Nah 1:12 is any indication, Assyria was still quite "strong" at the time the prophet was writing, in which case we could reasonably assign a date before about 625 B.C., just before the empire began its gradual decline toward dissolution.

II. CONTENTS

I. *The Anger and Majesty of Yahweh (1:1–15)*
II. *The Coming Fall of Nineveh (2:1–13)*
III. *The Judgment of Nineveh Explained (3:1–19)*

III. PURPOSE AND THEMES

The book of Nahum emphasizes the absolute sovereignty of God over the world: he holds in his hands the fate of all nations and peoples. While nationalistic in celebrating the defeat of a great enemy, the text also has an important lesson for Judah. The wickedness of Nineveh and the inevitable doom that it brought to the Assyrian Empire served as a warning for Judah and the dangers that it faced as it plunged into sin. The lessons of Nahum were to be learned the hard way because after the Assyrians fell, new threats arose from the Babylonians, culminating in the destruction of Jerusalem in 586 B.C.

The style of the prophecy is rich and epic, applying some of the most vivid language in all the prophetic writings of the OT. Of special note is the sense of dread, terror, and confusion in Nineveh as the enemy moved upon its walls. Judah's hate for Nineveh is readily apparent, but while the citizens of Judah might have had reason to celebrate the downfall of so cruel an enemy, the prophecy of Nineveh's terrible fall could not have failed in evoking the horror of bloodshed and war.

NAIN A village in Galilee mentioned in Scripture only in Luke 7:11. There Jesus raised a widow's son back to life (Luke 7:11–17). The site of the village is probably the modern Nein.

NAIOTH A place near Ramah, north of Jerusalem, to which **David** fled from **Saul**, with the assistance of **Michal** (1 Sam 19:11–19).

NAME Scripture places great emphasis on a person's name, as well as the naming or renaming of individuals and places (Gen 2:23; 4:1, 25; 5:29; 11:9; 17:5; Matt 16:18). In the ancient world, the giving of a name implied an exercise of authority: a creator or dominant figure bestowed a name and so helped set the destiny of the person receiving the name. God named his works as he created them (Gen 1:5, 8, 10, etc.). Adam likewise "gave names to all cattle, and to the birds of the air, and to every animal of the field" (Gen 2:20), and in so doing he was exercising his royal dominion (Gen 1:28) over the entire animal kingdom (Gen 2:19).

A name, then, is more than a conventional form of identification that distinguishes one individual from another. A name itself is mysteriously representative of the person (CCC 2158). Knowing someone's name thus gave one a certain access to the person and opened the way for an intimate relationship to develop. The name was also important as the means by which a person might be remembered across the generations. To have a name that was forgotten or obliterated was considered a disaster (1 Sam 24:21; 2 Kgs 14:27) or a punishment for the wicked (Job 18:17; Prov 10:7). The changing of a person's name also marked a major change in the person's life and mission, as we see in the changing of the name of Abram to Abraham (Gen 17:5), Jacob to Israel (Gen 35:10), and Simon to Peter (Matt 16:18).

The name of **God** assumed a preeminent importance in the history of Israel, for when God revealed his Name he revealed his true identity. In patriarchal times, God was known by a variety of names (Gen 14:18; 16:13; 21:23; 31:13), most notably as 'ēl šadday, "God Almighty" (Gen 17:1, 28:3; Job 5:17). It was not until Moses crouched before the burning bush that God revealed himself as "the LORD" or "Yahweh" (Exod 3:1–15; 6:3). God thus revealed his name as part of his entering into a covenant relationship with Israel, as a means of making himself known and accessible. The name of God was one of power and majesty, a source of hope and assurance of salvation (cf. Ps 54:3; 72:19; 124:8; 148:13). To know the name of the Lord, *Yahweh*, is to encounter the Lord himself and to know him as he is.

Since a name carried the power of the person named, the name of God was to be spoken with respect and given the same reverence as God himself. So close was the connection between the Lord's name and his presence that Scripture speaks of his choosing a place for his "name" to dwell among his people, first in the **Tabernacle** and then in the **Temple** (cf. Deut 12:11, 16:11; 1 Kgs 8:16). In later Jewish tradition, the name of God was never pronounced: a reader who came across the letters YHWH in the Hebrew text spoke the word "Adonai" (Lord) instead. Many of our modern Bible versions keep up this tradition: the word LORD in small capitals translates the Name of God.

The sacredness of Yahweh's name in the Old Testament is likewise recognized in the New Testament (Matt 6:9; Luke 1:49; John 12:28; Rom 15:9). What is new, however, is the idea that the name of Jesus Christ is equal in holiness and power to the name of God. Since Jesus is divine, his name is divine, for he is Lord and Savior. Only in Jesus's name may salvation be found (Acts 4:12).

The use of the name of Jesus gives power to heal and perform miracles (Mark 16:17; Acts 3:6), to forgive sins (Luke 24:47; Acts 10:43), to exorcise (Luke 10:17), and to baptize (Acts 2:38; 1 Cor 6:11). Jesus's name is above every other name: "Therefore God has highly exalted him and bestowed on him the name which is above every name, that at the name of Jesus every knee should bow, in heaven and on earth and under the earth, and every tongue confess that Jesus Christ is Lord, to the glory of God the Father" (Phil 2:9–11; cf. Eph 1:21). To proclaim the Gospel is to preach the name of Jesus (Acts 5:40; 8:12; 9:15). Ultimately, the entire activity of the Church is undertaken in Jesus's name, because his name brings life to all who call upon it in faith (John 20:31; 1 John 5:13). The believer is thus called upon to do all things in Christ's name (Col 3:17), even if doing so provokes the opposition and persecution of the world (Mark 13:13; Acts 5:41; 1 Pet 4:14–16).

NAMES OF GOD *See under* **God**.

NAOMI (Hebrew, "my delight") The wife of Elimelech and a main character in the book of Ruth. She is also the mother-in-law of **Ruth** (Ruth 1:1–4) and Orpah, and the mother of Mahlon and Chilion. After her husband and sons died in Moab, Naomi returned to Judea with Ruth and survived through the aid of **Boaz**, a wealthy relative of her deceased husband (Ruth 2:1; 4:3, 5). Ruth married Boaz, and from this union was born Obed, the grandfather of **David** (Ruth 4:22).

NAPHISH The eleventh son of **Ishmael** (Gen 25:15; 1 Chr 1:31). His descendants lived in the **Transjordan** (1 Chr 5:19).

NAPHTALI The sixth son of **Jacob** and the second born to his concubine **Bilhah** (Gen 30:8); he was the ancestor of the tribe of Naphtali (Gen 49:21; Deut 33:23). Jacob's wife Rachel was barren, and she urged Jacob to have children by Bilhah (Rachel's sister, Leah, had by then given birth to four sons). The name Naphtali is a play on the Hebrew verb "to twist" or "to wrestle" (Gen 30:8).

The tribe of Naphtali comes last in several lists and events of the wilderness period (Num 1:15; 2:29; 7:78; 10:27). The territory received by the tribe was delineated in Josh 19:32–39: Naphtali was allotted the area west of the Sea of Galilee and the upper Jordan. Naphtali tried to expel the Canaanite inhabitants of Beth-shemesh and Beth-anath, but the effort proved unsuccessful. Nevertheless, the Canaanites in these cities were subjected to forced labor (Judg 1:33). **Barak** was Naphtali's greatest military leader, although he depended greatly upon **Deborah** in his campaign against Sisera at Mount Tabor (Judg 4:6–10, 14–16; 5:18). The Naphtalis also took part in **Gideon**'s effort against the Midianites and Amalekites (Judg 6:33–35). The lands of Naphtali were later occupied by **Ben-hadad** of Syria during the reign of **Baasha** of Israel (1 Kgs 15:20; 2 Chr 16:4) and were finally seized by the Assyrians around 734 B.C., at which time the bulk of the tribe was marched off into exile (2 Kgs 15:29; Isa 9:1; cf. Matt 4:13, 15).

NAPHTUHIM A people mentioned in the Table of Nations (Gen 10:13; 1 Chr 1:11). They are listed as descendants of Egypt, the Hamitic grandson of **Noah**.

NARCISSUS The name of a man whose household was greeted by Paul in Romans. Apparently some of the family members were Christians, because the apostle specifically singled out "those in the Lord" (Rom 16:11).

NARD A perfume extracted from the oil of the plant *Nardostachys jatamans* found in India and commonly referred to as spikenard in English. The perfume was expensive: it was used in cosmetics and as a medicinal stimulant (Song 1:12). It was also used in the preparation of bodies for the tomb; the woman at Bethany anointed Jesus with nard, and Jesus defended her action on the basis that she had anointed him in anticipation of his burial (Mark 14:3–9; John 12:3–8).

NATHAN The name of two men in the Old Testament.

1. A court prophet who was a contemporary of King **David**. Nathan first appeared when David expressed a desire to build a temple, and he informed the king that such a task was to be left to his son (2 Sam 7:1–7; 1 Chr 17:1–15). Nathan played a key role in three major events in David's reign. First, he made the Messianic prediction that David's dynasty would endure forever: "And your house and your kingdom shall be made sure for ever before me; your throne shall be established for ever" (2 Sam 7:16). Second, Nathan rebuked David sharply for his adultery with **Bathsheba** and for sending her husband, **Uriah**, off to his death at the battle front (2 Sam 12:1–15). Third, in the crisis surrounding the royal succession, Nathan informed David of the treacherous aspirations of **Adonijah** to seize the throne as David's successor (1 Kgs 1:22–27).

2. One of the sons of David born in Jerusalem (2 Sam 5:14; 1 Chr 14:4). Nathan is mentioned in the Lucan genealogy of Jesus (Luke 3:31).

NATHANAEL (Hebrew, "gift of God") One of the Twelve; the name appears only in John (1:45–51 and 21:2). A native of Cana in Galilee, Nathanael was presented by Philip to Jesus but reacted with skepticism to the claim that Jesus was the Messiah: "Can anything good come out of Nazareth?" (John 1:45). When he met Jesus, however, Jesus announced, "Behold, an Israelite indeed, in whom is no guile!" (John 1:47). Nathanael is apparently the same person as Bartholomew, whose name appears in the list of apostles immediately after Philip in the **Synoptic Gospels** (Matt 10:3; Mark 3:18; Luke 6:14).

NATHAN-MELECH A chamberlain who served King **Josiah** of Judah (2 Kgs 23:11).

NATIONS *See* **Gentile**.

NAZARENE A resident of Nazareth. There are two forms of the name in Greek, *Nazarēnos* and *Nazōraios*. The former is used only in Mark and Luke (e.g., Mark 1:24, 10:47; Luke 4:34, 24:19), while the latter appears in Matthew, Luke, John, and Acts (e.g., Matt 27:61; Luke 18:37; John 18:5; Acts 2:22). The name Nazarene is given to Jesus, not simply to identify his hometown, but also to distinguish him from others of the same name, since Jesus (a shortened form of the name Joshua) was a fairly common name in first-century Palestine. The evangelist Matthew sees in this name the fulfillment of a prophecy: "He shall be called a Nazarene" (Matt 2:23). Since no prophecy of the Old Testament matches this wording, it is believed that Matthew is relying on a wordplay between "Nazarene" and the Hebrew word *nēṣer* ("branch"), which appears in a famous Messianic oracle that begins at Isa 11:1. The motif of a Messianic "branch" appears elsewhere in the Prophets in Jeremiah (Jer 23:5; 33:14–16) and Zechariah (Zech 3:8; 6:11–13). In all these passages, the branch is an image for the Savior King destined to sprout from the royal line of **David**.

NAZARETH The town in Lower Galilee (modern en-Nasira), north of the valley of Jezreel, that was the residence of Mary and Joseph and the place where Jesus grew up (Matt 2:23; Luke 1:26, 4:16). Because he grew up there, Jesus was called "Jesus of Nazareth" (Matt 21:11; Mark 1:9; John 1:45; Acts 10:38; *see also* **Nazarene**). Jesus left Nazareth to embark upon his earthly ministry (Matt 4:12–17), although he returned to the town once. He spoke at the local synagogue in Nazareth but was not well received by his own people (Matt 13:53–58; Mark 6:1–6; Luke 4:16–30).

The town itself was small and not very important in Galilee. Thus the mention of Nazareth might provoke disdain or sarcasm even from fellow Galileans (John 1:45–46).

NAZIRITE (Hebrew, from a verb meaning "to separate" or "consecrate") A man or woman who has taken a special vow of consecration to the Lord according to the terms prescribed in Num 6:1–21. Nazirites did not consume anything produced by the grapevine, including juice, wine, or grape skins, and they avoided all contact with corpses (cf. Amos 2:11; 1 Macc 3:49–51; Acts 18:18, 21:23). The vow could be temporary or lifelong; after a temporary consecration expired, the person who made it was obligated to perform certain rituals and offer prescribed sacrifices. Nazirites who appear in the Bible include **Samson** (Judg 13:4–5), **Samuel** (1 Sam 1:11), **John the Baptist** (Luke 1:15), and possibly Saint **Paul** (Acts 18:18).

NEAH A city in the territory of the tribe of Zebulun (Josh 19:13). It was located between Rimmon and Hannathon.

NEAPOLIS (Greek, "new city") A seaport near the Roman colony of Philippi. Paul stopped there on his second journey (Acts 16:11). The same name was used for many other cities founded by Greek colonists, of which the most famous is the modern Naples.

NEBAIOTH The firstborn son of **Ishmael** (Gen 25:13; 1 Chr 1:29) and the founder of an Arabian tribe (Isa 60:7). His sister Mahalath married Esau (Gen 28:9; 36:3). Some have identified the descendant of Nebaioth with the Nabateans, but most modern historians reject that view.

NEBAT The father of **Jeroboam I**, first king of the northern kingdom of Israel (1 Kgs 11:26).

NEBO

1. A Babylonian deity mentioned only once in the Old Testament (Isa 46:1). The god was worshipped in the city of Borsippa, south of Babylon. Nebo, or Nabu, appears as part of the names of several prominent Babylonian officials mentioned in the Bible: King **Nebuchadnezzar** (2 Kgs 24:1), the official **Nebushaz-**

ban (Jer 39:13), and the officer **Nebuzaradan** (2 Kgs 25:8).

2. A city in Moab that figured in the final events of the Exodus journey to Canaan (Num 33:47). Following the conquest of the Transjordan, Nebo was allotted to the tribe of Reuben (Num 32:37–38; cf. 1 Chr 5:8). According to the **Mesha** Stele, which dates back to the ninth century B.C., the city was taken by the Moabites from Israel and was subsequently in Moabite hands (Isa 15:2; Jer 48:1, 22). Modern Khirbet el-Mekhayyat or Khirbet Ayn Musa is probably the location.

3. The mountain from which Moses obtained a panoramic view of Canaan (Deut 34:1–4). Nebo is part of the Abarim range directly northeast of the Dead Sea (Deut 32:49), and is often identified with modern Jebel en Nebu.

NEBUCHADNEZZAR (Akkadian, "Nabu has protected the country"; *see* **Nebo**) Also spelled **Nebuchadrezzar**. The king of Babylon from 605 to 562 B.C., and the son and successor to Nabopolassar. He is best known in Scripture for his conquest of Judah and Jerusalem in 586 B.C. The heir to the founder of the Chaldean Dynasty, Nebuchadnezzar first demonstrated his military prowess in 606 B.C. with a campaign in northern Assyria. This was followed the next year by his defeat of Egyptian armies under Pharaoh **Neco II** at Carchemish (2 Kgs 23:29; 2 Chr 35:20; Jer 46:2). Learning that his father had died, he wasted no time in returning to Babylon to claim the throne. He then embarked on a campaign against Syria, where he extracted tribute from the kings of Damascus, Tyre, and Sidon, as well as from Jehoiakim of Judah (2 Kgs 24:1; Jer 25:8–9).

Nebuchadnezzar launched another expedition against Neco II, but in about 602 B.C. Neco defeated him. In the wake of this setback, **Jehoiakim** rebelled against Babylon. Nebuchadnezzar reequipped his forces and set out against Arab tribes in 599–598 B.C. (Jer 49:28–33). This was merely a preparation for the march against Judah.

After two punitive strikes against Judah in 601 and 597 B.C., the Babylonian army stormed into Judah, besieged Jerusalem, and finally destroyed both the city and its **Temple** in 586 B.C. In the course of these events, Nebuchadnezzar hauled off great numbers of Jewish captives into exile and looted the Temple and treasuries of Jerusalem as spoils of war. Nebuchadnezzar directed the campaign from the town of Kiblah (Jer 39:5–6), and it was there that he exacted his cruel punishments. Around five years later, he ordered yet another deportation of Judeans to Babylon (Jer 52:30).

The remaining decades of his reign are not known with great certainty. He conducted a thirteen-year siege of **Tyre** (Ezek 26:7), waged another campaign against Egypt around 568–567 B.C. (Jer 43:8–13), and with his wife Amytis began a large building program in Babylon whose architectural achievements were later counted among the seven wonders of the ancient world. He rebuilt the temples of **Marduk** and Nabu (see **Nebo**).

Nebuchadnezzar is mentioned several times by the prophets. **Jeremiah** said that Nebuchadnezzar was God's instrument and that there could be no resistance to his advance (Jer 32:1–5, 28; 34:2, 21; 37:1–10; 38:17–23). Because he repeated this utterance Jeremiah was hated by officials in Judah, but he won favorable treatment by the conquering Babylonians (Jer 39:11–14). Jeremiah predicted Nebuchadnezzar would conquer Egypt (Jer 43:8–13; 46:13–26), as did **Ezekiel** (Ezek 30:10). Ezekiel portrays Nebuchadnezzar casting lots on whether to attack Ammon or Jerusalem, and the lot fell to Jerusalem (Ezek 21:18–22). In **Daniel**, Nebuchadnezzar persecutes the followers of the Lord, but finally acknowledges God's supremacy (Dan 1–4).

Nebuchadnezzar died in 562 B.C. and was succeeded by his son **Evil-Merodach** (Amel-Marduk in Akkadian). According to Jer 52:31–34 and 2 Kgs 25:27–30, Evil-Merodach released the imprisoned **Jehoiachin**, former king of Judah, and gave him an allowance.

NEBUCHADREZZAR *See* **Nebuchadnezzar**.

NEBUSHAZBAN A Babylonian official who took part in the siege of Jerusalem in 586 B.C. and served as the commander of the Babylonian royal guard in the subsequent destruction of the city (Jer 39:13).

NEBUZARADAN A Babylonian official who took part in the siege and destruction of Jerusalem in 586 B.C. He was the captain of **Nebuchadnezzar**'s bodyguard unit in charge of prisoners and the deportation of the inhabitants (2 Kgs 25:8–11, 18–21; Jer 52:30). Most notably, he was responsible for freeing **Jeremiah** from his confinement and handing him over to the care of **Gedaliah** (Jer 39:11–14; cf. Jer 41:10, 43:6).

NECHO *See* **Neco**.

NECO Egyptian pharaoh from 610 to 595 B.C. during the Twenty-sixth Dynasty. He was the son of Psammetichus I (r. 663–610 B.C.). Neco is best known for his defeat of King **Josiah** of Judah at **Megiddo** in 609 B.C. (2 Kgs 23:29–30; 2 Chr 35:20–27). In the wake of Josiah's death, **Jehoahaz** (Shallum) reigned over Judah for only three months; he was replaced by Eliakim, whom Neco renamed **Jehoiakim** to signify his vassal status (2 Kgs 23:30–35; 2 Chr 36:1–4). The chief objective of Neco was to march against the rising threat of Babylon. He was defeated, however, by **Nebuchadnezzar** at the battle of Carchemish in 605 B.C. (Jer 46:2). Neco still managed to repel a Babylonian campaign against him in about 602 B.C. and may have encouraged Jehoiakim to rebel against Babylon, although he provided no assistance in that ill-advised undertaking.

NECROMANCY See **Magic**.

NEGEB (Hebrew, "arid land" or "south") The vast expanse of parched and rugged land that spreads over southern Palestine and encompasses the northeast shoulder of the Sinai Peninsula. In Mosaic times, the Negeb was home to seminomadic peoples such as the Amalekites (Num 13:29) and even certain Canaanites (Num 21:1; 33:42). Later times witnessed the presence of other tribes and clans such as the Geshurites, the Girzites, the Jerahmeelites, the Kenites, and the Cherethites (1 Sam 27:8–10; 30:14).

Through the middle of the Negeb ran a trade and travel route that connected Palestine with Egypt; it was called "the way of Shur" (Gen 16:7). The presence of this road, along with the presence of natural resources such as copper, may explain why the patriarchs settled for a time in the region (Gen 12:9; 20:1; 24:62). The way of Shur was also the route most likely taken by the Holy Family on their flight from Bethlehem to Egypt (Matt 2:13–15).

NEGEV See **Negeb**.

NEHEMIAH (Hebrew, "the Lord comforts") The son of Hacaliah, Nehemiah was an exiled Jew in the service of King **Artaxerxes I** of Persia (r. 465–424 B.C.; Neh 1:1; 2:1) at Susa. Nehemiah became one of the leaders of the Jewish reconstruction of Jerusalem following the return from exile. Born in Babylon during the captivity, Nehemiah rose to a position in the court of Artaxerxes and became a "cupbearer" for the king. After learning of the sad situation in Judah and Jerusalem, in particular the destruction of the city's walls and the gates (Neh 1:3) by fire, he took advantage of the position of trust that his office afforded to request royal permission to journey to Jerusalem (Neh 2:1–10). Artaxerxes acquiesced and went so far as to provide him with letters of commendation to present to the Persian satraps of the region.

Nehemiah set out in the twentieth year of Artaxerxes I's reign (445 B.C.). In Jerusalem, Nehemiah was soon opposed by a party centered in Samaria headed by Sanballat the Horonite and his chief sycophant, Tobiah the Ammonite, as well as Geshem and others (Neh 2:10, 19). Nehemiah persevered, however, and examined the state of the walls, and soon he was using the same forceful personality that had swayed Artaxerxes to convince the leaders of the Jerusalem community that the walls needed repair (Neh 2:11–20). Sanballat and his party continued to oppose the project, even threatening war to stop the work (Neh 4:1–9). Nehemiah armed the workers and took steps to prevent attack (Neh 4:10–23). When it was clear that they could not stop the progress, Sanballat's party tried negotiations, asking Nehemiah to come forth and entreat with them. Nehemiah perceived this as a trap and finished the walls in an astonishing fifty-two days (Neh 6:10–15).

After completing the walls, Nehemiah determined that the population in Jerusalem was insufficient to support the city. He therefore arranged for the population in the surrounding areas to draw lots to select 10 percent of the people to relocate to Jerusalem (Neh 11:1). The walls were then dedicated (Neh 12:27–43), and Nehemiah returned to Persia around 433 B.C. (*See also* **Zerubbabel**.)

Nehemiah returned to Jerusalem some years later and discovered a series of abuses, including those of the high priest **Eliashib** (Neh 13:7–9). Nehemiah ensured that the Levites received proper support (Neh 13:10–13), commanded that the Sabbath and Temple rites be honored properly (Neh 13:15–22), and demanded that Jews give up their foreign wives, including a member of the family of the high priest (Neh 13:23–31). The latter requirement had the practical objective of preventing the gradual erosion of the Jewish identity and religious purity.

Nehemiah stands with **Ezra** as a key figure in the restoration of Israel after the Exile. Although a layman rather than a clergyman, Nehemiah helped restore Judah's national and religious fervor by inculturating the laws of Moses in the social and spiritual lives of the Jewish returnees. Significantly, Nehemiah served as a civil administrator and governor, whereas Ezra, as a priest, served as a spiritual figurehead for Israel. Nehemiah was praised in Sir 49:13 and 2 Macc 2:13. Sirach declared: "The memory of Nehemiah also is lasting; he raised for us the walls that had fallen, and set up the gates and bars and rebuilt our ruined houses" (Sir 49:13; *see also* **Ezra, book of**, and **Nehemiah, book of**.)

Another Nehemiah was the leader of the Jewish community that returned to Palestine with Zerubbabel around 538 B.C., at the end of the Babylonian Exile. This Nehemiah is listed in Ezra 2:2 in the third place on a list of twelve names, after Zerubbabel and Joshua (cf. Neh 7:7).

NEHEMIAH, BOOK OF One of the Historical Books of the Old Testament. It is set in the fifth century B.C. and tells the story of a Jewish exile named **Nehemiah** who made it his mission to rebuild the walls of Jerusalem and to restore the city to its former greatness.

Originally, the Hebrew text of Nehemiah was joined to the book of Ezra to form one continuous story. In the Greek **Septuagint**, this extended narrative was called 2 Esdras. By the third century A.D., that book was divided into two parts, into what we now know as Ezra and Nehemiah. The Latin **Vulgate** adopted this division and referred to the books as 1 Esdras and 2 Esdras.

I. AUTHORSHIP AND DATE

According to Jewish tradition, the author of both Ezra and Nehemiah was Ezra himself.

Some modern scholars suppose that Ezra and Nehemiah were written by the same historian who wrote 1 and 2 Chronicles, usually called the "Chronicler." This view is decreasing in popularity, however, as scholars come to acknowledge the unique perspective offered by Ezra and Nehemiah. In any case, the bulk of the book of Nehemiah seems to come from Nehemiah himself. First-person narration in chapters 1–7 and 12–13 strongly suggests that the text was composed from a collection of personal notes usually called "Nehemiah's Memoirs." Chapters 8–10 come from a similar collection called "Ezra's Memoirs."

Many dates for the final compilation have been suggested, from as late as 300 B.C. to as early as 420 B.C., within the lifetimes of Ezra and Nehemiah. The first-person parts of the narrative must have been written close to the time of the events they describe, although it is possible that the final form of the book took shape at a later time.

II. CONTENTS

III. PURPOSE AND THEMES

Nehemiah wrote to record his own work in restoring the defenses of Jerusalem and implementing social and religious reforms in the city. The editor of Nehemiah had a larger purpose as well. The book does not just present historical records; it shows the development of the ideal religious community among the Jews who returned from exile and centered their worship in the Temple. Through the reforms of Ezra and Nehemiah, the restored Jewish community affirmed itself as the true inheritor of Israel's covenant identity in the midst of a hostile Gentile world.

To accomplish his goal, the author has arranged his material less with an eye toward chronology and more to subject matter. For example, the narrative of Nehemiah is interrupted in chapter 8 for the insertion of Ezra reading the book of the Law of Moses. Ezra's activities continue through chapter 10, and then chapters 11 and 12 return the focus to Nehemiah, who repopulates Jerusalem and dedicates its newly refurbished walls. The writer thereby connects two key religious events, the reestablishment of the divine law by Ezra and the dedication of the walls by Nehemiah. The two events epitomize the key roles played by Nehemiah the governor and Ezra the priest, the civil and religious authorities working together to repair both the faith and the fortifications of the Holy City.

The renewed Jewish community is a chastened one that is struggling to take the spiritual and moral lessons of the Exile to heart. The aim of reformers like Ezra and Nehemiah is to make the fledgling community aware of the dangers posed to it by a pagan world, and by the risk that intermarriage with Gentile neighbors might result in infidelity to the covenant. Hope is not to be placed in the rebirth of the grand kingdom of David and Solomon. Instead, hope is placed in the life of faith centered in the Temple, in the fulfillment of the liturgical demands, and in meditation upon God's law. The ideal of the restored community is expressed in Nehemiah with the description of worship: "And they offered great sacrifices that day and rejoiced, for God had made them rejoice with great joy; the women and children also rejoiced. And the joy of Jerusalem was heard afar off" (Neh 12:43).

NEHUSHTA The wife of **Jehoiakim** and the mother of **Jehoiachin**, king of Judah (2 Kgs 24:8). She was the last Queen Mother of the Davidic line in the Old Testament and was one of the captives taken during the Babylonian invasion of 597 B.C. (2 Kgs 24:12, 15; Jer 13:18; 29:2).

NEHUSHTAN *See* **Bronze serpent**.

NEPHEG One of the sons born to David after he established Jerusalem as his capital (2 Sam 5:15; 1 Chr 3:7).

NEPHILIM The name Genesis gives to an ancient people of colossal height and fame. These giants were said to have walked the earth before and after the **Flood**, and their race was propagated in part by the intermarriage of the sons of God with the daughters of men (Gen 6:1–4). Most likely this refers to the righteous line of **Seth** (Gen 5:1–32) corrupting itself by taking wives from the wicked line of **Cain** (Gen 4:17–24). Another tradition, with roots in both Jewish and Christian antiquity, holds that the "sons of God" were fallen angels seduced by the beauty of earthly women (see, e.g., *1 En.* 6–7 and Saint Justin Martyr, *Dial.* 1.79). We hear that in Mosaic times the Anakim warriors of southern Canaan, also men of imposing stature, were thought to be descendants of the primeval Nephilim (Num 13:33).

NER The son of Abiel, the father of **Abner**, and the uncle of **Saul** (1 Sam 14:50–51).

NEREUS A Roman Christian who was greeted by Paul in Romans (Rom 16:15).

NERGAL (Babylonian, "lord of the great city") A Mesopotamian god of death and the underworld who was worshipped by the Cuthites, a people forcibly resettled in Samaria by the Assyrians (2 Kgs 17:30).

NERGAL-SHAREZER A Babylonian official who took part in the conquest of Jerusalem in 586 B.C. (Jer 39:3) and the subsequent release of **Jeremiah** from his imprisonment (Jer 39:13–14).

NERI According to the genealogy of Jesus in Luke, Neri is the father of Shealtiel and son of Melchi (Luke 3:27). The name does not appear in the genealogy of Matthew.

NERO Roman emperor from A.D. 54 to 68, the successor to Emperor Claudius, and best known for his persecution of Christians in Rome. Nero's reign began under the influence of such Roman statesmen as Seneca; the new emperor enacted a number of useful imperial reforms. This promising start was soon overshadowed by Nero's decline into megalomania and corruption. He murdered his own mother and executed a host of relatives and Roman officials. The political crisis that attended his tyranny climaxed with the revolt of the legions in A.D. 68. As Galba marched on Rome, Nero killed himself, but there was a widely held superstitious dread, called the *Nero redivivus* myth, that he would return from the dead. His death brought to an end the Julio-Claudian Dynasty of Roman emperors.

The most infamous event of his reign was the terrible fire that swept through Rome in A.D. 64 and destroyed much of the densely occupied city. To divert attention from rumors that he had started the fire for his own amusement and to make room for his grandiose building program, Nero claimed that the Christians were to blame. Thus Nero was the first emperor to launch an official persecution of Roman believers.

Christians in the capital were arrested, tortured, and executed, and victims were set ablaze as torches to illuminate the atrocities in the night (Tacitus, *Ann.* 15.44). Historically, the persecution marked the first clear separation of Christians from Jews in the eyes of authorities. Some speculate that this separation may have been encouraged by Nero's mistress Poppaea, who showed favor to the Jews and was a friend of Flavius Josephus. Although the persecution actually generated sympathy for the victims, it set the precedent that Christianity was an illegal cult.

Nero was also the emperor to whom **Paul** appealed as a Roman citizen (Acts 25:10–11). Paul's first imprisonment in Rome took place before Nero's persecution (Acts 28:30). But tradition tells us that Paul was later rearrested and beheaded in Rome on imperial orders. Tradition also holds that **Peter** was executed on the Vatican Hill during Nero's reign.

Nero himself may be mentioned in the book of Revelation under the numerical cryptogram "666" (Rev 13:18). Not only is this the number of a ferocious "beast" who attacks the Christian faithful, but it is also the numerical value of Nero's name in Hebrew: *nrwn qṣr* tallies up to 666. Interestingly, a few early manuscripts of Revelation give the number not as 666, but as 616, which is the numerical value of Nero's name transliterated from its Latin spelling: *nrw qṣr*.

NEW COVENANT *See* **Covenant**.

NEW JERUSALEM *See* **Jerusalem**.

NEW MOON The first day of each month in the Israelite lunar calendar. The new moon was a regular feast day celebrated with special sacrifices and rest from ordinary work (Num 28:11–15; Amos 8:5). (*See* **Moon** for other details.)

NEW TESTAMENT *See under* **Testament**.

NEW TESTAMENT APOCRYPHA *See under* **Apocryphal books**.

NICANOR (Greek, "conqueror") A commander in the Syrian army under **Demetrius I** and **Antiochus IV** who was known and much hated for his severe animosity toward the Jews. He took part in the campaign against **Judas Maccabeus**. With **Gorgias**, he was active in the battle of Emmaus and so shared in the Syrian defeat in 165 B.C. during the reign of Antiochus (1 Macc 3:38–4:25; 2 Macc 8:9–36). Nicanor was again in a prominent position under Demetrius I and was sent against Judas, although his resources were inadequate for the task. He failed to quell the revolt of Judas through negotiations (2 Macc 14:18–25) and finally entered into battle against Judas in 160 B.C. at Beth-horon. Nicanor was killed in the fighting and his head and right arm were cut off and displayed as trophies in Jerusalem. The memory of his defeat was celebrated every thirteenth of Adar as the Day of Nicanor (1 Macc 7:26–50; 2 Macc 15:1–36).

NICODEMUS (Greek "conqueror of the People") A Pharisee and member of the ruling class of Judea (John 3:1). Presumably this means that he sat on the Jewish high court known as the **Sanhedrin** (cf. John 7:48; 12:42). Jesus regarded him as a preeminent teacher in the country (John 3:10). Nicodemus is best known for his nighttime visit with Jesus (John 3:1–21), during which Jesus told him he must be "born anew" (or "born from above"). Nicodemus did not understand what Jesus meant, but he was sympathetic to Jesus's teachings and once tried to prevent the arrest of Jesus, arguing that the Law required that the accused receive a fair hearing (John 7:50–51). After the Crucifixion, Nicodemus and **Joseph of Arimathea** prepared Jesus's body for burial (John 19:38–42). Tradition says that Nicodemus eventually became a member of the Christian community.

NICOLAITANS A heretical sect repudiated twice in the book of Revelation (Rev 2:6, 15). Revelation does not tell us what the Nicolaitans believed, but references in Saint Irenaeus, Clement, and Tertullian identify their belief as an early form of Gnosticism. The Nicolaitans are sometimes linked with the deacon Nicolaus, who was ordained in Acts 6:5.

NICOLAUS One of the seven who were appointed to assist the apostles in the early Jerusalem community (Acts 6:5). Traditionally, these seven men are considered the first deacons of the Church.

NICOPOLIS A city where Paul hoped to meet up with Titus after the latter's departure from Crete (Titus 3:12). There were several cities named Nicopolis, but Paul describes this one as a good place to spend the winter. This Nicopolis was probably the one in Epirus on the Greek peninsula, facing the Adriatic, on the isthmus of the Bay of Actium.

NIGER (Greek, "black") A name used for Simeon, one of the leaders in the Christian community at Antioch (Acts 13:1). He may have been of African origin.

NIGHT The hours of the night were divided into three watches by the Mesoptamians and the Hebrews (Exod 14:24; Judg 7:19; Lam 2:19); the Greeks and Romans divided the nighttime hours into four watches (Matt 14:25; Mark 13:35). (*See also* **Light**.)

NIGHT HAG (Hebrew *lîlît*, from Akkadian, "evil spirit") A demon or evil spirit of Canaanite and Mesopotamian folklore that was said to infest desolate places (Isa 34:14). The demon was believed to attack women in childbirth, so amulets were devised to give protection from its influence. In later Jewish literature and folklore, Lilith was said to have been Adam's first wife, who left him to become a demon.

NILE The longest river in Africa and possibly the longest river in the world (the Amazon is nearly the same length, and the figures depend on how the rivers are measured). The Nile is tied inextricably to the history, culture, and very life of **Egypt**. Along its banks was formed virtually the whole of Egyptian civilization, one of the great cultures of the ancient world. The Nile flows north nearly 4,000 miles (around 6,400 kilometers) from Lake Victoria in Tanzania to the Mediterranean Sea, coursing through Ethiopia, Sudan, and Egypt.

The Nile was well known in biblical times for its central role in the survival of Egypt. Its waters supported crops and pasturelands (Gen 41:1–3, 17–18) and provided an abundance of papyrus and fish (Isa 19:8). To raise crops, however, the water of the Nile had to be distributed by laborious irrigation—in contrast, Deuteronomy notes, to **Canaan**, where the land is watered by rain (Deut 11:10).

The Nile figured in the dream of Pharaoh interpreted by **Joseph** (Gen 41:1–36) and especially in the events of the **Exodus** (Exod 2, 7–8). Moses was taken from the Nile (Exod 2:1),

and the river was the target of the Lord's first two plagues on Egypt: first he turned its waters to blood (Exod 7:15–24) and then he unleashed an army of frogs to trouble the land (Exod 7:25–8:11). In the Prophets, the arrogance of Egypt is compared to the annual rising of the Nile (Jer 46:7–8), and Egypt is also called a crocodile lying in the Nile (Ezek 29:3–5). The prophet might warn the Egyptians that the worst fate to befall them would be the drying up of the Nile (Isa 19:5–8; Ezek 30:12). The Assyrian conqueror Sennacherib once boasted that he had dried up the Nile (2 Kgs 19:24; Isa 37:25).

NIMROD The son of Cush and the grandson of Ham, listed in the **Table of Nations** (Gen 10:8; 1 Chr 1:10). He is described as the first of the heroes after the **Flood**, a mighty hunter and ruler of the cities of Babel (Babylon), Erech (Uruk), and Akkad (Agade), in the land of Shinar (Babylonia) (Gen 10:9–10); the land next to Assyria is termed the "land of Nimrod" (Mic 5:6). Some have tried to identify Nimrod with a Mesopotamian god such as Ninurta or Marduk, or with the mythological hero Gilgamesh, but this is little more than speculation.

NINEVEH The chief city and final capital of **Assyria**. The city was on the east bank of the Tigris River, next to modern Mosul, Iraq. According to Gen 10:11–12, Nineveh was one of four cities founded by Nimrod after his departure from Babylon. The site was inhabited from the fourth millennium B.C. and became the royal residence of the Assyrian kings in the eleventh century B.C. under Tiglath-pileser I. Under Sargon (r. 722–705 B.C.), the capital was moved to Dur Sharrukin (modern Khorsabad) but was moved back under Sennacherib (r. 705–681 B.C.). A massive palace complex was erected in the city as well as ambitious fortifications, and additional palaces were built by Esarhaddon (r. 681–669 B.C.) and Ashurbanipal (r. 669–630 B.C.). The city eventually shared in the collapse of the Assyrian Empire: it was besieged by the Babylonians and Medes in 614 B.C. and finally captured in 612 B.C. The city was utterly destroyed, and its remains were left to pass into history (Zeph 2:13–3:7).

In the Old Testament, the city of Nineveh is despised as the seat of the Assyrian kings, who several times invaded Israel, laid waste its towns and cities, and made off with thousands of Israelite captives. It is not hard to understand why **Jonah** was so indignant about the brief repentance of Nineveh, which spared the city from destruction in his own day (Jonah 3:1–4:5). The reform would not last, however, and so the Lord sent other prophets to announce its ultimate doom (Nah 2:10–3:19; Zeph 2:13–15). Warning of the city's future demise spurred **Tobit**, a captive taken to Nineveh, to urge his son to flee before the Lord's judgment finally came down (Tob 14:4, 8, 15).

NISAN The first month of the Israelite liturgical year; it corresponds to March–April. The celebrations of Passover and Unleavened Bread came in the month of Nisan (Lev 23:5–8). The original Canaanite name of Nisan was Abib (Deut 16:1–8).

NISROCH An Assyrian deity in whose temple the Assyrian king **Sennacherib** was assas-sinated (2 Kgs 19:37; Isa 37:38). Since this god is not otherwise known, attempts have been made to identify him with a deity such as Enlil, Marduk, Ashur, Nusku, or Ninurta.

NO *See* **Thebes.**

NOAH A tenth-generation descendant of **Adam** (Gen 5:1–31) who, along with his family, survived the **Flood** by constructing the ark (Gen 6–9). Noah was the son of Lamech, and was born when Lamech was 182 years old. Noah was the father of three sons: **Shem**, **Ham**, and **Japheth** (Gen 5:32).

The etymology of the name "Noah" is uncertain, although one of the common interpretations is that it is derived from a verb meaning "to rest." In Gen 5:29, the etymology is connected with the task of Noah to "bring us relief from our work and from the toil of our hands," from the verb *nḥm*, "to bring relief."

I. NOAH AND THE FLOOD

According to Gen 6:9, "Noah was a righteous man, blameless in his generation; Noah walked with God." He was a man of faith (Heb. 11:7) and a herald of righteousness (2 Pet 2:5). These positive attributes set him apart from his contemporaries, because the rest of humanity is described as follows: "the earth was corrupt in God's sight, and the earth was filled with violence" (Gen 6:11). No one except Noah's immediate family found refuge in the ark.

Having determined to wipe out the sinful from the earth, the Lord ordered Noah to construct an ark in which Noah, his wife, his sons, and their wives would be spared the Flood. Noah also followed the Lord in collecting representatives of all the animals, seven each of the clean animals and two each of the rest (Gen 6:13–22). The Flood that ensued destroyed all except those in the ark (Gen 7:7; 1 Pet 3:20). After the Flood, Noah built an altar to the Lord, took one of every clean animal and bird, and offered burnt offerings on the altar (Gen 8:20). The Lord then promised, "I will never again curse the ground because of man, for the imagination of man's heart is evil from his youth; neither will I ever again destroy every living creature as I have done. While the earth remains, seedtime and harvest, cold and heat, summer and winter, day and night, shall not cease" (Gen 8:21–22).

Noah lived for a very long time. He was 500 years old at the time of his first son's birth (Gen 5:32), he was 600 years old when the Flood occurred (Gen 7:11), and he died at the age of 950 (Gen 9:28–29). (For details of the Flood, *see under* **Flood**.)

II. THE NOAHIC COVENANT

The covenant made between God and the world—with Noah as covenant mediator—was made ten generations after the covenant God made with Adam. The covenant with Noah was granted because of Noah's righteousness (Gen 6:9; 7:1) and obedience (Gen 6:22; 7:5). By its terms, God promised to maintain the stability of the created order forever and not to flood the earth again (Gen 9:11). The Noahic covenant represents a renewal of the original creation covenant established by God with the world in the beginning; in fact, the Genesis narrative sets forth several literary parallels to show that the Flood represents a "new creation" (cf. Gen 8:20–22; 9:9–17; Gen 2:2; 6:18)

(CCC 71). (On the descendants of Noah, *see under* **Shem**, **Ham**, and **Japheth**; *see also* **Covenant**.)

NOB A town of Benjamin to the east of Jerusalem. **Ahimelech** resided there with other priests (1 Sam 21:1), who may have fled there after the capture of the **ark of the covenant** and the destruction of Shiloh (1 Sam 4:11). **David** made his way to Nob and met with Ahimelech (1 Sam 21:1–6). Upon hearing of this meeting, **Saul** massacred Ahimelech and eighty-five other priests and then turned the sword of his rage against the residents of Nob and their livestock (1 Sam 22:9–19). **Isaiah** also placed Nob among the cities that would be conquered by the advancing Assyrians at the end of the eighth century B.C. (Isa 10:32). According to Neh 11:32, Nob is one of the cities that were reinhabited after the Exile.

NOD A region east of Eden (*see* **Garden of Eden**) where **Cain** resettled after he murdered **Abel** and was marked by God (Gen 4:14–16). The name means "wandering," an allusion to God's punishment of Cain as "a fugitive and a wanderer (*nād*) on the earth" (Gen 4:12).

NOMAD One who leads a wandering life. In the ancient Near East, the Akkadians, Amorites, Arameans, and later the Nabateans and Arabians all began as nomads, as did the tribes of Israel.

Nomads supported themselves chiefly through flocks and herds of sheep, goats, camels, and also donkeys, from which were derived milk, clothing, and fabrics for tents. Nomads also practiced some forms of cultivation, usually of fast-growing crops that could be harvested quickly. While they spent most of their time on the fringes of civilization, the nomads still had contact with settled peoples and maintained generally cordial relations with them. For example, in times of drought and famine, nomads might request permission to pitch camp temporarily on suitable pasture-lands. Something like this took place when Jacob and his clan moved from Canaan to Egypt (Gen 25:19–35:29).

Since nomads have no permanent association with any particular locality, family connections are extraordinarily important. Members of a tribe were connected by close blood ties, and those ties were strengthened by the common commitment to the defense of the tribe, its members, and its unity. This cohesiveness was needed for practical survival. Customs that kept the tribe together had the force of law; violations would be punished by the entire community and might in extreme forms entail exile from the tribe, meaning almost certain death because of the harshness of the environment (cf. the story of Cain in Gen 4:11–16; and the story of Ishmael in Gen 21:8–14). Similarly, an attack on one member of the tribe or community elicited a response from the entire tribe (see **Avenger of blood**). A group of tribes might join together for the good of all. Such unions might be temporary or broken in the best interests of the members (e.g., Abraham and Lot, Gen 13:5–13).

The first named nomad in the Old Testament is Cain (Gen 4:11–16), and a number of nomadic tribes are mentioned in the **Table of Nations** (Gen 10:2–31). The **patriarchs** were seminomadic chieftains, and the Israelites were nomads again on their long **Exodus** journey from Egypt to Canaan. The time they spent in the wilderness also showed how much the Israelites had become sedentary in Egypt: they needed divine assistance for their survival and longed for the luxuries of Egypt.

The wilderness period was seen by later prophets as an ideal one, a time prior to the corruption of the Israelites by Canaanite idolatry, because the Lord revealed himself to his people on Sinai and it was a time of better spiritual health (Jer 2:2; Hos 13:5). Hosea foresaw a time when the Lord would lure Israel back to that happy state, when he would "bring her into the wilderness, and speak tenderly to her" (Hos 2:14–15).

After the conquest of Canaan, the tribes settled down and soon became subject to the predations of nomadic enemies such as the Midianites and Amalekites. Israel made contact with a variety of nomadic peoples, such as the Arabs (Isa 13:20, 21:13; Jer 3:2, 25:23–24; Ezek 27:21).

NOPH *See* **Memphis**.

NUMBERS Israel, like its neighbors, used the decimal system of counting. Symbols for numbers were not used until after the **Exile**; before then, the word for the number was normally spelled out, although archaeology has found evidence of some number symbols borrowed from neighboring cultures, such as the Egyptians. By Maccabean times, the twenty-two consonants of the Hebrew alphabet were assigned numerical values, so they could represent numerals as well as letters.

Numbers often had symbolic significance

for ancient cultures, including the Israelites. The number 1 expressed the idea of uniqueness, especially when referring to the uniqueness of the God of Israel (Deut 6:4). Two was a symbol of unity but also of division, exemplified by the unity of the first family, Adam and Eve (Gen 1:27; 2:20, 24). Three was symbolic of perfection and completion, and in Christian tradition it became a symbol of the Trinity (cf. Matt 28:19; 2 Cor 13:14). Seven is the most significant of the sacred numbers in Scripture. God created the world in seven days (Gen 1:1–24) and sanctified every seventh day as a holy day (Exod 20:8–11). Using multiples of seven, the **Law** made every seventh year a holy year (Deut 15:1–6), and every seventh occurrence of the seventh year was a Jubilee year (Lev 25:1–55). Revelation uses the number 7 extensively, referring to the seven churches (Rev 1:4), the seven spirits (1:4), the seven torches (4:5), the seven seals (6:1), the seven angels (8:2), the seven trumpets (8:2), the seven heads of the dragon (12:3), the seven heads of the beast (13:1), the seven plagues (15:1), the seven bowls of wrath (15:6). Twelve is associated closely with the elective power of God: there were twelve tribes of Israel (Gen 49:28) and the twelve apostles selected by Jesus (Matt 10:1). After the death of Judas, the apostles considered it necessary to elect a successor to complete their number (Acts 1:26).

Forty is connected with times of tribulation or testing: the forty days of the Flood (Gen 7:4), the forty years the Israelites spent in the wilderness (Exod 16:35; Num 14:33), the forty days of Elijah's journey (1 Kgs 19:8), and the forty days Jesus spent in the wilderness (Matt 4:2; Mark 1:13; Luke 4:2). Jesus also spent forty days on earth after the Resurrection (Acts 1:3). Seventy is associated with the governance of the world by God: the sons of Israel were seventy (Gen 46:27; Exod 1:5); there were seventy elders of Israel (Exod 24:1; Num 11:16); and the Exile endured for seventy years (Jer 25:11; 29:10).

Since by New Testament times each letter in the Hebrew alphabet could stand for a number, names had numerical values. **Matthew**'s genealogy of Jesus Christ is divided into three groups of fourteen, which is the numerical value of the name "David" in Hebrew. The number of the beast in Revelation is 666, which is the numerical value of the name "Nero Caesar" in Hebrew (*see* **Nero** for details).

NUMBERS, BOOK OF The fourth book of the **Pentateuch** in the Old Testament. Numbers takes its name from the censuses recounted at the beginning and near the end of the book (chaps. 1–4 and 26). This book continues the story of the **Exodus** and ends with the arrival of the Israelites just outside the Promised Land. It combines a narrative of the Israelites' desert pilgrimage from **Sinai** to the border of Canaan with laws that supplement those presented in Leviticus.

The Hebrew title of the book is "In the Wilderness." The **Septuagint** called the book "Numbers," and that title has passed through the **Vulgate** into English.

I. AUTHORSHIP AND DATE

The text of Numbers does not identify its author, but the Jewish and the Christian traditions are in agreement that the Pentateuch was composed by **Moses**. Numbers itself mentions that Moses wrote down an account of the Israelites' journey at the command of the Lord (Num 33:2). Modern scholars generally prefer to think of the book of Numbers as a composite of different documents or traditions written by different authors at different times.

If, as long tradition asserts, Moses was the author, then the earliest possible date of composition would have been in the fifteenth century B.C. (or perhaps in the thirteenth century B.C., depending on the date of the **Exodus**). Scholars who read the book as a patchwork of various traditions date its earliest elements to around the tenth century B.C. and see its final form taking shape in the fifth century B.C., but even those scholars see much older traditions incorporated in the book.

II. CONTENTS

The loose structure of Numbers defies an easily organized outline. The narrative nevertheless falls generally into three main divisions constructed around Sinai (Num 1:1–10:10), Kadesh (10:11–20:13), and Moab (20:14–36:13). Based on these key locations, Numbers has the following structure.

I. *Sinai (1:1–10:10)*
  A. *The Census of the First Generation (1:1–54)*
  B. *The Arrangements of the Camp (2:1–34)*
  C. *The Census of the Levites and Firstborns (3:1–4:48)*
  D. *The Laws on Cleanness and Jealousy, and the Legislation for the Nazirite Vows (5:1–6:27)*
  E. *Consecration of the Tabernacle (7:1–89)*
  F. *Preparations for the Journey (8:1–10:10)*
II. *The Journey from Sinai to Kadesh (10:11–12:16)*

III. *Kadesh (13:1–20:21)*
  A. *The Twelve Spies (13:1–14:45)*
  B. *Miscellaneous Laws (15:1–41)*
  C. *Korah, Dathan, and Abiram (16:1–17:28)*
  D. *The Priests and Levites (18:1–32)*
  E. *Purification (19:1–22)*
  F. *The Death of Miriam (20:1–21)*
IV. *The Journey from Kadesh to Moab (20:22–21:35)*
V. *Moab (22:1–36:13)*
  A. *Balaam (22:1–25:18)*
  B. *The Census of the Second Generation (26:1–65)*
  C. *The Inheritance of Zelophehad's Daughters (27:1–23)*
  D. *Offerings, Feasts, and Vows (28:1–30:17)*
  E. *Revenge Against the Midianites (31:1–54)*
  F. *The Allotment of Land in the Transjordan (32:1–42)*
  G. *The Encampments (33:1–56)*
  H. *The Cities of Canaan (34:1–35:34)*
  I. *The Marriage of Zelophehad's Daughters (36:1–13)*

III. PURPOSE AND THEMES

Numbers tells the story of the long wanderings of the Israelites through the wilderness, from Mount Sinai to the very edge of Canaan. It also gives us important information about their lives while they were in the wilderness, including two censuses taken a generation apart.

The first part details the preparations of the Israelites for their departure from Sinai. It includes the census of the laymen, Levites, and firstborn sons and the arrangements for camping and marching in the wilderness. It also enumerates assorted laws regulating social life and worship.

The second part shows God's constant care for his people and their continual rebellion. For their stubborn refusal to seize the Promised Land, the Exodus generation of Israelites was required to wander for forty years and die outside the borders of Canaan. The second part also includes various laws, in particular on offerings and the **Sabbath**.

The third part follows the journey of the Israelites to Moab and the settlement of the tribes of Reuben, Gad, and Manasseh on the lands east of the Jordan. The book concludes with a second census, this time of the second generation, and a presentation of the laws intended to govern the settlement of Canaan.

Numbers gives us only highlights of the long journey, the stories that impart key lessons. First, Numbers is a meditation on God's working through history to form his people and to teach them obedience through difficult and arduous trials. He displays his love and concern for them in many ways, most notably by guiding them across the wilderness with the pillar of cloud and fire (Num 9:15–23), feeding them with both food and drink (11:4–9, 31–35; 20:2–9), and saving them from the evil magic of their enemies by transforming curses to blessings (22:1–24:25). In return, the Israelites proved ungrateful. They complained throughout the journey (11:1; 21:4–5) and they demanded meat instead of manna (11:4–6). Above all, the Israelites looked back longingly to their days in Egypt and often wished to go back to the land of their enslavement (11:5, 18, 20; 14:3–4; 20:5; 21:5).

Because of this doubt and criticism, the Israelites are punished in order to teach them the fruits of disobedience and to give them proper discipline (11:1, 18–20; 12:9–10; 16:31–35, 41–50; 20:12; 21:4–6; 25:1–9). The apostasy of the Israelites was so severe that an entire generation was condemned to die in the wilderness without reaching the Promised Land (14:20–25). What should have been a brief journey was stretched out over decades so the penalty could be paid through the deaths of the disinherited generation. Only after a second generation was born and had grown to adulthood were the Israelites permitted to enter the land of Canaan (33:50–56).

Numbers is rich in typology and lessons for the Christian life. The bronze serpent that was raised as a sign of salvation serves as a type for the Crucifixion of Jesus by which Christ was raised upon the Cross as a seal of salvation to believers (Num 21:4–9; John 3:14–15). The rock that gave water to the Israelites in the desert (Num 20:10–11; 1 Cor 10:1–4) and the manna that fell from heaven (Num 11:7–9; John 6:31–35) anticipated the Eucharist. The failings of the Israelites at Kadesh and Moab serve as a caution for believers not to fall into the same sins of idolatry and immorality that were such plagues to the Israelites (Num 14:1–12, 25:1–9; 1 Cor 10:6–11; Heb 3:7–4:10). Finally, the journey through the wilderness foreshadows the earthly pilgrimage of the Church as it moves toward the inheritance of the heavenly Promised Land (Num 10:33, 33:50–54; Heb 4:1–10, 11:13–16).

NUN The fourteenth letter of the Hebrew alphabet (נ).

NUN The father of Joshua (Exod 33:11) and the son of Elishama the Ephraimite (1 Chr

7:26–27). Note that Joshua's original name was Hoshea (Num 13:8, 16), and after the **Exile** his new name was sometimes spelled Jeshua (Neh 8:17).

NUNC DIMITTIS (Latin, "now you are dismissing") The first words of the Latin Vulgate version of the canticle sung by **Simeon** in Luke 2:29–35. The hymn of praise was recited in thanksgiving after Simeon saw the infant **Messiah**. The canticle consists of two parts. The first part expresses Simeon's recognition of Jesus as the Messiah: "Lord, now let your servant depart in peace, according to your word; for my eyes have seen your salvation which you have prepared in the presence of all peoples, a light for revelation to the gentiles, and for glory to your people Israel" (Luke 2:29–32). It also includes a second part, a prophecy spoken to Mary: "Behold, this child is set for the fall and rising of many in Israel, and for a sign that is spoken against (and a sword will pierce through your own soul also), that thoughts out of many hearts may be revealed" (Luke 2:34–35). The mood of the prophecy contrasts to the mood of the first part of the canticle, but the prophecy also advances Luke's purpose in expressing precisely what kind of Messiah Jesus will be: a Suffering Servant. The Nunc Dimittis is used as an evening prayer in the *Apostolic Constitutions* (7.48).

NUZI Also Nuzu, a city in Mesopotamia southeast of Kirkuk in modern Iraq. Occupied by the Hurrians in the second millennium B.C., the city was excavated from 1925 to 1931, and more than 3,500 cuneiform tablets were found detailing the commerce, law, administration, and social structure of the period. Close study of the tablets demonstrated notable points of contact between ancient Hurrian culture and the **patriarchs**, especially with regard to such activities as slave ownership, marriage customs, contracts, and adoption.

OAK A common tree in Palestine, with a variety of species. The oak—like other large trees, such as the terebinth—was a symbol of powerful fertility to the pagan Canaanites. Oaks can grow very large and live for centuries, making them ideal landmarks. There were, consequently, several famous oaks mentioned in the Old Testament, such as the oaks of Mamre (Gen 18:4, 8), the oak of Moreh (Gen 12:6), and the oaks of Bashan (Isa 2:13; Ezek 27:6; Zech 11:2).

OATH The solemn invocation of God to assert the veracity of a pledge or the truth of one's claim. An oath contained a conditional self-curse. Taking an oath entailed using sacred words and symbolic acts (Gen 31:50, 32:40; Num 5:22; Judg 8:19; 2 Kgs 2:2; Jer 42:5; Matt 5:34–36, 23:16; Rev 10:5–6) and was part of legal proceedings (1 Kgs 8:31; 2 Chr 6:22). An oath was especially connected with the ratification of a **covenant** (Gen 26:28; Ezek 16:59, 17:13–19; Hos 10:4). The two words in Hebrew used for a covenant pledge are šĕbûʿâ ("oath") and ʾālâ ("curse"). The former, along with its cognate verb šbʿ ("swear"), share the same consonantal root as the word for the number seven.

The number seven was exceptionally sacred to the Israelites. God created the world in seven days, establishing his covenant with creation (cf. Gen 6:18; Isa 24:5). In Gen 21:22–34, **Abraham** offers seven lambs to **Abimelech** as a symbol of the covenant of mutual peace forged between Abraham and Abimelech following a dispute over a well. The covenant followed the pattern of a Near Eastern kinship covenant that entailed a solemn oath from both parties during the ratification ceremony (Gen 21:31), including invoking God's name (Gen 21:23) and expressing mutual commitment through declaration by word (Gen 21:30) and ritual act (Gen 21:28). The well was given the name Beer-sheba, "well of seven" or "well of the oath."

The second term, ʾālâ, was a reminder of the conditional self-curse imposed by the oath should one's word prove false or should the terms under which the oath was pledged be violated (1 Sam 3:17, 14:24; Ruth 1:17; Ezek 17:16; Zeph 2:9). Sometimes the declaration of the curse was omitted in oath-taking, but even if unspoken, it could be ritually enacted by a symbolic gesture.

Oaths played a prominent part in the covenants made between God and his people. In God's covenant with Abraham, the broken covenant with **Adam** is renewed and the divine pledge is made for a new homeland (Gen 15:18; 17:8) and a future dynasty of kings (Gen 17:6, 16). God swears an oath in response to Abraham's faith and obedience, promising to restore his blessings to the world through Abraham's offspring (Gen 22:16–18), a pledge that represents the divine plan of redemption fulfilled in Jesus Christ (Acts 3:25–26; Gal 3:10–29) (CCC 706). The covenant pledge was renewed with **Isaac** and **Jacob** (Gen 26:3–5; 28:13–14; 35:9–12), and Moses appealed to the covenant oath that God had sworn concerning his promise to rescue the Israelites from slavery and grant them a homeland. Notably, where men swore oaths by invoking the name of God, the Lord has no superior to invoke and so swore by his own name to guarantee the fulfillment of his pledge (cf. Heb 6:13–18).

The **Sinai** covenant was sealed by an oath ceremony that included splashing blood on the altar (Exod 24:6) and on the people (Exod 24:8) to ritualize both the blessings and the curses (cf. Lev 8:24, 30; Matt 26:28; 1 Cor 11:23–25) (CCC 613). The Deuteronomic covenant (Deut 27:15–26) included a litany of twelve curses invoked by the twelve tribes and administered by the priests (Deut 27:14) and accepted with the solemn antiphonal refrain "Amen" (Deut 27:15, 16, 17). Deuteronomy gives a list of sins that will break the covenant and put the curses into effect: idolatry (Deut 27:15); failing to honor one's parents (Deut 27:16); stealing (Deut 27:17); mistreatment of the disabled and disadvantaged (Deut 27:18–19); sexual perversions (Deut 27:20–23); and murder of the innocent (Deut 27:24–25). The curses were listed in Deut 28:15–68.

Jesus taught that we should be so honest that no oaths should be necessary: "Again, you have heard that it was said to those of ancient times, 'You shall not swear falsely, but carry out the vows you have made to the Lord.' But I say to you, Do not swear at all, either by heaven, for it is the throne of God, or by the earth, for it is his footstool, or by Jerusalem, for it is the city of the great King. And do not swear by your head, for you cannot make one hair white or black. Let your word be 'Yes, Yes' or 'No, No'; anything more than this comes from the evil one" (Matt 5:33–37; cf. Jas 5:12). Paul swore an oath on several occasions (2 Cor 1:23; Gal 1:20) (CCC 2150–54; *Code of Canon Law*, can. 1199). (*See* **Covenant**.)

OBADIAH (Hebrew, "servant of the Lord") The name of several men in the Old Testament.

1. One of the twelve minor prophets. (*See* **Obadiah, book of.**)

2. The chief official in the royal household during the reign of Ahab, king of Israel (1 Kgs 18:1–16). He is listed as a protector of the Lord's prophets (1 Kgs 18:4) during Jezebel's persecution.

3. The son of Izrahiah (1 Chr 7:3).

4. A warrior who joined David at **Ziklag** (1 Chr 12:9).

5. A prince of Judah who was chosen by **Jehoshaphat** to take part in the effort to teach "the book of the law of the LORD" to the people of Judah (2 Chr 17:7).

6. A Levite who labored on the repairs made to the Temple under **Josiah** (2 Chr 34:12).

OBADIAH, BOOK OF The shortest book in the Old Testament at only twenty-one verses, Obadiah is counted as the fourth of the twelve minor prophets and is included in the Catholic canon among the prophetic writings. This prophecy is one of the sternest in Scripture; it speaks against the Edomites, the invaders of southern Judah and the enemies of those returning from the **Exile** to their homeland.

I. AUTHORSHIP AND DATE

Nothing is known of the author of Obadiah except what is noted from the text. While later Jewish tradition identified him with the official Obadiah in 1 Kgs 18, this connection seems unlikely. The date of the book is also a source of some disagreement among scholars. Jewish tradition in the Talmud dates Obadiah to the ninth century B.C. and the reign of Ahab. Most scholars consider the time frame for Obadiah to be after the destruction of Jerusalem in 586 B.C. and its occasion the harsh treatment of Jews who remained in Palestine during the **Exile** (cf. Lam 4:21; Ps 137:7). The latest possible date for its composition is the late fourth century B.C., when Edom was overrun by the Nabateans.

II. CONTENTS

I. *Title (v. 1)*

II. *The Judgment on Edom (vv. 1–14)*

  A. *The Prediction of Edom's Doom (vv. 1–4)*

  B. *The Destruction of Edom (vv. 5–9)*

  C. *The Reasons for the Judgment (vv. 10–14)*

III. *The Universal Judgment (vv. 15–16)*

IV. *The Triumph of Israel (vv. 17–21)*

III. PURPOSE AND THEMES

The "Vision of Obadiah" (verse 1; cf. Isa 1:1; Nah 1:1) is summed up almost entirely in the line that follows immediately: "thus says the LORD concerning Edom." The book of Obadiah is divided into two principal parts. The first is the pronouncement of judgment upon Edom (vv. 2–7, 10, 14, 15), and the second is the assurance of Israel's triumph. The oracle is a common one found in other prophetic declarations (cf. Isa 34:5–17, 63:1–6; Jer 49:7–22; Lam 4:21–22; Ezek 26:12–14; Joel 3:19; Amos 1:11–12). The similarities between Obadiah verses 1–9 and Jer 49:7–22 have led some scholars to see in them a literary relationship, and some have suggested that Jeremiah used elements of Obadiah rather than that Obadiah used Jeremiah. It is also possible that both were adopting an older oracle against Edom. There are also phrases found in both Obadiah and Joel: Obad 10 and Joel 3:19; Obad 11 and Joel 3:3; Obad 15 and Joel 1:15; 2:1; 3:4, 7, 14; Obad 18 and Joel 3:8. As with Jeremiah, it is likely that Joel used Obadiah rather than the other way around.

Although it is the shortest book of the OT, Obadiah is noted for its strong, acerbic, and aggressive language. It boldly assures Edom of destruction and uses vivid, sharp imagery to accomplish its prophetic purpose (e.g., vv. 3–4). It reiterates the assurance of the Lord's protection of his people and the promise of vengeance upon those who plague them: "You should not have entered the gate of my people on the day of their calamity; you should not have joined in the gloating over Judah's disaster on the day of his calamity" (v. 13). The text also reflects belief in the restoration of Israel and takes nationalistic pride in that certainty, but underneath such fervor is the deeper conviction in the final triumph of God's Kingdom.

OBLATION *See* **Sacrifice**.

OFFERING *See* **Sacrifice**.

OG The king of **Bashan** in Transjordan who was defeated and slain by the Israelites at Edrei (Num 21:33–35; Deut 1:4; 3:1–13). His defeat by the Israelites became a cherished memory and a symbol of the Lord's assurance of victory (Deut 4:47, 31:4; Josh 2:10, 9:10; Ps 135, 136:20; Neh 9:22). Following Og's destruction, Bashan was divided among the tribes of Reuben, Gad, and Manasseh (Num 32:33; Deut 29:6; Josh 13:29–30). Og is described as the last member of the Rephaim, a race of giants, and his bed of iron was displayed at Rabbah (Deut 3:11): it was 4 cubits wide and 9 cubits long. Some scholars prefer to interpret "bed of iron" as a tomb or sarcophagus.

OIL Olive oil was by far the most common oil in the ancient Mediterranean world, since the olive tree (*Olea europaea*) was abundant in many areas, including Palestine (Deut 7:13, 11:14, 31:12, 33:24; 2 Kgs 18:32; Jer 31:11; Joel 2:19). The oil was created by pressing olives in mills of various sizes (Exod 27:20; Deut 33:24) and was stored in containers (1 Sam 10:1; 1 Kgs 17:12; 2 Kgs 4:2, 9:1; Matt 25:4). The olive-oil trade was significant in ancient times, especially olive oil produced in Palestine (Ezek 27:17; Hos 12:2; Rev 18:12–13). King Solomon, for example, paid Hiram of Tyre for the construction of the Temple in olive oil (1 Kgs 5:11; Ezek 27:17). Likewise, Egypt imported great amounts of olive oil (Hos 12:1).

Olive oil was valuable for its wide variety of uses, including in medicine (Isa 1:6; Luke 10:34), cosmetics (Ps 104:15; Matt 6:17), and food (Deut 32:13; Judg 9:9; 1 Kgs 17:12–16; Ezek 16:13; Hos 2:7) and as fuel for oil lamps (Exod 27:20; Lev 24:2). Mixed with a perfume such as nard or myrrh, it was used for anointing priests (Exod 29:2) and in other ceremonies such as the purification of lepers (Lev 14:10–18) and the conclusion of the **Nazirite** vow (Num 6:15). Above all, olive oil was used for the anointing and installation of a king (1 Sam 10:1; 1 Kgs 1:39). Oil was also applied to the body after ablutions (Ruth 3:3; 2 Sam 12:20) and was used in the anointing of the sick (Jas 5:14). The words of a betrayer are described as "softer than oil" (Ps 55:21).

OLD GATE A gate on the wall of Jerusalem on the western side of the Temple Mount (Neh 3:6, 12:39; cf. Zech 14:10).

OLD TESTAMENT *See under* **Testament**.

OLIVE An evergreen tree (*Olea europaea*) found in great abundance and variety in Palestine and throughout much of the Mediterranean world. The olive tree provides **olive oil** and thus was absolutely essential to the economy and daily life of much of the biblical world. Because of its importance, the olive tree was much esteemed (Deut 8:8; Judg 9:8; 2 Kgs 18:32; Hag 2:19). First mentioned in Gen 8:11 (when the dove returned to Noah's ark bearing an olive branch), the olive tree also was featured in parables, and was a common symbol of strength and vitality (Ps 52:8; Hos 14:6). It is said that the restored Israel will be like the olive in its beauty (Hos 14:6; cf. Ps 52:10; Jer 11:16). In light of the story of Noah, the olive branch became a symbol of peace and conciliation (Ps 52:8). (*See* **oil**.)

OLIVES, MOUNT OF A hill to the east of Jerusalem that overlooks the city across the Kidron Valley and the river Kidron (2 Sam 15:30; Zech 14:40). Also called Olivet, the mount is famed for the large number of olive trees that grew there during the time of Jesus, although most of the trees were destroyed during the bloody siege of Jerusalem in A.D. 70.

The Garden of **Gethsemane** was located on the western slope of the mount (Matt 26:30; Mark 14:26; Luke 22:39), and the villages of **Bethany** and **Bethphage** were situated on the eastern slope.

The Mount of Olives is mentioned twice in the Old Testament. The first time is in the account of David's flight from Jerusalem in the face of the rebellion of his son Absalom: as he fled he passed over the Mount of Olives barefoot, with his head covered (2 Sam 15:30–32). The second mention is in Zechariah: "On that day [the **Day of the Lord**] his feet shall stand on the Mount of Olives which lies before Jerusalem on the east; and the Mount of Olives shall be split in two from east to west by a very wide valley; so that one half of the Mount shall withdraw northward, and the other half southward . . . then the LORD your God will come, and all the holy ones with him" (Zech 14:4–5). Other possible references include 1 Kgs 11:7–8; 2 Kgs 23:13; Ezek 11:23; and Neh 8:15.

Jesus raised Lazarus from the dead at Bethany (John 11; cf. John 12:1; Matt 26:6–12; Mark 14:3–9), and stayed in Bethany during the final week before his Passion, perhaps at the home of Mary and Martha or possibly in the residence of Simon the leper (Mark 11:11, 14:3; Luke 21:37). The Mount figured prominently in the events of the Passion. Jesus made his triumphal entry into Jerusalem from the Mount of Olives (Matt 21:1–11; Mark 11:1–10; Luke 19:28–39; John 12:12–15). Jesus wept for the Jewish nation on the Mount while heading into Jerusalem (Luke 19:41–44). He also delivered his eschatological discourse with the city before his eyes (Matt 24; Mark 13). The cursing of the fig tree took place the day after the triumphal entry (Matt 21:17–19; Mark 11:11–14, 19–20). According to Luke, Jesus spent his evenings on the Mount (Luke 21:37), including the night of the Last Supper (Matt 26:30; Mark 14:26; Luke 22:39; cf. John 18:1) and the Agony in the Garden of Gethsemane (Matt 26:30, 36; Mark 14:26, 32; Luke 22:30; Jn 18:1). Here, too, Jesus was betrayed by Judas and arrested (Matt 26:47–57; Mark 14:43–50; Luke 22:47–54; John 18:12). Finally, the Ascension took place on the Mount of Olives (Acts 1:12).

OLIVET *See* **Olives, Mount of**.

OLYMPAS A Roman Christian to whom Paul sent greetings in Rom 16:15.

OMEGA The twenty-fourth and last letter of the Greek alphabet (Ω). (*See* **Alpha and Omega**.)

OMER A dry measure used by the Hebrews; the omer was one-tenth of an ephah, or about half a gallon (Exod 16:36).

OMRI The king of Israel in the ninth century B.C. (probably r. 885–874 B.C.). His time on the throne is covered in 1 Kgs 16:15–28, with the focus on his accession. He served as a general under his predecessor **Elah** and came to the throne after Elah was assassinated by **Zimri**. With the death of Elah, Omri's troops proclaimed him king, and a civil war began that did not end with Zimri's defeat and death because another rival, **Tibni**, put up four years of resistance until he finally died (1 Kgs 16:15–23). Omri had taken up residence at the royal city of Tirzah, but after six years he transferred his capital to Samaria (1 Kgs 16:24).

Politically, Omri was one of the most successful rulers of Israel. He managed not only to cement his own rule but also to establish a comparatively long-lasting dynasty. He established good relations with **Tyre** through the marriage of his son **Ahab** to **Jezebel**, and with Judah by the marriage of his daughter **Athaliah** to King **Jehoram** (2 Chr 22:2). He encouraged trade and commerce and waged a successful campaign against Moab, as attested in the inscription of King **Mesha** of Moab (Omri was the first king of Israel to be named in an extra-biblical source). But he also encouraged idolatry, and the sacred writers depict him as being even worse than his predecessors in doing what was displeasing to the Lord (1 Kgs 16:25–28; Mic 6:16).

ON (Egyptian *Iwnw*, "city of the pillar"; Hebrew *'ōn*, "house of the sun"; Greek *Heliopolis*, "city of Helios [the sun]") A city in ancient Egypt identified with modern Matariyeh, a suburb of Cairo. The name was taken from the role the city played as a center for the worship of solar deities by the Egyptians, especially of the gods Re and Atum. Little remains of the original city, save for two obelisks dating to the reign of Sesostris I. Developed as early as the predynastic period, On received the attentions of the dynasties of the old kingdom and became a highly influential priestly city. The city was mentioned in Genesis (41:45; cf. 41:50; 46:20) as the place where **Potiphera** served as a priest; **Joseph** was married to Potiphera's daughter **Asenath**. On was also the object of animosity by **Jeremiah** in an oracle of destruction (Jer 43:13).

ONAN The second son of **Judah** and the Canaanite woman Shua (Gen 38:2–4) and the brother of Er and Shelah. Judah had arranged the marriage between Er, his firstborn, and **Tamar**, but Er died prematurely because he had been displeasing to the Lord (Gen 36:7). As Er died childless, Tamar was left a widow and Onan was compelled to enter into a levirate marriage (*see under* **Marriage**) with Tamar to ensure the continuation of Er's line (Gen 38:8). Although Onan entered into the levirate marriage, he was unwilling to father a child who would not be his own; hence, when he engaged in sexual relations with Tamar he made his seed to fall to the ground (Gen 38:9) to avoid making Tamar pregnant. For his evil actions, God brought about his death (Gen 38:4–10).

ONESIMUS (Greek, "useful") The slave of **Philemon** who fled from his master's household in Colossae, met **Paul**, and was converted to the Christian faith (Phlm 10). Paul refers to him as "the faithful and beloved brother" (Col 4:9). Onesimus was sent back to Philemon with Tychicus carrying a letter of recommendation and the letter to the Colossians. His name was a common one for slaves, and Paul punned on it in his letter to Philemon: "Formerly he was useless to you, but now he is indeed useful to you and to me" (Phlm 11). Paul added that he sent Onesimus back with the plea to "receive him as you would receive me. If he has wronged you at all, or owes you anything, charge that to my account. I, Paul, write this with my own hand, I will repay it— to say nothing of your owing me even your own self" (Phlm 17–20). The mention of Onesimus provides a clear link between Colossians and Philemon.

ONESIPHORUS A Christian of **Ephesus** mentioned in 2 Tim 1:16–18. He had assisted Paul in Ephesus and had later searched out Paul during his captivity in Rome. There is also a greeting to the household of Onesiphorus in 2 Tim 4:19, along with the prayer that the Lord grant mercy to the household. Onesiphorus himself received the commendation, "may the Lord grant him to find mercy from the Lord on that Day—and you well know all the service he rendered at Ephesus" (2 Tim 1:18). Although he is not mentioned elsewhere in the New Testament, Onesiphorus figured prominently in the apocryphal *Acts of Paul* (3.2–7, 15, 23–26, 42).

ONIAS The name borne by several members of a high priestly family during the late fourth century to the middle of the second century B.C. Onias I was the son of Jaddua and served as high priest in Jerusalem during the period after **Alexander the Great**'s conquests. He served as high priest around 300 B.C. and was likely the Onias who reached an agreement with the Spartan king Areus (1 Macc 12:7, 19–23). He was the father of **Simon I**.

Onias II was the son of Simon I. He did not immediately succeed his father as high priest—that honor fell to his uncle Eleazar and then his grandfather's brother Manasses (Josephus, *Ant.* 12.44, 157). Onias II served as high priest around 227 B.C. He entered into disagreement with Ptolemy III Euergetes of Egypt (r. 246–221 B.C.), owing to his refusal to pay tribute (Josephus, *Ant.* 12.158–59). His son was the high priest Simon II.

Onias III was the son and successor to the high priest **Simon II** and served around 195 or 190 B.C. He benefited from the prestige that surrounded the high priesthood under his father, but his excellent relations with the Seleucid rulers were wrecked when the official **Heliodorus** attempted to seize the treasures of the Temple. Heliodorus was prevented from this deed by a horseman clad in gold, and an offering made by Onias healed Heliodorus from his injuries (2 Macc 3). This event led to

Onias's journey to Anitoch to defend himself on charges that he had arranged the entire affair (2 Macc 4:1–6). As these events transpired, Menelaus conspired to win the post of high priest and, with the assistance of **Andronicus**, Onias was assassinated. Andronicus was subsequently arrested by the king and put to death for the murder (2 Macc 4:30–38).

Onias IV was a son of Onias III but never served as high priest. He is not mentioned in the Old Testament but is known through Josephus (*Ant.* 13.62–73; cf. *Ant.* 12.387–88; 20.236).

OPHEL The southeastern ridge of Jerusalem, site of the original City of David. Various kings built projects in the area (2 Chr 27:3; 33:14). The walls of Ophel were repaired after the **Exile** (Neh 3:26–27; cf. 11:21).

OPHIR The son of Joktan according to the **Table of Nations** (Gen 10:29; 1 Chr 1:23). The region of Ophir was the source of large amounts of gold that were imported by Judah, especially during the reign of **Solomon** (1 Kgs 9:28, 22:49; 2 Chr 8:18). Ophir also exported fine wood and precious stones (1 Kgs 10:11; 2 Chr 9:10; Job 28:16), as well as silver, ivory, apes, and peacocks (1 Kgs 10:22). The goods were transported to Israel by merchant fleets through the port of Ezion-geber on the Gulf of Aqaba. Such was the quality of the gold that Ophir became synonymous with fine gold itself (Job 22:24; Ps 45:10; Isa 13:12). The location of Ophir is uncertain, although a number of sites have been proposed: western Arabia, Oman, Somalia, and even India.

OPHNI A town in Benjamin (Josh 18:23).

OPHRAH The name of two places in the Old Testament.

1. A town in Benjamin (Josh 18:23; 1 Sam 13:17), probably the modern et-Tayibeh north of Bethel. Ophrah was also later known as Ephron (2 Chr 13:17; 2 Sam 13:23; John 11:54).

2. A town of the clan of Abiezer in Manasseh associated with the judge **Gideon** (Judg 6:11, 24; cf. Josh 17:2; 1 Chr 7:18). Gideon not only lived there, he built an altar to the Lord there (Judg 6:24) and an ephod (Judg 8:27). Gideon was also buried in the town (Judg 8:32), and his son Abimelech slew all his brothers except Jotham there (Judg 9:5). The exact location for this Ophrah is unclear.

ORACLES *See* **Divination**; **Prophecy**; *see also* **Urim and Thummim**.

ORDEAL An ancient form of determining a legal case or accusation by submitting an accused person to some kind of pain or personal risk. In effect, the guilt or innocence of a person was left in the hands of a deity, so the accused who survived the trial by fire, water, or torture was declared innocent. A primitive and brutal form of legal examination, the ordeal was found to be practiced in some areas of the ancient Near East, but it found expression in Hebrew custom only in the case of adultery. Numbers 5:11–31 stipulated that a woman accused of adultery should be forced to drink "the water of bitterness that brings the curse." This form of ordeal is significantly milder than the ones found elsewhere in the Near East.

ORDERS, HOLY, SACRAMENT OF *See* **Priest, priesthood**.

OREB, ROCK OF *See* **Oreb and Zeeb**.

OREB AND ZEEB Two princes or chieftains of Midian who oppressed the Israelites during the time of Gideon. They were defeated and slain by the men of Ephraim under Gideon (Judg 7:25, 8:3; Ps 83:12) at "the rock of Oreb" and "the winepress of Zeeb."

ORIGINAL SIN *See* **Sin**.

ORION A constellation of stars (Job 38:31; Amos 5:8).

ORNAN *See* **Araunah**.

ORPAH A Moabite woman who became the wife of Chilion, son of Elimelech and Naomi; she was the sister-in-law of **Ruth** (Ruth 1:4; 4:10). After the deaths of Elimelech and his sons, Orpah chose to remain in Moab and returned to the family of her father while Ruth journeyed to Bethlehem with Naomi (Ruth 1:13–17). Orpah stands in contrast to Ruth in her decision to return to her "people and her gods" (Ruth 1:15), whereas Ruth declares to Naomi, "Your people shall be my people, and your God my God" (Ruth 1:16). Ruth then benefits from the rewards of that fidelity.

OSNAPPAR The Assyrian king who was responsible for transporting a number of Mesopotamian peoples to the region of Samaria (Ezra 4:10). It is not known which historical Assyrian ruler is meant: most likely Osnappar is an alternative name or title for Ashurbanipal.

OSTRACON (plural *ostraca*; Greek, "shell, sherd") A potsherd on which was written a short inscription. Ostraca were sometimes used for documenting official proceedings, but chiefly they were used because they were less expensive than other writing materials (e.g., papyrus or leather), and they were used for writing brief messages and letters, notes, receipts, and lists. Ink was normally used for writing on ostraca. Owing to their durability, large numbers of ostraca have been preserved.

OSTRICH A bird commonly found in the desert regions, especially in Africa (Isa 13:21, 43:20; Jer 30:29, 50:39). The ostrich is considered an unclean bird according to Hebrew law (Lev 11:16; Deut 14:15). The presence of the ostrich on the land was taken as an indication that the territory was uninhabitable. Job gave a meditation on the ostrich (Job 39:13–18) and called the bird cruel to its young.

OTHNIEL The son of Kenaz and the brother (or nephew) of **Caleb** (Judg 3:9; cf. Josh 15:17), and the first of the Judges of Israel (Judg 3:9–11). Othniel won the hand of Caleb's daughter Achsah by capturing the town of Kiriathsepher (Judg 1:11–15; cf. Josh 15:15–19). The name "Othniel" is also used as a clan or tribal name (1 Chr 27:15) of the tribe of Judah.

OUR FATHER *See* **Lord's Prayer**.

OX One of the most important domestic animals in the biblical world. It had a wide variety of uses: as a beast of burden, for plowing, and as a draft animal. Oxen were also used for threshing grain, and the owner was not permitted to place a muzzle on them (Deut 25:4; cf. 1 Cor 9:9). The care of the animal was subject to legislation (Exod 21:28–22:18), including requirements for rest and nourishment (Exod 23:12; Deut 5:14, 25:4). Considered a pure animal (Deut 14:4), the ox was ranked as a most precious animal for sacrifice (Exod 20:24; Lev 3:1).

P

P The letter used by scholars to designate the Priestly source, one of the hypothetical sources of the **Pentateuch** in the modern Documentary Hypothesis. (*See* **Pentateuch**.)

PAARAI One of the Thirty warriors in the service of King **David** (2 Sam 23:35); he was called "the Arbite" after his home village in Hebron, formerly called Kiriath-arba (Josh 15:54).

PADDAN-ARAM The plain of Aram, the name given to the region around **Haran** in upper Mesopotamia, where **Abraham**'s family lived before traveling to Canaan (Gen 25:20; 28:2; 31:18; cf. Gen 24:10). Here too lived **Laban**, whom **Jacob** served, and here most of Jacob's sons were born (Gen 29:31–30:24; cf. Gen 35:26; 46:15). The same general area is also called Aram-Naharaim.

PAGANS *See* **Gentile**.

PALESTINE The land at the eastern end of the **Mediterranean Sea**, north of Sinai and south of Lebanon. Palestine derived much of its importance from its location between the great river civilizations of the Near East: Mes-

opotamia and Egypt. But it was also a battle-ground for ambitious empires. At various times the region was ruled by **Egypt**, **Assyria**, **Babylon**, **Persia**, **Greece**, and **Rome**.

The region was also the stage on which the drama of salvation history unfolded. It was the land God gave to Abraham and his descendants (Gen 15:18–21). Its desirability and richness was expressed in Deuteronomy: "For the LORD your God is bringing you into a good land, a land with flowing streams, with springs and underground waters welling up in valleys and hills, a land of wheat and barley, of vines and fig trees and pomegranates, a land of olive trees and honey, a land where you may eat bread without scarcity, where you will lack nothing, a land whose stones are iron and from whose hills you may mine copper" (Deut 8:7–9).

Palestine was known historically by several designations, including **Canaan**, Israel, Judah, and Philistia. "Canaan" in the **Table of Nations** stretched from Sidon in the north to Gaza in the south and as far to the east as the Cities of the Plain (Gen 10:19; cf. Num 34:1–2; Josh 13:4). After the conquest of Canaan, the region was known as Israel (1 Sam 13:19; 1 Chr 22:2); it was later divided into Israel and Judah around 930 B.C., when the united kingdom of Solomon divided into two separate states. Under the Romans the name Judah, or Judea, was sometimes applied to the whole region (Strabo, *Geogr.* 16.2). The term "Palestine" came through Greek from the Hebrew for the land of the Philistines, Philistia (Herodotus, *Hist.* 7.89). The name became especially common after the Roman province was renamed Syria Palestina, to differentiate it from Coele-Syria and upper Syria. During the Middle Ages the term "Holy Land" came into common usage.

I. GEOGRAPHY

The traditional extent of the land settled by the tribes of Israel was "all Israel from Dan to Beer-sheba" (1 Sam 3:20; 2 Sam 17:11); when including the **Transjordan**, it was described as "from Dan to Beer-sheba, including the land of Gilead" (Judg 20:1).

Palestine is a relatively small area, forming a rectangle of approximately 9,700 square miles; its length is around 150 miles, and its width is as narrow as 25 miles in the north and as wide as 80 miles in the south. The northern boundary of Palestine is Mount Hermon—the southernmost mountain in the Anti-Lebanon range. The Mediterranean marks the western boundary; the eastern boundary is formed by the deserts beyond the Jordan River and the Dead Sea. The southern boundary is the Wadi el Arish, called the Brook of Egypt (Num 34:5). At times, land promised to Israel extended to the upper Euphrates (Gen 15:18; Exod 23:31; Deut 1:7; Josh 1:4). But the whole territory was never truly possessed until David's northern conquests gave Solomon a kingdom that reached such an extent (1 Kgs 4:21).

Palestine offers one of the most varied environments on the planet, from the heights of Mount Hermon, which dominates the valley of Lebanon, reaching over 9,000 feet in height (more than 2,700 meters), to the Dead Sea, the lowest spot on earth, that sinks to depths of 1,290 feet (about 400 meters) below sea level; Mount Hermon and the Dead Sea are little more than 150 miles apart. Palestine is described as "a land of hills and valleys, which drinks water by the rain from heaven" (Deut 11:11)—as opposed to Egypt, where little rain falls and the water comes from the Nile. Of particular note is the Jordan depression, a rift that cuts from the Gulf of Aqaba to northern Syria.

Geographers divide Palestine into five zones:

1. The coastal plain, which stretches along the Mediterranean, although it is cut into by Mount Carmel;
2. The **Shephelah**, the rolling hills between the coastal plain and the central mountains;
3. The central range, which runs north to south through Lebanon to Jerusalem and south into the arid region of the Negeb;
4. The Great Rift or Jordan Valley, including the Sea of Galilee and the Dead Sea;
5. The Transjordan, the area east of the Jordan, which is now part of the kingdom of Jordan.

II. CLIMATE

Because of its geographical diversity, Palestine's climate varies widely. A traveler can pass from subtropical conditions in the southern Jordan Valley to the colder mountaintops of the central range. Temperatures range from highs of 120°F (49°C) in the Jordan Valley to the more temperate coastal plain with an annual average of 67°F (19°C).

The year is divided into dry and rainy seasons (generally from June to October and October to June, respectively), with annual amounts varying from 20 to 28 inches (51 to 71 centimeters) on the coasts to significantly smaller amounts in the eastern desert regions and the southern Jordan Valley; the mountain ranges receive over 20 inches (51 centimeters) a year, and the average for Palestine is 20–22 inches (51–56 centimeters) annually.

Prevailing winds are from the west, but in early autumn and late spring a brutal east wind (cf. Gen 41:6; Isa 27:8) fills the air with choking dust.

PALM The date palm (*Phoenix dactylifera*) is found in abundance throughout the Middle East, from Mesopotamia across Palestine and into Egypt. In Palestine, its growth is limited to the coastal plain and the Jordan Valley, around Jericho (which is called the "city of palms," Deut 34:3; 2 Chr 28:15). Palm branches were signs of rejoicing (Lev 23:40). Crowds greeted Jesus with palm branches at his triumphal entry into Jerusalem: "The next day a great crowd who had come to the feast heard that Jesus was coming to Jerusalem. So they took branches of palm trees and went out to meet him, crying, 'Hosanna! Blessed is he who comes in the name of the Lord, even the King of Israel!'" (John 12:12–13). On this basis (cf. Rev 7:9), the palm is one of the symbols of the martyr.

PALM SUNDAY The Sunday before Easter and the beginning of Holy Week: it commemorates the triumphal entry of Jesus into Jerusalem (John 12:12–13).

PAMPHYLIA A region on the southern coast of Asia Minor between Pisidia, Cilicia, and Lycia. Its chief cities are Attalia, Coracesium, Perga, and Aspendus. According to tradition, Pamphylia was colonized by Greeks under Amphilochus and Calchas after the fall of Troy. Initially governed by kings, it passed into the control of the Persians until the conquest of Alexander the Great. Although it was briefly under the Ptolemies, it was mainly under the control of the Seleucids until 189 B.C., when the Romans took over. Pamphylia was attached to various Roman provinces, including Cilicia, Asia, and Galatia. In A.D. 43, Emperor Claudius created the province of Lycia-Pamphylia. The region had a sizable Jewish population (1 Macc 15:23; Acts 2:10). **Paul** and **Barnabas** evangelized in Pamphylia during Paul's first missionary journey (Acts 13:13; 14:24).

PAPAL PRIMACY The authority of the Bishop of Rome as pastor of the universal Church, inherited from **Peter**, to whom Christ gave the keys of the Kingdom (Matt 16:19). The pope has supreme jurisdiction over the Church and is always free to exercise this power over the Church's pastors and faithful. As the Second Vatican Council declares,

For our Lord placed Simon alone as the rock and the bearer of the keys of the Church, and made him shepherd of the whole flock; it is

evident, however, that the power of binding and loosing, which was given to Peter, was granted also to the college of apostles, joined with their head. This college, insofar as it is composed of many, expresses the variety and universality of the People of God, but insofar as it is assembled under one head, it expresses the unity of the flock of Christ. (LG §22; cf. 23)

Scripture teaches the primacy of Peter on a number of occasions. In the Gospels, the two key texts are Matt 16:16–19 and John 21:15–17. In Matthew, Peter was promised the primacy when Christ told him that he was to be the "rock" ("Cephas" and "Peter" both mean "rock") on which Christ would build his Church (Matt 16:18; cf. John 1:42): "And I tell you, you are Peter, and on this rock I will build my church, and the powers of death shall not prevail against it. I will give you the keys of the kingdom of heaven, and whatever you bind on earth shall be bound in heaven, and whatever you loose on earth shall be loosed in heaven." No other apostle was singled out to receive such blessings and responsibilities.

Peter's headship over the Church was confirmed in John 21:15–17:

When they had finished breakfast, Jesus said to Simon Peter, "Simon, son of John, do you love me more than these?" He said to him, "Yes, Lord; you know that I love you." He said to him, "Feed my lambs." A second time he said to him, "Simon, son of John, do you love me?" He said to him, "Yes, Lord; you know that I love you." He said to him, "Tend my sheep." He said to him the third time, "Si-

mon, son of John, do you love me?" Peter was grieved because he said to him the third time, "Do you love me?" And he said to him, "Lord, you know everything; you know that I love you." Jesus said to him, "Feed my sheep."

In Matt 10:2, Peter is listed as the "first" of the apostles. In Acts, Peter clearly acts in a leadership role over the Christian community: he initiates the effort to replace Judas (Acts 1:15); he is the first to preach after Pentecost (2:36–41); Jesus's healing power is manifest in him (5:14–15); he receives the revelation regarding the inclusion of the Gentiles (10:9–13); and he acts as the spokesman for the Christian faith in the Council of Jerusalem (15:1–12) (CCC 880–87).

The authority entrusted to Peter in the Gospels and exercised by him in the book of Acts was not meant to be his exclusive possession. In other words, his role as the chief shepherd of the Church amounts to an office designed to be filled by successors. That Jesus intended this can be seen in Matt 16:19, when he promises to give Peter "the keys of the Kingdom." Scholars generally recognize in this statement an allusion to Isa 22:22, where the "key" of the Davidic kingdom is passed from one officeholder to the next. In the days of the Davidic monarchy, it was the steward or prime minister (the Hebrew title translates as "the one who is over the house") who possessed this key and all the authority it symbolized. The prime minister was thus established as the highest-ranking official in the kingdom next to the king himself. The significance of Jesus's alluding to this episode in Isaiah is that the prophet describes the *succession* of the keyholder from one steward, Shebna, to the next, Eliakim (Isa 22:15–25). It is thereby understood that Peter, the first keyholder of Christ's Kingdom, would eventually pass his authority to a line of successors.

PAPHOS A city on the west coast of **Cyprus**. Paul visited Paphos on his first missionary journey (Acts 13:6–13). Here the apostle encountered the Roman proconsul Sergius Paulus and had a dispute with the Jewish magician Elymas.

PAPYRUS An aquatic reed (*Cyperus papyrus*) that grows in great abundance in Egypt and was used as a common writing material from around 3000 B.C. The name is derived from the Egyptian word for "river plant," as the reed was usually found in the marshes of the Nile Delta and to a lesser extent along the banks of the Nile River. Papyrus sheets were made by slicing the pith of the reed stalk into thin strips that could be laid out in a crisscross pattern and then pressed together. Sheets were then attached end to end to create a long strip of paper that could be rolled up to form a scroll. Papyrus scrolls were common in the Mediterranean world, and Egypt profited from its rich papyrus trade to the Near East and elsewhere.

PARABLE (Greek, "comparison") A short pictorial narrative designed to impart a lesson or truth in a memorable way.

Jesus's parables resemble those found in the Old Testament and rabbinic literature. The OT utilizes varied kinds of metaphors, proverbs, and riddles, but it also contains parables, such as Jotham's parable of the trees (Judg 7–15), the parable of the lamb that Nathan relayed to David (2 Sam 12:1–4), Isaiah's song of the vineyard (Isa 5:1–2), and Ezekiel's eagle and vine (Ezek 17:3–10). Like Jesus's parables, these stories evoke an immediate response, forcing the audience to think.

There are at least thirty parables preserved in the **Synoptic Gospels**, depending on how we define a parable. In John there are a few allegories that might be called parables—the Good Shepherd (John 10) and the Vine and the Branches (John 15:1–7) are the most prominent.

When Jesus's disciples asked him, "Why do you speak to them in parables?" he answered,

"To you it has been given to know the secrets of the kingdom of heaven, but to them it has not been given. For to him who has will more be given, and he will have abundance; but from him who has not, even what he has will be taken away. This is why I speak to them in parables, because seeing they do not see, and hearing they do not hear, nor do they understand. With them indeed is fulfilled the prophecy of Isaiah which says: 'You shall indeed hear but never understand, and you shall indeed see but never perceive. For this people's heart has grown dull, and their ears are heavy of hearing, and their eyes they have closed, lest they should perceive with their eyes, and hear with their ears, and understand with their heart, and turn for me to heal them.' But blessed are your eyes, for they see, and your ears, for they hear. Truly, I

say to you, many prophets and righteous men longed to see what you see, and did not see it, and to hear what you hear, and did not hear it." (Matt 13:10–17; cf. Mark 4:10–12; Luke 8.9–10)

The parables of Jesus were filled with vivid imagery and deep insights into personality, and they could be remembered easily. Deceptively simple, they proclaimed aspects of the Kingdom of God to the audience of the time and to people of all succeeding generations, while at the same time concealing the full depth of the mysteries of that Kingdom from the unbelieving.

THE PARABLES OF JESUS
The Sower (Matt 13:1–9; Mark 4:1–9; Luke 8:4–8)
The Seed Growing Secretly (Mark 4:26–29)
The Mustard Seed and the Leaven (Matt 13:31–32; Mark 4:30–32; Luke 13:18–19)
The Hidden Treasure (Matt 13:44)
The Pearl of Great Price (Matt 13:45–46)
The Wheat and the Weeds (Matt 13:24–30)
The Net (Matt 13:47–50)
The Lamp (Mark 4:21–23; Luke 8:16–18)
The Two Debtors (Luke 7:40–43)
The Friend at Midnight (Luke 11:5–8)
The Barren Fig Tree (Luke 13:6–9)
The Unjust Judge (Luke 18:1–8)
The Pharisee and the Publican (Luke 18:9–14)
The Unmerciful Servant (Matt 18:23–35)
The Good Samaritan (Luke 10:25–37)
The Lost Sheep (Matt 18:12–14; Luke 15:4–7)
The Lost Coin (Luke 15:8–10)
The Prodigal Son (Luke 15:11–32)

The Unjust Steward (Luke 16:1–9)
The Rich Fool (Luke 12:16–21)
The Two Builders (Matt 7:24–27; Luke 6:47–49)
The Laborers in the Vineyard (Matt 20:1–16)
The Two Sons (Matt 21:28–32)
The Wicked Tenants (Matt 21:33–46; Mark 12:1–12; Luke 20:9–19)
A Great Supper (Luke 14:15–24)
The Marriage Feast (Matt 22:1–14)
The Watchful Servants (Mark 13:33–37; Luke 12:35–38)
The Thief in the Night (Matt 24:42–44; Luke 12:39)
The Faithful Servant (Matt 24:45–51; Luke 12:41–48)
The Ten Bridesmaids (Matt 25:1–13)
The Pounds (Luke 19:11–27)
The Talents (Matt 25:14–30)

PARACLETE (Greek, "advocate," "counselor") A title given to Christ and the Holy Spirit. The term is used in the New Testament only five times (John 14:16, 26; 15:26; 16:1–14; 1 John 2:1); the RSV translates "Paraclete" as "Counselor" or "Advocate." In traditional Greek usage, the paraclete was a person who provided aid or assistance, especially in legal affairs. A paraclete thus was a kind of helper, as well as one who speaks on behalf of another. In John's writings, "Paraclete" is used both for Christ and for the Holy Spirit. It is applied once to Christ (1 John 2:1), "an advocate with the Father, Jesus Christ the righteous." Elsewhere the word refers to "the Holy Spirit, whom the Father will send in my name" (John 14:26). The Paraclete will bear witness to Jesus Christ

(John 15:26), will prove the world wrong about sin and righteousness and judgment (John 16:7–10), and will guide the apostles into all the truth (John 16:13). (*See* **Spirit, Holy**.)

PARADISE (A loan word from Persian, "garden" or "park") A "paradise" was an enclosed park usually attached to a royal palace; in it there would be trees, streams, pools, and even game animals. In essence, a paradise was a place of peace and beauty, so that the Greek word *paradeisos* was used in the **Septuagint** for the **Garden of Eden**, starting with Gen 2:8.

In later prophetic writings, the Messianic age is foreseen as a return to the paradise of Eden (Isa 11:6–9, 51:3; Ezek 36:35). The New Testament develops this concept further by situating true Paradise, not as a place on earth, but in a supernatural and heavenly realm. Paradise is the dwelling place of God, the abode of the saints (Rev 2:7), where Jesus and the good thief went after death (Luke 23:43); it is the place beheld by Paul in his mystical vision (2 Cor 12:3).

PARAN A wilderness in the eastern Sinai, south of Israel. **Hagar** and **Ishmael** came to Paran after they were expelled from Abraham's camp (Gen 21:21). The area was also traversed by the Israelites on their **Exodus** journey (Num 10:12; 12:16), and from there spies were sent out by **Moses** to inspect Canaan (Num 13:3). Numbers also describes Paran as the location of Kadesh, modern Tell el-Qudeirat (Num 13:26). David journeyed "to the wilderness of Paran" after the death of Samuel (1 Sam 25:1), but this Paran may have been a different place.

PARCHMENT The skin of an animal (sheep, goat, antelope, pig, cow, etc.) subjected to a lengthy process of washing, stretching, and scraping until it could be used as a writing surface. According to the Roman writer Pliny the Elder, parchment was supposedly invented by Eumenes II (197–159 B.C.) of Pergamum, owing to the need to find a substitute for papyrus during a conflict with the Ptolemies of Egypt, who had imposed a boycott. Sheets of parchment were generally stacked, folded, and bound along one side as a "codex," like a modern book. Parchment is mentioned in Scripture at 2 Tim 4:13.

PARMENAS One of the seven men appointed to care for the needs of Christian widows (Acts 6:1–5).

PAROUSIA A Greek term used in the Bible to mean "coming" or "presence." Sometimes the word refers to a person's arrival at a particular place (Jdt 10:18; Phil 1:26; 2 Cor 7:6). In other passages, it denotes a person's presence as distinct from his absence (1 Cor 16:17; 2 Cor 10:10; Phil 2:12). More important, the term is employed by New Testament writers to refer to the future coming of Christ as Judge, either in the first Christian generation (Matt 24:3) or at the end of time (1 Thess 4:15). Theological reflection also points to a connection between the coming of Christ in history and the presence of Christ in the liturgy of the **Eucharist**.

I. FIRST-CENTURY PAROUSIA

One meaning of *parousia* is developed in the apocalyptic discourse of Jesus. When Jesus shocks his disciples with a vision of the **Temple** in ruins, its massive stones thrown down in a heap of destruction (Matt 24:2), the question is put to him: "Tell us, when will this be, and what will be the sign of your coming and of the close of the age?" (Matt 24:3). Jesus answers with a dramatic description of chaos descending upon the world; for the prelude to his coming will be a time of unparalleled deception, persecution, and tribulation. After this, the tribes of the earth "will see the Son of man coming on the clouds of heaven with power and great glory" (Matt 24:30). The exact day and hour of this mighty event is not revealed. Nevertheless, Jesus does point to a time in the earliest days of the Church: "Truly, I say to you, this generation will not pass away till all these things take place" (Matt 24:34).

Such language indicates that Jesus was predicting the Roman conquest of Jerusalem that occurred some forty years later in A.D. 70. To the Jews of the first century, this was an event of unimaginable consequence, for not only did it involve the death or enslavement of more than a million Jews, but it ended with the fiery destruction of the Jerusalem Temple and spelled the end of Mosaic religion in terms of its sacrificial worship. Beyond that, Jesus gives himself the leading role in bringing this about, for his coming as the Son of Man is a coming in judgment of the city that rejected his Messianic claims (cf. Matt 26:63–65; Luke 19:41–44; John 19:15). This was not a visible coming, such that Jesus himself was seen at the head of the Roman army; rather, it was the spiritual coming of Christ in his Kingdom as Judge over the deeds of men (Matt 16:27–28).

II. THE FINAL PAROUSIA

Christians from earliest times also believed in the Second Coming of Christ, that final *episode* of history when Jesus will return in glory to judge the living and the dead. This belief too has its basis in the NT. It is perhaps best summarized in the book of Acts, where Luke writes about the day on which Jesus withdrew his visible presence from the world: "This Jesus, who was taken up from you into heaven, will come in the same way as you saw him go into heaven" (Acts 1:11). The notion that Christ would make his return "in the same way" implies a belief that Jesus will come again in his physical body—visibly, tangibly, gloriously, wrapped in the heavenly cloud that had taken him to the right hand of the Father (Acts 1:9; 2:32–33).

Additional revelation about the Second Coming and associated events is given in the Epistles. There we learn that Christ will come as Savior, for when he descends from heaven at the blast of the Lord's trumpet, he will raise the dead to life (1 Cor 15:23) and gather up the saints on earth to be with him forever (1 Thess 4:15–17). He will also come as the divine Warrior, for he will slay the man of lawlessness, often called the **Antichrist**, a villainous figure who will appear at the end of days to deceive the unbelieving world with demonic power (2 Thess 2:8). At that time, too, the present world will be transformed by fire into a new heaven and a new earth (2 Pet 3:12–13). Jesus's closest disciples—**Peter**, **James**, and **John**—caught a glimpse of his coming when they witnessed the unveiling of his glory at his

Transfiguration on the mount (2 Pet 1:16–18; cf. Mark 9:1–8).

Believers are to concern themselves, not with predicting the time of the final Parousia, but with preparing themselves for the event. They must be patient in waiting for the Lord to right the wrongs of the world, so that their hearts may be ready to receive him (Jas 5:7–8). This means they must be established in holiness (1 Thess 3:13), thoroughly sanctified in body, soul, and spirit (1 Thess 5:23). In the meantime, no one should be unsettled by claims that Jesus has already returned (2 Thess 2:1–2), nor should they be surprised when scoffers arise in the last days to mock the apparent delay of his coming (2 Pet 3:4).

III. THE LITURGICAL PAROUSIA

The NT never uses the Greek term *parousia* in connection with the Eucharist or with the rites of Christian worship in general. Still, the notion that Jesus "comes" to his people and is truly "present" in the Eucharist made such a connection both logical and meaningful in the minds of the early Christians. Indeed, the basis for linking the coming of the Lord in history with the presence of the Lord in sacrament is solidly grounded in Scripture.

The teaching of Christ is the starting point for developing a theology of the Real Presence along these lines. First, the synagogue discourse of Jesus in John 6:35–59 establishes with flesh-and-blood realism the presence of Christ's humanity in the Eucharist. Having stressed the necessity of placing faith in him as "the bread of life" (John 6:35–47), Jesus then insists that faith is manifested through eating this bread, which is none other than his "flesh" (John 6:51). He goes on to make powerful statements, made the stronger by force of repetition. Jesus calls for the consumption of his flesh and blood as the sacrament of everlasting life (John 6:53–58).

How his humanity would be given to believers as food is revealed in the Last Supper accounts (Matt 26:26–29; Mark 14:22–25; Luke 22:14–20). On this occasion, Jesus transforms the Jewish Passover meal into the central liturgy of Christian worship. He does this by consecrating bread and wine, which brings about a transformation of the bread and wine into his "body" and "blood" (1 Cor 11:24–25). Thus, without using the word *parousia*, the Gospels make it clear that Jesus makes his presence real in the elements of the Eucharist and so comes to his disciples as true food and true drink each time the Eucharistic liturgy is celebrated.

The teaching of **Paul** confirms this interpretive deduction. Regarding the presence of Jesus's humanity in the sacrament, the apostle asserts that Eucharistic communion is a genuine participation in both the "blood of Christ" and the "body of Christ" (1 Cor 10:16). Regarding the coming of Jesus in relation to the sacrament, he declares: "For as often as you eat this bread and drink the cup, you proclaim the Lord's death until he comes" (1 Cor 11:26). At one level, Paul contends that the Eucharistic liturgy is oriented to the return of Christ in glory. But this does not make the Eucharist a sacrament of the Lord's absence—a ritual the Church engages in while waiting around for his final coming. Certainly the Lord will come again; and when he does, he will come as

Judge (1 Cor 4:5). Yet Paul is aware that Jesus comes as Judge in the meal itself, for the one who partakes of the Eucharist unworthily profanes "the body and blood of the Lord" (1 Cor 11:27) and consequently "eats and drinks judgment upon himself" (1 Cor 11:29). In other words, Jesus the Judge comes to the world in the Eucharist before he comes to the world to reveal his glory. Both instances of Christ's true presence constitute a true *parousia* of Jesus Christ, the one being a sacramental anticipation of the other.

PARSHANDATHA One of the sons of **Haman**, the archenemy of the Jews in the book of Esther (9:7).

PARTHIANS An Iranian people who established a formidable empire in the Near East that endured from the middle of the third century B.C. to the late third century A.D. The Parthian Empire was a longtime rival of the Roman Empire. Jews lived in the territory of the Parthians, according to Josephus (*Ant.* 15.14), having been exiled there, and Parthian Jews were present in Jerusalem at the **Pentecost** (Acts 2:9).

PARVAIM A place that produced the gold used in Solomon's Temple (2 Chr 3:6). The location of Parvaim is uncertain; some suggest Farwa in Yemen or el-Farwein in Saudi Arabia.

PASCH *See* **Passover, feast of**.

PASHHUR (Egyptian, meaning perhaps "son of Horus" or "portion of Horus") The name of two men in the book of Jeremiah.

1. The son of Malchiah (Jer 21:1). With Zephaniah the priest, he was sent to **Jeremiah** by King **Zedekiah** to ask the prophet if there was any hope at all that Judea might be saved from the advancing Babylonians (Jer 21:1–10).

2. The son of Immer and a priest in charge of the Temple during the reign of **Zedekiah**. He had Jeremiah flogged and imprisoned for making dire predictions of the fall of Jerusalem. Jeremiah prophesied the doom of Pashhur and his family as exiles (Jer 20:1–6).

PASSION OF CHRIST The Gospel accounts of the suffering and death of Jesus Christ.

The Passion was a climactic event in salvation history. It took place "according to the definite plan and foreknowledge of God" (Acts 2:23), a plan that was willingly assented to by Christ (Mark 14:36; John 12:27; Phil 2:8). Christ thereby achieved the redemption of humanity as "the Lamb of God, who takes away the sin of the world" (John 1:29) (CCC 599–618).

The Passion narratives in each of the four Gospels are as follows: Matt 26–27; Mark 14–15; Luke 22–23; John 18–19. Scholars commonly consider these narratives to be the earliest part of the written Gospels. The narratives were almost certainly the result of an effort to record in written form what was already a well-established part of oral tradition concerning the death of the Messiah. The structure and content of the narratives were thus clearly in place before the literary work of the evangelists. According to the Pontifical Biblical Commission,

The sacred authors, each using an approach suited to his specific purpose, recorded this

primitive teaching in the four Gospels for the benefit of the churches. Of the many elements at hand they reported some, summarized others, and developed still others in accordance with the needs of the various churches. They used every possible means to ensure that their readers would come to know the validity of the things they had been taught . . . From the material available to them the Evangelists selected those items most suited to their specific purpose and to the condition of a particular audience. And they narrated these events in the manner most suited to satisfy their purpose and their audience's condition. (On the Historical Truth of the Gospels IX)

Because each of the four writers had his own purpose and audience in mind, the accounts differ slightly. Details important to one of the Evangelists might not have been important to another writing under different circumstances. Nevertheless, all four narratives are essentially the same; each Gospel's differences complement rather than contradict the other accounts.

I. HARMONY OF THE PASSION NARRATIVES

Because the narratives are basically the same, we can build a single narrative outline, noting the differences as we go:

- The conspiracy against Jesus (Matt 26:1–3; Mark 14:1–2; Luke 22:1–2; John includes the conspiracy [John 11:47–53] but omits it from his Passion narrative).
- The anointing at Bethany (Matt 26:6–13; Mark 14:3–9).

- The betrayal by Judas (Matt 26:14–16; Mark 14:10–11; Luke 22:3–6; John does not include this incident).
- The preparation of the Paschal meal (Matt 36:17–19; Mark 14:12–16; Luke 22:7–13; John omits the preparations).
- The Last Supper with a brief account of the institution of the Eucharist (Matt 26:26–29; Mark 14:22–25; Luke 22:14–23).
- The prediction of Peter's denial (Matt 26:30–35; Mark 14:26–31; Luke 22:31–34; John 13:36–38).
- The Agony in the Garden (Matt 26:36–46; Mark 14:32–42; Luke 22:40–46; John does not include this event).
- The arrest of Jesus (Matt 26:47–50; Mark 14:43–50; Luke 22:47–53; John 18:2–11; Mark adds the flight of the young man from the garden).
- Jesus appearing before Caiaphas and the Council and the denial of Peter (Matt 26:57–75; Mark 14:53–72; Luke 22:54–71).
- Jesus appearing before Pilate (Matt 27:1–2; Mark 15:1; Luke 23:1; John 18:28–32).
- The trial of Jesus before Pilate (Matt 27:11–14; Mark 15:2–5; Luke 23:2–5; John 18:33–38; only Luke [23:6–12] has Jesus appearing before Herod).
- Jesus is condemned to die (Matt 27:15–26; Mark 15:6–15; Luke 23:13–25; John 18:39–19:16; the details of the trial vary among the Evangelists—e.g., Luke omits the scourging, Matthew alone includes the dream of Pilate's wife and the washing of Pilate's hands, and John has a much more detailed sequence).

- Jesus is mocked (Matt 27:27–31; Mark 15:16–20; Luke omits this scene and John [19:2–5] includes it after the scourging and before the condemnation).
- The Crucifixion (Matt 27:33–44; Mark 15:22–32; Luke 23:33–43; John 19:17–27; Luke alone includes the exchange between Jesus and the thief, and John alone uses the dialogue between Pilate and the Jews concerning the titulus; John also is unique in reporting that Jesus consigned the care of Mary to the beloved disciple).
- The death of Jesus (Matt 27:45–56; Mark 15:33–41; Luke 23:44–49; John 19:28–37; all but John report darkness coming over the land; Matthew uses an earthquake to add to the upheaval of nature, adding to the tearing of the veil in Mark; Luke and John report neither of these events).
- The burial of Jesus (Matt 27:57–61; Mark 15:42–47; Luke 23:50–56; John 19:38–42).

II. UNIQUE DETAILS IN EACH VERSION

As we have seen elsewhere, there are many minor differences among the Gospel accounts.

Unique to Matthew is the washing of Pilate's hands, the dream of Pilate's wife, the earthquake, and the death of Judas.

Unique to Mark is the story of the young man who fled naked, the description of the Temple as "made with hands," the explanation that Simon of Cyrene was "father of Alexander and of Rufus," and Pilate's asking for proof of the death of Christ.

Luke is the only Evangelist to record the presence of the angel in Gethsemane, Christ's sweating of blood in the Garden, the appearance before Herod, and three of the seven utterances from the Cross: the prayer for Jesus's executioners; the episode of the penitent thief; and the final declaration, "Father, into thy hands I commend my spirit." Luke is also alone in writing of the impact of the Crucifixion upon those who witnessed the event.

John, who almost certainly wrote his account after the Synoptic Gospels were already in circulation, differs the most in his presentation of the Passion. Probably assuming that his readers were familiar with the events of the Synoptics, John felt free to omit the institution of the Eucharist, the Agony in the Garden, and the trial before Caiaphas. Yet John incorporated various events that were not found in the Synoptics: Pilate's desire to release Jesus; the presence of Mary at the foot of the Cross, including Jesus's placing her in the care of the beloved disciple; the piercing of his side by the soldier's lance with the subsequent issue of blood and water; and the breaking of the legs of those on the crosses beside Jesus. Many scholars believe that John had the Gospel of Luke before him when he wrote his narrative, and they cite numerous parallels (John 13:2 and Luke 22:3; John 13:4–20 and Luke 22:24–27; John 18:23 and Luke 22:67–68; John 18:38, 19:4, 6 and Luke 23:4, 14, 22; John 19:12 and Luke 23:2; John 19:25–26 and Luke 23:40–43; John 19:30 and Luke 23:46).

PASSOVER, FEAST OF One of the most important feasts of the Israelite calendar. The word "Passover" is an echo of the verb *pāsaḥ*, "pass over," indicating that the feast was instituted to commemorate the deliverance of Israel from Egypt when the angel of death passed over the Israelites' firstborn (Exod 12:13, 23, 27). According to the Law, after nightfall on Nisan 15, the Israelite family gathered together and ate the Paschal lamb that had been slaughtered (the lambs were slaughtered in the final hours of Nisan 14 but not eaten until after the twilight gave way to nightfall and hence in the first hours of Nisan 15). The entire ceremony commemorated the departure from Egypt, and the family ate while dressed for a journey, sandals upon their feet and staff in hand ready for an immediate departure. The final celebration of the Passover by Jesus marked the institution of the Eucharist and the priesthood of the New Law (CCC 1362–66).

I. THE PASSOVER CELEBRATION

The chief requirements for the celebration of Passover are found in Exod 12:1–28. In this context, Passover was a solemn ritual to be performed in order to protect Israel from the last plague on Egypt—the visitation by the angel of death who claimed the lives of every Egyptian firstborn. The ritual required that a lamb be slaughtered on the fourteenth day of the first month (Exod 12:1–6). Its blood was to be smeared on the doorpost so that the angel would recognize the sign and pass over to the next house (Exod 12:7). The roasted lamb was served with unleavened bread and bitter herbs (Exod 12:8–11). The remains were then ritually burned before the next day.

Every generation to come was required to celebrate the annual feast of Passover, and part of the ritual was reciting the reason for the ritual: "It is the sacrifice of the LORD's passover,

for he passed over the houses of the people of Israel in Egypt, when he slew the Egyptians but spared our houses" (Exod 12:27). In its retelling, the Passover event would be brought alive for each generation so that there would be a direct link between the saving actions of God in the past and his saving deeds in the present.

In the Passover celebration of later times, Ps 113–118 were sung at different points during the course of the meal. The gathering of the family for the meal was the occasion that permitted the head of the family to teach the children about the nature and purpose of the festival (Exod 12:25–27; 13:6–10). Other ritual requirements stipulated that no one who was not circumcised should be permitted to eat the Passover meal (Exod 12:43–49). According to Deuteronomy (which ordered the feast around the central sanctuary), every male Israelite was obliged to make a pilgrimage to Jerusalem each year to participate in a national celebration of Passover (Deut 16:2).

II. PASSOVER CELEBRATIONS IN OLD TESTAMENT HISTORY

Passover was celebrated at **Gilgal** when the Israelites first entered Canaan (Josh 5:10–12). When Jerusalem became the center of Israelite religion, the Passover sacrifice had to take place at the central sanctuary (Deut 16:1–8). In order to accommodate the centralizing of the feast, lambs were slaughtered throughout the afternoon before the feast, which began at sundown. Also, the sacrificial animal no longer had to be a lamb or a goat (Exod 12:5) but could be a cow from the herd (Deut 16:2). Families would still regularly share in the Passover meal together, but the feast was placed within the context of the sanctuary where the meal was to be eaten. Passover had become the chief national feast, which celebrated the election of Israel as the people of God.

In spite of the explicit provisions of the Law, the celebration of the Passover was neglected. Two great revivals of the Passover feast are linked with the two great reforms of the monarchical period: the reforms of King **Hezekiah** (2 Chr 30:1–27) and King **Josiah** (2 Kgs 23:21–23; 2 Chr 35:1–19).

III. PASSOVER AND THE NEW TESTAMENT

By New Testament times, the Passover had regained its place as the great feast of the Jewish nation (Mark 14:1; John 2:13, 18:28; Acts 12:4). Luke 2:41, for example, notes that the Jews normally celebrated Passover in Jerusalem with many thousands of other pilgrims. The eating of the Passover happened in the midst of this throng.

Christ's death and Resurrection took place during the celebration of the Passover, and the NT depicts Jesus as the new Passover Lamb. The **Eucharist** that was instituted at the Last Supper serves as the memorial of Christ's Passover and makes real and present his sacrifice (Luke 22:14–23; 1 Cor 11:23–26). Hence, because it makes the Exodus event real and present, the traditional memorial of Passover assumed a new significance and meaning when the celebration of the Eucharist was instituted. Christ remains ever present through the Eucharist: "he is able for all time to save those who draw near to God through him, since he always lives to make intercession for

them" (Heb 7:25). Christians commonly refer to Easter, the feast of the Resurrection, as the Paschal Feast.

IV. THE DATE OF CHRIST'S PASSOVER

The date of the Passover in the Gospel accounts is debated. All four Gospels agree that Jesus died on a Friday; he lay in the tomb throughout the Sabbath, and on Sunday the tomb was discovered to be empty (Matt 28:1; Mark 16:1; Luke 23:1; John 20:1). It would appear, however, that there is a disagreement between John and the Synoptic Gospels as to whether that Friday was Passover (John) or not (the Synoptics). The Synoptic Gospels state that Jesus celebrated Passover with his disciples (Matt 26:17–20; Mark 14:12–17; Luke 22:7–15) and died the next afternoon (Matt 27:45; Mark 15:33; Luke 23:44). John says that Jesus died on the afternoon before Passover, noting that the Jewish officials could not enter the Roman praetorium for fear of becoming unclean (John 18:28; 19:14, 42). Passover appears to be on Thursday night in the Synoptics, but on Friday night in John.

Calendrical studies now seem to indicate that the chronology of John is correct with respect to the lunar calendar followed by the authorities of the Jerusalem **Temple**. Calculations indicate that Passover fell on Friday night in both A.D. 30 and 33, and in fact it never fell on a Thursday night between A.D. 27 and 34. Since nearly all scholars place the death of Jesus in A.D. 30, and none but the most radical historians would place it outside the window of A.D. 27–34, it follows that John's account accurately depicts the date of Passover accepted by mainstream Jerusalem.

What, then, of the Synoptic Gospels, which have Jesus and his disciples celebrating a Passover meal before Good Friday? One possibility, though difficult to account for, is that Jesus celebrated an anticipatory Passover a day ahead of the official calendar of the Temple. Another possibility is that Jesus celebrated the Passover meal of the Last Supper according to a different Jewish calendar from the one observed in the Temple.

It is a fact that not all Jews of the first century followed the lunar calendar of the Temple. Some, like those who wrote the Dead Sea Scrolls, followed a solar calendar instead. One distinctive feature of the solar calendar is that Jewish feasts always fell on the same weekday year after year. Passover, for example, always began on Tuesday night. Some scholars who have worked to reconcile John and the Synoptics have theorized that Jesus may have celebrated the Last Supper on Tuesday night of Holy Week rather than Thursday night. This would explain why the Synoptics insist that Jesus's final meal was in fact a Paschal meal in a true sense, even though most Jews would not have eaten the Passover until Friday night of that week (as John indicates). Hypothesizing that Jesus observed a Tuesday Passover is attractive but not entirely certain. Still, there is some early Christian tradition that indicates that this was the case (*Didascalia Apostolorum* 5.12–18; Saint Epiphanius, *Panarion* 51.2; and Victorinus of Pettau, *De Fabrica Mundi* 3).

PASTORAL EPISTLES The name usually given to the three Pauline Epistles addressed to individuals rather than to congregations (1 and 2 Timothy and Titus).

PATARA A seaport in the region of Lycia, in southwestern Asia Minor (modern Turkey). The city was located at the mouth of the Xanthus River. Paul made a brief stopover at Patara when returning from his final missionary journey (Acts 21:1–2).

PATHROS (Hebrew, from the Egyptian for "south country") Upper Egypt, meaning the region south of the Delta. According to the Table of Nations (Gen 10:14), the Pathrusim were descendants of Egypt, the grandson of **Noah** and the son of **Ham**. The region was also a destination of Israelites after the fall of Jerusalem in 586 B.C. (Isa 11:11; Jer 44:1) and was named as a place of divine judgment (Ezek 30:14).

PATMOS One of the Sporades Islands in the Aegean Sea off the western coast of Asia Minor. The island is best known as the place to which **John** was banished for having preached the Gospel. It was here that he received the visions that are recorded in Revelation (Rev 1:9). The banishment of John is consistent with Roman custom of sending prisoners to islands, and the craggy Sporades Islands were one of the known destinations (Pliny, *Nat.* 4:69–70; Tacitus, *Ann.* 4:30).

PATRIARCH The head of a tribe, family, or clan in biblical history. More narrowly, the prominent male figures of the book of Genesis, especially **Abraham**, **Isaac**, and **Jacob**. The book of Acts also gives the title "patriarch" to the twelve sons of Jacob and to King **David** (Acts 2:29) (CCC 61, 205).

The main history of the patriarchs is narrated in Gen 12–50, which may be divided into three broad parts focusing on the stories of Abraham (Gen 12–25), Isaac (Gen 25–26), and Jacob and his descendants (Gen 27–50).

The patriarchs were the first bearers of God's promise to future generations (see **Covenant**). Genesis 12–50 narrates a series of linked promise episodes that trace the beginnings of the plan of salvation in human history. The remaining books of the Bible chart the fulfillment of these promises as they build up to a final fulfillment in Christ (CCC 704–6, 2570–74). The patriarchs are thus more than the genealogical fathers of Israel: they are the spiritual fathers of all who believe (Heb 4:1–28). Thus Abraham's righteousness made him "the father of all who believe" (Rom 4:11; cf. Gen 12:2, 15:5–6).

PATROBAS A Christian of Rome who received greetings from Paul in Romans (16:14).

PATROCLUS The father of **Nicanor**; he was an official in the Seleucid army (2 Macc 8:9).

PAU The royal city of King Hadar of Edom (Gen 36:39; cf. 1 Chr 1:50).

PAUL, OR SAUL OF TARSUS One of the greatest theologians, writers, and missionaries in the history of the Church. Paul had a decisive role in the spread of the Christian faith and was known as the apostle to the Gentiles (Rom 11:13).

Paul's letters make up approximately one-third of the New Testament. The letters attributed to Paul are Romans, 1 and 2 Corinthians, Galatians, Ephesians, Philippians, Colossians, 1 and 2 Thessalonians, 1 and 2 Timothy, Titus, and Philemon; the Letter to the Hebrews may also have connections with the apostle. (*See also under individual letters for other details on Paul.*)

I. *Life of Paul*
   A. *Early Life and Conversion*
   B. *Missionary Labors*
   C. *Imprisonment*
   D. *Final Years*
II. *Paul's Theology*
   A. *Theology of the Trinity*
   B. *Theology of Salvation*
   C. *Theology of the Church*

I. LIFE OF PAUL

A. Early Life and Conversion

The book of Acts and his own writings give us little information about the early life of Paul. Born Saul in the town of Tarsus, in the Roman province of Cilicia, he was a Jew of the tribe of Benjamin (Rom 11:1; Phil 3:5), but he also possessed Roman citizenship—a useful privilege that entitled him to important legal rights (Acts 22:25–29). He was sent at some time to Jerusalem, where he studied "at the feet of Gamaliel," the famous rabbi (Acts 22:3), and became a zealous member of the **Pharisees** (Acts 26:5). Paul thus received an excellent education and was one of the most erudite and learned figures in the early Church.

He first encountered the Christian faith in Jerusalem, where the Church had taken root. Saul was an inveterate enemy of the Church and was present at the martyrdom of Saint Stephen, "consenting to his death" (Acts 7:58–

8:1). He was still a young man when he assumed a leading role in the persecution of the Christians (Acts 7:58, 26:10; 1 Cor 15:9; Gal 1:13).

He was "still breathing threats and murder against the disciples" when he set out for Damascus to arrest Christians (Acts 9:1–2). On his way he was stopped by a vision of the risen and glorified Christ, an event that is recounted three times in the book of Acts (Acts 9:1–19; 22:5–16; 26:12–18). With overwhelming clarity he understood that the Jesus who was worshipped by the Christians he had persecuted was the divine Messiah. This extraordinary event forever changed his life and mission.

Left blind by the light, Saul was taken to Damascus where he sat in darkness for three days. After he was baptized by **Ananias** (Acts 9:17–18), Saul accepted the challenge offered to him by God, and his sight was restored. Leaving Damascus (an event described in Gal 1:17 but not mentioned in Acts), Saul withdrew into Arabia, presumably for prayer and meditation. He then returned to Damascus and began preaching the faith. Owing to the danger of being seized by the governor under King **Aretas** of Nabatea and possibly being murdered by the local Jews (Acts 9:23–25; 2 Cor 11:32), Saul made a secret escape from the city, being lowered over the wall in a basket.

B. Missionary Labors

Three years later he came to Jerusalem to spend more than two weeks with the apostle Peter (called "Cephas," Gal 1:18). Perhaps around A.D. 46, Saul was at Antioch in Syria where the Holy Spirit declared: "Set apart for me Barnabas and Saul for the work to which I have called them" (Acts 13:2).

Here Acts mentions that Saul "is also called Paul" (Acts 13:9), and from here on the narrative calls him Paul. He may well have had both names most of his life: even today, many orthodox Jews retain the custom of having a Jewish name for family and synagogue, and a Gentile name for business with the outside world. Acts thus begins to call Paul by his Gentile name when his mission to the Gentiles gets under way.

The First Missionary Journey

Paul and Barnabas, along with **Mark**, set out on what is called the first missionary journey to Cyprus and southern Asia Minor (Acts 13:4–14:28). Paul preached and founded Christian communities in Antioch, Pisidia, Iconium, and elsewhere.

His strategy was to seek out the local synagogue as the base of his missionary operations and move on from there. In this way he was able to reach both Jews and Gentiles with the Gospel message. At Lystra, where he cured a cripple, Paul and Barnabas were revered by the crowd as gods (Acts 14:8–18). His labors also caused local disturbances, and at one point he was stoned by a mob and left for dead (Acts 14:27). Nevertheless, the return of Paul and Barnabas to Antioch (ca. A.D. 49) brought with it Paul's joyous declaration that the Gentiles were eager for conversion and that "he had opened a door of faith" to them (Acts 14:27).

At the end of this first mission, which was one of the early efforts at systematic outreach to non-Jews, Paul was forced to confront the theological question of whether Gentile converts needed to be circumcised according to the **Law** of Moses. Since some Jewish Christians insisted on circumcision, Paul brought the matter to Jerusalem, where the Church's first council convened in about A.D. 49. Paul's stance was vindicated when Peter and the elders made it clear that circumcision was *not* to be forced on Gentile believers who had come to embrace the Gospel (Acts 15:1–11).

Second Missionary Journey

Paul set out on the Second Missionary Journey (around A.D. 50) with **Silas** (Acts 15:36–18:22). It lasted about two years. He traveled to Tarsus and then revisited the churches of Asia Minor. **Timothy** joined him at Lystra (Acts 16:1–3). It is possible that at this time he converted the Galatians of central Asia Minor (*see* **Galatians, Letter to the**). Paul was then told in a vision to go to Macedonia. He crossed the Hellespont and thus brought the faith into Europe. Reaching Philippi, he made his first convert, a Macedonian named Lydia, who came from Thyatira (Acts 16:14–15). After being imprisoned briefly for exorcising a slave girl of a "spirit of divination" (Acts 16:16–18), Paul journeyed to Thessalonica, Beroea, and then Athens. In Athens he encountered Greek philosophers, including Stoics and Epicureans. They listened to his words but were largely unmoved (Acts 17:16–34), and Paul moved on to Corinth. He stayed there for some time, well over a year, firmly establishing the Christian community there (Acts 18:1–18). Leaving Greece, he sailed to Palestine and rejoined the church in Antioch.

Third Missionary Journey

The Third Missionary Journey began soon after (around A.D. 53) (Acts 19:1–21:16). He paid another visit to Asia Minor and then went to Ephesus, where he stayed for two years and taught in the "hall of Tyrannus" (Acts 19:4–10). While at Ephesus, he also wrote his First Letter to the Corinthians. His departure proved necessary owing to the rioting of silversmiths who were upset at the shrinking business in the shrine of the goddess Artemis (Acts 19:23–41).

Going on to Philippi, in Macedonia, he wrote his Second Letter to the Corinthians. Proceeding to Corinth, he wrote his magnificent letter to the Romans, but he kept his sojourn a short one, his intention being to gather money to relieve the hunger then afflicting the Christians in Judea (Rom 15:25–26; 1 Cor 16:3). On his way back to Jerusalem, he met the elders of the church at Ephesus in Miletus, bidding them a tearful farewell with the premonition of his impending imprisonment and martyrdom (Acts 20:17–37).

C. Imprisonment

Back in Jerusalem, he was attacked by his Jewish enemies, beaten by a mob, and rescued from death by a squad of Roman soldiers (Acts 21:27–36). When he was subsequently brought before the Sanhedrin on charges of bringing Gentiles into the Temple, he skillfully divided the council by appealing to the Pharisees' belief in the resurrection against the Sadducees' denial of it (Acts 22:30–23:10). Invoking his rights as a Roman citizen, he was sent to Caesarea for trial before the governor. The procurator Felix put him in prison for two years (ca. A.D. 58–60), and the trial was held only under Felix's successor Porcius Festus. Paul, as was his right, appealed to Caesar; so off to Rome he went, after meeting and much impressing King **Herod Agrippa** (Acts 25–26). Under Roman guard, Paul sailed for Rome and was shipwrecked on the island of Malta (Acts 27:1–28:10). When he finally reached Rome, he was warmly received but kept under house arrest for about two years (ca. A.D. 60–62, Acts 28:11–31). He probably wrote his letters to the Colossians, the Philippians, Philemon, and perhaps the Ephesians (the so-called captivity Epistles) while in Rome.

D. Final Years

Details about his final days are not given in the NT. Some maintain that Paul must have been martyred at the end of his imprisonment in Acts 28. Others give a more probable account—namely, that Paul must have been released to continue his missionary activity, traveling perhaps as far west as Spain (*1 Clem.* 5.7) and as far east as Crete (Titus 1:5). Arrested again, he was taken back to Rome, kept in close confinement, and apparently knew his death was imminent, as is clear from his Second Letter to Timothy (in particular 2 Tim 4:6–8). He was martyred around A.D. 67 by Emperor Nero, most likely beheaded as reported by Tertullian. According to the apocryphal *Acts of Paul*, his place of martyrdom was on the left bank of the Tiber; he was said to have been buried in a cemetery on the Via Ostia owned by a Christian named Lucina, the site where the Basilica of S. Paolo Fuori le Mure (St. Paul-Outside-the-Walls) was built.

II. PAUL'S THEOLOGY

Paul's theology is not found systematized and set forth in a single treatise; it must be gleaned from his many epistles. Indeed, he is often considered the greatest theologian of early Christianity, and his teaching has had an enormous influence on Christian thinking ever since.

A. Theology of the Trinity

Several times Paul affirms the Jewish doctrine of monotheism—the belief that God is "one" and has revealed himself as the God of the Bible (Rom 3:30; Gal 3:20; 1 Tim 2:5). However, he discovered in the Gospel another truth, namely, that God, who is Father, has an eternal Son (Gal 1:16). The Son of God is likewise the divine Lord, and through him the created world came into being (1 Cor 8:4–6). He humbled himself and came into the world as the man Jesus Christ, so that all might be saved through him (Phil 2:5–8; 1 Tim 1:15). Christ is thus the image of the unseen God (Col 1:15), the one in whom "the whole fullness of deity dwells bodily" (Col 2:9). His death for the sins of the world was a powerful sign of God's love for the world (Rom 5:8).

The mystery of God unfolded still more when Paul realized that the Spirit was also the divine Lord (2 Cor 3:17). The Spirit, like the Son, was sent forth from the Father for a saving mission to the world (Gal 4:4–7). Indeed, the divine Spirit is both the "Spirit of God" and the "Spirit of Christ" (Rom 8:9). As such, he alone can be said to search out and comprehend the thoughts of God (1 Cor 2:10–11). Through his indwelling in the believer, the love of God is poured out in the human heart, producing in our lives a fruitful harvest of "love, joy, peace, patience, kindness, goodness, faithfulness, gentleness, self-control" (Gal 5:22–23).

In essence, Paul teaches that God is a trinity of divine persons (2 Cor 13:14), through whom the gifts of God are given to men (1 Cor 12:4–6) and the whole drama of salvation is orchestrated and brought to fulfillment (Eph 1:13–14).

B. Theology of Salvation

Paul is rightly known for his teaching on salvation, which is fuller in his writings than in any other writings of the NT. Its essence is set forth in the Pauline doctrine of **justification**—that is, his teaching that believers are made righteous in Christ (Rom 5:19) and made sons of God through the Spirit (Rom 8:14–15). Justification constitutes a salvation from sin and death and separation from God (Acts 13:38–39; Rom 5:9–11). It is the world's rescue from the fallen condition of Adam and the dominion of darkness to a state of peace with God in the Kingdom of his Son (Rom 5:1, 12–21; Col 1:13–14). Justification takes place in the liturgical context of **baptism** (1 Cor 6:11).

On the one hand, Paul insists that salvation is not a human achievement; it is not something we can earn or merit for ourselves by good works (Rom 3:28; Eph 2:8–9; Titus 3:5). His point is that no human action, nothing but the grace of God can establish us in Christ or make us sons of God. On the other hand, the gift of salvation must be received by faith (Rom 3:21–26; Gal 2:15–16, 3:26), which in Paul's theology involves not only mental

acceptance of the Gospel, but also an obedient response to the full range of the demands it makes upon the Christian (Rom 1:5; 2:13; 6:17–22). This includes such things as keeping the commandments of God (Rom 13:8–10; 1 Cor 7:19) and submitting to the leading of the Spirit (Rom 8:1–7).

C. Theology of the Church

In several places, Paul expounds a theology of the Church. His is not an individualistic vision of each believer being in a private relationship with Christ, but a collective vision of all Christians bound together in union with the Lord. No one image or metaphor can capture the full breadth of Paul's doctrine, and so we see varied depictions of the Church throughout his letters.

Most prominently, Paul depicts the Church as the body of Christ. In this vision, Christ is the head of the body, and the baptized are members of this body, each one taking its direction from the head and having a unique role to play (1 Cor 12:12–31; Eph 4:15, 5:23). Related to this, the Church is also the Bride of Christ, united with him in the most intimate ways; Christian marriage is a visible image of this greater reality (Eph 5:21–33; cf. 2 Cor 11:2). The background of this notion is the Old Testament image of the Lord as the husband of his covenant bride, Israel (Isa 54:5; Jer 3:1; Ezek 16; Hos 2:16).

The Church, according to Paul, is also intimately united to the Holy Spirit, not just individually, but again collectively. Just as the Spirit dwells within each believer, thereby making him or her a temple of the Spirit (1 Cor 6:19), so the assembly of the faithful together constitutes the living temple of the Spirit (1 Cor 3:16; 2 Cor 6:16). This image brings out the holiness of the Church as a dwelling place of Almighty God (Eph 2:19–22).

The family of God is perhaps the most pervasive image of the Church in Paul. Unlike other prominent notions, the familial description is not confined to particular pockets in the Pauline letters; it is something that extends throughout. For instance, every time the apostle addresses his readers as "brothers," he is working with the assumption that every Christian is a spiritual sibling of the next. The basis for this is not in the realm of metaphor at all. Rather, it is a consequence of the grace of adoption that makes all believers "sons" and "children" of God in relation to the Father (Rom 8:14–17; Gal 4:4–6). The gift of divine sonship in Christ was intended by God from before the foundation of the world (Eph 1:4–5). Paul's many references to Christians as "heirs" are also connected with this theology of spiritual kinship (Rom 8:17; Gal 4:7; Eph 1:14; Col 3:24; Titus 3:7).

PAULINE Having to do with **Paul**; an adjective often used to describe his theology or his writings.

PAULUS, SERGIUS The Roman proconsul of Cyprus and a convert to the Christian faith through Paul during the apostle's first missionary journey (Acts 13:7–12). (*See also* **Elymas**.)

PE The seventeenth letter of the Hebrew alphabet (פ).

PEACE Harmony between persons and especially between God and man. Peace in the Bible is more than the absence of conflict or war: it signifies completeness, well-being, and what Saint Augustine called the "tranquility of order" (*City of God* 19.13).

The Hebrew word generally translated "peace"—*šālôm*—was understood in a host of senses. It was a common greeting and expression of regards and best wishes (cf. Gen 43:27; Exod 4:18). It also expressed a state of affairs between men characterized by peace that was achieved by treaties and covenants (cf. Josh 9:15; 1 Kgs 5:12). Above all, peace was the blessing that came from living faithfully to one's **covenant** with God (Lev 26:3–13). The Lord desires peace and welfare for his people (Ps 35:27).

Peace is the gift of God, so Israel hoped for a Messiah to restore peace (Zech 9:9; cf. Isa 2:2–4, 11:1–9; Hag 2:7–9); the Messiah was called the Prince of Peace (Isa 9:6). Hence, peace truly is more than the mere end of fighting; it is more closely related to spiritual well-being. Prosperity and health are good, but they likewise are not peace without righteousness (Isa 48:18; 60:17).

In the New Testament, the term for peace, *eirēnē*, is used ninety-two times, mainly with the Old Testament understanding of *šālôm*. Peace is offered to another in greeting (John 20:19), and it is stressed as an expression of order and harmony (Luke 19:42; 1 Cor 14:33). The deeper themes of the OT are also still present, but they are elevated in light of the Gospel: "Peace I leave with you; my peace I give to you" (John 14:27). Christ is the fulfillment of the Messianic expectations.

The peace offered by Jesus is a peace between God and man. We are reconciled to God through Christ's suffering and death (Col 1:20), so the soul of the Christian enjoys peace (Rom 5:1) and is left undisturbed by the strife of the world (John 14:27; 16:33). The Christian must follow Christ by wishing peace to all he or she meets (Matt 10:12) as Christ greeted the disciples with "Peace be to you" (Luke 24:36; John 20:21, 26). Christians must live in peace with one another (Rom 12:18; Eph 4:3; Heb 12:14) and proclaim the Gospel in the world and so bring peace among individuals, families, and nations (Matt 5:9; Heb 12:14; Eph 2:14–18; Jas 3:18), especially peace between Jews and Gentiles (Eph 2:14–16) (CCC 1716, 1829, 1832, 1941, 2302–17). (*See also* **Repentance**.)

PEACE OFFERING. *See* **Sacrifice**.

PEARL A gem largely unknown in the ancient world until the fourth century B.C. and the campaigns of Alexander the Great. The pearl is therefore not mentioned in the Old Testament. In the New Testament, the pearl is viewed as something of enormous value (Matt 7:6). Jesus compared its worth to the Good News of the Kingdom: "Again, the kingdom of heaven is like a merchant in search of fine pearls, who, on finding one pearl of great value, went and sold all that he had and bought it" (Matt 13:45).

PEKAH The king of Israel from around 740 to 732 B.C., and the son of Remaliah. He was a soldier in the service of King **Pekahiah** and succeeded to the throne after assassinating the king (2 Kgs 15:23–25). His chief policy was to oppose the Assyrians, and toward that end he allied himself with Rezin of Syria and put pressure on King **Jotham** and his successor **Ahaz** to join their alliance. Pekah marched on Jerusalem and tried unsuccessfully to besiege it (2 Kgs 16:5; Isa 7:1–9). In the face of this onslaught, Ahaz made himself a vassal of Tiglath-pileser III of Assyria. The Assyrians invaded Syria, captured Damascus, and then invaded Israel. In the wake of this catastrophe, a conspiracy emerged in the palace. Pekah was assassinated by **Hoshea**, quite possibly with the connivance of the Assyrians (2 Kgs 15:25–31).

PEKAHIAH The king of Israel from around 742 to 740 B.C., and the son and successor of **Menahem**. His reign proved a brief one (2 Kgs 15:22–26) owing to a conspiracy that culminated in his assassination and the succession of the soldier **Pekah**, son of Remaliah. Pekahiah continued his father's vassal relations with the Assyrians, who were then advancing westward and claiming tribute from subject states (2 Kgs 15:19–20). This foreign policy was a source of great irritation to many in the kingdom of Israel, and it was probably the reason for his assassination.

PEKOD An Aramean tribe that lived to the east of the Tigris River (Ezek 23:23). Assyrian records show that an Aramean tribe, the Puqudu (probably the same tribe), were defeated by the Assyrian kings Tiglath-pileser III, Sargon II, and Sennacherib, and were vassals thereafter, although they did not lose their fiercely independent spirit. The Pekod were mentioned by Jeremiah in his predictions of Babylon's fall (Jer 50:21).

PELEG (Hebrew, from a root meaning "divide") The son of Eber, the brother of Joktan, and the father of Reu (Gen 10:25; 11:16–19; 1 Chr 1:19, 25). During his long life "the earth was divided" (Gen 10:25)—an expression that could refer to the geographical dispersion of different peoples or possibly to the development of artificial irrigation through canals (cf. Isa 30:25).

PELETHITES A group of mercenaries who served King David. (*See* **Cherethites and Pelethites** for details.)

PELUSIUM A city in Egypt, east of the modern Suez Canal, that was mentioned by Ezekiel in his oracle against Egypt (Ezek 30:15–16).

PEN A tool for writing. The typical writing instrument of the ancient world was the stylus, made of bone, metal, or ivory with a sharpened tip used to inscribe text on wax, clay tablets, or even stone (cf. Job 19:24; Jer 17:1). The ink pen is not mentioned with great frequency (Ps 45:1; Jer 8:8), but typically it was a reed cut at an angle toward the bottom to create a tip and used on such surfaces as parchment, vellum, or papyrus (3 John 13). A scribe normally carried a penknife that was used to sharpen the reed to maintain its point (Jer 36:23).

PENANCE *See* **Repentance**.

PENINNAH One of the two wives of **Elkanah**, the father of **Samuel** (1 Sam 1:2, 4). It is possible that she was married to Elkanah because his other wife, **Hannah**, was barren (1 Sam 1:2). As she gave birth to several children, Peninnah mocked Hannah because she had as yet produced no children (1 Sam 1:6–7). Hannah, thanks to blessings from God, gave birth to four sons and two daughters (1 Sam 1:21; 2:21).

PENTATEUCH The name Christian tradition gives to the first five books of the Bible: Genesis, Exodus, Leviticus, Numbers, and Deuteronomy. In Hebrew, they are known collectively as *tôrâ*, meaning "instruction" or "teaching." "*Tôrâ*" was routinely translated *nomos*, "law," in the Greek Septuagint. The Greek title *pentateuchos*, meaning "five volumes," was coined in the second century A.D.

I. UNITY AND DIVISION

The five books of the Torah constitute a single, continuous work with an unbroken story line that extends from the Creation of the world to the threshold of Israel's conquest of Canaan. Some scholars maintain that the text's original author(s) did not envision the fivefold division we are familiar with today. Whether or not this is so, the separation of the text into five books is first evidenced in the Greek Septuagint, a translation that was undertaken in the third century B.C. Perhaps the division was made for the sake of convenience, since a typical papyrus scroll could contain only about one-fifth of the total text of the Pentateuch. Since that time, the division of the text into five books has been the norm.

II. MOSAIC AUTHORSHIP

The great majority of Jewish and Christian scholars down through the centuries have believed that **Moses** was the author of the Pentateuch. For the most part, the basis for this judgment is found in the Pentateuch itself, where Moses is depicted as an author who kept a written record of Israel's triumph over the Amalekites (Exod 17:14) and a travelogue of Israel's Exodus journey through the wilderness (Num 33:2). He is also the alleged author of the Song of Moses (Deut 31:19), of various laws revealed at Sinai (Exod 24:4; 34:27), and of the extensive law code embodied in Deuteronomy (Deut 31:9, 24). No claims are made in the Pentateuch that an author other than Moses composed any of its parts.

Outside the Pentateuch, the law of Israel is exclusively identified with the figure of Moses (Josh 8:32; 1 Kgs 2:3; Ezra 6:18; Neh 8:1). Jewish tradition took this to mean that the Law was not only mediated by Moses but also written down by him (e.g., Josephus, *Ant.* 4.326; Mishnah, *Aboth* 1.1). The tradition that Moses authored the Torah is likewise evidenced in the New Testament in statements made by Jesus (John 5:46–47), Paul (Rom 10:5), and the Sadducees (Mark 12:19).

The corollary of Moses's authorship is the dating of the composition of the Pentateuch in the time of the lawgiver. Depending on how one dates the early history of Israel, this would place the composition of the work in the latter half of the second millennium B.C., either in the 1400s or possibly in the 1200s.

III. MULTIPLE AUTHORSHIP

Adherence to the traditional view of Mosaic authorship eventually began to wane as the European Enlightenment got under way. Questions had been occasionally raised before this time about perceived problems and odd-ities in the text, but these queries had little impact on the thinking of most theologians. A turning point came in the eighteenth century, when a French physician named Jean Astruc published a theory in 1753 that Moses had used two main sources (along with other sources) in putting together the book of Genesis. These sources were differentiated based on what form of the divine name was used in the Hebrew narrative—whether it was Elohim (God) or Yahweh (Lord). Soon others began to theorize about the possibility that additional oral and written sources might underlie the present form of the Pentateuch.

The critical figure in refining and advancing these new developments was the German scholar Julius Wellhausen (1844–1918). He reworked earlier theories that were already in circulation and formulated his own classic synthesis called the Documentary Hypothesis (also called JEDP). According to this paradigm, the five books of Moses have nothing to do with Moses at all. Wellhausen contends, rather, that the Pentateuch was pieced together from four different sources that date to four different periods in Israel's history. The alleged documents were named the Yahwist source (J), the Elohist source (E), the Deuteronomist source (D), and the Priestly source (P).

The story of composition told by Wellhausen and later advocates runs as follows.

1. The Yahwist source (J) is the oldest of the four and appeared in Judah in the tenth century B.C. It was a long document in the form of an epic narrative that highlighted the connection between Abraham and the rise of the Davidic monarchy. Its style was simple, it pre-

ferred to use the name Yahweh for God, and it tended to describe Yahweh in anthropomorphic terms.

2. The Elohist source (E) originated in northern Israel around the ninth century B.C. It too was an epic narrative—though shorter and more fragmentary than J—and it highlighted the importance of persons and places connected with northern Israel. It tended to be moralistic, it preferred the Hebrew name Elohim for God, and it viewed God as distant and transcendent. After the final collapse of the northern kingdom in 722 B.C., refugees from the north fled to the south with the E document, at which time it was joined to the J document.

3. The Deuteronomist source (D) arose in the seventh century B.C. out of Levitical circles in Israel. Although it retells part of the Exodus story, it is more concerned with preaching the fundamentals of Mosaic religion and centralizing the worship of Israel in the Jerusalem Temple. It is said that an early form of Deuteronomy, which embodies most of the D source, was planted in the Temple archives to be discovered during Josiah's reform in 622 B.C. (the "book of the law" mentioned in 2 Kgs 22:8). Not long afterward the D source was joined to the JE narrative.

4. The Priestly source (P) is the latest of the four documents and dates to the time of the Exile in the sixth century B.C. It is largely concerned with genealogies, with priestly rubrics of worship, and with cultic notions of holiness. Most of the P material is embodied in the book of Leviticus, although parts of it are found in various places in Genesis, Exodus, and Numbers as well. Those responsible for incorporating P into the JED text are regarded as the final editors of the Pentateuch. The appearance of the Torah in its final form could thus be dated to the fifth or fourth century B.C.

Nineteenth-century scholars also developed critical theories along different lines. Some advocated a Fragmentary Hypothesis, which envisioned the Pentateuch as a collage of small, independent stories that an editor strung together into a coherent chronological narrative. Others formulated a Supplementary Hypothesis, which preferred the idea of one main story line underlying the Pentateuch, to which supplements of tradition were added over time. Nevertheless, the Documentary Hypothesis advanced by Wellhausen and others proved to be the most influential account of Pentateuchal origins in the twentieth century.

IV. MODERN DEVELOPMENTS

The Documentary Hypothesis has undergone some modification since its original formulation, yet it continues to dominate Pentateuchal studies in many academic sectors. Still, in the minds of many, it reigns like a king without an heir; that is, it no longer has the consensus that it once had, but no large-scale, alternative hypothesis has arisen to take its place. Instead, many scholars have redirected their energies away from the question of hypothetical sources in favor of looking at the text in its final, canonical form. Literary critical studies, for instance, prefer to examine the text holistically, tracing themes and motifs that stretch across large segments of narrative, rather than breaking the text down atomistically into its pre-canonical parts. Such approaches are more interested in the literary strategy of the Pentateuch than in the literary strata that have long occupied the attention of source critics.

Catholic scholarship has dealt with the rise of modern Pentateuchal theories in different ways at different times. In the early twentieth century, when the Documentary Hypothesis was taking the academic world by storm, the Pontifical Biblical Commission addressed the origin of the Pentateuch and defended a fundamentally conservative view of its composition. Unwilling to sweep aside the tradition of Mosaic authorship, the Commission explored ways to maintain the tradition and still account for the phenomena of the text as it stands. The Commission allowed for the possibility that Moses made use of secretaries, that he may have incorporated oral and written traditions into the work, and that later scribes may have updated the work in several places to make it more intelligible to later readers (Pontifical Biblical Commission, *On the Mosaic Authorship of the Pentateuch*, June 27, 1906). This declaration, though not infallible or strictly doctrinal, served as a standard of Catholic orthodoxy until the 1940s, when Pope Pius XII allowed Catholic scholars to make cautious use of historical-critical methods in the interpretation of the Bible (*Divino Afflante Spiritu*, 1943). Although optimistic scholars remained confident that such study would support rather than undercut the role

of Moses in the formation of the Pentateuch (Pontifical Biblical Commission, *Letter to Cardinal Suhard*, 1948), and Pope Pius XII himself had to insist that Genesis 1–11 was uniquely but authentically historical (*Humani Generis*, 1950), an alarming number of Old Testament scholars quickly went the way of rationalist criticism, which meant embracing the critical theories that were in vogue at the time and severing the link between Moses and the composition of the Pentateuch.

Where Catholic and non-Catholic scholarship will go from here is uncertain. It is certain only that debates about the authorship, date, and formation of the Pentateuch will go on. Likewise, methods of biblical interpretation, so central to this issue, will continue to be critiqued, refined, and, in some cases, replaced. So long as believers maintain focus on the canonical text and remain attentive to its message, new discoveries and insights can be expected to come forth to enrich our understanding of Scripture's first five books.

PENTECOST The feast of the **Law** of Moses originally known as the feast of Weeks (Deut 16:10) or the feast of Harvest (Exod 23:16). Later, among Greek-speaking Jews, the feast came to be called Pentecost (Tob 2:1). The Greek *penētkostē* means "fiftieth" and refers to the timing of the festival, which took place fifty days after the spring celebration of **Passover** (Lev 23:15–16). Pentecost became a Christian feast when the Holy Spirit rushed down on the apostles seven weeks after Jesus celebrated his final Passover (Acts 2:1–4).

In the Old Testament, the feast of Weeks

(Pentecost) is one of three major feasts listed in Exod 23:14–17 (where it is known as the harvest festival), along with the festival of Unleavened Bread and the festival of Ingathering at the end of the year (cf. Exod 34:22). In Lev 23:15–21, the feast is calculated to occur seven weeks from the day of the presentation of the first sheaf of the barley harvest during the Passover celebration. In Num 28:26–31 and Deut 16:9–12, it is known as the "feast of Weeks." Tobit 2:1 and 2 Macc 12:32, as well as Josephus (*Ant.* 3.252), refer to it to as the festival or feast of Pentecost.

In ancient Israel, the feast of Weeks was a harvest festival. Loaves of bread baked with wheat from the spring harvest were offered to the Lord as a gift of the first fruits (Lev 23:15–17). It was also a day of sacred rest and worship with prescribed sacrifices (Num 28:26–31). The Deuteronomic **covenant** made it a pilgrimage feast requiring participants to celebrate the holy rites in the Jerusalem sanctuary (Deut 16:9–12). In later times, the feast of Pentecost was also a time to remember the giving of the **Law** on Mount **Sinai**.

The Christian feast of Pentecost is celebrated on the seventh Sunday after Easter. According to Acts, on the day of Pentecost the apostles were gathered in one house in Jerusalem when the Holy Spirit descended upon them, sounding like a mighty wind and appearing as tongues of fire upon each of them. The apostles then miraculously spoke in foreign languages, went forth preaching the gospel without fear or hesitation, and Peter delivered a sermon that resulted in the conversion and baptism of some three thousand people (Acts 2:1–47). Pentecost is thus remembered as the founding of the Church as the bearer of God's Spirit to the world (CCC 731–32, 767, 1076, 1287, 2623).

PENUEL (Hebrew, "face of God") A place just east of Palestine where the Jabbok River meets the Jordan River; it is best known as the place where Jacob wrestled with the angel (Gen 32:22–32). In memory of the event, Jacob named the place Penuel, "the face of God." The people who settled on the site refused to assist **Gideon** with food during his pursuit of the Midianite kings, Zebah and Zalmunna. Angered by this, Gideon returned to Penuel and destroyed the city tower and slaughtered the male inhabitants (Judg 8:8–9, 17). The site is probably the modern Tell edh-Dhahab esh-Sherqiyeh.

PEOPLE OF GOD *See* **Church.**

PEOR A mountain in **Moab** northeast of the **Dead Sea** and across from **Jericho**. Its precise location is not certain. **Balaam**, who was hired by **Balak** to curse Israel and ended up imparting his blessings instead (Num 22–23), gave his final blessing from the top of Peor (Num 23:28). The Israelites were camped upon the plain below (Num 24:2). Peor was also the site of Israelite apostasy when the generation who grew up in the wilderness worshipped the god **Baal** according to the local pagan rites (Num 25:1–3; cf. Deut 4:3; Josh 22:17).

PERAZIM, MOUNT *See* **Baal-perazim.**

PEREA The name of the territory east of the lower Jordan during New Testament times. It is not mentioned by name in the Gospels but is designated by the expression "beyond the Jordan" (Matt 4:25, 19:1; Mark 3:8, 10:1; John 3:26).

PERESH The son of Machir and his wife, Maacah, of the tribe of Manasseh (1 Chr 7:16).

PEREZ (Hebrew, "breach") The son of **Judah** and his daughter-in-law **Tamar** (Gen 38:29; 1 Chr 2:4, 4:1) and the brother of Zerah (Gen 38:30). His birth provided the origin of his name. When the time came for Tamar to give birth to her twins, "one put out a hand; and the midwife took and bound on his hand a scarlet thread, saying, 'This came out first.' But as he drew back his hand, behold, his brother came out; and she said, 'What a breach you have made for yourself!' Therefore his name was called Perez" (Gen 38:27–29). Perez appears in the genealogy of Jesus in the New Testament (Matt 1:3; Luke 3:33).

PERFECT Complete and without flaw.

The Old Testament witnesses to the utter perfection of God. God's works are perfect (Deut 32:4; Ps 18:30), as is his **Law** (Ps 19:7). God wills us to blameless perfection as well. Perfection consists in faithful observance of the **covenant** with all its precepts for liturgy and life (Gen 17:1; Deut 18:13; cf. Gen 6:9; 1 Kgs 8:61).

In the New Testament, Christ demands of his followers: "You, therefore, must be perfect, as your heavenly Father is perfect" (Matt 5:48). This requirement includes faithful obedience to the commandments (Luke 1:6), making a constant effort to live for Christ (Phil 3:12),

and enduring trials while remaining steadfast in faith (Jas 1:4). For some, Christ's call can even mean renouncing property to live in poverty of spirit (Matt 19:21). The bond of perfection is love: "And above all these put on love, which binds everything together in perfect harmony" (Col 3:14).

PERGA A city in Pamphylia on the southern coast of Asia Minor (modern Turkey). Perga was the main religious center for Pamphylia and boasted a temple of Artemis. The city was visited by **Paul** and **Barnabas** on Paul's first missionary journey (Acts 13:13; 14:25). There John **Mark** left Paul and Barnabas and returned to Jerusalem.

PERGAMUM A major city in western Asia Minor (modern Bergama in Turkey) and one of the seven churches addressed in Revelation (Rev 1:11; 2:12–17). Pergamum was located north of Smyrna and was reached from the Aegean Sea by ships sailing up the Caicus River. Aside from its many temples and its importance as a commercial center, Pergamum was also widely known for its parchment industry.

PERIZZITES One of the pre-Israelite tribes of **Canaan** (Gen 15:20; Exod 3:8; Deut 7:1; Josh 3:10). The Perizzites were not driven from the land (Judg 3:5), but King Solomon subjected them to forced labor in the time of the Israelite monarchy (1 Kgs 9:20–21).

PERSEPOLIS (Greek, "Persian city") An ancient capital of the Persians, along with such cities as Susa, Ecbatana, and Babylon. It is identified as modern Takht-i Jamshid. The city was conquered and destroyed by Alexander the Great after he defeated the Persian Empire. Persepolis is mentioned in the Bible only in 2 Macc 9:2.

PERSIA The largest single empire ever to have spread across the ancient Near East. It succeeded the Neo-Babylonian kingdom in the sixth century B.C. and continued until its conquest by Alexander the Great in 330 B.C. The Persians were an Indo-European people who migrated into the Iranian plateau in the late second millennium B.C. At some point, they settled Parsua, west of Lake Urmia; they are mentioned in ninth-century B.C. Assyrian records as sending tribute to Shalmaneser III. From these obscure beginnings, the Persians gradually grew strong and positioned themselves to overthrow the Babylonian Empire.

The first truly significant Persian ruler was Hachmanish (Greek Achaemenes), who founded the Achaemenid Dynasty in the late eighth century. His successors extended Persian influence into Anshan, northwest of Susa, and under Cyrus I (r. 640–600 B.C.), they were able to establish themselves east of the Persian Gulf. This territory henceforth bore the name of Persia. The Persian Empire was forged by **Cyrus** II the Great (r. 559–530 B.C.). He rebelled against his overlords, the Medes, and seized the Median royal city of Ecbatana in 550 B.C. The Medes nevertheless exercised considerable influence on the language and customs of the Persians. Cyrus then marched westward and conquered Croesus of Lydia in 547 B.C., thereby claiming supremacy over Asia

Minor, including the Ionian Greeks who had settled in Anatolia. From there, he marched against the Babylonians. The dilapidated Babylonian Empire fell before his armies, and Babylon itself was captured in 539 B.C. after a siege of seventeen days.

The rise of the Persians had a direct influence on events of the Old Testament. With the collapse of the Babylonian Empire, Cyrus II became ruler over all of the conquered peoples who had long lived under the domination of the Babylonians. Among them were Jewish exiles. Cyrus departed radically from the customs of the Near Eastern rulers who had preceded him. Rather than adopt the practice of forced migrations of defeated peoples, Cyrus instead treated vassal states with respect and even permitted deported groups to return to their homelands. This policy had momentous ramifications for the Jews, large numbers of whom had been forcibly moved by the Babylonians. Cyrus issued a decree in 538 B.C. permitting the Jews to return to Palestine and was generous in his terms: the Temple could be rebuilt, and the vessels plundered by **Nebuchadnezzar** were to be returned to Jerusalem (2 Chr 36:22–23; Ezra 1:1–11). The official text of the edict is presented in Ezra 6:2–5. The prophets saw Cyrus as God's chosen instrument; Isaiah even calls him the Lord's anointed (Isa 45:1; *see* **Messiah**).

Under Persian king Darius I, the decree of Cyrus was confirmed, the rebuilding of the Temple was finished, and the Temple was dedicated in Jerusalem in 515 B.C. Many of the Jews, however, preferred to remain in the land of exile, where they had prospered, especially under the Persians. Esther became the royal wife of Xerxes I (**Ahasuerus**; Esth 2:16–17), and Nehemiah was commissioned by Artaxerxes I to be governor of Jerusalem (Neh 5:14). Likewise, Ezra was an important advisor at the Persian court (Ezra 7:12) and was sent as a special envoy to Jerusalem. The Persians were thus crucial in the restoration of Judah and Jerusalem in the period after the Exile.

PERSIANS *See* **Persia**.

PERSIS A Roman Christian who received greetings from Paul in Romans (Rom 16:12).

PESHITTA *See* **Versions of the Bible**.

PETER (Greek *petros*, "rock") Simon Peter, apostle of Jesus Christ, leader of the Twelve, and chief shepherd of the early Christian Church. He is seen and heard frequently in the Gospels and Acts and is the alleged author of two New Testament epistles, 1 and 2 Peter (1 Pet 1:1; 2 Pet 1:1).

I. DISCIPLE OF JESUS

Peter was originally known as Simon the son of John (John 1:42) and the brother of Andrew (John 1:40). He was a fisherman from **Bethsaida**, a small community just north of the Sea of Galilee (John 1:44) and was married (Matt 8:14). He also had a residence in **Capernaum** (Mark 1:21, 29).

Jesus called Simon to be a disciple at the beginning of his ministry. In Matthew, Mark, and Luke, Simon receives the summons to follow Christ while he is fishing (Matt 4:13–20;

Mark 1:16–18; Luke 5:1–11). In John, we learn of another encounter arranged by Simon's brother Andrew (John 1:40–42). On this occasion we discover that Jesus had intentions to change Simon's name to Peter: "So you are Simon the son of John? You shall be called Cephas" (John 1:42). "Cephas" is an Aramaic term that means "rock" and is rendered in Greek as *petros* or Peter. The formal change of his name comes later in the ministry when Simon confesses the divine sonship of Jesus (Matt 16:16). In response, Jesus makes Simon the foundation of the future Christian community: "I tell you, you are Peter, and on this rock I will build my church" (Matt 16:18). Hereafter the apostle is known mostly as Peter or Simon Peter, although Paul also refers to him by the Aramaic designation Cephas (1 Cor 1:12; 9:5; 15:5; Gal 2:9, 11, 14).

The change of Simon's name signals a change in Simon's mission. He was not to be one apostle among others, but the one who ranked "first" among the Twelve (Matt 10:2). He thus enjoyed an especially close relationship with Jesus (Matt 17:24–27) and was privileged, along with James and John, to witness such marvels as the raising of Jairus's daughter (Mark 5:37) and the Transfiguration (Matt 17:1–8). Peter likewise acted as the spokesman for the twelve apostles (Matt 15:15; Mark 9:5, 10:28; Luke 12:41; John 6:67–69).

The prominence of Peter in the Gospels is much more than honorary. Jesus conferred great responsibilities on him. As the "rock" and foundation of the Church, he was entrusted with the "keys of the Kingdom" and given the authority of heaven itself to "bind" and "loose" as the chief steward and teacher of Christ's disciples on earth (Matt 16:19). Confirmation of Peter's role is given after the Resurrection, when Christ commissions Peter to "Feed my lambs . . . Tend my sheep . . . Feed my sheep" (John 21:15–17). He is thus to represent and act on behalf of Jesus "the good shepherd" (John 10:14). No other apostle is singled out by Jesus for such an exalted mission.

Yet Peter struggled to remain faithful to Christ as the events of the Passion began to unfold. When authorities came to arrest Jesus in Gethsemane, Peter reacted with violence and cut off the ear of a man named Malchus (John 18:10–11). When questioned about his ties with Jesus as he lingered in the high priest's courtyard, Peter three times denied even knowing Christ (Matt 26:69–75). Jesus had foreseen this bout with cowardice (Mark 14:29–30) and had encouraged Peter to "strengthen" the brethren once Peter had turned back again after his fall (Luke 22:31–32).

Finally, Peter was the first apostle to inspect the empty tomb (Luke 24:12; John 20:3–7) and the first of the Twelve to see Jesus risen again (Luke 24:34; 1 Cor 15:5) (CCC 442, 552–53, 765, 880–81, 1429).

II. SHEPHERD OF THE CHURCH

Peter also features prominently in the early chapters of the book of Acts, which describe the founding of the Church in Jerusalem and the initial spread of the Gospel (Acts 1–12). His role in these earliest days is precisely what one would expect after reading the Gospels: he stands out among the apostles as the principal teacher, shepherd, and decision maker of the early Church.

His leadership played out in a variety of circumstances.

1. After the Lord's Ascension, Peter made the decision to replace Judas Iscariot with another qualified eyewitness, in order to reestablish the number of apostles at twelve (Acts 1:15–26).

2. On the day of Pentecost, when the Spirit rushed upon the disciples in the upper room, it was Peter who took the lead in preaching to the crowds as the Church's head evangelist (Acts 2:14–36), urging them to receive baptism (Acts 2:37–41).

3. The first person in Christian history to be healed in the name of Christ was healed by Peter (Acts 3:1–10).

4. Peter was recognized as the acting head of the Church when he was arrested by the Sanhedrin (with John) and was pressed to give an account of his evangelism (Acts 4:1–12).

5. Church discipline was first administered by Peter, who caught two members of the early community, Ananias and Sapphira, telling lies (Acts 5:1–11).

6. When the Samaritans first embraced the Gospel, Peter was called upon to approve their becoming members of the Church and to confer the Spirit upon them (Acts 8:14–17).

7. Peter was the first Christian authority to evangelize and baptize the Gentiles after the Lord revealed his will regarding the Gentiles in a vision (Acts 10:1–48).

8. Peter played the most decisive role in the earliest ecclesiastical council, the Council of Jerusalem (Acts 15; *see* **Jerusalem, Council**

of). Though others such as James assumed leadership roles in proposing a pastoral strategy for Christian fellowship (Acts 15:13–21), it was Peter, as the chief spokesman for the faith, who ended the lengthy debate about circumcision with a solemn doctrinal pronouncement: "we believe that we shall be saved through the grace of the Lord Jesus, just as they will" (Acts 15:11).

Outside of these main episodes, little else is recorded in the NT regarding Peter's ministry and movements. The book of Acts indicates that Peter moved on from the church in Jerusalem to another place in the early forties A.D. (Acts 12:17). The Pauline Epistles indicate that Peter played host to Paul in Jerusalem soon after the latter's conversion (Gal 1:18), that he later spent time in the Syrian city of Antioch, an occasion when Paul was forced to rebuke Peter for compromising his message under pressure from others (Gal 2:11–14), and it appears that Peter had come to Corinth in southern Greece sometime before the mid-fifties A.D. (1 Cor 1:12). Peter's two epistles, most likely written in the mid-sixties A.D., reveal his pastoral concern for churches in northern Asia Minor (1 Pet 1:1; 2 Pet 3:1) and indicate that he was writing from Rome (under the code name "Babylon" in 1 Pet 5:13).

III. FINAL DAYS

The NT says nothing about the end of Peter's life. Christian tradition, however, fills in some of the details. Eusebius of Caesarea, a fourth-century historian, relays a tradition that Peter first came to Rome during the reign of Emperor Claudius between A.D. 41 and 54 (*Hist. Eccl.* 2.14), and many ancient writers agree that Peter spent the final years of his life in the imperial capital (in agreement with 1 Pet 5:13). Eusebius later says that Peter was martyred in the Roman capital; he was crucified upside down at his own request (*Hist. Eccl.* 3.1). Saint Irenaeus of Lyon, a second-century churchman, makes the claim that Peter and Paul were cofounders of the Church of Rome (*Against Heresies* 3.3). Peter's martyrdom has been dated in the reign of Emperor Nero around A.D. 67.

PETER, LETTERS OF Two letters in the New Testament allegedly written by **Peter**. Together with the letters of James, John, and Jude, the two letters of Peter are called "Catholic Epistles" because they appear to be addressed to all Christians rather than to particular communities. Both of Peter's letters are addressed to Christians in Asia Minor, and both are exhortations to persevere in the faith despite difficulties arising from pagan influences, isolation from other Christians, and false teaching.

1 Peter

I. AUTHORSHIP AND DATE

The author of this letter describes himself as "Peter, an apostle of Jesus Christ" (1 Pet 1:1) and indicates that he is a witness of the sufferings of Christ and an elder who tends the flock of the Lord (5:1–2). Christian tradition from the earliest times has accepted the claim that the author was Peter the apostle. Modern scholars, however, have called that authorship into question. The principal arguments for an author other than Peter are the excellent Greek of the epistle (unlikely for an uneducated fisherman from Galilee who spoke Aramaic, cf. Acts 4:13), its use of the Greek translation of the Old Testament, and the reference to the sufferings of the Christian community (1 Pet 2:19–20; 4:12–16; 5:9–10), which some think occurred only later during the reign of Emperor Domitian (r. A.D. 81–96), years after Peter's death. On the basis of these claims, scholars suggest that the real author is either unknown or possibly Silvanus, the apostle's secretary (5:12).

The objections are insufficient to discard the long-standing tradition regarding Peter's authorship. As the letter was dictated to Silvanus, it is likely that he as secretary gave it its polish and expansive vocabulary. The writer's knowledge of the Greek OT may also be ascribed to Silvanus's assistance. As for the suffering mentioned in the letter, there is nothing that proves it was a form of imperial persecution conducted by Roman authorities. Christian persecution had long been instigated at the hands of the unbelieving Jews and Gentiles in the mission field (cf. Acts 8:1; 14:4–6; 16:19–24).

The date of the letter depends chiefly on the issue of authorship. Scholars who adhere to apostolic authorship normally place its composition to the early sixties A.D., not long before Peter's death in A.D. 67. Scholars who think the letter was written in Peter's name by a later disciple date the letter toward the end of the first century.

II. CONTENTS

I. Salutation (1:1–2)

II. Thanksgiving (1:3–12)

III. Holy Living (1:13–2:10)

IV. Christian Relationship (2:11–3:12)

V. Suffering (3:13–4:19)

VI. Shepherds and Their Flock (5:1–11)

VII. Closing Benediction (5:12–14)

III. PURPOSE AND THEMES

The letter is written and sent from "Babylon" (1 Pet 5:13), probably a symbolic name for Rome, which is consistent with the ancient tradition that Peter ministered in Rome in the years before his martyrdom. The letter is addressed to "the exiles of the Dispersion in Pontus, Galatia, Cappadocia, Asia, and Bithynia," meaning the communities in the Roman provinces of northern and western Asia Minor (1:1). The letter has an epistolary form with a salutation, a thanksgiving, and a conclusion.

The letter is intended to encourage Christians in the young communities to persevere in the face of mounting hostility from the world. The foundation for this encouragement is the Resurrection: "Blessed be the God and Father of our Lord Jesus Christ! By his great mercy we have been born anew to a living hope through the resurrection of Jesus Christ from the dead" (1:3). The readers are reminded of the reward that awaits them in heaven (1:3–5) and the value of enduring in the face of troubles to reach the glory of hope anticipated by the prophets of the OT (1:10–12).

The Christian life, with all its challenges and demands, is thus oriented toward the promises of Christ: "set your hope fully upon the grace that is coming to you at the revelation of Jesus Christ" (1:13). He goes on to point to specific attributes of the Christian and then offers examples of living as servants of God

(2:11–3:12) as "a chosen race, a royal priesthood, a holy nation, God's own people" (2:9).

Peter then devotes his attention to suffering persecution for the name of Christ—which he sees as a blessing (3:14; 4:14). Patient endurance during persecution is a sure sign of the genuine Christian, and rather than being discouraged in hard times, the follower of Christ should rejoice in following Christ's example (4:13). The basis of Christian hope is baptism: Peter cites the example of Noah's ark, in which souls were saved through water. Baptism, he writes, "which corresponds to this, now saves you, not as a removal of dirt from the body but as an appeal to God for a clear conscience, through the resurrection of Jesus Christ, who has gone into heaven and is at the right hand of God, with angels, authorities, and powers subject to him" (3:21–22).

2 Peter

I. AUTHORSHIP AND DATE

The writer of 2 Peter identifies himself as "Simon Peter" (2 Pet 1:1) and claims to have witnessed the Transfiguration of Jesus (1:16–18) and to have written an earlier letter (3:1). He also implies that he is a colleague of Paul (3:15). From these statements, the writer of the letter clearly makes the claim that he is the apostle Peter. Nevertheless, 2 Peter was not universally accepted as canonical until the fifth century.

Many modern scholars, as well as some ancient ones, claim that the letter was composed and given literary shape, not by Peter himself, but by a later disciple. Their arguments are based on the significant stylistic differences between 1 and 2 Peter, the literary dependence of 2 Peter on the book of Jude, and a possible reference to the passing of the first generation of Christians (2 Pet 3:4), which would indicate that the letter was composed after Peter's death.

On the other hand, as Saint Jerome suggested, the stylistic differences between 1 and 2 Peter could be accounted for by Peter having dictated the second epistle to a secretary other than Silvanus (*see* **Silas**), to whom 1 Peter was dictated (1 Pet 5:12). Giving the letter a late date because of its dependence on Jude assumes that Jude was also from a later period, which has not been conclusively proved. Finally, although 2 Peter was not universally accepted as canonical until the fifth century, the letter did find much support in the early Church and was used in the liturgy of many churches. Taken together, the arguments against Peter as author are far from conclusive.

Dating the letter depends on settling the question of authorship. If the letter was written by Peter, then the date of composition was likely to have been in the mid-sixties A.D., while Peter was ministering in Rome before his martyrdom. If the letter was written by someone else, the date is harder to determine; many scholars date it to around the end of the first century A.D., and some would even push its composition into the second century A.D.

II. CONTENTS

III. PURPOSE AND THEMES

The second letter of Peter begins as a letter with a salutation, "To those who have obtained a faith of equal standing with ours in the righteousness of our God and Savior Jesus Christ" (2 Pet 1:1), and an address and greeting (1:1–2), but the remainder of the text is more of a homily. The author encourages Christians to persevere in their faith and to live in the hope of Christ's Second Coming, even if that Second Coming does not happen as soon as they might expect. The letter was presumably sent to the churches of Asia Minor (1 Pet 1:1), meaning that it was meant for the same readers as those for whom 1 Peter was written (2 Pet 3:1).

The author is concerned with exhorting the Christians to be abundant "in the knowledge of God and of Jesus our Lord" (1:2). The lives of Christians must reflect the divine power that has been given them (1:3, 4). "For this very reason make every effort to supplement your faith with virtue, and virtue with knowledge, and knowledge with self-control, and self-control with steadfastness, and steadfastness with godliness, and godliness with brotherly affection, and brotherly affection with love" (1:5–7). The foundation of hope in this life is the awareness of eternal life (1:8–11) and the promise and hope of Christ's coming again in glory (1:12–21). Peter reminds his readers of what they already know (1:12–15; 3:1) but exhorts them to grow even more deeply in their knowledge (1:3; 3:18).

The theme of the Second Coming is coupled with a polemic against false teachers who are posing a threat to Christians (2:1–22). Their teachings are full of deceit, errors, and lies, and the teachers themselves are licentious (2:2), greedy (2:3, 14), and lustful (2:10, 14, 18); they oppose authority (2:10) and slander the angels (2:10–11). The author compares them to irrational animals (2:12) and sees them sharing the fate of the fallen angels, the sinful generation of **Noah**'s time, and the inhabitants of ancient **Sodom** (2:4–6).

Regarding the Second Coming, Peter calls upon his readers to remember the necessity of preparing for its eventuality by leading a blameless and virtuous life. He concludes by reiterating one last time his exhortation that Christians focus on knowing God: "You therefore, beloved, knowing this beforehand, beware lest you be carried away with the error of lawless men and lose your own stability. But grow in the grace and knowledge of our Lord and Savior Jesus Christ. To him be the glory both now and to the day of eternity" (3:17–18).

PETHOR A city in Mesopotamia, near the Euphrates River in the land of Amaw. It was the home of **Balaam**, the seer hired by **Balak** to place a curse on the Israelites (Num 22:4–7; Deut 23:4).

PHANUEL The father of **Anna** the prophetess; he was a member of the tribe of Asher (Luke 2:36).

PHARAOH (Egyptian, "great house") The title used for the king of Egypt from the time of the Eighteenth Dynasty of Egypt (ca. 1550–

1295 B.C.). Initially the title "Pharaoh" was not used for the rulers of Egypt, but for the massive royal palace complex at Memphis from the third millennium B.C. Early in the Eighteenth Dynasty, the name became attached to the actual person of the king, in much the same way that the phrase "White House" represents the U.S. president or the honorific "Majesty" might designate a monarch. By the eleventh century B.C., the title "Pharaoh" was given formal recognition and included among the official titles claimed by the rulers of Egypt. By the eighth century B.C., it was listed on the royal cartouche and thenceforth was synonymous with "king." "Pharaoh" in the Old Testament is always used in reference to a king of Egypt (Gen 12:15 and chaps. 37–50; Exod 1–14; 1 Kgs 3:1; 7:8; 9:16, 24; 11:1; Jer 25:19; 37:5, 7, 11; Ezek 17:17; 29:2–3).

PHARISEES (Hebrew, "separated ones") A religious sect or party within Judaism that flourished from the second century B.C. to the first century A.D. In the early first century A.D., there were over six thousand Pharisees, according to Josephus (*Ant.* 17.42). The name is linked to the Hebrew term meaning "separated ones," because they separated themselves from all forms of religious and ceremonial uncleanness. They were known for their strict observance of ritual piety, purity, and tithing, and for their determination to prevent the Jewish faith from being contaminated by foreign religious practices, to which end they insisted on strict separation from the Gentiles. The Pharisees are mentioned in Josephus, rabbinical literature, and the New Testament.

I. ORIGINS OF THE PHARISEES

The origins of the Pharisees are obscure. Josephus (*Ant.* 13.288–300) first mentions them in association with the reign of **John Hyrcanus** (r. 134–104 B.C.; *see* **Hasmonean Dynasty**), although it is likely that they were established earlier than his time. They considered themselves heirs of Ezra and emulated his vigorous commitment to the teachings of the Law. They opposed the policies of **Alexander Jannaeus** (r. 103–76 B.C.), and such was their hostility that Alexander crucified eight hundred of them (Josephus, *Ant.* 13.380). Pharisees also opposed the later Hasmoneans and **Herod** on the basis that the rulers did not adhere to the Law. Pragmatic in political matters, the Pharisees grudgingly accepted Roman domination, although some among them were more inclined to armed resistance. After the Jewish revolt against Rome (A.D. 66–70) was put down, Emperor Vespasian permitted the Pharisaic leader Yohanan ben Zakkai to found a rabbinical school at Jamnia. Pharisaic teachings became the basis of rabbinic Judaism thereafter.

II. THE PHARISEES' BELIEFS

The Pharisees were laymen, in contrast to the Sadducees, who were the priestly party. The Pharisees were allied closely to the scribes, those learned members of the community who studied and interpreted the Law. They enjoyed influence among the masses in Palestine during the NT period, but were openly contemptuous of the "people of the land" who were ignorant of the Law and failed to adhere to the Pharisaic observances.

The doctrines of the Pharisees deviated from those of the Sadducees in a number of ways. The Sadducees acknowledged only the Torah as having full religious authority, whereas the Pharisees also used, in addition to the Hebrew Scriptures, oral traditions that were designed to reinforce the observance of the **Law** (Matt 15:2; Mark 7:5). The oral traditions served as a crucial guide in the interpretation of the Law and a protection against violations. The Pharisees believed in angels and demons and upheld the doctrines of the Resurrection and the future life, all of which were rejected by the Sadducees.

III. JESUS AND THE PHARISEES

Jesus approved some of what the Pharisees taught but found their actions hypocritical. "The scribes and the Pharisees sit on Moses' seat; so practice and observe whatever they tell you, but not what they do; for they preach, but do not practice" (Matt 23:2). Pharisees are portrayed in the NT as being more concerned with outward than with inward purity (Luke 11:37–41), as neglecting the most important matters of the Law (Matt 23:23; Luke 11:42), as being proud and excessively scrupulous (Luke 18:9–14), and as being concerned with keeping themselves distant from sinners, tax collectors, and others deemed to be religiously unclean (Matt 9:11; Luke 7:36–39, 15:1–2).

The Pharisees' hostility toward Jesus is a major aspect of the Gospels; in this they are allied with the chief priests (the Sadducees, their traditional enemies), as well as the scribes and all the other enemies of Jesus. Their opposition to Jesus began early in his ministry.

The picture presented is a harsh one. John the Baptist called them a "brood of vipers" (Matt 3:7–10; Luke 3:7–9).

In their hatred for Jesus, the Pharisees tried to trap him with doctrinal questions designed to discredit him (Matt 22:15; Mark 12:13; Luke 20:20). Needless to say, the Pharisees were outraged by the teachings and actions of Jesus, including his claims to teaching authority, and especially his setting aside the precepts of the Sabbath (Matt 12:2; Mark 2:24; Luke 6:2, 14:1–3; John 5:9) and purifications against uncleanness (Matt 15:1–2; Mark 7:1–5), teachings that were utterly inviolable in the eyes of the Pharisees. Jesus also scandalized them by associating with sinners and tax collectors (Matt 9:9–13; Mark 2:13–17; Luke 5:27–32, 7:36, 15:2). They dismissed Jesus's exorcisms as the work of Beelzebul (Matt 12:24). Unable to contain or silence him, they sought his destruction and death (cf. Matt 12:14; Mark 3:6; John 11:46–57).

Jesus called the Pharisees a wicked and adulterous generation (Matt 12:38, 15:1; Mark 7:1), deliberately blind (John 9:40–41), and blasphemers against the Spirit (Matt 12:31; Mark 3:28).

On the other hand, not all the Pharisees stood against Jesus. Among their ranks was **Nicodemus**, who became a follower of Jesus (John 3:1–15; 7:45–51; 19:39–42), and **Gamaliel**, who advised the Sanhedrin not to persecute the Christians (Acts 5:34–39). The Christians in Jerusalem also included Pharisees among their ranks, and their greatest theologian turned out to be **Paul**, who was educated as a Pharisee (Acts 23:6; Phil 3:5).

PHARPAR A river near Damascus in Syria. The prophet **Elisha** advised **Naaman**, the Syrian commander, to bathe in the Jordan River to cure his leprosy. At first Naaman was perplexed, and complained that the Abana and Pharpar rivers of Damascus were "better than all the waters of Israel" (2 Kings 5:1–12).

PHICOL The army commander of **Abimelech**, who had dealings with the **patriarchs** (Gen 21:22, 32; 26:26).

PHILADELPHIA (Greek, "brotherly love") A leading city in Asia Minor (modern Turkey), in the region of Lydia. It was near the upper end of a broad and fertile plateau and on the route through Sardis to the sea. The church in Philadelphia was one of the seven addressed in Revelation (Rev 1:11; 3:7–13). Prosperous and well-situated, Philadelphia was nevertheless troubled by earthquakes, including an especially severe one that occurred in A.D. 17 (Strabo, *Geog.* 12.8.18, 13.4.10; Pliny, *Nat.* 2.86.200; Tacitus, *Ann.* 2.47.3–4). Such was the level of destruction that the imperial government granted the city dwellers a five-year remission of tribute. Philadelphia was also the name of one of the cities of the **Decapolis**, east of the Jordan River (modern Amman, Jordan).

PHILEMON, LETTER TO The shortest of Paul's letters in the New Testament. Paul addresses Philemon, a wealthy man from Asia Minor, concerning a runaway slave, **Onesimus**, who had escaped from Philemon. Paul appeals for Philemon's mercy and kind treatment of Onesimus on his return.

I. AUTHOR AND DATE

The author identifies himself as Paul three times in the epistle (Phlm vv. 1, 9, 19). Most scholars have accepted Paul's authorship.

Scholarly opinion is less unanimous on the date of the letter. Paul wrote his epistle from prison (vv. 1, 9–10, 13, 23), but it is not known from which of Paul's incarcerations the letter may have originated—Caesarea (Acts 23:31–35), Rome (Acts 28:16–31), or some other location (2 Cor 11:23). The likeliest date for the composition of the letter is between A.D. 60 and 62, during Paul's first Roman imprisonment. Philemon is thus counted along with Ephesians, Philippians, and Colossians as a "captivity Epistle," a letter written by Paul most likely from Rome.

II. CONTENTS

I. Greeting (vv. 1–3)

II. Thanksgiving (vv. 4–7)

III. The Plea for Onesimus (vv. 8–21)

IV. A Request for Hospitality (v. 22)

V. Greeting from the Friends of Paul (vv. 23–24)

VI. Blessing (v. 25)

III. PURPOSE AND THEMES

The letter is addressed to a Christian convert and slave owner by the name of Philemon, along with Apphia (perhaps Philemon's wife) and a leader in the Christian community named Archippus (possibly Philemon's son). Because of the close connection between this letter and Colossians, it is likely that Philemon and his household resided in or near the city of Colossae (cf. Col 4:9, 17). The letter speaks of Onesimus, a slave who had fled from the service of Philemon, had met up with Paul during the latter's captivity, and had been converted to the Christian faith.

Paul refers to Onesimus as "the faithful and beloved brother" (Col 4:9) and sends him back to Philemon with Tychicus carrying the letter to the Colossians. The slave's name (Greek *Onēsimos*, "useful") is the basis of a memorable pun: "Formerly he was useless to you, but now he is indeed useful to you and to me" (Phlm v. 11). A master had the right to exact the most terrible punishment upon a slave who had fled, especially one who might have been guilty of stealing money or property (vv. 11, 18), so Paul adds a plea to "receive [Onesimus] as you would receive me. If he has wronged you at all, or owes you anything, charge that to my account. I, Paul, write this with my own hand, I will repay it—to say nothing of your owing me even your own self" (vv. 17–20).

The brief epistle gives us a glimpse of Roman slavery and the Christian response to it. Paul is aware that Philemon is within his rights to put Onesimus to death, but he sends the slave home anyway. He does so because Onesimus must make amends for his misdeeds, and Paul expresses a willingness to pay Philemon the amount owed to him by the slave to make certain that justice is done (vv. 18–19). Paul challenges Philemon to be a true Christian and to recognize that he has obligations that go beyond the harsh laws of the Roman Empire. Paul urges the rich man to forgive the slave, and adds in subtle tones the suggestion that Philemon should emancipate Onesimus (vv. 16, 21). The old relation between slave and

master is not overthrown, but transformed, just as Onesimus and Philemon are no longer slave and master but brothers in Christ.

Ancient tradition says that Onesimus was indeed freed and later became a Christian bishop.

PHILETUS A Christian who denied the resurrection of the body. With Hymenaeus, he "swerved from the truth by holding that the resurrection is past already" (2 Tim 2:18).

PHILIP The name of six men in the Bible.

1. One of the twelve apostles. He is mentioned in Acts 1:13 and in John 1:43–51, which says he came from Bethsaida, the city of Andrew and Peter. Jesus called Philip to join him with the words, "Follow me." Philip then brought Nathaniel to Jesus, convinced that Jesus was the Messianic deliverer. In John, Philip is present in several episodes, including the feeding of the multitude (John 6:5–7); when several Greeks express the wish to meet Jesus and Jesus proclaims the coming of his hour (John 12:21–23); and when, during the Last Supper Discourses, Philip said to Jesus, "Lord show us the Father, and we shall be satisfied," and Jesus replied, "Have I been with you so long, and yet you do not know me, Philip? He who has seen me has seen the Father . . ." (John 14:8–9). Elsewhere in the Gospels, Philip is included among the twelve apostles sent out by Christ, and is ranked fifth in three different lists, after the brothers Peter and Andrew and James and John (Matt 10:2–4; Mark 3:14–19; Luke 6:13–16).

Philip's activities in later years are uncertain, with doubts being compounded by the confusion in tradition of Philip with Philip the Evangelist, one of the seven deacons appointed in Acts 6. Bishop Polycrates of Ephesus (second century A.D.) said Philip was buried in Hieropolis with his two daughters. The manner of his death is uncertain, although there is a tradition that he suffered crucifixion. In one tradition, Philip is said to be the disciple who wished to bury his father before following Jesus (Matt 8:21; Saint Clement of Alexandria, *Strom.* 3.4.25, 4.9.73). Philip's feast day is May 3, with Saint James the Less.

2. One of the seven Christians chosen by the apostles to care for the poor widows of Jerusalem (Acts 6:1–7). In the wake of the martyrdom of **Stephen**, Philip left Jerusalem and carried the Gospel to Samaria, where he was instrumental in the conversion of Samaritans, among them the famous magician Simon Magus (Acts 8:4–13). Philip also baptized a eunuch who served as the treasurer to Candace, queen of Ethiopia (Acts 8:26–39). Philip then went on to the onetime Philistine city of Azotus (Ashdod) and preached throughout the coastal cities until finally he took up residence in Caesarea (Acts 8:40). There **Paul** stayed with him for a time (Acts 21:8–9). Philip had four daughters who were prophetesses (Acts 21:8–9). Later tradition sometimes confused him with the apostle Philip.

3. Philip V of Macedon (r. 221–179 B.C.). He was defeated by Rome at the battle of Cynocephelae in 197 B.C. (1 Macc 8:5).

4. Regent and tutor to Antiochus V Eupator (r. 164–160 B.C.; *see* **Seleucids**), son of Antiochus IV Epiphanes (r. 175–164 B.C.). He lost his position to **Lysias** (1 Macc 6:14–18; 2 Macc 9:29).

5. The son of **Herod the Great** and his wife Mariamne. He wed **Herodias**, the mother of **Salome**, who left him in favor of **Herod Antipas**, his half brother (Matt 14:3; Mark 6:17; Luke 3:19).

6. The son of Herod the Great and his fifth wife, Cleopatra of Jerusalem. He was raised in Rome (according to Josephus, *Ant.* 17.21) and was granted the tetrarchy of Gaulanitis, Trachonitis, Auranitis, Batanaea, and Iturea (Luke 3:1) from around 4 B.C. to A.D. 34. He was noted—in stark contrast to his often reprehensible relatives—for his moderate rule. He rebuilt the cities of Caesarea Philippi (Matt 16:13; Mark 8:27) and Bethsaida Julias (Josephus, *Ant.* 18, 28).

PHILIPPI A city in Macedonia (northern Greece) a few miles inland from the seaport of Neapolis (modern Kaválla). It was originally called Krenides, meaning "spring," in honor of the rich streams in the surrounding area. Philippi was renamed after Philip II of Macedonia (r. 359–336 B.C.). When the city was conquered by the Romans in 167 B.C. it was made part of the Roman province of Macedonia. It was the site in 42 B.C. of the battle during the Roman civil war between Brutus and Cassius and Mark Antony and Octavian. After that it was made a Roman colony populated with large numbers of army veterans and subject to the Italian laws of Rome.

The church at Philippi was the first church to be founded by Paul on European soil. **Paul** visited Philippi with **Silas** during his second missionary journey (Acts 16:12) after he had a dream in which a Macedonian begged him to visit (Acts 16:9–12). The two were given welcome from **Lydia** of Thyatira, a convert of Paul (Acts 16:13–15). It was here that Paul cured a little girl with a divining spirit; and here he and Silas were charged with illegal religious practices and imprisoned. An earthquake opened the doors of the prison, but Paul refused to escape; the guard was so moved that he was baptized (Acts 16:25–34). After being freed, Paul and Silas set out for Thessalonica. Paul visited Philippi again during his third missionary journey (Acts 20:6–8). The Letter to the Philippians was addressed to the church in the city.

PHILIPPIANS, LETTER TO THE A letter written by the apostle Paul to instruct the Philippians on the need for unity and to thank them for their kindness to him while he was being held in prison.

I. AUTHORSHIP AND DATE

The apostle Paul is almost universally accepted as the author of Philippians (Phil 1:1). The tiny minority of scholars who question Paul's authorship have not persuaded the majority, although some have argued that parts of the letter may have been assembled from other epistles. The strength of the internal evidence for Paul's authorship is considerable, including personal references that are consistent with known events in Acts and other letters, the literary style, and especially the theology. The letter is distinctive in its warmth and heart-to-heart tone.

The date for the epistle depends on the time of Paul's imprisonment, which is mentioned in the letter (1:7, 13–14, 16–17). Paul was imprisoned on several occasions (cf. Acts 16:23–40, 21:32–23:30, 28:30; 2 Cor 11:23), and there are several possible locations of the letter's composition: Rome, Ephesus, or Caesarea. The most likely place of imprisonment is Rome (Acts 28:16, 30), given Paul's mention of the "praetorian guard" (Phil 1:13) and "Caesar's household" (4:22), as well as Paul's anticipation of his impending trial (1:26; 2:24). If Rome was the place of the letter's composition, then the letter was likely written around A.D. 62.

II. CONTENTS

III. PURPOSE AND THEMES

Paul writes to the community at **Philippi** (a major city in Macedonia) in intimate and personal terms. He is not concerned with a specific doctrinal or disciplinary problem, but wishes to give his greetings and encouragement to those he calls "my beloved" (Phil 2:12; 4:1) as well as news about himself. He expresses his gratitude for their generosity. When the Christians in Philippi learned that Paul had been imprisoned, they sent **Epaphroditus** to him with money (4:18). Epaphroditus fell ill while serving Paul in captivity, and upon his recovery, Paul sent him home and expressed the hope that he (Paul) might send Timothy to the Philippians soon (2:19–30). The Philippians were exemplary in their charity and generosity

(4:15–16), and Paul is exuberant in his praise. Paul assures them of God's blessing (4:19).

Paul is aware of the persecutions the Philippians have faced (1:29–30; cf. Acts 16:20, 21), most likely at the hands of civil authorities. He is concerned chiefly with the question of unity among the faithful and the attitude of humility and charity that make possible endurance in the face of tribulations. Paul proposes Christ as their supreme example (Phil 2:1–5). Paul includes in his exhortation a description of the Incarnation (2:5–11) that is one of the most beautiful in all his writings; he notes that Christ "emptied himself, taking the form of a servant, being born in the likeness of men" (2:7) and for his obedience on the Cross God exalted him and "bestowed on him the name which is above every name" (2:9). Paul also offers himself as a model for the Philippians to emulate. For Christ, Paul has "suffered the loss of all things" (3:8) and is eager to "know him and the power of his resurrection," so that Paul "may share his sufferings, becoming like him in his death" (3:10).

Philippians is deeply personal in its tone and is remarkable for its abundant joy. As he is not confronting some doctrinal or disciplinary problem, the structure is much looser than the other Pauline epistles. In his looser style, Paul gives readers a glimpse into his life and mind as well as his abiding fondness for the church at Philippi.

PHILISTIA The land occupied by the **Philistines** on the southwestern coast of Palestine.

PHILISTINES A maritime people who migrated into **Canaan** in the early twelfth century B.C. The Philistines became the chief enemies and oppressors of Israel in the days of the Judges and beyond (Judg 3:4). Philistia, their region in southwest Canaan, extended roughly from Gaza to Joppa. The Philistines embraced the local Canaanite deities, including Dagon (Judg 16:23; 1 Sam 5:2; 1 Chr 10:10), Ashtaroth (1 Sam 31:10), and Baal-zebub (2 Kgs 1:1–16).

The origin of the Philistines is complex. According to the **Table of Nations** they were descended from Egypt (Gen 10:13–14). Other texts more specifically link them with the Caphtorim (Deut 2:23), the Sea People from the island of Caphtor (Jer 47:4; Amos 9:7). The general view is that Caphtor is Crete, or it was a location more broadly in the Aegean basin. The Philistines were probably among the Sea People who were responsible for the Doric invasions in the twelfth century B.C. The Sea People were repulsed by Egypt under Ramses III (1184–1153 B.C.), and so the Philistines settled along the southwestern coast of Canaan. Once in Canaan, they established a five-city confederation based in **Gaza**, **Ashkelon**, **Ashdod**, **Gath**, and **Ekron**. The locations of three of those cities are known with certainty: Gaza, Ashkelon, and Ashdod. Ekron is perhaps the modern Khirbet el-Muganna, but no specific location is agreed upon for Gath.

Until around 1000 B.C., the Philistines were the dominant power in the region owing to their monopoly on iron technology, which gave them military superiority over their neighbors. The art of iron making was guarded jealously by the Philistines (1 Sam 13:19–21).

The expansion of the Philistines' influence brought them into conflict with the Israelites. The struggle that followed is detailed in the books of Judges and Samuel. It continued off and on until the Philistines were finally subjugated by King **David** (2 Sam 8:1). The presence of the Philistines allowed God to test Israel and discipline the people for their continued infidelity to the **covenant** (cf. Josh 13:2–3; Judg 3:1–3).

The Israelites produced many anti-Philistine heroes, such as **Shamgar** (Judg 3:31) and **Samson** (Judg 13–16), but the Philistines were a relentless and implacable enemy that brought Israel both misery and severe hardship. The degree of pressure created by the Philistine onslaught is seen in the forty years of domination (Judg 13:1; 14:4) that forced the tribe of Dan to migrate northward and caused great suffering in Judah.

The war between Israel and the Philistines included the defeat of the Israelites at Ebenezer, during which the **ark of the covenant** was captured and Shiloh was destroyed (1 Sam 4:1–11; cf. Ps 78:60–61; Jer 7:12–14). The Israelite victory at Mizpah (1 Sam 7:3–14) did little to ease the situation, and the establishment of the monarchy was deemed essential for the proper conduct of the war. The chosen king, **Saul**, devoted much of his reign to waging war against the Philistines (1 Sam 13–14). It was written, "There was hard fighting against the Philistines all the days of Saul" (1 Sam 14:52).

David's early life was also filled with the wars against the Philistines. The victory of David over **Goliath** and the Philistines aroused Saul's jealousy (1 Sam 17:41–54; 18:6–9, 25–27, 30; 19:8). David subsequently was forced to flee Saul, and he found refuge with **Achish**,

the Philistine king of Gath, under whom David served as a vassal (1 Sam 27:1–28:2). David did not take part in Saul's final engagement with the Philistines at Mount Gilboa (1 Sam 31).

David fared far better than Saul with his hostile neighbor. When the Philistines attacked, they were routed "from Geba to Gezer" (2 Sam 5:25). David went on to additional triumphs and established Israel as the foremost power in Canaan (2 Sam 8:1; 1 Chr 18:1). Gath apparently became a vassal city to Israel, and some of the Philistines entered into the service of the king as mercenaries, including membership in the royal bodyguard, the Cherethites and the Pelethites (2 Sam 8:18; 15:18; 20:7, 23; 1 Kgs 1:38, 44; 1 Chr 18:17).

The defeats suffered by the Philistines ended their dominion, although some resistance may have continued (cf. 2 Sam 21:15–22; 23:8–39). The city-states of Philistia were subject to Israel during the reign of Solomon. Conflict resumed during the time of the Divided Monarchy (cf. 1 Kgs 15:27, 16:15; 2 Chr 21:16–17, 28:18; Isa 9:12). The bitterness of the age-old enmity is seen in the oracle of Amos 1:6–8 against Gaza, Ashdod, Ashkelon, and Ekron (cf. Joel 3:4–8; Zeph 2:4–7).

The Assyrians had reduced the Philistines to vassal status in the ninth century B.C. under the Assyrian ruler Adad-nirari III, who mentioned the tribute he had received from Philistia. The Philistines fell under direct attack by Assyria in 734 B.C. after the conquest of Syria by **Tiglath-pileser III**. Succeeding Assyrian rulers such as Sargon II, Sennacherib, and Esarhaddon faced rebellions from the Philistine cities.

By the sixth century B.C., the Babylonians brought an end to the nation of Philistia. **Nebuchadnezzar**, as was the Babylonian policy, deported the population in response to an ill-advised alliance between Philistia and Egypt to resist Babylonian imperialism (cf. Jer 25:17–20, 47:2–7; cf. Zech 9:5–6).

PHILOLOGUS A Roman Christian who was greeted by Paul in Rom 16:15.

PHINEHAS The name of two priests in the Old Testament.

1. The son of **Eleazar** and the grandson of **Aaron** (Exod 6:25; Num 25:7; Judg 20:28; 1 Chr 6:4, 50; Ezra 7:5). He was known for his zeal and fidelity to the worship of the Lord, which he demonstrated on the plains of Moab when Israel committed apostasy by worshiping Baal-Peor, at which time Phinehas thrust a spear through a man of Simeon engaged in sexual impurity with a woman of Moab (Num 25:1–14; cf. Ps 106:28–31; Sir 45:23; 1 Macc 2:26). Phinehas was rewarded for this heroism with a covenant of perpetual priesthood in Israel (Num 25:10–13; Sir 45:24; 1 Macc 2:54). He was later involved in the holy war against Midian (Num 31:1–20), which climaxed with the slaughter of all males and females, except for the virgin girls (Num 31:17–18).

After the conquest of Canaan, when the tribes of Reuben, Gad, and the half-tribe of Manasseh built a massive altar in **Transjordan** (Josh 22:10), Phinehas, with ten other leaders, condemned its construction, although the builders claimed that it was an altar of memorial and not of sacrifice (Josh 22:11–34). Phine-has was also the chief priest in the early period of the Judges (Judg 20:28). His faithfulness to God earned him a place as the model of holy zeal for the Lord and his covenant.

2. A son of **Eli** and the brother of Hophni (1 Sam 1:3), with whom he served as priest. These two brothers were priests like their father, but they wickedly abused their positions (1 Sam 2:12–17). They were killed at the battle of Aphek when the Philistines captured the **ark of the covenant** (1 Sam 4:11).

PHLEGON A Roman Christian who was greeted by Paul in Rom 16:14.

PHOEBE A Christian woman from Cenchreae, near **Corinth**, who was recommended by Paul to the community in Rome (Rom 16:1–2). Paul describes her as "sister," "deaconess," and "helper." (*See also* **Deacon**.)

PHOENICIA (Greek, "purple" or "crimson") The coastal strip directly north of Palestine (modern Lebanon). It encompassed the ancient port cities of **Tyre**, **Sidon**, **Gebal**, and **Ugarit**. Its name was derived from the dyes that made the inhabitants famous around the ancient world. Phoenicia was also a renowned trading and maritime center, owing to the abundant natural harbors that dotted the coastline and the great fertility of the land. As a cultural and political entity, Phoenicia was not a country but a conglomeration of city-states formed by a Semitic people associated closely with the Canaanites. The Phoenicians enjoyed excellent relations with the Egyptians (who wielded a degree of control over Phoenician affairs) owing to the trade that developed in such commodities as cedar, and the ancient Phoenicians won justified fame as maritime and commercial experts. The zenith of their economic influence was reached from around 1500 to 700 B.C. They succeeded in avoiding domination by Assyria by paying tribute, and also managed to avoid the control of the Babylonians despite the long siege of Tyre by **Nebuchadnezzar** from around 585 to 573 B.C. They later became willing members of the Persian Empire and provided ships and logistical support in the Persian campaigns against Greece. **Alexander the Great** conquered Phoenicia as part of his defeat of the Persian Empire, and his capture of Tyre was a bloody struggle. The city—like Phoenicia—recovered its prosperity, but the political power of Phoenicia was gone. Phoenicia was subsequently annexed to the Roman Empire after the campaigns of Pompey the Great in 64 B.C.

Phoenicia was part of Canaan to the Israelites (Gen 10:15). During the time of **David** and **Solomon**, the ruler of Tyre, **Hiram I**, was an economic ally of Israel (2 Sam 5:11; 1 Kgs 5:1) who sent Phoenician commodities such as wood, ships, craftsmen, and artisans for the building of the Jerusalem **Temple** (1 Kgs 5:1–12; 2 Chr 2:3–16). Phoenician sailors and sea masters helped develop the commercial fleets of Israel that sailed in and out of **Ezion-geber** (1 Kgs 9:27). A later Phoenician king, **Ethbaal**, forged an alliance with Israel through the marriage of his daughter, **Jezebel**, to King Ahab (1 Kgs 16:31). The result was the destabilization of the northern kingdom of Israel and the proliferation of the worship of Baal (1 Kgs 18:19). (*See also* **Sidon** and **Tyre**.)

PHOENIX A harbor on the southern coast of Crete where **Paul** hoped to winter while traveling to Rome (Acts 27:12).

PHRYGIA A region in western Asia Minor (modern Turkey) bounded by Bithynia, Galatia, and the western half of the province of Asia. The name "Meshech" in the Old Testament probably refers to Phrygia (Gen 10:2; 1 Chr 1:5; Ezek 27:13; 32:26; 38:2, 3; 39:1). Philip, a Phrygian, was named a governor of Jerusalem by Antiochus IV in 168 B.C. (2 Macc 5:22). In the New Testament, Phrygian Jews were present in Jerusalem during Pentecost (Acts 2:10), and **Paul** preached the Gospel on two short trips into Phrygian territory (Acts 16:6; 18:23).

PHYGELUS A Christian from Asia who, with Hermogenes, "turned away" from **Paul** during his second Roman imprisonment (2 Tim 1:15).

PHYLACTERIES Small leather boxes or capsules containing biblical passages that are tied to the forehead and left arm of the Jew during morning prayers (Exod 13:16; Deut 6:8, 11:18). The phylactery is mentioned only once in the New Testament, in Matt 23:5, where Jesus criticizes the hypocrisy of the Pharisees: "They do all their deeds to be seen by men; for they make their phylacteries broad and their fringes long."

PHYSICIAN *See* **Luke**; *see also* **Medicine**.

PILATE, PONTIUS The fifth Roman prefect, or governor, of Judea, from ca. A.D. 25 to 36. The time he served as Roman governor included the trial and Crucifixion of Jesus of Nazareth. What is known about Pilate comes mostly from Flavius **Josephus**, Philo, and the New Testament. References by classical writers (e.g., Tacitus, *Ann.* 15.44) are generally brief notices connected with the death of Christ. Despite these various sources, the life of Pilate is not known in great detail.

Pontius Pilate was a member of the Roman equestrian class. Around A.D. 25 or 26, he was assigned by Emperor Tiberius as prefect of Judea. He soon earned a reputation for cruelty and indecision that became hallmarks of his time as governor. According to Josephus (*Ant.* 18.55; *B.J.* 2.169), upon settling in Jerusalem he immediately antagonized the Jews by setting up Roman standards adorned with the image of Caesar—a clear violation of the Jewish prohibition of images. A delegation of Jewish authorities journeyed to Caesarea to petition the removal of the standards; after five days he permitted his soldiers to execute many in the crowd that had gathered in protest, but on the sixth day, he prudently ordered the standards taken back to Caesarea. He then used money from the Temple treasury to construct an aqueduct to bring water to Jerusalem (Josephus, *Ant.* 18.60; *B.J.* 2.175); it was a practical project, but the Jews erupted in riots with the result that more blood was spilled when he sent troops in disguise against them. Some think this may have been the massacre mentioned in Luke 13:1–2. In A.D. 36, he at last overreached himself by slaughtering a large number of Samaritans who had gathered at Mount **Gerizim**. The Samaritans sent a delegation to the Roman governor in Syria, Vitellius, who ordered Pilate to answer the charges.

Marcellus was sent to Judea to replace Pilate (Josephus, *Ant.* 18.85–89). Pilate was on his way to Rome when Tiberius died in A.D. 37, and nothing is known of what followed. Eusebius reported that Pilate was forced to commit suicide by Emperor Gaius Caligula after A.D. 37 (*Hist. Eccl.* 2.7); an ancient Eastern tradition, on the other hand, says that he became a Christian convert.

The Gospels emphasize Pilate's indecision as much as his cruelty (Matt 27; Mark 15; Luke 23; John 18–19; cf. Acts 3:13, 4:27, 13:28; 1 Tim 6:13). All four Evangelists suggest that Pilate considered Jesus to be innocent, and tell of how Pilate took steps to secure Jesus's release by offering the crowd a choice between Jesus and the murderer Barabbas. Matthew alone tells us that Pilate's wife warned Pilate to have nothing to do with "that righteous man" (Matt 27:19) and that Pilate washed his hands in front of the crowd (Matt 27:24). John points out the threats made by the Temple leaders that pushed Pilate to condemn Jesus (John 19:12). John also develops more fully the questioning of Jesus by Pilate, so that we see Jesus controlling the dialogue and imparting a teaching on the real nature of his Kingdom—vexing Pilate, who was unable to comprehend Jesus's teaching on Truth (John 18:33–38). Pilate also took the unusual step of permitting Jesus's body to be turned over to **Joseph of Arimathea** (the bodies of criminals were normally hurled into a pit or common grave) and ordered guards to be posted at the tomb (Matt 27:57–66).

Pilate is the subject of many legends and apocryphal writings, including the Acts of Pilate and the Death of Pilate, which recount, unreliably, his attempted suicide and later conversion. Up to the 1960s the Orthodox Church of Abyssinia celebrated a feast in Pilate's honor on June 25, and another for his wife on October 27.

PIRATHON A town in Ephraim that was the home of the judge **Abdon** (Judg 12:13–15) and David's warrior **Benaiah** (2 Sam 23:30; 1 Chr 11:31, 27:14). The site is probably the modern Farata, southwest of Shechem.

PISGAH Either the peak or the slopes of Mount **Nebo** (Deut 34:1). It rises in the **Transjordan** northeast of the Dead Sea (Num 21:20; Deut 3:17, 4:49; Josh 12:3, 13:20). Pisgah was one of the mountaintops on which **Balaam** attempted to put a curse on Israel (Num 23:14). Pisgah was also the peak from which **Moses** surveyed the Promised Land before his death (Deut 3:27; 34:1). The plateau below it, Ras Siyagha, is a lower ridge that some scholars consider the likelier place of Moses's vision as it affords a clearer view of the lands beyond.

PISHON One of the four rivers that flowed from the **Garden of Eden** (Gen 2:11). The Pishon circled the land of Havilah. No effort to identify the river has succeeded, although some scholars have attempted to place it in Arabia. The river is also mentioned in Sir 24:25, where it is compared with wisdom.

PISIDIA A mountainous region in south-central Asia Minor (modern Turkey). The rugged terrain was the home of fiercely independent tribes whom both the Persians and the Greeks found difficult to subjugate. The

Romans succeeded in taking control of the hill country under a campaign headed by Sulpicius Quirinius in 25 B.C. Once a permanent peace was achieved, Pisidia was attached to the province of Galatia, and its chief city was Antioch, called Antioch of Pisidia to differentiate it from Phrygian Antioch.

Pisidia is mentioned twice in the Acts of the Apostles (Acts 13:14; 14:24) in conjunction with **Paul**'s evangelization of southern **Galatia**. The suggestion has also been made that 2 Cor 11:26 may refer to the dangerous environment of Pisidia.

PIT *See* **Sheol**; *see also* **Abaddon**; **abyss**.

PITHOM A city in Egypt built by enslaved Israelites (Exod 1:11). The city was intended to serve as a storage facility. Suggestions for its location have included eastern Delta sites such as Tell el-Maskhuta, Tell el-Ratabah, and even the famous city of Heliopolis. Scholars now strongly favor Tell el-Ratabah as the location of the biblical Pithom.

PLAGUE The most famous plagues in the Bible are the **plagues of Egypt**, but others are recorded in Scripture as well. Both times Israel committed apostasy in the wilderness, at Sinai and later at Peor, the Lord sent a plague to discipline his people (Exod 32:35; Num 25:9). Likewise, David's census unleashed a plague or pestilence upon the people of Israel (2 Sam 24:15). Revelation says that plagues will come upon the unbelieving world (Rev 15:5–16:21). The plague is always seen as a judgment of God, either on the enemies of God's people, or on God's own people for their faithlessness.

PLAGUES OF EGYPT The ten plagues inflicted on the Egyptians to impel the stubborn Pharaoh to permit the Israelites to leave Egypt (Exod 7:14–12:32).

The purpose of the plagues in Egypt was to break the chains of bondage that enslaved Israel and to demonstrate the Lord's power over the "gods of Egypt" (Exod 12:12, 18:11; Num 33:4). Eventually, these scourges forced Pharaoh to admit that such events were not merely tricks, but were "the finger of God" (Exod 8:19; 10:7).

Collectively, the first nine plagues are grouped into three cycles of three plagues; the tenth plague, the death of the firstborn, is the capstone to the whole cycle. Each triad of plagues commences with the clear issuing of a warning from Moses to the Pharaoh (Exod 7:15; 8:20; 9:13). The third plague in each cycle is sent suddenly without warning.

God is imposing his judgment upon not just Egypt but "the gods of Egypt" and manifesting his superiority over them (Exod 12:12, 18:11; Num 33:4; Wis 12:24–25). The Egyptian deities were tied closely to natural and cosmic forces. The plagues attested to the impotence of the Egyptian gods in the face of the God of the Israelites; thus the plagues showed the Egyptians the power of God and the Israelites the folly of idolatry. According to some scholars, the plagues are aimed directly at the power of Egyptian gods and goddesses: Hapi, god of the Nile; Heket, frog goddess; Apis, bull god; and Hathor, cow goddess. Two notable deities were Re, god of light and the sun, who was judged in the plague of the darkness, and Osiris, the god of life, who was judged in the final plague.

For the Israelites the plagues were an enduring testimony to the power of God, remembered for all the generations to come: "you shall say to your son, 'We were Pharaoh's slaves in Egypt; and the LORD brought us out of Egypt with a mighty hand; and the LORD showed signs and wonders, great and grievous, against Egypt and against Pharaoh and all his household, before our eyes; and he brought us out from there, that he might bring us in and give

THE PLAGUES OF EGYPT

First Plague	Exod 7:14–25	Turning the Nile into Blood
Second Plague	Exod 8:1–15	Frogs
Third Plague	Exod 8:16–19	Gnats
Fourth Plague	Exod 8:20–32	Flies
Fifth Plague	Exod 9:1–7	Death of Livestock
Sixth Plague	Exod 9:8–12	Boils and Sores
Seventh Plague	Exod 9:13–35	Fiery Hailstorm
Eighth Plague	Exod 10:1–20	Locusts
Ninth Plague	Exod 10:21–29	Three Days of Darkness
Tenth Plague	Exod 12:29–36	Death of Firstborn

us the land which he swore to give to our fathers'" (Deut 6:21–22; cf. Deut 4:34, 7:19, 26:8; Josh 24:5; Ps 78:43–51, 105:27–36). (*See also* **Exodus; Moses; Passover, feast of;** CCC 62, 700.)

PLEDGES *See* **Loan**.

PLEIADES A constellation of stars closely associated with Orion (Job 38:31; Amos 5:8).

PLOW A tool that cuts furrows in the ground for planting seed. Most plows of the biblical period were made either entirely or almost entirely of wood; some plows were tipped with iron. The larger varieties were designed with a wooden frame to which metal tips were attached, the whole machine being pulled by a team of animals, usually oxen. On smaller farms or on slopes, a handheld hoe was common. Farmers usually waited to plow until the first heavy rains of autumn helped soften the ground.

POETRY Any composition—including songs, prayers, oracles, proverbs, and hymns—that uses figures of speech and powerful imagery to express the emotions of life and worship. Biblical poetry played a major part in Hebrew literature and worship, and poetic forms were used to express both the maxims of wisdom literature and the oracles of the prophets.

The sharp distinction between poetry and prose that is common to readers and students of modern literature was less pronounced in Hebrew literature. The ancient Israelite did not conceive of the two literary forms as being entirely distinct, and the speaker was apt to move between the two as part of a discourse or formal address. Such poetic speeches or utterances were called "sayings." These are found in a variety of occasions and settings, such as weddings (Gen 24:60), the launching of wars (Exod 17:16), and the celebration of triumphs (Exod 15:20; 1 Sam 18:7; and especially Judg 5, the famed Song of Deborah). Literary experts do not always agree as to what should be classified as prose and what as poetry.

I. SECULAR POETRY

The majority of poems and poetic works in Scripture are religious in nature. Nevertheless, Scripture excerpts or refers to secular poetry composed as songs for wine making (Isa 16:10), harvests (Judg 9:27), drinking (Isa 5:11–12; 22:13), and well digging (Num 21:17–18). In addition, the Old Testament preserves a number of elegies and laments, such as the elegies of David for Saul and Jonathan (2 Sam 3:33–34) and Abner (2 Sam 3:33–34).

II. CHARACTERISTICS OF HEBREW POETRY

A typical characteristic of Hebrew poetry is balance or symmetry, a repetition in the second line of the same idea or image that was used in the first. Scholars call that balance "parallelism." The second part (or colon) can either repeat the first line in different words, or develop the idea conveyed in the first part with additional information. For example:

> *Blessed is the man who fears the* Lord,
> *who greatly delights in his commandments.*
> *(Ps 112:1)*

Students of Hebrew poetry distinguish at least three kinds of parallelism.

1. *Synonymous* parallelism (also called synthetic parallelism) repeats the first line in slightly different words in the second line:

> Does God pervert justice?
>> Or does the Almighty pervert the right?
>> (Job 8:3)

> Deliver me from my enemies, O my God;
>> protect me from those who rise up against
>> me. (Ps 59:1)

2. *Antithetic* parallelism expresses its point by establishing a contrast between the two lines. Antithetical parallelisms are found especially in Proverbs:

> The wicked flee when no one pursues,
>> but the righteous are as bold as a lion.
>> (Prov 28:1)

3. *Climactic* parallelism is a broad category for poetic stanzas that are neither synonymous nor antithetic. In general, the second and following lines complete or develop the idea of the first line:

> I fear no evil;
>> for you are with me;
> your rod and your staff,
>> they comfort me. (Ps 23:4)

> My son, keep your father's commandment,
>> and forsake not your mother's teaching.
> Bind them upon your heart always;
>> tie them about your neck. (Prov 6:20–21)

III. LITERARY DEVICES AND FORMS

Like all poetry, Hebrew poetry is full of simile, metaphor, alliteration, and assonance. Acrostic or alphabetic poems are also common, particularly in the Psalms, in which the successive letters of the Hebrew alphabet begin successive lines, couplets, or strophes. Psalm 119 has stanzas of eight verses each: a letter of the alphabet is placed before each stanza, and each verse begins with this letter. Meter was apparently not used, as Hebrew poets preferred instead a variable rhythm and a more free-flowing style.

Wisdom literature is most commonly written as poetry, such as that found in Proverbs, Job, Ecclesiastes, and Sirach. Its function is to impart to the reader the results of long contemplation on life and the experiences of living. Wisdom poetry tends to be more reflective than polemical or confrontational.

IV. NEW TESTAMENT POETRY

The New Testament contains little in the way of poetry, but isolated examples can be found. There are four significant songs that were adopted by the early Church in her liturgical life: the Magnificat (Luke 1:46–55); the Benedictus (Luke 1:68–79); the Gloria (Luke 2:14); and the Nunc Dimittis (Luke 2:29–32). Poetic compositions have also been identified in Rom 11:33, 1 Cor 15:54–55, Eph 5:14, and Phil 2:6–11, among other places. Hymns likewise appear in Col 1:15, 1 Tim 3:16, and throughout the book of Revelation (Rev 4:8, 11; 5:9–10; 11:17–18; etc.).

The NT writers were intimately familiar with the OT writings and used a large number of quotations from OT poetry. Some were also familiar with Greek poetry, as indicated by quotations from Aratus of Cilicia (Acts 17:28), Menander (1 Cor 15:33), and Epimenides (Titus 1:12).

POISON The Hebrew name for poison, *ḥēmâ*, meaning "heat," probably signifies the terrible burning sensation that can be experienced when one is poisoned. Among the animals that were feared for their poisons were serpents (Deut 32:33; Ps 140:3). Poison was also used in imagery for the wicked (Ps 58:4, 140:3; Rom 3:13; Jas 3:8). One-passage refers to poison-tipped arrows (Job 6:4).

POLYGAMY *See* **Marriage**.

PONTIFICAL BIBLICAL COMMISSION

A papal commission created by Pope Leo XIII on October 30, 1902, through his apostolic letter *Vigilantiae*. Its stated purpose was to promote Catholic biblical studies, to resist errors in biblical scholarship, and to study and answer questions that might arise.

Originally, the Commission consisted of a small group of cardinals, appointed by the pope, along with a group of consultors, chiefly Catholic biblical scholars from various countries (most were in Rome and taught at Pontifical universities). In the early twentieth century, the Commission devoted most of its efforts to issuing *Responsa* ("answers") to questions that were submitted from around the world. Among the more memorable were those related to the narratives in the Historical Books (1905), the Mosaic authorship of the **Pentateuch** (1906), and the historical character of the first three chapters of Genesis (1909). One of the primary concerns of the Commission at this point was to resist the rise of modernist ideas.

In the years before the Second Vatican Council, the *Responsa* encouraged serious and responsible biblical studies, especially in the wake of Pope Pius XII's encyclical *Divino Afflante Spiritu* (1943). The Commission's instruction *Sancta Mater Ecclesia* (1964), on the historicity of the Gospels, had some influence on the Second Vatican Council's Dogmatic Constitution on Revelation, *Dei Verbum* (1965).

In 1971, Pope Paul VI established new norms for the organization and function of the Biblical Commission. The first change was the adjustment to include biblical scholars (not just cardinals) as the primary membership. Second, the Commission was attached to the Congregation for the Doctrine of the Faith. The president of the Biblical Commission is now the cardinal prefect of the Sacred Congregation for the Doctrine of the Faith, and membership is limited to twenty scholars from various schools and nations, chosen from among those noted for their "learning, prudence and Catholic regard for the Magisterium."

Among the various documents issued by the Commission since 1971 have been *Fede e cultura alla luce della Bibbia* (1981, Faith and Culture in Light of the Bible); *Bible et Christologie* (1984, The Bible and Christology); *Unité et diversité dans l'Eglise* (1989, Unity and Diversity in the Church); *L'interprétation de la Bible dans l'Eglise* (1993, The Interpretation of the Bible in the Church); and *Le peuple juif et ses Saintes Ecritures dans la Bible chrétienne* (2001, The Jewish People and Their Sacred Scriptures in the Christian Bible).

PONTIUS PILATE *See* **Pilate, Pontius**.

PONTUS A region in northern Asia Minor (modern Turkey) along the Black Sea. A mountainous area, Pontus was a conglomeration of Greek states and Iranian noble territories that was forged into a kingdom that pushed out the Romans in the first century B.C. After the conquest of the kingdom by the Roman governor Pompey the Great in A.D. 64, the western part of Pontus was attached to the Roman province of Bithynia while the eastern part was retained under a Greek dynasty as a client state to Rome. Both Jews and Christians lived in Pontus in the first century A.D. (Acts 2:9; 1 Pet 1:1).

POOR Deprived of wealth and prosperity by various social, political, and economic circumstances. Poverty was fairly common in the biblical world, because of frequent wars, famines and droughts, and the accepted practice of debt slavery. Concern for the poor is mandated for Israel in the Old Testament and for Christians in the New Testament. In addition to material poverty, the Church also recognizes the reality of spiritual and cultural poverty.

The **Law** of Moses specified certain requirements for the protection of the poor and those stricken with misfortune, including the Jubilee year during which debts were forgiven, prohibitions of interest on loans and the collection and keeping of collateral, and the right to glean vines and fields (Lev 25; Deut 15:7–10; 23:19–20; 24:10–15, 19–22): "For the poor will never cease out of the land; therefore I command you, You shall open wide your hand to your brother, to the needy and to the poor, in the land" (Deut 15:11; cf. Tob 4:7–11; Sir 17:22). Oppression of the poor was strenuously denounced by the prophets (Amos 2:6–7).

Jesus was born to poor parents (Luke 2:24) in a humble stable (Luke 2:6–7) and shared the life of the poor. He said that he was sent to "preach good news to the poor" (Luke 4:18; 7:22), declared them "blessed" (Luke 6:20), and established an active love for them as one of the preconditions for entry into the Kingdom (Matt 25:31–46).

"The poor you always have with you," Jesus said (John 12:8). In light of this fact, the Christian is required to perform works of mercy, including giving aid to our neighbor, feeding the hungry, giving shelter to the homeless, clothing the naked, and caring for the sick. Almsgiving is pleasing to God because it is a work of justice (Matt 6:2–4; Luke 3:11, 11:41; Jas 2:15–16; 1 John 3:17–18). The theological implications of poverty were expressed by the Congregation for the Doctrine of the Faith in its document *Libertatis conscientia* (§68):

> *In its various forms—material deprivation, unjust oppression, physical and psychological illness and death—human misery is the obvious sign of the inherited condition of frailty and need for salvation in which man finds himself as a consequence of original sin. This misery elicited the compassion of Christ the Savior, who willingly took it upon himself and identified himself with the least of his brethren. Hence, those who are oppressed by poverty are the object of a preferential love on the part of the Church which, since her origin and in spite of the failings of many of her members, has not ceased to work for their relief, defense, and liberation through numerous works of charity which remain indispensable always and everywhere.*

The Christians in Jerusalem were attentive to the needs of the poor in the city (Acts 2:44–45; 4:34–35), and Paul during his journeys labored to raise money for the poor in Jerusalem (Rom 15:25–29; Gal 2:10). Paul also wrote the most detailed examination of poverty in the NT in the Second Letter to the Corinthians, building his teachings around the key idea, "For you know the grace of our Lord Jesus Christ, that though he was rich, yet for your sake he became poor, so that by his poverty you might become rich" (2 Cor 8:9). The disciple is thus called to emulate Christ by a generous life of sharing our blessings with those who have little or none (Luke 14:33, 21:14; Mark 8:35).

POSSESSION, DIABOLICAL *See* **Demon**.

POTIPHAR An Egyptian official who was the first master of the patriarch **Joseph** (Gen 37:36) and who named Joseph his chief steward (Gen 39:4). Potiphar is described as "an officer of Pharaoh, the captain of the guard" (Gen 39:1). The wife of Potiphar became enamored of Joseph; when he refused her advances, she falsely accused him of attempted rape (Gen 39:6b–18). The false claim was the occasion of Joseph's being hurled into prison (Gen 39:19–20) and his subsequent interpretation of dreams (Gen 40:1–23).

POTIPHERA An Egyptian priest of On, the father of Asenath, and the father-in-law of the patriarch **Joseph**. His daughter was given by the Pharaoh to Joseph for his wife (Gen 41:45), and their marriage produced two children, **Manasseh** and **Ephraim** (Gen 41:50–52; 46:20). The name is a longer version of the name Potiphar (Gen 39:1).

POTSHERD GATE One of the gates of Jerusalem in the City of David (Jer 19:2). It is probably the same as the Dung Gate (Neh 2:13; 3:13, 14; 12:31).

POTTER'S FIELD *See* **Akeldama**.

POTTER'S GATE *See* **Potsherd Gate**.

POTTERY Pottery appeared for the first time in the Near East during the Neolithic period (6000–5000 B.C.). Plates, jugs, bowls, cups, lamps, jars, utensils, and even toys were shaped out of clay. Pots were created from finely graded red clay mixed with water and then shaped. Early pots were shaped by hand. From the time the potter's wheel was invented in the late fourth millennium B.C., the wet clay could be turned and shaped into the desired form. The wheel was spun by either the potter or an assistant. The activity of the potter is described in detail in Sir 38:30:

> *So too is the potter sitting at his work*
> *and turning the wheel with his feet;*
> *he is always deeply concerned over his work,*
> *and all his output is by number.*
> *He moulds the clay with his arm*
> *and makes it pliable with his feet;*
> *he sets his heart to finish the glazing,*
> *and he is careful to clean the furnace.*

Pottery was universally used and easily broken, but the broken pieces lasted almost indefinitely. Pottery remains, therefore, are a valuable source of knowledge for archaeologists. Palestinian sites offer few stone monuments that preserve records or inscriptions, but potsherds (broken pieces of pottery) are found in such abundance that they provide a useful record of the habitation of a site. Archaeologists have used pottery remains to great effect for the study of ancient Palestinian history and the cross-dating of sites by comparing potsherds at one site with shards found in other sites. In their style and distribution, the pots also reveal patterns of trade and commerce.

The potter and his crafts provided rich symbolism for Scripture, starting with the image of God fashioning man out of clay in Gen 2:7. God is also depicted as a master potter who shapes peoples and nations (Isa 29:16, 45:9, 64:8; Jer 18:1–6; Sir 33:13; Rom 9:20–24). The smashing of fragile pots served as an image of utter destruction (Jer 19:10–11; Ps 2:9; Rev 2:27) and the cheapness of clay pots was a means of pointing to human frailty (Lam 4:2). For Sirach, "The kiln tests the potter's vessels; so the test of a man is in his reasoning" (Sir 27:5).

PRAETORIUM The headquarters of the praetorian prefect, a Roman official or governor who served in a region of the Roman Empire. The New Testament refers to several such residences. The praetorium of **Pilate** in Jerusalem is the place where Jesus's trial was conducted (Matt 27:27; Mark 15:16; John 18:28, 33; 19:9). Acts 23:25 mentions a praetorium in the coastal city of Caesarea that was built by **Herod** the Great (r. 37–4 B.C.), where Paul was incarcerated. The praetorium mentioned in Phil 1:13 is most likely the imperial Praetorium in Rome.

PRAISE Praise is defined in the Catechism as "the form of prayer which recognizes most immediately that God is God. It lauds God for his own sake and gives him glory, quite beyond what he does, but simply because HE IS" (CCC 2639). Praise encompasses other forms of prayer and directs them toward the object of our love, adoration, and thanks: "one God, the Father, from whom are all things and for whom we exist, and one Lord, Jesus Christ, through whom are all things and through whom we exist" (1 Cor 8:6). Scripture is full of praise for God, beginning with the first account of the Creation (Gen 1:1–2:4). God's works of creation resound with joy and praise in thanks (Job 38:4–7; Rev 4:6–11).

Praise is due from all for the life that has been given to them by God. Man was created to rejoice in God's bountiful works and to acknowledge his goodness (1 Chr 29:10–13; Ps 90:14–16; Phil 4:4). Rejoicing in the Lord was an essential part of Israel's festival and sacrificial observances (Lev 23:40; Num 10:10; Deut 16:11–12; Ps 42:4). It could take the form of song, dance, and music (Exod 15:20; 2 Sam 6:14; Ps 149:3, 150:4). The spirituality of praise is most perfect when it permeates the daily life of God's elect: "I will bless the Lord at all times; his praise shall continually be in my mouth" (Ps 34:1).

For those blessed to witness the saving power of Jesus, praise was a common reaction to being healed or cleansed (Mark 2:12; Luke 18:43). Likewise in the book of Acts, praise was the common response of those who were healed or who encountered the Gospel (Acts 2:46–47, 3:8–9, 4:21, 11:18, 13:48, 16:25; Eph 1:13–14). Early Christians gave praise in the Temple (Luke 24:53; Acts 3:1) and recited the Psalms (Eph 5:19; Col 3:16), but new forms of praise developed, including hymns and canticles that gave praise for Jesus's saving life, death, and Resurrection (cf. Col 1:15–20, 3:16; 1 Cor 14:26; Phil 2:6–11; Eph 5:14; 1 Tim 3:16; 2 Tim 2:11–13). Likewise, the doxology emerged as a profound means of praise (cf. Rom 11:36, 16:25–27; Jude 24–25), reaching a climax in the book of Revelation, in which the songs of the heavenly **liturgy** are so often heard (Rev 4:8–11; 5:9–10).

There is an intimate connection between praise and sacrifice (Ps 119:108; Hos 14:2). The supreme sacrifice for the praise and glory of God was offered by Christ (Matt 11:25–26; Mark 14:22–23, 26; John 17:1–2). The Church thus celebrates the **Eucharist** as the premier sacrifice of praise and thanksgiving: "The Eucharist, the sacrament of our salvation accomplished by Christ on the Cross, is also a sacrifice of praise in thanksgiving for the work of creation. In the Eucharistic sacrifice, the whole of creation loved by God is presented to the Father through the death and the Resurrection of Christ. Through Christ the Church can offer the sacrifice of praise in thanksgiving for all that God has made good, beautiful, and just in creation and in humanity" (CCC 1359; cf. CCC 2639–43).

PRAYER According to Saint John Damascene, "Prayer is the raising of one's mind and heart to God or the requesting of good things from God" (*De fide orthadoxa* 3.24). Through prayer God invites each person to enter into a personal encounter with the Creator. God's plan of salvation offers a reciprocal relationship between God and man, and prayer is integral to that reciprocity.

Prayer in Scripture encompasses the entire range of human emotions and expressions, from petitions and lamentations to meditations, benedictions, thanksgiving, praise, and adoration.

I. *Prayer in the Old Testament*
    A. *Kinds of Prayer*
    B. *Conversations with God*
    C. *Interceding with God*
    D. *Prayer in the Prophets*
II. *Prayer in the New Testament*
    A. *Jesus, the Model of Prayer*
    B. *Familiarity with God the Father*
    C. *Prayer in the Early Church*

I. PRAYER IN THE OLD TESTAMENT

A. *Kinds of Prayer*

In the **Pentateuch**, we read of conversations between God and the patriarchs and other persons. Whereas other ancient religions made petitions to a pantheon of divine beings, the prayers of Israel were addressed to Yahweh (Exod 20:2–3; Deut 6:4), earlier known as God Almighty (Exod 6:2–3). Discourse between God and individual persons was basic to the **covenant** relationship established by God with the patriarchs, who prayed when they called upon the "name" of the Lord (Gen 12:8; 21:33; 26:25).

There was, as well, a social and public dimension to Old Testament prayer. Emphasis was placed on sacred times and places set aside for worship. The Pentateuch notes such cult places as Shechem (Gen 12:6–7), Bethel (Gen 28:18–22), Mamre (Gen 13:18), and Beersheba (Gen 26:23–25) and sacred times such as the weekly Sabbath (Gen 2:1–3; Exod 20:8–11) and the yearly feasts (Exod 23:14–17; Lev

23; Deut 16:1–17). The chief place for liturgical prayer, however, was the **Tabernacle** and later the **Temple**, for that was where God dwelt with his people (Exod 25:8; Deut 12:5–7).

B. Conversations with God

The first mention of prayer in the OT is made in Gen 4:26, when, in the time of Enosh, "men began to call upon the name of the Lord." Even before this, however, we see Adam on speaking terms with the Lord (Gen 3:9–12). So, too, with Moses, for Exod 33:11 declares, "Thus the LORD used to speak to Moses face to face, as a man speaks to his friend."

Abraham and Moses are especially significant figures in OT prayer. Abraham is completely submissive to the will of God even to the point of being willing to sacrifice his own son (Gen 22:8; Heb 11:19) (CCC 2570–72). For his fidelity, Abraham receives God's promises that are renewed with Jacob, whose own struggle with the angel has been seen as a model for prayer as a struggle of faith (Gen 32:24–30) (CCC 2573).

C. Interceding with God

Intercessory prayer—prayer on behalf of others—is also important in the OT. Abraham prayed on behalf of Sodom (Gen 18:20–32) and Abimelech (Gen 20:17), but Moses is the foremost exemplar of intercessory prayer. Such prayer was part of his role as covenant mediator between the Lord and Israel. When the people sinned, he was there to plead for God's forgiveness (Exod 32:30–32; Num 14:13–19). When questions and uncertainties arose, he was there to inquire of the Lord (Num 27:1–5). He thus acquired a lasting reputation as one who stood before the Lord on behalf of others (Jer 15:1).

D. Prayer in the Prophets

The prophets were men of prayer because they were in frequent dialogue with the Lord. Sometimes they called out for him in their distress (Jonah 2:1–9) and despair (1 Kgs 19:4), and sometimes they professed their faith in the Lord even when they were struggling to comprehend his ways (Hab 3:1–19). Occasionally their oracles addressed the subject of prayer in the life of Israel. This is especially so in Isaiah, who had no patience for people who prayed yet whose hearts and lives were turned away from the Lord (Isa 1:15; 29:13). Still, he urged God's people to pray (Isa 55:6) in the confidence that the Lord would hear and give heed to their pleas (Isa 58:9). He also voiced the prayers of those who would give thanks for the Lord's salvation.

Job, Lamentations, and above all Psalms give us fine examples of OT prayer. The Psalms accentuate such key themes as liberation, wonder, instruction, and popular feasts. The Psalms also offer the ideal means of introducing prayer in the New Testament, for the Psalms were fulfilled in Christ (CCC 2596–97).

II. PRAYER IN THE NEW TESTAMENT

A. Jesus, the Model of Prayer

Jesus is the perfect model of prayer in the Bible. In him we see examples of solitary prayer, vigil prayer, conversational prayer, repetitious prayer, set prayer, and intercessory prayer. He prayed often in solitude in desert places and on mountains (cf. Matt 14:23; Mark 1:35, 6:46; Luke 5:16) and prayed in preparation for the most decisive and important moments of his ministry and life, including his baptism (Luke 3:21), the calling of the Twelve (Luke 6:12), his Transfiguration (Luke 9:28), and his Passion (Luke 22:41–45; cf. Matt 26:36–44). At the Last Supper, Jesus offered a long prayer of petition (John 17:1–26), and in the Garden of Gethsemane he prayed the same prayer three times in a row (Matt 26:36–44). On the Cross, he prayed the set words of the Psalms (Ps 22:2; cf. Ps 31:5 in Luke 23:46). (*See also* **Parable**; **Seven Words from the Cross**.)

B. Familiarity with God the Father

The prayer life of Jesus is marked by his use of the term "**Abba**" (Aramaic for "Father") to convey his intimacy and familiarity with God (Mark 14:36). Jesus thus serves as the supreme model of how to pray (Matt 6:5–15; Luke 18:9–14), especially in times of trial and suffering (Heb 5:7). When the disciples said to him, "Lord, teach us to pray" (Luke 11:1), Jesus replied by teaching his disciples the **Lord's Prayer**. He emphasized the need to approach God with faith: "whatever you ask in prayer, believe that you have received it, and it will be yours" (Mark 11:24). We should pray too with a disposition always to be obedient to the will of the Father (Matt 7:21) and thereby to cooperate with the plan of salvation. Jesus also taught that faith in the Son serves as the greatest means to enter into knowledge of the Father, for Jesus is "the way, and the truth, and the life" (John 14:6).

The prayer life of Jesus did not end when he ascended into glory, for even there, at the right hand of the Father, he lives to make intercession for the saints on earth (Heb 7:25).

C. Prayer in the Early Church

Early Christian prayer was offered in the name of Jesus (John 14:13; 1 Cor 1:2), confident that he was present among his disciples (Matt 18:20). Praying was done in a variety of contexts, both public and private: in the Jerusalem Temple (Luke 24:52; Acts 3:1), in people's homes (Acts 2:46), in prisons (Acts 16:25), and even on housetops (Acts 10:9). Calling upon the name of Jesus is likewise an integral part of liturgical and sacramental worship (Acts 2:38, 22:16; 1 Cor 6:11; Jas 5:14–15), and prayers of thanksgiving are clearly associated with the Christian celebration of the **Eucharist** (Acts 2:42; 1 Cor 11:23–26).

Apostolic catechesis teaches that prayer should be continual (1 Thess 5:17) and offered with confident faith in the Lord's ability to accomplish all things (Jas 1:5–8). It is likewise understood that one's prayer life is interconnected with one's moral life, for the prayers of the righteous are powerful (Jas 5:16), while the prayers of a sinner can be hindered (1 Pet 3:7, 12).

Theologically, the divine adoption of the believer *in* the Son and *through* the Spirit gives him or her access to the Father (Eph 2:18), whom he or she addresses on intimate terms as "Abba" (Rom 8:15–16; Gal 4:6). Not only that, but both Christ and the Holy Spirit are said to intercede for the faithful according to the will of God (Rom 8:26–27, 34).

PRAYER OF MANASSEH *See* **Manasseh**.

PREACHING *See Kerygma.*

PRESBYTER *See* **Elder**; *see also* **Priest, priesthood**.

PRIEST, PRIESTHOOD A priest is an authorized mediator who offers sacrifice to God on behalf of others. Christ is the perfect priest, for he is perfectly united to God in his divinity and fully united to us in his humanity. The Catechism of the Catholic Church teaches:

> *Everything that the priesthood of the Old Covenant prefigured finds its fulfillment in Christ Jesus, the "one mediator between God and men" (2 Tim 2:5). The Christian tradition considers Melchizedek, "priest of God Most High," as a prefiguration of the priesthood of Christ, the unique "high priest after the order of Melchizedek" (Heb 5:10; cf. Heb 6:20; Gen 14:18); "holy, blameless, unstained" (Heb 7:26), "by a single offering he has perfected for all time those who are sanctified" (Heb 10:14), that is, by the unique sacrifice of the cross. (CCC 1544)*

I. *The Priesthood in the Old Testament*
   A. *The Patriarchal Period*
   B. *Israel, a Nation of Priests*
   C. *The Levitical Priesthood*
II. *The Priesthood in the New Testament*
   A. *The Priesthood of Christ*
   B. *The Common Priesthood of the Faithful*
   C. *The Ministerial Priesthood*

I. THE PRIESTHOOD IN THE OLD TESTAMENT

We can see two principal periods of priesthood in the Old Testament: the patriarchal and the Levitical. The patriarchal period is detailed mainly in Genesis, and the Levitical period is presented in the rest of the **Pentateuch** and extends until the coming of Christ.

A. *The Patriarchal Period*

There was no professional class of priests in the age before the Levitical priesthood. The foundation for the religion of the patriarchs was the natural family order. In this context, authority passed from father to son, and sacrifices were offered not at designated sites, but at the discretion of the patriarchs, who practiced a form of natural religion. Sacred actions included building altars (Gen 12:8), planting trees (Gen 21:33), offering sacrifice (Gen 8:20), and erecting pillars (Gen 28:11–22).

The origins of the priestly office, then, can be traced to the unique spiritual authority, representative function, and religious service of the father in the family. At the same time, the office of kingship was the embodiment of the father's secular duties, most notably his role in leadership and governing. Thus priesthood is inseparable from fatherhood (cf. Job 1:5).

The archetype of the royal priesthood in the patriarchal period is **Melchizedek**, priest-king of Salem (i.e., Jerusalem; Ps 76:2). This mysterious figure is the first person in Scripture to be called a priest (Gen 14:17–20); he offers bread and wine to Abram (**Abraham**) and then gives his blessing to Abram and his men.

B. *Israel, a Nation of Priests*

The OT traces the progress of sin and its terrible impact upon the human family—from Adam's fall to Israel's enslavement in Egypt, which is described in the beginning of Exodus. We see a consistent pattern throughout the story: tragedy and sin lead to firstborn sons being disinherited (e.g., Cain, Ishmael, Esau, Reuben, Er, Perez, Manasseh). The pattern in individuals would be repeated in Israel as a nation. Moses was told at the burning bush: "Israel is my firstborn son" (Exod 4:22). The importance of the firstborn is revealed in stark terms at Passover when Israel's firstborn sons are redeemed by the blood of the Paschal lamb. Thereafter, firstborn sons are consecrated to the Lord's service (Exod 13:2; 22:29).

God commands Israel, his "firstborn son," to embrace its unique vocation and mission to be a "holy nation and a royal priesthood," to be a mediator between the Father and the family of nations. That status, however, is entirely conditional (as the earlier examples of disinherited sons demonstrate) upon the adherence of Israel to the covenant: "if you obey my voice and keep my covenant you shall be my special possession" (Exod 19:5–6). The Israelites soon broke their fidelity to God by worshipping the golden calf, and the blessing of the firstborn was forfeited to the Levites when they avenged the Lord at the command of Moses (Exod 32:25–29; see **Levi**). This event signaled the beginning of a second period of the priesthood in the OT, the Levitical priesthood.

C. The Levitical Priesthood

As the book of Exodus reveals, Israel's apostasy with the golden calf at Sinai required a renewal of the covenant—first with Moses alone (Exod 33–34), but then extended to Israel with the command to build a **Tabernacle** and consecrate **Aaron** as high priest (Exod 35–40). God only then commanded Moses to speak to Israel about the types of sacrifice (burnt, sin, peace) that Aaron and his sons would be instructed to offer on the people's behalf according to the priestly code (Lev 1–16). Finally, the holiness code was given for the Levitical priests to instruct the twelve lay tribes of Israel (Lev 17–26).

The result was an elaborate system of priestly mediation based on the hierarchical order of Moses, Aaron (and his sons), the Levites, and the twelve tribes of Israel. In the OT, this same priestly hierarchy (high priest, Aaronic priests, and Levites) continued (with some minor variations) throughout the history of Israel: the wilderness period, the conquest and settlement of Canaan, the monarchy, and the period after the **Exile**.

The result of Israel's second lapse into idolatry at Beth-peor (Num 25:1–13) was the imposition of the Deuteronomic covenant on the twelve tribes on the plains of Moab, the site of their new apostasy (Deut 3:29; 4:3). When the Deuteronomic covenant was ratified, a two-covenant structure was instituted over the twelve tribes (Josh 8:30–35). By its terms, Israel was placed under the administrative supervision of the Levites (Deut 27:9–26). The Levites for their part were bound by "the covenant of Levi" (Jer 33:17–26; Mal 2:4–8), which was made with them by Moses at Sinai after the incident of the golden calf. The Levitical covenant was then renewed with the grandson of Aaron, **Phinehas**, at the end of Israel's forty years of wandering in the wilderness. Phinehas was granted a "covenant of a perpetual priesthood" in recognition of his righteous zeal in avenging the second generation's idolatrous worship of Baal of Peor (Num 25:13).

In the time after the settlement of Canaan, the renewed covenant continued to exercise influence on the shape of the OT priesthood, climaxing with the collapse of **Eli**'s priestly house (1 Sam 2:27–36), the expulsion of **Abiathar** as high priest (1 Kgs 2:26–35), and the subsequent elevation of **Zadok** as high priest in Jerusalem (1 Kgs 2:35). Crucial in this development was proving genealogical descent from Phinehas, something possessed by Zadok (1 Chr 6:4–8) but missing in Eli and Abiathar (1 Sam 22:9–20). The Zadokite high priesthood in the Jerusalem Temple became one of the most distinctive features of the Davidic monarchy, at which time the Levites were given specialized ministries within the Temple (as liturgical musicians, singers, guardsmen, treasurers, etc.; 1 Chr 9:22–34; 23:2–28).

The importance of Israel's high priests after the **Exile** is foreshadowed in Ezekiel's visions of the restoration of Jerusalem under the (Zadokite) high priest (Ezek 43–45). This situation is one means of explaining Zechariah's seemingly incongruous description of the royal crowning of the high priest **Joshua** (Zech 6:9–13), instead of **Zerubbabel**, the Davidic descendant who played a pivotal role in the rebuilding of the Temple (Ezra 5:2).

Further, this view is seen in the praise reserved by Sirach for the priestly figures from Aaron down to the high priest of his day, Simon, who is honored as "the leader of his brothers and the pride of his people" (Sir 50:1). Sources outside the Bible further portray the Messiah as a combination of Davidic kingship and high priestly authority (*T. Sim.* 7:13; *T. Lev.* 2:10–11, 5:2, 8:2–15; cf. Ps 110:1–4). Messianic expectations and views of first-century A.D. Jewish Christians were seemingly influenced by this outlook, and the author of Hebrews makes it the basis of his argument concerning Christ's royal high priesthood "after the order of Melchizedek" (Heb 7).

The Zadokite high priesthood endured in Jerusalem until Antiochus IV Epiphanes (*see* **Seleucids**) deposed Onias II in 175 B.C. and replaced him with **Jason** (r. 175–172 B.C.). The Seleucid rulers then appointed non-Zadokites until they were defeated in 153 B.C. by the Hasmoneans, who continued the non-Zadokite rule until the Roman conquest in the first century B.C. The subsequent appointment of high priests was done only with the approval of the Herodian kings and the authority of Rome. This custom lasted until the destruction of the Jerusalem Temple in A.D. 70. With that event the last vestiges of the Levitical priesthood—and the Old Covenant—were extinguished (CCC 63, 1539–43). (*See* **Redemption**; **Sacrifice**.)

II. THE PRIESTHOOD IN THE NEW TESTAMENT

With the coming of Christ as God's firstborn Son (Heb 1:6), and royal High Priest (Heb 2:2–17; 5:1–10), the division of royal and priestly powers was brought to an end. By establishing his Church as "the assembly of the firstborn" (Heb 12:23), Christ reunited the offices of priesthood and kingship and restored the "royal priesthood" (1 Pet 2:9) of God's people, who now constituted the "Israel of God" (Gal 6:16).

The priesthood of Jesus must be seen in

light of the OT priesthood, and the full understanding of the New Testament priesthood should begin with the patriarchal period and the place of the firstborn son. Luke 2:7 refers to Jesus as the "firstborn," which indicates that Jesus is entitled to receive all of the rights and status of the firstborn under Mosaic Law (cf. Exod 13:2; Deut 21:15–17). It may be significant that, when Jesus was presented in the Temple (Luke 2:23), the redemption fee of five shekels (by which a Levite replaced a firstborn son in service to the Lord; Num 8:15–16) is not mentioned. If so, it indicates that Jesus is consecrated to the service of the Lord instead of being "bought back" by his parents. We would then see Jesus in the role of a priest by virtue of being a first son in the patriarchal sense.

A. The Priesthood of Christ

The Letter to the Hebrews gives us the fullest treatment of Christ's priesthood in the NT. According to its author, the priesthood of Jesus is defined in relation to the Levitical priesthood of Aaron, to which it is superior in every essential respect. Jesus is the *sinless* priest (Heb 4:15), whereas the Aaronic priests are sinners and must offer sacrifices for themselves as well as the people (Heb 5:1–3). Jesus is the *everlasting* priest (Heb 7:24), whereas the Aaronic priests are mortal and must be replaced by an endless line of successors (Heb 7:23). Jesus is the *heavenly* High Priest (Heb 4:14; 8:1–2), whereas the priests of the Old Covenant ministered in a sanctuary on earth (Heb 8:4–5). Jesus is the *royal* priest promised by oath in the Messianic Ps 110:4 (Heb 5:6; 7:17), whereas the Levitical priests took office without any oath at all (Heb 7:21).

As the more perfect priest, Christ offers the Father a more perfect sacrifice than any priests of the Levitical order could; Christ's sacrifice was offered once for all (Heb 10:10), in contrast to the continual cycle of sacrifices required under the Old Covenant (Heb 10:11). The reason is that Christ's sacrifice brought about a true remission of sins (Heb 9:11–14, 28; 10:12–18), in contrast to the Levitical offerings, which served as reminders of sin but were incapable of removing sins (Heb 10:4, 11).

The backdrop for these claims is the belief that Jesus belonged, not to the priestly order of Aaron, but to the patriarchal order of Melchizedek (Heb 5:6; 6:20). This idea is developed in Heb 7, and is based on Psalm 110, which envisions the **Messiah** both as an enthroned King (Ps 110:1) and as a Melchizedekian priest (Ps 110:4). The idea is that Christ belongs to the original order of priesthood that was exercised in pre-Levitical times.

This explains why the author of Hebrews puts such stress on the sonship of Jesus in relation to his priesthood (Heb 2:10; 5:5–10). In particular, he emphasizes that Christ is the "firstborn" of the Father (Heb 1:6), who stands in relation to believers as both a brother (Heb 2:11–12) and a father figure (Heb 2:13–14). It is even possible that Melchizedek, who is both a forerunner and a **type** of Christ, was viewed in such terms by the author and original readers of Hebrews, who would have known that Jewish tradition identified Melchizedek with **Shem**, the firstborn son of Noah (*see* **Melchizedek**).

Other aspects of Melchizedek's priesthood point to Christ as well. For instance, Melchizedek was the priest-king of Salem (Heb

7:1), which is an ancient name for Jerusalem or Zion (Ps 76:2). This priesthood-kingship of Melchizedek prefigures the royal priestly ministry of Jesus in the "heavenly Jerusalem" (Heb 12:22). So, too, just as Melchizedek the priest brought forth bread and wine (Gen 14:18), Christian reflection sees a prefigurement of the Eucharist, the sacrificial meal that Christ offers believers under the appearance of bread and wine (Matt 26:26–29).

B. The Common Priesthood of the Faithful

Christ, as High Priest and mediator, has made the Church "a kingdom, priests to his God and Father" (Rev 1:6). He has restored and fulfilled in himself the family priesthood of the firstborn, the vocation to which Israel was called, by sharing in that firstborn sonship and priesthood (cf. Exod 4:22; 19:6).

The people of God thus share in the dignity of Christ's priesthood through their baptismal participation in his mission as priest, prophet, and king, according to their individual vocations (1 Pet 2:5–9). By grace, the Church shares in the sonship of Christ, and thus shares also in his priestly mission. The Church is entrusted with the vocation that had been intended for Israel among the nations (CCC 897–903).

C. The Ministerial Priesthood

The second participation of the faithful in the priesthood of Christ is through the ministerial or hierarchical priesthood. The two forms of participation are ordered one to the other, as *Lumen Gentium* teaches (§10), but they are essentially different (in kind and not simply in degree). The common priesthood of the faithful is exercised through baptismal grace, whereas the ministerial priesthood serves and sanctifies the faithful and is passed on by the sacrament of holy orders.

Jesus chose the twelve apostles to serve as the heads of the new People of God (Matt 19:28; Rev 21:12–14). As sharers in the one priesthood of Christ, itself of the order of Melchizedek, the apostles were to serve as the priestly firstborn sons, acting as elder brothers and fathers to the communities under their charge (cf. Acts 15:23; 1 Cor 4:15). In turn, the apostles appointed to succeed them elders or presbyters over the churches they had founded (Acts 14:23). Strictly speaking, the NT does not refer to Christian ministers as "priests" (Greek *hiereis*) but as "bishops" (Greek *episkopoi*) and "presbyters" (Greek *presbyteroi*). Nevertheless, it is from this latter term that the English word "priest" is actually derived.

By virtue of the sacrament of holy orders, the priest acts in the person of Christ, the Head of the Church. As Thomas Aquinas wrote, "Christ is the source of all priesthood: the priest of the old law was a figure of Christ, and the priest of the new law acts in the person of Christ" (*Summa theologiae* III.22. 4c). Ordained ministers make the presence of Christ as Head of the Church visible to the community. As Pope John Paul II wrote in *Pastores Dabo Vobis*:

> In the Church and on behalf of the Church, priests are a sacramental representation of Jesus Christ, the Head and Shepherd, authoritatively proclaiming his Word, repeating his acts of forgiveness and his offer of salvation, particularly in Baptism, Penance and the

Eucharist, showing his loving concern to the point of a total gift of self for the flock . . . In a word, priests exist and act in order to proclaim the Gospel to the world and to build up the Church in the name and person of Christ the Head and Shepherd. (§15)

From the very beginning, bishops and presbyters of the Christian community offered the sacraments, taught and proclaimed sound doctrine, and governed as shepherds. By their ordination, they participated in the universal mission that Christ entrusted to the apostles. They were empowered not only to be at the service of the community but also to participate in the universal mission of salvation for the whole world (Acts 1:8). The exercise of priestly ministry is always measured against the supreme model of Christ (Mark 10:43–45; 1 Pet 5:3) (CCC 1544–68). (*See also* **Eucharist**; **Sacrifice**.)

PRINCIPALITIES A translation of the New Testament term *archai* used by Paul to designate angelic beings, usually in close conjunction with powers. Principalities are one of several angelic orders mentioned in Scripture, including *exousiai* ("authorities"), *archontes* ("rulers"), *thronoi* ("thrones"), and *kyriotētes* ("dominions"). According to Eph 6:12, principalities and powers are numbered among the evil spirits that pose a threat to believers. They are enemies of humanity, but their influence has been shattered by Christ. Similar notions appear in Eph 1:21, Col 2:15, and 1 Pet 3:21. Traditional names for angelic beings also appear in Old Testament pseudepigrapha such

as *1 Enoch* 61:10; *2 Enoch* 20:1; and *T. Sol.* 20:15. (*See also* **Demon**.)

PRISCA *See* **Priscilla**.

PRISCILLA Also Prisca, the wife of **Aquila**, both of whom were associates of the apostle **Paul**. Prisca and Aquila were early converts to the Christian faith and moved to Corinth after being expelled from Rome by a decree of Emperor Claudius (Acts 18:2). They gave welcome to Paul in Corinth, and the apostle labored alongside them as a tentmaker (Acts 18:2–3). Eventually the couple moved on to Ephesus (Acts 18:18–19) and then back to Rome (Rom 16:3–5). Prisca and Aquila were known to have generously opened their home to host Christian assemblies (Rom 16:5; 1 Cor 16:19).

PRISON In the ancient world, being held in prison was not usually a punishment in itself; rather, a prisoner was detained in prison while he awaited trial or execution. The first prison mentioned in Scripture is the one where **Joseph** was confined in Egypt (Gen 39:20). Joseph's brothers were also detained in a similar manner (Gen 42:17, 19). **Samson** was held in prison by the Philistines (Judg 16:21, 25).

Prophets who earned the enmity of rulers were placed under various forms of detention. **Jeremiah** was held in the guardroom of the palace (Jer 32:2; 37:21), the dungeon of the secretary of Jonathan (Jer 37:15), and an outdoor cistern, filled with sludge (Jer 38:6). **Hanani** was also imprisoned (2 Chr 16:10), as was **Micaiah** (1 Kgs 22:27; 2 Chr 18:26). For the vanquished, including kings, defeat was followed by a period of incarceration: **Hoshea** was held by the Assyrians (2 Kgs 17:4), **Jehoiachin** by **Nebuchadnezzar** (2 Kgs 25:27), and **Zedekiah** by the Babylonians (Jer 52:11).

In the New Testament, **John the Baptist** was imprisoned before his execution, probably in the fortress of Machaerus (Matt 11:2, 14:3; Luke 3:20). The apostles were held in a public prison at the command of the chief priests (Acts 5:18–19). **Paul** was held prisoner at various places (Acts 16:24; 22:24; 23:35), but once he had arrived in Rome he was permitted to live in his own lodgings, although a soldier was chained to him at all times (Acts 28:16; 30). Paul wrote that being an apostle brought the danger of imprisonment (2 Cor 6:5).

PROCHORUS One of the seven men who were chosen to care for the poor widows in Jerusalem (Acts 6:1–5).

PROCONSUL The governor of a Roman province; by the time of the New Testament, the proconsul was normally the governor of a senatorial province (as compared to the governor of an imperial province, which was under the direct authority of the emperor). Senatorial provinces were so designated under the imperial reorganization undertaken by Augustus (r. 27 B.C.–A.D. 14); these provinces did not require a Roman military presence. Several proconsuls are mentioned in the NT: L. Sergius Paullus of Cyprus (Acts 13:7–12) and L. Junius Gallio of Achaea (Acts 18:12–17).

PROCURATOR The governor, usually of equestrian rank, who was posted to a province of lesser rank in the Roman Empire (originally called a "prefect"). The most notable such provinces were Judea, Thrace, Rhaetia, Noricum, and Mauretania. A procurator might also be a financial officer or a personal representative of the emperor; hence the etymology of the word from the Latin *pro*, "on behalf of," and *curo*, "to care for." The procurator was usually under the authority of the nearest provincial governor; in the case of **Judea**, the procurator answered to the governor of Syria. The duties of the procurator included maintaining order, collecting taxes, and keeping tranquil relations with local religious leaders. In Judea, the procurator also had direct authority over capital cases and was responsible for appointing the high priest. Three procurators are mentioned by name in the New Testament: Pontius **Pilate** (Matt 27:2), Antonius **Felix** (Acts 23:26), and Porcius **Festus** (Acts 24:27).

Procurators of Judea (A.D. 6–66)

Coponius (r. 6–9)
M. Ambivius (r. 9–12)
Annius Rufus (r. 12–15)
Valerius Gratus (r. 15–26)
Pontius Pilate (r. c. 26–36)
Marcellus (r. 36–37)
Marullus (r. 37–41)
Cuspius Fadus (r. 44–46)
Tiberius Alexander (r. 46–48)
Ventidius Cumanus (r. 48–52)
Antonius Felix (r. 52–60)
Porcius Festus (r. 60–62)
Albinus (r. 62–65)
Gessius Florus (r. 65–66)

PRODIGAL SON The central figure in Jesus's parable in Luke 15:11–32. The prodigal son is the younger of two sons. He demands his inheritance and wastes it on profligate living, suffers poverty and hunger, repents, and then experiences the overwhelming power of forgiveness. (*See* **Parable**.)

PROMISE The biblical notion of promise is aptly summarized in the words of Samuel Johnson, who defines it as the "declaration of some benefit to be conferred."

God made promises in the very beginning and throughout the patriarchal period that laid the groundwork for universal salvation. Genesis chapters 12–50 offer a series of linked promise episodes in which God promises key things (e.g., covenants, sonship, progeny, blessings, divine assistance, and territory). The remainder of the Bible narrates how these various promises were fulfilled over time and culminate in the redeeming work of Christ.

I. *In the Old Testament*
  A. *The First Gospel*
  B. *Abraham*
  C. *David*
II. *In the New Testament*
  A. *Jesus Fulfills the First Gospel*
  B. *Jesus Fulfills the Promise to Abraham*
  C. *Jesus Fulfills the Promise to David*

I. IN THE OLD TESTAMENT

A. The First Gospel

The promise of salvation first came right after the **Fall**, when God pledged that the offspring of Eve would eventually prevail over the Satanic serpent. Christian tradition calls this promise in the Bible the first Gospel, in Latin the *protevangelium*.

B. Abraham

God made additional promises to Abraham (Gen 12:1–3). Eventually these were upgraded and guaranteed by divine covenant oaths (Gen 15:17–21; 17:1–21; 22:16–18). The promise to Abraham was born entirely out of God's goodness and willingness to assume responsibility for restoring the world to himself: "For when God made a promise to Abraham, since he had no one greater by whom to swear, he swore by himself, saying, 'Surely I will bless you and multiply you.' And thus Abraham, having patiently endured, obtained the promise" (Heb 6:13–15). The promise declared that to Abraham would come innumerable descendants, through the single son born of Sarah (namely, **Isaac**). The descendants would become a source of blessing for all the nations (Gen 12:3; 22:18) (CCC 2570–74). (*See also* **Covenant**.)

The promises seemed impossible. Sarah had been unable to bear children, and Abraham and Sarah were far too old to have children (Gen 15:1–6). Likewise, the captivity of Israel in Egypt stood in contrast to the promise of leading the people out of bondage and the settling of the people in a Promised Land (Gen 15:7–21). Nevertheless, both promises were realized within history; the obstacles were not insuperable for God. Sarah miraculously conceived and bore a son (Gen 21:1–3), and the many descendants of Abraham eventually took possession of the Promised Land (Josh 1–12).

C. David

To **David** the Lord promised an everlasting throne and kingdom. The promise was made in the famous oracle of Nathan, where the Lord swore an oath to establish David's kingship for all time (2 Sam 7:8–16; cf. Ps 89:3–4, 35–36). Beginning with the reign of Solomon, and continuing through a direct line of nineteen successors who occupied the throne of David and ruled over the kingdom of Judah, this promise too has a provisional, historical fulfillment in the lives of God's people. Nevertheless, the collapse of the Davidic monarchy in the sixth century B.C. raised important questions about the fulfillment of the divine promise in the future.

II. IN THE NEW TESTAMENT

A. Jesus Fulfills the First Gospel

Christian theologians from earliest times identified Christ as the "offspring" of the woman destined to trample down the devil. The overall message of the New Testament points in this direction when it describes Jesus's victory over Satan (John 12:31; Heb 2:14; 1 John 3:8). Specific allusions to the promise and its implications can be found in Rom 16:20 and Rev 12:9, 17.

B. Jesus Fulfills the Promise to Abraham

The promise of worldwide blessing is fulfilled in Jesus, a descendant of Abraham (Matt 1:1). In particular, Jesus is the "offspring" promised to Abraham who would channel the blessings of the covenant to all nations (Gal 3:15–18; cf. Acts 3:25–26). In one sense, Isaac was the initial fulfillment of this promise. But Isaac is himself a **type** of Christ, in whom the pledge to restore the world is fully realized (Gal 3:6–14, 29; cf. Rom 4:13–25; Heb 6:13–20).

C. Jesus Fulfills the Promise to David

The NT, and especially the **Synoptic Gospels**, stress Jesus's genealogical link with David. He is also grafted into the royal line of David that passes through Solomon by virtue of his legal relation to **Joseph** (Matt 1:1–16; Luke 2:4). Throughout his ministry he was addressed by the Messianic title "Son of David" (Matt 12:23; 15:22; 20:31), which evokes the expectation that he had come to restore the ancient kingdom of David in its earthly and historical form (Mark 11:10). However, we are told that Jesus fulfilled the Lord's oath to David, not by setting up an empire in Jerusalem, but by rising to an immortal life (Acts 13:32–37; Rom 1:1–4) and assuming the throne of David in heaven (Luke 1:32–33; Acts 2:29–36).

PROMISED LAND The land of **Canaan**, promised by God to **Abraham** and his offspring (Gen 12:7; 13:14–15; 17:8). The promise was renewed to the later patriarchs (Gen 26:3; 28:13) and Israel (Exod 13:5; 33:1–3). **Moses** was granted a view of the Promised Land from the top of Mount **Nebo**, but God did not permit him to enter (Deut 32:48–52). Theologically, the Promised Land is a **type** of heaven for which believers long (Heb 4).

PROPHECY *See* **Prophet**.

PROPHET One who speaks for God. In modern use, a prophet is one who foretells the future, but that is only one aspect of the biblical prophet's mission. Prophecy is a charism, a special gift of grace received for the benefit of the community.

Above all, the prophets helped prepare Israel for the coming of Christ and the institution of the New Covenant. The prophets called upon Israel to remember its covenant with the Lord and to turn away from sin before it was too late. They called upon Israel and all nations to turn to and trust in the Lord of history (CCC 64, 2595).

The prophets' predicting of future events reinforced the central message of repentance. Prophecies, therefore, were part of God's Providence, for God alone possesses knowledge of the contingent future. Just as miracles are an expression of God's omnipotence over matter and space, prophecies are the expression of God's providential control of time and history.

The phenomenon of prophecy was found elsewhere in the ancient Near East, including Egypt, Mesopotamia, and Canaan. Similarities between the Israelite prophets and the seers and diviners of the Near East are, however, entirely outward. Pagan seers used divination, trances, clairvoyance, and ritual actions to determine some decision, to interpret future events, and to discover the moods or whims of their gods. The prophets of Israel proclaimed the word of God to a people elected to fulfill a divine plan of salvation.

The legitimacy of a prophet was confirmed in the fulfillment of the prophet's short-term predictions (Deut 18:21–22) and the consistency of the prophecy with the known revelation of God (Deut 13:2–5; 2 Tim 4:3–8). Failure to meet these standards meant that one was a "false prophet" and was not to be trusted or followed.

I. *Prophets in the Old Testament*
   A. *Who They Were*
   B. *The Mission of the Prophets*
II. *Prophecy in the New Testament*
   A. *John the Baptist*
   B. *Jesus as Prophet*
   C. *Prophets in the Early Church*
III. *Christ's Prophetic Office*

I. PROPHETS IN THE OLD TESTAMENT

A. *Who They Were*

The first persons to be called prophets in the Old Testament were **Abraham** (Gen 20:7), **Aaron** (Exod 7:1), **Miriam** (Exod 15:20), and above all **Moses**, who is honored as the greatest prophet of all (Deut 34:10).

The first of the classic prophets of Israel was **Samuel** (1 Sam 3:20), who was instrumental in the establishment of the monarchy (1 Sam 7–10). Samuel likewise was the instrument for the deposition of Saul (1 Sam 13:8–15; 15:10–23). In his final public assembly, Samuel displayed his various roles as chooser of kings (1 Sam 12:1), judge of the people (1 Sam 12:3–5), and intercessor (1 Sam 12:17–19, 23–24). He was followed by the prophets who spoke to Israel over the next centuries.

Prophets in ancient Israel also existed in the form of professional groups or court prophets. Among the court prophets, **Nathan** stands out. He bore the word of the Lord to the king, in the form of both promises (2 Sam 7:8–17) and judgments (2 Sam 12:1–15). He also played a significant role in the political machinations surrounding the succession of the throne of **David**. Nathan served as a royal advisor (1 Kgs 1:22–27) and one of the three key figures in the coronation of Solomon—with **Zadok** the priest and **Benaiah** the soldier (1 Kgs 1:32–40). In this last function, Nathan was continuing to fulfill the role established by Samuel in anointing the divinely appointed ruler. The narrative shows the powerful status of Nathan, who enjoyed free access to the king and who displayed a willingness to speak openly, authoritatively, and boldly (1 Kgs 1:24–27).

Court prophets appear again in 1 Kgs 22:5–28 during **Ahab**'s preparation for a war against the Arameans. Three distinctive prophetic figures are present: the four hundred court prophets in attendance on Ahab (1 Kgs 22:6); **Zedekiah**, son of Chenaanah (1 Kgs 22:11); and **Micaiah** (1 Kgs 22:9). Ahab's prophets tell him only what he wishes to hear (1 Kgs 22:12). Similarly, Zedekiah performs a symbolic action in assuring the king of victory. The last prophet is Micaiah, who never prophesies good tidings for Ahab (1 Kgs 22:8). Micaiah dismissed the rest as false prophets who had spoken because the Lord had sent a lying spirit on them (1 Kgs 22:22). Micaiah predicted defeat for Ahab, speaking with divine authority. The price of his speaking the truth was that he suffered violence at the hands of Zedekiah (1 Kgs 22:24) and imprisonment (1 Kgs 22:26–27), but Micaiah declared that his words would be proven true (1 Kgs 22:28).

Another group of prophets is found in 2 Kgs 9:1–13. **Elisha** was the leader of a group of prophets (2 Kgs 9:1). Elisha served as a kind of father to the community, hence his position of authority to send forth the young prophet on his mission (2 Kgs 9:1–3; see also 2 Kgs 2–6). For his part, the young unnamed prophet was an obedient student to his master (2 Kgs 9:4) and faithful in the fulfillment of his task (2 Kgs 9:6–10).

Israel was often troubled by false prophets, who tended to speak only of peace and prosperity in times of great evil and impending judgment. False prophecy leads the people away from the will of God and not toward it (cf. Isa 28:7; Jer 5:31, 6:13, 23:9–40; Ezek 13:1–23; Mic 3:5–7; Zeph 3:4).

B. The Mission of the Prophets

True prophets were called and commissioned directly by God, not installed or appointed by kings or priests; nor was the office hereditary or acquired by special spiritual qualities or great intellect. Only the call of God set aside a prophet.

The prophets received the divine communication through visions, dreams, and audible encounters or locutions. In turn, they used a variety of means to deliver the Lord's message, including oracles, sermons, writings, and parables.

The divine commission and inspiration authorized—or even impelled—the prophets to speak and to act, and invested their words with divine power. This inspiration was termed variously "the spirit of the Lord" (1 Kgs 22:24; Isa 61:1) and "the word of the Lord" (Jer 1:2, 4;

Ezek 1:3). A prophet might be called from any walk of life, so they hailed from a variety of backgrounds. Elisha, for example, was called while plowing a field (1 Kgs 19:19). Prophets spoke the word of God wherever they were compelled to do so, from the marketplace to the royal court.

The prophets also spoke on behalf of God the Judge. Israel had failed in its fidelity, and the prophets spoke words of condemnation (Amos 2:6–7, 4:1; Isa 5:7; Mic 2:1–2, 3:1–3), demanding repentance for Israel's transgressions and its failure to adhere to its pledge to worship the Lord alone. Often the prophets saw the enemies of Israel as instruments of God, as when Isaiah prophesied that the plans of human beings would be destroyed by the rod of God's anger, namely, the Assyrians (Isa 8:5–8; 10:5–11). At the heart of the prophetic call was God's plea for the Israelites to return to their personal relationship with their Lord: they should "return" to their God (Isa 55:7; Ezek 18:30; Hos 6:1), "seek" the Lord (Amos 5:4–6), and "know" the Lord again (Hos 6:3; Jer 31:34).

Not infrequently, the prophets saw little hope of that repentance, and divine punishment—the consequence of infidelity—was inevitable (Amos 8:1–3). Prophets before the **Exile** (as well as the exilic prophets **Jeremiah** and **Ezekiel**) thus became concerned with what they saw was the guiding hand of the Lord in history, and encouraged their own people to accept the justice of the approaching punishment from God for their sins.

Often the prophets went beyond the proclamation of the word of God in history: they were involved directly and actively in the social and political events of their time. The court prophet Nathan took part in the struggle for Solomon's succession (1 Kgs 1:20–40), while Isaiah enjoyed influence at the court as an advisor to various kings (Isa 7:3–25; 37:21–35). After the Babylonian conquest, Jeremiah advised the exiles to accept the harsh reality of their lives in the land of their captivity (Jer 29:1–32). Further, where prophets before the **Exile** were preoccupied with the onset of divine judgment, postexilic prophets were more active in encouraging appropriate cultic conduct and serving as teachers of morality. **Haggai**, for example, saw it as his task to persuade the people to rebuild the Temple (Hag 1:4, 9).

II. PROPHECY IN THE NEW TESTAMENT

The New Testament represents the fulfillment of the words and oracles of the prophets of the OT (Matt 1:22, 26:56; Luke 1:70, 18:31; Acts 3:21). The prophets of old spoke words that have come to pass. Old Testament prophets are frequently mentioned or quoted, including Jeremiah, Daniel, Joel, Jonah, Hosea, Amos, Micah, Habakkuk, Haggai, Zechariah, and especially Isaiah, who is quoted or paraphrased nearly one hundred times in the NT (e.g., Matt 3:3, 8:17, 12:18–21; Mark 1:3; Luke 3:4–6; John 1:23; Acts 8:32–33; Rom 9:29).

A. John the Baptist

Jesus said that the OT period did not come to an end with Malachi but with **John the Baptist** (Matt 11:13). John the Baptist is the last and the greatest of the prophets, for he is the immediate precursor of the Messiah (Matt 3:3; Luke 1:76, 7:26; Acts 13:24–25): "he will go before him in the spirit and power of Elijah, to turn the hearts of the fathers to the children, and the disobedient to the wisdom of the just, to make ready for the Lord a people prepared" (Luke 1:17) (CCC 523, 717–19).

B. Jesus as Prophet

Jesus was widely considered a prophet by his contemporaries (Matt 16:14; 21:11, 46; Mark 6:15; 8:28; Luke 7:16; 9:8; 24:19; John 4:19; 6:14; 7:40; 9:17; Acts 3:22). Jesus did not use that word to describe himself, although he did not reject it. It was natural for others to see Jesus in this way, for he spoke the word of God with authority, he used prophetic modes of speech such as parables and judgment oracles, and he performed numerous miracles that recalled those of the prophets, especially Elijah and Elisha.

C. Prophets in the Early Church

Prophets played an important role in the early Church and were highly esteemed because of the special service they provided for the Christian community (Acts 11:27, 21:10; Eph 4:11; 1 Tim 1:18, 4:142). They were among the teachers of the early Church (Rom 12:6; 1 Cor 12:10; Eph 2:20). Paul writes of the gift of prophecy in Eph 4:11 and 1 Cor 12:28 and calls it the best of the spiritual gifts (1 Cor 14:3–5).

III. CHRIST'S PROPHETIC OFFICE

Jesus was anointed by the Holy Spirit as a priest, prophet, and king, and all the members of the Church share in these functions. The Second Vatican Council tells us about our share in Christ's prophetic office: "it spreads abroad a living witness to him especially by the life of faith and love and by offering to God a sacrifice of praise, the fruit of lips praising his name (cf. Heb 13:15). The whole body of the faithful who have an anointing that comes from the holy one (cf. 1 John 2:20, 27) cannot err in matters of belief" (LG §12). But the office and function of prophecy belong primarily to bishops, for they are the principal ministers of the word in preaching sacred doctrine.

The faithful participate in Christ's prophetic office first and foremost by bearing witness by their lives and, to the degree that they have the competence, by evangelization, as noted by the Second Vatican Council in the Decree on the Apostolate of the Laity: "The true apostle is on the lookout for occasions of announcing Christ by word, either to unbelievers to draw them towards the faith, or to the faithful to instruct them, strengthen them, incite them to a more fervent life" (*Apostolicam Actuositatem* §6) (CCC 64, 436, 702, 715, 785, 888–92, 904–7).

PROPHETESS A female prophet. Several women are named as prophetesses in the Old Testament: **Miriam**, the sister of Moses (Exod 15:20); **Deborah**, the judge and wife of Lappidoth (Judg 4:4); **Huldah**, the wife of the keeper of the royal wardrobe (2 Kgs 22:14); Noadiah (Neh 6:14); Isaiah's wife (Isa 8:3). In the New Testament, **Anna** gave praise to God at the arrival of Jesus (Luke 2:36); Philip's four daughters were called prophetesses (Acts 21:9). Paul notes also that the gifts of prophecy were exercised by Christians of both sexes in the early Christian community (1 Cor 11:4–5). In both Testaments, there are also false prophets and false prophetesses (Ezek 13:17; Rev 2:20).

PROPHETS, THE The name for the prophetic writings of the Old Testament. There are four major prophets—Isaiah, Jeremiah, Ezekiel, and Daniel—and twelve minor prophets—Hosea, Joel, Amos, Obadiah, Jonah, Micah, Nahum, Habakkuk, Zephaniah, Haggai, Zechariah, and Malachi. (These last twelve prophets are "minor" because their books are shorter, not less important.)

PROSELYTE (Greek, "one who approaches") A Gentile who embraced Jewish practices and teachings. By their preaching and also by the exemplary quality of their lives, Jews of the **Dispersion** in the Hellenistic world made Judaism an attractive faith and so found a population that was hungry for the truth.

Proselytes within the Hellenistic world took several forms. There were the so-called proselytes of justice—that is, the true proselytes who accepted Judaism in its totality, meaning they undertook rites of initiation including circumcision, ritual sacrifices, and a ritual bath (cf. Acts 2:10; 6:5; 13:43). Their numbers are not known with certainty. The second group—and the larger of the two—consisted of the so-called God-fearers (Acts 10:2, 22)—Gentiles who sympathized with the Jewish faith and accepted Jewish teachings and practices. They attended synagogue and observed a basic code of moral and ethical purity, but they did not take the decisive step of circumcision.

The God-fearers proved especially open to the Gospel (Acts 10:2; 13:126, 43; 14:1; 16:14; 18:4, 7). Owing to the success of Christian communities in converting the God-fearers, proselytism was forbidden by the Jewish community after the start of the second century A.D. (*See also* **Gentile**.)

PROSTITUTION A common institution throughout the ancient Near East. Cultic prostitution was a fertility rite in various Semitic religions and often took place in pagan temples and shrines. Professional prostitution was also widely known and practiced with little moral censure or societal disapproval.

In opposition to these practices, the Old Testament condemned prostitution (Jer 5:7; Hos 4:14) and warned young men to avoid the traps and snares of prostitutes (Prov 6:26, 7:6–27; Sir 23:16). Nevertheless, prostitution was practiced by some in ancient Israel (Gen 38:15–16; Judg 11:1, 16:1; 1 Kgs 3:16), and it was noted as well that the infidelity of Israel found expression in the embrace of the pagan customs of prostitution (Deut 23:17–18; 1 Kgs 14:24). Male cult prostitution became a concern under various kings (1 Kgs 15:12, 22:46; 2 Kgs 23:7). Not surprisingly, Israel's infidelity is compared to that of a harlot (Exod 34:16; Lev 17:7, 20:5; Deut 31:16; Judg 2:17, 8:27; Isa 1:21, 57:7–13; Jer 2:20, 3:1–4; Ezek 16:30; Mic 1:7). Such an image was used to contrast Israel's infidelity to the covenantal union of love and fidelity that should characterize Israel's relationship with the Lord.

Much as in ancient Israel, prostitution was prevalent in the Roman world of the New Testament period (Matt 21:31; Luke 15:30). Thus, in the NT, prostitution continues to be condemned as sinful (1 Cor 6:15–20; cf. Gal 5:19, 20; Eph 5:3; Col 3:5).

PROVERBS, BOOK OF One of the Wisdom Books of the Old Testament, consisting of collections of sayings attributed to **Solomon** and other persons on a wide variety of subjects, including wisdom and its nature, rules of conduct, duties with respect to one's neighbor, and the conduct of daily affairs. The Hebrew name of the collection is *mišlê šĕlōmōh*, "the proverbs of Solomon," taken from Prov 1:1. The title used in the **Septuagint** is *paroimiai*, while the **Vulgate** uses *Liber Proverbiorum*, from which was derived the common English title "Proverbs."

I. AUTHORSHIP AND DATE

Proverbs is a collection of wise sayings, compiled from a variety of sources from different periods. The book begins with the attribution of the collection to King Solomon, an attribution repeated in Prov 10:1. The presence of Solomon's name reflects his place as the greatest sage in the wisdom tradition and the reputed author of three thousand proverbs (1 Kgs 4:32). Solomon, however, was not the only author of the collection, as the book itself tells us. Proverbs brought together the sayings of many Israelite wise men and scribes. Most, if not all, of the wisdom material in the book is safely dated to the period before the **Exile**, with the oldest portion being the Proverbs of Solomon in Prov 10:1–22:16. Nevertheless, the final editing phase of the collection may have taken place in the fifth century B.C.

II. CONTENTS

III. PURPOSE AND THEMES

The purpose of Proverbs is stated at the very beginning, in Prov 1:2–6. The book is intended to impart the lessons of wise living. Thus it contrasts repeatedly the practice of wisdom against the life of folly. The sayings and wise adages offer a comprehensive and practical philosophy for life. The proverbs cover a vast number of topics, including justice, charity, self-discipline, drinking, indolence, prudence, and finding a good wife.

The first section notes the importance of wisdom (Prov 1:1–9:18) as an introduction to the pupil. For those who pursue the path of wisdom and avoid the snares of folly, there are the rewards of long life, wealth, happiness, and honors. The text combines morality and spirituality in such beautiful sayings as, "The fear of the Lord is the beginning of wisdom, and the knowledge of the Holy One is insight" (9:10).

The Proverbs of Solomon (10:1–22:16 and 25:1–29:27) have no obvious organizational structure. But the main theme is often repeated: the contrast of the wise man against the unwise man. Solomon's sayings are said to have been gathered by the scribes of King **Hezekiah** of Judah (25:1).

The Proverbs of the Wise Men (22:17–24:22 and 24:23–34) cover a variety of topics, including regard for the poor, the disciplining of children, temperance, and chastity. The section 22:17–23:11 shows striking affinities with the Sayings of Amenemope from Egypt. The second group of sayings in 23:12–24:34 is dedicated especially to the need for hard work, honesty toward neighbors, and opposing the wicked.

The Words of Agur (30:1–33) are the sage counsels of an otherwise unknown individual, identified as the son of Jakeh, while the Words of Lemuel, "which his mother taught him" (31:1–9), caution the wise man to avoid lust and excessive drink.

The Ode to a Capable Wife (31:10–31) is an acrostic composition, in which each saying begins with a successive letter of the Hebrew alphabet, thus signifying completeness. This section was intended in both form and content to echo the figure of Lady Wisdom in chapters 1–9, but in the form of a real woman. The poem describes the "woman of worth" and her virtues. A wife should be prized more for being pious, resourceful, industrious, wise, and charitable than for being charming or beautiful (cf. 31:30). Proverbs also warns against loose women, or foreign women, for an adulteress might cost a man his life (5:3–5; 6:24–35; 9:13–18). The sayings reflect the importance of the father and mother in transmitting religious values and wisdom (1:8; 13:1; 31:1).

PROVIDENTISSIMUS DEUS A papal encyclical of Leo XIII issued on November 18, 1893. Its aim was to clarify Catholic teaching on the nature of Scripture, to encourage its study in modern times, and to guard it against the attacks of rationalist scholarship and the careless practitioners of "higher criticism." This encyclical made a significant doctrinal contribution by defining the inspiration and inerrancy of the Bible, building on the teaching of the Council of Trent and Vatican I, and did much to insist that rigorous scholarship must still be reverent scholarship that acknowledges the divine origin and authority of Scripture as the written revelation of God. Pope Pius XII, writing fifty years later, called *Providentissimus Deus* "the supreme guide in biblical studies" (*Divino Afflante Spiritu* §2).

PSALMS, BOOK OF A collection of 150 religious songs that were used in the **Temple** liturgy of Israel before and after the **Exile**. They are the masterwork of prayer in the Old Testament. Called in the Hebrew *sēper těhillîm*, "book of praises," the Psalter is a work of praise and worship. It is likewise a vast treasury of theology, spirituality, and human emotion. The Psalms continue to play a significant part in the liturgical life of the Church and have a central role in the Divine Office.

The English title "Psalms" is derived from the Greek *psalmoi* ("songs of praise"). The Greek title for the book in the Codex Alexandrinus is *psaltērion*, which is the name of a stringed instrument used to accompany songs of worship. Rabbinic literature adopted the Hebrew title *sēper těhillîm*, "book of praises."

I. *Authorship and Date*
II. *Contents*
   A. *The Five Books*
   B. *Numbering*
III. *Types of Psalms*
IV. *Technical Terms and Directions*
V. *Liturgical Uses*
VI. *The Theology of the Psalms*

I. AUTHORSHIP AND DATE

David, whose name is associated with the whole book, certainly composed some of the

Psalms, but there were other authors as well. David was probably responsible, directly or indirectly, for seventy-three Psalms; other individuals who are named as contributors include **Asaph** (twelve Psalms; Ps 50, 73–83); the Sons of Korah (eleven Psalms; Ps 42–49, 84–85, 87–88); Solomon (Ps 72 and 127), Heman (Ps 88), Ethan (Ps 89), and **Moses** (Ps 90). Some are also associated with Jeduthun, one of David's musicians (Ps 39, 62, and 77; cf. 1 Chr 25:1–2; 2 Chr 5:12).

II. CONTENTS

A. The Five Books

The Psalter consists of 150 Psalms divided into five "books":

I. *Book One (Ps 1–41)*
II. *Book Two (Ps 42–72)*
III. *Book Three (Ps 73–89)*
IV. *Book Four (Ps 90–106)*
V. *Book Five (Ps 107–150)*

The division of the Psalms into five books dates back to the **Septuagint** and the third century B.C., but each section is clearly discernible because of the doxology that ends each of the five parts. The doxologies are found at Psalms 41:13; 72:20; 89:52; 106:48; Psalm 150 serves as the doxology for the fifth book and also for the entire collection. According to Jewish tradition, the division parallels the five-part division of the **Pentateuch**. Of the 150 Psalms, 116 have superscriptions (or titles) of varying length in the Hebrew text. The 34 Psalms that lack titles are Psalms 1–2, 10, 33, 43, 71, 91, 93–97, 99, 104–107, 111–119, 135–137, 146–150.

The Psalms can be grouped into three main collections: Davidic Psalms (Ps 2 or 3–41); Psalms by Asaph, Korahite, and Davidic authors, which scholars sometimes call the Elohistic Psalter owing to the frequent use of the Hebrew divine name "Elohim" (Ps 42–83; *see* "Names of God" *under* **God**), with an appendix added (Ps 84–89); and a body of miscellaneous Psalms concerned with various topics (Ps 90–150).

B. Numbering

Since the appearance of the **Septuagint**, the Psalms have been numbered in two different ways, so there are discrepancies between the Greek and Latin Bibles as compared to the Hebrew Bible except for Psalms 1–8 and 148–150. Most Protestant Bibles have used the Hebrew numbering system; earlier Catholic versions in English followed the Greek and Latin numbering, but the JB, RSV, NAB, and other more recent versions use the Hebrew numbering. The differences in specific Psalms are listed below for the Hebrew Bible (Masoretic Text) and the LXX (the Greek Septuagint):

HEBREW BIBLE	LXX (AND LATIN BIBLES)
Psalms 1–8	Psalms 1–8
9–10	9
11–113	10–112
114–115	113
116:1–9	114
116:10–19	115
117–146	116–145
147:1–11	146
147:12–20	147
148–150	148–150

III. TYPES OF PSALMS

Scholars have long noted the different types of Psalms that make up the canonical collection. Many of the Psalms were intended for public worship; others were meant for private devotion or piety. Broadly, the Psalms can be divided into several main categories—Thanksgiving and Praise, as well as Laments—and smaller categories, including Royal and Messianic Prayers, Pleas and Supplications, Wisdom, Alphabetic or Acrostic, "Songs of Ascent" (Ps 120–134, which were probably pilgrim songs or processional songs), and Imprecatory Psalms.

The chief literary feature of the Psalms is the parallelism (*see* **Poetry**). In addition, Psalms use alliteration and assonance, and there are also acrostic or alphabetic Psalms, in which the letters of the alphabet begin successive lines, couplets, or strophes, and rhymes can sometimes occur at the ends of lines and pauses.

IV. TECHNICAL TERMS AND DIRECTIONS

Many of the Psalms include technical notations whose exact meaning is not always clear to us. Most of the Psalms are described in the original Hebrew as *mizmôr*, a "psalm," probably suggesting that it was to be accompanied by musical instruments. A number of Psalms (e.g., Ps 46 and 48) are called "A Song" (Hebrew *šîr*). Thirteen Psalms (32, 42, 44–45, 52–55, 74, 78, 88–89, and 142) are labeled as a *maśkîl*, a word that suggests making wise or skillful. Such Psalms tend to be expressing experiences of suffering, except for Psalm 45,

which is a love song. Six Psalms (16 and 56–60) are termed *miktām* and are always said to be "of David"; the exact meaning of the term is uncertain. Psalm 7 is called *šiggāyôn*, apparently a particular type of song.

Some of the Psalms also include musical directions, such as Psalm 4 with its note, "To the choirmaster: with stringed instruments"; and Psalm 5 with its direction, "To the choirmaster: for the flutes." There are fifty-five Psalms containing such directions. The word "Selah" appears seventy-one times; its meaning remains a mystery. It may have been a direction to singers and worshippers as part of a refrain.

V. LITURGICAL USES

The precise use of the Psalms in the liturgy of Israel is uncertain. There is no question, however, that they were collected and used for worship, and Psalms of Thanksgiving and Praise were used especially for purposes of public declaration of God's glory, majesty, and mercy.

The Praise or Hallel Psalms (from the Hebrew *hālal*, "to praise") are those that include the acclamation "Praise the Lord," usually at the beginning or the end of the Psalm (Ps 104–106, 111–113, 115–117, 135, 146–150). These were traditionally chanted at the great pilgrimage feasts of Passover, Pentecost, and Tabernacles. The Hallel Psalms normally sung during a Passover Seder meal were Psalms 113–118 (despite the fact that Psalm 118 does not include the distinctive expression *halĕlû-yāh*, "Praise the Lord").

The practice of singing the Psalms as part of divine worship is termed "psalmody." Psalms were typically sung in a responsorial fashion in which a soloist chanted each verse of the Psalm and the assembly replied in refrain. The refrain could be a simple one, such as "Amen" or "Hallelujah," or a line taken from the Psalm being chanted. Christians adopted the practice at an early time. The Psalms thus became the foundation for the Church's public prayer, as well as a handbook for private devotion.

Jewish Temple worship also used antiphonal psalmody, in which the verses are chanted or sung by two alternating groups with a common refrain—the antiphon—sung before and after the Psalm proper. This form was adopted by monastic communities in the Church as early as the fourth century. The antiphon can be repeated every few verses of the Psalm, including its beginning and end. One of the most prominent antiphons was that featured in Psalm 136, "for his steadfast love endures forever."

In the revised Liturgy of the Hours, Psalms form one of the three principal parts with biblical and nonbiblical readings and are part of the Office of Readings, Morning, Daytime, Evening, and Night Prayer. The Psalter is spread out over a four-week period, although some Psalms, entirely or in part, are not recited. In the Order of the Mass, Psalms are a major element in the Liturgy of the Word.

VI. THE THEOLOGY OF THE PSALMS

The book of Psalms is renowned for its theology of God and its anticipation of the Messiah. It encapsulates the Old Testament's understanding of the existence and attributes of God, the pursuit of virtues, and the reality of death and judgment. Its theological message is expressed through a range of human emotions and sentiments, from joy and contentment to sadness and despair, and even to anger and indignation.

Even curses have their place in the Psalms. In Ps 69:23–25, for example, the poet pleads,

Let their eyes be darkened, so that they cannot see;
and make their loins tremble continually.
Pour out your indignation upon them,
and let your burning anger overtake them.
May their camp be a desolation,
let no one dwell in their tents. (cf. Ps 109:6–20)

The petitioner is calling upon the Lord as a plaintiff stands before a judge seeking justice. The Imprecatory Psalms represent the anguish of a nation beset by its enemies who do not acknowledge the One God. Even these "curse" Psalms are an acknowledgment of God's suzerainty over the whole world.

The full wonder of God's power and authority is revealed in the Psalms of Praise and Thanksgiving, be it his goodness (103, 115), his power revealed in nature (29, 104), or his strength as defender of Israel (11, 121).

The Psalms also have Messianic significance. God is praised as King (e.g., 47, 93–102), but so too is the special place of David and his descendants in the divine economy (2, 89, 110, 132). Messianic hope is woven throughout the Psalms dealing with the future of Israel, and a number of Psalms are well known to Christians as prophecies of Christ. For instance, in Psalm 110, Christ is foreseen as the Priest-King who will sit at the right hand of the Father. The Kingdom of the Messiah is predicted in Psalms 2, 18, 45, 61, 72, 89, and 132, while his betrayal and death are anticipated in Psalms 22, 41, and 69.

Christ quoted the Psalms in his teachings, most notably on the Cross, when he quoted Ps 22:1: "My God, my God, why have you forsaken me?" (*see also* **Eloi, Eloi, Lama Sabachthani**); and Ps 31:5: "Father, into your hands I commend my spirit." The Psalms were used by the Evangelists and gave comfort to believers (Acts 4:25–26) in time of suffering. The apostles used them to proclaim Jesus Christ (Eph 4:8; Heb 1:6, 10–13; 2:6–8; 5:6; 10:5–7) (CCC 2585–89).

PSALTER *See* **Psalms**.

PSEUDEPIGRAPHA *See* **Apocryphal books**.

PTOLEMAIS *See* **Acco**.

PTOLEMY The name of fourteen rulers who reigned in Egypt from ca. 323 to 30 B.C. The name is derived from the founder of the dynasty, Ptolemy I Soter (r. 304–285 B.C.); every male successor bore the same name.

With the death of **Alexander the Great**, Ptolemy, son of Lagus, one of Alexander's most capable generals, requested to be named the satrap of Egypt while giving recognition to Alexander's heirs, the dead conqueror's half brother Philip and Alexander's infant son, Alexander the younger. In 310 B.C., however, Alexander the younger was murdered and the nominal unity of the vast Macedonian Empire broke apart as the generals struggled to claim supreme power. The civil war led to the crea-

tion of several states, including the Seleucid and the Ptolemaic dynasties. Ptolemy claimed for himself the kingship of Egypt in 304 B.C. and bequeathed the throne to his son Ptolemy II Philadelphus (r. 285–246 B.C.). The first Ptolemies, especially Ptolemy I, II, and III Euergetes (r. 246–221 B.C.), were instrumental in establishing Ptolemaic Egypt as a genuine power in the East, and the furthest extent of the empire eventually reached across Palestine and into Coele-Syria and into the Mediterranean. Decline set in through the struggle of the Ptolemies with the Seleucid rulers, who pushed the Ptolemies out of Syria and Palestine in the late third and early second centuries B.C. The loss of Palestine set in motion the events of the Jewish rebellion against the Seleucids that feature in the books of Maccabees.

Internal strife divided the Ptolemies starting under Ptolemy VI Philometer (r. 180–145 B.C.; 1 Macc 10:51–58; 11:1–18; 15:16). Political decline characterized the succeeding reigns of the dynasty. Internal rivalries, assassination, and civil discontent were matched by the emergence of the Roman Empire as the true power in the Mediterranean. The Ptolemaic Dynasty reached its last fleeting moment of glory under the brilliant but erratic Queen Cleopatra VII, who charmed the Roman generals Julius Caesar and Marc Antony. With Antony, Cleopatra was defeated by the Romans under Octavian at the battle of Actium (31 B.C.). She committed suicide, and her son and heir by Julius Caesar, Ptolemy XIV Caesarion, followed her into death soon after. The Ptolemaic Dynasty thus came to an end and Egypt passed into Roman control.

THE PTOLEMIES (304–30 B.C.)

Ptolemy I Soter (r. 323–285 B.C.)

Ptolemy II Philadelphus (r. 285–246 B.C.)

Ptolemy III Euergetes (r. 246–221 B.C.)

Ptolemy IV Philopater (r. 221–205 B.C.)

Ptolemy V Epiphanes (r. 203–180 B.C.)

Ptolemy VI Philometer (r. 180–145 B.C.)

Ptolemy VII Neos Pilopator (r. 145 B.C.)

Ptolemy VIII Euergetes II (r. 145–116 B.C.)

Ptolemy IX Soter II Lathyrus (r. 116–108 B.C.)

Ptolemy X Alexander (r. 108–88 B.C.)

Ptolemy XI Alexander II (r. 80 B.C.)

Ptolemy XII Auletes (r. 80–51 B.C.)

Ptolemy XIII (r. 51–47 B.C.) and Cleopatra VII (r. 51–30 B.C.)

Ptolemy XIV (r. 47–44 B.C.) and Cleopatra VII (r. 51–30 B.C.)

Ptolemy XV Caesarion (r. 44–30 B.C.) and Cleopatra VII (r. 51–30 B.C.)

PUAH One of the midwives of the Hebrews in Egypt who refused to obey the Pharaoh's command to kill all the male infants of the Hebrews at birth (Exod 1:15).

PUBLICANS *See* **Tax collectors**.

PUDENS A Christian, presumably in Rome, who sent greetings to **Timothy** (2 Tim 4:21) along with Linus and Claudia.

PUL The throne name of **Tiglath-pileser III**, king of Assyria (745–727 B.C.). He received tribute from King **Menahem** of Israel (2 Kgs 15:19; 1 Chr 5:26).

PUNISHMENT *See* **Law**; *see also* **Sin**.

PUNON A place where the Israelites stopped during their journey to Canaan (Num 33:42–43). The location may be the modern Faynân, in the Wadi Arabah.

PURGATORY (Latin, "cleansing" or "purifying") Defined by theologians as the condition of those who have died in the state of grace but with lingering attachment to sin. In purgatory these souls are purified for a time before being admitted to the glory and happiness of heaven. In this period of passive suffering, they are purged of unrepented venial sins, satisfy the demands of divine justice for temporal punishment due for sins, and are made ready for the beatific vision.

The doctrine of purgatory is found in Scripture but is not fully developed. The two passages most clearly related to it are 2 Macc 12:45 and 1 Cor 3:12–15.

In 2 Maccabees, Judas Maccabeus sends twelve thousand drachmas to Jerusalem to have sacrifices offered for the sins of the dead. This action clearly supposes that forgiveness of faults and the expiation of guilt are still possible for the deceased. And not only that but the actions of Judas Maccabeus indicate that prayers and liturgical rites conducted by the living can benefit the deceased. Thus, Catholic tradition concludes that it is "a holy and pious thought" to make "atonement for the dead, that they might be delivered from their sin" (2 Macc 12:45).

In 1 Corinthians, Paul is discussing the Lord's scrutiny of our works on the Day of Judgment. Here it is said that each person's works will be tested with "fire" to see whether they are worthy of a reward (1 Cor 3:13). If not, the person will "suffer loss, though he himself will be saved, but only as through fire" (1 Cor 3:15). It is clear from this text that even persons who are saved, if their deeds in life are shady and imperfect, will pass through a fiery process of suffering on the way to glory.

A third passage, Matt 12:32, is likewise explained along these lines by Saint Gregory the Great: "As for certain lesser faults, we must believe that, before the Final Judgment, there is a purifying fire. He who is truth says that whoever utters blasphemy against the Holy Spirit will be pardoned neither in this age nor in the age to come. From this sentence we understand that certain offenses can be forgiven in this age, but certain others in the age to come" (*Dialogues* 4.39; cf. Saint John Chrysostom, *Hom. 1 Cor* 3.15; Saint Gregory of Nyssa, *De iis qui in fide dormiunt*) (CCC 1030–32, 1472).

PURIM (Hebrew, from the Assyrian *puru*, meaning "a pebble or small stone used for casting lots") A feast celebrating the deliverance of the Jews under **Esther** in the Persian realm (Esth 9:26–31). The name means "lots," from the fact that the wicked **Haman** had determined by lot the day of destruction for the Jews. It was later called "Mordecai's Day" (2 Macc 15:36). Purim is celebrated on the fourteenth and fifteenth days of the month Adar, during which the book of Esther is read to recount the festival's origins. (See **Esther, book of** for details.)

PURPLE *See* **Dye, dyeing.**

PUT The third son of **Ham**, the grandson of **Noah**, and the brother of **Cush** (Ethiopia), **Egypt**, and **Canaan**, according to the **Table of Nations** (Gen 10:6; 1 Chr 1:8). The name became associated with a place, most likely in Africa, and Put is mentioned as an ally of Egypt, and in connection with Ethiopia and Lud (both in northeast Africa; Jer 46:9; Ezek 30:5; Nah 3:9). Soldiers from Put also gave military support to **Tyre** (Ezek 27:10) and Gog (Ezek 38:5). The exact location of Put is uncertain. Somalia has been suggested, although the **Septuagint** and Vulgate translate the name in Ezekiel and Jeremiah as Libya. Some scholars have also associated Put with Punt, a country on the Red Sea that had ties to Egypt.

PUTEOLI (Latin, "little wells") A seaport on the Bay of Naples in Italy, today known as Pozzuoli. **Paul** and his companions landed at Puteoli on the way to Rome (Acts 28:13). By the time of Paul's arrival, there was already a Christian community in this area, and he stayed with them before setting out for Rome through Capua and along the Via Appia (Acts 28:14).

PYRRHUS Father of Sopater and a companion of **Paul** on his final journey to Asia Minor (Acts 20:4). He was from Beroea.

Q The abbreviation used to designate a hypothetical collection of Jesus's sayings that many scholars believe was used by the Evangelists Matthew and Luke. *Q* stands for the German word *quelle*, meaning "source." For details, *see* **Synoptic problem**.

QOHELETH *See* **Ecclesiastes, book of**.

QUAIL A bird, *Coturnix vulgaris*, that migrates back and forth between Arabia and the Mediterranean coast every fall and spring. The bird is a heavy one and sometimes falls from the sky from exhaustion. Quails "covered the camp" when the Israelites demanded meat in the wilderness (Exod 16:13; Num 11:31; Ps 105:40).

QUARTUS A Christian "brother," presumably at Corinth, who sends greetings through Paul to the church at Rome (Rom 16:23).

QUEEN The title of queen does not appear frequently in Scripture. Hebrew has several words that translate as "queen." The word *malkâ*, the feminine form of *melek* (king), most commonly serves to designate foreign queens and consorts such as the queens of Sheba (1 Kgs 10:1; 2 Chr 9:1) and Persia (Esth 1:9). Other words in Hebrew are used less frequently. The word *šēgal* appears twice, once in Neh 2:6, where it refers to the wife of King Artaxerxes of Persia; and once in Ps 45:9, referring to a woman who stands at the right hand of the king arrayed "in gold of Ophir." The word *gĕbîrâ*, the feminine form of *gebîr* ("lord" or "master"), is also applied to a foreign queen (1 Kgs 11:19), but it is most frequently used for the Queen Mother of the Davidic ruler (cf. 1 Kgs 15:13; 2 Chr 15:16; Jer 13:18, 29:2).

The role of the Queen Mother in **Judah** (see "Kingdom of Judah" under **Judah**) was very important. She enjoyed a position superior to all of the other women at the court, for unlike the wives of the king she sat at the right hand of the king (as **Bathsheba** did in 1 Kgs 2:19), adorned with a crown (Jer 13:18). One of the most powerful Queen Mothers in Judah was **Maacah**, who enjoyed her role under her son **Abijah** and remained in prominence even into the reign of her grandson **Asa** (1 Kgs 15:2, 10, 13; 2 Chr 15:16). The importance of the Queen Mother as a royal figurehead explains why the sacred writers always list the names of the Queen Mothers in Judah with the succession of each new king: a king might have many wives, but he had only one mother. Nevertheless, the Queen Mother could be deposed, as happened to Maacah (1 Kgs 15:13). (*See also* **Mary, the Mother of Jesus**.)

QUEEN OF HEAVEN The name of a pagan goddess worshiped in Judah and by the exiles in Egypt. The deity is mentioned only in the book of Jeremiah (Jer 7:18; 44:17–19). Jeremiah condemns the idolatry, which extended to the common people, kings, and officials, and was found in the towns of Judah and in the streets of Jerusalem (Jer 44:1–14, 24–30). After the fall of Jerusalem, the refugees in Egypt offered incense to the queen of heaven and poured out libations to her.

QUELLE *See* **Synoptic problem**.

QUIRINIUS, P. SULPICIUS The Roman legate of Syria beginning in A.D. 6. He is mentioned by name in Luke 2:2 in relation to the census of Augustus. Aside from the Gospel, he is known through various inscriptions, Tacitus's *Annals*, Josephus's *Antiquities of the Jews*, and Strabo's *Geography*. According to these sources, he was a long-serving soldier, a powerful political figure, and a friend of Emperor Tiberius (r. A.D. 14–37). He held the post of senator, governor of Crete and Cyrenaica and also in Asia, consul in 12 B.C., and legate in Syria in A.D. 6/7 for an uncertain amount of time. He died in A.D. 21.

As legate in Syria, he organized a census in Palestine that was mentioned by Josephus (*Ant.* 18.1–3, 26) and by Luke in Acts 5:37. This census was conducted for the purpose of taxation, as Judea was coming under direct Roman control in A.D. 6. The census discussed in Luke has long been the source of scholarly debate and speculation (see **census** for details). On the basis of his consulship in 12 B.C., it is deduced that he was born in the 50s B.C., meaning that he would have been active during the turbulent period of civil war between Octavian (later Emperor Augustus) and Marc Antony and Queen Cleopatra of Egypt. Quirinius's rise to political prominence was achieved almost entirely by his own skills as a soldier and politician.

The length of his term as legate is uncertain; in A.D. 12, Quintus Metellus Creticus is mentioned as legate, although it is not known if he was the direct successor to Quirinius.

QUMRAN, KHIRBET (Arabic, "the ruins at Qumran") The site of an ancient settlement in Palestine near the northwestern shore of the Dead Sea that became associated with the community that produced the **Dead Sea Scrolls** discovered in 1947.

I. ARCHAEOLOGICAL REMAINS

The area along the Dead Sea had been examined by general explorations in the period before 1947, but it was only with the discovery of the Dead Sea Scrolls that archaeologists paid serious attention to the site. The Qumran ruins, not far from where the initial scroll discoveries were made, were at first identified as the remains of a Roman fort. This judgment was altered when artifacts in the scroll cave (Cave 1) matched pottery remains unearthed at the Qumran complex. Since then it has been common for scholars to associate the settlement with the scrolls found in nearby caves. Adjacent to the ruins was a cemetery of obvious antiquity.

It is conjectured that the scrolls were placed in jars and stored in the caves in anticipation of trouble during the rebellion against Rome around A.D. 66. They remained hidden away in the caves because none of the members of the community survived the conflict to return and reclaim them.

II. THE QUMRAN COMMUNITY

As the archaeological research has indicated, at its peak the Qumran community numbered in excess of two hundred, with most residing in the main buildings. Their diet was varied, including meat (lamb, mutton, beef, veal, and goat). The specific identity of these inhabitants is still a matter of some debate, but general scholarly opinion is that they were members of the **Essenes**, a Jewish sect known to history from the writings of Flavius Josephus, Philo Judaeus, and Pliny the Elder. The latter, in his *Natural History* (5.15.73), mentioned that the Essenes lived on the western shore of the Dead Sea. They lived a heavily ritualized and communal existence that is mirrored to a large degree—with a number of minor differences—in the Qumran documents, in particular the "Community Rule" (1QS), also

called the "Manual of Discipline," the regulatory document that set out the community's government, requirements for admission, punishments, and assorted prescribed rituals. Worship was done at sunrise and sunset, and the day was spent mainly at manual labor. After ritual bathing, fully incorporated members ate as a group.

Leadership of the Qumran community was divided between a priestly and a lay class, according to the "Community Rule." The priests were termed the "sons of Aaron" (or the "sons of Zadok") and wielded effective administrative and judicial authority. Another ruling council was made up of twelve laymen—one for each of the tribes of Israel—and three priests. There were also several oversight officers. Membership was contingent upon two years of probation (Flavius Josephus wrote of three) that began with an oath-taking ceremony. After one year of probation, the candidate was granted admission into some of the community functions. If probationary membership was maintained, full admission followed. Discipline and punishment were decided by the community as a whole, and readmission was granted to those who had transgressed but who were also suitably repentant.

R

RAAMAH The son of Cush in the line of **Ham** and the father of Dedan and Sheba (Gen 10:7; 1 Chr 1:9). Raamah was later known as a small nation of traders in connection with **Sheba** (Ezek 27:22).

RAAMSES *See* **Rameses**.

RABBAH

1. A town in the northern hill country of Judah (Josh 15:60). Its precise location is unknown.

2. A city east of the Jordan that served as the capital of the ancient Ammonite kingdom. Also called "Rabbah of the Amorites," the city is identified with the modern city of Amman, the capital of the kingdom of Jordan (2 Sam 12:26, 17:27; Ezek 21:20, 25:5; Amos 1:14). According to Deut 3:11, Rabbah was the location of the giant "iron bedstead" of **Og**, the Amorite king who was vanquished by Israel at the start of the conquest of Canaan.

In the time of **David**, Rabbah was besieged and conquered by Israelite forces (2 Sam 11:1; 12:26–31). It was here that **Uriah** the Hittite was set up to be slain in battle (2 Sam 11:14–25). When David was later forced to flee to the Transjordan, **Shobi**, son of Nahash, from Rabbah, gave him aid (2 Sam 17:27–29).

After the death of **Solomon**, the Ammonites regained a large degree of their independence because of the collapse of Israelite unity and other political tribulations. The rise of Ammonite independence earned Rabbah several prophetic condemnations (Jer 49:2; Ezek 21:25, 25:5; Amos 1:14). In the time after the **Exile**, Rabbah was rebuilt and renamed Philadelphia under Ptolemy Philadelphus (285–246 B.C.) and became one of the cities of the **Decapolis**.

RABBI (Hebrew, "my great one") An honorific title used to address respected teachers of the Law. In modern Judaism, the title "rabbi" is used for an ordained clergyman authorized to teach the Law. The title is a form of the Hebrew word *rab*, meaning "great." In the New Testament, "rabbi" designated a teacher of the Law (Matt 23:7–8) and was used for John the Baptist (John 3:26). Jesus was also called "Rabbi" by the disciples (Matt 26:25, 49; Mark 9:5; 11:21; 14:45; John 1:38; 4:31) and by others (John 3:2). The emphatic form, *Rabboni*, is used to address Jesus in Mark 10:51 and John 20:16.

RABBITH A town in Issachar (Josh 19:20).

RABBONI *See* **Rabbi.**

RABSARIS The title of an Assyrian official who formed part of the delegation sent by **Sennacherib** to meet with King **Hezekiah** in Jerusalem (2 Kgs 18:17; cf. Isa 36:3). The Hebrew name is derived from the Assyrian for "chief eunuch." (*See also* **Rabshakeh** and **Tartan.**)

RABSHAKEH The title of an Assyrian official. The Hebrew word is derived from the Assyrian for "chief cupbearer." The Rabshakeh, with the Rabsaris and the Tartan, was sent by **Sennacherib** to meet with **Hezekiah** and demand the surrender of Jerusalem (2 Kgs 18:17–37; 36:2–22). (*See also* **Rabsaris** and **Tartan.**)

RACA An insult or term of abuse. It may represent the Aramaic *rêqāʾ* ("empty") and thus insinuate that someone is empty-headed or lacking sense and intelligence. Modern equivalents would probably be "idiot" or "numskull." The term appears only once in the Bible, where Jesus declares, "whoever insults his brother shall be liable to the council" (Matt 5:22). In Greek, the verb translated "insults" is literally "says 'Raca' to."

RACHEL The beloved wife of the patriarch **Jacob** and the mother of **Joseph** and **Benjamin**. She was also the daughter of **Laban** and the younger sister of Jacob's first wife, **Leah**. Her relationship with Jacob was one of the most romantic love stories in the Bible. In Jacob's estimation, Rachel was "beautiful and lovely" (Gen 29:17), and although he had to work seven years for her hand in marriage, "they seemed to him but a few days because of the love he had for her" (Gen 29:20).

Jacob first met Rachel after journeying to Paddan-aram (Haran) to find a wife (Gen 28:1–5). He encountered her at a well and immediately fell in love. He rolled away a heavy stone to water Laban's flock in a gesture that anticipated the many labors he would have to perform before finally winning her hand, but he also kissed Rachel and wept (Gen 29:9–11). The marriage proved difficult to arrange, for Laban demanded seven years of service and then through trickery substituted Leah as Jacob's first wife; before he would grant Jacob marriage to Rachel, Laban insisted upon another seven years of service (Gen 29:6–30). Jacob did wed Rachel following the week of marriage festivities with Leah (Gen 29:27), but he honored his word to serve for another seven years.

Once Rachel wed Jacob, she found that she was barren. Leah bore Jacob four sons before Rachel finally offered Jacob her maidservant Bilhah to act as her surrogate, and the sons from that union, Dan and Naphtali, were credited to Rachel (Gen 30:6–8). Only after Leah had borne six sons and a daughter (Dinah), and her maid Zilpah had borne Jacob two sons (Gad and Asher) did Rachel at last conceive a first child, Joseph, meaning "'May the LORD add to me another son'" (Gen 30:24).

Rachel died soon after the birth of her second son, Benjamin (Gen 35:16–18), a tragedy that Jacob would mourn for the rest of his life. She was buried between Bethel and Bethlehem, and Jacob gave a final testament of his abiding love for her by placing a memorial pillar on her grave (Gen 35:20). The Bible preserves two traditions about her burial place: one that locates the site in the territory of Benjamin at Zelzah (1 Sam 10:2) and one that locates it in the territory of Judah just outside Bethlehem (Gen 35:18–19).

Scripture honors Rachel as the matriarch of three tribes of Israel—Benjamin, Ephraim, and Manasseh (Ephraim and Manasseh being the sons of Joseph)—and she is counted with Leah as among those who "built up the house of Israel" (Ruth 4:11). She is likewise counted with **Sarah**, **Rebecca**, **Miriam**, **Deborah**, **Hannah**, **Judith**, and **Esther** as one of the outstanding women who kept alive the hope of Israel's salvation (CCC 64).

RAGES Also Ragae, a city in Media, the home of Gabael, to whom **Tobit** entrusted his money and from whom **Tobias** collected it (Tob 1:14; 4:1, 20; 5:5; 6:12; 9:2). The city (modern Rai) was located five miles to the southeast of Tehran, Iran.

RAGUEL The husband of Edna and the father of Sarah, the wife of **Tobias** (Tob 3:7; 6:10). Raguel drafted a marriage contract between Sarah and Tobias (Tob 7:14), but he also dug a grave for Tobias on the wedding night in anticipation of his imminent death (Tob 8:9). When Tobias did not die through the evil of the demon Asmodeus, Raguel blessed God's name and gave Sarah and Tobias half of his possessions (Tob 8:20–21). Outside the Bible, the name Raguel is also given to one of the holy angels who ministers alongside Michael and Raphael (*1 Enoch* 20:4).

RAHAB

1. A Canaanite woman and harlot from the city of **Jericho** who hid two of **Joshua**'s spies at the time of the conquest of Canaan (Josh 2:1–7; 6:17, 23–25). Rahab recognized the Lord's power and demanded from the spies the promise that she and her family would be spared when the Israelites conquered Jericho (Josh 2:18–14). Joshua was faithful to the pledge, and only Rahab and her family were spared after the city's capture (Josh 6:22–23). According to Josh 6:25, Rahab "dwelt in Israel to this day, because she hid the messengers whom Joshua sent to spy out Jericho." She is remembered as a heroine of faith (Heb 11:31) and was justified by her works (Jas 2:25). She is listed in Matthew's genealogy of Jesus as the wife of Salmon and the mother of **Boaz**, ancestor of **David** (Matt 1:5).

2. A mythological sea serpent mentioned several times in the Old Testament. Rahab, whose name in Hebrew means "arrogance," represents the forces of chaos and cosmic disorder that were overcome by God at creation (Ps 89:11; Job 9:13, 26:12); later, Rahab was used as a metaphorical name for Egypt (Ps 87:4; Isa 30:7). In Isa 51:9–10, the Lord's triumph over Rahab is also linked to the Red Sea crossing: "Was it not you that cut Rahab in pieces, that pierced the dragon? Was it not you that dried up the sea, the waters of the great deep; that made the depths of the sea a way for the redeemed to pass over?" God thus demonstrated his absolute power over nature and all those who might oppose his will.

RAIN The rainy season in Palestine falls mainly in the winter months between November and

February, though it can begin as early as October and taper off as late as April. Rain was a blessing that came from God above (Deut 11:14, 28:12; Ps 72:6–7; Joel 2:23; Jer 5:24, 14:22). As such, rain was an occasion for rejoicing, as the yearly rains were essential to maintaining a largely agricultural society. Rainfall was one of the blessings promised to Jacob's descendants (Gen 27:28; Deut 28:12). Drought was considered one of the most terrible of the covenant curses (Lev 26:19; Deut 28:23–24; cf. Jer 3:3).

The Israelites looked with much anticipation for the first rains of the early autumn, and the last rains in the spring, which signaled the end of the rainy season (cf. Deut 11:14; Joel 2:23; Hos 6:3; Zech 10:1; Jas 5:7). During the peak rain times, **Palestine** encounters violent downpours and torrential rains (1 Kgs 18:45; Ezra 10:13; Job 37:6). But gentler showers are also common (Deut 32:2; Ps 65:10; Mic 5:7).

RAINBOW The sign of the Noahic **covenant** that God made with creation after the **Flood**. In Hebrew, the word is *qešet*, which normally refers to a hunting or military bow (Gen 27:3; Isa 5:28). The sign of the rainbow thus evokes the image of God placing his weapon in the sky. This could mean that God was hanging up his bow and retiring it from service, having pledged to Noah that he would never again make war on the world by submerging it with a flood. On the other hand, it may represent the oath that God swore in establishing the Noahic covenant. Since oaths in biblical antiquity involved a conditional self-curse, the curved rainbow may be a sign that God threatened himself with a curse by pulling back the bow and aiming it toward heaven. Either way the rainbow was a guarantee of the Lord's pledge never to flood the earth again. Elsewhere in Scripture the rainbow and its vibrant colors appear in visions of God's glory (Ezek 1:28; Rev 4:3, 10:1).

RAKKATH A town in the tribal territory of Naphtali (Josh 19:35).

RAKKON A village of Dan near the port of Joppa (Josh 19:46).

RAM The name of two men in the Old Testament.

1. A descendant of **Jacob** through **Judah** and an ancestor of **David** (Ruth 4:19; 1 Chr 2:9, 10). His name appears as Aram in Matthew's genealogy of Jesus (Matt 1:4).

2. The firstborn of Jerahmeel and the nephew of Ram the son of Hezron (1 Chr 2:25, 27).

RAM *See* **Lamb**; *see also* **Sacrifice**.

RAMAH The name of a number of places in the Bible.

1. A town in the territory of Benjamin halfway between Jerusalem and Bethel (Josh 18:25). In Judg 4:5, the prophetess **Deborah** sat beneath a palm tree near Ramah. Later, a Levite traveling from Bethlehem considered spending the night at Ramah with his concubine (Judg 19:13). The city was also the site of a fortress built by **Baasha** of Israel during his conflict with **Asa** of Judah. Ramah was dismantled and its fortifications were used by Asa to build Geba and Mizpah (1 Kgs 15:17, 21–22; 2 Chr 16:1, 5–6). After the fall of Jerusa-

lem, the Babylonian commander **Nebuzaradan** assembled the Jewish captives at Ramah and freed **Jeremiah** (Jer 40:1); the city was occupied by the returnees after the Exile (Neh 11:33). Ramah was also mentioned by prophets (Hos 5:8; Isa 10:29; Jer 31:15). Ramah is probably the modern Er Ram, near Jerusalem, although Ramat Rahel is also suggested.

2. The hometown and burial spot of **Samuel** (1 Sam 1:1, 19; 2:11; 7:17; 8:4; 15:34; 19:18; 25:1; 28:3), located in the hill country of Ephraim. It was also called Ramathaim-zophim. Some scholars believe that Samuel was born in Ramah of Benjamin.

3. A village near the northern border of Asher (Josh 19:29).

4. A village in Naphtali (Josh 19:36), probably the modern Er Rameh.

5. A village allotted to Simeon on the outskirts of the Negeb desert (Josh 19:8; cf. 1 Sam 30:27).

6. See **Ramoth-gilead**.

RAMESES A city in the eastern Nile Delta named after Pharaoh Rameses II, ruler of Egypt from about 1279 to 1213 B.C. It served as the royal residence of the pharaohs of the Nineteenth and Twentieth Dynasties (ca. 1295–1069 B.C.). Modern archaeology locates Rameses at the site called Qantir.

It was in this region of the Delta that Joseph settled his father and brothers (Gen 47:11). The site became a store city for the Egyptians, and the Israelites were compelled to work on its construction (Exod 1:11). Rameses was thus the point of departure for the Israelites at the time of the Exodus (Exod 12:37; Num 33:3, 5). In the book of Judith, King **Nebuchadnezzar** summoned troops from Rameses to assist in his wars against Arphaxad (Jdt 1:9, 13–14).

RAMESES II Pharaoh of Egypt from about 1279 to 1213 B.C. and the third ruler of the Nineteenth Dynasty (after Rameses I and Seti I). Scholars who favor a thirteenth-century B.C. date for the Exodus often identify Rameses II as the unnamed pharaoh who was forced to let Israel leave Egypt (Exod 12:29–32). During his sixty-six-year reign, Rameses II sponsored numerous building projects on a grand scale. His name was given to one of the Delta storage cities that were built by Israelite slaves (Exod 1:11). Apparently his name was also used to identify the entire surrounding region, which the Bible normally calls "the land of Goshen" (Gen 47:1), but on one occasion calls "the land of Rameses" (Gen 47:11).

RAMOTH-GILEAD A fortress-city in the territory of Gad in Gilead, east of the Jordan (Josh 20:8). It was assigned to the Merarite Levites as one of the forty-eight Levitical cities (Josh 21:38; 1 Chr 6:80), and it was one of the six cities of refuge for those found guilty of unintentional homicide (Josh 20:8). When **Solomon** later organized the kingdom into twelve administrative districts (1 Kgs 4:7–19), Ramoth-gilead was used as the residence of Ben-geber, the governor of Gilead and part of Bashan (1 Kgs 4:13). The city was subsequently a battleground between the Syrians and the Israelites. The Syrians eventually captured it, since **Ahab** of Israel entered an alliance with **Jehoshaphat** of Judah to recover Ramoth-gilead from Aram (1 Kgs 22:3–4). This campaign was the occasion for the prophecy of **Micaiah**, son of Imlah, that only defeat would accompany such an expedition, despite the contrary assurances of the four hundred court prophets (1 Kgs 22:15–17). Another effort to recapture the city was made under **Joram** of Israel and **Ahaziah** of Judah (2 Kgs 8:28–29), an action that led directly to the overthrow of the Omride Dynasty by **Jehu** (cf. 2 Kgs 9:1–13). Ramoth-gilead is probably the modern Tell Ramith, on the border between Jordan and Syria.

RAPHAEL (Hebrew, "God heals") An angel who plays a major role in the book of **Tobit**. For most of the book Raphael is disguised as the man Azarias (Tob 5:12), whom Tobit hires to escort his son Tobias to Media and back (Tob 5:13–15). In the course of their adventure, Raphael helps to arrange the marriage of Tobias and Sarah (Tob 6:9–12) and prescribes the means to ward off a demon (Tob 6:15–17) that had long prevented Sarah from getting married (Tob 3:7–8). On their return, Raphael prescribes the means to restore the vision of Tobias's blind father, Tobit (Tob 11:1–15), and then finally reveals his true identity: "I am Raphael, one of the seven holy angels who present the prayers of the saints and enter into the presence of the glory of the Holy One" (Tob 12:15). Raphael does not appear in the New Testament but figures in Jewish theological writings outside the Bible as a healer and victor over demons (e.g., *1 Enoch* 10.4, 40.9; Dead Sea Scrolls, 1QM 9.15–16).

Raphael is one of the angels venerated by name in the Church, with Michael and Gabriel, and he is revered especially as an angel of healing. Christian lore sometimes identifies him as the head of the guardian angels, the angel of knowledge, and the angel of science. Raphael is also a prominent figure in the angelic traditions of Judaism; Jewish legend says that he was one of the three messengers who visited Abraham before the destruction of Sodom and Gomorrah (Gen 18:2).

RAPHAH A descendant of King **Saul** in the line of his grandson, Meribbaal, also called **Mephibosheth** (1 Chr 8:37).

RAPHON A city in Gilead, east of the Jordan, where **Judas Maccabeus** defeated a large army gathered by the Seleucid commander Timothy (1 Macc 5:37–44). Raphon is probably the modern er-Rafeh.

RAS SHAMRA *See* **Ugarit**.

RASSIS A site plundered by **Holofernes** in his lightning war of reprisal against Asia Minor and Syria (Jdt 2:23).

RAVEN A bird that is found in several species in Palestine. The raven was a carrion bird (Job 38:41) and was unclean (Lev 11:15; Deut 14:14). In the account of the **Flood**, **Noah** first sends out a raven to see if the waters have receded (Gen 8:7). The ravens also brought food to **Elijah** in the desert (1 Kgs 17:4–6) and were a sign of God's Providence (Ps 147:9; Luke 12:24). In Song 5:11, the hair of the beloved is black like a raven.

RAZIS An elder from Jerusalem who committed suicide rather than endure arrest and humiliation by the troops of **Nicanor** (2 Macc 14:37–46). He made several desperate attempts at suicide before he was successful.

RAZOR The razor was an important implement in various rites of purification and mourning. Levites used a razor to shave their entire bodies (Num 8:7), in a manner similar to the Sumerian and especially the Egyptian priests. Perhaps the most notable practice involving shaving was that of the Nazirite (Num 6:5), who took a vow not to shave until such time as the vow was completed. At its conclusion, the Nazirite shaved his hair, which was then burned. (*See* **Nazirite**.) Both **Samson** (Judg 13:5) and **Samuel** (1 Sam 1:11) were consecrated Nazirites. **Paul** also shaved his head (Acts 18:18) as a result of a vow. The razor was used in imagery, most notably by Isaiah when he described Assyria as the Lord's razor with which the Lord would shave the body hair (Isa 7:20). The sharp tongue is like a razor (Ps 52:2).

REBEKAH The wife of the patriarch **Isaac** and the mother of his two sons, **Jacob** and **Esau**. She was living in upper Mesopotamia with her father, Bethuel, and her brother **Laban** when **Abraham** sent one of his servants to find Isaac a wife, lest he have to marry a Canaanite woman (Gen 24:1–67). Like **Sarah** before her and **Rachel** after her, Rebekah began her married life struggling with the disappointment of infertility until the Lord intervened and enabled her and Isaac to conceive (Gen 25:21). Not only did she conceive, but she carried twin boys, Jacob and Esau, who wrestled for supremacy even in the womb. Rebekah had a preferential love for Jacob (Gen 25:28), and although he was the younger of the twins, she devised a clever ruse to procure the firstborn blessing from Isaac for Jacob (Gen 27:1–

29). Because of her success on Jacob's behalf, Jacob immediately had to flee the wrath of his older brother by escaping back to her relatives (Gen 27:42–45). Rebekah would never again lay eyes on her beloved son before dying and being buried in the cave of **Machpelah** (Gen 49:30–31). Christian tradition reveres Rebekah as one of the courageous women of the Bible (CCC 64).

RECHABITES An ultraconservative clan in Israel that seems to have idealized the nomadic life of the **Exodus** generation in the wilderness. The clan took its name from its ancestor, Rechab (cf. 1 Chr 2:55). The Rechabites were known for unwavering fidelity to Yahweh. The laws of the Rechabites were laid down by Rechab's son Jehonadab. According to 2 Kgs 10:15–31, Jehonadab encountered **Jehu** during Jehu's campaign against **Ahab**, and the general invited Jehonadab to join in his cause and "see my zeal for the Lord." The Rechabites followed their ancestor Jehonadab's example: even two hundred years later they rejected all aspects of settled culture— houses, agriculture, and wine from cultivated vines—choosing to live the life of the wilderness generation (Jer 35:1–19).

RECONCILIATION, SACRAMENT OF *See* **Repentance**.

REDACTION CRITICISM *See* **Biblical criticism**.

REDEEMER *See* **Jesus Christ**; *see also* **Redemption**.

REDEMPTION The payment of a ransom price to liberate someone held in captivity. In the biblical world, redemption was often a kinsman winning the release of a family member. In biblical theology, redemption is when God delivers a people from bondage and makes them his own by covenant. The liberation of Israel from slavery in Egypt is the preeminent act of redemption in the Old Testament (Exod 15:13). The salvation of the world from sin and death, made possible by the sacrifice of Jesus Christ, is hailed in the New Testament as redemption in the ultimate sense (Eph 1:7; Heb 9:11–12; Rev 5:9–10) (CCC 613, 616).

I. Redemption in the Old Testament
    A. The Blood Redeemer
    B. God as Redeemer of Israel
    C. Redeeming the Firstborn
    D. Redeeming Property
    E. Redemption as Liberation
    F. Future Redemption
II. Redemption in the New Testament

I. REDEMPTION IN THE OLD TESTAMENT

A. The Blood Redeemer

In ancient Israel, redemption was rooted in the family, where brothers and kinsmen were obligated by their blood ties to look after the welfare of the entire tribe or clan and each one of its members. For instance, the closest male relative served as the blood redeemer (Num 35:19–21; *see* **Avenger of blood**) to avenge the death of kin (Judg 8:18–21). The Hebrew word for "redeem" thus refers to the role of the nearest male relative (Exod 21:8; Ps 49:8): he assumed the responsibility for paying any ransom needed to free all family members from captivity or debt slavery (Lev 25:47–49).

B. God as Redeemer of Israel

As the divine Father of Israel, the Lord assumed the role of kinsman Redeemer (cf. Isa 41:14; 54:5–8; 63:16). He was the Israelites' deliverer, the one who ransomed his kin, the people he claimed as his firstborn son, from bondage in Egypt (Exod 4:22–23). In the OT, the stress on the redeeming activity of God is not on the notion that a ransom was paid but that liberation was accomplished through God's power (Deut 7:8; 15:15; 24:18) and also through his love (Ps 44:26).

C. Redeeming the Firstborn

In the **Law** of Moses, redemption in the sense of "buying back" became a standing duty with regard to the firstborn son in every Israelite family. Originally, every firstborn of Israel who was spared from the death of the tenth plague on Egypt (*see* **Passover, feast of**) was thereby consecrated to the service of the Lord (Exod 13:2; 22:9). But the zeal of the Levites in putting down the golden-calf rebellion at **Sinai** effected a change in clerical ministry (Exod 32:25–29). When the Sinai covenant was renewed, the firstborn sons were deconsecrated and the Levites replaced them as ministers of worship (Num 3:41, 44–45; 8:14–18). Thereafter, every firstborn son had to be bought back from the Lord with a redemption price of five shekels (Exod 34:20; Num 18:15–16).

D. Redeeming Property

Where redemption pertained to land, an Israelite was able to redeem property that he had been forced by economic hardship to sell. The land could be redeemed when the owner could afford to do so (Lev 25:26–28), or it could be reclaimed by next of kin (Lev 25:25). In a **Jubilee** year, property reverted automatically to the original owner or his heirs (Lev 25:28). Houses in walled cities were redeemable for a period of one year from the date of sale but not beyond that time. Houses outside of walled cities had no specific time limit for their redemption and were considered virtually the same as fields (Lev 25:31). Houses in Levitical cities were always redeemable only by Levites (Lev 25:32–33), and Levites were never permitted to sell their land to non-Levites (Lev 25:34; cf. Jer 32:6–15; Ezek 11:15).

E. Redemption as Liberation

In overtly theological contexts, the notion of redemption is basically equivalent to "deliverance" without any specific reference to a ransom price or monetary transaction. Redemption in this sense is epitomized by the **Exodus** liberation of Israel from Egyptian bondage (Exod 6:6, 7; Deut 7:6–8, 13:6, 15:15, 21:8). The Exodus was accomplished not through the payment of a ransom but through the exercise of God's divine power (cf. Ps 25:22; 130:7). By extension, the purpose of this redeeming act was to claim a people for God (Exod 6:6–7, 19:3–5; cf. 2 Sam 7:23; 1 Chr 17:21; Ps 74:2, 111:9) and lead them to the Promised Land. (*See* **Election**.)

F. Future Redemption

The Exodus from Egypt became a paradigm of salvation. It assured Israel that the Lord was a mighty Redeemer who could save his people from any earthly predicament. In the Prophets, the *first* Exodus created hope for a *new* Exodus in the future. Initially, this new Exodus refers to the return from the **Exile** in Babylon, but the promises were far too grand and glorious to be reduced to that one event (Hos 7:13, 13:14; Mic 4:10; Jer 31:11, 50:34). The new Exodus would ultimately have a Messianic fulfillment.

Isaiah assures the exiles in Babylon that they will receive the word of the Lord and will be liberated (Isa 41:14; 44:6; 47:4; 52:3). There were obvious parallels between the redemption of the Israelites from Egypt in the Exodus and the return of the Israelites from Exile in Babylon, because in both instances God fulfilled his role as the blood redeemer who brings vengeance for the ill treatment of his relatives (Isa 49:25–26; 51:9–11; 59:16–20; cf. Deut 19:6; Num 35:19, 21). Isaiah often shows God as both a relative and a father (Isa 43:1, 6; 44:24; 49:15; 63:16; 64:7; 66:9) and also as one with an obligation to assist the poor and suffering who are under his care (Isa 41:17; 49:13; 51:21; 54:11; 58:7; 66:2). In the postexilic period, Zech 10:8 delivered God's promise to his people: "I will signal for them and gather them in, for I have redeemed them and they shall be as numerous as they were before." At the same time, part of the redemption would entail a cleansing of sin (Isa 44:22, 53:5–6; cf. Jer 31:34; Ezek 36:27).

II. REDEMPTION IN THE NEW TESTAMENT

The heart of the NT message is the new redemption accomplished by Jesus Christ. At the cost of his own life, offered in sacrifice to the Father (Eph 5:2), Jesus expiated the sins of the world (John 1:29; 1 John 2:2) and delivered the human race from the dominion of darkness (Col 1:13–14) and its bondage to the devil (Heb 2:14–15). In his own words, Jesus came to offer his life "as a ransom for many" (Matt 20:28; Mark 10:45).

The theological language of redemption in the NT is deeply indebted to the concepts of liberation and salvation in the OT. It is primarily the Exodus that shapes the Christian understanding of Christ's redeeming work. Jesus himself plays the role of the Passover Lamb whose sacrifice brings salvation to the people of God (1 Cor 5:7; 1 Pet 1:18–19). The people's release is not from political bondage, as in Egypt, but from slavery to sin (Rom 6:16–18). The dignity that they are given through Christ is that of a "royal priesthood" and a "holy nation" (1 Pet 2:9; Rev 5:9–10; cf. Exod 19:6).

The Christian life is thus an Exodus adventure of passing through the waters of baptism into a wilderness of testing and trials, where believers are guided by the Spirit and sustained by a supernatural food (manna) and drink (water) as they make their way toward the heavenly Promised Land (1 Cor 10:1–111).

Redemption is also prefigured in the OT by the liturgy of the Day of Atonement (Lev 16:1–34; *see* **Atonement, Day of**), which anticipates how Christ, as High Priest and spotless victim, takes his own blood into the sanctuary of heaven to secure an eternal redemption (Heb 9:6–14). Among the prophets' texts none is more important than the fourth Servant Song in Isa 52–53, where the Messianic figure leads the iniquity of ages onto himself and pours out his life as an atoning sacrifice for many. Next to the new Exodus motif, which envisions the salvation of a people, the Suffering Servant sets the stage for the Savior himself and his vicarious act of life-giving sacrifice (Matt 8:17, 20:28; Luke 22:37; Acts 8:32–35).

RED HEIFER A red female cow. Its ashes were an essential ingredient in the purifying water used to cleanse persons and objects defiled by human death (Num 19:1–22). The ashes were both prepared and stored outside the camp of Israel, and all who took part in the slaughtering, burning, and collection of the heifer's remains were temporarily unclean. In the book of Hebrews, the ashes of a red heifer, which cleansed the Israelites from death and defilement, are surpassed by the greater power of Christ's blood, which cleanses the conscience of dead works (Heb 9:13–14).

RED SEA (Hebrew *yam sûp*, "Sea of Reeds") The inlet of water between the continent of Africa and the Arabian Peninsula. It is mentioned several times in the Old Testament, often in connection with the **Exodus**. The northern end divides into two gulfs: the Gulf of Suez, which separates the Sinai Peninsula from Egypt to the west; and the Gulf of Aqaba, which separates the Sinai Peninsula from Arabia to the east.

At the time of the Exodus, Moses led the Israelites to the shore of the "Red Sea" (Exod 13:18). There, by a miracle of divine might, God opened a path through the waters, allowing his people to cross, and then drove the waters back on the pursuing Egyptians (Exod 14:10–29; Ps 106:7–12, 136:13–15). The location of this sea crossing is debated. The Greek Septuagint takes *yam sûp* to be the Red Sea (*tēn erythran thallasan*), presumably the Gulf of Suez. This is not impossible, although a number of reed-supporting lakes lined the border between Egypt and the Sinai in the second millennium B.C., and any one of them (e.g., the Bitter Lakes or the El-Ballah Lakes) could qualify as the biblical "Sea of Reeds."

Other references in the OT suggest that *yam sûp* could also refer to the Gulf of Aqaba (Exod 23:31; Deut 1:40, 2:1; Judg 11:16; 1 Kgs 9:26; Jer 49:21). In 1 Kgs 9:26, we learn that **Solomon** docked his fleet of merchant ships at the northern tip of the Gulf of Aqaba at Ezion-geber.

REED An aquatic plant with rigid stalks, found in Palestine along the rivers and streams leading into the Jordan Valley. The reed was a symbol of weakness (cf. 1 Kgs 14:15; Isa 36:6; Ezek 29:6–7; Matt 11:7; Luke 7:24). Reeds were used for measuring rods (Ezek 40:3; Rev 11:1) and for walking sticks (2 Kgs 18:21).

REEDS, SEA OF *See* **Red Sea**.

REFUGE, CITIES OF Six cities that were set aside in Israel as places of asylum where someone who had unintentionally caused another's death could flee without fear of revenge until he could face a fair trial (Num 35:9–15;

Deut 4:41–43; Josh 20:1–9). The fugitive was to stand at the entrance of the gate of the city and explain the case to the elders of that city; the fugitive was then taken into the city and given sanctuary. If an **avenger of blood** (a kinsman of the victim) was in pursuit, the manslayer was not to be delivered up; he would remain in the city until a trial could be held. If there proved to be no evidence of malicious intent, he could live in the city of refuge "until the death of him who is high priest at the time: then the slayer may go again to his own town and his own home, to the town from which he fled" (Josh 20:6). The cities of refuge were listed in Josh 20:7–9 (cf. Deut 4:41–43; 19:1–13): three west of the Jordan (Kedesh, Shechem, and Hebron) and three east of the Jordan (Bezer, Ramoth, and Gilead).

REGENERATION The renewal of creation and its restoration to a state of grace. There is no specific term for this idea in the Old Testament, although a number of prophetic texts envision a rebirth of the covenant people in terms of resurrection (Isa 26:19; Hos 6:2; Dan 12:2) and the remission of sin (Isa 27:9; Jer 31:31–34; Ezek 36:25). Emphasis is often placed on the interior dimension of renewal; that is, the grace of regeneration touches man at the very heart of his being (Deut 30:6; Jer 31:33; Ezek 36:26–27). It likewise involves an outpouring of the divine Spirit upon the Lord's people (Isa 32:15, 44:2; Ezek 11:19; Joel 2:28).

The term for "regeneration" in the New Testament, the Greek *palingenesia*, appears twice. In one text, it refers to the "new world" or the renewed order that enters the world through the Christian economy of grace (Matt

19:28). In the other instance, it refers to the rebirth of the believer through baptism and the new life that comes through the Holy Spirit (Titus 3:5; cf. 1 Pet 1:3). Jesus himself referred to baptismal regeneration when he said, "unless one is born of water and the Spirit, he cannot enter the Kingdom of God" (John 3:5). In fulfillment of the prophetic hopes of Israel, regeneration entails the remission of sins (Acts 2:38; 22:16), the inner renewal of the heart (Rom 5:5; 2 Cor 3:3; Col. 2:11–12), and the anticipation of a bodily resurrection (Rom 8:11; 1 Cor 15:42–50) (CCC 1215, 1262).

REHOB

1. The father of **Hadadezer**, king of Zobah, who was defeated by **David** (2 Sam 8:3, 12).

2. A Levite who placed his seal on the covenant in Nehemiah (Neh 10:11).

REHOB Also Beth-rehob, the name of several places in the Old Testament.

1. The most northerly point in Canaan, near Hamath, that was surveyed by Joshua's spies (Num 13:21). It is probably the same place as Beth-rehob, an Aramean city in ancient Syria that allied with the Ammonites in their war against David (2 Sam 10:6, 8). The Rehob listed as a Canaanite city in the records of the Egyptian pharaohs Thutmose III and Shishak is probably this Rehob.

2. A town in Asher (Josh 19:28, 30) that was designated a Levitical city (Josh 21:31; 1 Chr 6:75). It was not conquered when Israel first took possession of the Promised Land (Judg 1:31).

REHOBOAM The son of **Solomon** and the successor to his father as king of a united Is-

rael. By a foolish policy decision, he incited the revolt of the northern tribes of Israel and was left with only two tribes under his dominion, Judah and Benjamin (1 Kgs 12:1–24). Rehoboam thus became the first ruler of the southern kingdom of Judah; Israel, the northern kingdom, was ruled by Jeroboam I. The date of Rehoboam's reign most likely covered the seventeen years from 930 to 913 B.C. (1 Kgs 14:21; 2 Chr 12:13).

In the reign of Rehoboam, the decline of the Davidic kingdom that had long been under way under Solomon reached its breaking point. Rehoboam perpetuated the tyrannical tendencies of his father's reign. The taxes and burdens imposed by Solomon to pay for his various royal projects were not only kept up by Rehoboam but increased, on the ill-considered advice of his counselors. This the northern tribes would not accept. The king attempted to assert his royal prerogative at the gathering at **Shechem**. The northern tribes rebelled and set up Jeroboam as king of the ten tribes of Israel (1 Kgs 12:1–20; 2 Chr 10:1–19). Rehoboam's effort to reassert his royal claim was circumvented by the prophet **Shemaiah** (1 Kgs 12:21–24).

Rehoboam also saw the invasion of Jerusalem by Pharaoh **Shishak** of Egypt, who plundered the city and carried off much of the treasure of Solomon (1 Kgs 14:25–28). The author of Kings judges Rehoboam harshly for allowing various religious abominations to flourish in Judah during his years in power (1 Kgs 14:22–24). In 2 Chr 12:5–8, 12, we read that the invasion by Egypt was a punishment for Rehoboam's apostasy, but the text adds that he repented.

REHOBOTH The name of three places in the Old Testament.

1. A well dug by **Isaac** (Gen 26:17–22) in the valley of Gerar. The location is generally identified with Wadi Ruhaybeh, to the southwest of Beer-sheba.

2. Rehoboth-Ir, one of the four cities in Mesopotamia built by **Nimrod** along with Nineveh and Calah (Gen 10:11).

3. Rehoboth on the Euphrates, the hometown of an ancient Edomite king (Gen 36:37; 1 Chr 1:48).

REHUM The name of three men in the Old Testament.

1. A leader among the first group of Jewish exiles to return from Babylon (Ezra 2:2). He is called "Nehum" in the parallel text in Neh 7:7.

2. A Persian commander in Samaria at the time of the return of the exiles from the Babylonian Captivity. He wrote to Artaxerxes I to oppose the proposed rebuilding of the walls of Jerusalem on the basis of the city's rebellious past. He received a favorable response and was authorized to halt the building effort by force (Ezra 4:17–22).

3. A Levite who helped **Nehemiah** in rebuilding the walls of Jerusalem (Neh 3:17).

REMNANT A biblical term for "those who are left" of a people or nation. Normally, this is either a faithful minority who refuses to join the apostasy of a majority, or it is the fortunate few who survive a catastrophe that overtakes the majority. Sometimes the remnant is both faithful and fortunate: theologically, it is often the case that the remnant is "chosen" by God and is the object of his special blessing and protection. The notion of a remnant left behind is a theme that recurs throughout the Bible.

REPENTANCE A conversion of heart away from sin and toward God. It begins with remorse for having offended God and entails both a change in one's life and a determination to avoid the further occasion of sin (CCC 1427–33). The call to conversion and true repentance is one of the central themes of the New Testament and a cornerstone of the Christian life.

I. *Repentance in the Old Testament*
    A. *Words for "Repentance"*
    B. *Turning Away from Sin*
    C. *The Prophets Call Israel to Repent*
II. *Repentance in the New Testament*
    A. *Echoing the Prophets*
    B. *Repent and Believe*
    C. *Conversion*
    D. *Paul Includes Repentance in Faith*
III. *The Sacrament of Penance*

I. REPENTANCE IN THE OLD TESTAMENT

A. Words for "Repentance"

The most commonly used term in the Old Testament for repentance is *šûb*, meaning literally "to turn" (in the **Septuagint** and NT, Greek equivalents are *apostrephō* or *epistrephō*; see also below). Another word is used, *nāḥam* ("to sigh" or "to grieve"), to express various forms of grief and remorse. *Nāḥam*, however, is often used in anthropomorphic descriptions of God's decision to bestow mercy on the repentant instead of carrying out his judgment against them (e.g., 1 Chr 21:15). Most notable in this sense is Jer 18:8: "and if that nation, concerning which I have spoken, turns from its evil, I will repent of the evil that I intended to do to it." Scripture declares that God does not repent in the way that humans do (Num 23:19; 1 Sam 15:29).

B. Turning Away from Sin

Repentance in the OT implied a genuine sorrow and turning away from sinful actions. For example, **Solomon** pleaded with God to show mercy upon those who repented and turned back to the Lord: "hear in heaven your dwelling place their prayer and their supplication, and maintain their cause and forgive your people who have sinned against you, and all their transgressions which they have committed against you; and grant them compassion in the sight of those who carried them captive, that they may have compassion on them" (1 Kgs 8:47).

Often this "turning" was expressed through penitential actions—fasting, lamenting, tearing of garments, wearing sackcloth and ashes, and openly confessing guilt (cf. Ezra 10:1–5; Neh 9:1–37; Isa 63:7–64:12; Hos 6:1–3, 14:1–3; Dan 9:3–19; Joel 2:15–18).

C. The Prophets Call Israel to Repent

The mission of the prophet in Israel is to call the people back to the Lord. Indictments of sin, threats of doom, promises of mercy for genuine conversion—all are part of the prophetic summons to repentance (Amos 4:6–13; Hos 5:15–6:5, 6:4–6; Isa 58:5–7).

In spite of repeated apostasy, the Lord seeks Israel's return as one seeks a wayward wife (Hos 2–3). Jeremiah 3:11–14 echoes the cries for Israel to turn and be repentant: "Return, faithless Israel, says the LORD. I will not look on you in anger, for I am merciful, says the LORD; I will not be angry for ever" (Jer 3:12; cf. Jer 4:1–2; 6:9; 31:3). Amos, in contrast, emphasizes the judgment that Israel's failure to repent—"yet you did not return to me"—makes inevitable. For this utter faithlessness, "prepare to meet your God, O Israel!" (Amos 4:12).

Hosea remains determined even in the face of such obduracy, so that the book ends with a final plea for repentance: "Return, O Israel, to the LORD your God, for you have stumbled because of your iniquity. Take with you words and return to the LORD; say to him, 'Take away all iniquity; accept that which is good and we will render the fruit of our lips'" (Hos 14:2). The prophets assure Israel of the great reward and happiness that will be found in such true repentance: salvation and deliverance (Isa 30:15; Jer 4:1, 26:3). The nation as a whole must repent, but each individual Israelite must also repent with a real change of heart (Ezek 18:31, 36:26–27; Hos 6:6; Amos 5:21–24; Joel 2:12–13; Isa 1:16–17).

II. REPENTANCE IN THE NEW TESTAMENT

A. Echoing the Prophets

The prophetic call to conversion reaches its climax in **John the Baptist**, the last of the prophets, who prepared the way of the Lord. John the Baptist appeared suddenly "in the wilderness, preaching a baptism of repentance for the forgiveness of sins" (Mark 1:4). John demanded more than mere contrition: he called for a deeper conversion that involved a change in the life of the penitent: "Bear fruits that befit repentance" (Luke 3:8; cf. Matt 3:2–11; Mark 1:4–6; Luke 3:1–14). John established the central theme that was reiterated by Jesus: "The time is fulfilled, and the kingdom of God is at hand; repent, and believe in the gospel" (Mark 1:15; Matt 4:17). The call of Jesus was a familiar one, rooted in the OT prophetic message of repentance and conversion that had been delivered repeatedly to Israel. In Jesus, the call to repentance becomes personal, for he asks people not only to embrace him as **Messiah**, but to imitate his generosity of life as the surest path to living out the Father's will (Matt 7:21–27; 10:37–39; 11:28–30).

B. Repent and Believe

Jesus came not for the righteous but for the sinner (Luke 5:32). The repentance of Nineveh at the preaching of Jonah (Matt 12:39–40; Luke 11:29–32) is what Jesus asks of his disciples (cf. Matt 1:20–24; Luke 10:13–15). The call of Jesus to repent implies more than mere sorrow for sin. He calls people also to believe (Mark 16:15–16). Repentance in faith is the beginning of the embrace of the new life that is offered by the Gospel (cf. Acts 5:31; 20:21).

Salvation is achieved by the forgiveness of sin through baptism and faith in Jesus (Acts 2:38). Those who reject faith reject the everlasting life that Christ offers to the world (John 3:36). Christian repentance is a complete transformation of the person from the life of sin to the life of Gospel charity. Thus we must proclaim repentance to the entire world:

"repentance and forgiveness of sins should be preached in his name to all nations, beginning from Jerusalem" (Luke 24:47).

C. Conversion

Jesus teaches the universality of sin and the need for all to undergo conversion. Baptism is fundamental to conversion, but there is also the ongoing conversion in the lives of believers. In Peter, we see a vivid example of initial conversion and ongoing conversion. In his initial conversion, Peter sinks to his knees and acknowledges his sinfulness: "Depart from me, for I am a sinful man, O Lord" (Luke 5:8). Then he drops everything and follows Jesus as a disciple (Matt 4:18–20). Later, having denied Christ three times, he weeps for his sin (Luke 22:62) and then reaffirms his love for Christ (John 21:15–19).

Christian conversion has both an interior and an exterior dimension. It begins in the mind and heart, where the conviction of sin arises and where the desire to draw closer to God takes place. It is significant that the NT word for "repentance" refers to a "change of mind" (Greek *metanoia*). The point is not that conversion can be reduced to a mental act, but that a change of perspective is essential to the redirection of one's life. The interior attitude thus leads to exterior actions such as fasting (Mark 2:20; Acts 9:9, 13:2) and various forms of self-discipline and mortification (Rom 8:13; 1 Cor 9:25–27).

Hebrews tells us that "it is impossible to restore again to repentance those who have once been enlightened, who have tasted the heavenly gift, and have become partakers of the Holy Spirit, and have tasted the goodness of the word of God and the powers of the age to come, if they then commit apostasy, since they crucify the Son of God on their own account and hold him up to contempt" (Heb 6:4–6). The passage has been the source of much theological discussion, but at its heart is the call not to presume upon the mercy of God and to recognize the seriousness of sin because it damages the relationship that exists between a person and God (CCC 1849–53).

D. Paul Includes Repentance in Faith

Paul seldom speaks of repentance directly. He does contrast godly versus worldly grief: "For godly grief produces a repentance that leads to salvation and brings no regret, but worldly grief produces death" (2 Cor 7:10), and he mentions "repentance" a few more times (Rom 2:4; 2 Cor 12:21; 2 Tim 2:25). It is not that Paul's theology has little room for repentance, but that repentance is included in Paul's doctrine of faith. For Paul, faith is far more than mental assent—that is, the acceptance of propositions about Jesus and his redeeming work. Rather, faith for Paul is our full response to God and his revelation in the person of Christ. Faith means embracing the totality of the Gospel, including its demands to turn from sin and live the life of Christian charity. And as faith is a gift of grace, so the transformation of life that constitutes the essence of repentance is a fruit of that grace.

III. THE SACRAMENT OF PENANCE

Christ instituted the sacrament of penance (also called the sacrament of reconciliation) when he proclaimed to the apostles on Easter Sunday night: "If you forgive the sins of any, they are forgiven; if you retain the sins of any, they are retained" (John 20:23). The Church is thus given the authority to confer the grace and mercy of God necessary for ongoing conversion in the lives of individual believers.

REPHAIM

1. A pre-Israelite people of **Canaan** concentrated mainly in the **Transjordan** (Deut 3:13; Josh 17:15). The Moabites called them "Emim" (Deut 2:11) and the Ammonites called them "Zamzummim" (Deut 2:20). According to Gen 14:5, **Chedorlaomer** and his allies defeated the Rephaim in Ashtaroth-karnaim with the Zuzim and Emim during the time of **Abraham**. The Rephaim are described as being men of tall and imposing stature, like the **Anakim** (Num 13:33). **Og** of Bashan is listed as the last of their race (Deut 3:11; Josh 12:4, 13:12).

2. Rephaim, translated "the shades" or "the dead" in the RSV, is also used to describe the inhabitants of Sheol (Ps 88:10; Prov 2:18; 9:18; 21:16; Isa 14:9; 26:14, 19). In Proverbs, the Rephaim are the dead who live in the netherworld; the house of folly leads to death and to "the shades" (Prov 2:18; cf. Prov 9:18; 21:16). The word also appears in Ugaritic.

REPHAIM, VALLEY OF (Hebrew, "valley of the giants") A valley to the southwest of Jerusalem that formed in part the boundary between Benjamin and Judah (Josh 15:8; 18:16). The valley was the site of remarkable victories of David's army against the Philistines (2 Sam 5:17–25; 1 Chr 14:8–17). According to Isa 17:5, the valley was known for its productive grainfields.

REPHIDIM The wilderness location where Israel last pitched camp before reaching Mount Sinai (Exod 19:2; Num 33:14–15). Rephidim was the place where **Moses** provided water for the Israelites after they complained; thus Rephidim became known as Massah, "testing," and Meribah, "contention" (cf. Exod 17:1–7; Deut 6:16, 9:22, 33:8). Here also the Israelites fought an engagement against the Amalekites (Exod 17:8–16). Victory was achieved only because Moses, aided by **Aaron** and **Hur**, kept his hands elevated. The location of Rephidim is uncertain, although suggested sites are the Wadi Refayid and Wadi Feiran.

RESEN A city founded in primeval times by **Nimrod** (Gen 10:11–12). It is described as "the great city." The location of the city is uncertain, although presumably it is near Nineveh and Calah on the Tigris River.

RESH The twentieth letter of the Hebrew alphabet (ר).

RESHEPH

1. A Canaanite god associated with pestilence or plagues. Resheph was worshiped in Palestine, Syria, and Phoenicia in the first millennium B.C., and the name came into use as a metaphor for pestilence (Deut 32:24; Ps 76:4; Hab 3:5). This god is sometimes depicted as fire or lightning (Job 5:7; Ps 78:48; Song 8:6).

2. A descendant of **Ephraim** (1 Chr 7:25).

REST See **Sabbath**; see also **Creation**; **Genesis, book of**.

RESTORATION See **Regeneration**.

RESURRECTION The reviving of a dead person to life again. Several persons are raised from the dead in the historical texts of the Bible, and all persons are destined to experience a resurrection, according to the prophetic texts of the Bible. The premier example is Jesus Christ, whose dying and rising to new life is the fulfillment of Jewish hopes and the foundation of the Christian faith.

I. *Resurrection in the Old Testament*
II. *The Resurrection of Christ*
  A. *The Resurrection as Historic Fact*
  B. *Christ's Risen Body*
  C. *Theological Significance*
III. *Resurrection of the Body*

I. RESURRECTION IN THE OLD TESTAMENT

In the Old Testament, the place of the dead is called Sheol and is envisioned as a place where the dead dwelt in utter silence and gloom (Ps 94:17; Prov 5:5, 7:27) and had no memory of their Creator (Ps 6:5; 88:12; 115:17). In the OT, since the human being was a composite of body and **soul** (Gen 2:7–8), **death** entailed the return of the body to the earth (Gen 3:19) and the dispatch of the immortal soul to Sheol. Thus resurrection meant a reunion of body and soul and a return to the realm of the living.

Both Elijah and Elisha raised individuals from the dead (1 Kgs 17:17–24; 2 Kgs 4:18–37; 13:20, 21). Beyond that, we have no other historical accounts of a resurrection in the OT.

Resurrection as a doctrine and hope for the future is a concept that developed gradually over time. The foundation of resurrection is the belief that God is the Lord of life and death; he can both "kill" and "make alive" (Deut 32:39). He can raise up from Sheol (1 Sam 2:6; Wis 16:13). Early prophets caught a glimpse of God's plan to raise Israel up from the dead (Isa 26:19; Hos 6:2) and even to destroy the power of death (Isa 25:8).

Resurrection can be used as a metaphor for "restoration from exile" (Ezek 37:14), but it was also a literal hope for Israel as a people (Dan 12:2) and especially for the heroically faithful (2 Macc 7:9, 11, 23).

II. THE RESURRECTION OF CHRIST

The Resurrection of Christ on the third day after his death and burial is the authenticating miracle of the Christian faith. From earliest times, Christ's Resurrection was proclaimed as a historical event verified by witnesses and preached along with the Cross as a central belief of the early Church (1 Cor 15:3–4; cf. Acts 9:3–18). Rising from the dead was the greatest of Christ's miracles and was the definitive proof of his divine mission. As Paul writes, "If Christ has not been raised, your faith is futile" (1 Cor 15:17).

A. *The Resurrection as Historic Fact*

None of the Gospels narrates the Resurrection itself, but there is no question that the Resurrection itself was a real, historical event that took place at a particular time and in a particular place in human history (Matt 28:1–15; Mark 16:1–18; Luke 24:1–49; John 20:1–29). **Paul** sums up what the Christians already knew: "For I delivered to you as of first importance what I also received, that Christ died for our sins in accordance with the scriptures, that he was buried, that he was raised on the third day

in accordance with the scriptures" (1 Cor 15:3–4). Paul goes on to declare that Jesus appeared to Cephas (**Peter**) and the other disciples, to five hundred, to James, and finally to Paul himself. Throughout the New Testament, the writers return to the Resurrection (Acts 1:22, 2:14–36, 3:11–26, 4:8–12, 8:37, 10:34–43, 13:16–37; Rom 10:9; 1 Cor 12:3; Eph 5:14; 1 Tim 3:16).

This testimony can be studied for its historical value. In the past, some historians have attempted to explain away or to refute the historicity of the Resurrection through a variety of theories (deceit, vision, symbolism, and apparent death); responsible scholars and historians have abandoned such alternative explanations as untenable and remain unable to explain the facts of Easter Sunday and its aftermath in an intellectually satisfying way (CCC 639–44).

The empty tomb in itself is not direct evidence of the Resurrection, as the absence of Christ's body from the tomb could be explained by other means (cf. Matt 28:11–15; John 20:13). Still, the empty tomb was a key moment in the discovery and acceptance by the disciples that their Lord had risen from the dead. It was women followers of Jesus who discovered the empty tomb (Matt 28:1–10; Mark 16:1–8; Luke 24:1–12) and then brought word of the event to the disciples, at least two of whom verified it for themselves (Luke 24:12; John 20:3–10).

The risen Christ was encountered by many witnesses, including Mary Magdalene, Mary the mother of James, Salome, Peter and the apostles, Cleopas and another disciple at Emmaus, Paul, and more than five hundred disciples. These encounters were not merely sightings: these witnesses spoke with Christ, dined with him, and even touched him (Matt 28:9; Luke 24:13–30, 36–43; John 20:24–29, 21:4–14). When Paul wrote, many of those literally hundreds of witnesses were still alive and were still able to verify what Paul said (1 Cor 15:6). The Resurrection of Christ was not a myth or a hallucination: it was a real event, witnessed and documented.

The chronological sequence of events is difficult to pin down, in part because of the different interests of the Evangelists. John and Luke narrate the appearances in Jerusalem; Matthew and Mark the ones in Galilee. The different writers used different appearances to emphasize the particular theological ideas they were trying to convey to their particular audiences.

At first the apostles did not recognize the risen Christ (Mark 16:12; Luke 24:16; John 20:14, 21:4), in keeping with their lack of understanding of Jesus's earlier predictions of his own death and Resurrection (Matt 16:21, 17:9, 17:23, 20:19; Mark 8:3, 9:9, 9:31, 10:34; Luke 9:22, 18:33). They understood fully what had happened only after **Pentecost**. The death of Jesus left some of the disciples so shaken that they were unable at first to believe the truth that Jesus had returned. The Lord gently scolded them for their hardness of heart in refusing to believe the words of those who had seen him (Mark 16:14; cf. Luke 24:38–41).

B. Christ's Risen Body

The Gospels attest to several miracles performed by Jesus in which he raised others from the dead: the daughter of Jairus (Matt 9:18–26; Mark 5:21–42; Luke 8:40–56), the son of the widow of Nain (Luke 7:11–17), and **Laz-** **arus** (John 11:1–44). Such miracles are not on par with the Resurrection of Christ. The recipients of Jesus's healing power were restored to life as they had known it before. This *revived* state was a distinctly different state from the *glorified* state of Jesus after the Resurrection and was different as well in comparison to the state of those who will rise in the general resurrection.

Jesus's Resurrection was indeed physical and bodily. He was not a ghost or spirit: he appeared to his followers in the same body that had died upon the Cross and had been buried. He was able consequently to show them the wounds he had received in the Passion (Luke 24:30, 39–40; John 20:20, 27; 21:9, 13–15) and to share a meal with them. On the other hand, he appeared and disappeared at will, and he entered and left closed rooms without opening the doors. His resurrected body was still physical, yet it was no longer limited by the laws of physics as we experience them on this side of death. In the Resurrection, Christ was not merely reanimated or resuscitated; he passed from death to a glorified state that was filled with the power of the Holy Spirit (1 Cor 15:35–50) and that was not limited by considerations of time and space (cf. Mark 16:2; John 20:14–16) (CCC 645–47).

C. Theological Significance

The Resurrection of Christ is a miraculous work of the Trinity in which "the three divine persons act together as one" (CCC 648). Thus, on the one hand, we find statements in the NT that Jesus was raised from the dead by God the Father (Acts 2:24; Gal 1:1). On the other hand, Jesus claimed for himself the unique power to surrender and reclaim his life (John 10:17–18). Paul adds that Christ's Resurrection from the dead "was according to the Spirit of holiness" (Rom 1:4).

With respect to Jesus, the miracle of Easter morning authenticates his Messianic claims, showing that God had made him "both Lord and Christ" (Acts 2:36). With respect to believers, the dying and rising of Jesus is the means of our redemption, which includes the forgiveness of transgressions as well as the infusion of justifying grace (Rom 4:25). The resurrection of the believer is actually a twofold process. The first is sacramental: in baptism we receive the risen life of Jesus, which restores the soul to a state of grace and supernatural life (Rom 6:1–11). The second is eschatological: at the general resurrection the risen life of Jesus raises our bodies to a state of glory and immortality (Rom 8:10–11; 1 Cor 15:35–57). This twofold passage from death to life, clearly articulated by Paul, is likewise the doctrine of resurrection expounded in the writings of John (John 5:25–29; cf. Rev 20:4–5).

III. RESURRECTION OF THE BODY

Proceeding from the Resurrection of Christ (cf. Acts 26:23; Rom 11:15–16), Paul teaches, "But if there is no resurrection of the dead, then Christ has not been raised; if Christ has not been raised, then our preaching is in vain and your faith is in vain" (1 Cor 15:13–14). Our bodies, Paul assures us, will be raised (1 Cor 15:20–23) and will be glorified and immortalized (1 Cor 15:35–50; also Rom 8:11; Phil 3:20–21; 1 Thess 4:16–18). For Paul, to deny the Resurrection is to deny the very heart of the **Gospel** (1 Cor 15:17–19).

The resurrection of the body, then, is the doctrine that the souls of all human beings, both good and evil, will be reunited to their bodies at the Second Coming of Christ and just before the Last **Judgment**. Through the power of God, the soul will be reunited with the same body that it had inhabited during earthly life—but a glorified body, differing from the earthly body as the plant differs from the seed (1 Cor 15:37–38). Although all will be raised from the dead, the just and the unjust will be subject to different ends in eternity. The good will take part in the resurrection of life, while the evil will rise to the resurrection of judgment (Dan 12:2; John 5:28–29; Acts 24:15). The resurrection will not be a return to earthly life as we know it now; it will be an entry into an everlasting glory free from all suffering and death—the completion of Christ's victory over sin and death. The risen will enjoy a condition similar to that of Christ's own glorified body (1 Cor 15:42–44; Phil 3:20–21).

REU A sixth-generation descendant of **Shem** after the **Flood**. He was the son of Peleg and the father of Serug, and he lived to the age of 239 (Gen 11:18–21).

REUBEN The firstborn son of **Jacob** and **Leah** (Gen 35:23; 46:8; 49:3) and the ancestor of the tribe of Reuben. His name—which means "see, a son"—is derived from the circumstances of his birth: "The Lord has seen my [Leah's] affliction" (Gen 29:31–32). Reuben is most remembered for having sexual relations with Bilhah, his father Jacob's concubine (Gen 35:22), an act that cost him his father's favor and his birthright (Gen 49:4; 1 Chr 5:1).

In the story of **Joseph**, Reuben displayed several positive attributes; most notably he made an effort to save the life of Joseph (Gen 37:21–22), he acknowledged that the family's adversity had been brought on by their betrayal of Joseph (Gen 42:22), and he offered his two sons to Jacob as surety for the return of **Benjamin** from Egypt (Gen 42:37).

The Reubenites were descended from Reuben through his four sons: Hanoch, Pallu, Hezron, and Carmi (Gen 46:9; Exod 6:14; 1 Chr 5:1). The territory the tribe of Reuben received after the conquest of Canaan is listed in Josh 13:15–23; it was located directly northeast of the Dead Sea in the **Transjordan**, north of the Arnon River (cf. Deut 3:12, 16). The tribe promised—along with Gad and Manasseh—to assist in the conquest of Canaan west of the Jordan (Num 32:28–32) and were accused of establishing an illicit altar for worship (Josh 22:10–34). In the days of **Deborah**, the tribe was remonstrated for its inaction in time of war (Judg 5:15–16), although 1 Chr 5:10, 19 mentions Reuben's efforts with Gad and Manasseh against the Hagrites in the days of **Saul**. Later, the tribe suffered deportation under the Assyrians and **Tiglath-pileser III** around 732 B.C. After this, the Reubenites disappear from the historical record of the Bible, although the tribe does figure in prophetic texts. In Ezekiel, the final vision of Israel's restoration includes a tribal territory reserved for Reuben (Ezek 48:6). Also, in the book of Revelation, the visionary sees a remnant of Reuben sealed for salvation in Messianic times (Rev 7:5).

REUEL (Hebrew, "friend of God") The name of two men in the Old Testament.

1. A son of Esau (Gen 36:4, 10, 13, 17; 1 Chr 1:35, 37).

2. Moses's father-in-law (Exod 2:18; Num 10:29), and a Midianite priest, also called Jethro. He welcomed Moses when the lawgiver fled from Egypt and gave Moses his daughter Zipporah in marriage (Exod 3:1; 4:18; 18:1, 5, 12). (*See* **Jethro** for other details.)

REUMAH The concubine of **Abraham**'s brother **Nahor** and the mother of Tebah, Gaham, Tahash, and Maacah (Gen 22:24).

REVELATION, BOOK OF The last book of the New Testament, also called the Apocalypse. The book's highly symbolic imagery and mysterious content have given rise to countless divergent interpretations about the drama of history's final days.

Although there are similar apocalyptic passages in the NT (e.g., Matt 24), Revelation is the only formal apocalyptic book of the NT. Revelation is also similar and yet uniquely dissimilar to Jewish apocalyptic works that appeared in the centuries immediately before and after the coming of Christ. It declares itself to be an apocalypse and gives the name of its author (Rev 1:1), whereas most apocalyptic works are pseudonymous, claiming the authorship of such long-deceased heroes of biblical history as Enoch, Abraham, and Ezra. In its content, Revelation is also in a class apart because of its use of liturgical hymns (cf. 4:8, 11; 5:9–10; etc.) and its clear focus on Jesus Christ as the Lamb (cf. 5:6–8; 7:10; 14:1–4).

I. Authorship and Date
II. Contents

I. AUTHORSHIP AND DATE

The author of Revelation tells his readers four times that his name is "John" (Rev 1:1, 4, 9; 22:8). He also calls himself God's "servant" (1:1) and states that he was exiled to the island of Patmos (1:9), where he received the visions of the book and wrote them down as commanded (1:11, 19; 2:1, 8, 12, 18; etc.). Tradition has identified the author "John" as the apostle John, the son of Zebedee (Mark 3:17). The earliest testimony to this effect comes from Justin Martyr around A.D. 140. Justin was followed by Saint Irenaeus (second century), Origen (early third century), Saint Clement of Alexandria (early third century), and many others.

Against this position, a handful of Christian writers from the East, such as Saint Dionysius of Alexandria (mid-third century) and Eusebius of Caesarea (early fourth century), opposed the apostle John's authorship on the basis of the book's peculiar style. In particular, the Greek found in Revelation is so markedly different from that found in the Gospel of John and the Johannine Epistles that Revelation was judged to have come from a different author.

Many modern scholars share the view of the Eastern writers and reject the authorship of John the apostle. Instead, they have proposed various alternatives, including the Evangelist John Mark, John the Baptist, John the Presbyter, an otherwise unknown prophet from Palestine named John, or an altogether anonymous writer who wrote pseudonymously in the name of John.

Claims against the apostolic authorship of Revelation are not decisive, however, and there are a number of points in favor of the mainline tradition. First, the stylistic differences between the other Johannine writings and Revelation can be attributed to the different literary genres employed: one is a Gospel, others are epistles, and the last is an apocalypse. Second, there are several similarities between the Gospel and Revelation, such as calling Jesus "the Word" (John 1:1; Rev 19:13) and Mary "Woman" (John 19:26; Rev 12:1), describing Jesus as a "Lamb" (John 1:29; Rev 5:6), and using the idea of "living water" (John 7:38; Rev 7:17). More broadly, the locations of the seven churches of Asia of Rev 2–3 are certainly consistent with the sphere of the apostle's known ministry.

Revelation was written during a time of Roman persecution, and two great outbreaks took place in the first century: during the reigns of Nero (A.D. 54–68) and Domitian (A.D. 81–96). On the basis of these two alternatives, scholars suggest the book was written either in the 60s or in the 90s; most scholars favor the later date, which is attested by various writers, including Saint Victorinus of Pettau (late third century), Eusebius of Ceasarea, Saint Jerome (late fourth century), and possibly Saint Irenaeus (late second century).

External support for the earlier date rests with the ancient Syriac versions of Revelation and perhaps also with Tertullian, who noted in his account of the persecutions in Rome under Nero that John was banished to an island after the Romans failed to kill him by lowering him into a vat of boiling oil—from which he had emerged unscathed. Internal evidence for dating the book to Nero's time is found in the apparent mention of the Roman emperors in Rev 17:9, with Nero as the fifth. Further, the number of the beast, 666, is taken by many scholars to refer to the name Nero Caesar (*see* **Nero** *for details*; *see also* **Numbers**). An earlier date for the book is often fixed in the late 60s A.D., not long before the Roman conquest of Jerusalem in A.D. 70.

II. CONTENTS

III. PURPOSE AND THEMES

The book of Revelation is arguably the most challenging in the whole of Scripture, owing to the very same imagery and apocalyptic language that make it a literary masterpiece. The complexity of its symbolism renders it exceedingly difficult to interpret. Even the learned Saint Jerome said that Revelation "has as many mysteries as words" (*Epist.* 53.9). Scholars have been divided in their approaches to its content and aims, but generally four views regarding the interpretation of Revelation have found support over the years, commonly called the futurist, preterist, historicist, and idealist views.

• The *futurist* view adopts the position that the book is a powerful prophecy of the end of the world—an intense tribulation, followed by the Second Coming of Jesus, the Last Judgment, and the final victory over evil. The prophecies, therefore, have yet to be fulfilled. This is probably the most popular view.

• The *preterist* supposes that the events described in the book are past history, having taken place within the time of the first readers of the book in the first century A.D. Many scholars see the book as an interpretation of Christianity's clash with pagan Rome in the late first century. Another preterist view reads the book against the backdrop of the Jewish War that led to the fall of Jerusalem. In the first view, the Roman political situation of the late first century is in view; in the second, the Church is given a theological vision of the end of the Old Covenant and the various factors that helped to bring this about.

• The *historicist* view sees Revelation as presenting the grand and sweeping landscape of the Church's history from the first century to the end of time. The contention that the progress of the Church in the world is presented is, however, difficult to substantiate due to a lack of consensus on the events that are supposedly presented.

• The *idealist* view contends that Revelation is a vivid portrayal of the spiritual life. Signs and symbols are used to give encouragement to the Christians who in the world face persecution and travails. The conflict between good and evil is timeless, and every Christian faces similar trials.

Each view supposes that Jesus is coming to right every wrong and bring about the definitive renewal and transformation of creation, and each view has something to contribute to an informed reading of Revelation. Yet no single view provides us with a comprehensively satisfying explanation of the whole. The most sensible course seems to be to accept some aspects of every one of them. For example, the historicist view opens readers to see the role of the Church in the ongoing drama of salvation; the preterist view adds the context of the time in which Revelation was composed; the idealist view focuses the reader on the profound spiritual teachings of the book; finally, the futurist view keeps in focus the Second Coming of Christ, the hope of all Christians. In effect, promises and prophecies are fulfilled in an ascending spiral: just as an event in the Old Testament may be a **type** of an event in the NT, so events now may be types of events to come.

IV. REVELATION AS LITURGY

Modern scholars are giving increasing attention to the *liturgical* dimensions of Revelation, both in its context and in its content.

A. Context

John receives his visions on the Lord's Day, the day when Christians everywhere celebrate the Liturgy (Rev 1:10). There is a "word" from God addressed to various churches, and intended to be read to them in the liturgical assembly. In Rev 1:3, for example, the "one who reads" and "those who hear" remind us of the lector and listeners during our Liturgy of the Word.

B. Content

Worship is both part of the plot and the primary action of the book. Revelation presents us with overtly Christian worship: it is directed both to God (chap. 4) and to the Lamb (chap. 5).

The visions are filled with the sights and sounds of the liturgy of Israel. John sees a **Temple** in heaven with the **ark of the covenant** (11:19), an altar of incense (8:3), golden lamp stands, priestly vestments, sacred gemstones, scrolls, trumpets, palm branches, harps, incense and libation bowls, and at the center of everything the sacrificial Lamb (5:6). There are songs of praise: "Holy, holy, holy, is the Lord God Almighty, who was and is and is to come!" (4:8).

All these sights, sounds, and even scents are familiar from the worship of ancient Israel: they are heavenly counterparts of earthly realities. The same liturgical actions continue in the Christian Church: Revelation shows us that the Christian liturgy on the Lord's Day is a participation in the eternal divine liturgy that never ceases in heaven.

REVELATION, DIVINE What God makes known about himself and his will through a supernatural intervention in history. The Catechism of the Catholic Church teaches: "Through an utterly free decision, God has revealed himself and given himself to man. This he does by revealing the mystery, his plan of loving goodness, formed from all eternity in Christ, for the benefit of all men. God has fully revealed this plan by sending us his beloved Son, our Lord Jesus Christ, and the Holy Spirit" (CCC 50).

I. THE NATURE OF REVELATION

God revealed himself numerous times and in numerous ways in the OT. As the author of Hebrews wrote, "In many and various ways God spoke of old to our fathers by the prophets; but in these last days he has spoken to us by a Son, whom he appointed the heir of all things, through whom also he created the world" (Heb 1:1–2). Divine revelation, then, came to the world incrementally in a series of interventions within the progress of history.

Each intervention is an encounter between persons—God who speaks and the human recipient who listens and responds. God reaches out to man, he communicates himself; man, in turn, accepts God and his will in faith and obedience. The Second Vatican Council's Dogmatic Constitution on Divine Revelation, *Dei Verbum*, said:

> In His goodness and wisdom God chose to reveal Himself and to make known to us the hidden purpose of His will (see Eph 1:9) by which through Christ, the Word made flesh, man might in the Holy Spirit have access to the Father and come to share in the divine nature (see Eph 2:18; 2 Pet 1:4). Through this revelation, therefore, the invisible God (see Col 1:15; 1 Tim 1:17) out of the abundance of His love speaks to men as friends (see Exod 33:11; John 15:14–15) and lives among them (see Bar 3:38), so that He may invite and take them into fellowship with Himself. This plan of revelation is realized by deeds and words having an inner unity: the deeds wrought by God in the history of salvation manifest and confirm the teaching and realities signified by the words, while the words proclaim the deeds and clarify the mystery contained in them. By this revelation then, the deepest truth about God and the salvation of man shines out for our sake in Christ, who is both the mediator and the fullness of all revelation. (DV §2)

The purpose of revelation, then, is to forge an intimate relationship between the Father and the human family. We experience the divine love and are made adoptive children of God (Gal 4:4–5; Eph 1:4–5) who share in the divine nature (2 Pet 1:4). That adoption occurs in Christ and means incorporation into the living body of Christ, the **Church** (1 Cor 12:12–13).

Revelation of the word of God is entirely gratuitous; it is an act of divine initiative and generosity. It is God who reaches out to man, even though man is entirely undeserving. Revelation as it culminates in Christ has as its object the establishment of the Church, which seeks to incorporate each person within it. Finally, revelation possesses an inherent saving property. God's choice to reveal himself was not undertaken merely to increase man's knowledge but to bring eternal salvation. "Through divine revelation, God chose to show forth and communicate Himself and the eternal decisions of His will regarding the salvation of men. That is to say, He chose to share with them those divine treasures which totally transcend the understanding of the human mind" (DV §6).

The response of man to this gratuitous communication of God is the "obedience of faith" (Rom 1:5; 16:26). This obedience of faith is to be an obedience by "which man commits his whole self freely to God, offering the full submission of intellect and will to God who reveals" (Vatican Council I, Dogmatic Constitution on Catholic Faith, *De fide*, c. 3).

II. NATURAL AND SUPERNATURAL REVELATION

Catholic theology, systematizing the teaching of Scripture, distinguishes between natural and supernatural revelation.

Natural revelation is what can be known about God by reflecting on creation with the tools of human reason. The beauty, order, and laws that govern the natural world can lead the mind upward to a perception of an all-powerful and all-wise Creator, apart from whom nothing would exist (Wis 13:5; Rom 1:19–20; cf. Acts 17:24–28). Natural revelation is therefore accessible to all people at all times.

Supernatural revelation is all that God makes known about himself and his will that is unknowable and undiscoverable by human reason alone. Truths of this order cannot be perceived in creation but are unveiled in unique historical events and encounters with God in history. The Bible shows us that supernatural revelation came to the world in measured amounts over long ages of time. Supernatural revelation is *incremental*, in that

God has made himself known in a gradual series of installments; but it is also *cumulative*, in that each new revelation is linked to preceding revelations in an intrinsic way. This gradual buildup of revelation—beginning with **Adam**, **Noah**, and the **patriarchs**—has continued for centuries until its final culmination in Jesus Christ, who is the definitive disclosure of God and his love in history (Heb 1:1–2).

Because of Jesus and his life and work, everything has been said about God; the New Covenant is established, and "the Christian dispensation, therefore, as the new and definitive covenant, will never pass away and we now await no further new public revelation before the glorious manifestation of our Lord Jesus Christ (see 1 Tim 6:14 and Titus 2:13)" (DV §3; CCC 66–67).

III. THE TRANSMISSION OF DIVINE REVELATION

Vatican II teaches that God has arranged for his revelation to "abide perpetually in its full integrity and be handed on to all generations" (DV §7). The transmission of divine revelation was first entrusted to the apostles with the command that they should preach the Gospel to all nations. This commission was accomplished "by their oral preaching, by example, and by observances" through which they "handed on what they had received from the lips of Christ, from living with Him, and from what He did, or what they had learned through the prompting of the Holy Spirit. The commission was fulfilled, too, by those apostles and apostolic men who under the inspiration of the same Holy Spirit committed the message of salvation to writing" (DV §7) (CCC 75–76).

This transmission continues through the apostolic succession of bishops, who continue the mission of the apostles and exercise their authority in every age.

IV. SACRED SCRIPTURE AND SACRED TRADITION

The revelation that each generation passes on to the next consists of Sacred Tradition and Sacred Scripture, both of which flow "from the same divine well-spring" (DV §9). Tradition is mainly the *unwritten* expression of divine faith embodied in the Church's liturgy and living institutions, whereas Scripture is the *written* expression of revelation as preserved in the inspired books of the Bible. Together these two "form one sacred deposit of the word of God committed to the Church" (DV §10).

V. THE MAGISTERIUM

Divine revelation is not self-interpreting (Acts 8:30–31; 2 Pet 3:15–16), and therefore "the task of authentically interpreting the word of God, whether written or handed on, has been entrusted exclusively to the living teaching office of the Church, whose authority is exercised in the name of Jesus Christ" (DV §10). The teaching office spoken of is vested in "the college of bishops (as successors to the college of apostolic witnesses) and to individual bishops united with the Bishop of Rome" (LG §§20–25; DV §10).

The Magisterium is not above the word of God, however, but serves it: "It teaches only what has been handed on to it. At the divine command and with the help of the Holy Spirit, it listens to this devotedly, guards it with dedi-

cation, and expounds it faithfully" (DV §10). In its exercise, the Magisterium is understood in two senses. The ordinary Magisterium is exercised on a day-to-day basis through the normal means of communication—spoken and written—as instruction to the faithful. The extraordinary Magisterium is exercised in a solemn way by a formal declaration of the pope or of an ecumenical council of bishops approved by the pope. The teaching of the extraordinary Magisterium is considered infallible when it takes the form of papal definitions or conciliar decisions binding on the consciences of all the faithful in matters of faith and morals (cf. LG §25; Congregation for the Doctrine of the Faith, *Mysterium Ecclesiae* §3; *Dignitatis Humanae* §14).

This service to Christian truth is intended for the benefit not only of the believing Church, but also of the unbelieving world. The Second Vatican Council provides the last word on the inherent unity of Tradition, Scripture, and the Magisterium:

> It is clear, therefore, that sacred tradition, Sacred Scripture and the teaching authority of the Church, in accord with God's most wise design, are so linked and joined together that one cannot stand without the others, and that all together and each in its own way under the action of the one Holy Spirit contribute effectively to the salvation of souls. (DV §10; cf. VS §110)

(*See* **Covenant**; **God**; **Inspiration**; **Interpretation of the Bible**; **Jesus Christ**; **Spirit, Holy**; **Redemption**; **Salvation history**.)

REVENGE *See* **Avenger of blood.**

REVISED VERSIONS *See* **Versions of the Bible**.

REZEPH A city in Syria that was captured and destroyed by **Sennacherib** and the Assyrians before 701 B.C. (2 Kgs 19:12; Isa 37:12). The city's fall was used to warn **Hezekiah** and Jerusalem of what might befall them should they resist the Assyrian advance.

REZIN An Aramean king from Syria who formed an alliance with **Pekah** of Israel against **Ahaz** of Judah (2 Kgs 15:37; 16:5, 9). Rezin was determined to lead an anti-Assyrian coalition, and the effort against Judah was intended to pressure Judah into joining that political alliance. Because Judah refused, Rezin and Pekah invaded Judah and besieged Jerusalem with the aim of deposing Ahaz in favor of an anti-Assyrian king (2 Kgs 16:5–9). The result was not as Rezin had hoped; rather, his efforts drove Ahaz into an alliance with Assyria (against Isaiah's advice; Isa 7:3–25); Ahaz became the vassal of **Tiglath-pileser III**. In 733 and 732 B.C., the Assyrian king turned his attention to Israel and Syria: "the king of Assyria marched up against Damascus, and took it, carrying its people captive to Kir, and he killed Rezin" (2 Kgs 16:9). The Aramean kingdom was thus added to the conquests of Assyria (cf. 2 Kgs 15:37, 16:1–9; Isa 1–8).

REZON The son of Eliada who became the ruler of Damascus and an enemy of **Solomon**. Described as an officer in the service of **Hadadezer**, king of Zobah, he left his post following the king's defeat by David (2 Sam 10:15–19) and then mounted a coup that ended with the seizure of Damascus and the proclamation of Rezon as king (1 Kgs 11:23–25).

RHEGIUM The modern city of Reggio di Calabria, in southern Italy on the Strait of Messina. Originally a Greek colony founded in the eighth century B.C. (Strabo, *Geog.* 6.1.6), Rhegium was superbly positioned for maritime trade. Immediately off the coast, however, were the notorious navigational hazards of the whirlpool of Charybdis and the rock of Scylla; ships would wait in Rhegium for a favorable southerly wind before setting sail, as was done by the sailors manning the ship carrying **Paul** northward to Puteoli (Acts 28:13). Paul had arrived at Rhegium from Syracuse.

RHODA (Greek, "rose") A servant girl in the house of Mary of Jerusalem, the mother of John **Mark** (Acts 12:12–17). She is remembered in Acts as the maid who recognized Peter's voice at the gate after his nighttime escape from prison. She was so excited that she ran to tell the houseguests before letting him in.

RHODES An island off the southwestern coast of Asia Minor. Rhodes was located advantageously on the main trade routes of the Aegean and the eastern Mediterranean. The capital of the island, also called Rhodes, was a port and trading city. **Paul** visited the city of Rhodes on his third missionary journey while heading back to Jerusalem (Acts 21:1). (*See also* **Rodanim**.)

RIBLAH A city in Syria near the source of the Orontes River. The Bible calls this region "the land of Hamath" (2 Kgs 23:33). The site is the modern Ribleh, to the northeast of Baalbek. Since the city was strategically located on the main routes for the region, it was considered ideal for military operations. Pharaoh **Neco II** of Egypt had his headquarters at Riblah when he killed King **Josiah** in 609 B.C. **Jehoahaz,** who was installed on the throne as successor, was summoned to Riblah by Neco and was deposed and replaced (2 Kgs 23:33–34).

Riblah was also used as a base of operations by **Nebuchadnezzar** during his fateful campaign against Judah (588–586 B.C.). Following the fall of the city, **Zedekiah**, the last king of Judah, was captured and brought to Riblah. There Nebuchadnezzar put to death Zedekiah's sons, gouged out the king's eyes, and deported him to Babylon in chains (2 Kgs 25:1–7; Jer 52:8–11). Other nobles of Judah faced the same fate at Riblah (2 Kgs 25:20–21; Jer 52:26–27).

RIDDLE A cryptic or symbolic saying that must be deciphered to be understood. Deciphering a riddle reveals a concealed meaning that is intended but only hinted at by the riddle maker. Riddles may also pose a simple and lighthearted challenge for social circumstances.

According to Num 12:6–8, God speaks to the prophets in visions and dreams, but he did not speak to Moses in such a way—rather, he spoke to him face-to-face, clearly, not in riddles. Proverbs 1:6 tells us that one of the purposes of the book is to help us "to understand a proverb and a figure, the words of the wise and their riddles." Similarly, Sirach noted the hidden meanings of parables (Sir 39:1–3). Wisdom literature does not preserve many of the riddles of the wise, although scholars suggest that elements of riddles can be detected in a number of wisdom writings, including Prov 5:15–23; 6:23–24; 11:22; 16:15; 20:27; 23:27, 29–35; 25:2–3, 27:20; Ps 49:5; 78:2; Song 4:12. Actual riddles were mentioned in the account of Samson, who bragged in a riddle of having killing a lion (Judg 14:12–19), and in the story of King **Solomon**, whose wisdom permitted him to answer the riddles of the Queen of Sheba (cf. 1 Kgs 10:1–5; 2 Chr 9:1–4).

RIGHTEOUSNESS *See* **Justification**.

RIMMON The name of a Semitic god worshipped in ancient Syria. His title means "thunderer," suggesting that Rimmon should be identified with the storm-god **Hadad** (Zech 12:11). **Naaman** the Syrian, who was cured of leprosy by **Elisha** and converted to the God of Israel, was concerned that as a Syrian commander he would still be required to worship in the temple of Rimmon (2 Kgs 5:17–18).

RIMMON (Hebrew, "pomegranate") The name of three places in the Old Testament.

1. Also En-rimmon, a spring in the Negeb near Edom assigned to Simeon (Josh 19:7; 1 Chr 4:32). The site was settled by Jewish returnees from Babylon after the **Exile** (Neh 11:29). It may be the modern Khirbet Umm er-Rammamin, north of Beer-sheba, although Tel Halif has also been suggested.

2. A village in Zebulun (Josh 19:13), probably the modern Rummanah, north of Nazareth.

3. The Rock of Rimmon, a rocky cliff or a cave "toward the wilderness," probably east of

Gibeah. In the days of the Judges, following a massacre at Gibeah by Israelite warriors, six hundred surviving Benjaminites found refuge at the Rock of Rimmon (Judg 20:45–47). Four months later, a reconciliation was achieved (Judg 21:13). The site is commonly identified today as the village of Rammun.

RISSAH A place where the Israelites camped during the **Exodus** journey through the wilderness (Num 33:21, 22).

RIZPAH A concubine of **Saul**, and the daughter of Aiah. After the death of Saul, Rizpah was seized by **Abner**, who probably meant to seize the throne for himself by controlling the royal harem (2 Sam 3:7; *see also* **Absalom** and **Adonijah**). But Abner's action sparked a quarrel with **Ish-bosheth**. Rizpah endured the execution of her sons, Armoni and **Mephibosheth**, along with the five sons of Merab, Saul's eldest daughter, in an effort to end a famine (2 Sam 21:1–14). She showed herself a model of maternal devotion by keeping vigil over the bodies until the rains finally came, and David ordered the corpses to be given a proper burial along with the remains of Saul and Jonathan (who had been buried in Jabesh-gilead) in the family tomb at Zela.

ROCK Mentioned often in the Bible as a metaphor for stability, solidity, and indestructibility. Usually it is a title given to the Lord, who is hailed as the everlasting Rock of Israel (2 Sam 23:3; Isa 26:4, 30:29). Having begotten Israel as his people (Deut 32:18), he marches to their aid as a rock of salvation (Deut 32:15; Ps 62:3, 95:1) and shelters them from harm as a rock of refuge (2 Sam 22:3; Ps 62:7; Isa 17:10). Others described as a "rock" in Scripture include **Abraham** (Isa 51:1–2), **Peter** (Matt 16:18), and **Jesus Christ** (1 Cor 10:4). (*See also* **Peter**.)

ROD A tall, slender staff used as a walking stick by travelers (Gen 32:10; Mark 6:8) and the old (Zech 8:4; Heb 11:21). The rod was also a sign of office or authority (Gen 49:10; Judg 5:14; Jer 48:17), as the rods of **Moses** (Exod 4:20) and **Aaron** (Num 17:8–11; Heb 9:4). In other contexts, a rod was used for correction of foolish behavior (Prov 10:13), but the rod of a shepherd, used to direct and defend his sheep, was a comfort to his flock (Ps 23:4).

ROD, AARON'S *See* **Rod**; *see also* **Aaron**.

RODANIM Descendants of **Noah's** son **Japheth** through **Javan** (1 Chr 1:7). Many scholars associate the Rodanim with the people of Rhodes, an island off the southwest coast of Asia Minor. In Gen 10:4, the name is given as "Dodanim," but this is probably the result of a copyist's error (the letters *R* and *D* are almost identical in Hebrew script).

ROGELIM A town in the **Transjordan** in Gilead that was the home of **Barzillai**.

ROMAN EMPIRE *See* **Rome**.

ROMANS, LETTER TO THE The longest letter of the apostle Paul, written to the Christians of Rome. It is hailed as one of the greatest works of Christian theology and has proved to be one of the most influential works in Christian history. Its master theme is the salvation of the world in Christ (chaps. 1–8). Other topics covered in the letter include the salvation of Israel (chaps. 9–11) and the moral responsibilities of the Christian faithful (chaps. 12–14).

I. AUTHORSHIP AND DATE

Few have seriously questioned Paul's authorship of Romans. His name stands at its opening (Rom 1:1), and its magnificent style and content are believed to reflect the mind of the great apostle to the Gentiles (11:13). Paul probably wrote Romans in the winter of A.D. 57–58 while in Corinth on his third missionary journey (i.e., when he passed through Greece, Acts 20:2). Presumably the letter was delivered to the Roman congregation by the deaconess Phoebe (16:1–2).

That being said, some modern scholars theorize that chapter 16 did not belong to the original letter but was added at a later time. Curiously, the oldest surviving manuscript of Romans does not include this chapter, and some find it odd that Paul should address so many individuals by name in 16:3–16 when he had never been to Rome before (cf. 1:10, 13). Still, arguments against the authenticity of chapter 16 are less than decisive. Whatever shorter versions of Romans did circulate in early times, they could well have been abridged texts designed for liturgical use. Likewise, the persons addressed in the final chapter were probably Christians who could vouch for Paul to a congregation that, for the most part, did not know him personally. Granted, the sheer number of greetings in Rom 16 is unusual for Paul, but in this case it suggests

he was smoothing the way for his arrival by establishing rapport with a community he hoped would support his missionary ventures to Spain and the West (15:23–24).

II. CONTENTS

I. *Salutation (1:1–15)*

II. *Justification in Christ (1:16–8:39)*

III. *The Salvation of Israel (9:1–11:36)*

IV. *The Standards of the Christian Life (12:1–14:23)*

V. *Personal Notes and Greetings (15:1–16:23)*

III. PURPOSE

Paul had several aims in mind when he wrote the Letter to the Romans. First, he needed to introduce himself to the community in advance of his planned arrival. This was necessary because the apostle had neither established nor visited the Roman church in person (Rom 1:10–13). Second, Paul hoped to resolve a pastoral problem in the community that was driving a wedge between Jewish and Gentile Christians. Statements in the letter suggest that Jewish believers saw themselves as especially blessed because of the historical and spiritual benefits granted to Israel that set them apart from other nations (2:1–3:20). Gentile believers, for their part, also struggled with pride; for it seems they viewed themselves as Israel's replacement as the new people of God (11:13–32). It was therefore important for Paul to establish that Jews and Gentiles are equal in sin (3:9) and therefore equal recipients of divine mercy (11:32). It is God's will that they worship one and the same Lord, side by side as brothers in the one family of faith (10:12; 15:7–12).

Finally, Paul hoped to gain the backing of the Roman church to launch a new missionary initiative into Spain (15:23–24).

IV. THEMES

Romans, though clearly an occasional letter, is the closest thing to a theological treatise that appears in the New Testament. Paul penetrates deep into the mysteries of sin and salvation, and he draws heavily on the Old Testament to help readers discover how the plan of God reached its historical zenith in the Person and work of Jesus Christ. For this reason, Romans is sometimes a difficult work to understand (cf. 2 Pet 3:16). Nevertheless, it is more fascinating than frustrating and has informed the thinking of many theologians throughout the centuries.

Sin, salvation, and sanctification dominate the discussion of chapters 1–8. Sin is the bad news that readies the world for the Good News of the gospel. Paul thus begins the letter with a stern condemnation of sin, which has spread like a deadly disease, not only among the pagans (Rom 1:18–32), but also among the covenant people (2:1–30). The result is that all nations, Jews and Gentiles alike, find themselves trapped in the clutches of sin (3:9). Salvation, so desperately needed by the world, is finally achieved by Jesus, who reveals the righteousness of God and offers it as a gift to be received by faith (3:21–26). The grace poured out through his dying and rising again brings about the justification of the sinner—the action of God that transfers the believer from the disgraced family of Adam to a state of righteousness in Christ (5:1–21). Sanctification

is part of this mystery and is the work of the Holy Spirit, who pours the love of God into the human heart (5:5) and enables Christians to obey the righteous laws of God (8:1–13). Through the Spirit, believers are filled with the grace of the divine sonship, by which God becomes their Father (8:14–17) and Christ becomes their elder brother (8:29).

The salvation of Israel is the subject of chapters 9–11. The issue needs to be addressed, one, because the Gospel met with widespread rejection among the Chosen People (9:1–5; 10:1–4), and, two, because certain Christians made the false inference that Israel as the Chosen People had been rejected by God and was now replaced by a predominately Gentile church (11:13–32). Paul thus had to explain the place of both Israel and the Gentiles in the plan of salvation. Israel has not been rejected by the Lord (11:1). On the contrary, it is God's intention to save "all Israel" (11:26)—and by this Paul means a representative remnant of all twelve tribes of Israel, not just Jews from the tribe of Judah (cf. Matt 19:28; Rev 7:1–8). As for believing Gentiles, they have not displaced Israel, but have been grafted like olive branches onto the trunk of an Israelite tree (11:17–19). They should therefore stand in awe at the mercy of God on their account, realizing that he stands ready to restore unbelieving Israel the very moment they come to faith in Christ (11:20–24).

Practical instructions on Christian living are given in chapters 12–15. Responsibilities are laid upon believers as members of the ecclesial body of Christ (12:1–21) and as members of the civil body of the state (13:1–7). The crowning imperative is to love one another (13:8–10) in a way that respects the freedom of others (14:1–23). In doing so, the believer will become more like Christ, who made himself a servant to all (15:1–13).

ROME One of the greatest empires in the ancient world, and one that shaped significantly the events of Scripture, in particular those of the New Testament. The world into which Jesus Christ was born, lived, and died was entirely dominated by the Roman Empire.

I. THE EMPIRE

According to tradition, the city of Rome was founded in 753 B.C. by Romulus upon an area of seven hills that was a gathering place in ancient Italy for the Etruscans, Latins, and Sabines. It was ruled until around 500 B.C. by Etruscan kings, the last of whom, Tarquinius Superbus, was replaced by the Roman Republic. The republic endured until the first century B.C., carving for Rome a vast Mediterranean empire. Increasingly corrupt, the republic was brought to an end by a civil war (49–45 B.C.) won by Julius Caesar, who became dictator. His assassination precipitated another series of wars (44–31 B.C.), ended by the triumph of Octavian (later Emperor **Augustus**) at the battle of Actium (31 B.C.) over Mark Antony and Cleopatra. Octavian ruled from 27 B.C. to A.D. 14, and did much to stabilize and bring peace to the new Roman Empire. The empire endured in the West until A.D. 476 and in the East (in the form of the Byzantine Empire) until 1453.

The Jewish population of Palestine saw the advance of Rome as a chance to free themselves from the oppression of the **Seleucids**, in particular Antiochus IV Epiphanes. The First Book of Maccabees speaks positively of the Romans (1 Macc 8:1–16) and records an alliance between Rome and the Jews (1 Macc 14:40; 15:15–21; 2 Macc 11:34–38).

By the turn of the first century B.C., Rome was the strongest power in the Mediterranean, and the campaigns of Pompey the Great in the sixties B.C. swept away the last vestiges of the Seleucid Empire. Syria was claimed as an imperial province to serve as a buffer against the Parthians to the East, and Judea was brought under Rome's jurisdiction.

Jesus was born during the reign of Emperor Augustus (Luke 2:1), whose decree of a census brought Mary and Joseph to Bethlehem (Luke 2:1–4). The Roman presence in Palestine was pervasive by the time Jesus reached manhood (Mark 12:13–14; Luke 3:14). His trial was before a Roman procurator, Pontius Pilate (Matt 27:1–2, 11–26), and his execution was carried out in the traditional Roman fashion by Roman soldiers (Matt 27:27–31; John 19:23).

Paul's evangelization efforts were undertaken across the Roman world, and he, like the many missionaries who followed him, used the empire's network of roads and communication to reach the corners of the Roman provinces. Paul also enjoyed the privilege of Roman citizenship (Acts 16:37–38) and used it to make a direct appeal to Caesar (Acts 25:11) after his arrest; in order to make his appeal, Paul was taken by authorities to Rome (Acts 27–28). Paul wrote one of his greatest epistles to the Christians of the Eternal City. (See **Romans, Letter to the**, for details.)

The book of **Revelation** deals in part with

Christianity's struggle for survival against Roman authorities. Clear allusions to that struggle can be found in Rev 13:18, where the number of the beast (666) is probably a cryptogram for Caesar Nero; and the harlot seated on seven hills in Rev 17:9 may be an image of Jerusalem and its leadership propped up on the authority of Rome, whose capital stands on the crests of seven hills. Nevertheless, following the teaching of Jesus, who refused to endorse a tax revolt against Caesar (Mark 12:13–17), the apostles insisted that the Christians of the first century must respect the governing authorities of Rome and show themselves exemplary citizens of the empire (Rom 13:1–7; 1 Pet 2:13–17).

II. THE CITY OF ROME

The city of Rome symbolized for the Roman people and indeed for the inhabitants of the empire the greatness of Roman civilization and achievement. It was literally true that all roads led to Rome, and the metropolis came to epitomize the political, artistic, architectural, and cultural accomplishments of the Roman people. It was also the center of all the social and religious innovations that arose within the empire and so, inevitably, Christianity found its way there. The faith was at first viewed by the cosmopolitan Romans as just another of the cults from the East that routinely became popular in the city.

It is unclear when Christianity was first established in the city. Some conjecture that Roman pilgrims who were present at the first Christian **Pentecost** might have taken the gospel back home with them (Acts 2:10). Tradition has it that Peter went to Rome and evangelized the city in the forties A.D. (see Eusebius, *Hist. Eccl.* 2.14). In any case, it is certain that Christianity was flourishing by the late fifties A.D. when Paul wrote his Letter to the Romans (Rom 1:7–8). The apostles Peter and Paul were both martyred in Rome about A.D. 67.

ROSE OF SHARON *See* **Sharon**.

ROSH The seventh son of **Benjamin** (Gen 46:21).

RUFUS The son of **Simon of Cyrene** (Mark 15:21) and the brother of Alexander. Based on the early tradition that the Gospel of Mark was written initially for the Roman church, it is possible that Rufus is the same person mentioned in Rom 16:13. Otherwise they are two distinct individuals.

RUTH, BOOK OF A book of the Old Testament that tells the story of a Moabite woman who became an ancestor of David. Ruth is included in the Hebrew Bible as one of the five Megilloth (rolls) in the third division of the Hebrew canon, called the Writings. Christian Bibles follow the lead of ancient translations into Greek (the **Septuagint**) and Latin (the **Vulgate**), both of which place the book of Ruth among the Historical Books between Judges and 1 Samuel.

I. AUTHORSHIP AND DATE

The book itself tells us nothing about its author. Jewish tradition, expressed in the **Talmud**, ascribed the work to Samuel, but this is uncertain, and in the eyes of many unlikely. The date is equally difficult to ascertain. Some scholars, saying that its language reflects the golden age of Hebrew, place it between 1000 and 700 B.C. Additional support for an early date is evidenced by its interest in King **David**, whose name appears last in the genealogy of Ruth 4:18–22. A later date has been argued on the basis of occasional Aramaisms, and some would read the book as an alternative solution to the problem of mixed marriages addressed by the reforms of Ezra and Nehemiah. As there is no agreement among scholars, we must regard the authorship and date of Ruth as unknown.

II. CONTENTS

I. *Naomi and Ruth Move to Bethlehem (1:1–22)*

II. *Ruth Gleans in the Field of Boaz (2:1–23)*

III. *Boaz Claims Ruth for Marriage (3:1–18)*

IV. *Ruth Marries Boaz (4:1–17)*

V. *Genealogy from Perez to David (4:18–22)*

III. PURPOSE

The book of Ruth tells the story of Ruth, a Moabitess who embraced the faith of Israel. She married Mahlon, son of Elimelech and Naomi. After the death of Naomi's husband and sons, she decided to return to the land of Israel, and Ruth chose to remain at her side. They settled in **Bethlehem**, and one day, as the women gleaned the fields of Boaz, a kinsman of Naomi's dead husband, Ruth encountered Boaz himself, who treated her with great kindness. His demeanor prompted Naomi to devise a plan to secure the marriage of her daughter-in-law. She urged Ruth to go to the threshing floor and ask Boaz to marry her by the law of affinity. Though willing, he first informed the nearest relative of the situation. When that relative declined the right of redemption, Boaz married Ruth.

By her marriage, Ruth became an ancestor of David. Elegantly written, the book has among its themes filial piety, faith and trust in the Lord, and the universality of God's salvation. The Lord is the protector of widows and rewards Naomi and Ruth with happiness in place of their sorrow. Above all, Ruth chose the Lord as her God and so she became a key figure in the history of Israel, as she became the great-grandmother of David. Ruth joins **Deborah**, **Judith**, **Esther**, and others among the exemplary women who prepared the way for Mary, the mother of Jesus (CCC 489). Ruth's conversion, expressed in the declaration, "where you go I will go, and where you lodge I will lodge; your people shall be my people, and your God my God" (Ruth 1:16), anticipates not only the incorporation of Gentiles into the kingdom of David but also the universal call of the gospel to bring all nations into the family of God (Matt 28:18–20).

SABAOTH *See* **Hosts of heaven**.

SABBATH The seventh day of the Jewish week, from sundown Friday to sundown Saturday (Exod 20:8–110). In the **Law**, the Sabbath is hallowed as a day of rest and a sign of the covenant between the Lord and Israel (Exod 31:12–17). Among Christians the Sabbath was moved from the seventh day of the week to the first day of the week, Sunday, in recognition of the new creation that was inaugurated by the Resurrection of Christ on Sunday (CCC 2168–76).

I. IN THE OLD TESTAMENT

A. A Fundamental Law for God's People

The Hebrew term *šabbāt* appears more than a hundred times in the Old Testament, forty-seven times in the **Pentateuch**, and is derived from a Hebrew root meaning "to cease or rest." The Sabbath's significance begins at creation (Gen 1:1–2:4), where the Sabbath is the climax of the Lord's labors, at which time he took rest (Hebrew *šābat*). The Sabbath was so important that observing it was one of the **Ten Commandments** (Exod 20:8–10; Deut 5:12–15). It is a day that is holy and blessed (Gen 2:3; Isa 58:13).

B. The Sign of God's Covenant

God did not merely rest on the seventh day; he also blessed and sanctified that day (Gen 2:2–3). He did not rest from exhaustion, but from the desire to establish the Sabbath as a sign of his **covenant** (Exod 31:12–17). The day serves not merely as a time of rest but as a time to reflect on the work of God as the Creator. Seen in this light, in the context of the OT the Sabbath elicited a sense of gratitude and also dependence upon and trust in God (CCC 345–47).

After the deliverance of Israel from Egypt in the **Exodus**, the Sabbath also became a sign of God's work of *redemption*: that is, his powerful intervention in history to give Israel rest from the burden of slavery. Thus the Sabbath commandment in Exodus links the Sabbath with God the *Creator*, and the one in Deuteronomy links the Sabbath with God the *Redeemer*.

The Sabbath came to rest at the heart of the Law of Israel; along with circumcision, its observance was an outward sign of one's membership in Israel (cf. Ezek 20:13; Neh 13:17–18). It was the day of religious assembly and worship (Lev 23:1–3). The Covenant Code (Exod 21–23; *see under* **Law**) enumerated assorted covenant statutes and demands, including rest on the Sabbath, the "seventh day" (Exod 23:12). Certainly this was a compassionate and practical law, but the main purpose of the Sabbath was to remember God and his saving deeds (Deut 5:15): "You shall remember that you were a servant in the land of Egypt, and the LORD your God brought you out thence with a mighty hand and an outstretched arm; therefore the LORD your God commanded you to keep the sabbath day."

All forms of unnecessary work were prohibited on the Sabbath. Even household servants and livestock had to rest (Exod 20:8–10, 31:13–17; Deut 5:12–14). Various specific regulations addressed cooking (Exod 16:23), plowing and reaping (Exod 34:21), gathering wood (Num 15:32–36), lighting a fire (Exod 35:3), trading and bartering (Neh 13:15–22), carrying loads (Jer 17:21–27), and loading animals (Neh 13:15). Since work was prohibited, food had to be prepared on the day before the Sabbath; the preceding day became known as the day of preparation (Matt 27:62; Mark 15:42).

C. The Prophets Call Israel to Observe the Sabbath

Violations of the Sabbath were punishable by death (Exod 31:14–15; Num 15:32–36), yet in spite of the penalty, nonobservance of the Sabbath was a problem both before and during the Exile (Jer 17:19; Ezek 20:13, 16, 21, 24; 22:8; 23:38). Amos describes the lamentable state of observance in the kingdom of Israel by noting the eagerness of merchants for the Sabbath to end at sunset (Amos 8:5). The prophets thus stressed proper observance (Isa 1:13, 56:6; Ezek 20:12). Isaiah sees the Sabbath not as a burden but as a joy and a delight:

> if you turn back your foot from the sabbath, from doing your pleasure on my holy day, and call the sabbath a delight and the holy day of the LORD honorable; if you honor it, not going your own ways, or seeking your own pleasure, or talking idly; then you shall take delight in the LORD, and I will make you ride upon the heights of the earth; I will feed you with the heritage of Jacob your father, for the mouth of the LORD has spoken. (Isa 58:13–14)

Jeremiah asserts that the survival of the kingdom of Judah was contingent upon obedience to the covenant and the demands of the Ten Commandments, including the Sabbath commandment (Jer 17:19–27; cf. Lam 2:6). Ezekiel, like Isaiah and Jeremiah, asserted that the Sabbath was the Lord's day (Ezek 20:12–13, 20–21, 24; 22:26; 23:38; 44:24) and a sign of the covenant (Ezek 20:12).

With the return of the exiles from Babylon, the Sabbath continued to be followed only loosely, a source of consternation to Nehemiah. Reforms followed, and a firm commitment to the Sabbath became a mainstay of recognized Jewish orthodoxy (Neh 13:15–22). Eventually, however, observance came to be characterized by a strictness that went beyond the Law. During the period of the Maccabees, some Jews allowed themselves to be slaughtered by the Seleucids rather than fight and defend themselves on the Sabbath (1 Macc 2:35–38; 2 Macc 8:26). Others, such as **Mattathias** and his friends, chose to defend themselves and adopt a less rigorous approach, although they would not go on the offensive on the Sabbath (1 Macc 2:39–41).

II. IN THE NEW TESTAMENT

A. "The Sabbath Was Made for Man"

Sabbath observance is also a topic of discussion in the New Testament, most often in the Gospels. Generally speaking, it is certain that Jesus, as a devout Jew, was accustomed to following the Sabbath laws, for we often see him attending synagogue services in Galilee (Mark 1:21, 3:1; Luke 4:16). His behavior on the Sabbath, however, became a source of tension with the scribes and Pharisees, for Jesus often chose to perform healings and miracles on the sacred day of rest (e.g., Matt 12:9–14; Mark 1:21–28; Luke 14:1–16; John 5:1–9). As far as the religious leadership was concerned, this was a form of unlawful work, and Jesus needed to be either discredited or eliminated (Matt 12:14; John 5:1–9). For the scribes and Pharisees, Jesus's noncompliance was proof that "This man is not from God, for he does not keep the Sabbath" (John 9:16).

Jesus responded to these accusations in ways that reveal the deeper mystery of his identity as well as the deeper meaning of the Sabbath itself. On the one hand, he claims to be "Lord of the Sabbath" (Matt 12:8; Mark 2:28). Because his heavenly Father is the Creator of the Sabbath, and the Father continues to work on the Sabbath, the divine Son can only do what his Father does (John 5:18). The Jews understood by these claims that Jesus was making himself "equal with God" (John 5:18). On the other hand, Jesus responds to charges that he is *breaking* the Sabbath with the claim that, on the contrary, he is *fulfilling* the true intent of the Sabbath (Luke 13:10–17). In other words, by healing and restoring, he is lifting burdens from the lives of the people, giving them rest from years of physical and spiritual bondage. The Sabbath is therefore something that frees rather than something that binds (Luke 13:10–17). It was "made for man," not the other way around (Mark 2:27). Acts of charity and necessity are thus in harmony with the Sabbath's deepest level of significance (Matt 12:1–6; Luke 6:9).

B. Sunday, the Christian Sabbath

Paul included the Sabbath among the Jewish ritual observances that were no longer obligatory to Christians (Col 2:16; Gal 4:9–10; Rom 14:5). Still, it was Paul's custom to attend synagogue services on the Sabbath, not because he was obligated to do so, but because he hoped to seize the opportunity for evangelization among his fellow Israelites. There was, apparently, no discussion of the Sabbath at the Jerusalem Council, but Gentile converts gathered on Sunday (Acts 20:7–12; 1 Cor 16:2), which became the day of Christian worship in memory of the Resurrection (CCC 349, 2174–76).

Finally, in Heb 4, there is an association between the Sabbath and the everlasting inheritance of the New Covenant. That rest was signified in the OT by the Sabbath rest at the end of creation (Gen 2:2), as well as the rest that Joshua gave Israel in the Promised Land.

SABBATH DAY'S JOURNEY The distance that Jewish tradition permitted a person to travel on the day of Sabbath rest. It was calculated on the basis of Old Testament passages such as Exod 16:29 and Num 35:5 and was set at 2,000 cubits—about 1 kilometer or two-thirds of a mile. Acts refers to this tradition in describing the distance between Jerusalem and the Mount of Olives as "a Sabbath day's journey" (Acts 1:12).

SABBATICAL YEAR A year of rest observed every seventh year in ancient Israel (Exod 23:10–11; Lev 25:1–7). On this year, the farmer was to let his fields, his orchards, and his vineyards lie fallow and unharvested. Deuteronomy adds to this that every sabbatical year is also a year of release when all debts in Israel were to be canceled (Deut 15:1–3).

If the Israelites did not adhere to the laws of the sabbatical year, God himself would cause the fields to lie fallow by means of exile (Lev 26:33–35; cf. 2 Chr 36:20–21). After the **Exile**, it appears that the Jewish community was more careful to observe the sabbatical year (Neh 10:31; 1 Macc 6:49, 53). While there were practical reasons for adhering to the law, namely, to promote the good of agriculture and soil chemistry, the deeper reason was to acknowledge that God provides us with food and that all human labor must be consecrated to him. (*See also* **Jubilee**.)

SACKCLOTH A rough fabric made of hair (usually from goats) and dark in color. Sackcloth could be used for grain sacks (Gen 42:25, 27, 35; Josh 9:4), although in Scripture it is most often associated with clothing. Sackcloth was worn as a sign of mourning for the deceased (Gen 37:34; 2 Sam 3:31; Joel 1:8). Wearing sackcloth next to the skin was also a disciplinary act of penance (1 Kgs 21:27; Neh 9:1; Jonah 3:5; Matt 11:21) or a devotional means of pleading to the Lord (2 Kgs 6:30; Ps 35:13). The wearing of sackcloth was coupled with other signs of mourning, such as wearing ashes (Isa 58:5; Jer 6:26; Luke 10:13) and shaving the head (Isa 22:12; Jer 48:37; Ezek 27:31). Wearing sackcloth was also part of a prayer for deliverance (Jdt 4:10–12; Bar 4:20; 1 Macc 3:47).

When used as clothing, sackcloth was worn around the waist, often under the clothing (1 Kgs 20:31–32; Isa 20:2; 2 Macc 10:25) and against the skin (2 Kgs 6:30; Job 16:15; 2 Macc 3:19). Shepherds wore sackcloth as a regular garment, because it was cheap and durable, but it was especially associated with prophets, who wore it as penitential garb (Isa 20:2; Rev 11:3). The heavens were also described as being dressed in sackcloth (Isa 50:3) as an omen.

SACRAMENT Defined by theologians as a sign and instrument of grace. Sacraments are liturgical rites instituted by Jesus Christ as channels of his salvation to the world. Catholicism has come to recognize seven sacraments, all of which have their foundation in the texts of the New Testament, although some appear more prominently than others. The seven are baptism, Eucharist, confirmation (or chrismation), reconciliation, matrimony, holy orders, and anointing of the sick.

I. TERMINOLOGY

Scripture does not use the word "sacrament." Rather, the term was adopted by ancient theologians to describe the defining actions of Christian worship. In referring to a sacrament, the Western Church used the Latin term *sacramentum*, meaning "oath," whereas the Eastern Church utilized the Greek term *mystērion*, meaning "mystery." It is sometimes said that the Latin expression highlights the exterior dimension of a sacrament as a sign of grace, whereas the Greek expression stresses the hidden, interior action that takes place when a sacrament is administered. The distinction is true as far as it goes, but the use of *sacramentum* to describe the rites of Christian liturgy is more closely tied to the biblical concept of the covenant.

II. BACKGROUND

In the biblical world, covenants were both ratified and renewed by oaths. In Israel and neighboring nations, covenants were made to forge kinship relationships be-tween two parties, and oaths were sworn by the two parties as a pledge of loyalty and fidelity to each other. Not only that, but oaths in Israel invoked the name of the Lord as a way of summoning him as a witness, and as a way of asking for his divine help in fulfilling one's commitments. Quite simply, oaths call God into action—to bring help to those who need it, to bring blessings upon those who are faithful, and to bring curses upon those who are not.

Though moderns think of oaths as juridical (or legal) acts, the ancients thought of oaths as sacred and liturgical acts, precisely because God was invoked and thereby involved in the proceeding. Scripture clearly attests to this fact, for it often describes the swearing of oaths and the making of covenants in the cultic context of worship and sacrifice (Gen 15:7–21, 22:13–18; Exod 24:3–8; Ps 50:5). On the one hand, covenants are ratified by oaths, as when the Deuteronomic covenant was sealed in the land of Canaan, with the twelve tribes swearing their "Amen" to the Lord while the Levitical priests offered up sacrifices on an altar (Deut 27:1–26; Josh 8:30–35). On the other hand, covenants are also renewed by oaths, as when the priest Ezra led the Jewish community in recommitting itself to the Lord's "firm covenant" (Neh 9:38) by swearing an "oath to walk in God's law" (Neh 10:29). These and other examples indicate that oaths are liturgical actions that function as both pledges of loyalty and pleas for divine help.

III. WITNESS OF THE NEW TESTAMENT

Given this backdrop, it is no surprise to see Jesus ratifying the New Covenant at the very moment that he instituted a sacrament. At the table of the Last Supper, he poured forth "the blood of the covenant" to be shed in sacrifice, and then summoned his apostles to partake of it for the forgiveness of sins (Matt 26:27–28).

Eucharistic communion, if received in faith, leads to abiding union with Christ through the blessing of eternal life (John 6:53–58), whereas unworthy communion—one that fails to discern the Lord's body and blood in the meal—leads to the curse of judgment and the threat of final exclusion from the covenant (1 Cor 11:27–32). Furthermore, the mandate of Jesus to "Do this in remembrance of me" indicates that the Eucharistic liturgy, which ratified the New Covenant in Christ's blood (Luke 22:19), is now celebrated as a renewal of the covenant in the ongoing life of the Church (1 Cor 11:24–25).

In a related way, all the sacraments of the New Covenant are celebrated by pledging our lives and our fidelity to the Lord. As actions of divine worship and covenant renewal, they serve as channels of God's help poured out for the covenant people in the form of grace. Following is a list of the seven sacraments and the primary passages of the NT that ground the Church's faith in these sacraments.

1. Baptism. The sacrament of new birth in Christ (John 3:3–5) and incorporation into the life of the Trinity (Matt 28:19). Baptism effects the forgiveness of sins (Acts 22:16), the sanctification and justification of the recipient (1 Cor 6:11), and the indwelling of the Holy Spirit (Acts 2:38). It also makes one part of the body of Christ (1 Cor 12:12–13) and a sharer in his Resurrection life (Rom 6:3–4). In short, baptism is a sacrament of salvation (1 Pet 3:21).

2. Eucharist. The sacrament that makes present the body and blood of Christ under the appearances of bread and wine (Matt 26:26–29; Mark 14:22–25; Luke 22:14–23; 1 Cor 11:23–25). In the Eucharist, it is truly his flesh and truly his blood given for the life of the world (John 6:53–58). Eucharistic communion is a participation in the body and blood of Jesus (1 Cor 10:16), and celebration of the Eucharistic liturgy is a proclamation of the Lord's death until he comes (1 Cor 11:26).

3. Confirmation. The sacrament that perpetuates the strengthening grace of Pentecost (Acts 2:1–4) by the laying on of hands (Acts 8:14–17, 19:6; Heb 6:2). It confers a special anointing of the Spirit (1 John 2:20, 27) to bear witness to the faith (Acts 1:8; Heb 2:4).

4. Reconciliation. The sacrament of confession and forgiveness (John 20:23; cf. Matt 16:19, 18:18). The ministry of reconciliation, through which God reunites the world to himself, is entrusted to the ordained shepherds of the Church (2 Cor 5:18–19).

5. Matrimony. The sacrament that elevates and enriches marriage, making it a living sign of the union between Christ and the Church (Eph 5:21–33; Rev 19:6–8). The sacramental bond between spouses is permanent and exclusive (Matt 5:32, 19:1–9; Luke 16:18; 1 Cor 7:10–11).

6. Holy Orders. The sacrament of ordained pastoral ministry, consisting of bishops, priests or presbyters, and deacons (Acts 14:23; Phil 1:1; 1 Tim 3:1–13, 5:17–20; Titus 1:5). It is conferred by the laying on of hands (1 Tim 4:14; 5:22; 2 Tim 1:6). Among other responsibilities, bishops and presbyters are preachers of the word of God (Acts 20:28–32) and celebrants of the Eucharist (1 Cor 11:23–25).

7. Anointing of the Sick. The sacrament of healing, sometimes in preparation for death. This sacrament stems from Christ's own healing ministry, which is handed on to his apostles (Mark 6:13). Its administration involves an anointing in the name of the Lord, the prayers of the Church's presbyters, commending the sick to God, and sometimes the confession and remission of sins (Jas 5:14–15).

SACRIFICE A ritual action of worship that is near-universally attested in ancient religions. So ubiquitous is sacrifice to the history of human culture that Christian theology considers it a precept of the natural law (e.g., Saint Thomas Aquinas, *Summa theologiae* II–II, q.85, a.1). Biblical religion is dominated by the practice of sacrifice in many and varied forms. Throughout the Old and New Testaments, sacrifice is one of the principal means of ratifying, renewing, and repairing the relational bond between God and his people.

I. THE PRACTICE OF SACRIFICE

Sacrifice has taken different forms at different times throughout the long centuries of biblical history. Distinctions in how it was practiced can be made between patriarchal, Mosaic, and Christian times. The first two phases are considered below, and the third is examined in part III.

A. Patriarchal Times

As witnessed in the book of Genesis, prayer and sacrifice are the signature forms of religious expression in patriarchal times. Prayer is usually described with the idiom "to call upon the name of the LORD" (Gen 4:26; 12:8; 21:33; 26:25). Sacrifice is described in a number of ways. Building altars, for example, implies the ritual offering of gifts to God (Gen 12:7–8; 13:18; 22:9; 26:25; 35:7). Objects of sacrifice include flock animals such as sheep and goats (Gen 4:4; 22:13), birds (Gen 8:20), crops of the field (Gen 4:3), libations of wine or oil (Gen 28:18; 35:14), and, in one instance, bread and wine (Gen 14:18).

Sacrifice during patriarchal times was a discretionary practice. That is, Genesis gives no indication that the patriarchs followed a religious calendar of feast days (though the agricultural seasons likely played a part in the timing), that they observed a canon of liturgical procedures, or that they felt compelled to worship within the precincts of a religious sanctuary. Matters of when, how, and where sacrifice should be offered were left to the discretion of the worshipper. Not only that, but all public actions of sacrifice were performed by the head of the family—the patriarch himself—instead of a clerical priest or cultic functionary set apart for this task. Patriarchal religion was thus a form of natural family religion that was quite distinct from the sacrificial cult instituted by Moses and seen throughout most of the OT writings.

B. Mosaic Times

Sacrifice became highly formalized and standardized in the Mosaic period. No longer a discretionary response to the natural law, it was now given precise definition in God's revealed Law to Israel. As part of the Sinai covenant, sacrifice came under extensive regulations that defined its many forms, objects, and procedures. So, too, the times and ministers of sacrifice were no longer entrusted to fathers and patriarchs in relation to the individual needs of their families, but were regulated by an annual calendar of religious feasts (Lev 23:4–44) and its attendant duties restricted to hereditary priesthood descended from Aaron and his sons (Exod 40:12–15). Sacrificial worship also came to be centered in a national sanctuary at this time—first in the Mosaic Tabernacle (Lev 17:1–7) and later in the Solomonic Temple (Deut 12:1–11).

The objects of Israelite sacrifice were heads of domestic livestock (cattle, sheep, goats) and a few species of birds (turtledoves, pigeons)—that is, only those animals that the Law declared "clean" and permissible to eat (Lev 11:1–47; Deut 14:3–21). Unclean animals, which included mainly wild animals, were never placed on the altar of worship. Among food offerings, sacrifices were made of wheat, barley, oil, and wine, with grain offerings being sprinkled with salt (Lev 2:13). Spices such as frankincense were also offered as an expression of worship (Exod 30:7–8).

Most of the Torah's sacrificial procedures are defined in Lev 1–7. In these chapters, a basic description is given of the five main types of sacrifice offered in biblical Israel. All such offerings were to be made at the central sanctuary, though each type had distinct liturgical rubrics for the officiating priest, the lay worshipper, and the gift to be offered.

1. *The Burnt Offering* (Hebrew *ʿôlâ*). The holocaust or ascending sacrifice outlined in Lev 1:3–7 and 6:8–13. In this sacrifice, the animal was drained of its blood, which was splashed against the sides of the altar, and then stripped of its hide, which was given to the officiating priest. The carcass was then cleaved into pieces and laid upon the fires of the altar hearth, from which point it ascended to God in the form of smoke and a savory scent. Because no part of the animal reverted to the worshipper, the burnt offering was considered the supreme oblation—a pure gift to the Lord. Its effect was atonement for sin (Lev 1:4; cf. Job 1:5). Holocausts could be voluntarily offered, though they were mandated for Israel's yearly festivals and for the twice-daily liturgy of the sanctuary (Exod 29:38–42).

2. *The Cereal Offering* (Hebrew *minḥâ*). The grain offering outlined in Lev 2:1–16 and 6:14–23. In this sacrifice, milled wheat or barley was mixed or spread with oil and brought to the sanctuary priest; it could be unbaked, baked, griddled, or otherwise cooked. The priest would throw a handful of the offering upon the fires of the altar as a memorial portion

to the Lord, while the rest he took as consecrated food to be eaten by the Aaronic priests. It seems that the cereal offering was conceived as a form of "tribute" to the Lord, for the Hebrew name given to this sacrifice is elsewhere used in Scripture for a gift or payment that a subject people renders to its overlord (e.g., Judg 3:15; 2 Sam 8:2). Evidence suggests that the bloodless cereal offering was not an independent form of sacrifice; rather, it appears as an auxiliary sacrifice that was meant to accompany various animal offerings.

3. *The Peace Offering* (Hebrew *šĕlāmîm*). Also called the fellowship or communion offering, which is outlined in Lev 3:1–17 and 7:11–36. In this sacrifice, a flock or herd animal was brought to the sanctuary and divided into several parts: the blood was collected and splashed on the sides of the altar, the fat portions and kidneys were placed on the fires of the altar, the breast and right thigh of the victim were given to the priests as consecrated food, and the rest of the sacrificial meat reverted to the worshipper and his family to be eaten as a communion portion. In general, the peace offering was conceived as a celebratory banquet shared with the Lord and intended to deepen that relationship. Presumably it was thought to reinforce the bond of fellowship and peace between God and his people, for scholars generally agree that the name given to this sacrifice is related to the Hebrew word *šālôm*, meaning "peace" or "well-being." Subtypes of the peace offering included the thank offering (*tôdâ*), the spontaneous free-will offering (*nĕdābâ*), and the votive offering given in payment for a vowel (*neder*).

4. *The Sin Offering* (Hebrew *ḥaṭṭāʾt*). The purification offering outlined in Lev 4:1–5:13 and 6:24–30. In this sacrifice, the animal offering is graded according to the person or persons in need of purification, whether a priest (bull), the whole congregation (bull), a ruler (male goat), or a layperson (female goat, lamb, turtledove, or pigeons). The fat portions and kidneys of the animal belonged to the Lord and were offered on the altar hearth; a meat portion was given to the priests as consecrated food; and the rest of the carcass was removed from the sanctuary and burned outside the camp. Central to the sin offering was the blood of the animal, which was conceived as a cleansing agent and was manipulated by the priest in a variety of ways (splashed, smeared, and sprinkled). The rite conferred forgiveness upon individuals (Lev 4:20, 26, 31), though many scholars contend that its primary purpose was the removal of ritual impurity from Israel and its sanctuary. Thus, in this context, sin is understood not only as a moral fault with its attendant guilt but also as a cultic transgression against the ceremonial laws of purity expressed in the Torah. Situations calling for purification included, among other things, childbirth (Lev 12:6), leprosy (Lev 14:19), and bodily emissions (Lev 15:1–33).

5. *The Guilt Offering* (Hebrew *ʾāšām*). The reparation offering outlined in Lev 5:14–6:7 and 7:1–7. In this sacrifice, an unblemished ram was brought to the sanctuary, its blood dashed against the sides of the altar, its kidneys and fat portions burned on the altar, and its meat given to the officiating priest as consecrated food. Besides this, the worship-

per confessed his sin to the priest and paid a 20 percent reparation fee to the sanctuary. The purpose of the guilt offering was to deal with the profanation of holy things as well as the unjust appropriation of personal property. Transgressions in this category included sins of omission as well as sins discovered some time after their commission.

On the one hand, these main types of sacrifice, along with auxiliary forms such as the drink offering (e.g., Num 15:5, 10), were occasional sacrifices offered as circumstances demanded in the life of the nation. Most, however, were mandated as part of the festival celebrations of Israel's liturgical calendar. An inventory of the sacrifices offered daily in the sanctuary, weekly on the Sabbath, and yearly during the annual festival times is given in Num 28–29.

II. THE PURPOSE OF SACRIFICE

A. Sacrifice and Representation

Sacrifice has many dimensions and levels of meaning in the Bible. In general, sacrifices are symbolic actions. They are liturgical rites that give outward and public expression to man's innermost acts of devotion toward God. By means of sacrifice, man recognizes his total dependence upon God and acknowledges the supreme authority of God over his life. The relation between the offerer and his offering is best understood in terms of "representation." In other words, the gifts that man surrenders to God on the altar and sends into heaven as smoke represent the worshipper offering himself to God. Some interpret this distinction between the worshipper and his gift

in terms of "substitution," so that the animal is slain *in place of* or *instead of* the person making the sacrifice. There is some truth in this notion, insofar as the priest and victim were always distinct in the OT period; nevertheless, it is reductionistic as an overall theory of sacrificial symbolism. More probable is the representation theory that sees the worshipper sacrificing his belongings *on behalf of* himself or others. After all, God had no real need of animal flesh or other foods (Ps 50:12–13); what he really wants is our lives and hearts in the form of obedience, thanksgiving, and repentance (1 Sam 15:22; Ps 51:16–17, 107:22). This is what the sacrifices of OT times make visible in a symbolic way.

B. Sacrifice and Covenant

The importance of sacrifice in the Bible goes together with the importance of the covenant theme that runs throughout Scripture. Indeed, covenants are often ratified and renewed by liturgical actions of sacrifice (Ps 50:5). The reasons for this are fairly clear. On the one hand, covenants in Israel as well as the wider Near East were sacred alliances, not mere political or commercial transactions. That is, covenants were made in the presence of God (or the gods) and its partners invoked God as a witness of the pledges sworn by oath and as a guarantor of the sanctions to be meted out to those who proved to be faithful and unfaithful (blessings and curses). At one level, then, sacrifice helped to sanctify and solemnize an event where human commitments were made in the name of God, in the presence of God, and in reliance upon God.

Still, the sacredness of the event only partially explains why sacrifice played a central role in the covenant ceremonies. To give a more complete account, one must consider the symbolism of the sacrifices themselves; for the blood that is shed in the ritual of ratification symbolizes both the blessings and the curses that are invoked upon the covenant partners. On the positive side, the lifeblood released from the animal victim symbolized the new relationship that bound the two parties together. In Israel and throughout the ancient Near East, covenants extended the rights and duties of "kinship" to persons genealogically unrelated. By slaying the victim and applying its blood to both of the pledging partners, the point was made that a new blood-relationship was being created. Thereafter, persons in covenant were not simply parties to a contract; they were now equivalent to family members on a legal and relational level of brothers and kinsmen. On the negative side, the ritual slaughter of animals symbolized the curse of death that the covenant threatened to impose on any partner who dared to violate its stipulations. Scholarship calls this a conditional self-curse or self-maledictory pledge. That is, in the act of swearing loyalty to each other, the covenant partners placed themselves under a curse sanction that was set to trigger on anyone who proved disloyal. The substance of this pledge is made visible in the sacrificial rite: if either partner chooses to break the covenant, he can expect to become like the animal victim that is slain and destroyed on the altar.

The ratification of the Sinai covenant in Exod 24 furnishes a clear example of this. Here the covenant between Yahweh and Israel was sealed by a sacrificial ceremony at the base of the mountain. Animals were slain, and their blood was collected in bowls. Then came the ritual enactment of the covenant: half of the blood was splashed upon the people, and the other half was splashed on the altar, representing the Lord (Exod 24:4–8). This first of all signified the blessing that Yahweh was becoming the divine Kinsman of Israel, the Father and Protector of Israel, who was declared his first-born son (Exod 4:22). At the same time, both God and the people were pledging their fidelity to the covenant under the pain of curse sanctions. These were tangibly presented by the slaughter of the animals, the shedding of their blood, and the application of that blood to the pledging partners.

C. Sacrifice and Idolatry

In addition to these functions and levels of symbolism, the sacrifices of the Mosaic Law call for special comment as to their intended purpose. For a new dimension of meaning unfolds at the time of the Exodus that relates sacrifice to the problem of idolatry. Narrative analysis of the Pentateuch indicates that the Levitical code of sacrifice was not part of the original covenant sealed at Mount Sinai; rather, it was added as a legal amendment to the Sinai covenant after the golden-calf apostasy of Israel (Exod 32:1–6). In other words, sacrifice became part of the Sinai covenant only in its renewed form after its original form was broken. Consider the story line: When Israel stood ready to make its Exodus journey out of Egypt, the Lord commanded the people to conduct a festival of sacrifice at Sinai (Exod 5:1–3) that would ratify the Sinai covenant (Exod 24:4–8). Notice that this *command* to sacrifice at the mountain was not a permanent *law* of sacrifice imposed on Israel for the duration of its national life. In the original terms of the covenant, expressed in the Decalogue (Exod 20:1–17) and the Covenant Code (Exod 21–23), the worship of Israel was envisioned more or less according to the patriarchal pattern—that is, with altars made of natural materials and reared in various places (Exod 20:24–26), coupled with a simple calendar of feasts that followed the rhythms of the agricultural seasons (Exod 23:14–17). Nothing in these stipulations defines or decrees the types and manners of sacrifice to be offered to Yahweh. The prophet Jeremiah was aware of this original situation when he addressed the issue centuries later: "For in the day that I brought them out of the land of Egypt, I did not speak to your fathers or command them concerning burnt offerings or sacrifices" (Jer 7:22). Likewise, Moses himself had reminded the people that, after the original Sinai laws were given, the Lord "added no more" stipulations (Deut 5:22).

The structure of the Sinai covenant changed dramatically, however, after the golden-calf incident. Some revisions were made to the original terms of the covenant, such as the change in status for the firstborn sons of Israel (cf. Exod 22:29 and 34:20). Mainly, however, the Law was expanded with a host of new requirements and institutions for worship. Israel, having disgraced itself before the calf idol, was now instructed to build a sanctuary (the Tabernacle) to ordain a professional order of clergymen to mediate the relationship between Yahweh and the lay tribes (the Aaronic priests assisted by non-priestly Levites), to observe a detailed calendar of festivals on an annual cycle (Lev 23:4–44), to maintain standards of ritual purity as a condition for participating in Israelite worship (Lev 11–15), and to follow a canon of sacrificial liturgies, taking the greatest care to ensure ceremonial precision (Lev 1–7). The context in which these additional laws were given—the aftermath of Israel breaking the original Sinai arrangement—points to a direct and causal connection with this antecedent tragedy. In other words, it implies that Yahweh responds to Israel's weakness for idolatry with strict guidelines for giving true worship to the true God. Viewed in this way, the Mosaic system of sacrifice, along with the ritual institutions that accompanied it, was a yoke of correction designed to steer Israel away from idolatry and to order their prayers, praises, and petitions to Yahweh alone. Serving as a safeguard against idol worship, it helped to reinforce the Mosaic doctrine of monotheism. This rationale for sacrifice was acknowledged in Jewish tradition (e.g., Moses Maimonides, *Guide for the Perplexed* 3.32) and is nicely summarized as a tenet of Christian interpretation by Saint Thomas Aquinas:

> *Wherefore another reasonable cause may be assigned to the ceremonies of the sacrifices, from the fact that thereby men were withdrawn from offering sacrifices to idols. Hence too it is that the precepts about the sacrifices were not given to the Jewish people until after they had fallen into idolatry, by worshipping the molten calf: as though those sacrifices were instituted so that the people, being ready*

to offer sacrifices, might offer those sacrifices to God rather than idols. (Summa theologiae I–II, q.102, a.3)

The same basic interpretation was put forward by early theologians such as Saint Justin Martyr (*Dial.* 19), Saint Athanasius (*Festal Epistles* 19.4), and Saint John Chrysostom (*Discourse against Judaizing Christians* 4.6.5). It is also expounded in ecclesiastical writings such as the *Constitutions of the Holy Apostles* (6.4.20) and the *Didascalia Apostolorum* (chap. 26).

Historically, then, sacrifice was seen as a form of "redirection" away from idolatry. But the ancient perspective did not stop there. Sacrifice in its Mosaic form was also seen as a "renunciation" of the idols themselves. In other words, the animals of Israelite sacrifice were animals revered in Egyptian religion as images of the gods and goddesses. Mnevis, for example, was worshipped under the form of a bull, Apis under the form of a bull calf, Hathor under the form of a cow, and Khnum under the form of a ram. To slay these animals in sacrifice was to declare war on Egyptian idolatry. The religion of Israel was thus defined in opposition to the religion of Egypt. All that Egypt revered in its idol cults, Israel renounced as false gods, and this in the very act of worshipping the true God.

The basis for this interpretation lies in the canonical narrative of Scripture. It involves, first, looking at Israel's situation before the Exodus and, second, examining the dialogue between Moses and Pharaoh.

The book of Exodus describes Israel's time in Egypt as a time of grueling oppression and state-sponsored enslavement (Exod 1:8–14). No direct statements are given, however, to inform the reader of Israel's spiritual condition in the pre-Exodus period. Insight into this matter comes later in the biblical tradition. For example, Joshua makes the curious statement that his ancestors "in Egypt" had served the foreign "gods" of the land (Josh 24:14). This is a claim that the Israelites, pressed under the yoke of Egyptian rule, had also placed themselves under the yoke of Egyptian deities. They had become not just slaves in need of liberation but idolators in need of spiritual reform. The same point is made by the prophet Ezekiel, who decries the fact that Israel, while still in bondage, refused to cast aside "the idols of Egypt" (Ezek 20:7). It is no surprise, given these explicit biblical testimonies, that Israel's attachment to idolatry in Egypt would be taken for granted in several works of Jewish (e.g., *Leviticus Rabbah* 22.5) and Christian (e.g., Eusebius, *Demonstration of the Gospel* 1.6) traditions.

Another side of this crisis comes into view when Moses negotiates with Pharaoh for the release of Israel. Before the decimation of Egypt with plagues, which finally broke the shackles of bondage for Israel, Moses had merely asked for a holiday in which the people could sacrifice to Yahweh at Sinai (Exod 5:1–3). Given Israel's assimilation to Egyptian culture, this was an opportunity to reclaim their ancient faith in Yahweh and to renounce the idols of Egypt once and for all. But Moses foresees a problem when Pharaoh permits them to sacrifice within the land of Egypt: "It would not be right to do so," he says, "for we shall sacrifice to the LORD our God offerings abominable to the Egyptians. If we sacrifice offerings abominable to the Egyptians before their eyes, will they not stone us?" (Exod 8:25–26). The unstated premise is that Yahweh is asking his people to sacrifice animals that represent Egyptian deities. Had Israel done so in the land of Egypt itself, it would have faced the violence of a nation outraged by perceived acts of sacrilege.

Admittedly, this interpretive view of sacrifice is not widely known or acknowledged among modern biblical scholars. Nevertheless, several ancient texts make precisely this point—namely, that Moses understands sacrifice as a cultic destruction of Egypt's idols. Consider the following quotations from Jewish antiquity, which give an expanded paraphrase of the Exodus passage in question:

> Then the Pharaoh summoned Moses and Aaron and said, "Go and sacrifice before your God in the land." And Moses said, "It is not proper to do so, because we are taking the cattle which the Egyptians worship to sacrifice before the Lord our God; here we will be sacrificing the cattle which the Egyptians worship and they would be seeing it; would they not intend to stone us? (Targum Onqelos at Exod 8.21–22)

> And Pharaoh called Moses and Aaron and said: "Go, sacrifice before the Lord your God in the land of Egypt." And Moses said: "It is not right to do so, because the idols of the Egyptians are an abomination, from which we must take to sacrifice before the Lord, our God. Behold, if we sacrifice the idols of the Egyptians in their presence, it is impossible that they should not stone us. (Targum Neofiti at Exod 8.21–22)

> And Moses said it is not right to do so, because the Egyptians worshipped cattle as gods. (Exodus Rabbah 11.3)

Similar statements can be found in ancient Christian texts that grapple with the meaning of sacrifice. Again, consider the following quotations.

> You should know . . . that because God determined concerning them that they should not worship calves, the gods of the Egyptians, he distinguished for them among foods and commanded them to sacrifice offerings of the very things they had feared in the land of Egypt. For the Lord had no need of sacrifices and offerings. But in order to restrain the Jews from sacrifices and offerings so that they should not worship the gods of the peoples—when they would enter the land and be mixed among the peoples—as they had worshipped the gods of the Egyptians when they had entered Egypt and been mixed among the Egyptians, he therefore forbade and restrained the Jews. (Saint Aphrahat, Demonstrations 15.6)

> In all respects mentioned, there was a suitable reason for these animals, rather than others, being offered up in sacrifice to God. First, in order to prevent idolatry. Because idolators offered all other animals to their gods, or made use of them in their sorceries: while the Egyptians (among whom the people had been dwelling) considered it abominable to slay these animals, wherefore they used not to offer them in sacrifice to their gods . . . For they worshipped the sheep; they reverenced the ram (because demons appeared under the form thereof); while they employed oxen for agriculture, which was reckoned by them as

something sacred. (Saint Thomas Aquinas, Summa theologiae *I–II, q.102, a.3)*

"Let us go on a journey of three days" (Exod 3:18). It does not say of one or two days, because this would not be sufficiently far enough away from the Egyptians, who would stone them if they knew they were sacrificing animals which they worshipped as gods. (Nicholas of Lyra, Postilla super totam Bibliam *at Exod 3.18)*

History reveals that even non-Jewish and non-Christian writers perceived the antagonism implicit between the worship of Israel and the cults of Egypt. The first quotation below comes from Manetho, an Egyptian priest of the Hellenistic period, whose work survives only in fragments. The second is by the famed Roman historian Tacitus. As both writers see it, Mosaic religion is intentionally and diametrically opposed to all things Egyptian.

He [Moses] then, in the first place, made this law for them, that they should neither worship Egyptian gods, nor should abstain from any one of those sacred animals, which they have in the highest esteem, but kill and destroy them all; that they should join themselves to nobody but to those that were of his confederacy. When he had made such laws as these, and many more such as were mainly opposite the customs of the Egyptians, he gave order that they should use the multitude of the hands they had in building walls about their city. (Manetho, quoted in Josephus, C. Ap. *1.26)*

Moses, wishing to secure for the future his authority over the nation, gave them a novel form of worship, opposed to all that is prac-

ticed by other men. Things sacred with us, with them have no sanctity, while they allow what with us is forbidden . . . They slay the ram, seemingly in derision of Hammon, and they sacrifice the ox, because the Egyptians worship it at Apis. (Tacitus, Hist. *5.4)*

In the end, it must be recognized that sacrifice in the OT period not only took various forms and served various functions, it was also layered with various levels of symbolism and meaning. Its positive aspects served to draw the covenant people toward the Lord and a fuller surrender to his will, while its negative aspects pulled them away from sin, especially from the corruption of idolatry.

III. THE PERFECTION OF SACRIFICE

Sacrifice finds its definitive meaning and efficacy in the NT period. Its perfection consists not of a last refinement of the Mosaic cult itself but of Jesus Christ offering his life as a vicarious sacrifice for the world. By extension, the Christian message also calls believers to a life of sacrificial service in imitation of the Lord.

A. Sacrifice of Christ

On the surface, the Gospel narratives seem to portray the death of Christ as little more than a criminal execution. The preacher from Nazareth was from the nonpriestly tribe of Judah, he was condemned as a blasphemer by the Jewish high priest, his blood was shed by a squad of Roman soldiers, and his life was finally surrendered outside the walls of Jerusalem, at some distance from the precincts of the Temple. Given these facts, it is legitimate to ask how the crucifixion of Jesus could be interpreted as a sacrifice at all, much less as the most perfect sacrifice of all. The question demands attention because this is the unanimous interpretation of his death in earliest Christianity.

The origin of the sacrificial interpretation is traceable to Jesus himself. On the night of his betrayal, Jesus both forewarned of his impending death and foretold of its sacrificial character. Consider his discourse at the Last Supper. In the words of consecration, Jesus said over the Eucharistic cup: "This is my blood of the covenant, which is poured out for many for the forgiveness of sins" (Matt 26:28). Certainly the shedding of his blood insinuates a violent death, a slaying and taking of his life. But to Jewish ears, these words also resonate with sacrificial implications. The reason for this is rooted in the narratives of the book of Exodus and the prophecies of the book of Isaiah.

The Exodus background is twofold. First, the expression "blood of the covenant" is an allusion to the words of Moses at Mount Sinai. The occasion is the ratification of the Mosaic covenant, which was sealed by a liturgy of sacrifice and these solemn words of interpretation: "Behold the blood of the covenant which the LORD has made with you" (Exod 24:8). For Jesus to apply this expression to himself indicates that the pouring out of his own blood will be a cultic sacrifice and the founding event of a new covenant. Second, since Christ spoke these words in the midst of a Passover meal, it must be remembered that the slaying of the Paschal lamb, which formed

the centerpiece of the Seder banquet, is described in Exodus as a "sacrifice" (Exod 12:27). The implications of this cultic backdrop for understanding both the death of Jesus and the sacrament of the Eucharist that anticipated it are inescapable.

The same could be said of Isaiah's influence on the words of Jesus. Again, looking at the Eucharistic consecration, several scholars have detected a reference to Isaiah's fourth Servant Song (Isa 52:13–53:12). This is the poem of the Suffering Messiah, the disturbing vision of Yahweh's beloved Servant submitting himself to the ridicule and rejection of his own people, even unto death. Why is this significant? Because the song comes to a climax with the Servant offering his life as a sacrifice for human sin. It is clear that Jesus had this oracle in mind when he uttered the words of consecration: he refers to his lifeblood being "poured out," just as the Servant "poured out" his life unto death (Isa 53:12); he offers himself for "many," just as the Servant was said to justify "many" (Isa 53:11) and bears the iniquity of "many" (Isa 53:12); and the effect of his sacrifice is the remission of "sins," just as the whole mission of the Servant was to make himself "an offering for sin" (Isa 53:10).

Little wonder, given the gospel traditions of the Last Supper, that the crucifixion of Christ was interpreted as a sacrificial offering. One often sees this tradition in Paul, where the memory of Jesus slain is the memory of a Paschal lamb having been sacrificed (1 Cor 5:7). So, too, the obedience of Christ the Servant results in "many" being made "righteous" (Rom 5:19), just as we see in the song of the Suffering

Servant (Isa 53:11). Several times Paul ventures beyond these traditional motifs and describes the crucifixion in words drawn from other sacrificial passages of the OT, as when he says: "Christ gave himself up for us, a fragrant offering and sacrifice to God" (Eph 5:2, recalling the Greek versions of Gen 8:20–21 and Exod 29:18). The apostle John likewise follows this line of interpretation with his claim that "the blood" of Jesus "cleanses us from all sin" (1 John 1:7). This, one should note, is the language of expiatory sacrifice, the victim's blood having been shed for the remission of sins (cf. 1 John 2:2; 4:10). Other passages could be cited as well that give witness to the sacrificial interpretation of Christ's death in the NT period (e.g., John 1:29; 2 Cor 5:21; 1 Pet 1:18–19; Rev 5:6–10).

Nowhere is the sacrifice of Jesus more extensively pondered than in the book of Hebrews. Everywhere the Christology of Hebrews is shot through with priestly and cultic significance. The point is to show that Jesus, by offering his sinless life to the Father, has made the definitive sacrifice that surpasses all others; and in doing so, he has sealed a new and eternal covenant (Heb 8:6–7; 13:20). In particular, the offering of Christ's "body" (Heb 10:10) and "blood" (Heb 9:12) relativizes the entire system of Mosaic sacrifice. This is because the sacrifice of Christ achieved a true expiation of sin that cleanses the conscience of the worshipper (Heb 9:14; 10:22) and need not be repeated (Heb 9:25–26; 10:14–18). It thus stands in contrast to the blood of animal sacrifices, which were incapable of taking away sins (Heb 10:1–4) and of purifying anything but the exterior

of the person from ritual defilements (Heb 9:9–10, 13). Of peculiar interest, Hebrews extends the reach of Christ's sacrifice beyond his death on the Cross to include his Ascension into the heavenly sanctuary (Heb 4:14; 9:24). The typology underlying this theology is the Day of Atonement liturgy, where the blood of the sacrificial victim was processed into the holy of holies (Heb 9:6–14; cf. Lev 16:1–19). Inasmuch as the inner sanctum of the Tabernacle was an earthly image of heaven (Heb 9:24), the idea is that Jesus, assuming the role of high priest and victim, has taken his blood once for all into the celestial sanctuary of God, thereby achieving an "eternal redemption" on our behalf (Heb 9:12).

B. Sacrifice of Christians

Sacrificial themes are not confined to the actions of Christ in the NT but are likewise applied to Christians. In one sense, this is implicit in the teaching of Jesus, who summons his followers to "take up the cross" in imitation of him (Matt 10:38; Mark 8:34; Luke 14:27). Once he describes his own crucifixion in cultic and sacrificial terms, it follows that the life of Christian discipleship would have this character as well.

This theme is developed mainly in the epistles of Paul, who uses sacrificial images and ideas to describe an array of Christian activities. For instance, he urges believers to present their "bodies as a living sacrifice, holy and acceptable to God" (Rom 12:1). This is an appeal for such things as chastity, temperance, mortification, and other actions of gospel morality and spirituality that surrender the body and its cravings to the will of the Lord. Other forms of sacrifice include monetary giving, such as the gift that Paul received from the church of Philippi, which he calls "a fragrant offering, a sacrifice acceptable and pleasing to God" (Phil 4:18). Missionary labor is likewise described in such terms, for Paul considered his ministry among the Gentiles a form of "priestly service" in which converts from the pagan world are made an "offering" to God (Rom 15:16). Similarly, his preaching is described as spreading "the fragrance" of Christ's message to the world, much like incense that wafts through the courts of the sanctuary (2 Cor 2:15). Finally, as Paul sees it, the prospect of martyrdom is a prospect of being "poured as a libation" upon the "sacrificial offering" of faith (Phil 2:17; cf. 2 Tim 4:6).

Similar encouragement is given later in the NT, where readers are summoned to "offer up a sacrifice of praise to God, that is, the fruit of lips that acknowledge his name" (Heb 13:15). Assurance is given that "such sacrifices are pleasing to God" (Heb 13:16).

Though sometimes unrecognized, the sacrificial character of Christian living is implied in depictions of the Church as the Temple of God (1 Cor 3:16–17; 2 Cor 6:16; Eph 2:19–22). The reason is that, in the ancient biblical world, temples were not simply dwelling places for God or another pagan deity, but houses of sacrificial worship. To take one example, Peter has this close connection between temples and priestly sacrifice in mind when he exhorts: "[L]ike living stones be yourselves built into a spiritual house, to be a holy priesthood, to offer spiritual sacrifices acceptable to God through Jesus Christ" (1 Pet 2:6).

Underlying these themes is a theology of participation. So far as the teaching of the NT is concerned, Christ is not viewed as a sacrificial substitute whose action on the Cross eliminates either the need or the propriety of additional offerings made by the Christian faithful. Rather, believers are called by the gospel to imitate the life of Jesus so far as this is possible with God's help. Sacrifice is a major part of this equation. No longer, as in OT times, is the sacrifice required of believers merely an animal or food that represents the worshipper before God. Now, by the perfect offering of Christ, the world is shown the ultimate meaning of sacrifice: it is a gift of loving obedience that surrenders the whole person—heart, mind, and body—to the altar of God's will.

SADDUCEES One of the major sects of Palestinian Judaism in New Testament times. The Sadducees may have derived their name from **Zadok**, high priest at the time of David and Solomon, or possibly from the Hebrew word ṣaddîq, "righteous." The Sadducees are known chiefly through Josephus and the NT Gospels and Acts. They were, with the **Pharisees**, one of the two major religious schools.

The Sadducees were an elite or aristocratic element in Judaism. They were largely members of the priesthood and came from the most powerful of the priestly families. They were disliked for their haughty demeanor and judgmental attitudes.

The teachings of the Sadducees differed from those of the Pharisees in a variety of ways. They denied the resurrection of the dead and the existence of angels and the soul

(Acts 23:6–8); they rejected the oral tradition and regarded only the Torah, written law, as authoritative; they opposed predestination in favor of free choice, with prosperity or misery resting in the hands of the individual; and they tended to be more conservative in the interpretation of penal laws. In Acts 23:6–8, the Sadducees sat on the **Sanhedrin**, or Jewish high court, with the Pharisees, and Paul used their disagreements on the resurrection of the dead to provoke a near riot. Although the Pharisees and Sadducees were ancient enemies, they united in their opposition to Jesus (cf. Matt 3:7; 16:1, 6, 11, 12; 22:23, 34; Mark 12:18; Luke 20:27; Acts 4:1; 15:17).

It's uncertain when the sect of the Sadducees first came into being. The first mention of Sadducees was under the early Hasmoneans, when the Sadducees held posts in the Senate (*gerousia*). They enjoyed considerable prominence through John Hyrcanus, who abandoned the Pharisees and joined the Sadducees.

SAKKUTH The planet Saturn (Amos 5:26). It was also known as Kaiwan, from "the steady one."

SALAMIS The largest city and port on the Mediterranean island of Cyprus, not to be confused with the Greek island of the same name. The book of Acts and Josephus (*Ant.* 13.284–87) attest to the presence of a Jewish population there in New Testament times. Salamis was the first stop for **Paul** and **Barnabas** on Paul's first missionary journey (Acts 13:5).

SALEM (Hebrew *šālēm*, "safe," "at peace") The city of the patriarchal priest-king **Melchizedek**

(Gen 14:18; Heb 7:1–2); it was later known as **Jerusalem**.

SALIM A site close to the Jordan River near the place where **John the Baptist** preached repentance and baptized (John 3:23). Its exact location is uncertain, though scholars have suggested several locations, including Tell Abu Sus, to the south of Beisan, and Tell Ridgha or Tell Sheikh Selim.

SALLU The name of two men in the Old Testament.

1. A priest who returned to Jerusalem after the Exile with Zerubbabel (Neh 12:7).

2. A Benjaminite who took up residence in Jerusalem in the days of Nehemiah (Neh 11:7).

SALMON The name of two men in the Old Testament (the name also appears as "Salma" or "Sala").

1. The son of Hur and the father of Bethlehem (1 Chr 2:51, 54).

2. The son of Nahshon, and the father of **Boaz**, who married **Ruth** (Ruth 4:21). He is the great-great-grandfather of David (1 Chr 2:11) and thus appears in the Davidic genealogies of Jesus (Matt 1:4–5; Luke 3:32).

SALOME The name of two women in the New Testament.

1. The mother of the apostles **James** and **John**, sons of Zebedee (cf. Mark 15:40 with Matt 27:56). Having become a disciple of Jesus in Galilee, Salome went with him to Jerusalem, stood by the Cross, and participated in his burial (Mark 15:40; 16:1). On one occasion,

she approached Jesus to request that her sons be given prominent seats on either side of him when he came into his kingdom. Jesus replied by asking whether they were willing to drink from the cup from which he had to drink (Matt 20:20–28).

2. The daughter of **Herodias** and **Herod Philip** (Josephus, *Ant.* 18.136), best known for her role in the death of **John the Baptist** (Mark 6:22). Salome (who is not named in the Gospel) became an accomplice in the plot of Herodias to kill John the Baptist. Her dance so entranced Herod Antipas that he offered her anything she wanted. Her reply was that she wanted the head of John the Baptist. Herod was obligated to fulfill the promise (Mark 6:14–29; Matt 14:1–12). According to Josephus, Salome married (Herod) **Philip** the Tetrarch and, after his death, Aristobolus. Nothing else is known of her later life.

SALT A vitally important mineral found in great abundance in the **Dead Sea** region, in particular at the Hill of Salt, a six-mile-long cliff area where ever-changing pillars of salt are shaped by the winds (Zeph 2:9). Salt was used for seasoning and as a preservative (Matt 5:13; Mark 9:50; Col 4:6). Job asks, "Can that which is tasteless be eaten without salt?" (Job 6:6). Salt was sprinkled on grain offerings and burnt offerings (Lev 2:13; Ezek 43:24). Children were also rubbed with salt in the hope of ensuring a long life (Ezek 16:4). The expression "a covenant of salt" stressed the durability or indestructibility of a covenant arrangement (Num 18:19; 2 Chr 13:5).

On the other hand, salt inhibits the fertility of the ground. **Abimelech** seeded the ground of **Shechem** with salt after capturing the city, as a symbol that it should remain barren forever after (Judg 9:45). Salt could therefore be associated with destruction and desolation (Deut 29:22–23; Ps 107:34; Jer 17:6; Zeph 2:9). A memorable example of this association is Lot's wife, who was turned into a pillar of salt because of her disobedience (Gen 19:26).

Jesus referred to salt as an image of the Church in the world. "You are the salt of the earth; but if salt has lost its taste, how shall its saltness be restored?" (Matt 5:13). Just as salt makes tasteless food palatable, so the followers of Jesus season the whole world: "Salt is good; but if the salt has lost its saltness, how will you season it? Have salt in yourselves, and be at peace with one another" (Mark 9:50; cf. Luke 14:34).

SALT, CITY OF A town of Judah near the **Dead Sea** (Josh 15:62). It was one of the six frontier cities for Judah "in the wilderness" (Josh 15:61–62): Beth-arabah, Middin, Secacah, Nibshan, the City of Salt, and En-gedi. The City of Salt is sometimes identified with Khirbet **Qumran**.

SALT, PILLAR OF *See* **Lot**; *see also* **Salt**.

SALT SEA The biblical name for the **Dead Sea**.

SALT, VALLEY OF A place in Edom near the southern end of the **Dead Sea**. The Israelites fought and won two battles in the valley against the Edomites. The first took place during the reign of **David** (2 Sam 8:13; 1 Chr 18:12). The second was fought in the eighth century

B.C. by King **Amaziah**, who conquered a large part of Edom (2 Kgs 14:7; 2 Chr 25:11). The precise location of this valley is uncertain. Traditionally, it was believed to be southwest of the Dead Sea, near the Hill of Salt (see **Salt**). Another suggested site is the Wadi el-Milḥ, to the east of **Beer-sheba**.

SALVATION HISTORY The story of God's plan to save the world from sin and death.

The divine origin of this history is the Holy Trinity. In this perfect divine family, God the Father loves the Son, the Son perfectly loves the Father, and the Holy Spirit is the bond of love between the Father and the Son. God intended that his creation, humanity, should share in this perfect communion of love by the grace of divine adoption.

But the original union of God with humanity was severed through the disobedience of Adam and Eve, by which sin was introduced into the world. The communion of humanity with God and the communion of men among themselves was destroyed. It was through God's plan of salvation in Christ that God sought a restoration of this family communion.

This restoration could not come all at once. Sinful and broken humanity had to be restored gradually to a state of blessing and union with God. Salvation history unfolds as a series of covenants (see **covenant**) made by God with the human race. Ever-broadening covenants in the Old Testament with Adam, Noah, Abraham, Moses, and David culminated in the New Testament with the everlasting covenant of Jesus Christ.

All of Scripture, then, although it is made up of many books with many styles and points of view, is really the story of God's plan to save us. It is history from God's perspective, and in it God reveals his own actions and their meaning. Scripture itself is part of salvation history: it bridges the gulf between the human and the divine and reveals in its pages the divine truths of salvation history that were unveiled by God in the history of Israel and the early Church.

SAMARIA, SAMARITANS Samaria was the capital city of the northern kingdom of Israel under the Omride Dynasty in the early ninth century B.C. (1 Kgs 16:23–24) until the city was conquered by the Assyrians around 722 B.C. The city of Samaria is normally identified with the modern Sebastiya (Sebaste). The Samaritans were the inhabitants of central Canaan surrounding the region of Samaria. Some scholars derive the people's name from the city, while others connect it with the Hebrew term for "guardians" or "keepers." (See **Israel** for other details.)

I. Samaria
  A. The City
  B. The Region
II. The Samaritans
  A. Disputed Origins
  B. Samaritan Religion
  C. Samaritans and Jews
  D. Jesus Among the Samaritans

I. SAMARIA

A. The City

The foundation of the city of Samaria is described in 1 Kgs 16:24: **Omri** "bought the hill of Samaria from Shemer for two talents of silver; and he fortified the hill, and called the name of the city which he built, Samaria, after the name of Shemer, the owner of the hill." From the seventh year of Omri's reign, the city served as the capital of the northern kingdom of Israel.

Samaria was expanded and beautified by King **Ahab** (r. 874–853 B.C.), who added an ivory palace (1 Kgs 22:39; Amos 6:4). But the Omride Dynasty was doomed, and the city endured the varying fortunes of the kingdom. The city was damaged by the sieges during the struggle with the Arameans (1 Kgs 20:1–2) and the revolt of **Jehu** (2 Kgs 10:1–36). The city eventually fell to the Assyrians under **Shalmaneser V** and **Sargon II** (2 Kgs 17:1–6) after a three-year siege from 725 to 722 B.C.

B. The Region

Assyrian records confirm that Sargon deported the population of the city of Samaria and the surrounding region (over 27,000 inhabitants) and settled new colonists in their place: "And the king of Assyria brought people from Babylon, Cuthah, Avva, Hamath, and Sepharvaim, and placed them in the cities of Samaria instead of the people of Israel; and they took possession of Samaria, and dwelt in its cities" (2 Kgs 17:24; cf. Ezra 4:2, 10). The result of this resettlement was a religious and cultural syncretism: the inhabitants continued to worship their native gods, but they also worshipped the Lord as the local god (2 Kgs 17:26–28). Later, King **Hezekiah** attempted to reform the cultic practices in Samaria (2 Chr 30:1–11), and Samaria was included in **Josiah**'s broad program of reform (2 Kgs 23:19).

Samaria was infamous for its wickedness. The prophets have nothing good to say about the city, but denounce it in the strongest terms. Isaiah 28:3 refers to Samaria as the "proud crown of the drunkards of Ephraim." He also prophesies its end: "and the fading flower of its glorious beauty, which is on the head of the rich valley, will be like a first-ripe fig before the summer: when a man sees it, he eats it up as soon as it is in his hand" (Isa 28:4); he was speaking of the Assyrian conquest (Isa 9:8–12; 10:9–11; 36:19). Amos refers to Samaria's women as the "cows of Bashan, who are in the mountain of Samaria, who oppress the poor, who crush the needy, who say to their husbands, 'Bring, that we may drink!'" (Amos 4:1). He likewise predicts the doom of Samaria (Amos 3:12; 6:1). Hosea 7:1 and 8:5 and Mic 1:5–7 refer to the wickedness of the city; the latter compares Samaria to Jerusalem in that Samaria was the center of the sinfulness of Israel, whereas Jerusalem was the center of the sinfulness of Judah.

After the Assyrian conquest of Samaria in 722 B.C., the city fell under the occupation of succeeding empires, including the Persians, Seleucids, and Romans. Eventually **Shechem** supplanted Samaria as the main city of the Samaritans, yet Samaria remained strategically important. In 109 B.C., it was destroyed during the siege of **John Hyrcanus** and subsequently rebuilt by the Romans. It was then enlarged and decorated by **Herod the Great** around 25 B.C. and renamed Sebaste (or, in Latin, Augustus, after Herod's imperial patron). Herod settled several thousand Roman veterans in the city. The district of Samaria was later attached to Judea and formed part of the ethnarchy of Archelaus. Following the deposition of Archelaus, administration passed to the procurator of Judea.

In the New Testament, mention is made of several places in the district, including Samaria (Sebaste), Shechem, Jacob's well, and Mount Gerizim (John 4:20, where it is only called "this mountain"). Samaria assumed some importance in the first days of the Church (Acts 1:8; 8:4–25; see below.)

II. THE SAMARITANS

A. Disputed Origins

The term "Samaritans" appears in the Old Testament only in 2 Kgs 17:29, where the people are described as idolators. Palestinian Jews saw all Samaritans as descendants of the foreign colonists who had been planted by the Assyrians—origins worthy of contempt, as far as Judeans were concerned. The Samaritans, on the other hand, asserted that they were the descendants of the Israelite tribes of Ephraim and Manasseh who had managed to survive the Assyrian destruction of the city.

In the judgment of 2 Kings, the religion of the Samaritans was a hybrid of idolatry and Israelite faith in Yahweh (2 Kgs 17:29–34). Because of this corruption of faith, the Samaritans and Judeans suffered centuries of mutual animosity. For instance, after the first wave of Jewish exiles returned from Babylon, and work on rebuilding the **Temple** was about to begin, the Samaritans offered to help with the reconstruction efforts, only to be rebuffed by the Jewish leadership (Ezra 4:1–4). The embittered Samaritans attempted to halt the construction by intimidation and political

interference (Ezra 4:5). Likewise, when Nehemiah later planned to rebuild the walls of Jerusalem, he faced dogged opposition from enemies, some of whom were Samaritans (Ezra 4:7–24; Neh 4:1–9).

The succeeding history of the Samaritans was an unhappy one. During the Maccabean struggle, the Samaritans allied themselves with the Seleucids (1 Macc 3:10). In 108 B.C., John Hyrcanus destroyed the Samaritan temple built on Mount Gerizim. Under the Roman occupation, the Samaritans suffered a terrible massacre at the command of Pilate in A.D. 35; the bloodshed was so extensive and excessive that Pilate was removed as procurator.

B. Samaritan Religion

In the time of Jesus, the Samaritans practiced an exclusively Mosaic religion, not accepting any of the traditions associated with the Davidic covenant. Thus they acknowledged only a version of the Hebrew **Pentateuch**, and possibly Joshua and Judges, but not the Prophets and later books. They did anticipate a coming Messiah (John 4:25); they also accepted the Sabbath, feasts, and circumcision. But they rejected the Jerusalem **Temple** and priesthood and set up the rival sanctuary of Mount Gerizim (John 4:20).

C. Samaritans and Jews

In Jesus's encounter with the Samaritan woman (John 4:4–42), the woman was surprised that a Jew would even speak to a Samaritan. "How is it that you, a Jew, ask a drink of me, a woman of Samaria?" It was regarded as obvious that "Jews have no dealings with Samaritans" (John 4:9). Even the apostles were shocked that Jesus would speak to her (John 4:27). Josephus reported the dangers posed to Jewish pilgrims from Galilee by Samaritans as they journeyed to and from Jerusalem. On one occasion, Samaritans refused hospitality to Jesus and the disciples on their way from Galilee to Jerusalem (Luke 9:52–56). Jesus rebuked James and John for their anger.

D. Jesus Among the Samaritans

In spite of the traditional hostility between Jews and Samaritans, Jesus spoke well of Samaritans and found several of them open to his message. He also used a Samaritan in the important parable (Luke 10:30–37) that contrasts the Good Samaritan with the priest and the Levite in the example of how to love one's neighbor. The Samaritan leper was also the only one of the ten healed by Jesus who thanked Jesus (Luke 17:16). Jesus at first commanded the disciples not to preach to the Samaritans (Matt 10:5), but only because the Gospel had to be preached first to Israel. When the apostles did preach among the Samaritans they found success, and a Christian community was founded at an early time among the Samaritans (Acts 8:4–17; 9:31; 15:3).

In Jesus's teaching, the Samaritans were a powerful means of expressing the truly radical call he was making in the Gospel. The Gospel belongs to the Samaritans as well, and Christian charity lays aside long-standing enmity and reaches out to all. As there was in first-century Palestine no greater feud than that between the Samaritans and the Jews, Jesus made the stunning demand that love of neighbor meant loving the Samaritan, and brotherhood included such a bitter enemy. Jesus the

Messiah reunited the divided kingdoms of Judah and Israel under the restored kingdom that he inaugurated with the New Covenant.

A small colony of Samaritans has endured over the centuries. They continue to celebrate the Passover each year on Mount Gerizim.

SAMARITANS *See* **Samaria**.

SAMEK The fifteenth letter of the Hebrew alphabet (ס).

SAMGAR NEBO A Babylonian military officer who, along with Nergal-sharezer, Sarsechim the Rabsaris, and Nergal-sharezer the Rabmag, was placed in charge of Jerusalem after its capture by **Nebuchadnezzar** in 586 B.C. (Jer 39:3).

SAMOS A large island in the Aegean, off the southwest coast of Asia Minor (modern Turkey). The name of the island means "height" or "mountain," describing its mountainous and rugged terrain. The Roman consul Lucius sent letters instructing the officials on the island to live at peace with the local Jewish population (1 Macc 15:23). Samos therefore must have had a recognizable community of Jews in the second century B.C. While returning to Judea from his third missionary journey, **Paul** "touched at" Samos, perhaps indicating that he stopped there for a night (Acts 20:15).

SAMOTHRACE A small mountainous island in the northern Aegean Sea. Its name was derived from *Samos*, meaning "height" or "mountain," and the nearby mainland of

Thrace. During the Greek and early Roman periods, Samothrace was comparatively unimportant. It gained independence in the early second century B.C. following the defeat of Antiochus the Great at Magnesia by the Romans in 190 B.C. The island later passed under Roman control in 133 B.C. **Paul** set sail from Troas for Europe across the Aegean Sea and was assisted by good winds to reach Samothrace in one day (Acts 16:11). It is possible that he made a short stop there at the end of his third missionary journey (Acts 20:6).

SAMSON (Hebrew, probably "sun") Perhaps the best known of the **Judges**. He was the instrument of deliverance from the Philistines at a time of prolonged Philistine domination (Judg 13–16).

Samson was the son of Manoah, of the village of Zoprah of the tribe of Dan. His mother had been barren, like **Sarah**, **Hannah**, and **Elizabeth**, and his birth was thus the result of a miracle that was announced by an angel (Judg 13:3). He was to be a **Nazirite** from birth (Judg 13:7).

Samson was famous for his incredible physical strength, but he had an equally incredible weakness for women and reckless behavior. His strong passions led to his marriage to a Philistine woman (Judg 14:1–15:8) in Timnah. The union proved a disaster as a result of the ongoing problems between the Israelites and Philistines; he lost his wife, and a bloody feud with the Philistines followed, including the episode of the foxes (Judg 15:2–5) and the slaughter of a thousand Philistines with the jawbone of an ass (Judg 15:14–17).

Samson's undoing was his sexual weakness. His involvement with a harlot in Gaza led to his being trapped by the enemy. He escaped by tearing off the city gates (Judg 16:1–3), but he soon became infatuated with **Delilah**, a woman living in the valley of Sorek (Judg 16:4). After learning from him that his hair was the secret of his strength, she betrayed him to the Philistines (Judg 16:5–20); he was blinded and made into a spectacle at a festival in Gaza. In one of the most famous episodes in Scripture, Samson brought down the temple of Dagon and killed everyone in it, including himself, but "the dead whom he slew at his death were more than those whom he had slain during his life" (Judg 16:30).

Samson often failed to control his own urges and weaknesses, and he showed little concern for his Nazirite commitment to God. For this reason the Spirit of the Lord withdrew from him (Judg 16:18–22). Nevertheless, he was the chosen instrument of God, despite his obvious failings, and in the end he was transformed into an admirable figure of faith (Heb 11:32).

SAMUEL (Hebrew, "his name is God") The last and one of the greatest **Judges** of Israel. He was a transitional figure who helped to end the tribal configuration of Israel and inaugurate the monarchy. Samuel fulfilled multiple roles in his lifetime: priest, seer, prophet, and judge.

I. THE ROLES OF SAMUEL

The story of Samuel is told in the book of 1 Samuel, and different parts of the narrative show Samuel in different roles.

Samuel is seen in the priestly role in the

early part of the narrative, ministering to the Lord at the sanctuary in Shiloh (1 Sam 2:11, 18; 3:1) and performing important sacrificial functions that are linked with the actions of priests (1 Sam 7:9; 9:13; 10:8; 16:1–5).

Samuel is declared a prophet in 1 Sam 3:20 (cf. 2 Chr 35:18; Sir 46:13–20), and he fulfilled this role by proclaiming the will of the Lord to his people (1 Sam 8:10–18; 15:1–2), interceding for them (1 Sam 7:8–9; 12:23), and declaring the judgment of God upon Saul (1 Sam 13:13–14; 15:22–23). Finally, Samuel used the traditional prophetic expression "Thus says the Lord" (1 Sam 10:18; 15:2).

Samuel can also be described as a "**covenant** mediator," mainly because of his leadership role in renewing the Deuteronomic covenant at Gilgal (1 Sam 11:14–15). Likewise, he put into effect the "law of the king" stipulated in Deut 17:14–20 by anointing Israel's first king (1 Sam 10:1) after reiterating the warnings of Deuteronomy about the dangers that come with kingship (1 Sam 8:4–18).

Similarly, Samuel was also known as a seer (1 Sam 9:5–21; cf. 1 Chr 9:22, 26:28, 29:29).

Samuel is above all noted as a judge; 1 Sam 7:15–17 declares that he judged Israel for as long as he lived, and 1 Sam 12:11 compares him favorably to **Barak** and **Jephthah**. Rather than being a warrior and deliverer like most of the judges who preceded him, Samuel was a judge who administered justice to Israel.

II. THE LIFE OF SAMUEL

Samuel was the son of **Hannah** and **Elkanah**. Because Hannah was barren she suffered cruel taunting by Elkanah's other wife, Peninnah (1 Sam 1:1–8). Hannah accompanied her husband on a pilgrimage to the sanctuary of Shiloh, where **Eli** was serving as priest. Begging God for a son, Hannah promised that if her request were granted she would give her son "to the Lord all the days of his life" (1 Sam 1:11). God heard her plea and granted her prayer. A child was born, and Hannah called him Samuel. True to her word, she dedicated him to the Lord's service (1 Sam 1:19–2:11).

Eli took the child and prepared him for the priesthood. While at Shiloh, Samuel received from God a prophecy that the house of Eli would be destroyed for its iniquity (1 Sam 3:11–14). He informed Eli of the coming judgment, and Eli was forced to watch events unfold as predicted: Eli's two sons were killed in the battle of Aphek by the Philistines, and the **ark of the covenant**, which they were carrying before the army, was captured. When Eli heard the news, he fell from his seat and broke his neck (1 Sam 4:1–18).

Samuel eventually emerged as a religious leader of Israel. Each year he made a circuit of the cities "to judge Israel." He also built an altar to the Lord in his home in Ramah (1 Sam 7:15–17). In later years, his sons became judges over Israel. But his sons were unworthy of the office, taking bribes and perverting justice (1 Sam 8:3). The people rejected Samuel's wishes and demanded instead that a king be appointed over them (1 Sam 8:1–22). At the Lord's direction, Samuel anointed **Saul** the first king of Israel (1 Sam 10:1).

During the reign of Saul, Samuel continued to exercise priestly and prophetic functions, frequently speaking in God's name, in particular chastising Saul for his failings as king in keeping the commandments of the

Lord. Samuel passed the Lord's judgment on Saul and, at divine command, anointed **David** as Saul's successor (1 Sam 16:1–13). Samuel's death was mourned by all the people of Israel (1 Sam 25:1).

SAMUEL, BOOKS OF Two of the Historical Books of the Old Testament. They originally comprised a single work that focused on three key figures associated with the foundation of the Israelite monarchy: **Samuel**, **Saul**, and **David**.

The two books formed one work in Hebrew, but they were divided into two books by the Greek **Septuagint** around the second century B.C. The Septuagint further linked the two books together with the books of Kings to form 1–4 Kingdoms, and the **Vulgate** adopted that numbering to create 1–4 Kings. The Hebrew Bible placed Samuel third in the Former Prophets, after Joshua and Judges. Many scholars see the books from Joshua to 2 Kings as forming the so-called Deuteronomic History, a connected account that tells how Israel's covenant with God in **Deuteronomy** was fulfilled by God and then broken by Israel's unfaithfulness, finally leading to the **Exile**.

I. AUTHORSHIP AND DATE

Jewish tradition holds that Samuel himself was the author. Clearly, the two books display prophetic concerns, but his authorship is unlikely for at least two reasons. First, the period involved—the times of Samuel, Saul, and David—would preclude Samuel as the author of the entire work: he died before David came to the throne (1 Sam 25:1). And second, the use of the phrase "to this day" (cf. 1 Sam 27:6) would suggest that the composition or editing took place even later than the end of David's reign.

Doubtless a number of sources and documents were used in the composition of the books as we have them today. Some critics have tried to isolate the individual sources or traditions, such as histories of the ark of the covenant, the Israelite monarchy, and the Court of David. Whatever the sources were, the final editor assembled them with a definite purpose. In the judgment of most scholars, the final forms of 1 and 2 Samuel can be dated to the sixth century B.C., at the time of the Babylonian **Exile**.

II. CONTENTS

1 SAMUEL

I. *Samuel (1:1–7:14)*

   A. *Samuel and Eli (1:1–3:21)*

   B. *The Struggle with the Philistines (4:1–7:14)*

II. *Samuel and Saul (7:15–15:35)*

   A. *Saul Becomes King (7:15–12:25)*

   B. *The Struggle with the Philistines (13:1–14:52)*

   C. *The Defeat of Amalek (15:1–35)*

III. *Saul and David (16:1–31:13)*

   A. *David and the Court (16:1–17:58)*

   B. *David and Jonathan (18:1–20:42)*

   C. *The Fugitive Period of David (21:1–26:25)*

   D. *David and the Philistines (27:1–31:13)*

2 SAMUEL

I. *David's Early Reign (2:1–5:25)*

   A. *War against Ish-bosheth (2:1–4:12)*

   B. *David's Victories over the Philistines (5:1–25)*

III. PURPOSE AND THEMES

The books of Samuel describe the transition from Israel's life as a *nation* of twelve tribes to its life as a *kingdom* that rules over other nations. This was made possible by the founding of the monarchy, from its precarious start with King Saul to its stabilization under King David. The pros and cons of adopting this form of government, which made Israel just one more nation-state on the regional stage of Near Eastern politics, make up much of the drama of these two books.

At a theological level, the founding of the monarchy was a step backward for Israel: the people became inclined to put their trust in political and military institutions that were no different from those of the secular nations surrounding Israel. Samuel, for one, was disturbed by this development, for he recognized it as an implicit rejection of God's kingship over the people (1 Sam 8:4–18). Nevertheless, the Lord permitted the establishment of kingship and would use it to achieve a greater good. The step forward came with Nathan's oracle in 2 Sam 7:8–17, which formed the basis of the Davidic **covenant**. Through the prophet, God committed himself to establishing the royal line of David for all time and to raising up David's heir to build God a **Temple**. God would not allow Israel's secular ambitions to extinguish its spiritual vocation. The people could have a king, but the king must see himself as a spiritual leader who would put the Lord at the center of his kingdom.

David, unlike Saul, showed himself the model king by doing precisely this. As soon as he conquered Jerusalem, making the city his political capital (2 Sam 5:6–10), he immediately made it the spiritual capital as well by moving the **ark of the covenant** there in a grand liturgical procession (2 Sam 6:1–23). It was David's heart for the Lord that explained his extraordinary success in uniting the tribes (2 Sam 5:1–5) and extending his sovereignty over neighboring states (2 Sam 8:1–14). It was only when David succumbed to temptation (2 Sam 11:5) that he began to experience the bitterness of disunity and political revolt (2 Sam 13–20).

SANBALLAT (Akkadian, "Sin [the moon-god] gives life") Called the Horonite, Sanballat was a leading opponent of **Nehemiah** and his plan to rebuild the walls of Jerusalem (Neh 2:10–19) after the return from exile. According to the Elephantine Papyri, Sanballat was "governor of Samaria." He first mocked Nehemiah

(Neh 4:1) and then entered into a conspiracy with the Arabs, Ammonites, and Ashdodites to halt the rebuilding of Jerusalem (Neh 4:7–14). When these schemes failed, he and his allies attempted treachery by inviting Nehemiah to a meeting at Caphirim, but Nehemiah perceived the trap and declined to attend (Neh 6:1–14). Nehemiah expelled the son-in-law of Sanballat from Jerusalem (Neh 13:28).

SANDAL Standard footwear in the biblical world. The ancient sandal was simply a leather sole fastened to the foot by a leather thong and then tied around the ankle (Gen 14:23). Both the rich and the poor wore sandals, and the lack of sandals was a sign of utter destitution, such as that endured by one captured in war (Isa 20:2–4). To cast one's sandal upon someone was a sign of superiority and domination (Ps 60:8; 108:9).

Sandals were customarily removed when one entered a home. The one exception was at the Passover meal, when the sandals were worn by the diners as a sign that they were dressed for travel (Exod 12:11). Sandals were also removed during times of mourning (Ezek 24:17, 23) and when standing on holy ground (Exod 3:5; Josh 5:15). Servants untied the sandals of their master (Matt 3:11; Mark 1:7; Luke 3:16; John 1:27; Acts 13:25).

SANHEDRIN The Jewish supreme court, which gathered in Jerusalem before and during the New Testament period. The Greek term *synedrion*, which is used for the Sanhedrin in the NT, was also used for assorted lesser tribunals. The Sanhedrin served as the highest authoritative body for the Jews as well as a final court of appeal on religious questions. In the Hellenistic world, the Greek *synedrion* referred to gatherings or meetings of high officials, such as city councils in Athens and other Hellenic cities as well as the Roman senate; it was also applied to assemblies such as trade boards or municipal commissions. Josephus, for example, used the word *synedrion* to refer to the district councils of the province of Judea (*Ant.* 14.91). A similar usage appears in the NT, where the term is used not only for the Sanhedrin as such (Matt 26:59; Mark 14:55; John 11:47), but also for lesser local tribunals (Matt 10:17; Mark 13:9).

The exact origins of the Sanhedrin are uncertain. Jewish tradition traces it to the seventy elders who were appointed to assist Moses (Num 11:16–24), a body that seems to have been reconstituted after the Exile (Ezra 7:25–26; 10:14). Josephus first mentions the council as in existence during the time of the Seleucids under Antiochus the Great (r. 223–187 B.C.; Josephus, *Ant.* 12.142, 148). Clear references to an official governing body appear under the title *gerousia*, meaning "senate," in the books of Judith and Maccabees (Jdt 4:8, 11:14; 1 Macc 12:6; 2 Macc 1:10, 4:44, 11:27).

Under the Romans, the Sanhedrin enjoyed considerable authority, except for a time when **Herod the Great** succeeded in curbing its powers. Throughout the first half of the first century and during the period of the prefects and procurators (A.D. 6–66), the Sanhedrin was the effective governing body of the Jews, with both civil and religious jurisdiction. Its powers were recognized to some extent even by Jews of the Diaspora. At the time of Jesus, however, its jurisdiction was more or less limited to Judea. Still, the council could, apparently, send messengers to Jewish communities—such as the community at Damascus—to demand the apprehension of those judged to be criminals (Acts 9:2; 22:5; 26:12). The Sanhedrin ordered arrests and maintained its own police force (Matt 26:47; Mark 14:43; Acts 4:1, 5:17–18). Judgment was also rendered in criminal cases, except for capital punishment, which demanded the confirmation of the procurator, as in the case of Jesus (John 18:31). Although the Sanhedrin had broad powers, the Romans could curtail its authority at will, and many details of how the Sanhedrin functioned under the Romans remain uncertain.

The Sanhedrin was originally made up mainly of the Sadducees. This changed under Queen Alexandra in the early first century B.C., when Pharisees and scribes were included. By the NT period, the Sanhedrin was made up of seventy-one members—seventy chief priests, elders, and scribes, with the high priest at its head. It is not known how the members were chosen. In terms of party affiliation, both Pharisees and Sadducees sat on the council (Acts 23:6). The high priest served as president (Matt 26:57; Acts 5:17). Thus **Caiaphas** was president at the time of Jesus's arrest and trial; **Ananias** was president at the trial of Paul (Acts 23:2). The council met in a chamber adjacent to or within the Temple complex. On the night Jesus was arrested, the council gathered in the house of the high priest, probably because the gates of the Temple were closed (Matt 26:57; Mark 14:53).

When assembled for a trial, the Sanhe-drin sat in a semicircle with two clerks, one to record the votes for acquittal and the other the votes for condemnation. For capital cases, special rules were followed. The arguments for acquittal were first presented, then those for conviction. Anyone who had spoken for acquittal could not then change his vote, but those who had spoken for condemnation were permitted to change their mind. Two witnesses were necessary for conviction, and an acquittal was announced on the first day while condemnation was held over until the next day. A simple majority was needed for acquittal; conviction required two-thirds. When voting, each member stood, beginning with the youngest. Legally, the benefit of the doubt was supposed to rest with the accused.

SAPH A giant Philistine warrior slain by Sibbecai the Hushathite, one of David's champions (2 Sam 21:18). His name also appears as "Sippai" (1 Chr 20:4).

SAPPHIRA (Greek, "good" or "beautiful") A convert to Christianity in Jerusalem and the wife of **Ananias**. She and her husband sold a field and then decided to withhold some of the money from the community. **Peter** rebuked Ananias for lying to the Church about the money, and Ananias dropped dead. Sapphira—not knowing her husband's actions—repeated the lie and died herself in the same fashion (Acts 5:1–11).

SARAH (Hebrew, "princess") The name of two women in the Old Testament.

1. The wife of **Abraham** and the mother of **Isaac**; she is called Sarai from Gen 11:29 to

Gen 17:15. Her name was changed to reflect the new role that she and her husband were to play in history as recipients of the Abrahamic **covenant**.

Sarah was a half sister of Abraham by the same father but different mothers (Gen 20:12); Abraham could thus claim her as his sister as well as his wife (Gen 12:13; 20:2). She journeyed with him from **Ur of the Chaldeans** through Haran to **Canaan**. She is said to have been beautiful (Gen 12:11), but to Abraham's distress, she bore him no children (Gen 15:2; 16:1). Desperate to give her husband a biological heir, she gave Abraham her handmaid **Hagar**, who gave birth to **Ishmael**. Then, at the age of ninety, Sarai was blessed by God, who changed her name to Sarah; despite her advanced years, she conceived and bore a son, Isaac (Gen 21:1–3). To protect Isaac's birthright, she had Abraham repudiate Hagar and Ishmael (Gen 21:10). She died in Hebron and was buried by Abraham in the cave of Machpelah (Gen 23:1–20).

Sarah is described in Isa 51:2 as an example of God's miraculous blessings: "Look to Abraham your father and to Sarah who bore you; for when he was but one I called him, and I blessed him and made him many." In the New Testament, Sarah's faith is also praised (Heb 11:11), as is her loyal obedience to Abraham (1 Pet 3:6). In Rom 4:19 her barrenness is presented as a test of Abraham's faith; elsewhere Paul mentions the conflict between Sarah and Hagar, which he develops into an allegory of the Old Covenant and the New (Gal 4:21–31).

2. The daughter of Raguel and eventually the wife of **Tobias** in the book of Tobit. Initially she appears as the bereaved widow of seven husbands, all killed by the demon **Asmodeus** on their wedding night (Tob 3:7–9). But once Tobias arrives, the angel Raphael helps to arrange their marriage and instructs the young man on how to exorcise the demon (Tob 6:9–17). Sarah bore Tobias several sons in Nineveh (Tob 14:3, 12).

SARDIS A city in western Asia Minor that served as the capital of the ancient kingdom of Lydia. The city was northeast of Ephesus on the Hermus River. Conquered by the Persians under Cyrus II in 546 B.C., it passed to the Macedonians under Alexander the Great in 334 B.C., and then to the Romans in 189 B.C. Sardis became a leading center in the Jewish Diaspora; it was also one of the seven churches of Revelation (1:11; 3:1–6).

SAREPTA *See* **Zarephath**.

SARGON (Assyrian, "legitimate king") Sargon II, ruler of Assyria from around 722 to 705 B.C. The son of **Tiglath-pileser III** and the brother of **Shalmaneser V**, he succeeded the latter and is known chiefly through inscriptions in Khorsabad, Nineveh, and Nimrud. Although only mentioned by name once in the Old Testament, in Isa 20:1, Sargon nevertheless played a significant role in the history of Palestine through his depopulation and repopulation of **Samaria**. Shalmaneser besieged the city for three years (2 Kgs 17:5–6). Sargon, who followed him, dealt with the inhabitants in typical Assyrian fashion: he deported over 27,000 Israelites "and placed them in Halah, and on the Habor, the river of Gozan, and in the cities of the Medes" (2 Kgs 17:6). In their place he resettled people from Mesopotamia, "from Babylon, Cuthah, Avva, Hamath, and Sepharvaim" (2 Kgs 17:24). Sargon returned to Palestine to suppress a rebellion of Ashdod and the Philistines in 711 B.C., an uprising in which **Hezekiah** was dissuaded from participating by Isaiah (Isa 20:1).

SARSEKIM A Babylonian official who participated in the siege and conquest of Jerusalem in 586 B.C. (Jer 39:3).

SATAN (Hebrew, "adversary") The chief of the fallen angels, also called the devil. Sin entered the world through his temptation of **Adam** and **Eve** (Wis 2:24), and he always seeks to bring men to sin (Gen 3:1; 2 Chr 18:21; Job 1:11; Zech 3:1; Matt 8:28; Luke 8:12; Eph 6:11; Rev 2:10, 12:9).

I. IN THE OLD TESTAMENT

The Hebrew *śāṭān* is first of all a legal term for an "accuser" or "adversary." In the Old Testament, the adversary might be of a terrestrial origin or a heavenly or celestial one. Thus David was a "satan" to the Philistines (1 Sam 29:4); Abishai, an advisor of David, was called a "satan" (2 Sam 19:22) for his harsh judgment of Shimei, the Benjaminite who cursed David during the king's flight from Jerusalem during Absalom's uprising (2 Sam 16:5–14); and enemies of Solomon, such as Hadad the Edomite (1 Kgs 11:14) and Rezon of Syria (1 Kgs 11:23, 25), were "satans." These were political enemies sent by the Lord to bring punishment to Solomon for his sins. Finally, in Ps 109:6, the "satan" is an accuser at a courtroom trial.

In Num 22:22, an angel of the Lord stands in the road preventing Balaam's progress on the road. He is a "satan"—an adversary—to the plots of wicked men.

A more technical sense of "accuser" appears in the prologue to the book of Job. Here Satan is one of the angels who patrols the earth and is permitted to go forth from the heavenly court to turn Job against his God. Satan's tactics are to send Job crushing misfortunes that strike both his family (Job 1:6–22) and his very person (Job 2:1–10). Elsewhere we see this malevolent figure tempting David to conduct a census of Israel's army (1 Chr 21:1) and accusing the high priest Joshua before God (Zech 3:1). It is this notion of a spiritual and diabolical "satan" that is brought into sharp focus in the books of the New Testament.

II. IN THE NEW TESTAMENT

In the NT, Satan is synonymous with "devil" and is described as the archenemy of God and man. He is the evil one (Matt 13:19) and the tempter (1 Cor 7:5) who sought even to tempt Jesus (Matt 4:1–11; Mark 1:12–13; Luke 4:1–13) (CCC 538–40, 566, 2119). He disguises himself as an angel of light to deceive men (2 Cor 11:14), and he poisoned **Judas** against Jesus (Luke 22:3; John 13:2, 27). He filled the heart of Ananias with lies (Acts 5:3) and prowls around like a lion seeking prey (1 Pet 5:8).

Satan is the prince of demons (Matt 12:24–32; Mark 3:22–30; Luke 11:15–23) and the ruler of the world captive to sin (John 12:31, 14:30, 16:11; 2 Cor 4:4; Eph 2:2). He wields the ability to bring human suffering (Luke 13:16; 1 Cor 5:5; 1 Tim 1:20). He tormented Paul (2 Cor 12:7) and prevented him from traveling to Thessalonica (1 Thess 2:18). Disciples are encouraged to resist the devil (1 Pet 5:9; Jas 4:7) and be on guard against his traps and snares (Eph 4:27, 6:11; 1 Tim 3:7; 2 Tim 2:26). Above all, Satan is opposed to the will of God for the salvation of the world. When Peter discouraged Jesus from taking up his Cross, Jesus replied, "Get behind me, Satan" (Matt 16:23) (CCC 394–95, 398, 2851–52).

The NT teaches that Satan has already been defeated and remains only to be destroyed. His defeat is the victory of Christ crucified (John 12:31–32; Heb 2:14; Col 2:13–15), and his final demise will come at the end of history, when he will be cast into eternal fire (Matt 25:41; Rev 20:10). In the meantime, he is ever active in deceiving the world in a desperate attempt to take others down with him (2 Cor 2:11; 2 Thess 2:9–10; Rev 12:9–12) (CCC 421, 550, 1708).

SATRAP The official title given to the governor of a Persian province or satrapy (Ezra 8:36; Esth 8:9, 9:3; Dan 3:2, 6:1). Herodotus links the system of the satrapies first with Darius I, who reigned from 521 to 486 B.C. (*Hist.* 3.89–95). (*See* **Persia**.)

SAUL (Hebrew, "the one asked for") The first king of Israel. Saul was anointed king by **Samuel** (1 Sam 10:1), although ultimately he lost God's favor through disobedience. Saul was the son of Kish and a member of the tribe of Benjamin (1 Sam 10:21). His sons were Jonathan, Ish-bosheth (or Ishbaal), Malchishua, and Abinadab; his daughters were Merab and Michal. His wife was Ahinoam, the daughter of Ahimaaz (1 Sam 14:49–50; 1 Chr 8:33).

Saul was described as "a handsome young man. There was not a man among the people of Israel more handsome than he; from his shoulders upward he was taller than any of the people" (1 Sam 9:2). Saul consulted with Samuel in the hope of finding a lost group of donkeys that belonged to his father, and at the Lord's direction Samuel anointed Saul the first king of Israel in private (1 Sam 10:1) and presented him in a public ceremony (1 Sam 10:17–27).

At first Saul's victories seemed to promise a glorious reign. But when Saul refused to wait for Samuel to make priestly sacrifices and assumed that duty himself, Samuel forecast the demise of Saul's dynasty (1 Sam 13:13–14). But Saul was not yet removed as king. It was when Saul disobeyed the ban against **Agag**, the king of the Amalekites (1 Sam 15), and kept the king and the best livestock alive, that Samuel passed the Lord's judgment on Saul and, at divine command, chose and anointed **David** as Saul's eventual successor.

Saul pursued David for years to kill him, but although David had two opportunities to dispatch Saul, he refused to lay hands on the Lord's anointed (1 Sam 24, 26). In his final battle, Saul and his troops were routed by the Philistines at Mount Gilboa (1 Sam 16:14; 31:4–7). Saul's sons Jonathan, Abinadab, and Malchishua were killed, and after being wounded Saul, fearing capture, begged one of his men to take his life. Unwilling to slay an anointed king, the soldier refused; Saul took his own life by falling on his sword (1 Sam 31; 2 Sam 1). His head was cut off by the victorious Philistines and sent as a trophy to their towns, while his body and the bodies of his sons were hung on the walls of Beth-shan. The inhabitants of Jabesh-gilead stole the bodies and burned them, burying their ashes in the surrounding woods (1 Kgs 31).

The reign of Saul was mostly military. He introduced a rudimentary but stable group of professional soldiers into which David was admitted (1 Sam 18:1–9). The extent of his kingdom is unclear; his main support came from Benjamin, the Transjordan, and central Palestine. His royal headquarters was at Gibeah (1 Sam 10:26; 15:34; 22:6; 23:19; 26:1; Isa 10:29). There are no indications that his rule entailed much beyond serving as a general; he placed no emphasis on lawmaking, establishing royal organization, or offering justice. In this sense, Saul took only the first step in establishing the kingdom that David would build into a multinational empire.

Saul was ultimately undone in part by his own personality. Nevertheless, he had shown greatness as a warrior, and David himself composed the tribute to Saul in 2 Sam 1:19–26.

SAUL OF TARSUS The Jewish name of **Paul**, who was born in **Tarsus**. As with King Saul in the Old Testament, he belonged to the tribe of Benjamin (Rom 11:1; Phil 3:5).

SAVIOR *See* **Jesus Christ**.

SCAPEGOAT. *See* **Azazel**; *see also* **Atonement, Day of**.

SCARLET. *See* **Dye**.

SCEPTER A decorated rod or staff that was carried as a symbol of royal power (Ps 2:9, 45:6; Isa 14:5; Ezek 19:11). The same Hebrew term can also refer to the "staff" of a shepherd or herdsman (Gen 38:18; Lev 27:32; Ps 23:4; Mic 7:14). The scepter became a Messianic symbol linked with prophecies about a future ruler of Israel (Gen 49:10; Num 24:17).

SCEVA A "Jewish high priest" in Ephesus (Acts 19:14) who was the father of seven "sons" (perhaps disciples), who were itinerant Jewish exorcists. The sons attempted to use the name of the Lord Jesus to perform an exorcism, declaring to the evil spirit, "I adjure you by the Jesus whom Paul proclaims." The evil spirit, replied, "Jesus I know, and Paul I know; but who are you?" They were set upon by the afflicted person and forced to flee, naked and wounded (Acts 19:13–16).

SCORPION A venomous arachnid with a stinging tail, found in parts of Palestine and Syria. The scorpions in Palestine are poisonous, but the sting is not generally fatal. The scorpion is noted in Deuteronomy as one of the dangers of life in the desert, along with others, such as snakes (Deut 8:15). For obvious reasons, the scorpion was used metaphorically for the injurious words of a sinner (Ezek 2:6) and the painful regret of the man yoked to an evil wife (Sir 26:7). Rehoboam threatened to discipline the northern Israelites with scorpions, which may refer to a particularly stinging sort of whip (1 Kgs 12:11, 14; 2 Chr 10:11, 14).

SCOURGING A severe form of whipping or lashing, used as a means of correction or punishment in the biblical world. The **Law** of Moses allows whippings of up to forty consecutive lashes for persons judged guilty of wrongdoing. By New Testament times, it was customary to limit the maximum number of blows to thirty-nine, lest the administrators of the Law accidentally break the Law by miscounting. The apostle **Paul** experienced scourging several times in Jewish synagogues for preaching his Messianic convictions about Jesus (2 Cor 11:24). In nonlegal contexts, whips could be used to spur on forced laborers (1 Kgs 12:11, 14; 2 Chr 10:11, 14). Metaphorically, a scourge is a painful misfortune, whether national (Isa 28:15) or personal (Job 5:21).

In the NT, Romans carried out scourgings and torture as a regular part of law enforcement. The Roman citizen was not to be subjected to scourging; the punishment was reserved for slaves, prisoners, and those living in the provinces. Brutal treatment was a typical fate for a prisoner, and floggings were used as part of interrogations, as the penalty for various minor offenses, and above all as a preparatory punishment for condemned prisoners, such as those to be crucified. Typically, a prisoner was scourged with a whip, called a flagellum, made of leather thongs with embedded shards of metal, bone, or seashell. Such a flogging was imposed upon Jesus (Matt 27:26; Mark 15:15; John 19:1).

Another type of punishment for witnesses or malefactors was the *verberatio*, a beating that used not *flagella* but *fasces*, rods customarily carried by the escorts for Roman magistrates. Paul was beaten that way at Philippi (Acts 16:22); he received the punishment three times (2 Cor 11:25) despite his Roman citizenship. His citizenship did prevent his receiving a flogging at Jerusalem (Acts 22:24–29).

SCRIBE One who writes, especially in an official capacity. Only a small minority of experts could write in ancient times; the majority of the population was illiterate. Scribal duties included a wide range of services, such as recording the collection of taxes, lists for labor and armies, records of royal decisions and decrees, and records of building projects. Scribes often rose to hold positions of great power and influence as chief ministers.

In ancient Israel, as in other Near Eastern cultures, scribes formed an essential aspect of bureaucracy, public government, and commerce. Scribes served as secretaries to the royal court (2 Chr 24:11), maintained royal records (2 Sam 8:16), and held high positions of influence (1 Kgs 4:3; 2 Kgs 18:18; 22:3; Jer 37:15). One famous scribe was **Baruch**, the scribe to whom **Jeremiah** dictated his prophetic words (Jer 36:32). Senior scribes enjoyed the honor of having their own chambers in the palace or the **Temple**. In military affairs, scribes were appointed to compile the formal lists of armies and the booty that had been captured. The chief scribe in the army was mentioned specifically as a military official (2 Kgs 25:19; Jer 52:25).

After the **Exile**, the monarchy was gone, and with it all the official ministers that went with it, including royal scribes. At this point "scribes" were generally religious legal scholars rather than government officials. **Ezra** is the model of this new type of Jewish scribe, one who was "skilled in the law of Moses"

(Ezra 7:6, 11): he acted as a religious leader of the community and interpreted the Law to the people. These scribes came mostly from the priestly class.

The scribes by the New Testament period were experts in the **Law** (the Torah). In Jesus's era, it seems that most of them were drawn from among the Pharisees and so were quite strict in their interpretation of the Law. They were one of the three components of the Sanhedrin (with the elders and chief priests; cf. Mark 14:43, 53; Luke 22:66; Acts 4:5) and gathered around them students whom they instructed in the Law. Their pupils called them by the respectful title of **rabbi** (Matt 23:2–7) and were expected to pass on their learning without deviation. Scribes lectured in the Temple (Luke 2:46).

The scribes are often presented as enemies of Christ, whom they saw as a threat to their influence—for he taught with authority (Matt 7:28–29). Jesus declared that they sat, like the Pharisees, on the seat of Moses: "practice and observe whatever they tell you, but not what they do; for they preach, but do not practice" (Matt 23:3). Jesus condemned their external formalism, their vanity, and their hardness of heart, "because you shut the kingdom of heaven against men; for you neither enter yourselves, nor allow those who would enter to go in" (Matt 23:13; cf. Luke 20:46). Nevertheless, he expressed admiration for one scribe, telling him he was not far from the Kingdom (Mark 12:28–34).

Jesus ranked the scribes among those who were seeking his death (Matt 16:21, 20:18; Mark 8:31, 10:33; Luke 9:22). They called his forgiveness of sin blasphemy (Matt 9:3; Mark 2:6; Luke 5:21); accused him of being in league with demons (Mark 3:22); and condemned his association with sinners and tax collectors (Mark 2:16; Luke 5:30, 15:2). They tried to seize him (Luke 20:19), were active in the plot to bring about his death, and took part in the trial (Matt 26:57; Mark 14:43, 53; Luke 23:10). They mocked Jesus as he hung on the Cross (Matt 27:41; Mark 15:31). Later, the scribes were enemies of the apostles (Acts 4:5; 6:12).

SCRIPTURE *See* **Canon of the Bible; Bible.**

SCROLL *See* **Book.**

SCROLLS, DEAD SEA *See* **Dead Sea Scrolls.**

SCYTHIANS Nomadic tribes from Central Asia who migrated into northern Persia in the eighth century B.C. They became allies of the Assyrians against the Medes, and later they launched a large incursion through Palestine and reached Egypt, only to be bought off by Psammetichus I. Some of the Scythians settled in Beth-shan, east of Mount Gilboa, giving the city the name of Scythopolis by New Testament times. They were infamous for their savagery, a reputation presupposed in the Bible (2 Macc 4:47; Col 3:11).

SCYTHOPOLIS *See* **Beth-shan.**

SEA *See* **Mediterranean Sea;** *see also* **Dead Sea; Red Sea; Galilee, Sea of.**

SEAL The engraved seal was used extensively in the ancient world to authenticate documents in much the same way that seals are used today for official purposes. The value of the seal or signet is apparent in a world in which writing and reading were not common; it was a personalized symbol of authority and identification (Gen 38:18; 1 Kgs 21:8; Isa 29:11; Rev 5:1). Seals were witnesses to a contract or a covenant (Jer 32:1; Neh 9:38).

Seals were often made from semiprecious stones into which the bearer's name or title was etched, along with pictorial scenes or symbols. The seals were rolled or pressed into wax, or into wet clay that was then baked solid for permanent preservation. Seals and seal impressions found by archaeologists provide a host of names and titles and offer glimpses into government administration in biblical times.

In the New Testament, the "seal" shows God's approval, as an ordinary seal would show the approval of someone in authority (John 6:27), or would serve as a sign of ownership and protection (Rev 7:4). Through baptism, the Christian is incorporated into Christ and sealed with an indelible spiritual mark: "But it is God who establishes us with you in Christ, and has commissioned us; he has put his seal upon us and given us his Spirit in our hearts as a guarantee" (2 Cor 1:21–22; cf. Eph 1:13, 4:30) (CCC 698, 1272–74). (*See* **Spirit, Holy**; *see also* **Baptism**; **Confirmation, sacrament of**.)

SEA MONSTER *See* **Leviathan**.

SEA OF GALILEE *See* **Galilee, Sea of**.

SEA OF GLASS Mentioned in two visions in the book of Revelation. In the first vision, there is a sea of glass, like crystal, before the throne of God and the Lamb (Rev 4:6); in the second, the sea of glass is mingled with fire (Rev 15:2). The background of this imagery is the Old Testament, where the Lord appears in glory enthroned over a translucent pavement of sapphire or crystal (Exod 24:10; Ezek 1:22). In Rev 15:2, the martyrs sing the Song of Moses that was sung by Moses and the Israelites after their deliverance from Pharaoh at the **Red Sea** (Exod 15:1–18).

SEA OF TIBERIAS *See* **Galilee, Sea of**.

SEA PEOPLES *See* **Philistines**.

SECOND COMING *See* **Parousia**.

SECUNDUS A gentile Christian from Thessalonica who accompanied Paul from Macedonia to Jerusalem during his third missionary journey (Acts 20:4).

SEER *See* **Prophet**.

SEGUB The younger son of **Hiel**. Hiel was responsible for rebuilding the fortifications of Jericho (1 Kgs 16:34). He undertook this project "at the cost of" his two sons, Abiram and Segub, meaning that his sons died because he broke Joshua's curse (Josh 6:26).

SEIR The rugged, mountainous region of Edom (Deut 1:2, 44; 2:1; 33:2; Josh 11:17; 12:7; Judg 5:4; 1 Chr 4:42). The name is synonymous with Edom itself (Gen 32:3, 36:8–9; Num 24:18; Ezek 35:15). The mountains of Seir rise south of the Dead Sea and extend as far south as the Gulf of Aqaba. The area was originally occupied by the Horites (Gen 14:6), descendants of Seir the Horite (Gen 36:20–21). Later, the descendants of Edom (that is, **Esau**) established themselves in the same area and overcame the Horites (Deut 2:12; Josh 24:4).

SELA (Hebrew, "rock") A fortress of Edom conquered by **Amaziah**, king of Judah, and renamed Joktheel (2 Kgs 14:7). Scholars have long identified the site with the famous city of Petra, later the capital of the Nabateans. A more precise location is suggested at Umm el-Bayyârah, a rocky promontory nearby; the terrain ideally fits the description given of the Edomites living "in the clefts of the rock" (Jer 49:16; Obad 3). Scholars have suggested that es-Sela, northwest of Buseira, might also be the site.

SELAH A word that occurs over seventy times in the Hebrew Psalms and three times in Habakkuk (Hab 3:3, 9, 13). Scholars surmise that "Selah" is probably a musical or liturgical sign, although its precise meaning is not certain. It may be a kind of direction for musicians and singers to perform a crescendo or begin an instrumental interlude; it may also be a liturgical sign for the lifting up of the voice and hands in prayer.

SELEUCIA A city in northwest Syria named after Seleucid I Nicator, founder of the Seleucid Empire. The city was on the coast near the mouth of the Orontes River and served as a seaport for Antioch. Although it was strongly fortified, it fell to Ptolemy VI Philomotor in 146 B.C. (1 Macc 11:8), but the Syrians soon recaptured it. **Paul** set out from Seleucia with **Barnabas** on his first missionary journey (Acts 13:4). Several cities named Seleucia were also found in Asia Minor, including in Pisidia, Pamphylia, Caria, and Phrygia, as well as Seleucia in Mesopotamia on the banks of the Tigris.

SELEUCIDS The Greek dynasty founded after the death of Alexander the Great in 323 B.C. by one of his generals, Seleucus I Nicator. The Seleucids ruled an empire that encompassed Asia Minor, Syria, and Babylonia, until the Romans seized control in the first century B.C. As one of Alexander's chief commanders, Seleucus I Nicator was a member of the so-called Diadochi ("Successors") who divided up Alexander's mammoth empire at the conference held in 320 B.C. at Triparadisus (Riblah). Seleucus received Babylonia as his territory. War inevitably followed among the squabbling generals, and Seleucus was forced to flee to Ptolemy I when he was attacked by Antigonus. The joint campaign of Seleucus and Ptolemy that defeated Antigonus in 312 B.C. marked the start of the Seleucid Dynasty. Seleucus took the title of king in 305 B.C., and in 301 he won the battle of Ipsus in Asia Minor, by which he extended his empire to encompass Armenia, Cappadocia, and much of Syria. To provide some kind of political, cultural, and military cohesion to an empire that stretched from the Indus to the Mediterranean, Seleucus and his immediate heir, Antiochus I Soter (r. 280–261

B.C.), established numerous Greek colonies that were instrumental in spreading Hellenism throughout the Near East. These centers of Hellenism included Antioch in Syria, Antioch of Pisidia, Apamea, Edessa, Seleucia, Dura-Europus, and Laodicea.

The Seleucids soon entered into an intense rivalry with the Ptolemies of Egypt, and Syria and Palestine were a frequent battleground. Ptolemy II conquered much of Syria and Damascus in 301 B.C., and Seleucus was compelled to recognize Ptolemaic domination in Palestine. In 278 B.C., Ptolemy II attempted to take northern Syria and was defeated by Antiochus I. Wars ensued, but in 198 B.C., Antiochus III the Great (r. 223–187 B.C.) defeated the Egyptians at Paneas and secured control of Palestine. The holdings of the dynasty were soon crumbling, however, and the Seleucids suffered a crushing defeat by the Romans at Magnesia in 190 B.C., after which they gave up claim to Asia Minor west of the Taurus Mountains. The line of Seleucid kings could not long endure and broke apart after the death of Antiochus VII Sidetes in 129 B.C. in the face of rival claimants to the throne. Neighboring rivals, such as Tigranes of Armenia (r. 83–69 B.C.), grabbed portions of the empire until the Romans, under Pompey the Great, ended the Seleucid Dynasty and declared Syria a Roman province.

The Seleucid Dynasty enters the biblical record mainly because of its involvements in Palestine. Seleucus IV Philopator (r. 187–175 B.C.) sent his minister Heliodorus to Jerusalem to plunder the treasury of the Temple (2 Macc 3:7–39; cf. Dan 11:20). Of particular significance was the effort on the part of Antiochus IV Epiphanes to Hellenize the Jews under his dominion (1 Macc 1:20–62; 2:1–48). His harsh policy precipitated the Maccabean War. (*See also* **Maccabees.**)

THE SELEUCID DYNASTY

Seleucus I Nicator (r. 312–281 B.C.)

Antiochus I Soter (r. 281–261 B.C.)

Antiochus II Theos (r. 261–246 B.C.)

Seleucus II Callinicus (r. 246–226 B.C.)

Seleucus III Soter (r. 226–223 B.C.)

Antiochus III the Great (r. 223–187 B.C.)

Seleucus IV Philopator (r. 187–175 B.C.)

Antiochus IV Epiphanes (r. 175–164 B.C.)

Antiochus V Eupator (r. 164–162 B.C.)

Demetrius I Soter (r. 162–150 B.C.)

Alexander Balas (r. 150–145 B.C.)

Demetrius II Nicator (r. 145–139 B.C.)

Antiochus VI Dionysus (r. 145–142 B.C.)

Antiochus VII Sidetes (r. 138–129 B.C.)

SELEUCUS I NICATOR *See* **Seleucids.**

SEMEIN The father of Mattathias and the son of Josech, in Jesus's genealogy (Luke 3:26).

SEMITE A descendant of **Noah**'s firstborn son, **Shem.** A large number of peoples spread across Syria, Palestine, Mesopotamia, and the Arabian Peninsula would be considered Semites according to the biblical data (Gen 10:21–32). Modern use of the term dates back to the eighteenth century, and today it is used mainly by linguists in reference to the Semitic family of languages (Hebrew, Aramaic, Akkadian, Arabic, etc.). Popular speech uses the expression "anti-Semitism" in a highly restricted way to describe both historical and contemporary animosity toward the Jewish people.

SENAAH The head of a family that returned from the Babylonian Exile with **Zerubbabel** (Ezra 2:35; Neh 7:38).

SENIR The Amorite name for Mount Hermon, northeast of the Sea of Galilee (Deut 3:9; cf. Song 4:8; 1 Chr 5:23). According to Ezekiel, Senir was known for its fir trees (Ezek 27:5–6).

SENNACHERIB (Assyrian, "Sin [the moon-god] has increased the brothers") The king of **Assyria** (r. ca. 705–681 B.C.), the successor of **Sargon II**. At the time of his accession, Sennacherib faced a series of serious rebellions among the various subjugated peoples in the Assyrian Empire and was compelled to devote his energies to their suppression. Uprisings in Babylon took place under **Merodach-baladan** and in Syria-Palestine under King **Hezekiah** of Judah (2 Kgs 20:12–19; Isa 39:1–8) with the assistance of Egypt. Sennacherib first put down the uprising in Mesopotamia and then in 701 B.C. marched into Palestine. Forty-six cities of Judah were captured, and Jerusalem itself was placed under siege (2 Kgs 18:13–19:34). The siege was broken by divine intervention: "And that night the angel of the LORD went forth, and slew a hundred and eighty-five thousand in the camp of the Assyrians; and when men arose early in the morning, behold, these were all dead bodies" (2 Kgs 19:35; Isa 37:36–38; 2 Chr 32:20–23). Faced with such mass casualties, Sennacherib broke camp and returned home. The event is sometimes in-terpreted as a sudden plague or epidemic that struck the Assyrian camp.

The reign of Sennacherib was brought to a violent end by his assassination at the hands of his sons, who then entered into conflict for the throne of Assyria. According to 2 Kgs 19:37: "And as he was worshiping in the house of Nisroch his god, Adrammelech and Sharezer, his sons, slew him with the sword, and escaped into the land of Ararat. And Esarhaddon his son reigned in his stead" (cf. Isa 37:38).

SENSES OF SCRIPTURE *See under* **Interpretation of the Bible**.

SEPHARAD A place to which captives from Jerusalem were sent (Obad 20). Its location is uncertain; scholars have suggested Sardis, in Asia Minor, as well as Sefarad, in Media. *Targum Pseudo-Jonathan* located the city in Spain, from which comes the name Sephardim to designate Spanish Jews.

SEPHARVAIM A city that was conquered by the Assyrians and whose people were settled by Sargon II in Samaria (2 Kgs 17:24). They worshipped the gods Adramelech and Anammalech (2 Kgs 17:31). The fall of the city was mentioned in the message from **Sennacherib** of Assyria to **Hezekiah** and the people of Jerusalem in 2 Kgs 18:34 (cf. Isa 36:19) and 2 Kgs 19:13 (cf. Isa 37:13). The location of Sepharvaim is uncertain, beyond the fact that it lay somewhere in Mesopotamia or Syria; scholars have suggested a variety of possible locations.

SEPTUAGINT (Latin *septuaginta*, "seventy") The most ancient and important translation of the Old Testament into Greek. It was produced between the third and first centuries B.C. Biblical scholars refer to the Septuagint as the LXX, which is the Roman numeral for seventy, for the seventy translators who allegedly worked on the text.

I. CONTENTS

The Septuagint is mainly a collection of biblical texts. All the books of the Hebrew Bible are represented (Genesis through Malachi); the deuterocanonical books accepted as biblical by Catholic and Orthodox Christians are represented (Tobit, Judith, Wisdom, Sirach, Baruch, 1 and 2 Maccabees, along with additions to Esther and Daniel); and a few books accepted as canonical only by Eastern Orthodox churches also appear in important ancient codices (1 Esdras, 3 Maccabees; also 4 Maccabees, which is included as an appendix in some Orthodox Bibles).

II. ORIGIN

The origin of the Septuagint is a difficult historical question. Jewish and Christian tradition, relying on a work from the second century B.C. called the *Letter of Aristeas*, held that King Ptolemy II Philadelphus of Egypt requested a copy of the Jewish Bible to be placed in his famous library at Alexandria (ca. 250 B.C.). Unable to read Hebrew, the king brought seventy-two scholars from Palestine to Alexandria to make a translation of the Hebrew Torah on an offshore island called Pharos. After the work was completed, the Alexandrians are said to have accepted it with great enthusiasm. Related traditions retain the basic shape of this story (Josephus), although some add miraculous elements (e.g., Philo says the scholars worked independently of one another, yet all came out with the exact same translation), while others correct matters of detail (e.g., the Babylonian Talmud says the work was done by seventy translators rather than seventy-two).

Many scholars reject the historicity of this tradition, though others accept the core of the story as credible. Alternative theories trace the need for a Greek translation, not to a curious king in Ptolemaic Egypt, but to the Jewish community itself. That is, throughout the Hellenistic and Roman periods, there were countless Jewish settlements in the Greek-speaking Mediterranean, and with the knowledge of classical Hebrew in progressive decline, the need must have been felt for a vernacular edition of the Jewish Bible to be used for preaching and teaching in Diaspora synagogues. This is certainly true, and it was probably a factor in calling forth a translation of the OT into Greek, although it does not discount the ancient tradition as such. By all accounts, uncertainties remain, and scholars are likely to debate the question of origin for some time to come.

III. RECEPTION

Evidence suggests that the Greek Septuagint was warmly received and revered by many Jewish communities of the first centuries B.C. and A.D. Still, it is unclear whether the translation had much appreciable influence in Palestine, and, in any case, we know that some Jews found fault with it. In fact, dissatisfaction with the Septuagint in certain quarters led to new translations of the Hebrew texts by Jewish scholars such as Aquila and Theodotian in the second century A.D. These new efforts probably arose out of tensions between Jews and Christians over the Messianic interpretation of passages as rendered in the Septuagint. Likewise, the text of the Hebrew Bible itself had become standardized about this time, so fresh translations of the OT were needed that more closely represented the biblical texts accepted as authoritative by rabbinic Judaism.

Early Christianity embraced the Septuagint as its OT. No doubt this was a practical decision, since only the churches in Palestine could have made any real use of the Hebrew OT. Beyond this, esteem for the Septuagint in the Jewish Diaspora made it quite natural for the apostles to rely on this translation when expounding the Scriptures out in the mission field. That Christian apostles and preachers used the Septuagint is a matter of record: the clear majority of OT quotations that appear in the New Testament are taken directly from the Septuagint. Far fewer citations represent the NT author's translation of the Hebrew text.

The influence of the Septuagint remained strong in the early Christian centuries. It was routinely cited in the Church Fathers and early Councils. Many patristic theologians even held that the Septuagint had been translated under the influence of the Spirit and had therefore surpassed the Hebrew Bible as the authoritative edition of the OT for Christians (e.g., Saint Augustine, *City of God* 18.43). In any case, only a few ancient scholars such as Origen and Saint Jerome were equipped to handle the Hebrew texts directly. Eastern Orthodox churches maintain both the divine inspiration and canonical authority of the Septuagint to this day.

IV. CONTEMPORARY SIGNIFICANCE

Modern scholarship continues to study and value the Septuagint for a number of reasons.

1. The Septuagint may preserve—in places, at least—a more original form of the OT than what is found in the standard Hebrew Bible (the Masoretic Text or MT). This is so, not only because the Greek translation was done in pre-Christian times, much earlier than the date of most extant Hebrew manuscripts, but also because biblical texts discovered among the Dead Sea Scrolls occasionally agree with the wording of the Septuagint and not with the MT. The Septuagint is thus an important witness in reconstructing the text of the OT, although its usefulness varies from book to book, and scholars continue to debate its precise significance for textual criticism.

2. To the extent that every translation involves some degree of interpretation, the Septuagint provides insight into Jewish understandings of the Bible in the first centuries B.C. At times it reveals the distinctive perspectives of Hellenistic Judaism vis-à-vis Palestinian Judaism.

3. Study of the Septuagint is likewise an integral part of NT scholarship. Its use by the Evangelists and apostles requires investigation in order to understand their interpretive insights and techniques. Just as important, the theological vocabulary of the NT is heavily indebted to the language of the Septuagint. Most notable are instances where Greek terms, known and used since classical times, take on new and different shades of meaning derived from the Hebrew terms they trans-

late. For these and other reasons the Septuagint remains a monument of great historical and theological importance into modern times.

SEPULCHER *See* **Burial**.

SERAIAH (Hebrew, "the Lord has prevailed") The name of several men in the Old Testament.

1. A royal secretary of **David** (2 Sam 8:17). He is also known as Sheva and Shavsha (2 Sam 20:25; 1 Chr 18:16).

2. The head priest in Jerusalem, who was executed in Riblah by the Babylonians in 586 B.C. (2 Kgs 25:18–21; Jer 52:24–27). He was the son of Azariah and the father of Jehozadak (1 Chr 6:14).

3. The son of Neriah, and a high-ranking official at the court of **Zedekiah**. He journeyed to Babylon with Zedekiah in the king's fourth year, to give assurance of Judah's loyalty to **Nebuchadnezzar** (Jer 51:59). Before the journey, **Jeremiah** commanded Seraiah to take with him prophecies of Babylon's doom (Jer 50–51). Seraiah's brother was **Baruch**, the personal secretary of Jeremiah (Jer 32:12).

4. A son of Kenaz and a member of the tribe of Judah (1 Chr 4:13).

5. The son of Asiel, the father of Joshibiah, and a member of the tribe of Simeon (1 Chr 4:34–43).

6. The son of Azriel and an official at the court of **Jehoiakim** (Jer 36:26). He was ordered to arrest the prophet Jeremiah and his secretary, Baruch, following the reading of Jeremiah's scroll.

7. The son of Tanhumeth and a commander of soldiers who joined with **Gedaliah** at Mizpah (Jer 40:8; 2 Kgs 25:23).

SERAPHIM (Hebrew, "fiery ones") A class of heavenly angels mentioned in Isa 6:2–3: "Above him stood the seraphim; each had six wings: with two he covered his face, and with two he covered his feet, and with two he flew. And one called to another and said: 'Holy, holy, holy is the LORD of hosts; the whole earth is full of his glory'" (Isa 6:3). A seraph (singular) also took a live coal from the altar, and with it touched and purified the prophet Isaiah's lips (Isa 6:6–7). Catholic theology traditionally ranks the seraphim just above the cherubim as the highest of nine choirs or orders of angels.

SERGIUS PAULUS *See* **Paulus, Sergius**.

SERMON ON THE MOUNT The traditional name for the discourse of Jesus in Matt 5–7. A parallel discourse appears in Luke 6:20–49, which is often called the Sermon on the Plain because it was delivered on a "level place" (Luke 6:17).

I. SOURCES OF THE SERMON

The name "Sermon on the Mount" was first used by Saint Augustine, who was the first to examine the discourse as a distinct literary unit (*On the Sermon on the Mount*, ca. 395). Scholars in the twentieth century suggested that Matthew composed the sermon from sayings of Jesus preserved in the hypothetical Q document (*see* **Synoptic problem**). The text in Matthew shares some notable material with the Sermon on the Plain in Luke. Both begin with the Beatitudes (Matt 5:3–12; Luke 6:20–26) and end with the Parable of the Two Houses (Matt 7:24–27; Luke 6:46–49). Whatever the sources—written or oral or both—most critical scholars agree that the Sermon on the Mount preserves authentic teachings of Jesus.

II. OUTLINE

I. *Introduction (Matt 5:1–2)*

II. *The Beatitudes (5:3–12)*

III. *The Salt of the Earth (5:13–16)*

IV. *Jesus as the Fulfiller of the Law (5:17–20)*

V. *The Six Antitheses (5:21–48)*

VI. *True Piety (6:1–18)*

VII. *Wealth, Anxiety, and God (6:19–34)*

VIII. *Judgment and the Golden Rule (7:1–12)*

IX. *The Narrow Gate (7:13–14)*

X. *The Tree and Its Fruits (7:15–20)*

XI. *True and False Disciples (7:21–23)*

XII. *The Parable of the Two Houses (7:24–27)*

XIII. *Conclusion (7:28–29)*

III. CONTENT

The Sermon on the Mount is a manifesto of the Kingdom of Heaven. It is a compendium of the moral code of Christianity. It contains some of the best-known material in the New Testament (e.g., the Beatitudes and the Lord's Prayer). Jesus declares at the beginning of the Sermon on the Mount, "Think not that I have come to abolish the law and the prophets; I have come not to abolish them but to fulfil them" (Matt 5:17). Jesus explains how the New Law fulfills and deepens the directives of the Old Law. He teaches on anger, adultery, marriage and divorce, oaths, retaliation, love for enemies, and almsgiving. He gives us the

Lord's Prayer as the way we should approach the Father (Matt 6:9–13). He lays out the Golden Rule as the summation of the Christian ethic.

The demands of the Sermon on the Mount are challenging ones, but they are key to the authentic life of the Christian. They are delivered with a *divine* and *Messianic* authority that surpasses that of **Moses**, who first delivered the **Law** to Israel at Mount Sinai. As Matthew declares at the end of the sermon, "Now when Jesus had finished saying these things, the crowds were astounded at his teaching, for he taught them as one having authority, and not as their scribes" (Matt 7:28–29). Saint Augustine declared that the Sermon offers "the perfect way of the Christian life . . . This sermon contains . . . all the precepts needed to shape one's life" (*Serm. Dom.* 1.1). As Pope John Paul II wrote, the Sermon on the Mount is the Magna Carta of gospel morality (VS §15), specifically in the way that the Sermon "demonstrates the openness of the commandments and their orientation toward the horizon of the perfection proper to the Beatitudes. These latter are above all promises, from which there also indirectly flow normative indications for the moral life" (VS §17) (CCC 1965–66, 1968, 1454, 1724, 1966, 2153, 2262, 2336, 2608, 2830).

SERPENT Various species of snakes are native to Palestine and the Near East. Venomous serpents, then as now, were greatly feared as a threat to human life (Gen 49:17; Exod 4:2–3). Snakebites could even be seen as signs of God's punishment for sin (Num 21:4–6; Jer 8:17). The movements and tactics of the reptile make it a poignant symbol of shrewdness and deceit (Gen 3:1; Sir 21:2; Matt 10:16; 2 Cor 11:3). In nonliteral texts, the schemes of the wicked are compared to the venom of the serpent's fangs (Deut 32:33; Ps 58:4, 140:3).

More than anything, the serpent is pre-eminently a symbol of evil in the Bible. This association appears at the very beginning, where the devil takes the form of a cunning reptile in the Garden of Eden (Gen 3:1). It re-appears at the very end, where Satan is called the "ancient serpent" (Rev 12:9) and is depicted as a huge red dragon (Rev 12:3). This association between serpent and dragon can be traced back to prophetic and apocalyptic texts of the Old Testament (Isa 27:1; Amos 9:3) and may allude to the seven-headed sea dragon of Canaanite mythology called Lotan (cf. Ps 74:13).

SERVANT OF THE LORD The title given to an important figure appearing in Isa 40–55. The word "servant" appears twenty times in those chapters (once in the plural). Subsections of these chapters where the servant appears prominently are called the "Servant Songs." Scholars usually speak of four Servant Songs.

I. THE CONTENT OF THE SERVANT SONGS

The location and content of the Servant Songs are as follows:

Isaiah 42:1–9: God speaks and states the call of his servant, whom he has prepared and who has received the Spirit. He will bring forth justice to the nations.

Isaiah 49:1–7: The servant speaks and stresses that "the LORD called me from the womb, from the body of my mother he named my name" (Isa 49:1). He will come to feel that he has toiled in vain, but the strength of the Lord will sustain him, and the Lord will use him to proclaim salvation to Israel and the Gentiles alike.

Isaiah 50:4–11: The servant says that he will endure suffering, but he will remain steadfast in his obedience and trust in the Lord.

Isaiah 52:13–53:12: A complex poem. The first part (Isa 52:13–15) expresses almost brutally the full weight of what it will mean to be a Suffering Servant: "his appearance was so marred, beyond human semblance, and his form beyond that of the sons of men" (Isa 52:14). Yet in the midst of his agonies, the Lord declares that his Servant will "prosper" and "be exalted" (Isa 52:13). The second part (Isa 53:1–12) says that "he had no form or comeliness that we should look at him, and no beauty that we should desire him" (Isa 53:2), and expresses his rejection, condemnation, and death despite his innocence. The language in this passage is vivid: "Surely he has borne our griefs and carried our sorrows"; "he was wounded for our transgressions, he was bruised for our iniquities"; "he was oppressed, and he was afflicted." But the Lord is bringing salvation out of this suffering: "Yet it was the will of the LORD to bruise him; he has put him to grief; when he makes himself an offering for sin, he shall see his offspring, he shall prolong his days; the will of the LORD shall prosper in his hand" (Isa 53:10; cf. Dan 11:33–12:10).

II. THE SERVANT'S IDENTITY

The word for "servant" in the Hebrew is *'ebed* ("slave" or "servant"). It was used for a person of trust and honor who was the special servant to the king; this title was then applied to certain persons who held this post in relation to God, who were chosen by God to accomplish a specific task or mission, including **Moses** (Exod 14:31; Num 12:7), **Elijah** (1 Kgs 18:36), **David** (2 Sam 3:18; 1 Kgs 11:34), and several of the prophets (cf. Amos 3:7; Jer 25:4).

Who, exactly, is the servant of the Lord envisioned by Isaiah? At one level, the servant is a representative of Israel (Isa 49:3). However, the two cannot simply be equated as though the servant and the nation were one and the same. Although the servant, like Israel, is "chosen" by God (Isa 49:7), the servant is also given a mission to raise up and restore the tribes of Israel (Isa 49:5–6). Like a prophet, the servant is given a mouth to speak the will of the Lord to his people (Isa 49:2; 50:4, 10). At the same time, the servant is the Lord's envoy to proclaim justice and salvation to all nations (Isa 42:4, 6; 49:6). Not only does the servant speak like a prophet, but he also suffers like a prophet by enduring the insults and injuries inflicted by those who despise him (Isa 50:6; 53:3, 7). Yet he suffers innocently (Isa 50:5; 53:9) and indeed vicariously for the sins of others (Isa 53:4–6, 12). And he does so willingly, for Isaiah says that the servant "makes himself an offering for sin" (Isa 53:10). We thus have a picture of a righteous man and prophet who represents Israel and yet works for the salvation of Israel and the world by preaching and ultimately surrendering his life as an expiatory sacrifice for sin.

III. THE SERVANT OF THE LORD IN THE NEW TESTAMENT

The witness of the New Testament is unanimous in identifying the Servant of Isaiah with Jesus Christ. At his baptism in the Jordan we hear echoes of the first Servant Song (cf. Isa 42:1 and Matt 3:17). In his Passion predictions we sense that Jesus understands both his mission and his fate in terms of the Suffering Servant (Matt 16:21, 20:18–19; Mark 10:45, 14:24). Sometimes he, or one of the NT writers, will make the connection explicit: note Isa 53:4 in Matt 8:17; Isa 53:7 in Acts 8:32; and Isa 53:12 in Luke 22:37.

The title of Servant is applied to Jesus throughout the NT (e.g., Acts 3:13, 26; 4:27, 30; Rom 15:21). It is implied elsewhere, such as in 1 Tim 2:6; Heb 9:28; 1 Pet 2:21–25; 1 John 2:2 and 4:10. Jesus himself does not use the title "Servant of the Lord." Instead, he embraces all that is implied in the title and applies it to the "Son of Man" (CCC 440, 539, 601, 615, 713). (*See* **Son of Man.**)

SETH The third son of **Adam**, born after the murder of **Abel** when Adam was 130 years old (Gen 5:3–8). His name (in Hebrew, *šēt*) is a play on Eve's declaration, "God has appointed [*šāt*] for me another child instead of Abel, because Cain killed him" (Gen 4:25). Seth fathered Enosh at the age of 105 and lived to the age of 912. In Seth is established the genealogy that led to **Noah** and so down to Jesus (Luke 3:38; cf. Sir 49:16). A comparison between Gen 4:17–24 and Gen 5:1–32 reveals a stark contrast between the righteous line of Seth and the wicked line of **Cain**. It is through Noah and his family that the Sethite line survives the devastation of the **Flood** while the wicked Cainite line is wiped out completely by the waters of judgment.

CAIN'S LINE	SETH'S LINE
Bigamy (Gen 4:19)	Prayer (Gen 4:26)
Murder (Gen 4:23)	Walking with God (Gen 5:24)
Fratricide (Gen 4:8)	Righteousness (Gen 6:9)

SEVEN, THE *See* **Deacon**.

SEVEN CHURCHES Seven Christian communities in seven cities of Asia Minor: Ephesus, Smyrna, Pergamum, Thyatira, Sardis, Philadelphia, and Laodicea. The churches are addressed in Rev 1:4, 11, 20, and individual letters are sent to them in Rev 2–3. All seven churches were geographically in the region that tradition associates with the mission field of **John**, the apostle and evangelist; William Ramsay in 1904 suggested that these seven in particular were chosen because a courier traveling from Patmos would have reached those seven along the postal highway in the order given in Revelation. The seven golden lamp stands in Rev 1:12 symbolized the seven churches, suggesting that they burned with the fire of the Holy Spirit (cf. Zech 4:2). Nevertheless, the churches are warned: "I will come to you and remove your lamp stand from its place, unless you repent" (Rev 2:5). Not one of those places has a significant Christian community today.

SEVENTY WEEKS, THE *See* **Daniel, book of**.

SEVEN WORDS FROM THE CROSS The Seven Last Statements that Christ made before his death:

1. "Father, forgive them; for they know not what they do" (Luke 23:34).
2. To the penitent thief: "Truly, I say to you, today you will be with me in Paradise" (Luke 23:43).
3. To **Mary** and his apostle **John**: "Woman, behold, your son! . . . Behold, your mother" (John 19:26–27).
4. *"Eli, Eli, lama sabacthani?"* ("My God, my God, why have you forsaken me?") (Matt 27:46; cf. Mark 15:34).
5. "I thirst" (John 19:28).
6. "It is finished" (John 19:30).
7. "Father, into your hands I commend my spirit" (Luke 23:46).

SHAALBIM Also Shaalabbin, a city in the lowlands of western Canaan near Mount Heres. It was allotted to the tribe of Dan in the conquest of Canaan, but Dan failed to conquer it (Josh 19:42). The people of Shaalbim were later subjugated by Ephraimites and became forced laborers (Judg 1:35). The city was later part of Solomon's second administrative district (1 Kgs 4:9). Based on excavations in 1949, the modern Selbit is considered the likely place for Shaalbim.

SHAALIM An area probably in the territory of Ephraim, south of Shiloh. It was crossed by Saul as he looked for his lost donkeys (1 Sam 9:4). Some scholars think that Shaalim may refer to Shaalbim (Judg 1:35; 1 Kgs 4:9) or Shual (1 Sam 13:17). (*See also* **Shalishah**.)

SHAARAIM The name of two towns mentioned in the Old Testament.

1. A town in the western hills of Judah (Josh 15:36); it was mentioned in relation to the flight of the Philistines after **David** killed **Goliath** (1 Sam 17:52). The precise location of Shaaraim has not been identified.

2. A town that was part of the inheritance of Simeon in the **Negeb** (1 Chr 4:31). It is called Sharuhen in Josh 19:6.

SHAASHGAZ A eunuch in the court of the Persian king **Ahasuerus**. He was in charge of one of the two royal harems (Esth 2:14).

SHABBETHAI A Levite who supported **Ezra**'s plan to separate Jewish men from unions with foreign women (Ezra 10:15).

SHADDAI *See* **God**.

SHADRACH The Babylonian name of Hananiah, who, with **Meshach** and **Abednego**, was one of the three young Jewish men who were made administrators when **Daniel** was named governor of the province of Babylon. The Babylonian names were given to the Jewish men by King Nebuchadnezzar's chief eunuch Ashpenaz (Dan 1:7; 2:49). The three refused to worship a golden image set up by Nebuchadnezzar and were hurled into a fiery furnace. For their faithfulness, they were miraculously saved by a messenger of God and subsequently honored by the king (Dan 3:12–30; 1 Macc 2:59).

SHALIM *See* **Shaalim**.

SHALISHAH A region mentioned with Shaalim in conjunction with Saul's search for the lost donkeys (1 Sam 9:4). Its location is uncertain. (*See also* **Shaalim**.)

SHALLUM The name of a number of men in the Old Testament.

1. The son of **Jabesh** and the king of Israel for only a month in 752 B.C. after the assassination of **Zechariah**, the last king of the dynasty of **Jehu** (2 Kgs 15:10, 13–15). Shallum was himself murdered by **Menahem**.

2. The son of Tikvah and the husband of the prophetess **Huldah** (2 Kgs 22:14; 2 Chr 34:22).

3. The fourth son of **Josiah**, and the king of Judah in 609 B.C. His throne name was **Jehoahaz** (2 Kgs 32:31–34).

4. The uncle of the prophet **Jeremiah** (Jer 32:7); his son, **Hanamel**, sold Jeremiah a field at Anathoth.

5. The son of **Zadok** and the father of **Hilkiah** (1 Chr 6:12–13; Ezra 7:2; Bar 1:7).

6. The son of Colhozeh (Neh 3:15). He was responsible as administrator over the Mizpah district for repairing the Fountain Gate and the wall of the pool of Shelah in 445 B.C.

SHALMANESER (Assyrian, "the god Šulmānu is prince") The name of five kings of Assyria. The most important of these in the

Old Testament was the last, Shalmaneser V (r. 727–722 B.C.). The son and successor of **Tiglath-pileser III**, he marched on Samaria when **Hoshea** of Israel made overtures to Egypt in the obvious hope of throwing off the Assyrian yoke. Shalmaneser besieged and eventually sacked Samaria after three years (2 Kgs 17:1–41; 18:1–12). The Israelites were then forced into exile in Assyria, and the Assyrians transferred other peoples to Israel. The siege of Samaria was the principal event of Shalmaneser's reign, although historians sometimes place the final capture of the city in the time of his successor, **Sargon II**. Shalmaneser was also mentioned in the book of Tobit (1:2, 13, 15, 16).

SHALOM *See* **Peace**.

SHAMGAR The son of Anath and one of the minor judges who helped save Israel from Philistine oppression (Judg 3:31; 5:16). Shamgar slew six hundred Philistines with a metal-tipped oxgoad. His tribal affiliation is nowhere mentioned in Judges.

SHAMIR The name of two towns mentioned in the Old Testament.

1. A town in the hill country of Judah (Josh 15:48). The site is probably Khirbet es-Sumara, southwest of Hebron.

2. A town in the hill country of Ephraim, best known as the burial place of Tola, the first of the minor judges (Judg 10:1–2). The location of the town is uncertain, although some identify it with the later site of Samaria.

SHAMMAH The name of several men in the Old Testament.

1. The third son of Reuel and the grandson of **Esau** (Gen 36:13, 17; 1 Chr 1:37).

2. Also called Shimea, the third son of **Jesse** and the older brother of **David** (1 Sam 16:9; 1 Chr 2:13; 20:7).

3. The son of Agee the Hararite, and one of David's famed warriors (2 Sam 23:11).

4. One of David's famed warriors (2 Sam 23:25). He is also known as Shammoth (1 Chr 11:27).

SHAMMUA

1. One of the twelve spies sent by Moses to reconnoiter the land of Canaan (Num 13:4). Shammua was a member of the tribe of Reuben.

2. One of the sons of David who was born in Jerusalem (2 Sam 5:14; 1 Chr 14:4).

3. A Levite who lived in postexilic Jerusalem (Neh 11:17).

SHAPHAM A leader from the tribe of Gad (1 Chr 5:12).

SHAPHAN A royal secretary under **Josiah**, king of Judah (2 Kgs 22:3, 8–10, 12; 2 Chr 34:8, 15–16, 18, 20). He was commanded by Josiah to distribute funds for the repair of the Temple in Jerusalem; while the work was being done, the book of the Law was discovered, and Shaphan brought it to Josiah. Josiah began his reforms based on that discovery. Shaphan was also part of the delegation that consulted **Huldah** the prophetess on the discovery (2 Kgs 22:14; 2 Chr 34:22). Ahikam was named as a son of Shaphan (2 Kgs 22:12; 2 Chr 34:20; cf. Jer 26:24, 39:14). Similarly, Jer 29:3 mentions Elasah, son of Shaphan.

SHAPHAT (Hebrew, "to judge") The name of two men in the Old Testament.

1. The son of Hori and one of the spies sent by **Moses** to reconnoiter the land of **Canaan** (Num 13:5).

2. The father of the prophet **Elisha** (1 Kgs 19:16, 19; 2 Kgs 3:11; 6:31).

SHARAI One of the exiles who returned to Jerusalem and put away his foreign wife (Ezra 10:40).

SHARAR Also Sachar, the father of Ahiam and one of **David**'s famed group of Thirty warriors (2 Sam 23:33; 1 Chr 11:35).

SHAREZER One of the sons of the Assyrian king **Sennacherib** (2 Kgs 19:37; Isa 37:38). Sharezer and his brother Adrammelech assassinated their father. (*See* **Sennacherib**.)

SHARON (Hebrew, from a root meaning "level") The coastal plain of northwest Palestine extending from Mount Carmel in the north to Joppa in the south. It has a maximum width of around twelve miles. Although mentioned only rarely in Scripture, the plain of Sharon was noted as a fertile pastureland (1 Chr 27:29; Isa 65:10), which earned it mention in poetic writings (Isa 33:9; 35:2). Peter preached the gospel there (Acts 9:35). The so-called rose of Sharon (Song 2:1) refers to the flowers that grew in the plain of Sharon; some have suggested that they might be crocuses.

SHARUHEN A city in southern Palestine allotted to the tribe of Simeon (Josh 19:6). The town was mentioned in Egyptian sources as a Hyksos stronghold conquered by Pharaoh Ahmose I (r. 1550–1525 B.C.) after a siege of three years. It was later used by the Egyptians as a base of operations in Palestine, after which it was occupied by the Philistines. The site is the modern Tell el Farah, near Gaza.

SHAUL The seventh king of the Edomites (Gen 36:37; 1 Chr 1:48).

SHAVEH, VALLEY OF A valley near Jerusalem where **Abraham** met with **Melchizedek** and the king of Sodom (Gen 14:17–18) after rescuing Lot from the hands of **Chedorlaomer** and his allies. Also called "the King's Valley," it was the site of the memorial pillar raised by **Absalom** (2 Sam 18:18).

SHAVEH-KIRIATHAIM A location east of the Jordan where **Chedorlaomer** and his allies defeated the Emim, a pre-Moabite tribe (Gen 14:5).

SHAVSHA A royal secretary in the court of King **David** (1 Chr 18:16). His name suggests that he was a foreigner. He had two named sons, Elihoreph and Ahijah, who likewise served as scribes under Solomon (1 Kgs 4:3). His name is also given as Seraiah (2 Sam 8:17), Sheva (2 Sam 20:25), and Shisha (1 Kgs 4:3).

SHAVING See **Razor**; *see also* **Beard**.

SHEALTIEL The son of Jeconiah (**Jehoiachin**), king of Judah (1 Chr 3:17), and the father of **Zerubbabel** (Ezra 3:2, 8; 5:2; Neh 12:1; Hag 1:1, 12, 14; 2:2, 23). He is named in the genealogy of Jesus in Matthew (1:12) and Luke (3:27).

SHEAR-JASHUB (Hebrew *šě'ār yāšûb*, "a remnant will return") One of the sons of Isaiah (Isa 7:3). The name was a symbolic advertisement that God would save a remnant of his people from Assyrian invasion (*see* **Remnant**).

SHEBA The name of two places mentioned in the Old Testament.

1. A city in the territory allotted to Simeon (Josh 19:2). It was located near Beer-sheba in southern Canaan. Scholars have suggested that Sheba may have been part of Beer-sheba.

2. The land from which the Queen of Sheba journeyed to meet Solomon. Scholars generally locate Sheba at the southern tip of the Arabian Peninsula, in modern Yemen. (*See* **Sheba, Queen of**).

SHEBA, QUEEN OF The royal lady from Sheba who traveled to Jerusalem to visit the court of Solomon. She intended to test the wisdom of the king and reached Jerusalem with camels, spices, gold, and gems (1 Kgs 10:1–2; 2 Chr 9:1). She was amazed both at Solomon's wisdom and at the opulence of the court and Temple (1 Kgs 10:4–8; 2 Chr 9:3–7). She praised God for both, and the story shows how the wisdom of Solomon led all nations toward the Lord.

She gave Solomon gold, spices, and precious stones (1 Kgs 10:10; 2 Chr 9:9), while Solomon gave her an even greater amount in return (1 Kgs 10:13; 2 Chr 9:12). She then went back home.

In Matt 12:42 (cf. Luke 11:31), Jesus calls her "Queen of the South" and contrasts her eager acceptance of Solomon's wisdom with the complacency of his fellow Jews who showed little interest in the one who was greater than Solomon. She also figured prominently in Ethiopian legends.

Traders from Sheba were well known in the ancient Near East, and the Old Testament references to trade goods from Sheba include gold (Ps 72:15; Isa 60:6; Ezek 38:13), stones (Ezek 27:22), and incense (Isa 60:6; Jer 6:20).

SHEBANIAH One of the priests who blew trumpets before the **ark of the covenant** as it was carried in procession into David's new capital of Jerusalem (1 Chr 15:24).

SHEBAT The eleventh month of the Hebrew calendar; it corresponded approximately to January–February.

SHEBNAH, SHEBNA A royal official in the court of **Hezekiah** of Judah who held the position of prime minister or royal steward ("over the household"; Isa 22:15), after serving for a time as the royal secretary (2 Kgs 18:18; 19:2; Isa 36:3). He was a member of the delegation that met with the Assyrian representatives of **Sennacherib** during the siege of Jerusalem in 701 B.C. (2 Kgs 18:13–19:7). Isaiah (22:15–25) recounts how Shebnah was removed from his office and replaced by **Eliakim** son of Hilkiah because of some scandal. Isaiah berated Shebnah for building himself an ornate tomb carved out of the rock.

SHEBUEL The name of two men in the Old Testament.

1. A Levitical musician whose brothers were commanded by David to prophesy with musical instruments (1 Chr 25:4; cf. 1 Chr 25:9–31).

2. A Levitical descendant of Gershom and Moses who was given charge of the Temple treasuries (1 Chr 23:16; 26:24).

SHECHEM

1. The son of Hamor. Shechem raped **Jacob**'s daughter **Dinah** (Gen 34:2). After the crime, Shechem fell in love with Dinah and asked to marry her (Gen 34:3). The union was agreed to on the condition that Shechem and the men of the town accept circumcision. They thought that was a small price to pay for a marriage and alliance that would bring them prosperity (Gen 34:22–23). As the men lay recovering from the surgery, however, **Simeon** and **Levi** massacred them and recovered their sister (Gen 34:25–26).

2. A city in central Palestine, at one end of a pass between Mount **Gerizim** and Mount **Ebal**. The site is today identified with Tell Balatah in Nablus. It is the first city in Palestine mentioned in the Bible (Gen 12:6). Abram (later **Abraham**) journeyed to Shechem, to the oak of Moreh, and built there an altar to the Lord, who had appeared to him (Gen 12:7).

Jacob, upon his return from Haran, went to Shechem, pitched his tent before the city (Gen 33:18–19) and purchased a parcel of land from Hamor. Like Abraham, Jacob raised an altar to the Lord (Gen 33:20). The sons of Jacob were known to pasture their flocks near Shechem. After the initial conquest of Canaan, the bones of Joseph were brought there from Egypt (Josh 24:32).

Shechem became an important site of covenant renewal under **Joshua**. Before his death, Joshua gathered the elders of the Israelites at Shechem so that Israel could formally recommit itself to the Lord and the demands of his covenant (Josh 24:1–28). As part of the allotment to the tribes, Shechem was in the territory of Ephraim (1 Chr 7:28) and was a city of refuge and a Levitical city (Josh 20:7, 21:21; 1 Chr 6:67).

The town after the conquest of Canaan was still a place of Canaanite worship, as it hosted the temple of Baal-berith (Judg 9:4). **Abimelech** was the son of a Shechemite woman and managed to convince the citizens of the city to elect him king, whereupon he slaughtered potential rivals except for Jotham, who told the Parable of the Bramble Bush (Judg 9:8–15). When the people of the city finally renounced Abimelech, he destroyed Shechem (Judg 9:45).

After the ten northern tribes rebelled against **Rehoboam**, **Jeroboam** restored the city and made it the capital of the northern kingdom (1 Kgs 12:25). The city's fortunes declined thereafter, although it was later inhabited by the Samaritans (Sir 50:26).

SHEDEUR The father of Elizur, chief of the tribe of Reuben at the time of the **Exodus** (Num 1:5, 20–21; 2:10–11; 7:30, 35; 10:18).

SHEEP *See* **Lamb**.

SHEEP GATE A gate in the northeast wall of Jerusalem. It was repaired under **Nehemiah** (Neh 3:1, 32; 12:39). The pool of Beth-zatha was just inside the gate (John 5:2). (*See also* **Beth-zatha**.)

SHEKEL *See* **Money**; **Weights and measures**.

SHEKINAH *See* **Glory**.

SHELAH The name of two men in the Old Testament.

1. A descendant of Shem and the father of Eber (Gen 10:24; 1 Chr 1:18, 24). Shelah lived to an age of 433 years. The biblical genealogies indicate that he was an ancestor of Abraham (Gen 11:12–15) and ultimately of Jesus (Luke 3:35).

2. The third son of **Judah** (Gen 38:5, 46:12; 1 Chr 1:18, 2:3, 4:21). After the deaths of Er and Onan, he was promised by Judah to **Tamar** (Gen 38:11, 14, 26). He is the father of the Shelanites (Num 26:20), a Judahite clan.

SHELAH, POOL OF A pool near the King's Garden in Jerusalem; Shallum repaired its wall under Nehemiah (Neh 3:15). It is probably the modern Birket el-Hamra.

SHELUMIEL The son of Zurishaddai and the leader of the tribe of Simeon at the time of the **Exodus** (Num 1:6, 2:12, 7:36, 10:19; Jdt 8:1).

SHEM (Hebrew, "name") The eldest son of **Noah** (Gen 5:32, 6:10; 1 Chr 1:4; Sir 49:16; Luke 3:36). He and his brothers survived the **Flood** by joining Noah on the ark with their wives (Gen 7:13–15) and so shared in the Noahic covenant that followed (Gen 9:1–17). With Japheth, he showed respect for their father, Noah, when he became intoxicated and lay naked in his tent. So Noah gave each of them a blessing (Gen 9:20–27). The benediction is

the first time in Scripture that God is identified as the patron of an individual; such a privilege will be granted later to the patriarchs.

Shem had five sons (Elam, Asshur, Arpachshad, Lud, and Aram; Gen 10:22) and is honored as the father of the Semitic peoples. (*See* **Semite**.) He is the lineal ancestor of the Israelites and a descendant of the righteous line of **Seth** (Gen 5:1–32) that stretches from **Adam** to **Jacob** (Israel) through the righteous figures of Seth, Noah, and Shem (Gen 1–11) and then through **Abraham** and **Isaac** to Jacob (Gen 12–50); the genealogy of Luke traces the line of Jesus through Shem (Luke 3:35–36). The **Table of Nations** (Gen 10:1–32) lists a total of seventy nations, twenty-six of which stem from Shem (Gen 10:21–31). (*See also* **Melchizedek**.)

SHEMA

1. A descendant of Judah (1 Chr 2:43–44).

2. A descendant of **Reuben** (1 Chr 5:8).

3. A city in southern Judah, near its border with Edom (Josh 15:21, 26).

SHEMAIAH (Hebrew, "the Lord has heard") The name of two prophets in the Old Testament.

1. A prophet who warned **Rehoboam** not to use strength of arms to reunite the northern and southern tribes after the death of Solomon (1 Kgs 12:22–24; 2 Chr 11:2–4). He also interpreted the raid of Pharaoh **Shishak** against Judah as the price of Rehoboam's infidelity to God (2 Chr 12:5–8). In addition, he wrote a chronicle of the period that was apparently used by the Chronicler (2 Chr 12:15).

2. A false prophet who wrote from Babylon after the **Exile** against **Jeremiah** (Jer

29:24–32). He wrote that Jeremiah should be punished for encouraging those in exile to accept that the period of exile would endure for some time. In reply, Jeremiah declared that Shemaiah and his family would not survive to see the Lord's restoration of Israel from exile. The name "Shemaiah" was also borne by some twenty other minor figures in the OT.

SHEMEBER The king of Zeboiim (Gen 14:2), one of the five cities that rebelled against **Chedorlaomer**.

SHEMER The name of three men in the Old Testament.

1. The owner of the hill that was purchased by **Omri**, king of Israel, on which was built the city of Samaria. His name was used in the naming of the city (1 Kgs 16:24).

2. A Levite of the clan of Merari (1 Chr 6:46).

3. A descendant of **Asher** (1 Chr 7:34).

SHEMIRAMOTH The name of two men in the Old Testament.

1. A Levite and musician who took part in the procession of the **ark of the covenant** to Jerusalem (1 Chr 15:18; 16:5).

2. A Levite commissioned by **Jehoshaphat** to help instruct Judah in the teachings of the **Law** (2 Chr 17:8).

SHENAZZAR *See* **Sheshbazzar**.

SHEOL The Hebrew name for the place of the dead, where they dwelt in utter silence and gloom (Ps 89:48; Prov 5:5, 7:27). Their existence was without "work or thought or knowledge or wisdom" (Eccl 9:10). It was a place where there was neither worship of God nor memory of him (Ps 6:5, 115:17; Isa 38:18). Nevertheless, God's power extended over Sheol (Ps 139:7–8; Prov 15:11; Job 26:6; Wis 16:13) even if his presence was not felt there. There was also the genuine hope that God would not abandon his people (Ps 16:10) and that God would bring redemption for the people who were there (Ps 49:16; cf. 1 Sam 2:6).

In the New Testament, "Sheol" was translated by the Greek word Hadēs, which likewise denotes the underworld of the dead (cf. Phil 2:10; Acts 2:27; Rev 1:18; Eph 4:9). Sheol was a state for both the evil and the righteous while they awaited the Redeemer (Gen 44:31; Ps 9:17; Luke 16:22–26; *see also* **Abraham's bosom**). The lot of those in Sheol, however, was not identical, because on Holy Saturday Jesus descended into Hades to deliver the righteous souls of Old Testament times; he did not deliver the damned (cf. Council of Rome [A.D. 745]; Benedict XI, *Cum dudum* [A.D. 1341]; Clement VI, *Super quibusdum* [A.D. 1351]; Council of Toledo IV [A.D. 625]). (CCC 632–35.) (*See also* **Death**; **Gehenna**.)

SHEPHATIAH The name of several men in the Old Testament.

1. The son of King **David** by Abital; he was born at Hebron (2 Sam 3:4; 1 Chr 3:3).

2. A warrior of Benjamin who joined David at Ziklag (1 Chr 12:5).

3. One of the sons of King **Jehoshaphat** (2 Chr 21:2). After his eldest brother, **Jehoram**, inherited the throne, Jehoram executed Shephatiah and his other brothers (2 Chr 21:3–4).

4. The son of Mattan and an official in the

court of King **Zedekiah** (Jer 38:1). He was an enemy of **Jeremiah**, and during the siege of the city he urged the king to put the prophet to death for encouraging the inhabitants of the city to surrender to **Nebuchadnezzar** and the Babylonians. Zedekiah acted on this advice and had Jeremiah hurled into an empty cistern (Jer 38:2–6). The prophet was rescued through the intervention of **Ebed-melech** (Jer 38:7–13).

SHEPHELAH The lowlands of western Canaan between the coastal plain and the central hill country (Deut 1:7; Josh 10:40, 12:8; Judg 1:9). The Shephelah of Judah bordered the traditional Philistine territory (Josh 15:33). The Shephelah of Israel (Josh 11:1–3, 16) denoted the area of hills between the mountains of Samaria and the coastal plain of Sharon.

SHEPHERD Sheep herding was one of the most common professions in the ancient world. **Abel** was the first shepherd mentioned in Scripture (Gen 4:2). The shepherd led a nomadic existence with few possessions (1 Sam 17:40) and a tent for his dwelling place (Song 1:8). He was assisted by dogs (Job 30:1).

The shepherd was often depicted as the self-sacrificing caretaker of sheep who was dedicated to their well-being, brought back strays, and kept them safe from the many dangers in the world (cf. 1 Sam 17:34–35; Ps 23:2; Amos 3:12; Matt 18:12). Thus the Lord was the Shepherd of Israel in poetic language (Gen 49:24; Ps 80:2). He led his people through the desert like a shepherd leading his flock (Ps 77:20; 78:52). The trust that the Israelite should have in the Lord is epitomized by Psalm 23. He

might also scatter his flock in anger or gather it together once more in forgiveness (Ps 74:1; Isa 40:11). The leaders and kings of Israel are also called shepherds (2 Sam 5:2; Jer 23:1–6).

Unfaithful shepherds will be punished (Jer 10:21; 49:19). The supreme scriptural example of the false shepherd is found in Ezek 34: "Ho, shepherds of Israel who have been feeding yourselves! Should not shepherds feed the sheep? . . . My sheep were scattered, they wandered over all the mountains and on every high hill; my sheep were scattered over all the face of the earth, with none to search or seek for them" (Ezek 34:2, 6). God, the true shepherd, will provide for his flock and will set up over them one shepherd, the Messianic descendant of David, who will feed them: "he shall feed them and be their shepherd" (Ezek 34:23).

Ezekiel 34 anticipates Christ the Good Shepherd, who laid down his life for his sheep. Christ said: "I am the good shepherd; I know my own and my own know me, as the Father knows me and I know the Father; and I lay down my life for the sheep" (John 10:14–15). The Good Shepherd theme is expressed elsewhere in the New Testament (Matt 18:12–14; Mark 6:34; Luke 15:3–7; Heb 13:20). Jesus confided his flock to Peter (John 21:15–17), and Christ's ministers are to be shepherds (Acts 20:28; Eph 4:11; 1 Pet 5:2–4).

SHEPHERD, GOOD *See* **Shepherd**.

SHESHACH A cryptogram or word cipher that is used for Babel (Babylon) in Jer 25:26 (where it is translated "Babylon" in the RSV). The cipher relies upon the rabbinic device called the athbash, in which the word is formed by substituting the last letter of the alphabet for the first. In English, for example, we would substitute *z* for *a*, *y* for *b*, and so forth. Thus the Hebrew consonants *š-š-k* are substituted for *b-b-l* to create a cryptogram for Babylon. The cipher is not meant to obscure the meaning, but was probably a wordplay, since Babylon is named specifically later (Jer 51:41).

SHESHBAZZAR A prince of Judah who was named the first governor of Judah by **Cyrus the Great** after the Babylonian Exile, and who was commissioned to return to Jerusalem the Temple vessels that had been plundered by **Nebuchadnezzar** (Ezra 1:8–11). He was responsible for starting the reconstruction of the Temple (Ezra 5:14–17). Many modern scholars have identified Sheshbazzar with Shenazzar of 1 Chr 3:18, called an uncle of **Zerubbabel**.

SHETH *See* **Seth**.

SHETHAR One of the seven princes of Persia and Media who served as counselors to King Ahasuerus (Esth 1:14).

SHETHAR-BOZENAI Also Sathrabuzanes, a Persian official in the province "Beyond the River" (which included Judea) who became involved in the question of whether the Jews were authorized to rebuild the Temple in Jerusalem (Ezra 5:3, 6; 6:6, 13).

SHEVA *See* **Seraiah**.

SHEWBREAD *See* **Bread of the presence**.

SHIBBOLETH A word most frequently meaning "ear of grain"; the word could also mean "floodwaters" (Ps 69:15). Its pronunciation was used as a test in the struggle between the Ephraimites and Gileadites in Judges (12:1–6). The Gileadites took control of the fords of the Jordan River and asked those trying to cross the river to pronounce the word "shibboleth." The Ephraimites vocalized the initial consonant slightly differently; they said "sibboleth," giving themselves away. As their identity was revealed, the Gileadites seized them and put them to death. The episode shows that there were local differences in the pronunciation of ancient Hebrew.

SHIELD A form of protective armor common in ancient warfare. Shields varied considerably in size, shape, and construction. The typical shield was a round buckler made of leather stretched around a wooden frame and anointed with oil (2 Sam 1:21; Isa 21:5; Ezek 39:9). When Saul died, David declared that his shield had been anointed with blood, not with oil. Later shields became far more sturdy and durable, especially in the time of the Romans. The Israelites used two types of shields: the buckler, *māgēn*, and a larger rectangular shield, the *ṣinnâ*. When carried in large numbers, the large shields could be used to form a strong defensive formation that could resist missile attack from above and on the flanks (Ezek 26:8). Solomon had two hundred large shields and three hundred bucklers made of gold mounted in the house of the forest of Lebanon (1 Kgs

10:16–17; 2 Chr 9:15). Metaphorically, the Lord is a shield who faithfully protects his people (Gen 15:1; Ps 3:3, 5:12, 18:2, 28:7, 33:20, etc.). Paul urged the Ephesians to take "the shield of faith, with which you can quench all the flaming darts of the evil one" (Eph 6:16).

SHIHOR (Hebrew, "waters of Horus") A branch of the Nile River in the eastern Delta of Egypt (Josh 13:3; Isa 23:3). In 1 Chr 13:5, the Shihor is used to denote the southern boundary of the Davidic kingdom.

SHILHI The father of Azubah and the grandfather of **Jehoshaphat**, king of Judah (1 Kgs 22:42).

SHILOAH, WATERS OF See **Siloam**.

SHILOH A city in the mountains of Ephraim, located "north of Bethel, on the east of the highway that goes up from Bethel to Shechem, and south of Lebonah" (Judg 21:19). It is probably the modern Seilūn. Shiloh was a place for sacred assembly among the Israelites in the period before the monarchy. For a time, it was the home of the **Tabernacle** and the **ark of the covenant** after the conquest of Canaan (Josh 18:1; 22:9), and it was here that Joshua made the allotments of land for the tribes (Josh 19:51). Shiloh was still the place of sanctuary in the time of the **Judges** (Judg 18:31). One festival there provided the men of Benjamin with the opportunity to seize wives for themselves (Judg 21:19). Eventually a shrine was established there that was served by priests from the line of Eli (1 Sam 1:3; 1 Kgs 2:27). The ark was eventually taken from Shiloh to Aphek, where it was lost in the crushing defeat of the Israelites by the Philistines (1 Sam 4:11). The shrine at Shiloh was later destroyed or abandoned (Jer 7:12–14, 26:6–9; Ps 78:60). After that, the priest moved the sanctuary from Shiloh to Nob (1 Sam 22:11), but the city of Shiloh was still inhabited (cf. 1 Kgs 14:2; Jer 41:5). Shiloh was also the birthplace of the prophet **Abijah** (1 Kgs 11:29).

SHIMEA The name of two men in the Old Testament.

1. Also Shimeah, the older brother of **David**, and the third son of Jesse (1 Chr 2:13). Called Shammah in 1 Sam 16:9, he was present at the fight between David and **Goliath** (1 Sam 17:13). His son Jonadab later gave advice to Amnon on the seduction of **Tamar** (2 Sam 13:3). His other son Jonathan killed one of the Philistine giants (2 Sam 21:21).

2. A son of David by Bathsheba, born in Jerusalem (1 Chr 3:5). He is also called Shammua (2 Sam 5:14; 1 Chr 14:4).

SHIMEI The son of Gera, a Benjaminite from Bahurim, and a member of **Saul**'s clan. When **David** was forced to flee Jerusalem during the revolt of **Absalom**, he went to Bahurim and encountered Shimei, who hurled stones, dirt, and curses at the king and his officer (2 Sam 16:5–13). Shimei declared that David was at last facing vengeance for the death of Saul and his kinsmen. **Abishai** urged the king to execute Shimei, but David commanded that he be spared. Later, when David returned to the throne, Shimei gave him an utterly abject apology (2 Sam 19:17–20). Once again, Abishai wished to kill Shimei, but David again granted him clemency (2 Sam 19:21–23). On his deathbed, however, David urged **Solomon** to punish Shimei (1 Kgs 2:8–9). Solomon ordered Shimei not to leave Jerusalem; when Shimei disobeyed his order, Solomon had him put to death (1 Kgs 2:36–46).

SHIMRON

1. The fourth son of the patriarch **Issachar** (Gen 46:13; 1 Chr 7:1). He migrated to Egypt during a great famine in Canaan (Gen 46:8–27).

2. Also Shimron-meron, a Canaanite city that joined the coalition of King **Hazor** against the Israelites (Josh 11:1). It was defeated by **Joshua** (Josh 12:20) and listed among the cities allotted to Zebulun (Josh 19:15).

SHIMSHAI A Persian official who opposed the rebuilding of Jerusalem and sent a letter to Artaxerxes I that accused the Jews in Jerusalem of entering into rebellion against the Persian Empire (Ezra 4:8–9, 17, 23).

SHIN The twenty-first letter of the Hebrew alphabet (ש), with the variant phonetic values of *sh* (š) and *s* (ś).

SHINAB (Hebrew, "Sin [the Babylonian moon-god] is the father") The ruler of Admah in the time of Abraham, and one of the five kings defeated by **Chedorlaomer** and his allies (Gen 14:2).

SHINAR The central Mesopotamian plain (Gen 10:10) on which were built the great cities of Babel (Babylon), Accad (Agade), and Erech (Uruk). Genesis 11:2 tells about ancient peoples migrating to the land of Shinar, gathering together, and beginning construction of the Tower of Babel (*see* **Babel, Tower of**). When the king of Shinar, **Amraphel**, joined a coalition against the cities along the Dead Sea, he came into conflict with **Abraham** (Gen 14:1, 9). Shinar, understood as Babylonia, was a place of exile for the Israelites (Isa 11:11; Dan 1:2).

SHIP *See* **Ships and boats**.

SHIPHRAH One of the two Hebrew midwives mentioned in Exod 1:15–20. She was commanded, with Puah, to slay all Israelite boys at the time of their birth. They were to permit the birth of girls. The two refused to obey out of fear of the Lord, and God showed favor to them for their faith (Exod 1:21).

SHIPS AND BOATS Trade and communication along the Nile in Egypt and the rivers of Mesopotamia necessitated raft building and wooden boats; later, oar-powered ships were built for sailing the Red Sea and the Mediterranean.

I. IN THE OLD TESTAMENT

For the most part, the Israelites were not a seafaring people: the Philistines and the Phoenicians were major maritime powers and thus controlled the waters of the eastern Mediterranean during their periods of greatness. The Israelites did have experience with the water, however, as several tribes—Zebulun, Issachar, and Asher—lived near the sea. The lack of experience in water travel is seen in Prov 30:19, with its description of "the way of a ship on the high seas" as too wonderful. Similarly, Ps 107:23–30 describes those who "went down to the sea in ships." The Israelites controlled the major port of Ezion-geber, at the northern tip of the Gulf of Aqaba, only during the reigns of David and Solomon.

Typical ships from the Old Testament period were merchant vessels jointly sailed by Phoenician and Israelite crews (1 Kgs 10:22). The Phoenicians were advanced sailors for their time, and their ships proved durable in the face of the harsh conditions and storms that plagued the Mediterranean. The ship on which **Jonah** sailed was a large one, with a cargo hold (Jonah 1:5). Other vessels were smaller merchant ships intended for cargo delivery to shorter distances. There were also warships (Isa 33:21; Ezek 27:8; Dan 11:30).

II. IN THE NEW TESTAMENT

By the time of the New Testament, the chief naval power in the Mediterranean was **Rome**. There were many sailing vessels of different sizes and purposes sailing the Mediterranean and the Red Sea as part of the vital trade and transport lines of the Roman Empire. The best description of ocean travel in the NT period was provided by Luke in Acts. Paul undertook most of his missionary travels at sea in small and squalid coastal vessels that hugged the coastlines to avoid the storms and strong waves. These ships took few passengers, being mostly cargo boats, and jumped from port to port along the coast. On his journey to Rome, however, Paul sailed in a much larger ship that carried grain from Egypt to Rome. The ship carried a complement of 276 crew and passengers (Acts 27:37).

During winter storm season from mid-November to mid-February, ships were dismasted and kept in harbors (Acts 20:3, 28:11; 1 Cor 16:6; 2 Tim 4:21; Titus 3:12). Not only did storms pose a threat to the craft, but the clouds that accompanied the storms also rendered navigation by the stars and sun impossible. The Mediterranean was still a danger outside of the winter season, and ships often sank in squalls and unexpected storms. Paul's first ship was wrecked at Malta, and the dangers posed by travel are described in detail in Acts 27.

In Palestine, smaller boats and rafts were used chiefly for fishing (Matt 4:21; Mark 1:19; John 21) and communications (Matt 8:23; 9:1; 14:13). Jesus preached from a boat in order for the crowds to hear him fully (Mark 4:1; Luke 5:2). The lakes, too, suffered from storms (Mark 6:48; John 6:19).

SHISHAK Founder of the Twenty-second Dynasty of Egypt (known to Egyptologists as Shoshenq I; r. ca. 945–924 B.C.). He belonged to a Libyan line of chieftains who had settled in Egypt near the end of the New Kingdom period. The reign of Shishak marked a resurgence of Egyptian power and influence, including engagement in the affairs of Palestine. Shishak gave sanctuary to **Jeroboam** (1 Kgs 11:40) and marched against Jerusalem during the reign of **Rehoboam**, looting both the Temple and the royal treasury (1 Kgs 14:25); the action against Jerusalem was interpreted as punishment for Rehoboam's infidelity (2 Chr 12:2–9). His campaign against Judah is confirmed by the presence of a victory stele found at Megiddo as well as inscriptions found at Karnak claiming the capture of 156 cities.

SHITTIM (Hebrew, "the acacias") The location of Israel's last Exodus encampment before taking possession of Canaan. It lay in ancient Moabite territory northeast of the Dead Sea. It was here that the final events of Numbers took place. Here, too, Israel broke faith with the Lord and took part in the idolatrous cult of **Baal** (Num 25:1–9). Shittim is also probably identical to Abel-shittim (Num 33:49) and has been identified with Tell el-Kefrein and Tell el-Hamman. The Shittim mentioned in Joel 3:18 is probably a different place, perhaps the Kidron Valley directly east of Jerusalem.

SHOA A people or tribe in Mesopotamia who are mentioned in Ezek 23:23 in the context of a judgment oracle against Judah; it was predicted that they would take part in an attack on Jerusalem. They may be the Sutu or Su people, who lived east of the Tigris.

SHOBAB A son of **David** by Bathsheba, born in Jerusalem (2 Sam 5:14; 1 Chr 3:5, 14:4).

SHOBACH A Syrian general in command of **Hadadezer**'s forces (2 Sam 10:16–18; 1 Chr 19:16–18; where he is called Shophach) during the time of **David**'s war with the Ammonites. While marching to the aid of the Ammonites, Shobach was routed in the engagement with David at Helam in the **Transjordan** and was killed along with over forty thousand men (2 Sam 10:15–19; 1 Chr 19:16–18).

SHOBAL The name of two men in the Old Testament.

1. The son of Seir, and a Horite chieftain who lived in Edom (Gen 36:20; 1 Chr 1:38). He was the father of Manahath (Gen 36:23; 1 Chr 1:40).

2. A son of Caleb the Judahite and apparently the founder of Kiriath-jearim (1 Chr 2:50).

SHOBI The son of King Nahash of the Ammonites (2 Sam 17:27). His father had enjoyed good relations with **David** (2 Sam 10:2; 1 Chr 19:2); thus Shobi gave assistance to David during the revolt of **Absalom** by sending supplies to David's weary troops (2 Sam 17:27–29).

SHOE *See* **Sandal**.

SHOW BREAD *See* **Bread of the presence**.

SHUA The name of two individuals in the Old Testament.

1. The daughter of Heber of the tribe of Asher (1 Chr 7:32).

2. A Canaanite and the father of **Judah**'s wife (Gen 38:2, 12).

SHUAH A son of **Abraham** by **Keturah** (Gen 25:2; 1 Chr 1:32).

SHUAL A region in the northern territory of Benjamin. It is mentioned in the context of a Philistine raid (1 Sam 13:17).

SHUMATHITES One of the Judahite families that lived in Kiriath-jearim (1 Chr 2:53).

SHUNEM A town in the territory of Issachar, north of Mount Gilboa (Josh 19:18). The Philistines camped at Shunem before the battle with **Saul** at Gilboa (1 Sam 28:4). The town was also the home of **Abishag**, the beautiful maiden who became the caretaker of David in his old age (1 Kgs 1:3–4). **Adonijah** made the fatal mistake of asking for her hand (1 Kgs 2:17, 21–22). **Elisha** visited the town and was shown generous hospitality by a Shunammite woman; he also raised her son from the dead (2 Kgs 4:8–37).

SHUR A wilderness region in the northern Sinai between southern Canaan and Egypt (Gen 16:7, 20:1, 25:18; Exod 15:22; 1 Sam 15:7, 27:8). The name of the region is derived from the Hebrew for "wall" (cf. Gen 49:22; 2 Sam 22:30). Some think "Shur" may refer to a series of Egyptian fortresses that ran across the top of Sinai. **Abraham** lived for a time between Kadesh and Shur (Gen 20:1), and the angel appeared to **Hagar** on the road to Shur (Gen 16:7). The region was also used by various nomadic groups (Gen 25:18; 1 Sam 15:7, 27:8). The Israelites traveled into the western part of Sinai during their **Exodus** journey from Egypt (Exod 15:22).

SIBBECAI Also called Mebunnai. One of David's Thirty elite warriors (1 Chr 11:29), called a Hushite from the village of Hushah (2 Sam 23:27). He killed Saph, one of the "descendants of the giants" (2 Sam 21:18; 1 Chr 20:4).

SIBBOLETH *See* **Shibboleth**.

SIBMAH Also Sebam. A town taken from Sihon, king of the Amorites, and given by **Moses** to the tribe of Reuben (Josh 13:19). It was famous for its grapevines and summer fruit. After it came into the hands of the Moabites, Isaiah prophesied against it (Isa 16:8–13; cf. Jer 48:32–33).

SICKNESS *See* **Medicine**.

SIDDIM, VALLEY OF The site of an ancient battle where five kings from the Dead Sea region were routed by a coalition of four kings from Mesopotamia (Gen 14:3, 8). Its location is somewhere in the valley of the Dead Sea (called the Salt Sea in Genesis); Gen 14:10 notes that the valley was full of bitumen pits.

SIDON A city on the Mediterranean coast of ancient Phoenicia (modern Lebanon). With Tyre to the south, Sidon was one of the major seaports of the Phoenicians and was perhaps the oldest (cf. Strabo, *Geogr.* 16.2.22); it is mentioned in Egyptian documents in the first half of the second millennium B.C.

Sidon was considered the northern extent of Canaanite territory, as well as the northern limit of the tribes of Israel and the kingdom of **David** (Gen 10:19, 49:13; Josh 19:28; 2 Sam 24:6). **Jezebel**, a princess of Sidon, was married to **Ahab** of Israel; she promoted the worship of the **Baal** cult in Israel (1 Kgs 16:31–33). Sidon was mentioned also in a number of judgment oracles against the nations (Isa 23; Jer 25:22, 27:3–6; Ezek 28:20–23).

Jesus journeyed to the region of Sidon and Tyre (Matt 15:21; Mark 7:24, 31) and healed the Syrophoenician woman's child (Mark 7:24–31). Many Sidonians listened to his words (Luke 6:17; 10:13–14). Jesus admired their acceptance of his message when he said, "Woe to you, Chorazin! Woe to you, Bethsaida! For if the deeds of power done in you had been done in Tyre and Sidon, they would have repented long ago in sackcloth and ashes" (Matt 11:21). A delegation from Sidon went to **Herod Agrippa** at Caesarea (Acts 12:20), and **Paul** visited friends in Sidon at the beginning of his journey to Rome (Acts 27:3).

SIEGE *See* **War and warfare**.

SIGN An act, event, or object that points beyond itself to something else, often a greater or unseen reality. Signs can serve to impart a message or key image, to give a reminder or memorial, to give an omen or portent, or to display the loving and powerful work of God.

I. IN THE OLD TESTAMENT

A sign in the Old Testament (Hebrew *'ôt*) could be a mark of protection or identification, such as the mark of Cain (Gen 4:15), the standards for a tribe (Num 2:2), or a military standard (Ps 74:4).

A sign could also be a memorial. Sometimes a sign was a visible or tangible demonstration that a **covenant** was in force. The rainbow, for example, was the sign of the covenant of God with Noah (Gen 9:13–16); circumcision was a sign of the covenant of God with Abraham (Gen 17:11); and the Sabbath was a sign of the covenant of God with the Is-

raelites (Exod 31:13). Past events were memorialized by signs, such as the stones signifying the crossing of the Jordan (Josh 4:6) and the rod of Aaron as a symbol of priestly authority (Num 17:25).

God's miracles were also "signs" of his presence among the people. The signs and wonders of the **Exodus** demonstrated the saving power of God, especially the ten **plagues** that were visited upon Egypt (Exod 4:8–9, 17, 28, 30; 7:3; 10:1; Num 14:11, 22; Deut 4:34; 7:19; 26:8; 29:3; 34:11; Josh 24:17; Neh 9:10; Ps 78:43; 105:27; 135:9; Jer 32:20). God's righteousness—that is, his perfect conformity to the covenant—was also signified in the curses of the covenant that were visited upon the Israelites because of their infidelity (Deut 28:46; Ezek 14:8).

II. IN THE NEW TESTAMENT

As in the OT, a sign in the New Testament (Greek *sēmeion*) is a mark of identification or certification (Matt 26:48; Luke 2:12; Rom 4:11). Signs and wonders attest to God's saving power and affirm the truth of what his ministers preach (Mark 16:17; Acts 2:22, 43; 4:16, 30; 5:12; 6:8; 14:3; 15:12; Rom 15:19; Heb 2:4). The **Pharisees** demanded signs (Matt 12:38, 16:1–4; Mark 8:11; Luke 11:29), a demand criticized by **Paul** (1 Cor 1:22).

The Gospel of John places special stress on "signs," always in reference to the miracles of Jesus. John enumerates seven signs performed by Jesus, culminating in his Resurrection:

1. Changing water into wine at **Cana** (John 2:1–11)
2. Healing the official's son (John 4:46–54)

3. Healing the sick man at **Beth-zatha** (John 5:2–9)
4. Feeding the five thousand (John 6:1–14)
5. Healing the blind man (John 9:1–41)
6. Raising **Lazarus** (John 11:17–44)
7. The **Resurrection** of Jesus (John 2:18–22; 20:1–10)

John declares, "Now Jesus did many other signs in the presence of the disciples, which are not written in this book; but these are written that you may believe that Jesus is the Christ, the Son of God, and that believing you may have life in his name" (John 20:30–31). Authentic faith sees the signs pointing to the true identity of Jesus; inauthentic belief accepts Jesus only as a wonder-worker (John 2:23–3:2; 4:48; 6:2, 14, 30; 7:31; 9:16; 12:18). As John testifies, such signs serve to point to the deeper reality that Jesus Christ is the Son of God (cf. John 2:11; 6:26; 12:37; 20:30), who has wrought our salvation by his death, Resurrection, and Ascension.

In the end times, there will be *true* signs that show God's plan unfolding in history as foretold in the Gospels (Matt 24:30; Luke 21:11; Acts 2:19; Rev 12:1, 3; 15:1). There will also be *false* signs and false Messiahs that lead people away from the Gospel and its promise (Matt 24:24; Mark 13:22). The **Antichrist**, the beast, the demonic spirits, and the false prophets will use false signs (cf. 2 Thess 2:9; Rev 13:13, 16:14, 19:20).

SIHON The Amorite king of Heshbon in **Transjordan**. He established his kingdom by seizing territory from the Moabites, and his territory extended from the Arnon River to the Jabbok and from the Arabian desert to the Jordan. The Israelites requested his permission to pass through his lands on their way into **Canaan**, but Sihon attacked them and was utterly defeated (Num 21:21–32). This victory was the first step toward the Israelites' conquest of Canaan. They took possession of Sihon's territories and distributed them to the tribes of Reuben and Gad, and half of the tribe of Manasseh (Num 32:33; Josh 13:21, 27). The defeat of Sihon was remembered thereafter (Deut 31:4; Josh 2:10, 9:10; Judg 11:19–21; Neh 9:22; Ps 135:11, 136:19; Jer 48:45).

SILAS A Jewish Christian and a leading member of the community in Jerusalem who was blessed with prophetic gifts (Acts 15:22, 32). He is also known as Silvanus (2 Cor 1:19; 1 Thess 1:1; 2 Thess 1:1; 1 Pet 5:12). Silas was sent with Judas by the Jerusalem church to Antioch to give welcome to Gentile Christians (Acts 15:22–35). He then became a companion of **Paul** on his second missionary journey (Acts 15:36–41) after a falling-out took place between Paul and **Barnabas** over John **Mark**. Silas was thus one of the first Christians to proclaim the Gospel in Europe (Acts 16:10). He shared imprisonment and a beating with Paul at Philippi (Acts 16:19–24), and we learn in the telling of this event that Silas, like Paul, was a Roman citizen (Acts 16:37). He also traveled with Paul to Thessalonica (Acts 17:1–9). Silas stayed at Beroea after Paul left (Acts 17:10–15) and later rejoined him at Corinth (Acts 18:5).

SILOAM An aqueduct and pool that was one of the chief water sources for the city of Jerusalem. The Siloam brought water from the

Gihon spring on the southeastern slope of the city along an open canal to the Lower Pool, the pool of Siloam (cf. Isa 22:9). This water-supply system was greatly improved when **Hezekiah**, king of Judah (r. 729–686 B.C.), ordered a tunnel to be constructed that was 1,749 feet (533 meters) long, extending from Gihon to a new reservoir on the western side of the hill of Sion (2 Kgs 20:20; 2 Chr 32:30). The pool that today bears the name Siloam is a later creation, although it is still fed by the tunnel of Hezekiah. In the New Testament, the pool of Siloam was the site where the man born blind regained his sight (John 9:7–11). A tower connected with or near the pool collapsed in the time of Jesus, killing eighteen people (Luke 13:4).

SILVANUS *See* **Silas.**

SILVER A precious metal that was more common and less valuable than gold and was used for currency (Gen 20:16; Matt 25:18, 28:12; Mark 14:11; Luke 22:5). Silver was also used for making trumpets (Num 10:2), plates and bowls (Num 7:13), cups (Gen 44:2), and utensils. Israelites were forbidden to use silver in the making of idols (Exod 20:23; cf. Rev 9:20). Silver was imported by the Phoenicians from Spain, but it was also mined in Armenia, Asia Minor, and Attica. God tested the faithful like silver (Ps 66:10), and his promises are like silver purified seven times over (Ps 12:6). The silversmiths of Ephesus rioted against Christian missionaries out of fear that their profitable trade in miniature silver temples would be threatened by conversions (Acts 19:23–41).

SIMEON The name of three men in the Bible.

1. The second son of **Leah** and **Jacob** (Gen 35:23); the full brother of Reuben, Levi, Judah, Issachar, Zebulun, and **Dinah**; and the founder of the tribe of Simeon. His name in Hebrew is a play on the verb "to hear," as indicated in the words of his mother, "Because the Lord has heard" (Gen 29:33).

Simeon is known chiefly for his act of revenge, with Levi, against **Shechem** for the rape of their sister Dinah (Gen 34:1–31). For this Jacob would curse their anger on his deathbed (Gen 49:5–7), as a result of which Simeon's tribe would be scattered. Simeon also played a part in the account of **Joseph** in Egypt. Simeon was imprisoned as a hostage to ensure that the rest of the brothers would return to Egypt with Benjamin. He was chosen perhaps because he was involved in Joseph's being sold into slavery.

The sons of Simeon were Jemuel, Jamin, Ohad, Jachin, Zohar, and Shaul, son of a Canaanite woman (Gen 46:10; Exod 6:15). The first generation of Simeonites to come out of Egypt was numbered at 59,300 (Num 1:22–23), and the second generation at 22,200 (Num 26:14). The reason for this striking reduction in numbers is probably that the tribe of Simeon played a leading role in the apostasy at Baal-Peor that left 24,000 dead (Num 25:1–9; note especially Num 25:14).

The inheritance given to Simeon in Canaan was basically a pocket of land and cities within the territory of Judah (Josh 19:1–9), and Simeon seems to have been assimilated into Judah over time. Simeon is not mentioned after the **Exile** until Rev 7:7, where the tribe is seventh in the list of the sealed.

2. An ancestor of Jesus (Luke 3:30).

3. A man in Jerusalem who "was righteous and devout, looking for the consolation of Israel" (Luke 2:25–35), meaning he anticipated the Messianic restoration of Israel. He was guided by the Spirit into the Temple and beheld Jesus. He took Jesus in his arms and praised God by proclaiming the **Nunc Dimittis**.

Simon **Peter** is also called Simeon or Symeon (Acts 15:14; 2 Pet 1:1), as is **Simon** son of Mattathias (1 Macc 2:65).

SIMON The name of a large number of men in the Bible.

1. Also Simeon. The second son of **Mattathias**, the brother of **Judas** and **Jonathan**, and a key figure in the Maccabean revolt who established the Hasmonean Dynasty. Also known as Thassi, he was praised as a man "wise in counsel" (1 Macc 2:65) and went to Galilee to organize resistance against the Gentiles (1 Macc 5:17, 20–23, 55). He fought with distinction against the Seleucids (1 Macc 9:65–68; 10:82; 11:65; 12:33–38) and the Nabateans (1 Macc 9:33–42). Simon assumed a major position in the rebellion and eventually succeeded his brother Jonathan after the latter was captured by **Trypho**. Trypho negotiated but did not fulfill his promises and, after murdering Jonathan, withdrew (1 Macc 13:15–19).

By 142 B.C., Simon had effectively secured the political independence of Judea (1 Macc 13:41), "and the people began to write in their documents and contracts, 'In the first year of Simon the great high priest and commander

and leader of the Jews'" (1 Macc 13:42). He added to his prestige and the stability of his leadership by capturing the citadel at Jerusalem (1 Macc 13:49–53) and renewing the alliances crafted by Jonathan with Rome and Sparta (1 Macc 14:16–24). Under the **Seleucid** ruler Antiochus VII Sidetes, a final effort was launched to regain Seleucid control over Judea. Military operations culminated in the attack under Antiochus's general Cendebeus, but Simon's sons Judas and John routed the enemy at Modein in the Judean hills.

Simon's six-year reign ended in 134 B.C. at the hands of his son-in-law Ptolemy, son of Abubus, who had been appointed governor of Jericho. Simon died with his two sons; one son, John, survived the assassination attempt and secured himself politically in time for the inevitable invasion by Antiochus. John thus succeeded his father as high priest, leader (r. 134–104 B.C.), and a key figure in the Hasmonean Dynasty.

2. Simon the Benjaminite, the captain of the Temple under the high priest Onias III (2 Macc 3–4). Owing to his hostility toward the high priest, Simon gave an exaggerated report to the governor Apollonius that led to the raid on the Temple by Heliodorus (2 Macc 3). He went on to make further accusations to the royal court (2 Macc 4). His brother, **Menelaus**, became high priest.

3. The original name of the apostle **Peter** (John 1:42; 21:15–17; Matt 16:17).

4. One of Jesus's closest relatives (Matt 13:55; Mark 6:3).

5. A Pharisee in whose house Jesus was anointed (Luke 7:36, 40, 43–47). He may be

the same person as Simon the Leper (see below).

6. A leper who lived in Bethany and who hosted Jesus. During his visit, Jesus had his feet and head anointed by a woman (Matt 26:6; Mark 14:3).

7. The father of Judas Iscariot (John 6:71; 13:2, 26).

8. A Jew from Cyrene who was forced by the Romans to carry Jesus's cross (Matt 27:32; Mark 15:21; Luke 23:26).

9. A tanner and Christian from Joppa. He lived along the seashore and hosted Peter (Acts 9:43; 10:6, 32).

10. Simon the Zealot, one of the Twelve (Luke 6:15; Acts 1:13). Matthew and Mark call him "the Cananean," but the underlying term is probably a Semitic equivalent of "zealot," referring to Jewish freedom fighters who wanted to liberate Palestine from Roman rule. According to the tradition in the West, he preached in Egypt and Mesopotamia, going to Persia with Saint Jude, where they were both martyred. There are other traditions about him in the East, including one that asserts that he died peacefully in Edessa. His feast day is October 28.

SIMON MACCABEUS *See* **Simon.**

SIMON THE MAGICIAN *See* **Simon Magus.**

SIMON MAGUS A magician of Samaria whose followers proclaimed him to be "that power of God which is called Great" (Acts 8:9–24). He and his followers were eventually baptized by **Philip**, and Simon "continued with Philip. And seeing signs and great miracles performed, he was amazed" (Acts 8:13). Simon, obsessed with power, offered to buy the power of communicating the Holy Spirit from **Peter** and **John** (from which the sin of "simony," buying and selling of Church offices, is named). Their rebuke caused Simon great alarm (Acts 8:19–24).

Simon became the subject of examination by Saint Justin Martyr (*Apol.* 26; *Dial.* 120), who asserted that Simon had come from Gitta, had performed wonders in Rome under Emperor Claudius, and had as his companion a former prostitute named Helen. He enjoyed a wide following in Samaria and Rome. Saint Irenaeus considered him the first major heretic, and indeed the founder of Gnosticism (*Against Heresies* 1.23–27). Hippolytus relates that Simon prophesied that he would rise again three days after his death, but he never did (*Haer.* 6.2, 4–15).

SIMON PETER *See* **Peter.**

SIN Defined by theologians as any thought, word, or deed that transgresses the law of God. In the famous words of Saint Augustine, sin is "something said, done, or desired that is contrary to the eternal law" (*Con. Faust.* 22.27).

I. *Definition*
II. *In the Old Testament*
   A. *Terminology*
   B. *Theology*
III. *In the New Testament*
   A. *Terminology*
   B. *Theology*

I. DEFINITION

Sin is first and foremost an offense against God through a failure to love. It is also an action against reason, truth, and conscience; oftentimes it involves a failure to love one's neighbor as well. In all cases, sin damages personal relationships, whether between man and man, or between man and God. The Old Testament describes sin as a breaking of the covenant that was meant to bind the Lord and his people together in family unity. The New Testament shows how Jesus Christ came to repair the damage of sin and to reconcile the human family with the heavenly Father.

II. IN THE OLD TESTAMENT

A. Terminology

The most common term for "sin" in the OT is *ḥāṭā'*, which means "to miss the mark." It can describe the breach of a contract between peoples or tribes (Judg 11:27), the violation of proper obligations toward a kinsman (Gen 31:36), the disloyalty of a servant to his master (1 Sam 19:4), or the rebellion of a vassal against his covenant overlord (2 Kgs 18:14). Another significant term is *'āwôn*, which refers both to "iniquity" and to the burden of "guilt" that results from it (Gen 15:16; 1 Sam 25:24). Another is *pešaʿ*, which denotes willful "rebellion" against a higher authority (1 Kgs 12:19; 2 Kgs 8:20).

B. Theology

Sin is decried by the prophets as brazen rebellion against God (Isa 1:2; Jer 2:29; Hos 7:13).

It is no mere disagreement between creature and Creator, but constitutes a personal offense against the Lord, who calls man to a personal communion with himself in the bonds of a covenant (Ps 51:4). In fact, sin is basically a failure to love God and neighbor as the covenant demands (Lev 19:18; Deut 6:4–6). The tragedy of sin can thus be compared to an unfaithful wife who betrays her husband and turns her affections to another man (Jer 3:1–14; Hos 1:2, 3:1, 4:1–19). Although the God of the Bible is transcendent and not controlled by human-like emotions, still he is said to grieve and regret the disobedience of his people (Gen 6:6; 1 Sam 15:35; Isa 63:10).

The book of Genesis makes it clear that sin had its beginning at the dawn of creation. Not that sin is part of creation, or that God is responsible for its first appearance, but that sin entered the world when the first human couple turned away from God in the Garden of Eden. Despite being enveloped in grace and established in friendship with the Lord, the first man and woman, Adam and Eve, succumbed to the temptations of the devil (Gen 3:1–6) and breached the original covenant (Gen 2:16–17). This was the "Fall" of the human race, which resulted in man's shame (Gen 3:7), suffering (Gen 3:16–19), and separation from God (Gen 3:23–24).

The effects of the Fall ripple down through history. Its most obvious result is what theologians call "original sin"—the fallen state of human nature, which is inclined toward sin and is deprived of God's grace. This is not a personal fault on the part of Adam and Eve's descendants, but nevertheless it is a wounded condition that is bequeathed to every human person in history. Sin thus spread throughout the world by human generation. Subsequent chapters in Genesis illustrate this well. Already in the earliest generations after Adam we see fratricide (Gen 4:3–8), bigamy (Gen 4:19), revenge (Gen 4:23–24), and uncontrollable violence (Gen 6:11). Not even the Flood, which cleansed the earth of a wicked humanity, could expunge the evil rooted in man's heart (Gen 8:21). Centuries later, the Psalmist would continue to see the propagation of sin in the human condition as such: "Behold, I was brought forth in iniquity, and in sin did my mother conceive me" (Ps 51:5) (CCC 386–409).

III. IN THE NEW TESTAMENT

A. Terminology

Several Greek terms are used in the NT to describe the mystery of sin. The most pervasive verb is *hamartanō*, which means "miss the mark" and is used in a theological sense to denote any act of disobedience against God (Luke 15:18; Rom 3:23). Related to this is the noun *hamartia*, which can refer to a forbidden action (Matt 12:31; Jas 1:15), to an inclination within man that leads to such actions (Rom 7:8, 23), to the guilt that results from such actions (Mark 2:5; 1 Cor 15:17), or to lawlessness in general (1 John 3:4). In imitation of Hebrew, it can also serve as a shorthand expression for a "sin offering" (2 Cor 5:21). Other terms for sin include *paraptōma*, meaning "trespass" (Matt 6:14; Rom 5:16–18), and *parabasis*, meaning "transgression" (Rom 4:15; Gal 3:19).

B. Theology

The central message of the NT is that Jesus Christ "came into the world to save sinners" (1 Tim 1:15). This is the rationale behind his Incarnation as well as his mission of healing, teaching, and offering his life in sacrifice. Even his name, Jesus, is a shortened form of the Hebrew *yĕhôšuaʿ*, meaning "Yahweh saves." His name indicates that he came "to save his people from their sins" (Matt 1:21).

Building on OT revelation, the NT recognizes the universality of sin. Jesus contends that men are generally "evil" (Matt 7:11), and Paul declares that "all have sinned and fallen short of the glory of God" (Rom 3:23), by which he means that both Jews and Gentiles have fallen victim to the power of sin (Rom 3:9). The primary culprit—the one who joined his wife in bringing sin into the world—is the first man, Adam, whose act of disobedience bequeathed a disastrous legacy to all future generations (Rom 5:12–21). Men and women thereafter come into the world as "children of wrath" in need of God's mercy (Eph 2:3).

The causes of personal sin are manifold. On the one hand, Satan remains as dangerous to humanity today as in the days of Adam. He moves about unseen, tempting persons to betray Christ (Luke 22:2–3) and to lie to the Holy Spirit (Acts 5:3). The devil is successfully at work in the unredeemed world, where he dominates the lives of "the sons of disobedience" (Eph 2:2) and makes them slaves to his sinful will (John 8:34, 44). Believers are not immune to this danger, for they too are targets of his attacks and temptations (Eph 6:12; 1 Pet 5:8).

On the other hand, man is still free to resist the devil (Jas 4:7), but he faces a mighty struggle with the flesh—that is, with the fallen inclinations of his nature that ever incline him toward sin and selfishness (Gal 5:16–21). Evil desires do not all come from outside, but often come from deep within the human heart (Matt 15:19); and unless one fights against these enticements, the desire gives birth to sin (Jas 1:14–15). Paul calls this interior corruption "the law of sin" (Rom 7:25) and laments its influence in our lives (Rom 7:7–24). Catholic tradition refers to it as the law of concupiscence.

It is precisely this predicament that Jesus Christ came to remedy. And he is uniquely qualified for the task, since he himself is untouched by sin (2 Cor 5:21; 1 Pet 2:22; 1 John 3:5). The devil made his attempts to turn Christ away from God, but he was unsuccessful (Matt 4:1–11; Luke 4:1–13; Heb. 4:15). On the contrary, Jesus came into the world to destroy the works of the devil (1 John 3:8). He did this by offering himself as the unblemished sacrifice that expiates or takes away the sins of the entire world (John 1:29; Heb 2:17; 1 John 2:1–2). The forgiveness of sins merited by Christ is dispensed to the world through the sacraments of baptism (Acts 2:38), the Eucharist (Matt 26:28), reconciliation (confession) (John 20:23), and the anointing of the sick (Jas 5:14–15).

SIN, WILDERNESS OF A desert region between Elim and Mount **Sinai** through which the Israelites traveled during the Exodus (Exod 16:1, 17:1; Num 33:11–12). The location of the wilderness may be Debbet er-Ramleh, below Jebel Tih, or the coastal plain of el-Markha, depending on where we place Mount Sinai.

SINAI The place where Israel entered into a **covenant** with God after leaving Egypt and where **Moses** received the **Law** from God (Exod 19:1–Num 10:11). Sinai is also called the "mountain of God" (Exod 3:1), the "mount of the Lord" (Num 10:33), and "Horeb" (Exod 33:6; Deut 1:6, 5:2; 1 Kgs 8:9; etc.). Upon Mount Sinai, God made the covenant that offered Israel the choice to be a royal priestly nation in service to the world (Exod 19:5–6). The location of Mount Sinai is uncertain and has been the subject of considerable discussion among scholars.

I. IN THE OLD TESTAMENT

The Israelites reached Mount Sinai three months after their departure from Egypt (Exod 19:1). They established a camp at its base, but were not permitted to go to the top of the mountain (Exod 19:12). The Lord, in a cloud of fire and smoke, summoned Moses to the mountaintop (Exod 19:20) to give him the **Ten Commandments** (Exod 20:1–7; 24:12). During the forty days and forty nights that Moses was on the mountain, the Israelites made a golden-calf idol (Exod 32:2), and when he discovered it Moses broke the two tablets (Exod 32:15–19). The people were spared from God's wrath by Moses (Deut 9:8–29). New stone tablets were then inscribed, and the **ark of the covenant** was constructed to serve as a repository (Deut 10:1–5). Other events included the setting up of the **Tabernacle** (Exod 40:1–33) and the census of the Exodus generation (Num 1:1). When the Israelites left the mountain almost a year later (Num 10:11–12), they carried the ark with them (Num 10:33).

II. IN THE NEW TESTAMENT

In Heb 12:18–29, Mount Sinai is not named directly, but it is clear that it symbolized the Old Covenant and stands in sharp contrast to Mount Zion and the institution of the New Covenant. In Gal 4:21–31, **Paul** allegorically identifies Abraham's concubine Hagar with the covenant on Mount Sinai: "Now Hagar is Mount Sinai in Arabia; she corresponds to the present Jerusalem, for she is in slavery with her children. But the Jerusalem above is free, and she is our mother" (Gal 4:25–26). **Stephen** refers to Mount Sinai and God's appearance to Moses (Acts 7:30, 38).

III. THE LOCATION OF MOUNT SINAI

From the time of Eusebius of Caesarea, Christian tradition has identified Mount Sinai with Jebel Musa in the southern Sinai Peninsula. The same is attested in the fourth-century *Peregrinatio Egeriae* and is still accepted by many modern scholars. Jebel Musa has at its base the monastery of Saint Catherine. The scriptural data are not detailed enough to pinpoint the exact location of Sinai. Deut 1:2 states: "By the way of Mount Seir it takes eleven days to reach Kadesh-barnea from Horeb." This information supports Jebel Musa, but it does not exclude other possible sites. Some scholars favor Ras es-safsafeh, which is near Jebel Musa, since its plain is large enough to support the Israelite camp (CCC 62, 204, 2810).

SINAITICUS, CODEX *See under* **Codex**.

SIN OFFERING *See* **Sacrifice**.

SION, MOUNT *See* **Hermon, Mount**.

SIRACH, BOOK OF Also called the book of Ecclesiasticus (not to be confused with Ecclesiastes) and occasionally the Wisdom of Jesus Son of Sirach or Jesus ben Sira. Sirach is a **deuterocanonical** book of the Old Testament, accepted as Scripture by Catholics and the Orthodox, but not found in the Bibles of Protestants and modern Jews. The title Ecclesiasticus (Latin for "pertaining to the Church") is used in some editions of the **Vulgate** and in the writings of the Latin Fathers; it was adopted because the Church used Sirach extensively for moral instruction. Sirach presents a collection of sayings offering a variety of wisdom exhortations and eulogies of patriarchs and other figures in Israelite history. Its moral maxims apply to individuals, the family and community, relations with God, friendship, education, wealth, the Law, and divine worship. Its theme is that true wisdom is embodied in the Law. Owing to the author's stress on divine law and God's wisdom, the book is counted among the Wisdom Books of the OT.

Originally written in Hebrew, the work was translated into Greek by the author's grandson. The translator added a foreword that contained information about the origins of the book and the reasons behind its translation. The Hebrew copies of the book disappeared early on, but in 1895 fragments of the original Hebrew were found in a synagogue in Cairo, followed in 1931 by the discovery of more frag-ments, and later even more among the **Dead Sea Scrolls**. Approximately two-thirds of the original Hebrew text has now been recon-structed; the Hebrew version that survives dif-fers both in its arrangement and in some of its material from the Greek translation.

I. AUTHORSHIP AND DATE

The book of Sirach opens with a clear attribu-tion of authorship by the author's grandson: "The Wisdom of Yeshua son of Eleazar son of Sira." The Greek title is "The Wisdom of Je-sus son of Sirach." At the end of the book, the name is repeated: "Jesus, son of Sirach, Eleazar of Jerusalem" in the Greek, and "Simeon, son of Jesus, son of Eleazar, son of Sirach" in the Hebrew (Sir 50:27). The author was probably born and grew up in Jerusalem; he wrote his book "after devoting himself especially to the reading of the law and the prophets and the other books of our fathers, and after acquiring considerable proficiency in them" (Prologue).

The book was composed between 200 and 175 B.C. and was translated into Greek around 132 B.C. The translator states that he "came to Egypt in the thirty-eighth year of the reign of Euergetes" (Prologue), suggesting Ptolemy VIII Euergetes II (r. 145–116 B.C.).

II. CONTENTS

III. PURPOSE AND THEMES

The book of Sirach defends and promotes the wisdom of the Jewish Law along with the Jew-ish way of life. The author wrote in the face of increasing Hellenization and considered his work a contribution to the wisdom tradition of Israel. The claim of the translator that his grandfather was learned in the Law and the Prophets is affirmed throughout the text, as the book is filled with quotations from and al-lusions to earlier biblical writings.

Sirach is deeply concerned with moral problems and offers guidance for all aspects of human existence. It is similar to Proverbs in its vast number of admonitions on wealth and poverty, friendship, speech, the treatment of slaves, women and marriage, legal proce-dures, and hospitality. The topics are grouped together into collections of sayings.

The author also uses—like Proverbs, Job, and Ecclesiastes—poems in praise of Wis-dom (Sir 1:1–20; 4:11–19; 14:20–15:8; 51:13–29), and like Proverbs, Sirach begins with a hymn to Lady Wisdom (Prov 1–9; Sir 1:1–20) and ends with an acrostic poem (Prov 31:10–31; Sir 51:13–30). Like Proverbs and Wisdom, Sirach considers the relationship of the wise man to woman in a host of roles: wife, mother, daugh-ter, adulteress, or prostitute (cf. Sir 3:2–6; 7:19, 24–26; 9:1–9; 19:2–4; 22:3–5; 23:22–26; 25:1, 8, 14–25; 26:1–18; 28:15; 33:20; 36:26–31; 40:19, 23;

42:6, 9–14). Sirach 25:24 is notable for being one of the most explicit references in the OT to the Genesis account of Paradise (Gen 2–3).

Always the focus is on the conduct of daily life and the proper management of personal affairs. The author sought to provide the young reader with comprehensive formation in proper duties, the pursuit of virtue against vice, and leading a good life in such areas as self-control, the use of money, the care and education of children, the value of silence, and the selection and proper treatment of a wife.

Death for the author is a fact of life: "The Lord created human beings out of earth, and makes them return to it again. He gave them a fixed number of days, but granted them authority over everything on the earth" (Sir 17:1–2). The passing of men is one aspect in the wider wisdom of God in Creation (16:24–30), and he exhorts his reader to remember that "death will not delay, and the decree of Hades has not been shown to you" (14:12–13). Sirach expresses nothing about the next life, and the author offers only resignation in the face of death (14:18; 40:11; 17:26–27).

SIRAH, CISTERN OF A well to the north of Hebron where the messengers of **Joab** found **Abner**. Joab subsequently murdered Abner (2 Sam 3:26).

SIRION Another name for Mount **Hermon** used by the Sidonians (Deut 3:9; Ps 29:6).

SISERA

1. The commander of the Canaanite king Jabin of Hazor in the time of the Judges. He was from Harosheth-ha-goiim (Judg 4:2); its exact location is unknown, although several sites have been proposed, including Tell el-ʿAmr or Tell el-Harbaj just east of Mount **Carmel**. Sisera has a more prominent place in the account of the war against Israel than does Jabin, and his defeat at the hands of **Deborah** and **Barak** at Mount Tabor near the brook Kishon is described in detail in prose narrative (Judg 4) and poetry (Judg 5). Sisera had a sizable force at his disposal, including nine hundred chariots, but he was still defeated and forced to flee on foot. He went to the tent of **Jael**, the wife of Heber the Kenite, and was welcomed. He fell asleep, and she killed him by driving a peg into his skull with a mallet (Judg 4:17–21; 5:24–27). Jael then invited Barak to come and view his corpse (Judg 4:22).

2. The family name of a group of Temple servants, the sons of Sisera, who returned from the Exile (Ezra 2:53; Neh 7:55).

SITNAH (Hebrew, "enmity" or "hostility") The name of a well dug by **Isaac**'s servants near Gerar (Gen 26:21). The well derived its name from the disagreement over the well that erupted between the shepherds of Isaac and the Philistine ruler **Abimelech**.

666 *See* **Numbers**.

SKULL *See* **Golgotha**.

SLAVERY Slavery—by which one person owns another as property—was an accepted institution in the ancient world. The practice of slavery was nevertheless subject to laws and regulations, and slaves had rights defined by the Law.

1. IN THE OLD TESTAMENT

The Israelites practiced slavery, as did virtually every ancient Near Eastern culture. The institution was subject to legislation, and there was a distinction between foreign slaves and Israelites who lived as slaves for various reasons. Generally, all slaves were viewed as property and could thus be disposed of as their masters saw fit. Although a slave was entirely at the disposal of his or her master, a slave still lived under the protection of the Law to some extent. A master who beat a slave to death was subject to a penalty, but if the slave lived for a few days then no penalty had to be paid (Exod 21:20–21). Mutilation of a slave, such as gouging an eye, breaking teeth, or cutting off an appendage, resulted in the manumission of the slave (Exod 21:26–27).

If a person became a debtor and was unable to pay, he might be made a slave, but only for six years, after which time he was freed (Exod 21:2–4; Deut 15:12; Jer 34:14) or allowed to remain a slave by choice (Exod 21:5–11; Deut 15:13–18). A Hebrew slave who was married at the time of his entry into slavery was permitted to take his wife with him into freedom after a six-year period (Exod 21:3; Lev 25:40–42). If such a slave had been given a wife by his master, the wife and any children remained part of the master's household and only the male slave was freed (Exod 21:4). The slave then had the option of remaining with his family; if he chose that option, the owner brought him to the doorpost and pierced his ear with an awl, after which the slave was owned for life (Exod 21:6; Deut 15:16–17).

When an Israelite sold himself to a fellow Israelite (Lev 25:39–46), freedom was to be granted as soon as the slave's family was able to raise sufficient funds for his manumission (Lev 25:47–55). If such a ransom could not be paid, the Israelite remained committed to his master as a hired laborer until the **Jubilee** year, when he gained freedom, along with his family (Lev 25:53–54).

The laws regarding manumission were not always observed. One famous case occurred during the reign of **Zedekiah**, when a decree was issued granting freedom to the slaves of Hebrew descent. A change of heart soon followed, and the Israelites re-enslaved those who had been set free. For this action, the Lord threatened to abandon Zedekiah into the hands of his enemies (Jer 34:8–22).

The typical slave lived as part of the family of his master and took part in the religious life of the household (Deut 12:12, 18; 16:11, 14). Slaves could even share in the Paschal meal, provided they were circumcised (Exod 12:44). Slaves also rested on the **Sabbath** (Exod 20:10).

Foreign slaves were typically acquired as a result of war (Num 31:26–47; Deut 20:10–14; 21:10–14). Foreign slaves were also purchased from slave traders (Lev 25:44; Ezek 27:13), and the Law permitted them to be kept in permanent servitude and passed on with the rest of family property (Lev 25:44–46). A woman who was taken in war could be accepted as a wife by a Hebrew, but the marriage ended her status as a slave. If she was divorced then she received her freedom and did not once more become a slave (Deut 21:10–14).

The conditions under which a typical slave lived depended almost entirely on the disposition and temperament of the owner. An owner might be loving and generous (cf. Sir 33:25–31; Job 31:13–15), or cruel and harsh. Discipline and punishment could be brutal. Slaves who ran away were considered fugitives and could be dragged back to their owners. In addition, those who assisted them to escape were subject to legal penalties, and treaties among states often included extradition agreements regarding slaves.

II. IN THE NEW TESTAMENT

In the Greek and Roman worlds, slaves were seen as part of the natural order of society. Every household of prominence had large numbers of slaves, as slaves were a sign of wealth and influence. When there were a lot of slaves, there was specialization of tasks and duties by slaves. Less affluent slaveholders might own two or three slaves who worked side by side with their owners in the fields and in maintaining property. The state also used vast numbers of slaves for virtually every type of public works.

Slavery in the Roman Empire expanded rapidly from the second century B.C. when the boundaries of Roman territory were extended across the Mediterranean through war and trade. With new conquests, slaves were brought to Rome and its colonies from the East, and many of these slaves were Jews, Syrians, Greeks, or Egyptians; slaves later came from Gaul, Spain, and the Rhine and Danube regions.

There were two forms of Roman slavery: private and public. Some forms of public slavery were often preferable to private slavery, as the public slaves enjoyed a degree of personal freedom, were rarely sold, and could even own property under certain conditions. Private slaves lived as part of a *familia*, a body of slaves under the hand of one master. Of great value were the *literati*, who were prized as secretaries for the household because of their education and language skills. Other professionals, such as doctors and teachers, were sometimes slaves.

As with slaves in the Old Testament, Roman slaves lived entirely at the behest of their owners. Life could be pleasant or utterly hellish. By various laws, a slave was to be guaranteed fair living conditions and the right to protest harsh treatment.

Manumission of slaves was generally up to the discretion of the owner, and the tendency to free slaves in the late first century B.C. created social problems in the eyes of Roman officials—too many foreign slaves were receiving their freedom and diluting the body of Roman citizens. Laws were passed that restricted manumissions, including the creation of magistrate boards to decide the fitness of a slave for manumission.

The Church was founded at a time when slavery was both accepted by society and essential to the economic survival of the Roman Empire. Although the Gospel principles were at odds with the institution of slavery, the first Christians recognized that a social and political revolution was not their principal objective but the proclamation of true liberation, from sin. The equality of all in Christ was far greater than any social distinction (1 Cor 12:13; Gal 3:28; Col 3:1).

Jesus and the apostles often spoke of slavery in theological terms. Habits of sin were thus a form of slavery to sin (John 8:34; Rom

6:5–7; 2 Pet 2:19), just as yielding oneself to the demands of the Gospel makes one a slave of righteousness (Rom 6:15–19). It is thus a positive notion of slavery of God or Christ that underlies the self-description of several New Testament authors (the term "servant" can also mean "slave" in Rom 1:1; Jas 1:1; 2 Pet 1:1; Jude 1; and Rev 1:1).

Nevertheless, the institution of slavery is also addressed in the NT writings. Paul was direct in urging Christian slaves to remain in their present state of life: "Were you a slave when called? Never mind. But if you can gain your freedom, avail yourself of the opportunity. For he who was called in the Lord as a slave is a freedman of the Lord. Likewise he who was free when called is a slave of Christ" (1 Cor 7:21–22). At the same time, Paul strives to remind slave owner and slave that their relationship has been transformed by their new life in Christ and the demands of their new faith (Eph 6:5–9; Col 3:22–4:1). A particular case in point is that of Onesimus, a slave who had fled the household of **Philemon**. Paul writes to the slave owner and begs him to receive back Onesimus. Paul is aware of the laws of slavery in the Roman Empire, but he reminds Philemon of his greater obligations as a Christian: "So if you consider me your partner, receive him as you would receive me. If he has wronged you at all, or owes you anything, charge that to my account" (Phlm verses 17–18) (CCC 407, 421, 549, 601, 635, 1733, 1741, 2057, 2097, 2414, 2744). (*See* **Sin**.)

SLING A simple weapon that launches a projectile. A pocket of leather or fabric is attached to leather cords; the cords and pocket (with a rock or missile placed in it) are twirled, and then one of the cords is released to launch the object. With training and experience, the slinger can achieve considerable accuracy. **David** killed **Goliath** with a sling (1 Sam 17:40, 49). Shepherds knew how to use the sling to defend their sheep, and the sling was a common weapon for soldiers in the ancient world even into the Roman period (cf. 2 Kgs 3:25; 2 Chr 26:14). Warriors from the tribe of Benjamin were noted for their skill with the sling (Judg 20:18; 1 Chr 12:2).

SMITH A worker in metals. According to Gen 4:22, the father of all metalworkers or smiths was **Tubal-cain**, son of **Lamech**. Before the turn of the second millennium B.C., the Israelites in Canaan did not have a single smith (1 Sam 13:19–22) and so were at a severe disadvantage against the Philistines, who enjoyed a monopoly over working iron and metal. In the time of the monarchy, however, the Israelites acquired the skills of metallurgy (1 Kgs 6:7; 2 Chr 24:12; Isa 41:7). Solomon used a smith from Tyre to work on the bronze in the Temple (1 Kgs 7:14). Smiths were deported by the Babylonians after the fall of Jerusalem (2 Kgs 24:14). The work of the smith was exacting and difficult toil, so much so that in Sirach it is noted that the smith is one of the professions that prevents leisure and so does not promote wisdom (Sir 38:28). Isaiah mocks the smith who makes an idol and then bows down before the work of his own hands (Isa 44:12). (*See* **Gold**; **Silver**.)

SMYRNA A city in Asia Minor, on the Aegean Sea at the mouth of the Melas River; the modern name is Izmir. One of the most ancient places colonized by the Greeks, it was captured and destroyed by the Lydians toward the end of the seventh century B.C. In the early third century B.C., the city was refounded by Lysimachus and became one of the foremost cities in Asia Minor. Under the Roman Empire it was known for its many beautiful buildings and as a center of learning. The Gospel arrived in Smyrna most likely from Ephesus, and the church in Smyrna was the recipient of one of the seven letters in Revelation (1:11; 2:8–11).

SNOW There are few references to snow in Scripture, since snow is scarce in Palestine (cf. 2 Sam 23:20; 1 Macc 13:22). In the central highlands, light snow falls in January and February, although heavier snow will occur every few years. Snow is virtually unknown in the Jordan Valley and along the Mediterranean coast. In contrast, snow is proverbial on the mountains of Lebanon (Jer 18:14).

Snow in Scripture is mentioned most often in theological and metaphorical contexts. It represents God's power and command over nature (Job 37:6, 38:22; Ps 147:16, 148:8). In other cases, it is mentioned in similes that describe something as stark or brilliantly white (Exod 4:6; Num 12:10; 2 Kgs 5:27; Lam 4:7; Dan 7:9; Matt 28:3; Rev 1:14).

SO An abbreviated form of the name Osorkon IV (r. ca. 730–715 B.C.), the Egyptian king of the Twenty-second Dynasty who entered into a conspiracy with King **Hoshea** against the Assyrians (2 Kgs 17:4). The result was a sharp Assyrian retribution against Israel.

SOAP The cleaning agent in the Bible is probably lye, a solution made of potash, soda, and water. It appears rarely in Scripture (Jer 2:22; Mal 3:2).

SOCO, SOCOH The name of three towns in Judah.

1. A town in the western lowlands of Judah, near Jarmuth, Adullam, and Azekah (Josh 15:35). The engagement between the Israelites and the Philistines that resulted in **David**'s victory over **Goliath** occurred in the Valley of Elah between Azekah and Socoh (1 Sam 17:1). The town may have been fortified by **Rehoboam** (2 Chr 11:6; see also below) and was attacked by the Philistines during the reign of **Ahaz** (2 Chr 28:18). The site is identified with Khirbet Abbad.

2. A town in the southern hill country of Judah (Josh 15:48); it may have been the city fortified by Rehoboam, rather than the first Soco (2 Chr 11:7). It is identified with the modern site of Khirbet Shuweikeh southwest of Hebron.

3. A town in Solomon's third royal district (1 Kgs 4:10). It is probably the modern Shuweiket er-Ras.

SODOM AND GOMORRAH Two of the five cities of the plain (with Admah, Zeboiim, and Zoar) in the area of the **Dead Sea** that were destroyed by God's wrath (Gen 10:19; 19:24–25; Deut 29:23; Wis 10:6). When Lot and Abraham separated, Lot chose the Dead Sea valley as his home and pitched his tent near Sodom (Gen 13:10–13). The five cities took part in a campaign against **Chedorlaomer** and his Mesopotamian allies but were soundly defeated and captured (Gen 14:8–11). Taken in the victory were Lot and the kings, including Kings Bera of Sodom and Birsha of Gomorrah. They were all rescued, however, by Abram (later **Abraham**), who set upon the enemy with 318 men of his household and drove them as far as Dan (Gen 14:13–16). The king of Sodom offered Abraham the booty from the war, but he refused (Gen 14:21).

The fate of Sodom and Gomorrah is decided in Gen 18, and their fiery destruction is recounted in Gen 19. Their fate hung on whether any righteous person or family lived within their gates, for the inhabitants of these cities were abominable sinners before the Lord (Gen 18:16–33). Since none but Abram's nephew Lot and his family were undeserving of heaven's wrath, angels were sent to hurry them out of the area before God's justice hammered down in fury (Gen 19:1–24). Once they were out of harm's way, "the LORD rained on Sodom and Gomorrah brimstone and fire from the LORD out of heaven; and he overthrew those cities, and all the valley, and all the inhabitants of the cities, and what grew on the ground" (Gen 19:24–25).

Sodom and Gomorrah were among the proverbial examples in Scripture of wickedness, and their destruction showed forth the just anger and judgment of God destined to come on all sinners (Deut 32:32; Isa 1:9, 10; Jer 20:16; 23:14; 49:18; Amos 4:11; Wis 10:6; Lam 4:6; Zeph 2:9). Sodom and Gomorrah also figured in the New Testament as a prophetic image of divine judgment (cf. Luke 17:29–33; 2 Pet 2:6–10) and as an instantly recognizable example of sin and depravity (Matt 10:15; 11:23–24; Luke 10:12; Rev 11:8). (*See also* **Sin**.)

SOLOMON (Hebrew, "peaceful"). One of four sons born to **David** by **Bathsheba** (1 Chr 3:5), and David's successor as king of all Israel (r. 970–930 B.C.). It was Solomon who made the kingdom of Israel one of the great military and economic superpowers of the ancient world (1 Kgs 5–10), and he himself acquired a legendary reputation as one of the wisest men who ever lived (1 Kgs 3:9–14; 42:29–34). His name in Hebrew (*šĕlōmōh*) is a play on the word for "peace" (*šālôm*). The Chronicler makes this explicit: "for his name shall be Solomon, and I will give peace and quiet to Israel in his days" (1 Chr 22:9).

I. EARLY LIFE AND ACCESSION

Solomon was one of nineteen sons born to David by his royal wives (1 Chr 3:1–9). He was also given the name Jedidiah, "beloved of the Lord" (2 Sam 12:25).

By command of the Lord, Solomon was chosen to be David's successor on the throne (1 Chr 22:6–16). Not long before his death, David assured **Bathsheba** that Solomon would succeed him despite the claims of Solomon's older brother, **Adonijah** (1 Kgs 1:17–18, 30), whom the people expected as David's successor (1 Kgs 2:15). Adonijah had the support of **Joab**, the chief of David's army, and the priest **Abiathar** (1 Kgs 1:7). Solomon was backed by his mother, Bathsheba, the priest **Zadok**, the prophet Nathan, and the head of the royal guard, **Benaiah** (1 Kgs 1:5–31).

The struggle for succession that ensued ended with Solomon's triumph, thanks in large measure to the swift action of his supporters. Solomon was anointed king (1 Kgs 1:38) and given instruction by David as to his royal duties and obligations (1 Kgs 2:1–9). Solomon thus came to the throne while David still lived (1 Kgs 1:32–40). Solomon initially spared Adonijah's life, although after Adonijah continued his scheming, Solomon finally had him executed, along with Joab. Abiathar was also deposed from the priesthood and supplanted by Zadok (1 Kgs 2:27, 35).

II. ROYAL ADMINISTRATION

Solomon's reign was characterized by the expansion of the royal government, and by a focus on massive construction that added to the fame of his kingship. Although the workings of government received little attention under **Saul**, David had built a sound organization for administration (2 Sam 8:15–18), and Solomon expanded this structure (1 Kgs 4:1–6).

The kingdom of Solomon was divided administratively into twelve districts and the land of Judah, with local government in the hands of a provisions officer (1 Kgs 4:7–19). Overseeing the prefects was **Azariah**, the son of Nathan (1 Kgs 4:5). The extent and configuration of the administrative districts is not known exactly, and despite correspondences with the twelve tribes, the twelve districts did not match the tribal territories. Some have thus conjectured that Solomon had in mind the deliberate weakening of the tribal structure. The administrative system relied on the collection of taxes and levies, and the burden was a heavy one, including requirements for forced labor (1 Kgs 5:13–16, 9:23; cf. 2 Chr 8:10). These burdens were a vexing problem for **Rehoboam** when he sought to assume the throne of Israel (1 Kgs 12:3–4). His refusal to ease the demand of forced labor contributed to the division of the kingdom between Israel and Judah.

The purpose of the taxes was to provide the royal court with a regular food allowance (1 Kgs 4:7) and to support Solomon's ambitious building program, which included forts for national defense across Palestine (1 Kgs 10:26) and above all the massive royal complex of Jerusalem encompassing the **Temple** (1 Kgs 6–7). The Temple compound in Jerusalem was "sixty cubits long, twenty cubits wide, and thirty cubits high" (1 Kgs 6:2). Though grand for the times, it was dwarfed by the royal palace (1 Kgs 7:1–12). The entire complex took twenty years to complete (1 Kgs 9:10), the Temple itself requiring seven years (1 Kgs 6:38). In this endeavor, Solomon emulated the mighty kingdoms of the Near East, providing a seat of rule that boasted palaces, houses, and gardens. The project also required the expenditure of vast sums of money, thousands of workers, and the leading craftsmen of the period.

III. SOLOMON'S EMPIRE

According to 1 Kgs 4:21–24, Solomon ruled over a territory stretching from the upper Euphrates to the border of Egypt. He clearly enjoyed influence in the region, using the stability of his kingdom to promote wide-ranging diplomatic and trade opportunities. Solomon's dealings with Egypt resulted in a negotiated treaty that included Solomon's marriage to the daughter of the pharaoh (1 Kgs 3:1; 7:8; 9:24). Similar marriages were arranged with other foreign women and princesses, including Ammonite, Edomite, Hittite, Moabite, and Sidonian women (1 Kgs

11:1). The marriages reflected Solomon's diplomatic abilities, but they also introduced a corrupting religious influence into the kingdom (see below). Solomon also brought in chariots and horses from Egypt and Cilicia, which formed the basis for his army of fourteen hundred chariots and twelve thousand horses (1 Kgs 10:26–29). Chariots and horses were also exported by the king's traders to the Hittites and the kings of Syria (1 Kgs 10:29).

Solomon's relations with Hiram of Tyre consisted of trade exchanges (wheat and oil in return for cedar and cypress from Lebanon, as well as craftsmen; 1 Kgs 5:1–12, 18; 9:11). There were also joint shipping ventures to East Africa and Arabia for gold, silver, ivory, monkeys and apes, and peacocks (1 Kgs 9:26–28; 10:11, 22). These were undertaken by Solomon's fleet at Ezion-geber (1 Kgs 9:26), where remains have been discovered of a copper foundry dating back to the Solomonic period. The extravagance of his wealth impressed even the **Queen of Sheba**, who exchanged gifts with him (1 Kgs 10:1–13; 2 Chr 9:1–12).

Further economic growth was achieved by Solomon's control over the main trade routes running through the coastal plain between Egypt and Damascus, and the King's highway, connecting the Red Sea with Damascus. Tariffs were probably imposed on all goods passing across the routes (cf. 1 Kgs 10:15; 2 Chr 9:14). The historians of his reign could express the splendor of it only by hyperbole: "And the king made silver as common in Jerusalem as stone, and he made cedar as plentiful as the sycamore of the Shephelah" (1 Kgs 10:27; cf. Matt 6:29; Luke 12:27).

IV. RELIGIOUS POLICY

Solomon's greatest accomplishment was building the Temple in fulfillment of the Davidic **covenant** (1 Kgs 8:14–21; 2 Chr 6:3–11). The **ark of the covenant** was placed in the holy of holies in the Temple (1 Kgs 8:1–13), to show the continuity of the Davidic and Sinai covenants (1 Kgs 8:21).

At the same time, Solomon perpetuated the role of covenant mediator that David had filled. Solomon spoke with God (1 Kgs 3:5–14; 6:11–13; 9:1–9; 11:9–13) and served in a priestly capacity, following in the footsteps of David by acting as both *king* and *priest* (1 Kgs 3:4, 15; 8:14–66).

By the end of his reign, however, Solomon had begun to fail in his fidelity to the covenant, and the collapse of the once-proud empire was the result. He had seven hundred wives and three hundred concubines (1 Kgs 11:3), and Solomon allowed his foreign wives to lead his heart away from the Lord and his covenant. Indeed, Solomon built "high places" for the worship of foreign gods that were still in existence during the reign of King Josiah (2 Kgs 23:13). According to 1 Kgs 11:11–12, Solomon was warned by the Lord: "Since this has been your mind and you have not kept my covenant and my statutes which I have commanded you, I will surely tear the kingdom from you and will give it to your servant. Yet for the sake of David your father I will not do it in your days, but I will tear it out of the hand of your son." Thus Solomon sowed the seeds for the collapse of the kingdom. Combined with the discontent of the north over issues of administration and forced labor, Solomon bequeathed to his successors social, religious, and political problems that proved insoluble. (*See also* **Jeroboam**.)

These failures came in spite of Solomon's unrivaled wisdom. He had won the Lord's favor when he asked humbly that wisdom be granted him as king (2 Chr 1:10–12). The testimony of his wisdom was preserved in famous decisions, such as the case of the two women who each claimed the same child as their own (1 Kgs 3:16–28). He was also ranked as the greatest sage in the Old Testament, and is credited with the composition of 3,000 proverbs and 1,005 songs (1 Kgs 4:29–34).

SOLOMON, PORTICO OF A colonnade running along the eastern side of the Temple complex of Herod's **Temple** in Jerusalem. It was part of a colonnade that surrounded the outer courtyard of the Temple and was used as a meeting place to discuss Scripture. Jesus and the disciples gathered there, as did members of the first Christian community in Jerusalem (John 10:23; Acts 3:11, 5:12).

SOLOMON, SONG OF *See* **Song of Solomon**.

SOLOMON, TEMPLE OF *See* **Temple**.

SON *See* **Family**; *see also* **Discipleship**; **Jesus Christ**.

SON OF GOD The divine title and identity of **Jesus Christ**. Jesus, although a historical man, is truly the Son of God who possesses a unique and eternal relationship with God,

his Father (Matt 11:25–27; John 1:14, 18; 3:16–18; 17:1–5). The Christian faith hinges on the belief that Jesus Christ is the Son of God (John 20:31; 1 John 4:14–15). Statistically, Jesus is called the Son of God some one hundred times in the New Testament. The title "Son of God" is found in both the Old Testament and the NT (CCC 441–45).

I. In the Old Testament
    A. The Nation of Israel as Son of God
    B. The King of Israel as Son of God
II. In the New Testament
    A. Jesus as "Son of God" in the Old Testament Sense
    B. Jesus as "Son of God" in a Divine Sense

I. IN THE OLD TESTAMENT

A. The Nation of Israel as Son of God

In the OT, "son of God" is a title given to a variety of people or beings, including angels (Job 1:6, 38:8; Ps 89:6) and just and righteous men (cf. Job 1:6, 2:1; Ps 88:7; Wis 2:13).

Most significant is the OT use of the title for the children of Israel. In Exod 4:22, Moses is commanded to tell Pharaoh, "Thus says the LORD, Israel is my firstborn son." In Deut 14:1, the Israelites are called the "sons of the LORD your God." The term denotes God's **election** of Israel, the divine initiative of choosing Israel to enjoy the privileges and responsibilities of adoptive sonship through the **covenant** (cf. Isa 2:1; Jer 3:19, 31:9; Hos 11:1, 13:13).

B. The King of Israel as Son of God

The monarchs of Israel were also called sons of God (2 Sam 7:14; 2 Chr 22:10; Ps 2:7, 89:28).

This was not, as was common with Near Eastern monarchs, a claim to divinity on the part of the kings of Israel. Rather, the claim to being son of God was an extension of the sonship of Israel; the king was son of God because he was leader and representative of Israel before God. More specifically, royal *adoption* was a blessing of the Davidic covenant (2 Sam 7:14). By adopting them, God chose the royal descendants of David to serve his purposes of salvation and the future hopes for the **Messiah**: "When your days are fulfilled and you lie down with your fathers, I will raise up your offspring after you, who shall come forth from your body, and I will establish his kingdom. He shall build a house for my name, and I will establish the throne of his kingdom for ever" (2 Sam 7:12–13) (CCC 441).

II. IN THE NEW TESTAMENT

A. Jesus as "Son of God" in the Old Testament Sense

In the NT, the title "Son of God" is understood in part to denote Jesus as the expected Messiah and king of Israel, "who was descended from David according to the flesh and designated Son of God in power according to the Spirit of holiness by his resurrection from the dead" (Rom 1:3–4). Such a traditional understanding may be visible in the words of Nathaniel, at his first meeting with Jesus, when he called him the Son of God (John 1:49).

B. Jesus as "Son of God" in a Divine Sense

The NT writers, however, understood Christ to be much more than the expected Messiah, in fidelity to Jesus's own claim of divine sonship (e.g., Matt 11:27, 21:33–41, 24:36; Mark 13:32; Luke 10:22, 20:9–16; John 3:16, 10:36). Jesus was the fulfillment of the Messianic expectations of Israel, but in this fulfillment, Jesus revealed a much deeper aspect of his divine sonship, for he is the one who enjoys a unique and eternal relationship with God the Father as his only Son (Matt 7:21–23; 10:32; 11:25–30; 24:30, 31; 27:25; 28:19, 20; Mark 12:2, 6, 37; 14:61–62; Luke 2:49; John 6:40; 16:1, 5; 20:17, 20–23). Two passages are especially important confirmation of Jesus's divine sonship. The first describes his baptism (Matt 3:13–17; Mark 1:9–11; Luke 3:21–22): "and lo, a voice from heaven, saying, 'This is my beloved Son, with whom I am well pleased'" (Matt 3:17; cf. Mark 1:11; Luke 3:22). The second tells of the **Transfiguration** of Christ (Matt 17:5–13; Mark 9:2–13; Luke 9:28–36; 2 Pet 1:16–18): "This is my beloved Son, with whom I am well pleased; listen to him" (Matt 17:5; cf. Mark 9:6; Luke 9:35).

When Peter makes his dramatic confession to Jesus, "You are the Christ, the Son of the living God" (Matt 16:16; cf. Matt 14:33), Jesus responds, "Blessed are you, Simon Bar-Jona! For flesh and blood has not revealed this to you, but my Father who is in heaven" (Matt 16:17), indicating that Peter has expressed faith in the divinity of Jesus as well as his Messiahship.

But it is only in the Paschal mystery that the truest meaning of Son of God can be comprehended by the believer: "And when the centurion, who stood facing him, saw that he thus breathed his last, he said, 'Truly this man was the Son of God!'" (Mark 15:39). In Gal 4:4–5, Paul writes, "But when the time had fully come, God sent forth his Son, born of woman, born under the law, to redeem those who were under the law, so that we might receive adoption as sons" (cf. Rom 8:14–15; Eph 1:5; Col 1:13). It is through Jesus's death and Resurrection that he shows himself truly the Son of God, and that he makes us children of God as well. John tells us that he wrote his Gospel "that you may believe that Jesus is the Christ, the Son of God, and that believing you may have life in his name" (John 20:30). John establishes the intimate connection between the sonship of Jesus and the grace of divine generation that makes us children of God (John 1:12; 1 John 3:1–2, 9; 5:1) (CCC 442–45).

SON OF MAN A title that Jesus frequently gave himself. His preference for the expression may be linked with its different possible meanings. At one level, "son of man" is nothing more than a Semitic way of referring to a human being—that is, one who shares in the limitations of a mortal human existence (Job 25:6). Sometimes, Jesus seems to use the phrase in this customary way, as, for example, when parallel passages in the Gospels treat it as a third-person equivalent of the first-person pronoun "I" (compare Matt 16:13 with Mark 8:27). At another level, however, the title "son of man" has definite ties with the Messianic vision of Dan 7, where "one like a son of man" rides the clouds of heaven and is given an everlasting kingdom (Dan 7:13). No doubt Jesus also intended to identify himself with this figure in Daniel and thus to use the title in a fully Messianic sense. This is clearest in passages where Jesus speaks of the "son of man" in connection with related imagery such

as the "clouds of heaven" (Matt 24:30; Mark 14:61–62) (CCC 440).

I. OLD TESTAMENT BACKGROUND

In the Old Testament, "son of man" can serve as a poetic synonym for man as a mere mortal (Num 23:19; Ps 8:4; Sir 17:30). It is used extensively in Ezekiel, where the prophet is addressed some ninety times by God as "son of man" (Ezek 2:1, 3; etc.). The only other similar use is in Dan 8:17. In Dan 7, after the appearance of four beasts, the Lord is seated upon his throne as the "Ancient of Days" (Dan 7:9) and into his presence comes "one like a son of man," with the clouds of heaven (Dan 7:13). "And to him was given dominion and glory and kingdom, that all peoples, nations, and languages should serve him; his dominion is an everlasting dominion, which shall not pass away, and his kingdom one that shall not be destroyed" (Dan 7:14).

The Son of Man is clearly presented here as a Messianic figure who reveals the Lord's wisdom and whose power will signal the inevitable defeat of the Lord's enemies. Jewish apocryphal writings amplified the role of the Danielic Son of Man. The Son of Man presented in the parables of *1 Enoch* 37–71 is a powerful Messianic ruler, an eschatological figure who will come at the end of time to sit in judgment. Until then, he is hidden away with God, although he was chosen before all creation, and he will bring with him salvation for the whole of the created order. The essential roles of the Son of Man were Judge (*1 Enoch* 49.4; 51.1–3), Messiah (*1 Enoch* 48.10), Light to the Gentiles (*1 Enoch* 48.4), and the Righteous One (*1 Enoch* 46.3).

II. NEW TESTAMENT USAGE

Jesus calls himself "Son of Man" throughout his ministry. Sometimes he speaks of himself in distinctively human terms, engaging in such activities as resting (Matt 8:20; Luke 9:58), eating and drinking (Matt 11:19; Luke 7:34), and suffering (Mark 8:31). Jesus, however, also claims divine or superhuman powers for himself, including the right to forgive sins (Matt 9:6; Mark 2:10; Luke 5:24) and suspend the demands of the Sabbath (Matt 12:8; Mark 2:28; Luke 6:5). In John, the Son of Man stands as a judge (John 5:27) and as one who descended from heaven and will ascend there once more (John 6:62); he is the mediator between heaven and earth (John 1:51) and is glorified by God whom he glorifies (John 13:31).

Jesus makes unmistakable allusions to the "Son of Man" from Dan 7:13 when he refers to his glorious enthronement in heaven (Matt 19:28; 25:31) and the Kingdom that belongs to him (Matt 16:28; Luke 9:26–27). In two contexts he mentions the "clouds of heaven" that figure prominently in Daniel's vision: once when he prophesies his future coming (Matt 24:30; Mark 13:26) and once when he prophesies his vindication before the high priest who is ready to condemn him (Matt 26:64; Mark 14:62).

What is most unique about Jesus's self-description as the "Son of Man" is not his ability to evoke both its mundane and its Messianic aspects, but the fact that he connects his status as Son of Man with his redemptive mission of suffering. In fact, his many predictions of the Passion mentioned in the Gospels are cast in terms of what will happen to "the Son of Man" (Matt 12:40; 17:12, 22; 20:18;

Mark 9:31; 10:33; Luke 9:44; 18:31). Although it is possible that readers of Daniel might have seen a connection between the "son of man" in Dan 7:13 and the "anointed one" who is cut off in Dan 9:26, it is also the case that Jesus wanted his disciples to identify the son of man from Daniel with the Suffering Servant of Isa 52–53. Followers would thus come to see that his humiliation unto death was the necessary prelude to his exaltation and enthronement in heaven.

SONG OF SOLOMON Also called the Song of Songs and the Canticle of Canticles, a collection of love poetry that celebrates the drama of romantic attraction between a man and a woman. The title "Song of Songs" is taken from the superscription in 1:1, *šîr haššîrîm*, a superlative expression implying the "greatest of songs." The name "Song of Solomon" is derived from the tradition that Solomon was the author, and "Canticle of Canticles" is taken from the **Vulgate** (the Latin title is *Canticum Canticorum*). In the Hebrew Bible, the Song of Solomon follows Ruth as the first of the five "Scrolls" and is read on the feast of Passover. In the Catholic canon, it follows Ecclesiastes and is counted among the Wisdom Books.

I. AUTHORSHIP AND DATE

The Song of Songs is traditionally attributed to Solomon on the basis of the opening verse (Song 1:1). Solomon himself is mentioned several times in the book (1:5; 3:7, 9, 11; 8:11), and the male lover of the book is identified as a "king" (1:4, 12; 7:5). We read in 1 Kgs 4:32 that Solomon's "songs were a thousand and five." Some scholars maintain the tradition of Solomonic authorship, although most scholars are of the view that the author is unknown.

The canonicity of the book was never questioned in Christian tradition, but there was some dispute regarding its inclusion in the Hebrew canon. According to a tradition in the Talmud, there was a debate over the book at the Council of Jamnia around A.D. 100. The questions were whether it was genuine and whether its contents were unsuitable for the canon. The great rabbi Akiba (d. A.D. 135) settled the debate by declaring that the universe is not as valuable as the day the Song of Songs was given to Israel; all the writings are holy, and the Song of Songs is the holy of holies. The objection was probably raised because of the sensual content of the poetry, but this was answered by the claims of Solomonic authorship.

The date for the composition of the book is uncertain. If Solomon was the author, then it would date to his reign in the tenth century B.C. Most scholars are of the view that the Song of Songs dates to a later period, although arguments for dating the book well after the time of Solomon are not particularly strong.

II. CONTENTS

The structure of the Song of Songs has long been the subject of debate among scholars. The following is a basic division of the chapters according to the breaks created by the refrain "I adjure you, O daughters of Jerusalem," appearing at Song 2:7; 3:5; and 8:4.

III. PURPOSE AND THEMES

The Song of Songs is a collection of romantic poetry that dramatizes the passion between a lover and his beloved. The poems constitute a dialogue between the lovers. Changes in mood and scene suggest to some that separate poems were collected and woven together. A key bridge phrase is used to unite the poems: "I adjure you, O daughters of Jerusalem"; it appears at Song 2:7; 3:5; and 8:4.

At first glance, the Song of Songs appears to be little more than a celebration of natural love between a man and a woman. The imagery is quite physical and explicitly sexual. Besides this, there is no mention of God, nor is there any apparent reference to spiritual or religious matters.

Part of the key to understanding the Song of Songs is understanding that human love and attraction are gifts of God oriented toward the bond of matrimony—an understanding that is implicit in the book itself. The Song of Songs is a rich and vivid commentary on the intimacy between a man and wife within that marital bond.

Jewish and Christian tradition also finds a deeper meaning in the Song of Songs. When the book is read allegorically, it is a celebration of the love of God for his people—the love of Yahweh for his Chosen People and of Christ for his Church. It is expressive of the great prophetic themes in Hos 1–3, Isa 1:21 and 62:5, Jer 3:1, and Ezek 16 and 23, all of which describe the **covenant** in terms of a marriage relationship. This theme is carried forward in the New Testament in Matt 25:1–13, Eph 5:21–22, and Rev 21:9.

The spiritual interpretation of the Song of Songs has been a stimulating source for Christian mystical theology. Among the most famous commentaries in this regard are the fifteen homilies by Saint Gregory of Nyssa on the first six chapters, the commentary of Theodoret, Saint Ambrose of Milan, the Venerable Bede, Honorius of Autun, the eighty-six homilies of Saint Bernard, and Saint John of the Cross.

SONGS OF DEGREES *See* **Psalms**.

SONS OF GOD *See* **Covenant**.

SONS OF LIGHT *See* **Light**.

SONS OF THE PROPHETS *See* **Prophet**.

SONS OF THUNDER *See* **Boanerges**.

SONSHIP *See* **Covenant**; *see also* **Israel**; **Jesus Christ**; **Son of God**.

SOOTHSAYER *See* **Divination**.

SOPATER A Christian from Beroea, the son of Pyrrhus (Acts 20:4). With several others, Sopater journeyed with **Paul** from Greece to Jerusalem on the final leg of Paul's third missionary journey. Sopater and several others sailed ahead of Paul to Troas; Paul soon reached them (Acts 20:5–6). Sopater's name is a shortened form of Sosipater, for which reason he may be identical to the Sosipater mentioned in Rom 16:21.

SOPHIA *See* **Wisdom**.

SORCERY *See* **Magic and sorcery**.

SOREK, VALLEY OF A valley in the low hills west of Jerusalem that was the home of **Delilah** (Judg 16:4); it is probably the modern Wadi al-Sarar between Jerusalem and Jaffa. The valley stood on the dividing line between the territories of Dan and Judah (Josh 15:9–12; 19:40–49). (*See* **Samson**.)

SOSIPATER The name of two men in the Bible.

1. A general in the army of **Judas Maccabeus** who fought against **Timothy**, a Seleucid commander, in the Transjordan. With Dositheus, he took Timothy prisoner but let him go free in order to prevent retributions against Jewish hostages held by the enemy (2 Macc 12:19–25).

2. A Christian mentioned by **Paul** in Rom 16:21, along with Lucius and Jason, and described as a "kinsman." Sosipater may be identical to **Sopater** (Acts 20:4).

SOSTHENES A "ruler of the synagogue" in Corinth (Acts 18:17) and the successor to **Crispus** after the latter's conversion through **Paul** (Acts 18:8; 1 Cor 1:14). When "the Jews" brought Paul before the Roman proconsul **Gallio**, the Roman official refused to pass judgment as the charges against Paul were an internal Jewish affair touching on Jewish Law (Acts 18:12–16). Frustrated by this decision, the crowd set upon Sosthenes and beat him before the courthouse. He too may have become a Christian, since a man of this name is listed after Paul as a co-sender of 1 Corinthians (1 Cor 1:1).

SOSTRATUS The **Seleucid** governor of the fortress or citadel in Jerusalem during the reign of Antiochus IV Epiphanes (2 Macc 4:27–29). Sostratus was charged with collecting taxes owed to the king by the high priest.

SOUL The spiritual principle of human life and the subject of human consciousness and freedom. The soul and the body together form one human nature, and each human soul is individual, immortal, and immediately created by God. The soul does not die with the body; rather, it is separated from the body at death and will be reunited with the body in the final resurrection.

I. IN THE OLD TESTAMENT

The Hebrew word *nepeš*, occurring over 750 times in the Old Testament, is sometimes translated "soul" (1 Kgs 17:21–22), although also frequently it is translated "life" (1 Sam 19:5; 2 Sam 1:9; Ps 72:14). It is difficult to tell whether the ancient Israelites made a clear distinction between the body and the soul, since both terms were used to describe a living being. Hence, *nepeš* was used for animals (Gen 1:20, 24; 9:12, 15–16; Ezek 47:9). Breath (Gen 2:7) and blood (Lev 17:11) serve as vital principles of life and were seen not merely as biological components. The soul is associated with the blood (Gen 9:4; Lev 17:10–14; Deut 12:22–24). Elsewhere in the OT, *nepeš* describes the seat of the appetites (Num 21:5; Deut 12:15; Job 33:20; Ps 78:18; Mic 7:1) and the seat of the moral will (Gen 49:6; Deut 4:29; Ps 24:4, 119:129).

The term *nepeš* also could mean a human person (Exod 1:5; Deut 10:22; Lev 7:21; Ezek 18:4), as delineated clearly in the Genesis account of the creation of Adam: "then the Lord God formed man from the dust of the ground, and breathed into his nostrils the breath of life; and the man became a living being" (Gen 2:7). The passage points to the two compositional elements of the human being: body and soul. The *nepeš* is seen to depart from the body at death (Gen 35:18; cf. Eccl 12:7).

II. IN THE NEW TESTAMENT

The Greek word for "soul" is *psychē*. Sometimes it refers to human life or the human person (Matt 2:20; Acts 2:41; Phil 2:30), but it can also mean the spiritual principle of a person (Matt 10:28, 26:38; John 12:27). It is likewise recognized that the body and soul are sometimes at war with each other, the passions of the flesh in conflict with the rational faculty of the soul (1 Pet 2:11).

Paul uses *psychē* in several senses, including "life" and "self" and even "mind" (Rom 16:4; Phil 1:27; 1 Thess 2:8). Paul also uses the word *pneuma*, "spirit": "may your spirit and soul and body be kept sound." Scholars have suggested that his use of "spirit" refers not to a compositional substance that is joined to body and soul, but to man's spiritual capacity for worship and communion with God (Rom 1:9; 1 Cor 14:14) (CCC 362–68, 1703).

SOURCE CRITICISM *See* **Biblical criticism**.

SPAIN The Iberian Peninsula was brought under Roman control in the second century

B.C. The First Book of Maccabees 8:3 lists Spain as a conquest of Rome, noting Rome's control of the region's gold and silver mines.

Paul intended to travel to Spain (Rom 15:24, 28), but the New Testament never confirms whether he accomplished this objective. Saint Clement of Rome declared that Paul had reached "the boundary of the West," a location generally assumed to be Spain, which marked the western extreme of the Roman Empire (*1 Clem.* 5.5–7).

SPARTA A city in southern Greece, on the Peloponnesian Peninsula. With Athens, Sparta was one of the chief city-states of ancient Greece, especially after the Peloponnesian War (which ended in 404 B.C.). The Spartans under King Arius established an alliance with **Jonathan Maccabeus** (1 Macc 12:2–23) that was renewed by Simon Maccabeus (1 Macc 14:16–23). In 1 Macc 15:16–23, a letter is mentioned from the proconsul Lucius to the king of Egypt and other states (including Sparta) affirming the Roman alliance with the Jews and discouraging any other states from hostilities toward Israel (Josephus, *Ant.* 14.145–55).

SPEAR A weapon with a shaft and point: a javelin, spike, or lance might also be called a "spear." A soldier might carry several spears into battle (1 Sam 17:6). A long spear or javelin was struck into the ground to denote the place chosen for the tent of the king (1 Sam 26:7).

SPIRIT, HOLY The divine Spirit of God, also called the Paraclete (Advocate) and Spirit of Truth. The Holy Spirit is active together with the Father and the Son from the beginning to the completion of the divine plan of salvation. Christian doctrine asserts that the Holy Spirit is co-substantial, coequal, and coeternal with the Father and the Son. The Personhood of the Spirit was foreshadowed in the Old Testament and is clearly revealed in the New Testament.

I. THE SPIRIT IN THE OLD TESTAMENT

The Hebrew word for "spirit" (*rûaḥ*) can also mean "wind" (Gen 8:1; Num 11:31; 1 Kgs 18:45) or "breath" (Gen 7:15; Eccl 3:19; Jer 10:14). The two images can also be combined to suggest that the wind is the breath of God (2 Sam 22:16; Ps 18:15; Isa 40:7).

"Breath" is a common expression in Scripture for the human spirit of man (Gen 41:8; Exod 6:9; Ezek 3:14). The start of life is seen as divinely willed, and the end of life as the return of man's spirit to God, the one who gave it in the first place (Eccl 12:7). The spirit, however, was not perceived to be a separate entity from the **soul** (cf. Gen 2:7). Like the soul, the spirit is the seat of the appetites and the seat of the moral will. God also has his spirit, and it was described in the OT chiefly in terms of his divine power at work in the world (1 Sam 16:13).

The power of God was visible in myriad ways, but it was seen especially in the charismatic leaders of the Israelites, the prophets, and those who fulfilled God's saving will. God's Spirit was evident in **Moses** and the seventy elders (Num 11:17, 25) and was imparted to his successor, **Joshua** (Deut 34:9). It was seen in the charismatic labors of the **Judges** (Judg 3:10; 6:34; 11:29; 13:25; 14:6, 9; 15:14; 1 Sam 11:6). The prophet was termed "a man of the spirit" (Hos 9:7).

In the eschatology of the prophets, the Spirit of the Lord is envisioned pouring down upon the world with his blessings and life (Isa 32:15, 44:3; Joel 2:28–29). The Spirit who brings forth creation (Gen 1:2) will bring renewal to the face of the earth (Ps 104:30) by a spiritual transformation of man that enables him to walk faithfully with the Lord (Ezek 11:19–20; 36:23–28). The time of this outpouring is implicitly linked with the coming of the Davidic **Messiah**, who is anointed with the fullness of the Spirit and his gifts (Isa 11:1–2). Isaiah also speaks of this Messianic figure as the Servant of the Lord, the suffering Redeemer who is likewise anointed with the Spirit (Isa 42:1; 61:1).

II. THE SPIRIT IN THE NEW TESTAMENT

As with the Hebrew *rûaḥ*, the Greek word *pneuma* can likewise mean "wind," "breath," or "spirit." But in the NT, we also see explicitly what was hinted at in the OT: that the Spirit is not an impersonal force but a divine Person, who is neither the Father nor the Son. The Spirit was present at key moments in Jesus's life and ministry. The Spirit brought about the virginal conception of Jesus (Matt 1:18, 20; Luke 1:35). Matthew 3:16 (cf. Mark 1:9–11; Luke 3:12–13) records that at the baptism of Jesus, "behold, the heavens were opened and he saw the Spirit of God descending like a dove, and alighting on him." Among other things, the event confirmed Jesus as the Servant of the Lord in the sense of Isa 42:1, and Peter described the baptism as an "anointing" when he told the household of **Cornelius** "how God anointed Jesus of Nazareth with the Holy Spirit and with power; how he went about do-

ing good and healing all that were oppressed by the devil, for God was with him" (Acts 10:38). Jesus was driven by the Spirit into the wilderness where he was tempted (Mark 1:12; Luke 4:1). Christ's healings and exorcisms, the signs of the inauguration of the Kingdom, are achieved through the power of the Holy Spirit (Matt 12:28; Luke 11:2), and those who claim that such gifts come from the devil or Beelzebul commit unforgivable sins against the Spirit (Matt 12:32; Mark 3:29; Luke 12:10).

At the end of Matthew's Gospel, Jesus tells the disciples the formula by which they should baptize: "Go therefore and make disciples of all nations, baptizing them in the name of the Father and of the Son and of the Holy Spirit" (Matt 28:19). Here, in what Christians call the Great Commission, the doctrine of the Holy **Trinity** is encapsulated by Christ himself (CCC 152, 683, 687, 689, 702, 727–30, 739, 747, 797, 1108).

John writes of the Advocate or Paraclete in connection with the promise of the Holy Spirit. Jesus declares, "And I will pray the Father, and he will give you another Counselor, to be with you for ever, even the Spirit of truth, whom the world cannot receive, because it neither sees him nor knows him; you know him, for he dwells with you, and will be in you" (John 14:16–17). Jesus calls the indwelling Spirit the Spirit of truth (John 15:26; 16:7, 13–15) who could not be given to the world until Christ was glorified (John 7:39).

The coming of the Spirit on believers takes place at **Pentecost** (Acts 2:14–21), and thereafter the Spirit is the principle of the Church's vitality in Acts (CCC 2640): "Being therefore exalted at the right hand of God, and having received from the Father the promise of the Holy Spirit, he has poured out this which you see and hear" (Acts 2:33). Having descended at Pentecost, the Spirit bestows wisdom (Acts 6:3), strengthens faith (Acts 6:5), guides labors (Acts 8:29), and inspires new prophets (Acts 11:28; 13:9). The Spirit also grants some to speak in tongues (Acts 2:4; 10:44–47) and prophesy (Acts 19:6) (CCC 799, 951, 1508, 1824, 1830–32). The Spirit descended on Cornelius and his family, an event that was decisive in convincing Peter that the Gentile Cornelius should be baptized and brought into the Church (Acts 10:44–48). Those, then, who are baptized receive the gift of the Spirit (Acts 2:32), as do those who receive the imposition of hands (Acts 8:18) (CCC 738–41, 747, 749, 767–68, 797–801, 852, 867).

Paul observes in 1 Cor 2:12–13, "Now we have received not the spirit of the world, but the Spirit which is from God, that we might understand the gifts bestowed on us by God. And we impart this in words not taught by human wisdom but taught by the Spirit, interpreting spiritual truths to those who possess the Spirit." He adds that because of the indwelling of the Spirit, we are made God's temple: "Do you not know that you are God's temple and that God's Spirit dwells in you?" (1 Cor 3:16; cf. 1 Cor 6:19) (CCC 1197, 1265).

For Paul, the work of the Spirit is closely linked with baptism: "you were washed, you were sanctified, you were justified in the name of the Lord Jesus Christ and in the Spirit of our God" (1 Cor 6:11). As a result, "God's love has been poured into our hearts through the Holy Spirit which has been given to us" (Rom 5:5) (CCC 1987–95, 2003). The Spirit is the source

of graces and gifts (1 Cor 12:3–11), our sanctification (1 Cor 3:16; 6:19), and it is the giver of a new life (Rom 8) that confirms that we are God's adoptive children (Rom 8:14–16; 2 Cor 1:22, 5:5; Gal 4:6). The Holy Spirit is both the Spirit of God and the Spirit of Christ (Rom 8:9) (CCC 686, 706, 759, 1076, 1229). The Spirit teaches us to pray and intercedes for us (Rom 8:26, 23) (CCC 741, 2600, 2623, 2625, 2630, 2644, 2650, 2670, 2681, 2711, 2726, 2736, 2756, 2766, 2803). He is the "guarantee" of our hope to receive God's blessings in full one day (2 Cor 1:22, 5:5; Eph 1:13–14), and God's indwelling Spirit will restore our mortal bodies to life—the same Spirit that raised Christ (Rom 8:11). The divine Spirit knows all divine mysteries hidden in God (1 Cor 2:10–11).

Paul's letters make it plain that he considered the Spirit to be a separate Person, as evidenced by his various Trinitarian formulae (cf. 1 Cor 12:4–6; 2 Cor 13:13; Gal 4:6; Rom 8:9, 11). His benediction at the end of the Second Letter to the Corinthians is especially eloquent: "The grace of the Lord Jesus Christ and the love of God and the fellowship of the Holy Spirit be with you all" (2 Cor 13:14). (*See also* **Baptism; Confirmation, Sacrament of; Temple**.)

SPIRITUAL GIFTS See **Grace**; *see also* **Spirit, Holy**.

SPIRITUAL SENSE See *under* **Interpretation of the Bible**.

SPRING GATE See **Fountain Gate**.

STAFF A branch or wooden rod used mainly for walking. The staff was both the support and the weapon of the shepherd (Ps 23:4; Mic 7:14). It was also considered essential equipment for a journey on foot, no matter what the health or age of the walker. The poor traveler carried nothing but a staff (Gen 32:10), and when Jesus told the apostles to take no staff (Mark 6:8), he meant that they should journey with nothing. The staff or rod inflicted punishment (Isa 10:5; Prov 10:13; 22:8, 15; 1 Cor 4:21) and oppression (Isa 10:24; 14:29), but the staff of the wicked was broken by God (Isa 14:5). God also performed wonders using the staff of Moses (Exod 4:2–3, 9:23, 10:13; Num 20:8).

STARS Created by God to separate the night from the day and to function as signs in the heavens (Gen 1:14). Although stars are objects of wonder and admiration (Ps 8:3), Genesis makes it a point to insist that the stars are part of creation, in order to distinguish Israelite faith from beliefs in the wider Near East, where the hosts of heaven were often worshipped as gods (Deut 4:19; Amos 5:26). Along with the sun and moon, representing father and mother, the stars can also represent the children of a large family (Gen 37:9–10; cf. Gen 15:5; 22:17). In some cases, they can represent the angels of heaven (Job 38:17; Rev 9:1).

In theological contexts, the stars function as signs of salvation and judgment. For instance, the prophetic oracle of Balaam in Num 24:17 envisions a Messianic King rising out of Israel as a "star." Many scholars believe that the star of Bethlehem that guided the **Magi** to the infant Jesus has some relation to this Old Testament promise (Matt 2:2, 7–11). Although many have tried to link the star of Bethlehem

with a comet or planetary conjunction that might have been visible at the time, the most likely explanation is that the star was an angel, brilliantly white (cf. Matt 28:2–3), leading the Magi to their Savior and King. This would explain why, in the Gospel of Matthew, the star is said to appear and disappear, as well as move forward and stand still.

In times of judgment, the stars of the sky are depicted in apocalyptic terms as darkening or falling out of the sky (Isa 13:10; Joel 3:15; Matt 24:29; Mark 13:25; Rev 6:13; 8:10, 12; 12:4).

STEPHANAS A Christian from Corinth. **Paul** called his household "the first converts in Achaia" (1 Cor 16:15); they were baptized by Paul himself (1 Cor 1:16). The members of the household of Stephanas are praised by Paul for "they have devoted themselves to the service of the saints" (1 Cor 16:15). With Fortunatus and Achaicus, Stephanas visited Paul in Ephesus (1 Cor 16:17).

STEPHEN One of the seven men chosen by the apostles to care for the needs of the widows within the community in Jerusalem (Acts 6:1–6). Described as "a man full of faith and of the Holy Spirit," he was the first Christian martyr (Acts 6–7). As his name is Greek, it is likely that he was a Hellenist Jew whose native language was Greek. Nevertheless, there is a tradition dating from the fifth century that "Stephen" was merely a Greek equivalent of the Aramaic *Kelil*, possibly Stephen's original name, since "Kelil" was inscribed on a stone slab found in his tomb. In any case, his ministry as a deacon appears to have been centered among Hellenist converts.

A remarkable preacher, Stephen performed miracles and was described as being full of grace and power (Acts 6:8). A group of Jews in Jerusalem debated with him but could not get the better of him, so they arranged to falsely accuse him of blasphemy. He was brought before the **Sanhedrin**, where he delivered the profound speech in Acts 7:2–53. His enraged enemies seized him, dragged him out of the city, and stoned him to death. The witnesses laid their garments at the feet of the young man named Saul, later known as **Paul** (Acts 7:55–60). Just before his death, Stephen had a vision of the glorified Christ and prayed, "Lord, Jesus, receive my spirit" (Acts 7:59), asking that Christ forgive his attackers. Stephen was buried by "devout men" who "made great lamentation over him" (Acts 8:2). His tomb was long forgotten until it was discovered by Lucien in A.D. 415, and a church was built in his honor just beyond the Damascus Gate (dedicated in 460). His feast day is December 26.

STEWARD A servant in charge of a house or estate. The steward was often given considerable authority over the household and served as a manager (Gen 39:4; Luke 16:1–8; 1 Cor 4:1–2).

STONING The most common method of execution in ancient Israel; it was applied for such serious crimes as idolatry (Deut 17:5), blasphemy (Lev 24:14–16), apostasy (Deut 13:11), sorcery (Lev 20:27), violations of the **Sabbath** (Num 15:32–36), child sacrifice (Lev 20:2), rebellion against one's parents (Deut 21:20), and adultery (Deut 22:13–24). The condemned person was taken outside the camp or town (Lev 24:14, 23; Num 15:36; 1 Kgs 21:10, 13; Acts 7:58), and the first stones were cast by the witnesses to the crime (Deut 13:9; 17:7). Jesus was threatened with stoning for blasphemy (John 8:59; 10:31, 33). He saved a woman who was about to be stoned for adultery (John 8:2–11). **Stephen** was accused of blasphemy and was executed by stoning (Acts 7:55–60), and **Paul** survived one attempted stoning (Acts 14:19; 2 Cor 11:25).

SUCCOTH (Hebrew, "booths" or "tabernacles")

1. The first site reached by the Israelites during the Exodus; it was located in the Nile's eastern delta between Rameses and Etham (Exod 12:57, 13:20; Num 33:5–6). The site is probably Tell el-Maskhuta in the Wadi Tumilat.

2. A city located in **Transjordan** just north of where the Jabbok meets the Jordan. **Jacob** stopped there when he returned from Aram and "built himself a house, and made booths for his cattle; therefore the place is called Succoth" (Gen 33:17). Once part of the kingdom of Sihon, it was apportioned to the tribe of Gad at the time of the conquest of Canaan. (Josh 13:27). **Gideon** inflicted a severe retribution upon the inhabitants of Succoth when he was refused assistance there during his pursuit of the Midianites (Judg 8:4–17). The bronze vessels for Solomon's **Temple** were cast near Succoth (1 Kgs 7:46; 2 Chr 4:17). The site of Succoth is probably Tell Deir Alla.

SUKKOTH *See* **Booths, feast of**.

SUN Created by God to mark days and years (Gen 1:14) and to give light to the world (Gen 1:15). The sun was an object of worship by ancient civilizations such as Egypt and Mesopotamia. Sun worship was specifically forbidden in the **Law** (Deut 4:19; 17:3). At the time of the Divided Monarchy, worshipping the sun became part of the idolatry that infested Judah, and **Josiah** ordered the destruction of all objects of worship related to the sun. The cult had been introduced under the influence of the Assyrians (2 Kgs 23:11; Ezek 8:16).

Jesus's face at the Transfiguration is compared to the shining sun (Matt 17:2), but the glory of God and of Jesus is greater than the sun (Isa 60:19; Acts 26:13; Rev 21:23, 22:5). Scripture shows the sun as part of creation; it exists for the benefit of the created order (Deut 33:14; 2 Sam 23:4; Matt 5:45). The sun is admired for its constancy (Ps 72:17; 89:36), but the sun stood still during **Joshua**'s battle at Gibeon (Josh 10:12–14), and the shadow of the sun was turned back ten steps on the dial as a sign for Hezekiah (2 Kgs 20:8–11). The sun also hid itself at the death of the Lord on the Cross (Matt 27:45; Luke 23:44–45). Times of judgment are often described as times when the sun was darkened (Exod 10:21–29; Isa 13:10; Joel 2:31; Matt 24:29; Mark 13:24; Rev 6:12, 8:12, 9:2).

SUPPER, LAST *See* **Eucharist**.

SUPPER, LORD'S *See* **Eucharist**.

SUSA One of the capital cities of ancient Persia (modern Shush in Iran) located on the river Karun at the foot of the Zagros Mountains. Susa served as the capital of Elam. The city enjoyed considerable political prominence under Elam and successor states until it was sacked in 645 B.C. by the Assyrians under Ashurbanipal. Under the Persians, Susa was one of the three chief royal cities (Neh 1:1; Dan 8:2). Darius I constructed a palace in Susa that was restored by Artaxerxes I and II and that figured in the book of Esther (1:2, 5; 2:3; 3:15). Excavation of the site, starting in 1851 and continuing through the twentieth century, discovered—among other treasures—the famous Code of Hammurabi preserved on a basalt column.

SUSANNA The name of two women in the Bible.

1. The central character in Dan 13, a chapter that is found only in the Greek version of Daniel (*see* **Deuterocanonical**). She was the daughter of Joakim, a wealthy Jew in the Babylonian Exile. Two elders who had been appointed judges over the Jewish community lusted after her. When she refused their improper advances, they falsely accused her of adultery, and she was condemned to death on the basis of their testimony. As her execution approached, Daniel intervened and cross-examined the two elders. He exposed the falsehood of their testimony and Susanna was released. The elders were then stoned to death. The story not only demonstrates Daniel's wisdom but also advocates trusting that God will deliver his people from injustice.

2. A wealthy benefactress who traveled with Jesus and his entourage; she is mentioned only in Luke 8:3.

SWEAR *See* **Covenant**; **Oath**.

SWEATING BLOOD *See* **Gethsemane**.

SWINE Defined by the **Law** of Moses as unclean animals (Lev 11:7; Deut 14:8), swine could not be eaten (Isa 55:4; 66:17) or sacrificed (Isa 66:3). Abstaining from eating swine became especially important during the period of the Maccabees, when Antiochus IV Epiphanes imposed an aggressive program of Hellenization (1 Macc 1:47). Those who refused to eat pork were tortured and executed. Eleazar (2 Macc 6:18–31) and the seven brothers (2 Macc 7:1–42) were among the Jewish martyrs.

The swine represents something despised by the religious Jew. Jesus said, "do not throw your pearls before swine" (Matt 7:6). He allowed the demons possessing a man in the territory of the Gerasenes to take possession of a herd of swine that was then driven into the sea (Matt 8:30–32; Mark 5:11–13, 16; Luke 8:32). In the Parable of the Prodigal Son, the unfortunate son had to herd swine, which was about the lowest station he could reach in life (Luke 15:15). The Second Letter of Peter 2:22 uses an old proverb, "the sow is washed only to wallow in the mire" as an image of the sinner returning to sin.

SWORD A long-bladed weapon, often with both edges filed sharp. The swords wielded by the patriarchs were probably made of bronze (Gen 27:40; 31:26; 48:22). By the late second millennium B.C., iron replaced bronze for swords, and in Palestine the Philistines' monopoly on iron technology gave them a for-midable advantage over the Israelites, most of whom did not have swords (1 Sam 13:19–22).

The sword was used as a metaphorical image for a sharp tongue, slander, and cutting words (Ps 55:21; Prov 12:18, 30:14). It is used to suggest war and death (Lev 26:25; 2 Sam 11:25; Jer 5:12; Ezek 7:15). God's word is compared to a two-edged sword (Heb 4:12; Rev 1:16) and a weapon by which God punishes sinners (Ps 7:12; Isa 66:16; and especially Ezek 21:18–22). In the Messianic days of peace, swords will be beaten into plowshares (Isa 2:4; Mic 4:3); conversely, in the terrible **Day of the Lord** in Joel 4:10, plowshares will be beaten into swords.

Peter wielded a sword to defend Jesus at the time of his arrest (Matt 26:51; Mark 14:47; Luke 22:49; John 18:10), but Jesus told him that those who live by the sword shall die by the sword (Matt 26:52; cf. Matt 5:38–48; Luke 6:27–30, 32–36; 22:35–28). In this statement, Jesus makes clear his opposition to the use of violence to promote or defend the Kingdom of God.

SYCHAR *See* **Jacob's well**.

SYENE An Egyptian town, perhaps modern Aswan, on the Nile. Isaiah 49:12 mentions it as a place from which the Lord's people will return. Ezekiel 29:10 and 30:6 use it to describe the southern frontier of Egypt.

SYMEON *See* **Simeon**.

SYNAGOGUE (Greek, "meeting place") A Jewish place of assembly, prayer, and religious instruction. Synagogues were established in the period after the destruction of Jerusalem in 586 B.C. and the **Dispersion** of the Jewish people across the Mediterranean world. The synagogue served as a means of preserving Jewish faith and worship in a world where Temple attendance was relatively infrequent.

I. ORIGINS

In the Greek Old Testament, the term "synagogue" is used to refer to the assembly of the people of Israel (Num 16:3; Josh 22:16; Ps 74:2). Although the general meaning did not change, by the New Testament period the word was also applied to the place where the gatherings of people occurred. When exactly the synagogue first appeared as a house of prayer and worship is uncertain, except that it developed from a need felt as early as the period of the **Exile** (mid-sixth century B.C.; cf. Ezek 11:16, 20:1). The first synagogues were probably informal gatherings in private homes.

By the time of the NT, synagogue buildings were found in Palestine and in the lands of the Dispersion (Luke 7:5; Acts 13:14, 17:17). In the Scriptures, synagogues served as places of prayer and instruction (Matt 6:5; Luke 4:16; Acts 15:21), as well as places where judicial questions and community discipline were addressed (Matt 10:17, 23:34; Luke 12:11). Synagogues were found throughout Palestine and in places where there was a large community of Jews (Acts 13:5, 14; 14:1). Larger cities, such as Jerusalem, often had several synagogues (Acts 6:9); according to legends, there were 394 or even 480 synagogues in Jerusalem at the time that Jerusalem was destroyed by the Romans in A.D. 70. According to the Gospels, Jesus taught in synagogues in Nazareth (Matt 13:54; Luke 4:16) and Capernaum (Mark 1:21; Luke 7:5; John 6:59). **Paul** found synagogues in many cities of Asia Minor and Greece.

II. FEATURES

Unlike the Temple, the synagogue was not a dwelling place of God. There were no sacrifices, and participation in religious services was open to members of the congregation and even to visitors and guests (Matt 4:23; Luke 4:16; Acts 13:15). Members were invited to lead prayers, and guests were shown the utmost courtesy.

Government (cf. Josephus, *Ant.* 19.291) was in the hands of the synagogue elders, who were probably the same as the elders of the community. They had the duty to enforce discipline by lashing and even expulsion (cf. Matt 10:7, 23:34; Mark 13:9; Luke 12:11; 21:12; Acts 9:2, 22:19; 26:11). The administration and maintenance of the synagogue were entrusted to the "ruler of the synagogue" (cf. Mark 5:22; Acts 13:15; 18:8), who also ensured that worship was properly conducted according to tradition.

The synagogue held services on the **Sabbath** and on feast days. Worship began with the recitation of the Shema (Deut 6:4–9, 11:13–21; Num 15:37–41), the profession of faith, followed by a prayer recited by a member of the community that was initially improvised but became standardized. The prayers were followed by a reading from the **Law** in Hebrew (Acts 15:21); the reading was then translated into or paraphrased in the vernacular and discussed in a homily by a member of the congregation (Acts 13:15). A reading from the Prophets was added later. The readings from the Pentateuch were arranged according to a three-year cycle. A benediction completed the services (Num 6:24–26).

The synagogue was constructed along simple lines, perhaps on the model of the Temple, with a rectangular hall, a nave, and two side aisles. Entrance was accessed by one or more doors. Later synagogues were designed to segregate the sexes. A portable ark or chest in which the scrolls of the Law and Prophets were kept was given a position of prominence against the front wall. There were also a table, lamps, horns, and trumpets for use in ceremonies. Seats facing the ark were reserved for the chief figures of the synagogue (Matt 23:6). Few archaeological remains of synagogues in Palestine date before the third century A.D.; most older Palestinian synagogues were probably destroyed in the terrible wars of the first and second centuries A.D. The oldest archaeological remains of a synagogue found so far were excavated in Alexandria, Egypt, and date from the second half of the third century B.C.

III. IMPORTANCE

The synagogue was a place of worship, but it was also a gathering place of the Jewish people that helped preserve the Jewish faith and culture, especially when Jewish communities were spread across the Greek and Roman world. The synagogue helped the Jewish people maintain their unique identity over against the powerful cultural influences of **Hellenism**. At the synagogue Jewish people in cities everywhere were able to meet together, to consult, and to maintain the structure for community life in the Dispersion.

The synagogue also played a significant role in the spread of the Christian faith. Jesus attended the synagogue and regularly taught there (Matt 4:23, 9:35, 12:9; Mark 1:39, 3:1; Luke 4:15, 6:6, 13:10; John 18:20), using his homilies to proclaim the Gospel (Mark 1:21; Luke 4:16–21; John 6:59). Paul started his ministry by preaching in the synagogue at Damascus (Acts 9:20) and visited synagogues on his journeys, preaching the Gospel when he was invited to deliver the homily (Acts 13:14, 15; 14:1; 17:1, 10; 18:4; 19:8). Eventually Christians abandoned (or were thrown out of) the synagogues, but these houses of worship were absolutely crucial in the early proclamation of the faith in the lands of the eastern Roman Empire. (*See also* **liturgy**.)

SYNOPTIC GOSPELS The Gospels of Matthew, Mark, and Luke. They are so called because they tell the story of Jesus's life from a similar point of view. The three Gospels have a great deal of material in common, the incidents are often in the same order, and sometimes the same words are use to describe events. (*See* **Synoptic problem**.)

SYNOPTIC PROBLEM The name biblical scholars give to the apparent relation between the Gospels of Matthew, Mark, and Luke. These Gospels are called "synoptic" because their contents can be arranged in parallel columns and compared at a glance (Greek *synopsis* means "view together"). The "problem" is how to account for their similarities and differences. In the judgment of most scholars, the Synoptic Gospels are interdependent at a literary level; that is, their presentation of Jesus is so remarkably similar in content, order, and expression that it seems likely that the Evangelists relied on one another's work. The Synoptic problem is thus the quest to ascertain, on the basis of painstaking analysis, which of the Gospels appeared first, second, and third, and therefore, which evangelist made use of the work of his predecessor(s).

I. EARLY HISTORY

For the most part, the Synoptic problem is a modern problem that occupies the attention of modern scholars. Ancient scholars were more concerned with preaching and harmonizing the texts of Matthew, Mark, and Luke. Few were interested in questions about the "sequence" of Gospel composition or the "sources" of information the Evangelists may have utilized. Still, the witness of history indicates that a handful of Christian writers did address these issues at some level.

1. *Luke.* The evangelist Luke states in the prologue to his Gospel that he researched the life of Jesus before setting it down in writing, and that others had attempted to put the story of Jesus into narrative form before him (Luke 1:1–4). It is clear that Luke made use of sources—oral or written or both—and that other authors had previously made attempts to preserve information about Jesus in written form. Scholars have not identified these anonymous authors or their works with certainty, but the possibility exists that Luke consulted the Gospel of Matthew or Mark or both in the course of his research.

2. *Early Christians.* Early Christian testimony is unanimous in claiming that the Gospel of Matthew was the first Gospel to be written. This was more or less an unquestioned tradition from the second century A.D. until the dawn of the eighteenth century. It is important to recognize, however, that the early transmitters of this tradition contend that Matthew wrote his Gospel in a Semitic language, either Hebrew or Aramaic (Saint Irenaeus, *Against Heresies* 3.1.1; Origen, in Eusebius's *Hist. Eccl.* 6.25; Saint Jerome, *Vir. Ill.* 3; Saint Augustine, *Harmony of the Gospels* 1.4). Unfortunately, no such edition survives, and it is unclear how such a Semitic original would relate to the canonical text of Matthew found in the New Testament, which is written in Greek.

3. *Papias.* An early bishop named Papias, who lived only a generation after the apostles, claims that the evangelist Mark composed his Gospel as a written summary of Peter's preaching delivered in Rome (see Eusebius, *Hist. Eccl.* 3.39). This could be taken to mean that Mark relied solely on the oral catechesis of Peter and thus never made use of any written sources at all.

4. *Saint Clement of Alexandria.* Writing in Egypt around A.D. 200, Saint Clement of Alexandria says that he learned from elder churchmen that the two Gospels containing genealogies of Jesus were written first (see Eusebius, *Hist. Eccl.* 6.14). This is a claim that Matthew (1:1–16) and Luke (3:23–38) were the first two Gospels to be written, and that Mark and John appeared later.

5. *Saint Augustine of Hippo.* Writing about A.D. 400, Saint Augustine of Hippo made an intensive study of Gospel parallels and passed on a tradition that Matthew wrote first, then Mark, then Luke (*Harmony of the Gospels* 1.3). On his authority, medieval Christendom came to view the order of the canon as the order of Gospel composition (Matthew, Mark, Luke, John). This view was advanced earlier by the Greek theologian Origen of Alexandria (see Eusebius, *Hist. Eccl.* 6.25).

II. MODERN HISTORY

The surge in critical scholarship of the Bible in the eighteenth century was attended by a surge of interest in Synoptic relations. Whereas earlier scholars had applied themselves to harmonizing the Gospels and resolving apparent discrepancies, modern exegetes developed a greater interest in uncovering the oral and written sources behind the canonical texts. This research inevitably involved them in questions about the composition of the first three Gospels. Methodologically, the new spirit of inquiry led to a diminished regard for tradition and early Christian testimony in the name of scientific objectivity. For these scholars, defining the relationship among Matthew, Mark, and Luke would require primarily, if not exclusively, the most minute examination of the texts by themselves.

Statistical analysis was very much part of this new procedure. Having determined that Matthew contains 1,068 verses, Mark 661 verses, and Luke 1,150 verses, it was discovered that the three Synoptic Gospels have about 330 verses in common (called "the tri-

ple tradition"). Matthew and Luke, however, have about 230 verses in common that have no parallel in Mark (called "the double tradition"). Each of the first three Gospels also has material unique to itself (called "the single tradition"). The order in which events were narrated was also taken into account, as was the degree of verbal agreement.

German scholarship, which first posed the question of Synoptic relations and began to wrestle with it, developed a myriad of hypotheses in the eighteenth and nineteenth centuries to explain the data. The canonical texts were said to arise from such things as protogospels, from the prevalence of oral tradition, from lost documents, and from different sectors of early Christianity. By the end of the nineteenth century, Synoptic studies had taken firm root in other countries beyond Germany, most notably in England. In twentieth-century scholarship, these earlier developments and experiments crystallized into three main hypotheses.

1. *The Augustinian Hypothesis.* This hypothesis maintains that the compositional order of the Synoptic Gospels is the same as the canonical order: Matthew, Mark, and Luke. Thus, advocates claim that Matthew wrote first, then Mark abbreviated Matthew, and then Luke relied on the work of both of his predecessors. The strength of the Augustinian paradigm is that it claims significant support from Christian antiquity—not only the unanimous tradition that Matthew wrote first, but also the tradition that puts Mark second and Luke third. Besides this, the hypothesis nicely ac-

counts for the Jewishness of the Gospel of Matthew—a trait one would expect in the earliest Gospel to be written but not from a later Gospel that used a less Jewish source. The weakness of the argument, according to some, is that the literary features peculiar to Mark are absent from Luke, yet certain literary features from Luke seem to show up in Mark. Only a small minority of scholars maintain the Augustinian hypothesis today.

2. *The Two-Gospel Hypothesis*. This hypothesis defines the order of composition as Matthew, Luke, and Mark. Matthew is said to have been written first; Luke is said to have used Matthew, making several passes through the text so as to follow a different sequence of presentation; then Mark is said to have produced a selective abridgment of Matthew and Luke, with his focus more on the actions of Jesus than on his teachings. The strength of the Two-Gospel paradigm is the unanimous tradition that Matthew wrote first as well as the fact that literary features of Luke's style show up in Mark, but not vice versa. The main weakness of the argument is the question of relevancy: If practically all of Mark's content already appears in Matthew and Luke, why did Mark write at all? The Two-Gospel hypothesis is sometimes called the Griesbach hypothesis, after the German scholar J. J. Griesbach who first popularized it. Due to a spike in popularity in the latter half of the twentieth century, this hypothesis is held by a growing minority of scholars today.

3. *The Two-Source Hypothesis*. This hypothesis contends that Mark was the first Gospel and that Matthew and Luke both made independent use of Mark as well as a hypothetical source document that preserved significant sayings of Jesus, conventionally called Q (an abbreviation for the German word *quelle*, meaning "source"). Matthew and Luke are said to have drawn additional material from their own unique sources, generally called M and L. The key to the development of this paradigm is the "double tradition"—that is, the 230 verses that Matthew and Luke have in common but that Mark does not contain (the vast majority of which are "sayings" of Jesus rather than recorded events). To account for this material, scholars have posited the existence of a source document that supplied sayings to Matthew and Luke but of which Mark had no knowledge. Likewise, the fact that Mark is the shortest Gospel led many to infer that it must have been the first to be written, since stories tend to expand and grow as they are retold rather than shrink and contract. The strength of the Two-Source hypothesis is the simplicity with which it explains why Matthew and Luke wrote their much longer Gospels: to provide more information than Mark had given. Mark is also the roughest of the Synoptic Gospels in terms of style—and it is difficult to account for this quality if Mark was drawing from Matthew and Luke, which are more elegantly written and composed. The weaknesses of this argument, however, are fairly pronounced: there is no ancient tradition that puts Mark first; the Q document is purely hypothetical—that is, there is no hard evidence of its existence; and most important, there are a number of so-called minor agreements between Matthew and Luke against Mark, and this makes it difficult to maintain that Mat-

thew and Luke copied Mark independently of each other. Still, the Two-Source hypothesis, also known as the Marcan Priority hypothesis, was the most widely accepted solution to the Synoptic problem in the twentieth century and remains so to this day.

In the end, it is fair to say that no one hypothesis answers all the questions raised by the Synoptic problem. Each has its strengths, and each has its weaknesses. Debates about the historical value of early tradition, the soundness of methodological criteria, and the uncertain role of oral tradition are destined to make the Synoptic problem a lively issue for many years to come.

SYNTYCHE A Christian woman in the community at Philippi. **Paul** implored her to settle differences with another member, Euodia, after some apparent quarrel (Phil 4:2–3).

SYRACUSE A Greek city on the coast of Sicily where the ship taking **Paul** to Rome landed after wintering on the island of Malta (Acts 28:11–12).

SYRIA The region directly north of Palestine and southeast of Asia Minor. In Old Testament times, Syria was the home of the Arameans, and later the seat of the Seleucid Empire. Syria became a Roman province in 64 B.C. after the conquests of Pompey the Great. In New Testament times, Syria was governed by an imperial legate of Rome who wielded considerable influence and power in the eastern part of the Roman Empire (Luke 2:2; Acts 15:23, 41; 18:18; 20:3; 21:3; Gal 1:21). (*See* **Antioch**; **Aram**; **Damascus**; **Seleucids**.)

SYRIAC VERSION *See* **Versions of the Bible**.

SYROPHOENICIAN An inhabitant of the region of **Phoenicia** in the Roman province of Syria. To Jews, Phoenicians were basically Canaanites. A Syrophoenician woman implored Jesus to expel the demon from her daughter's body (Mark 7:24–30; Matt 15:21–28 calls her a Canaanite). Jesus tested the woman by treating her with the typical Jewish contempt for Canaanites: "Let the children first be fed, for it is not right to take the children's bread and throw it to the dogs." She replied, "Yes, Lord; yet even the dogs under the table eat the children's crumbs." Jesus told her then that her daughter was cured. The Gospel writers use this incident to show Jesus bringing hope not just to the Jews but also to the Gentiles—even the hated Canaanites.

SYRTIS A gulf off the North African coast, west of Cyrenaica, that was known for its shallow waters (Acts 27:17).

TAANACH A Canaanite town often identified with the modern Tell Ti'innik. It was situated directly west of Mount Gilboa near the southern end of the plain of Megiddo. The Canaanite ruler of the town was defeated by **Joshua** (Josh 12:21), but the tribe that received the city, Manasseh (1 Chr 7:29), could not gain control of it (Josh 17:12; Judg 1:27). The victory song of **Deborah** mentions the city in the context of the battle with the Canaanites under Sisera (Judg 5:19). Later, the inhabitants were subjugated and compelled into forced labor (Judg 1:28); under Solomon, the town was part of the fifth administrative district of the kingdom (1 Kgs 4:12). Taanach was also designated a **Levitical city** (Josh 21:25).

TABEEL The name of two men in the Old Testament.

1. The father of the unnamed person chosen by **Pekah**, king of Israel, and Rezin, king of Damascus, to replace **Ahaz** as king of Judah (Isa 7:5–6).

2. A Samaritan official in the service of the Persians (Ezra 4:7). He and his associates dispatched a letter to Artaxerxes I urging the king to halt the rebuilding of Jerusalem that had begun under the Jews returned from the Exile (Ezra 4:11–16).

TABERAH One of the locations where the Israelites camped on their **Exodus** journey in the wilderness (Deut 9:22). The complaints of the Israelites brought the anger of the Lord on them, and a fire was sent down that burned one end of the camp—thus the name "Taberah" ("burning"; Num 11:1–3).

TABERNACLE (Latin *tabernaculum*, "tent") The tent-sanctuary that Israel transported through the wilderness. The Tabernacle was manufactured at Mount Sinai and used as the central place of Israelite worship until the building of the **Temple** of Solomon. The Tabernacle was built at the express orders of Moses and according to very specific instructions from God. Exodus provides a detailed blueprint of its floor plan and furnishings (Exod 25–27) and then describes the actual creation of the Tabernacle (Exod 36–39, 40). Prior to this Tabernacle, Moses had a provisional "tent of meeting," which was used not for sacrifice but for meeting with God (Exod 33:7–11) whose presence was manifested in the form of a cloud (Exod 33:9).

I. CONSTRUCTION AND PLAN

The plan for the structure was based on a heavenly pattern revealed to Moses on Sinai (Exod 25:9, 40). The people provided the materials used for the construction, and the actual building of the Tabernacle was supervised by Bezalel and Oholiab (Exod 31:1–11). Exodus 40 recounts the solemn dedication of the Tabernacle, climaxing with the descent of a splendid cloud that "covered the tent of meeting, and the glory of the Lord filled the tabernacle . . . throughout all their journeys the cloud of the Lord was upon the tabernacle by day, and fire was in it by night, in the sight of all the house of Israel" (Exod 34, 38).

During the wilderness period, the Tabernacle stood in the center of the Israelite camp (Num 2:1–4), reminding the people of Israel that the Lord must be at the center of their lives. The Hebrew of the Old Testament uses different terms for the Tabernacle. One term, *miškān*, meaning "dwelling," conveyed the idea that the Lord dwelt there among his people; another, *'ōhel mô'ēd*, meaning "tent of meeting," referred to the Tabernacle not as a place of gathering for the Israelites but as a place where God and Israel met through the mediation of Moses (Exod 29:42). In effect, the Tabernacle was the place of God's presence with his people.

The interior of the Tabernacle had two rooms. The larger room, closer to the entrance, was a double square, 15 by 30 feet (about 4.5 by 9 meters), and the smaller room was a perfect cube of 15 feet (about 4.5 meters) in each dimension, separated from the other by a suspended veil or curtain. The larger room, called the "Holy Place," contained the altar of incense placed in front of the veil, the table for the **bread of the presence** on the north, and the golden seven-branched candlestick or lamp stand on the south. The smaller room was called the "most holy place" or the "holy of holies"; it was the earthly dwelling place of God Himself. The only item in the room was the **ark of the covenant**.

The exterior of the Tabernacle was enclosed in a court 100 by 50 cubits (about 150 by 75 feet or 46 by 23 meters). The entrance faced east; the outer perimeter consisted of curtains supported by sixty posts. Each post was seven and a half feet high. The Tabernacle itself was set in the western part of the court, with the great bronze altar of burnt offerings between it and the entrance to the court. Between the altar and the Tabernacle, toward the south, was a bronze basin of water, called the laver, that was used for various rites of purification.

II. KEY MOTIFS

The Tabernacle accompanied the Israelites throughout their wandering in the desert. Offerings were made daily on the bronze altar and the altar of incense (Exod 29:38–42). The task of maintaining and transporting the tent was placed in the hands of the Levites. Once the Israelites reached the Promised Land, the Tabernacle was set up for a time in **Shiloh** (Josh 18:1, 19:51; 1 Sam 1:3; Ps 78:60). Later, it was moved to **Gibeon** (1 Kgs 3:4; 1 Chr 16:39, 21:29). When David captured **Jerusalem** and brought the **ark of the covenant** into the city, a tent was constructed on Zion to receive it (2 Sam 6:17; 1 Chr 15:1). This tent, which sheltered nothing but the ark, was not the Tabernacle of Moses, according to 2 Chr 1:3–4. Solomon built his **Temple** to replace the Tabernacle, and elements of the Tabernacle were stored away in a room of the Temple (1 Kgs 8:4; 2 Chr 5:5) to demonstrate the direct link between the Temple and the Tabernacle. The essential design and arrangement of the Tabernacle were also preserved in the Temple, although on a grander scale.

The Tabernacle finally disappeared when the Temple was destroyed by the forces of King Nebuchadnezzar in 586 B.C.; 2 Macc 2:4–8 tells us that Jeremiah hid the ark, the tent, and the altar of incense in an unmarked cave on Mount Nebo.

III. THE TABERNACLE IN THE NEW TESTAMENT

References to the Tabernacle in the New Testament are mainly concentrated in the book of Hebrews. For example, in Heb 9:1–5, the activities performed within the Tabernacle are contrasted with Christ, the mediator of the New Covenant, who "entered once for all into the Holy Place, taking not the blood of goats and calves but his own blood, thus securing an eternal redemption" (Heb 9:12).

Hebrews shows us how the Mosaic Tabernacle was merely a model of the heavenly Tabernacle (Heb 8:2, 5; cf. Wis 9:8). The outer tent, Hebrews says, represented the Mosaic covenant while the inner tent, the holy of holies, represented the New Covenant brought by Christ. In the earthly Tabernacle, the high priest alone was authorized to enter the holy of holies once a year, but "Christ has entered, not into a sanctuary made with hands, a copy of the true one, but into heaven itself, now to appear in the presence of God on our behalf" (Heb 9:24). In Rev 21:3, the Tabernacle again appears as the dwelling place of God in the New Jerusalem.

Occasional references to the Tabernacle appear elsewhere in the NT as well. For instance, the Gospel of John describes the mystery of the Incarnation by saying that the divine Word "dwelt among us" (John 1:14). The Greek verb *skēnoō*, here rendered "dwelt," also means "to pitch a tent or tabernacle." The idea is that Israel's tent-sanctuary prefigures God dwelling in the midst of his people in the Person of Jesus Christ. Likewise, when Paul contrasts the "earthly tent" of our mortal bodies with the eternal "house" that awaits us in heaven, he is probably alluding to the Tabernacle giving way to the more permanent Temple (2 Cor 5:1). Finally, the climactic vision of Revelation declares that God's "dwelling" (or "tabernacle") is forever with the saints of the New Covenant (Rev 21:3) (CCC 433, 592, 662). (*See also* **Ark of the covenant**.)

TABERNACLES, FEAST OF *See* **Booths, feast of**.

TABITHA *See* **Dorcas**.

TABLE OF NATIONS The genealogical list of seventy nations descended from **Noah** in Gen 10 (cf. 1 Chr 1:4–24). It traces each of the nations known to the Israelites back to one of Noah's three sons. It is notable that Israel's most hated enemies are listed as descendants of **Ham**, the cursed son of Noah who "saw the nakedness of his father."

TABLES OF THE LAW The two stone tablets on which were inscribed the Ten Commandments that God gave to Moses on Mount Sinai (Exod 24:12; 31:18; 32:15, 16, 19; 34:1, 28; Deut 4:13; 5:22; 9:9, 10, 15, 17; 10:1, 2, 4, 5; 1 Kgs 8:9). Two sets of tablets were actually made, since Moses destroyed the first set of tablets after he saw the Israelites worshipping the golden calf (Exod 32:19; Deut 9:17). The second set was cut by Moses and carried up the mountain to receive the divine writing (Exod 34:1, 28); these tablets were stored in the **ark of the covenant** (Deut 10:8; Exod 25:16; 1 Kgs 8:9). (*See* **Ten Commandments**.)

TABOR The name of two places in the Bible.

1. A Levitical city in the territory of Zebulun (1 Chr 6:77).

2. A mountain in lower Galilee five miles (eight kilometers) east of **Nazareth**, known today as Jabal al-Tur (Jer 46:18; Ps 89:13). The mountain commands a strong position on the main axis leading north and south across the plain of Esdraelon. The Israelites who took part in the mustering of **Barak** gathered at Mount Tabor (Judg 4:6). It was also the site of idolatry (Hos 5:1). Christian tradition places the Transfiguration of Jesus on Mount Tabor, although the mountain is not named specifically in the New Testament (Matt 17:1–8; Mark 9:2–8; Luke 9:28–36).

TABRIMMON The father of **Ben-hadad I**, the Syrian king of Damascus (1 Kgs 15:18). His name means "[the god] Rimmon is good."

TADMOR An oasis settlement that was fortified by Solomon (2 Chr 8:4). It is also known as Palmyra, which is identified with modern Tudmor, northeast of Damascus. Some schol-

ars suggest that the Tadmor of 2 Chr 8:4 is the same as the Tamar of 1 Kgs 9:18, but this is uncertain.

TAHPANHES A settlement in the eastern Nile Delta of Egypt (Jer 2:16, 46:14; Ezek 30:18), probably the modern Tell ed-Defenna. After the destruction of Jerusalem in 586 B.C., a band of surviving Jews fled to Tahpanhes, taking Jeremiah with them (Jer 43:7–9; 44:1). At Tahpanhes, Jeremiah was commanded by the Lord to hide stones at the entrance of the pharaoh's palace as a symbolic prediction of the imminent threat of **Nebuchadnezzar**, who would construct his throne on that site after conquering Egypt (Jer 43:8–13).

TALENT An ancient unit of weight and value, normally that of metals such as silver and gold. The Hebrew talent (*kikkār*) was about 75.7 pounds or 35 kilograms (1 Kgs 9:14; 20:39). The Greek talent (*talanton*) was also a large amount of money, but the unit varied greatly depending on the time, place, and metal (Matt 18:24; 25:15–18).

TALITHA CUMI The Aramaic expression uttered by Jesus when he healed Jairus's daughter (Mark 5:41). It means "little girl, get up"; the word for "girl" is derived from the Aramaic for "lamb" and was used as an affectionate address.

TALMAI The name of two men in the Old Testament.

1. One of the giant Canaanite warriors who lived in Hebron before the conquest of Canaan (Num 13:22). He and his kinsmen,

Ahiman and Sheshai, were driven out by Caleb and the Judahites (Josh 15:14; Judg 1:10).

2. The king of Geshur, the son of Ammihud; his daughter, **Maacah**, bore **David**'s third son, **Absalom** (2 Sam 3:3; 1 Chr 3:2). After the murder of Amnon, Absalom found refuge with his grandfather Talmai in Geshur for three years (2 Sam 13:37–38).

TALMUD (Hebrew, "study" or "learning") The vast collection of rabbinic teaching consisting of the Mishnah and the Gemara. The Talmud functions as a body of Jewish law and is considered binding for Orthodox Jews.

The Mishnah, meaning "repetition" and "study," denotes the collection of oral traditions and laws that were compiled by Judah the Patriarch about A.D. 200. The Gemara (from the Aramaic "to learn") is basically an Aramaic commentary on the Mishnah. It presents detailed interpretations of the words and sentences of the Mishnah, comparisons of individual elements of the Mishnah with others, stories related to the rabbis, and interpretations of Scripture. Most of the Gemara is written in Aramaic, although some traditions are in Hebrew.

The Talmud exists in two collections, the Palestinian Talmud (called *Yĕrûšalmî*) and the Babylonian Talmud (called *Babli*). The Palestinian Talmud was compiled by the rabbinical schools and dates from the fifth century A.D. Also known as "the Talmud of the land of Israel" and "the Talmud of the West," it is not a complete commentary but focuses only on the first parts of the Mishnah. The Babylonian Talmud is the larger collection; it was finished around the middle of the sixth century

A.D. Additions and revisions were made over the next centuries. The Babylonian Talmud became authoritative for most of Judaism and exercised an enormous influence over much of European and American Judaism; the Jewish populations of the Mediterranean follow the Palestinian Talmud.

The Talmuds are a major source of historical information about Judaism as it was practiced in the last centuries of the ancient world.

TAMAR The name of three women in the Old Testament.

1. The Canaanite wife of Er, **Judah**'s first son (Gen 38:6); after Er was slain by God for his wickedness, she was married to Judah's second son, **Onan**, in keeping with the custom of the levirate marriage (cf. Deut 25:5–6). Onan, however, refused to father children by her and so he died (Gen 38:7–10). When Judah delayed marrying his last son to her, Tamar disguised herself as a prostitute and had relations with Judah (Gen 38:12–19). By this union she bore twin sons, Perez and Zerah (Gen 38:27–30); through Perez she was an ancestress of **David** (Ruth 4:12, 18–22) and ultimately of **Jesus Christ** (Matt 1:3). (*See* **Marriage**.)

2. The daughter of David and Maacah and the full sister of **Absalom** (2 Sam 13:1–22). She became the object of the intense passion of **Amnon**, her half brother. Amnon used the pretense of sickness to lure her to his chambers and then raped her. Absalom avenged this act by arranging the murder of Amnon (2 Sam 13:23–33).

3. The only daughter of David's son Absalom, described as beautiful (2 Sam 14:27).

TAMMUZ A Mesopotamian deity of vegetation. Myth had it that Tammuz was married to the goddess Ishtar, who went into the underworld after his death to secure his release and restore fertility to the earth. Worship of the deity included rites of lamentation that were described by Ezekiel (8:14).

TANIS *See* **Zoan**.

TAPPUAH

1. One of the sons of Hebron of the tribe of Judah (1 Chr 2:43).

2. A town in the low western hills of Judah (Josh 15:34, 53). It is probably the modern Beit Natif.

3. A town in Ephraim, in the hill country of Samaria (Josh 16:8) on the southern border of Manasseh (Josh 17:7–8). It is probably the modern Sheikh Abu Zarad.

TARGUM (Hebrew, "translation") An Aramaic translation of the Hebrew Bible. Targums are found for every book of the Old Testament except for Ezra, Nehemiah, and Daniel. The Targums emerged as a direct result of the **Babylonian Captivity**. After the Exile, Aramaic replaced Hebrew as the common language of the Jewish people, and the custom developed for the Hebrew readings to be followed by an oral paraphrase of the readings in Aramaic for the benefit of the community. The earliest versions would have been loosely and informally undertaken, but over time, they assumed a more structured form and became traditional readings.

The Targums are invaluable for providing a picture of Jewish interpretation of the OT during the New Testament period, as well as useful evidence of the vernacular of ancient Palestine.

TARSHISH

1. One of the sons of Javan and a descendant of **Noah** through Japheth (Gen 10:4; 1 Chr 1:7).

2. The name is used also for a place, although the precise location is uncertain. According to references in the Old Testament, Tarshish was a coastal nation or settlement, presumably on the Mediterranean (Jonah 1:3, 4:2; Isa 66:19). The region had an abundance of silver (Jer 10:9), tin, lead, and iron (Ezek 27:12). Solomon constructed a fleet of merchant vessels called the "ships of Tarshish" (1 Kgs 10:22; 22:48), which means they were designed for distant sea voyages as far as Tarshish. The implication that Tarshish lies quite a distance from Israel lends credence to the view that it was on the coast of Spain at the other end of the Mediterranean.

3. One of the sons of Bilhan of the tribe of Benjamin (1 Chr 7:10).

4. A prince of Persia and Media who served as a royal advisor to King **Ahasuerus** (Esth 1:14).

TARSUS The chief city of the Cilician plain on the southeastern coast of Asia Minor; the city is best known as the home of **Paul** (Acts 22:3). Tarsus was fed by the river Cydnus and was situated some thirty miles south of the famous Cilician Gates, a pass through the Taurus Mountains. The city rebelled against the

Seleucid king Antiochus IV Epiphanes in the second century B.C. (2 Macc 4:30), and by New Testament times, the city was the capital of the Roman province of Cilicia. A rich commercial center, Tarsus could justifiably be called "no mean city" (Acts 21:39). After Paul's conversion and the dangers he faced at Jerusalem, the apostles sent him to Tarsus (Acts 9:30). There **Barnabas** sought him out to assist in the ministry of the church at Antioch (Acts 11:25).

TARTAN The title of a high-ranking Assyrian official. A Tartan was sent by **Sargon II** to besiege Ashdod (Isa 20:1); likewise, a Tartan was part of the delegation of officials sent by **Sennacherib** to demand the surrender of Jerusalem in 701 B.C. (2 Kgs 18:17).

TATTENAI The governor of the Persian province or satrapy called "Beyond the River," which was made up of the lands west of the Euphrates, including Syria, Palestine, and Phoenicia. Tattenai appears in Ezra when he inquired of the Persian king **Darius I** whether it was lawful for the Jews to rebuild the Temple in Jerusalem (Ezra 5:3, 6). As it turned out, the governor was instructed not to interfere with the reconstruction; instead, he was to help finance the effort with monies from his provincial treasury (Ezra 6:6–13).

TAX COLLECTORS Officials who collected monies from taxpayers on behalf of governing authorities. Typically, a tax collector was a private businessman who paid the government a fixed amount estimated according to various calculations. Any amount collected over the calculated estimate could be kept by the tax collector as a personal commission, but the fixed amount had to be paid, whether that amount was actually collected or not. For obvious reasons, the system was open to abuse, and tax collectors in first-century Palestine were despised (cf. Matt 5:46; Luke 6:32) along with sinners and Gentiles (Matt 9:11; 11:19; 18:17). Tax collectors represented an especially despicable aspect of Roman rule and oppression.

Jesus shocked the Pharisees with his willingness to interact with tax collectors, and in the face of the accusations that he was a friend of publicans and sinners, he replied to the Pharisees that he had come to call not the righteous but the sinner (Mark 2:15–17; Luke 7:34). Tax collectors listened to both **John the Baptist** (Matt 21:32; Luke 7:29) and Jesus (Luke 15:1). **Matthew**, or Levi, was a tax collector and was at his tax collector's table when Jesus called him to become an apostle (Matt 9:9; Mark 2:14; Luke 5:27–38). Likewise, **Zacchaeus**, the chief tax collector in Jericho, invited Jesus into his home (Luke 19:1–10). In a parable, Jesus uses the tax collector as a model of humility that calls forth the mercy of God (Luke 18:9–14).

TEKEL *See* **Mene, Mene, Tekel, Parsin.**

TEKOA A town in Judah, south of **Bethlehem**, now called Khirbet Tequa. Tekoa was the hometown of the prophet **Amos** (Amos 1:1); of Ira the son of Ikkesh, one of **David's** great warriors (2 Sam 23:26; 1 Chr 27:9); and of the wise woman chosen by **Joab** to convince David to reconcile with **Absalom** after he had killed Amnon (2 Sam 14:2). King **Rehoboam** strengthened the town's fortifications (2 Chr 11:6). People from Tekoa assisted later in the rebuilding of the city wall of Jerusalem (Neh 3:5, 27).

TEL-ABIB A site in Babylonia near the river Chebar to which exiled Jews were sent after the fall of Jerusalem (Ezek 3:15).

TELAIM A city in Judah where **Saul** gathered his army in preparation for war against the Amalekites (1 Sam 15:4). It may be the same as Telem, a site in the **Negeb** given to Judah (Josh 15:24).

TELASSAR An Aramean city populated by the people of Eden, one of the nations conquered by Assyria in the eighth century B.C. The city was destroyed and listed with Gozan, Haran, and Rezeph in **Sennacherib**'s message to **Hezekiah** that compelled the king to surrender (2 Kgs 19:12; Isa 37:12). It was located on the Euphrates.

TELL In Near Eastern archaeology, a hill or mound created by a long succession of human occupation. Typically, the site began as a small village that was established because of available nearby water or a strong defensive position. Over the course of centuries, the village might be destroyed or abandoned and another built on top of the old one because the geographical features or available resources were still useful. The tell is thus the creation of successive inhabitation and construction, but it is also the product of time. For archaeologists, the tell is a valuable source for information on the history of human civilization and culture, and contains vital remains, including buildings, potsherds, and debris. (*See also* **Archaeology**.)

TEMA A region in northern Arabia (Isa 21:14; Jer 25:23; Job 6:19). It was the home of the descendants of Ishmael (Gen 25:15; 1 Chr 1:30).

TEMAN The son of Eliphaz and a descendant of **Esau** (Gen 36:11, 15; 1 Chr 1:36, 53). It is also the name of a region in Edom (Ezek 25:13; Amos 1:12) that was well known for the wisdom of its inhabitants (Jer 49:7; Obad 8).

TEMPLE The central sanctuary where God dwelt in the midst of his people. The Temple in Jerusalem—the heart of Israel's religious life and worship—was not constructed until the emergence of the monarchy, but the idea of a central sanctuary was a feature of the Deuteronomic covenant.

I. *The Origins of the Temple*
II. *The Temple of Solomon*
III. *The Second Temple*
IV. *The Temple of Herod*
V. *The Temple in the New Testament*
   A. *The Gospels and Epistles*
   B. *Hebrews and Revelation*

There were three Temples constructed in Jerusalem:

1. The Temple of **Solomon** (ca. 960–586 B.C.), which was destroyed when the Babylonians conquered Jerusalem.
2. The Second Temple (ca. 515–19 B.C.), built on the ruins of the first after the **Exile**.
3. The Temple of **Herod** (19 B.C.–A.D. 70), an extensive renovation and enlargement of the Second Temple.

The place of the Temple in the life of Israel was recognized and respected by Jesus, who participated in its worship and feasts of pilgrimage. The Temple prefigured his own mystery, and his prediction of its destruction anticipated Jesus's own destruction and the establishment of the new and definitive Temple in his own glorified body (Matt 12:6; John 2:19–22).

I. THE ORIGINS OF THE TEMPLE

The beginnings of the Temple are remotely connected with the patriarchal period, when the people of God hallowed specific locations by calling upon the Lord in prayer and erecting altars at a number of worship sites (Gen 12:7–8; 13:18; 26:25; etc.). Yet the primary antecedent of the Temple is the Mosaic **Tabernacle**, the collapsible tentlike shrine that Israel manufactured at Mount Sinai (Exod 35–40) and transported through the wilderness (Num 4:1–33; 9:15–23) into the Promised Land (Josh 18:1). This sanctuary was believed to be an earthly replica of the Lord's heavenly dwelling (Exod 25:9, 40) and served as a centralized location for Israelite worship during the wilderness period (Lev 17:1–9).

The Deuteronomic covenant, which regulated Israel's life as a settled people in Canaan, envisioned a transition from a movable Tabernacle to a more permanent Temple. Once Israel established peace on its borders, it was to begin construction of a central sanctuary at a site chosen by God (eventually Jerusalem). As part of the Law given to Moses on the establishing of a central sanctuary, Moses declared,

> But when you go over the Jordan, and live in the land which the LORD your God gives you to inherit, and when he gives you rest from all your enemies round about, so that you live in safety, then to the place which the LORD your God will choose, to make his name dwell there, thither you shall bring all that I command you: your burnt offerings and your sacrifices, your tithes and the offering that you present, and all your votive offerings which you vow to the LORD. And you shall rejoice before the LORD your God, you and your sons and your daughters, your menservants and your maidservants, and the Levite that is within your towns, since he has no portion or inheritance with you. (Deut 12:10–14)

Centralizing worship in this way was a means of safeguarding the purity of Israel's faith. Pagan shrines dotted the landscape of ancient Canaan, and if the nation of Israel was going to keep its worship properly focused on the one true God, it would have to assemble and sacrifice at the one sanctuary consecrated for that purpose.

The conditions for building this sanctuary would not be met until the rise of the Israelite monarchy. In particular, it was David who gave Israel "rest" from its enemies (2 Sam 7:1) by conquering all the surrounding nations that shared a border with Israel (2 Sam 8:1–14). It was to him that God revealed both the site he had chosen for the Temple (1 Chr 21:28–22:1) and the heavenly blueprints for its construction.

But David was prohibited from building the Temple himself because he was stained with the blood of war (1 Chr 22:8). Nevertheless, he prepared for the undertaking by assembling the materials and manpower that would enable his son Solomon to do the building (1 Chr 22:2–16). The actual construction began in the fourth year of Solomon's reign (1 Kgs 6:1); the Temple was completed seven years later (1 Kgs 6:37–38).

II. THE TEMPLE OF SOLOMON

Solomon's Temple was built on the site of the threshing floor of Araunah the Jebusite, where David had built an altar to end the plague that had struck as God's punishment for David's census (2 Sam 24:18–25; 1 Chr 22:1). The site was on the crest of Mount **Moriah** (2 Chr 3:1). The Mosque of Omar, or "Dome of the Rock," marks the site today. For the construction, Solomon solicited the assistance of Hiram, king of Tyre, who provided skilled craftsmen and materials in exchange for food, and laborers were levied from among the tribes of Israel (1 Kgs 5:1–18).

The chief sources for information on the Solomonic Temple are 1 Kgs 6–7 and 2 Chr 3–4; these are supplemented by the description of an eschatological sanctuary provided by Ezek 40–43. The structure followed a rectangular plan and was made of stone and cedar wood. The Temple building itself was 90 feet (27 meters) long, 30 feet (9 meters) wide, and 45 feet (14 meters) high, with a porch at the front. On either side of the Temple entrance were two freestanding bronze pillars. The one on the right was Jakin ("He will establish") and the one on the left was Boaz ("In him is strength").

The interior of the Temple was approached by going up a flight of steps and passing through an atrium or porch (vestibule), which led to two chambers of different dimensions. The first, larger chamber, called the holy place (nave), was 40 cubits long by 20 cubits wide (60 by 30 feet). The second, smaller chamber

was the sanctuary, the holy of holies (inner sanctuary), 20 by 20 cubits (30 by 30 feet).

The holy place housed the altar of incense (1 Kgs 6:20–21), the table on which was placed the **bread of the presence**, and ten lamp stands (five at the right and five at the left; 1 Kgs 7:48–49). The holy of holies contained the **ark of the covenant** under two figures of the cherubim carved of olive wood (1 Kgs 6:23–28; 8:6–7).

In the courtyard before the Temple stood the bronze altar of sacrifice (1 Kgs 8:64) and the bronze laver (or "molten sea") supported by twelve bronze oxen. The laver contained water for the cult services, especially the ablutions for the priests (1 Kgs 7:23–26; 2 Chr). Storage rooms lined the outside of the Temple building on three sides (1 Kgs 6:5).

The solemn dedication of the Temple was held by Solomon during the feast of Booths (1 Kgs 8:1–66). The Temple remained in use for the next centuries, but after three centuries, during the reign of **Josiah**, it was in need of repairs. Contributions from the worshippers paid for the repairs (2 Kgs 22:4). But the restored Temple did not long survive. With the fall of Jerusalem in 586 B.C., the Temple was destroyed by the Babylonians under **Nebuchadnezzar** (2 Kgs 25:8–9, 13–17).

III. THE SECOND TEMPLE

The Temple lay in ruins during the first fifty years of the **Exile**, but hope was given to those in exile by **Ezekiel** through his vision of a new Temple (Ezek 40–43). The construction of a new temple was permitted by the decree of **Cyrus the Great** to the repatriated Jews (Ezra 1:1–4). The returning Jews began work immediately around 537 B.C., at which time they set up the altar of sacrifice and laid the foundation stones for the sanctuary building (Ezra 3:1–13). But the work was halted for about seventeen years (ca. 537–520 B.C.) because of the opposition of the Samaritans (Ezra 4:1–5). After the legal validation of their right to rebuild, the Jewish community of Jerusalem returned to work and finished the restored Temple in 515 B.C. Nothing is known of its dimensions and form, but it was certainly not as magnificent as Solomon's Temple (cf. Ezra 3:12–13; Hag 2:3).

The Temple was profaned by Antiochus IV Epiphanes (*see* **Seleucids**) in 167 B.C. (1 Macc 1:54–55; 2 Macc 6:1–6), but was purified and rededicated by **Judas Maccabeus** in 164 B.C. (1 Macc 4:36–59), an event celebrated thereafter as the feast of the Dedication, or Hanukkah (John 10:22).

IV. THE TEMPLE OF HEROD

Herod the Great commissioned a monumental renovation and expansion of the Temple complex. Work began in 20 B.C., and the main sanctuary building, which adhered closely to the dimensions of Solomon's Temple, was completed in about eighteen months. The Temple platform, however, with its series of courts, colonnade porches, and massive retaining walls, was not completed until the sixties A.D., only a few years before the destruction of the Temple by the Romans in A.D. 70.

The Herodian Temple was a dazzling spectacle of marble, white limestone, and gold. Its overall size was twice that of the Second Temple. The Jewish historian Josephus tells us that its courtyard was divided into several zones of progressively more restrictive access (*Ant.* 15.11.3; *B.J.* 1.21.1; 5.5.2). The outermost court

was the Court of the Gentiles, which was the largest open space in the Temple and could be accessed by all. Beyond this was the Court of Women, into which only the Jews could pass (a sentence of death was imposed on any Gentile who penetrated into this or any of the other inner courts, Acts 21:28–30). Beyond this was the Court of Israel, into which only Jewish males were permitted to enter. Finally, the open expanse surrounding the main sanctuary building was the Court of Priests, where the clergymen of Israel had a right of access and where they ministered at the altar of sacrifice.

The perimeter of the Temple platform was lined with covered colonnade porches called porticoes. At the northwest corner stood the Fortress Antonia, which was manned by Roman soldiers. The southeast corner of the platform, which overlooked the steep descent into the Kidron Valley, may have been the so-called pinnacle of the Temple (Matt 4:5).

V. THE TEMPLE IN THE NEW TESTAMENT

A. *The Gospels and Epistles*

The life of Jesus is closely tied to the Temple. Forty days after his birth he was dedicated to God in the Temple (Luke 2:22–38), and his family made routine trips to the Temple for the main Jewish feasts (Luke 2:41–51). Jesus continued these pilgrimages as an adult and presumably took part in the liturgies of Temple worship (John 2:13; 5:1; 7:14; 10:22–23; etc.). Like every Jewish man, he also paid the annual Temple tax (Matt 17:24–27). His reverence for the sanctuary stood out clearest when he saw others profaning the sacredness of the Temple.

On one occasion, Jesus burned with righteous zeal at the sight of merchants doing their business in the Temple courtyard (John 2:13–22). He reacted by driving them out and toppling their tables because they had made his "Father's house" into a "house of trade" (John 2:16). In the Synoptic Gospels, we see Jesus angered that such activities amounted to robbery, and beyond that, they made it all but impossible for pilgrims to pray (Matt 21:12–13; Mark 11:15–19; Luke 19:45–46).

Interestingly, Jesus also prophesied the destruction of the Temple. The Temple had its place in the economy of the Old Covenant, but with the inauguration of the New Covenant through the dying and rising of Christ, the institutions of the old would have to be swept away. Jesus envisioned the fall of the Temple and the termination of its worship in the Olivet Discourse (Matt 24:1–51; Mark 13:1–27; Luke 21:1–38). There would be a siege and conquest of Jerusalem (Luke 21:20) within the first Christian generation (Matt 24:34), he predicted. The fulfillment of his words came in A.D. 70, when Roman legions laid siege to Jerusalem and eventually burned and leveled the Temple.

In prophesying this event, Jesus was not saying that Christianity was to be a religion without a temple. On the contrary, Jesus himself was a new and greater Temple (Matt 12:6), destined to be destroyed in death and then rebuilt in the Resurrection (John 2:19–21). This notion was picked up and developed by the apostles Peter and Paul. In Pauline theology, incorporation into the body of Christ means incorporation into a holy temple in which the Spirit dwells (1 Cor 3:16–17; 2 Cor 6:16; Eph 2:19–22). And what is true of the Church is also true of the individual Christian, whose body is a temple of God's presence (1 Cor 6:19). Peter likewise envisions believers as "living stones" who are built into a spiritual temple that gives pleasing worship to God (1 Pet 2:5) (CCC 583–86, 593, 756, 797–98).

B. Hebrews and Revelation

The Letter to the Hebrews sees the Temple of Jerusalem in a typological sense, as "a copy and shadow of the heavenly sanctuary" (Heb 8:5). The heavenly sanctuary is the true one: "For Christ has entered, not into a sanctuary made with hands, a copy of the true one, but into heaven itself, now to appear in the presence of God on our behalf" (Heb 9:24). The heavenly sanctuary is a sanctuary into which Christ has entered as High Priest forever according to the order of **Melchizedek** (Heb 6:20). Believers participate in this celestial worship through the Church's sacramental worship on earth (cf. Heb 10:19; 12:22).

Revelation locates the true Temple on the celestial Mount Zion, the New Jerusalem (cf. Rev 3:12; 14:1; 21:10), but the New Jerusalem does not possess an architectural Temple, "for its temple is the Lord God the Almighty and the Lamb" (Rev 21:22). The city itself is shaped like a cube, with each side measuring nearly 1,500 miles and its walls over 200 feet thick. The shape of the New Jerusalem is clearly modeled after the inner chamber of the Temple, the holy of holies (1 Kgs 6:20). The Trinity is thus the sanctuary of the heavenly city (chap. 21). (*See also* **Spirit, Holy.**)

TEMPLE SERVANTS Members of the Temple staff in Jerusalem appointed by David to assist the Levites in their ministry (Ezra 8:20). Most references to the Temple servants appear in Ezra and Nehemiah, because the Temple servants played a significant role in the community that returned from Babylon after the **Exile** (Ezra 2:43–54; Neh 7:46–56, 10:28; cf. 1 Chr 9:2). Most of them lived in the Ophal district of southeast Jerusalem (Neh 3:26; 11:21). Their name in Hebrew, *nĕtînîm*, means "those who are given"—that is, assigned to a particular task. It is quite possible that they were descendants of the Gibeonites, whom Joshua condemned to do menial labor in support of the sanctuary (Josh 9:16–27).

TEMPTATION *See* **Sin**; *see also* **Adam**; **Eve**.

TEMPTATION OF JESUS The confrontation between Jesus and the devil in the wilderness as recounted in the **Synoptic Gospels** (Matt 4:1–11; Mark 1:12–13; Luke 4:1–13). Immediately after his baptism, Jesus was driven by the Spirit into the desert for forty days of fasting; he was alone among the wild beasts, and angels ministered to him. During this time, Satan tempted him three times to abandon his mission from the Father.

The three Gospels agree in all the essential details, but tell the story in slightly different ways. For example, they identify the tempter by different names: "the tempter" in Matthew, "the Satan" in Mark, and "the devil" in Luke. Also, Luke's version differs from Matthew's in the order of the temptations, and Mark abbreviates the story by passing over the three specific temptations.

The temptation in the wilderness is a test of Christ's filial obedience as the Son of God. Hence the devil initiates his attack with the words, "If you are the Son of God . . ." (Matt 4:3, 6). The test of sonship recalls the temptation of **Adam**, who was also approached by Satan among the wild beasts, as well as the testing of the people of Israel, who spent forty years in the wilderness struggling with the desire for food and drink. But unlike Adam and Israel, who proved to be disobedient sons, Jesus holds firm to his trust in the Father and refuses to turn away from his Father's will.

The temptation in the wilderness is also a test of Christ's Messiahship. The devil would have Christ dazzle the world with miracles and attain earthly glory without the need for suffering, humiliation, and death. If only Jesus would bow before Satan, the way would be open and easy. But here, too, Christ uses Scripture to fight off his assailant and to reaffirm his filial love for the Father and his commitment to the difficult mission assigned to him. In the end, Jesus's triumph over Satan in the desert foreshadows his more decisive victory over evil achieved through his Passion.

The book of Hebrews draws out a practical implication from this and similar episodes in the life of Jesus: "For we have not a high priest who is unable to sympathize with our weaknesses, but one who in every respect has been tempted as we are, yet without sin. Let us then with confidence draw near to the throne of grace, that we may receive mercy and find grace to help in time of need" (Heb 4:15–16) (CCC 538–40).

TEN COMMANDMENTS The ten universal laws given to Moses on Mount Sinai (Exod 20:1–17). Also called the Decalogue, from the Greek for "ten words," the Ten Commandments constitute the moral foundation of the covenant between God and his people (Exod 34:27–28). For this reason, the Ten Commandments not only assumed a place of central importance in the religion of Israel, but were reaffirmed by Jesus and the apostles as a normative guide for the Christian life as well (Mark 10:17–19; Rom 13:8–10).

I. THE DECALOGUE IN ISRAEL

There are two listings of the Ten Commandments in the Pentateuch, one in Exod 20:1–17 and a second in Deut 5:6–21. The first list was spoken by Yahweh to the Exodus generation assembled at Sinai, and the second was spoken by Moses to the next generation of Israelites assembled on the plains of Moab forty years later before they conquered Canaan.

Scholars classify the Ten Commandments as a collection of "apodictic" laws. These are laws of universal scope and application that are not limited by the gender, age, or social situation of the persons addressed. Unlike "casuistic" or case laws, which govern human actions in strictly defined circumstances, and often prescribe specific penalties for infractions, apodictic laws are exceptionless demands that come directly from God and are implicitly enforced by him. The most common formulation of such laws is "Thou shalt . . . " and "Thou shalt not . . . "

The commandments of the Decalogue hold a place of preeminence within the collection of Mosaic Laws, as is implied by several considerations.

1. The Decalogue is the only portion of the Mosaic covenant that was written by the finger of God (Exod 31:18).

2. Of all the laws that make up the Torah, only the Decalogue was spoken by Yahweh directly to the people of Israel without the mediation of Moses (Deut 4:12–13; 5:22–25). In fact, it was precisely the terrifying experience of hearing the voice of the Lord speaking the commandments from the mountaintop that led to the election of Moses as mediator (Exod 20:18–19; Deut 5:4–5).

3. The two tablets of the Decalogue are the only portion of the Law that was stored inside the ark of the covenant (Exod 25:16; 1 Kgs 8:9).

4. The Decalogue represents the original stipulations of the Sinai covenant. That is, when Yahweh set forth his demands at Sinai, he revealed only the Ten Commandments (Exod 20:1–17), along with a short collection of civil and religious laws called the covenant code (Exod 21–23; *see under* **Law**). Apart from these, he added nothing more (Deut 5:22). It was only after Israel had broken the Sinai covenant by worshipping the golden calf (Exod 32:1–20) that Yahweh added the bulk of the ceremonial and sacrificial laws that we find in the later chapters of Exodus as well as in the books of Leviticus and Numbers (cf. Jer 7:22–23).

In terms of content, the Ten Commandments sum up the obligations of man toward God (commandments 1–3) and toward neigh-

---

THE TEN COMMANDMENTS FROM EXODUS 20:1–17 (RSV)

I am the LORD your God, who brought you out of the land of Egypt, out of the house of bondage.

You shall have no other gods before me. You shall not make for yourself a graven image, or any likeness of anything that is in heaven above, or that is in the earth beneath, or that is in the water under the earth; you shall not bow down to them or serve them; for I the LORD your God am a jealous God, visiting the iniquity of the fathers upon the children to the third and the fourth generation of those who hate me, but showing steadfast love to thousands of those who love me and keep my commandments.

You shall not take the name of the LORD your God in vain; for the LORD will not hold him guiltless who takes his name in vain.

Remember the sabbath day, to keep it holy. Six days you shall labor, and do all your work; but the seventh day is a sabbath to the LORD your God; in it you shall not do any work, you, or your son, or your daughter, your manservant, or your maidservant, or your cattle, or the sojourner who is within your gates; for in six days the LORD made heaven and earth, the sea, and all that is in them, and rested the seventh day; therefore the LORD blessed the seventh day and hallowed it.

Honor your father and your mother, that your days may be long in the land which the LORD your God gives you.

You shall not kill.

You shall not commit adultery.

You shall not steal.

You shall not bear false witness against your neighbor.

You shall not covet your neighbor's house; you shall not covet your neighbor's wife, or his manservant, or his maidservant, or his ox, or his ass, or anything that is your neighbor's.

---

bor (commandments 4–10). In the first three, the Lord demands our exclusive allegiance to him as God, and requires every person to revere his Name and to observe a weekly day of rest in his honor. In the next seven commandments, we learn that other persons, beginning with our parents, deserve our love and respect for their right to life, truth, and personal belongings. Most of the Ten Commandments prescribe or prohibit outward actions, but a few, such as those that forbid coveting, also place restrictions on the inner movements of the mind and heart. In the original Hebrew, the individual commandments are formulated with the singular pronoun "you," implying that God addresses himself to us as individuals who stand accountable to his will.

II. THE DECALOGUE IN CHRISTIANITY

The New Testament teaches that Jesus Christ fulfilled rather than abolished the precepts of the Law, including the Decalogue (Matt 5:17). Observance of these primary laws thus remains a standing duty for Christian disciples who wish to gain eternal life (Matt 19:16–19; 22:36–40). Such is the teaching of Jesus. The apostle Paul expounds this and similar teachings of Christ (e.g., John 13:34) by insisting that "love" is the fulfillment of the Mosaic moral Law (Rom 13:8–10). This ideal cannot be attained by the efforts of human nature alone, which is ever inclined toward sin (Rom 7:7–12), but it has been made possible by the Spirit, who has poured the love of God into the hearts of believers (Rom 5:5). It is the power of the Spirit that enables people to fulfill the righteous decrees of the Law (Rom 8:3–4). Our need for this grace is all the more essential given the intrinsic unity of the Decalogue, since to transgress one commandment is tantamount to transgressing all of them (Jas 2:8–13).

In the catechetical tradition of the Church, the Ten Commandments are basic to the moral instruction of the faithful. Upon these ten foundation stones are built the teachings of the Gospel, most notably the deeper interpretations that Jesus himself gave to the Mosaic precepts in the Sermon on the Mount (Matt 5:21–48). For the most part, the Church has followed Saint Augustine in preferring the order of the Decalogue recorded in Deuteronomy, where the precept against coveting a neighbor's "wife" comes before the precept against coveting the goods of his "house" (Deut 5:21; see Saint Augustine, *Quaestiones in Exodum* 17). In the Exodus version, the neighbor's "house" is listed before his "wife" (Exod 20:17).

Finally, Christian theology teaches that the precepts of the Decalogue summarize the precepts of the natural law, which are written on the heart of every human person (Rom 2:14–15). For this reason, all are bound to ob-serve the Ten Commandments, not only Jews and Christians. These laws are among the endowments that were given to man at Creation; they are "nothing else than an imprint on us of the Divine light" whereby "we discern what is good and what is evil" (Saint Thomas Aquinas, *Summa theologiae* I–II, q.91, a 4; Vatican II, GS §16) (CCC 2052–82).

TENT OF MEETING *See* **Tabernacle**.

TERAH

1. The son of Nahor, and the father of Abram (later **Abraham**), Nahor, and Haran (Gen 11:24–32; 1 Chr 1:26). Terah lived to the age of 205 and died in Haran, to which he migrated from **Ur of the Chaldeans**. Unlike Abraham, he is said to have served gods other than the Lord (Josh 24:2).

2. A site where the Israelites encamped during their **Exodus** journey through the wilderness (Num 33:27–28).

TERAPHIM Cultic images or statues used in divination (Ezek 21:21; Zech 10:2). Such things were condemned in Israel as idols (1 Sam 15:23; 2 Kgs 23:24). Apparently teraphim could be different sizes, some small enough to hide in a saddle pack (Gen 31:34) and some large enough to look like a man (1 Sam 19:13).

TEREBINTH *See* **Oak**.

TERTIUS The scribe to whom **Paul** dictated his epistle to the Romans while in Corinth. He introduced himself with the words, "I Tertius, the writer of this letter, greet you in the Lord" (Rom 16:22).

TERTULLUS An orator who teamed up with Ananias and other Jerusalem elders to prosecute **Paul** before the Judean governor **Felix** (Acts 24:1).

TESTAMENT The name given to the two principal divisions of the Christian Bible. The Latin term *testamentum*, from which it is derived, is basically equivalent to "covenant." The designations Old and New Testament are inspired in part by Paul's distinction between the "new covenant" and the "old covenant" in 2 Cor 3:6, 14. The Latin **Vulgate** renders these expressions *novum testamentum* and *vetus testamentum*, respectively.

The OT is a collection of forty-six books, written mainly in Hebrew, that covers a stretch of salvation history from creation to the threshold of Messianic times. The NT is a collection of twenty-seven books, written entirely in Greek, that records the culmination of salvation history in Christ and the growth of the Church in the first Christian century.

Vatican II, in its Constitution on Divine Revelation, *Dei Verbum*, speaks of the OT as an indispensable part of Sacred Scripture, whose divinely inspired books retain a permanent value: "the economy of the Old Testament was deliberately so oriented that it should prepare for and declare in prophecy the coming of Christ, redeemer of all men" (DV §15). In addition, the books of the OT "are a storehouse of sublime teaching on God and of sound wisdom on human life, as well as a wonderful treasury of prayers; in them, too, the mystery of our salvation is present in a hidden way" (DV 15). Regarding the NT, *Dei Verbum* says, "The Word of God, which is the power of God for salvation to everyone who has faith, is set forth and displays its power in a most wonderful way in the writings of the New Testament" (DV §17).

According to the Church, the OT and NT together bear witness to the unity of the divine plan of salvation (cf. 1 Cor 10:6, 11; Heb 10:1; 1 Pet 3:21). Christians thus read the OT as preparing the way for Jesus Christ, and the NT is read as the comprehensive fulfillment of the OT. Saint Augustine summed this up in the memorable words, "the New Testament lies hidden in the Old and the Old Testament is unveiled in the New" (Saint Augustine, *Quaest. Hept.* 2.73; cf. DV §16) (CCC 121–30). (*See* **Bible**; *see also* **Covenant**; **Typology**.)

TETH The ninth letter of the Hebrew alphabet (ט).

TETRARCH A title literally meaning "ruler of one fourth." In Hellenic usage, it referred to a ruler of lesser rank than a king, such as a prince. Under the Romans, the tetrarch was a ruler over an eastern territory or province who enjoyed less autonomy than a king. In Palestine in the early first century A.D., there were several tetrarchs, chiefly as a result of the decision of Emperor Augustus to divide the kingdom of **Herod the Great** after his death in about 4 B.C. among his sons and successors. **Herod Antipas** was named tetrarch of Galilee and Peraea (Matt 14:1; Luke 3:19, 9:7; Acts 13:1); **Philip** was appointed tetrarch of Trachonitis, Ituraea, Batanea, Gaulanitis, and Auranitis (Luke 3:1); **Lysanias** was tetrarch of Abilene (Luke 3:1).

TEXT CRITICISM *See* **Biblical criticism**.

TEXTS OF THE BIBLE The original manuscripts of the Bible composed by the biblical authors have not survived. What survives are a vast number of handwritten copies of Scripture that were made in Jewish and Christian antiquity. These are the primary witnesses to the text of the Bible. Secondary witnesses include the many quotations of scriptural passages that appear in the works of ancient writers as well as the various translations that were made of the biblical books at an early date (called "versions"; *see* **Versions of the Bible**).

Reconstructing the text of the Bible is the work of textual criticism. Its aim is to recover, to the best of human ability, the original wording of the biblical books as they came forth from the hands of the sacred writers. This is a challenging and painstaking task, not only because the manuscripts produced by the authors (called "autographs") have perished, but also because the many copies that survive contain a great number of differences in wording (called "variant readings"). Most of these variants have little or no effect on the meaning of the text. Some, however, do affect the sense of the passage involved. Textual critics have to compare the vast number of extant copies and versions, assign them probable dates, and establish what relations may exist among them. Only then can they attempt to judge which manuscripts most likely preserve the original form of a given text.

I. THE TEXT OF THE OLD TESTAMENT

The text of the Old Testament is based mainly on manuscripts that date to the late Middle Ages. Generally speaking, these handwritten copies represent a uniform text and exhibit only minimal variation and corruption. Medieval texts of the greatest importance are those with ties to the Ben Asher family and include the following: the Aleppo Codex (A), which dates to A.D. 925 and includes the entire Hebrew Bible, although most of the Pentateuch is now missing; the Leningrad Codex (L), which dates to A.D. 1008 and includes the entire Hebrew Bible; the British Museum MS 4445 (B), which dates to A.D. 925 and preserves most of the Pentateuch intact; and the Cairo Codex (C), which dates to A.D. 896 and contains the Prophets. These manuscripts represent the achievements of Jewish traditionalists, called the Masoretes, who worked during the early Middle Ages to preserve the text of the Hebrew Bible along with its traditional pronunciation and punctuation. The standard version of the Hebrew Bible still in use today is thus called the Masoretic Text (MT). This standardized text first appeared in printed form in Soncino, Italy, in 1488. Several editions of all or part of the MT followed, culminating in the publication of the second Rabbinic Bible in Venice, Italy, in 1525.

Textual criticism of the Hebrew Bible entered a new era with the discovery of the **Dead Sea Scrolls** in the middle of the twentieth century. Among the finds were complete or partial copies of every book of the Hebrew Bible except Esther, along with Semitic versions of the other books that are part of the Catholic and Orthodox canon of the OT (Tobit, Sirach, Baruch). Several books of the Bible survive in multiple copies or fragments; the best represented are Genesis, Deuteronomy, and Isaiah.

The value of the scrolls for textual scholarship is inestimable, not least because the manuscripts date to the first and second centuries B.C., which makes them at least a thousand years older than the medieval texts copied out by the Masoretes and their successors. On the one hand, there is a remarkable conformity between the MT and the majority of the biblical manuscripts found among the scrolls, despite the centuries of hand-copying that separate them. The most celebrated example is the great Isaiah Scroll (IQIsaᵃ), a complete copy of the book of Isaiah that differs only in small and incidental ways from the copies of Isaiah preserved by the Masoretes. Examples such as this give eloquent testimony to the rigor of Jewish scribal practice in preserving the exact wording of the Hebrew Bible. On the other hand, a small percentage of the Dead Sea texts exhibit a form of the Hebrew Bible that differs slightly from the traditional MT. Some of the Dead Sea texts show close affinities with the Greek **Septuagint** translation of the OT (LXX), while others preserve a text that agrees with the Samaritan version of the Pentateuch (SP).

For the most part, then, the traditional MT is confirmed as a reliable witness to text of the OT. Nevertheless, the Dead Sea discoveries also indicate that matters are more complex than previously known, and scholars have come to acknowledge that readings found in the Dead Sea Scrolls seem, on occasion, to preserve older and more original forms of the Hebrew Bible. It is left to present and future scholarship to determine where and to what extent this is the case.

II. THE TEXT OF THE NEW TESTAMENT

The New Testament is by far the best attested work that has come down from antiquity. Of the mass of surviving witnesses, over three thousand are in Greek, about five thousand are in Latin, and roughly one thousand are from translations into other languages (Syriac, Coptic, Armenian, Gothic, etc.). Beyond this, another two thousand selections are preserved in ancient lectionaries, and almost all of the NT survives in the form of quotations in the writings of the early Church Fathers.

For a number of reasons, the primary witnesses are the surviving Greek texts, although occasionally one or another of the ancient versions can be used to establish a more original reading. The Greek witnesses are grouped into three major classes: the papyri, the uncials, and the minuscules.

1. The *papyri* are fragments of NT texts that were written on papyrus. Almost one hundred of these survive and are dated between the second and eighth centuries A.D. The most notable are the John Rylands Papyrus (P⁵²), which dates to A.D. 125 and preserves the text of John 18:31–33, 37–38; the Chester Beatty Papyrus II (P⁴⁶), which dates to circa A.D. 200 and preserves most of the Pauline Epistles; and the Bodmer Papyrus II (P⁶⁶), which also dates to circa A.D. 200 and preserves most of the Gospel of John.

2. The *uncials* are parchment manuscripts written in rounded uppercase letters and bound on one side like a book (called a "codex"). Some three hundred of these survive and date from

the fourth to the tenth century A.D. Several are very important for establishing the text of the NT. These include Codex Sinaiticus (ℵ), which dates to the fourth century and includes the complete NT; Codex Vaticanus (B), which also dates to the fourth century and contains most of the NT, minus the pastoral Epistles, Revelation, and parts of the Letter to the Hebrews; Codex Alexandrinus (A), which dates to the fifth century and preserves most of the NT, minus sections of Matthew, John, and 2 Corinthians; and Codex Bezae (D), which dates to the sixth century and includes the Gospels, Acts, and 3 John in both Greek and Latin.

3. The *minuscules*, which number over twenty-eight hundred witnesses, are written in a lowercase cursive script, and date from the ninth to the fourteenth centuries.

Printed editions of the Greek NT began to appear in the sixteenth century. The first was that of Cardinal Ximenes of Toledo, printed in 1514, although not officially released until 1522. Erasmus of Rotterdam, the renowned Catholic humanist, issued his famous edition in 1516 (the third edition of which appeared in 1522). Although based on a handful of witnesses no older than the twelfth century, the Greek text established by Erasmus was eventually hailed as the "Received Text" (in Latin, *textus receptus*) of the NT. Major translations were made from this Erasmian text, including Martin Luther's translation into German in 1522, William Tyndale's translation into English in 1525, and the King James Version of 1611. For the most part, it remained the authoritative Greek text until the gradual accumulation of older manu-

scripts forced scholars in the nineteenth century to set aside the "Received Text" and to reconstruct the Greek NT on the basis of new and better evidence. The most acclaimed of these critical editions was that of B. F. Wescott and F. J. A. Hort published in 1881.

Scholarship today continues to wrestle with the text-critical issues related to modern manuscript discoveries. Most scholars are convinced that the papyri, and especially the uncial codices of the fourth, fifth, and sixth centuries, must be taken seriously in establishing the original text of the NT. But a few scholars continue to retain confidence in the value of the "Received Text." Modern translations of the Bible since the late nineteenth century have been based mainly on the more ancient texts. Some would say, thanks to the overwhelming wealth of evidence available in our time, along with significant progress made in the science and art of textual criticism, that the Greek text accepted by most scholars today is about 98 percent secure as a witness to what the authors of the NT originally wrote down in the first century.

TEXTUAL CRITICISM *See* **Texts of the Bible**; *see also* **Biblical criticism**.

THADDAEUS One of the twelve disciples of Jesus (Matt 10:3; Mark 3:18). Luke calls him "Judas son of James" instead of Thaddeus (Luke 6:14–16; Acts 1:13). Some ancient manuscripts of Matthew and Mark give his name as "Lebbaeus."

THANKS, OFFERING *See* **Sacrifice**; *see also* **Eucharist**.

THEATER The traditional Greek theater was one of the centers of any major city and the place where theatrical performances were staged. The size of the theater depended only on the financial means of the city and the specific limitations of local topography. Large theaters were common, and their capacity to hold thousands of spectators made them useful for other civic activities, including religious ceremonies and large public gatherings. **Herod the Great**, seeking to emulate the classical Greek cities, constructed theaters in a number of cities, including Caesarea, Damascus, Jerusalem, and Gadara. In the New Testament, a theater is mentioned in Acts 19:29, 31 as the public stage where rioters clamored against the Christian missionaries at Ephesus. Paul also used the word in the sense of a "spectacle" to describe himself as an apostle whose sufferings were on display before the world (1 Cor 4:9; cf. Heb 10:33).

THEBES A renowned city of upper Egypt; it ranked with Memphis in importance. It was located on the present sites of Luxor and Karnak on the east bank of the Nile. Thebes was sacked by the Assyrians under Ashurbanipal in 663 B.C., and was again attacked by the Persians in 525 and 343 B.C. The city was the center of anti-Hellenic sentiment during the Ptolemaic period, after which Thebes declined sharply. The city was the object of prophetic judgment oracles (Jer 46:25; Ezek 30:14–16). Nahum 3:8 refers to its destruction by the Assyrians.

THEBEZ A town near Shechem in central Canaan. There **Abimelech** was mortally wounded when a millstone was hurled from a tower by a woman (Judg 9:50–53). His humiliating death in this fashion—at the hands of a woman in the context of a military conflict—became proverbial (2 Sam 11:21). Thebez is probably the modern Tubas to the northeast of Shechem.

THEOPHANY (Greek, "appearance of God") A supernatural manifestation of God in the world. Normally a theophany is a dramatic display of divine glory in a way that is visible (e.g., fire, clouds, lightning), audible (e.g., thunder, trumpet blast, divine voice), or otherwise sensible (e.g., earthquake, strong winds). Like miracles, theophanies demonstrate the power of God over the order and forces of nature.

I. IN THE OLD TESTAMENT

Theophanies can take place in the natural environment—in or by trees or bushes (Gen 12:6–7; Exod 3:1–12), near springs and rivers (Gen 16:7–14; 32:23–33), and above all on mountains (Exod 19:16–20). They are also accompanied by spectacular natural events, including earthquakes (Judg 5:4; Ps 18:8, 68:8, 77:18; Isa 6:4; Nah 1:5), wind (Ps 18:10, 50:3, 104:3; Ezek 1:4; Nah 1:3), rain (Judg 5:4; Ps 68:8, 77:17), thunder (Exod 19:16, 19; Ps 18:13), and lightning (Ps 18:14). Naturally, theophanies evoke a sense of awe and terror in those who behold them (Gen 28:17; Exod 3:6, 19:16; Lev 9:24; Deut 5:24–27; Judg 6:22–24, 13:21–23).

These spectacular appearances have a purpose: they demonstrate that God is in control of the most powerful forces of nature, and they instill a "holy fear" of God (Exod 20:18–20). Theophanies were occasions when God intervened in history to disclose his will, to issue divine decrees and commands, to pass judgment on tribes and nations, and especially to act as savior for his people.

The best-known theophany is the one at Mount Sinai (Exod 19). God appeared with clouds, earthquakes, and thunder, which showed his power to his people. The cloud continued to be present throughout the next events in the progress of the Israelites (Exod 24:15–18, 40:34–38; Num 9:15–23; Deut 1:33; 1 Kgs 8:10–13; *see also* **Tabernacle**). The Catechism of the Catholic Church explains the theophany within the context of the **Ten Commandments** and God's self-revelation as a gift: "The gift of the Commandments is the gift of God himself and his holy will. In making his will known, God reveals himself to his people" (CCC 2059).

II. IN THE NEW TESTAMENT

Theophanies in the New Testament share certain common features with those of the Old Testament. The main difference is that most theophanies in the NT were Christophanies— that is, manifestations of the divine glory of Jesus Christ. For example, the **Transfiguration** of Jesus is a visible revelation of his divine dignity, symbolized by the images of a cloud and brilliant light, while the voice of the Father is an audible revelation of Christ's divine sonship (Matt 7:1–8; Mark 9:2–8; Luke 9:28–36). The same can be said for the baptism of Jesus, described by Pope John Paul II as "a Trinitarian theophany which bears witness to the exaltation of Christ on the occasion of his baptism in the Jordan. It not only confirms the testimony of John the Baptist but also reveals an-

other more profound dimension of the truth about Jesus of Nazareth as Messiah. It is this: the Messiah is the beloved Son of the Father" (*Dominum et Vivificantem* §19). Other Christophanies, where the risen Jesus grants a vision of his heavenly glory, include his appearances to **Stephen**, the first martyr (Acts 7:55–56), and to the apostle **Paul** on the road to Damascus (Acts 9:3–6; 22:6–11; 26:12–18).

Theophanies of the Spirit also occur in the NT. The most notable example is the first **Pentecost**, with its flames of fire and the roar of a mighty wind (Acts 2:1–4), which call to mind the Sinai theophany in Exodus. The visions of God's glory in the book of Revelation are permeated with traditional theophanic imagery, although strictly speaking they are visions of heaven and not revelations of God in the context of nature and history.

THEOPHILUS (Greek, "friend of God") The man to whom Luke dedicated both his Gospel (Luke 1:3) and the Acts of the Apostles (1:1). This friend's identity is uncertain and has been the subject of considerable discussion. Some suggest the name refers not to a specific person, but to any and every believer who is God's friend. More likely, given the use of the honorary title "most excellent," which is borne by government officials in Acts (Acts 23:26; 26:25), Luke was addressing a well-to-do believer who acted as the patron for his work.

THESSALONIANS, LETTERS TO THE

Two epistles attributed to **Paul** and written within a short time of each other, most likely while the apostle was in Corinth. Both are pastoral letters, although they do touch on matters of doctrine, most notably the Second Coming of Christ (*see* **Parousia**). The letters are addressed to the Christians in **Thessalonica**, the capital of the province of Macedonia. The Christian community had been established by Paul, Silvanus (*see* **Silas**), and **Timothy** (1 Thess 1:1) around A.D. 50 on Paul's second missionary journey (Acts 17:1–9). Because of hostility in the city, the nascent community of Christians was a target of ongoing persecution (1 Thess 1:6, 2:14; 2 Thess 1:4). Most of the Thessalonian Christians were Gentiles (1 Thess 1:9).

I. AUTHORSHIP AND DATE

Both the First and Second Letters to the Thessalonians claim to be letters of Paul. His name stands at the beginning of both, and tradition from ancient times supports his authorship. Both letters also list Silvanus and Timothy as co-senders, a fact that explains why Paul usually speaks in the first person plural ("we," "us," "our").

Few scholars have questioned the authenticity of 1 Thessalonians. The authorship of 2 Thessalonians has been more debated. Paul's name appears both at the start (2 Thess 1:1) and the end (2 Thess 3:17), and tradition accepted his authorship going back to a very early time. But some modern scholars have suggested that the letter was composed pseudonymously by a later writer. They base their claims, first, on the perceived difference between the emphasis on the suddenness of Christ's coming in 1 Thessalonians and the apparent remoteness of that event in 2 Thessalonians; and, second, on the notable similarities between the two letters, which seem to suggest that the second was written in imitation of the first.

The traditional attribution, however, seems safest. Regarding the timing of Christ's coming, the discrepancies can be attributed to emphasis rather than real differences in theology. Paul declares that Jesus's return will come suddenly, and misunderstandings regarding that very statement made necessary the second letter (2 Thess 2:1–3). As for the similarities between the two letters, those are best accounted for by assuming that Paul wrote both letters in his usual style. Finally, scholars writing in defense of Pauline authorship point out that a writer impersonating Paul would hardly warn the Thessalonians against forged letters that claimed to come from Paul himself (2 Thess 2:2).

Most scholars are in agreement that 1 Thessalonians is the oldest of Paul's letters. The likeliest date for its composition is late A.D. 50 or early A.D. 51 (cf. 1 Thess 3:1–5; Acts 17:1–18:5). If Paul was, indeed, the author of 2 Thessalonians, then it was written around the same time as 1 Thessalonians, perhaps only a few months later. The Second Letter to the Thessalonians mentions the first epistle (2 Thess 2:15), but it is unclear how long before 1 Thessalonians had been sent.

II. CONTENTS

1 THESSALONIANS

I. *Greeting (1:1)*

II. *The Situation in Thessalonica (1:2–3:13)*
    A. *Thanksgiving (1:2–10)*
    B. *Paul's Defense (2:1–16)*
    C. *The Mission of Timothy (2:17–3:10)*
    D. *Prayer for Reunion (3:11–13)*

III. *Encouragement to the Thessalonians (4:1–5:22)*

III. PURPOSE AND THEMES

The First Letter to the Thessalonians was the result of the circumstances surrounding the establishment of the Christian community in Thessalonica. Paul had planted the faith there (Acts 17:1–10) but had departed the city in the face of harsh reactions. Paul later learned that the Thessalonian Christians were enduring persecution from the same parties that had forced him to leave. He thus sent his disciple Timothy to assess the situation; Timothy reported back to Corinth (Acts 18:5) of the zeal and steadfast faith of the converts. Paul wrote his letter to express his joy at their growth (1 Thess 1:8), to encourage them in their time of troubles (3:3–5), to remind them of the importance of chastity and charity (4:1–12), and to answer certain questions that had arisen concerning the Resurrection.

Paul speaks of the Christian dead in relation to the Second Coming and notes that the Resurrection of Christ is a pledge of our own hope of resurrection: "For since we believe that Jesus died and rose again, even so, through Jesus, God will bring with him those who have fallen asleep. For this we declare to you by the word of the Lord, that we who are alive, who are left until the coming of the LORD, shall not precede those who have fallen asleep" (1 Thess 4:14–15). Those who have died, Paul assures them, will be at no disadvantage, because "we who are alive, who are left, shall be caught up together with them in the clouds to meet the LORD in the air; and so we shall always be with the LORD" (1 Thess 4:17). When that time will be is unknown, and the fact of its uncertainty should be the motivation for the careful maintenance of virtue (1 Thess 5:1–11).

The Second Letter to the Thessalonians was sent as a follow-up to Paul's earlier letter and was intended to expand and clarify the teaching on the Second Coming that had been discussed in the earlier epistle. Paul had learned that there were still some misunderstandings and misapprehensions after the first letter, due in part to misrepresentations of his own teachings (1 Thess 4:13–5:12). Some in the community were so convinced of the imminence of the Parousia that they saw little point in continuing to work. He felt obligated to correct these errors.

In the Second Letter, Paul again gives thanks for the constancy of his flock (2 Thess 1:1–12) and proceeds to a more detailed presentation on the expectations of the Second Coming. He insists that the Second Coming cannot be now, as Christ will not return until a series of signs and events take place first. Among the signs will be the man of sin (often referred to as the **Antichrist**) who will amaze the wicked with his power (2 Thess 2:3, 9–10) and will rule as though he were God. A force, unnamed by Paul, restrains the Antichrist until the appointed time (2 Thess 2:7–8), and only after this period of trials will Christ come again to destroy him and judge the evil (2 Thess 2:8).

After renewing his thanks for their conversion, Paul asks the Thessalonians for their prayers and promises them his own (2 Thess 3:1–5). He then moves on to exhort his readers to proper moral conduct. He indicates (2 Thess 3:6–15) that some Thessalonians had stopped working because they expected the Second Coming at any moment. This Paul rejects, and he scolds these Christians as freeloaders who live off of other able-bodied members of the community. Not only must Christians work, but their fellow Christians must lead them from error when they become deluded or follow an improper path. He says that those who will not follow his urging should not be regarded as enemies; rather, they should be warned as believers (2 Thess 3:15).

THESSALONICA A city in Macedonia at the head of the Thermaikos Gulf. It was founded in 316 B.C. by Cassander, the son of Antipater, who had been left in charge of Macedonia by **Alexander the Great**. It was named in honor of Cassander's wife, Thessalonike, a stepsister of Alexander and the last surviving member of the Macedonian royal family. By New Testament times, Thessalonica was a free city.

Paul reached Thessalonica during his second missionary journey (Acts 17:1–13) and attracted many followers from among the local Jewish populations and the local Greek Gentiles. The resulting counterreaction by the Jews of the city was harsh, so Paul and **Silas** went to Beroea. The Jews, however, sent representatives to follow them to Beroea and accuse them of crimes. The First and Second Letters to the Thessalonians were written not long after Paul left Thessalonica; Paul also mentioned the city in Phil 4:16 and 2 Tim 4:10.

THEUDAS The leader of a failed rebellion in Judea after the death of **Herod the Great** in the first year of the first century A.D. The rebellion was mentioned in Acts 5:36, including that he had about four hundred followers, that Theudas was killed, and that all who followed him were dispersed and disappeared. Josephus (*B.J.* 20.5.1) also detailed the activities of Theudas, whom he calls an "imposter" (or "wizard"). According to Josephus, Theudas had promised to separate the waters of the Jordan River to permit the crossing of his supporters. The Romans crushed the rebellion and brought Theudas's head to Jerusalem.

THIEF *See* **Dysmas**; **Gestas**.

THOMAS (Aramaic, "twin") One of the twelve disciples of Jesus included in the lists of the apostles (Matt 10:3; Mark 3:18; Luke 6:14; John 20:24, where he is called also Didymus; Acts 1:13). Remembered for his doubts and skepticism, Thomas is mentioned in four detailed episodes in John (11:16; 14:5; 20:24–28; 21:2). In the first, he was willing to die with Christ, saying on the way to Bethany, "Let us also go, that we may die with him" (John 11:16). He next told Christ, "Lord, we do not know where you are going; how can we know the way?" to which Christ declared, "I am the way, and the truth, and the life; no one comes to the Father, but by me" (John 14:5–6). Third, he doubted his fellow apostles when they told him of having seen the risen Christ and examined his wounds on his glorified body (John 20:25). When he met Christ, however, Thomas cried out, "My Lord and my God!" (John 20:28), to which Christ replied, "Blessed are those who have not seen and yet believe" (John 20:29). Thomas's confession of Christ's divinity marks the theological climax of the Gospel of John.

Stories from early Christian times say that Thomas went to India and was martyred there. There he is revered as the founder of the Malabar Christians, who are also called Saint Thomas Christians. Every Western tradition agrees in placing Thomas in India, and the oral tradition of the Thomas Christians is firm and very ancient. Thomas's feast day is July 3.

THOMAS, GOSPEL OF An apocryphal Gospel written in Greek and found in a Coptic version among the papyri discovered in Nag Hammadi in Egypt during 1945–1946. The original Greek version probably dates to the latter part of the second century A.D., while the Coptic version is dated to around A.D. 400. The text is made up of 114 short sayings and parables supposedly by Jesus. The Gospel of Thomas is a work of Christian **Gnosticism** and is of interest chiefly in the study of that tradition.

THORNS Thornbushes are found throughout Palestine. They are an annoyance to farmers, who try to keep their fields clear of such weeds (Prov 24:30–31; Matt 13:7). **Adam** was told that as a consequence of his **Fall**, thorns and thistles would plague his efforts at agriculture (Gen 3:18). They are found in uncultivated areas (Job 30:7; Isa 5:6, 7:23, 32:13, 34:13, 55:13; Hos 9:6) and were used for fuel in areas where wood was not common (Ps 58:9; Eccl 7:6). **Jeremiah** warns that one should not sow among the thorns (Jer 4:3). A crown of thorns was forced onto the head of Jesus before the Crucifixion (Matt 27:29; Mark 15:17; John 19:2). Along with the scepter made of a reed and the purple robe, Jesus was mocked as King of the Jews.

THORNS, CROWN OF *See* **Thorns**.

THRONE Normally the seat of a king or judge, from which he exercises his authority to rule or administer justice (1 Kgs 22:10; Prov 20:28; Dan 7:9–10). Occasionally other royal figures had a throne as well, such as the Queen Mother (1 Kgs 2:19) and possibly the steward or prime minister (Isa 22:23). The Lord too has a throne, which is heaven itself (Isa 66:1), though in ancient Israel its earthly counterpart was the **ark of the covenant**, where the Lord sat enthroned on the wings of the cherubim (2 Sam 6:2; Isa 37:16). Perhaps the most prominent throne to appear in the biblical narrative is the royal throne of **David**, which the Lord swore to establish forever through the Davidic **covenant** (2 Sam 7:13; 1 Chr 17:12; Ps 89:3–4, 35–37; 132:11–12). In time, the throne of David would be associated with Israel's Messianic hope for a coming Davidic ruler (Isa 9:7; Jer 33:14–22). The New Testament addresses this hope by insisting that Jesus Christ, risen from the dead and raised into heaven, is now forever seated on the throne of David as **Messiah** and Lord. Jesus as the Son of Man will judge from his throne (Matt 25:31) through the Twelve who exercise authority in his name (Matt 19:28; cf. Luke 22:30).

The most elaborate descriptions of a throne in the Bible are of the throne of **Solomon** in the Old Testament and that of God in the book of Revelation. **Solomon**'s throne was made of ivory, overlaid with the finest gold: "The throne had six steps, and at the back of the throne was a calf's head, and on each side of the seat were arm rests and two lions standing beside the arm rests, while twelve lions stood there, one on each end of a step on the six steps. The like of it was never made in any kingdom" (1 Kgs 10:19–20).

THUMMIM *See* **Urim and Thummim**.

THUNDER Thunder in the Old Testament often appears as an element in a **theophany** (Exod 19:16; 20:18; 2 Sam 22:14; Ps 18:14). The voice of God is like the booming sound of thunder (Job 37:4; Sir 43:17; Isa 30:30; Jer 10:13). Again in the New Testament the voice of God is heard as thunder (John 12:29), and thunder accompanies appearances of God (Rev 4:5; 8:5; 11:19; 16:18).

THUNDER, SONS OF *See* **Boanerges**.

THYATIRA A city in Lydia, in western Asia Minor between Sardis and Pergamum. The city was well known for its brassware and its wool trade. **Lydia** of Thyatira, "a seller of purple goods," was **Paul**'s first convert at Philippi (Acts 16:14). The church of Thyatira was one of the seven churches addressed by the Lord in the book of Revelation (Rev 1:11; 2:18–29).

TIBERIAS A city on the western coast of the Sea of Galilee, now called Tabariya. It was founded in A.D. 20 by **Herod Antipas**, tetrarch of Galilee, to serve as his administrative capital. Herod named the city in honor of the Roman emperor **Tiberius**. Tiberias is mentioned only once in Scripture, in a reference to boats from Tiberias carrying people who were looking for Jesus (John 6:23), yet because of the prominence of the city, the Sea of Galilee was sometimes called the "Sea of Tiberias" (John 6:1; 21:1).

TIBERIAS, SEA OF *See* **Galilee, Sea of**.

TIBERIUS, EMPEROR Roman emperor from A.D. 14 to 37. Known as Tiberius Claudius Nero, he was the son of the powerful Roman lady Livia and the stepson of Emperor **Augustus**, whom he succeeded. His reign was marked by a long period of steady rule that carried forward the imperial policies of Augustus but that ended with Tiberius's isolation on the island of Capri. Luke 3:1 mentions that the reign of Tiberius was in its fifteenth year when John the Baptist began his ministry.

TIBNI The son of Ginath and a rival of **Omri** for the throne of Israel as successor to **Zimri** (1 Kgs 16:21–22). The struggle for the crown that followed lasted for four years, but ultimately Omri grew stronger and Tibni died in a conflict with his rival's supporters.

TIDAL The king of Goiim and one of the allies of the Mesopotamian king **Chedorlaomer** who waged war on the cities of the Transjordan in the days of **Abraham** (Gen 14:1, 9).

TIGLATH-PILESER III The Assyrian king from around 745 to 727 B.C. He was the successor to Adad-nirari III and resurrected the fortunes of the Assyrian Empire and more than once invaded the kingdom of Israel (2 Kgs 15:19–20, 29; 16:5–18). Known also as Tiglath-pilneser (1 Chr 5:6, 26; 2 Chr 28:20) and Pul, he established himself on the Assyrian throne and launched a campaign against **Babylon**. He conquered the Aramean tribes and declared himself king of Babylon with the intention of forging a Pan-Mesopotamian state. This ambition was furthered by Assyrians' deportations of conquered peoples to other regions to shatter nationalist or tribal unity and reduce the chances of local rebellions. Tiglath-pileser next marched on the northern Urartians in Armenia but failed in his effort. He had more success against the northern Syrian states and Palestine.

To halt the relentless advance of the Assyrians, Kings **Rezin** of Damascus and **Pekah** of Israel sought to compel **Ahaz** of Judah into an alliance (Isa 7:1–9). Instead of going along with that idea, Ahaz appealed to the Assyrians and made himself a vassal of Tiglath-pileser (2 Kgs 16:7–9; 2 Chr 28:20). Assyrian armies claimed Galilee and Gilead (2 Kgs 15:29), which were added to the empire, and **Samaria** (2 Kgs 15:19–20) and other major cities including **Tyre** paid tribute to Assyria. Soon after, Pekah was assassinated and succeeded by the Assyrian vassal **Hoshea**. Damascus was captured in 732 B.C., Rezin was killed, and much of the Syrian population was deported to Assyria (2 Kgs 16:9). Tiglath-pileser also built a palace at Calah and gave so much power to his successors that the empire endured for another century. (*See* **Assyria**.)

TIGRIS One of the two major rivers of Mesopotamia, with the Euphrates. Its headwaters are in the Armenian mountains, and the river flows southeast across the Mesopotamian plain until it joins the Euphrates to form the Shatt al Arab, which flows into the Persian Gulf. The Tigris is listed in Genesis as one of the four rivers of **Eden** (Gen 2:14). Daniel (10:4) had one of his visions near the Tigris, and from its waters came the fish used to heal Tobias's father of his blindness and to liberate Sarah from the demon Asmodeus (Tob 6:1–8).

TIMAEUS The father of the blind beggar **Bartimaeus** of Jericho who was healed by Jesus (Mark 10:46).

TIME Various measurements of time are found in the Bible. Primary units or divisions of time include the day, week, month, and year. The general notion of time, considered either as a point or period of history, is expressed in Hebrew by the term ʿēt and in Greek by the terms *chronos*, *kairos*, and *aiōn*.

I. TIME IN THE OLD TESTAMENT

In the biblical world, time was measured by the movements of the sun and moon (Gen 1:14).

THE HEBREW MONTHS

	Canaanite	Babylonian	Modern Equivalent
1.	Abib	Nisan	March–April
2.	Ziv	Iyyar	April–May
3.	——	Sivan	May–June
4.	——	Tammuz	June–July
5.	——	Ab	July–August
6.	——	Elul	August–September
7.	Ethanim	Tishri	September–October
8.	Bul	Marheshvan	October–November
9.	——	Chislev	November–December
10.	——	Tebet	December–January
11.	——	Shebat	January–February
12.	——	Adar	February–March

The "day" was defined both as the daylight hours before nightfall (Gen 1:5) and as a complete cycle from sundown to sundown (Gen 1:5, 8, 13, etc.). The "week" was measured as the passage of seven consecutive days, with the seventh being a day of rest (Gen 2:1–3). The "month" was calculated by the phases of the moon and lasted approximately thirty days, which is the time that elapses between each new appearance of the moon (cf. Num 28:11; Ps 81:3). The biblical "year" was a rotation of twelve months, the first being the springtime month of Abib (Exod 12:2; Deut 16:1). Because the lunar year is 354 days, and is thus eleven days short of the 365-day solar year, it became necessary to intercalate an extra month every two or three years to correct the difference (this unit of time was eventually called "second Adar"). Other chronological units in the Old Testament include the "single moment" (Exod 33:5) and the three "watches" of the night (Judg 7:19).

The twelve months of the year were given different names in different historical contexts. In Israel before the **Exile**, the names of the months probably represented those of the ancient Canaanite calendar. In postexilic Israel, the names followed those of the ancient Babylonian calendar. Not all the months were represented by name in the biblical texts.

In addition to its segmentation, time in the OT was also sanctified. That is, the Mosaic Law singles out certain units of time for spiritual contemplation and worship. On a weekly cycle, the people of God were expected to observe the Sabbath rest, the seventh day of the week set aside to remember God's work in creation (Exod 20:8–11) as well as his redemption of Israel in the Exodus (Deut 5:12–17). On a yearly cycle, the Israelites observed a calendar of festivals such as **Passover**, the feast of Unleavened Bread, the feast of Weeks or **Pentecost**, the Day of Atonement, and the feast of Tabernacles or **Booths** (Lev 23:4–44; Num 28–29; Deut 16:1–17). Festivals later added to the annual calendar include the feast of Purim (Esth 9:20–28) and Hanukkah (1 Macc 4:36–59). Beyond this annual schedule, every seventh year was a sabbatical year of rest and remission of debts (Deut 15:1–6), and every fiftieth year was a Jubilee year of freeing lands, slaves, and debtors of unpaid balances (Lev 25:1–55).

II. TIME IN THE NEW TESTAMENT

In the New Testament, it is generally true that the Greek *chronos* denotes the passage of time in general (Acts 1:6; Gal 4:4), that *kairos* has the nuance of an appointed or opportune time (Mark 1:15; Luke 4:13), and that *aiōn* refers to an age or epoch of time (Matt 12:32; 1 Cor 10:11).

The calculation of time as it appears in the NT follows both Jewish tradition and Roman custom. Standard units such as days, weeks, and years were the same as those in the Hebrew Scriptures. Likewise, in a Palestinian context, the passage of one day to the next seems to have been calculated from sundown to sundown (e.g., the end of the Sabbath in Mark 1:32). One also sees the Roman system in play, as when the nighttime hours were divided into four watches (Mark 6:48; 13:35) and the daylight from sunrise to sunset was divided into twelve hours (e.g., the third hour, Acts 2:15; the sixth hour, John 4:6; the ninth hour, Mark 15:34; the eleventh hour, Matt 20:6).

Time in the NT, as in the OT, also has a sacred and theological dimension. From earliest times, Christians held their communal worship on Sunday, the first day of the Jewish week (Acts 20:7; 1 Cor 16:2), rather than on Saturday, the Jewish Sabbath, which was reckoned as the seventh and final day of the week (Exod 20:8–11). The reason is that Christian worship is a celebration of the Lord's Resurrection, which took place on the first day of the week (Luke 24:1–12; John 20:1–18). Christianity also adapted the traditional Jewish belief in the "present age" of distress and the "coming age" of Messianic fulfillment into a vision of time and eternity (Matt 12:32; Eph 1:21). With the Messianic age now in progress, the coming age (or ages) is transferred to the future stretch of eternity that awaits the faithful (Mark 10:29–30; Luke 20:34–36; Eph 2:7), who yearn to escape the sufferings of "the present evil age" (Gal 1:4). This deliverance will come at the consummation of time, when Jesus returns in glory to judge the living and the dead (John 6:40; 1 Thess 1:10). Events connected with the end of days include a time of deception (Rev 20:7–10); the appearance of a man of lawlessness, often called the Antichrist (2 Thess 2:3–4); the resurrection of the dead (1 Cor 15:51–57); and the gathering of the saints into heavenly glory (1 Thess 4:16–17).

TIMNAH A town in the low hills of western Canaan, roughly 20 miles (32 kilometers) west of Jerusalem. In the time of Joshua, it was allotted to the tribe of Dan (Josh 19:43), although it seems to have remained under the control of the **Philistines** for much, if not all, of the Israelite settlement period. It was the home of **Samson**'s first wife (Judg 14:1). Presumably it became an Israelite town in the days of the kings, but eventually the Philistines took it back (2 Chr 28:18). The town of Timnah mentioned in connection with the patriarch **Judah** may be the same settlement as we have been discussing, but this is uncertain (Gen 38:12).

TIMNATH-SERAH Known in the Bible as the hometown of **Joshua** and the place of his burial (Josh 19:50; 24:30). It was located in the hill country of Ephraim, and was also called Timnath-Heres (Judg 2:9).

TIMOTHY The name of two men in the Bible.

1. The Seleucid commander in Palestine who was defeated by **Judas Maccabeus** (1 Macc 5:6–13; 2 Macc 8:30, 9:3, 10:24, 12:2).

2. A missionary, disciple, and trusted companion of Paul. Born at Lystra in Asia Minor, he was the son of a Jewish woman, Eunice, and a Greek father (Acts 16:1; 2 Tim 1:5). Deeply respected by the other members of the Christian community in Lystra and Iconium, he was attached to the small company of Paul during the apostle's second missionary journey (Acts 16:2–3). He was thereafter a constant and invaluable companion of Paul, who called him "our brother" (2 Cor 1:1; 1 Thess 3:2; Phlm 1), "fellow worker" (Rom 16:21), and "my beloved and faithful child in the Lord" (1 Cor 4:17; cf. 1 Tim 1:2). Timothy was also a co-sender of six of Paul's letters (1 Thess 1:1; 2 Cor 1:1; Phil 1:1; Phlm 1; cf. 2 Thess 1:1; Col 1:1).

Timothy traveled with Paul on the second missionary journey, was sent by him to Thessalonica to encourage the community of Christians there (1 Thess 3:2), and then rejoined Paul at Corinth (Acts 18:5). He was sent to Macedonia with Erastus (Acts 19:22) and was with Paul upon his return from the third missionary journey (Acts 20:4). Timothy is next mentioned when Paul wrote, as a prisoner, the letters to the Colossians (Col 1:1), Philemon (Phlm 1), and the Philippians (Phil 1:1). Paul speaks highly of him in Philippians (Phil 2:19–22). At Ephesus (1 Tim 1:3) Timothy had the task of confronting false teachers and assisting in the organization of the Christian community in that city. Later, it seems that Timothy himself was imprisoned (Heb 13:23), but nothing specific is known of his later ministry except that tradition says he was martyred in Ephesus in old age. Paul described Timothy as timid in personality (1 Cor 16:10–11; 2 Tim 1:7). Nevertheless, Paul had an abiding fondness for him and commended him especially for his loyalty (Phil 2:19).

TIMOTHY, LETTERS TO With the Letter to Titus, the First and Second Letters to Timothy form the "Pastoral Epistles," so called from their focus on Pastoral ministry. The letters are often dated in Paul's final years and reveal much of the great Evangelist's mind as he prepared to hand over the care of the Christian communities to a new generation. The First and Second Letters to Timothy were addressed to Paul's trusted assistant, Timothy, who was then in Ephesus with the task of reforming the Christian community (1 Tim 1:3). The First Letter to Timothy emphasizes pastoral responsibility for preserving unity of doctrine, and the Second Letter to Timothy is Paul's final testament during his imprisonment in Rome.

I. AUTHORSHIP AND DATE

According to 1 Tim 1:1, the author of the epistle is Paul; the same authorship is claimed for 2 Timothy (2 Tim 1:1). Christians accepted the authenticity of these letters from the earliest time, and several prominent figures in the first Christian centuries referenced the letters as Paul's: Saint Clement of Rome (A.D. 95) and Saint Polycarp (A.D. 120). Saint Irenaeus (A.D. 180), Tertullian (A.D. 200), and Saint Clement of Alexandria (A.D. 200) are among those who support the tradition.

The universal acceptance of Paul's authorship remained unchallenged until the nineteenth century. After that, some scholars termed the letters pseudepigraphical—meaning that the letters were written in Paul's name by one or more of his admirers many years after his death. Reasons for this claim include differences in language between the pastoral Epistles and some of Paul's other letters; the description of an ecclesiastical state of affairs that the scholars thought was not in place during Paul's lifetime; and the absence of the typical Pauline doctrinal themes.

On the other hand, there are still clear traces of Paul's thinking woven throughout these letters. Stylistic differences can be attributed to the more personal content of the letters, which were addressed to individuals in the service of the Church, whereas other epistles were for the benefit of young Christian communities. Other letters universally accepted as Paul's hint at the same kind of Church leadership (cf. 1 Cor 12:28; Phil 1:1; 1 Thess 5:12). Finally, the lack of Paul's favorite doctrinal themes is again attributable to the personal nature of the epistles: Paul would not need to reiterate essentials of the faith to one of his most trusted assistants. Taken together, the objections to Pauline authorship are not conclusive, and the uncontested attestation of Pauline authorship in the early Church can still be defended.

For those scholars who deny the Pauline authorship of the pastoral Epistles, the date of 1 Timothy is usually placed between A.D. 80 and 110. If 1 Timothy is genuinely written by Paul, the date for the letter can be estimated in the mid-sixties A.D., sometime between Paul's first imprisonment in Rome and his martyrdom. The date for 2 Timothy depends on the context of Paul's stated imprisonment in Rome (2 Tim 1:8, 17). Most would identify this as Paul's second detainment in Rome, which is not elsewhere mentioned in the New Testament, but which is attested in early Christian tradition. It is likely that the letter was written soon before his martyrdom in Rome around A.D. 67.

II. CONTENTS

1 TIMOTHY

2 TIMOTHY

III. PURPOSE AND THEMES

1 Timothy

The First Letter to Timothy was written to Paul's associate Timothy at Ephesus. Timothy, young and sometimes unassertive, needed encouragement to take bold action against various troublemakers in the Ephesian church who had exchanged sound doctrine for personal speculations that at best were pointless and at worst were dangerous. The letter is thus Paul's attempt to lend his apostolic authority to the difficult reforms that Timothy was charged with carrying out.

Most of the letter is taken up with the variety of pastoral duties that Timothy should fulfill: teaching sound doctrine (1 Tim 4:6–7; 6:20), appointing trustworthy pastors (3:1–13; 5:22), encouraging prayer (2:1–8), delineating proper conduct and dress on the part of women (2:9–15), fulfilling liturgical duties (4:13), caring for widows (5:3–16), and remaining pure (4:12; 5:22; 6:11–14).

2 Timothy

Paul wrote the Second Letter to Timothy to encourage Timothy and to summon him to Rome. As would be expected in a letter to a friend, this letter assumes Timothy's solid credentials in the faith. Paul's respect for Timothy—his frequent calls for him to be strong and steadfast notwithstanding—is apparent in his hope for Timothy to make his way to Paul's side (2 Tim 4:9, 21). In areas of doctrine, Paul is most preoccupied with the transmission of solid teaching (1:13–14; 4:3). He also declares that discipleship entails suffering (2:3; 3:12).

There is a sense in the epistle that Paul is saying farewell to those closest to him: "For I am already on the point of being sacrificed; the time of my departure has come. I have fought the good fight, I have finished the race, I have kept the faith. Henceforth there is laid up for me the crown of righteousness, which the Lord, the righteous judge, will award to me on that Day, and not only to me but also to all who have loved his appearing" (4:6–8). As death approached, Paul placed his confidence for the future in the hands of Timothy (and Titus) and gave fatherly advice to those who would succeed him.

TIPHSAH A city, probably the modern Dibse, that marked the northern boundary of Solomon's kingdom (1 Kgs 5:4). It was located in northern Syria on the west bank of the Euphrates.

TIRAS The youngest son of **Japheth** and the brother of Gomer, Magog, Javan, Tubal, and Meshech (Gen 10:2; 1 Chr 1:5).

TIRHAKAH The king of Egypt of the Twenty-fifth (Ethiopian) Dynasty (r. 690–664 B.C.). The son of Piye (Piankhi), he succeeded his kinsman Shebitku and embarked on a vigorous reign that included military ventures into Libya and Palestine. When the Assyrian king Sennacherib campaigned against Judah (2 Kgs 19:9; Isa 37:9), Tirhakah—then still a military officer, not yet king—marched against him (2 Kgs 19:9; Isa 37:9).

TIRZAH The name of a person and a city in the Old Testament.

1. One of the five daughters of Zelophehad (Num 27:1–11, 36:1–12; Josh 17:3–6; cf. 1 Chr 7:15).

2. A city in central Canaan that was captured by **Joshua** (Josh 12:24) and later became a royal residence of several northern kings of Israel, namely, **Jeroboam** (1 Kgs 14:17), **Baasha** (1 Kgs 15:21; 16:6), **Elah** (1 Kgs 16:8), **Zimri** (1 Kgs 16:15), and **Omri** (1 Kgs 16:23) until he moved the capital to **Samaria** (1 Kgs 16:24). Tirzah was also the home of **Menahem**, who later claimed the throne of Samaria (2 Kgs 15:14–16). The city was noted for its beauty (Song 6:4). It is probably the site now called Tell el-Far'ah, northeast of Nablus.

TISHBE The home of **Elijah**, east of the Jordan (1 Kgs 17:1). Its present location is unknown.

TISHRI The seventh month of the Israelite calendar, formerly known as Ethanim. It corresponds approximately to September–October.

TITHE A religious offering consisting of a tenth part of one's harvest or income. Tithing was a conventional means in the ancient Near East of rendering payment for cultic services. The tithe was paid to a sanctuary or directly to its ministers.

In the Bible, tithing is first mentioned in patriarchal times. For instance, **Abraham**, after a successful military venture, gave a tenth of his spoils to the royal priest **Melchizedek** (Gen 14:20). Later on, **Jacob** vowed to give his tithes to the Lord, provided he would be granted a safe return to Canaan (Gen 28:20–22). In these ancient times, tithing was something that was both customary and discretionary.

The practice of tithing became institutionalized in Mosaic times. The **Law** thus requires the lay tribes of Israel to pay tithes of their grain, wine, oil, and livestock to the ministerial tribe of Levi (Num 18:21–24). This tithe was given over to the non-priestly Levites, who in turn gave 10 percent of the offering, called "a tithe of the tithe," to the Aaronic priests (Num 18:25–32). Every third year, the Levitical tithe was shared with the poor and needy in Israel (Deut 14:28–29). The tribe of Levi received tithes, not only as compensation for spiritual service, but also as a steady food allowance, since Levi was the one tribe in Israel that received no land inheritance in Canaan (Josh 13:14).

Disregard for the tithe laws became a serious problem after the **Exile**. As one of his efforts at reform, **Nehemiah** made it a policy for the restored community in Judea to observe faithfully the practice of tithing (Neh 10:37). Later, the prophet **Malachi** accused the Jews of robbing God by withholding the tithe (Mal 3:8–9). He responded by challenging the people to give what was due, for this would bring the blessings of heaven upon their nation (Mal 3:10–12).

In the New Testament, the **Pharisees** were proud of their scrupulous observance of tithing and considered it proof of their exceptional piety (Luke 18:12). Jesus, however, rebuked the Pharisees on this count, not because the practice of tithing was irreligious, but because they gave more attention to tithing the smallest herbs of the garden than to the most important matters of the Law, namely, "justice and mercy and faith" (Matt 23:23).

TITIUS JUSTUS *See* **Justus**.

TITUS A Gentile Christian (Gal 2:3) who became one of **Paul**'s fellow laborers (2 Cor 8:23). Early on he appeared with Paul in Jerusalem at the time when circumcision was a matter of debate (Gal 2:1–5). Titus was later sent as Paul's representative to the Corinthian community (2 Cor 2:13; 7:6, 13–14; 8:6, 16, 23; 12:18). He was sent once more to oversee the collection for the church in Jerusalem (2 Cor 8:6) and was the recipient of the Letter to Titus (Titus 1:4). The letter suggests that Titus journeyed to Crete with Paul (1:4), as he was instructed to organize the community there and then proceed to Nicopolis (3:12). Later we find him in Dalmatia, where he was serving at the time of the writing of 2 Timothy (2 Tim 4:10). Tradition tells us that

he returned to Crete and served there as bishop (Eusebius, *Hist. Eccl.* 3.4.6).

TITUS, LETTER TO One of the three so-called pastoral Epistles (with 1 and 2 Timothy). Addressed to one of Paul's close collaborators, it is concerned with the pastoral care of the early Christian community. The Letter to Titus also provides valuable insights into Paul's ministry and thought during his last years.

I. AUTHORSHIP AND DATE

The unanimous conviction of Christians until the nineteenth century was that the Letter to Titus, along with the other pastoral Epistles, was written by the apostle Paul, as is claimed in the letter (Titus 1:1; cf. 1 Tim 1:1; 2 Tim 1:1). Some scholars in the nineteenth century questioned the apostolic authorship of the pastoral Epistles, citing linguistic differences with the undisputed Pauline Epistles, the absence of typical Pauline doctrinal concerns, and the historical situation that seems to underpin the letters. The arguments against Pauline authorship are the same as those for 1 and 2 Timothy (*see* **Timothy, Letters to**), and once again the traditional attribution to Paul remains a viable opinion that explains the data as well as any alternative hypothesis.

The date of the Letter to Titus is uncertain, and internal evidence provides few clues to compare the events with the chronology in the book of Acts. Tradition has it that Paul set out on a fourth missionary journey after his first Roman imprisonment (A.D. 60–62; cf. Acts 28:16) and before his martyrdom (A.D. 67); it is possible that the Letter to Titus may have been composed around the same time that

Paul wrote 1 Timothy, between A.D. 63 and 66. Scholars who argue that the pastoral Epistles are the work of a later Pauline disciple posit a date between A.D. 80 and 110.

II. CONTENTS

I. *Opening Address to Titus (1:1-4)*

II. *The Qualifications for Christian Leadership (1:5-9)*

III. *The Problem of False Teachers (1:10-16)*

IV. *Christian Behavior (2:1-10)*

V. *Christian Commitment (2:11-3:1-7)*

VI. *Conclusion (3:8-15)*

III. PURPOSE AND THEMES

Paul's letter is sent to Titus on the Mediterranean island of Crete where Paul and Titus had proclaimed the Gospel; Paul had continued to travel on his missionary labors, but Titus had remained behind to serve the island's inhabitants, who included both a Jewish community (Titus 1:10) and a large number of pagans who were noted for their moral decadence (1:12).

The body of the letter (1:5-3:11) is taken up with Paul's command that Titus organize the Christian converts and appoint leaders to provide pastoral care for the community (1:5). As he does in 1 Timothy (1 Tim 1:3), Paul exhorts Titus to provide the community with strength and leadership in the face of false teaching (Titus 1:10-16; 1 Tim 1:3-7).

Paul starts by commanding Titus to appoint reliable leaders (Titus 1:5-16), urging that they be capable teachers. One of the characteristics required of these leaders is the practical ability to maintain their own household (1:6). He then provides a code of behav-

ior (2:2-10) for the community and implores Titus to confront the troublemakers (2:15-3:11). He expresses full confidence in Titus, and following the fulfillment of his tasks on Crete, Titus is to rejoin Paul in Nicopolis for the winter (3:12).

TITUS MANIUS One of two Roman envoys (with Quintus Memmius) sent to the Jews in 164 B.C. (2 Macc 11:34-38).

TOB A region east of the Sea of Galilee where **Jephthah** took refuge after being driven out by his legitimate brothers; there he formed a gang of bandits (Judg 11:3). The Arameans of Tob marched to assist the Ammonites against **David**, but they shared in the defeat handed them by Joab (2 Sam 10:6-13). In the time of the Maccabees, the Jews of the region were slaughtered by the Gentiles (1 Macc 5:13).

TOBIAH The name of two men in the Old Testament. (**Tobias** in the book of Tobit is called Tobiah in some English versions.)

1. The head of a family that returned from the **Exile** (Zech 6:9-14). The clan was unable to prove its Israelite ancestry (Ezra 2:60; Neh 7:62).

2. An enemy of **Nehemiah** who is called "the servant, the Ammonite" (Neh 2:10) and who was perhaps a royal official or governor. Tobiah was a foreigner who, with **Sanballat** the Horonite and **Geshem** the Arab, opposed Nehemiah's plans to restore the walls of Jerusalem (Neh 2:19). Tobiah and his allies tried to thwart every move Nehemiah made. Tobiah enjoyed close relations with the nobles of Judah (Neh 6:17-19) and had ties to a priestly

family (Neh 13:4); from the priests he received chambers in the Temple for his own use. Nehemiah expelled him from these quarters and hurled his belongings out of the sacred precincts (Neh 13:4–9). It is likely that Tobiah was connected to the influential family of the Tobiads.

TOBIAS (Hebrew, "my good is the Lord")

1. The son of Tobit and the chief figure in the book of **Tobit**.

2. The grandfather of Hyrcanus (2 Macc 3:11).

TOBIT, BOOK OF The story of two Israelite families whose lives were touched by God in the Assyrian Exile. They were brought together by marriage and the intervention of the angel Raphael. Tobit is one of the **deuterocanonical** books of the Old Testament that is deemed scriptural by Catholics but not by modern Jews or Protestants.

I. AUTHORSHIP AND DATE

The author of Tobit is unknown, as is the place where it was written. Modern scholarship generally assigns a date for its composition around 200 B.C., though conservative judgments have dated its origin, and sometimes its composition, as early as the seventh century B.C. Tobit is preserved intact only in the Greek **Septuagint**, and the Greek manuscripts display a considerable variety. The original text was in Aramaic or perhaps in Hebrew. Three fragmentary copies of an Aramaic text were found in Qumran among the **Dead Sea Scrolls**, along with a fragment of a Hebrew text. Saint Jerome claims to have translated Tobit into the Vulgate

from an Aramaic version, but his translation was done in such haste—one day's work—that it does not offer sufficient information for a critical reconstruction of the Semitic text from which he worked (cf. *Praefatio in Tobiam*).

II. CONTENTS

III. PURPOSE AND THEMES

The book of Tobit resembles in style and spirit the familial history books such as Ruth and the latter parts of Genesis. It relates the personal history of Tobit, a devout and charitable Israelite in exile, and those persons connected with him, such as his son Tobias, his kinsman Raguel, and Raguel's daughter Sarah. In narrating several examples of faithfulness, it shows readers how to live as covenant people in exile and relies upon the principal themes of patience under trial and trust in divine Providence. The fidelity of the Lord is beautifully symbolized by the presence and action of the angel **Raphael**.

The account begins with the testimony of Tobit, son of Tobiel, of the tribe of Naphtali, telling how he was exiled from Israel to **Nineveh** and lived there during the reign of the

Assyrian king Shalmaneser V. In Nineveh, Tobit observed the law of God and demonstrated a deeply charitable nature. His good works included acts of mercy to captives and the dead. His life took a radical turn, however, when he was stricken with blindness in old age. But in the face of his hardships, Tobit turned to God in prayer (Tob 3:1–6). For this, God remained faithful to him and sent aid when Tobit and his family were most in need. Likewise, Sarah, daughter of Raguel, in Ecbatana, endured taunts by her maid because she was the widow of seven husbands (3:7–10). Sarah turned to God in prayer (3:11–23) and her prayers, like Tobit's, were answered (3:24–25).

The means of divine assistance was the angel Raphael, disguised as a man named Azarias (5:1–12:22). Raphael assisted Tobias on his journey to Rages of Media to obtain the ten talents of silver left in bond by his father (4:1–9:12); helped free Sarah from the evil of the demon **Asmodeus**, who had killed her seven previous husbands (8:1–24); helped arrange the marriage of Tobias and Sarah; prescribed a cure to heal the blindness of Tobit; and finally revealed his true identity (10:2–12:31).

The narrative offers one of the greatest examples of an angelophany in Scripture. The story is one of the most popular from the OT as a model for simple, sincere, and unflagging devotion to the Lord, the mercy of God, and the strength of perseverance in the face of life's troubles.

TOGARMAH The third son of Gomer and the grandson of the patriarch Japheth (Gen 10:3; 1 Chr 1:6). The region named Togarmah supplied horses to **Tyre** (Ezek 27:14).

TOI The king of Hamath in lower Syria and a contemporary of King **David** (2 Sam 8:9–10). He sent his son Joram to David with a gift in celebration of David's defeat of **Hadadezer** of Zobah. His name appears in 1 Chronicles as "Tou" (1 Chr 18:9).

TOMB *See* **Burial**.

TONGUE The Hebrew and Greek words for "tongue" were used both for the physical organ and for a spoken language. The tongue may be good or evil. On the one hand, it could be mendacious and deceitful (Ps 109:2; 120:2), seductive (Prov 6:24), whetted like a sword (Ps 64:3; 140:3), and wielded like a bow and arrow (Jer 9:3, 8). On the other, the wise man understands the power of the tongue to do good or evil (Sir 6:5; 20:1–8, 18–23; 23:7–15; 28:13–16). The tongue has the power of life and death (Prov 18:21; Jas 3:1–12). More positively, the healing tongue is a tree of life (Prov 15:4), and the tongue is called silver among the righteous (Prov 10:20). (*See also* **Tongues, gift of**.)

TONGUES, CONFUSION OF *See* **Babel**.

TONGUES, GIFT OF A spiritual or charismatic gift that enables a believer to speak to God in a language other than his own. Tongues first appeared as a manifestation of the Spirit on the first **Pentecost**, when the apostles began preaching the Gospel in a variety of different languages and dialects (Acts 2:4–11). Thereafter in Acts the gift of tongues is always associated with the descent of the Holy Spirit on those who came to believe (Acts 10:44–46; 19:6). In this context, speaking in tongues is a sign that the Christian message is a universal message to be preached to all nations (Mark 16:15–17).

Significant attention is given to charismatic tongues in 1 Cor 14. Here Paul describes the phenomenon as speaking "to God" and uttering "mysteries in the Spirit" (1 Cor 14:2). Also, the one who speaks in tongues "edifies himself" (1 Cor 14:4). This is fine as far as it goes, and personal edification has its place, but Paul counsels that tongues should not be exercised in the context of public worship unless someone with the charism of interpretation is present to share the meaning of the words with the assembly (1 Cor 14:5, 9–12). For this reason, Paul subordinates tongues to other charisms such as prophecy, because the latter provides encouragement for all in attendance (1 Cor 14:1–5, 39).

TONGUES OF FIRE *See* **Pentecost**.

TOPHEL A location east of the Jordan near where Moses gave Israel the law code of Deuteronomy (Deut 1:1). The location is uncertain, although some scholars have identified it with the modern Tafileh.

TOPHETH The location of a cultic sanctuary or "high place" in the Valley of **Hinnom**, south of Jerusalem. Child sacrifices were offered there to the Semitic god **Molech**. The site was condemned by **Jeremiah**, who prophesied that it would become a cemetery (Jer 7:32; 19:6–13). King **Josiah** defiled or destroyed the furnace in the valley with the aim of eradicating idolatrous child sacrifice (2 Kgs 23:10).

TORAH The **Pentateuch**. The name transliterates the Hebrew *tôrâ*, meaning "instruction."

TOWER OF ANTONIA *See* **Antonia, Tower of**.

TOWER OF BABEL *See* **Babel, Tower of**.

TOWER OF SHECHEM *See* **Shechem**.

TRACHONITIS A region northeast of the Sea of Galilee and south of Damascus that was under the tetrarchy of **Herod Philip** (Luke 3:1). (*See* **Bashan**.)

TRADITION *See under* **Revelation, divine**.

TRADITION CRITICISM *See* **Biblical criticism**.

TRANSFIGURATION The revelation of Jesus's divine glory witnessed by the apostles **Peter**, **James**, and **John** on a mountain (Matt 17:1–9; Mark 9:2–10; Luke 9:28–36). The Transfiguration took place after Jesus's discourse in response to Peter's declaration at Caesarea Philippi that Jesus was the Messiah (Matt 16:13–28; Mark 8:27–9:1; Luke 9:18–22). In the Transfiguration, Jesus's face shone brilliantly like the sun, and his clothing appeared white as light. Moses and Elijah appeared; Peter offered to build three tents (or booths) for Jesus and the prophets who appeared with him. A bright cloud then overshadowed them all and a voice was heard declaring, "This is my Son, my Chosen; listen to him!" (Luke 9:35).

In the Transfiguration, Jesus disclosed his divine glory for a brief moment, giving confirmation to Peter's confession. The presence of Moses and Elijah as witnesses implies that the Law and the Prophets testify to the coming of the Messiah, now identified as Jesus. The cloud, so consistent with the theophanies of the Old Testament, revealed the presence of the Holy Spirit. As Saint Thomas Aquinas noted, the Transfiguration included the whole of the Trinity: "The Father in the voice; the Son in the man; the Spirit in the shining cloud" (*Summa theologiae*, III, q.45, a.4, ad 2). Traditionally, the mountain on which the Transfiguration took place is said to have been Mount Tabor in lower Galilee (CCC 554–56). (*See also* **Son of Man.**)

TRANSJORDAN The area east of the Jordan Rift Valley as far as the Arabian desert. The term is not used in the RSV.

TRANSLATIONS OF THE BIBLE *See* **Versions of the Bible**.

TREE OF THE KNOWLEDGE OF GOOD AND EVIL One of the two primeval trees in the middle of the **Garden of Eden** (Gen 2:9). The "knowledge of good and evil" is not an awareness of the difference between good and evil, but rather, in the judgment of many scholars, *moral autonomy*—that is, the legislative right to decide for oneself what is good and evil. Eating from this tree means asserting one's independence from the Creator.

God had forbidden **Adam** and **Eve** to eat the fruit of this tree, as doing so would bring about their death. Eve yielded to the temptations of the serpent, ate the fruit, and gave it to Adam, who also ate it (Gen 3:1–6). The con-

sequence of this act was their expulsion from the Garden and all of the consequences of the **Fall**. The tree served to represent that the Creator has placed limits on all creatures. These limitations must be recognized and respected as part of our dependency upon the Creator, and we must exercise our human freedom within the moral norms established for our benefit (CCC, 396–97).

TREE OF LIFE One of the two primeval trees in the middle of the **Garden of Eden** (Gen 2:9). The tree bestowed immortality upon those who ate of its fruit (Gen 3:22), but **Adam** and **Eve**'s expulsion from the Garden owing to the **Fall** ended their access to the tree's life-giving fruit. In the book of Proverbs, the Tree of Life is a metaphor for wisdom (Prov 3:18), righteousness (Prov 11:30), fulfilled desire (Prov 13:12), and the gentle speech of the tongue (Prov 15:4). In Isaiah, the Tree of Life is a sign of longevity (Isa 65:22). In Rev 2:7 and 22:2, the Tree of Life may be seen as a type of the **Eucharist**. In the context of Rev 21:9–22:5, the tree appears as part of the vision of the New Jerusalem and grows on the sides of the river flowing beneath the divine throne (Rev 22:2). The tree offers "twelve kinds of fruit, producing its fruit each month; and the leaves of the tree are for the healing of the nations," and the righteous "will have the right to the tree of life and may enter the city by the gates" (Rev 22:14).

TRIBES OF ISRAEL The largest family units of the nation of Israel. Each of the tribes traced its ancestry back to one of the twelve sons of Jacob (Israel). The twelve sons were, according to the order of their birth: **Reuben, Simeon, Levi, Judah, Dan, Naphtali, Gad, Asher, Issachar, Zebulun, Joseph,** and **Benjamin** (Gen 29:31–20:24; 35:16–18). There was no tribe by the name of Joseph, because Jacob adopted the two sons of Joseph, **Manasseh** and **Ephraim,** as his own sons (Gen 48:1–20), and each became the ancestor of an Israelite tribe.

Following the conquest of **Canaan,** the land was divided up among the tribes (Josh 13–19), although Levi, because of its sacred function, was granted no territory; instead, forty-eight cities were given to Levi (Josh 21:1–42) along with the right to receive support from the other tribes in the form of **tithes** (Num 18:21–24).

TRINITY The greatest revealed mystery of the Christian faith. It is the claim that the God of the Bible is a communion of three divine Persons in one divine nature. The word "Trinity" is part of the Church's theological vocabulary (Greek *trias*; Latin *trinitas*) and was coined in the second century A.D. to express this distinctively Christian belief. The doctrine was disclosed to the world in two historical stages: the Old Testament reveals the oneness of God, and the New Testament reveals the tri-personal nature of God as Father, Son, and Holy Spirit.

I. THE OLD TESTAMENT

The God of the Bible is revealed in the OT as "one" (Deut 6:4). This was the fundamental creed of ancient Israel. At one level, it was a strictly theological claim that Yahweh was the only true God and Creator of the world, and that no other gods existed but him (Deut 4:35, 39; 32:39; Isa 45:5, 18). But more was implied

than simply the doctrine of monotheism. At another level, it was a covenant claim that Israel must give exclusive allegiance to Yahweh as the Lord of the covenant (Exod 20:2–3; 23:32; Deut 10:12–21). To worship or pledge fidelity to any other god would break the covenant and unleash its curses upon the nation (Exod 20:4–5; Deut 6:14–15, 28:20).

Essentially, the doctrine of God's unicity or oneness is a counterclaim that distinguishes the Israelite faith from the rampant polytheism of the biblical world. Apart from a single short experiment with monotheism in fifteenth-century Egypt, the ancient Near East was thoroughly dominated by the belief in a pantheon of gods and goddesses. It was thus logical and practical, given the religious mind-set of the wider culture, for the Lord to reveal himself as "one" before disclosing his inner life as "three." To do otherwise would have invited confusion, and the faith of Israel would hardly have seemed distinct from that of pagan religions.

It cannot be said, therefore, that the OT reveals the mystery of the Trinity in its literal sense. It is true that Christian theologians, looking back on the sacred books with the benefit of additional revelation, did indeed see reflections and hints of the Trinity in the Hebrew Scriptures, but these do not represent the literal meaning of the texts intended by the original authors. Christian tradition has seen traces of the Trinity in the Creation narrative (the Father speaks, the Son is spoken, and the Spirit hovers above the waters, Gen 1:1–3), in the use of the first-person plural with reference to God speaking ("let us make man in our image" Gen 1:26), and in the Lord's appearance to Abraham in the form of three men (Gen 18:1–2), among many other examples.

II. THE NEW TESTAMENT

The teaching of the NT represents a development rather than a departure from OT faith. It not only assumed the doctrine of monotheism, but Jesus and the apostles explicitly reaffirmed that God is "one" (John 17:3; Rom 3:30; Gal 3:20; 1 Tim 2:5).

Nevertheless, the oneness of God is opened in the NT to reveal a deeper mystery, namely, that the one God is a family of three divine Persons—Father, Son, and Spirit. Some of the first glimpses of this revelation come during the public ministry of Jesus at his baptism and Transfiguration. On both occasions, God declares that Jesus is his beloved Son and manifests the Spirit in visible form, as a dove (Matt 3:16–17) and as a glorious cloud (Matt 17:1–5), respectively. Jesus was thus accustomed to speak of God as his Father in the most intimate terms (Matt 11:25–27), declaring such things as "I and the Father are one" (John 10:30). Some Jews were offended by this because they understood it as a claim to divinity on the part of Jesus (John 10:33).

The Trinitarian teaching of Jesus is perhaps best summarized in the baptismal formula given as part of his missionary mandate to the apostles after the Resurrection: "Go, therefore, and make disciples of all nations, baptizing them in the name of the Father and of the Son and of the Holy Spirit" (Matt 28:19). Nevertheless, the most concentrated revelation on the Trinity was given in the hours before Jesus's arrest (John 14–17). In the course of his long discourse in the upper room, Jesus revealed his relationship to the Father and the Spirit, and the Spirit's relationship to the Father and the Son. The Son came "from" the Father (John 16:28) and possessed the "glory" of the Father before the world was created (John 17:5, 24). Because the Son is "in" the Father, and the Father is "in" the Son (John 14:11), it follows that to know Jesus is to know the Father (John 14:7), and to see Jesus is to see the Father (John 14:9). The Spirit too "proceeds" from the Father (John 15:26) and is "sent" into the world by both the Father (John 14:26) and the Son (John 16:7). Just as the Father glorifies the Son (17:1), so the Spirit glorifies the Son through his ministry of revealing the truth (John 16:13–14). The magnificence of this revelation for the Christian is the promise of being united with the three Persons of the Trinity: the Spirit comes to dwell within believers (John 14:16–17), as do the Father and the Son (John 14:23).

The apostle Paul embraced this new understanding of God as well. He came to recognize that, even though Christians believe in "one God, the Father" (1 Cor 8:6), they believe as well that Jesus Christ is also the "Lord" (1 Cor 12:3), as is the Spirit (2 Cor 3:17). From this insight Paul came to see Jesus as a divine Person come in the flesh (Col 2:9). Not only that, but he developed a doctrine of Christ as the Preexistent One who, with the Father, brought all things into being (1 Cor 8:6; Col 1:15–20; cf. John 1:1–18). The Spirit, like the Son, was also sent into the world from the Father (Gal 4:4–6). And he is no mere impersonal force, but is the One who probes, understands, and reveals the mind of God (1 Cor 2:9–13). Being a divine Person, he can be grieved by the sins of

God's people (Eph 4:30). The classic summary of Paul's belief in the Trinity is the benediction that closes 2 Corinthians: "The grace of the Lord Jesus Christ and the love of God and the fellowship of the Holy Spirit be with you all" (2 Cor 13:14).

TRIPOLIS An ancient port city on the Phoenician coast to the north of modern Beirut (1 Macc 7:1–4; 2 Macc 14:1).

TROAS A seaport city in northwestern Asia Minor, near the ruins of ancient Troy. The city was established by the successors of Alexander the Great and thus became known as Alexander Troas; the city by New Testament times was called Troas, especially after its designation as a Roman colony during the reign of Emperor Augustus (27 B.C.–A.D. 14).

Paul visited Troas several times but apparently did not spend much time there. While at Troas he received the vision of the man of Macedonia and sailed for Macedonia from there (Acts 16:7–12). Paul passed through Troas again on the third missionary journey (2 Cor 2:12) and found an "open door" for preaching the Gospel. On his return trip (Acts 20:5–6), Paul and his companions spent a week in Troas, during which time Paul broke bread with the members of the community and revived Eutychus after he fell out of a window (Acts 20:8–12). In 2 Tim 4:13, Paul asks Timothy to bring his personal possessions—a cloak and scrolls—that he had left at the house of Carpus at Troas.

TROPHIMUS A Christian from Ephesus and a companion of **Paul**. He joined up with Paul on his final trip to Jerusalem (Acts 20:4). Jews from the province of Asia, having seen Paul and Trophimus together in Jerusalem, assumed that Paul had taken Trophimus into the inner courts of the **Temple**, and so defiled the Temple, because they assumed that Trophimus was an uncircumcised Gentile convert to Christianity (Acts 21:27–29). Trophimus was the innocent cause of Paul's arrest and set in motion the events that ultimately brought Paul to Rome. At some later point, near the end of Paul's life, we hear that he left Trophimus behind in Miletus because he was ill (2 Tim 4:20).

TROPOLOGICAL SENSE See "Senses of Scripture" *under* **Interpretation of the Bible**.

TRUMPET An instrument that, in biblical times, could be used in civic, military, and liturgical contexts. Trumpets were made of cast metal or the hollow horns of a ram. Announcements were made with the trumpet, such as the beginning of a Jubilee year (Lev 25:9) or the accession of a newly crowned king (1 Kgs 1:34). On the battlefield, trumpets were sounded both to commence an attack (Josh 6:20; Judg 7:20) and to call off an attack (2 Sam 2:28; 18:16). As a liturgical instrument, the trumpet provided musical accompaniment for the praises of Israel sung to the Lord (1 Chr 15:28; 16:6, 42; 2 Chr 29:28). Most important, trumpets herald the anticipated interventions of God in history. That is, they signal the coming judgment of God (Zeph 1:26), the gathering of the saints (Matt 24:31), the resurrection of the dead (1 Thess 4:16), and the definitive arrival of the Kingdom of God (Rev 8:1–9:21; 11:16–18).

TRUTH Reality as correctly perceived by man or made known by God through revelation. In the Bible, truth is often connected with the tenets of Israelite or Christian faith. Religious truth includes the ideas of "facticity" as well as "fidelity." In other words, in biblical terminology (Hebrew *ĕmet*; Greek *alētheia*), truth tells us the way things really are, whether in reference to God, man, or the created order in general, and it does so in a way that is completely reliable and trustworthy. Knowledge of the truth has the power to set us free from the cynicism and skepticism and nagging uncertainties that plague the world (John 8:31–32).

I. IN THE OLD TESTAMENT

"Truth" in the Old Testament suggests constancy, faithfulness, and something worthy of our confidence and hope (Gen 24:27, 47:29; Josh 2:14; 2 Sam 2:6, 15:20; 2 Kgs 20:19; Hos 2:20). The OT proclaims that God is the source of all truth and guarantees his words, promises, and faithfulness, which "endures to all generations" (Ps 119:90; cf. Ps 31:5, 119:142; Jer 10:10). God's word is true; in fact, it is the standard of truth (2 Sam 7:28; Ps 119:89). Truth is his wisdom and commands and governs all of creation (Prov 8:7; cf. Wis 13:1–9).

Since God is truth, those who live in fidelity to him are called upon to live in truth and to bear witness to the truth. Thus the eighth commandment forbids bearing false witness (Exod 20:16; Deut 5:20) (CCC 2471–73). There is truth to be apprehended in the investigation of facts or events (Deut. 17:4; 1 Kgs 10:6). Truthfulness is also an attribute of a person: "Let one of you go and bring your brother, while the rest of you remain in prison, in or-der that your words may be tested, whether there is truth in you" (Gen 42:16).

II. IN THE NEW TESTAMENT

Truth has the same meanings in the New Testament as in the OT, but under the influence of Greek philosophy it can be more intellectual; it is a reality to be apprehended by the mind. The concrete understanding of truth as stability and dependability is still present (2 Cor 7:14), especially as it pertains to God (Rom 3:7, 15:8; 1 Pet 5:12). But the abstract sense of "truth," the correct perception of reality, is also very important to NT writers (Mark 5:33; John 5:34; 16:7, 13; 19:35; Acts 26:25; Rom 9:1; 2 Cor 12:6; Eph 4:25).

The NT proclaims that in Jesus Christ the whole of God's truth has been revealed, for Jesus is the truth (John 1:14; 8:12): "I am the way, and the truth, and the life" (John 14:6). By following Jesus, the disciple is led by the Spirit of truth, and "he will guide you into all the truth; for he will not speak on his own authority, but whatever he hears he will speak, and he will declare to you the things that are to come" (John 16:13).

The Christian faith is the truth (Gal 2:5; Eph 1:13), and believers are challenged to live in conformity with it—for "If we say we have fellowship with him while we walk in darkness, we lie and do not live according to the truth" (1 John 1:6). To find this truth, one need only believe in the Gospel (1 Tim 2:4), "and you will know the truth, and the truth will make you free" (John 8:32; cf. John 17:17) (CCC 1741). That freedom is possible by the power of Christ, and it brings with it the inner transformation of the person by freedom's encounter with the truth (Jas 1:18; 1 Pet 1:22; 2 Pet 1:12) (CCC 215–17; 2465–92).

TRYPHAENA AND TRYPHOSA Roman Christian women who received greetings from **Paul** in Rom 16:12.

TRYPHO The surname of Diodotus, an officer under **Alexander Balas**. A native of Kasiana, near Apamea, he served as general but then faced political difficulty when Demetrius II defeated Alexander and claimed the **Seleucid** throne. Trypho seized Balas's son, Antiochus VI Epiphanes, crowned him king in 145 B.C., and defeated Demetrius's army; as regent, Trypho controlled Antioch and central Syria (1 Macc 11:54–56). Trypho had the young king confirm **Jonathan** as high priest, and he proved a good ally: Jonathan twice defeated Demetrius's army. These successes alarmed Trypho, however, because he recognized that he could not defeat Jonathan militarily. So he lured Jonathan to Ptolemais and took him prisoner. After accepting a ransom for Jonathan, Trypho killed him anyway (1 Macc 13:12–24). Trypho then killed Antiochus and declared himself king (1 Macc 13:31–32). Meanwhile, Demetrius was killed in battle, leaving Trypho sole ruler of Syria. Demetrius's brother, Antiochus VII Sidetes, next claimed the crown for himself. He confirmed **Simon** as high priest and so gained Jewish assistance. In 139 B.C., he defeated Trypho and besieged him at the seaport of Dor. Trypho escaped, but he was captured at Apamea, where he committed suicide (1 Macc 15:10–14, 25). Trypho was much hated and was known for his cruelty, duplicity, and rapaciousness.

TRYPHOSA *See* **Tryphaena and Tryphosa**.

TUBAL One of the seven sons of Japheth and a grandson of **Noah** (Gen 10:2; 1 Chr 1:5). The name was used as a geographical designation for a people who inhabited the Black Sea region and who traded in slaves and bronze with **Tyre** (Ezek 27:13; cf. Isa 66:19). In Ezek 38:2–3 and 39:1, **Gog** is named the "chief prince of Meshech and Tubal."

TUBAL-CAIN The son of **Lamech** by his second wife, Zillah, and the brother of Naamah (Gen 4:22). Tubal-cain is called the ancestor of metalworkers.

TWELVE APOSTLES, THE *See* **Apostle**.

TWO-SOURCE HYPOTHESIS *See* **Synoptic problem**.

TYCHICUS A Christian from Asia Minor and a companion of **Paul** on his third missionary journey (Acts 20:4). Tychicus was later sent to deliver Paul's letters to the Colossians (Col 4:7–9) and Ephesians (Eph 6:21–22). At a later time, he was sent to Ephesus by Paul (2 Tim 4:12) and was a candidate, with Artemas, to replace **Titus** on the island of Crete (Titus 3:12).

TYPE (Greek *typos*, "impression," "copy," or "example") In a biblical and theological context, a type is any person, place, event, or institution in Scripture that foreshadows a greater reality yet to come. Normally something in the Old Testament points forward to something in the New Testament. For example, Paul teaches that Adam is "a type of the one who was to come," namely, Jesus Christ (Rom 5:14). The idea is that Adam prefigures Christ as one who came into the world without sin and as one whose actions affected the entire human race. Nevertheless, the greater of the two is Christ, for he succeeded where Adam failed, and Christ restored grace to the world by his obedience after mankind had lost grace because of Adam's rebellion (Rom 5:12–21). (*See* **Typology**.)

TYPICAL SENSE *See* "Senses of Scripture" *under* **Interpretation of the Bible**.

TYPOLOGY The study of persons, places, events, and institutions in the Bible that foreshadow later and greater realities made known by God in history. The basis of such study is the belief that God, who providentially shapes and determines the course of human events, infuses those events with a prophetic and theological significance. Typology thus reveals the unity of salvation history as a carefully orchestrated plan that God unfolds in stages of ever-increasing fulfillment. The movement from "types" to the realities they signify, called "antitypes," is always a movement from the lesser to the greater. Typology can be understood in prophetic (promise/fulfillment), metaphysical (matter/spirit), eschatological (time/eternity), or anagogical terms (earth/heaven).

Typology is not simply applied *to* the Bible; it is something applied *within* the Bible. Because typology was used by the authors of the Bible, studying the Bible in terms of typology is a valid approach to understanding salvation history. The point is important to stress, since typology is sometimes confused with a method of biblical interpretation that Christian theologians adopted from the world of classical antiquity—for example, from the philosophical speculations of Plato, or from the practice of allegorizing the poetry of Homer and Virgil. No doubt some early Christian writers, having been educated in these Greco-Roman traditions, approached the interpretation of the Bible in such ways. But typology is first and foremost grounded in the Semitic world of Scripture, because the biblical authors themselves made extensive use of typology in explaining the actions of God in history (CCC 128–30).

I. TYPOLOGY IN THE OLD TESTAMENT

Typology first appears in the books of the Old Testament, although the word "typology" is not used to describe the practice. In the Historical Books, we see the biblical authors highlighting parallels between significant figures and events in a way that invites the reader to ponder their deeper meaning. For example, the story of **Joshua** is deliberately worded to evoke memories of the story of **Moses** and to suggest to the reader that Joshua himself was a new Moses who acquired for his people what his venerable forebear could not, namely, possession of the Promised Land. This is nowhere stated explicitly in the book of Joshua, yet the typology at work is unmistakable to anyone familiar with the **Exodus** story of the Pentateuch. Consider, for instance, how Joshua parted the waters of the Jordan so that Israel could cross over on dry ground (Josh 3:14–17; 4:23), just as Moses had done at the Red Sea (Exod 14:16, 21–22). Consider too how Joshua sent spies into Canaan (Josh 2:1; 7:2) just as Moses had done while Israel was roaming in the wilderness (Num 13:2, 17). These and other parallels form the foundations of a "Moses typology" that will reappear several times in the Old Testament and then again in the New Testament.

Similar use of typology is made in the prophetic books. Perhaps the most obvious example is the "Exodus typology" of Isaiah. In looking ahead to Israel's release from captivity in Babylon, Isaiah recalls the drama of Israel's former release from captivity in Egypt. His description of the return from exile is thus colored with images and ideas drawn from the Exodus story, hinting that God's deliverance of old is a pattern or type of what God intends to do for his people again. Indications that Isaiah foresaw a new Exodus can be seen in his reference to dividing the "sea of Egypt" in order that "men may cross dryshod" (Isa 11:15; 51:10–11; cf. Exod 14:22). Other allusions include the "east wind" (Isa 27:8; cf. Exod 14:21), the "way" in the wilderness (Isa 35:8; 40:3; cf. Exod 13:21), the "wings like eagles" (Isa 40:31; cf. Exod 19:4), and the "water" that Yahweh gave his people to "drink" in the desert (Isa 43:20, 48:20–21; cf. Exod 17:6). The implicit idea underlying this and other examples is that God acts in similar or "typical" ways each time he intervenes to redeem his people.

II. TYPOLOGY IN THE NEW TESTAMENT

Typology comes into full bloom in the teaching of Jesus and the apostles. Not only is it more pervasive in the NT than in the OT—far more so than the seldom occurrence of words like "type" (Greek *typos*) and "typologically"

(Greek *typikōs*) might suggest—but typology reaches a certain crescendo of fulfillment. That is, many typological themes of the Hebrew Scriptures, which were fulfilled in partial degrees in the history of Israel, give way to the definitive antitypes that God had intended to prefigure from the beginning. In the Person and work of Jesus Christ, the full significance of the persons, places, events, and institutions of biblical history is finally revealed.

A. The Teaching of Jesus

Jesus found in the Bible a treasury of types that prepared the way for his coming. Several examples of this appear in Matthew 12, where he claims "something greater than the temple is here" (Matt 12:6), and "something greater than Jonah is here" (Matt 12:41), and again "something greater than Solomon is here" (Matt 12:42). His words indicate what is intrinsic to all typology, namely, that antitypes resemble the types that foreshadow them, yet they also surpass them because they are something greater than the original. In this case, Jesus placed himself above the holiest place known to Israel (the Temple), above the prophet who miraculously emerged from a three-day entombment (Jonah), and above the wisest king ever to rule the People of God (Solomon). Christ is a new and living temple, for in him dwells the divine presence more intensely than in the sanctuary (cf. John 2:21). He is likewise a new Jonah, for his Resurrection after three days in the grave would be the one miracle that outshines all others (cf. Matt 16:4). And he is also a new Solomon, a king from the royal line of David and a man of legendary wisdom who will draw the world closer to the Lord (Luke 11:31).

It is clear in the Gospels that Jesus also made typological claims through his actions. For example, when Christ spent forty days in the wilderness, he was knowingly reenacting the Exodus experience of Israel, who endured forty years of testing in the desert. The difference is that Jesus, in assuming the role of a new Israel, succeeded where historical Israel had failed because he fulfilled his filial obedience to the Father. To make the link unmistakable, he countered the devil's attacks by quoting passages from Deut 6–8, a portion of Scripture wherein Moses reflects on the Lord's faithfulness in contrast to Israel's many failings during the long wilderness period (Deut 6:13, 16; 8:3). In similar fashion, Jesus represented himself as a new and greater **Elisha** by performing miracles that recalled and yet exceeded the mighty acts of the prophet. Remember that Elisha once multiplied twenty "loaves of barley" to feed one hundred men and had some left over (2 Kgs 4:42–44). Jesus mimicked this action on a grander scale when he multiplied a mere five "barely loaves" to feed over five thousand people and still had twelve baskets full of bread left over (John 6:5–14). As a final example, Jesus reinforced his claim to be a new and greater Solomon by making his triumphal entry into Jerusalem on the back of a donkey amid shouts that he was "King" (Luke 19:28) and the "Son of David" (Matt 21:6). No one familiar with the OT would miss the typological symbolism of the event, which was deliberately staged in imitation of Solomon's coronation ride into Je-

rusalem on the back of David's mule (1 Kgs 1:38–40).

B. The Teaching of the Apostles

Jesus's approach to Scripture likewise became the apostles' approach to Scripture. This can be seen in the writings of Paul and Peter. Paul is perhaps most noted for expounding a typology of Christ as a new and greater **Adam** in Romans and in the First Letter to the Corinthians. The idea is that Adam foreshadowed Christ inasmuch as both men made a significant impact on the world. However, Christ is the counterimage of Adam: the first man Adam brought sin and death to the world by his rebellion (Gen 3:6; 1 Cor 15:22), whereas the God-Man Jesus compensated for the damage done by Adam's disobedience through his righteousness (Rom 5:12–21). Likewise, Adam possessed a living body made from the substance of the earth (Gen 2:7), but Christ, by his rising from the dead, now possesses a life-giving spirit endowed with the gifts of heaven (1 Cor 15:44–49).

In addition to this Christological typology, Paul also developed an ecclesiological typology to explain the mystery of the Church. For example, he several times refers to the community of believers as the temple of the living God (1 Cor 3:16–17; 2 Cor 6:19). The point is to show that the Church is holy through the indwelling of the Spirit and firmly established on Christ as the cornerstone of the whole structure (Eph 2:19–22). These statements are truly remarkable when we consider that Paul was writing when the Temple, the very thing that prefigured the Church as the dwelling place of

Yahweh, was still standing in Jerusalem. Another example in Paul compares the Church to the Exodus pilgrims of Israel in the wilderness. Like the Israelites, who passed through the sea (Exod 14:21–22) and were fed with manna from heaven (Exod 16:35) and water from the rock (Exod 17:6), so believers who make up the Church have passed through the waters of baptism and are now nourished on their journey by the food and drink of the Eucharist (1 Cor 10:1–5). In this instance, the typology serves as a warning, for most of the Israelites who received these blessings eventually spurned the Lord and thereby excluded themselves from the Promised Land (1 Cor 10:6–12).

Along with Christological and ecclesiological typology, one also finds sacramental typology in the NT. One clear instance is found in the First Letter of Peter, where Peter compares the **Flood** in the days of **Noah** to the waters of **baptism** in the liturgy of the Church. By heeding the Lord and boarding the ark, Noah and his family "were saved through water" (1 Pet 3:20). So, too, believers are saved by "Baptism, which corresponds to this" (1 Pet 3:21). Cleansing the world of a sinful generation is thus a type of cleansing the conscience of sin and guilt.

Many other examples could be cited to show how the NT writers developed Christological, ecclesiological, and sacramental typology. For that matter, examples could be marshaled to show that typology also proceeded along Mariological and anagogical lines, showing how the Mother of Jesus was prefigured by various persons and institutions of the OT, as were the celestial realities of heaven revealed in the book of Hebrews and the book of Revelation. Small

wonder that the Church Fathers spent so much time digging for OT types to explain the great mysteries of the NT. Whatever excesses the Church Fathers can be charged with, it is certain that the foundation of such a pursuit was valid, for they had as their example and guide the inspired authors of the Bible.

TYRANNUS An Ephesian who owned a hall where Paul preached every day for two years (Acts 19:9–10). Paul had initially taught at the synagogue, but opposition forced him to move to the hall of Tyrannus (Acts 19:1, 8–10).

TYRE One of the principal seaport cities on the Phoenician coast. Tyre was located south of **Sidon** and north of **Acco**. Part of the city was on an offshore island, and the other part was on the mainland. It has been inhabited since the third millennium B.C. and was one of the greatest cities and seaports in the first millennium B.C.

After foreign invasions in the late second millennium B.C., which led to the sack of Sidon, Tyre emerged as the chief Phoenician port; it was called the "daughter of Sidon" (Isa 23:12) because so many refugees from Sidon fled to the safety of its walls. The fortifications of Tyre were known throughout Palestine (Josh 19:29; 2 Sam 24:7). Tyre reached the zenith of its power in the tenth century B.C., during the reign of **Hiram I** (ca. 980–947 B.C.). It was at this time that **David** and Hiram began a close commercial and political relationship. Hiram sent cedar and workmen to assist in the construction of the royal palace of David (2 Sam 5:11).

Solomon continued the alliance and made

a contract with Hiram for the construction of the Temple in Jerusalem (1 Kgs 5:1–12; 2 Chr 2:1–16). The two kings also embarked on a joint effort in overseas trade through Eziongeber on the Gulf of Aqaba to **Ophir** (1 Kgs 9:26–28, 10:11–12; 2 Chr 8:17–18, 9:10–11), since Tyre enjoyed immense prestige and influence upon the seas (Isa 23:8; Ezek 27:1–4). Tyrian ships sailed to foreign ports and traded in, among other things, glass and famous dyes, called Tyrian (*see* **Dye, dyeing**). Hiram built a causeway to connect the island with the mainland, renovated the temples, and spread Tyrian power through an aggressive policy of colonization. Later, in the ninth century B.C., **Ethbaal** came to the throne and secured the marriage of his daughter **Jezebel** to **Ahab** of Israel (1 Kgs 16:31). The union led to the increase of **Baal** worship in Samaria and close ties between Tyre and Samaria until the death of Jezebel (1 Kgs 16:32–33; 2 Kgs 9:30–37).

The decline of Tyre began with the rise of the Assyrians, who extracted tribute from Tyre around 841 B.C. Eventually the city fell to the Assyrians in 724 B.C. under Sargon II and then submitted again to the Assyrians in 701 B.C. under **Sennacherib**. Esarhaddon installed an Assyrian on the Tyrian throne and extracted various concessions. In return, Tyre received extensive trading privileges in the Mediterranean. The prophets more than once pronounced the Lord's judgment on Tyre (Amos 1:9–10; Joel 3:4–8; Zech 9:2–4).

Following the destruction of Jerusalem in 586 B.C., the Babylonians under Nebuchadnezzar besieged Tyre for thirteen years, after which the city submitted (586–573 B.C.). Later, under the Persians, Sidon rose to greater prominence than Tyre. The last major event in the history of the famed city came in 332 B.C. when Alexander the Great besieged it for seven months and finally captured the island city after a near-legendary struggle. Tyre played little part in the New Testament. Jesus attracted followers from Sidon and Tyre (Mark 3:8). Jesus also visited the area (Mark 7:24) and remarked that it would have repented if it had witnessed the mighty works he had done in Palestine (Matt 11:21–22). **Paul** also stopped there briefly (Acts 21:3).

U

UCAL One of the recipients to whom Agur addressed his wisdom (Prov 30:1). Nothing else is known of him.

UGARIT A commercial seaport on the coast of ancient Syria that was the capital of a major city-state in the second millennium B.C. At the location now identified with Ras Shamra the remains of the ancient city were discovered by chance in 1928 and excavations were undertaken by a team of French archaeologists under the direction of C. F. A. Schaeffer (1929–1939 and 1948–1973). Over one thousand inscriptions were discovered dating from around 1400 B.C., and the texts proved of enormous interest to biblical scholars. Ugarit provided information on Canaanite language and religion and firsthand testimony on the Canaanite culture that the Israelites encountered during the conquest and settlement of ancient Palestine. (*See* **Canaan**; *see also* **Baal**.)

ULAI A river that flowed east of **Susa**, the capital of Elam (modern Iran). It was beside the Ulai that **Daniel** received his vision of the two-horned ram and the he-goat (Dan 8:2, 16).

ULAM The name of two men in the Old Testament.

1. The son of Sheresh of the tribe of Manasseh (1 Chr 7:16–17).

2. A tribal leader and member of Benjamin. His sons were skilled warriors and archers (1 Chr 8:39–40).

UMMAH A town in the territory of Asher (Josh 19:30). It may be the same as the coastal city of **Acco**.

UNCIRCUMCISED *See* **Circumcision**.

UNKNOWN GOD When Paul visited **Athens**, he found an altar inscribed, "To an unknown god" (Acts 17:23). He mentioned the altar when he addressed a gathering of Athenian intellectuals at the Areopagus (Acts 17:22–31). It was said that the philosopher Epimenides had once stopped a plague in Athens by directing that sacrifices be made to unknown local gods; Diogenes Laertius says that "even now" there were altars in and around Athens with no names inscribed on them, in memory of Epimenides' success (Diogenes Laertius, *Lives and Opinions of the Eminent Philosophers* I.110). Philostratus also speaks of "altars to unknown divinities" in Athens (*Life of Apollonius of Tyana* 6.3.5). Paul was familiar with Epimenides, whom he quotes in Acts 17:28 and Titus 1:12.

UNLEAVENED BREAD *See* **Leaven**; *see also* **Passover, feast of**.

UPHAZ An ancient mining colony noted for its gold (Jer 10:9; Dan 10:5). The location is unknown, and some scholars have suggested that it might refer to **Ophir**, which may have been in western Arabia. Others have theorized that the name may be related to the term for "refined gold" (e.g., Hebrew *mûpāz* or *paz*; cf. Song 5:11).

UPPER ROOM *See* **Eucharist**.

UR The father of Eliphal and one of King **David**'s elite warriors called "mighty men" (1 Chr 11:35).

UR OF THE CHALDEANS A city on the Euphrates River in lower Mesopotamia; the chief city of the Sumerian civilization. The site is now called Tell el-Muqayyar. Ur flourished in the third millennium B.C. but declined with the rise of Babylonia in the second millennium B.C. According to Gen 11:28–31 and 15:7 (cf. Neh 9:7), the family of **Terah** and Abram (later **Abraham**) migrated from Ur to **Haran** in upper Mesopotamia. According to tradition, recounted in Jdt 5:6–8, Abram's family was "driven out" because they refused to worship pagan gods. The name "of the Chaldeans" is a modernization of the text inserted by a later scribe: the "Chaldeans" emerged onto the world stage in the ninth century B.C., long after the time of Abram.

URBANUS A Roman Christian who received greetings from Paul (Rom 16:9). He was the only Christian in Rome to be termed a "fellow worker" by Paul, except for Aquila and Priscilla (Rom 16:3).

URIAH The name of three men in the Old Testament.

1. A Hittite warrior in the service of **David** and a member of David's elite corps of "mighty men" (2 Sam 23:39; 1 Chr 11:41); his wife was **Bathsheba**, daughter of Eliam (2 Sam 11:3). While Uriah was away with the army at Rabbah, King David committed adultery with Bathsheba in Jerusalem (2 Sam 11:1–4). When David found that Bathsheba was pregnant, he tried to arrange for Uriah to spend the night with Bathsheba, but Uriah refused (2 Sam 11:6–13). Seeing that there was no way to hide his adultery, David arranged Uriah's death. He gave Uriah a letter addressed to **Joab** that commanded the general to place Uriah up front in the battle and allow him to be killed in the fray. Uriah was slain by the enemy as planned (2 Sam 11:6–21). Bathsheba mourned for her husband and then married David (2 Sam 11:26–27). Through a parable **Nathan** showed David that he had sinned against the Lord, and the king accepted the rebuke. (2 Sam 12:1–14).

2. A priest and one of the two reliable men chosen by **Isaiah** to witness the prophecy concerning **Maher-shalal-hash-baz** (Isa 8:2).

Uriah built an altar at the request of King **Ahaz**, modeled on one the king had seen at Damascus (2 Kgs 16:10–16).

3. The son of Shemaiah of Kiriath-jearim and a prophet. He prophesied against King **Jehoiakim** and the kingdom of Judah in agreement with **Jeremiah** and was forced to flee to Egypt to escape the king's wrath. He was extradited to Jerusalem and put to death (Jer 26:20–23).

URIEL (Hebrew, "God is my light") The name of two men in the Old Testament.

1. The leader of the Levitical clan of the Kohathites, commissioned by **David** to assist in moving the **ark of the covenant** from the house of Obed-edom to Jerusalem (1 Chr 15:1–5, 11).

2. The father of **Micaiah**, the Queen Mother of Judah during the reign of King **Abijah** (2 Chr 13:2).

URIM AND THUMMIM Sacred lots worn on the breastpiece of the high priest (Exod 28:30; Lev 8:8). The lots, possibly marked sticks or stones, were cast in order to obtain guidance from God when the people were facing problems (Num 27:21; Deut 33:8). The etymology and meaning of the words are uncertain, and the references to the Urim and Thummim provide little description. The lots were seen as a means of consulting the Lord (1 Sam 28:6). **Abiathar** brought the priestly ephod to David (1 Sam 23:6), presumably with the Urim and Thummim, by which David asked direct questions and received yes or no answers (1 Sam 23:9–12). Consultation of the Urim and Thummim was almost never mentioned in the days of the Israelite monarchy, although their continued significance is noted in the period after the **Exile** (Ezra 2:63; Neh 7:65). Beyond the spare details offered in the passages involving the Urim and Thummim, little is known with any certainty.

USURY *See* **Loan**.

UZ

1. The homeland of **Job** and the setting of the book that bears his name (Job 1:1). Biblical references to Uz suggest that it was near Israel, although its exact location remains uncertain (Jer 25:20). Lamentations 4:21 seems to put the area near Edom, southeast of Israel, and the book of Job says it was exposed to raids from desert marauders (Job 1:15, 17), which suggests a location east or northeast of Israel on the edge of the Arabian desert.

2. The son of Aram and the grandson of **Shem** (Gen 10:23; 1 Chr 1:17).

3. The son of Dishan and the grandson of Seir the Horite (Gen 36:28).

UZAL An Arabian mentioned among the descendants of **Shem** (Gen 10:27; 1 Chr 1:21).

UZZAH (Hebrew, "O Lord my strength")

1. The son of Abinadab. He and his brother, Ahio, drove the cart that carried the **ark of the covenant** from Kiriath-jearim (2 Sam 6:3–4; 1 Chr 13:7). When the oxen stumbled, Uzzah reached out to steady the ark and was struck dead (2 Sam 6:6–7; 1 Chr 13:9–10).

2. The man who owned a garden in which **Manasseh** and Amon were buried (2 Kgs 21:18, 26).

3. A Benjaminite and descendant of Ehud (1 Chr 8:7).

4. The head of a family of Temple servants who were among the first of those to return from the **Exile** (Ezra 2:49; Neh 7:51).

UZZIAH (Hebrew, "the Lord is my strength") The ninth king of Judah and the son and successor to **Amaziah** following his father's assassination around 767 B.C. He is also known in Scripture as Azariah (2 Kgs 15:1–2); his reign lasted for fifty-two years (2 Chr 26:3), from around 792 to 740 B.C. Uzziah strengthened the fortifications of Jerusalem and reorganized the army, making certain that the soldiers were properly equipped. He campaigned successfully against the Philistines, Arabs, and Ammonites (2 Chr 26:6–8). By his military efforts, he extended the borders of Judah, reclaiming the port of Elath at the northern end of the Gulf of Aqaba (2 Kgs 14:22). At home, he promoted agriculture and herding and dug cisterns. In his last years, he was said to be inflated with pride (2 Chr 26:16). When Uzziah usurped the priestly function by offering incense, he was stricken with leprosy, and so named his son **Jotham** to be his co-regent (2 Chr 26:16–21).

VAIZATHA One of the sons of **Haman** (Esth 9:9).

VASHTI The wife of **Ahasuerus (Xerxes I)** and the queen of the Persian Empire at the start of the book of Esther (Esth 1:9, 11, 12, 15–19; 2:1, 4, 17). Little is known about her except that she refused the king's order to make a public appearance (Esth 1:11). Ahasuerus consulted his counselors for advice on the best way to deal with this affront, and they urged him to remove her from her place as queen. The king agreed, and when the king sought a replacement for Vashti, he loved **Esther** more than the other candidates. Once Esther became queen, she was in a position to assure the deliverance of the Jews from a decree for their destruction. Vashti disappears from the account upon the accession of Esther (Esth 2:17). It is uncertain how Vashti is connected to the notoriously devious Amestris, the wife of Xerxes I according to the Greek historian Herodotus.

VATICANUS, CODEX *See* **Codex**.

VEIL The fabric that curtained off the presence of the Lord and his ark in the innermost chamber of the **Tabernacle**, the "holy of ho-lies" (Exod 30:6). The veil was made of linen, colorfully embroidered and decorated with images of winged cherubim. The veil separated the **ark of the covenant** from human contact, and no one was permitted to pass beyond the veil, including the Levitical priests (Num 18:7). Once a year, on the Day of Atonement (*see* **Atonement, Day of**), only the high priest was permitted to penetrate the veil, but only after being cleansed (Lev 16:1–17). When the Tabernacle was disassembled and moved, the veil was draped over the ark (Num 4:5). The veil is described in detail in Exod 26:31–33 (cf. Exod 36:35–36, 40:21; Lev 4:17): "And you shall make a veil of blue and purple and scarlet stuff and fine twined linen; in skilled work shall it be made, with cherubim; and you shall hang it upon four pillars of acacia overlaid with gold, with hooks of gold, upon four bases of silver. And you shall hang the veil from the clasps, and bring the ark of the testimony in thither within the veil; and the veil shall separate for you the holy place from the most holy." The **Temple** had a similar veil. At Jesus's death, the veil was torn in two (Matt 27:51; Mark 15:38; Luke 23:45)—a sign that the Temple was doomed to destruction, and that the sacrificial religion of Moses was destined to pass away with it. But it was also a sign that a new intimacy had opened between God and his people: the ancient barrier of sin, which stood between the people and God, was taken away by Jesus's sacrificial death.

VENGEANCE *See* **Avenger of blood.**

VERSIONS OF THE BIBLE The Old Testament was written mainly in **Hebrew**, and some portions were composed in **Aramaic** and **Greek**, while the New Testament was written entirely in Greek. The original readers of the biblical texts had no need of translations, of course, but various circumstances arising over time made it necessary to produce translations or "versions" in different languages. For the Jewish people, the need to produce translations developed because classical Hebrew was gradually phased out as a spoken language in the postexilic period. The need for this in early Christianity was even more acute because the Gospel spread quickly to lands beyond the Hellenistic world.

I. *Ancient Versions*
    A. *Translations of the Hebrew Bible*
    B. *Translations of the Christian Bible*
II. *English Versions*
    A. *Translations in the Middle Ages*
    B. *Translations of the Reformation Era*
    C. *Modern Translations*

I. ANCIENT VERSIONS

A. *Translations of the Hebrew Bible*

The earliest translation of the OT was the Greek **Septuagint**, or LXX, which was done between the third and first centuries B.C. At least some of the translation was done in Egypt, and the purpose was to serve the needs of the synagogue in the lands of the Jewish **Dispersion** where Greek was spoken as the language of culture and commerce. The situation in Palestine and Mesopotamia was different, because there the language of daily life was Aramaic. To meet the needs of Jews in these areas, Aramaic paraphrases of the Bible, called Targums, were written down for the religious instruction of the masses. The Targums are notoriously difficult to date, but there is reason to believe that the earliest compositions were done in the first and second centuries A.D.

In later centuries, the Aramaic of Syria and Mesopotamia developed into the Syriac language. Important translations of the OT were thus made into classical Syriac, and these in two main forms. One version, called the Peshitta, was made from the Hebrew texts at an uncertain date. The earliest surviving manuscripts of the Peshitta version date to around the ninth century. The Peshitta continues to be used today by the Syriac churches (Syrian Orthodox, Maronite, Church of the East). A second version, called the Syro-Hexapla, was made from Origen's revision of the Greek Septuagint and dates back to the seventh century.

B. *Translations of the Christian Bible*

The earliest translation of the Old and New Testaments together was probably the Old Latin version. It dates back to the second century A.D. and found acceptance in parts of Gaul and North Africa. The translation is generally considered mediocre in quality and accuracy, and considerable differences are found among the surviving manuscripts of these earliest Latin renditions. The desire for a new Latin Bible eventually prompted Pope Damasus I to entrust Saint Jerome with the task of revising the Gospels in A.D. 382. Having completed this work in 384, Saint Jerome would go on to translate almost the entire OT from the Hebrew (and Aramaic) and possibly also the rest of the NT. Jerome's monumental version, completed in 406, became known in later centuries as the **Vulgate** (the Latin *vulgatus* means "common" or "public"). The Council of Trent endorsed the Vulgate as the official Latin translation of the Roman Catholic Church in 1546.

Other translations were made for Christian communities in the East where neither Greek nor Latin was known on a wide scale. These include Coptic translations, which were produced for Christians in Egypt from at least the third century. Syriac translations of the NT were made in the fourth and fifth centuries. The Syriac churches use the Peshitta version of the NT, which includes all the books recognized by the Catholic Church except 2 Peter, 2 and 3 John, Jude, and Revelation. These versions, along with others translated into Gothic and Slavonic, were made directly from the Greek NT. These became the basis, in whole or in part, for other ancient versions translated into Armenian, Arabic, Persian, Ethiopic, and so forth.

II. ENGLISH VERSIONS

A. Translations in the Middle Ages

Partial translations of the Bible into Old English (Anglo-Saxon) were reportedly done by a secular brother named Caedmon of the monastery of Whitby, England, around 680. These were more paraphrases than strict translations; they covered the Creation, Exodus, and conquest stories of the OT as well as the Incarnation, Passion, and Resurrection narratives of the NT. Caedmon's original work does not survive, but a metrical version from the tenth century housed in the Bodleian Library is often attributed to him.

The Venerable Bede supposedly produced a translation of the Gospel of John in the early eighth century, although it has not survived. Aldhelm of Malmesbury rendered the Psalms into Anglo-Saxon around 700. Others from this time period also produced partial translations: Egbert made a translation of the Gospels; and another individual named Cuthbert, this one a disciple of King Alfred the Great, is credited with producing a rendition of the Ten Commandments and an unfinished translation of the Psalms. The Gospels and Psalms, then, chiefly because of their liturgical importance, were the first portions of Scripture to be rendered into vernacular English.

One notable figure in the early history of English versions is John Wycliffe, who was put to death in 1384 and whose followers became the Lollards. Popular lore credits him as the first person to translate the entire Bible into English. Many scholars do not accept this, however. It is said that the two versions attributed to him were more likely the work of Nicholas of Hereford and John Purvey. In any case, these translations were made from the Latin Vulgate and had an important influence on succeeding versions.

B. Translations of the Reformation Era

Numerous versions of the Bible appeared in English translation between the years 1525 and 1611. The most important and influential are the following.

The Tyndale New Testament. The first printed edition of the NT in English. It was the work of William Tyndale, who was burned as a heretic in 1536. His version was full of polemical notes advancing tenets of Lutheran theology; but he was a master of English prose and his work had an appreciable impact on just about every English version that came after his.

The Coverdale Bible. The first printed edition of the complete Bible in English. It was the work of Miles Coverdale in 1535. For the NT, he used Tyndale's translation, and for the OT, he drew from both the Zurich Bible and portions of the text that were translated by Tyndale. The Coverdale Bible was the first to organize the books of the Bible according to the Hebrew canon, which meant that the deutero-canonical books of the Catholic canon were translated but not treated as Scripture; they were separated from the canonical books.

The Great Bible. Printed in 1539, this version was Miles Coverdale's revision of an earlier Bible (the Matthew's Bible of 1537). The book was named for its immense size. It was a compilation drawn from the Münster Bible of 1534 and Erasmus of Rotterdam's Latin NT of 1516. By a decree of King Henry VIII, a copy was placed in every church in England. The Psalms from this edition were later used in the Book of Common Prayer.

The Geneva Bible. The English edition produced by William Whittingham and his colleagues. Whittingham was an English exile living in Geneva, Switzerland; his NT appeared in 1557, and his complete Bible came out in 1560. The Geneva Bible stands out for the bitter sectarianism of its notes, which proved to be unacceptable to Elizabeth I and the Anglican bishops of England. Nonetheless, it became the most popular English Bible until the release of the King James Version. The Geneva Bible is the translation most often quoted by Shakespeare.

The King James Bible. The English translation of the complete Bible published by the Church of England in 1611. It derives its name from King James I (d. 1625), who made the decision to sponsor a new translation of the Bible; it is sometimes called the Authorized Version for this reason. Eventually it became the standard version used by most English-speaking Protestants, with whom it is still popular today.

The Douay-Rheims Bible. The first English translation of the complete Bible sanctioned by the Catholic Church. It was first published in two parts: the NT came out of Rheims, France, in 1582 (modern Reims), and the OT came out of Douay, France, in 1609 (modern Douai). This version was translated from the Latin Vulgate and was intended for English Catholics, who at that time had need of a vernacular translation that contained all the books of the Catholic canon. Most of the translation was done by a group of former students from Oxford who had fled England because of persecution: William Allen, Gregory Martin, Richard Bristowe, and Thomas Worthington. The students settled in Douai, where Allen had founded a college for training priests to minister to English Catholics.

The translators were meticulous scholars, but some complained that the translation was too literal for English ears. A revision was undertaken in 1750 by Richard Challoner, vicar apostolic of London. The revision was so extensive that, in the words of Cardinal Newman, it was "little short of a new translation." English-speaking Catholics knew Challoner's Bible until well into the twentieth century.

C. Modern Translations

Protestant scholars of the nineteenth century found the King James Version deficient in a number of ways. Revisions were undertaken by a committee of English and American scholars, who produced a revised NT in 1881 and a revised OT in 1885. Afterward, the American committee members published their own edition in 1901, reflecting their own preferences; it was called the American Standard Version. Changes were made again several decades later, resulting in the Revised Standard Version. The RSV version of the NT came out in 1946, and the OT came out in 1952. The RSV was acclaimed for its accuracy as well as its beautiful English, and a special Catholic edition, called the RSVCE, was completed in 1966.

Meanwhile, the Confraternity of Christian Doctrine released an edition of the Bible in 1941 that included a revision of the Rheims-Challoner NT, but it was based on the Latin Vulgate. The 1943 encyclical of Pope Pius XII, *Divino Afflante Spiritu*, called for new translations of Scripture to be made from the original languages. In the United States, this resulted in the publication of the New American Bible (NAB) in 1970, of which a revised NT appeared in 1986 and a revision of the Psalms in 1991.

Other significant translations appeared in the twentieth century as well, including the Jerusalem Bible (JB), the New Jerusalem Bible (NJB), the New Revised Standard Version (NRSV), the New International Version (NIV), and the New King James Version (NKJV).

VINEGAR Fermented and soured wine. Vinegar is most noted for its strong and sometimes bitter taste (Ps 69:21; Prov 10:26). **Ruth** was invited by Boaz to dip her bread in the vinegar (Ruth 2:14). Christ was offered vinegar while on the Cross (Mark 15:36; John 19:29–30), not to be confused with the gall that he was offered earlier (Matt 27:34; Mark 15:23). People who had taken a Nazirite vow were forbidden to consume anything produced by the grapevine, including vinegar and new wine (Num 6:3).

VINEYARD *See* **Wine**.

VIRGIN, VIRGINITY The Hebrew term is *bĕtûlâ*, which in biblical terms means a female "whom no man had known" in a sexually intimate way (Gen 24:16; Judg 21:12).

The term was used as a figure of speech or as an image for nations and peoples, such as Israel and Zion (2 Kgs 19:21; Jer 18:13, 31:4; Lam 2:13; Amos 5:2), Babylon (Isa 47:1), Sidon (Isa 23:12), and Egypt (Jer 46:11).

I. LAWS ON VIRGINITY

The **Law** presupposes that sexual relations outside of marriage are unlawful: virginity is the proper state of unmarried persons. Laws concerning the virginity of daughters were especially important in ancient Israel (Deut 22:13–28), and virgins were set apart from the rest of the community on certain occasions (cf. Judg 21:10–14; Num 31:18). A promised bride was expected to be a virgin, and should her husband discover that she was not a virgin, he was to make an accusation before the elders of the town; they then were to take her to the entrance of her father's house and stone her to death (Deut 22:20–21). In the event that such an accusation was made unjustly, her parents were permitted to prove her virginity, whereupon the bridegroom was to be flogged and fined a sum of 100 shekels of silver that were to be given to the girl's father; the husband was also never permitted to divorce his wife once he had so unfairly accused her (Deut 22:18–19).

When a man seduced a virgin who was not betrothed, he was fined 50 shekels, which were then paid to the girl's father; the seducer was obligated to marry the girl without the option of divorcing her at a later time (Deut 22:28–29). Should a father give his refusal to the girl's marriage to the seducer, the man would still have to pay the father the fine (Exod 22:15–16).

II. VIRGINITY AS A STATE OF LIFE

Virginity was not esteemed for its own sake in Old Testament times: it suddenly burst on the scene as a *desired* state in life and a path to spiritual fulfillment with the coming of the New Covenant. Jesus, unlike his rabbinic contemporaries, was celibate, as were **John the Baptist** and the apostle **Paul**. Christian tradition has held from the beginning that **Mary** was a lifelong virgin in spite of her lawful marriage to Joseph and her having brought Christ into the world.

Perfect chastity or continence—defined as the firm intention of abstaining from all sexual pleasure licitly in marriage or illicitly—is a moral virtue. It was given clear approval in the teaching of Christ. Jesus revealed that marriage is proper to earthly life, but not to heavenly life (Matt 22:30). When asked if marriage was no longer expedient or advisable, Jesus said, "Not all men can receive this saying, but only those to whom it is given. For there are eunuchs who have been so from birth, and there are eunuchs who have been made eunuchs by men, and there are eunuchs who have made themselves eunuchs for the sake of the kingdom of heaven. He who is able to receive this, let him receive it" (Matt 19:11–12). The unmarried state is the most conducive to serving the Lord with undivided attention. Paul highly recommended virginity to both men and women, although he did not require it of believers; he suggested that the unmarried are better suited to give of themselves completely to God than their married counterparts (1 Cor 7:25–35; 1 Tim 5:22).

Virginity for the sake of the Kingdom is rooted in the recognition of Christ as the center of Christian life. Our bond with him takes precedence over all other bonds, including those of the family. The Church recognizes that from the earliest days in the proclamation of the Gospel men and women have chosen to renounce marriage and give themselves entirely to God. Such a choice flows from baptismal grace and is a sign of a bond with Christ. Like marriage, virginity comes from Christ, and it is Christ who provides the grace necessary for the faithful living in the state of marriage or the state of virginity. Perfect virginity means total consecration to God in body and soul, of which the supreme example in a human person is the Blessed Virgin Mary, even though she was also a mother (CCC 496–507). (On the virginity of the Blessed Virgin Mary, *see under* **Mary, the Mother of Jesus**.)

VIRGIN BIRTH *See under* **Mary, the Mother of Jesus**.

VISION *See* **Prophet**.

VISITATION, THE The Gospel episode in which **Mary, the Mother of Jesus**, travels to the home of her kinswoman **Elizabeth** to serve her needs throughout the final three months of Elizabeth's pregnancy (Luke 1:39–56). The words of Elizabeth at this meeting were adopted by the Church as part of the text of the Hail Mary (Luke 1:42), and Mary's response to Elizabeth's greeting is known as the Magnificat (Luke 1:46–55).

VOW *See* **Oath**.

VULGATE The translation of the Bible into Latin by Saint Jerome (340–420) in the fourth and early fifth centuries. The name "Vulgate" has been given to Jerome's version since at least the Council of Trent in the sixteenth century; in Jerome's day, the expression "vulgate edition" referred to the Old Latin translation that had been produced in the second century A.D. Saint Jerome's translation became the most widely used Latin text for centuries even before the Council of Trent in the sixteenth century designated it as authentic and suitable for use in public reading, controversy, preaching, and teaching. Because of its authoritative character, it became the basis for many translations into other languages.

Before Jerome, many Latin translations had been produced in the Western regions of the Roman Empire. Concerned by the multiplicity of translations and the variations among the texts, Pope Damasus decided around A.D. 383 that a reliable standard Latin text was essential, and he commissioned Jerome to begin the revision and correction of the Latin version. All told, his Latin translation of both the Old and New Testaments required about twenty-two years of labor (ca. A.D. 384 to 406).

Jerome is responsible for the bulk of the Vulgate, but not all of it. In the NT, Jerome corrected the older Latin versions according to the Greek manuscripts that were available to him. He made changes only when the meaning of the Latin did not correspond to the meaning or style of the Greek text. Some scholars believe that Jerome revised only the Gospels, and that the revisions of the other books were done by someone known as Rufinus the Syrian.

The Vulgate OT is mostly Jerome's work. Of the thirty-nine books of the Jewish canon, thirty-eight are Jerome's Latin translations made directly from the original Hebrew. The Psalms are Jerome's revision of the Old Latin Psalms made in light of studying the **Septuagint** Greek Psalter. Five of the **deuterocanonical** books (Wisdom, Sirach, Baruch, and 1 and 2 Maccabees) are taken unrevised from the Old Latin version. Jerome translated Tobit and Judith from Aramaic manuscripts, and he translated the deuterocanonical portions of Daniel from the Septuagint.

The completed Vulgate is made up of the following:

- The NT revised according to the Greek;
- The protocanonical books of the OT translated from the Hebrew;
- Jerome's translation of Tobit, Judith, and additions to Daniel and Esther;
- The five deuterocanonical books not translated by Jerome (Wisdom, Sirach, Baruch, 1 Maccabees, 2 Maccabees) from the Old Latin version; and
- The Gallican Psalter corrected by Jerome on the basis of the Septuagint.

The Vulgate was the first printed book in Europe—the famous Gutenberg Bible. The Council of Trent (1545–1563) declared that the Vulgate was the authentic Latin translation. Nevertheless, the Council also decreed that a new corrected version should be undertaken. The result was the Sixto-Clementine Vulgate in 1592, named after two popes who played roles in its completion, Sixtus V (r. 1585–1590) and Clement VIII (r. 1592–1605). In 1907, Pope Saint Pius X established a special commission to publish a revised critical edition. The work was entrusted to the Benedictines of the Abbey of Saint Jerome. The Pontifical Commission for the Revision and Emendation of the Vulgate was established in 1984 by Pope John Paul II to take over the work formerly done by the Benedictines.

WAR AND WARFARE Palestine was right at the intersection of several major trade routes in the Near East, and for most of its history it was the borderland between giant empires. Wars and invasions have therefore been constant threats to the region.

I. RELIGIOUS WAR

God gave the Israelites the land of **Canaan**, but first they had to conquer it to possess it. For that reason, the Law gave particular regulations for the holy war against the Canaanites, especially since the idolatrous culture of Canaan posed a significant threat to the spiritual welfare of Israel. All men were to answer the summons to war, and only those who were newly betrothed, fearful at heart, or ineligible for a few other reasons could receive dispensation from service. Should a city bordering Canaan refuse terms of surrender, it was to be besieged, and after its capture its male inhabitants were to be put to the sword (Deut 20:10–14). But in the cities of Canaan itself, all inhabitants were targets of destruction, soldiers and civilians alike, in order "that they may not teach you to do according to all their abominable practices which they have done in the service of their gods, and so to sin against the LORD your God" (Deut 20:16–18).

The Israelites practiced *ḥērem* warfare, in which whole cities and their inhabitants were devoted to destruction. The ban meant that no Israelite was permitted to claim any item or person from the conquered city for his own use or ownership: everything belonged to God as the fruits of his victory. The penalties for violating this ban were severe, as we see in the case of **Achan** (Josh 7; cf. 1 Sam 15). Jericho was burned down along with everything in it, except that the silver and gold and the vessels of bronze and iron were "put into the treasury of the house of the LORD . . . Joshua laid an oath upon them at that time, saying, 'Cursed before the LORD be the man that rises up and rebuilds this city, Jericho. At the cost of his first-born shall he lay its foundation, and at the cost of his youngest son shall he set up its gates'" (Josh 7:24, 26). The ban might also be imposed on an Israelite settlement for lapses into idolatry (Deut 13:12–18). This holy war was a concession of the Deuteronomic covenant, announced after the Israelites had twice lapsed into idolatrous worship during the wilderness period; its stern provisions were necessary because God knew that otherwise his people were too weak to resist the attraction of Canaanite idolatry.

War was frequent for the Israelites from the time of the wandering in the wilderness; battles were fought against the Amorites (Num 21:23–26) and the Midianites (Num 31:1–54), among others. The books of Joshua and Judges detail the wars for the conquest of Canaan. More fighting followed with the **Philistines** and continued into the time of **David**.

The peaceful reign of **Solomon** was followed by the division of the kingdom and the wars between Judah and Israel (1 Kgs 15:4; 2 Kgs 14:8–12), against Egypt (2 Kgs 23:29–36), the Moabites (2 Kgs 3:21–27), the Edomites (2 Kgs 8:20–22), Syrians (1 Kgs 15:20; 20:1–21), and Assyrians (2 Kgs 15:27–29; 17:3–6; 19:9–36; 24:10–20; 25:1–21). The Old Testament ends with the struggles of the Maccabees against the Syrians.

II. ARMIES

In patriarchal times, kinsmen banded together to defend their tribe or clan against outside aggression; these fighting forces were made up of tribal fighters rather than professional soldiers. When necessary, tribal leaders mustered all able-bodied men (Gen 14:13–16). The forces of Israel assembled in the time of **Moses** were organized by the tribes with their own standards and leaders (Num 1–4; 10:14–27). In the time of the **Judges**, the military forces lacked central organization; tribal militias fought under the leadership of capable and charismatic chieftains.

Saul brought together the first organized army in Israel—an organization made necessary by the threat of the Philistines and the need to meet that threat effectively. Saul's army consisted of only three thousand picked men (1 Sam 13:2), a force on which he could rely in the heat of battle; any other forces were mustered from the tribal militias (1 Sam 14:52). David developed the army further. It consisted of regular units and militia. There was also a contingent of mercenaries, the so-called Cherethites and Pelethites, who served as a royal bodyguard (2 Sam 15:18–22). Under David, military leadership was entrusted to a commander-in-chief, **Joab**, who was "over the army" (2 Sam 8:16) and an elite corps of distinguished warriors called the "mighty men" (2 Sam 23:8–39).

Under Solomon, the army had a variety of ranks (1 Kgs 9:22). There were light infantry (bowmen and slingers) and heavy infantry (armed with sword and spear or javelin). Solomon's chariot corps was the first of its kind in Israel (1 Kgs 4:26; cf. 1 Kgs 10:26; 2 Chr 9:25).

III. WEAPONS AND ARMOR

A variety of weapons are mentioned in the Bible, including the **bow**, used especially by kings and princes (2 Sam 22:35); the **sling** (Judg 20:16; 1 Sam 17:40, 49; 1 Chr 12:2; 2 Chr 26:14); the **sword** (Gen 31:26; 2 Sam 2:16; 1 Kgs 3:24); and the **spear** and javelin (1 Sam 17:6; 18:10–11; 20:33; 22:6; 2 Sam 2:23). Larger weapons like catapults were used to launch arrows, fire, and stones, especially in sieges (2 Chr 26:15; 1 Macc 5:30; 6:37; 6:51).

For defensive armor, soldiers went into battle with **shields** and bucklers (Ezek 39:9;

2 Sam 1:21; Isa 22:6) and wore a helmet (1 Sam 17:38; 1 Macc 6:35), coats of mail (1 Sam 17:5; Neh 4:16; 1 Kgs 22:34; Jer 46:4), and greaves on the legs (1 Sam 17:6).

WARS OF THE LORD, BOOK OF THE A written collection of Israelite war songs mentioned in Num 21:14. It was probably an account of the Lord's "Holy War" waged against Israel's enemies during the time of Moses. It is possible that the Song of the Sea in Exod 15:1–18 and similar poetic texts of the Pentateuch are taken from this now lost work.

WATER For the inhabitants of Palestine, water was precious, and **rain** was seen as a blessing from God (Deut 11:14). The absence of water, rain, or drinkable water was sometimes considered a form of divine punishment and a sign of displeasure (Exod 15:23, 17:2; Deut 28:23; 1 Kgs 17:1–7; Isa 19:5; Jer 14:3; Rev 8:11). Unlike Egypt and Mesopotamia, Palestine is not suited for extensive irrigation, as Deuteronomy made clear: "For the land which you are entering to take possession of it is not like the land of Egypt, from which you have come, where you sowed your seed and watered it with your feet, like a garden of vegetables; but the land which you are going over to possess is a land of hills and valleys, which drinks water by the rain from heaven" (Deut 11:10–11). Springs were valuable locations for towns and cities, and with engineering water could be brought to the inhabitants. Rain was crucial for survival, and the Israelites greatly anticipated the rainy season (cf. Deut 11:14; Job 29:23; Hos 6:3; Zech 10:1). **Wells** were also

used as water supplies (Gen 21:19; Exod 2:15–17; Num 21:16).

Armies besieging cities normally tried to cut off the water supply (cf. 2 Kgs 3:25; Jdt 7:12–13). To safeguard against this possibility, King **Hezekiah** ordered the construction of an aqueduct to ensure a constant supply of freshwater even under dire circumstances (2 Kgs 20:20; 2 Chr 32:30; *see* **Siloam**).

Water was also an important symbol. It represented God's blessings and spiritual refreshment (Ps 23:2; Isa 12:3, 32:2, 35:6–7, 41:18; Jer 2:13; Ezek 47:1–11). The lack of water was a symbol of spiritual need (Ps 63:1; Amos 8:11). In the New Testament, water continued to represent blessing and spiritual nourishment (John 4:14; Rev 7:17, 21:6, 22:1). Water is the life of God that comes to us in the **Spirit** (John 7:38–39; 1 Cor 12:13). "Living" water meant the running water of a spring and represented fresh and pure water against sitting or stagnant water. When Jesus told the Samaritan woman that he would have given her "living water," she understood him in that sense, but Jesus revealed that "living water" was a symbol of eternal life (John 4:10–11; cf. Song 4:15).

Water was used as part of the ritual of purification and cleansing. Priests were washed at their consecration (Exod 40:15), and various ablutions were included as part of ceremonies and feasts (Lev 16:4, 24, 26). Water was used to remove legal defilement and impurity (Lev 11:40, 15:5, 17:15, 22:6; Deut 23:11). The purifying power of water in the Old Testament anticipated the place of water in the sacrament of **baptism**, which cleanses the conscience (Heb

10:22; 1 Pet 3:21) and washes away sin (Acts 2:38, 22:16; Eph 5:26).

WAY The term "way" is used in several senses in Scripture, reaching a culmination point in Christ, who is "the way, and the truth, and the life" (John 14:6).

I. In the Old Testament

    A. The "Way" as a Way of Life

    B. The Way of the Lord and the Way of the Wicked

II. In the New Testament

    A. The Two Ways

    B. Christ, the Way

    C. The Church Also as the Way

I. IN THE OLD TESTAMENT

A. The "Way" as a Way of Life

In the Old Testament, the word "way" (Hebrew *derek*) often means a literal road or journey, but it is also commonly used as a figure of speech for the direction of one's life (Josh 1:8; Job 23:10, 31:4). Man's journey through life is a mystery (Prov 20:24) that ends ultimately in physical death, which is the "way" common to all (1 Kgs 2:2; Prov 14:12). The days of men must come to an end (Josh 23:14; Job 16:22). A contrast is made between the ways of God and the ignorance of men. The gulf between the designs of God and those of humans is noted in Isa 55:8–9: "For my thoughts are not your thoughts, neither are your ways my ways, says the LORD. For as the heavens are higher than the earth, so are my ways higher than your ways and my thoughts than your thoughts."

B. The Way of the Lord and the Way of the Wicked

There is also a strong contrast between the righteous ways of God and the wicked ways of men (Ezek 18:25). In this sense, God's commandments are called his way (Gen 18:19; Exod 18:20; Judg 2:22), as opposed to the corrupt ways of men. The way thus can also denote human conduct (1 Kgs 2:4, 8:25; 2 Chr 6:16; Ps 119:1–9), described as good or bad (Job 31:7; Ps 1:1, 6; cf. Matt 21:32); both good and bad are known to God (Job 24:23; Ps 119:168). Two ways are before us: one that leads to life, peace, and happiness; and the other to difficulty, unhappiness, and death (Prov 3:17, 7:27; Jer 21:8; cf. Matt 7:13).

One must pay the price for one's conduct (Jer 4:18), but the Lord hopes that the wicked will turn away from the way of evil and travel on the way of salvation. "As I live, says the LORD God, I have no pleasure in the death of the wicked, but that the wicked turn from his way and live; turn back, turn back from your evil ways; for why will you die, O house of Israel?" (Ezek 33:11). Similarly, the prophet Ezekiel reminds us, "Yet your people say, 'The way of the LORD is not just'; when it is their own way that is not just. When the righteous turns from his righteousness, and commits iniquity, he shall die for it. And when the wicked turns from his wickedness, and does what is lawful and right, he shall live by it. Yet you say, 'The way of the LORD is not just.' O house of Israel, I will judge each of you according to his ways" (Ezek 33:17–20).

The righteous heed the words of the wise

(Prov 6:23), the way of peace (Isa 59:8). The way of wisdom is none other than the way declared by the Lord to his people (Exod 32:8) and the way that is pleasing to him (Prov 16:7; cf. 1 Sam 12:23). Above all, in anticipation of the New Testament, Ps 16:11 declares: "You show me the path of life; in your presence there is fulness of joy, in your right hand are pleasures for evermore" (cf. Isa 11:16, 40:3; Mal 3:1). The prophets announce the "way of the LORD" as the great coming of the Lord to his people (Isa 40:3; Mal 3:1).

II. IN THE NEW TESTAMENT

A. The Two Ways

In the NT, the theme of the two ways—one leading to life and the other to death—is defined in the Gospels according to one's acceptance or rejection of Christ. Acceptance is the way that leads to life (Matt 3:3; Mark 1:2; Luke 3:4, 7:27; John 1:23), the way of peace (Luke 1:79; Acts 13:10; 2 Pet 2:2). Above all, Christ himself is called the way to the heavenly Father (John 14:6; Heb 9:8, 10:20). *Didache* 1–6 repeats the idea of the two ways, with the knowledge that the way of life is Christ: "There are two ways, the one of life, the other of death; but between the two, there is a great difference" (CCC 1696).

The way of the Christian disciple is love (1 Cor 12:31). This way of salvation is proclaimed by the apostles (Acts 16:17) and is taught to converts. That the way is still a difficult one is noted in Matthew: "Enter by the narrow gate; for the gate is wide and the way is easy, that leads to destruction, and those who enter by it are many. For the gate is nar-row and the way is hard, that leads to life, and those who find it are few" (Matt 7:13–14; cf. Luke 13.24).

B. Christ, the Way

Jesus called himself the way, replying to a question in John with the key phrase "the way, and the truth, and the life" (John 14:6). As the incarnate God, Christ is himself the way that leads to life: "Therefore, brethren, since we have confidence to enter the sanctuary by the blood of Jesus, by the new and living way which he opened for us through the curtain, that is, through his flesh, and since we have a great priest over the house of God, let us draw near with a true heart in full assurance of faith, with our hearts sprinkled clean from an evil conscience and our bodies washed with pure water" (Heb 10:19–22).

C. The Church Also as the Way

As Christ established the **Church** as the sacrament of his presence and grace in the world, it too is called the way. The word was adopted early as a name for the Christian movement itself (Acts 9:2; 19:9; 22:4). The Vatican II Constitution *Lumen Gentium* declares that "the Church, a pilgrim now on earth, is necessary for salvation: the one Christ is the mediator and the way of salvation; he is present to us in his body which is the Church. He himself explicitly asserted the necessity of faith and baptism (cf. Mark 16:16; John 3:5), and thereby affirmed at the same time the necessity of the Church which men enter through baptism as through a door" (LG §14; cf. Decree *Ad gentes* §7; *Unitatis redintegratio* §3) (CCC 846–47). Likewise, Pope John Paul II wrote that "it is necessary to keep these two truths together, namely, the real possibility of salvation in Christ for all mankind and the necessity of the Church for this salvation" (*Redemptoris Missio* §9; Congregation for the Doctrine of the Faith, *Dominus Iesus* 20).

WEALTH Riches were seen in both the Old Testament and the New Testament as blessings from God (Ps 1:3; 112:1–3) and so were not necessarily to be condemned. We must recognize that such blessings come from God (Deut 8:17–18; Hos 2:8), and wealth therefore obliges us to pursue a good life and generosity (1 Tim 6:17–18; 2 Cor 8–9). The possession of wealth is also attended by the dangers of materialism (Rev 3:17) and placing excessive confidence in wealth (Ps 52:7). After all, wealth is fleeting and can be taken away at a moment's notice; dependence on God is the only lasting security (Luke 12:16–21). Those who have gained their wealth by unjust means will pay a price (Isa 5:8–10), as will the idle rich (Amos 6:1). The love of money is described as the root of evil (1 Tim 6:9–10).

Christ warned of the dangers of wealth by observing how difficult it would be for the rich to enter the Kingdom of Heaven (Matt 19:14; Mark 10:23). In the Sermon on the Mount, Jesus tells his disciples not to store up treasure on earth where it can be stolen (Matt 6:19–21), but to serve God (Matt 6:24) without being overly anxious about the necessities of life (Matt 6:25–34). True wealth is found in the spiritual blessings bestowed by God (Luke 12:33; 16:11). (*See also* **poor**.)

WEDDING *See* **Marriage**.

WEEK *See* **Sabbath**.

WEEKS, FEAST OF *See* **Pentecost**.

WEIGHTS AND MEASURES There was no universal standard for measurement in the ancient world, and common measurements varied not only from region to region but sometimes even between cities and villages. The absence of standardized measurements made for fraud through various unscrupulous practices, such as doubling or falsifying weights, a problem in Israel (Deut 25:13; Mic 6:11). Corrupt business practices were condemned by the prophets (cf. Amos 8:5) and in a number of places in the Old Testament (cf. Lev 19:35–36; Deut 25:13–15; Prov 11:1, 16:11, 20:23; Ezek 45:10–12; Hos 12:7; Sir 42:4).

Many unanswered questions remain as to the actual weights and measures referred to in the Hebrew and Greek texts of the OT, so the figures given here and elsewhere are approximations rather than strictly precise calculations.

I. OLD TESTAMENT

• *Weight.* The basic unit was the *shekel*, weighing approximately 11.5 grams. Fifty shekels equaled a *mina*, weighing approximately 575 grams. Sixty minas made a *talent*, weighing approximately 75 pounds or 34 kilograms.

• *Capacity.* The names of capacity measurements were derived from the vessels used to make the measurements. The *seah* was the equivalent of around 7 quarts (7.3 liters). Three seahs equaled 1 *ephah* and measured around 22 liters. Five ephahs equaled a half *homer*, approximately 110 liters; ten ephahs (or 2 half homers) equaled a full *homer* (220 liters). The most common liquid measures were the *bath* (about 6 gallons or 23 liters) and the *hin* (about 1 gallon or 4 liters).

• *Length*. The main instrument for measuring distance or length was the human body, so, for instance, four fingers equaled one *palm* (about 3 inches or 8 centimeters) and three palms equaled one *span* (about 9 inches or 23 centimeters). Two spans equaled one *cubit*, the distance from the elbow to the tip of the middle finger (about 18 inches or 45 centimeters). Six cubits equaled one *reed* (about 9 feet or 2.7 meters).

II. NEW TESTAMENT

• *Weight*. Only two weights are mentioned in the New Testament: the *pound* (John 12:3; 19:39), which was a Roman measurement of around a little less than an English pound (about 0.4 kilogram); the *hundred-weight* is used in Rev 16:21 to describe hailstones that were just about 100 pounds.

• *Capacity*. When measuring dry weight, the *choinix* ("quart"; Rev 6:6) served as the starting unit; it was approximately a liter. Forty-eight *choinikes* equaled a *medimnos*, and ten *medimnoi* equaled a *koros*. When measuring liquid weight, the starting measurement was the *sextarius* (likely the Greek *xestēs* of Mark 7:4, "pot"), about half a liter. Sixteen *sextarii* equaled one *modius*, and four and a half *modii* equaled one *batos* (or *metrētēs*), about 10 gallons or 40 liters. Six *modii* equaled one *medimnos*.

• *Length*. The basic units of measurement in NT times, as in the OT period, were taken from the human body. Hence the basic unit was the cubit, the length of the forearm. Four cubits equaled the *orgyia* ("fathom"; Acts 27:28), which was the length of outstretched arms from fingertips to fingertips. One hundred fathoms equaled one *stade*, and eight *stades* equaled one *mile*. For measuring a land area, two basic measurements were used: the *iugerum* was about 2/3 of a modern acre (about 1/4 hectare), estimated by the amount of land an ox could plow in one day; and the *actus*, or furrow, which equaled approximately half a *iugerum*.

WELL A shaft dug into the earth in order to reach water underground. In arid Palestine, wells were of great importance. The Old Testament is rich with allusions to the importance of wells, cisterns, reservoirs, and other water supplies. Disagreement over wells could lead to violence and fighting (Gen 21:25, 26:21; Num 20:17), and wells could also serve as symbols of covenant-making (Gen 21:25–32). Wells were connected so closely to water—and so to life—that Christ's encounter with the Samaritan woman at the well of Jacob assumed great symbolic importance (John 4:6–15). Here the whole scene of a man encountering a woman at a well recalls how wives for **Isaac, Jacob**, and **Moses** were secured at a well. (*See also* **Baptism**; **Water**.)

WESTERN SEA *See* **Mediterranean Sea**.

WIDOW A woman whose husband has died. The woman who had lost her husband was permitted to remarry (Lev 21:14) and was subject to legal protection and special concern by society (Isa 1:17) and especially by God (Deut 10:18; Jer 49:11; Mal 3:5; Ps 68:5, 146:9; Prov 15:25). The maltreatment of widows provoked divine wrath (Deut 27:19; Ps 94:6; Jer 7:6; Zech 7:10).

According to Old Testament law, a childless widow was given the option of marrying the brother of her deceased husband, in order that the name of the deceased man might not end; this was the so-called levirate law (Deut 25:5–10; *see* **marriage**). If the brother chose not to marry her, she returned to her paternal home (Lev 22:13; Ruth 1:8). A notable exception was **Ruth**, who chose to remain with her mother-in-law, Naomi (Ruth 1:16).

In the New Testament, Jesus decried the scribes who extorted the houses of widows (Mark 12:40). Jesus displayed special care for widows by raising the widow's dead son to life (Luke 7:11–17), by praising the widow for giving from her substance (Mark 12:41–44), and by condemning those who oppress widows (Luke 20:45–47). Although it was not necessary that widows remarry, and in some cases it was not advisable, **Paul** recommended that younger widows do so to avoid sins of immaturity (1 Tim 5:11–15). Caring for widows remains a religious duty for Christians as it was for the Israelites (Acts 6:1, 9:39; Jas 1:27). In 1 Tim 5:3–16, Paul gives detailed instructions for the care of widows, including a role that should be created for mature widows who had demonstrated their faith and good works by caring for children, showing hospitality, and so forth. Paul advised caring for widows in different ways: those with family should be supported by them (1 Tim 5:4); younger widows were encouraged to remarry (1 Tim 5:14); and older widows without family were to receive material help from the local church (1 Tim 5:16).

WIFE *See* **Family**; *see also* **Marriage**.

WILDERNESS *See* **Desert**.

WINE First mentioned in connection with **Noah**, who planted a vineyard after the **Flood** (Gen 9:20–21). Wine was counted among the first fruits owed by the Israelites to God (Num 18:12), along with cereal, oil, and animals, and was used in various sacrifices as a ritual offering and for penance (Exod 29:40; Num 15:5). Priests were not to drink alcohol before ministering in the **Tabernacle** (Lev 10:8); the **Nazarites** and the **Rechabites** were entirely forbidden to drink wine (Num 6:1–4; Jer 35:6). Immoderate consumption of wine was condemned (Prov 20:1, 21:17, 23:20; Sir 19:1; Joel 1:5; Rom 13:13; 1 Cor 5:11, 6:10; Gal 5:21). Drunkenness can bring severe spiritual and moral consequences for the one who drinks (Hos 4:11; Amos 6:6; Isa 5:11, 56:11) and for his or her family (Prov 20:1; 23:20–21, 29–35). Scripture promotes temperance rather than strict abstinence; consumed in moderation, wine is allowed and occasionally recommended (Sir 31:27; 2 Macc 15:40; John 2:3; 1 Tim 5:23).

Wine serves as a symbol of life and happiness; it is counted among the greatest gifts of creation and one of the chief enjoyments of life (Ps 104:15; Sir 31:27, 39:26–27). God's anger is symbolized by those who disobeyed his Commandments being compelled to drink the wine of his fury (Jer 25:15; cf. Rev 14:10, 19:15).

Jesus changed water into wine at the marriage feast of **Cana** (John 2:1–11). In his teachings, Jesus used wine as an image, as in his mention of the need to pour new wine into new wineskins (Matt 9:17). At the Last Supper, celebrated as a traditional **Passover** meal, Jesus used bread and wine for the institution of the **Eucharist** (Matt 26:27–28; Mark 14:23–24; Luke 22:20; 1 Cor 11:25).

WISDOM

WISDOM Wisdom in human beings derives from the perfect wisdom of God.

I. *Wisdom in the Old Testament*
   A. *Practical Knowledge*
   B. *Wisdom Comes from God*
II. *Wisdom in the New Testament*

I. WISDOM IN THE OLD TESTAMENT

A. Practical Knowledge

In the Old Testament, wisdom was most often a matter of practical knowledge, and other senses of wisdom derived from this primary sense. The Hebrew word translated "wisdom" often referred to the skill of the tradesman. For example, the bronze worker on Solomon's **Temple** was described as having wisdom (1 Kgs 7:14; cf. Exod 28:3, 31:1–5). Likewise, there were references to the wisdom of the artisan (1 Chr 22:15–16), the sailor (Ps 107:27), and the weaver (Exod 35:35), with wisdom in this specific sense expressing notions of skill or ability.

By a simple extension, the administrative skill of the able government leader or judge was also called wisdom (Gen 41:39; Deut 1:13, 34:9). Conversely, the false wisdom of leaders who brought the people into error or ruin was condemned by the prophets (Isa 5:21; Jer 8:9).

Finally, "wisdom" could refer to the skillful discernment of the righteous in making godly moral choices. Those who were most knowledgeable were also accounted among the wise, and the wisest of all was **Solomon**. His wisdom was legendary and earned him the admiration of all who met him (1 Kgs 4:29–34).

B. Wisdom Comes from God

The wisdom of the laborer, poet, or artisan was traced not to mere human experience but to the working of God. Those who are wise are filled with God's spirit (Exod 31:3; 35:31); ultimately, it is only the Lord who is wise, because he is the wise Creator of all things (Job 28:20–28; Prov 3:19; Sir 42:15–43). God's wisdom is closely connected with his creation. God not only brought all things into existence but also chooses to direct the course of human events (Job 11:1–12; Ps 104:24–30; Sir 16:24–18:14; Jer 10:12).

The wise men—the sages who encouraged others and showed them how to live—placed great stress on observance of the **Ten Commandments**. For Israel, wisdom entailed adhering to the laws of the covenant (Deut 4:6; cf. Sir 24:23–34, 38:24–39:11). Always in sight, however, was that wisdom is found by the righteous and is a gift from God to those who earnestly desire it (Wis 1:4–5; 7:15; 8:3–4, 21). Wisdom gives the promise of a long and fulfilling life (Wis 8:16; cf. Prov 3:7–10, 4:10–13, 9:10ff., 10:27; Sir 4:11–19, 15:1–6). Although evil is all around us, and the sinner seems to enjoy triumph and prosperity, the righteous gifted with wisdom understand that the future will bring rewards to those who live prudently (Prov 8:32–36; 23:17ff.; 24:13ff.). For these reasons, one should prize wisdom above all things, in contrast to those who despise wisdom or refuse to search for it (Wis 7:8–12, 30; 8:5–9); they will be doomed to unhappiness (Wis 3:11).

In wisdom literature, Wisdom is often personified. Wisdom might be seen as a patient teacher or a preacher, or as the moral or created order itself, overseeing the functioning of the world (Job 28; Prov 1:20–28; 8:1–3, 12–16; 9:1–5; Bar 3:9; 4:4).

Wisdom is often personified as a woman, in part because the terms used for "wisdom" in Hebrew (ḥokmâ) and Greek (sophia) are grammatically feminine (Job 28; Prov 1, 8, 9; Sir 24; Wis 7:7–9:18). Wisdom is described as a divine attribute and as the action of divine intelligence and skill that created the world. In Prov 8:30–31, Wisdom personified speaks of being God's "delight," while further on, she calls upon humans to listen to her as children (Prov 8:32–33), speaking in a voice that echoes that of the wise mother. As such she contrasts herself with the "foolish woman" (Prov 9:13–18), who is loud and who lures the simple from the straight way. The righteous man seeks Wisdom to be his bride and falls in love with her beauty just as "the Lord of all loves her" (Wis 8:2–5).

Wisdom existed with God before creation itself came into being. Wisdom was at his side at the creation of the world, the mirror of the power and goodness of God (Wis 7:23–27; 8:3, 21; 9; 10:1–21).

II. WISDOM IN THE NEW TESTAMENT

In the Gospels, Jesus is the new teacher of wisdom who surpasses even the illustrious Solomon (Matt 12:42). He summons the wise disciple to build on the foundation of his teaching (Matt 7:24–27) and to accept his yoke of gentle instruction (Matt 11:28–30), recalling the ancient summons of Wisdom (Sir 51:23–27).

In the Epistles, **Paul** marvels at God's wisdom as something beyond the ability of man to comprehend (Rom 11:33–36). Faithful to the OT tradition, he declares that wisdom is a gift from God (Eph 1:9, 17; Col 1:9). Paul writes that the faithful should delineate between true and false wisdom (Col 2:23), and that true wisdom is seen in right conduct (Rom 16:19). Against such true wisdom, the foolish think themselves wise (Rom 1:22); Paul also pits the wisdom of the world (1 Cor 1:17–2:6) against true Christian wisdom (1 Cor 2:7–16). Paul asks:

> Has not God made foolish the wisdom of the world? For since, in the wisdom of God, the world did not know God through wisdom, it pleased God through the folly of what we preach to save those who believe. For Jews demand signs and Greeks seek wisdom, but we preach Christ crucified, a stumbling block to Jews and folly to Gentiles, but to those who are called, both Jews and Greeks, Christ the power of God and the wisdom of God. For the foolishness of God is wiser than men, and the weakness of God is stronger than men. (1 Cor 1:20–24)

Likewise, James contrasts the wisdom of the Gospel, which comes "from above" (Jas

3:17) with mere "earthly" wisdom (Jas 3:15). The one who lacks heavenly wisdom is urged to ask God for such a gift, assured that the Father will give it generously (Jas 1:5).

WISDOM, BOOK OF Also called the Wisdom of Solomon and counted among the Wisdom Books of the Old Testament. Being one of the **deuterocanonical** books, it is part of the Catholic canon but not included in the modern Jewish or Protestant canon.

I. AUTHORSHIP AND DATE

The book of Wisdom was written originally in Greek and probably in Alexandria, Egypt. The author of the book writes in the guise of Solomon (Wis 1:1; 6:1–11; 8:9–16), but this is merely a literary device to connect the work to the older wisdom tradition. The author is unknown, but was probably a well-educated Greek-speaking Jew.

There is no agreement on the precise date of composition. Most scholars place the date in the first or second century B.C.

II. CONTENTS

I. *The Immortality and Destiny of Man (1:1–6:21)*

II. *Solomon and Divine Wisdom (6:22–9:18)*

III. *Divine Wisdom and the History of Israel (10:1–19:21)*

IV. *Conclusion (19:22)*

III. PURPOSE AND THEMES

The author of the book of Wisdom encourages his fellow Jews to take pride in their faith and to remain committed to it in the face of oppression. He wrote at a time when the Judaism of the **Dispersion** was struggling to maintain its identity amid the temptations and attacks of an altogether pagan culture. The book is steeped in the earlier Wisdom Books such as Proverbs and Psalms, uses phrases and language from those writings, and skillfully applies the literary tradition of personified Wisdom. At the same time, the book looks beyond this life to a blessed immortality and **resurrection**.

The book begins with a study of justice and immortality. The treatment is notable because it represents the first detailed discussion of life after death in the OT. Regarding immortality, Wisdom declares, "But the souls of the righteous are in the hand of God, and no torment will ever touch them. In the eyes of the foolish they seemed to have died, and their departure was thought to be an affliction, and their going from us to be their destruction; but they are at peace" (Wis 3:1–3). It adds, "In the time of their visitation they will shine forth, and will run like sparks through the stubble" (3:7). Justice is likewise immortal (1:15) and ready to judge the ungodly. The wicked have summoned death and have made a covenant with it (1:16). Here the author develops the teachings presented in Ps 73:21–26, entrusting himself to the Lord's care and protection. The righteous will be vindicated in the afterlife while the unrighteous will be laughed at by the Lord, and "After this they will become dishonored corpses, and an outrage among the dead for ever" (4:18).

In the second major section of the book, Wisdom is personified in a way similar to that found elsewhere in Job 28; Prov 1, 8, 9; and Sir 24. Wisdom is described variously as a divine attribute and a mediatrix of creation (cf.

Wis 7:23–27; 8:3, 21; 9; 10:1–21). She is also "easily discerned by those who love her, and is found by those who seek her. She hastens to make herself known to those who desire her" (6:12–13). One who sought her was Solomon. Solomon's desire for Wisdom is described in terms of courtship: he sought Wisdom to be his bride and fell in love with her beauty just as "the Lord of all loves her" (8:3). The author goes on to write of Wisdom's attributes (7:22–8:1) and to describe her many gifts, including the cardinal virtues: self-control, prudence, justice, and courage (8:7). Chapter 9 presents an eloquent prayer for Wisdom written as though Solomon were the speaker.

Personified Wisdom is often identified in the Christian tradition with the *Logos*, the Word coeternal with the Father, and so the book anticipates the New Testament and the embodiment of wisdom in Christ, the "Word made flesh" (cf. Wis 1:5–7; 2:13; 3–5; 7:22, 24; 9:1–17). The description of the *Logos* in the Prologue of John's Gospel (John 1:1–18) shows similarities with the description of wisdom in chapter 7 of Wisdom.

The third part of the book of Wisdom takes up the role of divine Wisdom in the history of Israel. It interprets Israelite history as a series of moral and theological lessons. The section studies the work of Wisdom in guiding history from Adam to Moses and into the **Exodus** journey toward Canaan. At every stage, God intervened to advance salvation history, most dramatically in the plagues visited upon the Egyptians.

Idolatry is condemned in a long digression that stretches across Wis 13:1–15:17. The author mocks the irrationality of idolatry, and those who fall into such folly are treated with biting satire and sarcasm. Against idolatry is hailed Israel's faith in the one True God. The discussion is distinctly reminiscent of the prophets and their contempt for idols and idolatry (cf. Isa 44:9–20; Jer 10:1–16; Bar 6).

A superb achievement of Hellenistic Judaism, the Wisdom of Solomon stands in the tradition of the Alexandrian Jews who expressed classical Hebrew theology in Hellenistic philosophical terms, such as Philo of Alexandria, Josephus, and others. For them, Judaism was presented as a universal religion that could be grasped by all and that offered answers to the problems of life and death. The author was acquainted with Greek philosophy, in particular Platonism and Epicureanism, and was unafraid to use the weapons of Greek thinking to his own purposes. The book is thus a bridge between the world of the Jews and the world of the Gentiles among whom the Jews lived.

WISDOM LITERATURE Writing whose aim is to give practical advice on the well-lived life. Wisdom literature is found throughout the ancient Near East; among the Israelites, **Solomon** was considered the father of wisdom literature, and several books of the Old Testament in that style are attributed to him.

The Hebrew word for "wisdom" (*ḥokmâ*) appears over 300 times in the OT; there are 183 occurrences just in Proverbs, Job, and Ecclesiastes; the Greek word for "wisdom" (*sophia*) appears in Sirach and the Wisdom of Solomon over 100 times. Seven books of the OT are commonly called Wisdom books: Job, Psalms, Proverbs, Ecclesiastes, Song of Songs, Wisdom, and Sirach.

Examples of wisdom teachings survive from Egypt and Mesopotamia. In Egypt, wisdom texts included the instructions of Ptah-hotep (ca. 2450 B.C.) and Meri-ka-re (ca. 2100 B.C.). Various Akkadian maxims have also survived. These writings and aphorisms offered guidance on how to lead a good life, how to behave in public, and how to cultivate honesty, chastity, loyalty, and other practical virtues.

Hebrew wisdom literature closely resembles the wisdom literature of the Near East generally, and even includes some of the same types of sayings. But there is an essential difference. In the wisdom literature of the Israelites, "The fear of the LORD is the beginning of knowledge" (Prov 1:7).

We can see, then, that the wisdom literature of Israel has a theological purpose that goes beyond mere practical instruction. It is the literary expression of the **covenant** with **David**. As the multinational empire of **Solomon** was a first step in leading the nations to the knowledge of God, so the intellectual genius of Solomon had that same mission (1 Kgs 4:32). Just as meeting Solomon led the **Queen of Sheba** to praise God for his wisdom (1 Kgs 10:9), so the wisdom literature traced to and inspired by Solomon and his successors—expressed in terms familiar and pleasing to the surrounding nations—pointed the way for the Gentiles toward the true God.

WISDOM, PERSONIFICATION OF *See* **Wisdom**.

WISE MEN, THREE *See* **Magi**.

WITCHCRAFT *See* **Magic and sorcery**.

WITNESS A person or thing that gives verbal or visible testimony to something else. In the legal system of the Old Testament and New Testament, a witness would be called in a variety of cases. Witnesses provided third-party verification of legal and commercial transactions (Gen 23:1–16; Isa 8:1–2; Jer 32:12).

In criminal proceedings, persons were called as witnesses to provide testimony regarding adultery, murder, idolatry, and other crimes (Prov 14:25; 1 Kgs 21:10, 13). For the court to reach a verdict, two corroborating witnesses were needed (Deut 19:15; 2 Cor 13:1), especially in cases involving capital crimes (Num 35:30; Deut 17:6). Once the sentence had been passed, the witnesses were also required to assist in the execution of a death sentence (Deut 13:6–4, 17:6–7; Acts 7:57–58). The foremost witness to be invoked is God, who is called upon to witness to the truth of testimony or to a covenant that has been forged (cf. Gen 31:49–50; 1 Sam 12:5; Jer 29:23; Rom 1:9; 2 Cor 1:23).

Those giving testimony were also aware that perjury or bearing false witness was forbidden and made them subject to the same punishment allotted to the criminal (Exod 20:16; Deut 19:16–21; Prov 6:19; Dan 13:61–62).

A witness could serve as a messenger who bears a message for another person. The apostles, for example, served as witnesses of Jesus and his Resurrection (Acts 1:8, 22; 2:32; 10:39–42; 13:31). This meant telling the world about what they had seen and heard and experienced. **Paul**, having seen the risen and glorified Christ, was commissioned by Jesus to be a witness of Jesus's name (Acts 22:15, 26:16; 1 Cor 9:1, 15:5–8). (*See also* **Apostle**.)

Very early in Christian history, "witness" came to have a specialized meaning: a "martyr" (from the Greek word for "witness") was one who gave testimony to Christ to the point of death (Acts 22:20). The sense of witness as martyrdom is most probable in the book of Revelation, where Jesus is the model for all those who offer their lives for him (Rev 1:5) and who choose to go to their deaths rather than deny him (Rev 2:13; 11:3–7; 17:6).

Inanimate objects were also used to provide witness or evidence. In the OT, stones were set up as monuments to record the establishment of a **covenant**, both between people and between God and his people (Gen 21:30, 31:44–50; Josh 22:26–28, 24:25–27).

WOMAN "So God created man in his own image, in the image of God he created him; male and female he created them" (Gen 1:27). Because man and woman were both created in the image of God, they possess an equal dignity that is bestowed by the Creator. Woman is equal in dignity with man, despite being sexually distinct from man in her physical and psychological constitution. Woman and man were created and willed for each other (Gen 2:18–24). In marriage, man and woman are united to form "one flesh" (Gen 2:24). The Catechism underscores this equal dignity of woman by linking it with the image of God stamped onto both sexes:

> Above all, the fact that human beings are persons needs to be underscored: "Man is a person, man and woman equally so, *since both were created in the image and likeness of the personal God*" (Pope John Paul II, Mu-

lieris Dignitatem *6). Their equal dignity as persons is realized as physical, psychological and ontological complementarity, giving rise to a harmonious relationship of "uni-duality," which only sin and "the structures of sin" inscribed in culture render potentially conflictual. (Congregation for the Doctrine of Faith, "Letter to the Bishops of the Catholic Church on the Collaboration of Men and Women in the Church and in the World" §8) (CCC 369–73, 2331–35)*

I. WOMEN IN THE OLD TESTAMENT

The world of the Old Testament was, for the most part, a patriarchal world. Genesis shows the subjection of women to men as a consequence of the **Fall**: "your desire shall be for your husband, and he shall rule over you" (Gen 3:16). Women were subject to men, but Genesis tells us that this was part of the consequence of sin, not the original intention of creation.

In general, women in the ancient world were under the domination of men both socially and legally. In the Near Eastern cultures, there was a disparity in rights that extended to virtually every aspect of life. A woman possessed few rights in her own regard and was always subject to some form of male authority, be it from the father of her family, her brothers, or her husband. When a woman became a widow, she passed under the protection of her brother or nearest male relative. If she had no children as a widow, she returned to the protection of her original family. Women who had no living male family members were left abandoned, and prostitution or slavery was often their only viable options.

Under the Mosaic **Law**, women were also

secondary to men, but they did have some legal protection. A husband was permitted to divorce his wife, but he was not permitted to remarry the same woman if she had been remarried since the original divorce (Deut 24:1–4; *see also* **Marriage** for other details). Nevertheless, a woman was not allowed to file for divorce, and a married woman was legally the equivalent of her husband's property (Gen 12:12–20, 20:2; Exod 20:17; Judg 19:24–27). On the other hand, in matters of religious law, women shared many rights in common with men, although they were prohibited from the priesthood.

While their status was an inferior one, women did enjoy a position of great respect because of their culture's esteem for motherhood. This was a reflection of the importance of family in Hebrew society, but it was also in fidelity to the fundamental teachings of Genesis on the cooperative roles of man and woman to "multiply" and "fill" the earth (Gen 1:28) and the particular mission of woman to be man's "helper" (Gen 2:18). Not surprisingly, the majority of references to women in the OT are to mothers or motherhood, with a woman's status dependent upon her ability to bring children into the family (Gen 30:20; 1 Sam 1:2–8). In contrast, it was considered a tragedy to be barren (Gen 30:1–2; 1 Sam 1:5; 2 Sam 6:20–23), and it was often viewed as a sign of divine displeasure.

Wisdom literature presented lessons on how to lead a good life, and finding a suitable wife was one of the most important decisions a man could face. In the acrostic poem in Prov 31:10–31, the "good wife" is described as one who will do a man "good, and not harm"

(Prov 31:12; cf. Sir 26:1–18). A wife should also be prized more for being resourceful, industrious, wise, and charitable than for being charming or beautiful (Prov 31:30). Beauty, the poem laments, can be "deceitful" and "vain." Proverbs also warns against loose women, or foreign women, for an adulteress might cost a man his life (Prov 5:3–5; 6:24–35; 9:13–18).

The mother was required to care for the children of the family and oversee the running of her household. In social settings, women were active participants in the festivals (Judg 21:19–21) and the celebrations of victories (Exod 15:20; Judg 11:34; 1 Sam 18:6–7; Ps 68:25).

Although women were subservient, the OT relates the activities of multiple women noted for their intelligence, bravery, and dedication to the Lord. The most memorable of the heroines are **Deborah**, **Judith**, and **Esther**. (*See* **Abigail**; **Hagar**; **Leah**; **Michal**; **Rachel**; **Rahab**; **Rebekah**; **Rizpah**; **Ruth**.)

II. WOMEN IN THE NEW TESTAMENT

The social and legal status of women in the Roman Empire was sometimes better and sometimes worse than it was for Jewish women. Women in Roman Egypt, for example, had rights and opportunities outside the sphere of the home, whereas women in Roman Greece were subject to many of the same restrictions placed on women in Jewish Palestine. Although the Christian faith did not completely revolutionize the social status of women at once, it did acknowledge women as persons in God's image and equal candidates for baptism and membership in the Church of Christ.

Jesus was never reluctant to talk with

women, nor did he prevent them from speaking to him or from honoring him (Matt 26:6–13; Mark 14:3–9). Jesus's encounter with the Samaritan woman in John 4:4–42 shows his surprising new attitude. Not only is she a woman, but she is also a Samaritan; yet he speaks to her as though she, too, might become a disciple.

Not only did Jesus challenge some of the traditional limitations imposed on women, but he saw women as equal recipients of grace. For instance, he made no distinction in the performance of miracles—healing Peter's mother-in-law (Matt 8:14; Mark 1:29–31; Luke 4:38), the daughter of Jairus, the woman with the hemorrhage (Matt 9:18–26; Mark 5:21–43; Luke 8:40–56), the woman with a deformed back (Luke 13:10–17), and the son of the widow of Nain (Luke 7:11–17). He also accepted the support of more than one benefactress (Luke 8:1–3) and enjoyed a close relationship with the women of the first community of his followers (e.g., Martha and Mary; Luke 10:38–42). Women likewise displayed courage and devotion by standing near him in his agony (Matt 27:55–56; Mark 15:40) and preparing to reverence his entombed body after death (Mark 16:1–3; Luke 23:55). Above all, women discovered the empty tomb (Matt 28:1–10; Mark 16:1–8; Luke 24:1–10; John 20:1).

The full equality of discipleship that Jesus emphasized in his ministry continued in the early Church, as we see in Acts (1:14; 12:12; 16:14–15; 17:4), where women are accepted as active members of the community. Priscilla (with her husband Aquila) was a notable participant in Paul's missions (Acts 18:18; Rom 16:3–4; cf. 1 Cor 16:19; 2 Tim 4:19). We also hear of at least one deaconess, **Phoebe** (Rom 16:1–2).

Paul also emphasizes the equality of discipleship between men and women. Although he does not permit women to teach in church in an official capacity as pastors or homilists (1 Cor 14:34–35; 1 Tim 2:12), women are equally heirs of Abraham according to the promise, in which there is no distinction between women and men (Gal 3:28–29).

Paul, like Jesus, sees the grace of God working to redeem not just individual persons, but relationships as well, marriage in particular. Paul's approach makes a direct connection between the Paschal mystery and the hearts of Christian spouses who, through grace, overcome the subjugation of sin and no longer need the accommodations of the Mosaic Law regarding divorce (cf. Matt 19:3–9).

For Paul, marriage is a mutual giving, an opportunity to serve rather than to be served. Marriage is a living parable of Christ's relationship to the Church, which is entitled to the care and comforting love of her spouse.

At one level, Paul affirms the traditional structure of Jewish marriage with its emphasis on male headship (Eph 5:22–31; Col 3:18–25; 1 Cor 11). On the other hand, "there is neither male nor female; for you are all one in Christ Jesus" (Gal 3:28). He repeatedly stresses the role of women in the Christian community (1 Cor 11:5; 16:19; Rom 16:1, 3, 7; Phil 4:2–3).

The role of women within the family was reaffirmed, but it was also to be seen in light of the restoration wrought by the Cross. Marriage is part of the natural order: it came before the Law of Moses (1 Cor 11:3–15), but it had fallen under the curse of sin. The consequence of this sin was a complete rupture of the original state between Adam and Eve, and among the punishments faced by Eve were the pains of childbirth and subjection to her husband (Gen 3:16; cf. 2 Cor 11:3; 1 Tim 2:13). In the life of faith, marriage is transformed through Christ, and the submission of women to their husbands becomes a voluntary one that is no longer an expression of sin and servitude (Col 3:18; Titus 2:5; 1 Pet 3:1). Paul affirms the mutual interdependence and equality of woman and man in 1 Cor 11:11–12: "Nevertheless, in the Lord woman is not independent of man nor man of woman; for as woman was made from man, so man is now born of woman. And all things are from God."

Marriage for the Christian is seen with the eyes of faith and in recognition of the power of the Resurrection. Husband and wife are equal partners who share in the freedom from sin and in the joyful and mutual self-giving of marriage (cf. LG §56; Pope John Paul II, *Mulieris Dignitatem* 6–10) (CCC 1601–42). (*See also* **Mary, the Mother of Jesus**.)

WOOL One of the most common materials for clothing in biblical times (Job 31:20; Prov 31:13; Ezek 34:3). It was used in trade (Ezek 27:18) and for paying tribute (2 Kgs 3:4), and it was often mentioned along with **linen**. The **Law** of Moses prohibited wearing cloth made of linen and wool joined together (Deut 22:11). In places where water was difficult to find, a herdsman would spread out shearings of fleece to collect the morning dew (Judg 6:36–40).

WORD In biblical Israel, a spoken utterance was a powerful and even sacred reality. It said something about the speaker himself, and the spoken word itself had a kind of existence beyond the "sound" that it made. Ancient society, in many ways, revolved around the power of the spoken word to bring order to the world (e.g., in oaths, marital vows, judicial pronouncements, liturgical prayers, etc.).

I. IN THE OLD TESTAMENT

In the Hebrew of the Old Testament, the word *dābār* can denote both a word and a thing, a dual meaning that largely captures the Israelites' idea of the power of the word. "The word of the Lord" appears throughout the OT as an extension of the divine power that must be followed obediently. The word of God is seen also as synonymous with the Law (Deut 8:3; Ps 119). The word spoken by God possesses the same power as its speaker (Isa 55:11); the word is the creative power of God that brought creation into existence (cf. Gen 1:3; Ps 33:6; Wis 9:1).

The same "word of the Lord" was the message conveyed by the **prophets**. The word was truth; what the Lord spoke would come to pass (Isa 38:7). God's word is not only his creative power, but also his means of reaching humanity, of intervening in history to save his people. The word is, in part, God's revelation of himself.

II. IN THE NEW TESTAMENT

God's word is still his revelation and his power, but in the New Testament we learn the most astonishing fact of God's self-revelation: that "the Word became flesh and dwelt among us" (John 1:14). God has said all that he intends to say to us through the incarnate life and death of Christ. The words of Jesus Christ are thus the words of God (cf. John 5:24; 12:48; 18:32; Acts 8:25; 12:24; 13:44, 48–49; Col 3:16). Now the "word" of God means specifically the Gospel: "But many of those who heard the word believed" (Acts 4:4; cf. Acts 4:31; 13:5; 18:11).

In theology, the identity of Jesus Christ as the Word (Greek *Logos*) is also one way of comprehending the inner life of God, whereby the Father generates the Son. From all eternity, God generates his Word, who is the coequal and consubstantial Son. As Thomas Aquinas wrote, "The eternal generation or begetting of the Son is likened to the process by which the human intellect generates the concept or mental word. Hence the Word of God is the Person begotten by the Father. It is the personal name for God the Son" (*Summa theologiae* I, q.34 a.2).

WORKS *See* **Justification**.

WORLD The whole of **creation** existing in time and space. The world is good, having come from the hands of God (Gen 1:4, 10, 12, 18, 21, 31), but it now suffers death and decay, owing to the rebellion of the human race (Rom 8:19–23).

I. IN THE OLD TESTAMENT

To refer to the totality of the created universe, Genesis uses the phrase "the heavens and the earth" (Gen 1:1). In poetical texts, descriptions sometimes follow the Near Eastern conception of the world as sitting on the primeval waters (Isa 40:22; Job 26:10; Prov 8:27; cf. Job 26:7, 38:13) or on pillars (1 Sam 2:8; Ps 104:5; Job 38:4). The cosmological map also included an underworld, **Sheol**, variously described as a pit, cave, or grave (1 Sam 28:13; Ps 71:20; 106:17; Isa 29:4).

The Creation narrative in Genesis also gives us a striking image of creation as a great temple of God, of which the earthly sanctuaries of Israel are merely smaller images. Thus creation is accomplished by God's utterances in seven days; the **Tabernacle** is built according to seven commands (Exod 40:16–33); and the **Temple** is built in seven years (1 Kgs 6:38). The whole created universe is a sanctuary filled with the presence of the Creator: "Heaven is my throne and the earth is my footstool" (Isa 66:1; cf. Exod 31:17; Ps 102:26; Isa 48:13, 51:13).

The place of God as Creator and Sustainer of the world is affirmed repeatedly in the Old Testament (e.g., Gen 1:1–2:4; Ps 121:2, 124:8, 146:6; Isa 45:18, 48:13). There are no limits to God's Lordship over the world (1 Sam 2:10; 2 Chr 16:9; Job 28:24; Ps 139:7–12; Isa 41:5, 45:22, 49:6, 52:10). The Greek notion of the *kosmos* as an ordered reality is found in the latest books of the OT, which were written in Hellenistic times (cf. 2 Macc 7:23; 12:15; 13:14). However, even these books firmly keep the biblical doctrine of creation at the beginning of time. The *kosmos* is not eternal.

II. IN THE NEW TESTAMENT

The world (Greek *kosmos*) has at least three distinct meanings in the New Testament writings.

1. The first meaning is the *created universe*. The NT continues to affirm the sovereignty of God over his creation (Matt 5:35, 11:25; Luke 10:21; Acts 4:24, 7:49, 17:24; 1 Cor 8:5–6, 10:26; Rev 11:4, 14:7). Echoing the OT, Paul tells the Athenians: "The God who made the world and everything in it, being Lord of heaven and earth, does not live in shrines made by man, nor is he served by human hands, as though he needed anything, since he himself gives to all men life and breath and everything" (Acts 17:24–25). The world was created through the **word** of God the Father (John 1:1–3), and thus had a definite beginning in time (Matt 24:21, 25:34; Luke 11:50; John 17:24; Rom 1:20; Eph 1:4; Heb 4:3, 9:26; Rev 13:8). Equally, the created order of the world reveals the power and majesty of God (Rom 1:19–20). The world is not eternal; in its present form, it will have an end (Matt 5:18; Mark 13:31; 1 Cor 7:31; 2 Pet 3:7, 10; 1 John 2:17). When that time will come is hidden from man (Mark 13:32). At that time, the world is destined to undergo a transformation. The present form of the world, suffering as it is from death and decay, will pass away, as God refashions the universe into a new heaven and a new earth (Rom 8:19–21; 2 Pet 3:13; Rev 21:1, 5).

2. The "world" is also the worldwide family of *fallen humanity*. Although the world was created and entrusted to men and women, made in the image of God, human sin corrupted the world (Rom 5:12; cf. 1 Cor 6:2, 11:32). Thus "the world" comes to mean the world of sin, and the lives of unredeemed men and women who are still in bondage to sin (John 1:29; 1 John 5:19; 1 Pet 5:8–9). This world tempts the Christian to be caught up in its concerns and anxieties and so turn away from God (Jas 4:4). The task for the believer is to remain free of excessive entanglements, to be in the world but not of the world: "If with Christ you died to the elemental spirits of the universe, why do you live as if you still belonged to the world?" (Col 2:20; 1 Cor 7:31). It is this world to which Jesus brought redemption (Matt 18:7; John 12:31, 15:18, 16:8–11, 17:9). Christ is the light of the world (John 1:9; 3:19; 8:12; 9:5; 12:46), yet he is also not of the world (John 8:23). The Son, the Word, entered into the world (John 3:17; 9:39; 10:36; 16:28; 18:37) to take away the sins of the world (John 1:29; cf. Mark 2:10) (CCC 295–301, 337–49).

3. Thus the "world" also comes to mean the *world of sin*: the realm where sin and evil have dominion over the lives of fallen humanity. The "world" of sin is implacably hostile to God and the inexpressible love that sent Christ into the world to bring salvation (John 3:16); it rejects both the Father and the Son (John 1:10; 17:25). John writes of "the ruler of this world"—Satan—who has been condemned (John 16:11) and who has no power over Jesus (John 14:30–31). It is certain that sin will not triumph, for the "ruler of the world" is already judged. In believing, therefore, the disciples are themselves considered by Christ not to be of the world: "I have given them your word; and the world has hated them because they are not of the world, even as I am not of the world. I do not pray that you should take them out of the world, but that you should keep them from

the evil one. They are not of the world, even as I am not of the world" (John 17:14–16).

WORM Commonly associated in Scripture with death, wretchedness, and destruction (Ps 22:6; Sir 7:19; Isa 41:14, 66:24). Moses, delineating the curses of the covenant, warned the people that their crops would be consumed by the worms (Deut 28:39). Job lamented the prospect of dying and called the worm his "mother" (Job 17:14), while Bildad replied that man is a maggot and a worm (Job 25:6). In the New Testament, Herod Agrippa died and was eaten by worms as a sign of divine punishment (Acts 12:23). Jesus describes hell as a place where the damned are forever eaten by worms (Mark 9:48).

WORMWOOD Any of several plants belonging to the genus *Artemisia*. The wormwood appearing in the Bible is probably *Artemisia herba-alba*, the most common of the varieties found in Palestine. In Scripture, wormwood represents poisonous bitterness and woe. Especially notable is its use by the prophets, including **Amos** (Amos 5:7; 6:12) and **Jeremiah** (Jer 9:15). In Lamentations, wormwood is used to describe the painful distress that came with the destruction of Jerusalem (Lam 3:15, 19). Wormwood is mentioned only once in the New Testament, in Rev 8:11, as the name of the star that falls to the earth: "A third of the waters became wormwood, and many men died of the water, because it was made bitter."

WRATH *See* **Anger**.

WRITING *See* **Book**; **Ink**; **Greek**; **Hebrew**; **Papyrus**; **Parchment**.

XANTHICUS The name of the sixth month in the Macedonian calendar. According to Josephus (*Ant.* 1.81, 3.248), it corresponded to Nisan (March–April), the first month of the Jewish calendar (2 Macc 11:30, 33, 38).

XERXES The king of Persia from 486 to 465 B.C. This Greek form of the name, by which he is usually known in secular history, does not appear in the RSV; instead the name is given as **Ahasuerus** (Ezra 4:6; Esth 1:1; etc.), the Hebrew rendering of the same Persian name. The book of Esther is set at his court. Outside the Bible, Xerxes's reign is best known for his colossal invasion of Greece in 480–79 B.C. His massive army fought an engagement at the famous pass of Thermopylae; he then suffered a crushing naval defeat at Salamis, one of the ancient world's greatest sea battles. The following year, after he had returned to Persia, his army was routed by the Greeks at Plataea. The defeat in Greece colored the rest of his reign, which was perceived thenceforth as a time of decline. Eventually he was assassinated by a court conspiracy.

YAHWEH *See* **God**; *see also* "The Names of God" *under* **God**.

YEAR *See* **Calendar**.

YHWH *See* **God**; *see also* "The Names of God" *under* **God**.

YOD The tenth letter of the Hebrew alphabet (׳).

YOKE A heavy wooden beam laid across the shoulders and fastened around the neck of a team of animals, usually oxen, and tied by rope or straps. The yoke enabled the team to pull a plow or a cart (Deut 21:3; Num 19:2). Yokes were also used on slaves and prisoners (Jer 28:10; Lam 1:14; 1 Tim 6:1). Metaphorically, the yoke was used both positively and negatively as a symbol of servitude. Thus Paul spoke of the "yoke" of slavery (Gal 5:1). Israel broke the "yoke" of the Lord in refusing to abide by the **Law** (Jer 2:20), and Peter speaks of the "yoke" of the Law—that is, the ceremonial laws of Israel—as a burden even the Jews had not been able to bear (Acts 15:10). In contrast, it is no great burden to serve Christ: "My yoke is easy, and my burden light" (Matt 11:30).

YOM KIPPUR *See* **Atonement, Day of**.

Z

ZAANAN A village mentioned in Mic 1:11. It may be the same as Zenan, located in the western lowlands of Judah (Josh 15:37).

ZAANANNIM A settlement in Naphtali, west or northwest of the Sea of Galilee (Josh 19:33). It is remembered as the place where Heber the Kenite camped and where his wife, **Jael**, killed **Sisera** (Judg 4:11).

ZABAD A member of **David**'s elite corps of mighty warriors (1 Chr 11:41). The name belongs also to various other men (1 Chr 7:21; 2 Chr 24:26; Ezra 10:27, 33, 43).

ZABDI The name of two men in the Old Testament.

1. The grandfather of **Achan**, whose infamous violation of a holy war ban brought death and dishonor to his family in the time of Joshua (Josh 7:1, 17–18).

2. An official of **David** who was in charge of wine production and storage (1 Chr 27:27).

ZACCHAEUS A wealthy **tax collector** from Jericho who became a disciple of Jesus (Luke 19:1–10). Small in stature, he climbed a sycamore tree to see Jesus. Jesus then invited him to come down and host him in his house. Zacchaeus was delighted to accept this request; he promised to give half of his belongings to the poor and to give back fourfold everything that he had ever taken in a dishonest fashion. The crowd was displeased that Jesus went into the home of a hated tax collector, but Jesus reminded them that he had come to save the lost. Through the story of Zacchaeus's conversion, Luke reminds us of one of the important parts of the Gospel message, detachment from the love of money, especially as it is expressed in giving to the poor. According to one ancient tradition, Zacchaeus was eventually named bishop of Caesarea by **Peter**.

ZACHARIAS *See* **Zechariah**.

ZACHARY *See* **Zechariah**.

ZADOK A priestly descendant of Aaron through his third son, Eleazar (1 Chr 6:50–53). He was a son of Ahitub and the father of Ahimaz (2 Sam 8:17, 15:27; 1 Chr 6:8). Zadok was priest at David's court with **Abiathar**. In 2 Sam 15:24–29, Zadok, with Abiathar, was in charge of the **ark of the covenant**. During the rebellion of **Absalom**, Zadok (and Abiathar) remained loyal to the king (2 Sam 15:24–35; 17:15) and proved helpful in dealing with the elders of Judah; thus they made it possible for David to return to Jerusalem (2 Sam 19:12–15). When David was old and his sons were fighting over the succession, Zadok supported **Solomon** and anointed him as king (1 Kgs 1:8, 32–40). Abiathar supported the claim of **Adonijah** and so was banished to Anathoth by King Solomon (1 Kgs 2:26–27). The banishment of Abiathar put Zadok in a position to become the sole high priest in Jerusalem (1 Kgs 2:26–27).

Zadok and his descendants were responsible for the exercise of the high priesthood in Jerusalem until the destruction of the **Temple** in 586 B.C. and the **Exile** (2 Chr 31:10). After the Exile, **Ezekiel** proposed that the priesthood be restricted to Zadokites, because they had never committed apostasy during the time of the monarchy (cf. Exod 40:46; 43:19; 44:15; 48:11). The Zadokites remained in charge of the priesthood in the second Temple until 171 B.C. when Antiochus IV Epiphanes gave it to **Menelaus**. After that, some Zadokites stayed on in Jerusalem and presumably formed the party of the **Sadducees**. Others left the city and regrouped in Leontopolis, Egypt, and still others withdrew into the wilderness to form the priestly core of the Qumran community (Dead Sea Scrolls, 1QS 5.8).

ZALMON

1. One of David's elite warriors. He was a member of the clan of Ahoh of Benjamin (2 Sam 23:28).

2. A mountain in the tribal territory of Ephraim, near **Shechem** (Judg 9:48), possibly related to Mount **Ebal** or Mount Gerizim, which rise directly north and south of Shechem. **Abimelech** and his men gathered brushwood from Mount Zalmon to burn his political enemies who had taken refuge in a temple near the mountain.

ZALMUNNA

One of the kings of Midian, with Zebah, who was killed during **Gideon**'s war against the Midianites (Judg 8:5–12).

ZAMZUMMIM

The name used by the Ammonites for a people, also called the **Rephaim**, whose lands east of the Jordan they had conquered and claimed for themselves (Deut 2:20–23).

ZAPHENATH-PANEAH

The Egyptian name given to **Joseph** by the pharaoh when he was appointed vizier of Egypt (Gen 41:45). The name may mean "the god speaks and he lives," or possibly "he who is called Ip-ankh," the latter being a fairly common name among Egyptian men in the second millennium B.C.

ZAPHON

A city in the tribal territory of Gad (Josh 13:27) in the Jordan Valley near Succoth and Beth-nimrah. The city was a scene in the feud between **Jephthah** and the Ephraimites over the expedition against the Ammonites (Judg 12:1).

ZAREPHATH

A Phoenician coastal town south of **Sidon**, the modern Sarafand. It was a possession of Sidon at the time of its capture by **Sennacherib** in 701 B.C. and later belonged to **Tyre**. It was here that **Elijah** went during a severe famine in Palestine under **Ahab**. In the town he was shown hospitality by a widow and restored her son to life (1 Kgs 17:8–24; Luke 4:26). **Obadiah** also prophesied that Zarephath would serve as the northern boundary of Israel when the Lord regathered the exiles of Israel into the land (Obad 20).

ZARETHAN A city east of the Jordan River. According to Josh 3:16, the water flow of the Jordan was stopped at Adam, which is said to be a neighboring settlement near Zarethan, to permit the passage of the Israelites. The exact location is uncertain, but Tell es-Sa'idiyeh is one candidate; another possibility is Qarn Sartabeh.

ZAYIN The seventh letter of the Hebrew alphabet (ז).

ZEALOTS A party of Jewish religious nationalists during the first century A.D. They were noted for determined resistance, sometimes militarily, to the Roman occupation of Palestine. The Zealots were founded by Judas the Galilean, the leader of a Jewish revolt against the Romans in A.D. 6, on the grounds that taxes should not be paid to a pagan emperor. Both the group's name and its inspiration can be traced back to the zeal (in Greek, *zēlos*) displayed by **Phinehas** in the wilderness (Num 25:11) and by **Mattathias** and his sons in their revolt against Antiochus IV Epiphanes in defense of the Mosaic Law (1 Macc 2:24–27). The rebellion of A.D. 6 was crushed by overwhelming Roman force, but the spirit of Judas did not expire. Two of his sons were subsequently crucified by the Roman procurator Alexander around A.D. 46, and a third son tried to claim the leadership of the Jewish War against Rome that began in A.D. 66.

During the bloody fighting that ensued, the Zealots played a leading part, but their fervor proved no match for the strength of the Roman legions. Jerusalem fell in A.D. 70, and the Zealot stronghold of Masada was captured in A.D. 74, although the Zealot spirit survived and remained strong into the second century. Simon, one of the apostles, was called the Zealot (Luke 6:15; Acts 1:13), which may indicate that he was once affiliated with the Zealot resistance movement. Paul refers to his own exceptional zeal for religious Judaism, but in his case it was expressed as a Pharisee and not as a member of the Zealot party (Acts 22:3; Gal 1:14).

ZEBADIAH (Hebrew, "the Lord has given a gift") The name of several men in the Old Testament, including a descendant of Benjamin (1 Chr 8:15); the Benjaminite son of Jeroham (1 Chr 12:8), who joined **David** at Ziklag with his brother Joelah; a Levite, the third son of Meshelemiah (1 Chr 26:2) and a gatekeeper; and a Levite who was sent by King **Jehoshaphat** to teach in the cities of Judah (2 Chr 17:8).

ZEBAH One of the two kings of Midian, with Zalmunna, who was defeated and killed by Gideon in revenge for the death of his brother (Judg 8:5; Ps 83:11).

ZEBEDEE The father of the apostles **James** and **John** according to the Synoptic Gospels (Matt 4:21, 10:2, 26:37; Mark 1:19) and the husband of Salome (Matt 27:56; Mark 15:40).

Zebedee was a fisherman in Galilee with his sons and hired employees; they worked together with Simon **Peter** and **Andrew** (Luke 5:10). In the Gospel of John, the brothers James and John are mentioned not by name but as "the sons of Zebedee" (John 21:2).

ZEBOIIM One of the cities of the plain associated with **Sodom and Gomorrah** and destroyed with them. The destruction account in Genesis (19:24–29) does not name Zeboiim explicitly, but Deut 29:23 makes it clear that Zeboiim and Admah were also destroyed. Zeboiim stood near the southern border of **Canaan** (Gen 10:19). Before the city's destruction, Zeboiim was defeated and despoiled at the hands of the Elamite king **Chedorlaomer** and his Mesopotamian allies (Gen 14:2, 8).

ZEBOIM The name of two places mentioned in the Old Testament.

1. A valley near Michmash in the tribal territory of Benjamin (1 Sam 13:18).

2. A Benjaminite settlement after the **Exile** (Neh 11:34).

ZEBUL The appointed ruler or mayor of **Shechem** in the days of **Abimelech** (Judg 9:30–41). Being loyal to the ambitious Abimelech, he warned him of the revolt of Gaal, son of Ebed; thanks to his warning, Abimelech routed Gaal and his supporters.

ZEBULUN The tenth son of **Jacob** and the sixth son born to **Leah** (Gen 30:20). The tribe of Zebulun is often counted as the sixth tribe of Israel (Gen 35:23, 46:14; Exod 1:3). The tribe's territory is described in Josh 19:10–16 as being north of the plain of Jezreel and west of the Sea of Galilee. The blessing of Jacob (Gen 49:13) promised Zebulun an inheritance as far north as the Phoenician coastal city of Sidon. In the blessing of Moses, Zebulun shared a holy mountain with Issachar (Deut 33:19). The Zebulunites were praised for courage in battle against the Canaanites and aided **Gideon** in battle against the Midianites and Amalekites (Judg 4:6, 10; 5:14, 18; 6:35). The tribe fielded a sizable army in the time of Moses (Num 1:30–31) and later supported **David** (1 Chr 12:33). It endured terrible losses in the Assyrian invasion under **Tiglath-pileser III** in about 734 B.C. (2 Kgs 15:29). **Isaiah** promised an age of Messianic glory for Zebulun (Isa 9:1; cf. Matt 4:12–16), and **Ezekiel** speaks of its future restoration (Ezek 48:26–27). Zebulunite survivors of the Assyrian conquest took part in **Hezekiah**'s celebration of the Passover (2 Chr 30:10–22). The prophet **Jonah** probably belonged to this tribe, since his hometown of Gath-hepher (2 Kgs 14:25) was in the territory of Zebulun (Josh 19:13).

ZECHARIAH The name of twenty-eight men in Scripture. Among them are the following.

1. The king of Israel in about 753 B.C., the son and successor of **Jeroboam II** (2 Kgs 14:29; 15:8–12). Zechariah reigned for only six months before he was assassinated. His death brought an end to the dynasty of **Jehu** and anticipated the fall of the kingdom of Israel a few decades later.

2. The Benjaminite uncle of **Saul** (1 Chr 9:37).

3. A Levitical musician who played the harp in the procession of the **ark of the covenant** into Jerusalem (1 Chr 15:18–20).

4. A priest and trumpeter who took part in the procession of the ark of the covenant into Jerusalem (1 Chr 15:24).

5. The son of **Jehoiada**, a priest who led a palace coup against **Athaliah** to install **Joash** as king of Judah (2 Chr 24:20). When Joash reverted to idolatry, Zechariah delivered a prophetic oracle against him and was stoned to death in the court of the Temple (2 Chr 24:22).

6. The eleventh of the minor prophets (see **Zechariah, book of**).

7. The father of **John the Baptist** (Luke 1:5; 3:2) and a priest of the division of **Abijah** (1 Chr 24:10). Zechariah and his wife, **Elizabeth**, were old and without children when he was informed by the archangel **Gabriel** that God had answered their prayers: they would have a son, and his name would be John. Zechariah expressed doubt as to the possibility and so was rendered unable to speak until John was born (Luke 1:8–25). He confirmed John's name at the child's circumcision by writing it on a tablet, whereupon his voice returned to him. Once more able to speak, Zechariah declared the Messianic hope of Israel in the Benedictus (Luke 1:68–79).

ZECHARIAH, BOOK OF Zechariah was a contemporary of **Haggai** who prophesied to encourage the faith of the Jewish people and the rebuilding of the Temple after the **Exile**. Among several significant oracles, he relates a vision of the coming of the **Messiah**, who would bring peace to the nations. The book of Zechariah is the eleventh book of the twelve minor prophets in both the Hebrew Bible and the **Septuagint**. It is the also the longest of those twelve books, and in the opinion of many—including Saint Jerome—the hardest to understand.

I. AUTHORSHIP AND DATE

Zechariah, son of Berechiah, son of Iddo, is almost universally accepted as the author of Zechariah chapters 1–8. At least these chapters can be securely dated to around 520 B.C.

More complicated is the question of who wrote chapters 9–14. Many modern scholars believe those chapters were written by another author in a later period, perhaps in the fourth century B.C. Among the reasons cited for this opinion are the sharp divergences in tone and language between chapters 1–8 and 9–14. Chapters 1–8 are written in prose, chapters 9–14 in poetry. Chapters 1–8 address the historical situation after the **Exile**; chapters 9–14 consist of eschatological texts that seem to point to the future.

On the other hand, the two parts, 1–8 and 9–14, might represent different periods in the prophet's ministry. The later chapters could have been written at a time when the leadership in Jerusalem was sadly lacking and the atmosphere was gloomy. The weakness of the multiple-author argument is its unstated assumption that a single writer always writes in only one way. An author is not always concerned with only one subject throughout his career and does not always write in the same style about different subjects. The difference between prose and poetry might account for much of the difference in language and grammar.

In the end, the hypothesis of two different authors is possible, but not decisively proved.

II. CONTENTS

III. PURPOSE AND THEMES

The book of Zechariah sought to stimulate the faith of the Jews in the postexilic period, especially in the rebuilding of the Temple of Jerusalem. The prophet Zechariah, son of Berechiah, son of Iddo (Zech 1:1; cf. Ezra 5:1, 6:14; Neh 12:16), was a member of a priestly family and began his prophetic ministry in the year 520 B.C., soon after Haggai received his own call to be a prophet of the Lord. Both were concerned with the spiritual welfare of the Jews who had returned from captivity in Babylon, and both urged them to rebuild the Temple as the center of worship. Enthusiasm had at first been high among the returnees, but gradually the spiritual ardor cooled and enthusiasm for rebuilding the Temple waned. Opposition from the Samaritans, scheming at the Persian court, and a lack of leadership in the Jerusalem community all discouraged the people, and the reconstruction ground to a halt. For his part, Zechariah called upon the Jews to recognize their own failings, to repent of their sins, and to place their trust in a merciful God.

The first part of the book, chapters 1–8, is taken up with Zechariah's eight visions that prepared him to instruct those responsible for rebuilding the Temple. The occurrence of these visions is also dated exactly: the eighth month of the second year of Darius (Zech 1:1, October/November 520 B.C.), the twenty-fourth day of the eleventh month of the same year (1:7, February 519 B.C.), the fourth day of the ninth month of the fourth year of Darius's reign (November 518 B.C.). The visions are recounted in the first person and follow a literary pattern similar to that of **Ezekiel**, in which the prophet receives a vision, asks a question, and then is given an explanation by an angel. These visions begin with a call to repentance (1:2–6) and end with a reflection on past sin and a promise of an eschatological future that will bring a better time for the righteous.

The visions reveal a clear Messianic program of restoration of the Temple (1:7–17) and Jerusalem, the Holy City (2:5–17), that includes the promise of destruction for those who have persecuted God's people (2:1–4) and the eventual salvation of the Gentiles (2:1–13). The role of the high priest is stressed, embodied by **Joshua**, who is invested and vindicated by God against the accusations of Satan (3:1–10). Beside the high priest stands the descendant of David, **Zerubbabel**, who served as governor of Judah under Darius I and began the reconstruction of the Temple (Hag 1:1–2; Zech 4:9). Because of his Davidic lineage, Zerubbabel's efforts stirred the Messianic hopes of the Jewish community after the Exile (Hag 2:21–23; Zech 4:6–10). The vision of the seven-branched candlestick, representing the "eyes of the LORD" that range across the earth (4:10), fed by two olive trees, "the two anointed who stand by the LORD of the whole earth" (4:14), was likely intended to encourage the two leaders, Joshua and Zerubbabel, as the pillars of the restored community. The concluding vision, of Joshua's coronation, provides a symbol of the divine approbation of the restored priesthood at Jerusalem (6:9–14).

Chapter 8 is full of Messianic hope that was given its foundation in the rebuilt and repopulated Jerusalem. It reiterates the universal scope of redemption in the Messianic future: "Many peoples and strong nations shall come to seek the LORD of hosts in Jerusalem, and to entreat the favor of the LORD" (8:22).

The second part of Zechariah is made up of two sections, chapters 9–11 and chapters 12–14. Chapter 9 gives a prophetic description of the Messiah as a royal but humble king entering Jerusalem on a donkey and inaugurating an era of peace (9:9–10). The passage was fulfilled in Christ's entry into Jerusalem on Palm Sunday (Matt 21:1–9; Mark 11:1–10; Luke 19:28–38; John 12:14–15). Chapter 12 begins with the promise of Jerusalem's triumph over its enemies (Zech 12:1–9), followed by a further Messianic prophecy (12:10–14). The Gospel of John reads Zech 12:10, with its reference to "him whom they have pierced," as a reference to the Crucifixion of Jesus (John 19:37). Concluding the second half of the book is chapter 14's apocalyptic imagery of the **Day of the Lord**. The oracle in chapter 14 envisions the fall of Jerusalem (14:2), the judgment of the Lord's enemies (14:3), and the conversion of the nations to the worship of the Lord (14:16). Jerusalem's enemies will gather against the Lord and be destroyed, and "every one that survives of all the nations that have come against Jerusalem shall go up year after year to worship the King, the LORD of hosts, and to keep the feast of booths" (14:16).

ZEDEKIAH (Hebrew, "the Lord is my righteousness") The name of several men in the Old Testament.

1. The son of Chenaanah. He was one of the four hundred court prophets under **Ahab**; he promised Israel a sure victory against the Arameans at Ramoth-gilead (1 Kgs 22:1–28; 2 Chr 18:1–27). **Micaiah**, on the other hand, foresaw defeat, including the death of Ahab. Zedekiah called Micaiah a liar and struck Micaiah on the cheek, but Micaiah's prophecy came true (1 Kgs 22:29–40).

2. The son of Hananiah and a royal official under King **Jehoiakim** of Judah (Jer 36:12).

3. The son of Maaseiah and a prophet at the time of **Jeremiah**. Jeremiah accused him of

prophesying falsely, and foretold his death at the hands of **Nebuchadnezzar** (Jer 29:21–23).

4. The last king of Judah (r. ca. 597–586 B.C.), the third son of **Josiah** (1 Chr 3:15) and Hamutal (2 Kgs 24:18), younger brother of **Jehoahaz** and **Jehoiakim**, and the uncle and successor of **Jehoiachin** (2 Kgs 24:17). Originally known as Mattaniah, he was installed on the throne at the age of twenty-one after the deposition and deportation of Jehoiachin by Nebuchadnezzar and given the name Zedekiah as a symbol of his vassalage.

Zedekiah's accession came after Nebuchadnezzar had already deported many of the kingdom's leading citizens to Babylon (2 Kgs 24:15–16). Relying on the poor advice of his counselors, Zedekiah committed to an ill-advised rebellion to throw off the Babylonian yoke. His decision led to the final destruction of the kingdom. Nebuchadnezzar laid siege to Jerusalem (2 Kgs 25:1; Jer 39:1), and Jeremiah advised the king to surrender, as the Babylonian conquest was divinely ordained (Jer 27:1–22). According to Jeremiah, three times Zedekiah asked Jeremiah for direction (Jer 37:1–10, 16–21; 38:14–28), but under the thrall of his advisors, the king proved too weak to accept the prophet's call to offer no resistance to the Babylonians.

With the fall of the city, Zedekiah fled only to be captured and brought to Nebuchadnezzar at Riblah. As part of the Babylonian ruler's vindictive revenge upon Judah, the royal sons and many of the leading citizens of the kingdom were executed before Zedekiah. The fallen king was then blinded and sent in chains to Babylon and exiled (2 Kgs 25:4–7;

Jer 39:4–6, 52:2–30). With his fall and the destruction of Jerusalem, the kingdom of Judah was no more.

ZEEB *See* **Oreb and Zeeb**.

ZELOPHEHAD The son of Hepher of the tribe of Manasseh (Num 26:33; Josh 17:3; 1 Chr 7:15) and the father of five daughters: Mahlah, Noah, Hoglah, Milcah, and Tirzah. His daughters requested rights to the inheritance of their father before **Moses** and **Eleazar**, as Zelophehad left no male heirs (Num 27:1–4). In their successful claim, they established the precedent that the property of a man without male heirs should pass to his daughters (Num 27:5–11). In order for the property to continue in Zelophehad's name and tribe, however, the daughters were required to marry within their father's tribe (Num 36:1–11).

ZENAS A Christian lawyer stationed on the island of Crete with **Apollos**; **Titus** was told to assist Zenas and Apollos with supplies and send them on their way from Crete (Titus 3:13).

ZEPHANIAH, BOOK OF The ninth of the twelve minor prophets. Zephaniah exercised his ministry in the second half of the seventh century B.C., during the reign of King **Josiah**. The period was one of widespread idolatry, superstition, and religious degradation, and Zephaniah prophesied the Lord's impending judgment on Jerusalem and its people. But he also prophesied that a holy remnant of the people would be spared.

I. AUTHORSHIP AND DATE

Scholars are in general agreement that the author of Zephaniah was the prophet of that name. Little is known about him beyond the opening genealogy that identifies him as son of Cushi, son of Gedaliah, son of Amariah, son of Hezekiah (Zeph 1:1). This **Hezekiah** is probably the king of Judah by that name, as this would account for the effort made to trace the prophet's line of ancestors. Zephaniah performed his ministry in Jerusalem. While some scholars prefer to attribute only parts of the book to the prophet, the majority opinion holds that most of the work should be considered to be by his hand.

The date for the work is placed sometime during the reign of King Josiah. It is difficult to say whether Zephaniah's oracles should be placed before or after Josiah launched his religious reform in 622 B.C. The prophet's condemnation of corruption and idolatry seems to favor a date before the reform got under way, but it is also possible that the king's effort to purge Judah and Jerusalem was a project that took several years to complete, and so a date after 622 B.C. cannot be ruled out.

II. CONTENTS

III. PURPOSE AND THEMES

Zephaniah begins with oracles of judgment, followed by oracles of eschatological blessing—a pattern followed by Isaiah, Ezekiel, and other Old Testament prophets. The book's prophecies commence with a grim vision of universal judgment (Zeph 1:2–3): "I will sweep away man and beast; I will sweep away the birds of the air and the fish of the sea." The prophecies proceed to a judgment on Judah that condemns the impiety and idolatry of the kingdom (1:4–6). Zechariah 1:7–18 develops the theme of the **Day of the Lord**, a time of divine wrath and severe judgment and punishment.

The next oracle is against the nations (cf. Amos 1–2; Isa 13–23; Jer 46–51). Coming on the heels of the promise of punishment for Judah, the oracle was a reflection in part of the looming international crises that eventually engulfed Judah. The rise of the Babylonian Empire brought an end to the Assyrian dominance of the Near East. Zephaniah 2:4–15 speaks against the surrounding nations who were then enemies of God's people: the Cherethites (Cretans) and Philistines (2:4–7); the Moabites and Ammonites (2:8–11); the Ethiopians (Cushites; 2:12); and the Assyrians (2:13–15).

Another oracle (3:1–7) is against Jerusalem for its failure to heed the word of the Lord, and the result will be the judgment and conversion of the nations (3:8–10). Zephaniah 3:12–13 describes the remnant of Israel, a "people humble and lowly," who take refuge in the name of the Lord. The remnant will survive the calamity that is coming and will be reformed and renewed. In the climactic oracle, the remnant sings and rejoices because the Lord has chosen to dwell in its midst and restore its fortunes (3:14–20). Thus the central theme of the last section is joy: the Lord will take away the judgments against Israel and promises to make his people "renowned and praised among all the peoples of the earth" (3:20). Several scholars have seen this oracle (3:14–20) as the backdrop to the **Annunciation** scene in Luke 1:26–38, as Mary is the faithful daughter of Israel in whom dwells the presence of God.

ZEPHTHAH *See* **Hormah**.

ZERAH The name of several men in the Old Testament.

1. The son of Judah by Tamar (Gen 38:30) and the father of the Zerahite clan of Judah (Num 26:20; 1 Chr 2:4, 6). Achan was a member of the clan, and his doom was a warning for those who sinned against the ban placed on Jericho (Josh 7:1; 22:20).

2. A clan belonging to the tribe of Simeon (Num 26:13; 1 Chr 4:24).

3. The son of an Edomite chieftain named Reuel (Gen 36:13, 17; 1 Chr 1:37).

4. An Ethiopian general who engaged Judah in battle but whose army was routed to the last man (2 Chr 14:9–15).

ZERED A brook or seasonal stream, the natural border between **Moab** and **Edom**, that was crossed by the Israelites in the final year of the **Exodus** wanderings (Deut 2:13–14). It flows into the Arabah Valley near the southeastern end of the Dead Sea; it is probably the stream now called the Wadi Hasa.

ZERESH The wife of Haman (Esth 5:10). She advised him to erect a gallows for the hanging of Mordecai (Esth 5:14), only to have her husband hanged there instead (Esth 7:9–10).

ZERUBBABEL The son of Shealtiel and the grandson of King **Jehoiachin** (Ezra 3:2; Hag 1:1; Matt 1:12); according to 1 Chr 3:19, he was the son of Pedaiah. The two different fathers may indicate that a levirate marriage took place (*see* **Marriage**). Zerubbabel returned to Palestine after the **Exile** (Ezra 2:2) and served as governor of Judah under **Darius I**. He and the high priest Joshua initiated the reconstruction of the Temple at the encouragement of the prophets **Haggai** and **Zechariah** (Hag 1:1–2; Zech 4:9). Owing to his Davidic lineage, Zerubbabel's efforts stirred the Messianic hopes of the Jewish community (Hag 2:21–23; Zech 4:6–10). He appears in Matt 1:12 as a Davidic ancestor of Jesus Christ.

ZERUIAH The sister of **David** and the mother of **Joab**, **Abishai**, and **Asahel**, the "sons of Zeruiah" (1 Chr 2:16).

ZEUS The supreme god of the Greek pantheon; he was identified in Roman religion as Jupiter. One of the causes of the Maccabean revolt was the proposal to dedicate the **Temple** at Jerusalem to Olympian Zeus (2 Macc 6:2). After the healing of a crippled man in Lystra, the inhabitants thought **Paul** and **Barnabas** were the gods Hermes and Zeus in disguise (Acts 14:12). The local pagan priests thus urged the people to offer sacrifices to them (Acts 14:18).

ZIBA A servant of King **Saul** (2 Sam 9:2) and the father of fifteen sons (2 Sam 9:10). After the death of Saul and his sons, Ziba won the confidence of **David** and was given the task of farming and managing the estate of **Mephibosheth**, the crippled son of **Jonathan** (2 Sam 1–13). He gave provisions to David after the king fled Jerusalem during the revolt of **Absalom**; he also informed the king that Mephibosheth had turned against David in the hope of becoming king himself. David informed Ziba that Mephibosheth's property would be given over to him (2 Sam 16:1–4), but when David returned to power, Mephibosheth in his turn accused Ziba of deceit and lies and claimed that he did not greet the king on account of his lameness. In a quandary, David divided the property between them, and Mephibosheth replied, "Oh, let him take it all, since my lord the king has come safely home" (2 Sam 19:30). In the end, Mephibosheth was not interested in pressing his case against Ziba, who was truly the treacherous one, but was only concerned with the welfare of King David.

ZIKLAG A frontier town in the territory of Simeon in southwest Judah (Josh 19:5). The town was seized by the Philistines during the reign of **Saul** and was given to **David** by **Achish**, the Philistine king of Gath, for his loyalty (1 Sam 27:6). After that, David and his forces utilized Ziklag as a base of operations (cf. 1 Sam 30:1–3, 26; 2 Sam 1:1–9). The town remained a possession of the Davidic kings until the Exile and was later resettled by Jewish returnees from Babylon (cf. 1 Sam 27:6; Neh 11:28). Among the sites considered possible locations for Ziklag are Tell el-Khuweilfeh and Tell esh-Sharia.

ZILLAH The second wife of **Lamech**. She became the mother of **Tubal-cain** and his sister Naamah (Gen 4:19–22).

ZILPAH The handmaid of Jacob's first wife, **Leah**. She was given to Leah by **Laban** at the time of her marriage to **Jacob** (Gen 29:24). Leah later gave Zilpah to Jacob as a concubine (Gen 30:9), and Zilpah bore **Gad** and **Asher** by him (Gen 30:10–13; 35:26). Sixteen descendants of Zilpah are listed among those who journeyed to Egypt (Gen 46:16–18).

ZIMRI The name of three men in the Old Testament.

1. The eldest son of Zerah and the grandson of **Judah** and **Tamar** (1 Chr 2:6).

2. The son of Salu and a clan leader of the tribe of Simeon during the wilderness period (Num 25:6–18). He was executed for engaging in religious prostitution with a Midianite maiden, Cozbi.

3. The king of Israel around 885 B.C. He came to the throne through a coup and the assassination of **Elah** (1 Kgs 16:9–20). Zimri was toppled after only a week in power by **Omri**, the commander of the army, who besieged Tirzah. Despairing of survival, Zimri set fire to the palace and died in the flames. The name Zimri soon became a pejorative (2 Kgs 9:31).

ZIN A desert region traversed by the Israelites during their **Exodus** wanderings in the wilderness. It was probably in the **Negeb** south of Canaan and included **Kadesh** (Num 13:21; 20:1; 27:14; 33:36). The wilderness of Zin is also called the wilderness of Kadesh; it should not be confused with the wilderness of **Sin** (Exod 16:1).

ZION The original name of the citadel of Jerusalem that was taken from the Jebusites by David (2 Sam 5:6–9). It was on the eastern ridge of the Jerusalem elevation, south of the site where the Temple was later built. The name was subsequently applied to the entire mountain crest on which Jerusalem was built (Ps 2:6) and even to the city of Jerusalem itself (Ps 147:12; Isa 1:27). It was also understood allegorically as heaven itself (Heb 12:22; Rev 14:1). (*See* **Jerusalem.**)

ZION, DAUGHTER OF A poetic personification of the city of **Jerusalem**, perhaps better translated as "Daughter **Zion.**" The name is used more than twenty-five times in the Old Testament; it accounts for over one-quarter of the descriptions of Jerusalem in the OT. The similar expression "daughter of Jerusalem" also occurs (2 Kgs 19:21; Isa 37:22; Lam 2:18; Mic 4:8; Zeph 3:14).

The name "daughter of Zion" occurs in many passages expressing exultation and joy (Isa 16:1, 52:2, 62:11; Jer 6:2; Mic 4:13; Zeph 3:14; Zech 2:14; Lam 4:22). It also occurs in passages foretelling or lamenting the destruction of the city (Lam 1:6, 2:1, 2:13; Isa 1:8, 10:32; Mic 1:13, 4:10; Jer 6:23). In both uses, the term expresses the Lord's tender affection for the city, whether in joy or in sorrow.

ZIPH

1. A city in southern Judah, southeast of Hebron (Josh 15:55), probably the site now called Tell Zif. **David** spent time with his army in the "wilderness of Ziph" to the east of the city and was visited there by **Jonathan** (1 Sam 23:14–16). The people of the city, however, betrayed him to **Saul** (1 Sam 23:19–24; 26:1) who went to Ziph. It was here that David had the opportunity to slay Saul while the king slept and was entirely at David's mercy, yet David spared his life (1 Sam 26:6–25). The city was fortified later by **Rehoboam** (2 Chr 11:8).

2. A city of Judah near Edom (Josh 15:24).

ZIPPORAH The Midianite daughter of Reuel (Jethro) who became the wife of **Moses.** She was the mother of Moses's two sons Gershom and Eliezer. Once when Moses's life was in danger because he had failed to circumcise one of their sons, she performed the circumcision herself (Exod 4:24–26). Zipporah remained with her father and children when Moses returned to Egypt to free his people (Exod 18:1–5).

ZIV The second month of the Canaanite calendar; it corresponds approximately to April–May.

ZIZA The son of King **Rehoboam** and Maacah. He had three brothers born of the same mother: Abijah, Attai, and Shelomith (2 Chr 11:20).

ZOAN A major Egyptian city in the eastern Nile Delta (Num 13:22; Ps 78:12). It was established seven years after Hebron was built in southern Palestine (Num 13:22). Known in Greek as Tanis, it is probably to be identified with Avaris, the capital of the Hyksos rulers in the first half of the second millennium B.C. Under the Twenty-first to the Twenty-third Dynasties in Egypt (ca. 1069–727 B.C.), the city was the effective capital of the kingdom. It underwent decline after the conquests of Alexander the Great in the fourth century B.C.

ZOAR A city of the Jordan Valley south of the Dead Sea (Gen 13:10; Deut 34:3). Genesis 14:2, 8 makes reference to the king of Zoar (also called Bela), who joined the alliance of five kings that was defeated by **Chedorlaomer** and his allies from Mesopotamia. **Lot** successfully implored the two angels to spare the city from the doom that fell upon **Sodom and Gomorrah** (Gen 19:18–23).

ZOBAH Also Aram-Zobah, an Aramean kingdom in southern Syria. The kingdom flourished during the period of the Israelite monarchy, especially in the eleventh century B.C., when it extended to the Euphrates and Damascus. It entered into conflict with Israel at least twice during the reign of **David** (2 Sam 10:6–19; 1 Chr 18:3–8; 19:1–19). Despite his aggressions, King **Hadedezer** of Zobah suffered defeat and plundering by David's forces (2 Sam 8:3–8). Decline set in beginning in the tenth century B.C., and the kingdom was subjugated by the Assyrians in 732 B.C. (cf. 2 Kgs 16:9).

ZOHAR The father of Ephron the Hittite (Gen 23:8). His son sold **Abraham** a field that included the cave of **Machpelah**, which became the burial place of Sarah (Gen 23:17–19) and Abraham (Gen 25:9–10).

ZORAH A town in the Sorek Valley, in the lowlands of Judah (Josh 15:33). It has been identified with modern Sarʿa north of Beth-shemesh. Manoah, the father of **Samson**, was from Zorah (Judg 13:2; 16:31).

ZUR *See* **Beth-zur.**

ZUZIM One of the ancient peoples of the **Transjordan** defeated by **Chedorlaomer** and his allies in patriarchal times (Gen 14:5). They may be the same people as the Zamzummim (Deut 2:20).

Chronology of the Old Testament

The timeline presented below is based on the internal chronology of the Old Testament. Differences between this and other reconstructions of biblical history are fairly minor when it comes to dating the kings of the Israelite Monarchy and the events of the postexilic period leading up to the New Testament. Significant differences arise in connection with the early history of Israel in the second millennium B.C. Most notably, the Old Testament puts the Exodus in the fifteenth century B.C. (based on 1 Kgs 6:1) and the Patriarchal period more than four hundred years before that (based on Exod 12:40–41). Many scholars, however, prefer a shortened timeline based on a reading of modern archeological data. Accordingly, one often sees the Exodus dated in the thirteenth century B.C. and the patriarchs in the middle of the second millennium.

From Creation to the Exodus

Pre-Abrahamic History	Dates Uncertain	Gen 1–11
Abraham migrates to Canaan	c. 2090 B.C.	Gen 12:1–3
Jacob migrates to Egypt	c. 1876 B.C.	Gen 46:8–27
Exodus of Israel from Egypt	c. 1446 B.C.	Exod 12–3

Israel Conquers and Occupies Canaan

The Wilderness Wanderings	c. 1446–1406 B.C.	Num 14:34–35; Deut 2:7
Beginning of the Conquest	c. 1406 B.C.	Josh 1–12
The Time of the Judges	c. 1350–1050 B.C.	Judg 1–1 Sam 9; cf. Judg 11:26

The United Monarchy

The Kingship of Saul	1050–1010 B.C.	1 Sam 13:1; Acts 13:21
The Kingship of David	1010–970 B.C.	2 Sam 5:3–5
The Kingship of Solomon	970–930 B.C.	1 Kgs 11:42
Foundations laid for the Temple	966 B.C.	1 Kgs 6:1

The Divided Monarchy

United Kingdom becomes Divided	930 B.C.	1 Kgs 12
Assyrian conquest of Israel (north)	722 B.C.	2 Kgs 17
Babylonian conquest of Judah (south)	586 B.C.	2 Kgs 24–25

Return from Exile and Restoration

Edict of Cyrus—Exiles free to Return	538 B.C.	Ezra 1
Reconstruction of Jerusalem Temple	520–515 B.C.	Ezra 6:14–15
Reconstruction of Jerusalem Walls	445 B.C.	Neh 1–6

The Maccabean Period

Antiochus Epiphanes IV outlaws Judaism	167 B.C.	1 Mac 1:20–64
Judas Maccabeus rededicates Temple	164 B.C.	1 Mac 4:36–61
Romans seize control of Palestine	63 B.C.	——

Chronology of the Kings of Israel and Judah

It is a challenging task to ascertain the dates of the biblical kings. There are several reasons for this. For one, fathers and sons sometimes reigned at the same time during overlapping periods of co-regency. For another, the kingdoms of Israel and Judah used different methods of calculation at different times in their history. Two different methods were adopted from the systems in use in the empires of the ancient Near East. One was the accession-year system of ancient Egypt, in which the year of the king's coronation was counted as a full year in the final calculation of his reign. The second was the nonaccession-year system of ancient Mesopotamia, in which only the first full year of a king's reign was counted as his first year on the throne. Despite these irregularities, which make synchronizing the dates of the biblical kings a painstaking task, the overall picture is fairly secure: Solomon's kingdom split apart about 930 B.C., and the rival kingdoms set up in the north and south fell to foreign invaders in 722 B.C. (Assyrian conquest of Israel) and 586 B.C. (Babylonian conquest of Judah). Both kingdoms saw the rise and fall of nineteen kings in succession.

Northern Kingdom of Israel		
	KINGS	DATES B.C.
1.	Jeroboam I	930–910
2.	Nadab	910–909
3.	Baasha	909–886
4.	Elah	886–885
5.	Zimri	885
6.	Omri	885–874
7.	Ahab	874–853
8.	Ahaziah	853–852

Southern Kingdom of Judah		
	KINGS	DATES B.C.
1.	Rehoboam	930–913
2.	Abijam	913–911
3.	Asa	911–870
4.	Jehoshaphat	873–848
5.	Jehoram	848–841
6.	Ahaziah	841
——	(Athaliah)	841–835
7.	Joash	835–796

Northern Kingdom of Israel (cont'd)

	KINGS	DATES B.C.
9.	Jehoram	852–841
10.	Jehu	841–814
11.	Jehoahaz	814–798
12.	Joash	798–782
13.	Jeroboam II	793–753
14.	Zechariah	753
15.	Shallum	752
16.	Menahem	752–742
17.	Pekahiah	742–740
18.	Pekah	740–732
19.	Hoshea	732–722

Southern Kingdom of Judah (cont'd)

	KINGS	DATES B.C.
8.	Amaziah	796–767
9.	Azariah/Uzziah	792–740
10.	Jotham	750–731
11.	Ahaz	735–715
12.	Hezekiah	729–686
13.	Manasseh	696–642
14.	Amon	642–640
15.	Josiah	640–609
16.	Jehoahaz	609
17.	Jehoiakim	609–598
18.	Jehoiachin	598–597
19.	Zedekiah	597–586

The list of biblical references is not exhaustive. Normally only one reference is given to a single chapter even though the name occurs in it several times.

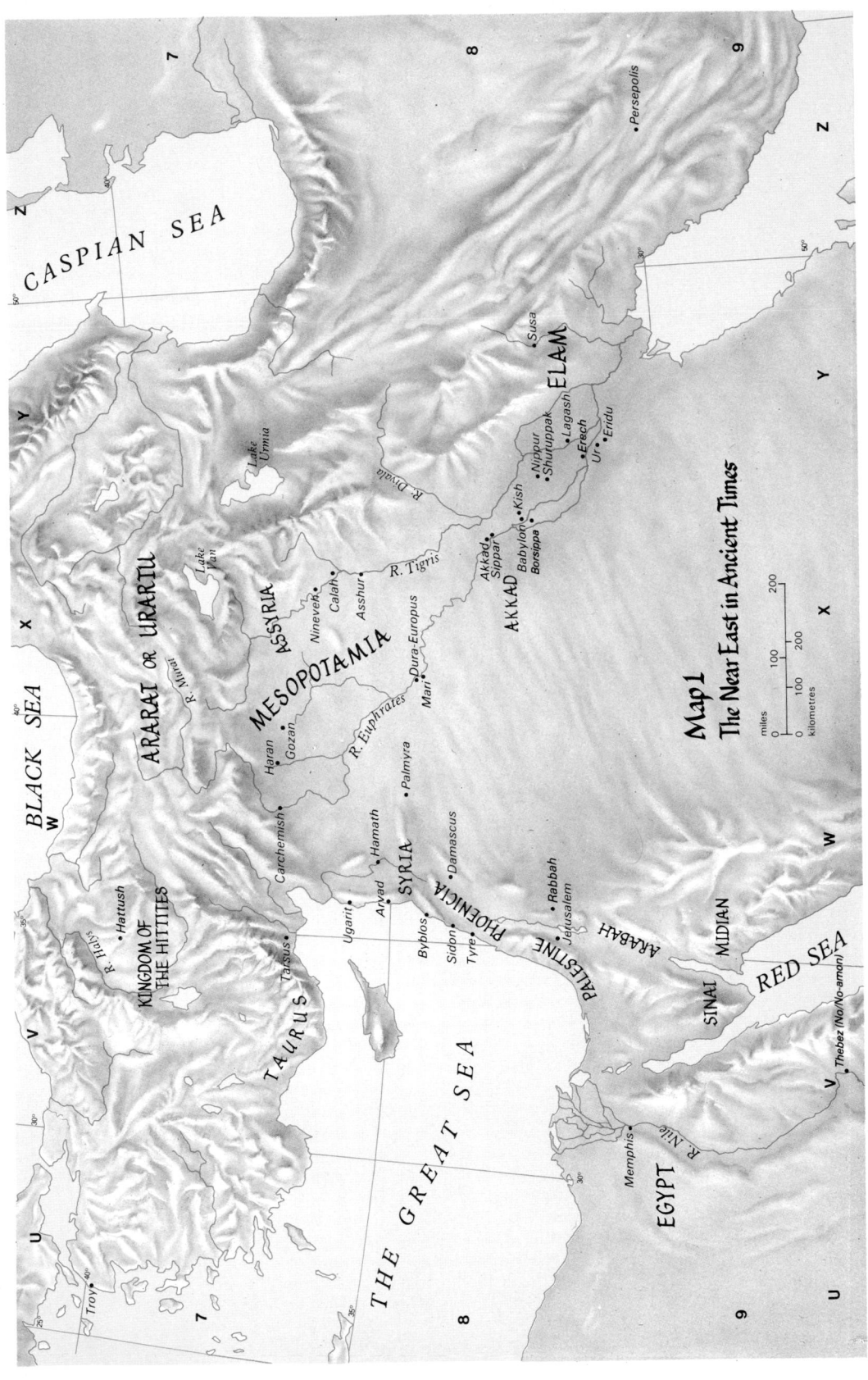

Map 1
The Near East in Ancient Times

CASPIAN SEA

BLACK SEA

CISPIAN SEA

KINGDOM OF
THE HITTITES

ARARAT or URARTU

ASSYRIA

MESOPOTAMIA

ELAM

Troy

Hattush

Tarsus

Carchemish

Ugarit

Arvad

Byblos

Sidon

Tyre

Hamath

Palmyra

Damascus

Rabbah

Jerusalem

SYRIA

PHOENICIA

PALESTINE

ARABAH

MIDIAN

SINAI

EGYPT

Memphis

Thebez (No/No-amon)

RED SEA

THE GREAT SEA

Haran

Gozan

Dura-Europus

Mari

Nineveh

Calah

Asshur

Akkad

Sippar

Babylon

Borsippa

Kish

Nippur

Shuruppak

Lagash

Erech

Ur

Eridu

Susa

Persepolis

Lake
Urmia

Lake
Van

R. Diyala

R. Tigris

R. Euphrates

R. Halys

R. Murat

R. Nile

TAURUS

AKKAD

miles   0   100   200

kilometres   0   100   200   300

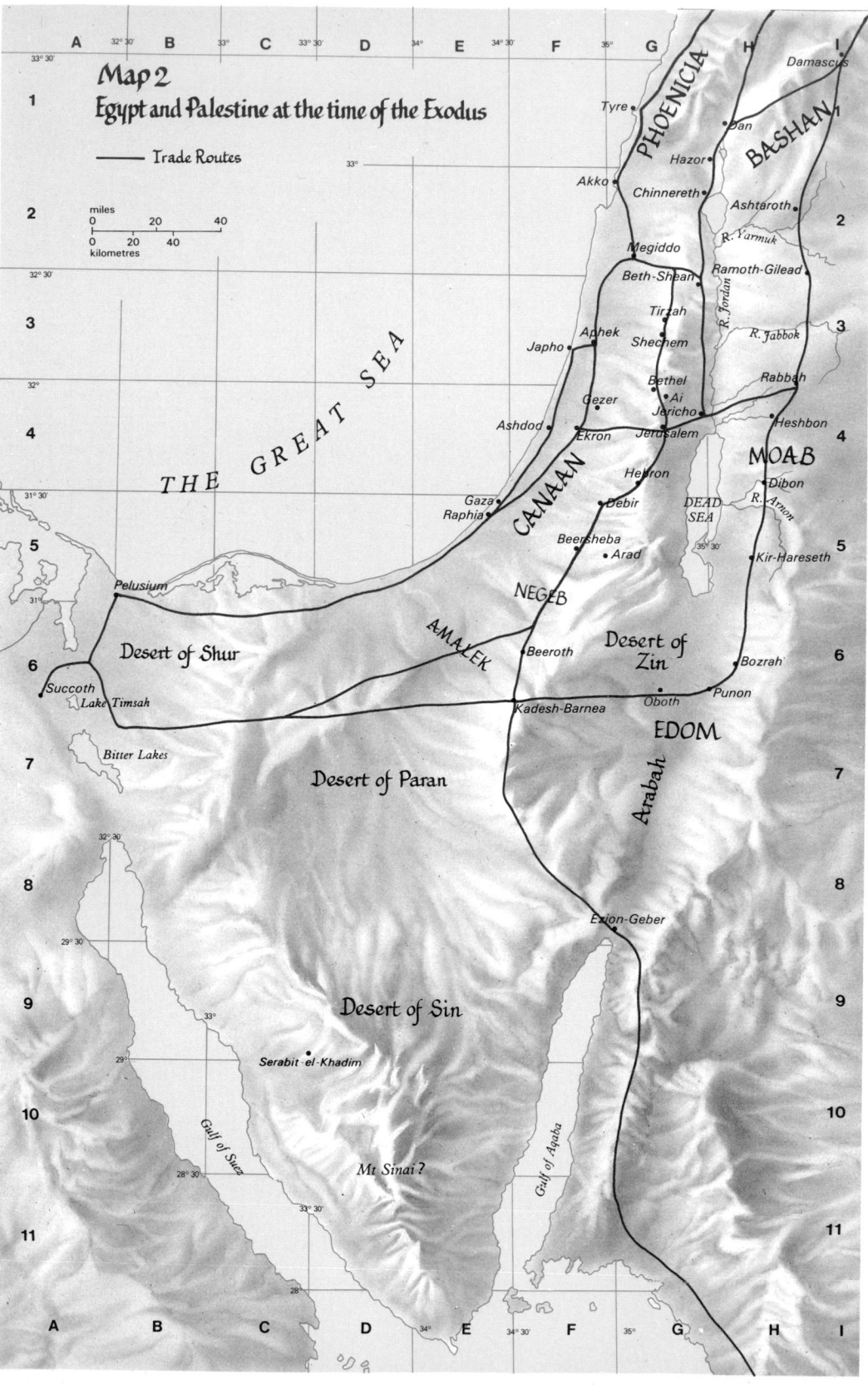

Map 2
Egypt and Palestine at the time of the Exodus

Trade Routes

miles
0   20   40
0 20 40
kilometres

A · 32° 30' B · 33° C · 33° 30' D · 34° E · 34° 30' F · 35° G H I

PHOENICIA
BASHAN

Damascus

Tyre

Dan

Hazor

Akko

Chinnereth

Ashtaroth

R. Yarmuk

Megiddo

Beth-Shean

Ramoth-Gilead

Tirzah

R. Jordan

Japho

Aphek

Shechem

R. Jabbok

Bethel

Rabbah

Gezer

Ai

Ashdod

Jericho

Heshbon

Ekron

Jerusalem

MOAB

CANAAN

Hebron

Dibon

Gaza

Debir

R. Arnon

Raphia

DEAD SEA

Beersheba

Arad

Kir-Hareseth

THE GREAT SEA

NEGEB

Pelusium

AMALEK

Desert of Shur

Beeroth

Desert of Zin

Bozrah

Succoth

Lake Timsah

Punon

Kadesh-Barnea

Oboth

EDOM

Bitter Lakes

Desert of Paran

Arabah

Ezion-Geber

Desert of Sin

Gulf of Suez

Serabit el-Khadim

Gulf of Aqaba

Mt Sinai?

A B C D · 34° E · 34° 30' F G · 35° H I

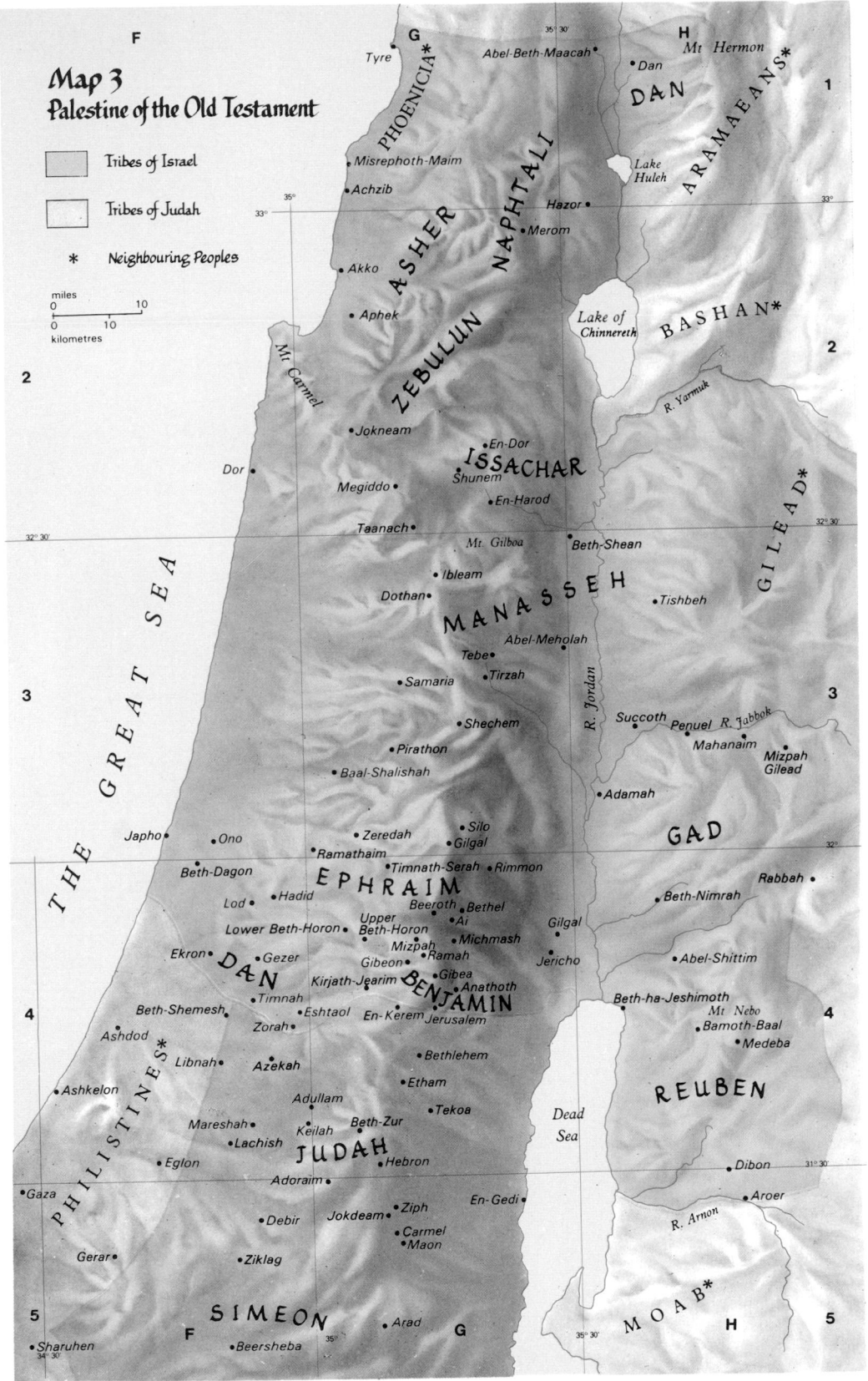

Map 3
Palestine of the Old Testament

Tribes of Israel

Tribes of Judah

* Neighbouring Peoples

miles
0   10
0   10
kilometres

F   G   H

Tyre
PHOENICIA*   Abel-Beth-Maacah   Dan   Mt Hermon*   1
DAN   ARAMAEANS*

Misrephoth-Maim   Lake
Achzib   Huleh
35°   Hazor   33°
33°   ASHER   NAPHTALI   Merom

Akko   BASHAN*
Lake of
Aphek   Chinnereth
ZEBULUN   R. Yarmuk

2   Mt Carmel   2

Jokneam   En-Dor
Dor   ISSACHAR   GILEAD*
Megiddo   Shunem
En-Harod
32° 30'   Taanach   Mt. Gilboa   Beth-Shean   32° 30'
Ibleam   MANASSEH   Tishbeh
THE   Dothan   R. Jordan
Abel-Meholah
Tebe
3   Samaria   Tirzah   Succoth   Penuel R. Jabbok   3
GREAT   Shechem   Mahanaim   Mizpah
Pirathon   Gilead
Baal-Shalishah   Adamah

SEA   GAD
Silo   32°
Japho   Ono   Zeredah   Gilgal
Ramathaim   Rimmon   Rabbah
Beth-Dagon   Timnath-Serah
EPHRAIM   Beeroth Bethel   Beth-Nimrah
Lod   Hadid   Upper   Ai   Gilgal
Lower Beth-Horon   Beth-Horon   Michmash   Jericho   Abel-Shittim
Ekron   Gezer   Mizpah
DAN   Gibeon   Ramah   Beth-ha-Jeshimoth
Kirjath-Jearim   Gibea   Mt Nebo   4
4   Timnah   BENJAMIN   Anathoth   Bamoth-Baal
Beth-Shemesh   Eshtaol   En-Kerem   Jerusalem   Medeba
Ashdod   Zorah
PHILISTINES*   Libnah   Azekah   Bethlehem   REUBEN
Ashkelon   Etham
Adullam   Tekoa   Dead
Mareshah   Beth-Zur   Sea
Keilah
Lachish   Dibon
Eglon   JUDAH   Hebron
Gaza   Adoraim   Aroer
Ziph   En-Gedi
Debir   Jokdeam   R. Arnon
Gerar   Carmel
Ziklag   Maon
MOAB*
5   SIMEON   Arad   5
Sharuhen   Beersheba   35°   34° 30'
F   G   H

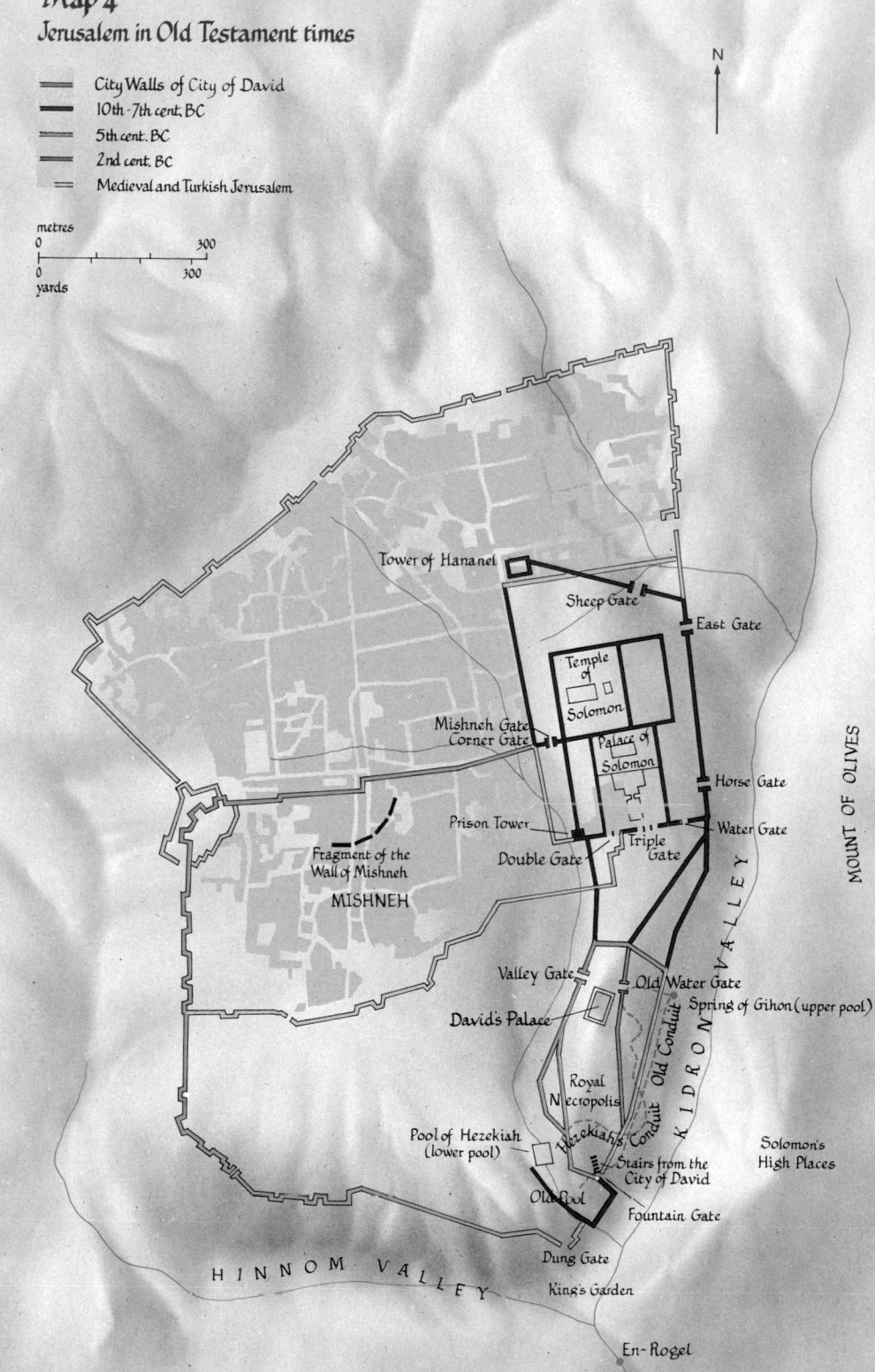

Map 4
Jerusalem in Old Testament times

City Walls of City of David
10th–7th cent. BC
5th cent. BC
2nd cent. BC
Medieval and Turkish Jerusalem

metres
0   300
0   300
yards

N

Tower of Hananel
Sheep Gate
East Gate
Temple of Solomon
Mishneh Gate
Corner Gate
Palace of Solomon
Horse Gate
Prison Tower
Water Gate
Fragment of the Wall of Mishneh
Double Gate
Triple Gate
MISHNEH
Valley Gate
Old Water Gate
David's Palace
Spring of Gihon (upper pool)
Royal Necropolis
Solomon's High Places
Pool of Hezekiah (lower pool)
Hezekiah's Conduit Old Conduit
Stairs from the City of David
Old Pool
Fountain Gate
Dung Gate
King's Garden
En-Rogel

MOUNT OF OLIVES
KIDRON VALLEY
HINNOM VALLEY

Map 5
Jerusalem at the time of Jesus
Herod the Great
Medieval and Turkish Jerusalem
N
+ Place of Stephen's Martyrdom
metres
0
300
0
300
yards
Pool of Bethesda
Sparrow Pool
Pool
Antonia
Sheep Gate
Gethsemane
Jewish Tombs
+ Golgotha
TEMPLE
Solomon's Portico
Court of Gentiles
Pool
Bridge
Royal Portico
Royal Palace
Hasmonean Palace
Double Gate
Triple Gate
KIDRON VALLEY
Spring of Gihon
Conduit
Herodian Street
Aqueduct
Pool of Siloam
Gate of the Essenes
Solomon's Pool
HINNOM VALLEY
+ Haqeldama

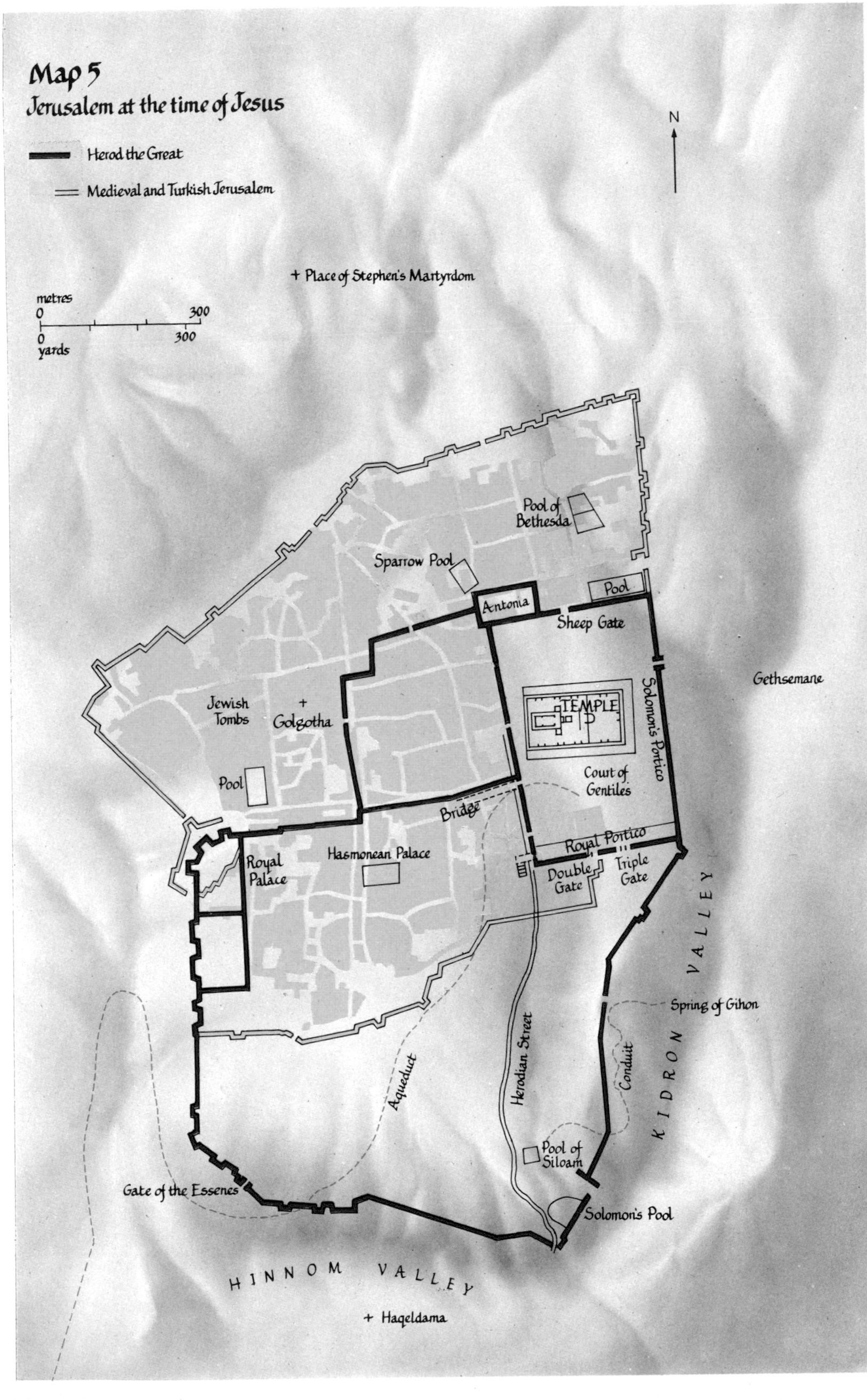

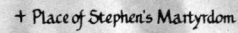

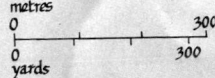

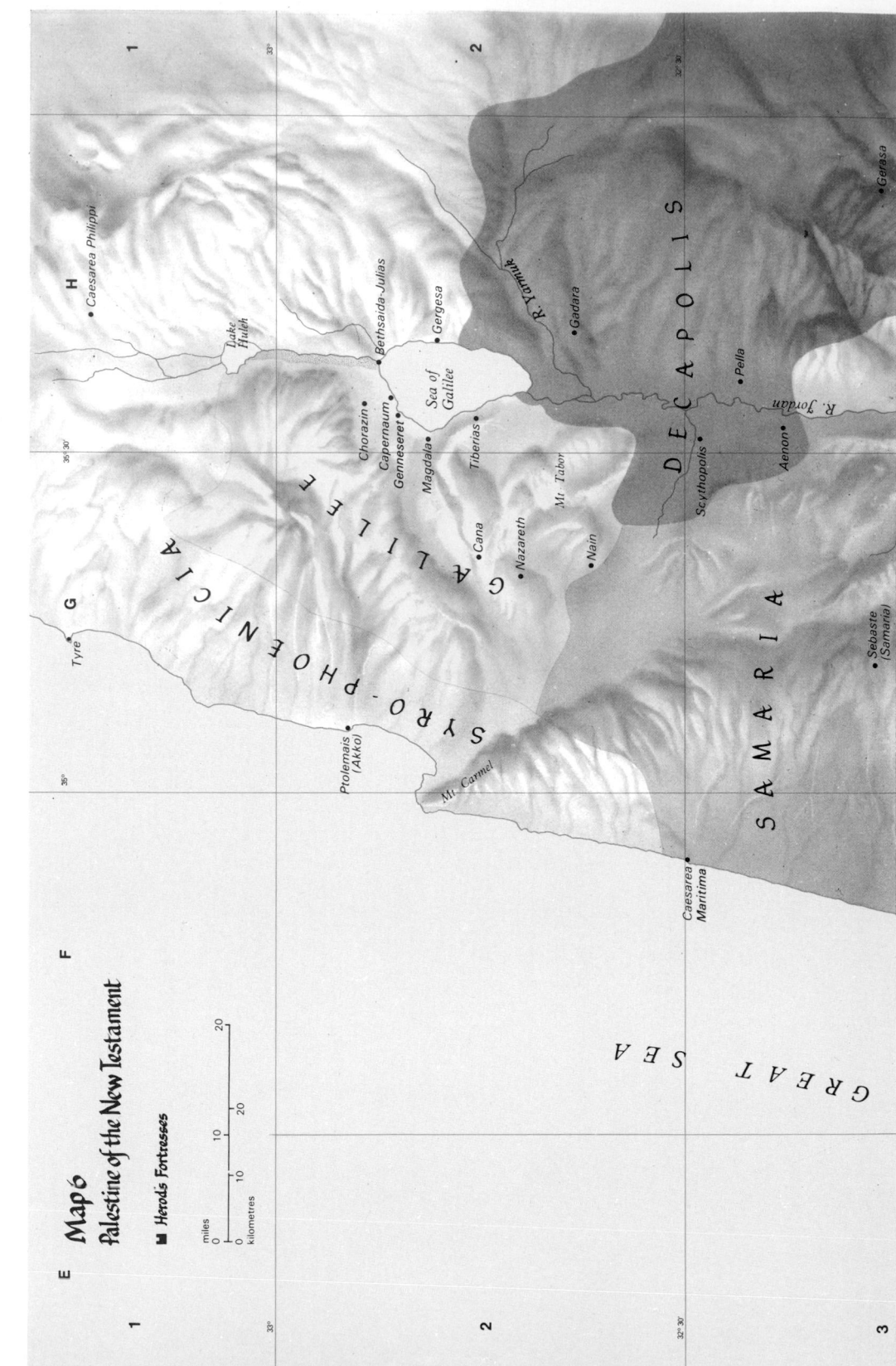

E

Map6
Palestine of the New Testament

■ Herod's Fortresses

miles
0   10   20

kilometres
0   10   20

F

G

SYRO-PHOENICIA

Tyre•

Ptolemais
(Akko)•

Mt Carmel

Caesarea
Maritima•

G A L I L E E

Chorazin•
Capernaum•
Genneseret•
Magdala•
Tiberias•
Cana•
Nazareth•
Mt Tabor
Nain•

Sea of
Galilee

Bethsaida-Julias•
•Gergesa

Lake
Huleh

H

•Caesarea Philippi

R. Yarmuk

•Gadara

Scythopolis•

•Pella

R. Jordan

Aenon•

•Gerasa

D E C A P O L I S

S A M A R I A

•Sebaste
(Samaria)

G R E A T   S E A

1

2

3

33°

35° 30'

35°

33°

32° 30'

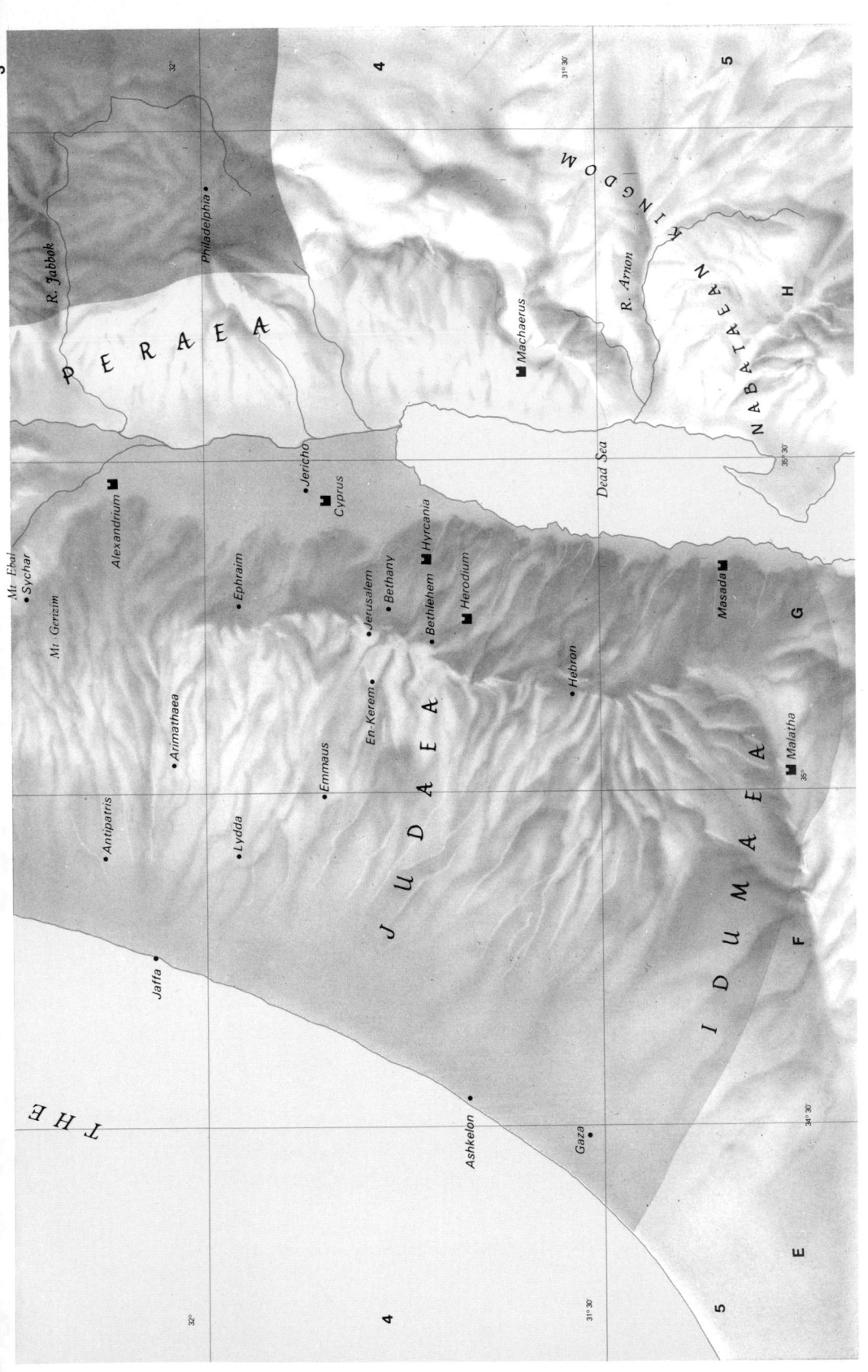

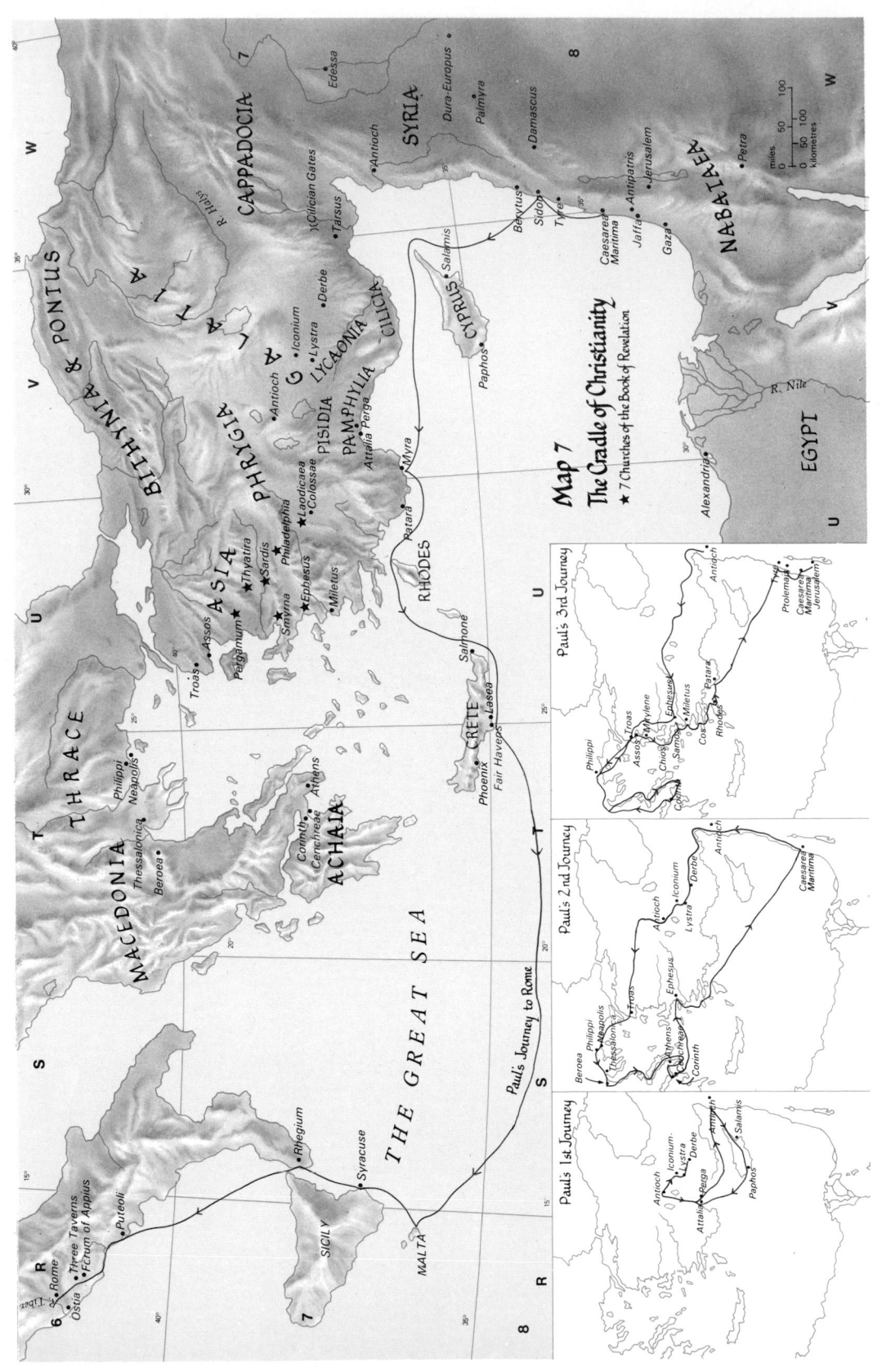

Map 7
The Cradle of Christianity
★ 7 Churches of the Book of Revelation

THE GREAT SEA

THRACE

MACEDONIA
ACHAIA

BITHYNIA & PONTUS

GALATIA

ASIA

PHRYGIA

PISIDIA
LYCAONIA
PAMPHYLIA
CILICIA

CAPPADOCIA

SYRIA

NABATAEA

EGYPT

CRETE
RHODES
CYPRUS
SICILY
MALTA

Paul's Journey to Rome

Paul's 3rd Journey

Paul's 2nd Journey

Paul's 1st Journey